THE OXFORD ENCYCLOPEDIA

OF THE

Modern Islamic World

THE OXFORD ENCYCLOPEDIA OF THE Modern Islamic World

John L. Esposito
EDITOR IN CHIEF

VOLUME 3

New York Oxford
OXFORD UNIVERSITY PRESS
1995

Oxford University Press

Oxford New York
Athens Auckland Bangkok Bombay
Calcutta Cape Town Dar es Salaam Delhi
Florence Hong Kong Istanbul Karachi
Kuala Lumpur Madras Madrid Melbourne
Mexico City Nairobi Paris Singapore
Taipei Tokyo Toronto

and associated companies in
Berlin Ibadan

Published by Oxford University Press, Inc.,
200 Madison Avenue, New York, NY 10016

Library of Congress Cataloging-in-Publication Data

The Oxford encyclopedia of the modern Islamic world
John L. Esposito, editor in chief
p. cm.
Includes bibliographic references and index.
1. Islamic countries—Encyclopedias. 2. Islam—Encyclopedias.
I. Esposito, John L.
DS35.53.095 1995 909'.097671'003—dc20 94-30758 CIP
ISBN 0-19-506613-8 (set)
ISBN 0-19-509614-2 (vol. 3)

Grateful acknowledgment is made to grantors of permission to use the following illustrations in this volume. Metalwork: *figure 1, courtesy of Board of Trustees of the Victoria and Albert Museum; figure 2, courtesy of Metropolitan Museum of Art, New York; figure 3, courtesy of Museum of Turkish and Islamic Art, Istanbul.* Mosque, *article on* Mosque Architecture: *figures 1-3, photographs by Walter B. Denny; figures 4-6, courtesy of Aptullah Kuran.* Painting: *figure 1, courtesy of Topkapı Palace Museum Library, Istanbul; figure 2, courtesy of Istanbul Painting and Sculpture Museum; figure 4, by permission of A. D. Pirous; figure 5, photograph by John G. Ross, courtesy of* Aramco World.

Printing (last digit): 9 8 7 6 5 4 3 2 1

Printed in the United States of America
on acid-free paper

L

CONTINUED

LIBERATION MOVEMENT OF IRAN. A political party whose program is based on a modernist interpretation of Islam, the Liberation Movement of Iran (LMI) was founded in May 1961 by leaders of the former National Resistance Movement (NRM). A few days after the ouster of Prime Minister Mohammad Mossadegh (Muḥammad Muṣaddiq) in August 1953, with his close collaborators either under arrest or surveillance, some of Mossadegh's less politically prominent followers founded the NRM as a secret organization to uphold the nationalist cause under the repressive conditions of the new dictatorship. Among its leaders were the cleric Sayyid Riẕā Zanjānī, Mehdi Bāzargān, the lawyer Ḥasan Nazīh, and Muḥammad Raḥīm ʿAṭā'ī. The NRM had two social bases: the bazaar and students. Key NRM leaders came from a bazaar background, which facilitated contacts with Mossadeghist merchants who financed the movement; students, for their part, demonstrated. Based in Tehran, the NRM was also present in a few provincial centers, most notably Mashhad, where ʿAlī Sharīʿatī was active.

The NRM organized protest demonstrations against the regime on the occasions of Mossadegh's trial (fall 1953), Vice President Richard Nixon's visit to Iran (December 1953), sham parliamentary elections (winter 1954), and the new oil agreement that resolved Iran's dispute with Great Britain (spring 1954). Internal disagreements—between secular and Islamist activists, between opponents and proponents of collaboration with the communists—weakened the movement, and after 1954 the increasing efficiency of the shah's security apparatus caused NRM activity to decline, until the organization was crushed in 1957 when all top activists were arrested and held prisoner for eight months.

When in 1960 Mossadeghists became active again in the course of the shah's liberalization policies, carried out in response to President John F. Kennedy's election, conflict arose between erstwhile NRM leaders and the National Front's old guard of former cabinet members. Two issues were at stake. First, NRM veterans and their young sympathizers in the National Front wanted to target the shah personally, whereas the more moderate National Front leaders tried to spare him, hoping that he would become a constitutional monarch. Second, the core members of the former NRM, most of whom were also active in Islamic circles, wanted to mobilize Iranians by appealing to their religious values, a policy the National Front's secular leadership rejected. The dispute came to a head in May 1961 when Mehdi Bāzargān, Sayyid Maḥmud Ṭāleqāni, Ḥaṣan Nazīh, Yad Allāh Ṣaḥābī, and eight other men formed a separate party, the LMI. The party was defined as Muslim, Iranian, constitutionalist, and Mossadeghist.

During the nineteen months of its activity, the LMI opposed the shah's regime and its policies, calling on the ruler to respect the constitution. When the shah named the independent politician ʿAlī Amīnī prime minister, the LMI tried to accommodate him so as to weaken the shah, unlike the National Front, which considered Amīnī too pro-American. Amīnī's resignation in July 1962 heralded the end of liberalization in Iran. In January 1963 the shah had the entire leadership of the LMI and the National Front arrested, after both had sharply criticized his planned referendum on what would become the "White Revolution." Although the secular politicians were soon released, the LMI leaders were sentenced to several years imprisonment.

After the violent repression of the June 1963 riots, which propelled Ayatollah Ruhollah Khomeini into the political limelight and in which certain lower level LMI activists participated, the shah's rule became increasingly autocratic. This made any oppositional party activity in Iran impossible. Several young LMI militants concluded that the legal constitutional methods of their elders having failed, armed struggle was now called for: they formed the Mujāhidīn-i Khalq [*see* Mujāhidīn, *article on* Mujāhidīn-i Khalq]. Others decided to continue the struggle against the shah abroad and formed an LMI-in-exile. The chief initiators of this move were ʿAlī Sharīʿatī, Ibrāhīm Yazdī, and Muṣṭafā Chamrān. The first was active in Paris until his return to Iran in 1964. Yazdī's base was Houston, Texas, but he was also in close contact with Khomeini in Iraq. Chamrān first worked in the United States but then moved to Lebanon, where he had a leading role in the formation of the Amal movement [*see* Amal].

The LMI reconstituted itself in 1977 with Bāzargān as chairman. In 1978 the party would have preferred to accept the shah's offer of free elections, but recognizing Khomeini's hold on Iranian public opinion, it went along with Bāzargān's rejection of elections. In the last weeks of the shah's regime, LMI figures played a leading role in negotiating with striking oil workers, military leaders, and U.S. diplomats to smooth the transfer of power to the revolutionaries. In 1979 most LMI leaders held key positions in the provisional government. After its ouster in the wake of the seizure of the U.S. hostages in November, the LMI gradually became an oppositional force. It was represented in the first parliament of the Islamic Republic but barred from presenting candidates in subsequent elections. After 1982 it sharply criticized Khomeini's unwillingness to end the Iran-Iraq War. Since then its activities have been sharply restricted, and many of its leaders have been in and out of prison.

Remarkable continuity characterizes the LMI in its two periods of activity. The party's program derives from a liberal interpretation of Shīʿī Islam that rejects both royal and clerical dictatorship in favor of political and economic liberalism, which are both considered more conducive to the flowering of Islamic values than coercion. Based on a relatively narrow constituency of religiously inclined professionals, the party's major weakness has been its inability to engender mass support.

[*See also* Iran; Iranian Revolution of 1979; *and the biographies of Bāzargān, Khomeini, Pahlavi, Sharīʿatī, and Ṭāleqānī.*]

BIBLIOGRAPHY

Chehabi, H. E. *Iranian Politics and Religious Modernism: The Liberation Movement of Iran under the Shah and Khomeini.* Ithaca, N.Y., and London, 1990. In-depth study of the history and ideology of the party.

H. E. CHEHABI

LIBRARIES. Like Islamic civilization in general, Islamic libraries have a glorious past to which present-day Muslims are struggling to measure up. The Muslims' love of learning naturally produced a culture of literacy and the preservation of books. The vastness of modern literature has brought different challenges as Muslim librarians seek adequate ways to manage it bibliographically.

The Qur'ān first spread the written word widely in the previously oral literary culture of the Arabs. As Muslims made pious donations of Qur'ān manuscripts to mosques, the practice of storing written materials developed. Literacy increased because of the religious necessity of reading the Qur'ān, and professional scribes flourished. The Qur'ān, with its command "Read!," provided the groundwork for the production of learning and literature, leading to the growth of organized, well-managed book collections—libraries.

The first library collections appeared in the Umayyad era. Few books from that time survive, but there are accounts of literary activity and book collecting. The Umayyad prince Khālid ibn Yazīd (d. 704) was a man of letters and a noted book collector. The earliest collections belonged to mosque libraries and private libraries; later came caliphal, academic, and public libraries. Mosques were often the chief suppliers of public library services.

The second ʿAbbāsid caliph al-Manṣūr (r. 754–775) established a translation bureau at Baghdad, which led to a seminal achievement of classical Islamic librarianship, the Bayt al-Ḥikmah, founded in 830 by the caliph al-Ma'mūn (r. 813–833). In addition to being the leading library of its time, it continued the translation of texts from other civilizations and included an academy for scholars; thus it was a central clearinghouse for the learning of the Islamic world. Other rulers in that era founded similar centers, such as the Fāṭimid Dār al-ʿIlm of al-Ḥākim at Cairo, and the great library of the Spanish Umayyads at Córdoba, which held some 400,000 volumes. The rise of the *madrasah* universities brought with it the important development of academic libraries.

The large-scale production of books and their acquisition by libraries in great numbers became possible only after paper replaced the more expensive parchment and vellum. The manufacture of paper was introduced to the Islamic world from China at Samarkand in the mid-eighth century. From there the technique spread west to Damascus, Cairo, and Spain. Once paper became widely available, the production and distribution of books had its nexus in the profession of the *warrāq*, a paper dealer, copyist, and bookseller, and frequently a scholar and author in his own right.

The famous *warrāq* Ibn al-Nadīm produced in 987 a monumental, landmark bibliography entitled *Al-fihrist*, a description of every book he had handled, seen, or otherwise learned of. It remains an invaluable source for the history of the literary culture of that era. A later bibliographic milestone was the work of Kâtib Çelebi (sometimes known as Ḥājjī Khalīfah) of Istanbul (1609–1657). Having visited all the great libraries of Istanbul, he wrote the *Kashf al-ẓunūn*, an annotated bibliography of some 14,500 titles in alphabetical order; it also included a general survey of the arts and sciences.

Over time, the great library collections became dispersed, either from lack of care or by incorporation of their books into other collections. Books were always subject to destruction by the usual natural hazards—fire, flood, decay, and so on. There was also deliberate, massive destruction of books by the Mongols at Baghdad and by Spanish Inquisitors after the Reconquista. The age of European colonialism saw the removal of many thousands of manuscripts from the Islamic world to the libraries and private collections of the West, most notably those of the British Library, France's Bibliothèque Nationale, and Princeton University.

Some notable manuscript collections in the Islamic world today include those of Topkapı Sarayı and Süleymaniye Kütüphanesi in Istanbul, the library of Ayatollah Marʿashī in Qom, and the Khuda Bakhsh Oriental Public Library in Patna, India. Such collections are an important link between the glorious past and the troubled present.

The printing of books came late to the Islamic world, and the traditional custodianship and cataloging of manuscripts bear scant relationship to the practices of modern librarianship and bibliographic control (systems permitting users to identify, locate, and get access to desired publications). Bibliographic control involves cataloging, classification, and indexing, as well as the production of bibliographies and accession lists. All such activities are called "documentation" in countries outside the United States.

Islamic librarianship has been in a generally sorry state during the twentieth century. The publication of books and other items in the Islamic world is flourishing, but the ability of Muslim librarians to handle the material adequately has been deficient—although not for lack of sincere, conscientious thought and discussion among concerned librarians.

In the colonial period, modern libraries in Muslim countries were set up and run by Europeans; in the early postcolonial period as well, professional British librarians dominated librarianship in the former British colonies. By now, however, library education has progressed enough in Muslim countries to enable Muslim librarians to assume leadership. Pakistan and Egypt are especially noted for their library education, and those two countries are major exporters of professionally trained librarians, especially to the Gulf region.

Issues that the Anglo-American world long ago settled, such as cataloging, classification, national libraries, and public library legislation, still pose some serious challenges for Muslims. An Islam-centered approach to classification and subject headings remains a dream that seems far from practical realization. The Dewey Decimal Classification (unsuitable as it is) has been widely used by Muslim countries, often with local tinkering, but the Library of Congress Classification with its attendant subject headings is now gaining in popularity. Muslims continue to propose Islamic classification schemes, but none has proved suitable for general use.

Most Muslim countries have managed to establish some form of national library, and some, particularly Egypt and Tunisia, are making serious attempts at national bibliographies. Unfortunately, public libraries seem to be a low priority throughout most of the Islamic world, and they are altogether too scarce in many countries. Often it is the national library, by default, that provides public library service. Turkey, Jordan, Pakistan, and Malaysia deserve mention for their establishment of public libraries; in Lahore and Kuala Lumpur there are even public libraries especially for children. The site of the Prophet's birthplace in Mecca is now a public library. The quality of academic libraries is varied, but in general they are showing slow, steady improvement.

The most important issues for librarians today—automation, freedom of access to information, and above all, library cooperation and networking—are especially challenging in the Islamic world. Saudi Arabia and other Gulf states have led the way in regional cooperation. Their GULFNET online database is the model for other Muslim countries. Malaysian libraries have also been automating and forming themselves into a network.

International cooperation, coordination of activities, and networking throughout the entire Islamic world constitute the biggest challenge, one that still seems far from solution, although it has seen plenty of discussion. The Congress of Muslim Librarians and Information Scientists (COMLIS), previously headquartered in Malaysia, was formed to address this issue. It has met three times but has been inactive much of the time. The Organization of the Islamic Conference has established the Research Center for Islamic History, Art and Culture (IRCICA) in Yıldız Sarayı at Beşiktaş, Istanbul; it has been doing some important work in international Islamic bibliography. There is still no international scholarly journal devoted to Islamic library science, though one is badly needed.

In Alexandria, Egypt, work is under way on the Bibliotheca Alexandrina, scheduled to open in 1998 and inspired by the memory of the great ancient library there (no one who wants to be taken seriously can any longer blame the Muslims for its destruction, because it was gone long before the Muslims arrived). Although there seems to be nothing specifically Islamic about it, it is intended to be one of the world's biggest repository libraries, with all the latest information technology; one may therefore hope that Islamic librarianship will benefit from it.

To meet these challenges, the knowledge exists, the technology is readily available, and the funding could be found. What bedevils Muslim librarians is a lack of organization and cooperation, and of initiative toward these goals. It is as if the political disunity of the Islamic world is reflected in its uncoordinated librarianship. There is progress, but it is slow.

[*See also* Book Publishing; Periodical Literature; Reference Books.]

BIBLIOGRAPHY

Aman, Muhammad M., and Shaʿbān Khalīfah. "Library and Information Services in the Arab Countries." In *Librarianship in the Muslim World 1984*, edited by Anis Khurshid and Malahat K. Sherwani, vol. 2, pp. 3–45. Karachi, 1985.

Anees, Munawar A. "Information Technology and Global Control System for Islamic Literature." *Pakistan Library Bulletin* 20 (June 1989): 21–36.

Anwar, Mumtaz Ali. "Towards a Universal Bibliographic System for Islamic Literature." *International Library Review* 15.3 (1983): 257–261.

COMLIS III: The Third Congress of Muslim Librarians and Information Scientists. Istanbul, 1989. Papers from the conference held at Istanbul in May 1989.

Ḥamādah, Muḥammad Māhir. *Al-maktabāt fī al-Islām: Nashʿatuhā wa-Taṭawwuruhā wa-Maṣāʿiruhā* (Libraries in Islam: Their Origin, Development, and Destiny). Beirut, 1970. Includes history as well as philosophy of librarianship.

Ibn al-Nadīm, Muḥammad ibn Isḥāq. *The Fihrist of al-Nadim: A Tenth Century Survey of Muslim Culture*. Edited and translated by Bayard Dodge. 2 vols. New York, 1970.

ʿIshsh, Yūsuf al-. *Les bibliothèques arabes publiques et semi-publiques en Mésopotamie, en Syrie et en Égypte au Moyen Age* (Arabic public and semipublic libraries in Mesopotamia, Syria, and Egypt in the Middle Ages. Damascus, 1967. Translated into Arabic by Nizār Abāẓah and Muḥammad Ṣabbāgh as *Dūr al-kutub al-ʿArabīyah al-ʿāmmah wa-shibh al-ʿammah li-bilād al-ʿIrāq wa-al-Shām wa-Miṣr fī al-ʿAṣr al-Wasiṭ* (Beirut and Damascus, 1991). Probably the best history of classical Islamic libraries. Unfortunately, there is no English translation.

Islamic Educational, Scientific and Cultural Organization (ISESCO). *Bibliothèques et Centres de Documentation = Libraries and Documentation Centers*. Rabat, Morocco, 1988. A directory of modern institutions. Incomplete but useful.

Kâtib Çelebi. *Kitāb Kashf al-ẓunūn ʿan asāmī al-kutub wa-al-funūn*. Edited by Mehmet Şerefeddin Yaltkaya. 2 vols. Istanbul, 1941–1943.

Muṭahharī, Murtaẓā. *The Burning of Libraries in Iran and Alexandria*. Translated by N. P. Nazareno and M. Nekodast. Tehran, 1983. A conclusive refutation of the myth of Muslims' culpability.

Newson, Jo, and Larry Luxner. "Rebuilding an Ancient Glory." *Aramco World* 45.2 (March–April 1994): 24–29. On the new Bibliotheca Alexandrina.

Pearson, J. D. "Maktaba." In *Encyclopaedia of Islam*, new ed., vol. 6, pp. 197–200. Leiden, 1960–.

Roman, Stephen. *The Development of Islamic Library Collections in Western Europe and North America*. London and New York, 1990. An interestingly written and detailed account of how so many Islamic manuscripts were removed from Muslim countries.

Sajjad ur-Rahman. "Information Resource Sharing and Network Projects." In *Building Information Systems in the Islamic World* (Papers presented at the Second Congress of Muslim Librarians and Information Scientists, held in Kedah, Malaysia, 20–22 October 1986), pp. 125–141. London and New York, 1988.

Sibai, Mohamed Makki. *Mosque Libraries: An Historical Study*. London and New York, 1987.

Siddiqi, Rashid. "The Intellectual Challenge of Islamizing Librarianship." *The American Journal of Islamic Social Sciences* 5.2 (December 1988): 275–278.

Sliney, Marjory. "Arabia Deserta: The Development of Libraries in the Middle East." *Library Association Record* 92 (December 1990): 912–914.

Yaḥyá Monastra

LIBYA. Islam in nineteenth-century Libya—known at the time as the regions of Cyrenaica, Tripolitania, and Fazzan—was marked by Sunnī orthodoxy in its urban areas (primarily Tripoli, Benghazi and the mercantile centers of Sabha and Murzuq in Fazzan) and by a number of heterodox and more populist interpretations in the rural hinterlands and among the nomadic tribes of the desert areas. The latter reinterpreted and adapted the austerity of Sunnī Islam to the Islamic practices of the regions' tribal communities. Small pockets of Ibāḍī Muslims dotted the Tripolitanian landscape.

The second Ottoman occupation of 1835, meant primarily to forestall European colonial designs after the French invasion of neighboring Algeria in 1830, resulted in the first manifestations of both anti-Ottomanism and anti-Western sentiments expressed in overtly Islamic terms. This identification of a popular expression of Islam with political opposition would become a defining characteristic of politics in Libya—a characteristic that not only marked the anticolonialist struggle and the Sanūsī monarchy after independence but has also played a significant role in Muʿāmmar Qadhdhāfī's Jamāhīrīyah, a political system run directly by the people.

Sanūsīyah. In part to escape foreign encroachments and defend Islam against them, and simultaneously to revitalize and purify the religion, Sayyid Muḥammad ibn ʿAlī al-Sanūsī, an Algerian religious scholar who had traveled to Mecca, founded the Sanūsīyah order. Isolated Cyrenaica—outside European influence and only nominally under Ottoman suzerainty—provided the ideal locale for a religious movement that relied in part on the doctrine of *hijrah* ("withdrawal" in emulation of the prophet Muḥammad's flight from Mecca to Medina) to settle among the tribes of the territory's hinterlands.

For almost nine decades the Sanūsīyah represented a powerful Islamic revivalist movement that combined both economic and religious elements as it spread across Cyrenaica, Fazzan, and parts of rural Tripolitania. Its economic importance, pointed out by Emrys Peters, resulted from the order's manipulation of tribal power over the trading routes that ran from the Sahara via Cyrenaica to the Egyptian coast. Peters (1990) delineates a system of alliance patterns among local tribal leaders and shaykhs that allowed the order to dominate both local and long-distance trade. The order's religious relevance to the local tribes was expressed through its incorporation of the *shurafāʾ* (descendents of the prophet Muḥammad who acquire thereby some of his qualities) and of *murābiṭūn* (locally acclaimed pious individuals endowed with saintly qualities).

By the end of the century the Sanūsīyah, centered first in Jaghbub and then retreating to the even more isolated desert oasis of Kufrah in 1895, became the dominant religious and political power in Cyrenaica. As part of its mission it imposed a previously unknown degree of Sunnī orthodoxy among its rural adherents and paved the way for the further spread of Sunnī practice into Waddai and Tibesti, areas now incorporated in modern Chad. The declining Ottoman Empire unofficially agreed to what Evans-Pritchard (1949) describes as a "Turco-Sanūsī Condominium." With its property officially recognized by the Ottomans as *waqf*, the order came to symbolize orthodox Islam wherever its *zawāyā* (lodges) were found.

By the early part of the twentieth century, only some of the *ʿulamāʾ* in the urban centers could challenge the hegemony the Sanūsīyah had established. Not surprisingly, the order led the local resistance, particularly in Cyrenaica, to the Italian invasion after the Ottoman Empire abandoned that effort in 1912. Although the Sanūsī leadership eventually fled to Egypt, it left behind a number of individual shaykhs, such as ʿUmar al-Mukhtār, who would continue the struggle against Italy until 1927.

Owing in part to the Sanūsī alliance with the British in World War II, and in part to the great powers' determination that Libya should not fall once more under Italian tutelage, the Kingdom of Libya was proclaimed in 1951 with King Idrīs al-Sanūsī, the grandson of the order's founder, as its head. More concerned with matters of religious importance—such as the creation of an Islamic university in Al-Bayda'—and with personal piety, Idrīs proved unable effectively to face both the demands of a younger generation imbued with a growing sense of nationalism, and those of an oil economy that grew at a phenomenal pace after the first marketing of oil in 1961. By the eve of the Qadhdhāfī coup in 1969 the monarchy had become a political anachronism, but, significantly, the confluence of religion and a growing political opposition (to the West) would remain a significant feature of the military regime that succeeded it.

Qadhdhāfī's Revolution and Islam. Colonel Muʿammar al-Qadhdhāfī's "revolution" was originally considered as one of the earliest examples of the political renewal of Islam since the North African countries obtained their independence in the 1950s and 1960s. The Libyan leader had not been trained in Islamic jurisprudence and had only a cursory knowledge of Islamic theology. His knowledge and interpretations of Islam reflected primarily the recent history of both his country and the Sanūsī kingdom.

The earliest pronouncements of the regime included a number of nationalist as well as Islamic references, and the substantive measures initially taken by the regime in its early days—among them the revival of Qur'ānic criminal penalties and the banning of alcohol and nightclubs—indicated an open admittance of Islam as a guiding force in the country's political life. But, although Islam would clearly be part of the revolution's ideology, it was mentioned only briefly in article 2 of the country's new constitution of 11 December 1969, and then simply as "the religion of the state." Despite the fact that Qadhdhāfī himself often referred to the importance of Islam to his revolution, the unveiling of his political program during the Libyan Intellectual Seminar in May 1970 made only perfunctory references to Islam—except in the context of Qur'ānic education, which the government initially left untouched.

Both events, however, hinted at the fact that if Qadhdhāfī and his revolutionary officers were to be considered Islamic reformers, this reformism—as events later confirmed—consisted of a highly idiosyncratic interpretation and a highly politicized version of Islam. The experience of Islam in Libya since 1969 can thus be characterized both as a conscious choice to promote political mobilization and as the embodiment of moral commitments by the revolution's leadership. The regime firmly believed that its search for legitimacy could only be achieved within Libya's conservative society if it could demonstrate its adherence to Islamic principles.

Simultaneously, however, this search for legitimacy would also entail the evisceration of all potential competitors, in particular the rural religious elites formerly affiliated with the Sanūsī lodges and the orthodox *ʿulamā'* in the urban centers. The imposition of a new bureaucratic structure after 1970—only partly successful—was meant to secure the first objective. The latter, although already foreshadowed by expressions of distrust made by the regime vis-à-vis the *ʿulamā'* during the 1970 Intellectual Seminar, would take until early 1975, when they were removed from committees set up to reform the country's legal system. By that time Qadhdhāfī had already taken a number of measures that put his experiments at odds with Sunnī Islamic practice elsewhere.

Qadhdhāfī's initiatives involved a series of legal reforms, dating back to a decree issued shortly after the 1969 revolution, that called for the implementation of *sharīʿah* law; this was extended by the islamization of Libyan law in October 1971. The new regulations, derived from Mālikī legal practice, called for the maintenance of existing laws if they agreed with *sharīʿah* principles, and for the use of customary law (*ʿurf*) when applicable. In essence, the regime devised a two-track approach by arguing that matters of religious doctrine were inviolable but that "secular" issues could be subjected to *ijtihād* (innovative reasoning). Similarly, Qadhdhāfī was less willing to accept *ḥadīth, sunnah, ijmāʿ* and *qiyās*, pronouncing them unnecessary accretions to Islam. In particular, he maintained that only part of the *sunnah* could be considered a constitutive element of *sharīʿah* and argued furthermore that *ijtihād* was an acceptable means of broadening its scope in the modern world. In a celebrated discussion with the country's *ʿulamā'* at the Mawlāy Muḥammad Mosque in Tripoli in July 1978 (reprinted in Barrada et al., 1984) Qadhdhāfī reiterated most of these points.

Islam, Qadhdhāfī argued, should not simply reassert traditional values but should become a progressive force. As such, the Libyan leader clearly saw the revival of *sharīʿah* in particular as a means for both ideological renewal and greater political legitimacy. It was this populist reinterpretation of Islamic law, devoid of input from specialized jurists, that assumed increasing importance throughout the 1970s and 1980s and that made every individual—in line with the regime's populist aspirations—a potential *mujtahid*, an individual capable of interpreting and innovating Islamic doctrine and law. These legal reforms in effect afforded the Libyan regime the opportunity carefully to control independent religious organizations. By taking control of *waqf* property through special legislation enacted in 1972 and 1973, the regime further reduced the already diminished impact of the urban *ʿulamā'*. The *ʿulamā'*, now bereft of the financial basis of the religious establishment, for all practical purposes became state employees and lost whatever cultural, financial, and political autonomy they had once possessed. The Libyan state assumed the role of patron of the religious establishment, heavily subsidizing religious life and observance after 1970, including financial support for pilgrims performing the *ḥajj* and the construction of a significant number of new mosques.

Qadhdhāfī started to conceptualize his ideas that would eventually result in the *Green Book* and its Third Universal Theory of political action based on Islam that would replace both capitalism and communism. At the April 1973 Zuwarah speech that ushered in his cultural revolution, Qadhdhāfī revealed the principles on which the country's political system would be based: Arab unity, direct popular democracy, and Islamic socialism. According to the Libyan leader, the new theory would solve once and for all the tension, inherent in a secular concept of the state, between *dīn* and *dawlah:* Islam would serve as the source of inspiration for political renewal and innovation, and as a means of legitimizing the regime's political institutions. Qadhdhāfī's vision of egalitarian individualism—visible now in the country's political institutions, which were run directly by the people represented in People's Congresses and in Islam through the application of individual *ijtihād*—was repeated in the *Green Book,* which was implicitly based on Islamic doctrine.

The creation of the Jamāhīrīyah in 1977 was the culmination of this egalitarian process and ushered in a new stage of Qadhdhāfī's interpretation of Islam. The economic aspects of his *Green Book*—which included the abolishing of private property—were judged by the *ʿulamāʾ* as contradictory to Islam; they objected that Qadhdhāfī seemed determined to use the *Green Book*'s principles as an alternative to the traditional teachings of *sharīʿah* law. In response, Qadhdhāfī further elaborated his interpretations of Islam, declaring, for example, in 1977 that the Libyan calendar now started with the death of the prophet Muḥammad in 632 rather than with the customary date of the Hijrah in 622. He finally mounted an all-out offensive against the power of the *ʿulamāʾ* in early 1978, arguing that since the Qur'ān was written in Arabic, there was no need for expert interpretation. The Qur'ān was declared the sole source of *sharīʿah* law, and the *sunnah,* as well as *qiyās, ijmāʿ,* and *ḥadīth* were now rejected as errors. The mosques were put under popular control; the status of women in divorce cases was declared equal to that of men; and the *ḥajj* to Mecca was no longer considered a pillar of Islam.

As on all other occasions, Qadhdhāfī's innovations served political as well as religious purposes: they afforded the regime greater legitimacy for whatever actions it took in secular matters and simultaneously freed it from the constraints of Islamic doctrine and tradition, which, Qadhdhāfī argued, were outdated and open to individual interpretation. Although the reaction of the *ʿulamāʾ* within Libya remained necessarily muted, Qadhdhāfī's actions in time would be labeled by the country's underground Islamist movements as *bidʿah* (heretical innovation). By the mid-1980s these movements' followers—among others, the Ḥizb al-Taḥrīr al-Islāmī and the local version of the Ikhwān al-Muslimīn—were increasingly targeted, and several were publicly executed by the regime. By the early 1990s they had been singled out as potentially the most dangerous opposition and were denounced in vitriolic terms by Qadhdhāfī, who declared them public enemies of the revolution.

Conclusion. Islam in Libya in the nineteenth and twentieth centuries has shown the lingering impact of the country's historical legacy. During the colonial period in particular, the two groups of competing religious establishments—the Sanūsī-allied shaykhs and the urban-based, orthodox *ʿulamāʾ*—cooperated with the British and the Italians respectively, and as a result undermined confidence among young Libyans who grew up during the Arab nationalist period that these established powers could serve as trustworthy political interlocutors.

Qadhdhāfī's pronouncements on Islam since 1969 have clearly referred to this earlier historical period; in particular, the pro-Western attitude and weak nationalist credentials of the Sanūsī monarchy indelibly impressed the Libyan leader as he grew up in the country's hinterland. This endowed him with a clear suspicion of any type of organized religious group in the country, and led eventually to their evisceration. It also resulted in his strong conviction, maintained consistently throughout his tenure in office, that religious affairs were both within the purview of government and subject to personal interpretation.

Soon after the 1969 coup Qadhdhāfī adopted a highly activist political stance in which he proclaimed himself a mediator between different interpretations of Islamic precepts. His insistence on the right of personal interpretation necessitated a number of doctrinal interpretations that pitted him both against his country's *ʿulamāʾ* and against much of the orthodox Sunnī religious establishment throughout the Arab world. In the end, it resulted in a political process where he simply imposed his own views on Libyan religious leaders and the country's population alike. The Islamic precepts that Qadhdhāfī had originally advocated as valuable in and of themselves assumed an evocative symbolism within Libya, anchored within the teachings of the Third Universal theory, that would allow them to become one of the regime's array of political instruments.

Despite this, Islam in the Jamāhīrīyah today is not an attempt to foster religious revivalism by radical means. Qadhdhāfī has sought simply to extend a long tradition of government that is based on and legitimated by religious precepts. If his attitude toward Islam is considered radical, it is primarily so because his overall political, secular ambitions are radical as well. The regime rejects Islamic tradition, relying instead on a popular reinterpretation of Islam steeped in the egalitarian tradition in which Qadhdhāfī himself had grown up.

[*See also* Sanūsīyah; *and the biographies of Mukhtār and Qadhdhāfī.*]

BIBLIOGRAPHY

Sanūsīyah

El-Horair, A. S. "Social and Economic Transformations in the Libyan Hinterland during the Second Half of the Nineteenth Century: The Role of Sayyid Ahmad al-Sharif al-Sanussi." Ph.D. diss., University of California–Berkeley, 1981. The only comprehensive study of Aḥmad al-Sharīf al-Sanūsī, who became one of Libya's national heroes for his stance against the colonial power.

Evans-Pritchard, E. E. *The Sanusi of Cyrenaica.* Oxford, 1949. Classic study of the Sanūsīyah.

Martel, André. *La Libye, 1835–1990: Essai de géopolitique historique.* Paris, 1991. Excellent essay on Libyan history, with some attention to the Islamic dimension of the country's background.

Peters, Emrys L. *The Bedouin of Cyrenaica: Studies in Personal and Corporate Power.* Cambridge, 1990. A much needed update and reinterpretation of Evans-Pritchard's earlier work, from an anthropological perspective.

Qadhdhāfī's Islam

Ayoub, Mahmoud M. *Islam and the Third Universal Theory: The Religious Thought of Muʿammar al-Qadhdhāfī.* London, 1987. Arguably the best explanation of Qadhdhāfī's thought and ideology, contained within a hagiography of the Libyan leader.

Barrada, Hamid, et al. *"Kadhafi: "Je suis un opposant à l'échelon mondial."* Lausanne, 1984. Contains several thoughtful interviews with the Libyan leader, as well as a number of important statements and debates engaged in by Qadhdhāfī.

Burgat, François, and William Dowell. *The Islamic Movement in North Africa.* Austin, 1993. Substantial treatment of North African, including Libyan, Islamist movements.

Mason, John Paul. *Island of the Blest: Islam in a Libyan Oasis Community.* Athens, Ohio, 1977. Excellent study of the effect of Qadhdhāfī's revolution and his interpretation of Islam on one Libyan oasis.

Mayer, Ann Elizabeth. *Islamic Law in Libya: Analyses of Selected Laws Enacted since the 1969 Revolution.* London, 1977. The best available interpretation of some of Qadhdhāfī's edicts and statements on Islam and Libya's legal system.

Qadhdhāfī, Muʿammar al-. *The Green Book.* 3 vols. Tripoli, 1980. The Libyan leader's thoughts bundled into three slim volumes.

DIRK VANDEWALLE

LIFE CYCLE. *See* Rites of Passage.

LOYA JIRGA. Councils summoned by Afghan rulers over the past century to consolidate their authority and nationalist programs have been called by this term, which means "grand assembly" in Pashtu. Modernist Afghans and historians have attempted to trace *loya jirga* into the distant past and indigenous tribal custom, but *loya jirga* differ from tribal *jirga* in fundamental ways. Tribal *jirga* are a Pashtun custom of communal assembly for deciding on collective undertakings or settling internal conflicts. Decisions are reached by a consensus of those attending. *Loya jirga* are bodies of delegates summoned by the ruler and limited to his initiatives; they include religious leaders, who have only ratifying roles in tribal *jirga.* A more proximate model would be the *majlis,* for *loya jirga* belong to the history and centralization of government in modern Afghanistan.

The format was set by Amir ʿAbd al-Raḥmān Khān (1880–1901), who initiated several consultative bodies to check the quasifeudal *jāgīr* system of titleholders adopted by previous amirs and to assert power over officeholders and local leaders. His arrangement of *loya jirga* as "national" assemblies alongside assemblies of titleholders (*darbārī shāhī*) and of local leaders (*khawānīn mulkī*) was formalized in the first constitution of Afghanistan proclaimed by Amir Amanullah (1919–1929) in 1923.

Boundaries of the nation and the ruler's authority have been the constants of *loya jirga.* ʿAbd al-Raḥmān held three, according to Hasan Kakar, to affirm his negotiations of Afghanistan's modern borders and his paramount authority within them. Amanullah summoned a *loya jirga* in 1921 to ratify his treaty with Britain recognizing Afghanistan's independence, again in 1924 after a rebellion against his efforts to modernize Afghanistan, and in 1928 to press reforms; the last provoked a civil war. After its conclusion, Nādir Shāh (1930–1933) called a *loya jirga* in 1930 to affirm his proclamation as ruler by a *jirga* of tribal militia; another was summoned in 1941 to accept British demands (to expel Axis nationals) that infringed Afghan sovereignty. *Loya jirga* were convened again in 1949 and 1955 to press nationalist claims to tribal territories in Pakistan; these were reaffirmed by a *loya jirga* summoned in 1964 to ratify a new constitution.

The last provides a picture of *loya jirga* at work. Of more than 450 delegates, 176 were elected for the event, to offset 176 who were members of the National Assembly, with the balance drawn from appointed legislators, officials, and the committees that had drafted the constitution. Although the delegates were not "king's men," it was the ruler's assembly; it was composed to check entrenched interests and to establish the authority of the center.

Whatever *loya jirgas* employ of regional traditions and techniques, their specific features belong to the history of modern Afghan government, not to tribal models. *Loya jirga* have never assembled to settle conflicts or to decide a course of collective action, but only on a ruler's initiative, and then more for communication than for consultation between the ruler and constitutent communities. Apparently formulated by Amir Abd al-Raḥmān as a check on title-holders and local leaders, the *loya jirga* has been a device for nationalizing the boundaries of the country and authority within it.

[*See also* Afghanistan; Majlis.]

BIBLIOGRAPHY

Gregorian, Vartan. *The Emergence of Modern Afghanistan.* Stanford, Calif., 1969. The most comprehensive and balanced political history of Afghanistan.

Kakar, M. Hasan. *Government and Society in Afghanistan.* Austin, 1979. Provides a detailed study of Emir ʿAbd al-Raḥmān's government.

Poullada, Leon B. *Reform and Rebellion in Afghanistan, 1919–1929.* Ithaca, N.Y., 1973. Places the Amanullah period in a tribal context.

Dupree, Louis. *Afghanistan.* Princeton, 1978. Contains a lively account of the 1964 *loya jirga*.

Jon W. Anderson

M

MADANĪ, ʿABBĀSĪ (b. 1931), Algerian Islamic activist and political leader. ʿAbbāsī Madanī was born in Sīdī ʿUqbah, in southeastern Algeria. The son of a religious teacher and imam, Madanī committed the Qur'ān to memory at an early age. He then received his Arabic and Islamic education in Biskra at one of the schools of the Association of Algerian Scholars.

In 1954 Madanī joined the National Liberation Front (FLN) and participated in an armed operation against the French occupation. This led to his arrest and imprisonment for eight years. Following his release, Madanī resumed his religious and political activism through the Qiyām (Values) Society, which was established in 1963 and advocated a reformist orientation that sought to reassert Arab and Islamic values in post-independence Algeria. The activities of the society were restricted in 1966, following a demonstration by its members protesting the execution of Sayyid Quṭb of Egypt's Muslim Brotherhood; eventually, in 1970, Qiyām was outlawed.

Madanī grew increasingly critical of the FLN for its adoption of a socialist orientation. Deciding to continue his education, he obtained degrees in philosophy and psychology. In 1978 he received a British doctoral degree in comparative education and was appointed professor at the University of Algiers.

Madanī became a public figure in 1982 during the violent clashes between the state and Islamist students at the main campus of the University of Algiers. Along with Shaykhs ʿAbd al-Laṭīf Sulṭānī and Aḥmad Saḥnūn both eminent religious scholars, he signed a fourteen-point statement criticizing the secular policies of the state and demanding the promotion of Islam in government and society. Madanī was then arrested and imprisoned for two years.

Subsequently the new Algerian regime permitted a margin of freedom for the Islamists, who managed to increase their activities in the mosques, schools, and universities and to broaden their following. When a new constitution allowing the formation of political parties was adopted in February 1989, Madanī announced the establishment of the Islamic Salvation Front (known by its French initials, FIS). Headed by Madanī, the FIS was legalized in September of that year. Madanī led the party through the June 1990 municipal and provincial elections, in which it won a large majority of the seats. He pushed for early parliamentary and presidential elections and organized a general strike in May 1991 protesting the new electoral law, which favored the FLN. In June 1991 Madanī was arrested along with his deputy ʿAlī Bel Ḥajj. Both were tried before a military court and in July 1992 received a sentence of twelve years for leading an armed conspiracy against state security.

As an education specialist, ʿMadanī has written studies on pedagogy and philosophy and contributed numerous articles to the FIS's periodicals *Al-munqidh* and *Al-furqān*. Reflecting the concerns of an Islamic modernist, he attempts to delineate the nature of the Islamic solution to the crises of modern societies. Madanī holds that contemporary Western thought suffers from ideological and moral predicaments that have emanated from a misperception of the incompatibility of science and religion. Like many other Islamic revivalist intellectuals, he regards Islam as a humanistic and universal message that presents a worldview counter to Western ideologies.

Madanī is known for his moderation and political skills. He managed to integrate into his party several Islamic groups with various orientations; in a relatively short time he transformed the FIS into a potent political force in Algeria, challenging the historic political monopoly of the FLN and presenting itself as a viable alternative. Throughout his leadership of the FIS, Madanī was able to steer his party toward effecting change from within the system through legal and constitutional processes.

[*See also* Islamic Salvation Front.]

BIBLIOGRAPHY

Burgat, François, and William Dowell. *The Islamic Movement in North Africa.* Austin, 1993. Excellent and thorough analysis of the phenomenon of Islamic revival in North Africa.

Madanī, ʿAbbāsī. *Azmat; al-fikr al-ḥadīth wa-mubarrirāt al-ḥall al-Islāmī* (The Crisis of Modern Thought and the Reasons for The Islamic Solution). Mecca, 1989. Critical analysis of Western thought containing Madanī's views of the nature of the Islamic alternative.

Madanī, ʿAbbāsī. "Nurīdu taghyīr al-Barlamān wa-al-ibqā' ʿalā al-ra'īs" (We Want to Change the Parliament but Keep the President). *Al-Muslimūn* 279 (8–14 June 1990). Interview with Jamāl Aḥmad Khashūshjī.

Shahin, Emad Eldin. "Algeria: The Limits to Democracy." *Middle East Insight* 6 (July–October 1992): 10–19.

EMAD ELDIN SHAHIN

MADHHAB. *See* Law, *article on* Legal Thought and Jurisprudence.

MADĪNAH AL-FĀḌILAH, AL-. The term *al-madīnah al-fāḍilah* ("virtuous city") reminds one first, and most properly, of the famous book written by the illustrious Abū Naṣr Muḥammad ibn Muḥammad ibn Tarkhān al-Fārābī (AH 257–339/870–950 CE). Designated as "the second teacher"—second, that is, after Aristotle—al-Fārābī may also be called the founder of Islamic political philosophy. He wrote commentaries on Aristotle, some of which are extant, and several other works on various aspects of philosophy, but none of these seems to have as much fame as the work entitled *Mabādi' ārā' ahl al-madīnah al-fāḍilah* (Principles of the Opinions of the People of the Virtuous City).

Formally, the work is divided into six sections comprising nineteen chapters. It seems possible to group these sections and chapters in three major parts, the first having to do with the world around us (sections I–III and chapters 1–9), the second with human beings and human nature (section IV and chapters 10–14), and the third with political association as well as good and bad (sections V–VI and chapters 15–19). Most scholars hold it to be the writing in which al-Fārābī sets forth his idea of the best regime (as with Richard Walzer and his descriptive title of the work, *Al-Fārābī on the Perfect State*), but they thereby neglect al-Fārābī's explicit and precise title with its emphasis on opinions.

Indeed, in the first sixteen chapters, al-Fārābī sketches out what the correct opinions about the universe, human beings, and the city should be and shows what is wrong with other kinds of cities as well as with some of the opinions held by those in wrongly guided cities. Then, in chapter 17, that is, the last chapter of section V, he shows how important it is to link these opinions about natural science, the soul, and politics with religion. In section VI, chapters 18–19, he presents opinions that inhabitants of yet other misguided cities might have, along with what makes them fallacious, and he indicates above all the undesirable political actions to which they lead. We see, then, that to have a truly desirable political rule, one that is good and leads to what al-Fārābī deems real happiness, one must have opinions like those set forth earlier. In this work he does not, however, explain the ordering of such a desirable political regime nor how it can be brought into being.

The term *al-madīnah al-fāḍilah* also brings to mind the actual city of Madīnah (Medina), originally called Yathrib, which the prophet Muḥammad reached on 12 Rabīʿ al-Awwal (1 or 24 September) 622, following his flight or emigration from Mecca, and in which he died a decade later (13 Rabīʿ al-Awwal, 11 or 8 June, 632). Yathrib is mentioned once in the Qur'ān (surah 33.13), but al-Madīnah is mentioned four times (9.101 and 120, 33.60, 63.8)—albeit each time in a negative context (see, in contrast, surah 90 with its praise of Mecca, though not mentioned by name). Still, it was in Medina that the Prophet established the first community of Muslims. Moreover, it came to be known among Muslims as the city of the Prophet *(madīnat al-nabī).* Though there is no Qur'ānic allusion to Medina as "virtuous" or to Yathrib as a "virtuous city" *(madīnah fāḍilah),* historians, political scientists, and Muslim activists and reformers look to the Prophet's governance of the city and especially to what has come to be known as the Constitution of Medina for guidance and inspiration.

They do so, however, only obliquely. Either because al-Fārābī's stimulating treatise had little or no circulation until very recent times, or because the rhetorical appeal of the phrase "virtuous city" has no resonance for them, one finds no explicit references to it among writers of the nineteenth and twentieth centuries. Even when someone as gifted as Jamāl al-Dīn al-Afghānī calls for greater attention to the wisdom of the medieval Islamic philosophers, and especially to the understanding of the relationship between religion and science put forth by someone like al-Fārābī, he does so without hearkening back to al-Fārābī's *Mabādi' ārā' ahl al-madīna al-fāḍilah* or to anything that evokes the idea of a virtuous city. Indeed, for al-Afghānī, his student and associate ʿAbduh, and all those who followed them (al-Bannā', Mawdūdī, Quṭb, Sharīʿatī, and Khomeini), political goals were expressed more in terms covering many nations than in terms of a single city, however virtuous.

[*See also* Islamic State; Medina.]

BIBLIOGRAPHY

Ali, A. Yusuf, *The Holy Qur'ān: Text, Translation, and Commentary*. Brentwood, Md., 1983.

Fārābī, Abū Naṣr Muḥammad al-. *Mabādi' ārā' ahl al-madīnah al-fāḍilah*. See Walzer, below.

Walzer, Richard. *Al-Farabi on the Perfect State: Abū Naṣr al-Fārābī's Mabādi' Ārā' Ahl al-Madīna al-Fāḍila, a Revised Text with Introduction, Translation, and Commentary*. Oxford, 1985.

CHARLES E. BUTTERWORTH

MADRASAH. An establishment of learning where the Islamic sciences are taught, the *madrasah* is a college for higher studies. During the tenth and eleventh centuries, the *madrasah* was devoted primarily to teaching law, and the other Islamic sciences and literary philosophical subjects were optionally taught. Today, however, the designation *madrasah* is ambiguous. Although originally the *madrasah* was created as an institution of Islamic higher learning in contrast to the *kuttāb* or *maktab*, the children's schools in the Middle East, currently the term *madrasah* is sometimes used for establishments for elementary teaching of Qur'ānic knowledge.

History. Related to the *madrasah*, in particular to the pre-*madrasah* institutions, is the *masjid* (mosque), which was the first institution of learning in Islam. The *jāmiʿ* (congregational mosque) had its *ḥalaqāt* (study circles): the *dār*, *bayt* and *khizānah* are three terms that mainly designate libraries. Other institutions similar to the *madrasah* are the *ribāṭ*, *khānqāh*, *zāwiyah*, *turbah*, and *duwayrah*, all types of monastery colleges in medieval Islam.

At earlier stages the instruction in the *madrasah* was linked with the mosque: at a later stage the mosque-*khānqāh* complex developed and served to house students. The final step was the creation of the *madrasah* as a distinct institution. A *madrasah* was an edifice used for study and as a residence for teachers and students; annexed to it was usually a library. *Madrasah*s were subsidized with permanent sources of income, such as land or rent-bearing urban property in the form of the *waqf* (religious endowment). The *waqf* provided for salaries for the faculty and scholarships for students. For a long time there was much overlap between the mosque and the *madrasah*. The regular mosques continued to be seats of learning even after the creation of *madrasah*s, and the word *madrasah* also signified a room in a mosque dedicated to teaching. In Mecca, for example, the *madrasah*s were often built near the large mosques. There is much debate about the history of the *madrasah* and its association with teaching in the mosque. Although *madrasah*s existed before Niẓām al-Mulk, he is nevertheless given credit for having institutionalized and created a vast network of these schools. According to Asad Talas (1939), the *madrasah* served as an institution to combat anti-Shīʿī propaganda. Niẓām al-Mulk ordered that the Niẓāmīyah *madrasah* be constructed in AH 457 (1065 CE), and the school was completed two years later in Baghdad. During the time of Niẓām al-Mulk and immediately afterward, *madrasahs* spread in Iraq, Khurasan, al-Jazira and other leading cities of the Muslim world.

The *madrasah*s were established mainly to teach law, and originally each institution was devoted to a single school of law. The ordinary *madrasah*s, however, included other subjects in addition to *fiqh* (jurisprudence). The phenomenon of "traveling students" who strove to sit at the feet of scholars to collect the Prophet's sayings applied equally to *madrasah*s. In fact medieval Muslim scholars were great travelers.

As Louis Gardet has noted (1977), many of the students frequenting the *madrasah* and university mosques originated from the poorer strata of society. The *madrasah* was a path to escape manual work, and many strove to obtain the meager stipends given by the mosque or *madrasah*. Until completing their studies, such students lived modestly in lodges of the school and were given a daily ration of bread. C. Snouck Hurgronje (1931) has pointed to the decaying state of *madrasah*s in Mecca during the late nineteenth century. Government officials treated the schools as abandoned property; the only university building in Mecca where lessons were taught was the great mosque.

In Muslim India the *madrasah*s were establishments of higher learning that produced civil servants and judicial officials. One of the most important events in terms of the revival of the of the *madrasah* during the latter part of the nineteenth century was the founding of the Deoband school by Rashīd Aḥmad and Muḥammad Qāsim in 1867 in British India. This led to the establishment of many *madrasah*s modeled on Deoband. Deoband itself remained a center for Islamic studies. Its *madrasah* was created in the old Chattah mosque as a distinct institution with a central library and was run by professional personnel. The students were required to take examinations. The school aimed at spreading reformist Islam. Some methods of instruction in Deoband differed from those of other *madrasah*s. Deoband was thus considered as a successful example of how the *ʿulamāʾ* might propagate their message through modern organizational style and innovative educational methods.

Decline. With the advent of colonialism in Muslim countries, the introduction of Western curricula and teaching, and subsequent independence movements, the *madrasah*s experienced tremendous changes, varying from country to country. First, most Muslim countries adopted modern educational institutions in the form of universities, academies, colleges, and institutes. Quite often modern Islamic institutes, centers, and faculties of theology were created to counterbalance the old *madrasah*s. In some countries the *madrasah*s themselves adapted by introducing secular subjects. At the same time they lost potential students to secular institutions. This fact constitutes one of the most important reasons for social change.

Turkey is a case in point. When Mustafa Kemal Atatürk was elected president, the new republican regime undertook measures to control religious institutions. The Kemalist secularist reforms between 1924 and 1928 aimed, among other things, to close the *medrese*s (the Turkish term).

Al-Azhar University in Cairo likewise witnessed successive reforms since the end of the nineteenth century in the government's attempts to stabilize the standards of education. Cairo University and Dār al-ʿUlūm, as modern institutions of learning attracting the rising elites, certainly competed with al-Azhar. In particular, a 1961 law, Article 103, led to the secularization of al-Azhar through the introduction of secular faculties. The idea was to produce graduates who would have "multiple exposure", meaning both a scientific and a religious perspective, so that religion would cease to be a profession. The al-Azhar certificates were standardized vis-à-vis the national system. This law recomposed the institution and created new colleges in such areas as business and administration, Arabic studies, engineering and industries, agriculture, and medicine, in addition to the existing Islamic Colleges. [*See* Azhar, al-.]

In Iran, after the introduction of a Western-influenced educational system, the *maktab* or Qur'ānic school witnessed a significant decline; the only institution that survived the modernizing policies of Reza Shah was the *madrasah,* although the number of students in *madrasah*s declined. Even the sons of prominent mullahs were attracted to the secular schools because of the economic advantages of such degrees.

There is much debate among social scientists regarding the dual system of education in Muslim countries. It is viewed as having generated an antagonism between the *ʿulamāʾ*, who are the product of the traditional religious educational system, and the Western-trained intelligentsia who dispute with them about the legitimate interpretations of religious texts. ʿAlī Sharīʿatī, one of the most distinguished ideologues of the Iranian revolution, expressed criticism of traditional education in the *madrasah;* he considered that the alternative Ḥusaynīyah Irshād Islamic Institute, established in the 1960s by reformist ayatollahs, offered a more stimulating education.

Despite such conflicts, both the *ʿulamāʾ* and the intellectuals who teach in Western-style universities have in most Muslim countries been integrated into the state bureaucratic apparatus and have become professionalized; they simply function through different educational channels. Thus the significance of al-Azhar University in Cairo rests not only in its being the most important Sunnī center in the Muslim world, but equally because it is a huge bureaucratic apparatus providing organizational status, income, teaching facilities, publications, and international networks for a wide range of *ʿulamāʾ* and religious officials.

Renewed Interest. Only in recent years, with the success of the Iranian revolution and the growing impact of the *ʿulamāʾ*, has a renewed interest among scholars concerning the significance of "traditional intellectuals" and their channels of transmission of knowledge been observed. Dale Eickelman (1985) considers that although traditional intellectuals place a particular value upon the past they are not necessarily stagnant, and that traditional social thought is revealed to be politically dominant. He recounts the social biography of a rural Moroccan *ʿālim* who received his education in a rural *madrasah* and *zāwiyah*, an exclusively male student community, and later in a mosque-university in Marrakesh, revealing the intellectual vitality of this traditionally educated class.

With renewed interest in Islam and with further islamization launched by both Muslim state and the religious opposition, there has been a revival of the *madrasah.* For example, under the islamization policies of Zia ul-Haq in Pakistan the *dini madaris* witnessed a flowering; they underwent reforms and their degrees were recognized by the national system. In recent years, a significant Muslim migration from the Indian subcontinent to England, from North Africa to France, and from Turkey to Germany has been accompanied by the establishment of muslim religious schools in Europe. There has been a proliferation of private *madrasahs* as Qur'ānic schools for the European-born children of Muslim migrants.

Turkey has also seen an increase in the number of Imam Hatip schools, which were created in 1951 and which operate as both middle- and high-school levels. In 1986 there were 386 of these schools. Parallel to this, the Muslim world has witnessed the creation of alternative colleges and religious centers of education. For example the African Islamic Centre in Khartoum, Sudan, was founded in 1977. Various faculties of theology were newly established in many Muslim countries, including two faculties of divinity in Turkey; the Islamic Research Institute and the Faculty of Sharīʿah at the University of Damascus, Syria, which was founded some thirty years ago and was influenced by the methods of teaching practiced at al-Azhar; the International Islamic University in Islamabad, Pakistan, and the similar institution in Kuala Lumpur; the International Institute of Islamic Civilization in Kuala Lumpur, Malaysia, established in 1987 as a continuation of the *madrasah* tradition; and the IAIN (Institut Agama Islam Negeri) in Indonesia. These are all examples of contemporary attempts to promote higher Islamic education.

Southeast Asia. In discussing the *madrasahs* of Indonesia it is crucial first to mention the *pondok pesantren,* an educational system spread generally in Malaysia and particularly in the regions of Kedah and Kelantan as well as in Southern Thailand. The word *pondok* comes from the Arabic word *funduq,* meaning "inn"; it is a boarding school for Qur'ānic and other religious subjects. The word *pesantren* comes from *santri,* "religious students." In such a school there is a teacher-leader, the *kijaji/kiyayi,* and a group of male pupils—ranging in number from three or four to a thousand—called *santris.* The *santris* reside in the *pondok* in dormitories, cook their own food, and wash their own clothes. There are also *pesantren* for female students and others with segregated male and female quarters. The students travel from one *pesantren* to another to obtain a certificate *(ijazah)* in various religious subjects, but they always return to the mother *pesantren* once a year to maintain the link. The *santris* lead a very disciplined and regulated religious life. Lombard has pointed out (*Le carrefour javanais,* vol. 2, *Les reseaux asiatiques,* Paris, 1990) that the functioning of most of the *pesantrens* in Indonesia relies heavily on the person of the *kiyayi.* The *pesantren* usually faces decline with the death of the *kiyayi* and thus lacks continuity. In Indonesia there are around forty thousand *pesantren* teaching eight million students. Most of these schools are in rural areas.

Perhaps what makes a *pesantren* different from the traditional Middle Eastern *madrasah* is the fact that the former never belonged to royal patrons, nor did they rely on *waqf* funding; they are instead dependent on personal contributions. Recently important changes have occurred in some *pesantren* with the introduction of classes, chairs, and tables. Special attention should be drawn to the famous Gontor Pondok Moderen, "Pendidikan Darrusalam" at Gontor Ponorogo in East Java. This *pesantren* is significant for sending a number of students to the Middle East. Arabic and English are the medium of instruction. The *pesantren* itself has many returning Indonesian graduates from the Middle East who teach there. The certificate offered by Gontor is recognized by al-Azhar University.

The *madrasah diniya* are a special category of *madrasah* that provide religious instruction to pupils within the state school system. After completion of state secondary schooling, these students are admitted to religious studies at a tertiary level. These schools are divided into *madrasahs* for elementary and higher education, called the *madrasah ibtida'iya* ("primary school"), *madrasah thanawiya* ("secondary school"), and *madrasah ʿaliya* ("high school"). The *madrasah ibtidaʿiya negeri* (M.I.N.) is a six-year elementary state *madrasah.* Since the 1970s the government has introduced secular subjects into the *madrasahs*; in 1994 religious subjects constitute 30 percent of the elementary curriculum, while in the *ʿaliya* religious subjects constitute 70 percent. In recent years the modernization of the *pesantrens* and *madrasahs* under the auspices of one of the largest religious movements in Indonesia, the Nahdatul Ulama, has been perceived as a positive step toward the integration of *madrasah* and *pesantren* graduates into the national higher-education system.

In Singapore there are now thirty-six Islamic religious schools and *madrasahs*, of which only four offer both primary and secondary education. Since 1971 these schools have introduced mathematics, science, and English, and their students can sit for the same examinations as students from secular schools. These *madrasahs* are a link to the Middle East, and their students' success is measured by their admission to study at al-Azhar or any other Middle Eastern institution. Al-Azhar recognizes only the certificates from Madrasah al-Junied al-Islamiiah, and any student wanting to travel to the Middle East must complete one year in this *madrasah*. As a result of financial problems, MUIS (Majlis Ugama Islam Singapora, the Islamic Religious Council of Singapore) recently placed the *madrasahs* under its auspices in order to support the system.

In the early 1960s the *pondoks* of Thailand underwent state intervention that transformed them into regular private schools with special emphasis on religious education. The most important contributions the students of the *pondok* make while studying is preaching in remote areas. The *pondoks* have recently come under the control of the Thai state, and further government intervention in the *pondok* curriculum has led to students being sent abroad to study in Middle Eastern countries. These students have become a channel through which external Islamic influence has been brought into Thailand.

[*See also* Education; Khānqāh; Mosque; Pesantren; Universities; Zāwiyah.]

BIBLIOGRAPHY

Boland, B. J. *The Struggle of Islam in Modern Indonesia*. The Hague, 1971. Insightful overview of the role of Islam in contemporary Indonesia since the Japanese invasion.

Eccel, A. Chris. *Egypt, Islam, and Social Change: Al-Azhar in Conflict and Accommodation*. Berlin, 1984. Extensive and rich study of the evolution of Al-Azhar University and mosque.

Eickelman, Dale F. *Knowledge and Power in Morocco: The Education of a Twentieth-Century Notable*. Princeton, 1985. Brilliant study of the education of a Moroccan notable, with information about the *madrasah* in Morocco.

Faruqi, Zia-ul-Hasan. *The Deoband School and the Demand for Pakistan*. London, 1963. One of the best studies of the Deoband school.

Feillard, Andrée. "Les oulema indonésiens aujourd'hui: De l'opposition à une nouvelle légitimité." *Archipel*, no. 46 (1993): 89–111.

Gardet, Louis. *Les hommes de l'Islam: Approche des mentalités*. Paris, 1977. Interesting "history of mentalities" approach to Islamic history.

Geertz, Clifford. *The Religion of Java*. New York, 1960. Excellent study of the various religions in Java, with outstanding information on the *pesantren* and *madrasah*.

Kepel, Gilles, and Yann Richard. *Intellectuels et militants de l'Islam contemporain*. Paris, 1990. Collection of essays about the tensions between traditional and Western-trained intellectuals in contemporary Muslim societies.

Lapidus, Ira. *A History of Islamic Societies*. Cambridge, 1989. Excellent historical survey of Islamic institutions, politics, and culture in the Muslim world.

Lombard, Denys. *Le carrefour javanais: Essai d'histoire globale*, vol. 2, *Les réseaux asiatiques*. Paris, 1990. Fascinating study of Javanese spiritual and material culture, with insightful data on religious education in Indonesia.

Makdisi, George. *The Rise of Colleges: Institutions of Learning in Islam and the West*. Edinburgh, 1981. The best study to date of the growth of colleges, their methods of teaching, and various types of institutions in medieval Islam.

Malik, S. Jamal. *Islamisierung in Pakistan, 1977–84: Untersuchungen zur Auflösung autochthoner Strukturen*. Stuttgart, 1988. Perceptive study of politics, religion, and changing educational patterns in Pakistan.

Metcalf, Barbara D. *Islamic Revival in British India: Deoband, 1860–1900*. Princeton, 1982. The best study to date of the Deoband school and the role of the Indian *ʿulamāʾ* in politics and education.

Mottahedeh, Roy P. *The Mantle of the Prophet: Religion and Politics in Iran*. New York, 1985. Excellent biography of an Iranian Muslim scholar, with descriptions of the evolution of the *madrasah* in Iran.

Pedersen, Johannes, et al. "Madrasa." In *Encyclopaedia of Islam*, new ed., vol. 5, pp. 1123–1154. Leiden, 1960–.

Pitsuwan, Surin. *Islam and Malay Nationalism: A Case Study of the Malay-Muslims of Southern Thailand*. Bangkok, 1985. The best study to date of the Muslims in Thailand.

Reed, Howard A. "Ataturk's Secularizing Legacy and the Continuing Vitality of Islam in Republican Turkey." In *Islam in the Contemporary World*, edited by Cyriac K. Pullapilly, pp. 316–339. Notre Dame, Ind., 1980. Insightful data on the role of the state and religion in Turkey.

Richard, Yann. *L'Islam Chiʿite*. Paris, 1991. Overview of Iranian Islam and contemporary intellectual trends.

Saint-Blancat, Chantal. "Hypothèse sur l'évolution de l'Islam transplanté en Europe." *Social Compass* 40.2 (1993): 323–342.

Snouck Hurgronje, Christiaan. *Mekka in the Latter Part of the Nineteenth Century: Daily Life, Customs, and Learning; The Moslims of the East-Indian-Archipelago*. Translated by J. H. Monahan. Leiden and London, 1931. Lively anthropological study of Meccan life, containing insights into the religious teachings and customs of the Meccans and other communities.

Talas, Asad. *La madrasa Nizamiyya et son histoire*. Paris, 1939. Exemplary study of the most important *madrasah* in medieval Islam.

MONA ABAZA

MAGAZINES. *See* Newspapers and Magazines.

MAGIC AND SORCERY. According to Henri Hubert and Marcel Mauss ("Esquisse d'une théorie générale de la magie," in Mauss's *Sociologie et anthropologie*, Paris, 1950, pp. 1–141), magic must be distinguished from religion. While religious rites and prayers are conducted by special clergies for the sake of the community, magic is usually practiced privately for individual purposes. Indeed, the practice of magic has tended to be regarded as an antisocial, malevolent activity, and magicians, wizards, witches and sorcerers have often been accused of being followers of the devil, punished, and executed (though there have usually been other political, economic, and historical reasons for these persecutions).

A similarly negative attitude toward magic exists in various Muslim societies. Educated people in particular, whether traditionalists or modernists, have been apt to look down on magical practices as mere superstitions of the ignorant and to criticize them as *bidʿah* or heretical innovation. [*See* Bidʿah.] However, there remain various types of magical practices among Muslim communities, some of them apparent survivals of pre-Islamic belief and practice, and they have in fact played a significant role in popular Islam.

Classification. In his detailed ethnography of the Egyptian people in the early decades of the nineteenth century (*An Account of the Manners and Customs of the Modern Egyptians*, London, 1836), based mainly on the people of Cairo, Edward W. Lane observed that intellectual Muslims in those days distinguished two kinds of magical practices. The first, called *al-rūḥānī* or spiritual magic, depended on the mysterious supernatural power possessed by spiritual agents such as angels, *jinns*, and certain names of God. *Al-rūḥānī* was considered to be true magic and was subdivided into "high" or divine magic and "low" or satanic magic. High magic, which depended on the mysterious power of God, angels, and other good spiritual agents, was always practiced for a good purpose, such as using a charm to avert misfortunes. Low magic, on the other hand, was said to be used for sinister purposes through the agency of the devil or evil spirits. Its practitioner was called *sāḥir,* a sorcerer. This division roughly corresponded to that between white and black magic.

Second, there was *al-sīmiyā* or natural magic, in which natural materials like certain perfumes and drugs were used rather than supernatural agents. Lane also discussed astrology, geomancy, and alchemy, which at that time were popular and widely studied by many Egyptians. These "sciences" were generally regarded as being different from magic. There was also a wide range of folk practices that were not based on the forms of magic or the "sciences" mentioned above. These were called "distaff" science or wisdom *(ʿilm al-rukkah)* and were practiced predominantly by women.

Magicians and Amulets. Magic is mostly practiced by experts who are believed in some way to acquire special knowledge and techniques for controlling supernatural agencies, which they use in response to requests from their clients. As Winifred S. Blackman described in her ethnography *The Fellahīn of Upper Egypt* (London, 1927), there was at least one magician living in every village of Upper Egypt in the early decades of the twentieth century. Formally they were respected as possessors of esoteric knowledge who could contribute to the villagers' welfare. In some contexts, however, they were greatly feared as sinister sorcerers who could use the same power for the opposite purpose of destroying people's fortunes. There is evidence that the magician generally plays a morally ambiguous role in various parts of the Muslim world.

In Upper Egypt these magicians have usually been called *shaykh* if male, or *shaykhah* if female. A Sudanese magician is generally called a *faqī*, a local term supposed to be derived from a combination of two Arabic words, *faqīr* (a mystic or Ṣūfī) and *faqīh* (a jurist or one of the *ʿulamāʾ*). Not only teachers in the Qurʾānic schools but also leaders of Ṣūfī orders *(ṭarīqah)* could be called *faqī*. [*See* Faqīh.] Some of them provide clients with magical medicine or amulets that contain mainly excerpts from the holy scriptures, and they thus play the role of magician in their communities. (There are also magical specialists without any relationship to *ʿulamāʾ* or to Ṣūfī orders.) One *faqī* who is also the head of the Qādirīyah Ṣūfī order in a town in the Northern Sudan writes excerpts from the Qurʾān on small pieces of paper after the collective prayers on Friday, in compliance with clients' requests. After returning home, the clients may burn them in order to rub their bodies with the smoke or soak them in water to dissolve the ink, which is then drunk. These magical papers are also used as the principal elements in amulets. Similar forms of magical practice are found in many Muslim societies, though with subtle differences. For example, a magician may write a passage from scripture on the inner surface of an earthen bowl in ink, pour water in it and stir it to dissolve the writing. The client is then asked to drink the liquid as a cure for illness.

Certain passages from the Qurʾān are frequently used in magical practice. They include passages such as surahs 1, 112, 113, and 114, and single verses such as surah 12.64 or surah 61.11 for an amulet, and surah

9.14 or surah 10.58 for a cure. The ninety-nine epithets of God, the ninety-nine names of the Prophet, and the names of the "companions of the cave" (Aṣḥāb al-Kahf) as well as copies of the Qur'ān itself *(muṣḥaf)* are believed to have supernatural power that can be effective in a variety of magical practices.

Besides these holy scriptures and writings, some objects are believed to have supernatural power and can be used as effective amulets. Among them are water from the Zamzam Well in Mecca and pieces of the cloth cover of the Kaʿbah *(kiswah)*. Relics of Muslim saints are treated as sacred in the same way.

Sorcery. Many Muslims believe in the existence of black magic or sorcery in their own societies. Blackman in the account cited above mentions a case in which a man who wanted to divorce his wife asked a magician to make her hate him, and another in which a magician, at a client's request, used magic to kill one of the client's enemies. She cites a story that in one village a marriage notary who fell in love with the beautiful wife of a villager asked a magician to write a charm to drive her husband insane. It is noteworthy that in these magical practices, the name of the victim's mother must be referred to in the charm and incantation, not that of the victim's father; this is inconsistent with the usual emphasis on patrilineality in Arab societies.

According to Edward Westermarck (1926), sorcerers in Morocco called *saḥḥār* (male) or *saḥḥārah* (female) practiced magic related to sex, for instance to make a man impotent or to protect the virtue of an unmarried girl. This type of magic was named *thaqāf*.

Cursing and the Evil Eye. Folk belief in the evil eye can be distinguished from ordinary magic and sorcery and is widespread in Middle Eastern societies. The evil eye, which is called *ḥasad* ("envy") or *ʿayn* ("eye") in Arabic and *chashm-i shūr* ("salty eye") in Persian, is a folk belief that some persons can glance or stare at someone else's favorite possession and, if they are envious of the latter's good fortune, can hurt, damage, or destroy it. Although some people, especially the educated, tend to disdain this belief as mere superstition, others insist that the evil eye really exists because of a reference to it in surah 113.5 of the Qur'ān.

There are a number of ways to defend oneself against the evil eye. One of the best ways to avert the misfortunes it can cause is to use the holy scriptures and other forms of writing mentioned above. Since the hand is believed to be effective in warding off its attacks, hand-shaped amulets made of metal or plastic are popular forms of protection. It is said that a boy is much more vulnerable to attack than a girl, and some parents may disguise a boy in girl's clothes or call him by a name other than his real one to protect him.

Although the evil eye attacks its target secretly, people can put a curse on their enemies openly by speaking. A person may curse another by invoking the names of a supernatural being, either God or a saint. Unlike an ordinary curse that resembles sorcery in its function, curses that use the names of God or saints are generally considered as punitive attacks on sinners rather than malevolent attacks on the innocent.

In Morocco, people can put a conditional curse called *ʿār* on others in order to compel them to comply with requests. Even though the *ʿulamā'* often criticize *ʿār* as non-Islamic, among the Moroccans, it appears that one can cast an *ʿār* on the Prophet or the saints, or even on God.

[*See also* Popular Religion.]

BIBLIOGRAPHY

Ibrahim, Hayder. *The Shaiqiya: The Cultural and Social Change of a Northern Sudanese Riverain People*. Wiesbaden, 1979. Ethnography of an ethnic group of the northern Sudan which includes information about the Sudanese *faqī*, *jinn* (spirit), and the evil eye in villages.

Westermarck, Edward. *Rituals and Belief in Morocco*. 2 vols. London, 1926. Encyclopaedic study of Moroccan folk beliefs and rituals based on the author's field research at the turn of the century, from which we can obtain valuable information about magic, sorcery, evil eye, and *ʿār*.

Winstedt, Richard. *The Malay Magician (1951)*. Kuala Lumpur, 1982. Account of magical practices in a Muslim country of Southeast Asia, a region not covered in this article.

KAZUO OHTSUKA

MAHDI. The term *mahdī* ("divinely guided one") has come to denote an eschatological figure whose presence will usher in an era of justice and true belief prior to the end of time. The origin of the word cannot be traced to the Qur'ān, where in fact it is never mentioned, but rather to a strictly honorific title applied to the Prophet and first four caliphs by the earliest Muslims. The term was further developed by the Shīʿīs, who applied it to Muḥammad ibn al-Ḥanafīyah (a son of the caliph ʿAlī) who organized a revolt in 685. A Shīʿī sect later came to revere this "rightly guided one" and deny his death, believing him to be in hiding. Other events in the history of Shiism paralleled this example—the Twelfth

Imam, Muḥammad ibn Ḥasan al-ʿAskarī, who disappeared in 878, was designated a Mahdi—and so the idea evolved of a messianic deliverer *(al-Mahdī al-muntaẓar)* who would return to champion the cause of his adherents.

Although the idea of a Mahdi came to play a central part in Shīʿī belief, it enjoyed no such recognition in Sunnī Islam, where trust in the consensus of the learned and faith in the community's capacity for self-reform made such a figure doctrinally unnecessary. Rather, the concept took hold strictly in popular Sunnī belief during the early centuries of political unrest. Supporting various contenders in their claims was a large and ever-growing body of prophetic traditions *(ḥadīth)* regarding the Mahdi. Certain common themes run through these developing traditions: the Mahdi will be of the Prophet's family, he will bear the Prophet's name, and his father will bear the Prophet's father's name (i.e., he will be called Muḥammad ibn ʿAbd Allāh); he will appear when the world has reached its worst state of affairs; his reign will be a time of natural abundance, and he will spread justice, restore the faith, and defeat the enemies of Islam; miraculous signs will accompany his manifestation, and he will be generous and divide the wealth. On many matters the traditions disagree—hence their broad applicability. In general, the Sunnī notion of a Mahdi came to represent more a restorer of the faith than the Shīʿī incarnation of God, and one who would be chosen for office rather than returning from hiding. Important vehicles for the spread of this idea were the writings of various Ṣūfī sages, including the influential Ibn al-ʿArabī (d. 1240).

Attesting to the popularity of the Mahdi idea is the abundance of claimants to that title in Islamic history. Muḥammad ʿUbayd Allāh (d. 934), the first Fāṭimid caliph, came to power in North Africa through a manipulation of Mahdist expectations and Shīʿī sentiment. Manifesting himself at Jabal Massa in the Maghrib—thereafter an expected site of the Mahdi's appearance—he claimed descent from the Prophet's daughter Fāṭimah and was alleged to be the brother of the hidden Twelfth Imam. The founder of the Almohad reform movement in the twelfth century, Muḥammad ibn Tūmart (d. 1130), also claimed to be the Mahdi with descent from the Caliph ʿAlī. In particular, the arrival of the thirteenth Islamic century (1785–1883 CE), which had long been expected as a time of great messianic importance, increased Mahdist belief. During that period at least three leaders of reform movements in West Africa—Shaykh Usuman dan Fodio of Sokoto, Shaykh Aḥmadu Bari of Masina and al-Ḥājj ʿUmar Tal of the Tukolor empire—exploited Mahdist tendencies to launch their *jihāds*. Expectations of the Mahdi's arrival from the east attracted waves of West African emigrants to the Nile and facilitated the rise and success of the Sudanese Mahdi Muḥammad Aḥmad (d. 1885). [*See the biographies of Dan Fodio and ʿUmar Tal.*] Several Mahdis meanwhile arose in Egypt, leading uprisings against both French occupation and Egyptian government rule. By the end of the 19th century, Mahdist revolts against European imperialism were almost commonplace, occurring for example in India, Algeria, Senegal, Ghana, and Nigeria. Common to all such movements was the perceived corruption of Islamic ideals and nefarious influence of Western political and cultural hegemony. More recently, such thinking inspired the 1979 seizure of the Grand Mosque of Mecca by a Saudi Arabian Mahdi; Shīʿī criticism of the American-led "New World Order" has also been couched in Mahdist terms. Given the emotive power of messianism and the flexible conditions of the Mahdi's appearance, claims to that authority may be expected wherever Islamic interests are perceived to be threatened.

[*See also* Eschatology; Messianism; Revival and Renewal.]

BIBLIOGRAPHY

Holt, P. M. "Islamic Millenarianism and the Fulfillment of Prophecy." In *Prophecy and Millenarianism*, edited by Ann Williams, pp. 337–347. London, 1980. Overview of the Sudanese Mahdīyah within the context of Islamic ideas of a Mahdi.

Ibn Khaldūn. *The Muqaddimah*. 3 vols. Translated by Franz Rosenthal. New York, 1958. Classic study of the philosophy of history and sociology, written in 1377 by the North African Arab scholar. Chapter 3 contains an important discussion of Muslim popular beliefs in a Mahdi, with emphasis on Ṣūfī and Shīʿī influences.

Sachedina, A. A. *Islamic Messianism: The Idea of Mahdī in Twelver Shīʿism*. Albany, N.Y., 1981. The most complete study to date of the idea of a Mahdi in Islam, emphasizing Shīʿī beliefs but also treating the development of the idea in Sunnī Islam.

ROBERT S. KRAMER

MAHDĪ, AL-ṢĀDIQ AL- (b. 1936), Sudanese Islamic-Mahdist theologian and contemporary political leader. As great-grandson of the Sudanese Mahdi, Muḥammad Aḥmad ibn ʿAbdallāh (d. 1885), Ṣādiq was born into a leading Islamic family and trained for his leadership role from birth. [*See* Mahdi; Mahdīyah.] He received a broad traditional Muslim education and later a modern one at Victoria College in Alexandria. He then studied at the University of Khartoum and graduated from St. Johns College, Oxford, where he read philosophy, politics, and economics. Ṣādiq rose to prominence in 1961 following the death of his father, Imam Ṣiddīq al-Mahdī. The *shūrā* council of the Anṣār decided that he was too young to become their imam and appointed his uncle al-Hādī instead. With the leadership divided and Ṣādiq heading the Ummah party, a split within the Ummah and the Anṣār became unavoidable. It paved the way for a long-term pact between Ṣādiq and Ḥasan al-Turābī, the leader of Sudan's Muslim Brothers. This was probably one of the factors that led Ṣādiq, a presumed liberal, to announce his intention, on becoming prime minister in 1966, to promulgate an Islamic constitution and found an Islamic state. Ṣādiq and his followers were defeated in the 1968 elections and had to seek a reconciliation with his conservative uncle. This seems to have turned him into a conservative, and the Ummah-Anṣār complex in the 1980s was as autocratic as it had been under previous imams. As prime minister after the 1986 elections, Ṣādiq was in full control of both the Anṣār and the Ummah. His failure to lead on the most crucial issues, the Islamic nature of the state and its interethnic and interreligious relations, probably caused his downfall in June 1989.

Ṣādiq was the most prominent leader to oppose the so-called *sharīʿah* laws implemented by President Jaʿfar Nimeiri in September 1983. He denounced them as un-Islamic because *sharīʿah* could only be implemented in a just society in which Muslims were not forced to steal in order to survive. He failed to abolish these laws, however, while he was prime minister in 1986–1989, owing both to his ambivalence and to his weak leadership. His ambivalence was the result of his reluctance to abolish the existing Islamic laws, which after all he too had advocated, without introducing alternative ones first. He assumed that he would lose popular support if he submitted to southern and secularist demands for unconditional abrogation.

Ṣādiq has expressed his views on the Islamic state in many of his writings, and in these his ideology is by far more liberal and progressive than his political career would suggest. He rules that modern formulation of *sharīʿah* should be entrusted to universities, with lay scholarly supervision; otherwise *sharīʿah* will wither away, and Muslim leaders will have abdicated their trust. Islamic states may be traditional, modernizing, or revolutionary, as long as they abide by the general constitutional principles of Islam and as long as their legal systems are based on a traditional or modern formulation of *sharīʿah*. In the sphere of economics, two principles should be applied. First, wealth is collectively owned by humanity, and while individual ownership is legitimate, society has to provide for the poor. Second, it is mandatory to implement special injunctions such as *zakāt*, inheritance laws, and the prohibition of usury. Hence there is no contradiction in an economic system that is both Islamic and modern. Islamic international relations, according to Ṣādiq, are to be based on peaceful coexistence; war is justified to deter aggression and is not permitted as a way of enforcing Islam. Even pagans are not to be converted by force. In Islamic international relations there are four basic principles: human brotherhood, the supremacy of justice, the irreversibility of contracts, and reciprocity. Finally, Ṣādiq regards *taqlīd*, or the uncritical adoption of a tradition or a legal decision, as a major curse; he claims that when non-Muslim opinion refers to Islamic fundamentalism, it is *taqlīd* they have in mind, which therefore should be abolished.

[*See also* Anṣār; Sudan; Ummah-Anṣār; *and the biography of Turābī.*]

BIBLIOGRAPHY

Mahdī, Al-Ṣādiq al-. *Yas'alūnaka ʿan al-Mahdīyah*. Beirut, 1975.

Mahdī, Al-Ṣādiq al-. "The Concept of an Islamic State." In *The Challenge of Islam*, edited by Altaf Gauhar, pp. 114–133. London, 1978.

Mahdī, Al-Ṣādiq al-. "Islam—Society and Change." In *Voices of Resurgent Islam*, edited by John L. Esposito, pp. 230–240. New York and Oxford, 1983.

Mahdī, Al-Ṣādiq al-. *Al-dīmuqrāṭīyah fī al-Sūdān, ʿā'ida wa-rājiḥah*. Khartoum, 1990.

Gabriel R. Warburg

MAHDĪYAH. In the last twenty years of the nineteenth century, the northern territories of the present-day Democratic Republic of the Sudan were dominated by a politico-religious movement that aimed initially to reform worldwide Islam, but that was ultimately realized in the formation of a territorial state along the Nile. Although its fortunes and ideals changed with the fluctuating political conditions within and outside the Sudan, the movement—popularly called the Mahdīyah after its founder—succeeded in creating symbols and evoking an ethos that have had lasting importance to Sudanese identity.

Turco-Egyptian rule of the Nilotic Sudan, which had been established by the armies of the Egyptian viceroy Muḥammad ʿAlī Pasha from 1820 to 1822, began to unravel with the spread of a revolutionary movement led by Muḥammad ʿAhmad al-Sayyid ʿAbd Allāh, a shaykh of the Sammānīyah Ṣūfī brotherhood originally from the region of Dongola, who in 1881 declared himself to be the "Expected Mahdi" (al-Mahdī al-Muntaẓar) and called for the overthrow of Turkish rule. Muḥammad Aḥmad's millenarian message of an age of justice and equity prior to the end of time was readily accepted by a Sudanese people suffering the dislocating effects of Turco-Egyptian rule; moreover, the timing of the Mahdi's mainfestation at the end of the thirteenth Islamic century accorded with messianic expectations long held across the Sudanic belt of Africa and along the Nile River Valley. Asserting his conformity with Sunnī doctrines of the Mahdi contained in the authoritative *ḥadīth* literature (doctrines numerous and contradictory enough to establish almost any claim), Muḥammad Aḥmad confounded his critics from the *ʿulamāʾ*, and his military successes against government troops sent to arrest him enhanced his credibility among both sedentary and nomadic populations. After an initial victory in August 1881 at his base on Abā Island, the Mahdi moved from the White Nile region to the more defensible highlands of the Nuba Mountains in the west-central province of Kordofan. In a deliberate reference to the Prophet's own experience, the Mahdi termed this withdrawal a Hijrah and named his followers *anṣār* ("helpers"), while calling for a *jihād* against all "unbelievers" who opposed him. The name of his sanctuary in Kordofan, Jabal Qadīr, was changed to Māssa in further conformity to messianic tradition. Two more government expeditions sent to capture him were defeated in 1881 and 1882. As pastoral Arab tribesmen of the west (Baqqāra) flocked to his banner, the Mahdi laid siege to the provincial capital al-Ubayyid, which surrendered in January 1883. After destroying a British-commanded Egyptian force at Shaykān in Kordofan in November 1883, the Mahdi accepted the surrender of the remaining Egyptian garrisons in the west; by early 1884 he was effectively in command of at least the northern provinces of the Egyptian Sudan. The capital city Khartoum alone held out against the Mahdi's forces, but after the fall of the city of Berber in May 1884 and the closure of the Nile escape route, Khartoum's fate was sealed. On 25 January 1885, Khartoum was taken, its British governor General Charles Gordon being killed in the fighting. The Mahdi next retired to his army's encampment at Omdurman on the western bank of the Nile, anxious to avoid the spiritual contamination of "the city of the Turks." Six months later he was dead, the victim of a sudden illness, and his body was laid to rest in Omdurman. His tomb *(al-Qubbah)* towered over the city, a reminder of the Mahdi's teachings and a symbol of the movement he had launched.

The man who assumed the leadership of the Mahdist state, ʿAbd Allāh ibn Muḥammad of the Taʿāʾishah Baqqārah, had been one of the Mahdi's earliest followers as well as his most powerful general, commanding the huge western tribal levies. In official Mahdist ideology the Mahdi had represented the successor to the prophet Muḥammad (Khalīfat Rasūl Allāh), while ʿAbd Allāh represented the successor to the first caliph, Abū Bakr (Khalīfat al-Ṣiddīq); two further leaders, ʿAlī ibn Muḥammad Ḥilw of the White Nile Arabs and the Mahdi's cousin Muḥammad Sharīf ibn Ḥāmid, respectively represented the successors to the caliphs ʿUmar (Khalīfat al-Farūq) and ʿAlī (Khalīfat al-Karrār). (Succession to the caliph ʿUthmān, offered to Muḥammad al-Mahdī of the Libyan Sanūsīyah, was declined.)

ʿAbd Allāh's identification as *khalīfat al-ṣiddīq* helped solve the ideological problem of the Mahdi's premature death; however, the more practical problems of governing the Sudan plagued Khalīfah ʿAbd Allāh throughout his reign. On two occasions, in 1886 and 1891, he faced overt challenges to his leadership from the Mahdi's jealous kinsmen the Ashrāf, led by the junior *khalīfah* Muḥammad Sharīf. Throughout the period an underlying tension between the settled riverine population *(awlād al-balad)* and the western pastoralists who had emigrated to the Nile *(awlād al-ʿArab)* eroded the Mahdist ideal of a unified community and intensified economic and political competition within the state. A famine in the years 1888–1890, originating in natural causes but exacerbated by the Khalīfah's policy of forced migration to the capital, decimated the population. Meanwhile the Khalīfah's tendency to concentrate authority in his own hands and those of his brother, Amīr Yaʿqūb, robbed his subordinates of needed initiative and led to serious administrative failings. The institutional development of the state did not advance much beyond what the Mahdīyah had inherited from the previous regime (many Mahdist officials had in fact earlier served the Turks), and leadership of both the judiciary and the state treasury often fell victim to political expediency. Finally, the *jihād* itself, the original raison d'être of the Mahdīyah, came to an effective end with the destruction of a Mahdist army by the Anglo-Egyptians at Tushki, north of Wadi Halfa, in August 1889. Although fighting continued along the state's borders for the remainder of the period, no further effort was made to export the Mahdist movement.

To his credit the Khalīfah was able to convince most Sudanese of his personal integrity long after they had grown disaffected with his regime; his status as Khalīfat al-Mahdī continued to carry supreme moral and political authority. However, just as the Mahdīyah was beginning to coalesce into a socioreligious and political order, foreign powers were planning its destruction. An Anglo-Egyptian invasion of the Sudan, carried out on behalf of larger British imperial interests, began with the occupation of Dongola province in 1896. Within a year a railway had been built across the Nubian desert, safeguarding Anglo-Egyptian supply lines, and the invasion proceeded steadily up the Nile. The end of the Mahdīyah came at the battle of Karari, north of Omdurman, on 2 September 1898. The Khalīfah himself survived the battle and fled with a small following into Kordofan, only to be hunted down and killed by a British force one year later. For the next fifty-six years the Sudan was ruled by an Anglo-Egyptian Condominium, though Mahdist belief persisted: F. R. Wingate, governor-general from 1899 to 1916, was regarded by some former *anṣār* as the Antichrist (al-Dajjāl), who in theory was supposed to follow the Mahdi; and numerous neo-Mahdist revolts erupted in the first two decades of the new regime.

Viewed in the context of modern Sudanese history, the Mahdīyah represents an acceleration of the ongoing process of arabization and islamization, as the Mahdi's practice of Islam—essentially the normative Islam of the riverine population—was adopted by other Sudanese peoples. With the creation of powerful symbols of common identity (e.g., the Mahdi as leader and Omdurman as capital), a degree of national coherence was imparted to the otherwise disparate provinces of the region. The obvious legacy of the period has been the Anṣār religious movement, established by the Mahdi's posthumous son ʿAbd al-Raḥmān (1885–1959), and its political branch the Ummah Party (founded in 1945). Both derive their chief support from the former Mahdist strongholds of Kordofan, Darfur, and White Nile provinces, though reverence for the Mahdi's family and observance of his collection of prayers *(rātib)* are common throughout the northern Sudan. In a wider context, the Mahdīyah has been interpreted variously as a fundamentalist movement within the Islamic tradition of reform and renewal, a protonationalist and anticolonial movement, or even an example of "Semitic messianism."

[*See also* Anṣār; Mahdi; Revival and Renewal; Sudan; Ummah-Anṣār.]

BIBLIOGRAPHY

Bedri, Babikr (Badrī, Bābakr). *The Memoirs of Babikr Bedri.* Translated by Yousef Bedri and George Scott. London, 1969. This translation of the first volume of a three-volume autobiography covers the author's life up to the defeat of the Mahdist state in 1898, and provides the fascinating perspective of a loyal follower of the Mahdi on the events of the period.

Holt, P. M. *The Mahdist State in the Sudan; 1881–1898.* 2d ed. Oxford, 1970. The most scholarly treatment of the subject, focusing on the institutional development of the Mahdist state and the political history of the period, stressing the importance of the Mahdīyah in its Islamic and African contexts. Contains an extensive and critical bibliography.

Sanderson, G. N. *England, Europe, and the Upper Nile, 1882–1899.* Edinburgh, 1965. Excellent study of the European diplomatic and political contexts of events during the Mahdist period, taking into account the larger region of the Nile River Valley.

Shaked, Haim. *The Life of the Sudanese Mahdi.* New Brunswick, N.J., 1978. Summary translation of the official Mahdist biography of the Mahdi, Ismāʿīl ibn ʿAbd al-Qādir's *Kitāb saʿādat al-mustahdī bi-sīrat al-Imām al-Mahdī* (The Book of the Bliss of Him Who Seeks Guidance by the Life of the Imam the Mahdi). The original work, completed in November 1888, reflects official Mahdist thinking on the Mahdi's life and times, and hence provides a useful comparison to the memoirs of Babikr Bedri.

Shuqayr, Naʿūm. *Tārīkh al-Sūdān al-qadīm wa'l-ḥadīth wa jughrāfīyatuhu* (The Ancient and Modern History of the Sudan and Its Geography). 3 vols. Cairo, 1903. The most important contemporary work on the Mahdist period, written by a former officer of the Egyptian Military Intelligence who had unrivaled access to both written materials and oral accounts. Much of the primary source material provided in volume 3 is unique.

ROBERT S. KRAMER

MAḤKAMAH. Meaning a "place of judgment," the term *maḥkamah* has come to refer to all forms of law court in the Arabic-speaking world. In traditional Islamic settings, emphasis was placed on the individual judge, for instance the *qāḍī* or the *amīr,* rather than on the institution. Often there was no specialized building which might be referred to as a court; judges heard cases in marketplaces, mosques, private dwellings, or the audience chambers of palaces. Sometimes the judge was assisted by a consultative council *(majlis)* made up of legal scholars. Discrete judicial institutions with their own distinct space emerged gradually in response to increases in the volume of cases, the complexity of the judicial apparatus, the emphasis on record keeping, and the independence of the judiciary.

Beginning in the nineteenth century, westernizing indigenous regimes and European colonial administrations accelerated this process of institutionalization, eventually creating complex integrated structures of courts under the supervision of a central ministry of justice. This process was accompanied by the substitution of European for indigenous bodies of law (not only *sharīʿah* but also *qānūn*, *ʿādat*, and *ḥukm*), especially in criminal, commercial, and administrative matters. Only personal status law remained Islamic, and even here, the local *qāḍī*'s court was made subject to a European-style hierarchy of appellate courts and centralized regulation. With independence from colonial rule and the spread of nationalism in the mid-twentieth century, the personal status courts in many Islamic countries lost their separate identity and became, at least in theory, fully integrated into national court systems under such rubrics as *maḥkamah juz'īyah* (Egypt) or Area Court (northern Nigeria). In most cases, however, they continued to apply the *sharīʿah*.

Of the various types of court within a national system, it is the *qāḍī*'s court (whatever its official bureaucratic appellation) which has the most bearing on the daily lives of ordinary people through its jurisdiction over marriage, divorce, guardianship, inheritance, and minor civil cases. It also provides notarial services of the *ʿudūl* (sg., *ʿādil*) or certified witnesses. The *qāḍī*'s *maḥkamah* is likely to employ a scribe, a doorkeeper or usher, and sometimes specialists with technical knowledge in matters frequently brought before the court. Sometimes a professional legal representative *(wakīl)* may appear in the court with or on behalf of a client. Many observers have noted that the people who appear in the *qāḍī*'s court are frequently poor and often female. This court is the forum in which they pursue their negotiations over rights and obligations, no matter how apparently trivial.

The close integration of the *qāḍī*'s court with popular life, and the fact that other courts tend to be identified with a distant, alien bureaucratic state, have contributed to demands voiced by Islamist political movements in the late twentieth century for a reislamization of the law, especially in criminal matters. These calls for reislamization, however, tend to emphasize the content of the law, demanding replacement of Western-style codes by the *sharīʿah,* rather than challenging the bureaucratic structure and style of modern courts.

[*See also* Qāḍī.]

BIBLIOGRAPHY

Azmeh, Aziz al-, ed. *Islamic Law: Social and Historical Contexts*. London, 1988.

Christelow, Allan. *Muslim Law Courts and the French Colonial State in Algeria*. Princeton, 1985.

Hill, Enid. *Mahkama! Studies in the Egyptian Legal System*. London, 1979.

Rosen, Lawrence. *The Anthropology of Justice: Law as Culture in Islamic Society*. Cambridge, 1989. Study of the relation of courts to their cultural environment in Morocco.

Starr, June. *Law as Metaphor: From Islamic Courts to the Palace of Justice*. Albany, N.Y., 1991. Examines the emergence of the secular Turkish legal system in a region of western Anatolia.

ALLAN CHRISTELOW

MAḤMŪD, MUṢṬAFĀ (b. 1921), leading Egyptian Islamist philosopher, author, and scientist. Many scholars argue that Islamism in the Middle East is, among other things, a reaction against Marxism and that ex-Marxists have turned increasingly to Islam as an antimodernist ideology. Egypt's Muṣṭafā Maḥmūd, a widely known and generally respected figure, might appear to represent just such a trend. Maḥmūd has indeed rejected Marxism and has distinguished himself as an Islamist; but he is far from an antimodernist. Trained as a physician, Maḥmūd has gained prominence as an Islamic entrepreneur: scientist, television personality, author of more than sixty books, cardiologist, and founder of a successful charitable organization. One of his early books, *God and Man,* was censored by the regime of President Gamal Abdel Nasser for its overemphasis on "materialism."

Raised and educated in Tanta in the Egyptian Delta, Maḥmūd attended medical school at Cairo University. After graduation, he practiced medicine from 1952 to 1966. He also began to write. Turning to Islam after years of adhering to belief in Western values (especially secularism and materialism) and leftist modes of thought, he wrote his autobiography, *Riḥlatī min al-shakk ilā al-'īmān* (My Journey from Doubt to Faith), which became a national bestseller in Egypt in the 1970s. He also initiated a television program—*Al-ʿilm wa al-īmān* (Science and Faith)—dedicated to the precept that Islam and science are completely compatible and self-supportive. He founded the Muṣṭafā Maḥmūd

Society much in compliance with this theory—in the name of Islam, to promote the general welfare, and to maintain his extensive health center.

This Islamic organization, founded in 1975, contains an aquarium, library (for the study of Islam), observatory (to mark the precise dates for the beginning and ending of holy days), geological museum, seminar hall, health center (polyclinic) and hospital. The society also conducts tours to Islamic monuments, presents lectures and films, and sends relief aid abroad, for example, clothes and medicine to Afghan refugees; thousands of dollars to the Red Crescent in Sudan for victims of floods. In 1979, the society's Office of Social Services began providing sociomedical services. By the early 1990s, approximately eight thousand families annually were receiving financial aid—monthly stipends, medical services (related to kidney, chest, cancer, cardiac, and leper illnesses), aid to poor students and to blind and disabled individuals.

Located on the main street of the upper-middle class district of Muhandisīn, the Muṣṭafā Maḥmūd Society links a mosque with a hospital, the former raising funds through *zakāt* (wealth tax, alms), the latter providing health services. Beyond local contributions, Maḥmūd's activities receive special assistance from his personal friends from Gulf Arab states, providing his society with hundreds of thousands of dollars annually. The health services these funds help to provide run the gamut from physical exams, blood testing, urinalysis, and diagnoses to kidney dialysis, appendectomies, CT-scans, and heart treatment. Dental and psychological services are also provided. In the late 1980s, a high-rise apartment building in Muhandisīn was donated by a friend of Maḥmūd and is the society's hospital.

The hospital has sixty beds, half of which are for charitable and low-price services. The medical staff consists of more than ninety physicians—perhaps the largest group among the thousands of Islamic societies throughout Egypt. Doctors and physicians receive anywhere from 20 to 50 percent of the value of their treatment.

This capitalist enterprise founded in the name of Islam is hardly representative of the vast number of Islamic societies in Egypt, but it is a model of achievement with financial benefits accruing to the staff and low-cost health care for thousands of patients. Through these achievements, Maḥmūd has provided tangible evidence for his theories linking Islam with scientific and socioeconomic advancement.

BIBLIOGRAPHY

Ayubi, Nazih N. *Political Islam: Religion and Politics in the Arab World.* London and New York, 1991. Compares Muṣṭafā Maḥmūd Mosque/Society to Islamic banks, companies, and other providers of social services. Also discusses Muṣṭafā Maḥmūd along with other popular Islamists, such as Shaykhs Kishk and Shaʿrāwī.

Hammady, Iman Roushdy. "Religious Medical Centers in Egypt." Ph.D. diss., American University in Cairo, 1990. Compares and contrasts Muṣṭafā Maḥmūd Medical Center with other Islamic and Coptic facilities in Egypt.

Maḥmūd, Muṣṭafā. "Islam vs. Marxism and Capitalism." In *Islam in Transition: Muslim Perspectives,* edited by John J. Donohue and John L. Esposito, pp. 155–159. New York, 1982. Proposes Islam as an alternative to communism and capitalism, Islam being the nonmaterialist, spiritual, and humanist solution to the problems besetting developing nations. This article is based on his *Al-Mārksīyah wa-al-Islām* (Marxism and Islam) (Cairo, 1975).

Sullivan, Denis J. *Private Voluntary Organizations in Egypt: Islamic Development, Private Initiative, and State Control.* Gainesville, Fla., 1994. Presents the Muṣṭafā Maḥmūd Society as a successful model of Islamic entrepreneurialism and charity in comparison with scores of other nongovernmental organizations promoting development and providing services the government has failed to support.

DENIS J. SULLIVAN

MAI TATSINE (1927?–1980), leader of a separatist sect in Kano, Nigeria. Mai Tatsine was the nickname given by people in Kano to Muhammadu Marwa (also known as Muhammadu ʿArab), the leader of an Islamic sect that was involved in violent disturbances in that city in December 1980. The name is derived from a Hausa phrase he commonly employed against his detractors, *Alla ya tsine maka albarka,* "May God deprive you of his blessing." His followers were known as the 'Yan Tatsine. Because the group was intensely suspicious of outsiders, and because the disturbances gave rise to many wild rumors and apocryphal stories, little reliable knowledge exists of the movement or its leader.

Muhammadu Marwa was reportedly born in the region of Marwa, a city in northern Cameroon, probably in the 1920s. (A Nigerian passport that he acquired gave the date 1927.) He is commonly thought to have been Kirdi by origin, a member of one of the small hill peoples, followers of indigenous religions, who inhabit the region, the plains of which have been dominated by Muslim Fulani since the *jihād* of the early nineteenth century. But there are also reports that at least one of his parents belonged to the Shuwa, an Arabic-speaking group living in the region. In the 1920s and 1930s there was a large-scale emigration of young Kirdi men from the hills to the plains, driven by poverty and, in 1931, by a severe famine; the young Muhammadu Marwa may have been among them. He reportedly became the servant of a Muslim scholar who inspired his conversion to Islam. On that occasion, he took his Muslim name, Muhammadu. He may have been exposed to Mahdist ideas; in the 1890s this region had served as the base for the Mahdist movement led by Ḥayāt Bin Saʿīd (d. 1899), a member of the Sokoto royal family.

Muhammadu Marwa is said to have come to Kano in 1945, but nothing is known of his activities there until the early 1960s. By this time he had acquired a reputation for *tafsīr,* or Qur'ānic commentary, and so was given the nickname "Mallam Mai Tafsīrī." This presumably was the origin of his later derogatory nickname. The political and religious life of Kano in the years just after Nigeria's independence in 1960 was turbulent, and Muhammadu Marwa joined in the fray. In 1962 Emir Muhammadu Sanūsī (r. 1953–1963) had him brought before a Muslim judge on charges of illegal preaching and an offense known in the Arabic legal records as *shatīmah,* or abusive language. The latter offense was severely—and frequently—punished in Kano at the time, since the exchange of insults by political or religious groups often led to violence. The judge gave Marwa a three-month prison term, to be followed by deportation to his native Cameroon.

The Nigerian military takeover of 1966 brought an end to the formal powers of the emirs and in general weakened traditional social controls. This change made it possible for Marwa to return to Kano in the late 1960s. In 1971 he was issued a Nigerian passport in order to perform the pilgrimage to Mecca.

By the late 1970s the petroleum boom had brought a major new injection of wealth to Kano, and with it came rapid social change. For many of the established residents of the city this meant accelerated incorporation into the modern sector of Nigerian society, especially through the state-run secular school system. At the same time, young men were drawn from the countryside in increasing numbers. Many of them followed a traditional pattern in the region, leaving their families to become Qur'ānic students (Hausa, *almajirai*) and supporting themselves and their teacher through begging (Hausa, *bara*) and casual labor. The economic and educational changes of the 1970s made this group increasingly marginal. Such youth were the main recruiting ground for the 'Yan Tatsine. Groups affiliated with them sprang up in other towns in northern Nigeria and developed their own separate ritual centers.

Starting in 1977, the aggressive preaching of Marwa's disciples and the growth of his community of followers inspired vociferous public complaints. The approach of the turn of the Islamic century (fourteenth century AH) in 1979, an event associated with the arrival of a renewer of the faith, apparently inspired Marwa to announce his claim to prophethood. In 1978, as Nigeria returned to civilian rule, Kano state elected a governor from the People's Redemption Party, Abubakar Rimi. The Nigerian presidency, however, was captured by this party's conservative rival in northern politics, the National Party of Nigeria. The distrust between the federal and state levels of government hampered efforts to control the 'Yan Tatsine.

On 26 November 1980, Governor Rimi issued an ultimatum demanding the dispersal of the large group of followers who had gathered around Marwa's compound in 'Yan Awaki Quarters, just outside the old walled city. At this time, the arrival of Libyan troops in the Chadian capital of Njamena added to public anxiety. Governor Rimi took no immediate action on the expiration of the ultimatum. Rumors circulated that the 'Yan Tatsine planned to take over the city's two main mosques at congregational prayers on Friday, 19 December. The day before, however, a group of 'Yan Tatsine entered into a violent confrontation with the police at Shahuci Field, near the emir's palace. With bows and machetes, they drove off the police, captured weapons, and burnt trucks.

Ten days of heavy fighting ensued in which more than four thousand people were killed. Many were victims of vigilante groups that sprang up around the city and attacked anyone they suspected of belonging to the 'Yan Tatsine. The Nigerian army finally was called in to quell the disturbances. Marwa and his followers fled their stronghold on 29 December. Marwa himself was killed in the process and some one thousand of his followers arrested. In October 1982 violent disturbances linked to the 'Yan Tatsine occurred in the city of Maiduguri in northeastern Nigeria. Other disturbances followed at Yola (March 1984) and Gombe (April 1985).

The 'Yan Tatsine follows a pattern common in Muslim West Africa that may be termed "religious separatism," or, in the phrase of Jean-Paul Charnay (1980), "closed Islam." Such groups embrace heterodox practices and esoteric interpretations of the Qur'ān. They emphasize their own purity and refuse contact with the rest of society. Muhammadu Marwa was especially known for his condemnation of all modern innovations from bicycles to radios and buttons. He reportedly accepted only the Qur'ān as a valid source of religious teaching, yet as a prophet claimed the right to issue new religious injunctions, or at least new interpretations of the Qur'ān. He had no known links with other Islamic groups of either Ṣūfī or Wahhābī orientation.

[*See also* Nigeria.]

BIBLIOGRAPHY

Abba, Isa A. "*Bara* by Some *Almajirai* in Kano City in the Twentieth Century." In *Studies in the History of Kano*, edited by Bawuro M. Barkindo, pp. 193–206. Ibadan, 1983. Sharply critical view of traditional Qur'ānic education.

Charnay, Jean-Paul. "Islam et négritude: Quelques réflexions sur l'Afrique noire." *L'Afrique et l'Asie Modernes*, no. 126 (1980): 3–16.

Christelow, Allan. "Religious Protest and Dissent in Northern Nigeria: From Mahdism to Quranic Integralism." *Journal Institute of Muslim Minority Affairs* 6 (1985): 375–393.

Christelow, Allan. "The 'Yan Tatsine Disturbances: A Search for Perspective." *Muslim World* 75 (April 1985): 69–84.

Clarke, Peter B. *West African Islam: A Study of Religious Development from the Eighth to the Twentieth Century*. London, 1982.

Hajj, Muhammad A. al-. "Hayatu Bin Saʿid: A Revolutionary Mahdist in the Western Sudan." In *Sudan in Africa*, edited by Yusuf Fadl Hasan, pp. 128–141. Khartoum, 1971.

Hiskett, Mervyn. *The Development of Islam in West Africa*. London, 1984.

Lubeck, Paul. *Islam and Urban Labor in Northern Nigeria: The Making of a Muslim Working Class*. Cambridge, 1987. Study of the role of Islamic education in forming working-class consciousness.

Paden, John N. *Religion and Political Authority in Kano*. Berkeley, 1973. Essential reference for study of religion and politics in Kano up to late 1960s.

ALLAN CHRISTELOW

MAJALLAH. *See* Mecelle.

MAJLIS. An Arabic term that seems to have been used in pre-Islamic Arabia to indicate either a tribal council or council of tribes, *majlis*, after the advent of Islam and the foundation of the caliphate, denoted the audience chamber of the caliph and, later on, that of one of the sultans. It also referred to a gathering of a select group of people in the presence of a leading notable, a religious dignitary, or a well-known poet.

In modern times, *majlis* has been primarily used as the name of an institution set up to deal with matters pertaining to the public interest or domain. Hence, in the first half of the nineteenth century, *majlis* was virtually restricted to governmental institutions and organs, formally known as *dīwāns*. These new institutions were established during the age of reform, particularly as a result of the Tanzimat movement associated with a number of Ottoman sultans, ministers, and officials. [*See* Dīwān; Tanzimat.] It was perhaps the Egyptian Ibrāhīm Pasha (d. 1848), Muḥammad ʿAlī's son, who popularized the use of the term after his occupation of Syria between 1831 and 1840. He thus set up a central council in Damascus (*majlis al-shūrā*) and other local councils in every city and town. The central and local councils dealt with civil, financial, and administrative matters, although ultimate authority was reserved for the military governor of the country.

In the second half of the nineteenth century, *majlis* entered the vocabulary of modern Islam in order to denote a particular type of institution. Its most outstanding characteristic was the fact that it signified an organization which had clearly defined aims and equally precise internal regulations. Moreover, it often referred to institutions that had official functions in society and served a common purpose. This type of institution, governed by procedural rules and set up for the benefit of the community, came into being as part of the belief in the necessity of an orderly system of government. In Egypt, for example, Khedive Ismāʿīl (r. 1863–1879) set up in 1866 a consultative chamber of deputies (*majlis shūrā al-nuwwāb*) and introduced a system of indirect elections. In 1876 the sultan Abdülhamid II (r. 1876–1909) promulgated a new constitution which stipulated the creation of an elected chamber of deputies (*meclis-i mebʾusan*) and an appointed senate (*meclis-i a'yân*).

In the twentieth century, the term *majlis* has gained widespread currency in all Islamic countries. Used in various combinations, it refers to a variety of official, private, and social institutions. Thus, a board of directors of a commercial company is generally called in Arabic *majlis al-idārah*. However, its most frequent use is reserved for parliamentary institutions endowed with legislative authority or deliberative functions, as in the cases of Turkey, Iran, and most Arab countries.

A new type of *majlis* began to emerge, particularly in the Arab world, following the proliferation of coups d'état between 1949 and 1970. Once in power, the military officers would invariably set up a new institution—*majlis qiyādat al-thawrah* (Revolutionary Command Council)—and invest it with ultimate authority.

BIBLIOGRAPHY

Gilsenan, Michael. *Recognizing Islam*. New York and London, 1982. Articulate anthropological insights on *majlis* as a reception room.

Hudson, Michael. *Arab Politics: The Search For Legitimacy*. New Haven, 1977. Analytic study of institution building in the Arab context.

Kedourie, Elie. *Politics in the Middle East*, New York and Oxford, 1992. Provocative diagnosis of parliamentary life in a number of Islamic countries.

Maʿoz, Moshe. *Ottoman Reform in Syria and Palestine, 1840–1861*. London and New York, 1968. Accurate descriptive sections on the role of *majlis* (meclis) in Ottoman Syria.

YOUSSEF M. CHOUEIRI

MAJLISĪ, MUḤAMMAD BĀQIR AL- (1628–1699/1700), leading Iranian Shīʿī scholar of the late Ṣafavid period. He was born in Isfahan, the capital of the Ṣafavid state, into a family of *ʿulamāʾ* (religious scholars). His father, Muḥammad Taqī al-Majlisī, was a noted religious figure. It is said the Majlisīs were related to the ʿĀmilīs of south Lebanon (Jabal ʿĀmil) who, when Shah Ismāʿīl founded the Shīʿī Ṣafavid state in Iran in 1501, flocked to Iran to participate in the flowering of a new era of Shīʿī scholarship. Al-Majlisī's life and works marked the end of this "golden age." He died in Isfahan and was buried in the great old mosque of the city.

The most readily accessible biography of Majlisī is to be found in Muḥammad Bāqir Khwānsārī's well-known nineteenth-century biographical dictionary, *Rawḍāt al-jannāt*, (vol. 2, pp. 78–93). In narrating the life and works of Majlisī, Khwānsārī, as is his usual style, quotes from contemporary and later sources. He refers to him as "Shaykh al-Islām" of the Ṣafavid capital, adding that "he was the chief figure [*raʾīs*] in religious and secular matters." During the reign of the last Ṣafavid ruler, Shah Sultan Ḥusayn, the affairs of the state had deteriorated to such a degree that it was only thanks to Majlisī's activities that the country maintained a semblance of unity. The end came soon after Majlisī's death.

Aside from his religious duties as a member of the *ʿulamāʾ*, which the sources describe in exaggerated detail, Majlisī's position in regard to the government and the shah is unclear. He was not a statesman.

In addition to the material in Khwānsārī's work, the earliest life of Majlisī is included in *Mirʾāt al-aḥvāl-i Jahān-namā*, written by Aḥmad ibn Muḥammad ʿAlī Bihbahānī (d. 1819 or 1820) and recently published in Tehran, edited by ʿAlī Davvānī (only pp. 112–26 deal specifically with Majlisī). This work served as the basis for a more elaborate biography of Majlisī written in 1884 by Ḥusayn ibn Muḥammad Taqī ibn ʿAlī ibn Muḥammad al-Nūrī al-Ṭabarsī, entitled *Al-fayḍ al-qudsī fī tarjamat al-ʿAllāmah al-Majlisī*. This work was published as part of volume 105 of the new edition of Majlisī's *Biḥār al-anwār*. After a short introduction, the biography deals with Majlisī's personal characteristics, his works, his teachers and students, his ancestors, his descendants, and his life and visions of him after his death.

The sources stress two aspects of Majlisī's life: his strong opposition to Sufism and his attempt at popularizing Shīʿī thought among Iranians by writing several of his works in Persian rather than Arabic. His major work, however, *Biḥār al-anwār*, a compendium of Shīʿī knowledge, is in Arabic. A new (second) edition of this work, which began to appear in Tehran in the 1960s is in 110 volumes. Karl-Heinz Pampus wrote a doctoral dissertation on *Biḥār al-anwār* in 1970. The first 134 pages of Pampus's work is a comprehensive life of Majlisī; the rest (pp. 135–229) is a detailed analysis of *Biḥār*. An index (*Safīnat al-biḥār*) to the first (1887) edition of *Biḥār al-anwār*, composed by ʿAbbās Qummī, is useful inasmuch as the new edition awaits a comprehensive index.

Majlisī is said to have written as many as thirteen books in Arabic and fifty-three in Persian. Some of these compositions are short treatises dealing with such topics as belief, prayer, ethics, and morality, many of which intended to teach the common person. In Shīʿī thought and scholarship, Majlisī represents the culminating point in the Ithnā ʿAsharī revival that can be said to have begun with the rise of the Ṣafavid dynasty. The continuity in Shīʿī learning that the Ṣafavid rulers provided for Ithnā ʿAsharī scholars (thus linking them with their predecessors of the late Middle Ages, such as Ibn al-Muṭahhar al-Ḥillī, Ibn Makkī al-ʿĀmilī, Ibn Fahd al-Ḥillī, and others) is counterbalanced with the continuity that Majlisī himself provided for future generations of Shīʿī scholars, linking the Ṣafavid period with that of the Qājār dynasty in the nineteenth century—all the way to the present Islamic Republic of Iran. No modern scholar today dealing with Islamic thought, Shīʿī or otherwise, can afford to ignore the writings of Muḥammad Bāqir al-Majlisī. Majlisī, al-Ḥurr al-ʿĀmilī, and Mullā Muḥsin Fayḍ constitute the so-called Three Later Muḥammads who, with the "Three Early Muḥammads"

(Kulaynī, Ibn Bābūyah, and Shaykh al-Ṭā'ifah al-Ṭūsī), share among themselves the most important writings of the teachings of the Shīʿī tradition of Islam.

[*See also* Shīʿī Islam, *historical overview article.*]

BIBLIOGRAPHY

General and uncritical material on the life and times of Majlisī may be found in Shīʿī biographical works such as Muḥammad Bāqir Khwānṣārī, *Rawḍāt al-jannāt* (Tehran, n.d.), and Mīrzā M. Tunkābunī, *Qiṣaṣ al-ʿulamā'* (Tehran, n.d.). For basic information and a proper evaluation of Majlisī and his works, consult Āghā Aḥmad ibn Muḥammad ʿAlī Bihbahānī, *Mir'āt al-Aḥvāl Jahān-namā*, edited by ʿAlī Davvānī (Tehran, 1370/1992), and Ḥusayn ibn Muḥammad Taqī al-Nūrī al-Ṭabarsī, "Al-fayḍ al-qudsī fī tarjamat al-ʿAllāmah al-Majlisī," in volume 105 of Majlisī's *Biḥār al-Anwār*, new ed., vol. 105, pp. 2–165 (Tehran, 1391/1971). Volume 1 of the new edition of *Biḥār* contains an extremely useful introduction, as does the Persian translation of volume 13 by ʿAlī Davvānī.

The following may be consulted for useful insights about this learned scholar:

Browne, Edward G. *A Literary History of Persia*. Vol. 4. Reprint, Cambridge, 1969.

Hairi, Abdul-Hadi. "Madjlisī, Mullā Muḥammad Bāḳir." In *Encyclopaedia of Islam*, new ed., vol. 5, pp. 1086–1088. Leiden, 1960–.

Momen, Moojan. *An Introduction to Shiʿi Islam*. New Haven, 1985. Contains a reconstructed family tree of Majlisī and his descendants on pages 132–134.

Pampus, Karl-Heinz. *Die Theologische Enzyklopädie Biḥār al-Anwār des Muḥammad Bāqir al-Mağlisī (1037–1110 A.H. = 1627–1699 A.D.): Ein Beitrag zur Literaturgeschichte der Šīʿa in der Ṣafawīdenzeit*. Bonn, 1977. Published doctoral dissertation on Majlisī and his *Biḥār*.

Shaybī, Kāmil Muṣṭafā al-. *Al-fikr al-shīʿī wa al-nazaʿāt al-ṣūfiyah*. Baghdad, 1386/1966.

Michel M. Mazzaoui

MAKKAH. *See* Mecca.

MALAY AND INDONESIAN LITERATURE.

Ever since the emergence of the Srivijaya empire on the east coast of Sumatra around 700 CE, the Malay language has played a dual role in Southeast Asia. It has first been the language of *alam Melayu*, the Malay world—the coastal areas around the Strait of Malacca, the South China Sea, and the Java Sea whose common narrative traditions, religious practices, and rituals make them the heartland of a distinctly Malay culture. Malay has also been the language of communication in Southeast Asia among people of different cultures, not only for natives of the archipelago but also for travelers from India, China, and the Middle East. Traders and travelers, preachers and monks, administrators and soldiers have used Malay (or Malay pidgins and creoles) as their second language; they also wrote in it, often to escape from local tradition and create something novel.

Malay has thus been both a vehicle of ideas and concepts that originated in the Malay heartland and a language associated with novel ideas introduced by travelers and migrants. This duality, or even ambivalence, has made Malay a dynamic language with an undefined and open identity. Actively supported by Dutch and British administrators in colonial times, it has become the national language of the Republic of Indonesia where it is called *(Bahasa Indonesia)* and the kingdom of Malaysia (under the name *Bahasa Malaysia*) as well as of the Republic of Singapore and the Sultanate of Brunei.

Literacy and Orality. The first evidence of Malay writing is in inscriptions found on the Malay Peninsula and on the islands of Kalimantan and Sumatra. Written in a script that originated in southern India, these short texts are an amalgam of older form of Malay and Sanskrit, suggesting a predominant presence of Hinduism and Buddhism in Southeast Asia. With the arrival of Islam in the twelfth and thirteenth centuries, when it was introduced by merchants and priests from India and China, the Arab/Persian script called Jawi was adapted for writing Malay. Jawi is still widely used in some parts of the Malay heartland.

Islam was readily accepted by the local population, who were attracted by its notions of equality and democracy. Neither did local rulers hesitate to adopt the new religion; they saw in its rituals and philosophy a novel way to support their authority and easily assimilated the idea that the ruler is God's shadow on earth and a "perfect man"—a concept developed in the Muslim kingdoms of southern Asia (see Milner, 1983).

With its strong focus on the scriptures, Islam must have stimulated the respect for writing and thus the production of manuscripts *(naskah)* and letters *(surat)*. Owing to the scarcity of surviving materials, however, it is impossible to determine how widespread literacy really was in the Malay heartland and neighboring regions before the advent of printing and nationalism. It was a highly valued commodity in court circles, often supplied by relative outsiders including Arabs, Indians, and Chinese. Within Islamic educational institutions (the *madrasah, pondok,* and *pesantren*) literacy may have been more common, which at times made the scholars an aggressive alternative to the political and cultural authority of the courts over the local population. In general, literacy remained a relative rarity until the end of the nineteenth century (see Amin Sweeney, *A Full Hearing*, Berkeley, 1987).

In a context that was so strongly organized by orally transmitted knowledge, the term "literature" is an unfortunate one; not until 1930 had Malay itself assimilated the words *sastra, sastera,* and *kesusastraan* to refer to intentionally fictional texts. Before that, words like *karangan, tulisan, gambar,* and *surat* were used to refer to various genres of writing; *ceritera, kisah, pantun,* and *riwayat* were common terms for orally transmitted stories.

Since its introduction into Southeast Asia, Islam-inspired writing has always remained closely associated with Malay; it was considered the best language in which to read and write about the Qur'ān, tradition, law, and knowledge. In the twentieth century a corollary argument has often been proposed in the Malay heartland: Malay is associated with Islam, and therefore every Malay-speaking person should be a good Muslim. In Indonesia, where Malay is the second language for much of the population, this statement has never been accepted as self-evident; not all people who use Malay (or "Indonesian") feel obliged to be staunch defenders of Islam. In modern literary life, discussions are conducted along similar lines of differentiation: the assumption that a Malay author has to work from an explicit Islamic stance is generally accepted in Malaysia, but this has rarely been the case in Indonesia.

Prelude to Modernity. The fifteenth-century Sultanate of Malacca is usually seen as the Islamic heir of the empire of Srivijaya. Malacca's authority was brought to an end by European colonialists in 1511; in the memory of people in the Malay heartland it remained the period of greatest Malay glory, sanctified and described in many narratives. Materials from the days of Malacca are rare and none of its writings have been preserved. Contemporary reports of European visitors picture Malacca as an international city with a great sphere of influence; no doubt the activities developed under the aegis of its Muslim rulers had great impact on cultural life in Southeast Asia as a whole and on the Malay heartland in particular. At the fall of Malacca in 1511, Islam was strongly established on the coasts around the Java Sea and the Straits of Malacca. Religious and juridical treatises *(kitāb)* and tales of the prophets *(hikayat),* partly translations from Arabic and Persian originals and partly adaptations to local ideas, left a strongly Islamic stamp on Malay culture. Islamic ideas have since taken a central position in Malay intellectual life and writing.

The oldest known Malay texts of some length originate from the Sultanate of Aceh on the north coast of Sumatra, where Malay played an important role in administration, trade, and culture alongside the local Acehnese language. A vivid intellectual life existed there in the first half of the seventeenth century; this is particularly manifest in its the religious writings, which find their climax in the works of Nuruddin ar-Raniri (Nūr al-Dīn al-Rānīrī), Samsuddin al-Sumatrani (Shams al-Dīn al-Sūmātrānī), and Hamzah Pansuri (Ḥamzah Fanṣūrī). The most authoritative Islamic scribe was ar-Raniri, born and raised in Rander in Gujarat, India; he came to the archipelago with a great knowledge of Persian and Arabic texts and propagated this knowledge in the numerous texts he wrote in his somewhat idiosyncratic Malay. Ar-Raniri stayed at the court of Aceh between 1637 and 1644, long enough to ensure that his writings would have a lasting influence on Malay Islamic thinking. Some of his texts are still consulted today in Malaysian and Indonesian religious schools. The best known of his works is *Sirat al-mustakim (Al-ṣirāṭ al-mustaqīm).* Mention should also be made of the *Bustan as-Salatin (Bustān al-Salāṭīn),* an encyclopedic compendium of seven volumes in which the history of the world is presented following Persian models, with numerous references to works from the Islamic heartland.

Ar-Raniri is usually viewed as an orthodox mystic who apparently met with great resistance and even hostility among local intellectuals. In religious treatises like *Hujjat as-siddik li-dafᶜ as-zindik (Ḥujjat al-ṣiddīq li-dafᶜ al-zindīq)* and *Tibyan fi maᶜrifat al-adyan (Al-tibyān fī maᶜrifat al-adyān)* written in a mixture of Malay and Arabic, he tried in particular to refute the writings of the Wujūdīyah movement. The leaders of this movement had developed an erudite philosophy the essence of which was the claim that man's being and God's being, the world and God, are identical. The most respected author of theological texts in defense of the Wujūdīyah was Samsuddin al-Sumatrani (d. 1630), who tried to bring Islamic teachings about the seven grades of being (as developed by authors like Ibn al-ᶜArabī and ᶜAbd al-Qādir al-Jilānī) into accordance with local religious notions (see C. A. O. van Nieuwenhuijze, *Samsu 'l-din van pasai*, Leiden, 1945).

In literary terms, ar-Raniri's greatest opponent was Hamzah Pansuri, whom he accused of having heretical ideas close to those of Samsuddin. Hamzah Pansuri expressed his ideas about God and the world in a mathematically constructed form of written poetry called *syair;* he appears to have had a rather random knowledge of Persian and Arabic writings, which he very ably incorporated into his own work. It has not been determined whether Hamzah invented this genre of poetry or merely perfected a form already known in Malay. Using images, metaphors, and similes that were novel at the time, his *syair* had a far-reaching effect on Malay literature. *Syair* became a generally accepted form that—at least after Hamzah Pansuri's experiments—could be used for every possible topic; it was to remain very popular among all Malay speakers until the late twentieth century. Poems like *Syair dagang* and *Syair burung pingai,* which are attributed to him, have remained a source of inspiration; even after *syair* as a form lost its authority, the echoes of Hamzah can be found in the modern Malay poetry of both Indonesia and Malaysia. The question whether Hamzah was a heretic and his work deserved to be burnt (as it was as a result of Raniri's endeavors) need not concern us here (see Naguib al-Attas, 1970; and G. W. J. Drewes and L. Brakel, *The Poems of Hamzah Fansuri,* Leiden, 1987). Discussions between scholars like ar-Raniri, who defended so-called orthodox mysticism on the basis of al-Ghazālī's work, and those who tried to combine mystical notions from the Islamic heartland with local ideas and rituals, remained a source of tension in Islamic circles. To what degree and at what pace should foreign elements be accepted and assimilated into Malay writing?

Malay authors in the tradition of ar-Raniri and Hamzah often appear to have a more or less solid knowledge of Persian and Arabic texts; they translated and adapted many narratives *(hikayat)* and treatises *(kitāb)* that in turn had a far-reaching impact on Malay culture. Many prose works elaborate and explain stories from the Qur'ān, are for instance the *Hikayat anbiya* and *Hikayat jumjumah;* others are tales about the Prophet *(Hikayat nur Muhammad* and *Hikayat Nabi bercukur)* or about his contemporaries *(Hikayat Raja Khandak, Hikayat Amir Hamzah,* and *Hikayat Muhammad Hanafiyyah).* Most of these *hikayat* are anonymous, and in this they joined the existing Malay tradition transmitted in an uneasy mixture of oral and written forms. *Hikayat* became as familiar in the archipelago as its more serious counterpart, called *kitāb* and including theological works in the strict sense of the word, dealing with the law and other religious topics. Unlike *hikayat, kitāb* were usually attributed to specific authors. At courts and schools, these Islamic writings must have been appreciated as exemplary texts for behavior and thinking. A prime example is the seventeenth-century text *Taj us-Salatin (Tāj al-Salāṭīn),* a 1603 adaptation of a Persian text in which the prerogatives of rulers and the correct behavior of human beings are described (see P. P. Roorda van Eysinga, *De Kroon aller koningen van Bocharie van Djohore naar een oud Maleisch handschrift vertaald,* Batavia, 1827).

Texts of both genres were copied again and again, the *kitāb* more meticulously than the *hikayat* owing to their differences in content and function. To the enjoyment and edification of all they were distributed over the archipelago, giving a new impetus to the knowledge of Malay. Toward the end of the nineteenth century many of them were lithographed and printed in the Malay heartland. In this process of writing and copying, reading and reciting, the narratives that had been inspired by Indian and Javanese examples and local traditions were gradually pushed to the margin; the same was happening to the orally transmitted tales, which in the days of Malacca must still have played a prominent role in shaping the central values of the Malay-speaking world.

After Aceh, other authoritative centers of Muslim writing in Malay emerged and disappeared in the archipelago—Palembang, Banjarmasin, Patani, Trengganu, and Riau. A few of the authors and texts that traveled through the archipelago in the company of *hikayat,* constantly restating the configuration of Malay cultural life were Abdul Samad al-Palembani, who wrote, most notably, *Hidayat as-Salikin* (Hidāyat al-Sālikīn), *Sair as-Salikin* (Sayr al-Sālikīn), and *Bidayat al-hidayat* (*Bidāyat al-hidāyah,* strongly based on work by al-Ghazālī); Kemas Muḥammad ibn Aḥmad al-Palembani, author of *Hikayat Syaik Muhammad Samman;* and Daud ibn Abdullah al-Patani, who wrote *Ghayar al-Tallab al-murid marifat* (see Drewes, 1977). In new editions, many of these older *kitāb* are still being consulted in religious schools.

Arguably the center of religious writing in Malay with the most lasting radiance was Penyengat, a small island in the Riau Archipelago where the prestigious family of the vice-rulers of Riau-Lingga had its residence in the nineteenth century. In particular, Raja Ali Haji (1810–1874) should be mentioned. Inspired by Dutch and British examples, he wrote a Malay grammar *(Bustan al-Katibin)* and a dictionary of Malay *(Pengetahuan Bahasa)* based on Arabic models; at the same time he inspired members of his family, female as well as male, to write. His contacts with Dutch scholars enabled him to have some of his texts printed. Print being the key to modernity, Raja Ali Haji can be seen as one of the first modern Muslim authors in Malay; his example was taken up by his descendants, who set up a publishing house on the island.

Modernity. In the course of the nineteenth century contacts between Southeast Asia and the Middle East, most importantly Mecca and Cairo, were intensified owing to the introduction of steamboats, the telegraph, and printing techniques. In the shadow of developments in the Middle East where intellectuals like Muḥammad ʿAbduh and Muḥammad Rāshid Riḍā propagated a moral and religious reformation of Islam, tensions and discussions in the British-controlled peninsula and the Dutch Indies took a new shape (Roff, 1967). Until now the relationship between individual and God and between man's being and God's being had been the predominant subject of discussion and writing, but subsequent discussion focused on the question of to what extent Islamic law and the Qur'ān and *ḥadīth* could and should be directly applied in everyday life, and to what extent local customs should be permitted.

In the Malay heartland, this conflict between modern Islamic responses to the intrusions of the British and more traditional Islamic practice syncretized with local customs and beliefs is usually presented in terms of the conflict between the *kaum muda* (the reformists, literally "the group of the young") and the *kaum tua* (the traditionalists, literally "the group of the old"). Printed materials were to play an important role in this conflict. As in so many other parts of the Muslim world, the *kaum muda* were far better equipped than their opponents to take control over modernity; in the first half of the twentieth century they made very effective use of printing to persuade their fellow-believers to hold more strictly to the rules and regulations of Islam and at the same time to be more open to Western innovations, if only to withstand the West's power—and even better, to keep it at bay.

The first modern author, Abdullah bin Abdul Kadir Munsyi (1796–1854), had died before the conflict between the *kaum muda* and the *kaum tua* took serious form in Southeast Asia. Born in Malacca of mixed Arabic and Indian descent, Abdullah was a pious Muslim and a great admirer of British achievements. His autobiography, *Hikayat Abdullah* (Singapore, 1849) shows him to be fully aware of the possibilities western culture had to offer to the Muslim people of the Malay-speaking and -writing world, and nowhere did he hide his contempt for what he considered the unwillingness of Malays to be more open to the outer world. Abdullah had made himself familiar with printing techniques by working for Christian missionaries, but he did not succeed in convincing Malays of its usefulness. It was another fifty years before Malay literates more carefully read Abdullah's book and took his plea for printing seriously. In the meantime, people of Chinese, Indian, European, and Arab descent who felt only thinly connected with the Malay heritage had become the main initiators of innovation and modernization in the urban areas of Singapore, Penang, Batavia, and Surabaya. These were places on the margin of the Malay heartland, to be followed only much later by those who saw themselves as the "real" Malays.

Another pioneer in publishing was Syed Syeikh Ahmad al-Hadi, an intellectual of Arab descent who had been given a religious education in Penyengat and Mecca before settling in the peninsula. With some religious friends he published the journal *Al-imam* (1906–1909), mouthpiece of the *kaum muda,* in Singapore; later he established his own printing press, Jelutung Press, in Penang, where he published his first novel. *Setia Asyik kepada Maksyuknya atau Shafik Afandi dengan Faridah Hanom* (1926/27) is a Malay adaptation of an Egyptian novel in which Muslim ideas about modernity are carefully explored and propagated. *Faridah Hanom* was not the first novel to appear in the Malay heartland, yet it was of exemplary importance in the fictional literature *(sastra)* that emerged; subsequent novelists like Ahmad Rashid Talu (*Iakah Salmah?,* 1928) took inspiration from both its content and its form in realistic novels and novelettes in which the Malays were pictured as lacking moral strength and were urged to develop more religious fervor.

Malay prose authors in the peninsula experimented on the model of English and Dutch Indies examples and presented the teachings of Islam as the appropriate moral and ethical frame of reference for their protagonists and readers alike. From that perspective, it is justifiable to call all modern Malay literature produced in the peninsula "Islamic literature"—a point that was explored in great depth in the Islamic reorientation *(dakwa)* of the 1970s and 1980s (see Judith Nagata, *The Reflowering of Malaysian Islam: Modern Religious Radicals and their Roots*, Vancouver, 1984). Many of the modern authors in the Malay heartland had a Muslim upbringing; at least they appreciated the fact that being a Malay meant being a Muslim, and sooner or later every Malay had to come to terms with Islam. Islam thus became a strong catalyst to nationalism once the writings of the *kaum muda* and their descendants made the growing number of literate Malays aware of the fact that non-Islamic Chinese and Indian immigrants on the peninsula were gaining control over economic life and pushing the children of the soil *(bumiputra)* into the countryside. The statement that Malayness should be identical with Islam was an almost inevitable consequence of this growing self-awareness; only a few intellectuals had the courage to question and challenge this.

Different Concepts of Islamic Literature. Literacy in the Malay-speaking world as a whole increased owing to colonial programs of education, and so did the demand for reading materials. In the British-controlled areas the *kaum muda* competed with the *kaum tua* as well as with secularists to gain the upper hand in cultural and literary life. In the Dutch Indies, Islam was hardly a theme at all in the literature that came into being in the twentieth century.

Politically speaking, the Straits of Malacca and the South China Sea were the main boundaries between the Dutch Indies and the British Malay States (and Straits Settlements). Culturally speaking, however, they were inland seas within the Malay world, over which continuous migrations back and forth were taking place. This explains, for instance, why many of the leading authors and journalists in present-day Malaysia are of Sumatran descent. Parallel to the ambivalent position of Malay, at once the language of the heartland and the language of novelties, two traditions were taking shape in the centers of political and economic authority—in Kuala Lumpur, Singapore, and Medan on one hand, and in Jakarta and Surabaya on the other. Authors who saw themselves as part of the Malay heartland with its distinct heritage tried to explore their "Malay-ness" by way of Islam; others, more secularly oriented and as much tied to their local heritage and Western culture, preferred following Western examples to combining their writings with Muslim teachings.

In the Malay States and Straits Settlements and later in Malaysia, a well-defined cultural policy was a very important tool for the Malays in constructing a national and unifying culture on Malay terms. In the 1950s and 1960s "Malay power" was the predominant slogan in enforcing Malay ideas and values on the new state and its national ideology. In the 1970s and 1980s Malay authors reformulated their stance; more than ever, they emphasized the importance of Islam as the essential element of Malay culture and to this end the Islamic part of the Malay heritage was retrieved and strengthened. A wide variety of Islam-inspired organizations succeeded in uniting Malays under an Islamic banner. The Malay intelligentsia discussed how to reach their readers with *sastra Islam* (Islamic literature), a kind of writing that was to contain Islamic values, project Islamic concepts, and be created by pious Muslims with pure hearts.

The discussions between Shahnon Ahmad, undisputedly the most respected prose author of the second half of the century, and the literary critic and scholar Kassim Ahmad are generally considered exemplary for the problems and questions involved in defining *sastra Islam.* The task of a Muslim author, according to Shahnon, is to discover the order that God has created in this world, to acquire insight in his truth, his beauty, and his will, and then to use it as the main force in creating literature. This is only possible and conceivable if one carefully follows the Qur'ān, the *ḥadīth*s, and the law. Writing literature, claim Shahnon and his followers, is a form of *ʿibādah,* a religious duty; neither "art for art's sake" nor "art for society" (two slogans with which everybody literate in the Malay world had become familiar in the 1950s) should be the maxim, but rather "art because of God" *(seni karena Allah);* such art could only be made when the heart was pure and all rituals were appropriately performed. The objections of Kassim Ahmad to Shahnon's views can be summarized in two main points. First, living as a good Muslim and trying to fathom God's design does not suffice; those who try to shape and defend *sastra Islam* should be more explicit about the rules, concepts, sources, principles, devices, and prescriptions that are to regulate the writing of works of art—and that may be impossible without smothering the vitality of the act of creation. Second, Muslim authors too readily disregard literature written by non-Muslims: there are many literary works not written by Muslims that still contain values useful for the Muslim community and for humanity in general. Such considerations led Shafie Abu Bakar, another prominent discussant, to suggest that it may be best not to attempt an exact definition of what *sastra Islam* is and is not; perhaps writing with a pure heart and pious intentions could suffice after all. It is obvious that such discussions are not merely about literature and its required qualities; they also have to do with politics in that they are yet another effort to strengthen the position of the Malays and their culture within the multiracial society of Malaysia. This explains the heat and intensity of the debates.

The concept of Islamic literature is not only disputed, of course, but also explicitly tested in works of prose and poetry scattered through all sorts of periodicals and journals with a wide and varied readership. The most highly regarded works of prose and poetry have occasionally been collected; notable anthologies of short stories include *Tuhan, bagaimana akan Kucari-Mu* (1979) and *Sebuah lampu antik* (1983). Among novels, *Muhamad Ahkhir* by Anas K. Hadimaja (1984), and *Al-Syiqaq I* (1985) and *Tok Guru* (1988) by Shahnon Ahmad are often named as interesting examples of *sastra Islam*. At least as influential as this prose is the poetry that emerged in the late 1970s; popular poems can be found in the anthology *Tuhan, kita begitu dekat* by Hamzah Hamdani (1984) and in collections of individual poets, for example *Manifesto* by Suhor Antarsaudara (1976), *Cahaya* by Ashaari Muhammad (1977), and *ʿAyn* by Kemala (1983). The prose works of *sastra Islam* usually focus on a protagonist who after a deep crisis repents and becomes a devout and good Muslim; the poetry is usually more concerned with the question of the relationship between God and the individual—in the tradition of Hamzah Pansuri and Amir Hamzah, it is often couched in monologues addressed by the author to God in deep and painful striving toward self-definition.

In Indonesia, authors who explicitly claim to find inspiration in Islamic teachings and experiences have played a less prominent role in shaping the canon of the national literature. Before World War II, Islam was not supposed to play any role in the government-censored cultural life in which *sastra* came into being; activities in Islamic circles were mainly restricted to editing and printing older texts and to writing new *kitāb*-like treatises. Islam was only a marginal theme (if it was a theme at all) in the literary work published in Batavia. The secularists in control were of the opinion that religious experiences were a personal, not a societal matter. Two exceptions should be made, Amir Hamzah and Hamka, and it is no coincidence that both are from Sumatra. The poet Amir Hamzah (1911–1946), a Malay prince from the east coast of Sumatra, found his inspiration in his Malay heritage, using metaphors and similes that circle around his personal search for God and strongly echo Hamzah Pansuri's poems. Caught between tradition and modernity, his poems (collected in *Njanji soenji*, 1937, and *Boeah Rindoe*, 1941 are still discussed and recited in Malaysia as well as in Indonesia. An even more intermediate figure is Hamka (1908–1981), who grew up in reformist circles in Sumatra and became a leading religious teacher. His numerous books on religious affairs seem in form and content like continuations of the *kitāb* of Malay heritage, but he also took part in the emerging literary life with novels like *Di bawah lingkungan Ka'bah* (1938) and *Merantau ke Deli* (1939). These novels focus on Islamic questions; they are still widely read in the Malay world, and in Malaysia they are now seen as early manifestations of the *sastra Islam*. [*See the biography of Hamka.*]

In the first period of Indonesian independence between 1945 and 1965, Muslim intellectuals were given ample opportunity to formulate their ideas about literature. They formed a number of organizations that were more or less directly affiliated with political parties, but the various Muslim organizations never succeeded in taking a central place in the literary scene of Jakarta and beyond. In the last years of the so-called Old Order, they were increasingly criticized by communists and nationalists for not being wholehearted supporters of President Sukarno's efforts to construct a national culture. This criticism came to a climax in 1962 when Hamka, already a revered and respected religious leader, was accused of plagiarism. Opponents claimed that his novel *Tenggelamnya Kapal van der Wijck* (originally published in 1938) was a shameless translation of an Egyptian novel by Manfaluthi (who had himself taken a novel by the French author A. Carre for his model). Hamka had acted within a tradition of adaptation and translation going back to Raniri and beyond, but this was not much appreciated by his enemies, who found his defense as lukewarm as his support for the national non-Islamic culture Sukarno envisaged.

In the early years of the New Order adherence to religion was strongly advocated by the new government as an effective antidote to the banned communist movement. Once more, Islam was given ample opportunity to develop a higher profile in the literary scene. Islamic thinking in Indonesia never took on the intense forms that are so characteristic of the Malaysian situation; in general intellectuals, critics, and authors remained aloof from the dogmatic teachings that began to be propagated in the Malay heartland. This moderation was most dramatically shown in the famous case of *Langit makin mendung*, a short story written by Ki Panji Kusmin and published in the literary journal *Sastra* in 1968. Muslims considered the story blasphemous because it depicts

Muḥammad and God as human beings. Eventually H. B. Jassin, the editor of the journal and himself a good Muslim, was brought to court, and after a much-publicized trial the case eventually ended undecided. The Muslims who were invited to support the accusations of blasphemy, Hamka among them, were unable to present their accusations in a unified and convincing manner. As it turned out, many leading Muslim intellectuals were of the opinion that artistic freedom should be respected and that religious life was a personal affair that should not pervade public life.

In spite of this defeat, Islam has gradually taken a more prominent place in Indonesian literary life, concurrent with the expanding role Islam is playing in political and cultural life as a whole. As in Malaysia, the traditional dichotomy between poetry and prose seems relevant. In the shadow of Amir Hamzah, poets like D. Zawawi Imron (*Nenekmoyangku airmata*, Jakarta, 1985), Emha Ainun Nadjib (*99 untuk Tuhanku*, Bandung, 1983), and Sutarji Calzoum Bachri (*O amuk kapak*, Jakarta, 1981) continue to explore the relationship between the individual and God in terms of personal emotions and experiences in a lyrical tone and language that easily lends itself to public recitation. As in Malaysia, Islam-inspired poetry by both famous and unknown poets can be found in many newspapers and journals. The oral element in modern poetry is further explored in public poetry readings where poems are sung and recited in dramalike fashion (the so-called *bazanji* are a good example of these performances). As for prose, short stories and novels explicitly inspired by Islam and the Qur'ān play only a very limited role in modern Indonesian literature. In this connection the work of short story writers like Muhammad Diponegoro, Jamil Suherman, and in particular Danarto (*Adam ma'rifat*, 1982) should be mentioned; it is to be expected that with the resurgence of Islamic values, the number of authors who try their hand at this particular kind of literature will grow.

Indonesian literature as a whole is generally appreciated as being more challenging, sophisticated, and playful than the rather predictable and rigid prose and poetry of Malaysia, an evaluation usually extended to work considered a manifestation of *sastra Islam*. The intensity is of a different kind, so to speak, the irony and ambiguities of the margin being substituted for the grimness of the heartland. The relevant essays of A. A. Navis, another Indonesian author who was once accused of blasphemy, are a fine illustration of the gap that grew between the margin and the heartland in the conceptualization of *sastra Islam*. An author should never follow rules and regulations, Navis claims; on the contrary, set rules and regulations should be seen as problems, and it is the task of an author to challenge and question readers' opinions rather than to confirm them.

Present Situation. In this Indonesian plea for *sastra Islam* as a subversive element lies its main difference from Malaysian literature as a whole, and this difference can be explained largely from the position literature plays in these two states. In Malaysia literature is primarily regarded as a tool in the creation of a national culture and, in a wider sense, in the political struggle; it is supposed to strengthen the position of the Malays vis-à-vis the other groups in a multiracial society, and authors feel intensely involved in societal developments. In Indonesia literature is given only a very marginal social role, and this very marginality offers authors the freedom to experiment. The language is the same; function and intent, however, are different, as they circle around different points of reference. There is irony in the fact that the work of Indonesian authors on the margin is often taken by Malaysian authors in the heartland as exemplary, rather than the other way around. Tensions between the Malay heartland and the margins of "Malay-ness" remain, as does the ambivalent role of the Malay language. Islam has filled the gap of these tensions again and again.

[*See also* Islam, *article on* Islam in Southeast Asia and the Pacific.]

BIBLIOGRAPHY

Abdullah, Munshi. *The Hikayat Abdullah* (1849). Translated by A. H. Hill. Kuala Lumpur, 1970.

Drewes, G. W. J. *Directions for Travellers on the Mystic Path*. The Hague, 1977.

Hamka. *Tenggelamnya kapal van der Wijck dalam polemik*. Jakarta, 1963.

Ismail Hamid. *The Malay Islāmic Ḥikāyat*. Bangi, Selangor, Malaysia, 1983.

Jassin, Hans B. *Polemik: Suatu pembahasan sastera dan kebebasan mencipta berhadepan dengan undang 2 dan agama*. Kuala Lumpur, 1972.

Kratz, Ernst U. "Islamic Attitudes toward Modern Malay Literature." In *Cultural Contact and Textual Interpretation*, edited by C. D. Grijns and S. O. Robson. Dordrecht, 1986.

Maimunah Mohd and Ungku Tahir. *Modern Malay Literary Culture: A Historical Perspective*. Singapore, 1987.

Milner, A. C. "Islam and the Muslim State." In *Islam in South-East Asia*, edited by M. B. Hooker, pp. 23–49. Leiden, 1983.

Naguib al-Attas, Syed. *The Mysticism of Hamzah Fansuri*. Kuala Lumpur, 1970.

Roff, William R. *The Origins of Malay Nationalism*. New Haven, 1967.
Shahnon Ahmad. *Kesusasteraan dan Etika Islam*. Malakka, 1981.

HENDRIK M. J. MAIER

MALAYSIA. The Malay Peninsula before the imposition of British rule in the late nineteenth century was made up of traditional Malay states under the control of hereditary Malay sultans. In these states Islam, which spread to this part of the world during the twelfth to fourteenth centuries, was already strongly established at all levels of society. Aspects of Islamic law were observed to varying degrees, although elements of pre-Islamic culture were still prevalent among the people as a whole. Among the sacral powers of the Malay rulers was responsibility for the defense and good governance of Islam as the state religion. In some states, such as Johore-Riau, Malacca, Kelantan, and Trengganu, certain rulers were well known for their patronage of Islamic religious learning and scholarship.

The role of the religious scholar was essentially that of faithfully preserving, transmitting, translating, and commenting on the classical Arabic texts from Mecca that he had learned, mastered, and to a large extent memorized. The intellectual tradition and paradigm of religious *taqlīd* (faithful preservation and imitation of traditional opinions regarded as authoritative and orthodox) that was nurtured in the Malay kingdoms prior to the twentieth century had roots in the intellectual environment of Mecca in the seventeenth and eighteenth centuries. The inclination toward taṣawwuf (Islamic mysticism) and popularity of Ṣūfī *ṭarīqah*s (brotherhoods) among the Malays was due to the widespread influence of Ṣūfī-oriented Muslim preachers and scholars—hence the preeminent position of al-Ghazālī's thought in the Malay-Indonesian archipelago. Owing to the unifying and integrating thrust of al-Ghazālī's intellectual contributions, many great figures of Islamic learning in the Malay states from the seventeenth century through the nineteenth pursued a tradition of Islamic learning in which *fiqh* (jurisprudence), *taṣawwuf*, and *kalām* (theology) were integrated.

What formal education existed during the early part of the nineteenth century for the Malay community was purely Islamic religious education revolving around the reading and memorization of the Qur'ān and the learning of basic religious rituals such as prayer, fasting, *zakāt*, and the *ḥajj*. The mosque was the only site of such education until the emergence of the *pondok* (private residential religious seminary) in the late nineteenth century and the *madrasah* (school) in the beginning of the twentieth century.

The Muslim states of the Malay Peninsula outside the three Straits Settlements (the island of Penang acquired in 1786, the island of Singapore in 1819, and Melaka [Melacca] in 1824) remained free from British interference until the latter part of the nineteenth century. The Pangkor Treaty of 1874 signaled the imposition of British rule on the Malay states of the peninsula. It provided for the appointment of a British resident to the Malay state; it was incumbent upon the Malay ruler or sultan to ask for his advice and act upon it in all matters "other than those touching Malay Religion and Custom." This led to the creation of a new religio-legal bureaucracy subservient to the royal palace and subordinate to the traditional Malay elites close to the palace. This bureaucratization of Islam served to strengthen the control of the Malay sultan and the secular traditional elite over the religious life of the people.

Perceiving British rule as essentially one of *kāfir* dominance supported by Christian evangelism, the Malay religious leaders and scholars generally adopted a hostile attitude toward western culture. Consequently they mobilized their resources to strengthen and defend the Islamic identity of the masses by building their own *pondok*s and *madrasah*s with independent curricula and financial resources. Except in areas where the spirit of *jihād* against British colonialism or Siamese expansionism in the north was generated by a few prominent religious scholars around the turn of the century, an attitude of resignation and submission to British rule prevailed among both the Malay rulers and the masses.

The beginning of the twentieth century witnessed the emergence of an Islamic reformist *(iṣlāḥ)* movement that began to criticize the socioeconomic backwardness and religious conservatism of traditional Malay society of the time. This new socioreligious activism began when several religious scholars studying in the Middle East came under the powerful influence of the revivalist and reformist ideas of Jamāl al-Dīn al-Afghānī and Muḥammad ʿAbduh at the close of the nineteenth century; others were earlier exposed to the puritanical teachings of the Wahhābī movement. The leader of the Malay reformist movement, Shaykh Ṭāhir Jalāl al-Dīn (1869–1957), a student of ʿAbduh, founded *Al-imām* in 1906, the first periodical to spread the message of Islamic reformism in the Malay-Indonesian archipelago. From their base in Singapore and later in Penang, the reformers pioneered the establishment of modern Islamic schools (*madrasahs*) whose curriculum differed radically from the *pondok* system with the introduction of several modern subjects and a new method of learning and teaching religion. This modernization of religious education and the spread of reformist writings and thought through the new media of magazines and newspapers had far-reaching social and political consequences.

The religious bureaucracy and the traditional *ʿulamāʾ* were used to some religious practices regarded by the reformists as *bidʿah* (unlawful innovation), and they tolerated some degree of accommodation with local traditions that were perceived by the reformists as *khurāfāt* (superstitions and accretions). They opposed the views and activities of the reformists, popularly called Kaum Muda (the Young Group). The call for greater exercise of independent religious reasoning *(ijtihād)* with direct reference to the Qur'ān and the *sunnah* and less reliance on a single *madhhab* (legal sect) was strongly resisted by the traditionalists, who came to be known as Kaum Tua (the Old Group). In their efforts to rouse the Malay community from its intellectual slumber and socioeconomic inferiority to the immigrant non-Muslim communities in the urban centers, the reformists also came to criticize and challenge the political order of the British colonialists. Indeed, the seeds of Malay nationalist consciousness were sown by the reformists. However, the fruits of their labor were to be reaped by the next elite who emerged from the new schools, as well as by the scions of aristocratic families who led the anticolonial struggle in the 1940s and 1950s. Seriously inhibited by British colonial policy coupled with opposition from both the traditionalists and Malay secular elites, Islamic reformism in British Malaya was unable to become an effective social force.

The Japanese interregnum during World War II, though traumatic for the masses, did not seriously alter the position of Islam among the Malays. The Islamic reformist spirit was suppressed while Malay nationalist sentiments were gathering momentum. Postwar Malay nationalism of a conservative orientation saw the foundation of the United Malay Nationalist Organization (UMNO) in 1946. The British formed the Federation of Malaya in 1948 after its Malayan Union proposal was rejected by the Malays. They arrested both the radical Malay nationalist leaders and the proponents of an Islamic political party, Hizbul Muslimin, which was banned a few months after its formation in 1948. The Pan-Malayan Islamic Party (Partai Islam Se-Malaysia, better known as PAS) originally developed from the defection of the *ʿulamāʾ* faction in UMNO in 1951 and became a registered political party in 1955. Its emergence marked another turning point in the development of Islamic thought in the Malay states. The idea of establishing an Islamic state in British Malaya was propagated and articulated for the first time as mainstream Malay nationalists in UMNO pressed for the independence of the country from British rule. The British granted independence to the Federation of Malaya in 1957, with Singapore becoming a separate colony, and thus began the era of parliamentary democracy and constitutional monarchy. In 1963 Malaysia came into being, with the inclusion of Singapore (until mid-1965) and the two Bornean states of Sabah and Sarawak.

The total population of Malaysia in mid-1990 was estimated to be 17,755,900, compared with 13,764,352 in mid-1980. According to 1990 estimates, the Muslim Malays in peninsular Malaysia constituted 58 percent of the total population, the Chinese 31 percent, and the Indians 10 percent. The 1980 census put Muslims at 53 percent, Buddhists at 17.3 percent, Confucians, Taoists, and traditional Chinese believers at 11.6 percent, Christians at 8.6 percent, and Hindus at 7 percent.

Although the position of Islam as the official religion of post-independence Malaysia—with the Malay rulers of each state serving as the guardians of Islamic religion and Malay custom—was guaranteed in the constitution, only some aspects of the life of the Muslim community and the nation were influenced by Islamic values and norms. The government under the leadership of Tunku Abdul Rahman with the support of the British was committed to a secularistic vision of the new nation and vigorously opposed the Islamic political struggle and ideals. As such, it came under strong attack from the PAS and Islamically oriented Malay organizations. Five years after the 1969 racial riots, the PAS joined the coalition government of the National Front. As a result, the government under the second prime minister of Malaysia, Tun Abdul Razak, established the Islamic Centre, which formed an important part of the Islamic Religious Affairs section of the Prime Minister's department. Tun Abdul Razak's government gave increased attention to the educational, social, and economic development of the Malay Muslims to accommodate the demands coming from PAS within the government and from the *daʿwah* movement outside it.

The assertive and generally anti-establishment *daʿwah*

(Islamic proselytization) movement emerged in the 1970s through the activities of youth organizations in secular educational institutions, including PKPIM and ABIM (the Muslim Youth Movement of Malaysia, established in 1971). It represented a new phase in Islamic thought and action, but its vision of Islam as a complete and holistic way of life was in fact a continuation and elaboration of earlier reformist and revivalist movements in the Middle East and Pakistan. Complementing the Islamic political movement in the country, the youth-led *daʿwah* organizations pressed for the greater application of Islamic laws and values in national life and articulated the holistic Islamic perspective of social, economic, and spiritual development. While the scope of Islamic religiosity was widened to embrace all aspects of human life, the intensity of religious life was simultaneously emphasized by *daʿwah* proponents. Thus the form and content of Islamic life were noticeably affected. The government under Tun Hussein Onn at first viewed the new phenomenon negatively and was extremely wary of the political effect of assertive, Malay-dominated *daʿwah* on the multiracial nation and its own political strength. One of the central government's responses was to initiate its own *daʿwah*-oriented institutions and activities under the aegis of the Islamic Centre and in cooperation with government-linked Muslim missionary organizations such as PERKIM, USIA in Sabah, and BINA in Sarawak. The Ministry of Education was also progressively improving and upgrading the teaching of Islam in the schools; it established the Faculty of Islamic Studies in the National University of Malaysia in 1970, opening up new opportunities for Islamically committed graduates to work in the civil service.

The resurgence of the holistic Islamic consciousness spearheaded by the *daʿwah* movement, with its call for Islamic alternatives, continued to influence the Malay community as well as the state authorities. It reached a high point around 1979–1982 with the victory of the Islamic revolution in Iran. The demand for the establishment of more Islamic institutions in the country was raised by several organizations in national seminars and international conferences held in Malaysia. The government under Tun Hussein Onn's premiership made some concessions and decided to conduct a feasibility study for the establishment of an Islamic bank in Malaysia; when Dr. Mahathir Mohamed became prime minister in 1981, this was one of the projects that received his immediate attention.

Under Mahathir's leadership the government took a more conciliatory and positive approach toward the demands of the *daʿwah* movement. PAS had been forced to leave the National Front coalition government in 1977 and had continued its struggle for complete implementation of the *sharīʿah* and the establishment of an Islamic state in Malaysia as an opposition party. It regarded Mahathir's Islamic initiatives and efforts as "cosmetic islamization" aimed at undermining the influence of the Islamic party. Anwar Ibrahim, the charismatic leader of ABIM and an articulate spokesman of nonpartisan *daʿwah* in the 1970s, decided to support Mahathir by joining his government in 1982 in order to achieve his Islamic objectives from within the administration. Anwar Ibrahim's support gave a new lease on life to Mahathir's Islamic initiatives. The creation of the Islamic Bank and the establishment of the International Islamic University in 1983, followed by the that of the International Institute of Islamic Thought and Civilization in 1987, were the immediate results of Anwar's direct involvement in Mahathir's administration.

Under Mahathir the islamization process in Malaysia entered yet another important new phase. This included the institutionalization of concrete Islamic programs within the government; the inculcation of Islamic values in the administration; the encouragement of Islamic intellectual discourse in government departments and institutions of higher learning; the reform of national education by incorporating Islamic perspectives and values; the initiation of changes in the legal system to facilitate the growth and expansion of Islamic *sharīʿah* court administration; the removal of glaringly un-Islamic practices from the official ceremonies of government departments; finding ways and means to cease the practice of charging interest on government loans to Muslims; and the establishment of an Islamic insurance company, an Institute of Islamic Understanding (1992), and interest-free banking facilities in conventional commercial banks (1993). In foreign relations the Mahathir administration strengthened its pro-Palestinian and anti-Israel policy. It became more vocal and consistently critical of the superpowers.

The widening scope of Islamic consciousness outside the government framework also affected the world of Malay literature and journalism, which had formerly been under the influence of socialist as well as secular humanist trends. The urgency for an Islamic paradigm in economics and other social sciences in the universities was articulated in the late 1970s and 1980s as part of a new realization among Muslim intellectual circles worldwide. Thus the mission for the "islamization of human knowledge" came into being, and the International Islamic University, Malaysia, was entrusted with pursuing it without any government obstruction. [*See* International Islamic University at Kuala Lumpur.] Meanwhile, the ABIM leadership decided to change its approach of sloganeering and Islamic rhetoric to one of "problem-solving" and "corrective participation" in cooperation with the government. The emphasis on solving immediate social problems and direct involvement in community development seemed to be the order of the day in the early 1990s. All the major Islamic *daʿwah* organizations, such as ABIM, Darul Arqam, and JIM (Jamaah Islah Malaysia, established in 1991), have embarked on active educational programs for preschool, primary, and secondary school children nationwide.

PAS, as an opposition party, and some Islamic factions continued to dwell on the ideal of an Islamic state, the abolition of secularism, and the complete implementation of the *sharīʿah,* including that of capital punishment (*ḥudūd*) in the state of Kelantan. The Muslim community in the 1990s, however, is confronted with many new issues, such as efficient management of big businesses, increasing whitecollar crime, environmental degradation, serious drug abuse, AIDS, the plight of Muslim female workers in factories, widespread corruption and fraud, negative influences of the electronic media, and increased interreligious dialogue. As Malaysia moves toward the goal of becoming an industrialized nation by the year 2020, the place of ethics and spiritual values in an industrial society will certainly become more crucial. Several Muslim leaders and Islamic groups are beginning to realize that the challenges of industrializing Malaysia are far too numerous and complex to be handled by any one group or party. The future demands greater unity, cooperation, and interdependence among all groups within the Muslim community.

[*See also* ABIM; Dar ul Arqam; Daʿwah, *article on* Modern Usage; Madrasah; Malay and Indonesian Literature; Partai Islam Se-Malaysia; PERKIM; United Malays National Organization; *and the biography of Ibrahim.*]

BIBLIOGRAPHY

Ahmad Ibrahim, ed. *Readings on Islam in Southeast Asia.* Singapore, 1985.

Bastin, John, and Robin W. Winks. *Malaysia: Selected Historical Readings.* Kuala Lumpur, 1966.

Deliar Noer. *The Modernist Muslim Movement in Indonesia 1900–1942.* Singapore, 1973.

Funston, John. *Malay Politics in Malaysia: A Study of United Malays National Organization and Party Islam.* Kuala Lumpur, 1980.

Holt, P. M., ed. *The Cambridge History of Islam.* Vol. 2. Cambridge, 1970. Chapters 2 and 3 are extremely useful.

Hooker, M. B., ed. *Islam in South-East Asia.* Leiden, 1983.

Lyon, M. L. "The Dakwah Movment in Malaysia," *Review of Indonesian and Malayan Affairs* 13.2 (1979).

Mauzy, D. K., and R. S. Milne. "The Mahathir Administration in Malaysia: Discipline Through Islam." *Pacific Affairs* 56.4 (Winter 1983–1984): 617–648.

Means, G. P. "The Role of Islam in the Political Development of Malaysia." *Comparative Politics* 1 (1969): 264–284.

Mohd, Nor bin Ngah. *Kitab Jawi: Islamic Thought of the Malay Muslim Scholars.* Singapore, 1982.

Morais, J. V. *Anwar Ibrahim: Resolute in Leadership.* Kuala Lumpur, 1983.

Muhammad Kamal Hassan. "The Response of Muslim Youth Organizations to Political Change: HMI in Indonesia and ABIM in Malaysia." In *Islam and the Political Economy of Meaning,* edited by W. R. Roff, pp. 180–196. New York, 1987.

Muhammad Kamal Hassan. *Moral and Ethical Issues in Human Resource Development: Old Problems and New Challenges.* Kuala Lumpur, 1993.

Naguib al-Attas, Syed Muhammad. *Some Aspects of Sufism as Understood and Practised among the Malays.* Singapore, 1963.

Naguib al-Attas, Syed Muhammad. *Preliminary Statement of a General Theory of the Islamization of the Malay-Indonesian Archipelago.* Kuala Lumpur, 1969.

Revival of Islam in Malaysia: The Role of ABIM. Kuala Lumpur, n.d.

Roff, W. R. *The Origins of Malay Nationalism.* Kuala Lumpur, 1967.

Snouck Hurgronje, Christiaan. *Mekka in the Latter Part of the Nineteenth Century.* Leiden and London, 1931.

M. Kamal Hassan

MALCOLM X (1925–1965), born Malcolm Little, also known as El-Hajj Malik El-Shabazz; African American Muslim leader, civil and human rights advocate, Pan-Africanist and Pan-Islamist. The life of America's most conspicuous Muslim in the 1960s was shaped by resentment of white (European American) racism and a determination to improve the lives of African Americans. Malcolm was born in Omaha, Nebraska, to uneducated, poor, Christian, "black nationalist" (Garveyite) parents whose unfortunate destinies affected him throughout his life. He believed that whites had murdered his father and unjustly placed his mother in an insane asylum and himself and his siblings in different foster homes (Malcolm X and Alex Haley, *Autobiography of Malcolm X,* New York, 1965, pp. 2, 12–13, 17–18, 21, 22). At the age of fifteen, when Malcolm finished the eighth grade, he knew that he was disinclined toward formal education and established religion. He chose a life of vice and crime.

Malcolm's imprisonment for larceny (1946–1952) marked the beginning of his intellectual and social transformation. Prison was the "academy" where he read Western and Eastern philosophy and literature, works on Christianity, genetics, and American slavery, and improved his oral skills. The scope of his readings may have exceeded that of the average American undergraduate (Bruce Perry, *Malcolm: The Life of a Man Who Changed Black America,* Barrytown, N.Y., 1991, p. 118). His informal studies introduced him to Islamic precepts and Muslim heroic history.

Encouraged by his siblings and an inmate, Malcolm converted in 1948 to the doctrines of the Honorable Elijah Muhammad (d. 1975), leader of the Nation of Islam. Malcolm was attracted by Muhammad's principal claims that God is a black man (often called Master W. F. Muhammad) who will liberate African Americans and destroy Satan, their white oppressors (Armageddon), and that Elijah Muhammad was his messenger. Malcolm was equally fascinated by Muhammad's verbal boldness and his sanction of retaliatory, not aggressive, violence. Malcolm's social experiences, intellectual accomplishments, and dedication to his leader qualified him for an ascendant position in the Nation.

Muhammad's appointment of Malcolm X to the leadership of Temple Number Seven (mid-1954) in the Harlem district of New York City was crucial to his and the Nation's fame. As Third World and American political activism expanded in the late 1950s and early 1960s, Malcolm became increasingly brazen in his denunciation of racism, and publicly supportive of African American, African, and Muslim liberation. Some of his speeches tested his leader's protective policies of political inaction and avoidance of unnecessary contact with Sunnī Muslims. Nonetheless Muhammad recognized the benefits of giving him a margin of freedom, provided Malcolm's loyalty was evident.

From 1959 onward, Malcolm allowed his eagerness for modification of Muhammad's policies and his own popularity to make his loyalty questionable. His short visits to Saudi Arabia and African countries, as Muhammad's emissary, and the national broadcast of "The Hate That Hate Produced" (1959), his most effective television interview, strengthened his political attraction. Malcolm was disappointed that Elijah Muhammad's visit to Muslim countries (1959), and his performance of the Lesser Pilgrimage (*ʿumrah*), did not result in significant political changes in the Nation (Akbar Muḥammad, in Yvonne Y. Haddad et al., eds., *The Islamic Impact,* Syracuse, 1984, p. 205).

Under the watchful eyes of envious officials of the Nation, Malcolm gradually modified his administration of Muhammad's Mosque Number Seven. Although he continued to respond sharply to Sunnī Muslim condemnation of the Nation's theology, he instituted regular Arabic instruction and maintained close contact with Muslim diplomats. Furthermore, Malcolm deemphasized the Nation's doctrine of "the satanic nature of whites" and instructed his assistant ministers in African and Asian cultures and current affairs (Malcolm X and Haley, 1965, p. 298; Benjamin Karim et al., *Remembering Malcolm,* New York, 1992, pp. 97, 98, 128, 146–147). These modifications were indicative of the less-restrained, sociopolitical activist role he wished to perform.

Malcolm provided his detractors in the Nation and Elijah Muhammad with an excuse to rid themselves of what they perceived as a threat to their power. Contrary to his leader's directive not to comment on the murder of President John F. Kennedy (November 1963), Malcolm compared it to "chickens coming home to roost." Although he claimed that his remark was inadvertent (Malcolm X and Haley, 1965, p. 305; Louis E. Lomax, 1968, pp. 126–127), it reflected his impatience with Muhammad's political restrictions. Yet he was neither organizationally nor financially prepared for his suspension (December 1963). His withdrawal from the Nation (March 1964) represented his realization that he was not indispensable to Muhammad's movement and his determination to be an effective political activist. His vindictive exposure of Muhammad's immorality, about which he had heard in the 1950s (Malcolm X and Haley, 1965, p. 299; Peter Goldman, *The Death and Life of Malcolm X,* New York, 1973), did not augment much his meager following or his prestige.

Malcolm's public confrontation with Muhammad was not essentially doctrinal. Months after his withdrawal from the Nation, he continually acknowledged Muhammad as his spiritual leader, and he asserted that their differences were primarily political and moral.

Among Malcolm's most urgent concerns were his Islamic credibility, funds, and his racist image. He probably thought his conversion to Sunnī Islam and his pilgrimage, (*ḥajj*) in 1964 would help to resolve these problems and reconcile him with Muslims internationally. Now known as El-Hajj Malik El-Shabazz, his acts of piety, his celebrated letter from Mecca, and his meetings with Muslim heads of state and Islamic officials apparently were not given much laudatory coverage in the Arabic press. Malcolm knew that Muslim dignitaries wished him well and recognized the Islamic legitimacy of his sociopolitical concerns, but their belated and parsimonious response to his need for material and moral support negatively affected the growth of his short-lived Muslim Mosque, Inc., and Organization of Afro-American Unity (founded in March and June 1964, respectively, now apparently defunct).

Immigrant Muslims, whom Malcolm had charged two years earlier with deliberate disinclination toward proselytization among African Americans (Louis E. Lomax, *When the Word is Given . . .* , New York, 1963, pp. 140–141), were unconvinced of his Islamic sincerity. Most American Sunnī Muslims were similarly unresponsive. Despite their admiration of his advocacy of civil and human rights, which the Organization of African Unity resolved to support in the United Nations, Malcolm's recent past and his conversion attracted few of them to the Muslim Mosque, Inc.

It is debatable whether Malik completely abandoned the notion of an organic relationship between European and American whites and Satan. Malcolm had seen phenotypically white Muslims—and African Americans—and accepted them as brothers long before his travels abroad. Minimally, his post-pilgrimage statements indicate his increased preparedness not to offend potential supporters.

The influence of Malcolm X, rather than El-Hajj Malik El-Shabazz, is most observable among non-Muslims and Muslims. Under pressure from mainly non-Muslim African Americans, New York City is to dedicate as a municipal monument part of the Audubon Ballroom, where assassins' bullets cut short Malcolm's last speech. His birthday and his assassination on 21 February 1965, by members of the Nation of Islam, with the apparent complicity of American authorities, are widely remembered. He was given a Muslim burial by an obscure African American Sunnī organization (Heshaam Jaaber, *The Final Chapter. . . . I Buried Malcolm (Haj Malik El-Shabazz)*, Jersey City, N.J., 1993, pp. 64–68, 80–81). The Sunnī Muslim community was conspicuously underrepresented at his funeral, which was held in a church. He is immortalized by reprints of his best-selling *Autobiography*, his speeches, and biographies; streets, schools, and other buildings, including the former Mosque Number Seven, bear his name. Muslims reproach non-Muslims for their projection of El-Hajj Malik El-Shabazz as an ethnocentric revolutionary whose primary concern was civil and human rights, not Islamic proselytization *(daʿwah)*.

Spike Lee's internationally acclaimed film *Malcolm X* (1992), generated the most varied discussion of Malcolm since his death. Many immigrant and American Muslims, notably Imam Warith Deen Mohammed, have confirmed Malcolm's Islamic genuineness. Minister Louis Farrakhan continues to speak ill of Malcolm's attitude toward Elijah Muhammad's immorality; he cautions that Lee's film may cause further division in the present Nation of Islam, which he leads. Both Imam Mohammed and Minister Farrakhan claim to continue Malcolm's social and political work. Although both "Malcolm X" and "El-Hajj Malik El-Shabazz" are considered martyrs, the life of "Malik" was too brief, and thus his Islamic legacy too meager, to compete with "Malcolm" for an exalted place in the collective Muslim memory.

[*See also* Nation of Islam *and the biography of Elijah Muhammad.*]

BIBLIOGRAPHY

Speeches and Interviews

Malcolm X. *Malcolm X Speaks*. Edited by George Breitman. New York, 1965. Useful collection of his post-Nation religious and political thought.

Malcolm X. *The End of White World Supremacy: Four Speeches*. Edited by Benjamin Goodman. New York, 1971. Rare representation of his doctrinal and social thought before his conversion to Sunnī Islam.

Malcolm X. *February 1965: The Final Speeches*. New York, 1992. The latest and most useful compilation of Malcolm's last presentations abroad.

Works about Malcolm X

Carson, Clayborne. *Malcolm X: The FBI File*. Edited by David Gallen. New York, 1991.

Clarke, John Henrik, ed. *Malcolm X: The Man and His Times* (1969). Trenton, N.J., 1993. The best collection to date of essays by persons who were associated with Malcolm in the United States and abroad, including his widow.

Cone, James H. *Martin & Malcolm & America: A Dream or a Nightmare?* Maryknoll, N.Y., 1991. Outstanding analysis by a renowned African American exponent of Christian liberation theology.

Evanzz, Karl. *The Judas Factor: The Plot to Kill Malcolm X*. New York, 1992. Ambitious, informative attempt to analyze the motives for Malcolm's assassination.

Kly, Y. N., ed. *The Black Book: The True Political Philosophy of Malcolm X (El Hajj Malik El Shabazz)*. Atlanta and Ottawa, 1986. A Muslim's interpretation of Malcolm's religio-social and political doctrines.

Lomax, Louis E. *To Kill a Black Man.* Los Angeles, 1968. The earliest and fullest comparative analysis of the thoughts of Malcolm X and Martin Luther King by a close associate of both men.

AKBAR MUḤAMMAD

MALI. The region now within the Republic of Mali has been exposed to Islam for more than nine hundred years. In present-day Mali the Islamic presence has grown to the point where 80 to 90 percent of the population of approximately 9 million is Muslim, the most significant minority faiths being Catholic Christianity and so-called "paganism." Islam has always been more entrenched in the north, mainly because of its transmission from the Maghrib through trans-Saharan trade and the Moroccan invasion of Songhay in the sixteenth century.

By the early nineteenth century the major centers of learning—Timbuktu, Gao, and Jenne—had long been in decline in terms of Islamic scholarship, largely because of insecurities brought about by conquest and fluctuations in trade. More popular versions of the faith, based on rote recitation of the Qur'ān and adherence to the Qādirīyah brotherhood, were practiced in the northern countryside, especially among the nomadic Tuareg, Fulani, and Moors. The south remained largely resistant to Islam, with the Bambara and Dogon being known for their adherence to local polytheistic religious systems.

As in other parts of the Sahel in the nineteenth century, a social context that combined the expanded popularity of Islam with reduced scholarly rigor and frontier societies resistant to the faith became fertile ground for historically significant reform efforts. The *jihād* of Usuman Dan Fodio from 1804 to 1810 did not penetrate far into the territory, but it did lead to settlement by a vanguard of Fulani warriors on the eastern portion of the Niger bend near Ansongo. The *jihād* of ʿUmar Tal in the mid-nineteenth century had a greater effect on the Islamic heritage of Mali. Although ʿUmar Tal was defeated and killed in battle in 1864, his holy war did result in a widened influence of the Tijānīyah. Through much of the nineteenth century a more peaceful revival of the Qādirīyah was largely inspired by the Kunta jurists Sīdī al-Mukhtār (d. 1811) and Shaykh Sīdīyah al-Kabīr (d. 1868). With their close links with the Berber and Arab traditions of North Africa, Kunta jurists are largely responsible for the present-day dominance of Maghribi influence throughout West Africa. [*See* Tijānīyah; Qādirīyah; *and the biographies of Dan Fodio and ʿUmar Tal.*]

Like other parts of French West Africa, this region underwent an Islamic resurgence that increased in momentum through the period of colonial occupation. This was expressed in a number of reform movements, most notably the Hamallīyah and the Wahhābīyah.

The Hamallīyah was an offshoot of the Tijānī brotherhood that developed in the Nyoro region in the early 1940s. Aside from veneration of its founder Shaykh Hamallah, its main distinguishing characteristic was a revised formula of recitation *(wird)* that used an eleven-bead rosary. Despite Shaykh Hamallah's espousal of pacifism, his followers became involved in a massacre directed against a rival nomadic group, resulting in harsh suppression by the French. The scattering of the Hamallīyah resulted in two very different successors to the movement: a quietist Ṣūfī tradition exemplified by Cerno Bokar, and more overtly enthusiastic, short-lived uprisings, including the abortive *jihād* of Musa Aminu in his natal village of Wani north of Bourem.

In the postwar phase of colonization, more lasting reform efforts were initiated by West Africans who had been educated in the Middle East. One of the central platforms of these reformers was opposition to the perceived excesses of the brotherhoods, including veneration of holy men and dependence on "Islamic magic," such as the manufacture of amulets, for worldly aid. As with some medieval reformers of Christian Europe, their reforms have hinged on scriptural literacy and a basic understanding by the laity of the original sacred texts. This reformist trend was to become known as Wahhabism because the French saw a negative similarity between these reformers and the puritan followers of Ibn ʿAbd al-Wahhāb of the eastern Arabian Peninsula (d. 1787). One important West African reformer, ʿAbd al-Raḥmān al-Ifrīqī, a native of the Ansongo region, became a fulltime resident of Saudi Arabia, where he taught in the Islamic schools Dār al-Ḥadīth and al-Maʿhad al-Ilmī. Many of his students were West African pilgrims who returned to their natal areas with greater religious knowledge and commitment. More significant was the return to Bamako of a group of students from al-Azhar University in Cairo who established the Muslim youth organization Subbanu al-Muslimīn in the 1950s.

Trading groups were central to the development of the Wahhābīyah, particularly in Bamako, a strategically situated trading center. Since independence, however, there has been an expansion of reformed Islam into a wide range of social groups, including students, administrative officials, and peasants. An increase in the popularity of the Wahhābīyah during the later phase of colonialism and the first decades of independence was marked by disputes and occasional violence between adherents of the Ṣūfī orders and the reformers. Such disputes often hinged on the outward symbols of change, such as the fact that the reformers pray with arms folded across the chest rather than hanging at the sides. [*See* Wahhābīyah.]

The first independent government (1960–1968) led by Modibo Kieta promoted radical state socialism; although its ideology was moderated by a Pan-African Islamic identification, this regime had a dampening effect on the development of Islam. Islamic reform efforts sponsored by Malian clerics, however, continued to make progress, especially in the migrant communities or *zongo*s of West African coastal cities. The military government of Mousa Traore (1968–1991), while remaining nominally secular, was more tolerant of the development of Islam. In 1971, however, the Traore government disbanded the Union Culturelle Musulmane, the main organizational body of reformers in Bamako, and in the 1980s it made efforts to bring religious organizations under government control, first in 1981 by creating the Association Malien pour l'Unité et le Progrès de l'Islam, sponsored by the state to the exclusion of other formal Islamic organizations, and then by regulating Islamic education, sanctioning only officially recognized *madrasahs*. Despite such efforts to coopt Islamic reform, independent movements such as the Jamāʿat Anṣār al-Sunnah of the Gao region have continued to exist on the margins of state control.

BIBLIOGRAPHY

Brenner, Louis. *West African Sufi*. London, 1984. Detailed examination of the historical background and teaching of Cerno Bokar, which provides some material on the Hamallīyah.

Kaba, Lasiné. *The Wahhabiyya: Islamic Reform and Politics in French West Africa*. Evanston, Ill., 1974. Considers the development and political involvement of Islamic reformers in the postwar colonial period.

Launay, Robert. *Traders without Trade*. Cambridge, 1982. Good case study of the place of trading groups in the development of West African Islam.

Niezen, R. W. "The Community of Helpers of the Sunna: Islamic Reform among the Songhay of Gao (Mali)." *Africa* 3 (1990): 399–424.

Robinson, David. *The Holy War of Umar Tal: The Western Sudan in the Mid-Nineteenth Century*. Oxford, 1985. The most thorough historical study of ʿUmar Tal's background and career.

Saad, Elias N. *Social History of Timbuktu: The Role of Muslim Scholars and Notables, 1400–1900*. Cambridge, 1983. The best study to date on the political background of Timbuktu, but not as strong in its sociological analysis.

Stewart, C. C., and E. K. Stewart. *Islam and Social Order in Mauritania*. Oxford, 1973. Excellent study of the scholars and Islamic traditions of Mauritania whose influence reached much of present-day Mali.

RONALD NIEZEN

MALIK. *See* Monarchy.

MĀLIKĪ. *See* Law, *article on* Legal Thought and Jurisprudence.

MALKOM KHĀN (1833/34–1908), or Malkum Khān, an enigmatic figure in late nineteenth- and early twentieth-century Iranian history. He was an advocate of progress and reform, but he was often motivated by self-aggrandizement and self-interest. He called for political and governmental changes as well as cultural ones that included Persian language and alphabet reform. As one of the first to write in a recognizably modern prose idiom and as an editor of *Qānūn,* his influential newspaper, Malkom Khān's most important historical contribution is perhaps to be found here, even though he has not been regarded as a major literary figure or stylist. It was in Turkey rather than Iran that alphabet reform was achieved. The liberal political values expressed in *Qānūn* found expression in the Iranian Constitution of 1905–1906.

Malkom Khān was born into an Armenian family in Julfa Isfahan. Malkom, like his father, Yaʿkūb Khān, studied abroad, learned French, served as an interpreter and translator, established useful patronage links, was a self-professed Muslim with interests in freemasonry and an advocate of cultural change including alphabet reform. Malkom returned from Paris at the age of eighteen to work as an interpreter in Dār al-Funūn, the new college in Tehran, where he also taught geography and natural science. Five years later, through patronage ties with Nasīr al-Dīn Shāh and his prime minister, Malkom returned to Europe as the member of a diplomatic mission to conclude peace with Britain. This was the beginning of his diplomatic career and European travel that convinced him of the superiority of European civilization and the value of westernization. In Paris, he was initiated into a Masonic lodge.

Malkom Khān returned to Iran in 1858 and was involved with the introduction of the telegraph in Iran and wrote his first treatise on political and administrative reform, which was influenced by Ottoman models. He advocated, among other general principles, the separation of the legislative from the executive branch, codification of law, equality before the law, and freedom of belief. In addition, he also spelled out specific recommendations for the implementation of these principles in Western-style ministries, comprehensive education, the development of roads, increased government revenues, a reformed military, and a national bank. He established a freemasonry-type society and used it as a base for political action and reform. The shah forced the closure of his lodge because of its secrecy and membership that included potential rivals for the monarchy.

In late 1861 Malkom Khān was sent into exile, first in Baghdad and then Istanbul, where he was assigned as counselor at the Iranian embassy. In 1868 he was dismissed and given Ottoman nationality but was reappointed to his position in the Iranian embassy, which he held until 1871. From 1873 to 1889 he served as Iran's minister in London. In 1889, he was involved in a financial scandal relating to a proposed national lottery in Iran, which resulted in his final dismissal and the loss of his titles. In 1890, he began publishing his influential newspaper, *Qānūn*, which attacked Qājār despotism, stressed westernization as the means for saving Iranian sovereignty, and called for a constitution and parliamentary government. *Qānūn*, influenced by Turkish newspapers in Istanbul, was printed in London and smuggled into Iran, where it was widely circulated and read by like-minded clerical and secular anti-Qājār reformers. It ceased publication in 1898. Malkom died on a visit to Switzerland in 1908.

[*See also* Qājār Dynasty.]

BIBLIOGRAPHY

Algar, Hamid. *Mīrzā Malkum Khān: A Study in the History of Iranian Modernism.* Berkeley, 1973.

Keddie, Nikki, and Mehrdad Amanat, "Iran under the Later Qajars, 1848–1922." In *The Cambridge History of Iran, 7, From Nadir Shah to the Islamic Republic,* edited by Peter Avery, Gavin Hambly, and Charles Melville. pp. 174–212. Cambridge, 1991.

GENE R. GARTHWAITE

MAMLŪK STATE. A regime controlled by slave soldiers (sg. *mamlūk*, pl. *mamālīk;* "one owned") governed Egypt, Syria, southeastern Asia Minor, and western Arabia (*al-Ḥijāz;* the Hejaz) from 1250 to 1517 CE. Founded by officers (*amīrs*) of the last Ayyūbid sultan al-Ṣāliḥ Ayyūb (d. 1249), the Mamlūk State was born under the shadow of usurpation. Fearing their displacement by al-Ṣāliḥ's heir Tūrān-Shāh, these officers, who had attained high rank in their former master's Baḥrīya regiment, assassinated the legitimate claimant and designated one of their own as sultan. The first two sultans, Aybak and Quṭuz, were preoccupied with quelling internal rebellion by their own subordinates and external rivalry by surviving Ayyūbid princes in Syria. Quṭuz's lieutenant Baybars won renown following his victory over invading Mongols at ʿAyn Jālūt (Spring of Goliath) in Palestine, but soon thereafter he murdered his sovereign and began to formalize his administration.

Sultan Baybars (r. 1260–1277) spent much of his reign battling the Crusader states in Syria-Palestine and securing his eastern frontiers against invasions from Il-khānid Iran. Yet he did not neglect the infrastructure of his regime. The Nile Valley's agrarian resources were inventoried, and the Ayyūbid system of land allotments to militarists (*iqṭāʿ*s) was restructured. In consequence of Baybars's policies and those of his major successors, Qalāwūn (r. 1279–1290) and al-Nāṣir Muḥammad (r. 1310–1341), a state far more centralized than its Ayyūbid predecessor was created in the central Arab lands. Moreover, Baybars offered haven in Cairo to an uncle of the last ʿAbbāsid caliph in Baghdad (dispatched by the Mongols in 1258), and so the orthodox caliphate was revived in Egypt—but under the Mamlūk sultan's strict control. The caliph now functioned solely as the sultan's legitimator, thereby mitigating the seizure that had sullied the origins of his office.

Until the mid-fifteenth century, the Mamlūk State flourished as the undisputed military power of the central Muslim world. Although the regime recruited its ruling oligarchy from men who were imported as slaves, and therefore never surmounted the sedition and intrigue that had given it birth, the Mamlūk sultanate stabilized the political order in this turbulent zone for 267 years. Until around 1340, when the Black Death decimated the populace of both Egypt and Syria, the regime enjoyed an era of prosperity. Agrarian productivity was high, and the trade linking South Asia with the Mediterranean poured copious revenues into the government's coffers. The Mamlūk autocrat was acknowledged as the paramount monarch of Sunnī Islam because of his dominion over all four holy cities (Mecca, Medina,

Jerusalem, and Hebron). No foreign competitor in Europe or Southwest Asia posed any tangible threat to Mamlūk suzerainty until the final decade of the fifteenth century, when the international balance of power altered radically. Because Mamlūk factional quarreling was confined largely to the military elite, the mass of the population and its productive sectors remained unscathed until insurmountable fiscal crises compelled the regime to adopt predatory measures to stave off bankruptcy. Cairo, Damascus, and Aleppo flourished as brilliant centers of culture, while the literary arts experienced a "silver age" of refinement. The Mamlūk elite invested heavily in charitable endowments (*waqf*s) that supported a sophisticated religio-academic class in these urban centers. Cairo in particular cast a cosmopolitan lure across the Islamic world, attracting scholars to its schools from afar.

The sultanate's economy never recovered fully from the famines and plagues of the later fourteenth century. Whether the regime could have devised long-term strategies rather than short-term expedients to surmount these disasters—had its elite been less preoccupied with disputes among cadres—remains a debated issue. Certainly the emergence of the formidable Ottoman military threat in Asia Minor, plus the growing maritime menace from Europe, transcended the Mamlūks' powers of deterrence. Thus, after more than one hundred years of stop-gap efforts to recover its former glory, the Mamlūk sultanate was defeated in 1516 at Marj Dābiq in Syria by the Ottoman monarch Selim I. Cairo fell to Selim the following year. Today, historians castigate the Mamlūk State for its acceleration of economic decline in the central Arab lands. Yet this regime indelibly shaped the bureaucracy and administrative profile of Egypt into modern times. The sultanate imparted a legacy of security to these regions that later governments have sought with less success to emulate.

[*See also* Egypt; Ottoman Empire.]

BIBLIOGRAPHY

Ayalon, David. *Studies on the Mamlūks of Egypt, 1250–1517*. London, 1977. *The Mamlūk Military Society*. London, 1979. Collected articles by the leading authority on the Mamlūk institution.

Irwin, Robert. *The Middle East in the Middle Ages: The Early Mamluk Sultanate, 1250–1382*. London, 1986. Political survey of the Baḥrī Mamlūk era.

Lapidus, Ira. *Muslim Cities in the Later Middle Ages*. Cambridge, 1967. Insightful description of urban society under Mamlūk rule, with an extensive bibliography.

Petry, Carl F. *The Civilian Elite of Cairo in the Later Middle Ages*. Princeton, 1981. Quantitative analysis of the scholastic elite (*ʿulamāʾ*) during the Mamlūk period.

CARL F. PETRY

MARĀGHĪ, MUṢṬAFĀ AL- (1881–1945), Egyptian reformist and rector of al-Azhar (1928–1929 and 1935–1945). Shaykh Muṣṭafā al-Marāghī is the link between the reforms of his mentor Muḥammad ʿAbduh and such subsequent leaders of al-Azhar as Muṣṭafā ʿAbd al-Rāziq, ʿAbd al-Ḥalīm Maḥmūd, and Maḥmūd Shaltūt; the last, his professed disciple, later transformed al-Azhar by compromising with the secular nationalist regime of Gamal Abdel Nasser.

He was described by his contemporaries as a unique man of strong character and leadership abilities. Marāghī's dismissal by King Fu'ād in 1929 caused a revolt among the Azhari *ʿulamāʾ* that resulted in the dismissal of seventy of them.

As a reformer, Marāghī believed in Islam's flexibility and ability to adapt to the needs of modernity. He called for social, legal, and educational reforms and pursued an aggressive campaign-begun by ʿAbduh and finished by Shaltūt—to integrate the modern sciences into al-Azhar's curriculum. To that end he organized committees to reform the university's regulations and curriculum and created a supervisory department for research whose responsibilities included publishing and translation.

Maraghi called for the exercise of *ijtihād*, reinterpretation, and opposed *taqlīd*, the blind following of tradition. He worked for the reconciliation of different Muslim *madhhab*s (schools of law) and cooperated with the Aga Khan in setting up Islamic educational and research associations to arbitrate between various *madhhab*s and strengthen ties among them. He also waged a campaign against Christian missionaries and the schools they opened in Egypt, which he felt were comprising Islam and undermining Islamic society. He also participated in international religious conferences, where he asked for recognition of the equality of all religious groups.

Marāghī was in several senses an enigmatic figure. Although a leader at conservative al-Azhar, he was nevertheless a close associate of Aḥmad Luṭfī al-Sayyid and the liberal Aḥrār Dustūrīyūn Party. He opposed British rule, yet he often cooperated with the British. He refused to support King Fu'ād's bid for the Islamic caliphate after its 1924 cancellation by Atatürk, yet later he joined Miṣr al-Fatāt's Aḥmad Ḥusayn in calling upon

King Fārūq (who reinstated him as Shaykh al-Azhar in 1935) to claim it. His professed desire for a greater role in government for the clergy did not stop him from proposing a reform program that, if fully implemented, could have weakened them, since it included closure of Dār al-ᶜUlūm and the school for *sharīᶜah* judges. It is also reported that he proposed the translation (to other than Arabic languages) of the Qur'ān to King Fārūq.

As Shaykh al-Azhar, Marāghī exerted a final effort to keep that institution under full clerical authority at a time when the *ᶜulamā'* were losing authority to a new bureaucratic and intellectual order whose discourse was secularly oriented. Students of Egyptian social history also note his provincial origin in the small Upper Egyptian town of Maragha near Tahta as a reminder of the often-forgotten importance of the periphery in the transformation of the center.

[*See also* Azhar, al-; *and the biographies of* ᶜ*Abduh and Shaltūt.*]

BIBLIOGRAPHY

Bayyūmī, Muḥammad Rajab al-. *Al-Azhar Bayna al-Siyāsah wa-Ḥurrīyat al-Fikr.* Cairo, 1983.

Bāz, Niᶜam al. *Al-Bāqūrī: Thā'ir taḥta al-ᶜimāmah.* Cairo, 1988.

Qurrāᶜah, Sanīyah. *Tārīkh al-Azhar fī alf ᶜām.* Cairo, 1968.

AMIRA EL AZHARY SONBOL

MARJAᶜ AL-TAQLĪD. The term *marjaᶜ al-taqlīd* designates the highest ranking authorities of the Twelver Shīᶜī community. They are usually few in number. In local or national communities (Iraq, Iran) the term can be loosely applied to between four and eight high-ranking jurists (or ayatollahs). On a world scale, and at particular times, the term is more stringently used to refer to only one or two such jurists. The position is informally acquired and depends on patterns of loyalty and allegiance which vary with time, geography, politics (clerical and national), and the perceived conduct of the jurist. In the two decades after 1970, the Shīᶜī community was dominated by two ayatollahs of immense stature: Ayatollah Ruhollah Khomeini (1902–1989), a majority of whose followers were found in Iran, though he had followers elsewhere; and Ayatollah Abū al-Qāsim al-Khū'ī (Abol-Qāsem Kho'i; 1899–1992), whose followers included most Arabic-speaking Shīᶜīs (those in Iraq, the Gulf states, Lebanon, and Syria) and probably a majority of those in India, Pakistan, and East Africa and some in Iran. Their divergent views of how Islam should respond to the crises of the late twentieth century neatly illustrates the breadth of possibilities in an ancient juristic tradition. Their deaths have left the community in a position not historically unprecedented where there are between six and nine possible claimants to the title, most of them in Najaf, Iraq, or in Qom, Iran. If the patterns of the past are repeated, there will probably be a gradual convergence of public opinion on a more limited number. Not the least factor will be the collegial opinion of the Shīᶜī clerics, pupils to previous masters, potentially divided by training and national allegiance but sharing a sense of the international and unified nature of the Twelver Shīᶜī community.

The authority and power that have come to be associated with the *marjaᶜ al-taqlīd* depend on the historical convergence of two theoretical structures. The first is that of *ijtihād.* Although it has origins that go back to the *ḥadīth* collections of Kulīnī (d. about 940) and earlier, the Shīᶜī theory of *ijtihād* found its first systematic exposition in the works of ᶜAllāmah al-Ḥillī (d. 1325). It is a theory which combines an epistemology and a structure of authority. It states that although the fundamentals of *sharīᶜah* (the divine law) are definitively known, the bulk of its details are uncertain and difficult of access, a matter of (informed) opinion, not knowledge. Those who have the training, the skills, and (ideally) the piety to exercise the utmost possible effort *(ijtihād)* to derive a ruling on questions of the law within this area are *mujtahids.* Those who do not belong to this group (the *ᶜāmmī*s, the common people) are dependent on the *mujtahid*s and must submit to their rulings. This submission is known as *taqlīd* and should be offered to the most learned jurist. Historically, this was a matter of local rather than national or international authority. The concept of *taqlīd* and the idea of recourse (to authority, from *rajāᶜah,* hence *marjaᶜ*) have always been a part of the theory of *ijtihād,* but the term *marjaᶜ al-taqlīd* and the notion of a sole *marjaᶜ* for the whole community emerged only in the nineteenth century. [*See* Ijtihād *and the biography of Ḥillī.*]

Sunnī and Shīᶜī theories of *ijtihād* are not markedly different (the stress on the closing of the door of *ijtihād* which has marked Western perception of the Sunnī tradition is wrong), but the Shīᶜī jurists added a second set of ideas related to juristic authority. These ideas were derived exegetically from a number of *ḥadīth,* the most famous of which is that known as the *ḥadīth* of Ibn Ḥanẓalah. In this *ḥadīth* the sixth imam, Jaᶜfar al-Ṣādiq, is seen to transfer judicial authority to those of his followers who know and understand *ḥadīth.* Over time, the Shīᶜī jurists interpreted this as meaning that, if there was any rightful executor of the *sharīᶜah* during the period of the imam's absence (the Ghaybah), it was the qualified jurist, acting in his capacity as *ḥākim sharᶜī* (legitimate judge) and *nā'ib al-imām* (representative of the imam). In the sphere of *sharᶜī* taxes, there was convergent agreement that the just and learned *faqīh* was the rightful manager of *zakāt* (alms) and *khums* (the "fifth," a ritual tax on specified products). Of these, the latter (usually assessed as 20 percent of income and voluntarily submitted) became and still is a major source of financial patronage for high-ranking jurists, ensuring political independence and real power. (Sunnī jurists had no corresponding access to an independent income.) [*See* Zakāt; Khums.] In the sphere of political authority, the Shīᶜī theory ensured that the actual governor could never be seen as the rightful executor of *sharīᶜah,* although the community might accommodate itself to his rule. A jurist, however, might be the ideal and real executor of the *sharīᶜah,* depending on the implications of *al-niyābah al-ᶜāmmah* (general deputyship to the imam), and, possibly, in virtue of *wilāyat al-faqīh* (the jurist's general guardianship to the community). These concepts were much debated throughout the nineteenth and twentieth centuries. They found one of their most politically activist formulations in the works of Ayatollah Khomeini, whose political career culminated in his acquired leadership of the Iranian Revolution in 1978–1979. They found one of their most quietist formulations in the works of the Ayatollah Khū'ī, whose writings and activities stressed the spiritual dimension of the *marjaᶜīyah* and the social and educational imperatives of the worldwide Shīᶜī community. [*See* Wilāyat al-Faqīh; Iranian Revolution of 1979.]

The convergence of the theories of *ijtihād* and of general deputyship secured and guaranteed the increasing authority of the great *marjaᶜ*s of the nineteenth and twentieth centuries. Available to the jurists of the Ṣafavid period (1501–1722), these ideas were not exploited both because accommodation offered political advantages and because, beginning in the early seventeenth century, the community was divided, precisely on the question of *ijtihād,* between the Akhbārīs (who denied its validity) and the Uṣūlīs. From the mid-seventeenth until the late eighteenth century, Shīᶜī clerics were engaged in a painful academic dispute about *ijtihād* which had perennial social consequences. For most of that period, the Akhbārīs dominated the centers of learning in Iraq and elsewhere. Biographical sources indicate that the scholarly genius and the political skills of one man, Muḥammad Bāqir ibn Muḥammad Akmal al-Bihbahānī (d. 1791), changed this. He is responsible for a general realignment of scholarship in Najaf, which ensured the dominance of the Uṣūlī tradition of thought until the present day and created the conditions for the decisive emergence of the great *marjaᶜ*s. Among his immediate pupils was Jaᶜfar ibn Khiḍr Kāshif al-Ghiṭā' (d. 1812), a jurist remarkable for his political skills (he mediated between the Ottoman authorities and the Qājār shah in Iran and was influential at the Qājār court) and for his decisive restatement of traditional political theory. The Russian wars of the early nineteenth century led Fatḥ ᶜAlī Shāh to look for support and legitimacy to the clerical class. Shaykh Jaᶜfar offered it in a sophisticated statement of the law: as *mujtahid* and representative of the Hidden Imam, he gave his permission to the sultan of Iran to undertake the management of *jihād* (war against nonbelievers). It was an ad hoc response to a political situation, but a significant development of theory and not untypical of how such developments took place. Its implications reverberated in the works and imaginations of succeeding generations of jurists. [*See* Akhbārīyah; Uṣūlīyah.]

Retrospectively, the Shīᶜī tradition has liked to assert a sequence of sole *marjaᶜ*s going back to the time of the imams. In fact, it was the events and personalities of the early nineteenth century, together with improving communications, that made the emergence of a sole *marjaᶜ* a possibility. Bihbahānī and Kāshif al-Ghiṭā' had many of the prerequisites for this authority but do not seem to have attracted the title. It is the two great scholars of the next generation who are associated with its earliest use: Muḥammad Ḥasan al-Najafī (d. 1850) and Shaykh Murtaḍā Anṣārī (d. 1864). The reputations of both depend on their scholarly rather than their political achievement. Najafī's magnificent restatement of the Uṣūlī tradition of legal writing, the *Jawāhir al-kalām,* was succeeded and to some extent displaced by the methodological subtlety and discretely innovative thinking of Anṣārī. His epistles on hermeneutic theory (*uṣūl al-fiqh*) represent the beginnings of a new phase in the history of this discipline. His *Kitāb al-makāsib* is a finely structured analysis of only one section of the law that manages to integrate an astonishing diversity of legal issues. His discussions are massively detailed, formally organized, and appropriately equivocal about the implications of a sophisticated juristic tradition. He may be the first major jurist to devote a special section to the question of the jurist's right of guardianship. Although he uses the same material, he is much less convinced about the jurist's right to government than was Khomeini, who, more than a hundred years later, converted the same topic into a political ideology.

After the death of Anṣārī it became gradually evident that the senior *mujtahid* was Muḥammad Ḥasan ibn Maḥmūd al-Shīrāzī (d. 1895). He was recognized as sole *marjaʿ* only after the obscure events that led to his move from Najaf to Samarra. The decisive action that revealed general acknowledgement of his status was his famous intervention in the affair of the Tobacco Regie in 1891. It is another example of opportunistic involvement in politics which, whether through judgment or luck, transformed a particular jurist into a symbolic figure of immense political stature.

In the generations following Shīrāzī it is difficult to pinpoint sole *marjaʿ*s. The senior jurists of Najaf continued to dominate, as did Iranian politics, especially during the period of the Iranian Constitutional Revolution of 1905–1909. A majority of jurists in Najaf supported the constitution, but some, both in Najaf and Iran, did not, notably Shaykh Faẓlullāh Nūrī (who was executed shortly after the success of the constitutionalists). The informal nature of the *marjaʿīyah*, and the absence of any institutions to embody its authority, made it difficult for a jurist simply to command; rather, he had to acquire and hold authority. This sometimes meant following rather than dictating the mood of the people. Grand political gestures had little effect if they were not accompanied by significant acknowledgment and success. Mīrzā Muḥammad Taqī Shīrāzī (d. 1920) issued a decree calling for a *jihād* against the British in Iraq, but it had little resonance at any level. [*See* Constitutional Revolution *and the biography of Nūrī.*]

The 1920s and 1930s saw the emergence of Qom as a center of learning that rivaled Najaf. In both cities it was possible to discern a number of leading *marjaʿ*s who divided between them the allegiance of the Shīʿī world. Only with the arrival of the Ayatollah Burūjirdī (Moḥammad Ḥosayn Borujerdi; 1875–1962) in Qom in 1945 did there gradually emerge again a near-universal consensus that here was the sole *marjaʿ* for the whole community. (It is unclear, however, how the Arabic-speaking Shīʿīs reacted to Iranian leadership during this period.) Burūjirdī was politically a quietist and scholarly. Like most of the *marjaʿ*s before him, the bulk of his activity was devoted to the day-to-day juristic problems of his followers, an unspectacular activity ensuring the quiet accommodation of the Shīʿī world to the exigencies of twentieth-century life. Owing to the focus of Western scholarship on narrowly political issues, it is still difficult to assess the importance of this activity.

Burūjirdī's death in 1962 precipitated another period in which there were from eight to twelve significant *marjaʿ*s, in Najaf, Qom, Tehran, and Mashhad, each of whom had a measure of community allegiance. The period saw some formal lay and religious discussion about the post and the possibilities of reforming or institutionalizing it. But political events and traditional loyalties proved more important than academic discussion. In Iran, the political activities of Ayatollah Khomeini in the early 1960s gave him a substantial prominence which survived his exile in Najaf and increased in proportion to dissatisfaction with the Pahlavi government. The period of exile (1965 to 1978–1979) gave him time to develop and propagate his theory of government, based on the idea of *wilāyat al-faqīh*. Inside Iran the routine business of giving and developing juristic rules depended on the day-to-day activity of the three senior ayatollahs, Muḥammad Kāẓim Sharīʿatmadārī, Muḥammad Riẓā Gulpāygānī, and Shihāb al-Dīn Marʿashī Najafī. Even in the late 1970s, Khomeini's leadership had not acquired universal assent, not among the educated young who were often indifferent, cynical, and more attracted by socialist and communist ideologies, nor among the old who, resisting clerical pressure to follow only a living *marjaʿ*, would sometimes cite Burūjirdī as their favored authority. Those with Ṣūfī affiliations would sometimes transfer the term to the leader of their Ṣūfī order. The events of the revolution and its long-term aftermath gave Khomeini political power and international prestige. Since his death, however, the position of the *marjaʿ* is at least, again, clearly separate from political structures. Religious leadership in Iran after Khomeini's death is uncertainly focused and complicated by political involvement.

In the Arabic-speaking Twelver Shīʿī community, the name of Ayatollah Khū'ī has been dominant since the early 1970s. His stature grew, as it became evident that his political and religious stance was an alternative to that of Khomeini. It is probably true of Khomeini, in spite of his great fame, that he did not achieve a truly international significance as *marjaʿ*; he was perceived too much as Iranian. Revolutionary movements of course adopted him as their symbol, and political movements entered into alliance with his government. But the piety, learning, seriousness, and political quietism of Ayatollah Khū'ī gained him a broad international following and, consequently, control of immense wealth. This he administered with a quiet institution-building skill. Living in Najaf, his indifference to political power was always interpreted as distaste for the Iraqi leader, Saddam Hussein, and may have become active opposition during the Shīʿī revolt in southern Iraq which followed the Gulf War of 1990–1991. His institutional legacy lies in an extraordinary international network of mosques, schools, libraries, and other charitable institutions, which, through his rulings, have been integrated into the existing structures of national and international bodies, from London and New York to Bombay, Islamabad, Malaysia, and Thailand. How this will survive is still uncertain. The enduring legacy of his thought is likewise uncertain, but markedly pragmatic and eirenic, it might turn out to be more significant for the needs of the Shīʿī community in the twenty-first century than that of Khomeini.

[*See also* Ayatollah; Ithnā ʿAsharīyah; Najaf; Qom; Shīʿī Islam; *and the biographies of Borujerdi, Kho'i, and Khomeini.*]

BIBLIOGRAPHY

Algar, Hamid, *Religion and State in Iran, 1785–1906: The role of the Ulama in the Qajar Period*. Berkeley and Los Angleles, 1969.

Arjomand, Said Amir, *The Shadow of God and the Hidden Imam*. Chicago and London, 1984.

Lambton, Ann K. S. "A Reconsideration of the Position of the *marjaʿ al-taqlīd* and the Religious Institution." *Studia Islamica* 20 (1964): 115–135.

Lambton, Ann K. S. "The Tobacco Regie: Prelude to Revolution." *Studia Islamica* 22 and 23 (1965): 119–157 and 71–90.

Lambton, Ann K. S. "A Nineteenth-Century View of Jihād." *Studia Islamica* 32 (1970): 181–192.

Martin, Vanessa. *Islam and Modernism: The Iranian Revolution of 1906*. London, 1989.

Momen, Moojan. *An Introduction to Shīʿī Islam*. New Haven and London, 1985.

Norman Calder

MARKET. *See* Bazaar.

MARRIAGE AND DIVORCE.

[*To articulate religious values and traditions reflected in marriage and divorce in modern Islamic societies, this entry comprises two articles:* Legal Foundations *and* Modern Practice. *For related discussions, see* Family Law; Mutʿah; Polygyny; Women and Islam, *article on* Role and Status of Women.]

Legal Foundations

The Qur'ān is the foundation of all Islamic laws, including laws of marriage and divorce. Where a matter is not addressed specifically there, or where the application of a verse to a certain situation permits several reasonable interpretations, jurists look to the *sunnah* of the Prophet (including *ḥadīth*) for additional guidance. Where neither the Qur'ān nor *sunnah* address a matter explicitly, jurists resort to *ijtihād,* a system of reasoning and interpretation for which they have articulated several basic principles. Chief among these is the principle that laws vary with time, place, and circumstance. This principle was adopted to emphasize the fact that Islam is a religion for all times and all people, and that therefore each culture is permitted, within the bounds of Qur'ānic injunctions, to have a reasonable degree of flexibility in interpreting and applying Islam to its own community.

The *ijtihād* of jurists on matters of marriage and divorce was significantly influenced by their milieu. Often local gender, class, and political preferences filtered into Islamic consciousness and were incorporated as part of regional Islamic legal tradition.

Originally, Muslim family law was not codified. Judges who were faced with an issue relied directly on the Qur'ān and *ḥadīth* and, where necessary, on their own *ijtihād*. As the schools of legal thought gained prominence, Muslim states began selecting the jurisprudence of one of these schools as the basis of their legal systems. There are significant jurisprudential differences not only among the schools, but also among scholars within each school.

Most Muslim countries today have codified their family laws. In each case, the code was based primarily on the jurisprudence of a single school; however, for a variety of reasons, a code sometimes combined this jurisprudence with that of other schools. Such an approach, when consistent and properly reasoned, is fully permissible in Islam because the Prophet stated that differences among the various jurists were a sign of divine mercy and that Islam is a religion of facilitation, not complication. Unlike the majority of Muslim countries, Saudi Arabia and some other Gulf states continue to follow an uncodified system of family law. Cases are not published, and, since the system relies in each case on the *ijtihād* of the individual judge, it is possible that similar cases there result in significantly different judgments.

Although in early Islam ʿĀʾishah, the wife of the Prophet, and other Muslim women played a leading role in the interpretation of law, women were later increasingly excluded from the field of jurisprudence until they were finally declared unfit for judicial positions. This view has survived to the present in most Muslim countries, although recently it has again become the subject of debate. The barring of women from judicial positions, however, has significantly affected the development of Islamic jurisprudence, especially in the area of family law. Despite their differences, the various schools appear to base their jurisprudence on a traditional patriarchal view of males as rational, courageous, and firm and of females as emotional, weak, and rash. Consequently, many of the laws have been justified explicitly on this basis, although exceptions do exist.

For example, the major schools (Mālikī, Ḥanbalī, Ḥanafī, Shāfiʿī and Jaʿfarī) generally agree that a Muslim woman needs a *walī* (guardian, usually her father) to enter into a marriage, but they disagree significantly as to the extent, nature, and duration of the *walī*'s authority. Most major schools agree that a father acting as *walī* can force his virgin daughter to marry a man of his choice, regardless of her age. This position was justified on the basis that virgins lack experience in men and may be subject to emotion in making their marriage decision. However, if a father declares his daughter mature or if she was previously married, then under the Mālikī view the daughter cannot be forced into marriage regardless of her age; in that case she must reach the marriage decision jointly with her *walī*.

A well-established Ḥanafī line of thought views the mature woman who has reached puberty as capable of contracting her own marriage, with the *walī* playing a merely advisory role. However, if the woman ignores the *walī*'s advice and marries someone "unsuitable," then the *walī* immediately acquires remarkable powers. He can move to void the marriage if no pregnancy has occurred. Ḥanafīs and Mālikīs imbued the notion of "suitability" with culturally based class distinctions that were not present in its original articulation, which was based on piety.

Jaʿfarīs view a mature woman who has reached puberty, whether a virgin or otherwise, as a full legal entity coequal with her male counterpart. She is considered legally competent to make her own marriage decisions and even to conclude her own marriage contract, regardless of her father's approval and the social station of the prospective husband.

Modern family codes sometimes present new permutations of old positions. For example, the Syrian Personal Status Code (1953, as amended), which is basically Ḥanafī, modifies the Ḥanafī position by limiting the *walī*'s ability to unfairly block, delay, or cause the avoidance of the marriage of a daughter who has reached majority. The Moroccan Personal Status Code (1957), which is basically Mālikī, departs from the traditional Mālikī position by prohibiting a *walī* from forcing his female ward into marriage, whether she is virgin or otherwise, if she has attained the age of majority. It does, however, instruct the woman to delegate her right to contract a marriage to her *walī*. Mālikī and other jurists have explained the need for such delegation as emanating from a desire to shield the woman from the indignity of being present among men to negotiate and execute her own marriage contract.

The Tunisian Personal Status Code (1956, as amended), which is also basically Mālikī, departs more fundamentally from such jurisprudence by abandoning the notion of *walī* altogether and adopting a position akin to that of the Jaʿfarīs. Once the prospective parties reach the age of majority, they may contract their own marriage or delegate that power to another, at their option. The consent of both husband and wife is required for a valid marriage, and the notion of "suitability" is absent from the code.

All schools of thought have interpreted the Qurʾān as permitting polygyny as long as certain conditions of fairness are observed. The Tunisian code prohibits it. This prohibition, along with other departures like the ones discussed above, has been viewed by many as a reflection of Western colonial influences. Tunisian jurists in fact relied on the Qurʾān and other basic sources in developing their arguments for prohibiting polygyny, but it is probably true that their desire to reexamine past *ijtihād* on this issue was motivated by external Western influences. Still, even under a traditional analysis of polygyny, there are legal approaches that enable a woman to guard against it in her own marriage.

One such method is for the woman to specify in the marriage contract that her prospective husband may not marry a second wife. Unfortunately, the validity of this condition varies with the school. Jaʿfarīs and Shāfiʿīs, for example, reject it as, respectively, contrary to Islamic law and contrary to marital rights flowing from the marriage contract; but in either case, both schools view the rest of the contract as valid. This result is quite harsh for a woman bent on protecting her marriage from polygyny.

Ḥanafīs also regard this condition as null and void; but as an inducement for women to marry, they recognize the validity of a condition in the marriage contract that reserves for the woman the right to divorce her husband at her option. Mālikīs accept the condition not to take a second wife as valid, but they discourage it. The condition giving the woman the right to divorce is also acceptable to them, but it is so bound to various formal and procedural requirements that it is hard for the average woman not to forfeit (or even fail initially to acquire) such right inadvertently. In all jurisdictions, a woman may obtain divorce by giving up her dower *(khulʿ)*, quite a hardship for a woman of modest means. She can also request a judicial divorce, which can be a lengthy procedure.

The attitude of one line of thought among Ḥanbalīs toward a marriage condition preventing the husband from taking a second wife is closest to that of the Prophet, who stated that one's *ʿuhūd* (promises or undertakings) must be fulfilled and that the *ʿuhūd* most worthy of fulfillment are those of the marriage contract. Not only do Ḥanbalīs view as valid this and all other conditions which are not incompatible with Islamic law or the object of marriage; they also signal the seriousness of violating such *ʿuhūd* by giving the party whose marriage condition has been violated the option of voiding the marriage *(faskh)*. By contrast, Ḥanafīs, for example, specify a limited monetary remedy for such violations.

Other laws relating, for example, to *mutʿah* marriage (a form of temporary marriage accepted by Shīʿīs), spousal maintenance, the ability of the wife to work outside her home, the role of the husband in the family, the duties of the wife in a marriage, and child custody, have posed challenging questions to Muslim jurists in modern societies. In response, a movement to reinvigorate *ijtihād* and modernize family law in accordance with the Qur'ān and *sunnah* is taking root around the Muslim world.

[*See also* Family; Family Law; Mutʿah; Polygyny; *and* Women and Islam, *article on* Role and Status of Women.]

BIBLIOGRAPHY

Abū Zahrah, Muḥammad. *Muḥāḍarāt fī ʿaqd al-zawāj wa-āthāruh.* Cairo, 1971. Excellent modern work on marriage in Islam.

Bardīsī, Muḥammad Zakarīyā al-. *Al-aḥkām al-Islāmīyah fī al-aḥwāl al-shakhṣīyah.* Cairo, 1965.

Dardīr, Aḥmad al-. *Al-sharḥ al-Ṣaghīr.* Vol. 1. Cairo, 1962.

Dijwī, Muḥammad al-. *Al-aḥwāl al-shakhṣīyah lil-Miṣrīyīn al-Muslimin fiqhan wa-qaḍā'an.* Vol. 1. Cairo, 1969.

Hibri, Azizah al-. "A Study of Islamic Herstory." In *Women and Islam*, edited by Azizah al-Hibri. Oxford, 1982. Feminist discussion of certain Islamic laws and principles relating to women.

Hibri, Azizah al-. "Marriage Laws in Muslim Countries." *Family Law and Gender Bias: International Review of Comparative Public Policy* 4 (Fall 1992): 227–244.

Hooker, M. B. *The Personal Laws of Malaysia: An Introduction.* Kuala Lumpur, 1976. Orientalist but comprehensive study of family laws in Malaysia.

Jazīrī, ʿAbd al-Raḥmān al-. *Kitāb al-fiqh ʿalā al-madhāhib al-arbaʿah.* Vol. 4. Beirut, 1969. Rich classical source of information on family law under Ḥanafī, Shāfiʿī, Mālikī, and Ḥanbalī jurisprudence.

Khamlīshī, Aḥmad al-. *Al-taʿlīq ʿalā Qānūn al-aḥwāl al-shakhṣīyah.* Rabat, 1987.

Maghnīyah, Muḥammad Jawād al-. *Al-fiqh ʿalā al-madhāhib al-khamsah.* Beirut, 1960. Excellent presentation of the position of each of the five major schools of Islamic jurisprudence on a host of issues.

Maḥmaṣānī, Ṣubḥī. *Al-awḍāʿ al-tashrīʿīyah fī al-duwal al-ʿArabīyah.* Beirut, 1981.

Nasir, Jamal J. *The Status of Women under Islamic Law and under Modern Islamic Legislation.* London, 1990.

Rahman, Fazlur. "A Survey of Modernization of Muslim Family Law." *International Journal of Middle East Studies* 11 (1980): 451–465.

Shalabī, Muḥammad Muṣṭafā. *Aḥkām al-Usrah fī al-Islām.* 4th ed. Beirut, 1983. Good source for Jaʿfarī jurisprudence.

Zuhaylī, Wahbah al-. *Al-fiqh al-Islāmī wa-Adillatuh.* Vol. 7. Damascus, 1984.

AZIZAH Y. AL-HIBRI

Modern Practice

Rules and procedures regarding marriage and divorce are stipulated in the Qur'ān and regulated through the *sharīʿah.* Laws relating to marriage and divorce are thus part of the body of Islamic personal status law, the only aspect of *sharīʿah* law that has been retained nearly intact at the close of the twentieth century.

Marriage in Islamic law is formalized by a contract *(nikāḥ)* between the legal guardian of the bride—always a male and usually the bride's father—and the prospective husband. By custom, marriage partners are usually determined by arrangement through families: women work through social alliances to seek out suitable wives for their sons and to introduce unmarried daughters to the mothers of eligible sons. Men who are guardians of women assume the formal arrangements for a marriage, which include the offer and acceptance and the drawing up of the marriage contract, specifying such conditions as the amount of the *mahr* (see below), the location of the marital home, or the right of the wife to divorce should the husband take a second wife.

In *sharīʿah* law, the legal guardian of the bride has the power to contract his ward in marriage to any man of his choice without her knowledge or permission, and he can also refuse to allow her to marry at all. In practice, parents usually ask their daughter whether or not she agrees with their choice of a spouse. To a large extent, in the Middle Eastern Muslim world, the realities of modern life have superseded the traditional mode of arranged marriages, as men and women now meet and choose each other through contact in universities, in the workplace, through mutual friends, or during travel abroad. Modern legislation in most countries has further eroded the prerogatives of the guardian by forbidding compulsion in marriage. Even among professional and well-educated groups, however, the desire to preserve parental guidance in the choice of a marriage partner remains strong. Among Pakistani Muslims in the United States, for example, arranged marriages continue to take place even in the American-born younger generation. Arranged marriages also persist among tribal groups that insist on marriages back into the family, and among economically or politically powerful families for whom marriage alliances are viewed as an extension of family interests.

The marriage contract usually stipulates the *mahr*, an amount of money or property that must be given by the prospective husband in order legally to validate the marriage. The *mahr* may be given all at once or may be divided into two parts, one to be paid before consummation and the other stipulated for future payment in the event of divorce or death. Ideally and by law the *mahr* is intended as a gift to the bride from her husband for a purpose of her choice, whether to furnish her marital home or to establish her financial independence. In practice, however, the *mahr* has sometimes been assumed by the guardian for his own use. In bedouin communities especially, women almost never receive the *mahr* or even know its amount.

The amount of the *mahr* is individually determined and traditionally is commensurate with the economic or social standing of the bride's family. Among many westernized and especially two-income couples, however, no money is transferred at all, as the *mahr* is considered as only a token payment to be stipulated in the contract in order to satisfy the terms for a legally validated marriage. For most other people, the *mahr* remains a considerable factor in determining marriage alliances, and in some regions the cost has risen to the point that the *mahr* now constitutes a barrier to marriage. In the Gulf region, where value of the average *mahr* may be from U.S. $10,000 to $25,000, private Muslim charities and government agencies offer contributions toward the *mahr* for the benefit of men who would otherwise have no hope of marriage. The rationale for these donations is that marriage is considered a religious duty in Islam.

In *sharīʿah* law rules concerning divorce favor the interest of males. A man is entitled to repudiate his wife without cause in *ṭalāq* divorce, by which a man repeats the formula "I divorce you" three times before witnesses, constituting a formal termination of the marriage relationship. Repudiation by a husband does not entitle the wife to financial compensation other than the *mahr* as designated in the marriage contract, and maintenance for a period of time (*ʿiddah*) during which she may not contract a new marriage—the purpose being to establish paternity in the event the former wife finds herself pregnant in the months immediately following divorce.

Women do not have the same right of repudiation, but they are entitled to two other kinds of divorce, one costly and the other potentially humiliating for the woman and her family. *Khulʿ* divorce, also known as divorce through ransom, entitles a woman to buy herself out of the marriage by paying her husband an agreed-upon sum of money, by returning the *mahr*, or by waiving her right to the delayed *mahr*. The second type of divorce that can be initiated by the wife, known as *tafrīq*, entitles the wife to petition the court for divorce, but such divorce is allowable on very limited grounds, such as impotence on the part of the male or desertion. Modern legislation in some countries has codified and slightly expanded the grounds on which a woman may petition for divorce to include injury or discord, a physical defect on the part of the husband, failure to pay maintenance, and absence or imprisonment of the husband.

Women are at a disadvantage not only by virtue of legal impediments to obtaining a divorce but also in regard to obtaining custody of their children. In *sharīʿah* law custody of children goes first to the mother, but only during early childhood; custody then reverts to the father, since as a man he is deemed better qualified to oversee the child's education. Schools of law vary on the exact age at which a mother's right to custody of her children terminates in favor of the father, but the age range in Sunnī practice is seven to ten for a boy and nine to the onset of puberty or time of marriage for girls. Shāfiʿī law grants children the right to choose the custodial parent at age seven. In Twelver Shīʿī law the father gains custody of a boy at age two and of a girl at age seven. In all schools of law, if the mother remarries at any time while her children are in her care, she jeopardizes her right to retain custody. Modern legislation in most countries codifies but does not significantly alter these custody arrangements that favor the father: the principle that custody should be determined according to the best interests of the child has been explicitly incorporated into modern legislation in a few countries, but courts tend to presume that the child's best interests are served in applying *sharīʿah* rules.

With the exception of Turkey, where the *sharīʿah* was abrogated in 1926 and replaced by a Swiss civil code, the most far-reaching reforms in family law in the Middle East are to be found in Tunisia. A Tunisian Code of Personal Status was enacted in 1956 that provided for a minimum age for marriage, abolished polygyny and the right of guardians to contract marriage without the woman's consent, abolished male *ṭalāq* divorce outside of court, and granted court-registered *ṭalāq* to women. More recently the minimum age for marriage has been raised to seventeen for women, and mothers have been granted automatic guardianship over their children in the event of the father's death. In 1992 further reforms guaranteed child-support payments for divorced women and granted mothers the right to be considered legal guardians of minor children along with the father, so that the marriage of a minor daughter cannot proceed without her mother's consent.

On the whole, modern legislation regarding marriage and divorce has had limited effect in altering the inequalities between men and women in *sharīʿah* family law. The first reason is that modern legislation may be difficult to implement where there is a lack of desire or ability to comply. Many countries, for example, have established a minimum age for marriage. Some countries, such as Syria, Jordan, and Morocco, have also made attempts to control the contracting of marriages between very young girls and much older men by setting limitations on the allowable age difference between the bride and prospective husband. In Jordan, for example, marriage contracts cannot be validated if a woman under eighteen is to be married to a man more than twenty years her senior. However, especially in rural areas, enforcing conditions of age on marriage contracts is difficult since the age of either party may be undocumented; moreover, government intervention in what are considered private family matters may be viewed as unacceptable and therefore may be ignored.

Another reason that modern legislation has done little to correct the inequalities between men and women is the fact that, for the most part, modern legislation tends to codify *sharīʿah* law rather than to modify it. In most countries today, for example, legislation on divorce requires that *ṭalāq* divorces be registered in a government court. Legal documentation of a divorce assures the wife that she will be informed that she has in fact been divorced, and it provides the legal structure through which she can petition for child custody, payment of maintenance, or the delayed *mahr*. Court registration, however, in no way impedes the husband's absolute right of repudiation without any grounds, as allowed in the *sharīʿah*.

Similarly, the practice of polygyny, which among Middle Eastern countries has been abolished only in Tunisia and Turkey, is now subject to certain government-imposed conditions. In Egypt, for example, the first wife must be notified through the courts if a second marriage has taken place, and the wife is then entitled to apply for a divorce if she feels that the new marriage has caused her to suffer "a material or moral injury." She is not, however, entitled to any additional financial compensation that would make divorce feasible for her and costly for the husband. Thus the man's right to take up to four wives at a time, as granted in the *sharīʿah*, remains virtually unfettered in modern legislation.

As another example, the *sharīʿah* provision that a Muslim woman cannot marry a non-Muslim man, even though a Muslim man is entitled to marry a Christian or a Jew, is codified in all modern Muslim legislation. Furthermore, in some countries this principle is extended into the realm of nationality of prospective spouses. In Kuwait, for example, a Kuwaiti man who marries a non-Kuwaiti woman retains all the privileges of citizenship, whereas the children of a Kuwaiti woman who marries a foreign national are not entitled to Kuwaiti citizenship. In Saudi Arabia, a male citizen may petition the government for permission to marry a non-Saudi, but that right is absolutely denied to women. In Tunisia, by contrast, a new provision of the Tunisian Code of Nationality allows a Tunisian woman married to a foreigner to give Tunisian nationality to her children, where previously the privilege of citizenship for the children of mixed marriages was granted only to those whose father was Tunisian.

A third reason that modern legislation has not diminished the inequalities between men and women in marriage is that in codifying *sharīʿah,* modern legislation also codifies and thus helps to preserve traditional attitudes that reinforce men's power over women. For example, the Moroccan Code (article 35) states that a wife has the right to visit her parents, which is considered a special privilege because in traditional practice a wife does not have the right ever to leave her home without her husband's permission. The implication of the code, however, is to recognize and confirm in law that the wife does not otherwise have the right to leave the home whenever she wishes.

As another example, in the *sharīʿah* a man is obligated to provide maintenance for a legally contracted wife, but only under two conditions: that she be physically available to him at all times, and that she obey him in all lawful things. The obligation of the husband to maintain his wife, as well as the conditions of absence or disobedience on the part of the wife that terminate his obligation, are recognized in modern legislation in most countries. This poses a dilemma for working women. Does absence due to working without the husband's permission constitute a failure to make oneself available to one's husband? Jordanian, Syrian, Iraqi, and Egyptian legislation says that it does and releases the husband from the obligation of maintenance, even if the wife went to work because she has a profession that cannot be interrupted at will, or because the family is in need of her income. Modern legislation, therefore, rather than allowing traditional attitudes to evolve along with changing conditions, can have the opposite effect of imposing on men's power over women a seal that is impervious to women's individual achievement or rising expectations.

The effect of contemporary Islamist political movements has been to limit further reforms in family law. All these movements, including those in Pakistan, Algeria, Egypt, and Sudan—and in both strictly shariatic Saudi Arabia and secularizing Tunisia—call for strict application of *sharīʿah* family laws. In Iran, the fundamentalist government of Ayatollah Ruhollah Khomeini abrogated what had been one of the most progressive family law codes in the Muslim Middle East. The Family Protection Act put into effect under the shah in 1975 set limits on a man's right to contract a second marriage, gave the spouses equal right to divorce by removing the man's right to *ṭalāq,* raised the minimum age for marriage, and placed the decision for child custody at the discretion of the courts to be determined on the basis of the child's best interests. One of Ayatollah Khomeini's first acts on coming to power in 1979 was to lower the minimum age for marriage from eighteen to thirteen and to reenact Twelver Shīʿī law, by which fathers and paternal relatives regained the right to have custody of children in case of divorce or death of the father, and husbands the right to polygyny and divorce at will.

The formulation of marriage and divorce laws in the contemporary Middle East is inseparable from an ongoing debate that has persisted since the late nineteenth century over the perceived need for progress and reform in Muslim society and the role of women in shaping the future of that society. In the nineteenth century Western critics of Muslim society, most notably colonial rulers and Christian missionaries, targeted the condition of women as the central cause of the perceived degradation and backwardness of Muslim society.

Indigenous spokesmen held similar views. Muḥammad ʿAbduh, *muftī* of Egypt, recognized in the late nineteenth century that the unrestricted right to polygamy and divorce created an unstable home life and an inauspicious environment for raising children. In *The Liberation of Women,* published in 1899, Qāsim Amīn brought the question of women's rights and Muslim family law into public discussion. Amīn argued that a transformation in the role and status of women was a necessary prerequisite for the Muslim world to progress; he called for primary school education for girls, the abolition of the veil, and reform in laws regarding polygyny and divorce. Other writers, including women, took up the same call. Malak Ḥifnī Nāṣif (1886–1918), for example, worked toward reform in marriage laws, denouncing polygamy, early marriage for girls, *ṭalāq* divorce, and the custom of marriage between older men and young girls; the feminist activist Hudā Shaʿrāwī called in 1935 for the abolition of polygamy. Even the Muslim Brotherhood, founded as a movement to reassert religious tradition in the face of British occupation, sought reform in *sharīʿah* laws of marriage and divorce, arguing that polygyny was incompatible with both the Qur'ānic view of marriage—an institution created for love and mercy between two people—and the Qur'ānic directive to treat one's wives equally. The brotherhood also opposed the abuse by men of the absolute right to divorce, on the grounds that unfettered divorce was incompatible with the moral premises of true Islam.

To a considerable extent, the goals of both traditionalists and westernizing secularists who sought reforms in family law were the same, although one sought reform within Islamic tradition and the other change in emulation of Western values. Even though the desire for reform has been articulated within a religious tradition as well a secular one, and by indigenous voices as well as by Western critics, the feminist movement has never been able to extricate itself from the taint of its origins in colonial discourse. Today calls for reform tend therefore to be associated with foreign occupation and cultural imperialism. With the Islamist revival gaining strength, those who advocate family law reform run the risk of being labeled "secularist" or "infidel," and are thus silenced. At the same time, Middle Eastern governments, with few exceptions, appease Islamist sentiment by reasserting controls over women enshrined in family law. In 1993 liberalization in marriage and divorce laws in the region as a whole does not look promising.

[*See also* Family Law; Polygyny.]

BIBLIOGRAPHY

Abderrazak, Moulay R'chid. *La femme et la loi au Maroc*. Casablanca, 1991.

Ahmed, Leila. *Women and Gender in Islam: Historical Roots of a Modern Debate*. New Haven, 1992. Discusses family law and legal reform in historical perspective and social context, including the effects of fundamentalism.

Chamari, Alya Chérif. *La femme et la loi en Tunisie*. Casablanca, 1991.

Esposito, John L. *Women in Muslim Family Law*. Syracuse, N.Y., 1982.

Fluehr-Lobban, Carolyn. *Islamic Law and Society in the Sudan*. London, 1987. Excellent discussion of Islamic family law in theory and in practice, based on actual court cases.

Mayer, Ann Elizabeth. *Islam and Human Rights: Tradition and Politics*. Boulder, 1991.

Nasir, Jamal J. *The Status of Women under Islamic Law and under Modern Islamic Legislation*. London, 1990. The title aptly describes the contents; a manual, with select reference to legal concepts and countries in the Middle East.

Saadi, Nouredine. *La femme et la loi en Algérie*. Casablanca, 1991.

ELEANOR ABDELLA DOUMATO

MARTYRDOM. Islam accords a special status to those who lose or sacrifice their lives in the service of their religion. This is clear from the earliest sources (Qur'ān, *ḥadith*) and the auxiliary sources (*sīrah, maghāzī, ʿilm al-rijāl* and *tafsīr*). The word which these sources agree on for designating a martyr is *shahīd* ("witness"). The most usual meaning of *shahīd*, which appears no less than fifty-six times in singular, plural, and adverbial forms in the Qur'ān, is "eyewitness" or "witness" in a legal sense. A. J. Wensinck's pioneering study (1941) observed a close relationship between Islam and Christianity that centered on this meaning; the Christian technical term *martyr* also means "witness." This correspondence led Wensinck to conclude that both traditions share a similar development involving ancient Semitic and Hellenistic religious motifs. Whatever the previous development that lead to the choice of "witness" to designate a believer who has made the ultimate gesture in the path of religion, it is clear that the idea of martyrdom in Islam was thoroughly at home in the early religion.

The problem for philologists resides in the fact that the Qur'ān does not appear to use the word *shahīd* in any completely unambiguous way, at least in the singular form, although there is one instance of the use of the plural which has readily lent itself to the martyrdom interpretation. But apart from the direct reference to the plural *shuhadā'*, the Qur'ānic glorification of *ṣabr* (endurance in times of difficulty) and the related theme of the suffering of apparently all the prophets at the hands of persecutors, to name only two motifs, blends perfectly with the Islamic admiration of martyrdom, long suffering, and patience. This theme would reach apotheosis in the poetic expressions of the mystics of Islam who saw as their starting point in this regard such *ḥadīth qudsī* as: "Who My beauty kills, I am his blood-money," or Ḥallāj's "Happiness is from Him, but suffering is He Himself" (Schimmel, in Chelkowski, 1979, p. 217).

Sacred Texts on Martyrdom. One anchors a discussion of martyrdom in the Qur'ān, rather than in history as such, because of the central position of scripture in Islam. It is through the Qur'ān that Islam gained its general understanding of the shape and purpose of history—not to mention many historical details and facts—whether that history be of the Jāhilīyah period or of the epochs of various previous religions and cultures. Ayoub (1978) has pointed out that even in the earliest portion of the Qur'ān, that is, in those revelations that came even before the duty of *jīhād* was made incumbent on Muslims, there is a divine confirmation of the ideal of martyrdom, namely, Qur'ān 85.3–8, which many commentators say refers to the famous Christian martyrs of Najran. But regardless of the actual identities of the persons and events being alluded to, the meaning of the text is unambiguous.

The most important verse to do with martyrdom is one in which *shuhadā'* ("witnesses") has come to mean martyrs for so much of exegesis. Qur'ān 4.69 runs as follows: "Whosoever obeys God, and the Messenger—they are with those whom God has blessed. Prophets, just men, martyrs [*shuhadā'*], the righteous; good companions they!" (Arberry trans.). Arberry, faithful to the exegetical tradition, unhesitatingly uses "martyrs" to translate *shuhadā'*, whereas other translators, for example, Yusuf ʿAli, more cautiously use the English word "witnesses" instead. This verse is the locus classicus for the later exegetical and theological discussions about the hierarchy of the inhabitants of Paradise. About the rank of "witness" *(shahīd)*, Yusuf ʿAli offers the following comment: "[These] are the noble army of Witnesses, who testify to the truth. The testimony may be by martyrdom, as in the case of the Imams Ḥasan and Ḥusain. Or it may be by the tongue of the true Preacher or the pen of the devoted scholar, or the life of a man devoted to service." Thus *shahādat*, translated as "martyrdom" depending on the context, in its strict sense takes in much more in Islam than the sacrificing of life in the path of God *(sabīl Allāh)*, indeed it is also the word for the act of confessing adherence to Islam by uttering, "There is no god but God and Muḥammad is the messenger of God." Nonetheless, *shahādat* as martyrdom is regarded as highly praiseworthy. The Qur'ān has many passages which indicate an authentic appreciation and inchoate theory of martyrdom: "Say not of those who die in the path of God that they are dead. Nay rather they live" (2.154); "Count not those who were slain in God's way as dead, but rather living with their Lord, by Him provided, rejoicing in the bounty of God has given them, and joyful in those who remain behind and have not joined them, because no fear shall be on them, neither shall they sorrow, joyful in blessing and bounty from God, and that God leaves not to waste the wage of the believers" (3.169–171; see also 9.20–22, 47.4, 61.11, and 3.157–158). These few verses suffice to illustrate that even though the word "martyr" as such is not found in the Qur'ān and that the subject is represented through circumlocutions, nonetheless the virtue is emphatically and dramatically taught in the verses of the Holy Book. The Islamic ideal of martyrdom can be thought to be the logical adjunct to the overall Qur'ānic view of death as illusory. This view is perhaps nowhere more succinctly represented in the Qur'ān than at 62.6–7. "Say: 'You of Jewry, if you assert that you are the friends of God, apart from other men, then do you long for death, if you speak truly.' "

The doctrine of the Hereafter *(ākhirah)* caused Muḥammad a great deal of trouble with his early audiences, who stubbornly refused to accept the idea of life beyond the grave. So in Islam death is paradoxical (cf. the famous statement of the Prophet: "Die before you die."), and it is the paradox which supplies the energy for the strong belief in the spiritual station of martyrs. Thus the pre-Islamic Arab literary and cultural motif of *fakhr*, honor or pride in prowess on the field of tribal warfare found throughout the Ayyām literature, was deemed by Islam "vainglory" and replaced by a glorification of the pious dedication to the struggle for the promotion of the Word of God. In Muslim's *ḥadīth* collection we find the following statement by the prophet Muḥammad: "Whosoever partakes of the battle from desire of glory or in order to show his courage, is no martyr; a martyr is only he who fights in order that Allāh's Word may be prevalent" (W95). Even though it remains to be seen whether or not the pre-Islamic phenomenon does not have a more positive relationship with the Islamic ideal of martyrdom, the change in ethos indicated here between the period of Jāhilīyah and the Islamic era is quite analogous to the change Christianity wrought in the pagan world (cf. Robin Lane Fox, *Pagans and Christians*, New York, 1989, p. 336).

As Wensinck has pointed out, the theme of martyrdom in Islam is intimately connected with the theme of the rewards of Paradise. This becomes quite clear in the *ḥadīth* literature which served as a basis for the final elaboration of the doctrine of martyrdom by the *fuqahā'* (religious scholars) of Islam.

The *ḥadīth* literature is vastly more supportive of and unambiguous about martyrdom than the Qur'ān. Countless explicit statements attributed to the Prophet exist in which it is quite clear that those who die for Islam enjoy a special rank. Here is a random example: "The Messenger of God said, The Prophet is in the Garden and the martyr is in the Garden and the newborn child is in the Garden and the new-born girl is in the Garden" (from *Musnad*, Smith and Haddad, 1981, p. 173). Most of the following *ḥadīth* are from Bukhārī as either translated directly or paraphrased by Wensinck: "Paradise [or the gates of paradise] lies under the shadow of the swords" (W90); "God is a guarantee to him who is zealous in His way [*li-man jāhada fī sabīlihi*] . . . that He shall make his enter paradise." On the topic of the ordeals of the tomb, from which martyrs are exempted, the Prophet was asked why those who have given their lives in battle will not have to endure the interrogation of the two angels Munkar and Nakīr, and his response is reported as: "They have been put to the test sufficiently by the flashing of swords over their heads."

On the theme that martyrs are those who are distinguished in Paradise by their desire to leave their bliss and return to earth to be martyred again (up to ten times), Muḥammad is credited with having said that had he followed his personal wish he would not have missed a single battle or campaign in order to be killed in the first and to return to life in each subsequent one. And on the general theme of desiring death, which would come to be neutralized in later centuries (see below) Bukhārī preserves a prayer ascribed to 'Umar in which the second caliph expresses the desire to be killed in the Prophet's country.

All Muslims, no matter what their *madhhab*, *ṭarīqah*, or *ṭā'ifah*, esteem martyrdom highly. This esteem can be ritualistic or devotional, as in the case of the *ta*ʿ*ziyah* commemorations in Shiism, or historical, as in the manner in which all Muslims idealize the formative struggle of the early band of Muslims under the leadership of Muḥammad. It can in fact be existential: that is, Muslims seek to become martyrs. All three responses to the ideal have existed at all times in Islamic history. The ideal of martyrdom can be read into the very name of the religion: *Islām* means submission to the will of God. And the primary, not to say archetypal, act of submission, according to the Islamic tradition, is Abraham's willingness to sacrifice his son, and, presumably, his son's willingness to comply, thereby rendering Ismāʿīl (or according to some traditions Isḥāq) a martyr, or more accurately, one who was willing to become a martyr. In its veneration of the individual act of self-sacrifice for a higher moral, ethical, spiritual idea or cause, Islam is no different from any of the other great religious traditions of the world. But Islam as a whole is distinguished from other traditions that have theologized away the challenging blade of the martyrdom ideal through metaphor and other abstractions. This fact accounts for the simultaneous feelings of unease and admiration which occur to the non-Muslim observer of the contemporary scene and its examples of *shahādah*. To put it bluntly: martyrdom has become very unfashionable in the West, at least any martyrdom associated with a religious purpose.

There have been times even within the Islamic community when the ideal of martyrdom was also emasculated. Within the larger Sunnī religious culture which was firmly consolidated no earlier than the late ninth century, the personal ethos and ideal of martyrdom had become quiescent as an urgent religious motif. Even though Sunnī theologians recognized the power of the idea and even perpetuated the veneration the early martyrs of Islam, such as Hamzah, the original *sayyid al-shuhadā'* or "Prince of Martyrs" (a title which is most familiarly attached to the hero par excellence of the Shīʿah, Ḥusayn ibn ʿAlī), and to venerate the various sacrifices made by the early community as acts of martyrdom, they nonetheless rigorously opposed the cultivation of a contemporary cult of martyrdom in their respective societies by emphasizing the illegality of suicide and equating the seeking of a martyr's death with this. This was no doubt at least partly in response to the activities of Khawārij and Shīʿīs whose activities were disruptive to the greater unity of Muslims, the *ahl al-sunnah wa al-jamā*ʿ. The seeking of martyrdom (*ṭalab al-shahādah*) thus was discouraged by theologians because of its easy confusion with suicide (and of course, the challenges an active doctrine of martyrdom poses to stable community life)—an act unequivocally forbidden in Islam. The same theologians elevated the accomplishment of moral and ethical challenges as equal if not preferable to death: (1) fasting; (2) regularity in prayer; (3) reading the Qur'ān; (4) filial devotion; and (5) rectitude in the collection of taxes. All of these count as valorous deeds in the way of God (*fī sabīl Allāh*). So now the rank of martyr could be sought in the normal acts of worship: the ritual perfection and purity of motive with which these were performed then determined how close a believer might come to being granted the prize of martyrdom. A typical *ḥadīth* from one of the Sunnī collections runs as follows (quoting the Prophet):

> Whoever believes in Allāh and his Apostle and performs the *ṣalāt* and fasts the month of Ramaḍān, Allāh is obliged to make him enter paradise, be it that he has been zealous in Allāh's way, or that he never left his birthplace.—Thereupon it was said to the Prophet: Are there no better tidings to be given to men (viz., to those who are zealous in Allāh's way). He answered: Certainly; in paradise there are a hundred degrees which Allāh has preserved for those who are zealous in his way. Between every two of them is a distance as there is between heaven and earth. If ye beseech Allāh, demand of him *firdaws;* it is in the middle of paradise and its highest point and above it is God's throne. (Wensinck, p. 91.)

In addition, books of *ḥadīth* also contains lists of categories of believers whose deaths occur in such a violent or painful way that they are counted as martyrs. According to Wensinck, this can be five, seven, or eight types of death. The most explicit list is from the *Muwaṭṭa'* of Mālik ibn Anas (d. 795):

> The martyrs are seven, apart from death in Allāh's way. He that dies as a victim of an epidemic is a martyr; he that dies by being drowned, is a martyr; he that dies from pleuresy, is a martyr; he that dies from diarrhoea, is a martyr; he that dies by fire is a martyr; he that dies by being struck by a wall falling into ruins, is a martyr; the woman who dies in childbed, is a martyr.

Such scriptural raw material would eventually produce doctrinal statements like the following one from the pen of the preeminent Sunnī theologian, Muḥammad Abū Ḥāmid al-Ghazālī (d. 1111):

> Every one who gives himself wholly to God *(tajarrada illāhī)* in the war against his own desires [*nafs*], is a martyr when he meets death going forward without turning back. So the holy warrior is he who makes war against his own desires, as it has been explained by the apostle of God. And the "greater war" is the war against one's own desires, as the Companions said: We have returned from the lesser war unto the greater one, meaning thereby the war against their own desires. (Wensinck, p. 95.)

It is indicative of this transition that none of the four Rightly Guided Caliphs, each of whom is recognized by Islamic tradition as having been murdered, is typically given the rank or title of martyr. This fact is interesting because Abū Bakr is the only one of the four Rashīdūn not to have been killed in an open act of violence and might mean that all four are regarded as martyrs, although it is not a common observation in discussing this early period of Islamic history. It is also true that Sunnī Islam has recognized as martyrs those who have died for Islam after the time of the Rashīdūn. In keeping with Islam's communal ethos, martyrdom is treated by the *fuqahā'* as not necessarily or foremost a means for individual salvation or felicity in the next world. Rather, it has the pragmatic value of ensuring the continued existence of the group through its being a mere by-product of communal defense (see Klausner, 1987).

Shī'ī Islam, however, is often identified by the way in which the ideal of martyrdom has been kept a vital if not essential element of belief. The potency of the ideal here can be seen by referring to the only Islamic movement of the modern period to have acquired a universally recognized distinct or non-Islamic identity—the Bahā'ī faith. In this religion, which began in a Shī'ī milieu, the ideal of martyrdom is retained as an important element of contemporary religious belief (Bethel, 1986). Shiism, particularly from the beginning of the sixteenth century, with the establishment of the Ṣafavids, took the motif of martyrdom to its bosom and cultivated it as a religio-cultural ideal to a degree unwitnessed earlier. The Twelver Shī'ī list of martyrs begins with Abel (Qābīl) and continues through history to include the prophet Muḥammad and eleven of the twelve imams, the exception being, of course, the expected twelfth Imam who has in fact never died. There is obviously no space here to fully examine the martyrdom tradition in Shiism. It is indisputable, for example, that the success of the 1978–1979 Iranian Revolution owes much to the Shī'ī veneration of martyrs and the concomitant willingness of the "average believer" to suffer martyrdom. The Shī'ī tradition has been the main guardian of the martyrdom ideal for the entire Islamic tradition, for it is within Shiism that the visiting of the graves of the martyrs—preeminently but not exclusively the imams—has special significance, that weeping for them, or even *pretending* to weep, has special religious value, and suffering similar distresses as for example Ḥusayn and his companions, such as thirst, in however slight a degree also has religious value. Indeed, according to some contemporary Shī'ī authorities, the true meaning of the erstwhile purely mystical term *fanā'* (annihilation, selflessness) is none other than the sacrifice of the physical life in the path of Islam (Abedi and Legenhausen, 1986, p. 68, in a speech by Ayatollah Sayyid Maḥmud Ṭāleqāni [d. 1979]).

Within Sufism the theme of martyrdom is also highly important. The Islamic world is adorned with thousands of shrines (s., *mashhad*) to pious Muslims who have been regarded as martyrs (see Björkman, Patton, and Arnold), although, it should be added, not all places known as *mashhad* claim for this reason to hold the remains of a bona fide martyr. (In Turkish, for example, a word for cemetery in general is *meshhed*.) In any case, these tombs are the objects of special veneration and pilgrimage, the practice of which is traced to the Prophet himself, who is said to have visited the graves of the martyrs of the Battle of Uḥud interred in al-Baqī' cemetery to pay special homage to them. The *shahīd ganj* in India is said to be the tomb of no less than 150,000 martyrs. However, in Sufism martyrdom acquires many of the same features associated with the type of the martyr hero most readily exemplified by Jesus in the Gospel accounts of the passion, the most important example here being of course Ḥusayn ibn

Manṣūr al-Ḥallāj (whose act of martyrdom is frequently conflated with Ḥusayn ibn ʿAlī's—see Schimmel, in Chelkowski, 1979, p. 213), who was crucified Baghdad in the early tenth century and has been "kept alive" as an ideal of piety and spiritual valor within not only the Ṣūfī tradition but in some aspects of the wider Islamic cultural context as well: Ḥallāj is the preeminent martyr hero (Massignon, 1982). But there have been many others, including his son Manṣūr, Suhrawardī of Aleppo, ʿAyn al-Quẓat of Hamadan, Nesimî in Turkey, Ibn Sabʿīn in Spain, and Sarmad in Mughal India, to name only a few of the most famous. It is important to note that even at the time of Ḥallāj's crucifixion, visitation to the tombs of martyrs was such a firmly established practice that Ḥallāj's remains were cremated and the ashes scattered on the Euphrates in order that no tomb to him could be erected which would then perhaps become the object of a cult. The recent study of the Ṣūfī martyr Masʿūd Beg in India of the late fourteenth century (Ernst, 1985) shows the literary process involved in the acknowledgment of a saint as also a martyr. Ernst makes the interesting observation that "Islamic historiography reverses the relationship between *passio* and *vita*. The Islamic martyrologies are later and derive their authority from the norms established by the Prophet and the Imams" (p. 313).

Martyrdom Today. The Islamic religion is based on "bearing witness" to the truth of God's most recent revelation through his last prophet Muḥammad, and that insofar as the most dramatic, and according to some most meaningful, form of bearing witness is to do so with one's "self" *nafs* ("self," soul, life), then Islam is also based on martyrdom. But, as we have seen, the act of bearing witness is accomplished in Islam in a number of ways, ranging from the uttering of the words *lā ilāha illā Allāh Muḥammad rasūl Allāh* to the ultimate act of witnessing, the sacrificing of one's own life in the pursuit of the establishment of Islamic ideals or the defense of those ideals. Between these two possibilities are a number of other acts and gestures that have been recognized by *fuqahā'* as constituting *shahādah* within the purview of the Islamic holy law, *sharīʿah*. Some of these other acts are: dying during pilgrimage, dying from a number of particularly virulent and painful diseases, for women dying during childbirth, and so forth. Today, Islam is distinguished among the world religions by the degree to which and the intensity with which the motif or ideal of martyrdom, in the sense of relinquishing one's life for faith, is consciously kept alive and cultivated. The motif within Sunnī Islam has been seen to reside chiefly in veneration of the struggles of the early Islamic community with the Meccan Arabs and their Jāhilī culture. With the severe dislocations experienced by a large part of the Muslim world since the eighteenth century, a new period of understanding martyrdom has come into being. In some ways, the importance of the theme in the contemporary world transcends the always somewhat misleading divisions of Sunnī, Shīʿī and Ṣūfī. See for example the Arabic book by ʿĀrif ʿĀrif, *The Scroll of Immortality: Names of the Martyrs Who Bore Witness with Their Lives in the Battles for Palestine, 1947–1952* (*Sijill al-khulūd: asmā' al-shuhadā' alladhina istashhadū fī maʿārik Filasṭīn;* Sidon, Lebanon, 1962), or the recent book on Egyptian history, *Martyrs of the 1919 Insurrection* (*Shuhadā' thawrat 1919;* Cairo, 1984). Martyrdom was a prominent theme in the recent Iran-Iraq War where both sides relied heavily on the ideal to motivate military troops.

From the point of view of the cultural tastes of the non-Muslim world, namely, Europe and North America, anyone who aspires to be a *shahīd* in the physical/existential sense is neither a witness nor martyr, but rather a terrorist or fanatic. From the point of view of Islamic religio-cultural presuppositions, these people, especially those who lose their lives in the course of an action, are seen as martyrs and knights (*fidā'iyīn*). However, in recent times, even the Western popular press has come to recognize the possible significance in such a disparity of interpretation of the same act. For example, those who have been indicted for conspiracy to commit acts of terrorism in North America and Egypt at considerable risk to personal life have also been recognized as belonging to organizations without whose existence the vast majority of impoverished Egyptians would have no health care, postal service, or education (Weaver, 1993).

In sum, a Muslim martyr, that is one who has died in the service of Islam, is distinguished from other Muslims in the life after death in a number of ways: (1) a martyr is spared the post-mortem interrogation by the two angels Munkar and Nakīr; (2) a martyr bypasses purgatory (*barzakh*) and proceeds directly on death to the highest station in Paradise, those locations nearest the divine throne; (3) this station is called in a *ḥadīth* the most beautiful abode and the *dār al-shuhadā'*; (4) martyrs' wounds will glow red and smell of musk on the Day of Judgment; (5) of all the inhabitants of Paradise, only the martyrs wish for and are theoretically allowed to return to earth for the purpose of suffering martyrdom; (6) by virtue of their meritorious act, a martyr is rendered free of sin and therefore does not require the Prophet's intercession *(shafāʿah);* (7) some traditions even portray notable martyrs as intercessors for others; (8) as a result of their purity, martyrs are buried in the clothes in which they died and are not washed before burial; (9) according to Ghazālī, a martyr enjoys the third highest position in post-mortem existence after the prophets and the *ʿulamāʾ* (religious scholars); according to an earlier authority (Abū Ṭālib al-Makkī, d. 996), the martyrs rank second as intercessors after the prophets.

[*See also* Jihād; Mashhad; Sainthood; Shīʿī Islam, *historical overview article;* Shrine.]

BIBLIOGRAPHY

Alserat: The Imam Husayn Conference Number 12 (Spring–Summer 1986). Contains a number of articles, many from a Shīʿī perspective, on the significance of the martyrdom of the Prophet's grandson, Ḥusayn.

Arnold, Thomas W. "Saints and Martyrs (Muhammadan in India)." In *Encyclopaedia of Religion and Ethics*, vol. 11, p. 68–73. Edinburgh, 1958.

Ayoub, Mahmoud M. *Redemptive Suffering in Islam: A Study of the Devotional Aspects of ʿĀshūrāʾ in Twelver Shīʿism.* The Hague, 1978. The first major Western study on the subject, shedding light on the martyrdom motif in both Sunnī and Shīʿī Islam.

Ayoub, Mahmoud M. "Martyrdom in Christianity and Islam." In *Religious Resurgence: Contemporary Cases in Islam, Christianity, and Judaism*, edited by Richard Antoun and Mary Elaine Hegland, pp. 67–77. Syracuse, N.Y., 1987.

Bethel, Fereshteh Taheri. "A Psychological Theory of Martyrdom." *World Order* 20.3–4 (Spring–Summer 1986): 5–25. Study of the martyrdom motif in the Bahāʾī Faith, based on the events following the 1978–1979 Iranian Revolution.

Björkman, W., "Shāhid." In *Shorter Encyclopaedia of Islam*, edited by H. A. R. Gibb and J. H. Kramers, pp. 517–518. Leiden, 1953.

Chelkowski, Peter, ed. *Taʿziyeh: Ritual and Drama in Iran.* New York, 1979. Classic study highlighting the importance of the martyrdom motif for the rise and development of *taʿziyah*, which has been called the only authentic Islamic drama.

Ernst, Carl W. "From Hagiography to Martyrdom: Conflicting Testimonies to a Sufi Martyr of the Delhi Sultanate." *History of Religions* 24 (May 1985): 308–327. Primarily a literary study of martyrdom, describing the transformation from saint to martyr.

Fischer, Michael M. J. *Iran: From Religious Dispute to Revolution.* Cambridge, Mass., 1980.

Kattabi, Ahmad. "Feeding the Iranian Need for Martyrdom: Mecca Massacre." *New Statesman* 14 (28 August 1987): 14–15.

Klausner, Samuel Z. "Martyrdom." In *The Encyclopedia of Religion*, vol. 9, pp. 230–238. New York, 1987.

Massignon, Louis. *The Passion of al-Ḥallāj: Mystic and Martyr of Islam.* 4 vols. Princeton, 1982. Classic study of the life, milieu, and works of Islam's most famous martyr.

Patton, Walter M. "Saints and Martyrs (Muhammadan)." In *Encyclopaedia of Religion and Ethics*, vol. 11, pp. 63–68. Edinburgh, 1958.

Peters, Rudolph, trans. *Jihad in Medieval and Modern Islam.* Leiden, 1977.

Sachedina, A. A. *Islamic Messianism: The Idea of the Madhī in Twelver Shīʿism.* Albany, N.Y., 1981. Pioneering study of the subject, demonstrating the importance of martyrdom in Shiism.

Sande, Hans. "Palestinian Martyr Widowhood: Emotional Needs in Conflict with Role Expectations." *Social Science and Medicine* 34.6 (March 1992): 709–717. Discusses the importance of martyrdom in Islam beyond sectarian boundaries.

Smith, Jane I., and Yvonne Yazbeck Haddad. *The Islamic Understanding of Death and Resurrection.* Albany, N.Y., 1981. Contains much useful information on the topic.

Swenson, Jill D. "Martyrdom: Mytho-Cathexis and the Mobilization of the Masses in the Iranian Revolution." *Ethos* 13.2 (Summer 1985): 121–149.

Ṭāleqāni, Maḥmud, Murtaẕā Muṭahharī, and ʿAlī Sharīʿatī. *Jihād and Shahādat: Struggle and Martyrdom in Islam.* Edited by Mehdi Abedi and Gary Legenhausen. Houston, 1986. Highly useful collection, especially for a Shīʿī perspective.

Vieille, Paul. "Notes on the Iranian Revolution followed by an Interview with the President of the Republic." *Peuples-Mediterraneens/Mediterranean Peoples* 12 (July–September 1980): 109–140.

Weaver, Mary Anne. "The Trail of the Sheikh." *The New Yorker*, 12 April 1993: 71–89.

Wensinck, A. J. "The Oriental Doctrine of the Martyrs." In *Semietische Studien uit de Nalatenschap*, pp. 91–113. Leiden, 1941. The first important Western study of the problem, by one of the greatest Islamicists in that tradition.

Zarandī, Muḥammad Nabīl. *The Dawn-Breakers* (1932). Translated and edited by Shoghi Effendi. Wilmette, Ill., 1974. Describes in graphic detail the ordeal of the early Bābī community in Iran and the way in which the ideal of martyrdom has remained important to Bahāʾīs.

Zonis, Marvin, and Daniel Offer. "The Psychology of Revolutionary Leadership: The Speeches of Ayatollah Khomeini." *Psycho-History Review* 13.2–3 (Winter 1985): 5–17.

B. TODD LAWSON

MARYAM JAMEELAH (b. 1934), revivalist ideologist. Maryam Jameelah was born Margaret Marcus to a Jewish family in New Rochelle, New York on 23 May 1934. She grew up in a secular environment, but at the age of nineteen while a student at New York University she developed a keen interest in religion. Unable to find spiritual guidance in her immediate environment, she looked to other faiths. Her search brought her into contact with an array of spiritual orders, religious cults, and world religions; she became acquainted with Islam around 1954. She was then greatly impressed by Marmaduke Pickthall's *The Meaning of the Glorious Koran* and by the works of Muhammad Asad, himself a convert from Judaism to Islam. Maryam Jameelah cites Asad's *The Road to Mecca* and *Islam at Crossroads* as critical influences on her decision to become a Muslim. Through her readings on Islam she developed a bond with that religion and soon became its spokesperson, defending Muslim beliefs against Western criticism and championing such Muslim causes as that of the Palestinians. Her views created much tension in her personal life, but she continued to pursue her cause. On 24 May 1961 she embraced Islam in New York, and soon after began to write for the *Muslim Digest* of Durban, South Africa. Her articles outlined a pristine view of Islam and sought to establish the truth of the religion through debates with its critics. Through this journal she became acquainted with the works of Mawlānā Sayyid Abu al-Aʿlā Mawdūdī (d. 1979), the founder and leader of the Jamāʿat-i Islāmī (Islamic Party) of Pakistan, who was also a contributor to the journal. Maryam Jameelah was impressed by Mawdūdī's views and began to correspond with him. Their letters between 1960 and 1962, later published in a volume entitled *Correspondences between Maulana Mawdoodi and Maryam Jameelah*, discussed a variety of issues from the discourse between Islam and the West to Maryam Jameelah's personal spiritual concerns. Maryam Jameelah's attachment to Islam created great difficulties for her in her family and community; her anguish was relayed to Mawdūdī, who advised her to move to Pakistan and live among Muslims.

Maryam Jameelah traveled to Pakistan in 1962 and joined the household of Mawlānā Mawdūdī in Lahore. She soon married a member of the Jamāʿat-i Islāmī, Muhammad Yusuf Khan, as his second wife. Since settling in Pakistan she has written an impressive number of books, which have adumbrated Jamāʿat-i Islāmī's ideology in a systematic fashion. Although she never formally joined the party, she became one of its chief ideologists. Maryam Jameelah has been particularly concerned with the debate between Islam and the West, an important, albeit not central, aspect of Mawdūdī's thought. She sharpened the focus of the Muslim polemic against the West and laid out the revivalist critique of Christianity, Judaism, and secular Western thought in methodic fashion. Her works often fall into the trap of citing the worst moral and ethical transgressions of the West—usually isolated incidents—to condemn the West in its entirety. Maryam Jameelah's significance, however, does not lie in the force of her observations, but in the manner in which she articulates an internally consistent paradigm for revivalism's rejection of the West. In this regard, her influence far exceeds the boundaries of Jamāʿat-i Islāmī and has been important in the development of revivalist thought across the Muslim world.

The logic of her discursive approach has recently led Maryam Jameelah away from revivalism and Jamāʿat-i Islāmī. Increasingly aware of revivalism's own borrowing from the West, she has distanced herself from the revivalist exegesis and has even criticized her mentor Mawdūdī for his assimilation of modern concepts into Jamāʿat-i Islāmī's ideology. Her writings in recent years embody this change in orientation and reveal the influence of traditional Islam. Today she lives in Lahore and continues to write on Islamic thought and life.

[*See also* Jamāʿat-i Islāmī *and the biography of Mawdūdi.*]

BIBLIOGRAPHY

Correspondences between Maulana Maudoodi and Maryam Jameelah. 4th ed. Lahore, 1986. Outlines Maryam Jameelah's first contacts with Jamāʿat-i Islāmī.

Maryam Jameelah. *Is Western Civilization Universal?* Lahore, 1969. Critique of modernism and its impact on Islamic societies.

Maryam Jameelah. *A Manifesto of the Islamic Movement.* Lahore, 1969. One of Maryam Jameelah's most lucid articulations of the objective of Islamic revivalism.

Maryam Jameelah. *Islam in Theory and Practice.* Lahore, 1973. Maryam Jameelah's account of the ideology and operations of Jamāʿat-i Islāmī.

Maryam Jameelah. "An Appraisal of Some Aspects of Maulana Sayyid Ala Maudoodi's Life and Thought." *Islamic Quarterly* 31.2 (1987): 116–130. Maryam Jameelah's recent critique of Mawdūdī.

Maryam Jameelah. *Islam and Orientalism.* Reprint, Lahore, 1987. Critique of Western conceptions of Islam.

Maryam Jameelah. *Islam and Modernism.* Reprint, Lahore, 1988. Representative of Maryam Jameelah's polemic against the West.

Maryam Jameelah. *Islam versus the West.* Reprint, Lahore, 1988. One of Maryam Jameelah's most celebrated works denouncing the West.

SEYYED VALI REZA NASR

MASHHAD. An Arabic word meaning "a place where a martyr died," *mashhad* is the gravesite of an imam of Ithnā ʿAsharī Shiism believed to have suffered *shahādah* (martyrdom). The Qurʿān attests that a martyr is granted special heavenly privileges, and the concept of exalting divine purposes by suffering violent death played an important role in the development of the belief in the sanctity of the imams' gravesites. The imam as *shahīd* (martyr) will be called on to bear witness on the Day of Judgment as to what was revealed to the

Prophet as well as to those who acknowledged him and those who charged him with falsehood. The first Shīʿī imam, ʿAlī ibn Abī Ṭālib, was abandoned and murdered by Muslims, and each of the imams after him was persecuted or poisoned by a caliph or his supporters. Thus all imams are revered as martyrs, and their tombs have become sites for *ziyārah* (annual visitation) by Shīʿīs, who believe that their *wilāyah* (devotion) to the martyred imams, expressed through these pilgrimages, will win forgiveness for their sins and a share in the final victory of the Mahdi, the messianic imam. Pious Shīʿīs also look on the shrines as places where they can share in the imam's sanctity.

Of all the imams, Ḥusayn ibn ʿAlī enjoys the status of Chief of Martyrs, having suffered the torments of thirst and hunger in the desert and having been slaughtered by his enemies at Karbala, in present-day Iraq. His tomb was probably the first *mashhad* in Shīʿī piety, and it was regarded as holy immediately after his martyrdom in 680. The ritual of *ziyārah,* salutations offered at the tombs of the imams, evolved from the concept of *mashhad.* Unlike the *ḥajj,* which has to be performed at a set time, the *ziyārah* can be performed at any time, although some special days, such as ʿĀshūrāʾ (the day of Ḥusayn's death), are recommended.

Following the one at Karbala, the tombs of other imams were also regarded as *mashhad.* The *mashhad* of ʿAlī at Najaf, Iraq, a town some six miles west of Kufa, was revealed to the public in the early ʿAbbāsid period (749–1258). The *mashhad* at Kazimayn, a town near Baghdad, enshrines the tombs of Mūsā al-Kāẓim and Muḥammad al-Jawād, the seventh and ninth imams. In Samarra, a city north of Baghdad, ʿAlī al-Hādī and al-Ḥasan al-ʿAskarī, the tenth and eleventh imams are buried; the eighth imam, ʿAlī al-Riḍā, is buried in Sanabad, in the district of Tus, which has given rise to the most celebrated city of the Shīʿah world, Mashhad, Iran.

The *mashhads* of other imams in Medina's Baqi graveyard were leveled by the Wahhābīyah in 1925. The Sunnī Wahhābī "puritans" regard the Shīʿī practice of venerating the *mashhad* as leading to a form of *shirk* ("associationism"), hence, grave sin against God.

The *mashhads* of all imams were richly endowed, and lavish gifts were bestowed by various Muslim rulers, especially those of Shīʿī dynasties. Towns grew up around them, and the *ḥaram* (sacred areas) were adorned with magnificent and costly ornamentation. All the shrines have some architectural features in common. The tomb lies in a courtyard surrounded by arched halls and cells. Its walls are decorated resplendently with colored tiles. The entrance to the main rectangular building is through a golden outer hall. In the middle of the central golden-domed chamber lies the shrine, surrounded by a *ḍarīh* (silver enclosure). Two golden minarets usually flank the entrance to the shrine.

The shrines are important centers of Shīʿī learning, and important *madrasahs* (seminaries) grew up around them. Every Shīʿī longs to find a last resting place in the holy precincts of the beloved imams, and this has resulted in the development of extensive cemeteries at all the shrines, especially at Karbala, Najaf, and Mashhad and in areas near these shrines.

[*See also* Ithnā ʿAsharīyah; Karbala; Martyrdom; Najaf; Qom; Shrine; Wilāyah; Ziyārah.]

BIBLIOGRAPHY

Algar, Hamid. *Religion and State in Iran, 1785–1906: The Role of the Ulama in the Qajar Period.* Berkeley, 1969. Discusses the *mashhads* of Najaf and Karbala in the politics of Muslim powers.

Ayoub, Mahmoud M. *Redemptive Suffering in Islam: A Study of the Devotional Aspects of ʿĀshūrāʾ in Twelver Shīʿism.* The Hague, 1978. Covers *mashhads* and Shīʿī piety.

Donaldson, Dwight M. *The Shīʿite Religion.* London, 1933.

Nöldeke, Arnold. *Das Heiligtum al-Husains zu Kerbelâ.* Berlin, 1909.

ABDULAZIZ SACHEDINA

MASHRŪṬAH. *See* Constitutional Revolution.

MASHWARAH. *See* Democracy.

MASJUMI. One of Indonesia's main political parties during the period of parliamentary democracy in the 1950s, the Masjumi (also spelled Masyumi under the new system of spelling introduced in 1972) can trace its origins to a body also called Masjumi, the Majlis Sjuro Muslimin Indonesia (Consultative Council of Indonesian Muslims), which was established in 1943 by the Japanese military administration that ruled the former Dutch East Indies during World War II. The Japanese-sponsored Masjumi included all the major Indonesian Muslim organizations and was intended to mobilize support for the Japanese occupation. Although it disintegrated with the Japanese surrender, a new Muslim political party named Masjumi was established in November 1945, three months after the Indonesian nationalists had proclaimed Indonesian independence. As with the original council, all the major Indonesian Muslim organizations joined the new Masjumi, including the modernist Muhammadiyah and the traditionalist Nahdatul Ulama (NU).

The Masjumi constituted a major, but by no means dominant, political force in the new republic. Although about 85 percent of Indonesians described themselves as Muslim, many among them, especially in Java, followed a syncretic combination of Islamic and traditional Javanese beliefs and practices. Orthodox Muslims usually identified with Muslim parties, but the Javanese syncretists, often referred to as *abangan,* tended to support the nonreligious parties. As a Muslim party, the Masjumi called for the establishment of an Islamic state, particularly the adoption of the so-called Jakarta Charter, which included "the obligation for Muslims to observe the *sharīʿah,*" a provision strongly opposed by the *abangan* Javanese as well as the Christian minority.

The Masjumi played a prominent role in the politics of parliamentary democracy between 1950 and 1957. Despite their advocacy of an Islamic state, most of the party's leaders were pragmatic in outlook and formed coalition governments with secular and Christian parties. The Masjumi's economic policies were generally conservative, perhaps reflecting the support it received from Muslim businessmen and landowners. Parliamentary democracy, however, was unable to produce strong and stable governments. Regular realignments among parties resulted in coalition governments rising and falling in quick succession. In the six coalition governments before the collapse of the system in 1957, the Masjumi held the prime ministership in three, a deputy prime ministership in two, and failed to be represented in only one.

Initially composed of virtually all the significant Muslim organizations, the Masjumi suffered from sharp internecine rivalries. Its top leaders were drawn largely from the Dutch-speaking, Western-educated intelligentsia, many of whom were affiliated with the Muhammadiyah and therefore sympathetic toward a modernist perspective on religious questions. A substantial part of the party's grassroots support, however, was mobilized by the traditionalist religious teachers of the NU, whose influence was strong in the rural areas of East and Central Java. The rivalry between the Masjumi leaders and the NU culminated in 1952 when the NU withdrew and constituted itself as a distinct party. This withdrawal reduced the Masjumi's popular support considerably. Subsequently, in Indonesia's first national election in 1955, the nonreligious Indonesian National Party, with 22.3 percent, was able to win the largest share of votes; the Masjumi came in second with 20.9 percent, closely followed by the NU with 18.4 percent. The 1955 election, however, showed the Masjumi to be by far the strongest party outside Java and in the ethnically Sundanese province of West Java. It polled poorly in East and Central Java, the home provinces of the ethnic Javanese who made up about 45 percent of the Indonesian population. After 1952, therefore, the Masjumi represented regional as well as religious aspirations.

During the 1950s discontent had been growing against what many non-Javanese claimed was "Javanese domination," and several rebellions had broken out. Former Masjumi activists were among the leaders of the Darul Islam Rebellion in West Java and similar movements in Aceh (northern Sumatra) and elsewhere. Regional dissent culminated in the mid-1950s when coordinated revolts took place in several provinces in Sumatra and Sulawesi. Although dissident military officers played leading roles in this rebellion, they were supported by local branches of the Masjumi, and three top Masjumi leaders, including two former prime ministers, fled from Jakarta to participate in the formation of the Revolutionary Government of the Republic of Indonesia (PRRI) in early 1958. The inability of the central government—a coalition that included the Masjumi—to deal with the rebellion led to the government's collapse, the introduction by President Sukarno of martial law, and the replacement of parliamentary democracy with a form of authoritarian rule known as "Guided Democracy" in 1959. The regional revolt was eventually put down by central government troops, but the involvement of sections of the Masjumi earned it the enmity of both President Sukarno and the military leadership—the twin pillars of the "Guided Democracy" system. The Masjumi further alienated the president by continuing to defend parliamentary democracy, and when it joined other parties in threatening to reject the government's budget in 1960, Sukarno dissolved the parliament and established a new, appointed body without Masjumi representation. A few months later the Masjumi was banned, and in later years several of its prominent leaders were detained.

After President Sukarno had been deposed in a gradual process between 1965 and 1967, former Masjumi leaders hoped that the military-dominated regime of President Suharto would agree to the revival of the party. However, the military had been alienated by the involvement of Masjumi elements in the regional revolt, which had cost the lives of several thousand soldiers. The new government did not allow the revival of the Masjumi but permitted instead the formation of a new party, Partai Muslimin Indonesia (Indonesian Muslims' Party), which was intended to represent the old Masjumi constituency but without its old leaders.

[*See also* Indonesia; Muhammadiyah; *and* Nahdatul Ulama.]

BIBLIOGRAPHY

Benda, Harry J. *The Crescent and the Rising Sun: Indonesian Islam under the Japanese Occupation, 1942–1945*. The Hague and Bandung, 1958. Comprehensive study of the position of Islam during the Japanese occupation, including the establishment of the original Masjumi.

Boland, B. J. *The Struggle of Islam in Modern Indonesia*. The Hague, 1971. Valuable survey of the political role of Islam in Indonesia.

Feith, Herbert. *The Decline of Constitutional Democracy in Indonesia*. Ithaca, N.Y., 1962. Standard work on the period of parliamentary democracy in Indonesia.

Geertz, Clifford. *The Religion of Java*. New York, 1960. Seminal study of religious affiliation in Java.

Kahin, George McTurnan. *Nationalism and Revolution in Indonesia*. Ithaca, N.Y., 1952. Classic study of Indonesian nationalism and the revolution against Dutch rule.

Lev, Daniel S. *The Transition to Guided Democracy: Indonesian Politics, 1957–1959*. Ithaca, N.Y., 1966. Detailed study of the politics of the late 1950s, with much information about the Masjumi's role.

HAROLD CROUCH

MAṢLAḤAH. Public interest (*al-maṣāliḥ al-mursalah*) is regarded in *sharī'ah* (the divine law) as a basis of law. According to necessity and particular circumstances, it consists of prohibiting or permitting a thing on the basis of whether or not it serves a "useful purpose" or *maṣlaḥah*. It can be defined as the establishment of legal principles recommended by reason of being advantageous. The jurists of different schools have used different Arabic words to describe it. Imām Mālik calls it *al-maṣāliḥ al-mursalah*, that is, the public benefit or public welfare. The Arabic word *mursalah* literally means to set loose from the texts, and *maṣāliḥ* means welfare. The Ḥanafīs call it *istiḥsān*, meaning equitable preference to find a just solution. It consists of disregarding the results of *qiyās* (analogy) when it is considered harmful or undesirable to meet the strict demands of theory, for example, where a strict *qiyās* would lead to an unnecessarily harsh result. The Ḥanbalī scholar Ibn Qudāmah as well as the Mālikī jurist Ibn Rushd also have occasionally used the term *istiḥsān*. Imām Aḥmad ibn Ḥanbal calls it *istiṣlāḥ*, meaning seeking the best solution for the general interest of the Muslim community. Unprecedented interests should be supported and protected so long as they fulfill the following conditions: they should not be related to religious observances; they should not be in conformity with *sharī'ah;* it should be a necessity and not a luxury. The only school that does not recognize *istiṣlāḥ* as a source is the Shāfi'ī school. According to Imām Shāfi'ī, if this is allowed, it can open the door to the unrestricted use of fallible human opinions, since the public interest will vary from place to place and from time to time.

The concept of public interest can be very helpful particularly in cases that are not regulated by any authority of the Qur'ān, the *sunnah*, or *qiyās*. In that case, equitable considerations can override the results of strict *qiyās*, taking into consideration the public interest. Shāfi'ī jurists have employed *istidlāl* to achieve similar results by avoiding merely the application of strict *qiyās*. *Istidlāl* is the process of seeking guidance, basis, and proof from the sources through deduction, although its dictionary meaning is merely "argumentation." As examples of juristic decisions based on *maṣlaḥah*, two juristic decisions of Imam Mālik ibn Anas are listed: (1) the Muslim ruler can exact additional taxes from wealthy citizens in periods of emergency; (2) sale of grapes (which is otherwise legal) is prohibited to a wine merchant.

Since contemporary *fiqhi* (legal) issues have arisen, it is important to evaluate the role *al-maṣāliḥ al-mursalah* can play to make life easier for ordinary Muslims who must confront legal issues unknown in the past. The first step in dealing with present-day legal problems is to establish the proper context for interpreting the *naṣṣ* ("text"; explicit provision of the Qur'ān or prophetic tradition) with a view to operate *al-maṣāliḥ al-mursalah*. I do not mean by "context" mere perspective, which focuses on the angle of vision of the interpreter of the *naṣṣ*. In fact, context refers to the environment of what is being interpreted. With *maṣāliḥ* of the *ummah* (community) in mind, *fuqahā'* (jurists) can add the perspective of *fiqh* (jurisprudence) to create a bridge to the modern scientific age and interpret not only the *naṣṣ* but also the very spirit of the *naṣṣ*.

Each new generation of interpreters of the Qur'ān and the *sunnah*, particularly the *fuqahā'*, will faithfully interpret the *āyah* (verse of the Qur'ān) and the *ḥadīth*s (prophetic traditions) for renewed illuminations on such new issues as using gelatin in the preparation of sweets and marmalade or adding certain animal products to cheese and margarine. In the best interests of the community, jurists have examined the molecular structure of gelatin both in its original form and after being processed before it can be used. They have noticed that the original structure of the substance changed while being processed. In juristic terms, this phenomenon is called *qalb al-māhiyah* (changing of the very property of the substance). Since a new substance has been formed, its consumption is considered permissible. The interpretation of *naṣṣ* does not and should not restrict the interpreter to any one particular exegetical method to arrive at certain solutions to modern-day problems.

Attempts to interpret and apply the spirit of the *naṣṣ* on various new issues, such as blood transfusion and organ transplant involving non-Muslims, became to some legal scholars an offense, as they insisted that *naṣṣ* must be understood in a particular context. The *fiqh* academy, with its headquarters in Mecca, offered solid liberal legal alternatives to make life easier for Muslims in the modern age; for example, blood transfusion and organ transplants were adjudged *mubāḥ* (permissible), considering that human life is sacred and that as human beings we must not remain silent spectators to human suffering, or even the suffering of animals, as can be vouchsafed from the *sunnah* of the Prophet.

Muslim minorities in non-Muslim lands will also have resort to juristic principles of *maṣlaḥah,* since the ruling power of their land operates a political system based on principles different from those that govern the running of an Islamic state, laid down by the Muslim jurists in such books as *Aḥkām al-sulṭānīyah* and many others. In the case of democracy, elections are held where Muslim citizens are encouraged to vote. Some *ʿulamāʾ* (religious scholars) have opined that since the ruling system is one of disbelief, Muslims may not participate in an election. Others apply the principle of *maṣlaḥah.* They concede that the political structure is *bāṭil* (based on falsehood and thus null and void) but also accept that it is an existing reality that elections will take place and certain candidates or parties will assume power. These scholars have therefore defined the exact nature and implication of voting. The casting of the vote can be interpreted as a form of *shahādah* (giving testimony). By voting for a certain candidate or party, the voters are indirectly testifying to the credibility of that candidate or party. Voting can also be viewed from the angle of *shafāʿah* (intercession). The voter is thus interceding for a party to come into power that is most likely to safeguard Islamic rights in particular and human rights in general. Voting is also explained as a form of representation. When one votes for a certain party, one is in essence appointing that party as a representative for one's Islamic and human rights. Voting is also a form of *mashwarah* (consultation). The voter is giving an opinion on who should be elected to run the government. Thus, purely *shari* (juristic) equivalents such as *shūrā* (counsel), *shahādah,* and *shafāʿah* are linked to some aspects of the nature of voting.

Similarly, the concept of modern banking seems to be somewhat foreign to the sections of *fiqh* dealing with *buyūʿ* (commerce). Banks are, however, an indispensable part of modern-day commerce. Muslims find it necessary to deal with these financial institutions in their day-to-day affairs. Banks are usually interest based, although Islam is strongly opposed to an interest-based economy with its resultant financial oppression. This situation puts the Muslim in a dilemma. With the principle of *maṣlaḥah* (best interest) in mind, the *fuqahāʾ* have thus promoted the idea of "Islamic banking," which runs on the principles of *sharikah* and *muḍārabah.* The dividends an investor receives are not from interest but from joint participation with the bank in various investment schemes.

Apart from these few examples, there are issues, such as those dealing with birth control, abortion in the case where the mother's life is in danger, artificial insemination, adoption of children, or inheritance of a child whose father has died in the lifetime of the grandfather, which can be addressed afresh to find meaningful solutions.

It would be a mistake to identify the *fuqahāʾ* of the past as too conservative or too orthodox and the *fuqahāʾ* of the present time as modern, but it is fair to say that the jurists of the past simply did not have to confront the issues that Muslims face in the modern scientific and technological age. The Qur'ān and *sunnah* were read, understood, and interpreted in the past in a certain setting, and then are read and interpreted in a different setting today. It is unfair to say that the earlier setting in which the *ʿulamāʾ* and *fuqahāʾ* worked is irrelevant for later generations. The historical continuity of the Muslim background offers a historical rationale to face new challenges—for the religion of Islam is for the past, present, and future, and so is *fiqh* and its *uṣūl.*

BIBLIOGRAPHY

Doi, Abdul Rahman I. *Shariah: The Islamic Law.* Kuala Lumpur, 1989.

Ghazālī, Abū Ḥāmid al-. *Al-Mustasfā min ʿilm al-uṣūl.* Cairo, 1937.

ABDUL RAHMAN I. DOI

MATHEMATICS. The mathematical sciences occupy a prominent place in Islamic intellectual history. Historically called *ʿulūm riyāḍīyah* or *taʿlīmīyah* (pedagogic mathematics), they comprised the four main branches—arithmetic, geometry, astronomy, and music— of the quadrivium of the ancient schools. The establishment of the classical scientific heritage in the first few centuries of the spread of Islam further brought such fields as algebra, trigonometry, mechanics, and optics—together with their practical, even experimental aspects—under this domain. Although fields considered mathematical did not have comparable status or existence throughout the Islamic world, mathematical subjects in all their manifestations drew the attention of a large number of Islamic scholars who produced impressive, often historically significant, works.

There is no shortage of sources in Islamic or European languages about the rich history of mathematics in the premodern Islamic world. *The Annotated Bibliography of Islamic Science (ABIS)* lists in its third volume devoted to mathematical sciences nearly eighteen hundred printed sources on the subject published before 1970 alone. Since that date, additional works equal to at least half of that number have appeared. Nonetheless, a comprehensive study on the history of mathematics in Islamic societies remains a distant dream. The current state of research is such that it is not possible to reconstruct such a history beyond the stage of theoretical and partial studies of the first half of the Islamic era, and the coverage of such crucial subjects as the social context of mathematics and the history of mathematics in the modern Islamic world is still limited and fragmentary. Attention to social context has been occasional (Hoyrup, 1987, 1990; Heinen, 1978; King, 1980, 1990; Berggren, 1992), that to modern history is just beginning (İhsanoğlu, 1992; Rashed, 1992). Such isolated studies, especially those of mathematics in modern Turkey, Iran, or other non-Arab countries of the region, are bound to extend the chronology and scope of our understanding of mathematics in the Islamic world.

Historical Meaning. Mathematics in the premodern Islamic world differed in its meaning and domain from that of the modern era (to which it is unquestionably bound), as well as that of the ancient world (from which it initially arose). Its disciplinary boundaries were changing even during the period in Islamic intellectual history that is commonly considered its peak. As the collective form *ʿulūm al-riyāḍīyah* indicates, these sciences existed as composite mathematical disciplines which had themselves evolved as a branch of the so-called "sciences of the ancients" *(ʿulūm al-awāʾil),* that is, the original, pre-Islamic sciences in contrast to Islamic sciences *(ʿulūm Islāmīyah).* The affiliation of these "rational" *(ʿaqlī)*—in contrast to "traditional" *(naqlī)*—sciences with the ancient sciences of Greece, India, or Persia was itself of a varied nature, and the practicing mathematical disciplines each inevitably had different elements of the classical heritage, different disciplinary encounters and boundaries, and naturally, different historical fates.

The science of arithmetic was not a single science. Of its main two divisions, the science of numbers *(ʿilm to al-ʿadad),* which was at the head of the seven divisions of mathematical sciences *(ʿulūm taʿālīm)* according to al-Fārābī's (d. AH 339/950 CE) *Iḥṣāʾ al-ʿulūm,* was more theoretical. It was cast in the tradition of the arithmetic books (vii–ix) of Euclid's *Elements* as well as Nichomachus's *Introduction to Arithmetic.* The science of reckoning *(ʿilm al-ḥiṣāb)* on the other hand, dealt more with arithmetical operations, and had its own distinct intellectual currents and systems of numerical calculation. One of unknown origin employed the fingers in the calculation process, and so was often termed "finger reckoning" *(ḥisāb al-ʿuqūd)*", or else "hand reckoning" *(ḥisāb al-yad)*" or "mental reckoning" *(al-ḥisāb al-hawāʾī);* it had a rhetorical mode of expression for numbers. In contrast, the so-called "Indian system of reckoning" *(ḥisāb al-Hindī),* also known as "board and dust calculation" *(ḥisāb al-takht wa-al-turāb)* was based on the place-value concept and expressed numbers in terms of ten figures including zero *(ṣifr)* as the empty place. In addition to the first system, which became the arithmetic of the scribes or secretaries, and the second system from which the medieval European "Arabic numerals" are supposed to have been derived, there was another system in which numbers were represented neither by fingers nor by figures but by letters; this third system was linked to the old Babyonian astronomical tradition according to which computations were performed in sexagesimals indicated by alphabetical symbols. This kind of treatment was known as the "arithmetic of astronomers or astrologers" (*ḥisāb al-munajjim*), "arithmetic of astronomical tables" (*ḥisāb al-zīj*), or "arithmetic of degrees and minutes" (*ḥisāb al-darā'ij wa al-daqā'iq*). Besides the *abjad* system of ciphered numeration with twenty-eight Arabic letters, there was also a *siyāq* style of representation used until very recent times in Iran and Turkey, according to which forty-five Pahlavi-style characters where employed for commercial purposes. Finally, books on reckoning included an algebraic section for the determination of unknown quantities from known ones, where the expression "algebra" (*al-jabr*), meant an operation, not the distinctint discipline it eventually became.

An independent science of algebra (*ʿilm al-jabr*), correctly associated with Muslim mathematicians, did in fact take form as such during the appropriation of ancient learning in Islamic lands. Its early character as an offshoot of applied arithmetic may explain why it was later classified under "the science of devices" (*ʿilm al-ḥiyal*) as an applied branch of mathematics. But algebra had an equally close association with geometry from the start, as the common method of supplying algebraic problems with geometrical demonstrations; this indicates the distinction between its methodology of proofs (*barāhīn*), and the method of checks (*mawāzin*) in arithmetic. As algebra seems to have been placed somewhere between geometry and arithmetic, a number of other related fields such as trigonometry and optics were considered intermediate between geometry and another of the four main mathematical disciplines, astronomy. Such intermediate fields were ultimately based on a series of Greek mathematical texts known as the "middle books" (*al-mutawassiṭāt*), because they were studied intermediately between Euclid's *Elements* and Ptolemy's *Almagest*, the two chief authorities on geometry and astronomy, respectively.

Geometry (*ʿilm al-handasah*) officially came to the Islamic intellectual world through Greek sources, and mainly through Euclid. Initially known as *jūmāṭrīyah*, Arabic geometry was predominantly Greek in origin as well as method, although it also reflects encounters with Indian works such as *Siddhantas* (*Sind hind* in Arabic) and with Persian sources—hence its designation *handasah* (geometry), from Persian *andazah* (measure).

Astronomy, by contrast, had more and stronger links to non-Greek ancient traditions, as the Babylonian heritage can now safely be added to Sanskrit, Pahlavi, and Syriac astronomical sources alongside Greek ones. Astronomy also started off as a much wider discipline than it later became, with a cluster of subfields including instruments and tables, star movements, chronology, and astrology. The existence of such designations as "the science of the figure of the heaven" (*ʿilm al-hayʾah*) as well as "the science of the heavens" (*ʿilm al-aflāk*) or "the science of stars" (*ʿilm al-nujūm*) by itself points to a historical distinction between observational and theoretical astronomy, exemplified in the respective traditions of Ptolemy's *Almagest* (*al-Majisṭī*) and *Planetary Hypothesis* (*Iqtiṣāṣ*). More curious, however, is the absence of an explicit historical distinction between the traditions of Ptolemy's *Almagest* and *Tetrabiblos* (*Arbaʿ maqālāt*), namely between the two fields of astronomy and astrology; not only were these designated by the common expression *nujūm*, but they also shared such terms as *al-ḥāsib* (computer) to refer to their practitioners. The historical affinity of astronomy and astrology to yet another of the mathematical propedeutical sciences, theoretical music (*mūsīqā*) in this same period is further indication of the invalidity of assuming fixed mathematical fields with distinct borders between them. There is another aspect to the historical meaning of mathematical sciences. Fields like astronomy and arithmetic acquired new meaning and domain as they continued to grow on Islamic soil, as the emergence of such categories as a *muwaqqit* (time-keeper) as an astronomer attached to the mosque, or a branch of arithmetic called *farā'iḍ* (dealing with the division of legacies) as part of the equipment of Islamic law attests.

Achievements. The achievements of mathematicians in the early Islamic world were of quite a varied nature and their most significant achievements were not always the most lasting. In the field of arithmetic there were few breakthroughs. The appearance of decimal fractions occurred as early as the work of the Damascene arithmetician Abū al-Ḥasan al-Uqlīdisī in his *Kitāb al-fuṣūl fī al-ḥisāb al-Hindī*, composed in AH 341/952–953 CE. These were much later reintroduced as *al-kusūr aʿshārīyah*, together with the first appearance of a unified place-value system for both integers and fractions, in the work of the Persian mathematician Jamshīd ibn Masʿūd al-Kāshī in *Miftāh al-ḥisāb* (*Key to Arithmetic*), composed in Samarkand in 830/1427. Although the earlier work of al-Uqlīdisī was of less impact, credit goes to him for the use of strokes for decimal signs, for the first successful treatment of the cube root, and for the alteration of the dust-board method to suit ink and paper. Other breakthroughs include notable steps toward considering irrationals as numbers, as in the work of the famous mathematician and poet ʿUmar Khayyām, as opposed to treating them as incommensurable lines as did those in the tradition of Book X of Euclid's *Elements*.

On the whole, developments in theoretical arithmetic (*ʿilm al-ʿadad*) are of less historical significance, and despite much theoretical treatment, e.g. arithmetic sections of Ikhwān al-Ṣafā's *Rasāʾil*, or works on "amicable numbers" (*aʿdād mutaḥabbah*) or pyramidal numbers, it is in the area of computation that more important contributions seem to have been made. Especially important in this category are treatises devoted to algebra, often including the term *ḥiṣāb* associated with practical aspects of arithmetic in their titles: *Kitāb mukhtaṣar fī al-ḥisāb al-jabr wa-al-muqābalah* by al-Khuwārizmī and *Ṭarāʾif al-ḥisāb* by Abū Kāmil al-Shujāʿ (d. 287/900), *Al-kafī fī al-ḥisāb*, by Abū Bakr al-Karajī (d. 390/1000), or *Al-bāhir fī ʿilm al-ḥiṣāb* by al-Samawa'l al-Maghribī (d. c.570/1175). Arabic algebra as contained in these and similar texts is often associated with the successful treatment of problems corresponding to quadratic—and occasionally third degree—equations, many of which combine the act of reducing rhetorical algebraic problems into canonical form with that of providing geometrical proofs.

The most significant achievement of Muslims in arithmetic may be characterized as the fusing together of various methods into a single unified system. But fusing by no means describes their achievements in other areas. In geometry, for example, attempts to prove Euclid's Parallel postulate by a number of mathematicians, culminating in the work of Naṣīr al-Dīn al-Ṭūsī, resulted in the formulation and proof of some non-Euclidean theorems assumed to have been known to European founders of non-Euclidean geometry. In another impressive and influential scientific movement a theoretical program of reaction against certain inconsistencies in Ptolemaic astronomy resulted in a series of complex non-Ptolemaic models that have been compared to those proposed in Europe by Copernicus a few centuries later. What is particularly remarkable about this astronomical movement, which ranged from Eastern Persia, to Damascus, and all the way to Andalusia, is its preoccupation with philosophical, rather than observational, concerns. Nonetheless, a strong observational program did exist as astronomical records were produced for many major Islamic cities from Baghdad, Damascus, and Cairo to Shirāz, Khwārazm, and Marāgha, as reflected in several tables (*zīj*). In fact, this same observational tradition produced a concept of testing, adopted and developed under the terms *miḥnah*, *imtiḥān* or *iʿtibār*, which converted the methodology of the neighboring science of optics from a theoretical to an experimental science.

As it turned out, the most significant contribution of the mathematical sciences of the Islamic world to modern science was not in the field of mathematics proper, but in optics. Belonging not to physics, but to mathematics—more specifically a field intermediate between geometry and astronomy—optics, was to be revolutionized in the hands of Muslims. This revolution occurred during the golden era of sciences in Islamic civilization through Ibn al-Haytham's (d. 432/1040) *Kitab al-manāẓir*, which put this science on a new foundation. His seven books on optics were translated into Latin and Italian, and being among the first scientific books to be printed, strongly influenced the works of medieval Latin, Renaissance, and seventeenth-century thinkers.

Finally, it should be remembered that the history of optics—like the history of other mathematical disciplines in this period—includes significant developments that were not transmitted to Europe. This is particularly true of the history of astronomy, where a large body of nontransmitted literature survives from late periods in Islamic intellectual history. A study of this late mathematical tradition—now beginning to emerge from Turkey, Iran, and India—is both needed and promising. But much more is needed, and many important mathematical texts and treatises in Islamic languages now only available in manuscript form throughout the world must be brought to the aid of constructing a history of the exact sciences with a fuller context and a broader time line in the hope of approaching a deeper understanding of the history of mathematics in Islamic societies.

[*See also* Astronomy; Numerology.]

BIBLIOGRAPHY

Berggren, J. L. "History of Mathematics in the Islamic World: The Present State of the Art." *Bulletin of the Middle East Studies Association* 19.1 (1985): 9–33.

Berggren, J. L. *Episodes in the Mathematics of Medieval Islam*. New York, 1986. Contains sections on arithmetic, geometry, algebra, trigonometry, and spherics.

Berggren, J. L. "Islamic Acquisition of the Foreign Sciences: A Cultural Perspective." *American Journal of Islamic Social Sciences* 9.3 (1992): 309–324.

Heinen, Anton M. "Mutakallimūn and Mathematicians: Traces of a Controversy with Lasting Consequences." *Islam* 55 (1978): 57–73. Considers the relationship between religious thought and mathematics, particularly the attitudes of al-Jāḥiz and al-Birūnī.

Hill, Donald R. "Mathematics and Applied Science." In *Religion, Learning, and Science in the ʿAbbasid Period,* edited by M. J. L. Young et al., pp. 248–273. Cambridge, 1990. A more updated work on the early history of mathematics in Islamic civilization which includes the practical as well as theoretical aspects of the discipline.

Hoyrup, Jens. "The Formation of 'Islamic Mathematics': Sources and Conditions." *Science in Context* 1 (1987): 281–329. "Subscientific Mathematics: Observations on a Premodern Phenomena." *History of Science* 28.1 (1990): 63–81. Particularly valuable pieces for the often ignored subject of the encounter between mathematics and Islamic society.

İhsanoğlu, Ekmeleddin, ed. *Transfer of Modern Science and Technology to the Muslim World.* Istanbul, 1992. Includes articles related to mathematics in fourteenth- to eighteenth-century Turkey (İhsanoğlu, pp. 1–120), and nineteenth-century Iran (Roshdi Rashed, pp. 393–404).

Iushkevich, Adol'f Pavlovich. *Les mathématiques arabes, VIIIe–XVe siècles.* Translated by M. Cazenave and K. Jaouiche. Paris, 1976. Reviewed in *Journal of the History of Arabic Science* 1 (1977): 111.

Kennedy, E. S. *Studies in the Islamic Exact Sciences.* Beirut, 1983. By the author of several earlier articles on the subject, including "The Arabic Heritage in the Exact Sciences," *Al-Abḥāth* 23 (1970); "The Exact Sciences," in *The Cambridge History of Iran,* vol. 4, *The Period from the Arab Invasion to the Saljuqs,* edited by Richard N. Frye, pp. 378–395 (Cambridge, 1975); and "The Exact Sciences in Timurid Iran," in *The Cambridge History of Iran,* vol. 6, *The Timurid and Safavid Periods,* edited by Peter Jackson and Laurence Lockhart, pp. 568–580 (Cambridge, 1986).

King, David A. "The Exact Sciences in Medieval Islam: Some Remarks on the Present State of Research." *Bulletin of the Middle East Studies Association* 4 (1980): 10–26.

King, David A. "The Sacred Direction in Islam: A Study of the Interaction of Religion and Science in the Middle Ages." *Interdisciplinary Science Review* 10 (1985): 315–328.

King, David A. *Islamic Mathematical Astronomy.* London, 1986.

King, David A. *Islamic Astronomical Instruments.* London, 1987.

King, David A. "Science in the Service of Religion." *UNESCO; Impact of Science on Society* 159 (1990): 245–262. This article along with "The Sacred Direction in Islam" (above) are valuable sources on this rarely studied interaction.

King, David A., and George Saliba, eds. *From Deferent to Equant: A Volume of Studies in the History of Science in the Ancient and Medieval Near East in Honor of E. S. Kennedy.* New York, 1987. Indispensable source that contains, in addition to a list of Kennedy's own publications, many specialized articles and an extensive bibliography.

Nasr, Seyyed Hossein. *An Annotated Bibliography of Islamic Science,* vol. 3, *Mathematical Sciences.* Tehran, 1991. Valuable volume containing 1,831 sources printed before 1970, arranged according to subject, some with annotations in English and Persian.

Rashed, Roshdi. *Optique et mathématiques: Recherches sur l'histoire de la pensée scientifique en Arabe.* London, 1992. Collection of previously published articles on the history of mathematics.

Sabra, A. I. "The Scientific Enterprise: Islamic Contributions to the Development of Science." In *The World of Islam,* edited by Bernard Lewis, pp. 181–199. London, 1976. Contains informative sections on various branches of mathematics: arithmetic, algebra, and geometry; applied mathematics (mechanics); and those involving testing and experimentation (astronomy, light, and vision).

Sezgin, Fuat. *Geschichte der arabischen Schrifttums,* vol. 5, *Mathematik;* vol. 6, *Astronomie;* vol. 7, *Astrologie, Meteorologie, und Verwandts.* Leiden, 1970–1979. Fundamental reference works for manuscript sources and bibliography of the exact sciences during the classical period of Islamic civilization. For a review of volume 5, see David A. King, "Notes on the Sources for the History of Early Islamic Mathematics," *Journal of the American Oriental Society* 99 (1979): 450–459, which lists sources for later periods.

See also articles "ʿIlm al-ḥisāb," "ʿIlm al-handasa," "ʿIlm al-hay'a," "al-Djabr wa al-muqābalah," and "Mūsiqā" in *Encyclopaedia of Islam,* new ed., Leiden, 1960–.

Elaheh Kheirandish

MAURITANIA. The place of Mauritania in the Islamic history of the Maghrib dates at least from the birth of the Almoravid dynasty, but it was the gradual southward migration of the Hilalian Banū Maghfar group, the Banī Ḥassān, that accounts for the arabization of nomadic populations in the territory by the sixteenth century. The traditional guardians and interpreters of Islamic culture in Mauritania are the *zāwiyah* lineages ("marabouts" in French colonial literature). They are said by tradition to have become institutionalized in this role following the *shurr bubba,* an event (or more likely, a series of events now telescoped) between 1645 and 1675, which pitted more recently migrant Ḥassanī warriors against a confederation of autochthonous peoples. The victorious Hassānīs (from whom the Arabic dialect spoken in Mauritania today, Ḥassānīyah, derives its name) are said thereafter to have maintained temporal authority and lived by raiding. The *zāwiyah* lineages (who also refer to themselves as Ahl al-Kitāb) are largely of Berber origin and pursued a pastoral lifestyle as well as serving as the repositories of literacy and Islamic learning. This division of labor, analogous to broad distinctions between bellicose and pacific lifestyles in other nomadic societies in the Islamic world, is fundamental to the social charter for both Hassānī and *zāwiyah,* who are collectively identified as *baydan* (in Ḥassānīyah, people of Arab descent; *bīḍān* in standard Arabic). Both further elaborated a strict hierarchy of nobles, tributaries, freed slaves *(haratine/ḥarrātīn),* slaves, smiths, and musicians/praise-singers. However, the historic horizontal transfer and merging of groups between

Ḥassānī and *zāwiyah* traditions, the internal vertical movement of individuals and families, and the evident upward flow of servile laborers into higher status both belies and explains the rigid ideology of class distinctions.

By the nineteenth century the names of the eponymous ancestors of particular Ḥassānī lineages had come to be identified with four major regions that they sought to dominate: Trarza in the southwest, bordering the Atlantic coast and the right bank of the Senegal River; Brakna, in the south and immediately east of Trarza; Tagant, also in the south on roughly the same longitude and east of Brakna; and Adrar, in the north and including the caravanserai Shinqiti, by which the entire territory was known in the Arab world. These were the Ḥassānī "emirates," so christened by French observers; but the cultural zone defined by the Ḥassānīyah dialect effectively extended from the mouth of the Senegal River eastward as far as Timbuktu on the Niger Bend, and from there northward in a gentle arc meeting the Atlantic near the southern border of Morocco. To the south of the Ḥassānī nomadic populations, on both sides of the Senegal River, lived pastoral and sedentarized Pular-speaking Toucoulor or Fulbe peoples. Toucoulor populations had been islamized from the time of the eleventh-century state of Takrur (which many early Arab writers identified with several West African Sudanese Muslim lands). To the east of the Toucoulor populations, at roughly the same latitude, lived Sarakole peoples, also islamized from at least the time of the sixteenth-century Songhay empire. Both these populations had long served as labor reservoirs for the nomadic economy and may have accounted for up to one-half of the non-*baydanī* lower classes in the nineteenth century. Tension between Arabic-speaking "Moors," a name first applied to the nomads by European visitors and used by themselves today, and their southern, black African neighbors has long accounted for a major divide in Mauritanian ethnic politics which even today is only occasionally bridged by their shared Islamic heritage.

During the nineteenth century the Fulbe and other southern populations were engaged in two major Islamic reform movements, the first centered on the Futa Toro region on the left bank of the Senegal River, which succeeded in asserting its autonomy from Moorish control from the 1770s until the opening years of the nineteenth century. The second, inspired in part by the Futa Toro experiment, was led by al-Ḥajj ʿUmar Tal, who had grown up in Toro and, following his pilgrimage, returned briefly to his natal village in the 1840s to enlist forces to wage *jihād* and to spread the Tijānīyah *ṭarīqah*. The subsequent movement led to a steady stream of recruits and material from western lands, including the Senegal basin. Northern, Moorish populations played only marginal roles in these events, although particular *zāwiyah* camps appear in accounts of the education of Toucoulor reformers and holy men. [*See the biography of ʿUmar Tal.*]

The main mid-century *zāwiyah* influence in the southern Sahara was a disciple of the Timbuktu Qādirī shaykhs, Sīdīyā al-Kabīr (1774–1868). Sīdīyā's twelve years of study in the Kunta camps (1811–1824) provided experience with an integrated economic and spiritual network, which he replicated in Trarza and Brakna after his return there in the mid-1820s until his death in 1868. In a society lacking institutionalized state political authority, Sīdīyā's juridical skills combined with his studies in mysticism to capitalize on the labor of disciples who sought him out for protection and catapulted him into a position of regional spiritual leadership in southwestern Mauritania. Although Sīdīyā was associated with the Qādirīyah/al-Mukhtārīyah of his Kunta teachers, there is no indication that adherence to Ṣūfī orders held any political significance in Moorish society at the time. Sufism in the nineteenth-century Moorish *zāwiyah* tradition generally constituted a final stage in intellectual formation and was regarded as a tool for gaining divine insight that might supplement advanced studies ranging from the Qur'ān and *fiqh* to grammar. This was in contrast to the growing confrontation on the Niger Bend between the Kunta shaykh Aḥmad al-Bakkā'ī, and the ʿUmarian state that was increasingly polarized around Qādirī and Tijānī confessional lines by mid-century. [*See the biography of Bakkā'ī al-Kuntī.*]

A contemporary of Sīdīyā, Muḥammad Fāḍil (c. 1797–1869), also a student of the Kunta camps, played a similar role in the Tagant, although he distanced himself from his Qādirī al-Mukhtārī masters, who criticized his eclecticism in Ṣūfī matters. The Fāḍilīyah was chiefly spread by two of Muḥammad Fāḍil's sons, Mā' al-ʿAynayn (1831–1910) and Saʿd Būh (c. 1850–1917). From the time of his settlement in 1870 in the Sāqiyat al-Ḥamrā', Mā' al-ʿAynayn was on good terms with the ʿAlawī sultans in Morocco, and he soon was recognized as the principal religious leader in the northern reaches of the Ḥassanī region. By the 1890s he was charged by Ḥasan I with the security of the kingdom's southern Atlantic coast against Christian intruders, and during the next two decades he became increasingly drawn into Moroccan politics as his natal lands were being occupied from the south by the French. His political career culminated in 1910 when he briefly claimed the throne in Marrakesh, was defeated by the French, and retreated to the Sūs where he died. Mā' al-ʿAynayn's voluminous writings range from grammar to ethics and from law to mysticism, but it is chiefly his resistance to infidel rule for which he is remembered today.

His half-brother Saʿd Būh also achieved a broad regional reputation in the southwest of the country (Trarza) as a Ṣūfī and, during the French occupation, as one who counseled cooperation with the colonial forces. Like his brother, Saʿd Buh freely dispensed both Tijānī and Qādirī *wird*s as well as Shādhilī and Nāsirī, but the significance of *ṭarīqah* affiliations as political networks appears to have been greater in the minds of the incoming French administration than in the experience of Moorish adherents.

The French military and administrators began the "pacification" of Mauritania in 1902, bringing their North African experience that had sensitized them to the political danger of Ṣūfī orders. Their efforts to contain such a threat in West Africa effectively heightened the prestige of Ṣūfī shaykhs in many Muslim communities during the first two decades of the twentieth century. In Mauritania the Qādirīyah/al-Mukhtārīyah was chiefly identified with Sīdīyā's grandson Sīdīyā Bābā (1862–1922). Like Saʿd Būh, Sīdīyā Bābā cooperated with the French administration and thereby preserved and consolidated much of the spiritual influence he had inherited; but unlike his peers who were expanding the influence of the Ṣūfī orders in the early colonial era, Bābā criticized the ritual excesses of the *ṭuruq*. In this he sought to distance himself from the traditional *zāwiyah* practice in the southern Sahara, and he thus marks a distinct departure from the nineteenth-century Ṣūfī shaykhs.

More typical of the direction in which Ṣūfī affiliation was moving in Mauritania during the interwar period was the confrontation between followers of a *sharīf* from Tichitt, Shaykh Ḥamallāh (1886–1943), and the French administration. The doctrinal issues that set Shaykh Ḥamallāh apart focused on his practice of the Tijānīyah in the eastern Nioro region on the Mauritania/Mali frontier. Civil disturbances led to the arrest and exile of Shaykh Ḥamallāh by French officials, first in 1925 and again soon after his return home in 1940, which effectively martyred him and led to the birth of a *ṭarīqah*, the Ḥamallīyah, that survived the shaykh's death in 1943.

The colonial experience in Mauritania was a relatively benign one. The major direct impact of French administration upon Islam was the sporadic encouragement given to a very few Franco-Arabic *madrasah*s, based on their experience in Algeria. Begun in Sīdīyā Bābā's village of Boutilimit in 1913, the first *madrasah* suffered from the low priority given to education in any form in the colony and was abandoned during World War I, reestablished in Mederdra, and then returned to Boutilimit in 1929. During the 1930s additional *madrasah*s were established at Timbera (1933), Atar (1936), and Kiffa (1939), largely with local scholars and a handful of instructors from Algeria; however, the total numbers enrolled in these schools (150 by the early 1940s) never compared favorably with those in other French schools along the river (780 in the early 1940s), nor with the several thousand students who remained in the hundreds of traditional *maḥaḍra*s for advanced studies in the Islamic sciences. In the 1950s the Ahl Shaykh Sīdīyā clan revived the *madrasah* in Boutilimit as a private venture, the Institut Musulman de Boutilimit, which became a government college in 1963, three years after independence, and remained the national center for advanced studies in the Islamic sciences until the early 1970s. In 1979 the Ministry of Islamic Affairs opened an Institut des Hautes Études Islamiques in Nouakchott in an effort to consolidate and formalize the *maḥaḍra* tradition. At the end of its first decade of activity the Institute enrolled nearly 500 students, and its staff of 25 included several non-Mauritanians.

Colonial jurisprudence essentially followed an indirect rule system by which the entire territory was administered, with the greater part of civil law dispensed by locally appointed *qāḍī*s under the supervision of regional French authorities. Their charge was to administer "customary law" (under which the *sharīʿah* was categorized); penal law along with an appeals process was regulated by the French code. One effect of the imposition of the French code was to undermine the *qāḍī*s' former responsibility for adjudicating economic matters (inheritance, contract law, and slavery), which led to their increased preoccupation with religious matters. Not until some years after independence was the *sharīʿah* reexamined as a system for adjudication in civil cases.

Education policy after independence, and in particular the language of instruction and bureaucracy, was one of the central issues in ethnic conflicts. Prior to the coup that brought the military to power in 1978, roughly one-quarter of the (mainly Moorish) schoolchildren followed an Arabic program in their studies, and three-quarters followed a francophone course (favoring riverine populations). Fifteen years later those ratios were reversed, the result of a concerted arabization plan under the military government and of increasing numbers of the majority, Arabic-speaking students entering the system.

At independence in 1960 the founders of the République Islamique de Mauritanie sought a common cultural ground in Islam. The intent was not so much to create an Islamic state as to serve the pragmatic objective of enshrining in the new republic's name a common ideology that might supplant ethnic constructions of national identity. The colonial judicial system was largely transferred to the independent state; the francophone educational system was little changed; and the external relations of the state were initially formulated to maintain a delicate balance between Mauritania's southern neighbors, Senegal and Mali, upon whom the country was economically dependent for labor and access to virtually all imports, and her Maghribi antagonist at the time, Morocco.

The combined effects of the Ṣaḥrāwī war, twenty years of drought, and the resulting urbanization beginning in the early 1970s provide the context in which internal tensions have been heightened. Changes in the educational system since the late 1970s and the increasing use of Arabic as the language of government and the local media have led to a latter-day Arabist movement in Mauritania that shares many of the implications and contradictions associated with the phenomenon seventy years earlier in the former Ottoman provinces. Although Mauritania is still heavily beholden to France for economic aid, it has increasingly turned to Arab (mainly Gulf state) financing. This and an acceptance by Maghribi governments of Mauritania's military rulers as poor cousins have given new weight to the country's Arab heritage and a new meaning to Islam in the national life of the country. The only internal ideological common ground has also become a bridge to legitimate external relations to offset postcolonial dependence on France, but at the cost of heightened internal ethnic tension. Embedded in this process has been a new meaning for Islam, which is no longer simply a set of local expressions of an abstract *ummah* presided over by noble guardians of orthopraxy, but a dynamic and accessible ideology that ties individuals to the marketplace of ideas throughout the Muslim world. Thus, thirty years after independence, the main streams of Islamic activity in the central lands are also to be found in Mauritania, mainly in the urban centers, alongside an aging but still highly influential traditional Islamic authority that is attempting to maintain a role in the dramatically changed economic and social circumstances since the 1970s.

[*See also* Qādirīyah; Tijānīyah; Zāwiyah.]

BIBLIOGRAPHY

Baduel, Pierre R. "Mauritanie entre arabite et africanite." Special issue of *Revue des Études du Monde Mediterrané Musulman* 54.4 (1989). Series of scholarly essays that examine contemporary ethnic problems and ties to the Arab world.

Brenner, Louis. "Concepts of *tariqa* in West Africa. The Case of the Qadiriyya." In *Charisma and Brotherhood in African Islam*, edited by Donal B. Cruise O'Brien and Christian Coulon, pp. 33–52. Oxford, 1988. While not touching directly on Mauritania, Brenner deals with the Kunta influence in Qādirī practice and describes the role of Sufism in the intellectual life of nineteenth-century West Africa.

Chassey, Francis de. *Mauritanie, 1900–1975*. Paris, 1984. Although not explicitly concerned with Islam, this may be the best overview of Mauritanian society and economy in the twentieth century, for which no comparable English-language work is available.

Martin, B. G. *Muslim Brotherhoods in Nineteenth-Century Africa*. Cambridge, 1976. Surveys the careers of al-Ḥājj ʿUmar and Māʾ al-ʿAynayn.

Norris, H. T. *Shinqītī Folk Literature and Song*. Oxford, 1968. Excellent survey of literary traditions in the Ḥasanīyah world.

Stewart, C. C. *Islam and Social Order in Mauritania*. Oxford, 1973. Life and times of Sīdīyā al-Kabīr, and politics in nineteenth-century southern Mauritania.

CHARLES C. STEWART

MAWDŪDĪ, SAYYID ABŪ AL-AʿLĀ (also rendered from Urdu as Abu'l-Aʿla Maudūdī; 1903–1979), Islamic ideologue and politician. Sayyid Abū al-Aʿlā Mawdūdī was one of the most influential and prolific of contemporary Muslim thinkers. His interpretive reading of Islam has contributed greatly to the articulation of Islamic revivalist thought and has influenced Muslim thinkers and activists from Morocco to Indonesia. His impact is evident in the exegesis of Sayyid Quṭb of Egypt, as well as in the ideas and actions of Algerian, Iranian, Malaysian, and Sudanese revivalist activists. In South Asia, where Mawdūdī's ideas took shape, his influence has been most pronounced. Jamāʿat-i Islāmī (the Islamic Party), the organization that has embodied his ideology over the course of the past five decades, has played a significant role in the history and politics of Pakistan, India, Bangladesh, Sri Lanka, and the South

Asian communities of the Persian Gulf states, Great Britain, and North America.

Mawdūdī was born in Aurangabad, Deccan (now Maharashtra), on 25 September 1903 (3 Rajab 1321) into a notable family of Delhi who traced their lineage to the great Chishtī Ṣūfī saints who had played a prominent role in the conversion of India to Islam. The Mawdūdīs had been close to the Mughal court, especially during the reign of the last ruler of that dynasty, Bahādur Shāh Ẓafar. The family had suffered greatly during the sack of Delhi by the British in 1858 and had witnessed a reversal in its fortunes following the suppression of Muslim power in the Indian subcontinent. It had, however, continued to identify with the glories of Muslim history in India and was not reconciled to British rule over the domain of the Mughals. Mawdūdī's mother was also from a notable family of Delhi who had settled in the Deccan and served generations of nizams of Hyderabad. The Indo-Islamic cultural roots of the family, its identification with the glorious heritage of Muslim rule over India, its aristocratic pretensions, and its disdain for British rule were to play a central role in shaping Mawdūdī's worldview in later years.

Mawdūdī's father, Sayyid Aḥmad Ḥasan, was among the first to attend the Muslim Anglo-Oriental College at Aligarh and to embark on Sayyid Aḥmad Khān's experiment with Islamic modernism. His stint at Aligarh, however, did not last long, since he left the school to complete his education in law in Allahabad. After completing his studies, Aḥmad Ḥasan settled in the Deccan, first in Hyderabad and later in Aurangabad. There he was initiated into Sufism and for a time abandoned his career to devote himself to worship at the shrine of Niẓāmuddin Auliyā in Delhi. Aḥmad Ḥasan's puritanical streak and love of Sufism created a strongly religious and ascetic environment in which his children were nurtured. Aḥmad Ḥasan, moreover, took great pains to rear his children in the Muslim notable *(sharīf)* culture and to educate them classically, intentionally excluding English from their curriculum. They were educated at home in Arabic, Urdu, and religious texts for a number of years. Mawdūdī's mastery of Arabic was such that at the age of fourteen he translated the Egyptian thinker Qāsim Amīm's work *Al-mar'ah al-jadīdah* from Arabic into Urdu.

At the age of eleven the young Mawdūdī was enrolled at the Madrasah-i Fauqaniyah in Aurangabad, where he encountered modern education for the first time. He was compelled to abandon his formal education at the age of sixteen because of his father's illness and death; however, he remained acutely interested in writing and politics. His interests were then secular and focused solely on the issue of nationalism. In 1918 and 1919 he wrote essays in praise of Hindu Congress leaders, notably Gandhi and Madan Muhan Malaviya. In 1918 he joined his brother Abulkhair in Bijnor to begin a career in journalism. Soon after that the brothers moved to Delhi, where Mawdūdī was exposed to the variety of intellectual currents in the Muslim community. He became acquainted with modernist writings as well as with the activities of the independence movement. In 1919 he moved to Jabalpur to work for the pro-Congress weekly *Taj*. There he became fully active in the Khilāfat movement and in mobilizing Muslims in support of the Congress Party. His passionate articles eventually led to the closure of the weekly by the authorities.

Mawdūdī then returned to Delhi, where he became acquainted with such important Khilāfat activists as Muḥammad ᶜAlī, with whom Mawdūdī briefly cooperated. He continued to show interest in the independence movement, albeit increasingly from a Muslim standpoint. For instance, he briefly joined the Tahrik-i Hijrat protest movement, which encouraged Muslims to emigrate from British India (*dār al-ḥarb*, "abode of war") to Muslim-ruled (*dār al-Islām*, "abode of Islam") Afghanistan. In 1921 Mawdūdī became acquainted with the senior leaders of the Jamᶜiyatul ᶜUlamā'-i Hind, Mawlānās Muftī Kifāyatullāh and Aḥmad Saᶜīd. The eminent *ᶜulamā'* recognized Mawdūdī's talents and invited him to edit the Jamᶜīyat's official newspaper, *Muslim*, and later its successor *Al-jamīᶜat*. Mawdūdī remained in the service of the Jamiyat until 1924. There he developed a more acute awareness of Muslim political consciousness and became more actively involved in the affairs of his faith. He began to write on the Muslim plight in India, the predicament of the Turks in the face of European imperialism, and the glories of Muslim rule in India. His tone was communalist and political; revivalism was not yet a central focus of his writings. [*See also* Khilāfat Movement; Jamᶜīyatul ᶜUlamā'-i Hind.]

These years were also a period of learning and intellectual growth for Mawdūdī. He learned English and became acquainted with Western works. His association with the Jamᶜīyat also encouraged him to acquire a formal religious education. He studied Arabic and commenced the *dars-i niẓāmī* (syllabus of education of *ᶜulamā'* in India) first with the renowned ᶜAbdussalām Niyāzī and later at Delhi's Fatihpuri Madrasah. In 1926 he received his certificate in religious training (*ijāzah*), thus becoming a Deobandī ʿ*alim*. Interestingly, Mawdūdī never acknowledged his status as one of the ʿ*ulamā*', and his education in the Deobandī tradition did not come to light until after his death.

The collapse of the Khilāfat movement in 1924 was a turning point in Mawdūdī's life. He lost faith in nationalism, which he believed had led the Turks and Egyptians to undermine Muslim unity, and became suspicious of the Congress Party's manipulation of nationalist sentiments to serve Hindu interests. His views became openly communalist, revealing an opprobrium for the nationalist movement and its Muslim allies. At this time he found himself at odds with the Jamʿīyat and decided to part ways with his Deobandī mentors, who had chosen to support the Congress Party in the interests of ridding India of British rule.

No less opposed to British rule, Mawdūdī advocated an Islamic anti-imperialist platform that asserted opposition to colonialism together with safeguarding Muslim interests. The communalist rhetoric, articulated in terms of religious symbolism, gave place to revivalist discourse when taken to its logical conclusion. This course of events, moreover, soon imbued Mawdūdī with a sense of mission, permitting him to articulate his views as a discrete religious and political platform. In 1925 a young Muslim activist assassinated the Hindu revivalist leader Swami Shradhanand. The swami, who had advocated reconverting low-caste converts to Islam back to Hinduism, had publicly slighted Muslim beliefs. The assassination led to widespread criticism of Islam as a religion of violence by the Indian press. Angered by this response and summoned to action by Muḥammad ʿAlī's sermon at Delhi's Jamiʿ Mosque encouraging Muslims to defend their faith, Mawdūdī took it upon himself to clarify to critics Islam's position on the use of violence. The result was his famous treatise on war and peace, violence and *jihād* in Islam, *Al-jihād fī al-Islām* (Jihad in Islam). This book was the only systematic explanation of the Muslim position on *jihād* in response to criticism by the press, and it remains one of the most articulate expositions of this theme by a revivalist thinker; it received warm accolades from the Muslim community and confirmed Mawdūdī's place among the Muslim literati.

Mawdūdī became convinced that his vocation lay in leading his community to political and religious salvation. The direction which this endeavor was to take was not, however, entirely clear. In 1928 Mawdūdī moved to Hyderabad and immersed himself in writing. He completed a number of translation projects, historical accounts of Hyderabad, and religious texts at the behest of the nizam's government, the most important of which was his seminal introduction to Islam, *Risālah-yi dīnīyāt* (later translated as *Towards Understanding Islam*). It was here that he first grew a beard, adopted Indo-Muslim attire, and underwent a conversion experience, one which was religious in content but motivated by his understanding of political imperatives. The political situation in Hyderabad, the last remnant of Muslim rule in India, was highly precarious at the time. The majority Hindu population had begun to assert itself, and the power of the nizam was on the wane. Mawdūdī did not remain unaffected by what he witnessed in his birthplace. He became convinced that the decline of Muslim power stemmed from the corruption and pollution of Islam, the centuries of dross that had obscured the faith's veritable teachings. Conversely, the salvation of Muslim culture lay in the restitution of Islamic institutions and practices, once the culture was cleansed of the unsavory cultural influences that had sapped its power. He therefore encouraged the nizam's government to reform Hyderabad's Islamic institutions and to promote the veritable teachings of the faith. The government's subsequent inaction disheartened Mawdūdī and led him to lose trust in the existing Muslim political structures and instead to look for a new, all-inclusive sociopolitical solution.

Mawdūdī's revivalist position was in fact radical communalism. It asserted Muslim rights, proposed a program for promoting and safeguarding them, and demanded the severance of all cultural, social, and political ties with Hindus in the interest of purifying Islam. He went so far as to advocate a separate cultural homeland for Indian Muslims.

In 1932 Mawdūdī purchased the journal *Tarjumān al-Qur'ān*, which became the forum for his views. The rapid changes that characterized the passing of the Raj, however, convinced Mawdūdī that the pen alone was unlikely to affect the course of events significantly. He thus became interested in an organizational expression of his ideas. In 1938 he agreed to head Darul-Islam, a religious education project conceived by Muhammad Iqbal at Pathankut, a hamlet in Punjab. At Darul-Islam Mawdūdī devised a model Islamic community, which he hoped would spearhead the reform of Islam in India. Meanwhile he remained intensely interested in politics. He became embroiled in the struggle between the Pakistan Movement and Muslims of the Congress Party, always maintaining his independence of thought from the two positions. He lambasted first the Muslim supporters of the Congress, many of whom were his mentors in the Jamʿīyatul ʿUlamā'-i Hind, for betraying the Muslim cause, and then turned his attention to the Muslim League, which he chastised for its secularist communalism. As a result of Mawdūdī's activism, the project acquired an increasingly political tone, leading him to leave Pathankut for more direct political activity in Lahore. There he taught at the Islamīyah College and joined in debates over the future of the Muslim community. It was at this time that the idea of an organizational expression for his ideas, combining a model community and a political party, found shape in Mawdūdī's thought and works. In August 1941, Mawdūdī, with a number of young *ʿulamā'* and Muslim literati, formed the Jamāʿat-i Islāmī (Islamic Party). The party soon moved its headquarters to Pathankut, where Mawdūdī and his cohorts articulated the party's ideology and plan of action. The Jamāʿat began to organize across India, but it did not evolve rapidly enough to have an impact on developments in the Muslim community there.

When India was partitioned, Mawdūdī divided the Jamāʿat into independent Indian and Pakistani units. He moved to Lahore to assume leadership of the Jamāʿat-i Islāmī of Pakistan. The communalist agenda was replaced by the campaign to establish an Islamic state. During the early years of Pakistan Mawdūdī did much to mobilize public opinion for the cause of Islam, pushing the *ʿulamā'* to demand an Islamic constitution. He soon became identified as an enemy of the state and was accused of opposing Pakistan and of being a tool of India and a subversive element. Between 1948 and 1950 he was imprisoned for refusing to lend religious legitimacy to the government's military campaign in Kashmir. In 1954 he was again imprisoned, and this time sentenced to death, for his role in instigating the disturbances against the Aḥmadīyah in Punjab in 1953–1954. His sentence was later commuted, and he was released from prison in 1955. He was incarcerated on two other occasions, in 1964 and again in 1967, for challenging the regime of Ayub Khan.

In 1969 Mawdūdī instructed the Jamāʿat to launch a national anti-left campaign to forestall the Awami League's effort to gain independence for East Pakistan, and to keep the Pakistan Peoples' Party out of power. The Jamaʿat failed on both counts; it lost the elections of 1970 and was overshadowed by the left in the first open elections in the country. Taking stock of the defeat, after serving thirty years at the helm of the Jamāʿat, Mawdūdī stepped down as the president *(amir)* of the party. Although he continued to exercise much power in the Jamāʿat as well as in national politics in subsequent years, most of his time was dedicated to writing. Mawdūdī died in Buffalo, New York, on 22 September 1979. His funeral later in that month in Lahore drew a crowd of more than one million. He was buried in his house in the Ichhrah neighborhood of Lahore.

Throughout his years of political activity Mawdūdī continued to produce an impressive number of articles, pamphlets, and books. His *oeuvre* has not only made him the foremost revivalist thinker of his time, but has also confirmed his place as an important force in traditional religious scholarship. His Qur'ānic translation and commentary, *Tafhīm al-Qur'ān* (Understanding the Qur'ān), begun in 1942 and completed in 1972, is one of the most widely read Qur'ānic commentaries in Urdu today. Although written in a popular style and with a revivalist agenda, it has found a place in the classical Islamic scholarship of the subcontinent. In his numerous works Mawdūdī elaborated his views on religion, society, economy, and politics. They constitute an interpretive reading of Islam that sought to mobilize faith for the purpose of political action. His ideological perspective, one of the most prolific and systematic articulations of the revivalist position, has been influential in the unfolding of revivalism across the Muslim world. The contours of Islam's discourse with socialism and capitalism were first defined by him, as was much of the terminology associated with Islamic revivalism, including "Islamic revolution," "Islamic state," and "Islamic ideology."

Mawdūdī's reading of Islam began with a radical exegesis. His vision was chiliastic and dialectic in that it saw the battle between Islam and un-Islam *(kufr)*—both the West and the Hindu culture of India—as the central force in the historical progression of Muslim societies. This struggle, argued Mawdūdī, would culminate in an Islamic state, which would in turn initiate broad reforms in society, thereby erecting a utopian Islamic order. With this agenda, Mawdūdī advocated a view of Islam that mobilized the faith according to the needs of political action. He rationalized Islam into a stringent belief system, predicated upon absolute obedience to the will of God and amounting to a command structure that aimed to transform society and politics. By reinterpreting such key concepts as divinity *(ilāh)*, god/lord *(rabb)*, worship *(ʿibādah)*, and religion *(dīn)* he recast the meaning of the Muslim faith so that social action became the logical end of religious piety, and religion itself became the vehicle of social action. Despite the radicalism of his vision and his polemic on Islamic revolution, Mawdūdī's approach to politics throughout his career remained irenic. He continued to believe that social change would not result from mobilizing the masses to topple the existing order, but from taking over the centers of political power and effecting wide-scale reforms from the top down. In Mawdūdī's conception, Islamic revolution was to unfold within the existing state structures rather than after their destruction. He disparaged the use of violence in promoting the cause of Islam and defined the ideal Islamic state as a "theodemocracy" or a "democratic caliphate." Moreover, education rather than revolutionary action was the keystone of his approach to Islamic activism. In this regard Mawdūdī's position, as manifested in Jamāʿat's politics, stands in contrast to Ayatollah Ruhollah Khomeini's example; it has provided Islamic revivalism with an alternate paradigm for social action that may prevail among revivalists in the years to come.

[*See also* Jamāʿat-i Islāmī; Pakistan.]

BIBLIOGRAPHY

ʿAbd, Chaudhrī ʿAbdurraḥmān. *Mufakkir-i Islām: Sayyid Abūlaʿlā Maudūdī* (Thinker of Islam: Mawlānā Sayyid Abū al-Aʿlā Mawdūdī). Lahore, 1971. Official account of Mawdūdī's life and thought.

Abūlāfāq. *Sayyid Abūlaʿlā Maudūdī: Sawāniḥ, Afkār, Taḥrīk* (Sayyid Abū al-Aʿlā Mawdūdī: Biography, Thought, and Movement). Lahore, 1971. Official rendition of Mawdūdī's life story.

Adams, Charles J. "The Ideology of Mawlana Mawdūdī." In *South Asian Politics and Religion*, edited by Donald E. Smith, pp. 371–397. Princeton, 1966. Authoritative examination of Mawdūdī's ideology.

Adams, Charles J. "Mawdūdī and the Islamic State." In *Voices of Resurgent Islam*, edited by John L. Esposito, pp. 99–133. New York, 1983. Useful account of Mawdūdī's views on the "Islamic state."

Ahmad, Aziz. "Mawdudi and Orthodox Fundamentalism of Pakistan." *Middle East Journal* 21.3 (Summer 1967): 369–380. Critical overview of the Jamāʿat's ideology and its impact on Pakistan.

Fārūqī, ʿAbdulghanī. "Ḥayāt-i Javīdān" (Eternal Life). *Haftrozah Zindagī*, Mawdūdī Number (29 September–5 October 1989): 23–31. Account of Mawdūdī's life by a close friend and ardent follower.

Gilani, Sayyid Asad. *Maududi: Thought and Movement*. Lahore, 1984. Official account of Mawdūdī's life.

Hasan, Masudul. *Sayyid Abul Aʿala Maududi and His Thought*. 2 vols. Lahore, 1984. Exhaustive account of Mawdūdī's life and politics.

Mawdūdī, Sayyid Abū al-Aʿlā. *Risālah-yi dīnīyāt* (Treatise on Religion). Hyderabad, 1932. Best representation of Mawdūdī's views on faith in Islam.

Mawdūdī, Sayyid Abū al-Aʿlā. *Musalmān aur mawjūdah siyāsī kashmakash* (Muslims and the Current Political Crisis). 3 vols. Lahore, 1938–1940. Mawdūdī's famous examination of the problems before Indian Muslims on the eve of partition.

Mawdūdī, Sayyid Abū al-Aʿlā. *Tajdīd va iḥyā'-i dīn* (Renewal and Revival of Religion). Lahore, 1952. Mawdūdī's celebrated argument for the revival of Islam.

Mawdūdī, Sayyid Abū al-Aʿlā. *Islām kā naẓarīyah-yi siyāsī* (Islam's Political Views). Delhi, 1967. Summary of Mawdūdī's views on Islam's role in politics.

Mawdūdī, Sayyid Abū al-Aʿlā. *Taḥrīk-i Islāmī kī akhlāqī bunyāden* (The Basic Ethical Principles of the Islamic Movement). Lahore, 1968. Outlines Islamic ethics with a view to placing political activity within the context of Muslim religious practice.

Mawdūdī, Sayyid Abū al-Aʿlā. *Islāmī riyāsat* (Islamic State). Lahore, 1969. Outlines the idea of the "Islamic state."

Mawdūdī, Sayyid Abū al-Aʿlā. *Jamāʿat-i Islāmī kī untīs sāl* (Twenty-Nine Years of Jamāʿat-i Islāmī). Lahore, 1970. History of the Jamāʿat as told by Mawdūdī.

Mawdūdī, Sayyid Abū al-Aʿlā. "Khud nivisht" (Autobiography). In *Maulānā Maudūdī: Apnī aur dūsroṇ ki naẓar meṇ* (Mawdūdī in His Own and Others' Views), edited by M. Yusuf Buhtah, pp. 23–39. Lahore, 1984. Mawdūdī's autobiography, covering the early part of his life.

Mawdūdī, Sayyid Abū al-Aʿlā. *Al-jihād fi'l-Islām* (*Jihād* in Islam). Reprint, Lahore, 1986. Mawdūdī's celebrated exposition on *jihād*.

Mawdūdī, Sayyid Abū al-Aʿlā. *Taḥrīk-i Islāmī kā ayandah lā'ihah-yi ʿamal* (Islamic Movement's Future Course of Action). Lahore, 1986. Outlines the objectives and duties of an Islamic movement.

Mawdūdī, Sayyid Abū al-Aʿlā. *Vaṣā'iq-i Maudūdī* (Mawdūdī's Documents). Lahore, 1986. Useful collection of various documents on the Jamāʿat's history and Mawdūdī's thought.

Mawdūdī, Sayyid Abū al-Aʿlā. *Tanqīḥāt* (Inquiries). 22d ed. Lahore, 1989. Series of responses to perceived problems confronting Muslims.

Tarjumānul-Qur'ān (Hyderabad) (1932–). Principal vehicle for the expression and dissemination of Mawdūdī's views on religion and politics from 1932 to 1979.

SEYYED VALI REZA NASR

MAWLĀ. Derived from *walā* ("to be close to, be friends with, have power over"), the term *mawlā* (pl., *mawālī*) has entered other languages as a loan word. Through history it has accrued a varied set of meanings, depending largely on whether it is used in the active or passive voice. Therefore, *mawlā* can have the reciprocal meanings of "master" or "slave, freedman," "patron" or "client," "uncle" or "nephew," and "friend." It is an epithet of God "the Protector" in the Qur'ān (e.g., 8.40, 47.11), and it is used today as a title for religious and political authorities. Its Persian form, *mullā* (commonly rendered in English as *mullah*), usually denotes anyone who has attained competence in a field of Islamic learning to teach, deliver sermons, and conduct rituals, especially within the lower reaches of the *ʿulamāʾ*.

The *mawālī* in pre-Islamic Arabia were clients of an Arab tribe. The appearance of Islam and the seventh-century conquests caused a shift in the significance of the term as Arab Muslims sought ways to normalize relations with their new subjects. Thus they used the term *mawālī* to designate foreign Arabs, Persians, Greeks, Copts, Jews, Africans, and others who allied with the community as clients in Arabia itself and in the Arab settlements of Syria, Iraq, Egypt, and Iran. These people entered the community voluntarily or as war captives who were subsequently emancipated. In either case, clientage was established with a specific Arab tribe, often through a male patron from that tribe; it also entailed conversion to Islam. As most of the *mawālī* were of foreign origin, the term came to denote non-Arab Muslims. Clientage afforded them the protection of members of the new Arab ruling elite—along with material benefits from the conquests—in return for loyalty, service, and gifts.

One study has estimated that 10 percent of the prophet Muḥammad's original following consisted of *mawālī*, such as Salmān the Persian, Bilāl the Ethiopian, and Ṣuhayb the Byzantine (Pipes, 1985). By 715 they had begun to play an active role in political life and formed separate units in the Arab armies that were crucial to the conquests in Andalus and Central Asia. The widely held theory that *mawālī* resentment of their second-class status in the early empire was a leading cause of the conflicts that brought about the ʿAbbāsid revolution in 750 has been disputed in recent years. Although many *mawālī* held servile status in relation to Arabs and were regarded as little better than slaves, others took leading positions in the army and government, remaining faithful to their Umayyad and ʿAbbāsid patrons and attaining higher status than Arab nobles *(ashrāf)*. Individuals of *mawālī* origins also contributed to the formation of Islamic law, Islamic tradition, and dialectical theology *(kalām)*, and to the development of Arabic grammar and letters. Such prominent early scholars as al-Ḥasan al-Baṣrī (d. 728), Abū Ḥanīfah (d. 767), Ibn Isḥāq (d. 767), Sībawayh (d. 791), and al-Bukhārī (d. 870) were remembered as having been of *mawālī* descent.

By the time of the ʿAbbāsid caliph al-Muʿtaṣim (r. 833–842), the practice of designating non-Arab Muslims as *mawālī* had largely lapsed with the decline of Arab elitism and with Arab detribalization in urban areas. Other forms of clientage emerged subsequently to play a decisive role in the organization of government, warfare, learning, and economy in Muslim lands, notably in the Mamlūk, Ottoman, Ṣafavid, and Mughal Empires. The place of *mawālī* in Islamic history continued to be acknowledged in later times, however. Reflecting on the fates of states and civilizations, Ibn Khaldūn (d. 1406) concluded that *mawālī* and other clients are vital to the continuity of dynasties once tribal solidarity has dissipated (*Muqaddima* II.8, III.2, 12, 17, 18).

In Islamic law, the early *mawlā* form of clientage survived only in vestigial form as *walāʾ*, which is seen as a kind of fictive kinship relationship. According to *fiqh*, it defines the automatic rights and duties of masters and their freedmen (in all the major Sunnī and Shīʿī schools), or the relations contracted formally between Muslim patrons and new client-converts (only in Ḥanafī and Imāmī law). The most important provisions of *walāʾ* are that it gives patrons some inheritance rights against the estates of their clients, and that it obliges patrons to agree to pay blood-money on their clients' behalf.

In later centuries, the active meaning of *mawlā*, "master," has prevailed as a title for rulers, religious figures, and, of course, God. The patron saint of Fez, Idrīs, and members of the Saʿdī (1511–1628) and ʿAlawī (1631–) dynasties of Morocco are designated by the title *mawlāy* ("my master"). Jalāl al-Dīn Rūmī (d. 1273), the Persian mystic, is remembered with the sobriquet *mawlānā* ("our master"), and in consequence, his Ṣūfī order is named the Mawlawīyah (Tk., Mevlevî). Its Persian form, *mullah*, usually denotes anyone who has attained competence in a field of Islamic learning to teach, deliver sermons, and conduct rituals, especially within the lower ranks of Shīʿī *ʿulamāʾ*. *Mawlā* is also a designation for Sunni scholars in India and Pakistan.

[*See also* Mawlawīyah; Mawlāy; Mevlevî; *and* Mullah.]

BIBLIOGRAPHY

Crone, Patricia. *Slaves on Horses: The Evolution of the Islamic Polity*. Cambridge, 1980. *Roman, Provincial, and Islamic Law: The Origins of the Islamic Patronate*. Cambridge, 1987. Two revisionist studies of *mawālī* in relation to the early Arab conquests and the *sharīʿah*, respectively. Summarized in her article, "Mawlā," in *Encyclopaedia of Islam*, new ed., vol. 6, pp. 874–882 (Leiden, 1960–).

Ibn Khaldūn. *The Muqaddimah*. 3 vols. Translated and edited by Franz Rosenthal. New York, 1958.

Morony, Michael. *Iraq after the Muslim Conquest.* Princeton, 1984. State-of-the-art exposition of Iraqi, Persian, Aramean, Jewish, Christian, and pagan communities and institutions on the eve of the conquests, and their subsequent transformations, with an extensive bibliography.

Pipes, Daniel. "Mawlas: Freed Slaves and Converts in Early Islam." In *Slaves and Slavery in Muslim Africa,* edited by John R. Willis, vol. 1, pp. 199–248. London, 1985.

JUAN EDUARDO CAMPO

MAWLAWĪYAH. The Turkish Ṣūfī order of the Mawlawīyah (Tk., Mevlevî) is known to Europe as the "Whirling Dervishes" in recognition of its distinctive meditation ritual. It derives its name from Jalāl al-Dīn Rūmī, known as Mawlānā (Mevlânâ in Turkish, meaning "Our Master"), whose life and writings had a profound influence on the development and ritual of the order.

Rūmī was born in 1207 CE (AH 604) in the Central Asian city of Balkh, where his father Bahā' Walad (d. 1231) was a religious scholar and Ṣūfī master of some renown. The uncertain religious and political situation under the Khwārazm-shahs forced them to leave for Anatolia in 1219, and Bahā' Walad and his family eventually settled in the Seljuk capital of Konya at the invitation of ʿAlā' al-Dīn Kayqubād. Bahā' Walad was given a prominent appointment as a legal scholar and preacher, a position that Jalāl al-Dīn inherited after his father's death. It is from his lengthy residence in Anatolia (Rūm) that Mawlānā Jalāl al-Dīn came to be known as Rūmī.

There can be little doubt that Rūmī was familiar with Sufism from childhood. Nevertheless, most sources insist that his formal Ṣūfī training began in 1232 with the arrival in Konya of Burhān al-Dīn al-Tirmidhī, a disciple of Bahā' Walad. Rūmī remained his disciple until Burhān al-Dīn's death nine years later.

The defining moment in Rūmī's life occurred in 1244 with the arrival of an enigmatic wandering mystic named Shams al-Dīn (commonly referred to as Shams-i Tabrīzī). Until this time Rūmī's public persona had been defined by his role as a legal scholar and judge, with little mention of his participation in any mystical activities; he now began to devote himself entirely to the company of Shams-i Tabrīzī, whom he identified as the ideal medium for gaining access to mystical knowledge of God.

Rūmī's infatuation with Shams-i Tabrīzī was a source of jealousy (and probably also embarrassment) to his family and students, who apparently forced Shams-i Tabrīzī to leave Konya after about two years. Rūmī rushed after him and convinced him to return, but soon after that Shams vanished forever, in all likelihood murdered by Rūmī's students with the connivance of both his son, Sulṭān Walad (d. 1312) and his principal disciple Ḥusām al-Dīn Chalabī (d. 1283). Following Shams's disappearance, Rūmī withdrew from public life and devoted himself entirely to the guidance of Ṣūfī disciples. He also began to compose exquisite and profuse poetry, the bulk of which is contained in two works—the *Masnavī-yi maʿnavī* (approximately 26,000 verses) and the *Dīvān-i Shams-i Tabrīzī* (approximately 40,000 verses). The *Masnavī,* written at the request of Ḥusām al-Dīn Chalabī, is a didactic work in six books that rapidly gained extreme popularity in the Persian- and Turkish-speaking world. It has been widely translated and commented on and has been used for prognostication, as a source of mystical inspiration, and as a religious text by countless individuals as well as by several mystical organizations such as the Iranian Khāksārs. It is on the basis of this work, which is the central mystical text of the Mawlawīyah, that Rūmī has become the best-known Islamic mystical poet. [*See* Devotional Poetry.]

It is probable that a Ṣūfī order gathered around Rūmī during his lifetime. One of his early biographers, Shams al-Dīn Aḥmad al-Aflākī al-ʿĀrifī, mentions an assembly room *(jamāʿat khānah)* attached to Rūmī's *madrasah* where learned conversations and musical concerts were held. Although Rūmī had already come to be known as Mawlānā, it is doubtful that his followers were called the Mawlawīyah at this early date: in his account of Konya, Ibn Baṭṭūṭah refers to them as the Jalāliyah (after Jalāl al-Dīn). Rūmī was succeeded by Ṣalāḥ al-dīn Zarkūb, who had originally been a disciple of Burhān al-Dīn al-Tirmidhī and who succeeded Shams-i Tabrīzī as a vessel in which Rūmī contemplated God. Zarkūb was followed by Rūmī's disciple Ḥusām al-Dīn Chalabī and finally by Rūmī's son Sulṭān Walad, although for the first seven years after Ḥusām al-Dīn's death the latter was under the care of a guardian, Karīm al-Dīn ibn Bektimūr. After Sulṭān Walad the leadership of the Mawlawīyah was almost invariably held by a descendant of Rūmī.

The two most distinctive features of the Mawlawīyah are their process of initiation through a lengthy orientation rather than the trials typical of other Ṣūfī orders, and the importance they give to *samāʿ* (audition) as a form of meditation. Some elements of the *samāʿ* are traceable to Rūmī, although major features continued to be added until the time of ʿĀdil Chalabī (d. 1460), a great-grandson of Sulṭān Walad. The only significant changes since that time concern the occasion and frequency of the *samāʿ;* these occurred under the reign of the Ottoman sultan Selim III (r. 1789–1807) and again in the period after the Turkish religious reforms of 1925.

The *samāʿ* of the Mawlawīyah is carried out in a wood-floored circular room called a *samāʿ khānah* (Turk., *semâhâne*). The room is normally surrounded by galleries for guests and a separate one for the musicians. Before the *samāʿ* begins, the officiating Ṣūfī (called *meydâncı dede*) places a skin, marking the seat of the *shaykh,* at the opposite end of the room from the *qiblah.* He then gives an order for the call to prayer to be sounded, after which the *shaykh* enters the room followed by the participants (referred to as *samāʿ zan;* Tk., *semâ zen*). After performing their ritual prayers the participants gather around the seated *shaykh* to listen to hymns and readings from the *Masnavī,* which are accompanied by music. The *shaykh* then recites the "prayer of the skin" *(pust duası).*

Following this prayer all participants, including the *shaykh* and the *meydâncı dede,* go through a complex and choreographed series of salutations. Accompanied by a simple beat from the musicians, the participants walk in a circle up to the skin with their arms folded under their cloaks *(khirqah).* On reaching the skin, each participant bows in salutation to the person in front of him, passes the skin while facing it and stepping over the diameter of the circle extending from the skin to the *qiblah,* turns around to face the person behind him, performs the identical salute, takes three steps back, turns around to face forward, and continues walking in a circle. Many outside observers appear to have been impressed by the sight of the *semâ zen*s wearing tall caps and black cloaks over white tunics, two of them facing each other across the skin and the remainder walking in a circle with their eyes lowered and heads bowed. After completing the round of salutations the *shaykh* sits on his skin and the *samāʿ* itself begins, comprising several cycles or rounds *(dawra;* Tk., *devre),* in which each *semâ zen* extends his arms to the side with the right palm facing upward and the left downward and whirls counterclockwise, using his left foot as a pivot.

The form of the *samāʿ* is imbued with mystical meaning for the Mawlawīyah: the upturned right hand symbolizes the mystic's receipt of divine grace, while the downturned left hand implies that what is received from God is passed on to humanity. Thus the *semâ zen* represents a conduit whereby God showers blessings upon the planet. A similar representation of the relationship between the celestial and the terrestrial is accorded to the hall itself, with the right half symbolizing the descent from God to human beings in the physical realm, and the left symbolizing ascent from the physical state to mystical union with God in the spiritual realm.

The Mawlawīyah has been an order of courtly art and culture since Rūmī's day and has always encouraged and nurtured court poets and musicians. As such, it is in contrast to more popular orders such as the Bektāshīs, which have been more in tune with the needs and aspirations of the Anatolian populace. This distinction was exploited by the later Ottoman sultans, who favored the Sunnī and courtly Mawlawīyah against the more populist and predominantly Shīʿī Bektāshīs favored by the Janissaries. By the beginning of the nineteenth century it became a tradition for the head of the Mawlawīyah to gird the imperial sword on the new sultan. [*See* Bektāshīyah.]

The importance of the Mawlawīyah to the development of Ottoman culture cannot be overemphasized. It has had a definitive impact on the development of art and music, and luminaries such as the court poets Nefʿī (d. 1635) and Şeyh Gâlib (d. 1799), and composers such as İtî (d. 1712) and Zekâ'î (d. 1897) were all Mawlawīs. In fact, the Mawlawīyah is so closely identified with Ottoman Turkish culture that it has enjoyed almost no success in non-Turkish societies. The only exceptions are certain cities in non-Turkish regions of the former Ottoman Empire, such as Damascus, Tripoli, Homs, Jerusalem, and Beirut in the Middle East, and a larger number of cities in Greece, Bosnia, and other parts of the Balkans. However, these were all towns with significant Turkish populations, and only the center in Beirut is known to have remained active into the latter half of the twentieth century. In contrast, the founder of the order still enjoys widespread fame and reverence rivaled by only one or two other Ṣūfī figures.

[*See also* Mevlevî; Sufism, *articles on* Ṣūfī Thought and Practice *and* Ṣūfī Orders.]

BIBLIOGRAPHY

Aflākī, Shams al-Dīn al-. *Manākib al-ārifin.* 2 vols. Edited by Tahsin Yazıcı. 2d ed. Ankara, 1976–1980. Translated into English by James W. Redhouse as *Legends of the Sufis.* 3d ed. Wheaton, Ill., 1976. Primary source on the early masters of the order.

Chittick, William C. *The Sufi Path of Love: The Spiritual Teachings of Rumi*. Albany, N.Y., 1983. Thematically arranged translation of selections from Rūmī's poetry.

Gölpinarlı, Abdülbâki. *Mevlânâ'dan Sonra Mevlevîlik*. 2d ed. Istanbul, 1983. Single most important study of the Mawlawīyah.

Jong, F. de. "Mawlawiyya." In *Encyclopaedia of Islam*, new ed., vol. 6, pp. 883–888. Leiden, 1960–.

Rūmī, Jalāl al-Dīn. *The Mathnawī of Jalālu'ddīn Rūmī*. 8 vols. Translated and edited by Reynold A. Nicholson. London, 1925–1940.

Schimmel, Annemarie. *Mystical Dimensions of Islam*. Chapel Hill, N.C., 1975. Excellent introduction to Sufism that balances readability with exhaustive scholarship.

Schimmel, Annemarie. *The Triumphant Sun: A Study of the Works of Jalāloddin Rumi*. London, 1978.

Trimingham, J. Spencer. *The Sufi Orders in Islam*. Oxford, 1971. The most expansive treatment of Ṣūfī orders available.

JAMAL J. ELIAS

MAWLĀY. The Arabic word *mawlāy* (also transliterated *moulay* and *mulay*) means "my lord" or "my master"; in North Africa it is frequently used in this sense, although the word is pronounced *mulay*. Various honorific titles are derived from the term *mawlā* in combination with pronominal or adjectival suffixes. *Mawlā* is in turn derived from the Arabic verb *walīyah*, "to be close to" or "to be connected with something or someone," and by extension to be proximate in terms of power or authority. In the Qur'ān, in the *ḥadīth*, and in early Islamic history, *mawlā* had several meanings. First, it was employed in the sense of "tutor," "preceptor," "trustee," or "helper"; for example, God is the *mawlā* of the community of the faithful, according to the Qur'ān. Second, it denoted "lord" or "master," and thus God is referred to as "Mawlānā" or "our lord"; here the term is synonymous with *sayyid*. Finally, it can signify "client," "affiliate," or "freedman," thus designating a relationship of inferiority or dependence. In the early Islamic period, *mawālī* (the plural of *mawlā*) referred at first to non-Arab converts to Islam who became clients of one of the Arab Muslim tribes and were regarded as socially inferior. In the ʿAbbāsid period, however, the term more commonly designated freedmen, although it had passed out of general use by the tenth century.

As a title or honorific, *mawlāy* has been and is still used in various regions of the Muslim world. In the Maghrib and Andalusia, it was applied to saints or Ṣūfīs, as well as to various ruling houses that based their legitimacy upon descent from the prophet Muḥammad. The Ḥafṣid dynasty of Tunisia (1207–1574) employed this title, as did high dignitaries both secular and religious. Originally in the Moroccan context, *mawlāy* was a title conferred upon all those belonging to the *shurafā'* (descendants of Muḥammad). Since the sixteenth century, however, it has been employed as a prenominal title applied to the sultans of the two Moroccan Sharīfī dynasties—the Saʿdīs (c.1510–1654) and the ʿAlawīs (c.1660–); both dynasties have claimed descent from Muḥammad through al-Ḥasan ibn ʿAlī.

In the Ṣūfī sense, *mawlāy* is related to the terms *walī* and *wilāyah;* the former is often inadequately rendered as "saint," although a better definition would stress the holy person as being close to God or His protege, while the latter signifies something approximating sanctity. In both Sufism and Shiism *mawlā* can be understood as a spiritual protector or patron as well as a client. The great thirteenth-century Persian Ṣūfī and poet Jalāl al-Dīn Rūmī is still referred to as Mawlānā, "our master," because of his immense piety and uncommon spirituality. In the Turco-Iranian world and in South Asian Islam, *mawlānā* (or *mawlawī*) is a title in widespread use even in the 1990s and can denote Muslims of high religious status, such as Ṣūfīs or members of the *ʿulamā'*. In the Indian subcontinent it is applied to scholars of the Islamic religious sciences—meaning once again "my tutor" or "my lord"—or to saints, implying spiritual lordship and hence protection.

[*See also* Mawlā; Sainthood; Sayyid; Sufism.]

BIBLIOGRAPHY

Trimingham, J. Spencer. *The Sufi Orders in Islam*. Oxford, 1971.

Westermarck, Edward A. *Ritual and Belief in Morocco*. 2 vols. London, 1926. Volume one contains a brief discussion of the various uses of *sayyid, sharīf,* and *mulay (mawlay)* in the North African context.

JULIA CLANCY-SMITH

MAWLID. Derived from the triliteral Arabic root *w-l-d*, *mawlid* means "birth." Al-Mawlid al-Nabawī al-Sharīf, for example, refers to the twelfth day of Rabīʿ al-Awwal of the Islamic calendar, believed to be the day of the prophet Muḥammad's birth, and celebrated (except in Saudi Arabia) by Muslims as a holiday marked by popular festivities and state ceremonies. In popular usage the term *mawlid* refers to a commemorative occasion of the anniversary of a deceased holy person, man or woman, Muslim, Christian, or Jewish. The Jewish *mawlid* of Shaykh Abū Hasira continues to be popular today. While Christian *mawlid*s honor the anniversary of a holy person's death, Sunnī Muslims celebrate the anniversary of his or her birth; some *mawlid*s are honored across religious lines.

Commemorative anniversaries take place around the holy person's tomb or at a spot believed to shelter a body or a relic, or to be the site of an important event. The spot then serves as a center for annual pilgrimages that occur throughout the Islamic world, with varying degrees of local or regional popularity. In some countries there are several hundred major and minor *mawlids*. Not all Muslims use the term *mawlid* for these pilgrimage anniversaries: in Tunis the term *zardah* is used, while other Arab countries use *mawsim*.

In the Muslim *mawlid* the holiness and legitimacy of the person whose life is remembered and honored derives from a real or presumed, blood or spiritual, lineal descent from the prophet Muḥammad, traced through his daughter Fāṭimah and his son-in-law and cousin ʿAlī ibn Abī Ṭālib. The title of such a descendant is *sharīf* or *sayyid* (female, *sayyidah* or *sitt*). This descent carries with it the *barakah* (blessing) that elevates the charismatic person into holy (but not divine) status and draws throngs to such pilgrimages, particularly from among ruralites, the poor, and the infirm who seek solace and healing.

The common title of the holy person is *walī* (pl., *awliyā'*), from the root *w-l-y,* meaning "to succeed or follow." *Walī* literally means "guardian" or "successor." While there may be superficial similarities between *walī* and the European *saint,* they are not identical, and using the term *saint* both blurs the significant differences and assumes the superiority of a Christian vocabulary and conceptual framework against which Islamic ideas are to be interpreted. Unlike Christian saints, who are believed to intercede with the divine on behalf of humans, *walī*s radiate goodness and blessing because of the holy status they have acquired by sharing ancestry that goes back to the Prophet. They are also popular exemplary models for religious life and teachings. The *walī* builds a reputation on the basis of personal qualities of charisma, religious teachings, piety, and miraculous happenings. Some *walī*s found a Ṣūfī *ṭarīqah* (order), but others acquire the status without this achievement.

A *mawlid* has its own dynamic and structure, which includes the Ṣūfī element but is not necessarily confined to it, so one must distinguish the phenomenon of *mawlid* from Sufi *ṭarīqah*. Thus, the most popular *mawlid* in Egypt is *mawlid* al-Sayyid Aḥmad al-Badawī of Tanta, the *walī* who founded the Aḥmadīyah, one of the major Ṣūfī orders in Egypt; but approaching the *mawlid* from the sole perspective of Ṣūfī practices would ignore significant aspects unique to *mawlids*. One can recognize the historical, ideological, and socioeconomic connections between *mawlid*s and *ṭarīqah*s without blurring them.

A characteristic quality of the *mawlid* is its blending of the mythical and the mystical, the ritual and the scripturalist, the religious and the political/economic, and all these aspects with popular traditional practices. It combines elements at the local, state, and regional levels into multiple events over a period of days marking the celebratory complex, which usually spans seven days, building in intensity by the Thursday evening before the *mawlid* (al-Laylah al-Kabīrah) and culminating on the *mawlid* day on Friday.

Central to a *mawlid* is the tomb around which activities occur. The *ziyārah* or visit to the tomb involves circling the tomb seven times, paying money or sacrificing an animal, and when possible touching the tomb. [*See* Ziyārah.] People come from all over the area, and Ṣūfī orders set up tents giving out food. The poor and the infirm hope for charity and healing. *Dhikr* (ritual chanting) is performed on the roofs of homes and in surrounding tents. [*See* Dhikr.] A market is established with stalls of foods, sweets, and trinkets, carts of hats and toys and incense, and traditional drink-sellers on foot. Booths are set up near the tomb of the *walī* in which circumcision is performed on young boys brought by parents who have made a *nadhr* (vow) to circumcise their sons at a particular *mawlid*. [*See* Circumcision.]

Following the Friday public prayer a *zaffah* (procession) representing all the principal elements in the *mawlid* begins and ends at the tomb of the *walī*. A leading figure in the procession is the *khalīfah,* the contemporary successor and lineal descendant of the *walī*. He leads the celebration as he mounts a horse and rides in the Ṣūfī procession. In the *mawlid* of Sayyid Aḥmad al-Badawī people touch his turban for blessing because it is claimed to contain cloth from the original veil of Aḥmad al-Badawī. Other participants include an elder and a youth representing the *walī*'s *ṭarīqah,* state military troops, other Ṣūfī *ṭarīqah*s marching on foot with banners, men and women of various vocations on carts and carriages, and finally carriages bearing the newly circumcised boys dressed in Arabian clothing, with their families. The vocational parade is a survivor of the medieval *ṭā'ifah* system of guilds that was closely intertwined with the Ṣūfī *ṭarīqah*s. The end of the *zaffah* marks the end of the seven days of the *mawlid*.

Some observers consider the phenomenon of *mawlids* to be rooted in ancient traditions, such as those of Egypt where gods were honored annually at harvest time when temples organized elaborate processions and festivities. A few trace the modern *mawlids* to Pharisaic influences and Jewish celebrations around the tombs of venerated persons in early Judaism and early Christianity. More scholars see the modern form of *mawlids* as rooted in Ṣūfī and/or Shīʿī traditions that emerged from the Maghrib and Mesopotamia and developed in Mecca. The latter proposal, however, does not account for the presence of similar, often identical practices among Christian and Jewish populations in the Middle East.

Mawlids comprise a richly complex phenomenon that operates at many different levels—religious, political, economic, and recreational—and speaks to many people in a variety of different ways. God is not only very real but very immediate, and he has always been and continues to be a vital force in people's lives. He is the source of the benevolent power called *barakah,* which cannot be translated simply as "blessing."

Although in Islam no official doctrine advocates a role of mediation for religious figures between God and mortals, deceased *walīs* as well as living *sayyids* and shaykhs are perceived by the faithful as the carriers of God's benevolence, which radiates from the holy place to everyone who comes in contact with it. *Barakah* continually flows from God and through his intermediary to the people. To get its blessing, the visitor at a *mawlid* touches the tomb, its *kiswah* (cover), or the *khalīfah* himself, and then wipes his hands down his face, transmitting the blessing to his body. The common call "Shillah yā sayyid" (give us something from God, O sayyid), confirms that the *walī* is considered intermediary in the flow of *barakah* from God. *Barakah* is needed and desired for purposes of healing and general wellbeing. A similar phenomenon occurs among Christians who touch the Pope and Jews who kiss and touch religious relics for blessing. A *mawlid* also reminds people of the *walī* and his behavior and beliefs, providing religious teaching for the people; it is a public statement about a particular religious/moral model for people to emulate in their lives. [*See* Barakah.]

From the point of view of scripturalist Islam, the popular practice of *mawlids* poses a religious challenge to orthodoxy and a political challenge to the established authority of al-Azhar. The state is also aware of the potential threat of revivalist opposition inherent in the building of a popular base. In reality, however, *mawlids* are interwoven with both popular Ṣūfī and orthodox scripturalist practices and beliefs.

The interrelationship between Ṣūfī practices and scripturalist Islam as represented through the mosque is manifest and alive in the *mawlid* and cannot be overlooked. For example, principal mosques are often built over the tombs of important *walīs*; thus Sayyid Aḥmad al-Badawī's *maqām* occupies a focal position inside the principal mosque of Tanta, a central town in Egypt's Delta and the capital of al-Gharbīyah governorate. *Mawlid* activities are intertwined with mosque activities: the *khalīfah* has a prominent presence in the mosque at the Friday prayer of the Badawī *mawlid.* These connections serve to legitimize the popular *mawlids* to people who might otherwise question their orthodoxy.

People go to *mawlids* for different reasons—commercial, social, recreational, charity, or religious. The infirm and the disabled seek blessing and hope for healing. The term *madad* is always invoked for divine aid or strength. Boys circumcised during *mawlids* are both blessed and initiated to masculinity. At the collective level, *mawlids* revitalize the local market at the same time as they reaffirm a collective sense of identity and a unity of spirituality.

[*See also* Shrine; Sufism, *article on* Ṣūfī Shrine Culture; Walī.]

BIBLIOGRAPHY

Biegmann, Nicolaas. *Egypt: Moulids, Saints, Sufis.* London, 1990. Photographic essay of Egyptian *mawlids* and *awliyā'*. Photos are aesthetically and technically beautiful and ethnographic in quality.

Canaan, Taufik. *Mohammedan Saints and Sanctuaries in Palestine.* Jerusalem, 1927. Rich description of the *walī* sanctuaries of Palestine, available in a facsimile of the edition originally published in 1927 as volume 5 of Luzac's Oriental Religions Series.

El Guindi, Fadwa. *El Moulid: Egyptian Religious Festival.* Los Angeles, 1990. Available from El Nil Research, 1147 Beverwil Drive, Los Angeles, CA 90035. Ethnographic film (16mm) of the popular seven-hundred-year-old *mawlid,* which celebrates the life and legacy of the *walī* Sayyid Aḥmad al-Badawī of Tanta, Egypt. The film vividly captures the festive and religious mood, and analyzes the *mawlid*'s structure and symbolism, revealing various levels of religious experience—scriptural, mystical, ritual, mythical—interacting with secular traditional life.

Gilsenan, Michael. *Recognizing Islam.* New York, 1982. Although this work does not deal directly with *mawlids,* it provides a sophisticated discussion that connects several aspects of Islam and Arab society, including Sufism and Ṣūfī-related phenomena, from a nonorientalist cultural perspective.

Keddie, Nikki R., ed. *Scholars, Saints, and Sufis: Muslim Religious Institutions since 1500.* Los Angeles, 1972. Collection of scholarly articles dealing with scripturalist Islamic concerns, particularly the

ʿulamāʾ, and including a section on Sufism as it relates to the phenomenon of *awliyāʾ*, ranging from the Sudan to the Maghrib to Iraq.

Kennedy, John, ed. *Nubian Ceremonial Life*. Los Angeles, 1978. Interesting collection of ethnographic field studies on Nubia, a culture often neglected in discussions about Islamic phenomena, containing articles about *mawālid*.

Manṣūr, Aḥmad Ṣubḥī. *Al-Sayyid al-Badawī bayna al-ḥaqīqah wa-al-Khurāfah* (in Arabic). Cairo, 1982. Written from an orthodox Sunnī perspective that is skeptical of "the holiness" of the *walī* Badawī, and associates the phenomena of veneration with Shiism.

McPherson, J. W. *The Moulids of Egypt*. Cairo, 1941. Detailed descriptive account of the *mawlids* of Egypt from an orientalist perspective.

Reeves, Edward B. *The Hidden Government: Ritual, Clientelism, and Legitimation in Northern Egypt*. Salt Lake City, 1990. In-depth sociological analysis of the *mawlid* of Sayyid Aḥmad al-Badawī, its history, politics, and economics, and the most recent account of the *mawlid* of Tanta, Egypt. Its value lies in its treatment of the *mawlid* as a phenomenon separable from Sufism, but the account is weak on cultural factors.

FADWA EL GUINDI

MECCA. A holy site since the beginning of Arab memory of the place, Mecca (Makkah) is the goal of the annual pilgrimage that the Qurʾān (2.196–198) requires every Muslim to perform once in a lifetime. Whatever the surmises regarding the origin of its sanctity, the Muslims traced the holiness of its sanctuary back to Adam, who was directed there and built a cubelike house *(kaʿbah)* directly beneath an identical structure in heaven. Adam's *kaʿbah* was destroyed in the Flood, but, according to the Qurʾān, at a later date Abraham, too, was directed to Mecca where he and his son Ishmael raised anew the foundations of the Holy House (2.127). Mecca was taken over by pagans in the generations after Ishmael, and idolatrous practices were introduced there, though without entirely obliterating what the Qurʾān calls the "religion of Abraham" (2.135). In the early fifth century CE, Ishmael's descendants, themselves now pagans, returned to Mecca under the name of Quraysh and took control of the city. They brought prosperity, probably by associating the bedouin pilgrimage to the shrine with the opportunity for trade at the local fairs.

Muḥammad was born around 570 CE in this Mecca: a town set down in a hot and inhospitable mountain defile, a settlement whose crude mud houses were prey to destructive flash floods during the occasional downpours in the vicinity. And in its midst was the Kaʿbah, a ramshackle construction that the Quraysh rebuilt and roofed during the early manhood of Muḥammad. Around the Kaʿbah was an undefined open space that was regarded as taboo *(ḥaram)* and in which a great many idols were set up. The Meccans were not sympathetic to Muḥammad's divinely dispensed "warning" of God's impending judgment; indeed, the reaction to his preaching was so hostile that in 622 he was forced to leave his native city and migrate to Medina. It took him eight years to force the Meccan Quraysh into submission. In 630 the Prophet reentered Mecca in triumph, cleansed the sanctuary of its idols, and reinstated the "religion of Abraham" in its pristine vigor. But he did not remain; Medina was now his home.

What Mecca gained in purity, it lost in commercial prosperity; the trade routes of the new Islamic empire did not pass through western Arabia, and the town descended to provincial status. Henceforth its chief resources derived from endowment income, gifts of the faithful to the shrine and its overseers, and the annual pilgrimage *(ḥajj)*. With the seats of imperial power removed elsewhere, Mecca returned to the control of its local aristocracy, now constituted of those who could claim descent from the Prophet through Fāṭimah, the Prophet's daughter, and her husband, ʿAlī. These were the *sharīf*s; one of them ruled Mecca and the Hejaz (Ḥijāz), with a nod of obeisance toward a distant caliph or sultan, from the tenth century onward.

Mecca participated again in the commercial life of the Islamic empire under the Mamlūks (1250–1517), when trade quickened between Indian and other eastern ports and newly prosperous consumers around the Mediterranean. This eastern trade passed through the Red Sea on its way to Egypt, and Mecca shared in both the wealth and danger of the enterprise, the latter arising from the Portuguese, European newcomers in eastern waters who from their Indian bases had begun to cast covetous eyes upon the Red Sea lands. The task of defending Islam's Holy Land fell to the Ottomans, who had wrested the guardianship of the Hejaz from the Mamlūks in 1517. They were successful: the ports of India remained in the grip of the Portuguese, but the Europeans were turned from the Red Sea.

Although the center of international Muslim pilgrimage, Mecca was closed early to outsiders, and although non-Muslims were for long periods banned from even entering Arabia, they were increasingly active in the affairs of Mecca in the nineteenth century. In the 1830s cholera appeared in Europe, an occurrence linked to *ḥajjī*s returning from Mecca; European pressure forced the Ottomans to cooperate in a number of international conferences regulating sanitary conditions in and en route to Mecca. The slave trade, too, which the British in particular opposed, directed European attention toward Mecca, which was still an emporium for African slavers. Finally, increasing numbers of pilgrims were colonial subjects of the British, Dutch, and French, and reports of their mistreatment by the grand *sharīf* quickly reached the ministries of Europe. By the late nineteenth century, most of the European powers had established consuls in the port city of Jeddah to lodge complaints with the *sharīf,* some 45 miles distant in Mecca.

In November 1914, when the Ottomans joined the war against the Allied Powers, the *sharīf* was Ḥusayn ibn ʿAlī, and the British were already testing his allegiance to the Turks. Ottoman rule in the Hejaz was neither agreeable nor very profitable for their subjects, and so the *sharīf,* armed with British encouragement and funding, declared an armed revolt against the Turks in June 1916. Mecca soon fell to the *sharīf*'s men, and the city became self-governing for the first time since the days of the Prophet. Later, Ḥusayn proclaimed himself king of the Hejaz, and though his ambition to head an independent Arab state in the Fertile Crescent was never fulfilled, he held onto his throne until 1926, when the Hashemite kingdom was brought to an end by Ibn Saʿūd and his Wahhābī "Brethren." [*See the biographies of Ḥusayn and Saʿūd.*]

In 1926 Mecca was still very much a medieval town of narrow streets, crumbling buildings (most of the endowments had long since dried up) and a sterile economy. The Saudis brought relief from the capricious rule of Sharīf Ḥusayn, but it was not until the oil revenues of the 1950s had their effect that the city began to change its face. In 1956–1957, the shrine was greatly enlarged, pilgrimage facilities were improved, and the city underwent rapid growth. Today, Mecca is a modern city, though still transformed annually by the pilgrimage, which, in the age of flight, brings enormous numbers of pilgrims to Islam's holiest place.

[*See also* Medina.]

BIBLIOGRAPHY

Burckhardt, John L. *Travels in Arabia* (1829). Reprint, New York, 1968. A sharp-eyed and judicious anglicized Swiss visitor to Mecca describes the city early in the nineteenth century.

Burton, Richard F. *A Personal Narrative of a Pilgrimage to al-Madina and Meccah* (1855). 3d ed. Reprint, New York, 1964. Celebrated British soldier-adventurer makes the pilgrimage in disguise in the mid-nineteenth century.

Farāhānī, Muḥammad Ḥusayn Ḥusaynī. *A Shiʿite Pilgrimage to Mecca, 1885–1886: The Safarnâmeh of Mirzâ Moḥammad Ḥosayn Farâhânî.* Edited, translated, and annotated by Hafez Farmayan and Elton L. Daniel. Austin, 1990. Mecca and the Hejaz through Shīʿī eyes in the late nineteenth century.

Firestone, Reuven. *Journeys in Holy Lands: The Evolution of the Abraham-Ishmael Legends in Islamic Exegesis.* Albany, N.Y., 1990. Muslim traditions on the patriarchal origins of Mecca.

Long, David E. *The Hajj Today. A Survey of the Contemporary Makkah Pilgrimage.* Albany, N.Y., 1979. Analysis of the effects of the modern pilgrimage on Mecca.

Ochsenwald, William. *Religion, Society and the State in Arabia: The Hijaz under Ottoman Control, 1840–1908,* Columbus, Ohio, 1984. Detailed analysis of nineteenth-century Ottoman rule of the Holy Cities and the Hejaz.

Peters, F. E. *Hajj: The Muslim Pilgrimage to Mecca and the Holy Places.* Princeton, 1994. Collection and analysis of the narrative sources on the Muslim pilgrimage to Mecca from earliest times to 1925.

Peters, F. E. *Mecca and the Hijaz: A Literary History of the Muslim Holy Land.* Princeton, 1994. Collection and analysis of the narrative sources dealing Mecca and the Hejaz from the earliest times to World War I.

Rutter, Eldon. *The Holy Cities of Arabia,* 2 vols. London and New York, 1928. Eyewitness account of Mecca and the pilgrimage during the first years of Saudi sovereignty.

Snouck Hurgronje, Christiaan. *Mekka in Latter Part of the Nineteenth Century.* Leiden, 1931. Translation by J. H. Monahan of *Mekka,* vol. 2, *Aus dem heutigen Leben* (1889). Dutch Orientalist resident in Mecca describes everyday life there in the 1880s.

F. E. PETERS

MECELLE. The Arabic term *majallah* originally meant a book containing wisdom or, by extension, any kind of writing; its Turkish derivative *mecelle* refers more specifically to the civil code in force in the Ottoman Empire from AH 1285/1869 CE onward. The *Mecelle-i Ahkâm-ı Adliye,* to cite the work's full title, covers contracts, torts, and some principles of civil procedure.

The *Mecelle* was important for numerous reasons. Derived from Ḥanafī jurisprudence, the code incorporated not always the opinions of the most prominent Ḥanafī jurists, but rather whatever Ḥanafī jurists' opinions seemed most suited to the times. Although the justificatory memorandum *(esbab-ı mucibe mazbatası)* submitted to the Ottoman Council of Ministers said that the authors never drew from non-Ḥanafī jurists, some of the opinions incorporated did in fact originate in non-Ḥanafī sources. This kind of eclecticism also characterized later efforts at reform of *sharīʿah* law and in itself provided added impetus for codification. The *Mecelle* represented the first attempt by any Islamic state to codify part of the *sharīʿah*. Moreover, since the *Mecelle* was applied in the Ottoman Empire's secular *(nizamî)* as well as *sharīʿah* courts, the code, as state law *(kanun;* Ar., *qānūn)* made provisions of the *sharīʿah* applicable to the empire's non-Muslim subjects as well as to the Muslims whom the code's *sharʿī* content would have bound in any case. Most significantly, the *Mecelle* is a case of successful resistance, unique in the late Ottoman Empire and Turkish republic, to the tendency to adopt European law.

The decision to draft the *Mecelle* emerged from a dispute over whether the Ottomans should adopt the French civil code. One of the greatest Islamic scholars of the period as well as a great historian and statesman, Ahmed Cevdet Paşa (1822–1895) championed the opposing view that a compendium of Ḥanafī jurisprudence should be adopted instead. The Council of Ministers entrusted the drafting of such a work to a commission and appointed Cevdet Paşa to chair it. The commission completed the sixteen books of the *Mecelle,* and they were placed in force by successive decrees of the sultan, dating from 1286/1870 to 1293/1876. The *Mecelle* was not solely the work of Ahmed Cevdet Paşa, but it bears his stamp more than anyone else's; the commission's poor results when he was called away proved that the successful outcome of the project depended on him.

The *Mecelle* opens with two sections that define *fıkh* (Ar., *fiqh;* Islamic jurisprudence) and its components and state its basic principles. Following these, the sixteen books successively deal—citing the subjects in Arabic rather than in their Ottomanized forms—with sales *(buyūʿ);* hire and lease *(ijārāt);* guaranty *(kafālah);* transfer of debts *(ḥawālah);* pledge *(rahn);* deposit *(amānāt);* gift *(hibah);* usurpation and property damage *(ghaṣb [wa-itlāf]);* guardianship, duress, and preemption *(ḥajr, ikrāh, wa-shufʿah);* joint ownership and partnership *(shirket);* agency *(wakālah);* compromise and remission of debt *(ṣulḥ wa-ibrā);* acknowledgment *(iqrār);* lawsuits *(daʿwā);* evidence and oaths *(bayyināt [wa-taḥlīf]);* courts and judgeship *(qaḍā')*.

The drafting commission intended to continue by codifying the law on family and inheritance; however, Sultan Abdülhamid II (1876–1909) prevented it from doing so. Not until enactment of the Ottoman Law of Family Rights (Hukuk-ı Aile Kararnamesi, 8 Muharrem 1336/24 October 1917) would these topics be codified. The Law of Family Rights again took an eclectic approach to *sharīʿah* sources; in this law, moreover, applicability to non-Muslims was achieved by incorporating provisions of the religious laws of the various communities.

Despite its bases in Islamic jurisprudence, the *Mecelle* differs from traditional *sharīʿah* law in several respects. These include its codification, its official promulgation, and the admission—a consequence of the intended scope of application—of non-Muslims as witnesses. The *Mecelle* also differs from European civil codes in omitting noncontractual obligations, types of real property other than freehold *(milk),* family law, and inheritance, as well as in including some procedural provisions from the *sharīʿah.*

According to Fazlur Rahman, the *Mecelle* stands as lasting proof that "a system of law can very well be built" on the *sharīʿah*—in effect, that Islamic law can be codified—and thus that "the efforts of some modern Muslim states to replace the *sharīʿah* with purely secular law are mainly the result of intellectual defeatism" (1982, p. 29). Precisely because the route of legal secularization has been widely taken, the importance of the *Mecelle* can also be measured by its durability in practice. In the secular *(nizamî)* though not the *sharīʿah* courts, the Ottoman Empire in 1879 did replace the procedural provisions of the *Mecelle* with a Code of Civil Procedure based on French law. Otherwise the *Mecelle* remained in force until the Turkish republic adopted the Swiss Civil Code in 1926. In some successor states, it survived much longer. The *Mecelle* remained in force in Bosnia-Herzegovina after the Austrian occupation of 1878, in Albania until 1928, and in Cyprus at least into the 1960s. Though never in force in Egypt, the *Mecelle* was not replaced by new civil codes until 1932 in Lebanon, 1949 in Syria, 1953 in Iraq (where many elements of it survived in the new civil code of that year), and 1977 in Jordan. It remained basic to the civil law of Israel, too, until 1984.

Not surprisingly, considering the scope of its application, the *Mecelle* gave rise to a number of commentaries and translations. Noted commentaries include those of Ali Haydar (1912) and Salim ibn Rustam Baz (1888–1889). Available translations include those into English by W. E. Grigsby (1895) and by Sir Charles Tyser et al. (1901), and one into French published by George Young in 1906.

[*See also* Law.]

BIBLIOGRAPHY

Ali Haydar. *Dürer ül-Hukkâm: Şerh Mecellet il-Ahkâm.* 4 vols. 3d ed. Istanbul, 1330/1912.

Amin, S. H. *Middle East Legal Systems*. Glasgow, 1985.
Bāz, Salīm Rustam. *Sharḥ al-Majallah*. 2 vols. Beirut, 1888–1889.
Berki, Ali Hikmet. *Açıklamalı Mecelle (Mecelle-i Ahkâm-i Adliye)*. Istanbul, 1982.
Grigsby, W. E., trans. *The Medjellè*. London, 1895.
Israel. "Repeal of *Mejelle* Law, 5744-1984." In *Laws of the State of Israel*, vol. 38, p. 212. Tel Aviv, 1984.
Liebesny, Herbert J. *The Law of the Near and Middle East: Readings, Cases, and Materials*. Albany, N.Y., 1975.
Mardin, Ebül'ulâ. "Mecelle." In *İslâm Ansiklopedisi*. Istanbul, 1940.
Mardin, Ebül'ulâ. *Medenî Hukuk Cephesinden Ahmed Cevdet Paşa*. Istanbul, 1946.
Mecelle-i Akhâm-i Adliye. 2d printing. Istanbul, 1305/1887–1888.
Onar, Sıddık Sami. "İslâm Hukuku ve Mecelle." In *Tanzimat'tan Cumhuriyet'e Türkiye Ansiklopedisi*. Istanbul, 1985.
Rahman, Fazlur. *Islam and Modernity: Transformation of an Intellectual Tradition*. Chicago, 1982.
Schacht, Joseph. *An Introduction to Islamic Law*. Oxford, 1964.
Tyser, Charles, et al. *The Mejelle Translated*. Nicosia, 1901.
Young, George. *Corps de droit Ottoman: Recueil des codes, lois, règlements, ordonnances et actes les plus importants du droit intérieur, et d'études sur le droit coutumier de l'Empire Ottoman*, vol. 6, pp. 169–446. Oxford, 1906.

Carter Vaughn Findley

MEDICINE. [*This entry comprises two articles. The first considers the roots and development of traditional Islamic medicine and its historic interaction with methods of healing and curing in non-Islamic cultures. The second focuses on medical practices in modern Islamic societies and its relation to Western scientific values. For related discussion, see* Natural Sciences.]

Traditional Practice

Medical thinking and practice in a society are often viewed in terms of a dominant tradition; in the case of traditional Islamic societies, that dominant tradition was, for almost a millennium, a humoral system representing a revival of Greco-Roman medicine. But in Islamic society at large this was not the only alternative available, and it was never so dominant as to suffocate other medical views. Indeed, one must think in terms not only of multiple medical alternatives, but of intermingling options as well, since thinking most characteristic of one approach to medicine could simultaneously play a role in others as well.

For purposes of discussion here, three principal categories can be identified—a popular medical folklore that can be traced to remote antiquity, a mechanistic humoral tradition inherited from the Greeks, and a religious tradition focused on the person of the prophet Muḥammad. These traditions differ in the areas they stress and the ways in which they are legitimated; but at the same time, there are significant degrees of overlapping and numerous shared ideas and beliefs. Islamic societies have tolerated them all in various ways and degrees, and overall, Islamic medical history presents a profoundly pluralistic face. Each of these traditions can be assessed in isolation but in the end only becomes meaningful in terms of the social context that allows all an important role.

Substrate of Popular Medicine. All societies possess a body of medical lore that makes sense to the members of that society and is considered efficacious by them, but that is legitimated not by formal structures of legal, scientific, or religious sanction but rather by established custom. In the Islamic world this "popular" medicine has roots in the usage and tradition of remotest antiquity, and certain customs still encountered today find their counterparts in, for example, ancient Babylonia or Egypt. This medical folklore is not specific to certain groups; it crosses religious and ethnic lines with little modification and may be encountered as fully among Christians as among Muslims, in settled as well as nomadic populations, and among Turks or Persians as well as Arabs.

Popular medicine in the Islamic world has always had both practical and magical dimensions. Cupping, venesection, and cautery were common procedures believed to be useful treatments for a wide range of disorders. Drug therapy consisted of an array of broths, elixirs, liniments, salves, and errhines (nasal powders), mostly prepared from herbal and other natural ingredients. Inorganic medicaments (such as minerals) are seldom encountered, but a wide range of animal products were used, including meat, gall, milk, and urine.

Many external and internal disorders were treated using these remedies, but little could be done in the case of serious physical injury; broken bones, for example, were massaged, rubbed with salves, and kept immobile to heal. Surgery was limited to simple procedures such as lancing boils, and any injury involving significant penetration of the body cavity was likely to be fatal.

Accompanying these measures was a broad range of animistic practices based on a belief—ubiquitous in premodern times—in the influence on personal health wielded by supernatural forces, especially the evil eye and spirit beings known as the *jinn*. To combat these powers, a vast array of charms, amulets, and talismans was used; stones, animal parts, or magical sayings were carried personally or kept in the home, and various charms and other magical procedures were used to seek protection, especially from epidemic disease, with which spirits were most closely associated. [*See* Magic and Sorcery.]

In the pre-Islamic period, this medical lore could be found in all the various pagan and monotheistic communities. Beginning probably in the eighth century, emerging circles of Muslim scholarship began to argue against some aspects of it in the form of traditions ascribed to the prophet Muḥammad, but in the main the lore is still widely encountered in the Islamic world. Epidemic disease, for example, is still considered by many to be the work of the *jinn;* recourse to amulets and charms for medical purposes is widespread; and manuals on how to deal with supernatural afflictions are frequently published and widely distributed.

Greek Humoral Tradition. Greek medicine is prominently linked with the name of Hippocrates of Cos, a physician of the fifth century BCE (who may not have written any of the many works later ascribed to him); it reached its high point with the work of Galen (d. c.216 CE). This medical tradition viewed health as a state of balance among four "humors"—blood, phlegm, yellow bile, and black bile—embodying various combinations of four primary qualities: warmth, cold, heat, and dryness (yellow bile, for example, was characterized as dry and hot). All diseases and health problems, including psychological disorders, were explained in terms of excesses or imbalance in the interplay among these humors and qualities, and remedies were sought in treatments believed to have a contrary effect, which by restoring balance would also restore health. For an illness considered to represent imbalance toward the cold and moist, for example, drugs believed to have warming and drying properties would be used. Such factors as sleep, emotional states, exercise, eating and drinking habits, evacuation and retention, and environmental conditions were also recognized as influential, and all were integrated into the humoral system.

The great master of this humoral medicine was Galen of Pergamum, who wrote more than 350 books and lesser essays on it, and whose colossal reputation (rarely questioned until early modern times) attracted spurious attribution to him of some eighty or ninety further titles. In the centuries following Galen, humoral medicine as set forth in this massive corpus was widely practiced and taught, but by the late sixth century it had significantly declined, challenged by major social, economic, and other changes in the Near East which were disruptive to traditional classical culture in general. The rise of Islam could have had little influence on this process, which was already far advanced by the time of the Islamic conquests in the early seventh century. Indeed, it was within the context of the efflorescence of Islamic culture in the early ʿAbbāsid caliphate (eighth to tenth centuries) that scholarship in general flourished, and that medicine, the sciences, and philosophy found special official favor. This solicitude was not so much for the practical utility of these fields as for their usefulness in confessional disputes with Christianity and (perhaps even more) with the dualist doctrines of Manichaeism.

In the ninth century, the revival of Greek humorial medicine was initially pursued by searching out and translating important Greek texts, especially those of Galen, either directly into Arabic or into Arabic through a Syriac intermediary. This translation movement not only made hundreds of medical works available in accurate Arabic renderings, but it also served to create a mode of discourse, complete with its own technical terminology, for pursuit of original medical research in Arabic.

Such research, already under way among the translators, produced a vast array of specialized monographs, comprehensive medical encyclopedias, teaching texts, commentaries, and popular self-help manuals through the medieval period. This scholarship was Galenic in inspiration and content, but the contribution of Islamic culture was nonetheless considerable. Major advances were made in pharmacology, ophthalmology, optics, and surgery, and certain ideas neglected by the Greeks (e.g., contagion) were raised to prominence only in Islamic times. Further, it was under Islamic auspices, and most particularly in the *Canon of Medicine* of Ibn Sīnā (known in the West as Avicenna, d. 1037), that the ideas of Galen, scattered through his many practical and theoretical works, were drawn together into a unified system. Latin translations of the *Canon* were the basis of the medieval European Galenism for the next six hundred years.

Many humoral medical authors and practitioners were Christians and Jews, but just as peoples of different religious persuasions adhered to essentially the same tradition of popular medicine, humoral writers and physicians all pursued the same Galenic tradition and produced works that were not specifically Muslim, Christian, or Jewish in orientation. Insofar as they had a religious agenda, it was usually of a general monotheistic character, and it is often impossible to determine the religious identity of a medical author from his works. This reflects a broader cosmopolitan outlook in Islamic society, at least where medicine was concerned: individuals sought out medical help, teachers, students, and books with little if any attention to religious affinities.

Humoral medicine was a system legitimated and sustained by its ancient scientific connections, by official patronage and support among elite groups, and by its role in intellectual and literary discourse among esteemed medical scholars. The presence of hospitals and collections of medical books, and eventually medical schools as well, also served to encourage humoral medicine as an urban-based system. Prominent at first in centers in the heartland of the Near East, it soon spread and was pursued with equal vigor and profit in the cities of Persia, Khurasan, and the Indian subcontinent in the East, and in Tunisia and Spain in the West. Both Persian and Turkish became vehicles for important medical scholarship, and from the fifteenth century on Istanbul was a major center for the study and teaching of humoral medicine.

The crucial roles played by the Islamic city and its political and social elites in nourishing humoral medicine can nowhere be seen so clearly as in the fact that the gradual impoverishment of urban centers and the declining power and prestige of their elites were accompanied by the recession of humoral medicine. This process was exacerbated by tendencies among political and administrative authorities of the nineteenth century and after to establish and promote medical institutions modeled after those of Europe, thus undercutting the social position of traditional humoral practitioners, their pedagogical and intellectual institutions, and their languages of scholarship.

The demise of humoral medicine was in many areas severe, but not complete. In the 1870s, when medieval Arabic medical encyclopedias were printed in the Islamic world (in Cairo) for the first time, this work was undertaken as a contribution to current medical scholarship, not medical history. Many of the herbal remedies of humoral medicine are still prepared today as—ironically enough—alternatives to modern Western biomedicine. And in India and Pakistan, where humoral medicine from the sixteenth century onward was associated with various saintly families and figures, it managed to survive under the rubric of *yūnānī ṭibb* ("Greek medicine"). It is still extensively studied and taught in this part of the Islamic world, and there its remedies are manufactured on a large scale and widely promoted and consumed.

Medicine of the Prophet. As discussions among Muslims led to the clearer definition and articulation of Islamic dogma and religious thought, many traditional practices and beliefs that had earlier aroused no objection gradually came to be regarded as suspect on religious grounds. Discussions on whether and in what ways these customs should be allowed to continue included debates on aspects of popular medical lore; and as in other such arguments, the authority of the Prophet was invoked by citing reports of sayings, deeds, or attitudes of his that reflected judgments on these matters. While it would be absurd to insist that Muḥammad never said anything relevant to medicine—or that if he did, no one would have remembered it and then passed it down on his authority—the repeated reworking of the material and its problematic transmission make it impossible to discern any authentically prophetic core. But while most of the reports appear to represent discussions unlikely to predate the late seventh century (Muḥammad died in 632), the fact remains that for more than twelve hundred years Muslims have viewed them as the genuine "Medicine of the Prophet."

Early collections of this material loosely organize reports under discrete but often arbitrary headings and discuss a wide range of subjects, ranging from the curative power of honey (asserted in the Qur'ān, 16.69) to the medical properties of wolf's gall (an old popular remedy); whether or not one should flee from the plague or use passages from the Qur'ān as charms; and whether ritually unclean or forbidden substances are allowed to someone whom they might restore to health. These collections do not appear as independent works, but rather stand as chapters in larger compendia of *ḥadīth*. The Iraqi scholar Ibn Abī Shaybah (d. 849) compiled the largest extant collection of this early material.

Stimulated by these medical chapters in *ḥadīth* works, new medical reports cited from the Prophet continued to appear over the centuries and were collected into independent works, culminating in the *Medicine of the Prophet* by the Syrian jurist Ibn Qayyim al-Jawzīyah (d. 1350). The genre came to incorporate both natural/herbal and faith/magical remedies, an extensive materia medica, and ethical and moral advice on topics ranging from doctors' fees to coitus and singing. Humoral physicians active in the formative stages of this literature seem to have despised it, but by the thirteenth century their objections had largely been overcome.

In modern times the Medicine of the Prophet has enjoyed great popularity; and as it is legitimated by direct appeal to the sanction of Muḥammad himself, its social role is closely linked to the strength of prevailing religious sentiments. A recent edition of Ibn Qayyim al-Jawzīyah's work is a bestseller in the Arab countries, and a recent survey shows that among Muslims in general there is both awareness of the specific contents of the tradition and willingness to use it. Natural and herbal cures are employed for such complaints as headache, gastrointestinal disorders, and coughs, but just as prominent are faith/magic-oriented procedures, such as pronouncing a prayer or charm over a cup of water or milk and then drinking it to achieve the desired result.

This prominent corpus of medical lore sanctioned by the Prophet has probably played a significant role in sustaining discussions of medicine from an Islamic perspective. The Qur'ānic attribution of curative power to honey, for example, became an important early topic in the Medicine of the Prophet; in modern times this is pursued not only in sizable works devoted to this subject, but further in books on the broader relevance of Islam, and Islamic scripture in particular, to modern medical issues. Medical journals and scientific publications in the Islamic world, though patterned after Western biomedical models, also take up such questions. Similar discussions are regularly laid before the general public in the press, which publishes the formal pronouncements (*fatāwā;* sg., *fatwā*) of religious scholars on issues of medical ethics, including birth control, artificial insemination, autopsy, organ transplants and cosmetic surgery, euthanasia, and medical aspects of Islamic worship (e.g., whether one's fast is broken by taking essential medication). Justifying precedents are almost always drawn from medieval Islamic legal texts.

Medical Pluralism. In a stimulating essay on cognitive aesthetics ("Gedanken zur kognitiven Ästhetik Europas und Ostasiens," *Geschichte in Wissenschaft und Unterricht* 12 [1990]: 735–744), Paul U. Unschuld observes that in China, medical options are viewed as complementary rather than exclusive: "not only/but also" as opposed to "either/or." This characterization also applies to attitudes toward medicine in the Islamic world in medieval and modern times, and it highlights the fact that descriptive labels such as those used above should not be assigned determinative value or be regarded as defining insulated medical categories or epistemologies. Some concluding examples may serve to clarify the nature and extent of this pluralism.

As observed above, the Medicine of the Prophet is defined in Islamic religious terms and comprises a distinct literary and scholarly genre. At the same time, however, it has firm connections to both popular and humoral medicine. Early works admit many magical customs and beliefs, and in one early text charms and incantations in fact account for the majority of the traditions it contains. In later centuries the influence of the humoral tradition is prominent, and such eminent personalities of Greek medicine as Hippocrates, Galen, and Dioscorides are all quoted and regarded with approval.

A similar attitude can be seen in humoral medicine. It is not uncommon to find that one physician began his career as an astrologer and fortuneteller, that another wrote a *Medicine of the Prophet* as well as works on humoral medicine and natural history, and that magical remedies appear in works which otherwise stand squarely within the Galenic tradition.

Such patterns pose important contradictions to an outsider, but from an internal perspective these lose much of their significance. As recent anthropological research shows, many societies readily accommodate multiple medical alternatives on a complementary basis, with little sense of fundamental conflict between them. Physicians trained in and practicing modern Western biomedicine, for example, may still wear charms and amulets for protection from spirits; a charm-peddler, however, may proceed directly to the Western-style clinic as soon as he becomes ill. Overall, popular medical folklore is followed because it is based on long-established tradition (including its supernatural dimension), the Medicine of the Prophet because it invokes the authority of Muḥammad among Muslim populations, humoral medicine because it is seen to represent an indigenous alternative with convincing Islamic credentials, and modern Western biomedicine because of its manifest efficacy and its associations with the authority of government and, in the end, modern science.

[*See also* Natural Science; Science.]

BIBLIOGRAPHY

Conrad, Lawrence I. "Arab-Islamic Medicine." In *Companion Encyclopedia of the History of Medicine,* edited by W. F. Bynum and Roy Porter, vol. 1, pp. 676–727. London, 1993. An effort to take a broader view of the medical history of the Islamic world, without the traditional bias in favor of the humoral tradition.

Conrad, Lawrence I., et al. *The Western Medical Tradition, 800 B.C.–*

1800 A.D. Cambridge, 1995. Chapter 4 of this textbook treatment of the subject considers the Islamic tradition.

Dols, Michael W. *Majnūn: The Madman in Medieval Islamic Society.* Oxford, 1992. Magisterial study of madness, with relevance to many other issues.

Elgood, Cyril. *A Medical History of Persia and the Eastern Caliphate.* Cambridge, 1951. Dated but still useful account of Islamic medicine, primarily in Persia.

Goitein, S. D. "The Medical Profession" and "Druggists and Pharmacists." In his *A Mediterranean Society: The Jewish Communities of the Arab World as Portrayed in the Documents of the Cairo Geniza,* vol. 2, pp. 240–272. Berkeley and Los Angeles, 1971. Fundamental study based on medieval documents found in a Cairo synagoque.

Leiser, Gary. "Medical Education in Islamic Lands from the Seventh to the Fourteenth Century." *Journal of the History of Medicine* 38 (1983): 48–75.

Morsy, Soheir A. *Gender, Sickness, and Healing in Rural Egypt.* Boulder, 1993. Important for its analysis of the interplay of medical perspectives.

Rahman, Fazlur. *Health and Medicine in the Islamic Tradition: Change and Identity.* New York, 1987. Learned Islamic perspective.

Rispler-Chaim, Vardit. *Islamic Medical Ethics in the Twentieth Century.* Leiden, 1993. Analysis of *fatwās* (largely Egyptian) on medical ethical issues.

Rosenthal, Franz. *Science and Medicine in Islam.* Aldershot, 1990. Collected studies by a leading historian of Islamic society, culture, and science.

Temkin, Owsei. *Galenism: Rise and Decline of a Medical Philosophy.* Ithaca, N.Y., and London, 1973. Masterful account of Galenism in both the Islamic world and Europe.

Ullmann, Manfred. *Islamic Medicine.* Edinburgh, 1978. Series of eight studies, valuable but traditional in their bias toward "real" medicine.

LAWRENCE I. CONRAD

Contemporary Practice

Medicine in modern Islamic societies must be understood in the context of Western political, economic, and scientific dominance. In the nineteenth century many Muslim rulers, convinced of European military and scientific superiority and anxious to defend and strengthen themselves and their societies, began to establish Western-style medical facilities. In 1822 Muḥammad ʿAlī, the ruler of Egypt, invited Antoine-Barthelemy Clot, a French physician, to organize his medical services. In 1827 Clot founded a hospital and medical school in Cairo where European medicine was taught. In 1839 the Ottoman sultan Mahmud II opened a Western-style medical school in Istanbul. Muslim rulers from Morocco to Indonesia recruited European physicians to serve them and often to organize their health services.

In the era of direct colonial rule, beginning for example in Algeria in 1830 and in Egypt in 1882, the French and British authorities administered medical services and usually placed their nationals in the highest positions. Medicine was not a priority for colonial administrators, who generally established modern hospitals and public health facilities only in the European quarters of larger cities. In Algeria and Egypt medical facilities came to reflect the class structure of the colonial societies, with the best hospitals for the French or British, second-class hospitals for Jewish or Italian communities, and third-class hospitals for the Muslims. The vast majority, in both urban and rural areas, did not have recourse to modern medicine and continued to consult herbalists, bonesetters, health barbers, midwives, spiritual healers, and other practitioners.

After political independence was won in the first part of the twentieth century, most Muslim governments began to require physicians to be trained and certified by Western-style medical schools, although some gave traditional practitioners a second-class medical status. Nationalist governments frequently made the extension of medical services an important political platform, and medical schools, hospitals, and other medical facilities and public health systems were expanded throughout the Muslim world. In Egypt, for example, the Department of Public Health was made into the Ministry of Health in 1936, and in the 1940s resources were increased in response to the recurrence of deadly epidemics. A system of rural and urban health units instituted in the 1940s was enlarged under the regime of President Gamal Abdel Nasser, and Egypt today has a vast network of medical services. Nevertheless, inequities and organizational difficulties have resulted in widespread deficiencies. Oil-rich nations such as Saudi Arabia have spent billions on importing ultramodern medical facilities; poorer nations like Pakistan, which spends less than 1 percent of its gross national product on health, have inadequate medical facilities. In many regions medical schools have produced more specialists than needed while the basic needs of the rural and urban populace go unmet. Programs to train physicians, public health nurses, and other personnel to practice preventive medicine in rural and urban health centers are, however, becoming more common.

As elsewhere in the world, modern medical technologies have not brought unmixed blessings. As a result of improved public health and medical services and the increased production of foodstuffs, populations have soared, outstripping resources. In some regions modern irrigation techniques now allow for the cultivation of two or three crops per year, but waterborne bilharzia (schistosomiasis) has spread into previously uninfected regions. Automobile and industrial pollution now chokes major cities of the Muslim world, resulting in a widespread deterioration of public health. The medical inequities of the preindependence era have continued and even become worse in many regions.

In recent years, however, many Islamic reformers have become disillusioned with modern medicine, claiming that its tendency to treat the patient symptom by symptom rather than as a whole person is inherently dehumanizing and medically unsound. Modern medicine, they argue, has become overly materialistic and technocratic, addressed to the financial interests of the medical industry rather than to the unique needs of the patient. They have called for a return to Islamic values to make modern medicine more humane and moral, based on preventive rather than curative medicine and addressed to the needs of the individual and his or her community. Medical reformers are trying to reinforce the concept of caring for the whole person rather than treating one organ or an isolated ailment, and for using natural remedies, nutritional regimens, and spiritual healing before more radical treatments and surgical intervention.

In 1982 the Second International Conference on Islamic Medicine, held in Kuwait, addressed many of these questions. Specialists in Islamic medicine from many parts of the world called for integrating Islamic medical ethics derived from the Qur'ān and *sunnah* with modern medicine. Some called for Muslim medical students to learn the medical ethics of Islam by studying the *sharīʿah* and *ḥadīth* and biographies of noted Muslim physicians. Others called for research programs to study the efficacy of the diverse traditional medicines of Islamic societies. The conference ended with recommendations to launch the World Islamic Medicine Organization established after the first conference, to publish Kuwait's Islamic Code of Medical Ethics, and to further study the role of Islam in medical education. The conference participants repeatedly expressed their discomfort with aspects of modern medicine and a nationalistic pride in the medical achievements of earlier centuries.

In addition to such academic specialists in Islamic medicine, many Islamic religious authorities, commentators, and philosophers have attempted to bring modern medicine into the framework of Islamic ethics. They generally argue that in Muslim societies, no activity of life, including the practice of modern medicine, should be secular. In many cases, the solution is to find sanctions for or prohibitions of modern medical practices within the Qur'ān or *ḥadīth*. For example, in Riyadh, Saudi Arabia, the religious authorities were asked to rule on the legality of organ transplants. In 1982 (6 Dhū al-Qaʿdah 1402) the senior *ʿulamā'* issued Decree Number 99, stating that organ donation and transplantation both during and after life are legal provided that written consent is available from the donor or the next of kin. In Egypt, Shaykh Muḥammad Mutawallī al-Shaʿrāwī, the prominent Islamic commentator, has given his views on the ethics of cosmetic surgery. He has reasoned that if it leads to modifications in God's creation it should be viewed negatively, adding that beauty is a gift of God that is beyond human understanding and should not be measured by humankind. On the other hand, he suggests, if such surgical intervention relieves suffering, including psychological suffering, it would be acceptable under Islamic ethics.

The late Fazlur Rahman, a noted Pakistani philosopher and Islamic reformer, argued that in the Qur'ān and *ḥadīth,* the needs of the living are more important that those of the dead, and therefore both dissection and organ transplants are legal (see Rahman, 1987). Regarding genetic engineering, he reasoned that although tampering with the will of God was not acceptable, the genetic improvement of plants and animals had been accepted since the beginning of history, and so should the genetic improvement of human beings as long as it involved no loss of human life or dignity. He argued that the technology involved in producing test-tube babies helped a husband and wife have children and so should be sanctioned. If, however, the reproductive cells were from donors rather than from the husband and wife, the procedure should be illegal, because under Islamic law adultery means not only extramarital relations but also confusing the genetic heritage of the child. Finally, regarding prolongation of life by artificial means, he reasoned that it was not acceptable because the Qur'ān emphasizes the quality of life over the quantity of life. If the quality of life was also improved it was acceptable, but this meant that the environment and food resources must be improved at the same time. Like many but not all Islamic authorities, he argued that family planning is acceptable in Islamic ethics, as is abortion within the first four months of pregnancy. He observed that even when the *ʿulamā'* have objected to medical advances, Muslim communities have often accepted them, providing an additional argument for them on the basis of community consensus. [*See* Family Planning; Abortion.]

One of the most intractable issues for contemporary medical practice is the worldwide spread of AIDS. Because of the officially prescribed ideals of Muslim sexual behavior, a number of Muslim governments have been reluctant to disseminate information or even to collect statistics on the epidemic, preferring to view it as a foreign danger to be stopped at the borders. Muslim physicians and social critics such as Munawar A. Anees, however, have argued convincingly that there is a gulf between ideals and realities, that the community is responsible for the welfare of all of its members, and that this "denial syndrome" must stop.

In response to the many calls for the integration of modern medicine within an Islamic framework, Islamic hospitals have been established in many cities in the Muslim world. In Amman, Jordan, for example, the Islamic Hospital is large, active, and modern, resembling any Western hospital except for the conservative Islamic dress worn by its employees, male and female physicians and staff members alike, and its insistence on conforming to Islamic values in its practices. Many of the Islamist (fundamentalist) movements have made medicine an important part of their social services, and their clinics and hospitals often dispense free medical and public health services.

In conclusion, many reformers have asked why Islamic civilization has not assimilated and advanced Western medicine as easily as it assimilated Greek, Persian, and Indian medicine in the early centuries of Islam. One common answer is that Islamic civilization was politically dominant over the more scientifically advanced civilizations, in contrast to the present situation, making it psychologically easier to incorporate new knowledge into the cultural framework. Another is that current medical research is far more complex and costly than in earlier centuries and thus more difficult to assimilate. Whatever the answer to this question, implicit in it is another question: how can Muslim societies end their dependency on the West and advance on their own terms? Some believe that the Muslim world must return to its Islamic roots, for example by instituting the Qur'ānic *zakāt* tax (a tithe on income) to fund regional medical research centers where the wealth and talent of the region can be concentrated. Others argue with equal conviction that the solution lies in secular and democratic political, social, and economic reforms that would combine the wealth and talents of the region in a secular atmosphere. This conflict between Islamist and secularist views of medical, public health, and other social reforms is perhaps the most crucial of the present era.

BIBLIOGRAPHY

Anees, Munawar A. "The Silent Killer: AIDS and the Muslim World." *The Minaret* (January–February, 1994): 33–35.

Faqih, S. R. al-. "The Influence of Islamic Views on Public Attitudes towards Kidney Transplant Donation in a Saudi Arabian Community." *Public Health* 105 (1991): 161–165.

Gallagher, Eugene B., and C. Maureen Searle. "Health Services and the Political Culture of Saudi Arabia." *Social Science and Medicine* 21.3 (1985): 251–262.

Gallagher, Nancy E. *Medicine and Power in Tunisia, 1780–1900*. Cambridge, 1983. Discusses the transition from Galenic-Islamic to Western medicine in Tunisia in the context of European political and economic expansion.

Gallagher, Nancy E. *Egypt's Other Wars: Epidemics and the Politics of Public Health*. Syracuse, N.Y., 1990. Shows how malaria, relapsing fever, and cholera became major political issues in the post–World War II era.

Good, Byron. "The Transformation of Health Care in Modern Iranian History." In *Modern Iran: The Dialectics of Continuity and Change*, edited by Michael Bonine and Nikki R. Keddie, pp. 59–82. Albany, N.Y., 1981.

Jundī, Aḥmad Rajā'ī, and Hakeem Mohammad Zahoorul Hasan, eds. *Proceedings of the Second International Conference on Islamic Medicine*. Kuwait, 1982.

Khan, Muhammad Salim. *Islamic Medicine*. London, 1986. Argues that the creative thought, balanced lifestyle, and healing forces known to the Islamic medical tradition can reform modern medicine.

Kuhnke, LaVerne. *Lives at Risk: Public Health in Nineteenth-Century Egypt*. Berkeley, 1990. Discusses epidemics of cholera, plague, and smallpox and Western medical institutions introduced by Muḥammad ʿAlī.

Morsy, Soheir A. "Towards a Political Economy of Health: A Critical Note on the Medical Anthropology of the Middle East." *Social Science and Medicine* 15B (1981): 159–163. Provides background to the study of traditional medicine.

Nanji, Azim A. "Medical Ethics and the Islamic Tradition." *Journal of Medicine and Philosophy* 13 (1988): 257–275.

Rahman, Fazlur. *Health and Medicine in the Islamic Tradition*. New York, 1987. Indispensable study of Islamic ethics, medicine, and health, beginning with a comprehensive analysis of "Wellness and Illness in the Islamic World View."

Rispler-Chaim, Vardit. "Islamic Medical Ethics in the Twentieth Century." *Journal of Medical Ethics* 15 (1989): 203–208.

Sonbol, Amira. *The Creation of a Medical Profession in Egypt, 1800–1922*. Syracuse, N.Y., 1992. Surveys the introduction of Western medical institutions into Egypt.

NANCY E. GALLAGHER

MEDINA. In pre-Islamic times called Yathrib, Medina (Madīnah) became Muḥammad's home after the Hijrah. An oasis 275 miles north of Mecca, it was originally an agricultural settlement, with widely scattered palm groves and armed farmsteads; among its inhabitants were both Arabs and Jews. The two groups lived in a complex political association, which began to unravel late in the sixth century CE, resulting in a grave civil war throughout the oasis. This condition led to Muḥammad's invitation to leave his native Mecca and migrate to Yathrib, where it was thought by some that this charismatic holy man might successfully arbitrate the woes of the oasis. The migration (Hijrah) took place in 622 CE and marks the beginning of the Muslim era.

Once settled in Yathrib, thereafter called "the City of the Prophet" (Madīnat al-Nabī), or simply Medina, Muḥammad began to set the subsequent course of Islam as a religious and political society. The courtyard of his residence served as the first mosque for the Muslims. Early on, he had a falling out with the Jews and, consequently, changed his direction of prayer from Jerusalem to the Kaʿbah in Mecca and modified his fasting practice, which had been based on a Jewish model.

Muḥammad first regulated the political problems of Medina by gaining assent to a document (the "Constitution of Medina") knitting all the inhabitants into a single polity. Soon, however, a more peremptory solution presented itself. In 624 Muḥammad and his Muslims successfully attacked a Meccan trade caravan at nearby Badr Wells. The results disheartened the Meccans and emboldened the rest of the Medinans to declare openly for their new leader and his prophetic claims. Other successes followed that of Badr Wells, and it became increasingly clear to the Medinans, and eventually to the Meccans as well, that Muḥammad and his message was a force to be reckoned with in western Arabia. By the time of Muḥammad's death in 632, the movement called Islam had not only won Arabia but stood poised to conquer the great but enfeebled superpowers of Byzantium and Iran.

Muḥammad's first four successors chose to remain in Medina, and so the oasis settlement became the capital of the new Islamic empire. The city remained, for all that, a simple place not much changed from the Prophet's own days there. During the next hundred-odd years the Muslim armies were on the march across North Africa and Iran; when they finally came to rest, and the booty of empire began to be invested in the adornment of its capital, that capital had moved elsewhere. Medina was not to be the seat of sovereignty, its rulers decided. Nor did sovereignty ever return to Medina, though eventually, under the Ottomans, it gained the ascendancy over its political rival Mecca.

The two cities also became rivals in sanctity. Muḥammad himself had constituted Medina a "sacred area" (*ḥaram*) like Mecca, though probably for commercial purposes since it had no shrine. But, with the Prophet's death, Medina possessed its shrine. Muḥammad was buried in the apartment of one of his wives in Medina, right off the courtyard that served as the first mosque in Islam. Later rulers began to invest in the expansion and beautification not only of the mosque but of the Prophet's own tomb. Other celebrated Muslims were buried nearby: his daughter Fāṭimah, Abū Bakr and ʿUmar (who lay next to the Prophet), and ʿUthmān as well. Their tombs also received secondary embellishment, but it was the Prophet's own sarcophagus, invisible inside a draped, grilled enclosure within the enlarged mosque, that began to attract Muslims to Medina. The *ḥajj* might be made only to Mecca, but a *ziyārah* or pious visit to the Prophet's tomb at Medina was on the itinerary of every Muslim pilgrim to the Hejaz (Ḥijāz).

Thus, Medina and Mecca became known as the Ḥaramān, the "Twin Sanctuaries," and the distant caliphs and sultans who ruled the Holy Cities of Arabia rejoiced in the title "Servant of the Ḥaramān." It was an expensive honor. The ruler was responsible for the caravans that set forth from within his domains on their long and dangerous journey to the Hejaz. They carried with them the annual allocations from the imperial budget and from private sources for the support of the personnel of the Ḥaramān, everyone from the grand *sharīf* who ruled them to the lowliest sweeper at the Prophet's mosque in Medina.

In medieval times Medina enjoyed little political importance. The *sharīf* lived in Mecca by preference, and the Egyptian or Ottoman governor usually chose to live in Jeddah on the coast. What indirectly changed the political fortunes of the city was the British establishment of themselves in Egypt, thus channeling the direct communication from Istanbul to the Hejaz overland through Syria, thence south through Medina to Mecca. The Turks, to strengthen the link, constructed a telegraph line to Medina and, in 1908, completed the Hejaz Railway, which was for political reasons extended no further than Medina. Medina thus became the chief communication center of Ottoman Arabia, and so its chief garrison town as well.

When Sharīf Ḥusayn ibn ʿAlī announced his revolt against the Turks in 1916, Mecca fell quickly; but Medina, with its garrison of regular Ottoman troops under the command of the redoubtable Fakhrî Pasha, held out against the Sharīf's forces until January 1919. With the end of the war, Medina formed part of Sharīf Ḥusayn's short-lived Kingdom of the Hejaz. Ḥusayn's bitter rival Ibn Saʿūd took the city without much difficulty in December 1925; it was absorbed with the rest of the Hejaz into the newly enlarged Saudi kingdom. There were misgivings at the time that the Wahhābī Saudis might extend their severe disapproval of the cult of the dead to the Prophet's own tomb in Medina, but the fears were groundless. The Saudis destroyed some minor shrines, but the Prophet's mosque and tomb they eventually made larger and more ornate than before. Medina today is a large modern city with few physical traces of its pre-Islamic or even medieval past.

[*See also* Mecca *and the biographies of Ḥusayn and Saʿūd.*]

BIBLIOGRAPHY

Burckhardt, John L. *Travels in Arabia* (1829). Reprint, New York, 1968. A sharp-eyed and judicious anglicized Swiss visitor to the holy cities early in the nineteenth century.

Burton, Richard F. *A Personal Narrative of a Pilgrimage to al-Madina and Meccah* (1855). 3d. ed. Reprint, New York, 1964. Celebrated British soldier-adventurer makes the pilgrimage in disguise in the mid-nineteenth century.

Farāhānī, Muḥammad Ḥusayn Ḥusaynī. *A Shīʿite Pilgrimage to Mecca, 1885–1886: The Safarnâmeh of Mirzâ Moḥammad Ḥosayn Farâhânî.* Edited, translated, and annotated by Hafez Farmayan and Elton L. Daniel. Austin, 1990. Mecca and the Medina through Shīʿī eyes in the late nineteenth century.

Ochsenwald, William. *Religion, Society and the State in Arabia: The Hijaz under Ottoman Control, 1840–1908,* Columbus, Ohio, 1984. Detailed analysis of nineteenth-century Ottoman rule of the Holy Cities and the Hejaz.

Peters, F. E. *Hajj: The Muslim Pilgrimage to Mecca and the Holy Places.* Princeton, 1994. Collection and analysis of the narrative sources on visits to Mecca and Medina from the earliest times to 1925.

Peters, F. E. *Mecca and the Hijaz: A Literary History of the Muslim Holy Land.* Princeton, 1994. Collection and analysis of the narrative sources dealing Mecca and Medina from the earliest times to World War I.

Rutter, Eldon. *The Holy Cities of Arabia,* 2 vols. London and New York, 1928. Eyewitness account of Mecca and Medina during the first years of Saudi sovereignty.

F. E. PETERS

MEDITATION. *See* Sufism, *article on* Ṣūfī Thought and Practice.

MERNISSI, FATIMA (b. 1940), Moroccan sociologist and writer. Born in Fez to a middle-class family, Mernissi studied at the Mohammed V University in Rabat and later went to Paris, where she worked briefly as a journalist. She pursued her graduate education in the United States and in 1973 obtained a Ph.D. in sociology from Brandeis University. Returning to Morocco, she joined the sociology department at Mohammed V University. Mernissi currently holds a research appointment at the Moroccan Institut Universitaire de Recherche Scientifique.

As one of the best known Arab-Muslim feminists, Mernissi's influence extends beyond a narrow circle of intellectuals. She is a recognized public figure in her own country and abroad, especially in France, where she is well known in feminist circles. Her major books have been translated into several languages, including English, German, Dutch, and Japanese. She writes regularly on women's issues in the popular press, participates in public debates promoting the cause of Muslim women internationally, and has supervised the publication of a series of books on the legal status of women in Morocco, Algeria, and Tunisia.

Mernissi's work explores the relationship between sexual ideology, gender identity, sociopolitical organization, and the status of women in Islam; her special focus, however, is Moroccan society and culture. As a feminist, her work represents an attempt to undermine the ideological and political systems that silence and oppress Muslim women. She does this in two ways, first, by challenging the dominant Muslim male discourse concerning women and their sexuality, and second, by providing the "silent" woman with a "voice" to tell her own story. Her book *Doing Daily Battle* (1989) is a collection of annotated interviews with Moroccan women who present a lucid account of the painful reality of their lives as they struggle against poverty, illiteracy, and sexual oppression.

From the writing of her first book, *Beyond the Veil: Male-Female Dynamics in Modern Muslim Society* (1975) Mernissi has sought to reclaim the ideological discourse on women and sexuality from the stranglehold of patriarchy. She critically examines the classical corpus of religious-juristic texts, including the *ḥadīth*, and reinterprets them from a feminist perspective. In her view, the

Muslim ideal of the "silent, passive, obedient woman" has nothing to do with the authentic message of Islam. Rather, it is a construction of the *'ulamā'*, the male jurists-theologians who manipulated and distorted the religious texts in order to preserve the patriarchal system.

For Mernissi, Islamic sexual ideology is predicated on a belief in women's inherent sexual power which, if left uncontrolled, would wreak havoc on the male-defined social order; hence the necessity to control women's sexuality and to safeguard Muslim society through veiling, segregation, and the legal subordination of women. Mernissi's work explores the impact of this historically constituted ideological system on the construction of gender and the organization of domestic and political life in Muslim society today.

Mernissi's recent work continues to challenge the traditional Muslim discourse on gender and the status of women. In her book *The Veil and the Male Elite* (first published in French in 1987), she critically examines the historical context of Muslim law and tradition and argues that the original message of the Prophet Muḥammad, which called for equality between the sexes, has been misrepresented by later political leaders and religious scholars. Turning her attention to the Arab world today, Mernissi situates the "woman question" within a more inclusive framework that links it to problems of political legitimacy, social stagnation, and the absence of democracy. Her most recent book, *Islam and Democracy: Fear of the Modern World* (1992), is an impassioned plea for Muslims to reclaim the best of their tradition and to cast off their fear of the West. This can only be accomplished, she maintains, through a radical overhaul of the political, ideological, and social structures that have for generations conspired to deny the majority of Muslims, men and women alike, the modern benefits of equality, democracy, literacy, and economic security.

[*See also* Feminism; Women and Social Reform, *article on* Social Reform in North Africa.]

BIBLIOGRAPHY

The following works by Fatima Mernissi are available in English:

Beyond the Veil: Male-Female Dynamics in Modern Muslim Society. Rev. ed. Bloomington, 1987.

Doing Daily Battle: Interviews with Moroccan Women. Translated by Mary Jo Lakeland. New Brunswick, N.J., 1989.

The Veil and the Male Elite: A Feminist Interpretation of Women's Rights in Islam. Translated by Mary Jo Lakeland. Reading, Mass., 1991.

Islam and Democracy: Fear of the Modern World. Translated by Mary Jo Lakeland. Reading, Mass., 1992.

AMAL RASSAM

MESSALI AL-ḤAJJ (1898–1974), more fully Ahmed Messali al-Ḥajj and often spelled Messali Hadj, the first Algerian nationalist leader in the twentieth century to call for the complete independence of Algeria from France. Born in Tlemcen, to a lower-middle-class Turkish-Algerian family, Messali attended a Qur'ānic school before being sent to a French school where he earned an elementary-school diploma. After joining the French army and serving three years in the Bordeaux region, Messali decided, in 1923, to live in France. He married a French woman, joined the French Communist Party, and became a leading member of the Etoile Nord Africaine (founded in 1926). In 1927 he set the agenda for the Etoile that included demands for Algeria's complete independence from France and the withdrawal of French troops of occupation; freedom of association and the press; and the election of an Algerian parliament and municipal councils through universal suffrage.

In the mid-1930s, Messali al-Ḥajj left the French Communist Party, which had condemned the demands of the Etoile Nord Africaine, and returned to Algeria to mobilize peasants and workers and to create new chapters of the Etoile Nord Africaine. In March 1937, two months after the French government dissolved the Etoile, he formed the Party of the Algerian People (PPA). When three thousand of his PPA supporters demonstrated in Algiers in July 1937, he was arrested and imprisoned for two years, until the outbreak of World War II. Messali al-Ḥajj was arrested again, however, and he spent most of the war in prison, and in 1945 his PPA was outlawed.

When released in 1946, he immediately created the Movement for the Triumph of Democratic Freedoms (MTLD) to replace the banned PPA. The MTLD's members won electoral seats in the Algerian National Assembly in 1946, but when they tried again in 1948 and in 1951, the elections were rigged by the colonial administration. By 1950 the MTLD had an estimated twenty thousand members and had become the largest opposition party in Algeria.

In 1947 Hocine Aït Ahmed, a member of the MTLD, built a paramilitary group, the Organization Speciale

(OS), within the MTLD. In 1950 when the MTLD leaders and many OS members were arrested by the French, Messali al-Ḥajj's fortunes within the MTLD began to decline. He and his supporters were ousted from the MTLD in 1954 for personal and ideological reasons, and the nationalist movement was permanently split. Attempts by a newly created Revolutionary Committee for Unity and Action (CRUA) of ex-OS members to mediate the conflict failed. On 31 October 1954 the CRUA announced the formation of the Front for National Liberation (FLN) and launched the war of independence the very next day. Messali al-Ḥajj, however, did not support the FLN. He renamed the branch of the MTLD still under his control the National Algerian Movement (MNA) and created a militia that fought the FLN in France until 1957. The movement was finally wrecked by deaths and defections, and although it continued to exist until independence it was no longer a political force.

Messali al-Ḥajj, who had fought so hard for Algeria's independence, found himself out in the cold politically when his dream was realized. He spent the last years of his life in Lamorlaye, France, writing his memoirs, surrounded by his family and a few loyal supporters. He died of cancer in 1974, and his body was carried back to Algeria for burial in Tlemcen, the city of his birth.

[*See also* Algeria.]

BIBLIOGRAPHY

Entelis, John P. *Algeria: The Revolution Institutionalized*. Boulder, 1986.

Ruedy, John. *Modern Algeria: The Origins and Development of a Nation*. Bloomington, 1992.

Stora, Benjamin. *Messali Hadj, 1898–1974*. Paris, 1982.

MARY-JANE DEEB

MESSIANISM. In the sense of divine intervention in human history—through the appointment of a *mahdī* (rightly guided person) to deliver the people from tyranny and oppression at the End of Time—messianism is a salient feature of Islamic soteriology. Messianic expectations were part of the early Muslim belief in the prophet Muḥammad as the *ākhir al-zamān* ("apostle of the End of Time"). In that eschatological position the Prophet was expected to usher humanity toward an ideal community with a universal mission. Such expectations were also part of the reformist and revivalist tendencies among the Judeo-Christian communities of Arabia in the sixth and seventh centuries. The Qur'ānic preoccupation with the impending Day of Judgment and the Signs of the Hour, which announced cosmic disorder and a period of terror and fear preceding the Final Days, can be understood within the cultural and ideological setting of the messianic prophecy in Abrahamic soteriology and eschatology.

The Qur'ānic Vision of the Messianic Future. The major this-worldly expression of Islam was its self-implementation in a religiopolitical community, the *ummah,* with a worldwide membership of all those who believe in God and the divine revelation through Muḥammad. Consequently, Muslim belief in the divinely guided messianic leader, the Mahdi, is rooted in the acknowledgment that Muḥammad's position and function as the divinely guided prophet was to create this ideal *ummah.* Islamic revelation sees itself actively engaged in assessing human conditions that obstruct the fulfillment of the ultimate divine purposes for humanity. Human civilization, as the Qur'ān maintains, is the record of the perpetual *jihād* (struggle) against human self-centeredness and self-cultivated pettiness, the two main sources of conflict and the attendant destruction of humanity. It is the enemy within that needs to be conquered, through *jihād akbar* ("greater struggle") before one can truly undertake to overcome the external enemy through *jihād aṣghar* ("lesser struggle") that impedes the creation of the just and peaceful human society. Islamic soteriology is an expression of the desperate human situation, and it provides the critically needed sense of common human destiny—the human saga of the search for justice and peace. This is the essence of Islamic messianism.

At different times in history God intervenes and provides living examples, the prophets, who can remind humanity of its true nature and its perfectibility through faith in God. Toward the End of Time, after having failed time and again, when humanity finds itself in need of spiritual-moral revival to assume its historical responsibility of creating the divine order on earth, God will send Jesus and the Mahdi to restore the pure faith and redress the wrongs committed against the righteous servants of God. In the meantime, human beings must continue to strive in order to recognize their primordial nature through *islām* ("submission"). This is the spiritual-moral expression of Islamic messianism.

Historical Messianism. The responsibility to create

an independent political community, the *ummah*, which carried within itself the revolutionary challenge to any inimical order which might hamper its realization, was historically assumed by the Prophet himself when he established the first Muslim policy in Medina in 622 CE. The decisive connection between the divine investiture to the prophetic mission and the creation of an Islamic world order is the integral facet of Islamic messianism. Hence, the Mahdi, through his investiture as the Prophet's successor and God's caliph, is awaited to implement the transcendental ideal on earth.

Historical and sociological factors in the first century, following the Prophet's death in 632, were instrumental in heightening the messianic expectations in the Muslim community, especially among those who were persecuted as Shīʿah—partisans of ʿAlī ibn Abī Ṭālib and sympathizers of his claim to the caliphate. The hopes of Banū Hāshim, the Prophet's clan, who had supported the claims of the descendants of ʿAlī, and who looked forward to the return of the prophetic "golden age," were greatly frustrated when the caliphate slipped out of their hands in 661. Thereafter, the idea of a perfect leader, the divinely appointed imam, continued to be emphasized more specifically among the religiously oriented Muslims in general, and among Shīʿīs in particular. Although both ʿAlī and his son Ḥusayn were regarded as *mahdī*, perhaps in a noneschatological sense, it was ʿAlī's son Muḥammad ibn al-Ḥanafīyah, who was declared to be the promised Mahdi. He was believed to have possessed the esoteric knowledge necessary to deliver his followers from oppression and to establish a just society.

The outbreak of the civil wars and the perturbed condition that followed greatly contributed to the notion of messianic savior whose function, in the first place, was to redress the wrongs committed against the downtrodden and establish justice, by which the Shīʿīs meant abolition of the caliphate of the oppressors and the return to a pure Islam; and, in the second place, to achieve the conversion of the world to Islam. Among the various factions of the Shīʿīs disagreement on the identification of the Mahdi was one of the chief factors separating sect from sect. Shīʿī hope for justice, in their oft-quoted phrase, "the world would be filled with justice as it is now filled with injustice" when the Mahdi emerges from the divinely imposed occultation, expressed radical social protest. The expectation meant not merely a hope for the future, but a revaluation of present social and historical life. Every generation found reason to believe that it was likely that the Mahdi would appear in their own time and test the faithful by summoning them to launch the great social transformation themselves under his command, with the promise of divine help when it would be needed. Hence, messianic tendencies became the source of heretical and even combative attitudes among the Shīʿīs. These revolutionary insurrections were feared and severely crushed by the ruling authorities for their potential destructive and chaotic repercussions.

Several adventurous individuals, of Shīʿī sympathies, organized and led revolutions from the last decades of the Umayyad rule. The most important of which was the ʿAbbāsid revolution, which carried on a very effective propaganda against the Umayyads on a largely Shīʿī basis, keyed to the messianic expectation. The ʿAbbāsids were able to overthrow the Umayyads and establish their own dynasty in the eighth century. The Fāṭimid revolution in the tenth century was another uprising with considerable popular support. It won a large number of adherents to its cause and established a Shīʿī state in North Africa. In this case also the emphasis was on the messianic anticipation for an ideal social order, and in it too the leader manipulated the Shīʿī ideology and even adopted the Shīʿī messianic title of *al-manṣūr* (the victorious) and *al-mahdī*.

However, all Shīʿī attempts were not successful, and once its adherents met with repeated failures and persecutions, they ceased to attempt revolutionary transformation. With this change in fortunes, the Shīʿī ideology became the chief vehicle for any Muslim who entertained radical change, and it was perpetuated in terms of esoteric messianic teaching. The title Mahdi ceased to connote immediate and direct political action. The frustration of the adherents of messianic prophecies gradually caused the shift in the emphasis of the Mahdi from political power to religious reform, which also touched the social and communal life of Muslims. It continued to express the idealism of the *ummah*, the hope that one day Islam, with all its political and social implications, will return to its pristine purity. The original historical mission of Islam, namely, the establishment of the ideal society under divine guidance, was believed to attain fulfillment under the Mahdi in future. In independent books of esoteric erudition about future events (*al-balāyah wa-al-manāyah*), in which narratives reported on the authority of the Prophet and the Imams were related, dark events to come were foretold in such a way that every new generation of Muslims could see its trials and hopes mirrored in them.

By the end of the eighth century, a majority of Muslims regarded the historical caliphate as the continuation of the Prophet's temporal position divested of any eschatological anticipation. The eschatological function was transferred to the future "caliph of God," the Mahdi. This formed the main thrust of the Sunnī conviction about the Prophet's messianic legacy.

However, different subdivisions of the Shīʿīs maintained the necessity for the continuation of the Prophet's temporal and spiritual authority in the person of a divinely appointed imam to guide the community to its ultimate deliverance. This was the cardinal doctrine of the Shīʿīs who rejected the historical caliphate as a human interference in the procurement of the divine plan, and awaited the appearance of the Mahdi, as the restorer of ideal Muslim order.

Messianic Legacy during and after the First Islamic Millennium. In the fifteenth century, owing to the approach of the first millennium after the advent of the Prophet, various groups began to revive their hopes for a better future. In the holy cities of Mecca and Medina a number of religious scholars wrote their opinions confirming the popular belief in the appearance of a *mujaddid* (reformer) at the turn of the century. A prominent Sunnī jurist, Ibn al-Ḥajar al-Makkī, declared that the advent of the Mahdi was to be expected in the millennium, and that such a messianic person would be a descendant of Fāṭimah, daughter of the Prophet, and that his name would conform to the Prophet's name and the names of his parents to those of his parents. The recognition of the true Mahdi was not going to be an easy task because of the manner in which the traditions predicting the emergence of the eschatological personage were multiplying. The problem of the identity of the Mahdi was too intricate for any religious authority or political ruler to solve.

The idea of the Mahdi was popular among the Sunnīs in India in the fifteenth century where the rise of the idea that Sayyid Muḥammad of Jaunpur was the Mahdi opens an entirely new chapter in the history of Islamic messianism. The sayyid opened his mission with the claim to be the Mahdi in 1495 at Mecca while performing the circumambulation of the Kaʿbah. On his return to India he reasserted his claim in the major mosque of Tāj Khān Sālar at Ahmedabad, followed by a reiteration of the claim with renewed vigor and force in 1499 in a village called Barhli in Gujarat. In the hagiographical sources on him the names of his parents have been given as those of the parents of the Prophet, ʿAbd Allāh and Amīnah, in order to justify his claim to be the Mahdi. The Ḥanafī jurists of Gujarat challenged him to prove his claim and took effective steps to put a stop in his growing popularity. A *fatwā* was consequently drawn up in which he was denounced as a heretic and condemned to death. The reason for this extreme denunciation was due to the fact that his revolutionary socialistic-moral interpretation of Islam, which redressed the corruption in Indian Muslim society, was contrary to the orthodox Sunnī understanding of the faith.

A further example of the intensity and impact of the messianic ideology among the Sunnīs is found in the Mahdīyah movement of the Mahdi of Sudan, Muḥammad Aḥmad ibn ʿAbd Allāh, during the last two decades of the nineteenth century. The Mahdīyah have been regarded as the last eruption in the series of religiously inspired movements in the Sunnī world that led to the establishment of the *sharīʿah*-based states of the Wahhābīyah in Arabia, the Fulbe of Usman dan Fodio in Sokoto, and the Sanūsīyah in Cyrenaica. The Mahdi of Sudan consciously tried to establish the ideal rule of God on earth based on the paradigm of the Prophet's ideal community, engaging in *jihād* against the British and Ottoman-Egyptian forces. The movement was also inspired by the Ṣūfī philosophy of moral life and was based on Shīʿī messianic lore.

In Twelver Shiism, where the twelfth imam is believed to be the awaited Mahdi and to live in occultation, belief in messianism has served a complex, seemingly paradoxical function. It has been the guiding doctrine behind both an activist political posture, calling on believers to remain alert and prepared at all times to launch the revolution with the Mahdi who might appear at any time, and behind a quietist waiting for God's decree, in almost fatalistic resignation, in the matter of return of this imam at the End of Time. In both cases the main problem was to determine the right course of action at a given social and political setting. The adoption of the activist or quietist solution depended on the interpretation of conflicting traditions attributed to the Shīʿī imams about circumstances that justified radical action. Resolution of the contradiction in these traditions in turn was contingent on acknowledgment of and the existence of an authority who could undertake to make the imam's will known to the community. Without such a learned authority among the Shīʿīs, it was practically impossible to acquire knowledge about whether a radical solution was an appropriate form of struggle against an unjust government.

It was in this Shīʿī messianic context that in Iran ʿAlī Muḥammad of Shiraz who called himself the Bāb ("gateway"), at the turn of the millennium since the disappearance of the twelfth Imam in 874, proclaimed himself to be the "gateway" to esoteric knowledge and a reformer in 1844. He preached a new and quite unconventional *sharīʿah* and promised a new prophetic dispensation of social justice. His followers, the Bābīs, came into open conflict with the Shīʿī religious establishment and then with the Qājār government. ʿAlī Muḥammad was arrested and imprisoned. There followed riots and finally extensive revolt. ʿAlī Muḥammad was executed and the Bābī movement was suppressed with much bloodshed in 1852.

The Bahāʾī faith proclaimed by Bahāʾ Allāh in 1863 retained the social mission of the Bābīs and the cultural symbols of Shīʿī Iran, but abandoned its chiliastic overtones in favor of a more general conversion of the people around the globe by the followers of the new order. Late in the nineteenth century Mirzā Ghulām Aḥmad of Qādiān, who claimed to be the Mahdi, undertook to reform traditional Sunnī Islam and succeeded in building an effective social organization, with economic cooperatives and other exemplary establishments, restricted to benefit his followers. Whereas the Bābīs and the Bahāʾīs were seen as heretical movements by the Twelver Shīʿī religious establishment, the Aḥmadīyah sect represented a breach in the sense of unity among the Sunnī Muslims and their activities, with claims of a sort of prophethood for its founder, were regarded by the Sunnī religious establishment as divisive and sectarian. Thus, as evinced in both the Bahāʾī and Aḥmadīyah movements, heretical ideas were ostensibly and inherently part of the esoteric nature of messianic lore. Moreover, this esoteric lore tended to be potentially catastrophic as foretold in numerous traditions about the Signs of the Hour.

Recent Messianic Hopes. Both during the Iranian Revolution of 1978–1979 and the Gulf Crisis of 1990–1991, messianic traditions foretelling the apocalyptic events and describing the cataclysmic outcome of the world were in wide circulation in the Middle East, feeding on the hopes and fears of Muslims. Several attempts were made to fit Ayatollah Ruhollah Khomeini's return from Paris on 1 February 1979 to the chiliastic tradition that foretold the "rise of a sayyid from Qom, as a precursor to the Mahdi, among the descendants of Mūsā al-Kāzim (the seventh Shīʿī imam to whom Khomeini is lineally related) and will summon people to the right path" at the time of political and social turmoil in Iran. On 20 November 1979, the holiest shrine of Islam in Mecca experienced the rise of the Saudi Mahdi, Jahaymin al-ʿUtaybī, fulfilling the prophecy foretold in many traditions about rise of the messianic leader in the grand mosque of Mecca. The insurrection that was crushed mercilessly by the authorities posed the most formidable challenge to the worldly and corrupt rulers of the Saudi royal family. Similarly, a tradition predicting the rise of a man as strong as a *ṣādim* (rock) in the month of Rajab (February 1991), was mysteriously circulating among the Muslim masses in Jordan and the Occupied West Bank in support of Saddam Hussein as a promised victor of that month.

A book that was published symbolically in 1979 (1400 AH), and which has found eager readers in Lebanon, Iraq, and many other places in the Muslim world, deals with the relevance of the Islamic messianism as preserved in the Shīʿī tradition. Its title *Yawm al-khalāṣ fī ẓill al-Qāʾim al-Mahdī* (The Day of Deliverance under the Protection of the Twelfth Imam) serves as a reminder to many Muslim governments in the world today that the Muslim public still awaits the ideal Islamic order to be established where oppression and tyranny will be replaced, through apocalyptic divine intervention, by justice and equity. In other words, chiliastic hope in the return of the Mahdi among Muslim masses reflects their heightened sense of expectation and remains a latent source of challenge to moral complacency and political tyranny in Muslim governments.

[*See also* Aḥmadīyah; Bābism; Bahāʾī; Eschatology; Mahdi; Mahdīyah.]

BIBLIOGRAPHY

Hodgson, Marshall G. S. *The Order of the Assassins: The Struggle of the Early Nizari Ismaʿilis against the Islamic World.* The Hague, 1955.

Kechichian, Joseph A., "Islamic Revivalism and Change in Saudi Arabia: Juhayman al-ʿUtaybi's 'Letters' to the Saudi People." *The Muslim World* 80.1 (1990): 1–16.

Rizvi, S. A. A., "Mahdavi Movement in India," *Medieval India Quarterly* 51 (1950): 1–25.

Sachedina, A. A. *Islamic Messianism: The Idea of Mahdi in Twelver Shiʿism.* Albany, N.Y., 1981.

Sachedina, A. A. "Activist Shiʿism in Iran, Iraq, and Lebanon." In *Fundamentalisms Observed,* edited by Martin E. Marty and R. Scott Appleby, pp. 403–456. Chicago, 1991.

Sulaymān, Kamīl. *Yawm al-khalāṣ fī ẓill al-Qā'im al-Mahdī*. Beirut, 1400/1979.

Voll, John O., "Fundamentalism in the Sunni Arab World: Egypt and Sudan." In *Fundamentalisms Observed*, edited by Martin E. Marty and R. Scott Appleby, pp. 345–402. Chicago, 1991.

ABDULAZIZ SACHEDINA

METALWORK. Traditional Islamic metalwork techniques, shapes, decorations, hardstones, and gems continued into the nineteenth and twentieth centuries with the same conservative styles of the Ottoman, Ṣafavid, and Mughal dynasties and their adjoining regions. Beginning in the eighteenth century, French, Italian, and Russian designs and techniques had a great impact, while Western industry and imports adversely affected Muslim handicrafts.

Political and economic changes have been cited for the decline of patronage, but a wealth of skillfully handcrafted plate, base metals, gems, and jewelry survive from this period, despite the periodic reuse or melting down of jewelry and plate. The World's Fairs in the second half of the nineteenth century created an interest in the East, and both tourism and exports stimulated local craft production. Artisans always respected earlier traditions but were not hesitant to adapt some modern innovations. The bazaars of the Muslim countries still contain sections for jewelry and metalwork. In addition, some governments have revitalized craft production.

Gold was reserved for royalty and controlled by the state. Plain or gilded silver served the daily needs of the court, nobility, and the wealthy. Gifts of precious and nonprecious metal objects were made to religious shrines, mosques, and the Holy Cities, and turban ornaments were often important diplomatic gifts. Examples exist in the treasuries of the Topkapı Sarayı and Tehran, and at auction sales.

Plate and base metals were made from sheet, worked in different techniques, and were inlaid or enameled and sometimes set with gems. Champlevé enamel on gold in India favored geometric, floral, bird, and animal patterns. Painted enamel figural scenes and portraits on gold or silver are found in Iran. A sun face was a common feature in both countries. In Turkey, floral motifs were executed in painted and cloisonné enamel.

Classical, rococo, baroque, and European shapes and decor were found in Turkish plate. Trophy motifs, rose-filled baskets and vases, volutes, garlands, ribbons, acanthus, and pine cone and rose finials were adapted from European models in major Islamic areas. Traditionally, Bosnia was the source of silver worked mainly in Istanbul, Trabzon (Trebizond), and Erzerum. Assay and hallmarks were used in Turkey and Egypt, but generally not in Iran, India (except for colonial silver), or the Maghrib, though makers' names are sometimes found. Mughal silver abounds and reflects the synthesis of native Indian, Islamic, and European styles. Iranian silver in the twentieth century is an amalgam of native and European styles. Isfahan and Shiraz were major silversmithing centers. European tea and coffee services, candlesticks, place settings, candelabras, and cigarette cases were copied.

Vessels and architectural elements were made of bronze, iron, and steel, along with the preferred brass and copper, the latter sometimes tinned enameled. Objects could be undecorated, inlaid with gold or silver in geometric or floral patterns, with figural and animal elements common to Iran. Few pieces were inscribed or dated, and now plastic has replaced many domestic vessels; aluminum is used for architectural decor. Gilded copper was highly esteemed in Turkey. Silver and brass vessels, inlaid with niello and jewelry, were made in Erzerum and Van in eastern Anatolia and the Caucasus, where they are still produced.

In Egypt and Syria from the late nineteenth to the first quarter of this century, copper inlaid with silver and brass inlaid with gold, silver, or copper, imitating Mamlūk (1250–1517) models, were produced in Cairo and Damascus. Cairo designs were faithful to the originals, but in Damascus more imaginative designs were created. Many pieces carried inscriptions, workshop names, and dates. Misunderstood inscriptions, titles, design variations, gouged rather than chased metal, and the use of copper wire betrayed the copies. This revival of Mamlūk designs derived from Westerners, interested in the Middle East, who commissioned the pieces, which were then copied in Europe in glass and ceramics.

Production in India of bidri, a zinc alloy inlaid with silver or brass, increased in the second half of the nineteenth century, and antique and modern shapes were produced in many centers. Today the craft is practiced in Bihar and Hyderabad, Andhra Pradesh. Later production can be identified by the thin silver inlay and the crowded, repetitive classical flower pattern. Steel inlaid with gold and silver in geometric or floral designs was also made.

FIGURE 1. *Bottle and Stopper Inlaid with Silver.* Bidar, India, c.1850; Victoria and Albert Museum, London.

In Iran, forged steel vessels, inlaid with gold or silver or silvered or gilded, and inscribed with texts and names derived from its Ṣafavid predecessors, exist in great quantity. A pear-shaped vessel with long spout and curved handle was copied in eastern Iran in brass inlaid with turquoise, and inlaid brass in the Caucasus. Inlaid steel birds, animals, harpies, and fruit seemed to have been inspired by birds found on processional standards. Their function has not been explained.

For jewelry, gold and precious gems were generally used in urban areas, and silver and more modest gems in the countryside. Sheet, filigree, wire, granulation, champlevé, painted or cloisonné enamel, chasing and engraving, stones, and pearls were employed. Jewelry is still indispensable for dowries, and jewelers abound in the bazaars. Traditional head and body adornments are still worn by women. However, anklets are no longer in general fashion. Traditional jewelry has died out in some areas, especially in urban settings where modern Western designs have become popular. Jewelry has even been ordered directly from Europe. Ethnographers have made detailed studies on regional variations of folk jewelry, but court jewelry studies are lacking.

In India, settings of sheet gold, stone-set (nine gems) on lac, are still used. Jewelry styles illustrated in the Gentil album of 1774 in the Victoria and Albert Museum are still made and can be purchased in bazaars. The Indian tradition of placing enamel on the reverse of jewelry items probably set the fashion in Iran and, perhaps, in Turkey. Pearls abound until the end of Mughal rule in 1858. The fashion for heavily pearled costumes among the late Mughal rulers may have been introduced by the Persians.

In Iran, pearled bandoliers, armbands, jewelry, crowns, and clothing, combined with precious gems, were traditional until the change in mid-nineteenth century. Elongated domed- or half-moon earrings and bird pendants were common. At the turn of the nineteenth century, miniature portraits and European orders and medals were first worn in Iran, and later in Turkey, but apparently not in Mughal India. Hanging ornaments of precious metals and gems were made for the palace and religious buildings until the end of Ottoman rule.

FIGURE 2. *Steel Ewer, Gilded and Silvered.* Iran, nineteenth century; Metropolitan Museum of Art, New York.

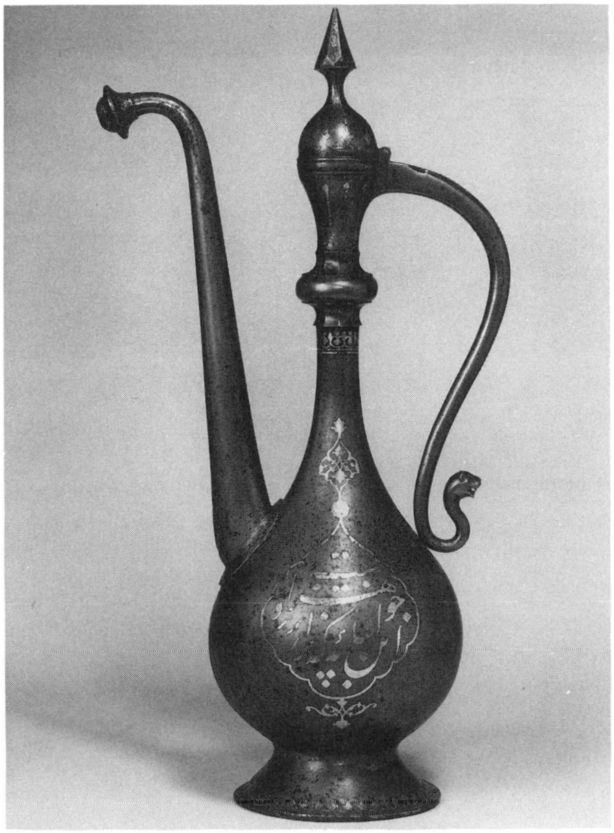

Precious and semiprecious stones included emerald, bloodstone, jade (inlaid with gold and gems in Turkey and India), rock crystal, garnet, turquoise, lapis lazuli, chalcedony, topaz, hematite, red and green jasper, amethyst, rose-cut and square diamonds, amber, spinels, rubies, garnet, sapphire, coral, and agate (the most common), as well as seed and baroque pearls, blue and green glass, plaster beads, imitation stones, and enamel-backed jewelry.

Many of these gemstones were used for seals, current until the mid-twentieth century, and talismans, but cornelian and agate predominated, as well as turquoise for talismans, which were also made in mother-of-pearl, quartz, metal, and jade. Bezels were made and mounted in precious and base metals and other materials, but bronze and brass were favored. Seals were also double-faced or cabochon-cut, and handled, bell-like signets exist in silver, gold, and enamel. Talismans were fashioned in a larger format than seals and carved in relief, differentiating them from seals, which were incised in reverse. Round, square, rectangular, oval, and the nineteenth-century teardrop bezel exist. The latter two shapes were the most popular. Talismans also had heart, shield, or cabochon shapes. Seals were carried in a bag placed in an inside pocket, suspended around the neck as a ring or hinged seal, or worn on the hand. Seals had political and social significance, indicating the investiture and power of a sultan or officeholder, and the wealth and social position of the owner, male or female. Traditionally they served to authenticate documents and ownership. Talismans, worn to protect or avert the evil eye, had metal mounts, sometimes enameled, and were worn as pendants, on armbands and bracelets, or sewn to clothing or bedding. The choice of stone and mount was personal, depending on wealth, local materials, magical properties, and qualities associated with the stone, and the text selected.

Inscriptions on seals contained Qur'ānic verses and religious formulas, including Shīʿī ones, but poetry, names, titles, dates, and engravers' names were included. Talismanic inscriptions were religious, rarely dated, and never contained personal names. Cursive and painted texts in Arabic, Turkish, or Persian were inscribed on plain, geometric, or floral and vegetal scrolls. Figures were rare, but the *tughrah* was used in Turkey. Maghribi script was used in that area. Combinations of talismanic formulas (i.e., words, letters, numerals) abound.

Gilded or nielloed silver or, rarely, gem-studded gold

FIGURE 3. *Silver Hanging Ornament.* Turkey, c.1876–1909; Museum of Turkish and Islamic Arts, Istanbul.

Qur'ānic amulet cases were made in hexagonal, octagonal, cylindrical, and triangular forms, and were decorated with incised floral scrolls.

BIBLIOGRAPHY

Content, Derek J., ed. *Islamic Rings and Gems: The Benjamin Zucker Collection.* London, 1987.

Edgü, Ferit, ed. *The Anatolian Civilisations: Istanbul, May 22–October 30, 1983.* Vol. 3. Istanbul, 1983.

Gluck, Jay, and Sumi Hiramoto Gluck, eds. *A Survey of Persian Handicraft: A Pictorial Introduction to the Contemporary Folk Arts and Art Crafts of Modern Iran.* Tehran, 1977.

Jenkins, Marilyn, and Manuel Keene. *Islamic Jewelry in the Metropolitan Museum of Art.* New York, 1983.

Meen, V. B., and A. D. Tushingham. *Crown Jewels of Iran.* Toronto, 1968.

Mughal Silver Magnificence (XVI–XIXth c.). London, 1987.

Rogers, J. M., ed. *The Topkapı Saray Museum: The Treasury.* Boston, 1987.

Scarce, Jennifer. "The Arts of the Eighteenth to Twentieth Centuries: Metalwork." In *The Cambridge History of Iran,* vol. 7, *From Nadir Shah to the Islamic Republic,* pp. 939–945. Cambridge, 1991.

Stronge, Susan. *Bidri Ware: Inlaid Metalwork from India.* London, 1985.

Stronge, Susan, Nima Smith, and James C. Harle. *A Golden Treasury: Jewellery from the Indian Subcontinent*. New York, 1988.
Türkische Kunst und Kultur aus osmanischer Zeit. Vol. 2. Recklinghausen, 1985.
Whelan, Estelle. *The Mamluk Revival: Metalwork for Religious and Domestic Use*. New York, 1982.

CAROLYN KANE

MEVLEVÎ. This Turkish/Ottoman Ṣūfī order, known also by its Arabic name Mawlawīyah, takes its name from the epithet of its founder Muḥammad Jalal al-Dīn Rūmī (1207–1273). He was the son of the famed scholar Bahā' al-Dīn Valad, and migrated as a child with his father from Balkh (in modern Afghanistan) to Konya in Rūm (modern Anatolia). Rūm was the capital of the Seljuk Empire, whose officials welcomed Bahā' al-Dīn and gave him the post of professor *(müderris)* in an institution of Islamic learning. In his early twenties Jalāl al-Dīn succeeded his father as teacher. The title "Mevlana" (Ar., *mawlānā*, "our master") by which Rūmī became known to later generations is a token of his brilliance not only in emulating his father but in surpassing him in the exposition of the spiritual and esoteric teachings of Islam. In contrast with the legalistic Islamic thinkers of his time, Rūmī was able through his poetic treatment of mysticism to attract a wider and more permanent audience. He also laid the foundations for an Islamic humanism that endured until the secularization of learning in twentieth-century Turkey. Rūmī's elaboration of the mystical "path of love" has attracted a number of Muslims in modern Turkey and Iran and has also stirred interest in his thoughts in the West. This has resulted in translations from the original Persian into Turkish and Western European languages of his works, including the *Dīvān*, the *Maṣnavī*, and the *Fīhi mā fīhi*.

The disciples of Mevlana became organized at the time of Rūmī's son Sulṭān Valad (d. 1312). The order, known as that of the Mevlevî dervishes, spread through Anatolia and other parts of the Ottoman Empire. All Mevlevî lodges *(tekke)* were responsible to a *çelebi* who resided in Konya and was chosen from among Mevlana's descendants. The influence of the order grew in spite of the *ʿulamā*'s interdiction of the teaching of Persian—the language of Rūmī's poetry—in *madrasah*s, the centers of Islamic instruction. The Mevlevîs' influence attracted the attention of the Ottoman government, which was suspicious of potential rivals to the state. Only with the government's control of the pious foundations that provided the income of the order was the situation stabilized.

Another aspect of the Mevlevîs' political role was their attempt to achieve influence in palace circles beginning in the seventeenth century. They finally seem to have secured this role during the nineteenth century, when they figured as "girders of the sword" at the enthronements of the of Ottoman sultans. In these years they received the support of Sultan Abdülmecid (r. 1839–1861) and (with some caution) of Sultan Abdülhamid II (r. 1876–1909) and Sultan Mehmed V (r. 1909–1918). Mevlevî lodges acted as cultural centers in Ottoman cities and were a key influence in the development of Ottoman upper-class culture. Some Mevlevî leaders are known to have been sympathetic to the Young Turks. Along with all other religious orders, they were disbanded in Turkey in 1925.

The Mevlevîs became well known to Europeans through their unorthodox use of music and dance, a feature they shared with the Bektāshī order, thus acquiring the name "whirling dervishes." Although the lodges were closed after 1925, their ceremonial practices were allowed again after 1950, and a yearly Mevlevî celebration now takes place in Konya. The attendance of a much wider audience at these tourist-oriented performances may not lower the quality of Mevlevî ceremonies, but it certainly detracts from its original mystical substance.

[*For additional information on the order, see* Mawlawīyah.]

BIBLIOGRAPHY

Berkes, Niyazi. *Türkiye'de çağdaşlaşma* (Modernization in Turkey). Istanbul, 1978.
Chittick, William C. *The Sufi Path of Love*. Albany, N.Y., 1983.
Friedlander, Shems. *The Whirling Dervishes*. 2d ed. Albany, N.Y., 1991.
Gölpınarlı, Abdülbâki. *Mevlânâ'dan Sonra Mevlevîlik* (The Mevlevî Order after the Time of Rūmī). 2d ed. Istanbul, 1983.
Inalcık, Halil. *The Ottoman Empire: The Classical Age 1500–1600*. London, 1973.
Pakalın, Mehmet Zeki. *Osmanlı Tarih Deyimleri ve Terimleri Sözlüğü* (Dictionary of the Expressions and Terminology of Ottoman History). 3 vols. 2d ed. Istanbul, 1971.

ŞERIF MARDIN

MILITARY FORCES. Warfare was central to the early history of Islam. The doctrine of *jihād*, or holy war, affirms that the true faith can be spread by conquest as well as by conversion; "commander of the faithful" *(amīr al-mu'minīn)* was one of the titles of the caliphs; and the territories ruled by Muslims and the regions beyond their borders were referred to, respectively, as the "house of Islam" *(dār al-Islām)* and the "house of war" *(dār-al-ḥarb)*.

In the century after the prophet Muḥammad, Muslim armies extended the realm of the caliphs from the Arabian Peninsula to Spain, Central Asia, and the Indian subcontinent. By the tenth century CE that empire had begun to fall apart, but Islam continued to spread by trade or military conquest as far as Mongolia, Indonesia, and parts of sub-Saharan Africa.

Ottoman and Colonial Legacies. By the fourteenth century the Ottoman Empire emerged as the most powerful of Islamic states, at its peak in the sixteenth century stretching from Hungary to Yemen and the Sudan and from the Caucasus to Algeria. The military remained at the very center of the Ottoman ruling establishment not only during its rise (1453–1683) but also after a century of defeats on its European frontiers and in Egypt (1683–1798). Those defeats spurred efforts to modernize the Ottoman military forces by bringing in European experts, such as Italian naval and Prussian army officers, or by sending Ottoman subjects for military training in Paris. The modernized armed forces soon required further administrative and educational reforms, culminating in the Tanzimat reforms of the mid-nineteenth century.

The newly westernized Ottoman officer corps had a wide base of recruitment in the empire's Islamic population, particularly in its Turkish-speaking regions from the Balkans to Anatolia; by the late nineteenth century military careers had become the most conspicuous channel for advancement by merit within the empire's social structure. Even when Sultan Abdülhamid II (r. 1876–1909) reversed most of the westernizing policies of the Tanzimat, he continued them in the military sector—a development that only pushed the officers further into the vanguard of westernization and into politics. The New Ottoman (or "Young Turk") revolution of 1908–1909, which deposed Abdülhamid II and reestablished the representative constitution of 1876, began with a conspiracy of middle-ranking officers in the Committee of Union and Progress (CUP). Growing disputes among Ottoman Turkish and Arab nationalists and defeats in the Balkan Wars of 1912–1913 prompted the CUP to transform that constitutional government into a military and party dictatorship.

By the nineteenth century most non-Ottoman Muslim countries had been incorporated into European colonial empires, including Central Asia (Russia), Indonesia (the Netherlands), and the Muslim parts of India (Britain). Colonial partition was soon extended to the Arab parts of the Ottoman Empire, including Algeria and Tunisia (occupied by France in 1830 and 1881), Egypt (placed under "temporary" British occupation from 1882 to 1946 and, along the Suez Canal, until 1956), Libya (conquered by Italy in 1912), and the Fertile Crescent from Palestine to Iraq (placed under British and French "mandates" in 1920–1921). By the 1920s Turkey, Saudi Arabia, Yemen, Iran, and Afghanistan were the only independent Islamic countries. Elsewhere in the Islamic world, from Mauritania to Pakistan and Indonesia, political independence was not reestablished until the European imperial withdrawal in the wake of World War II—or, in the Central Asian region from Azerbaijan to Kyrghyzstan, until the collapse of the Soviet Union in 1991. In both the post-Ottoman and post-colonial regions of the Islamic world, there resulted a political vacuum in which the military came to play a major political role; however, the specific patterns of military politics have been far from uniform.

Turkey from Independence to Democratization. In Turkey, which inherited most of the Ottoman officer corps, the military in 1919 organized a successful war of independence to counter a Greek invasion and Allied plans for further partition of the remnants of the defeated empire. Initially there was much disagreement within the independence movement between those loyal to Ottoman or Islamic traditions and those aspiring to Turkish (or pan-Turkic) nationhood. Hence the movement's leader Mustafa Kemal Pasha (later known as Atatürk) was careful to create a united political resistance, including representatives elected throughout the unoccupied parts of the country, bureaucrats and politicians who had fled from occupied Istanbul, and local *'ulamā'*. A "National Assembly" was convened in Ankara in 1920 without specifying the name of the nation it was to represent, and the Republic of Turkey was proclaimed only after the country's independence was internationally recognized by the peace treaty signed at Lausanne in 1923. Only in the following decade (1924–1935) did the Kemalist movement introduce secularizing reforms. [*See* Kemalism *and the biography of Atatürk.*]

Although the first presidents of the Turkish Republic, Kemal Atatürk (1923–1938) and Ismet Inönü (1938–

1950), had been military leaders in the war of independence, their Republican People's Party provided them with a broad civilian base. In its foreign policy, Ankara cultivated good relations with all neighbors, including the Soviet Union and even Greece, and pursued a careful course of neutrality in World War II. By the late 1940s Turkey's armed forces were vastly expanded in response to Moscow's threats that initiated the Cold War, and in 1952 Turkey became a member of NATO. Nonetheless, Turkey has not been at war since 1923, except for participation in the United Nations operation in Korea (1950–1953), military intervention on Cyprus in 1974, and support for the Allied action against Iraq in 1990–1991.

It was in the Cold War context and on President Inönü's initiative that Turkey in the late 1940s entered a period of transition from one-party dictatorship to multiparty democracy. In the following decades, as the country faced successive problems of reversion to authoritarianism, prolonged political stalemates, and rampant terrorism, the military intervened three times (1960–1961, 1971–1973, and 1980–1983). Government by civilian elections was restored after each military coup; and, since the 1987 referendum that readmitted all former party leaders banned by the military in 1982, democracy seems well established and renewed military intervention very unlikely.

Military Coups in the Post-Imperial Vacuum. In contrast to Turkey, military rule at home and external wars ending in defeat abroad have been the prevailing pattern in other post-Ottoman countries. Algeria is an exception among Arab countries in having fought a prolonged war of independence (1954–1962); political rifts soon developed in the independence movement, however, and military rule has been a recurrent pattern from the time of the 1965 coup by General Houari Boumédienne. In many other Arab countries military coups overthrew the governments left behind by European imperial powers. Thus after Iraq was released from its status as a British mandate in 1932, a military coup in 1936 was followed by six more in the next five years. In Syria, where the French withdrew in 1946, three military coups ensued in 1949. In Egypt, from most of which the British withdrew in 1946, the "Free Officers" under General Muḥammad Najīb (Mohammed Naguib) and Gamal Abdel Nasser seized power in 1952.

Other landmark military coups in post-colonial Arab or Islamic countries were those by Marshal Ayub Khan in Pakistan in 1958, General Suharto in Indonesia in 1966, and Muʿammar al-Qadhdhāfī in Libya in 1967. In Iran, along with Turkey and Saudi Arabia one of the few Muslim countries never to come under European colonial rule, Colonel Reza Pahlavi seized power in 1921, had himself proclaimed Shah in 1925, and passed the throne on to his son Muhammad Reza (1941–1979).

Militarization of the Middle East. These military coups followed what became a widespread pattern in the Third World, arising out of the power vacuum after the imperialists' departure and the unpopularity of the collaborationist governments they left behind. In the Middle East the pattern was reinforced by the Cold War, the Arab-Israeli conflict, the OPEC price revolution, and the lack of clear national identities in the Arab world.

The Cold War began with Soviet territorial demands against Turkey late in 1945 and Washington's response in the Truman Doctrine of 1947; soon Turkey built up the largest military forces in NATO except for those of the United States. In 1955 Nasser's Egypt set a dramatic precedent by importing weapons from the Soviet bloc, which in the following decades also supplied arms to Iraq, Syria, Libya, and South Yemen; the West countered with weapons exports to Israel, Pakistan, and Iran. Growing oil revenues led to a quadrupling of Middle Eastern military expenditures in the 1960s and a further tripling in the 1970s. The continuing Arab-Israeli conflict—erupting into full-scale war in 1948–1949, 1956, 1967, and 1973—also meant that the weapons supplied by the Cold War arms race were more likely to be used in the Middle East than elsewhere in the Third World. (For a summary of military expenditures, size of armed forces, and weapons imports of Middle Eastern countries, see Table 1.)

Although the Arab countries proved to be militarily weaker in all these encounters with Israel, their defeats further accentuated the political role of the military. Most notably, the initial defeat in 1948–1949 destroyed the slender base of popularity of the post-imperial governments and led to the military coups in Syria in 1949 and Egypt in 1952.

The only Arab countries where military forces have played no major political role are the hereditary monarchies, including Morocco, Jordan, Saudi Arabia, and the oil shaykhdoms from Kuwait to Oman. Indeed, the massive arms purchases by Saudi Arabia did not ensure its defense; if it had not been for the U.S.-led military intervention in 1991, that country would probably have

TABLE 1. *Military Manpower, Expenditures, and Imports of Selected Islamic Countries, 1985–1991*

COUNTRY	DEFENSE EXPENDITURES $ MILLION 1985	1991	% OF GDP 1985	1991	NUMBERS IN ARMED FORCES (IN THOUSANDS) 1985	1991	IMPORTS OF CONVENTIONAL WEAPONS, 1987–1991 (IN $ MILLIONS, 1990 PRICES)
Afghanistan	287	n.k.	8.7	n.k.	47.0	45.0	8,430
Algeria	953	971	1.7	1.4	170.0	139.0	1,009
Egypt	4,143	3,582	8.5	7.5	445.0	410.0	5,460
Indonesia	2,341	1,739	2.8	1.3	278.1	283.0	1,429
Iran	14,223	4,270	8.6	7.1	305.0	528.0	2,862
Iraq	12,868	7,490[a]	25.9	21.1[a]	520.0	382.5	10,320
Jordan	523	594	12.8	14.1	70.3	98.3	616
Kuwait	1,796	7,959	9.1	33.0	12.0	11.7	1,114
Libya	1,350	1,177[a]	n.k.	6.3	73.0	85.0	1,101
Malaysia	1,764	1,670	5.6	3.7	110.0	125.0	105
Morocco	641	730	5.4	4.3	149.0	195.5	551
Nigeria	1,251	814	1.3	0.8	94.0	76.0	373
Oman	2,157	1,182	20.8	12.3	2.5	35.7	602
Pakistan	2,076	3,014	6.9	7.0	482.8	580.0	2,299
Saudi Arabia	17,693	35,438	19.6	33.8	62.5	102.0	10,597
Somalia	46	n.k.	n.k.	n.k.	62.7	64.5	13
Sudan	207	222[a]	3.4	2.1[a]	56.6	82.5	228
Syria	3,483	3,095	16.4	13.0	402.5	408.0	3,447
Tunisia	417	323	5.0	3.3	35.1	35.0	65
Turkey	1,649	2,014	4.5	3.1	630.0	579.2	6,386
United Arab Emirates	2,043	4,249	7.6	14.6	43.0	54.5	1,790
Yemen[b]	792	910	8.9	13.1	64.1	63.5	367

[a] 1990 figures. [b] North and South Yemen combined. n.k. = not known.

SOURCES. For defense expenditures and armed forces: International Institute of Strategic Studies, *The Military Balance 1992–1993* (London, 1993), pp. 218–221; for arms imports: Stockholm International Peace Research Institute, *World Armaments and Disarmament: SIPRI Yearbook 1992* (London, 1993), pp. 311–314.

been overrun by Saddam Hussein's aggression as was Kuwait in 1990.

Identity Conflicts and Regional and Civil Wars. Another major factor in the growing role of the military has been a lack of clear political-geographic identity. The division of Arabic-speaking peoples among two dozen separate states has inspired resonant appeals to Pan-Arabism and, as in nineteenth-century Italy and Germany, strong temptations to resolve the problem by force. Thus Nasser after his military coup in 1954 proclaimed a United Arab Republic with Syria (1955–1958), although the scheme fell apart as soon as economic implementation was attempted. Similar appeals to Pan-Arabism came from aggressive military dictators such as Libya's Muʿammar al-Qadhdhāfī in the 1960s and 1970s, and Iraq's Saddam Hussein in justifying his invasions of Iran (launched first into the Arabic-speaking region of Khuzistan) and Kuwait. [*See* Arab Nationalism *and the biographies of Nasser and Qadhdhāfī.*]

Considering the close historic connection between Islam and the modern Arabic language, which was largely shaped by the Qurʾān, it is not surprising that Islamic movements also play an active role in this identity crisis. Thus Egypt's Muslim Brotherhood (al-Ikhwān al-Muslimīn) was organized by Ḥasan al-Bannāʾ as early as 1929, and Islamist opposition has been a major problem for the government of Hosni Mubarak in the 1980s and 1990s. The clash between the military and the Islamists has been sharpest in Algeria, where military intervention annulled the 1992 election victory of the Islamic Salvation Front.

Internal ethnic or religious divisions also have contributed to this militarization of Middle Eastern politics. Thus in Syria under the French mandate, most military officers were recruited from the ʿAlawī minority, amounting to about 13 percent of the total population, rather than from the Sunnī majority; it was this ʿAlawī officer corps that has established itself as the ruling elite in Hafez al-Assad's dictatorship since 1970. In Iraq there is sharp social and political cleavage among the ruling Sunnī-Arab minority, the Shīʿī-Arab majority, and the Kurdish-Sunnī minority; and although Saddam Hussein was not a professional officer, his Baʿth Party has long relied on Sunnī-Arab military forces for its major political support.

Religious divisions have been sharpest in Lebanon, where the multidenominational system of representation developed under the French mandate fell apart in civil war in 1958 and again in 1975–1976; Sunnīs, Shīʿīs, Maronites, Druze, and other religious groups developed their own armed forces, and outside powers such as the U.S. (1958, 1983), Israel (1978, 1981–83), and most decisively Syria intervened from time to time. A similar pattern of civil war developed in Afghanistan in the 1970s and 1980s, with warfare among ethnic or tribal groups aggravated by Soviet military intervention and covert U.S. support for Pakistan-based Islamist groups. Somalia since its independence in 1960 has imported arms first from the Soviet bloc and later also from the West, which in a context of weak government structure merely fueled the conflicts among tribal warlords.

Present Trends and Future Prospects. Although military rule has been the prevalent form of government in much of the Muslim world in recent decades, it should be noted that there has been an increasing pattern of stability. Thus in Egypt, although all presidents since 1953 have been of military background, there were peaceful and orderly successions in 1970 and 1981. Moreover, despite the many wars in the region, it is remarkable how few boundary changes have occurred in the Middle East since the unification of Najd and Hejaz into Saudi Arabia in 1926.

There are obvious dangers of renewed international crises, such as the continuing conflicts in Afghanistan and Somalia, the aggressive stance of Iran since the 1979 revolution of Ayatollah Ruhollah Khomeini, and above all the continuing military conflicts in the former Soviet republics from Abkhazia and Armenia-Azerbaijan to Tajikistan. Still, there are opposite trends that might reduce the importance of the military in the politics of Middle Eastern and other Islamic countries.

The end of the Cold War and the collapse of the Soviet Union are likely to reduce the competitive flow of arms into the region. Turkey seems secure in its transition to democracy and eager to act as a liberal-democratic role model for Central Asian states. Moves toward Arab-Israeli peace, from the Camp David agreement of 1979 between Egypt and Israel to that between Israel and the Palestine Liberation Organization in 1993, may move the political pattern of the Middle East from military competition toward economic cooperation. It should also be noted that Anwar Sadat's courageous moves to peace with Israel (1977–1979) in effect put Egyptian national interests above Nasser's Pan-Arabism. Similarly, the failure of the Pan-Arab aspirations of Nasser and Qadhdhāfī, and most recently the defeat of Saddam Hussein's aggressive wars, may presage a consolidation of political identities and loyalties within separate states—as occurred in nineteenth-century Latin America—and may thus provide a further incentive toward demilitarization.

[*See also the entries on individual countries mentioned.*]

BIBLIOGRAPHY

Brown, L. Carl. *International Politics and the Middle East: Old Rules, Dangerous Game*. Princeton, 1984. Suggestive analysis of forces making for conflict and regional balance from the 1870s to 1967.

Cordesman, Anthony H. *After the Storm: The Changing Military Balance in the Middle East*. Boulder, 1993. Detailed survey of weapons inventories from Morocco to Iran and Somalia.

Fisher, Sydney N., ed. *The Military in the Middle East*. Columbus, Ohio, 1963. Early analysis of the domestic and international role of the military in the Middle East since World War II.

Freedman, Robert O. *Moscow and the Middle East: Soviet Policy since the Invasion of Afghanistan*. Cambridge, 1991. Concise summary and analysis focusing on the 1980s.

Hourani, Albert. *A History of the Arab Peoples*. Cambridge, 1992. Scholarly and readable political-cultural history from the days of Muḥammad to the 1980s.

Hurewitz, J. C. *Middle East Politics: The Military Dimension*. New York, 1969. Excellent account of the militarization of politics and society from late Ottoman to Cold War days.

Khouri, Fred J. *The Arab-Israeli Dilemma*. 2d ed. Syracuse, N.Y., 1976. Analysis of the Israeli-Palestinian conflict from mandate days to 1973, including international efforts at settlement.

Lewis, Bernard. *The Emergence of Modern Turkey*. 2d ed. London and New York, 1968. Scholarly and readable political and cultural history of Turkey from the late Ottoman to the Kemalist periods.

Lenczowski, George. *The Middle East in World Affairs*. 4th ed. Ithaca, N.Y., 1980. Detailed scholarly summary of the region's domestic and international politics, especially from 1914 to 1945.

Nasser, Gamal Abdel. *Egypt's Liberation: The Philosophy of the Revolution.* Washington, D.C., 1955. Vivid memoir of the frustrations of defeat by Israel, leading to the seizure of power in the 1952 coup.

Parry, V. J., and M. E. Yapp, eds. *War, Technology, and Society in the Middle East.* London, 1975. Scholarly essays on the place of the military and of warfare in the modern Middle East.

Rustow, Dankwart A. *Oil and Turmoil: America Faces OPEC and the Middle East.* New York, 1982. Analysis of U.S. policy, focusing on oil interests and the Arab-Israeli conflict.

Rustow, Dankwart A. *Turkey: America's Forgotten Ally.* New York, 1987. Account of Turkey's sociopolitical and cultural scene, including its struggle for democracy.

DANKWART A. RUSTOW

MILLET. This term is most commonly used in Islamic history to mean "religious community." It is derived from the Arabic word *millah,* which was employed in the Qur'ān to mean "religion." Later the Qur'ānic usage was extended to include religious community and especially the community of Islam. By the time of the Ottoman Empire (1300–1918) its sense had expanded widely to include non-Muslim religious communities and, in the period of Ottoman decline, foreign merchants who entered the empire under special treaties called capitulations. During the nineteenth century a fundamental change in its usage occurred when the concept of nationalism entered the empire and Ottomans used the word to mean both "religious community" and "nation." With the collapse of the empire in 1918 and the division of its territories into nation-states, *millet* acquired its modern Turkish meaning of "nation," with only a vestige of the old religious sense.

The system of *millet*s was the institutional means by which the agriculturally based empires of Islam accommodated religious diversity. Its religious foundation rested on the concept of Islam as the culmination of a prophetic tradition emanating from Judaism and Christianity. Since Jews and Christians would eventually see the truth of Islam, their place in an Islamic society became one of subordinate and protected religious communities. Over centuries of expansion into non-Muslim lands the application of this institution created an elaborate structure of fairly autonomous communities whose religious leaders developed formal relations with the rulers of Muslim empires in a manner that guaranteed imperial peace at the price of religious and social fragmentation.

What completely transformed the Islamic system of handling religious diversity was the importation into the Muslim world of nationalism. This political ideology was brought into the Ottoman Empire and other Muslim areas from Europe in the nineteenth century, largely by non-Muslims, and was introduced to populations that had no previous experience with the separation of politics from religion or with the secular ideas associated with the European Enlightenment. It therefore followed that national movements, if they were to have any social basis at all, quickly became embedded in the *millet* system; and where Europeans did not establish a colonial regime, they had the opportunity to split up Islamic states along religious lines.

By the turn of the twentieth century the successes—and even the failures—of national movements within the Ottoman Empire had all but destroyed the idea of religious coexistence. Meanwhile, the political supremacy available to a centralizing, industrial European nation-state capable of mobilizing its culturally homogeneous populations encouraged national ideas to spread among the Ottoman elite. In this same period, Ottoman intellectuals became aware of the pre-Islamic history of the Turks. Alienated from an ineffectual government and armed with the image of a glorious national past, young army officers developed the foundation for Turkish nationalism during the last hours of the empire. When World War I resulted in the collapse of the Ottoman Empire (1918) and the rise of a Turkish opposition under Mustafa Kemal Atatürk to the dismemberment of the core, Turkish-speaking regions of the empire, a Turkish elite appeared with a new politics and a new social framework for which the language was national rather than religious. Under these conditions the word *millet* came, after 1923, to mean "nation" in modern Turkish.

[*See also* Capitulations; Dhimmī; Nation; Ottoman Empire; *and* Pan-Turanism.]

BIBLIOGRAPHY

Berkes, Niyazi. *The Development of Secularism in Turkey.* Montreal, 1964. Excellent study of the ideological transformation of Ottoman thought from medieval to modern worldviews.

Findley, Carter V. *Bureaucratic Reform in the Ottoman Empire: The Sublime Porte, 1789–1922.* Princeton, 1980. The best study of bureaucratic reform in the Ottoman Empire during the period of the impact of European ideas.

Jennings, Ronald. "Zimmis (Non-Muslims) in Early Seventeenth-Century Ottoman Judicial Records: The Sharia Court of Anatolian

Kayseri." *Journal of the Economic and Social History of the Orient* 21.3 (April 1978): 226–293. Excellent study of the absence of *millet* structures at local levels in rural Anatolia during the period before the impact of nationalism.

Lewis, Bernard. *The Emergence of Modern Turkey*. London, 1961. The major work on the subject.

Shaw, Stanford J., and Ezel Kural Shaw. *History of the Ottoman Empire and Modern Turkey*, vol. 2, *Reform, Revolution, and Republic: The Rise of Modern Turkey, 1808–1975*. London and New York, 1977. The most detailed study of the fall of the empire and the rise of modern Turkey.

ANDREW C. HESS

MILLÎ NIZAM PARTISI. *See* Refâh Partisi.

MILLÎ SELAMET PARTISI. *See* Refâh Partisi.

MINORITIES. [*This entry comprises two articles. The first is a historical survey of the status and treatment of non-Muslim minorities (principally Jews and Christians) in Muslim societies; the second considers the position of Muslim minorities in non-Muslim societies.*]

Minorities in Muslim Societies

The status and treatment of minorities in Muslim societies (or, more generally, under Islam) has always been of special concern to outside powers seeking to establish themselves as their protectors. It has also been a favorite subject of Western Orientalists. Non-Muslim neighbors and observers in the modern age no longer content themselves with traditional notions of tolerance and the absence of persecution, but expect full social, political, and legal equality of Muslims and non-Muslims. Their critical regard has not failed to call forth strong reactions from many Muslims who try to show that on this score, too, Islam has in fact a much better record than other civilizations, particularly the West. The subject therefore continues to be sensitive, raising considerable controversy.

Classical Legal Doctrines. The status and treatment of non-Muslims in Muslim societies (or in the *dār al-Islām*) have varied greatly over time and space. Legal theory has never been uniform throughout the Muslim world and has often been rather far removed from practice. Traditional rules and regulations clearly show the impact of history, particularly the experience of the Prophet and the conditions of Muslim conquest. Whereas relations between Muḥammad, his followers, and their pagan neighbors had almost from the outset been tense, if not openly hostile, relations with the Jews and Christians of the Arabian Peninsula passed through phases of understanding and cooperation to growing distrust, animosity, and finally confrontation.

Muḥammad had originally hoped to be acknowledged as Prophet by the guardians of the monotheist traditions. After his move (the Hijrah) to Medina in 622, the Muslims entered into a formal alliance with the local Jewish and heathen tribes, which was documented in the so-called Constitution (*ṣaḥīfah*) of Medina, granting all allies internal autonomy with Muḥammad acting as supreme head and arbiter of the newly established community. When recognition of his prophethood was denied and when, under pressure, the political loyalty of the Jewish tribes appeared to be in doubt, Muḥammad turned against them until they had been either expelled or killed. By the time of the Battle of Badr (624), the brief spell of political collaboration and unity had ended. Yet in spite of its limited historical relevance and validity, the Constitution of Medina has come to be widely regarded by contemporary Muslims as the blueprint or model of a political community (*ummah*) that is based on the Qur'ān and includes as its citizens both Muslims and non-Muslims.

Mirroring the concerns of the young and vulnerable community, the Qur'ān touches repeatedly on the question of whether it is lawful for Muslims to entertain friendly relations (*muwālāt*) with unbelievers. The guiding principle (see surahs 3.28, 5.51, 29.46 and 60.8–9) is that the believers should treat the unbelievers decently and equitably as long as the latter do not act aggressively toward them. A reactive principle linking the treatment of non-Muslims to their behavior toward the Muslims, this clearly reflects the conditions of the early period, when the Muslims were still a small minority facing large and partly hostile non-Muslim majorities.

The reactive principle appears less prominently in the provisions of Islamic law (*fiqh*). Underneath the rigid divide between *dār al-Islām* and *dār al-ḥarb* (non-Muslim lands) concerning territory, and between Muslims and non-Muslims concerning people, one finds the fine distinctions characteristic of Islamic legal reasoning. The basic distinction was between the pagans, idolaters, or polytheists (sg., *kāfir*) on the one hand, with whom there was to be no social intercourse, ranging from shared food to intermarriage, and who were to be fought until they either converted or were killed or enslaved; and the 'people of the book' *(ahl al-kitāb)* on the other, whose faith was founded on revelation, who were to be granted protection, and with whom social intercourse was allowed. In the course of Muslim conquest and expansion, their numbers were enlarged beyond the Jews, Sabaeans, and Christians mentioned in the Qur'ān to include the Zoroastrians (Majūs) and eventually the Buddhists and others.

The Ḥanafī law school extended protection to non-Arab pagans, and Mālik ibn Anas (d. 796), founder of the Mālikī school, even included Arab polytheists provided that they did not belong to the clan of the Prophet, the Quraysh. As a result, the category of polytheists was steadily reduced until, in the modern era, it had lost all practical relevance. At the same time, the state of those monotheist groups (e.g., the Bahā'īs in Iran or the Aḥmadīyah/Qādiānīs in India and Pakistan) that developed after Islam and were regarded by the respective Muslim majorities as renegades or apostates (sg., *murtadd*) remained precarious. In legal theory, they had to be fought until they either repented and (re-) converted or were killed.

The status of the "people of the book" was secured by a contract of protection *(dhimmah)*, which in principle was unlimited and which, in accordance with the Qur'ānic injunction, "No compulsion in religion" (surah 2.256), guaranteed their life, body, property, freedom of movement, and religious practice (if carried on discreetly). Protection was granted against the payment of tribute, dues, and taxes of various kinds. Out of these dues and taxes two main categories evolved, without, however, being consistently defined: a land tax *(kharāj)* often to be paid in kind, which soon came to be imposed on all owners of land thus categorized irrespective of their religious affiliation; and a poll tax *(jizyah)* levied on all able-bodied free adult *dhimmī* males of sufficient means. The various law schools varied considerably as to the precise definition of the legal rights and obligations of the protected people (*dhimmīs*). The most liberal among the Sunnī schools was the Ḥanafī one (dominant in the Ottoman Empire among other places), which granted *dhimmīs* equal rights with regard to property and parts of criminal law (notably *diyah*, or blood money), but not in the domains of family law, inheritance, or testimony.

The primary aim of all practical measures and legal provisions seems originally to have been to mark unmistakably the boundary between Muslims and non-Muslims. Basing themselves on the notoriously unclear text of surah 9.29 (". . . and fight the infidels until they pay the *jizyah* out of their hands while they are small/humble"), Muslim jurists tended to translate the submission of non-Muslims to Muslim rule into the requirement of humbleness and humiliation. Prevailing norms and expectations were mirrored in the so-called Pact of ʿUmar *(al-shurūṭ al-ʿumarīyah)*, attributed to the second caliph, ʿUmar ibn al-Khaṭṭāb (r. 634–644), but probably not formulated before the eighth century. This laid down a number of restrictions regarding dress and hairstyle, worship, the construction and repairing of churches and synagogues, the height of houses, the use of animals, and so forth, which served not only to identify the *dhimmīs*, but also to discriminate against them. Shīʿī thought and law went further in that it considered non-Muslims to be ritually impure *(najis)*, thereby banning (at least theoretically) social intercourse and intermarriage altogether.

Practice. Practice, however, frequently did not conform to the restrictive notions of the *ʿulamā'* (religious scholars). The actual situation of the *dhimmīs* was more closely conditioned by the economic and political circumstances prevailing within the various Islamic territories and by their relations with the major non-Muslim powers of the day, a correlation still largely valid in the modern age. Yet until well into the twentieth century, the legal norms essentially retained their normative force, and if at any specific moment the *dhimmīs* or individual members of their elites did in fact enjoy better conditions than those prescribed by the jurists, it was condemned as a deviation from how things ought to be. Umayyad Spain and Fāṭimid Egypt are widely seen as the golden age of harmonious coexistence among Muslims, Christians, and Jews, which mutually enriched their cultures and heritage. If from the thirteenth century onward, intercommunal relations deteriorated, it has been attributed to the impact of the Mongol invasion rather than the Christian crusades. By that time, the gradual spread of Islam had reduced the *dhimmī* populations of the Middle East from majorities to minorities. Still, community structures were left basically intact.

In return for submission to Muslim rule, non-Muslims enjoyed considerable autonomy in the fields of personal-status law, worship, and education, forming largely self-contained units with their separate religious, legal, social, educational, and charitable institutions. Although there was in most parts no forced segregation in terms of residence or occupation (Morocco and Iran at certain periods excepted), there was often professional specialization, which has been characterized by modern scholars as "ethnoreligious division of labor." Non-Muslims fulfilled complementary economic roles and functions, some of which were regarded as undesirable, lowly, or unclean by Muslims. Most important, non-Muslims were incorporated into Muslim society not as individuals, but as members of their religious communities. The principle found its clearest expression in the Ottoman *millet* system (derived from the Turkish term for ethnoreligious group or community) as it had evolved by the nineteenth century. It exerted administrative control through a number of legally recognized religious communities (notably the Greek Orthodox and Armenian Christians as well as the Rabbanite Jews) headed by their clergy with autonomy compensating for the absence of equal status and the denial of political rights.

In the nineteenth century, European influence and expansion, internal migration, social differentiation, and cultural change began to affect the *dhimmīs*' legal status, communal organization, and place in society. The Ottoman reform edicts of the Tanzimat period (issued in 1839 and 1856) proclaimed the principle of legal equality between Muslims and non-Muslims and replaced the *jizyah* by general conscription or the payment of an exemption tax *(bedel-i asker)*. Religious personal-status law as a powerful marker of communal separateness, however, was retained. Within the Ottoman and Persian empires, European powers assumed the role of protector of specific religious communities. Individual Christians and Jews managed to benefit from increased educational and economic opportunities, gaining access to legal protection (foreign passports) and privilege (under the system of capitulations). Within the various communities, a rising commercial and professional middle class began to challenge the rule of the clergy and notables. The communities as a whole broke out of the place assigned to them under the old order. But sociocultural change and closer contact also resulted in growing friction and competition, occasionally exploding in intercommunal violence. Even among the cosmopolitan elites, the vertical element of religious and ethnic identification became increasingly superseded but never fully supplanted by the horizontal element of social class.

The role of non-Muslims as intermediaries facilitated their economic advancement, but it also exposed them as dependents—not any longer on the Muslim ruler, but on the colonial system. The rise of nationalism made their position difficult, if not untenable. When religious and ethnic affiliation tended to merge, religious communities could be transformed into nations, and *millets* turned into minorities. Although certain nationalist movements, such as the Wafd in Egypt or Congress in India, attempted to overcome religious divisions and to unite Muslims, Christians, Jews, or Hindus under the banner of national unity, the tie between nationalism and religion was never entirely dissolved. It became more marked in the course of what has been widely termed the assertion, or surge, of political Islam that since the 1970s made itself felt in the entire Muslim world.

Most written constitutions of Muslim states now confirm the principle of equality of all citizens irrespective of religion, sex, and race. At the same time, however, they usually declare Islam to be the state religion and the *sharīʿah* (the divine law) the principal (or even exclusive) source of legislation. In most cases, the head of state must be a (male) Muslim. In some countries, such as Lebanon, Jordan, or the Islamic Republic of Iran, non-Muslim and other minority groups are guaranteed a fixed share of seats in representative political bodies.

Contemporary Debates. Given the fact that at least as far as constitutional theory is concerned, the principle of equality has been generally accepted, much of the contemporary debate about the status of non-Muslims in the ideal Islamic order has a certain ring of unreality. Individual thinkers, groups, and activists have adopted widely divergent views. Certain militant Islamic groups, such as al-Jihād in Egypt, advocate hostile suspicion toward non-Muslims and the reimposition of the *dhimmah* regulations. They refer themselves to the medieval scholar Ibn Taymīyah (d. 1328), who conditioned the toleration of non-Muslims on their utility to the Muslim community, and to the Indo-Pakistani activist Abū al-Aʿlā Mawdūdī (1903–1979) and the Egyptian Muslim Brother Sayyid Quṭb (1906–1966). They also engage in physical violence that is aimed at the regimes in power as much as at the minorities attacked.

At the other end of the spectrum, there are Muslim intellectuals seeking ways to legitimize full legal and political equality of Muslims and non-Muslims in Islamic terms. They clearly perceive the need for radical *ijtihād* (individual inquiry in legal matters) that takes into account the spirit or *maqāṣid* (intentions) of *sharīʿah* rather than the details of *fiqh,* looking at the public good *(al-maṣlaḥah al-ʿāmmah)* rather than the letter of the law. Their primary concern is to preserve the unity of the national or territorial community and to avoid *fitnah* (disorder) in its modern guise of sectarian violence *(fitnah ṭāʾifīyah)*. The dilemma rests in the fact that on this particular issue, *sharīʿah,* in order to allow for equality, would have to be literally purged of the provisions of *fiqh,* whose primary function is to demarcate between Muslims and non-Muslims and to ensure the superiority of the former in this world as well as in the hereafter.

Between the two extremes there is what might be called a mainstream position that proclaims the principle of "same rights, same duties" ("lahum mā lanā wa-ʿalayhim mā ʿalaynā"), but limits legal equality to the "non-religious domain." The decisive questions are, of course, how the religious sphere proper is defined and whether non-Muslims can hold public office in an Islamic state, which has as its primary raison d'être realization of the rule of Islam, particularly when the presidency (still frequently termed imamate), judicature, and military command are viewed as religious functions. Faced with the double challenge of traditional restrictive norms and modern egalitarian demands, Muslim reformists resort to a historical-functional approach: the *jizyah* is interpreted as the functional equivalent of a military tax (and here they have historical evidence on their side), and national liberation as the modern equivalent of *jihād* (war against nonbelievers). If and when non-Muslims participate in national defense or liberation, the *jizyah* is no longer incumbent on them; nor do they require any specific kind of protection. They can therefore be granted citizenship of the Islamic state *(al-jinsīyah al-islāmīyah),* including the right to vote and to participate in political decision making. But they continue to be debarred from the highest political, military, and judicial functions.

The commonly used term *muwāṭin,* therefore, is understood in its literal sense, describing non-Muslims as compatriots sharing the same *waṭan* (homeland), not as citizens sharing the same legal and political status. The emphasis is on justice that gives to everyone his or her due, rather than on equality which, so it is argued, attempts to make level or equal what should be kept apart.

[*See also* Christianity and Islam; Conversion; Dhimmī; Jizyah; Judaism and Islam; Millet; People of the Book.]

BIBLIOGRAPHY

Betts, Robert B. *Christians in the Arab East: A Political Study.* Rev. ed. Atlanta, 1978. Still useful overview of the situation of Christians in the modern Arab world, who have been much less intensively studied than the Jewish communities of the Middle East, past and present.

Braude, Benjamin, and Bernard Lewis, eds. *Christians and Jews in the Ottoman Empire: The Functioning of a Plural Society.* 2 vols. New York, 1982. Collection of essays examining among other things the evolution of the Ottoman *millet* system.

Bulliet, Richard W. *Conversion to Islam in the Medieval Period: An Essay in Quantitative History.* Cambridge, Mass., 1979. Detailed examination of the modalities and implications of conversion to Islam in the medieval period.

Esman, Milton J., and Itamar Rabinovich, eds. *Ethnicity, Pluralism, and the State in the Middle East.* Ithaca, N.Y., 1988. Collection of stimulating and in some cases controversial articles, covering the Ottoman legacy and the present situation in various Middle Eastern countries.

Fattal, Antoine. *Le statut légal des non-musulmans en pays d'Islam.* Beirut, 1958. Classic and detailed presentation of the classical legal doctrines, still useful as a general reference.

Goitein, S. D. *A Mediterranean Society.* 5 vols. Berkeley and Los Angeles, 1967–. Classic study of Muslim-Jewish relations in the "golden age" of Fāṭimid Egypt.

Khoury, Adel Theodor. *Toleranz im Islam.* Munich, 1980. Excellent presentation of classical Sunnī law and attitudes concerning the status of non-Muslims in Muslim societies as well as the doctrine of *jihād.*

Khuri, Fuad I. *Imams and Emirs: State, Religion, and Sects in Islam.* London, 1990. Stimulating analysis of the position of religious minorities as compared to Islamic sects in the modern Middle East.

Krämer, Gudrun. *The Jews in Modern Egypt, 1914–1952.* Seattle, 1989.

Lewis, Bernard. *The Jews of Islam.* Princeton, 1984. Judiciously balanced study of the evolution, decline, and end of Muslim-Jewish symbiosis.

Noth, Albrecht. "Möglichkeiten und Grenzen islamischer Toleranz." *Saeculum* 29 (1978): 190–204. Concise analysis of the concept of Islamic tolerance, emphasizing the relevance of historical reality rather than of legal theory.

Serjeant, R. B. "The 'Constitution of Medina' " and "The *Sunnah Jāmiʿah,* Pacts with the Yathrib Jews, and the *taḥrīm* of Yathrib." In *Studies in Arabian History and Civilisation.* Reprint, London, 1981. Very thorough, though not undisputed, examination of the so-called Constitution of Medina.

Stillman, Norman A. *The Jews of Arab Lands: A History and Source Book.* Philadelphia, 1979. *The Jews of Arab Lands in Modern Times.* Philadelphia, 1991. Exemplary and densely documented studies of one non-Muslim minority from the advent of Islam to the present day.

Tritton, A. S. *The Caliphs and Their Non-Muslim Subjects: A Critical Study of the Covenant of ʿUmar* (1930). London, 1970. Detailed, though rather unsystematic presentation of classical legal doctrines and the so-called Pact of ʿUmar.

Gudrun Krämer

Muslim Minorities in Non-Muslim Societies

About one third of the estimated 1.2 billion Muslims in the world today are living as religious and political minorities in non-Muslim societies. A more-precise estimation of the size of Muslim populations in many countries is difficult because of the absence of reliable demographic statistics. The problem is exacerbated by the lack of ethnic or religious classifications in most national statistics. Estimates of even relatively small Muslim minority populations vary widely: for example, in Hungary one estimate claims 6,000 Muslims and another claims 105,000; in Poland, 15,000 against 333,000; and in Romania, 35,000 against an estimate of 346,000. Even in countries with large populations much controversy exists—for example, in China estimates range from 14.6 to 144 million. The number and proportion of Muslims in countries where they are in the majority is generally known and accepted. It is only when they are in a minority status that not only their numerical strength (as in China) but their very existence (as in Albania) is questioned. (See Saleha Abedin, "Muslim Minority and Majority Countries: A Comparative Study of Demographic, Social and Economic Data," *Journal Institute of Muslim Minority Affairs* 10.2 [July 1989]: 375–424).

The etiology of Muslim minority communities is varied. Ali Kettani (*Muslim Minorities in the World Today*, London, 1986) has classified Muslim minority communities into three types based on their historical origins and current situation: they were once in the majority but later lost power and prestige and through attrition and absorption became a minority, as in Palestine, Ethiopia, and Bosnia-Herzegovina; they were in minority as rulers, but their rule ended, and they remained as religious minorities, as in India and the Balkans; they were non-Muslims who became converted to Islam in a non-Muslim environment, as in Sri Lanka.

Minorities are generally defined in terms of numbers, indicating that in their area of residence they are proportionately less than all the other groups combined, including the majority. However, Muslim minorities which constitute a small proportion of large populations, such as those of China, India, and the republics of the former Soviet Union, make up numerically significant communities and often exceed in population size many of the Muslim majority nations. Minority status, therefore, is not simply a game of numbers.

Minorities can also be defined in terms of ideological affiliations. Thus, minorities are those whose system of ideas or values are distinct, to a greater or lesser degree, from that of the majority around them. We might have religious or political minorities who form a subculture (such as Protestants in Europe, Catholics in America, Muslims in Europe and North America) and sometimes a counterculture (such as Catholics in Northern Ireland, Palestinians in Israel, Moros in the Philippines). Minorities are also identified in racial and ethnic terms, such as the classification of nationalities in Central and Eastern Europe, or under the euphemism of "visible minorities," as in Canada. Minorities are defined in terms of lesser degree of political participation or access to economic resources, as in the case of the colonies in Africa and Asia under British and French rule, or in South Africa, where until 1994 a disadvantaged majority remained subservient to a powerful political minority.

A particular minority might have one or a combination of the above characteristics and in varying degrees of intensity and relevance. Muslim minorities come in all of the above forms and in significant numbers and proportions that cannot be ignored in most countries of the world. The one common denominator that approximates a generic classification is their religious affiliation, professed or residual, current or historic, that gives them an identity with an onus of responsibility.

Besides having to contend with the hardships of minority living in the middle of an alien or alienated majority, Muslim minorities face the additional challenge of defining their own position in the context of the larger Muslim *ummah* (community). Ironically for them, the "in-group" is the physically distant *ummah* of which they consider themselves a part, and the "out-group" is seen as the majority non-Muslim community within which they reside.

The concept of *ummah* is very crucial to the understanding of the Muslim minority situation, contextually as well as topically. Muhammad Asad, in his well-known translation and commentary on the Qur'ān, explains, "the word *ummah* primarily denotes a group of living beings having certain characteristics or circumstances in common" (*The Message of the Qur'ān*, Gibraltar, 1980, p. 177). Thus, he points out, the term *ummah* is often used as synonymous with community, people, nation, genus, generation. In his brief but seminal article on the Qur'ānic concept of *ummah*, ʿAbdullāh al-Aḥsan (*Journal Institute of Muslim Minority Affairs* 7.2 [July 1986]: 606–616) identifies a number of usages from the Qur'an and classifies them as follows: the exemplar of an ideological group of people such as Abraham (16.120); a particular period or span of time that applies to a particular community (7.34 and 11.8); a group of more committed people within the larger community (7.159); a circumstantially or professionally unified group of people (28.23); a community based on common beliefs, law, and custom (5.48). Thus, *ummah* as a community based on shared beliefs and experiences is found in as many variations and forms as there are differences among nations and peoples. The Muslim *ummah,* however, has no variants, for it is based on one set of beliefs, focusing on the oneness of Allāh and the prophethood of Muḥammad and one code of practice guided by *sharīʿah* (the divine law) and shared experiences through common history of Islam and Muslims—the early persecutions, the trials and triumphs, the flowering and denouement, all have come to characterize the common Muslim experience leading to the emergence of an "*ummah* consciousness."

The Qur'ān defines the Muslim *ummah* as those who surrender to Allāh and follow his guidance as sent through the prophet Muḥammad who was chosen to be a messenger to all humanity. Muslims, therefore, are a group of people committed to a set of beliefs and entertaining a sense of mission and a special role in history. Allāh says in the Qur'ān: "And thus we have willed you to be a community of the middle way [*ummatan wasaṭan*] so that you may be a witness to the truth before all mankind" (surah 2.143).

The constitution adopted by the first Islamic state established by the Prophet in Medina declares in its first article: "Believers and Muslims of Quraysh and Yathrib and those who follow and meet them, and strive with them, constitute one single community [*ummatan wahīḍatan*] to the exclusion of all others in mankind [*min dūni al-nās*]." (For a concise discussion of the articles see W. Montgomery Watt, *Islamic Political Thought,* Edinburgh, 1968, especially pp. 130–134.)

In the Islamic tradition, then, all Muslims belong to the *ummah.* All non-Muslims, though living within the same territorial confines, are outside the *ummah.* However, when Muslims are the dominant community they are required to abide by the rules governing the rights and obligations of non-Muslim minorities, *al-dhimmī* (the protected ones), as specified in the Qur'ān and the *ḥadīths* (traditions of the Prophet). Thus the *dhimmī* are those nonbelievers who reside within the Islamic political domain. They live in *dār al-Islām* under the protection of the Muslims, and in lieu of rendering military service they make payment of a nominal tax called *jizyah* which entitles them to protection. (See AbdulHameed AbuSulayman, "Al-Dhimmi and Related Concepts in Historical Perspective," *JIMMA* 9.1 [January 1988]: 8–29). However, nonbelievers like believers are creatures of the One God, created to inherit the earth, *khalā'if al-arḍ* (vicegerents) with honor and dignity in their human person and with equal claims to the *rubūbīyah* (sustainership) of God. They are entitled to the *hidāyah* (guidance) from God and, like all children of Adam, are exalted with the power of choice (the ability to say no), thereby attaining a status higher than that of the angels. Murad Hoffman refers the collection of these rules and injunctions as the Qur'ānic Minority Statute (*Islam: The Alternative,* Reading, 1993, p. 168).

If Muslims are living as parts of non-Muslim communities, their treatment by the non-Muslim majority is subject to the varying conditions that are operational in that setting. There is an on-going debate, however, on what the *ummah* can expect from the Muslim minority and an equally strong debate on what can be expected from the *ummah* for the cause of those Muslims living under non-Muslim jurisdiction.

Since the Muslim minority community is often perceived by the majority of Muslims as an integral part of the larger Muslim community, albeit a part that is living outside its jurisdiction, minority status is often seen as a transitory phase, a redressable accident of history. Thus, as it was often done through history, the Muslim minorities might be encouraged or advised to pursue one of the following two courses: when subjected to the hardships of living in non-Muslim societies, Muslim minorities undertake *hijrah* (migration) to a Muslim or another more hospitable land or respond to repression and threats to their survival by *jihād* (taking up arms or undertaking extraordinary effort). The Qur'ānic sanction for this line of argument is sought in the following verse from the Qur'ān: "Those who believe and suffer exile and strive with might and main in God's cause with their goods and their persons, have the highest rank in the sight of God: they are the people who will achieve salvation" (surah 9.20).

It is obvious that in the areas where Muslim minorities live Islam is not a dominant religion or culture, and there is no positive inducement for the growth and nurture of Islamic values. In many of these areas Muslim minorities encounter active hostility against anything Islamic and complain of calculated efforts by the majority to ensure that Islamic norms do not prosper, and that even in their individual lives Muslims cease to render allegiance to Islam or to pursue the Islamic way of life. Such is the situation, sometimes mild, sometimes aggravated, in which one out of every three Muslims is living today.

In the early history of Islam we have two models for minorities to follow. One is the Mecca model, where Muslims facing persecution opted for *hijrah,* and the other is the Abyssinia model, in which a state of tolerance and peaceful coexistence is achieved within a non-Muslim majority context through exerting extraordinary effort. For Muslim minorities today, the adoption of one of these two models is inevitable. Both are viable, yet one might be more workable than the other. The third alternative of doing nothing will maintain a state of continuous belligerence which is neither necessary nor desirable. Thus a minority Muslim is expected to become a *muhājir* (migrant) or else become a *mujāhid* (one who strives for a cause). When Muslims are living in non-Muslim lands it is incumbent on them to organize with other Muslims to preserve and enhance their Islamic identity. Yet the isolationist approach to preservation is excluded on the basis of an equally important need and indeed duty of the Muslim to make *daʿwah* (invite people to Islam). Thus, dialogue with the non-Muslims is encouraged both for the purpose of mission and for the objective of attaining peaceful coexistence with non-Muslims in their lands.

Historically, the *dār al-Islām* has been confronted not only with the realm of the other, in principle hostile, not-yet Muslim world *(dār al-ḥarb),* but it has also been complimented by the realm of compromise *(dār al-ṣulh)* beginning with the famous armistice agreement which the Prophet signed with the people of Mecca two years before returning to that city in 628. Thus the options available to Muslim minorities are varied, Islamically valid and practically viable. Problems remain as to the role of the larger Muslim *ummah* in the affairs of the Muslim minorities living "beyond their jurisdiction." Should the *ummah* do something about this situation? Should the worldwide Muslim *ummah* be concerned about its constituents in diaspora?

Most Muslims would argue that the *ummah* has very little choice. If Muslims follow the spirit of their faith then they have obligations toward each other, wherever they reside, individually and collectively. These obligations derive from the Islamic concept of the brotherhood of the faithful. Although in doctrinal terms this concept is present in other faiths as well, in Islam it is spelled out in very clear terms: "And the believers, both men and women are the protectors of one another" (Qur'ān 9.7). Elsewhere the Qur'ān says, "All believers are but brethren" (10.49)

One of the most concise, yet regnant statements in the Qur'ān with regard to the obligations that faith imposes on individuals as well as collectivities is to be found in surah 103.3, which prescribes four categories of obligations: faith *(īmān),* action *(aʿmāl),* reinforcement in faith *(tawāṣī bi-al-ḥaqq),* and reinforcement in perseverance *(tawāṣī bi-al-ṣabr).* Faith and action are individual obligations. Since faith is not an acquisition which once acquired can thereafter be taken for granted, it needs continuous nurturing through action (see Qur'ān 2.214). This process of interaction of faith and action makes an individual into an Islamic "whole" and on him it becomes obligatory to reinforce others in preserving and enhancing their Islamic "wholeness."

The last two categories of obligations *(tawāṣī bi-al-ḥaqq* and *tawāṣī bi-al-ṣabr)* are social in nature, involving the individual within the larger Muslim community and requiring policies, plans of action, and methodology to implement them. In contemporary Muslim populations, majority as well as minority, many national and international organizations, formal associations, centers for learning and research, and even organized community groups have become active and outspoken in their efforts to serve Islam and Muslims. The crisis of minority living need no longer be embedded in a litany of woes; it can be confronted with the verve of the *mujāhid* and the elan of the *muhājir.* However, caution should be exercised in preserving the true nature of this resurgent "*ummah* consciousness" and preventing it from deteriorating into Pan-Islamic consciousness, the particular from determining the universal, the political from subverting the religious and social.

Most Muslims in Muslim majority countries postulate certain inescapable political obligations toward their coreligionists who reside as minorities in non-Muslim states. This impels them to energetic expressions of concern over the plight of these minority communities, generally in times of crisis. In some cases Muslim majority intervention antagonizes the perpetrators of the crisis who invariably resent this as interference from the outside.

Contemporary Muslim societies lack clear policies in respect to Muslim minority communities, and there is much confusion about the exact nature of the relationship that should obtain between the *ummah* and the

Muslim minorities. From the point of view of the minorities themselves the issue is not very clear and adds to their minority predicament. The Muslim *ummah* can thus elect one of two options: adopt a patron-client relationship in regard to the Muslim minorities, treating them as spiritual and cultural (and even economic and political) colonies of the Muslim world on alien soil; or treat minorities as autonomous bodies, sharing the attribute of sovereignty with their non-Muslim compatriots and at par with Muslim majority communities.

The first option is more favored and most widely accepted among Muslim majority communities who find in the Qur'ānic verse, "and the believers, both men and women, are the protectors of one another" (surah 9.71) an irrevocable obligation of the *ummah* toward the Muslim minorities. However, in terms of policy and action Muslim majorities are hedged in by the contemporary political and economic realities and are left with the second option.

What we euphemistically term as the Muslim world is actually a number (forty-six or thereabout) of national sovereign entities with independent political and economic structures, with policies and priorities defined by their national interests. These entities have no doubt formed several regional alliances or economic and trade agreements among themselves. But there is nothing particularly Islamic about them. They have their exact parallels, predating them, in the non-Muslim world. Even the largest of these, the Organization of the Islamic Conference (OIC), in its conception, structure, and functioning is not much different from the EEC, the OAS, or the UN with its various affiliates. They have no mandate for action even within their own member states. How can OIC then expect to be heard by sovereign entities outside the range of their membership? Nevertheless, it is generally agreed that there exists among all Muslims a sense of mutual belonging. It may not be institutionalized in form, but it can be invoked readily and forcefully whenever occasion arises, and it forms the characteristic feature of the Muslim community worldwide.

"*Ummah* consciousness" is an integral part of Muslim faith and belief and inheres in Islamic doctrine. It derives from the Qur'ānically imposed duty incumbent on those "who have attained to faith, enjoining upon one another patience in adversity [*sabr*] and enjoin(ing) upon one another compassion [*marḥamah*]" (surah 90.17). *Ummah* consciousness, then, is the epitome of that concern, that feeling of solidarity which Muslims everywhere feel for each other. Patience in *ṣabr* is not an argument in favor of inaction. In the Qur'ānic meaning *ṣabr* is a very positive concept which brings out the best in man, separating the weak from the strong (surah 2.45–46).

The exercise of *marḥamah* as the twin attribute of *ṣabr* ensures an individual's continued adherence to human values and acts as a brake against savage impulses. It reminds Muslims that whatever the provocation and however severe the crisis, they cannot adopt just any means to resolve their predicament. They have of necessity to be guided in their choices by *ṣabr* and *marḥamah,* and in practicing these principles they will be preserving their own humanity. To formulate these into plans of action in contemporary societies is the challenge of great magnitude facing the Muslim *ummah.*

Is it, however, possible to lead an Islamic life under the rule and control of non-Muslims? Muslims have rarely had this experience before in their history. If they were in numerical minority in non-Muslim lands they have either lived as rulers (in India, for instance, despite the fact that their population never exceeded 10 percent, they ruled the country for close to a thousand years), or they enjoyed the protection of a powerful Muslim state. For centuries Muslims were such a dominant world power, that non-Muslim states could not conceive of mistreating Muslims living within their jurisdiction. All Muslims are familiar with the *wa-iʿtaṣimah* syndrome in Islamic history. It signifies the *ummah*'s obligations toward Muslim minorities and is based on the historic launching of an army by Caliph Mutawakkil in the third/ninth century, in response to a lone woman in Sindh's call for help.

At the close of the twentieth century the situation is different. Muslims currently living as minorities can hardly expect any immediate change in their minority status or expect instant help from their Muslim majority brethren. The most relevant question to consider now is: how should they learn to adjust themselves, emotionally and religiously, as well as economically and politically, to their minority status? Thus, any deliberations on the status of Muslim minorities should candidly discuss ways in which Muslims living in non-Muslim states can learn to lead useful, productive, and comfortable lives, without in any way compromising their Islamic identity.

A second related subject of discussion emanates from the fact that Muslims, wherever they live, regard themselves as constituting one *ummah.* Under the present circumstances, when approximately one-third of them (350 million) live as minorities in sovereign, non-Muslim states, what should be the proper relationship between the Muslim minorities and the Muslim majorities? Should Muslim governments or Muslim international organizations continue to forcefully support every cause of Muslim minorities and condemn all non-Muslim governments whenever and wherever a Muslim minority in these regions feels that any of its rights is being violated? Would this be in the long term interests of the minority itself? What kind of climate of peace and harmony would this create at the international level? How would it affect the relations of Muslim states with non-Muslim states? What about economic, trade, and other relations between them? Should the minority communities be encouraged to expect from the *ummah* support in all matters of dispute with their non-Muslim countrymen? How would this affect the minority's day-to-day relationship with people with whom it is destined to live in perpetuity?

If any of these scenarios are not Islamically feasible, then what is the proper form of relationship between the *ummah* and the Muslim minority communities? A candid discussion of these and other related issues is necessary to understand the true nature of the Muslim minority problem in the contemporary world.

There are grounds to argue that no effort to uplift the condition, moral or material, of Muslim minorities anywhere is likely to bear fruit unless it also touches on and enriches the total life of their societies of residence. The minority problem is essentially a problem between the Muslim minority and the non-Muslim majority among whom it resides. Hence, there is a need for understanding and accommodation between these two parties. If the objective is to enhance and maintain the quality of Islamic life among Muslim minority communities and if these communities are to be strengthened in their steadfastness to Islamic practice as well as beliefs, the avenues of interaction and peaceful coexistence with the non-Muslim majorities must be explored.

It should be recognized that the problems of Muslim minorities are different in many ways from the problems of the Muslim world. To deal with their own particular situation Muslim minorities have to achieve a social and political identity that is distinct from the Muslim majority communities, and in this the Muslim majority communities should extend their assistance and support. This is ultimately in their best interests. The *ummah* deliberations should be future and solution oriented. Concrete and specific proposals should be formulated. Practical and functional ideas should be presented and examined. Muslim minorities in any country should not be used as pawns in the game of power between Muslim states and non-Muslim states.

Furthermore, the Muslim world should not only encourage the Muslim minorities to pursue justice and truth *(ta'marūna bi-al-maʿrūf)*, they should also caution and advise them when they appear to be taking the wrong path *(tanhawna ʿan al-munkar)*. Islam, being a code of conduct covering all aspects of human life, provides clearcut rules on how a struggle for rights and redress of wrongs is to be conducted. Finally, efforts to achieve a life of security, equality, and dignity for minorities in their societies of residence would be effective only if both Muslim majorities and minorities are truly convinced that minority living is not a historical or even a moral aberration.

Considering the fact that more than one-third of the 1.2 billion Muslims in the world today are living in the minority situation from which there are no imminent chances of an exit, a sincere and honest effort to engage in leading, under non-Muslim aegis, a fully rewarding Islamic life should not just be aspired for, but also attempted. Islam, as Muslims believe, is a way of life which encapsulates all human situations and vouchsafes guidance for spatial and temporal infinity. "We", God assures in the Qur'ān, "have neglected nothing in (this) Book" (surah 6.38).

[*See also* Institute of Muslim Minority Affairs; Ummah; *and entries on individual non-Muslim countries.*]

BIBLIOGRAPHY

Abedin, Saleha M. "Demographic Consequences of Muslim Minority Consciousness: An Analysis." *Journal Institute of Muslim Minority Affairs* 1–2 (Winter 1979–Spring 1980): 97–114. Relates minority consciousness to demographic conditions, and discusses its relevance for religious fertility differentials.

Abedin, Syed Z. "A Word about Ourselves." *Journal Institute of Muslim Minority Affairs* 13.1 (January 1992): 1–25. Written in the spirit of a "state of the union message," this article identifies problems faced by Muslim minorities and takes a long-term perspective, suggesting programs and policies for implementation.

Aḥsan, ʿAbdullāh al-. *OIC: The Organization of the Islamic Conference.* Herndon, Va., 1988. In this study of a modern-day Islamic political institution, the author provides an overview of Islamic political philosophy, with particular reference to the concept of *ummah.*

Denny, Frederick Mathewson. "The Meaning of *Ummah* in Qur'ān." *History of Religions* 15.1 (August 1975): 35–70. Excellent article on the subject of *ummah* and the Qur'ān.

Fārūqī, Ismāʿīl R. al-, and Lois Lamyā' al-Fārūqī. *The Cultural Atlas of Islam*. New York, 1986. Comprehensive coverage of the world of Islam and its legacy in art, science, law, and philosophy. A beautifully produced 512-page volume with three hundred photographs, drawings, and other illustrations, and seventy-five original maps.

Gibb, H. A. R. "The Community in Islamic History." *Proceedings of the American Philosophical Society* 107.2 (1963): 173–176. Succinct historical account of the emergence of Muslim *ummah* as a law-based community.

Ibn Hishām, ʿAbd al-Malik. *The Life of Muhammad*. Translated by Alfred Guillaume. Oxford, 1935. Well-received translation of a popular biography of the life of the Prophet.

Irving, Thomas B. *Islam Resurgent: The Islamic World Today*. Lagos, 1979. Reprinted as *The World of Islam*. Brattleboro, Vt., 1984. Historical account of Muslim communities around the world, with particular emphasis on the contributions of Muslims to science and art. Also includes a useful classification of countries and areas by percentage of Muslims in the population, although population figures should be updated and sources identified.

Islamic Council of Europe. *Muslim Communities in Non-Muslim States*. London, 1980. One of the first among recent books on Muslim minorities, containing a collection of essays on minority problems, human and constitutional rights, and Muslim personal law. Some of the papers were presented at the first world conference on Muslim minorities, held in London, 1980.

Kettani, M. Ali. "Muslims in Non-Muslim Societies: Challenges and Opportunities." *Journal Institute of Muslim Minority Affairs* 11.2 (July 1990): 226–233. Considers Muslim minority living as an opportunity for *daʿwah* (Islamic call).

Khalidi, Omar. "Muslim Minorities: Theory and Experience of Muslim Interaction in Non-Muslim Societies." *Journal Institute of Muslim Minority Affairs* 10.2 (July 1989): 425–437. Focuses on Muslim minority and non-Muslim majority relationships and provides recommendations for practical implementation.

Masud, Muhammad Khalid. "Being Muslim in a Non-Muslim Polity." *Journal Institute of Muslim Minority Affairs* 10.1 (1989): 118–128. Explores Muslim minority options in the light of three historical models.

Serjeant, R. B. "The Constitution of Madinah." *Islamic Quarterly* 8 (June 1964): 3–16. Interprets the nature of the document and the historical antecedents that influenced its formulation.

Syed Z. Abedin and Saleha M. Abedin

MIRACLES. *See* Muḥammad; Sainthood.

MIʿRĀJ. Muḥammad's ascent to God and return to the world is known as the *miʿrāj*, literally, "ladder." This specialized term is sometimes used synonymously with *isrā'* or "night journey," when God "carried his servant [Muḥammad] by night" (Qur'ān, 17.1). Qur'ānic commentators take this verse, along with surahs 53.1–21 and 81.19–25, to refer to the *miʿrāj*. From earliest times the ascent has been one of the grand themes of the Islamic popular and elite imaginations and the complement of that other grand theme, the descent of the Qur'ān. Western scholars have devoted a great deal of attention to the *miʿrāj*, typically struggling to distinguish various strands in the accounts and to identify the historical facts.

Most versions of the *miʿrāj* tell the story something like this. Gabriel came to Muḥammad at night, mounted him on a winged beast called Burāq, and took him to Jerusalem, where Muḥammad led all the prophets in prayer. Then Gabriel took Muḥammad up through the seven heavens, introducing him to the angels and the prophets residing in each of them, and then to hell and paradise. Finally Muḥammad went alone into the presence of God. On the way back down Muḥammad took leave from the prophets in each heaven. Moses, whose community has the heaviest legal prescriptions, sent Muḥammad back to God several times so that that the number of daily prayers might be reduced from the original fifty.

The significance of the *miʿrāj* for the Islamic tradition can be summarized on three levels, corresponding to practice, faith, and spirituality, or to the *sharīʿah*, Islamic thought, and Sufism. The connection with the *sharīʿah* appears most clearly in the role given to Moses in reducing the daily *ṣalāt*s (prayers) from fifty to five. Only after the *miʿrāj* were these *ṣalāts* instituted. A saying sometimes attributed to the Prophet suggests the inner meaning of the daily prayer: "The *ṣalāt* is the *miʿrāj* of the believer." Thus the fundamental pillar of Islam is a ladder that takes the believer to God and back to the world. Significantly, the ladder that the Prophet climbed is identified with that whereby believers mount up to God after death; in a similar way, the straight path (*ṣirāṭ)* established by the *sharīʿah* becomes embodied as the "bridge" (*ṣirāṭ)* over hell at the resurrection.

The *miʿrāj* raises important issues in Islamic thought. Was it simply spiritual, or was it corporeal as well? Did the Prophet see God, or did God remain veiled? The answers proposed to such questions by different thinkers had implications for many other theological issues, especially in the domain of eschatology. Another set of questions, important among philosophers and Ṣūfī thinkers, has to do with the structure of the cosmos and its mirror image, the human soul. Hence the *miʿrāj* becomes an important key to the Islamic understanding of both cosmology and psychology.

From early times, Ṣūfī authors looked upon the *miʿrāj* as the model for the return to God in this life. In *Miʿrāj al-sālikīn* al-Ghazālī takes the *miʿrāj* as the guide for the soul's rational development, pointing out that "proofs are the ladders by which creatures mount up to their Lord." Ṣūfī poets like Sanā'ī, ʿAttār, and Rūmī employed the *miʿrāj* accounts to describe the ascending levels of the soul's perfection. Ibn al-ʿArabī developed the cosmological, psychological, and spiritual implications of the *miʿrāj* in detail, especially in the works in which he describes how he himself ascended to God following in the Prophet's footsteps; but, he writes, "My journey was only in myself."

[*See also* Muḥammad, *article on* Life of the Prophet.]

BIBLIOGRAPHY

Böwering, Gerhard. "Miʿrāj." In *The Encyclopedia of Religion*, edited by Mircea Eliade, vol. 10, pp. 552–556. New York, 1987.

Morris, James. "The Spiritual Ascension: Ibn ʿArabī and the Miʿrāj." *Journal of the American Oriental Society* 107 (1987): 629–652; 108 (1988): 63–77.

Schimmel, Annemarie. *And Muhammad Is His Messenger*. Chapel Hill, N.C., 1985. See chapter 9.

Schrieke, Bertram, et al. "Miʿrādj." In *Encyclopaedia of Islam*, new ed., vol. 7, pp. 97–105. Leiden, 1960–.

WILLIAM C. CHITTICK

MODERNISM. Islamic modernists advocate flexible, continuous reinterpretation of Islam so that Muslims may develop institutions of education, law, and politics suitable to modern conditions. Modernizing tendencies appeared in the last decades of the nineteenth century in response to westernizing regimes and European rule. Elite Muslim culture was evolving into separate westernized and traditional spheres that modernists sought to unify. To validate their reexamination of Islam's sources among traditionalists, Muslim modernists declared that modernism constituted a return to true Islam as originally preached and practiced, a claim put forth by many reform movements throughout Islamic history. Modernism's distinction among such movements lies in the philosophical and political liberalism displayed by its expositors, in contrast to the tendency in late-twentieth-century Islamist discourse to regard liberalism as alien to Islam. To win the support of Muslims attracted to Western culture, modernists argued that the recovery of true Islam would generate the requisite dynamism needed to restore Muslim societies to an honored place in the world. Modernism, then, begins with the assumption widely held by nineteenth- and twentieth-century Muslims that the Muslim world had become backward in relation to the West and that in order to restore equilibrium between the two societies, it was necessary to adapt the practices, institutions, and artifacts associated with European power to an Islamic milieu.

Such adaptation began in Egypt and the Ottoman Empire during the first half of the nineteenth century. In the 1860s, some Muslims objected to the inclusion of manners and customs in the inventory of items borrowed from Europe. Such Muslims anticipated that indiscriminate imitation of Europe would lead to Western culture supplanting Muslim culture and to the erasure of Islam. These Muslims argued for a more judicious selection of features to be adopted, for distinguishing between the kernel of modern practices and the husk of Western culture. They held that the scientific and technological underpinnings of European power were reducible to categories of knowledge and practice that Muslims could learn without damaging Islam's integrity. Moreover, these modernists asserted that modern European science had developed on the basis of classical Islamic learning transmitted to Europe through Muslim Spain. Therefore, were Muslims to learn modern sciences, they would reclaim their own heritage.

This reference to Islam's Golden Age of learning is related to another element in modernist thought, namely, the revival of Islam's rationalist philosophical tradition, which distinguished between knowledge attained from revelation and knowledge acquired through the exercise of reason. Since Islamic beliefs and practices derived from revelation, they could not clash with any conclusions acquired through rational thought. One strain within modernism even asserted that revealed knowledge is essentially rational, that is, it could be attained by the exercise of reason.

Modernists authenticated their ideas with yet another appeal to Islamic history by claiming to return to Islam's original principles. In this respect they were putting their own stamp on the eighteenth-century tendency to emphasize strict adherence to beliefs and practices as defined by scripture: the Qur'ān and the *sunnah*. Early modern scripturalist movements included the Wahhābīs in Arabia, Shāh Walī Allāh's circle in India, and reformist Ṣūfī orders throughout the Muslim world. In modernist hands, the scriptural orientation legitimized criticism of current beliefs and practices as deviations from the pristine Islam of *al-salaf al-ṣāliḥ* (the pious ancestors).

The earliest formulations of Islamic modernism issued from Egypt and the Ottoman Empire, the first Muslim lands to initiate reforms of bureaucratic and military institutions along European lines. In the 1860s Rifāʿah Rāfiʿ al-Ṭahṭāwī (1801–1873), a leading Egyptian education official, restated classical Islamic philosophy's view on the complementary relationship between reason and revelation, thereby giving Islamic sanction to the study of European sciences, the striving for technological progress, and the rationalization of government institutions for the sake of advancing society. Al-Ṭahṭāwī also wrote that Muslims who studied modern science and technology would be retrieving knowledge Arabs had imparted to Europe centuries earlier. With respect to Islamic law, he urged religious scholars to exercise *ijtihād* (independent reasoning) in order to adapt religious law to changing conditions. Furthermore, al-Ṭahṭāwī called for educational reform, in particular the provision of primary education for all boys and girls. He argued that educating girls would benefit society, because educated women would be more suitable wives and better mothers, and they would contribute to economic production.

In North Africa Khayr al-Dīn al-Tūnisī's (1810–1889) position as a high minister in the reforming autonomous regime of Tunisia during the 1870s was comparable to al-Ṭahṭāwī's in Egypt. In 1875 Khayr al-Dīn established Ṣādiqī College, one of the first schools to combine Islamic and modern scientific topics. Its graduates provided the core of Tunisia's small modernist movement for the next few decades. In addition, Khayr al-Dīn introduced liberal political thought to modernism by claiming that parliamentary government and a free press accorded with Islam.

While Khayr al-Dīn and al-Ṭahṭāwī advanced modernist ideas as high officials in modernizing states, the modernist movement known as the Young Ottomans in Istanbul represented lower-level bureaucrats. The Ottoman movement to rationalize bureaucratic and military institutions, known as the Tanzimat (1839–1876), was dominated by a handful of high-ranking officials. The Young Ottomans agreed with the Tanzimat programs designed to rationalize administration in order to enable the Ottoman Empire to fend off European encroachments, but they objected to high officials' adoption of Western manners. In the late 1860s, the Young Ottomans called for a liberal political regime similar to European constitutional monarchies that limited sovereigns' powers with elected parliaments. Given their opposition to wholesale adoption of European ways, the Young Ottomans justified the introduction of liberal political principles by claiming that they were part of Islam. Thus, their leading writer, Mehmet Namık Kemal (1840–1888), interpreted the Islamic concepts of *shūrā* (consultation) and *bayʿah* (oath of allegiance) to mean an elected parliament and popular sovereignty. [*See also* Young Ottomans; Tanzimat; *and the biography of Kemal.*]

Modernist ideas were taken up by men outside official circles in the Ottoman Empire's Arab provinces toward the end of the nineteenth century. In Damascus, Beirut, and Baghdad a handful of progressive religious scholars (Jamāl al-Dīn al-Qāsimī [1866–1914], Ṭāhir al-Jazā'irī [1852–1920], ʿAbd al-Qādir al-Maghribī [1867–1956], and Maḥmūd Shukrī al-Ālūsī [1857–1924]) called for educational and legal reform, upheld the compatibility of Islam and reason, and favored a liberal political system in terms similar to those laid out by the Young Ottomans. The major impetus for modernism in these circles was alarm at the marginalization of religious scholars in the new Ottoman order. Their aim was to demonstrate the relevance of their expertise in Islamic law to a modernizing Ottoman state.

Jamāl al-Dīn al-Afghānī (1838–1897) brought to modernism a new sense of activism and political resistance to European domination. Born in Iran, he did not belong to any Muslim state's reformist bureaucracy or to a local corps of religious scholars: rather, he restlessly roamed from India to Istanbul spreading his call for an activist ethos and a positive attitude to modern science. Like al-Ṭahṭāwī, al-Afghānī drew on classical Islamic philosophy and promoted its revival to open Muslims' minds to the necessity of acquiring modern knowledge. His chief contribution to modernism was to imbue it with an anti-imperialist strain, because he lived during an era when European armies were conquering Muslim lands from Tunisia to Central Asia. To combat European aggression, Muslims had to shake off fatalistic attitudes and embrace an activist ethos, individually and collectively. This voluntaristic spirit became characteristic of modernism in the assertion that Muslims must take responsibility for their own welfare rather than passively accept foreign domination as a fate decreed by God. Al-Afghānī succeeded in spreading his views and reputation through political journalism and teaching, but he failed in his bids to gain influence over Muslim rulers. Without an organized base or institutional backing, his conspiratorial approach to political agitation proved fruitless. [*See the biography of Afghānī.*]

Islamic modernism underwent its richest development

in a Middle Eastern context at the hands of al-Afghānī's Egyptian disciple Muḥammad ʿAbduh (1849–1905). His formulations of modernist thought in the fields of law, education, and theology provided the intellectual bases for modernist trends throughout the Muslim world. ʿAbduh believed that European wealth and power stemmed from achievements in education and science. Consequently, Muslims could overcome European domination only by promoting a positive attitude to modern learning and its application in society. A few years after Great Britain occupied Egypt in 1882, his gradualist approach gained the support of British authorities, who secured his appointment to official positions to promote educational and legal reform. In his capacity as rector of al-Azhar (the Arab world's most prestigious center of Islamic learning), ʿAbduh attempted to bring together customary religious education and modern learning, but his opponents thwarted him. His theological writings asserted the harmony of reason and Islam, demonstrating that all rational knowledge, including modern science, accords with Islam. To substantiate this view, ʿAbduh's Qur'ānic exegesis claimed that the Qur'ān anticipated modern scientific knowledge: for instance, the prohibition of alcohol accords with modern medicine's conclusions about alcohol's damaging effects on health. As for such classic Islamic theological issues as the nature of God and His attributes, ʿAbduh discouraged speculation, because their subject lay beyond the limits of rational comprehension. In the legal sphere, where ʿAbduh served as chief jurisprudent *(muftī)* of Egypt, he flexibly interpreted Islamic law to show that Muslims could adapt to modern circumstances and still remain true to their faith. [*See the biography of ʿAbduh.*]

ʿAbduh's thought contained a tension between scrupulous adherence to the authority of religion and a willingness to accommodate to the demands of modernity. The generation of Muslims in Egypt influenced by ʿAbduh tended to emphasize one or another of these elements. Muḥammad Rashīd Riḍā (1865–1935), who came to Egypt from Syria in 1897 to join ʿAbduh's reformist circle, developed the religious element in his influential journal, *Al-manār*. In the first three decades of the twentieth century, Egypt's political and cultural elites leaned toward secularism, as they sought to separate religion from politics. Rashīd Riḍā reacted by reinforcing scriptural authority, thereby safeguarding the integrity of Islam. He particularly sought to demonstrate the suitability of Islamic law to modern government, and he stressed the reform of religious practices and beliefs. Most of ʿAbduh's disciples (lawyers, teachers, and government officials), however, traveled down the path to secularism, bending their interpretation of Islam to demonstrate its compatibility with modern life. It seems as though this split stemmed from opposing sources of authority: Islamic scripture and the exigencies of modern life. A second source for this split lay in modernists' call for a return to the way of the first generation of Muslims, the *salaf*. Modernists validated their views by calling for a return to Islam's scriptural sources, the Qur'ān and the *sunnah*. For Rashīd Riḍā, this meant close study of those sources to define a core of concepts that would safeguard Islam's integrity. This method, however, gave secularists license to interpret the sources to suit their liberal temperament. Hence, in 1925 ʿAlī ʿAbd al-Rāziq (1888–1966) cited scripture to justify Turkey's abolition of the caliphate and the separation of religion and politics. Islamic scripture contains enough general statements and ambiguities to allow for both secular and religious interpretations. [*See the biographies of Rashīd Riḍā and ʿAbd al-Rāziq.*]

As in the Middle East, Muslims in India confronted European domination, which became virtually complete when Great Britain abolished the Mughal dynasty following the 1857 Revolt. A second impetus to modernism in India lay in missionaries' criticisms of Islam, which led to a tradition of public debates between missionaries and Muslim scholars. Indian modernism emerged in full bloom in the works of Sayyid Aḥmad Khān (1817–1898), who aimed to convince the British to overcome their distrust of Muslims in the wake of the 1857 Revolt and to persuade Muslims to open their minds to Western ideas. Aḥmad Khān argued that Islam's teachings concerning God, the Prophet, and the Qur'ān are compatible with modern science, which involves discovery of "the work of God" in natural laws. Since God is the author of both natural laws and the Qur'ān, the two exist in harmony. In general, Aḥmad Khān would bend the meaning of scripture to suit the conclusions of reason to a greater extent than ʿAbduh, who often declared that only God knows the truth when reason and revelation appeared to conflict.

Aḥmad Khān's major achievement was the establishment in 1875 of the Muhammadan Anglo-Oriental College at Aligarh, which was intended to train Muslims for government service, thereby restoring them to the roles they filled in Mughal times as administrators and officials. Because Aḥmad Khān's religious ideas were so controversial, however, the task of teaching Islamic subjects was entrusted to more orthodox scholars, and the desired blend of modern learning with a modernist religious orientation did not emerge. Other Aligarh modernists introduced ʿAbduh's and Rashīd Riḍā's writings to the curriculum, worked for the flexible interpretation of Islamic law, and advocated improvements in women's status in matters of education, veiling, seclusion, and marriage. [*See* Aligarh *and the biography of Aḥmad Khān.*]

In the first half of the twentieth century, Indian modernists had to face the question of how to sustain the Muslim community under a non-Muslim regime, be it the existing British one or an envisioned Hindu majority state. One group, led by Muhammad Iqbal (1875–1938), argued that Indian Muslims comprise a distinct nation and must live in a Muslim state. Followers of this view struggled for the creation of Pakistan as a separate Muslim polity. The other group, whose spokesman was Abū al-Kalām Āzād (1888–1958), held that Muslims should join with Hindus to combat British rule and struggle for a unified, composite nation. Although this fundamental issue divided them, both groups interpreted the juridical concept of *ijmāʿ* (consensus) to indicate that whether Muslims form a separate state or live in a Hindu majority state, they should live under a democracy. [*See the biographies of Iqbal and Āzād.*]

Indonesia, at the eastern end of the Muslim world, gradually came under Dutch rule during the nineteenth century. Once again European domination and missionary activities stimulated rethinking among Muslims, and a modernist movement emerged. In addition, more regular steamship service to the Middle East increased the flow of Indonesian Muslims traveling for pilgrimage and study. On their return, many Indonesians brought with them the new reformist teachings circulating in Cairo and Mecca. Indonesia's most important modernist movement, the Muhammadiyah, was founded in 1912 in Jogjakarta by Hadji Ahmad Dahlan (1868–1923), who had resided in Egypt during the 1890s and met Muḥammad ʿAbduh. He resembled ʿAbduh and Aḥmad Khān in avoiding involvement in nationalist politics in order to avoid suppression by colonial authorities. The Muhammadiyah established a network of modernist schools to combine instruction in religion and modern sciences. To demonstrate support for improving women's status, it set up schools for girls. The Muhammadiyah also advocated legal reform through a return to the Qur'ān and the *sunnah* and the exercise of *ijtihād*. Because Indonesian Islam confronted local animist and Hindu traditions that survived among nominal Muslims, the Muhammadiyah tended over time to focus more on purifying religious practices and beliefs than on spreading modernist interpretations. [*See* Muhammadiyah.]

Around the turn of the twentieth century, modernists in Egypt, India, and Indonesia accommodated themselves to European rule because of their conviction that it was futile to seek independence until Muslims had thoroughly assimilated true Islam. Nationalists in each land would accuse the modernists of compromising with European powers and thereby prolonging foreign rule. This criticism cost the modernists dearly in the contest to influence popular opinion. In the first half of the twentieth century, nationalist forces grew stronger and eclipsed modernist influence. In large measure, modernism's limitations stemmed from its character as an elitist intellectual response to Western power, whereas nationalists used symbols and rhetoric designed to appeal to a broader spectrum of society.

After the achievement of independence, fundamentalism emerged to pose yet another challenge to modernism, because, like nationalism, fundamentalist ideas have greater popular appeal than those of modernism. This problem for modernism has appeared in Iran quite vividly in recent years. In the nineteenth century, Iran experienced neither a modernizing state nor direct European rule, the main stimuli to modernism in other Muslim lands. Rather, modernism emerged in the twentieth century in response to a despotic secularizing regime bent on importing Western culture. Iran's leading modernist is Mehdi Bāzargān (b. 1907), who founded the Liberation Movement of Iran in 1963. He tried to reconcile his nation's westernized and traditional religious cultures by bringing the former back to Islam and introducing the latter to modern science. Like modernists elsewhere, Bazargan and his associate Ayatollah Maḥmud Ṭāleqāni (1912–1979) called for a return to the Qur'ān, sought to demonstrate Islam's compatibility with modern science, and tried to inculcate the activist ethos. In response to the Pahlavi dynasty's despotism, the Liberation Movement of Iran argued for a liberal polity with an Islamic character. In the tumult of the Iranian revolution of 1978–1979, Bāzargān and his allies tried to provide a bridge between the religious-minded followers of Ayatollah Ruhollah Khomeini and the secular nationalist opponents of the Pahlavi dynasty. In the revolutionary regime's second year, however, the clerical fundamentalists toppled Bāzargān and thereafter relegated the modernists to the margins of Iranian politics. [*See* Liberation Movement of Iran *and the biographies of Bāzargān and Ṭāleqānī.*]

Modernism, then, has failed to extend its appeal beyond intellectual elites, whose advocacy of liberal ideas is portrayed by fundamentalists as a sign of infatuation with the West. By contrast, fundamentalists hold that Muslims need not look to the West for solutions to their problems. Nonetheless, modernist ideas survive among contemporary thinkers who hold that exercising independent reasoning in legal matters would lend Islamic law to flexible interpretation according to changing circumstances. Another enduring modernist notion is that public *maṣlaḥah* (public welfare) is the general principle that guides the evolution of Islamic law. Legal reform along lines advocated by the modernists has achieved modest results in laws affecting the status of women in marriage, divorce, and inheritance. The educational strain in modernism has prevailed in gradually bringing a degree of modern learning to some religious schools, such as Egypt's prestigious al-Azhar. However, the modernist education agenda in Pakistan succumbed to pressures from conservative quarters. In the view of Fazlur Rahman (1919–1988), a leading contemporary modernist who lost the battle for educational modernism in Pakistan, the integration of Islam with modern scientific education has not yet taken place. Rahman also believed that Islamic theology required a new formulation. Perhaps theological modernism has received less emphasis in recent years because of a decline in missionary attacks on Islam and because of a decline in fatalistic attitudes that nineteenth-century modernists felt compelled to combat. Rahman's work indicates that in the last decade of the twentieth century modernism is alive among Muslim thinkers but not widely influential in Muslim societies. [*See the biography of Rahman.*]

BIBLIOGRAPHY

Adams, Charles C. *Islam and Modernism in Egypt*. Reprint, New York, 1968. Classic study of the lives, work, and thought of Jamāl al-Dīn al-Afghānī, Muḥammad ʿAbduh, Rashīd Riḍā, and Egyptian modernists of the 1920s. Originally published in 1933, its account of al-Afghānī's early years has been revised by later scholarship.

Ahmad, Aziz. *Islamic Modernism in India and Pakistan, 1857–1964*. London, 1967. Outstanding survey; examines the thought of Sayyid Aḥmad Khān, Muḥammad Iqbal, Abū al-Kalām Āzād, and other leading modernists.

Boullata, Kemal. *Trends and Issues in Contemporary Arab Thought*. Albany, N.Y., 1990. Although not specifically devoted to Islamic modernism, its discussion of debates over the Arab heritage, Islam, and women's status reveals the continued relevance of modernists' ideas and the problems they confronted.

Chehabi, H. E. *Iranian Politics and Religious-Modernism: The Liberation Movement of Iran under the Shah and Khomeini*. Ithaca, N.Y., 1990. Study of Mehdi Bāzargān and Maḥmud Ṭāleqānī's movement for a liberal, modern application of Islam in contemporary Iran. Briefly describes the movement's intellectual positions and dwells at length on its political activities.

Commins, David. *Islamic Reform: Politics and Social Change in Late Ottoman Syria*. New York, 1990. Study of the modernist trend in Damascus, its political fortunes, and its traditionalist opponents.

Enayat, Hamid. *Modern Islamic Political Thought*. Austin, 1982. Excellent work. Considers both Sunnī and Shīʿī thinkers who have grappled with nationalism, democracy, socialism, and the nature of the Islamic state. Encompasses both modernist and fundamentalist trends.

Gibb, H. A. R. *Modern Trends in Islam*. Chicago, 1947. Engaged, critical analysis of al-Afghānī, ʿAbduh, Aḥmad Khān, Iqbal, and others from an avowedly Christian perspective.

Green, Arnold H. *The Tunisian Ulama, 1873–1915: Social Structure and Responses to Ideological Currents*. Leiden, 1978. Outstanding English-language monograph on religious trends during this period in a North African setting.

Hourani, Albert. *Arabic Thought in the Liberal Age, 1798–1939*. Rev. ed. London, 1967. The best single examination of religious, nationalist, and secularist trends. Includes sections on Ṭahṭāwī, Khayr al-Dīn al-Tūnisī, al-Afghānī, ʿAbduh, and Rashīd Riḍā.

Keddie, Nikki R. *An Islamic Response to Imperialism: Political and Religious Writings of Sayyid Jamāl al-Dīn "al-Afghānī."* Rev. ed. Berkeley, 1983. The best introduction to al-Afghānī's life and thought by the author of his definitive biography. Translations of four Persian texts, an Arabic text, and a French text.

Kerr, Malcolm H. *Islamic Reform: The Political and Legal Theories of Muḥammad ʿAbduh and Rashīd Riḍā*. Berkeley, 1966. For those interested in a detailed and critical examination of theological, political, and legal doctrines. Difficult for the general reader.

Lelyveld, David. *Aligarh's First Generation*. Princeton, 1978. Rich and engaging study of India's leading modernist Muslim institution of higher learning. Integrates social, cultural, and intellectual history.

Mardin, Şerif. *The Genesis of Young Ottoman Thought*. Princeton, 1962. Classic work on this small but highly influential circle.

Noer, Deliar. *The Modernist Muslim Movement in Indonesia, 1900–1942*. London, 1973. Comprehensive study of the social, intellectual, and political dimensions of modernism, and the reactions to it of traditional Muslims and the Dutch.

Peacock, James L. *Purifying the Faith: The Muhammadijah Movement in Indonesian Islam*. Menlo Park, Calif., 1978. Social anthropologist's account of the movement's history, current activities, and cultural significance.

Rahman, Fazlur. *Islam and Modernity: Transformation of an Intellectual Tradition*. Chicago, 1982. The best recent survey of Islamic modernism by an engaged participant who not only criticizes the movement's shortcomings but advances a methodology for modernist education and legal reform.

Troll, Christian W. *Sayyid Ahmad Khan: A Reinterpretation of Muslim*

Theology. New Delhi, 1978. Briefly reviews Aḥmad Khān's life and provides a detailed discussion of his thought. Includes translations of sixteen texts from the Urdu.

David Commins

MODERNIZATION AND DEVELOPMENT. Contemporary intellectual concepts with roots in the Western Enlightenment and denoting both ideological and socioeconomic processes, the concepts "modernization" and "development" have been subject to critique by theorists and scholars of the Islamic revival as part of an anti-imperialist project. The underlying assumptions of modernization—secularism, materialism, individualism, and a commitment to progress through science and technology—formed the core of Western intellectual polemic against Islam and the intellectual justification for Western political domination of Muslims. Likewise, development, defined as the control of nature for the benefit of man, proceeded according to principles of liberal market forces, leading inevitably to secular and individualist political outcomes.

Decolonization and the post-1945 political independence of Muslim countries has been characterized by the replacement of this fairly overt liberal economic and political agenda by either the equally overt one of Western socialism, or the implicit one of Western social science. The ideas of Western socialism have been variously reconceived as Arab or Islamic socialism, or Baʿthism. The tenets of these reformulations are derived from the European Enlightenment principles of materialism and rationalism, as well as the Marxist concept of class consciousness. Islamic development is here argued to be superior to Western forms of capitalism and socialism because it attends to both spiritual and material needs, and more effectively addresses the problem of equity (Kurshid Ahmad, "Economic Development in an Islamic Framework," in Ahmad, 1980).

Western social science has codified liberal Enlightenment principles in the technocratic discourse of modernization and development, and, until the 1970s, unquestioningly assumed the objectivity of its methods and universality of its application. An economic model of development, in which the increasing concentration of capital, investment, and productivity would improve the condition of all classes, was combined with a pluralist model of political enfranchisement, in which individuals would speak through the formal apparatus of liberal bourgeois democracy. Islamic societies were thus analyzed by Westerners through this economistic lens and their "needs" judged accordingly.

The social science literature has had important policy implications for both foreign economic assistance and development planning in Muslim countries. The materialist and individualist assumptions of the Enlightenment-derived "science of economics" governed the allocation of foreign aid until the 1970s. At that time, following on the radical upheavals of the sixties and in the face of a profound challenge to, among other things, notions of corporatism and scientific expertise, Western elites were forced to reevaluate economic and social policies vis-à-vis the domestic populations of their own countries and those deployed in their relations with the Third World. This is reflected in the shift from technocratic economism to "basic needs" policies, in which attention was directed toward greater economic benefits for lower-income groups and attempts were made to foster more inclusive political participation. But this interlude in the domination of Western classical economics has been followed in the 1980s and 1990s by a return to *laissez-faire* doctrine. The new orthodoxy, with its reverence for market forces, economic competition, and individual decision making, has been accompanied by an ideological commitment to democratization. However, "democracy," as envisioned by the new technocrats, may be criticized as an effort to substitute political equality in the Western liberal mode for economic equity through the management of the more dislocating effects of market forces.

The earlier, implicit, normative judgments of Western "scientific" social science regarding political pluralism, individual political participation, and government accountability, have now become explicit. Whereas the former, mutually enforcing relationship between scholarly and public policy approaches to modernization and development was covert and even denied, in the 1980s and 1990s it has become explicit and acknowledged, even celebrated. Intellectual efforts are now directed to the examination of what is termed "civil society," in order to determine the potential for democracy in Middle Eastern states (Norton, 1993). Scholars and U.S. foreign policy makers alike now collaborate in a common endeavor to identify and encourage the democratization of Muslim societies within the framework of market-driven capitalism.

The foregoing constitutes a critical view of a generally acknowledged phenomenon. What has not been sufficiently recognized is that, beginning in the 1970s, Western social science has begun to be modified and adapted to the realities of Middle Eastern society by an intellectually sophisticated and talented generation of indigenous scholars and researchers. (See, for instance, Mustapha Kamal al-Sayyid, "A Civil Society in Egypt," and Saad Eddin Ibrahim, "Crises, Elites, and Democratization in the Arab World," in Norton, 1993, and Binder, 1988). The dominant social science interpretations of modernization and development, however, have been subjected to an even more powerful challenge from indigenous Islamic forces, coinciding with the Islamic revival from the mid-1960s onward. The contemporary Islamic response to Western intrusion is not without historical precedent. From the time of the French Expedition to Egypt in the early 1800s, Muslims have resisted political, economic, and intellectual penetration by the West. These earlier struggles were, however, defensive in character, intended literally to safeguard and maintain the social and political positions of the *ʿulamāʾ*, or they assumed an apologetic tone, arguing that Islam had anticipated modernity and development. The recent revival of Islam may be traced, in part, to the 1967 military defeat of Egypt, which was viewed as a message from God and galvanized Muslims in Egypt and elsewhere in the Islamic world. Because the Egyptian *ʿulamāʾ* were virtually exhausted by the 1960s, the Islamic revival took on a populist character from its inception.

The contemporary Islamic revival has both majoritarian centrist and minority radical-oppositional factions. Advocates of an Islamic approach to development are now almost entirely identified with the former position, even though at one time some of them, including Sayyid Quṭb, Sayyid Abū al-Aʿlā Mawdūdī, and Ḥasan al-Turābī, were counted among the opposition. Their presence in the contemporary mainstream is an indication of the ideological success of the Islamic revival, even though its political agenda remains to be played out.

The revival has had two effects on the conceptualization of modernization and development. The first, and more significant, one has been a general claim by Islamic theorists as varied as Mawdūdī (Pakistan), ʿAlī Sharīʿatī (Iran), and Quṭb (Egypt) that modernization and development, or at least the latter, are in fact universal concepts that belong in effect to the age, not to the West alone. The ideas of the Islamic theorists are, consequently, less revolutionary than reformist. Structurally, the Islamic revival has occurred within already established nominally Muslim states, with the single exception of Iran. It is therefore not so much regime transforming as it is regime reforming. Moreover, in the theoretical writings of the revival related to issues of development, the criticism of the West is less polemical. This is both a reflection of the purpose of such writings—guiding fellow Muslims to religious awareness—and an intellectual self-confidence that is contributing to the creation of dialogue rather than confrontation. This dialogue is occurring between Islamic theorists and more secular Middle Eastern leaderships, as well as between Islamic and Western theorists.

In general, however, Islamic scholars dismiss the concept of modernization as being intrinsically Western ethnocentric. Thus it is argued that the criteria of modernization, particularly secularism, are peculiar to Western advanced industrial societies. In other words, modernization is equivalent to westernization itself, therefore politically and culturally unacceptable in an Islamic context (Al-Buraey, 1985). The tendency of Western theorists to emphasize the criteria of modernization further exacerbates the negative view of the concept.

Development, on the other hand, is considered a more flexible concept, containing within it a teleological dimension that permits an Islamist reformulation (Ahmad, 1980). But the Western definition of development is also treated critically, for reasons given by an American Muslim: "By concerning itself with 'process' and denying every teleological representation of reality, Western 'development' has turned man into a 'moment' of and within the cosmic process, rootless, anchorless, and destinationless. Development created a narcissistic exercise and invented an epistemology and science theory to explain and justify his predicament" (Ismāʿīl R. al-Fārūqī, Foreword to *Islam and Development,* 1977).

In their reconceptions of development, Islamic theorists have stressed the linkage between spiritual development and material improvement. The Qurʾān provides support in such passages as: "God does not change the condition of a people until they change their own inner selves" (surah 13.11; see Chapra, 1992, p. 197). Development is God's work, and His reward for spiritual improvement. Quṭb makes this point generally when he lays out a three-phase process of development, beginning with the spiritual cultivation *(tazkiyah)* of the good side of man, which simultaneously creates self-discipline against evil. This contributes to his wellbeing, or *falāḥ* (Chapra, 1992). Development then proceeds on a political front, to build the community of believers *(ummah)* within which good is pursued and evil is forbidden. Finally, since man lives in family and social networks, social reform is required. Quṭb then specifically begins to approach material development when he quotes the Qur'ān to the effect that, although the "earth is subservient to you," a balance must be sought between individual gain and the welfare of society (Sayyid Quṭb, "The Islamic Stages of Development," in *Islam and Development*, 1977).

These themes are supported by other scholars writing from a more technical perspective. Chapra notes that the teleology of Islamic development begins with the goals of revealed religious law *(maqāṣid al-sharīʿah)*, that is, the goals of God as expressed concretely in legal form (Chapra, 1992). It is the recognition of this relation between development and revelation that lies behind the insistent demand for the institution of *sharīʿah* law: there can be no economic progress until religious goals are institutionalized.

Development is also related to the theological imperative of unity, or *tawḥīd*. The term refers to the belief in the oneness of God as well as the oneness of existence with God, which suggests the organic solidarity, or corporatism *(takāfulīyah)*, of Islamic society (Cantori, 1990). The identification of God and society means that the needs of society must take precedence over those of the individual, that the collectivity of man is represented by the community of believers *(ummah)*. Individuals are related to the organic whole by the concept of *khilāfah*, or the vicegerency of the individual as the expression of God on earth, constituting the brotherhood of man in the sharing of this vicegerency. Accordingly, man is the custodian *(amīn)* of God's resources, meaning, in development terms, economic resources. Thus, individuals may acquire wealth in a capitalist fashion, but only with the understanding that such wealth does not belong to them, but to God.

The principle of *ʿadālah*, or justice, conditions the acquisition of wealth. Not only is the accumulation of capital part of the management of God's resources, but the individual must also be committed to the elimination of *ẓulm*, or inequity. Wealth must be produced from a respectable source with the employment of skill and as a reward for risk taking, but such accumulation is accompanied by a requirement to attend to the basic needs of those less fortunate. These needs are met through the provision of *zakāt*, or alms, dispensed by individuals through the family and neighborhood, rather than the state. The individual is thus free to pursue wealth and hence develop society because of his service to or representativeness of God and his responsibility to Him.

Family and neighborhood are the basis of the social solidarity, or corporativeness, of Islamic society, achieved via two concepts that, taken together, bind society to the state. These concepts, in turn, are related to an Islamic view of political development, or what might be termed Islamic democracy. The first is that of *shūrā*, or consultation. Political authority is to be exercised through a consultative process with those governed. In theory, and to a significant extent in practice, consultation is accomplished by representatives of constituent groups such as the *ʿulamāʾ*, professionals, businessmen, landowners, and leaders of trade unions (Javid Iqbal, "Democracy and the Modern Islamic State," in Esposito, 1983). Consultation may be extended more popularly through an elected parliament, but deliberation and consultation must characterize its proceedings, not divisiveness and contestation (Ḥasan al-Turābī, "The Islamic State," and Javid Iqbal, "Democracy and the Modern Islamic State," in Esposito, 1983).

The second concept binding society to the state is that of *bayʿah*. While the term essentially means allegiance, or even obedience, it also connotes agreement in the selection of a leader and a contract between leaders and followers (Osman, 1986). As a rhetorical device, *bayʿah*, in its latter connotations, may serve to legitimize a leader or a regime. More speculatively, it suggests that elections, especially presidential, are really plebiscitary in nature and not a matter of exercising political choice. What is being sought in elections is legitimacy and approval, with less consideration given to removing one political leader or expressing preference for another. Democratic practice in the Muslim world is characterized less by contentious competition among groups seeking to capture the citadels of political power, as in Western civil societies, than by disciplined deliberations within the framework of Islamic development. Sovereignty in Islamic democracy rests with God and not the individual.

All of this suggests that the role of the state in Islamic development is a minimal one. Traditionally, the state was responsible for the maintenance of order and the collection of taxes. The state *(dawlah)* and the ruler are also the *khilāfah*, or vicegerency, of God on earth. Thus, maintaining order involves upholding and enforcing His law and in general supporting and assisting the *ummah* in meeting its spiritual needs. But although the limited role of the state accords with the ethos of Islamic capitalism, it is also the case that the state is ultimately responsible for the enforcement of social and economic justice (*ʿadālah*). The Islamic theory of development is thus a conservative theory in its greater priority given to the revelations of God, yet is progressive in its recognition of the desirability of economic growth accompanied by attention to the problem of equity. At a minimum, the Islamic theory of development in the contemporary Islamic revival represents a set of modernized ethical standards by which the economic policy of Muslim states may be judged. Whether in the matter of interest-free Islamic investment companies in Egypt, the government policy of *zakāt* in Pakistan, or general economic policy in Malaysia, it appears that Islamic development theory is fast becoming practice.

[*See also* Economic Development.]

BIBLIOGRAPHY

Ahmad, Kurshid, ed. *Studies in Islamic Economics.* Leicester, 1980.

Association of Muslim Social Scientists. *Islam and Development: Proceedings of the Fifth Annual Convention of the Association of Muslim Social Scientists.* Plainfield, Ind., 1977.

Binder, Leonard. *Islamic Liberalism: A Critique of Development Ideologies.* Chicago, 1988.

Buraey, Muhammad al-. *Administrative Development: An Islamic Perspective.* London, 1985.

Cantori, Louis J. "Islamic Revivalism, Conservatism, and Progress in Contemporary Egypt." In *Religious Resurgence and Politics Worldwide,* edited by Emile F. Sahliyeh, pp. 183–194. Albany, N.Y., 1990.

Chapra, Mohammed Umer. *Islam and the Economic Challenge.* Leicester, 1992.

Choudhury, Masudul Alam, and Uzir Abdul Malik. *The Foundations of Islamic Political Economy.* New York, 1992.

Donohue, John J., and John L. Esposito, eds. *Islam in Transition: Muslim Perspectives.* New York, 1982.

Esposito, John L., ed. *Islam and Development: Religion and Sociopolitical Change.* Syracuse, N.Y., 1982.

Middle East Journal 47.2 (Spring 1993). Special issue entitled "The Future of Civil Society in the Middle East," edited by Augustus Richard Norton.

Osman, Fathi. "The Contract for the Appointment of the Head of an Islamic State: Bai'at al-Imam." In *State, Politics, and Islam,* edited by Mumtāz Aḥmad, pp. 51–85. Washington, D.C., 1986.

LOUIS J. CANTORI

MODESTY. Freedom from vanity (*al-tawaduʿ*) is a central concept in Islam, directly connected to the concept of *tawḥīd.* According to the Qur'ān, Satan's fall from grace was a direct result of his vanity. Having been ordered by God to bow to Adam, all angels complied except Satan. Satan explained his defiance as follows: "I am better than [Adam]; You created me from fire and created him from clay" (7.12).

Any Muslim who engages in vain and arrogant behavior, such as adopting an attitude of racial, gender, or class superiority, is embracing Satanic logic. The Qur'ān makes clear that, while God has bestowed on some humans more earthly gifts than he did on others, God created all humans from the same *nafs* (soul) and made them male and female, nations and tribes, so that they may come to know each other (49.13). Thus diversity was introduced into this world as a way of making the human experience more interesting and providing people with an incentive to communicate with one another. In the same passage, the Qur'ān also states that the most honored individuals in the eyes of God are the most pious.

The Qur'ān commends Christians and calls them "closest in friendship to Muslims" because "they do not act arrogantly" (5.82); the modesty of these believers evidences their faith in and submission to God. The Prophet said that a person with vanity in his heart, even if it weighs no more than a mustard seed, will not enter paradise. The Qur'ān is even clearer; it states that arrogant people are unjust, criminal, and nonbelievers (25.21, 45.31, 39.59), and that God will turn them away from divine revelation (or signs) and send them to hell eternally (7.146, 39.72).

Those who believe that they are more powerful than others install themselves as demigods on this earth, and their followers submit to them and not to God. This is *shirk,* believing in more than one god or in a god other than God. It negates *tawḥīd.* The Qur'ān is replete with examples of arrogant nonbelievers that God disgraced, defeated, or destroyed, among them the Pharaoh and his chiefs, and the people of ʿĀd and Madyan.

For these reasons, Muslim jurists discouraged all types of behavior that might constitute even early symptoms of arrogance. Muslims were enjoined not to strut vainly down the street, to raise their voices to impart superiority, or to indulge in excessive luxuries. The Prophet himself dressed and ate modestly; so did his companions. He also mended his own garments, participated in housework and child care, and helped others, including widows and maids, in their tasks when they sought his assistance.

The emphasis on discouraging early symptoms of arrogance, combined with an increasingly entrenched patriarchal tradition in the Islamic world, has led some jurists to demand that Muslim women veil their faces and avoid public life. In fact, women during the life of the Prophet were not required to do either. Today, some jurists have found such excesses unjustifiable and have called for a return to moderation, which the Qur'ān describes as the defining characteristic of the Muslim *ummah* (2.143).

[*See also* Dress; Seclusion; Shame; Tawhīd.]

BIBLIOGRAPHY

Abū Shuqqah, ʿAbd al-Ḥalīm Muḥammad. *Taḥrīr al-mar'ah fī ʿaṣr al-risālah.* 5 vols. Kuwait, 1990–. Excellent and thorough discussion of women and Islam. See volumes 3 and 4 for a discussion of the veil.

Esposito, John L. *Islam: The Straight Path.* Exp. ed. New York, 1991.

Ghazālī, Abū Ḥāmid al-. *Iḥyā' ʿulūm al-dīn.* Vol. 3. Cairo, 1939. Classic work with an extensive discussion of modesty.

Shīrāzī, Muḥammad al-Mahdī al-Ḥusaynī. *Al-fiqh: Mawsūʿah istidlālīyah fī al-fiqh al-Islāmī.* Vol. 96. 2d ed. Beirut, 1989.

AZIZAH Y. AL-HIBRI

MONARCHY. Islam's expansion faced the *ummah* (community) with the issue of *mulk* (royal authority). This term was already used, sometimes pejoratively, under the Umayyads (661–750), who were criticized for betraying an ideal. Qurʾān 2.247–249 cites the Hebrew prophet emphasizing that God alone made and unmade (3.26) kings, whom he endowed with knowledge and power, not wealth. Their *āyah* ("sign") was the Ark, a *sakīnah*, and Moses' and Aaron's relics. Shīʿī traditions mention the imams' *sakīnah* (the divine radiance), legitimating hereditary charisma.

God's throne overspreads heaven and earth (2.256; 25.60). The Last Day will mark *mulk*'s return to God (22.55). His law, *sharīʿah,* preexists any earthly law. Man's purpose is the exemplification and execution of *sharīʿah*, and the purpose of the *dār al-Islām* (Muslim lands) is the elimination of the *dār al-ḥarb* (non-Muslim lands). Except in Shīʿī doctrine, the Prophet died without nominating sucessors in his secular, leadership role. Those closest to him solved the dilemma by reference to Arab practice. By *ijmāʿ* (consensus) they selected the venerable among his companions, his first four deputies (*khulafā';* "rightly guided"), because they were best versed in the law revealed to the Prophet. Qurʾān 4.62, however, while primarily enjoining obedience to God and the messenger, affords some scope for flexibility by adding, "and those in charge among you."

The aim of such great jurists as al-Māturīdī (d. 944), Bāqillānī (d. 1013), Baghdādī (d. 1037), al-Māwardī (d. 1058), Juwaynī (d. 1085), al-Ghazālī (d. 1111), and Ibn Taymīyah (d. 1328) was adherence to revelation, maintaining Muslim piety, and, never more than in the paramount matter of leadership of the community, matching Muslim theory with practice. Muʿtazili rationalizations needed refuting, but, beginning in the ninth century, the Sunnī jurists had first to combat two extremes: Shīʿī doctrine that only the descendants of the Prophet's son-in-law ʿAlī were rightful leaders of the community and, notably after the occultation of the Twelfth Imam in 873, that in effect secular rulers were only tolerable under the aegis of the *fuqahā'* (those qualified to interpret the law); and the Khārijī doctrine that, if sound of body and mind, any Muslim might be elected caliph. Given that opposition to God's law and the consensus of the Prophet's people, "who can never agree on error," was heresy, the Sunnī jurists' watchwords were *maṣlaḥah* (commonweal for Muslims to fulfil God's purpose), *ittifāq al-ahwā'* (unanimous agreement on what is desirable), and on the negative side, *mafsadah* (what causes corruption), and especially, *fitnah* (economic and social disruption).

In a situation lacking dichotomy between spiritual and temporal authority, the jurists' problem was soon compounded by the rise of more than one caliphate, the ʿAbbāsid (749–1258) in Baghdad rivaled by others in Spain and Egypt. Although for reasons where theology and law were intertwined, the jurists sought the caliph's warrant, from 821 onward, provincial *amīrs* assumed and made hereditary local sovereignty as *malik* or *sulṭān,* and in 945, the Shīʿī Būyids captured the caliph's capital, Baghdad. They demonstrated pre-Islamic Iranian *kisrāwī* or khosroan influence by reviving Sassanian royal titles.

Such changes defied the Shīʿī theory of *naṣṣ* (imams by prophetic designation) as well as the Sunnī *bayʿah* (mutually agreed "bargain" between ruler and ruled). Al-Fārābī (d. 950), philosopher rather than jurist, anticipated developments by stipulating that a king should be skilled and powerful enough to be in fact philosopher-king, whether he were honored or not, rich or poor. Ibn Khaldūn (d. 1406) described the *inqilāb* (transformation) of the caliphate to *mulk* as "natural," but decadent, implying Arab Muslims' loss of *ʿaṣabīyah* (strong common feeling). Rūzbihān Khunjī (d. 1521) accepted kings as world managers provided that they protected *sharīʿah* and enabled the people to be dutiful Muslims.

The pre-Islamic Iranian *dīn* and *dawlah* (twinning of kingship and religion in mutual interdependence) as invoked, and crystalized in the Seljuk compromise with the caliphate. Under the Būyids, the jurist al-Māwardī said a restrained caliphate might function provided the restraining force upheld *sharīʿah*. New rulers' other primary duties related to taxes and defending Islamic territory. Al-Ghazālī was less concerned with the sultan-caliph relationship than with preservation of the religious life. Order, avoidance of *fitnah*, was vital.

When the Mongol Hülegü Khan ended the ʿAbbāsid caliphate, the symbol of authority from the Prophet's kinsmen and companions disappeared, though the Muẓaffarid Mubāriz al-Dīn Muḥammad (1313–1357) in Fars and certain North African aspirants to kingship sought legitimation from an ʿAbbāsid descendant in Cairo. The legal implications and Islam's exposure to unbelievers' infiltrations consequent on this not being lost on religious teachers around him, Il-Khānid caliph Ghāzān's conversion to Islam in 1295 appears to have initiated an attempt to fill the void. He was assiduously apostrophized by his minister and apologist, Rashīd al-Dīn, as Pādshāh-i Islām, and proof of the intention seems evident in the adoption of the ʿAbbāsid black banner.

For the Shīʿah the dilemma might have seemed resolved when, challenged by Sunnī Ottoman and Mughal neighbors, the Ṣafavids (1501–1722) made Shiism the religion of Iran, though both the shah and his Ottoman enemy styled themselves to each other as sovereign of Islam. Because Twelver Shiism claimed Ṣafavid descent from the seventh imam, Mūsā al-Kāẓim (d. 799), it might seem to have combined imamate and *mulk*. In effect, it caused tension between the *ʿulamāʾ* and king.

An Afghan Sunnī leader's defeat of the Ṣafavids and their subsequent final removal by their erstwhile liberator, Nādir Shāh, left Iran still officially Shīʿī. By 1979 a monarch had allowed his version of *kisrāwīyah* seriously to distort the delicate balance between the divine and mundane which Islam requires to be kept, at least as nearly as possible, in equilibrium. Ayatollah Ruhollah Khomeini replaced the shah in the Iranian Revolution. Enthusiastic followers called the ayatollah "imam," but he instituted what he termed, and depersonalized as, *vilāyat-i faqīh* (guardianship of the jurisprudent): one sufficiently knowledgeable in *sharīʿah* to be viable as curator of *maṣlaḥah* until the awaited Hidden Imam's return. Kingship banished, a fresh experiment in application of the ideal began: according to pure Islamic theory, not so much a political-social experiment as an attempt to retrieve from *mafsadah* God's purpose for man.

In Saudi Arabia, Ibn Saʿūd took the title of king in 1924. Foreign oil agreements, obviating dependence on local finance, consolidated his position. Morocco's old dynasty became a constitutional monarchy in 1962. Faced by modern Muslims' repurification concerns, these kingdoms' survival, owing much to their creators' abilities, largely depends on their heirs' capacity. Represented as "Western" innovations, these monarchies might, whatever their credentials, look beholden to forces threatening Islam.

[*See also* Authority and Legitimation; Caliph; Islamic State.]

BIBLIOGRAPHY

Ghazālī, Abū Ḥāmid al-. *Ghazali's Book of Counsel for Kings*. Translation of *Nasíhat al-Mulúk* by F. R. C. Bagely. Oxford, 1964. Maxims for "kings" on ideal government.

Gibb, H. A. R. *Studies on the Civilization of Islam*. Edited by Stanford J. Shaw and William R. Polk. London, 1962. Valuable discussion of Islamic legal and historical problems, based on extensive research.

Ibn Khaldūn. *The Muqaddimah: An Introduction to History*. Translated from the Arabic by Franz Rosenthal. New York, 1958. See especially chapter 3.

Lambton, Ann K. S. *State and Government in Medieval Islam*. Oxford, 1981. Useful, comprehensive introductory survey.

Levy, Reuben. *The Social Structure of Islam*. Cambridge, 1957. A picture of state and society under the ʿAbbāsid caliphs.

Niẓām al-Mulk. *Siyāsatnāmah*. Translated by Hubert Darke. London, 1960. Admonitions for secular rulers—the Seljuks—concerning how to rule according to both Islamic and what purport to be ancient Iranian principles, a key to practical as well as ideal statecraft.

Rosenthal, E. I. J. *Political Thought in Medieval Islam*. Cambridge, 1958. Essential and detailed study.

Rosenthal, E. I. J. *Islam in the Modern National State*. Cambridge, 1965. Survey of Islamic political thought in the context of secularizing movements and ideas of the nineteenth and twentieth centuries.

PETER AVERY

MONOTHEISM. *See* Tawḥīd.

MOROCCO. The population of Morocco, about 27 million (26,345,000 in mid-1991), is more than 99 percent Sunnī Muslim. There is a small Jewish minority of fewer than 8,000 people (mostly in Casablanca and other coastal cities). There is no indigenous Christian minority. There are no significant religious differences between the Berbers, found primarily in the mountains, and the Arabic-speaking population. Islamic "fundamentalist" movements have challenged the regime of King Ḥasan II since the 1970s. Educated Moroccans unsympathetic to these movements generally refer to them by the Arabic equivalent of the term "fundamentalist": *uṣūlī*. The members of these groups typically call themselves "Islamists" (Islāmīyin).

The most influential model of the history of Islam in Morocco is that of Ernest Gellner (1969), who sees Moroccan Islam as having oscillated throughout history between the puritanical, scripturalist religion of the literate urban bourgeoisie and the ritualistic, anthropolatrous religion of the illiterate rural tribes. He characterizes urban orthodox Islam as "Protestant" and the rural popular religion as "Catholic." Orthodoxy, says Gellner, revolved around holy scripture and thus entailed literacy. It was strictly monotheistic and egalitarian (among believers). It emphasized moderation and sobriety and abstention from ritual excesses. In this form of Islam, there were no intermediaries between the believer and God. The more anthropolatrous popular Islam, on the other hand, stressed hierarchy and mediation between the believer and God. The mediators were Ṣūfī shaykhs, saints, and *shurafā'*. This form of Islam was characterized by ritual indulgence, in contrast to the puritanism of urban orthodoxy.

Gellner concedes that popular Islam was not solely a rural phenomenon; it also existed among the urban poor. But whereas among the tribes it served as a kind of social lubricant making possible the resolution of conflicts, in the cities it provided ecstatic consolation for the poor. Orthodox Islam, on the other hand, served to ratify the style of life of the urban bourgeoisie. (This contrast is taken from Max Weber.)

The tribes of Morocco's mountains and deserts periodically revolted against the reigning dynasty in the name of the puritanical Islam normally associated, in Gellner's model, with the towns. This was possible because the ideals of urban orthodoxy were always present among the rural tribes, although they were subordinate to the norms of popular belief. Once successful, the puritanical revivalist movements would eventually revert to the anthropolatrous popular religion, once more vulnerable to puritanical revolt. Gellner sees this "pendulum swing" as having been unhinged by "modernity." The modern state monopolized violence whereas the precolonial one did not; as a result, the tribes atrophied, as did the saints who formerly mediated their conflicts.

Puritanical reformist movements, as Gellner points out, did periodically emerge to advocate a return to the pristine Islam of the Qur'ān and *sunnah*—Ibn Yāsīn's Almoravids and Ibn Tūmart's Almohads are the most obvious examples. But Gellner overlooks the fact that no such movements have managed to seize and retain control of the Moroccan state since the Almohads did so in the middle of the twelfth century, although many have tried.

More importantly, Gellner attempts to impose on the whole of Moroccan history the relationship between popular and orthodox Islam that he observed in the 1950s and 1960s. On the basis of his fieldwork among the High Atlas Berbers, he sees Sufism as a distinctive component of popular religion; in fact, it pervaded both popular and orthodox Islam at least from the fifteenth century through the first decades of the twentieth. Most of the *ʿulamā'* whom Gellner sees as embodying orthodoxy were themselves Ṣūfī mystics. It is true that some *ʿulamā'* periodically criticized Sufism in general, and that tension between orthodoxy and Sufism definitely existed. But the Ṣūfīs persecuted by *ʿulamā'* were typically renowned *ʿulamā'* themselves, often from the same urban elite as their persecutors. Gellner's model works as an "ideal type" conception of a recurrent tension in Islamic theology, but not as a model of its social manifestations.

There has always been a distinction between popular and orthodox Islam in Morocco—as there inevitably is in all world religions encompassing people of various social strata; however, both learned scholars and illiterate peasants have always prayed the same prayers every day of their lives. While there is much that is different in the ways they have interpreted their religion, there is also much that is the same. Moreover, Islam's "great" and "folk" traditions were even more intertwined in the past than they are in the late twentieth century. This becomes obvious when one examines the principal attempts at Islamic reform from the late eighteenth through the early twentieth century.

Forerunners of Twentieth-century Reformism. The history of Islamic reformism in Morocco may be said to begin with the revivalism of the Almoravids in the eleventh century and the Almohads in the twelfth. Modern reformism, however, is usually thought of as beginning with Sultan Sīdī Muḥammad ibn ʿAbd Allāh, who reigned from 1757 to 1790. Sīdī Muḥammad insisted on the strict application of Islamic law and the elimination of heretical innovations in both town and country. He condemned charlatans who used Sufism to exploit the gullible masses and "extremist Ṣūfīs" who did not conform to Islamic law; yet he was himself a member of the Nāṣirīyah Ṣūfī order and regularly visited saints' tombs and sent gifts to them. His attempts at reform did not constitute a fullfledged critique of Sufism and the veneration of saints.

Sīdī Muḥammad ibn ʿAbd Allāh's son Mawlāy Sulaymān (r. 1792–1822) is also cited as a forerunner of twentieth-century reformism. He too condemned heretical innovations (*bidʿah*) and stressed the need to conform to the Qur'ān and *sunnah*. He criticized the popular Ṣūfī orders and banned their festivals in honor of saints on the grounds that the rhythmic dancing, clapping, and mixing of men and women at such gatherings were all contrary to the Qur'ān and *sunnah*.

Although Mawlāy Sulaymān was more sympathetic to the Wahhābīs than most of the Moroccan *ʿulamā'* of his time, he insisted that visiting the shrines of saints to ask for their intercession was not only permitted but recommended by Islamic law, as long as people remembered that saints could not grant requests themselves but could only ask God to do so. Mawlāy Sulaymān never banned the visitation of saints in Morocco but rather specified the rules concerning such practices. Although he condemned many aspects of popular Sufism (including the use of musical instruments), he, like his father, belonged to the relatively orthodox Nāṣirīyah. Mawlāy Sulaymān's reformism was considerably less radical than that of the Wahhābīs or of Morocco's twentieth-century Salafī reformists. Yet even his relatively moderate demands for a return to the Islam of the Prophet disturbed many Moroccan *ʿulamā'*.

Salafī Reformism. The Salafīyah reformist movement spread to Morocco in the late nineteenth and early twentieth century. There is a widespread tendency to equate Salafī reformism in Morocco with nationalism. While it is true that reformism did become intertwined with nationalism in the 1930s, it is a mistake to assume, as many scholars do, that early Salafīs like Abū Shuʿayb al-Dukkālī (d. 1937) were nationalist heroes. On the contrary, al-Dukkālī never opposed the French Protectorate imposed in 1912; in fact, he amassed considerable wealth serving as an administrator in the colonial regime. Salafī *ʿulamā'* like al-Dukkālī did not enjoy seeing unbelievers control the Islamic world, and their country in particular, but they generally did nothing to stop the European onslaught. Even al-Dukkālī's student Muḥammad ibn al-ʿArabī al-ʿAlawī (d. 1964) did not openly oppose the French until 1944.

In contrast, Ṣūfī shaykhs such as Sīdī Muḥammad ibn ʿAbd al-Kabīr al-Kattānī (d. 1909) and Aḥmad al-Hībah (d. 1919) died trying to lead resistance to colonial rule. The conventional generalization that Ṣūfī shaykhs collaborated with the French and the Spanish (in the far north and the south) against the Salafī nationalists reflects the situation in the 1940s rather than that of the early decades of anticolonial resistance.

The inadequacy of much discussion of early twentieth-century Islam in Morocco is illustrated by the case of Sīdī Muḥammad ibn Jaʿfar al-Kattānī, best known for two books, *Salwat al-anfās* (Solace of the Souls), published in 1899, and *Naṣīḥat ahl al-Islām* (Frank Counsel to the People of Islam), first published in 1908. The first work celebrates the saints, Ṣūfīs, *shurafā'*, and *ʿulamā'* buried in Fez; the second calls for a return to the pristine Islam of the Prophet. Like most *ʿulamā'* of his day, Muḥammad ibn Jaʿfar al-Kattānī saw no contradiction between the two.

Very few *ʿulamā'* of the late twentieth century would still speak of saints as Muḥammad ibn Jaʿfar al-Kattānī did in 1899. But much of al-Kattānī's *Naṣīḥat ahl al-Islām* has a decidedly "modern" ring—at least in that much of its rhetoric and virtually all its reasoning remain commonplace among some Salafī reformists and most "Islamists" or "fundamentalists." This text is in fact a milestone in the evolution of the Islam of the precolonial *ʿulamā'* toward later, more ideological forms of reformism and fundamentalism. Its basic argument is that God enabled the first Muslims, "the righteous ancestors" (*al-salaf al-ṣāliḥ*), to thrive and conquer much of the world because they conformed to his laws. Then the believers deviated from those laws, and the unbelievers of Europe were therefore able to subjugate them. If believers return to "the straight path," they will once again thrive, and God will liberate them from the domination of the infidels and eliminate all social injustice. This argument has been the central theme of twentieth-century Muslim reformism and fundamentalism.

The Salafī movement did eventually merge with Moroccan nationalism, as embodied by the Istiqlāl party and its most famous leader, Muḥammad ʿAllāl al-Fāsī. Once Morocco regained its independence in 1956, King Muḥammad V (d. 1961) and his successor Ḥasan II managed to curb the political influence of this party. But as public education spread, so too did the Salafī conception of Islam. [*See* Salafīyah; Istiqlāl; *and the biography of Fāsī.*]

Fundamentalist Movements. During the 1970s a number of fundamentalist movements emerged in Morocco. The most important of these was led by ʿAbd al-Salām Yāsīn. In 1965, at the age of thirty-eight, Yāsīn had what he called a "spiritual crisis." After reading a wide range of mystical texts, Yāsīn joined the Ṣūfī brotherhood of the Būtshishīyah, becoming a follower of Shaykh al-Ḥājj al-ʿAbbās, who died six years later. It has been alleged that Yāsīn left the order in 1971 because he wanted to turn it into a political movement and was unable to do so. Yāsīn never renounced Sufism and refers to it repeatedly in his writings, in sharp contrast to the antipathy toward Sufism characteristic of most twentieth-century Muslim fundamentalists.

Yāsīn's attitude toward Islam was politicized in the early 1970s, in part as a result of reading the Egyptian writers Ḥasan al-Bannā' and Sayyid Quṭb. In 1974 he decided to write a *risālah* (epistle or letter) to King Ḥasan II entitled *Al-Islām, aw, al-ṭūfān: Risālah maftūḥah ilā malik al-Maghrib* (Islam, or, the Deluge: An Open Epistle to the King of Morocco). Its basic message is simple and familiar. The Muslims' problems are due to their having deviated from Islam. If they return to the laws of God and stop imitating the West, the oppression of the poor by the rich will vanish, as will the domination of Morocco by the West, the state of terror in which Moroccans live, and the squatter settlements ringing Morocco's cities. The caliph will be a man of the people instead of a potentate living indolently in his palaces. Everything that is bad will be good.

Ḥasan II was outraged by Yāsīn's epistle and asked the late ʿAbdallāh Gannūn, head of the league of Moroccan *ʿulamā'*, how he should respond to it. Gannūn told the king that Yāsīn should be put in a psychiatric hospital, since only a lunatic could address the king as Yāsīn had.

Yāsīn spent three and a half years (1974–1977) in an insane asylum because of his epistle. Once released, he resumed his campaign for a strictly Islamic polity in Morocco, but he no longer criticized the king directly. In 1979 he began publishing an Islamic review entitled *Al-jamāʿah* (The Group); no more than three thousand copies were ever published, and it was banned after the eleventh issue appeared in 1983. The government also forbade Yāsīn from preaching in mosques. In December 1983, he tried to publish another newspaper entitled *Al-ṣubḥ* (The Dawn), but this too was immediately banned, and he was sentenced to two years in prison. He was released in January 1986.

From 1986 until 1989, Yāsīn's home in Salé became the center of his movement, even though policemen always guarded it and often questioned visitors. The movement, now known as "Justice and Benevolence" (al-ʿAdl wa-al-Iḥsān) was itself reminiscent of a Ṣūfī order. Like a Ṣūfī shaykh, Yāsīn is regularly referred to as a *murshid* or "guide" by his followers. Like a shaykh, he stresses the importance of prayers involving "the remembrance of God" *(dhikr Allāh);* like some Ṣūfīs, Yāsīn's followers are allegedly expected to chant "There is no god but God" three thousand times a day and "God bless our Lord Muḥammad" three hundred times. This Ṣūfī aspect of Yāsīn's movement is unusual and is condemned by some fundamentalists.

In December 1989 the police stopped allowing visits to Yāsīn's house, where he remained under house arrest. The following month, six leaders of Justice and Benevolence were arrested. Their trial in May 1990 sparked a demonstration by some two thousand people; the center of Rabat was paralyzed for about three hours before the police finally dispersed the protestors, most of them university students. The fact that this demonstration was Yāsīn's most dramatic political success indicates just how unsuccessful his movement has been, at least through 1992.

One reason given for the weakness of Yāsīn's movement is the popular belief in the holiness of the Moroccan king. This belief, however, has ceased to exist among educated Moroccans, whose numbers have grown rapidly since independence.

[*See also* Islam, *article on* Islam in the Middle East and North Africa; Popular Religion, *article on* Popular Religion in the Middle East and North Africa.]

BIBLIOGRAPHY

Agnouche, Abdellatif. *Histoire politique du Maroc: Pouvoir-légitimités-institutions.* Casablanca, 1987. Good history of the political role of Islam.

Brown, Kenneth L. *People of Salé: Tradition and Change in a Moroccan City, 1830–1930.* Manchester, 1976.

Burke, Edmund, III. *Prelude to Protectorate in Morocco: Precolonial Protest and Resistance, 1860–1912.* Chicago, 1976.

Eickelman, Dale F. *Moroccan Islam: Tradition and Society in a Pilgrimage Center.* Austin, 1976. Classic ethnography of the Sharqawa *zāwiyah.*

El Mansour, Mohamed. *Morocco in the Reign of Mawlay Sulayman.*

Cambridgeshire, 1990. Good on early nineteenth-century Islam.
Geertz, Clifford. *Islam Observed: Religious Development in Morocco and Indonesia*. New Haven, 1968. Good discussion of the "ideologization" of religion.
Gellner, Ernest. *Saints of the Atlas*. Chicago, 1969. Contains Gellner's "pendulum swing" model of Islam.
Laroui, Abdallah. *Les origines sociales et culturelles du nationalisme marocain, 1830–1912*. Paris, 1977. Classic portrait of the precolonial social and political roles of Islam.
Munson, Henry, Jr. *Religion and Power in Morocco*. New Haven, 1993. Political role of Islam from the twelfth century through the early 1990s.
Westermarck, Edward A. *Ritual and Belief in Morocco*. 2 vols. London, 1926. Encyclopedia of popular Islam.

HENRY MUNSON, JR.

MORO NATIONAL LIBERATION FRONT.

To safeguard Moro (Philippine Muslim) interests and cultural identity, the Moro National Liberation Front (MNLF) was formed in 1969 by a group of young, progressive Moros headed by Nur Misuari, a former student activist at the University of the Philippines. The formation of the MNLF was in response to the historical manifestation of religious and political animosity between the Christian majority and Muslim minority in the Philippines. In addition, the acceleration of national integration and development programs during the 1950s and 1960s resulted in an influx of Christian settlers into Moroland (Mindanao, Sulu, and Palawan). The Moros suspected the government's motives behind integration and feared that it intended to destroy their Muslim community *(ummah)*.

When President Ferdinand Marcos imposed martial law in the Philippines in 1972, the conflict between Christians and Muslims intensified. The MNLF was able to obtain the support of Muslim leaders such as President Muʿammar al-Qadhdhāfī of Libya and Tun Mustapha Harun, Chief Minister of Sabah, Malaysia. In 1974, the Central Committee of the MNLF issued a manifesto declaring its intention to establish an independent Bangsa Moro Republik. With the support of Libya and other member countries of the Organization of the Islamic Conference (OIC), the MNLF was able to escalate the war during 1973–1976, which forced the Philippine government to sign the Tripoli Agreement conceding full autonomy to Moroland.

The rapid ascendancy of the MNLF, however, can be attributed not so much to effective organization as to a fortuitous combination of circumstances, including the prior existence of various Moro armed groups fighting against the government and the support of several Muslim countries in response to the plight of the Moros. The MNLF was a loosely knit organization and had been unable to establish a clear chain of command. The thirteen-member Central Committee contented itself with setting broad policy outlines.

The toll of the armed conflict was tremendous, and the MNLF's success was short-lived. The Philippine government failed to abide by the Tripoli Agreement, the ceasefire collapsed, and fighting resumed in late 1977. In the same year, Misuari's leadership was challenged and other factions—the Moro Islamic Liberation Front (MILF) and MNLF-Reformist Group (MNLF-RG)—emerged. Although the divisions within the movement reflected underlying ideological and ethnic differences, the various factions were founded on the basis of a common ideology, Islam. The MNLF is more socially progressive, with strong support from the ethnic Tausug, while the MNLF-RG draws its support from the more conservative Maranao, and the MILF from religious and conservative elements of the Maguindanao.

Under President Corazon Aquino, the Philippine government again failed to proceed with a negotiated settlement on the basis of the Tripoli Agreement but was committed to a constitutional provision granting limited autonomy to the Muslims in the south. The MNLF, however, dissociated itself from the institution of the autonomy provisions. Rather, it called on the different Moro factions to unite in a renewed armed struggle for an independent Moro state.

The MNLF-led movement must be credited with some success in terms of the recognition achieved for Muslims. For example, Muslims have been able to extract concessions from successive Philippine governments under Marcos and Aquino. These include the official recognition of Islam and Moro culture, the establishment of *sharīʿah* courts, and the granting of limited autonomy. The Muslims have also received educational and economic assistance from Muslim countries, and the MNLF itself has been given observer status in the OIC.

[*See also* Philippines.]

BIBLIOGRAPHY

Che Man, W. K. *Muslim Separatism: The Moros of Southern Philippines and the Malays of Southern Thailand*. Singapore and New York, 1990. Comparative study of the Moro and the Malay separatist struggle.

Gowing, Peter G. *Muslim Filipinos: Heritage and Horizon*. Quezon City, 1979. Comprehensive overview of the contemporary Moro community and its problems within the larger Philippine society.

Majul, Cesar Adib. *Muslims in the Philippines*. Quezon City, 1973. Excellent account of the history of Muslims in the Philippines.

W. K. CHE MAN

MOSQUE. [*This entry comprises five articles:*
Historical Development
Mosque Architecture
The Mosque in Politics
The Mosque in Society
The Mosque in Education
The first is a historical survey of the origin and development of the mosque as a socioreligious institution; the second is an essay on the genesis and development of mosque architecture. The companion articles consider the mosque as a center of political, social, and educational activity in the modern world.]

Historical Development

The word "mosque" is derived from the Arabic *masjid* "place for (ritual) prostration." *Jāmiʿ* is a designation for the congregational mosque dedicated to Friday communal prayer; in modern times it is used interchangeably with *masjid*. The term *muṣallā* designates informal areas set aside for prayers and open-air spaces used for prayer on the major feast days, outside cities or in town squares.

Mosques have served as the focal points for the religious and social life of the Muslim community throughout its history. Depending on circumstances, as is the case for places of worship in other religions, they may serve both as shrines for contact with the sacred and as meetingplaces for the community.

This combination of functions is evident from the earliest period in Islamic history. From the Qur'ān, we know that the Mecca mosque is God's "sacred house," a setting for ritual activity, and a "meeting place for the people" (2.125); It is even declared to be "the first house founded for people" (3.96). The founding of the prophet Muḥammad's house-mosque in Medina (622) was one of the first events connected with the establishment of an autonomous Islamic community. It served as a place of assembly for the conduct of mundane affairs and prayer alike. Later tradition would elevate the status of the Mecca and Medina mosques, together with that in Jerusalem, to cosmological proportions. Thus the Kaʿbah marked the spot where the earth was created and was an earthly image of the divine throne in heaven. Muslims are required to face toward it when they pray and to perform *ḥajj* rites there if they are able. The Medina mosque became the Prophet's mausoleum, and *ḥadīth*s instructed the faithful that this was one of the gardens of paradise; visiting it would win the Prophet's intercession on judgment day. The Jerusalem al-Aqṣā mosque was identified as the site of the Prophet's miraculous night journey and ascent through the heavens. While it should not be surmised that all mosques have obtained the stature that these three have, they nonetheless have tended to replicate such combinations of sacred and mundane attributes in varying degrees.

The Prophet is reported to have taught, "The earth is a mosque for you, so pray wherever you happen to be when prayer time comes" (Muslim, *Ṣaḥīḥ, Masājid* 1). Although prayer can be performed nearly anywhere, and mosques as prayer places can be built nearly anywhere, the fact is that both most commonly occur in cities, towns, and villages. Indeed, wherever Muslims have settled in large enough numbers, one of their first efforts has been to erect a mosque, often within or among their houses. During the seventh-century conquests of Iraq and North Africa Muslim troops would customarily create a space for the main mosque in the center of their camps, following the example of the Prophet in Medina. These prayer spaces evolved into buildings, as the garrisons evolved into the cities of Basra, Kufa, Fustat, and Kairouan (Qayrawān). This pattern would later be emulated in the founding of Baghdad (eighth century) and Cairo (tenth century). In the preexisting settlements of conquered peoples, such as Damascus, Jerusalem, Luxor, and Mada'in, Muslims would establish mosques on the sites of temples, churches, and palaces.

Ibn Khaldūn (d. 1406) observed that there are two kinds of city mosques: grand ones under state control, for Friday prayer and major communal assemblies, and small ones built and operated by different sectors of the civilian population. It was customary in the early period, following pre-Islamic practice and Muḥammad's example in Medina, for the caliph or his appointed governors to build their residence *(dār al-imārah)* next to the congregational mosque, while the common people would establish mosques in their tribal quarters. With the efflorescence of power and wealth in Islamic empires and kingdoms, as the ruler's residence and congregational mosque became physically detached, both state and non-state mosques proliferated. Both kinds of centers were usually founded and maintained by private charitable donations and *waqf* revenues.

For example, Fustat-Cairo started with one congregational mosque in the seventh century and had 130 by the fifteenth, supplemented by hundreds of common mosques, *madrasahs*, Ṣūfī convents, and mausoleums. Aleppo, Damascus, and Fez experienced comparable mosque growth. The same trend is evident in Iraq and Iran until the interruption of the Mongol invasions. After Constantinople fell to the Ottomans (1453), during the reign of Sultan Mehmed II alone 190 new mosques were built and 17 churches were converted.

In the history of Shīʿī Islam the significance of mosques and their power have waxed and waned. The Shīʿī tomb-mosques of Karbala and Najaf benefited from Buyid (tenth to eleventh centuries) and Ṣafavid (sixteenth to seventeenth centuries) sponsorship. The Ismāʿīlī Fāṭimid dynasty (tenth to twelfth centuries) established and supported mosques across North Africa to Egypt and the Hejaz. The Ṣafavids did the same in Iran and the gulf coast of Arabia. However, when Shīʿī populations have been subjugated by Sunnī powers, not only has their mosque-building decreased, but observance of Friday prayers has also been largely curtailed, with the concurrence of Shīʿī *ʿulamāʾ* opposed to acknowledging the legitimacy of Sunnī authorities.

A mosque exists ostensibly to serve as a place for formal worship in the daily and Friday prayers. Men are supposed to be its chief patrons, but women are permitted also, preferably in the back, segregated by a screen, in a separate chamber, or up in a gallery. According to some jurists, the preferred place for female prayers is at home, because of the distraction or ritual impurity women might otherwise bring. Because of the purity rules applying to prayer, most mosques have a spot set aside for performing ablutions away from the main prayer area. Mosques are also the sites for the delivery of Friday sermons, homilies, and Qur'ānic recitation. Ṣūfīs have sometimes used mosques for conducting *dhikr* rites.

Mosques are also the recommended locale for retreats and voluntary vigils, especially during Ramaḍān. They serve as centers for the collection and distribution of alms *(zakāt);* congregational mosques once served as the treasuries for the caliphs. The poor and homeless have often found shelter and sustenance there. Many pilgrims visit their local mosques when they depart for and return from the *ḥajj* and *ʿumrah* (minor pilgrimage). The dead are brought and placed before the *miḥrāb* for funerary prayers. The contracting of marriages and business agreements can also occur there.

The mosque also possesses functions with respect to the afterlife. Mosque-builders have been promised a house in paradise by the Prophet. Although *ḥadīths* decry the erection of tomb-mosques, by the twelfth century venerating the relics of the Prophet, his family, and other holy men and women at shrines had become an extremely widespread practice for people seeking saintly blessing and intercession. These tomb-mosques became pilgrimage sites; some even doubled as congregational mosques, such as Cairo's Ḥusayn mosque and Fez's Mawlay Idrīs mosque. The growth of Shiism and the spread of Ṣūfī orders played a major role in this development. [*See* Ziyārah.]

Another function of mosques, closely tied to worship, is that of education. Circles of religious scholars and their students have gathered in the courtyards or porticos to study the Qur'ān, *ḥadīth* literature, law, and grammar, and to hear the exhortations of preachers. Judges have also issued their rulings there, and respected religious authorities customarily have kept appointed hours to dispense advice and wisdom. In good times, mosques have provided employment to many skilled and semiskilled individuals, including imams, Qur'ānic reciters, *mu'adhdhins* (muezzins; those calling people to prayer), and caretakers. In times of crisis, students and common people have gathered in them for mutual support and to gain obtain guidance from religious leaders. Likewise, mosques have served as focal points for opposition to other groups and authorities.

The multiplicity of mosque functions, already evident in the time of the Prophet, reached an apogee in the Ottoman complex known as the *külliye*. The majestic Süleymaniye *külliye* (sixteenth century) in Istanbul, for example, consists of a monumental congregational mosque, five *medreses*, two preparatory schools, a hospital and medical school, a Ṣūfī lodge, a hostel or caravanserai, a public bath and fountains, a public kitchen, housing for mosque teachers and caretakers, a wrestling ground, cafes, shops, imperial mausoleums, and a cemetery.

Today many of the characteristics and functions of mosques in Islamic history are still evident in mosques from the Middle East to Africa, Asia, and the Americas; however, two significant changes have been occurring. First, new national regimes in Muslim lands have been incorporating mosques into highly bureaucratic administrative systems to centralize state control, further their nationalist political agendas, and acquire legitimacy. Second, mosque construction in the second half of the twentieth century has been occurring at an unprecedented rate, both in traditional Muslim homelands and among immigrant Muslim communities in Europe and North America. This cannot be attributed only to state involvement; rather, it is a result of the growth of Muslim populations and of their prosperity, enhanced by oil revenues. But it also suggests something more profound—a desire on the part of Muslims to form and maintain their identities, to define a place on which to stand in a tumultuously changing, uncertain global society.

BIBLIOGRAPHY

Campo, Juan Eduardo. *The Other Sides of Paradise: Explorations into the Religious Meanings of Domestic Space in Islam.* Columbia, S.C., 1991. Contains analyses of the symbolic relations between houses, mosques, and the cosmos, as expressed in the Qur'ān, *ḥadīth*s, and Egyptian culture.

Berger, Morroe. *Islam in Egypt Today: Social and Political Aspects of Popular Religion.* Cambridge, 1970. Chapter 2 reports the results of a 1962 Egyptian government mosque census, and describes government efforts to reorganize and redirect mosques to serve government aims.

Fahim, Hussein M. "The Ritual of the *Ṣalāt al-Jumʿa* in Old Nubia and Kanuba Today." In *Nubian Ceremonial Life,* edited by John G. Kennedy, pp. 19–40. Berkeley, 1978. Anthropological study of changes in communal prayer performance and mosque functions in Egyptian Nubia.

Goodwin, Godfrey. *A History of Ottoman Architecture.* Baltimore, 1971. Includes detailed descriptions of imperial mosque architecture and its functions.

Grabar, Oleg. *The Formation of Islamic Art.* 2d ed. New Haven, 1987. Chapters 3 and 5 are exceptionally informed essays about the forms and meanings of early Islamic religious architecture in the eighth century.

Haddad, Yvonne Yazbeck, and Adair T. Lummis. *Islamic Values in the United States: A Comparative Study.* New York, 1987. Based on a sociological survey of U.S. Muslims. Chapter 2 contains a discussion of American mosque forms, constituencies, and functions.

Ibn Khaldūn. *The Muqaddimah: An Introduction to History.* 3 vols. Translated by Franz Rosenthal. New York, 1958. Consult volume 1:449–450, and volume 2:249–266, for discussions of mosques.

Muslim ibn al-Ḥajjāj al-Qushayrī. *Ṣaḥīḥ Muslim.* 4 vols. Translated by ʿAbdul Hamid Siddiqi. Lahore, 1976. Volume 1 contains the quasi-canonical *ḥadīth*s pertaining to prayer and mosques.

Pedersen, Johannes, et al. "Masdjid." In *Encyclopaedia of Islam,* new ed., vol. 6, pp. 645–707. Leiden, 1960–. Detailed account of the history, functions, and administration of the mosque prior to the modern period. Concludes with sections on mosques in India, Southeast Asia, China, and Africa.

Turner, Harold W. *From Temple to Meeting House: The Phenomenology and Theology of Places of Worship.* The Hague, 1979. Insightful comparative study of Jewish, Christian, and Islamic concepts of religious space, despite a reliance on secondary sources for the Islamic data.

JUAN EDUARDO CAMPO

Mosque Architecture

There are two words for mosque in Arabic—*masjid* and *jāmiʿ*. Derived from *sujud* (prostration), *masjid* means a building for prayer; *jāmiʿ* denotes a place of gathering. Any conveniently located mosque, large or small, may be used for daily prayers, but at noon every Friday the community congregates in a *jāmiʿ* not only to pray but also to hear the prayer-leader deliver a sermon *(khuṭbah)* from the steps of the *minbar*. Emulating the stone platform that the prophet Muḥammad ascended to give his sermons, the *minbar* has been an essential feature of a congregational mosque since the year 750 CE. It stands next to the *miḥrāb*, an ornamental arched niche set into the *qiblah* wall to indicate the direction of Mecca.

Originally the *qiblah* was Jerusalem; Mecca became the focal center of Islam in 629. Another eighty years passed before the *miḥrāb* niche made its appearance in mosque architecture. Prior to that innovation, the orientation of prayer was indicated either by a spear standing upright in the sand in an open desert mosque without walls, or by a piece of rock, as in the Prophet's house in Medina. This house had a spacious courtyard enclosed by unfired brick walls with a row of cells on one side and sheltered areas set against the other two walls; the latter were covered by palm leaves resting on palm trunks. There is general agreement that the architectural organization and construction materials of the earliest congregational mosques, such as those built in Basra and Kufa during the first half of the seventh century, were direct descendants of the house in Medina in which the Prophet lived, led communal prayers, and preached.

Neither of these congregational mosques retained its original architectural characteristics for long. In 665, the governor of Basra, Ziyād ibn Abīh, ordered the Basra mosque reconstructed in sun-dried brick with stone columns and a teak roof. When Ziyadh moved to Kufa as governor five years later, he also rebuilt the congregational mosque in that city. The renovated Kufa mosque consisted of a *ḥaram* (prayer hall) with five rows of stone columns and a *ṣaḥn* (court) surrounded by double rows of *riwāq*s (porticos). Another early congregational mosque, the ʿAmr ibn al-ʿĀṣ at Fustat in Egypt, underwent similar changes when it was enlarged and renovated in 827. Rows of arches on classical columns gathered from Roman ruins replaced its original wooden supports.

The *riwāq*s constituted a significant development because they converted the nondirectional pillared *ḥaram* into a multi-aisled hall. Actually, the aisled *ḥaram* probably emerged a century before in the al-Aqṣā Mosque at Jerusalem. Built by the Umayyad caliph al-Walīd between 709 and 715, the al-Aqṣā was severely damaged in the earthquake of 747 and was almost entirely rebuilt and enlarged by al-Mahdī (r. 775–785), with aisles running perpendicular to the *qiblah* wall.

By contrast, the congregational mosque al-Walīd built at Damascus (705–715) had a lofty central hall flanked by gable-roofed wings that were divided into three lateral aisles by two rows of columns. The columns supported *riwāq* walls pierced by arched openings not unlike the clerestory windows in early basilica churches. (The elegant double-tiered *riwāq*s in ʿAbd al-Raḥmān I's Great Mosque at Córdoba [785] may well have been inspired by the high arched openings in the Damascus Great Mosque.) Yet another feature of early Christian derivation is mosaic decoration. Panels depicting landscapes cover the mosque's walls above the marble revetments up to the archsprings on the three sides of the two-story *riwāq*s surrounding the *ṣaḥn*. They resemble in style and workmanship the mosaic decoration in the sixth-century Church of Saint Apollinare Nuovo at Ravenna and were no doubt the work of Byzantine craftsmen.

The Damascus Great Mosque originally had four minarets, one at each corner of the building. Today, only two minarets—one rebuilt in the fourteenth century, the other in the fifteenth—occupy the southeast and southwest corners of the *ḥaram*. A third minaret, erected in the twelfth century, stands by the main gateway on the north, across from the domed central hall. This arrangement emulates the axial union of the *miḥrāb* and minaret, which made its appearance in the Great Mosque of Qayrawān (Kairouan) in Tunisia.

The Qayrawān Great Mosque was built in 670, but it acquired its present form after modifications in 724 and 836. Its vast prayer hall is sectioned into aisles by sixteen *riwāq*s that extend toward the *qiblah*. Not only is the center aisle wider and higher than those on either side of it, it is also emphasized by a dome at each end—behind the main entrance, and in front of the *miḥrāb*. These two small domes align with a third over the three-level, square minaret (which may be the earliest surviving minaret in Islamic architecture) that rises in the middle of the mosque's front wall, right in the center of the *qiblah* axis. (For a different example of a square minaret, see figure 1.)

The tradition of a monumental minaret standing in front of a congregational mosque on its *qiblah* axis continued during the ʿAbbāsid period. This is well illustrated by the two mosques that the caliph al-Mutawakkil built in Samarra in Iraq. The Great Mosque of Samarra dates from 852, and the Mosque of Abū Dulaf was probably built during the first few years of the following decade.

FIGURE 1. *Qarawīyīn, Fez.* Tenth century; view from the west, showing square minaret.

The mammoth ziggurat minaret of the Samarra Great Mosque (al-Manārah al-Malwīyah) is the largest minaret ever erected. It rises as a free-standing structure in front of the sanctuary on its center and consists of a tower with an external ramp that spirals to a 50-meter-high platform over a square base 33 meters on a side. The Malwīyah has survived in good repair; however, of the enormous sanctuary—240 meters long by 156 meters wide—only the outer walls buttressed by semicylindrical bastions are still standing: the interior is empty.

Although the outer walls of the slightly smaller (213

× 135 meters) Abū Dulaf were destroyed, its piers have not totally disappeared. They show what the Samarra Great Mosque's interior may have been like before its internal support system collapsed. The Abū Dulaf's sanctuary arches span slightly more than 3 meters and spring from nearby square piers in the front and back of the court and from rectangular ones on the sides. Originally both the Samarra Great Mosque and Abū Dulaf were surrounded by walled *ziyādah*s on all four sides. On the east, west, and south the enclosures were wide, and on the north there was only a narrow strip.

The *ziyādah*s of the Samarra Great Mosque and Abū Dulaf are known through documentary and archaeological evidence. That of the Ibn Ṭūlūn mosque at Fustat has survived intact. Built by the ʿAbbāsid governor of Egypt, Aḥmad ibn Ṭūlūn, during the 870s (it was completed in 879), the Ibn Ṭūlūn is surrounded on three sides by a *ziyādah* that functions as a buffer between the town and mosque. The *ziyādah* serves as additional prayer area when large crowds gather in the mosque on Fridays and special occasions. It also contains within its walls the ablution facilities and minaret; the latter is composed of a cylindrical shaft with a spiral staircase on the outside over a high, square base. As in Samarra, an elevated passageway connects the minaret to the mosque. (See figure 2.)

Doors lining the Ibn Ṭūlūn's northeastern wall lead to a spacious, square *ṣaḥn* with double aisles on three sides and a five-aisle-deep *ḥaram* on the fourth. The *riwāq*s forming the aisles have rectangular piers marked by engaged columns at the corners. They shoulder painted arches that alternate with small arch-openings pieced into arcade walls over the piers. The soffits of both types of arches are decorated with bands of ornament. There is also a frieze of rosettes in stucco that runs along the top of the *riwāq* walls just below the flat timber roof. The fenestration system of the mosque's crenellated walls, comprising a row of pointed arched windows with polyfoil arched niches between them, emulates the rhythmic pattern of the alternating large and small arch openings in the interior.

There is a kinship between the Ibn Ṭūlūn and the two congregational mosques in Samarra. The same observation cannot be made for the ʿAbbāsid mosques in Iran. As Islam penetrated eastward into Asia, old mosque forms were replaced by new ones, as illustrated by the Masjid-i Tārīkh at Dāmghān (first half of the ninth century). In plan the Masjid-i Tārīkh recalls the early mosques in Mesopotamia. Its heavy barrel vaults over stumpy, cylindrical pillars, however, derive from Sassanian architecture.

Another new mosque form appeared in the ʿAbbāsid mosque at Balkh in Afghanistan (ascribed to the ninth century), in which the square *ḥaram* was divided into

FIGURE 2. *Mosque of Ibn Ṭūlūn, Cairo.* Ninth century; view to the north.

nine smaller squares—three deep and three wide—and all nine squares were covered by individual domes. The domed superstructure reflected the secular building tradition of Central Asia.

More important was the incorporation of another secular architectural theme—the cross-axial plan—into sacred building. The cross-axial plan was formed by an *īwān*, an important element resembling a gateway, in the middle of each side of a covered or open quadrangular hall or court. This plan was used in the eighth century by the Umayyads in al-Qaṣr on the citadel of Amman in Jordan, and by the ʿAbbāsids a century later in the main reception room of the Jawsaq al-Kharqānī at Samarra; the Seljuks used it in the twelfth-century Masjid-i Jumuʿah at Isfahan and Masjid-i Jāmiʿ at Zawara.

As illustrated by the Great Mosque of Varamin (1326) and the Masjid-i Shāh at Isfahan (1638), the cross-axial plan persisted in Iran during the Il-khānid and Ṣafavid periods (see figure 3). Bībī Khānum Mosque at Samarkand (1406) and the Jāmiʿ Masjid at Fatehpur Sikri near Agra (c. 1570) show that the cross-axial plan also played a part in the formation of mosque architecture in Timurid Turkestan and Mughal India.

Actually, the oldest mosque in India was the Qūwat al-Islām at Delhi. Begun in 1193 by Quṭbuddīn Aibak, it consisted of a sanctuary built on the substructure of a Hindu temple and the Quṭb Minār, a freestanding minaret tower named after its founder. Successive stages of Quṭb Minār's round, tall, and tapering shaft were marked by four projecting balconies; the spacious *ṣaḥn* of Qūwat al-Islām featured the four accents of the cross-axial plan.

Although it was sometimes used in such buildings as *madrasah*s and *māristān*s, the cross-axial plan was not seen in Artukid and Anatolian Seljuk mosques. As illustrated by the Great Mosques of Diyarbakır, Silvan, and Kızıltepe (Dunaysir), the Artukids created variations on the laterally set theme of the Damascus Great Mosque, but they did not use the cross-axial plan in their mosques. Neither did the plan play a significant role in Anatolian Seljuk sacred architecture. Except in the Great Mosque of Malatya (begun in 1243), the *īwān* was not used at all by the Anatolian Seljuks. They preferred instead the *āpādānah* type of columnar mosque exemplified by the Old Mosque (now called the ʿAlāʾ al-Dīn Mosque) at Konya (begun c. 1155; see figure 4) and the Great Mosque of Afyon (c. 1272). More importantly, they developed the basilica mosque, which consisted of several aisles running in the *qiblah* direction, with a dome in front of the *miḥrāb* and a small inner court in the middle of the center aisle to serve as the *ṣaḥn*. Two examples of the basilica type are the Great Mosques of Divriği (1228) and Beyşehir (1299). The first is notewor-

FIGURE 3. *Masjid-i Shāh, Isfahan.* Seventeenth century; view of the north facade.

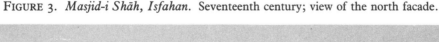

FIGURE 4. *ʿAlāʾ al-Dīn Mosque, Konya.* Twelfth century; view of the interior.

thy for its ornate stone portal and decorative vaults, and the second for its wooden columns with intricately covered capitals and its *miḥrāb* dome decorated with glazed tiles. The cross-axial plan did not find a favorable environment in Upper Mesopotamia and Anatolia, but another traditional element—the *miḥrāb* dome—became a significant feature in both regions. Artukids and Anatolian Seljuks emphasized their mosques with domes.

It was the Ottomans, however, who truly exploited the full potential of the dome in the mosque architecture. This development took place in three stages. The first stage was realized in the Great Mosque of Bursa (1399) when all but one of its twenty square bays were covered by domes of equal size (see figure 5). In the second stage, exemplified by the Üç Şerefeli Mosque at Edirne (1447), not only was a larger dome placed at the center of the *ḥaram,* but a *sahn* surrounded by domed arcades also preceded it. In the final stage, smaller bays around the larger central area of the *ḥaram* were integrated under half domes on one, two, three, or all four sides.

Among the Ottoman sultans' mosques dating from the sixteenth century, three are especially worthy of mention: the Şehzade Mehmed and Süleymaniye at Istanbul, and the Selimiye at Edirne. In the Şehzade Mehmed (1548), four half domes shoulder the central dome on four sides, while two minarets anchor the corners where the two squares that define the *ḥaram* and the *ṣaḥn* come together. The Süleymaniye (1557), with its upper structure highlighted by a central dome and two half domes before and after it on the *qiblah* axis, displays an Ottoman interpretation of the Hagia Sophia theme (see figure 6).

Unlike the minarets that mark the corners of the Süleymaniye's *sahn,* in the Selimiye (1575), four high, pencil-point minarets (the highest in Ottoman architecture) rise at the four corners of the *ḥaram,* which is covered by a large dome. It sits on eight elephantine pillars, bolstered by half domes on the diagonals. Within a quadrangular *ḥaram,* the Selimiye's central dome forms an octagonal baldachin. This was in keeping with the Ottoman preoccupation with searching for new mosque forms in the sixteenth century, which produced domical schemes over octagonal and hexagonal bases as well as square ones. The spirit of experimentation did not persist; by the seventeenth century the symmetrical and balanced form of the Şehzade Mehmed was accepted as the most suitable for a large imperial mosque, as shown by the Sultan Ahmed (1616), Yeni Cami (1667), and new Fatih (1771) mosques at Istanbul, as well as the Alabaster Mosque built by Muḥammad ʿAlī on the citadel of Cairo (1848).

FIGURE 5. *Great Mosque, Bursa.* Fourteenth century; plan.

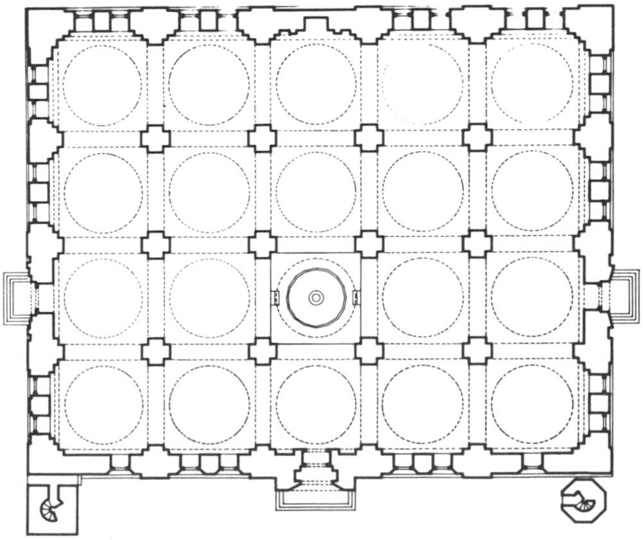

FIGURE 6. *Süleymaniye Mosque, Istanbul.* Sixteenth century; exterior.

Finally, it should be noted that the congregational mosque at Islamabad has a twentieth-century version of the cross-axial plan. The reinforced concrete folded plates of the *ḥaram*'s superstructure, with ridges pointing in the four directions, exemplify the happy union of contemporary building technology and a traditional architectural theme.

[*See also* Architecture.]

BIBLIOGRAPHY

Aslanapa, Oktay. *Turkish Art and Architecture.* London, 1971.

Brown, Percy. *Indian Architecture.* Bombay, 1949.

Creswell, K. A. C. *A Short Account of Early Muslim Architecture.* London, 1958.

Ettinghausen, Richard, and Oleg Grabar. *The Art and Architecture of Islam, 650–1250.* New York, 1967.

Gabriel, Albert. *Monuments turcs d'Anatolie.* 2 vols. Paris, 1931–1934.

Gabriel, Albert. *Voyages archéologiques dans la Turquie orientale.* Paris, 1940.

Godard, André. *The Art of Iran.* New York, 1971.

Goodwin, Godfrey. *A History of Ottoman Architecture.* London, 1971.

Hoag, John D. *Islamic Architecture.* New York, 1977.

Kuban, Doğan. *Muslim Religious Architecture.* Leiden, 1974.

Kuran, Aptullah. *The Mosque in Early Ottoman Architecture.* Chicago and London, 1968.

Kuran, Aptullah. *Sinan.* Washington, D.C., and Istanbul, 1987.

Michell, George, ed. *Architecture of the Islamic World.* New York, 1978.

APTULLAH KURAN

The Mosque in Politics

In recent decades the mosque has become a vital center of social and political activity wherever Muslims live. It has also become a visible and physical symbol of Islam, at times reduced to a journalistic cliché by the Western media. To understand Muslim society we need to understand the mosque in its midst.

Analysts discussing Christian revivalism in countries like the United States often compare the church to the mosque, but it is misleading to equate the mosque in Muslim society to the church in Christian society. The church, however central to Christian worship, does not have the same political or social influence today among Christians as the mosque has among Muslims. Moreover, the mosque performs many political functions the church does not.

At the outset it is important to point out that the idea of the mosque as a base for Muslim politics is not entirely a new or contemporary one. The mosque has always been at the center of political activity from the earliest days of Islam. The prophet Muḥammad helped build the first mosque in Medina next to his own house, and it became a center for discussion and debate. Among the first acts of most pious Muslim rulers was the building of a central mosque; later generations remembered the ruler through the mosque he built. According to folk tradition, whoever builds a mosque creates for himself or herself a place in paradise.

Inevitably, those seeking to express their discontent through violent means were able to do so also at the mosque. It is significant that two of the four righteous caliphs of Islam were assassinated in the precincts of the mosque. Given their pious nature, it was not difficult for the assassins to calculate where they would be during prayer time.

Mosques in Non-Muslim and Muslim Societies. Now more than ever the mosque is the hub and symbol of intense political and intellectual activity, whether Muslims are a majority or a minority in the region. In non-Muslim societies, the mosque has become a focus for the debate around Muslim identity.

In India the mosque in Ayodhya, built early in the sixteenth century, became the central symbol of the campaign of the Bharatiya Janata Party, the Hindu nationalist movement, to achieve power. It was argued that the Hindu deity Rama was born on the very spot on which the mosque was built; it had to be destroyed to build a temple in his honor. Underlying this was the feeling that the mosque had to be destroyed in order to prove Hindu superiority, to avenge Hindu defeats at Muslim hands, and to create Hindu cultural pride. In this milieu, where fact and fantasy fed into the communal passions of millions of people, Muslims became the ready victims of riots and police action (during the ten hours it took the Hindu mobs to demolish the mosque in December 1992, the police—almost entirely Hindu—stood idly by).

Soon other historical monuments were also being claimed by Hindu extremists. One is the Juma mosque in Delhi, built by the Mughal emperor Shāh Jahān, a descendant of the emperor who built the Ayodhya mosque, and a major center of Muslim political activity in India. Whenever there is a political crisis, the speeches there reflect it. Hindus now claim that the mosque was built on the site of a temple and must be destroyed so that a new temple can be built. The Taj Mahal (which also contains a mosque) is another target for extremists who claim it was once a Hindu palace. The threat is serious enough for the government to have posted armed security forces. Unlike the mosque in Ayodhya, the Taj Mahal is an internationally recognized tourist attraction, and damage to it would attract world attention.

Bosnia offers another example of violence against Muslims that focuses on the mosque. Although Muslims in Bosnia had over recent generations gradually been forced to give up the outward symbols of Islam—Arabic, prayers, and fasting—the first target of the Serbs was the mosque. It is estimated that by 1993 about eight hundred mosques had been destroyed. The standard procedure of the Serb offensive is to surround a village, blow up the mosque, and then plant trees on the site in the hope that the memory of it will be obliterated.

The destruction of a mosque evokes a highly charged and emotional response in Muslims. The notion of *shahīd* (martyr) has even been applied to the mosques that have been destroyed by non-Muslims. When the mosque in Ayodhya was destroyed by Hindus, Hindu temples in the neighboring Muslim countries of Pakistan and Bangladesh were attacked almost immediately.

Although mosques are safe from attack in Muslim countries, the mosque has become a focus of opposition to government in these societies and thus a target of official displeasure. The ideas that are generated in the network of mosques easily permeate the bazaar and the *sūq*, the *favela* and the village. In Egypt and Algeria the main opposition to what is seen as the corruption and incompetence of the government comes from the mosque; the Muslim parties that appeared poised to win the elections in Algeria in 1991 were thwarted by the imposition of martial law. In both Egypt and Algeria the state security apparatus has sometimes invaded mosques to try to crush Muslim opposition, creating a highly volatile situation.

In Egypt it is estimated that there are some forty thousand private mosques that are often the centers for militant antigovernment activities. The government is therefore attempting to incorporate these mosques, recently announcing that it would nationalize five thousand of them. Officials of the Ministry of Religious Endowments now write the sermons for the twenty thousand government-controlled mosques instead of allowing this to be done by local preachers.

Increasingly Muslim governments attempt to control the running of the mosque, the appointment of its officials, and the content of the *khuṭbah* or sermon. By doing so they hope to direct the nature of Islamic debate in society. They encourage the preachers to concentrate on innocuous religious topics, to talk of fasting and praying and of respecting elders and those in authority, in sermons that support ideal values and general principles not related directly to the demands of actual contemporary life. This kind of *khuṭbah* contrasts with those delivered in mosques not controlled by government, which serve as authentic, populist forums. Some of the most famous mosques in the Muslim world are directly under government control. An example is provided by one of the oldest university mosques in the world, the highly respected al-Azhar in Cairo. By incorporating the al-Azhar into its administrative structure, the government effectively removed its teeth.

Heightened Politicization. The mosque has become more politically relevant in recent decades for several reasons. First, many Muslim governments appear to have lost credibility in the eyes of the public. Few Muslims are prepared to believe the official statements of the government propaganda machine. The mosque, in contrast, provides a free forum for ideas that can challenge the corruption, inefficiency, and nepotism that mark many governments. In the sermon no one is spared who is seen as deviating from Islam—even a king or a military dictator. Under severely repressive regimes too the subtext of the sermon makes clear the message of opposition.

Second, from the 1970s on the central importance of the mosque was underlined by the emergence of enthusiastically Islamic rulers like King Fayṣal in Saudi Arabia, Ayatollah Khomeini in Iran, and General Zia ul-Haq in Pakistan. They made it a point to pray in the mosque, particularly on Fridays. These prayers became national events as they were shown on television. A sense of cultural pride was created, and the publicity encouraged people to go to the mosque themselves.

Third, the globalization taking place in Muslim society allows those in charge of the mosque to develop a global perception, a unified Muslim response to the times. It gives them the strength and courage to take on the establishment. Improvements in communication enable the person delivering the sermon to be well-informed and to relate local crises to international events. Thus a crisis in one part of the world can quickly be communicated to another and incorporated in sermons.

Finally, the importance given to the mosque over other forums gives the imams a sense of destiny to take up the challenge of leadership. They believe that they not only are on high moral ground, but also wear the legitimate mantle of political authority.

These points apply as well to the situation of Muslims living in predominantly non-Muslim societies. At Cambridge University in Britain until a few years ago, for instance, there was no place for Friday prayers. In the 1990s, however, there are three. The main mosque overflows on Friday with as many as two to three hundred people gathering, many spilling into the street. Women covered in their *ḥijāb* (Islamic dress) are present too, and according to Islamic custom they pray in a separate enclosure. The sermons are highly political and radical in content.

The mosque is also contributing in another significant manner to Islamic politics. There has been a tendency toward the universalization of Islam through the mosque. The sectarian barriers between Shīʿīs and Sunnīs, between Barelwīs and Deobandīs, may be starting to break down. Very often Muslims of different sectarian backgrounds gather at the central mosque for major occasions, when global issues can be raised and discussed. In the 1980s as such issues were identified and publicized, they reinforced a sense of Muslim identity. They included the controversy around Salman Rushdie's novel *The Satanic Verses,* the Gulf War, and the mass murders of Muslims in Bosnia. Such crises created anger among Muslims, but they also forged a global sense of identity. Through the sermon in the mosque, the imam was able to develop the arguments into a plausible worldview.

The mosque officials were therefore able to act as political leaders and to become spokesmen. For instance, the Bradford Council of Mosques in Great Britain became more or less the official voice for Muslims during the *Satanic Verses* controversy. Its members regularly appeared in the media explaining why Muslims were responding as they did. It gave the mosque officials a new sense of power and importance. The more westernized or less traditional Muslim leadership was bypassed and made almost irrelevant in the media. [*See* Rushdie Affair.]

Importance of Sermons. In order to understand the power of the mosque, it is essential to understand the nature of the sermon. The *khuṭbah* is often a highly emotional and topical speech discussing the crises in Bosnia, Palestine, or Kashmir and linking the failure of Muslim governments to solve them to the corrupting influences of the West. The corruption of Western society and the need for Muslims to protect themselves from its evil influences from a large part of the argument.

The *khuṭbah* is not necessarily an academic or structured discourse. It ranges from a high idealism that borrows from early Islam to a radical populism that appeals to the young. Unfortunately, few non-Muslim commentators understand this, and so they tend to turn to westernized Muslim journalists for political comment and analysis. They would do better to listen to the sermon in the mosque as the key indicator of social and political Muslim thinking, especially the Friday sermon.

A typical Friday sermon focuses on three areas: mainstream Islamic thinking, with well-known historical events recounted, supported by anecdotes and stories; national problems and crises, especially in the context of local politics; and international crises that link Muslims throughout the world. These help to form a coherent worldview.

Several themes are common in the sermons. One is the eternal and universal struggle between the forces of good and evil. The world is increasingly analyzed as being dominated by the power of the West, especially the United States, which is projected as representing moral and spiritual decadence. Sex, drugs, and violence are what the West offers, and Muslims must resist them with moral confidence. Another theme, also linked to the West, focuses on contemporary problems. It is here that ideas of justice and *jihād* or holy struggle are explicitly linked. The loss of Jerusalem and the fate of the Palestinians are prominent, as is the slaughter in Bosnia. It is significant that Bosnia itself has become a major and unlikely stick with which to beat Muslim governments. Even in a society like Saudi Arabia, *khuṭbahs* mention Bosnia to point to the ineffectual response of the government in providing tangible support to fellow Muslims, hinting that Muslim governments are submitting to the West in their silence on the issue. Among the nationalist issues that are raised in *khuṭbah*s, corrupt rulers, the inequality between rich and poor, and the inefficiency of government are highlighted. The West is shown as supporting incompetent and corrupt Muslim rulers in order to obtain concessions such as oil or military bases.

The main themes emerging in the sermons reflect an apocalyptic mood among many ordinary Muslims, fed by memories of the great days of Islam, its lofty ideals, and the nobility of early Muslims. The analysis is usually simplistic, the colors black and white, and the expression hyperbolic. The audience, often rural and illiterate, tends to respond with passion. Broad and familiar themes tend to comfort people in these times of rapid change. The mosque thus provides a secure, familiar base to Muslims bewildered by change, angry at the perceived injustices of a hostile world, and seeking solace in an increasingly secular and materialistic age.

[*See also* Imam; Khuṭbah.]

BIBLIOGRAPHY

Ahmed, Akbar S. *Postmodernism and Islam: Predicament and Promise.* London, 1992. Situates role of mosque in context of larger themes of globalization and politicization of religion.

Antoun, Richard. *Muslim Preacher in the Modern World: A Jordanian Case Study in Comparative Perspective.* Princeton, 1989. Study of the mosque sermon as a political and social institution in one Middle Eastern country.

Gaffney, Patrick D. "Authority and the Mosque in Upper Egypt: The Islamic Preacher as Image and Actor." In *Islam and the Political Economy of Meaning,* edited by William R. Roff, pp. 199–225. Berkeley, 1987. Examination of how the mosque and mosque preacher in Egypt exercise influence.

AKBAR S. AHMED

The Mosque in Society

The functions of a mosque may vary in different settings, but its importance as a ritual center remains paramount. Its defining feature resides in its symbolic expressions. Other activities related to education, legal procedures, counseling, conflict resolution, life-cycle celebrations, public communication, political mobilization, entertainment, and the provision of welfare assistance follow from this cultic *raison d'être*.

The types of rituals that occur in and around a mosque also vary, reflecting a diversity of doctrinal views and devotional practices. Nonetheless, two standard rituals predominate—the daily prayer and the Friday sermon, which ordinarily form the basis of a mosque's institutional structure. Other ceremonies (notably the dramatization of Imam Ḥusayn's martyrdom among Shīʿī congregations) may supplement or even overshadow the basic liturgical acts that most Muslims regard as obligatory.

The variety in the functions that link a mosque to society has its origin in the double image of Islam's initial place of worship. On the one hand, the prophet Muḥammad's original call to his fellow Arabs to convert from idolatry and heed the Qur'ān envisaged the *ḥarām* or sacred precinct, first in Jerusalem and then at Mecca, as its idealized focus. On the other hand, the mosque the Prophet himself founded and whence he directed the primitive community was the open courtyard beside his house in Medina, which hosted ritual gatherings as well as a broad range of practical operations. Hence two models appear in the Qur'ān and the *sunnah.* One portrays the mosque as a sacrosanct enclosure, a liminal perimeter, while the other depicts it as the exemplary hub of public affairs and the seat of just government.

Iconographically, most mosques combine aspects of both prototypes, but they often emphasize one or the other. The location, architecture, and ornament may exhibit either withdrawal or engagement. Mosques are sometimes set at the periphery of an inhabited area or at some remove where they are approached by a sort of pilgrim's journey. The rites at such a relatively isolated retreat tend to be personalized, often featuring the vows or petitions of single individuals; however, these solitary supplications may alternate with periodic exuberant assemblies or a colorful annual festival. In the main, there is little attention given to otherwise pronounced social distinctions based on age, sex, status and wealth.

A mosque stressing the activist aspect, by contrast, may be situated at the center of a village, on a major thoroughfare, or in the midst of a neighborhood. In another version, the principal mosque of a capital city usually stands adjacent to the ruler's palace or in the vicinity of the parliament, where it is the scene of national convocations or mass protests. Here, typically, key elements of a society's hierarchical structure are manifested by the mosque's spatial arrangements.

Mosques committed to participation in practical concerns often consist of an unpartitioned space that is informally demarcated to separate concurrent or consecutive activities. Thus the area used for congregational prayer may be taken over, perhaps regularly (as when a mosque doubles as a school), and put to other purposes. A mosque of this sort may also be designed as a composite complex with one portion devoted exclusively to prayer and preaching, while adjoining rooms are provided for classes, meetings, lodging, administration, or other needs. Formal supervision is inevitably greater under these expanded circumstances as, while rituals and other activities tend to follow a strict schedule and to be overseen by a certified and usually salaried leader.

Knowledge as the Source of Authority. According to Islamic tradition, in principle every knowledgeable Muslim who is capable of doing so is qualified to preside at the ritual prayer and to preach; but in any given company, the one who leads the others—the imam—is supposed to be the most learned among them or his delegated deputy. This shared premise also assumes tacitly that women do not lead men in prayer, although a woman may act as the imam where only females are present. It follows therefore that Islam does not recognize a clergy as the term is usually understood in the Christian context. Nevertheless, historically, ritual leadership has persistently been concentrated among certain definite social categories, and preaching has often been restricted by custom or edict to specifically authorized individuals.

Nonetheless, the definition of learning as the prerequisite qualification of authority is not univocal. A fecund ambiguity surrounds this ideal and has permitted two contrasting paradigms to emerge, coexist, and freely overlap. Both schools of thought maintain that *ʿilm* or knowledge is the foundation for authority in Islam, but they diverge significantly over what they understand by the concept and how it may be acquired, transferred, displayed, and enforced.

One view stresses the mastery of canonical texts, preferably by memorization. It sees the validation of such learning in the faithful reproduction and application of their contents, using prescribed rational techniques. The other view regards knowledge primarily as the mystical apprehension of hidden realities gained by divine illumination. Such knowledge is recognized intuitively as the product of infused grace or *barakah.*

Lately these perspectives connecting the mosque to expertise have been augmented and to some extent challenged by a possible rival in the form of modern scientific learning as manifested in the triumphs of Western technology. The claims flowing from this quarter, however, have largely been deflected from fundamental beliefs even as elements of modernity are selectively grafted onto received notions, often with dynamic impact on reform and revitalization movements. ʿAlī Sharīʿatī (d. 1977) is among the best known contemporary exemplars of this seminal adaptation. His "sociology of Islam", which had such forceful effect on the leaders of the Islamic revolution in Iran, draws heavily on French leftist themes. It is analogous in the domain of social theory to the cogent synthesis in the field of comparative philosophy of religion produced by Muhammad Iqbal (d. 1938) a half-century before. [*See the biographies of Sharīʿatī and Iqbal.*]

These different ways of knowing underlie two opposing approaches to the establishment of order. They are also objectified in contrasting forms of mosque leadership. First, in the classical frame of reference, a corps of scholars known as the *ʿulamāʾ*, *fuqahāʾ* (jurists), or occasionally *ṭalaba* (seminary students) have been widely recognized as the appropriate overseers of mosques. Furthermore, their functions in courts and schools as well as mosques historically placed them in a unique intermediate position between ruling elites and indigenous populations in stratified societies. Through their agency as an intermediary class, these scholars made the mosques rare channels of contact across the social and cultural boundaries that separated the upper echelons from the masses.

This intermediary role was most explicitly articulated in the Friday sermon, which bears extraordinary significance because the pulpit belongs by right to the successor of the Prophet. The scholar-orator who was nominated to preach was thus combining the authority of rational learning with his ritual function as the ruler's mouthpiece. In fact, however, this characterization of the mosque as the meetingplace for all levels of society, mediated by the *ʿulamāʾ*, vastly idealizes the past and is today patently antiquated. At best this pattern was restricted to the grand mosques of great cities where the authoritative pulpit or *minbar* was installed and where these scholars, who were almost exclusively an urban class, were essentially confined.

The second type of mosque and preacher has flourished especially in villages, within tribal societies, and among the populace in towns and cities, and revolves around views of divine power emanating from holy men or women who act as intercessors before God. These saints are said to bestow their favors, sometimes miraculously, to confer esoteric knowledge, protection, healing, and prosperity on those whom they choose. The veneration of a holy person, usually deceased, variously known as *ṣāliḥ, shaykh, walī, pīr, sayyid, murshid, murābiṭ*, or *āghā*, often incorporates magical and ecstatic elements. The site of these rituals is often a cupola shrine, lodge, mausoleum, or oratory, which may also serve as a mosque or be combined with a mosque. A chosen devotee or descendant of the saint, or perhaps the chief of a related Ṣūfī order, is usually understood to be the leader in such settings, even when someone else—perhaps one of the *ʿulamāʾ*—formally conducts the rituals. [*See* Sainthood.]

Mosques associated with saints and their cults frequently play an important part in life-crisis ceremonies within bounded communities, especially for males. Circumcisions, for instance, may occur under a saint's patronage. Induction into a mystical fraternity and progress through its graded stages may follow later. Marriages and funerals may also be orchestrated in a manner that affords participants the blessings of the interceding saint. In this sense, the mosque is used both to divide groups into social categories as it validates status transformation among individuals, and also to unite them by providing a base for undifferentiated solidarity. These simultaneous processes are conveyed in a Turkish proverb posed as a riddle: "What can a man do that a woman cannot?" The answer: "Go to the mosque." [*See* Rites of Passage.]

Popular and Official Reform. The recent changes that have so vastly reshaped Muslim society through modernization and all that it connotes have also profoundly influenced mosques. Thus, while the complementary paradigms of spiritual and practical emphasis persist, their priorities have been redirected. In general, both the appeal of the saints and respect for the *ʿulamāʾ* have declined markedly. The effects of Western-style schooling, mass media, improved communications, advanced technologies, universal military conscription, centralizing bureaucracies, political awareness, and exposure to the international marketplace have coalesced to undermine an uncritical confidence in these ancient religious institutions.

Efforts to reform the mosque, and especially to reinvigorate the pulpit, have pressed for change in both radical and moderate degrees, pointing in both conservative and liberalizing directions. Among the most important results of this sometimes contradictory process has been the emergence of a novel dichotomous scheme of classification that recasts and updates the rapport between the mosque and society.

In general, almost all reformers have encouraged the observance of ritual practices in closer conformity with the normative, literal *sharīʿah* codes. This has also meant a shift of attention, on a grand scale, toward interest in the style and content of preaching. In recent decades, often in the wake of anticolonial struggles, the Friday sermon has undergone dramatic revision and resurgence. The stilted rhetorical conventions and ossified language that traditionally constricted the expressive range of this idiom have steadily given way to direct speech, creative innuendo, and local vernaculars. Amateur preachers of all sorts—enthusiasts, pedants, ideologues, and militants—have moved in to fill the vacuum left as mosques abandon obsolete fixtures and the space becomes available for those who seek to reply to the questions arising from the confusion and frustration of an Islamic world that perceives itself to be under siege.

This new classification system defines mosques as falling under either government or private sponsorship. In the case of a government mosque (*masjid ḥukūmī*), the buildings and staff are all fully supported by the state. The preacher is a professional specialist trained either at a traditional *madrasah* such as al-Azhar in Cairo, Qarawīyīn at Fez, or one of Qom's many colleges, or at the faculty of Islamic studies of a university, or in an academy whose curriculum prepares students for careers in mosques and related institutions. This official imam (prayer-leader) and *khaṭīb* (preacher) is assigned to a mosque by the appropriate superior in the Ministry of Religious Affairs or its equivalent, which also details his job responsibilities, monitors his performance, and pays him in the manner of other government functionaries. Like clerks, such professional preachers are seen as interchangeable, and the ladder of promotion ascends first to larger and more prestigious pulpits and then into administration.

A private mosque *(masjid ahlī)*, by contrast, lacks government support, either because it was not offered or because it was rejected, and therefore it is not embraced by officialdom. Its autonomy is prized mainly because it permits the mosque's benefactor, or more normally its congregation, to set its agenda and to select its preacher. Most private mosques are relatively small and socially marginal. Some are used rarely or irregularly, erected spontaneously or for display; however, other private mosques are products of sustained initiative and extensive cooperation. Among the most influential mosques of this sort are those underwritten by a form of voluntary benevolent society known in Arabic as a *jamʿīyah khayrīyah* or charitable association.

Many groups of this flexible and pragmatic format have been in the vanguard of collective activism since this popular genre of organization was conceived in Egypt more than a century ago. Coinciding with the elimination of the notoriously corrupt system of religious endowments known as *waqf*, these voluntary societies arose as an innovative and self-sustaining framework whose success or failure depended almost entirely on the vision, skill, and motivation of the membership. A number of these private mosques attract sizable congregations; their preachers, who may include both *ʿulamāʾ* and laymen, come into prominence as important social and sometimes political voices. Thus in many places mosques affiliated with such associations have become rallying points for those eager to fashion alternatives to inefficient or inadequate public services. They have also at times fostered opportunities for dissent that some governments have in turn sought to curtail.

Given these qualities, one might suggest that such well-rooted private mosques are moving to recover that intermediary position that today is referred to as civil society, which in modified circumstances approximates the social role that classical theory accorded to the *ʿulamāʾ* and that popular piety entrusted to the saints. Such mosques appear to accomplish this mission by maintaining an equilibrium that avoids the extremes of both inert pompous ceremonialism and surrender to the self-justifying tactics of pure political competition. If the mosque is to preserve its role as a bridge between high and low, connecting the temporal and eternal realms of experience, it can do so only by providing the space for the reenactment of the sacred rituals and the presentation of the sacred book that recalls a community of believers to its origin and its end.

BIBLIOGRAPHY

Ahmed, Akbar S., and David M. Hart, eds. *Islam in Tribal Societies: From the Atlas to the Indus*. London, 1984. Brings good ethnographic data together with perspectives that go well beyond inherited stereotypes of limited usefulness.

Antoun, Richard. *Muslim Preacher in the Modern World: A Jordanian Case Study in Comparative Perspective*. Princeton, 1989. Indispensable and pioneering source on the study of mosque preachers in the context of changing peasant villages.

Campo, Juan Eduardo. *The Other Sides of Paradise: Explorations into the Religious Meanings of Domestic Space in Islam*. Columbia, S.C., 1991. Masterful exposition of the symbolic implications of spatial arrangements and decorations.

El-Zein, Abdul Hamid M. *The Sacred Meadows: A Structural Analysis of Religious Symbolism in an East African Town*. Evanston, Ill., 1974. Explores local Islamic myths and rituals on the island of Lamu, noting the symbolic linkages between the mosque and social relations.

Gaffney, Patrick D. "The Changing Voices of Islam: The Emergence of Professional Preachers in Contemporary Egypt." *Muslim World* 81 (January 1991): 27–47.

Gaffney, Patrick D. *The Prophet's Pulpit: Islamic Preaching in Contemporary Egypt*. Berkeley, 1995. Thorough description and analysis, notably of sermons, in their social and cultural context.

Gilsenan, Michael. *Saint and Sufi in Modern Egypt: An Essay in the Sociology of Religion*. Oxford, 1973. Exceptionally perceptive description and analysis of a recently founded and thriving urban Ṣūfī order.

Grabar, Oleg. "The Architecture of the Middle Eastern City from Past to Present: The Case of the Mosque." In *Middle Eastern Cities*, edited by Ira Lapidus, pp. 26–46. Berkeley, 1969. Instructive survey of continuities in mosque design from one era to the next.

Joseph, Roger. "The Semiotics of the Islamic Mosque." *Arab Studies Quarterly* 3 (July 1981): 286–301.

Khuri, Fuad I. "The Ulama: A Comparative Study of Sunni and Shiʿa Religious Officials." *Middle Eastern Studies* 23 (July 1987): 291–312.

Khuri, Fuad Ishaq. *Imams and Emirs: State, Religion, and Sects in Islam*. London, 1990. Comprehensive review of Islamic sects in the contemporary Arab world, with copious attention to the training and roles of religious leaders.

Mottahedeh, Roy P. *The Mantle of the Prophet: Religion and Politics in Iran*. New York, 1985. Brilliant account mixing fictive biography with detailed social history and portraying the build-up to the revolution from the perspectives of a traditional and modern student.

O'Brien, Donal Cruise, and Christian Coulon, eds. *Charisma and Brotherhood in African Islam*. Oxford and New York, 1988. Useful survey of the dynamics of religious leadership, concentrating on francophone West Africa.

Reeves, Edward B. *The Hidden Government: Ritual, Clientelism, and Legitimation in Northern Egypt*. Salt Lake City, 1990. Rich mine of details on the economic and political dimensions of the ritual life surrounding the mosque of Sayyid Aḥmad Badawī in Tanta.

Roff, William R., ed. *Islam and the Political Economy of Meaning*. Berkeley, 1987. Unusually engaging collection of anthropological and recent historical studies exploring the ways that Islamic discourse, including preaching, shapes and is shaped by various aspects of social experience.

PATRICK D. GAFFNEY

The Mosque in Education

In addition to being a place where preaching and worship take place and where the community assembles, the mosque has also been from the beginning a place of instruction in religion and its application in life. The Qur'ān speaks of religion as something that can be known and communicated with the help of reason. Muḥammad is said to have taught and answered questions in the mosque of Medina, and throughout Islamic history study of religion has been constantly encouraged.

The mosques that came into use after the Arab conquests were the natural places to learn about religion. On an elementary level this implied simply learning by heart verses from the Qur'ān and *ḥādith*s. Already at an early stage children were encouraged to memorize verses and passages of the Qur'ān, as they are still today. This tradition has spread to the *kuttāb*s (Qur'ānic schools) everywhere in the Muslim world, which are found mostly in or beside mosques, even in regions where Arabic is not spoken. Equally, up to the present day selections of famous *ḥadīth*s are' memorized and recited on numerous occasions.

On a less elementary level, mosques were also places of religious inquiry, discussion and debate, besides serving as places for communal worship and assembly, private study, and meditation. In other words, the mosque was the place where the religious aspects of things could be investigated and where people could look for religious truth, norms, and rules, and for religious guidance in the broader sense of the word, all centered around the Qur'ān.

Out of this kind of service and function of the mosque, it became the custom in early times that those possessing knowledge of religion and recognized as such were free to communicate their knowledge and to teach if they found an audience. This no longer consisted merely of learning by heart but extended to teaching the meaning of Qur'ānic verses, *ḥadīth*s that were not yet locally known, prescriptions as to how one should act in different situations of life, and answers to doctrinal problems related to knowledge of God and revelation. This advanced religious teaching started in the mosques and led eventually to the development of the religious sciences.

Thus from the beginnings of Islam mosques have functioned as centers of religious education, both in the sense of instruction *(ta'līm)* and in the sense of building a moral personality in the student who becomes an integrated member of the community *(tarbiyah)*. However mechanical and rational certain techniques may have been, this education created a communal sense and transmitted the basic truths by which the community distinguished itself from others. There was a close connection between what was held to be the true religion and the kind of education developed to transmit it. In Ṣūfī circles the learning process and education of the heart took place under the personal leadership of a *murshid*. The *'ulamā'* would teach the rational study of scripture and law, which required in the first place a good memory and intelligence. We are concerned here only with this second, formal kind of instruction and education as it was practiced in the mosques.

When Islam became institutionalized as a religion and its main prescriptions and doctrines had been fixed, knowledge of religion became more and more identified with knowledge of the Qur'ān and *sunnah* on one hand, and of the *sharī'ah* (religious law) on the other. Together with some less important disciplines, this became a corpus to be assimilated. To the construct of the religion corresponded a construct of knowledge of this religion, with particular ways of teaching and of studying that were in part indebted to existing educational traditions in the Near East.

The gradual acceptance of a certain corpus of knowledge to be acquired, embodied in texts that had to be read, did not exclude variety. And variety there was: regional cultural centers of religious learning, each with its own local *sunnah* (tradition), and different schools of *fiqh* (jurisprudence) and *kalām* (scholastic theology). There were majority views and the opinions of dissidents: Shīʿīs possessing their own chains of authority (*isnād*s) and their own corpus of traditions *(akhbār),* their own kind of education, and their own mosques; Ẓāhirīs with their literal conception of texts and the study of texts; or Muʿtazilīs making extensive use of reason and Aristotelian logic. The Sunnī majority, recognizing the established caliphate, needed only to defend itself by asserting that its idea and practice of religion was in line with established tradition *(sunnah).* But the Shīʿī minorities had to justify intellectually their specific ideas and practices as different from those of the majority; they may from the beginning have had a greater interest in good education because they were a minority, though a tolerated one.

It was Fāṭimid Ismāʿīlīs in late tenth-century Egypt who started to establish institutions for the education of their preachers and missionaries. Partly as a response to this, Sunnī authorities from the second half of the eleventh century promoted the establishment of Sunnī educational institutions (*madrasahs*) that assumed to a large extent the educational function of the mosques, at least beyond the primary level. These institutions, which quickly spread through the cultural centers of Islam, presented a coherent outlook on the world, humankind, and religion. At the time, the corpus of texts of authoritative religious knowledge according to the Sunnī perspective had been largely fixed, and religious education became more and more restricted to reading, learning, and explaining scripture, tradition, and texts according to authoritative commentaries. Hardly any new knowledge could be added; philosophy in the Sunnī institutions was largely reduced to the principles of Aristotelian logic; and the empirical disciplines, to the extent they were permitted, had only an auxiliary function with regard to the normative religious disciplines. Education in matters of religion, in both mosque and *madrasah,* had become the assimilation of knowledge essentially acquired in the past. Its aim was the simple transmission of religious truth known for a long time, to be inculcated into generation after generation of students. Basically, this orientation of *madrasah* and mosque education continued until the independence of many Muslim countries around the middle of the twentieth century, when national governments reorganized traditional institutions of Sunnī religious education. In some countries, such as Turkey, the reorganization occurred earlier; in others, such as India and Pakistan, where private institutions have continued to exist, it was less thoroughgoing. On the whole, Shīʿī religious education paid more attention to philosophy; its institutions enjoyed more political and financial independence. The mosque continues to play an educative role when Muslims migrate to the West.

I shall concentrate here on some major Sunnī mosques and the education given there around the turn of the nineteenth century: the Great Mosques in Mecca and Medina, the Azhar Mosque in Cairo, the Zaytūnah in Tunis, and the Qarawīyīn in Fez. Other mosques where religion was taught, as in Damascus, Aleppo, Kazan, Bukhara, Lahore, and Delhi, did not differ fundamentally from these. We also leave aside religious education given in *madrasah*s (Sunnī and Shīʿī), Ṣūfī *khānqah*s and *zāwiyah*s, and private associations founded in the nineteenth and twentieth centuries and concerned with the study of the Qur'ān and Islam generally. The following paragraphs note the features characteristic of the education promulgated in the great Sunnī mosques at the time.

Knowledge of classical Arabic was presupposed and further instruction in this language given according to traditional patterns that made such study, in particular of grammar, extremely difficult. Furthermore, a corpus of authoritative texts of the Islamic religious sciences *(ʿulūm al-dīn),* dating from the classical (medieval) period and offering the view of Islam at that time, had to be studied with the help of authoritative commentaries.

The teaching was offered by individual *fuqahā'* and *ʿulamā'* (shaykhs) to students who assembled in circles *(ḥalaqāt)* around them according to their own choice. After years of study with a particular shaykh a student could obtain a written statement *(ijāzah)* from him certifying that he had successfully studied certain texts with the teacher and was now allowed to teach these texts in his turn. Students might come from great distances in order to study in this way under highly reputed scholars; most students would come, however, from families living in the town or the surrounding countryside. In the teaching given at a particular mosque there was no coordination between the subjects actually taught, and there were no formal study programs and degrees or diplomas other than the individual *ijāzah.*

The pedagogy applied was based on the absolute authority of scripture, tradition, and the other texts studied, as well as on the authority of the masters of the past and the teachers of the present; both kinds of authority had to be respected. Such pedagogy required both the mental assimilation of the texts studied by means of memorization (printed texts were not yet available) and the sharpening of intelligence by putting and answering questions in discussions with the teacher.

As a result, a vision of Islam, the world, and humanity was presented that was supposed to be universally valid beyond time and space. At least in mosque education, no knowledge was provided about nature, society, history, or geography, not to speak of Western languages. A kind of self-sufficiency or at least a feeling of superiority prevailed among both teachers and students, proud of not only possessing the absolute religion but also knowing it, which made self-criticism and dialogue with others difficult.

The economic basis of this mosque education consisted principally of the revenues from *waqf*s (charitable endowments) that had made possible the foundation and upkeep of the mosques, and also of gifts, donations and legacies from people of the wealthier classes. Lodging and feeding of students was often provided in the same way, many students living in houses *(riwāq)* according to their regions of origin. At the time the mosques were practically independent of political authorities and governments at large, although there were often close personal links between the shaykhs and prominent personalities of public life through commercial and marriage alliances. It was rare for shaykhs to protest against government politics; they rather supported the regime in place, which would be able to offer appointments to gifted students and further the careers of ambitious *ʿulamāʾ*. Although there was a basic solidarity among the *ʿulamāʾ* as a class, they had no independent religious organization to defend the interests of their profession and themselves; they had to rely on their high social prestige among the population and the private wealth and influence of some members.

The social profile of the students was extremely broad. For many of them, coming from the countryside or the lower classes of the towns, mosque education hardly cost anything and was the only path to upward mobility. For sons of the urban upper classes and of the *ʿulamāʾ* themselves, this education gave access to important positions in the judiciary, state administration, and of course religious education itself. In a traditional Muslim society mosque and *madrasah* provided the education needed to fill the existing "intellectual" positions in the overall socioreligious structure.

Several explanations may be advanced for the major changes that occurred in this traditional mosque education between 1850 and 1950 and finally put an end to it. First, the modernist reform movement initiated by Muḥammad ʿAbduh (1849–1905) in Egypt and Sayyid Aḥmad Khān (1817–1898) in India was largely stimulated by educational concerns. Muslim thought had to come to terms with modern knowledge and the problems of the modern world, and Muslim students had to be prepared to face it. It was thought that a reform of Islam on the basis of a new, rational interpretation of its main sources, Qurʾān and *sunnah,* would make this possible. Much more than traditionalist Muslims, the reform movement had a vision of education as an engine to propel Muslim societies from the "backwardness" responsible for the success of foreign domination. The call for the reform of education was readily adopted by students committed to the reform of society and to nationalist movements, social development, and justice. It was also taken up by students who realized that finding a job in the society to come would be more difficult for those who came from the traditional educational system than for graduates of the increasing number of institutions offering a modern education.

New government policies also had their impact on traditional mosque and *madrasah* education. Muḥammad ʿAlī in Egypt, Khayr al-Dīn in Tunisia, and some enlightened sultans in Istanbul not only took the initiative in founding new educational institutions on a higher level; they also tried to limit private *waqf*s and to exert some control over the traditional educational institutions. Most nationalist movements were highly critical of a kind of education that was in fact a remnant of medieval times. Whereas most foreign colonial administrators were not allowed by their governments to meddle in the internal affairs of the Islamic institutions in the countries they ruled, the succeeding national and generally revolutionary governments could and did interfere with institutions sanctioned by traditional religion, like *waqf*s, mosques, and religious education. This was a natural consequence of the hard fact that, in order to survive, the newly independent countries needed to start planned economic development. To bring about the necessary changes, and for other reasons too, their societies were placed under complete governmental control. Moreover, in their efforts to modernize their countries the new nationalist governments reduced the spheres of influence of the traditional religious authorities, including the realm of education. Thinking along the same line, such governments have actively promoted modern educational institutions (including modern religious education) opposed to the traditional ones. They have also made concerted efforts to make the traditional educational institutions more functional, serving what they define as society's priorities.

Beyond the forces of Islamic reform and government policies, however, it was the changing economic and social structures of society that brought traditional mosque education to an end. Formerly students could exhibit their *ijāzahs* and find decent jobs in the traditional society of the time. In modern society people after their studies had to show diplomas and compete for a job. Those coming from traditional education often lost the battle because of their poor pragmatic qualifications compared with those of graduates from modern institutions who could show degrees and diplomas. The once-dominant traditional religious views had lost their monopoly in the minds of the people when nationalist and other secular ideologies offered themselves to the younger generation. Whereas the traditional mosque and *madrasah* education had been of great service to the traditional Muslim societies, rather closed to the outside world, they lost relevance once these societies were broken open not only by the penetration of the colonial powers, foreign capital, and Western ideas, but also by the efforts of new leaders—secular nationalists, military revolutionaries, socialists, and technocrats—not to speak of the many influences Muslim countries have undergone since independence. Traditional mosque education simply stood in the way of these new forces.

As a consequence, with the exception of certain regions of the Indian subcontinent, traditional mosque education at present persists only on the elementary level, that of learning the Qur'ān. This may be in the form of the traditional Qur'ānic school *(kuttāb)* where children learn parts of the Qur'ān and certain *ḥadīths* by heart, in addition to learning how to read and write. Or it may be listening to religious preaching or participating in study groups organized by mosques or other associations where adults receive instruction in Qur'ān and *sunnah,* no longer sitting in *ḥalaqāt* on the floor around the shaykh who leans against a pillar in the hall of the mosque, but now assembled in a room designed for the purpose under the roof of the mosque, provided with a library of printed books instead of the manuscripts found in the older mosques.

Religious education on higher levels has been mostly transferred to more or less modern Islamic university institutions. The Zaytūnah in Tunis finally became an Islamic university; so did Qarawīyīn in Fez. In 1961 even the venerable mosque university al-Azhar of Cairo became an Islamic university endowed with a great number of faculties similar to those found at modern universities, distinguished only by having faculties of Islamic law *(sharīʿah)* and theology *(ʿuṣūl al-dīn),* and also a women's faculty *(kullīyat al-banāt).* Al-Azhar has in addition an immense network of Islamic education on all levels throughout Egypt. In most Muslim countries, surviving *madrasahs* have been transformed into higher institutes for Islamic research or faculties of *sharīʿah* attached to universities.

In the course of the twentieth century higher education in Islamic religion in its Sunnī version has been shifting from the mosque to the university (whose Arabic names both have the same root, *j-m-ʿ*, meaning "coming together"). Of course, the mosques still have an important educational function, but not on the level of formal education in the religious sciences of Islam. As a result of the increasing interest in Islamic studies in Muslim countries today, new Islamic universities, higher Islamic institutes, and faculties of Islamic religious studies and *sharīʿah* have been opened in many countries during the past few years. Governments are attentive to how Islam is presented in these institutions, partly to counter interpretations of it that might be politically threatening.

[*See also* Azhar, al-; Education, *articles on* Religious Education *and* Educational Institutions; Madrasah; Zaytūnah.]

BIBLIOGRAPHY

Ahmad, Mohammad Akhlaq. *Traditional Education among Muslims: A Study of Some Aspects in Modern India*. New Delhi, 1985. Important survey of the content, form, and organization of present-day Islamic education in India.

Belambri, A. *Bibliographie systématique sur l'éducation islamique*. Paris, 1988. Indispensable for any research on Islamic education.

Berque, Jacques. "Ville et université: Aperçu sur l'histoire de l'école de Fès." *Revue de l'histoire du droit français et étranger* 27 (1949): 64–117. Contextualizes the Qarawīyīn mosque and its educational system in the social history of Fez.

Dodge, Bayard. *Al-Azhar: A Millennium of Muslim Learning*. Washington, D.C., 1961. Highly readable account of the history of the al-Azhar mosque and its educational aspects up to the reforms of 1961.

Dohaish, Abdullatif Abdullah. *History of Education in the Hijaz up to 1925*. Cairo, 1398/1978. Survey of the development of modern education and the history of traditional Islamic education up to the establishment of Saʿūdī rule.

Eccel, A. Chris. *Egypt, Islam, and Social Change: Al-Azhar in Conflict and Accommodation*. Berlin, 1984. Fundamental study with rich documentation on the nineteenth- and twentieth-century history of al-Azhar within the context of modernizing Egyptian society.

Fischer, Michael M. J. *Iran: From Religious Dispute to Revolution*.

Cambridge, Mass., 1980. Chapters 2 and 3 offer a description of religious teaching in Qom during the 1970s.

Jaʿfar, S. M. *Education in Muslim India*. Peshawar, 1936. Useful survey of traditional and modern education for Muslims in India.

Lemke, Wolf-Dieter. *Maḥmud Šaltut (1893–1963) und die Reform der Azhar: Untersuchungen zu Erneuerungsbestrebungen im ägyptisch-islamischen Erziehungssystem*. Frankfurt am Main, 1980. Careful study of the impact of modern reform thought, through the person of Shaykh Shalṭūt, on the reorganization of al-Azhar in 1961.

Rahman, Fazlur. *Islam and Modernity: Transformation of an Intellectual Tradition*. Chicago, 1982. Excellent introduction to various trends of thought with regard to educational renewal in Muslim countries during the last two centuries.

Shalabī, Aḥmad. *History of Muslim Education*. Beirut, 1954. Historical study of education in Muslim countries in the medieval period.

Snouck Hurgronje, Christiaan. *Mekka in the Latter Part of the Nineteenth Century: Daily Life, Customs, and Learning: The Moslims of the East-Indian-Archipelago*. Leiden and London, 1931. Fascinating account of Meccan life in 1884/85 by a Dutch scholar and eyewitness, with a discussion of educational institutions.

Tibawi, A. L. *Islamic Education*. London, 1972. Basic introduction to Islamic education and changes undergone with the rise of modern nation-states.

Tritton, A. S. *Materials on Muslim Education in the Middle Ages*. London, 1957. Historical study of education in Muslim countries in the medieval period.

Waardenburg, Jacques. "Some Institutional Aspects of Muslim Higher Education and Their Relation to Islam." *Numen* 12 (1965): 96–138.

Wayne, Keith Martin. "The Reformation and Secularization of Zaytuna University." Ph.D. diss., University of Utah, 1975. Useful study of transformations in the educational system of al-Zaytūnah in Tunis during the nineteenth and twentieth century up to 1975.

JACQUES WAARDENBURG

MOVIES. *See* Cinema.

MUFTĪ. A Muslim jurist capable of giving, when requested, a nonbinding opinion known as a *fatwā*, on a point of Islamic law is termed a *muftī*. During the formative period of Islam, learned Muslims whose counsel was sought on legal and ethical issues that arose in the community attempted to provide opinions and answers in the light of their understanding of the Qur'ān and in relation to the emerging body of *ḥadīth* (prophetic traditions). This activity subsequently crystallized to constitute the major Muslim legal schools. In its formal aspect, the position of *muftī* arose and became institutionalized as a response to the need for legal opinion and advice from scholars knowledgeable in early Islamic history among the various schools of law. In time, however, the *muftī* came to occupy a mediating position between the *qāḍī*, the judge who administered the law, and the *faqīh* or jurisprudent—that is, between actual courtroom situations where justice was administered and places of learning where the theoretical study of legal texts took place. The *muftī*'s opinions built on precedent and were incorporated in legal reference manuals such as the well-known *Fatāwā ʿĀlamgīrīyah*. The *muftī* also played an important role in the islamization of newly converted regions through education and counsel about legal norms.

Traditionally, a *muftī* was to be a person of integrity who possessed a thorough knowledge of established texts, traditions, and legal precedents. Although most were private scholars, some were appointed to official positions, notably in Mamluk Egypt and in the Ottoman Empire. In the Twelver Shiʿi tradition an analogous role came to be played by the *mujtahid*, who maintained continuity within the tradition after the *ghaybah* (occultation) of the twelfth imam in the ninth century. Under Ṣafavid rule the *mujtahid* held the office of *shaykh al-Islām*. The role of such jurist/theologians eventually led to the development of the concept of *wilāyat al-faqīh*, the "governance of the jurist." [*See* Shaykh al-Islām; Wilāyat al-Faqīh.]

In the nineteenth and twentieth centuries, as legal codes of European origin were introduced to the Muslim world, the *muftī*'s role became limited primarily but not exclusively to the sphere of personal law. But since a *muftī* often acted as a religious teacher in the local community, people continued to seek his opinions on a wide range of matters dealing with practice of the faith as well as on everyday life. This role has persisted in the many new nation-states that emerged after colonial rule. As many of these Muslim countries seek to integrate and institutionalize aspects of Islamic law in national life, new patterns are emerging for the *muftī*'s role in society. Some have been appointed as *muftī*s of the state; others provide consensus as part of advisory councils of religious scholars or constitutional assemblies of scholars. It is the private role of the *muftī*, however, that continues to be influential, offering possibilities for further evolution in their creative task as counselors and mediators for tradition in times of change.

[*See also* Faqīh; Fatwā; Qāḍī.]

BIBLIOGRAPHY

Coulson, Noel J. *A History of Islamic Law*. Edinburgh, 1964. Survey of Sunnī Muslim legal history, theory, and practice, up to the modern period.

Messick, Brinkley. "The Mufti, the Text, and the World: Legal Interpretation in Yemen." *Man* 21.1 (March 1986): 102–119. Analytic illustration of the methodology, conceptual framework, and social context of decision making by a Yemen *muftī*.

Sachedina, A. A. *The Just Ruler in Shiite Islam*. New York, 1988. Comprehensive treatment of the history of Shīʿī jurisprudence and its doctrine of the just ruler.

Schacht, Joseph. *An Introduction to Islamic Law*. Oxford, 1964. Standard work of Western scholarship on Muslim jurisprudence and law.

Shāfiʿī, Muḥammad ibn Idrīs al-. *Islamic Jurisprudence: Al-Shāfiʿī's Risāla*. Translated by Majid Khadduri. Baltimore, 1961. This translation makes available a pioneering work on Sunnī jurisprudence.

Azim A. Nanji

MUGHAL EMPIRE. The great Muslim empire on the Indian subcontinent was founded by Bābur (1483/84–1530), who was descended on his father's side from Timur and on his mother's from Chinggis Khan. Unsuccessful in reviving Timurid glories in Central Asia, he turned to India, where he established Mughal power in 1526. The empire reached its zenith under four great emperors: Akbar (r. 1556–1605), Jahāngīr (r. 1605–1627), Shāh Jahān (r. 1627–1657) and Awrangzīb (r. 1658–1707). Mughal rule embraced all India except the far south. After Awrangzīb died, power quickly waned; former provinces became independent states. By the mid-eighteenth century its power was finished. The last emperor was deposed by the British in 1858.

Akbar developed the administrative systems and policies on which Mughal power rested. He recruited into his administration not just members of the Turānī clans who had come with Bābur but also Persians, Indian Muslims, and Hindu Rajputs. These officials were granted *manṣab*s, military ranks expressed in numbers, which indicated their pay and their duties; these duties were fulfilled using revenues assigned to them from nonhereditary and transferable land grants (*jāgīr*s). Akbar developed a method of calculating revenue based on detailed knowledge of crops, land, productivity, and price fluctuations that yielded maximum return for minimum impact on the cultivator; revenue was collected by *zamīndār*s, for the most part Hindus, who kept a proportion for themselves.

Akbar integrated Hindus into the empire from the lowest levels of administration up to his own marriages with Rajput princesses. For this reason he adopted policies of religious toleration, abolishing for instance the *jizyah* tax on non-Muslims. As long as Akbar's administrative and religious policies were maintained, all was well. But Awrangzīb found he had to change them: faced with growing Hindu and Sikh opposition, he began to replace non-Muslims in government with Muslims; and under pressure from orthodox *ʿulamāʾ*, he ordered that the *jizyah* be reimposed and that the *sharīʿah* be followed. Then constant warfare and the expansion of the official class led to a crippling dearth of *jāgīr*s.

Like all rulers of India, the Mughals were primarily concerned about attack from the northwest, first from the Uzbeks of Central Asia and then from Ṣafavid Iran. The ultimate dangers, however, lay in India and beyond the seas; the British were the successors to the empire, first building on the Mughal legacy and then transforming it.

The Mughal Empire stands with those of the Ṣafavids and Ottomans as one of the three great "gunpowder" empires, in which some of the highest expressions of Islamic civilization were achieved. In religious belief it was the arena in which, in opposition to the Mughal policy of religious innovation and the liberal interpretation of Ibn ʿArabī's Ṣūfī understanding that then prevailed, Aḥmad Sirhindī emphasized strict obedience to *sharīʿah* and *sunnah* as the path to Ṣūfī realization, refocusing attention on the transcendance of God and the need for men to be guided by revelation; this development was to be carried by Naqshbandī Ṣūfīs through much of Central and Western Asia. Thus the empire marks the point at which India stopped being a mere receiver of Islamic ideas and took up its role as a major contributor to modern Islamic civilization as a whole.

[*See also* India *and the biography of Sirhindī.*]

BIBLIOGRAPHY

Athar Ali, M. *The Mughal Nobility under Aurangzeb*. Bombay, 1968. Classic analysis of the Mughal ruling class and its involvement in Mughal decline.

Gascoigne, Bamber. *The Great Moghuls*. London, 1971. Popular and well-illustrated introduction to the great Mughal emperors.

Journal of Asian Studies 35.2 (1976). Articles by Peter Hardy, M. N. Pearson and J. F. Richards debate the reasons for Mughal decline.

Raychaudhuri, Tapan, and Irfan Habib. *The Cambridge Economic History of India*, vol 1, *c. 1200–c. 1750*. Cambridge, 1982. The best introduction to the economy of the empire.

Schimmel, Annemarie. *Islam in the Indian Subcontinent*. Leiden and Cologne, 1980. Chapters 3–5 give an excellent overview of Islamic developments and Muslim practices in the Mughal period.

Francis Robinson

MUḤAMMAD. [*This entry focuses on the Prophet, or the Messenger of God, from whose activity the religion of Islam developed. It comprises three articles:*

Life of the Prophet
Biographies
Role of the Prophet in Muslim Thought and Practice

The first treats the historical details of his life and work; the second surveys the biographical literature on him; and the third considers him as the paradigm of the ideal person in Muslim thought and practice.]

Life of the Prophet

The Prophet of Islam was a religious and social reformer who gave rise to one of the great civilizations of the world. From a modern, historical perspective, Muḥammad was the founder of Islam. From the perspective of Islamic faith, he was God's Messenger (*rasūl Allāh*), called to be a "warner," first to the Arabs and then to all humankind.

Reconstructing the life of "the historical Muḥammad" is one of the most difficult and disputed topics in the modern study of Islam. The most valuable source for modern biographers of Muḥammad is the Qur'ān, the Islamic scripture, which records what he recited as revelation during the last two decades or so of his life. The Qur'ān responds constantly and candidly to Muḥammad's historical situation, but it is not in chronological order, and most surahs contain recitations from different parts of his life, making it difficult for nonspecialists to interpret as a historical source. Muḥammad in the Qur'ān is a real person, whose fears, anxieties, hopes, and eventual power show forth with clarity to the critical reader.

The fullest accounts of his life, however, are in the traditional biographies called collectively the *sīrah*. The most influential works in this genre are by Ibn Isḥāq (d. 768), al-Wāqidī (d. 822), and Ibn Hishām (d. 834). The *sīrah* is often supplemented by the *ḥadīth* collections, which contain thousands of accounts of things Muḥammad is reported to have said and done, allegedly going back to the "Companions of the Prophet," a technical expression that refers to those who were Muslims during Muḥammad's lifetime. and thus were trustworthy eyewitnesses. The most respected *ḥadīth* collections, which have a canonical status second only to the Qur'ān, are by al-Bukhārī (d. 870) and Muslim (d. 875). Similar accounts appear in the general histories by Ibn Saʿd (d. 845) and al-Ṭabarī (d. 923). These four types of writings—the Qur'ān, the *sīrah*, the *ḥadīth* accounts, and general histories—provide the source material for modern biographers and also for traditional views of Muḥammad. The last three contain miracle stories and other accounts that are inconsistent with statements and teachings about Muḥammad in the Qur'ān (see below).

The nature of the *sīrah* accounts changes dramatically over three main stages of Muḥammad's life. (1) For the period before the earliest passages in the Qur'ān, legends predominate; they probably arose after Muḥammad's death and have little historical value for the modern biographer. (2) For the period from the earliest Qur'ānic passages up to the Hijrah, the migration of Muḥammad and his followers from his native Mecca to Medina in 622 CE, exegetical stories, based on ambiguous or cryptic passages in the Qur'ān, are the most distinctive literary type. (3) It is only for the Medinan period, from the Hijrah to the Prophet's death in 632, that the life of the "historical Muḥammad" can be reconstructed with a moderate degree of certainty.

Early Meccan Period. The *sīrah* and *ḥadīth* literatures contain legends regarding Muḥammad that begin even before his birth. It is said that his father, called ʿAbd Allāh, was on his way to the home of Āminah to marry her when a woman standing in her doorway begged him to come into her house and make love. He refused, continued to Āminah's house, and consummated the marriage. Later, he passed by the house of the first woman, who this time said nothing to him. He turned back and asked why she had not invited him in again, and she said, "When you walked by before, a light shone from your face and I knew you were going to be the father of a prophet. Now, the light has disappeared from your face and I no longer desire to have you" (Ibn Isḥāq, Ibn Saʿd). Several stories say that throughout Āminah's pregnancy with Muḥammad a light or glow beamed from her face. During Muḥammad's birth, as he was emerging, a bright light beamed forth and lit up the city of Busra (Bostra) in Syria (Ibn Isḥāq). When Muḥammad was a young boy taking care of flocks of sheep and goats, a cloud formed over him and created a cool area that protected him from the heat of the sun. When he was twelve years old (Ibn Saʿd), or some say nine (Ṭabarī), he traveled with his uncle Abū Ṭālib on a caravan journey to Syria. When they arrived at Busra, a monk named Baḥīrā provided a meal for everyone and then announced that Muḥammad was going to be a prophet (Ibn Isḥāq, Ibn Saʿd, Ṭabarī). In another version, it was on the way north to Syria, before reaching Busra, that the caravan stopped at a restingplace, and the monk Baḥīrā saw certain physical signs on Muḥammad's back and proclaimed that he was going to be a prophet. He warned Abū Ṭālib not to take the boy to the land of the Byzantines (that is, Syria), since they would kill him (Ṭabarī). Another story says an unnamed monk made the same prediction, but warned that Jews in Syria would kill the boy if they knew who he was (Ibn Saʿd). It is said that when Muhammad was twenty-five years old, a well-to-do widow named Khadījah hired him to be in charge of her goods on a caravan to Syria. When the caravan arrived in Busra, Muḥammad sat beneath a tree to rest, and a monk named Naṣṭūr came out of a nearby monastery and said, "No one has ever sat beneath this tree before except prophets." He asked Khadījah's servant some questions about Muḥammad and then announced that he was going to be a prophet (Ibn Isḥāq, Ibn Saʿd, Ṭabarī). When Muḥammad was thirty-five, the Kaʿbah was repaired by men of the leading tribes in Mecca. When they got to the final task, lifting the Black Stone and replacing it in one corner of the Kaʿbah, the men quarreled over which tribe would have the privilege. After a while they agreed that the next person to enter the sanctuary would decide. The next one to enter was Muḥammad, who listened to each tribe's claim and then said that the stone should be placed on a blanket and that one person from each tribe should assist as they lifted it and set it in place together (Ibn Isḥāq, Ṭabarī).

These are representative *sīrah* and *ḥadīth* legends set in the period before Muḥammad's first vision or revelation. The stories usually stand alone, without any connecting narrative. Occasionally, narrative accounts or simple biographical statements appear between stories, for instance reporting the deaths of Muḥammad's mother and grandfather. Some of the narrative accounts and biographical reports are no doubt historical, but most are impossible to date, and differing details of the same event are often given.

Among the reports that can be accepted as historical are the following: that Muḥammad grew up as an orphan (see surah 93.6) in the clan of Hāshim; that an uncle Abū Ṭālib was his guardian; that he had other uncles named Ḥamzah, al-ʿAbbās, and ʿAbd al-ʿUzzā (nicknamed Abū Lahab); and that he married a well-to-do widow named Khadījah who bore him four daughters who grew to adulthood—Zaynab, Ruqayyah, Umm Kulthūm, and Fāṭimah. Questions remain, however, regarding most of the alleged events of this early period of his life. The exact year of his birth is not known, but the early 570s appear likely. He could not have been born in the Year of the Elephant (Ibn Isḥāq, Ibn Saʿd), since this expedition led by Abrahah, the ruler of southern Arabia, is now known to have occurred in the 550s or early 560s. Muḥammad's given name at birth is not certain. Ibn Saʿd reports that Āminah was told by God to name the child Aḥmad, a name that also occurs for Muḥammad in the Qur'ān (61.6). He is also often said to have been called Amīn before the revelations began. The name given his father, ʿAbd Allāh, is possibly a later, orthodox substitution for an original pagan name. The events of Muḥammad's infancy and early childhood are variously reported; for instance, several different women are said to have been his wet nurse. The accounts that say he lived with a desert tribe until after his mother's death are also highly suspect.

From the time of the legends of his childhood journey to Syria with his uncle Abū Ṭālib, the sources mention only one or two other events in Muḥammad's life until the time of his marriage to Khadījah, when he is said to have been twenty-five. They agree that he was twenty at the time of the Battle of Fijār and the so-called Oath of al-Fuḍūl. Some say he was present at this battle and took part in the oath (Ibn Saʿd), while others do not (Ibn Isḥāq, Ṭabarī). Finally, the number and names of Muḥammad's sons by Khadījah, all of whom died in infancy, are uncertain. Besides al-Qāsim, the eldest, two other names are mentioned (al-Ṭāhir and al-Ṭayyib, "the modest" and "the good"—Ṭabarī) but each boy is sometimes said to have been called ʿAbd Allāh, and other evidence suggests that one of the names may be a nickname for the other son.

Period of the Meccan Revelations. As mentioned above, the striking feature of this period in the *sīrah* works is the presence of exegetical stories based on cryptic or ambiguous verses of the Qur'ān. A few examples will illustrate this type of *sīrah* account.

Surah 96 begins: "Recite *(iqrā')*: In the Name of your Lord who created. . . . Recite: And your Lord is the Most Generous, who taught by the Pen, taught Man what he knew not." From this arose the story that when Muḥammad was forty or forty-three years old [Ṭabarī], Gabriel appeared to him and said "*Iqrā'* " ("read" or "recite"), but Muḥammad responded, "I cannot read." This exchange was repeated two more times, and then Gabriel recited surah 96 to him. Although often taken as historical, with the corollary belief that this surah was the first to be revealed, this story has the obvious purpose of affirming Muḥammad's illiteracy, a doctrine that arose in later Islamic theology and is not supported by an analysis of all the relevant passages in the Qur'ān.

Surah 74 begins: "O you shrouded in your mantle, arise and warn!" From this verse a story arose saying Gabriel came to Muḥammad's house, saw him sitting outside wrapped in a shroud (a custom of soothsayers and prophets while waiting for inspiration), informed him that God was calling him to be a prophet, and then recited this surah, which other sources say was the first to be revealed.

Surah 94 begins: "Did We not expand your breast for you and lift from you your burden, the burden that weighed down your back?" A story with several variations arose from this surah, saying that two angels (or Gabriel, or two birds) came to Muḥammad, "opened his breast," and removed or opened his heart. They "cleansed it like a receptacle" and "took the pollution of Satan out of it." Then they removed something black, washed it, and replaced it—or, according to other versions, they threw it away. Then they sewed Muḥammad's breast back up. This story is placed at different points in Muḥammad's lifetime: when he was a child, at the time of his first vision or revelation, and just before the Hijrah (Ibn Isḥāq, Ibn Saʿd; Bukhārī, Muslim). Harris Birkeland (*The Legend of the Opening of Muhammed's Breast*, Oslo, 1955) has reconstructed the stages in the development of this legend during the century following Muḥammad's death.

One of the most fascinating exegetical legends is based on surah 53.19–20, which mention three goddesses who were popular in and near Mecca: "Have you considered al-Lāt and al-ʿUzzā, and Manāt, the third, the other?" The story says that immediately following these two verses Muḥammad recited two others: "These are the high-flying ones *(gharānīq)*, whose intercession [on the Day of Judgment] is to be hoped for." This was taken by the Meccan polytheists as a sign that Muḥammad had accepted their goddesses into his belief system. A short time later, Gabriel informed Muḥammad that the two *gharānīq* verses had been placed in his mouth by Satan (leading Europeans to call this "the Story of the Satanic Verses"), and thus they were deleted from the Qur'ān (Wāqidī, Ṭabarī).

The story of Muḥammad's Night Journey *(isrā')* and Ascension *(miʿrāj)* to heaven grew from the opening verse of surah 17: "Glory be to Him, who carried His servant by night from the sacred place of worship *(al-masjid al-ḥarām)* to the farthest place of worship *(al-masjid al-aqṣā)*, the precincts of which We have blessed, that We might show him some of Our signs." The earliest explanation of this verse says Muḥammad ascended to heaven directly from the sanctuary in Mecca. The expression *al-masjid al-ḥarām* became the name of the sanctuary and later of the Great Mosque in Mecca. Later *al-masjid al-aqṣā* came to be associated with the Temple Mount in Jerusalem, and a mosque by this name was built at its southern end. At about this time, another story based on surah 17.1 arose: Muḥammad's Night Journey *(isrā')* from the sanctuary in Mecca to the Temple Mount in Jerusalem. His Ascension *(miʿrāj)* was then transferred from Mecca to Jerusalem and placed after the Night Journey. This combined story is placed at different points in Muḥammad's career, usually shortly before the Hijrah (Ibn Isḥāq, Ibn Saʿd), but occasionally at the time of his first vision or revelation (Ṭabarī). [*See* Miʿrāj.]

These are just a few representative exegetical stories that characterize the *sīrah* for this part of Muḥammad's life. To conclude that they are legends in their present form does not preclude the possibility that historical events might lie behind some of them. For instance, the basic elements in the story of the *gharānīq* or "the Satanic Verses" are consistent with many other statements in the Qur'ān that date from the time of its setting (see A. T. Welch, "Allāh and Other Supernatural Beings," *Journal of the American Academy of Religion* 47 [1979]: 733–753).

Very few historical facts are known for certain regarding events in the life of Muḥammad for the period of his public ministry in Mecca. One difficulty in reconstructing his life in Mecca is that major events reported in the *sīrah* for this period are not mentioned or even alluded to in the Qur'ān, whereas major events reported for the Medinan period are not only mentioned, but are discussed at length and are often corroborated in Medinan passages. For instance, the Qur'ān is silent on the emigration of Muḥammad's followers to Abyssinia (Ethiopia), the boycott of his clan of Hāshim, the deaths of his wife Khadījah and his uncle and protector Abū Ṭālib, the loss of his clan protection, his visit to al-Ṭā'if to seek refuge there, and, most surprising of all, the Hijrah to Medina—all of which are presented in the *sīrah* as major events of this period. Since dates are not given for most of these events, and since the *sīrah* and *ḥadīth* accounts vary in significant details, we are left with more questions than answers regarding their causes and circumstances.

Certain facts about Muḥammad's life and situation in Mecca can be known, however, from the Qur'ān. He proclaimed himself to be a "warner" *(nadhīr)* to the Arabs, called by the God of the Jews and the Christians to recite in "a clear Arabic recitation *(qur'ān)*" the same revelation that was brought by earlier Messengers *(rusul)*. The similarity in form of his early recitations to the messages of the soothsayers caused the Meccans to accuse him of being inspired by the spirits called *jinn* rather than by God. Preaching against the wealthy for not sharing with the poor brought severe persecution, especially to his followers. Valuable insights into Muḥammad's character and personality can be seen in the section that follows below.

The list of unanswered questions regarding this period in Muḥammad's life is long, and only a few examples can be given. Muḥammad's age at the time of his first vision or revelation is variously given, usually as forty or forty-three. This difference cannot be resolved by the alleged *fatrah* or "gap" in the revelations, usually said to have lasted three years, since this concept most likely was an invention of later biographers used to reconcile the different accounts. Also unknown are the causes of the "First Hijrah" to Abyssinia, where more than simple persecution must have been involved. Several unanswered questions also surround the boycott of Hāshim, where the traditional accounts differ in several significant aspects. Finally, Muḥammad's activities during his last two years in Mecca before the Hijrah are largely unknown. The few events that are reported for this period could not have taken up more than a fraction of his time.

Contrary to the images of Muḥammad that dominate the *sīrah* and *ḥadīth* literatures, the glimpses of Muḥammad in the Meccan parts of the Qur'ān consistently portray him as fully human with no supernatural powers. His opponents frequently challenged him to perform miracles: "We will not believe you until you make a spring gush forth from the ground" (17.90); the Qur'ān responds by commanding Muḥammad to say, "I am only a human being *(bashar)* like you" (18.110 and 41.6). He also had no supernatural knowledge. When his opponents challenged him to reveal things of the invisible world, the Qur'ān instructs him to say, "I do not know the Unseen *(al-ghayb)*" (6.50); and when they ask him when the end of time would come, the Qur'ān responds, "Say: Only my Lord has knowledge of it and He will not reveal it until its proper time" (7.187). His humanness is seen clearly when he is frequently comforted in times of persecution or disappointment—"Your Lord has not forsaken you [Muḥammad] nor does he hate you" (93.3); in times of grief—"We know indeed that the things they say grieve you" (6.33); and in times of doubt—"By your Lord's blessing you are not a soothsayer, nor are you possessed by *jinn*" (52.29). That he suffered periods of uncertainty and impatience in Mecca, when his message was met with rebuke and the people taunted him with accusations he could not refute, is shown by the many passages that urge him to be steadfast and patient: "So be patient . . . and do not let those who do not have sure faith make you unsteady" (30.60); "So be patient, for indeed God's promise is true" (40.55). According to the Qur'ān, Muḥammad's primary role in Mecca was simply that of "warner," usually *nadhīr* but sometimes *mundhir:* "He [Muḥammad] is a warner *(nadhīr)* of the warners of old" (53.56); "Now they marvel that a warner *(mundhir)* has come to them from among them" (38.4). This role appears frequently in the rhyme phrase, "I am/He is a clear warner *(nadhīr mubīn)*" (for instance, in 7.184 and 29.50).

Medinan Period. The life of Muḥammad can be reconstructed with much more confidence for the Medinan period. In addition to a wealth of biographical data in the Qur'ān, we have extensive reports of *maghāzī* ("military expeditions") that Muhammad led or organized and sent out. After the Qur'ān and some of the poetry preserved in the *sīrah*, modern historians regard the *maghāzī* works as the oldest sources for the life of Muḥammad and the foundation of the Medinan portions of the *sīrah,* which are fuller and more trustworthy than the Meccan portions. Also, the Qur'ān and the *sīrah* frequently corroborate each other for the Medinan period.

Narrative form in the Medinan part of the sīrah. For the period after the Hijrah, Ibn Isḥāq includes a detailed "chronological frame narrative" that gives the dates for Muḥammad's military expeditions and for the time he spent in Medina. This narrative form is seen in the following example that covers the one-year period from the end of the battle of Badr until the beginning of the battle of Uḥud (pages 360–369 in Guillaume's 1955 translation):

> The Messenger left Badr at the end of Ramaḍān or in Shawwāl [in AH 2]. He stayed only seven nights in Medina before

he led a raid against the Banū Sulaym. He got as far as their watering place called al-Kudr and stayed there three nights, returning to Medina without fighting. He stayed there for the rest of Shawwāl and Dhū al-Qaʿda. . . . Abū Sufyān made the raid of Sawīq ["barley meal"] in Dhū al-Ḥijja. . . . When the Messenger returned from the raid of al-Sawīq he stayed in Medina for the rest of Dhū al-Ḥijja, or nearly all of it. Then [in Muḥarram] he raided the Najd, making for [the tribe of] Ghatafān. This is the raid of Dhū Amarr. He stayed in the Najd through the month of Ṣafar, or nearly all of it, and then returned to Medina without fighting. There he remained for the month of Rabīʿ I or a day or two less. . . . Then he made a raid on Quraysh as far as Baḥrān, a mine in the Hijāz. . . . He stayed there for the next two months and then returned to Medina without fighting. . . . After his arrival from Baḥrān the Messenger stopped [in Medina] for the months of the Jumādā II, Rajab, Shaʿbān, and Ramaḍān. Quraysh made the raid of Uḥud in Shawwāl of AH 3.

The precise dates that are given in Watt's *Muhammad Prophet and Statesman* (1961) are taken from al-Wāqidī rather than Ibn Isḥāq. The two dating systems differ in detail but agree in assuming that the later Islamic calendar was projected back to the time of the Hijrah.

Muḥammad's problem with the Meccans. Soon after his arrival in Medina, Muḥammad, following the Arabian custom at that time, began to send out razzias or raiding parties against Meccan caravans. A wronged party was expected to take goods by force from an oppressor tribe. Muḥammad and his followers believed that the Meccans had forced them out of their homes and businesses and thus owed them redress. When a group of Muḥammad's men captured a Meccan caravan at Nakhlah in late 623 or early 624, this gave warning to the Meccans. Thus on their next trip north, in the spring of 624, the Meccans stayed together in Syria until everyone was ready to return home in one huge caravan led by Abū Sufyān, a wealthy and powerful leader of Mecca. Muḥammad led about 300 men out to intercept this caravan, and the Meccans sent a force three times as large to protect it. Abū Sufyān evaded Muḥammad and arrived safely back in Mecca, while Muḥammad's men and the Meccan force encountered each other by chance at Badr, where caravans stopped for water. The two forces engaged in battle and Muḥammad's men defeated the much larger polytheist army, killing about seventy Meccans. The Muslim victory at Badr (mentioned by name in surah 3.123) was taken by many as a sign that God was on Muḥammad's side, and this led to a large number of converts. A year later, in the spring of 625, Abū Sufyān led another Meccan army north to Medina for revenge. The two forces met on the hill of Uḥud, just north of the Medinan settlement, and Muḥammad and his men suffered a near disaster. After a fatal mistake by a flank of his archers, Muḥammad was injured but was able to rally his forces. Abū Sufyān, seeing that about seventy Muslims and their allies had been killed, declared a victory and returned to Mecca (surah 3.121-179 treat the battle of Uḥud). Two years later, in the spring of 627, the Meccans, again under the command of Abū Sufyān, made their last attempt to stop Muḥammad by force. This time the Muslims dug a trench across exposed areas into the settlement, which was sufficient to deter the Meccans and their allies, who withdrew after about two weeks (treated in 33.9–25). By this time Muḥammad was in complete control of Medina, and bedouin tribes in the surrounding area were making alliances with him and becoming Muslims.

Muhammad's problem with the Jews. It is clear from the Qur'ān, seen especially in surah 2, that Muḥammad expected the three main Jewish clans in Medina to accept him as a prophet sent by their God (2.40–41). Since Islamic beliefs and practices were just being formulated in the Qur'ān, flexibility within the nascent community allowed for the adoption of certain Jewish practices, some becoming permanent in Islam, while others were temporary. The Jewish fast on the Day of Atonement, called the ʿĀshūrā' fast, was adopted during the first year in Medina (Bukhārī and Muslim say Muḥammad followed the example of the Jews in adopting this fast), along with food restrictions that are close to those of the Jews (surah 2.172–173). The Muslims even adopted the Jewish *qiblah,* or direction one faces when performing the daily prayer rituals, facing north toward Jerusalem. About a year and a half after Muḥammad arrived in Medina, it became clear that the Jews there were not going to accept him as a prophet. The so-called "break with the Jews" thus occurred, marked dramatically by a "change of the *qiblah,*" when the Muslims began to face south from Medina toward the Kaʿbah in Mecca (2.142–150).

After each of the three battles mentioned above, one of the main Jewish clans was expelled from Medina. The primary justification was their failure to support Muḥammad, marked by their collaboration with his enemies in Medina and their possible conspiracy with the Meccans. After the battle of Badr, the clan of Qaynuqāʿ was forced to leave Medina, and some of the Emigrants *(muhājirūn)*, Muḥammad's followers from Mecca who had made the Hijrah, took over their marketplaces and soon controlled trade within the settlement. The clan of al-Naḍīr was expelled after the battle of Uḥud; they owned rich groves of palm trees that were distributed among Muḥammad's poor Emigrant followers and others (surah 59.2–10). The treatment of the third and last Jewish clan, the Qurayẓah, was much harsher because of evidence of a conspiracy during the battle of the Trench in which they made plans to attack Muḥammad's forces from the rear. If this fifth-column plot had been carried out, it could have ended his career. After a siege of their strongholds, they surrendered and Muḥammad put them on trial, appointing a judge from an Arab tribe that was allied to them. The verdict was that all the men of the clan were to be executed and the women and children were to be sold as slaves (surah 33.26–27). In this one action of his career, Muḥammad followed the customs and expectations of his day rather than his usual magnanimous treatment of his foes after battles and intrigues.

Muḥammad's last years and his death. In the spring of 628, guided by a dream or vision, Muḥammad led a massive group of Muslims on the 270-mile journey from Medina to Mecca to perform the pilgrimage ceremonies. They camped at al-Ḥudaybiyah on the edge of the Ḥaram, the sacred territory that surrounds Mecca. There Muḥammad negotiated a treaty in which he agreed not to press his claim to complete the pilgrimage ceremonies that season, while the Meccan leaders promised to open the city to the Muslims the following year. They also agreed to a ten-year truce when neither side would attack the other. In the spring of 629, Muḥammad led the first Muslim pilgrimage, an *ʿumrah* or "Lesser Pilgrimage" to Mecca. Later that year, a clan allied to the Meccans attacked a clan allied to Muḥammad, thus breaking the treaty. Abū Sufyān and other Meccan leaders rushed to Medina to dissuade Muḥammad from attacking their city, and they apparently agreed to surrender Mecca to him peacefully. Late in 629 Muḥammad and his forces set out for Mecca, and early in 630 his native city surrendered to him without a fight.

Just weeks after the surrender of Mecca, with Muḥammad now in command of all of west-central Arabia, a large confederation of tribes from south and east of Mecca made one last attempt to stop him by force. Muḥammad's 12,000 men fought an army twice that size at Ḥunayn (mentioned by name in the Qur'ān, 9.25), and once again the Muslims and their allies defeated a much larger force of polytheists. After dividing up the spoils, Muḥammad and his followers from Medina returned home, where he consolidated his position. In the spring, a son named Ibrāhīm (Abraham) was borne to Muḥammad by his Christian concubine, Māriyah the Copt, said to have been a gift to him from an Egyptian ruler. During the last part of 630, he undertook his largest and last military expedition, with a force said to number 30,000 men, to Tabūk, near the Gulf of ʿAqaba. Muḥammad encountered no army, but this show of force demonstrated his intention to challenge the Byzantines for control of the northern part of the caravan route from Mecca to Syria. Ibn Isḥāq and al-Wāqidī record twenty-seven expeditions, including pilgrimages to Mecca and the expulsions of the three Jewish clans, that Muḥammad led himself, but they say he actually fought in only nine. In addition to these, he organized and sent out more than fifty other expeditions. (For a complete list of these expeditions, see Watt, 1956, pp. 339–343.)

The following year, 631, is called "the Year of Deputations." Envoys from tribes all over Arabia traveled to Muḥammad's headquarters in Medina and surrendered to him. Some tribes may have seen these treaties as normal Arabian tribal alliances, but Muḥammad regarded them as including acceptance of Islam. The year 632 began on a sad note for Muḥammad with the death of his young son, Ibrāhīm. Later that spring the Prophet led to Mecca the largest number of Muslim pilgrims ever assembled during his lifetime on what came to be called his "Farewell Pilgrimage." On the return trip to Medina, Muḥammad contracted a fatal illness and knew his days were numbered. He appointed his longtime friend, Abū Bakr, to lead the daily prayers and the weekly worship service. Then he asked permission of his wives to be relieved of his duty of nightly rotation so he could spend his last days in the apartment of his youngest wife, ʿĀ'ishah, the daughter of Abū Bakr. It was there that he died, at about age sixty, in June 632.

Glimpses of Muḥammad in Medinan parts of the Qur'ān. Muḥammad is portrayed in terms just as personal and candid in Medinan passages as in the Meccan ones cited above. The Qur'ān continues to stress his completely human nature and limitations. Even after his victories over the Meccans and his success in winning converts among the tribes of the Ḥijāz (Hejaz), Muḥammad still agonized over those who did not believe: "O Messenger, let them not grieve you who vie with one another in unbelief" (5.41). A significant Medinan theme that is stated explicitly in several passages is Muḥammad's need to seek forgiveness for his sins: "[Muḥammad,] ask forgiveness *(ghafr)* for your sin *(dhanb),* and for [those of the] the believers, men and women" (47.19); and "Surely We have given you [Muḥammad] a manifest victory that God may forgive you your former and your latter sins and complete His blessing on you" (48.1–2). The later Islamic doctrine of Muḥammad's sinlessness has no foundation in the Qur'ān. His humanness is also seen in passages on his mortality: "You [Muḥammad] are mortal *(mayyit)* and they are mortal. Then, on the Day of Resurrection before your Lord you will dispute" (39.30–31). The candidness of the Qur'ān is striking in a number of Medinan passages on another aspect of Muḥammad's humanness, his attraction for the good things of this life, including women, wealth, and children: "Thereafter women are not lawful for you [Muḥammad], neither for you to take other wives in exchange for them, though their beauty please you, except what your right hand owns [female slaves, who may be taken as concubines]" (33.52); and "Do not let their wealth and their children please you [or cause you to desire to have them]" (9.85).

The most prominent difference between the Meccan Muḥammad and the Medinan Muḥammad involves his roles within the two communities and the explicit Medinan references to his considerable power and authority. One indication of this change in Muḥammad's circumstances is seen in his titles, especially where he is mentioned along with God. Contrary to popular belief, Muḥammad is never explicitly called a "prophet" *(nabī)* or "the Messenger of God" *(rasūl Allāh)* anywhere in Meccan passages of the Qur'ān. The Qur'ānic usage of Muḥammad's various titles and other evidence show his humility in that he is only gradually, and explicitly only after the Hijrah, portrayed as a "Messenger of God" equal to the great prophets of the past. Sometime after the battle of Badr a primary Medinan motif began to appear, for instance in 4.13: "Whoever obeys God and His Messenger will be admitted to gardens in which rivers flow [Paradise], therein dwelling forever"; this is coupled with a threat in verse 14, "But whoever disobeys God and His Messenger and transgresses His bounds will be admitted to a Fire, therein dwelling forever." An even stronger statement of this motif occurs in 4.80: "Whoever obeys the Messenger thereby obeys God." A frequently occurring variation on this theme occurs in 4.136: "O believers, believe in God and His Messenger and the Book He has sent down [revealed]," stated more strongly in 48.13: "We have prepared a Blaze [the hellfire] for whoever does not believe in God and His Messenger." The height of Muḥammad's power is portrayed nowhere more clearly than in several passages where he is told to be harsh in his treatment of those who oppose him, as in surahs 9.73 and 66.9, where the same statement occurs verbatim: "O Prophet, struggle with the unbelievers and the hypocrites, and be harsh with them. Their refuge is Gehenna [Hell], an evil homecoming!"

Even in the context of this new power and authority, Muḥammad's humility and even shyness continue to be portrayed vividly. As is often the case, it is the Qur'ān that instructs the believers on personal matters pertaining to Muḥammad, as in 49.2: "O believers, raise not your voices above the Prophet's voice, and be not loud in your speech to him as you are loud to one another"; and in one of the most fascinating verses in the Qur'ān on Muḥammad's character, 33.53: "O believers, do not enter the apartments of the Prophet, unless you are given permission for a meal, and wait for the proper time. But when you are invited, then enter, and when you have finished your meal, then leave. Do not linger for idle talk, for that would be an annoyance to the Prophet, and he would be shy to ask you [to leave]." What a graphic picture of the personality of the most powerful ruler in Arabia!

Concluding Comments. The verses quoted above as "glimpses" of Muḥammad in the Qur'ān represent only a small sample of the hundreds that provide insight into his life and character. Throughout these verses the single characteristic of his personality that predominates from the beginning to the end is his sincerity. Through periods of persecution and doubt, then reassurance, and finally complete confidence in his mission, there is no hint of deceit or dishonesty. Yet Muḥammad is often criticized by modern writers; the two accusations most often made against him involve his Medinan militarism and his alleged lasciviousness.

Regarding the first, it must be remembered that Muḥammad was a man of his time. The razzia or raiding party was a characteristic feature of life in Arabia in Muḥammad's time, so that his attempt to stop the Meccan caravan that resulted in the battle of Badr was accepted by all as customary and within his rights. Most other major battles in which he fought were initiated by the enemy, and the majority of the other expeditions he led did not make contact with any enemy tribe but were largely demonstrations of his growing power to the neighboring bedouin tribes. It is best to see Muhammad as using the customs of his day to mold a new social community. The idea of founding a new religion or being solely a religious leader would have been totally foreign to him. He was administrator, legislator, judge, and commander in chief as well as teacher, preacher, and prayer leader.

As for the second criticism, it must be remembered that Muḥammad had only one wife, Khadījah, until her death when he was about fifty years old. Shortly thereafter he married Sawdah, the widow of a Muslim who died in Abyssinia. It was only natural that he remarry after Khadījah's death, since he had a large household, with children, servants, and many duties that were usually assumed by the wife. These two were his only wives in Mecca before the Hijrah. In Medina most of his marriages fall into two categories: those with political significance, as when they established bonds between the Prophet and important tribes and clans; and those that resulted from his responsibilities as head of the Muslim community, as when he married widows of Muslim men who died in battle. He is usually said to have had fourteen wives in the proper sense, of whom nine survived him. Māriyah the Copt, as the mother of Ibrāhīm, had a special place in Muḥammad's life but was not regarded as a wife.

The quest for "the historical Muḥammad" is a modern task that is still in its infancy. Volumes on "the traditional Muḥammad," the exemplar for Islamic faith and practice, who was created in the process of the establishment of Islamic orthodoxy and orthopraxis, are as old as Islam itself. The Muslim world also knows many "popular Muḥammads," who vary from culture to culture and combine features of the traditional Muḥammad of Muslim faith and those of the ideal man or the shaman or priest of the various cultural areas. This Muḥammad is often a miracle-worker or a fortuneteller who can communicate with and control the spirits, and can call upon supernatural powers to heal or otherwise aid the believers. The glimpses of Muḥammad in the Qur'ān cited above make it clear that such beliefs, while worthy of study as part of popular Islam, are inconsistent with the teachings of Islamic scripture, which happens also to be the ultimate source in the quest for the historical Muḥammad.

[*See also* Biography and Hagiography; Ḥadīth; Mecca; Medina; Prophethood.]

BIBLIOGRAPHY

Sources: The Qur'ān (in English)

Arberry, A. J., trans. *The Koran Interpreted*. 2 vols. London and New York, 1955. Reprinted in one volume, but paginated as two. The most readable translation in English and, despite its title, the most literal.

Bell, Richard. *The Qur'ān Translated, with a Critical Re-arrangement of the Surahs*. 2 vols. Edinburgh, 1937–1939. Intended only as a preliminary, critical analysis of the composition of the Arabic text of the Qur'ān, this ground-breaking study has never been followed up except in peripheral works. Remains essential for any critical study of the chronology and composition of the Qur'ān. Invaluable for the quest for "the historical Muḥammad."

Pickthall, M. M. *The Meaning of the Glorious Koran: An Explanatory Translation* (1930). New York, 1953. Solid translation utilizing modern scholarship, while sometimes reading later, orthodox meanings into the text. A bilingual edition called *The Glorious Koran* (Arabic and English; London and Albany, N.Y., 1976) contains the Egyptian Standard text of the Arabic, with a renumbering of the English verses to agree with the Arabic.

Yusuf Ali, Abdullah, trans. *The Holy Qur'an: Text, Translation, and Commentary*. 3d ed. Lahore, 1938. Solid translation, influenced by earlier European ones, with extensive notes, often on Muḥammad but more frequently of a devotional nature or arguing for a later, orthodox interpretation of a verse or a key word.

Sources: *Sīrah, Ḥadīth,* and General Histories

Bukhārī, Muḥammad ibn Ismāʿīl al-. *Sahih al-Bukhari: The Translation of the Meanings of Sahih al-Bukhari* (Arabic and English). 9 vols. Translated by M. M. Khan. 3d rev. ed. Chicago, 1979. The most highly respected of all the *ḥadīth* collections (see comments on Muslim, below).

Ibn Isḥāq, Muḥammad. *The Life of Muḥammad: A Translation of Ibn Isḥāq's Sīrat Rasūl Allāh*. Translated with introduction and notes by Alfred Guillaume. London and Karachi, 1955. Ibn Isḥāq's *Sīrah* or *Maghāzī* is extant in two recensions, one by Ibn Hishām, used by Guillaume and often listed as the "author" of this translation, and another by Yūnus ibn Bukayr (d. 814). Guillaume has attempted to reconstruct Ibn Isḥāq's original work by beginning with Ibn Hishām's recension, placing all of his additions in the back as notes, and then inserting long excerpts that were deleted by Ibn Hishām, but have been preserved in works such as al-Ṭabarī's *Ta'rīkh*.

Ibn Saʿd, Muḥammad. *Ibn Saʿd's Kitab al-Tabaqat al-Kabir* (The Large Book of the Generations). Translated by Syed Moinul Haq, assisted by H. K. Ghazanfar. Karachi, 1967. Contains more variations of multiple accounts than Ibn Isḥāq's work, and also many anecdotes that have parallels in the canonical *ḥadīth* collections. Volumes 1 and 2 treat the life of Muḥammad.

Muslim ibn al-Ḥajjāj al-Qushayrī. *Ṣaḥīḥ Muslim: Being Traditions of the Sayings and Doings of the Prophet Muḥammad as Narrated by his Companions and Compiled under the Title al-Jamiʿ-uṣ-Ṣaḥīḥ*. 4 vols. Translated by ʿAbdul Hamid Siddiqi. Lahore, 1976. Often considered with al-Bukhārī's *Ṣaḥīḥ* as the two "canonical" *ḥadīth* collections, they are regarded as authoritative and definitive in matters of Islamic ritual and law.

Ṭabarī, Muḥammad ibn Jarīr al-. *The History of al-Ṭabarī (Ta'rīkh al-rusul wa-al-mulūk).* 38 vols. Edited by Ehsan Yar-Shater. Albany, N.Y., 1985–. The most important universal history produced in the Islamic world. Four volumes treat the life of Muḥammad, one of which (volume 8) has not yet been published. See volume 6, *Muhammad at Mecca,* translated and annotated by W. Montgomery Watt and M. V. McDonald (1988); volume 7, *The Foundation of the Community: Muhammad at al-Madina, A.D. 622–626/Hijrah-4 A.H.,* translated and annotated by Watt and McDonald (1987); and volume 9, *The Last Years of the Prophet: The Formation of the State, A.D. 630–632/A.H. 8–11,* translated and annotated by Ismail K. Poonawala (1990).

Wāqidī, Muḥammad ibn ʿUmar al-. *Kitāb al-Maghāzī lil-Wāqidī.* 3 vols. Edited by Marsden Jones. London, 1966. Fundamental work on the life of Muḥammad, which unfortunately has not been translated into English. Julius Wellhausen prepared an abridged German translation, *Muhammed in Medina: Das ist Vakidi's Kitab alMaghazi [sic] in verkürzter deutscher Wiedergabe* (Berlin, 1882).

Modern Biographies and Other Literature on Muḥammad

Andrae, Tor. *Mohammed: The Man and His Faith.* Translated by Theophil Menzel. London and New York, 1936. Rev. ed. New York, 1955. Translated from the German, *Mohammed: Sein Leben und Sein Glaube.* Göttingen, 1932. Originally published in Swedish. Translated into several languages, this classic study emphasizes the religious aspects of Muḥammad's life and, using insights from psychology, elucidates his experience of revelation.

Bint al-Shāṭi' [ʿĀ'ishah ʿAbd al-Raḥmān]. *The Wives of the Prophet.* Translated with an introduction by Matti Moosa and D. Nicholas Ranson. Lahore, 1971. Translated from the Arabic, *Nisā' al-Nabī.* Cairo, 1961. Exp. ed. Cairo, 1973. Vivid portrayals of the traditional views of Muḥammad's wives.

Buhl, Frants. *Das Leben Muhammeds.* Translated by H. H. Schaeder. Leipzig, 1930. Rev. and exp. German translation of the original Danish, *Muhammeds Liv.* Copenhagen, 1903. Remains the best historical-critical analysis of the sources, although dated in places. No English translation exists, but a summary is available in Buhl's "Muḥammad," in *Encyclopaedia of Islam,* vol. 3, pp. 641–657 (Leiden, 1913–).

Buhl, Frants, and Alford T. Welch. "Muḥammad." In *Encyclopaedia of Islam,* new ed., vol. 5, pp. 360–376. Leiden, 1960–. Completely revised and updated version of Buhl's article in the first edition, omitting long discussions of outdated topics. The co-author shares Buhl's conclusions on many major issues, which thus remain among the basic conclusions of the revised article.

Glubb, John Bagot. *The Life and Times of Muhammad.* London and New York, 1970. Demonstrates keen insight into the customs of desert life and warfare in Arabia that shed light on key events in Muḥammad's life.

Hamidullah, Muhammad. *The Battlefields of the Prophet Muhammad, with Maps, Illustrations, and Sketches: A Contribution to Muslim Military History.* Hyderabad (Deccan), 1973. Originally published as *ʿAhd-i nabvī ke maidān-i jang.* The only extended study of the topic, based on field research at the locations where Muḥammad's expeditions occurred.

Haykal, Muḥammad Ḥusayn. *The Life of Muḥammad.* Translated by Ismāʿīl Rājī al-Fārūqī. [Indianapolis], 1976. Translation of the eighth edition of the Arabic, *Ḥayāt Muḥammad.* 1st ed. Cairo, 1935. One of the most popular twentieth-century Arabic biographies of Muḥammad. Despite the author's claim to follow modern critical methods, this work presents the familiar traditional narrative of Muḥammad's life, interspersed with strong condemnations, although not refutations, of views by European scholars that differ from orthodox and traditional beliefs about Muḥammad.

Lings, Martin. *Muhammad: His Life Based on the Earliest Sources.* London and New York, 1983. Exceptionally well-written account of "the traditional Muḥammad" as depicted in the classical *sīrah* and *ḥadīth* works, with no critical analysis. Contains material not found in other modern biographies of Muḥammad.

Schimmel, Annemarie. *And Muhammad Is His Messenger: The Veneration of the Prophet in Islamic Piety.* Chapel Hill, N.C., 1985. Author's own translation of the original German, *Und Muhammad ist Sein Prophet.* Düsseldorf, 1981. The most penetrating study to date of "the popular Muḥammad" and his roles in Muslim piety, containing chapters on topics such as Muḥammad's physical beauty, his miracles, his role as intercessor, and his place in Ṣūfī thought and ritual. Also contains valuable translations of modern poetry on devotion to Muḥammad from several South and West Asian languages.

Watt, W. Montgomery. *Muhammad at Mecca.* Oxford, 1953. First of a two-volume work that constitutes the most recent major scholarly study of the life of Muḥammad, based on a thorough analysis of the Arabic sources. Adopts an intermediate position between those of Buhl and Lings regarding the sources by accepting as historical all accounts that cannot be refuted by strong evidence.

Watt, W. Montgomery. *Muhammad at Medina.* Oxford, 1956. The second of Watt's two-volume work goes far beyond a biography by including exceptionally valuable chapters on topics such as the tribes Muḥammad encountered in various parts of Arabia, the internal politics in Medina, the character of the new Islamic state, and Muḥammad's reform of the Arabian social structure. Twelve additional excurses, on topics such as marriage and family life in pre-Islamic times, Muḥammad's marriages, and a list (with dates and page numbers in Ibn Isḥāq and al-Wāqidī) of all the expeditions Muḥammad led and those he sent out, add to the value of this volume.

Watt, W. Montgomery. *Muhammad: Prophet and Statesman.* London and New York, 1961. Essentially an abridgment of the author's two-volume biography, except that the chronological order of Muḥammad's life is followed more closely and material that does not deal specifically with Muḥammad is omitted.

Welch, Alford T. "Muhammad's Understanding of Himself: The Koranic Data." In *Islam's Understanding of Itself,* edited by Richard G. Hovannisian and Speros Vryonis, Jr., pp. 15–52. Malibu, Calif., 1983. Study of Qur'ānic portrayals of Muḥammad in Meccan and Medinan contexts that provides analysis and additional references regarding topics treated in the present article.

Wensinck, A. J. *Muhammad and the Jews of Medina.* Translated by Wolfgang Behn. Freiburg im Breisgau, 1975. Translation from the original Dutch, *Mohammed en de Joden te Medina.* Leiden, 1908. Despite its age and a number of later books on related topics, this classic continues to present the clearest, most concise view of the relationship between Muḥammad and the Jewish clans of Medina.

ALFORD T. WELCH

Biographies

The "Life" of Muḥammad (c.570–632) has been one of the most important genres in the Islamic literary tradition from the earliest periods of Islam to the present. Numerous biographies exist in all Islamic languages in prose, poetry, and recently on film. Muḥammad's companions began collecting information about him while he was still alive, particularly about his military exploits (*maghāzī*) after the Hijrah (622). This material consisted of short prose accounts (*ḥadīth, khabar*) centered on one theme and sometimes accompanied by the name of a witness. The reports were anecdotal and modeled on the heroic genre of the pre-Islamic "Battle Days of the Arabs" (*Ayyām al-ʿArab*), although there was little poetry in the early collections. Very little about Muḥammad's childhood and early life can be found in the first biographies. No formal editions were made of this material until much later, and there is no evidence that any of it was put in chronological order before the middle of the first Islamic century.

The death of Muḥammad in 632 CE, the crises of succession, and the expansion of Islam beyond Arabia had a profound impact on the biographies of Muḥammad. In the social and religious turmoil of the first Islamic century, when Islam expanded to present-day France in the west and India in the east, many groups began to collect and organize real and fictitious traditions about Muḥammad to serve their religious, political, and social needs. Genealogical closeness to the Prophet or to his family played an important role for many groups, not the least of whom were the Shīʿīs. To this day, claiming to be a descendant of Muḥammad's tribe or family carries political or religious prestige in many parts of the Islamic world. By the end of the first Islamic century, claims to political power were being made not only on the basis of membership in the Prophet's family, clan, or tribe, but also on contending views that Muḥammad had designated ʿAlī, his closest male relative, or Abū Bakr, his father-in-law and close adviser, as his successor (*khalīfah*, caliph).

Intergroup accusations of falsification of traditions and the need to establish a solid basis for religious and political claims promoted an increase in the collection of stories about Muḥammad, his wives, and his companions. Muslims interested in establishing a basis for proper conduct and understanding of the Qur'ān insisted on making citations about Muḥammad more exact and scholarly. By the beginning of the second Islamic century and the ʿAbbāsid revolution, all traditions were expected to have a sound chain of attribution (*isnād*) reaching back through recognized and reliable transmitters. This requirement led to the collection of biographical data about the companions and subsequent transmitters of traditions as well as the writing of heresiographical treatises in which the reliability of individuals and groups was judged by their adherence to one religious norm or another. Because Sunnī and Shīʿī doctrines were only forming during this early period, many collections reflect attitudes that were later rejected. In spite of increased scholarly attention, or maybe because of it, traditions of dubious authenticity entered the major collections. This fact, coupled with the inevitable loss of historical material over time, has presented problems for both classical and modern scholars in reconstructing a picture of the historical Muḥammad. Some Western scholars are so skeptical as to deny the possibility of knowing anything about Muḥammad's biography. These problems were also faced by the early collectors of traditions: for example, the collector al-Bukhārī (d. 870) is said to have chosen only about 7,275 traditions as reliable from more than 600,000. Issues of the reliability of traditions and the veracity of transmitters remain a central issue in Muslim legal discussions and in intercommunal disputes between Sunnī and Shīʿī.

Toward the end of the first Islamic century, biographical materials about Muḥammad began to be grouped into two distinct types of collections—one historical, discursive, and narrative, called *sīrah*, and the other discrete, anecdotal, and ahistoric, called *sunnah*. The two terms had been used interchangeably but now came to designate separate functions for the sacred biography within the Islamic communities. *Sīrah* came to be used exclusively for narrative histories of Muḥammad and other prophets to whom he was compared. As a result it became the basis for the Muslim views of history. The *sīrah* written by Muḥammad ibn Isḥāq (d. 767) was an apology for the ʿAbbāsid revolution and a model for subsequent universal histories, such as that by the famous al-Ṭabarī (d. 923). It started with the creation and chronicled the history of the world up to Muḥammad, demonstrating how Muḥammad's life was the fulfillment of the divine mission. In this form, it matched Jewish and Christian hagiographic and apocalyptic works with which it shared many features. Muḥammad's life was compared to previous prophets and holy men in the Jewish and Christian traditions, in keeping with the Muslim view that Islam is the culmination of divine revelation. The comparisons served to aid Muslim missionary activities but also led to accusations among Christians that Muḥammad's similarity to Jesus meant that he was the Antichrist. A shorter form, edited by Ibn Hishām (d. c.827), rapidly became the standard biography in the Islamic world and the basis for most subsequent works.

Sunnah developed as the basis for Islamic law, *sharīʿah,* in which Muḥammad became the paradigm for proper behavior. In this genre, Muḥammad is represented ahistorically as explaining or acting out some aspect of correct behavior. Even in those traditions that can be dated to some part of Muḥammad's life, the emphasis is more on the universality of the action rather than on the historical specificity of the event. The Islamic use of sacred biography as a model goes beyond that found in Christianity or Judaism. As an example, we know in detail Muḥammad's favorite foods (honey and nuts), that he would not wear silk or gold, and when and how he performed oral hygiene. Many Muslims today will eat sweets made from honey, consciously aware that Muḥammad did so, and Muslim men will not wear silk and will cleanse their teeth as religious acts. Through *sunnah* (or more properly, through *ḥadīth*) it is possible to reconstruct a detailed picture of Muḥammad's life—but not a historical picture.

The few biographical references to Muḥammad found in the Qur'ān can be fully understood only by means of the independent biographical traditions, so the biography of Muḥammad serves in part as a commentary on the Qur'ān rather than the Qur'ān being a historical source for Muḥammad's life. The technical relationships between verses of the Qur'ān and *ḥadīth* are matters of Islamic legal theory, but by the second Islamic century, most Muslims had agreed generally on when passages of the Qur'ān appeared in Muḥammad's life. For the believing community, Muḥammad, conceived of as freed or protected from sin and error, was the key to understanding the difficulties in the sacred scripture. Even the legendary stories regarded with skepticism by pious Muslim scholars served a didactic function in the popular imagination and hence were preserved, embellished, and fixed in the biographical traditions.

Popular narrative and poetic biographies have long been associated with the celebration of the Prophet's birthday (ʿĪd al-Mīlād or Mawlīd). Such celebrations can include readings from the Qur'ān, recitations of poetry, songs, and the preparation of food, which is dedicated to Muḥammad and then donated to the poor. In South Asian Islamic communities some of the celebrations incorporate characteristics of the local culture. Some condemn these practices as non-Islamic innovations; for example, several *fatwāh*s have been issued by religious authorities in Saudi Arabia against the practice of women reciting poetry addressed to Muḥammad that implies that Muḥammad will be at least spiritually present at the celebration. Even the government-sponsored conference on the biography of Muḥammad held in Pakistan in 1982 was condemned by some Saudi religious authorities because it celebrated the Prophet's birthday. Other examples of adaptation of Muḥammad's biography to local literary forms can be seen in the "infancy poetry" *(pillaittamil)* written in Tamil in Southeast India, in which Muḥammad is depicted in the same manner as an infant Hindu god.

Biographies of Muḥammad proved to be as susceptible to the influences of modernism and colonialism as other Islamic institutions. In the face of Western scientific inquiry into the "historical" Muḥammad, many Muslims adopted either accommodationist or rejectionist attitudes toward such biographies. William Muir's *The Life of Muhammad From Original Sources* provoked strong reaction in the Indo-Muslim communities, presaging the recent reaction to Salman Rushdie's *Satanic Verses.* While the first work purports to be a scholarly inquiry into the historical Muḥammad and the second a work of imaginative fiction, they both share in their offense to the sensibilities among some Muslims that the "Life" of Muḥammad is almost as sacred as the Qur'ān. Similar criticism, although not so violent, has been leveled at Muḥammad Ḥusayn Haykal's *The Life of Muhammad.* One contributing factor to crystallizing the biography of Muḥammad has been the uses to which it has been put for Islamic modernism *(tajdīd),* for example in the establishment of a Ṣūfī Ṭarīqah Muḥammadīyah or "Way of Muḥammad" in the eighteenth century.

Until modern times, Western views of Muḥammad have, with rare exceptions, been hostile. (A contrary example is Thomas Carlyle's *On Heroes, Hero Worship, and the Heroic in History.*) The tendencies of Islamic biographies to portray Muḥammad as a spiritual isomorph of various prophets, including Jesus, have been seized on by Western polemicists who claimed that Muḥammad was merely a deceiver and that Islam started as a Christian (or Jewish) heresy. This bias is so pervasive that the reader must be cautioned about finding it in much material available in Western languages written before the mid-twentieth century. Some recent Western scholars, following an antipositivist interpretive stance, deny that we can know the historical Muḥammad at all and contend that all of his biography is a hagiographic fiction. [*See* Islamic Studies, *article on* History of the Field.]

Biographies of Muḥammad continue to be one of the most popular forms of literary expression among Muslims. They provide spiritual models for the individual Muslim and paradigms for community formation among emerging Islamic republics. Interest in the West has increased to include popular as well as scholarly biographies. Attempts to portray Muḥammad in film have been discouraged by opposition within Muslim communities, although a 1976 Lebanese film, *The Messenger,* starring Anthony Quinn, was widely distributed. Probably its most noted feature was the fact that no image of Muḥammad was shown, in keeping with an Islamic aniconic tradition. If past trends and current increases in the number of Muslims throughout the world are any indication, one can expect the popular and resilient genre of Muḥammad's biographies to incorporate most modern literary forms.

BIBLIOGRAPHY

Abbott, Nabia. *Aisha, the Beloved of Mohammed.* Chicago, 1942. Sympathetic view of Muḥammad based on original sources from the perspective of his favorite wife.

Crone, Patricia, and Michael Cook. *Hagarism.* Cambridge, 1977. Analysis of early Islam that strongly questions the reliability of available sources.

Haykal, Muḥammad Ḥusayn. *The Life of Muhammad.* Translated by Ismāʿīl R. al-Fārūqī. Indianapolis, 1976. English translation of an Egyptian journalist's biography of Muḥammad.

Ibn Hishām, ʿAbd al-Malik. *The Life of Muhammad.* Translated and edited by Alfred Guillaume. Lahore, 1967. Reconstruction and translation of the earliest biography of Muḥammad.

Newby, Gordon D. *The Making of the Last Prophet.* Columbia, S.C., 1989. Study of the early development of Muḥammad's biography, with bibliography.

Schimmel, Annemarie. *And Muhammad Is His Messenger: The Veneration of the Prophet in Islamic Piety.* Chapel Hill, N.C., 1985. Sympathetic discussion of the role of Muḥammad in popular Muslim piety.

Watt, W. Montgomery. *Muhammad at Mecca.* Oxford, 1953. Readable scholarly analysis of Muḥammad's early life, based on original sources.

Watt, W. Montgomery. *Muhammad at Medina.* Oxford, 1956. Noted Western Islamicist's analysis of Muḥammad's later career. Readable and accurate.

Waugh, Earle H. "Following the Beloved: Muhammad as Model in the Sufi Tradition." In *The Biographical Process,* edited by Frank E. Reynolds and Donald Capps, pp. 63–85. The Hague, 1976. Explains the role of Muḥammad as a paradigm for behavior among Ṣūfīs.

GORDON D. NEWBY

Role of the Prophet in Muslim Thought and Practice

During the first three centuries of Islamic thought, Muslims cast the prophet Muḥammad around key religious images. For the scholars of Islamic law, the Prophet was the legislator-jurist who defined the limits and possibilities of ritual observance; for the mystic, he was the ideal seeker on a journey to spiritual perfection; and for the philosopher and the statesman, he was the role-model of both a resolute conqueror and a just ruler. For most ordinary Muslims, the Prophet was a beautiful model, a source through whom flowed God's grace and salvation (Waugh, 1985; Schimmel, 1987).

These various images for the Prophet have since been repeated and refined in a continuing "biographical process" (Frank E. Reynolds and Donald Capps, Introduction to *The Biographical Process,* The Hague, 1976, pp. 1–33). Scholars have continuously refashioned the Prophet in extensive biographies, of which the earliest extant work is that of Muḥammad ibn Isḥāq (d. AH 150/767 CE) edited by Muḥammad Hishām (d. 238/833). Most ordinary Muslims, however, have learned about the Prophet at his birthday celebrations *(mawlīd),* the commemoration of his Night Journey and Ascension, and other special gatherings. On such occasions, the virtues, physical beauty, and spiritual position of the Prophet are extolled in prose, poetry, and even ritual movement.

In the modern period, the image of the prophet Muḥammad has undergone key changes in direct response to the rise of the powerful West and a corresponding decline in the material fortunes of Muslim society. From being the supreme symbol of a powerful and dominant civilization, the prophet Muḥammad has had to adapt to a community embattled on all sides.

Muslim conceptions of the Prophet have also been challenged by the rise of historicocritical scholarship in the West. The relentless search for the historical Muḥammad redeemed him from the vilified stereotype of Christian theology. At the same time, however, he is now viewed from an array of critical, often reductionist, perspectives; instead of being a Christian impostor, he was now a psychopath or a mere product of the material forces of seventh-century Arabia (Saunders, 1954).

These new developments in modern scholarship have influenced the new images constructed within the Muslim community by Muslims at the crossroads between the West and traditional Islam. It is these scholars who have refashioned the older images of the Prophet and produced new ones that have gradually affected ordinary Muslims' perceptions of the last Prophet of Islam. There are at least three identifiable images in modern Islamic thought: the universalization of the Prophet as a unique model of civilization in Muslim apologetic; the Prophet as a model of sociopolitical ideologies; and the deemphasis of the Prophet as the supreme spiritual font and presence.

The "universalization" of the prophet Muḥammad begins with the modernist reformers at the end of the nineteenth century and the beginning of the twentieth. The works of Syed Ameer Ali (*Spirit of Islam: A History of the Evolution and Ideals of Islam,* 1890), and Muḥammad Ḥusayn Haykal (*Ḥayāt Muḥammad,* 1935) are representative examples of modernist castings of the Prophet. In their hands, he becomes the ideal personality manifesting the values of modern civilization (Waugh, 1985, p. 53). They used the Prophet Muḥammad to claim the values they admired in the powerful West. This resulted in numerous volumes of apologetic in response to both the Christian theological images of the Prophet and the historicocritical theories of Western scholars.

Haykal's work discloses the mechanism of this universal and apologetic image of the Prophet. Haykal's decision to write a biography of the Prophet Muḥammad was a direct response to Émile Dermenghem's biography *La Vie de Mohamet* (Paris, 1928). The Egyptian novelist wanted to reproduce the latter's favorable approach to the Prophet Muḥammad in contrast to other more critical writings emerging from Europe (Smith, 1983, p. 115). In addition, Haykal was happy to blame the misrepresentations of the prophet Muḥammad on the fertile imagination and uncritical scholarship of earlier Muslims, particularly the *ʿulamāʾ* (Smith, pp. 114–116). In this way he could freely excise or reinterpret those aspects of the Prophet's life that were embarrassing to modern Muslims; aspects such as polygamy and slavery receive ingenious interpretations to maintain an esteemed image.

Although not all Muslims have felt the need to rebut the European image of the Prophet, there has been a general caution in approaching traditional Muslim sources. For example, Muḥammed al-Nuwayhī (1970) warns against the irresponsible use of Muslim sources and appeals for a reevaluation of the Prophet on the basis of "reason" and "good will." Not quite as modern, Shiblī Nuʿmānī's *Sirat al-Nabi* (Pakistan, 1970) also searches for a historical Muḥammad without the medieval accretions.

This universalistic view was incorporated in the second image of the Prophet as a model for sociopolitical development which received greater attention by Muslims during the period of nationbuilding, ranging from the struggles for independence to the call for an Islamic state. This image deemphasizes the apologetic of the early modernists. Now, however, there rages a battle over the particular ideology that the Prophet championed.

Muhammad Iqbal rejected the idea of nationalism within the particular Islamic notions of commitment and universality in Muḥammad's teachings. At the same time, however, he speaks of the *ummah* (Muslim community) inheriting the function and responsibility of the Prophet. This then become the basis of a special "Islamic nationalism" witnessed in, for example, the Islamic state of Pakistan (Schimmel, 1962, pp. 124–125). Later, under the impact of Gamal Abdel Nasser's socialist experiment in Egypt, the prophet Muḥammad was seen as a socialist revolutionary in Muḥammad Sharqāwī's *Muḥammad rasūl al-ḥurriyyah* (Muhammad, the Prophet of Freedom, 1962). This sociopolitical image has reached its climax in the work of Zakaria Bashier. In his *Sunshine at Madinah* (Leicester, 1990), Bashier deals mainly with the evolution of the state in the Prophet's time. It is an outstanding reflection of revivalist Islam's quest for an Islamic state.

The universal and sociopolitical images of the Prophet are accompanied by the suppression of his spiritual significance. Under the modern reformulations the Prophet loses his central spiritual station in material reality. Earlier modernists did in fact emphasize a hazy moral and spiritual legacy of the Prophet in the service of their secularist project. Under these conditions, however, the Prophet is granted spirituality on condition that he depart from the center stage of history.

In spite of the numerous biographies by Muslims in this century, then, there lurks a deep question about the religious presence of the Prophet. It is not surprising that the rise of the Aḥmadīyah (Qādiānīs), who accepted Mirzā Ghulām Aḥmad (1835–1908) as a new Prophet, accompanied strong modernist inclinations. Some Muslim thinkers have expressed this deep malaise in artistic form. Iqbal, for example, spoke of the Prophet as supreme doubter; he even suggested that the belief in the finality of the prophet Muḥammad carries the seed of its "own abolition." The Egyptian playwright Nagib Mahfouz (Najīb Maḥfūẓ) also addressed the issue in *Awlād ḥāratinā* (The People of Our Quarter, 1959), an allegorical account of religion and the end of religion, including Islam, in modern times.

Finally, these modern images have had an effect on the perception of the Prophet among ordinary Muslims participating in the birthday celebrations *(mawlīd)*, Night Journey and Ascension commemorations, and other gatherings. The image of the Prophet as the universal political hero takes its place alongside his presence as the spiritual center of the universe. More progressively, there is some evidence that the nature of the traditional patterns persists in modern reformulations. Both Tapper (1987) and Antoun (*The Muslim Preacher*, 1989, pp. 219–229) have shown the spread of the Prophet's image as a rational statesmen building a nation for the marginalized Muslims of the world.

BIBLIOGRAPHY

Nuwayhī, Muḥammad al-. "Towards a Re-Evaluation of the Muhammad: Prophet and Man." *Muslim World* 60 (1970): 300–313. A plea by a recent Muslim modernist on the image of the Prophet.

Saunders, John J. "Mohammed in Europe: A Note on Western Interpretations of the Life of the Prophet." *History* 39 (1954): 14–25. Concise account of Western interpretations of the Prophet, including the period after the emergence of historico-critical thought.

Schimmel, Annemarie. "The Place of the Prophet of Islam in Iqbal's Thought." *Islamic Studies* 1.4 (1962): 111–130. Excellent analysis of the rich repertoire of images in Iqbal's thought.

Schimmel, Annemarie. *And Muhammad Is His Messenger*. Chapel Hill, N.C., 1985. Exhaustive compendium of prophetic imagery in Muslim religious life.

Smith, Charles D. *Islam and the Search for Social Order in Modern Egypt: A Biography of Muhammad Husayn Haykal*. Albany, N.Y., 1983. Comprehensive account of the background and nature of the most widespread biography of the Prophet.

Tapper, Nancy, and Richard Tapper. "The Birth of the Prophet: Ritual and Gender in Turkish Islam." *Man* 22 (1987): 69–92. Analyses of the gender differentiation of contemporary prophetic images in Turkey.

Waugh, Earle H. "Images of Muhammad in the Work of Iqbal: Tradition and Alteration." *History of Religions* 23.2 (November 1983): 156–168. Analysis of how a modernist changes the traditional images of the Prophet.

Waugh, Earle H. "The Popular Muhammad: Models in the Interpretation of an Islamic Paradigm." In *Approaches to Islam in Religious Studies*, edited by Richard Martins, pp. 41–58. Tucson, 1985. Excellent use of models for understanding the changing interpretation of Prophet among Muslims.

Wessels, Antonie. "Modern Biographies of the Life of the Prophet Muhammad." *Islamic Culture* 49 (1975): 99–105. Focuses on the biographies of the Prophet in the Arab world.

ABDULKADER I. TAYOB

MUḤAMMAD ʿABDUH. *See* ʿAbduh, Muḥammad.

MUḤAMMAD ʿALĪ DYNASTY. A dynasty of Albanian-Ottoman origin that reigned in Egypt from 1805 until Gamal Abdel Nasser and the Free Officers deposed King Fārūq in 1952 and his infant son Aḥmad Fu'ād II the following year and established a republic. The rulers bore the titles *pasha* and *wālī* (governor) until 1867; they were called *khedive* (viceroy) until 1914, *sulṭān* until 1922, and finally *king* until 1953. Figure 1 shows their simplified genealogy and the order and dates of their reigns.

Muḥammad ʿAlī and Ibrāhīm (who ruled only a few months and predeceased his mentally incapacitated father) are usually depicted as able rulers, and Ismāʿīl and Fu'ād I as energetic if not unflawed ones. ʿAbbās I, Tawfīq, ʿAbbās II, Ḥusayn Kāmil, and Fārūq are generally seen as capricious, weak, or subservient to Western interests.

Arriving with an Ottoman force sent to expel Napoleon Bonaparte's French expedition (1798–1801), Muḥammad ʿAlī maneuvered until the sultan recognized a *fait accompli* by naming him governor of Egypt. The *ʿulamā'* of al-Azhar mosque helped him to power, but he soon curbed their political influence and economic autonomy. The hard-driving "founder of modern Egypt" dug irrigation canals, promoted cotton as a cash crop for export, centralized taxes, and established monopolies in industry and foreign trade. Western advisers helped him build a modern army and schools to train officers, administrators, and technicians. Muḥammad ʿAlī conquered parts of Arabia, the Sudan, and Greece in the name of the sultan, then rebelled in the 1830s and seized Palestine and Syria. The European powers forced him back to his Egyptian base and made him pare down his army, but he obtained the hereditary governorship of Egypt for his line.

A recent revisionist study (Toledano, 1990) has challenged the prevailing view of ʿAbbās I as a xenophobic and reactionary despot. The weak-willed Saʿīd went along with the Suez Canal project and opened wide the

FIGURE 1. *Genealogy of the Muḥammad ʿAlī Dynasty*

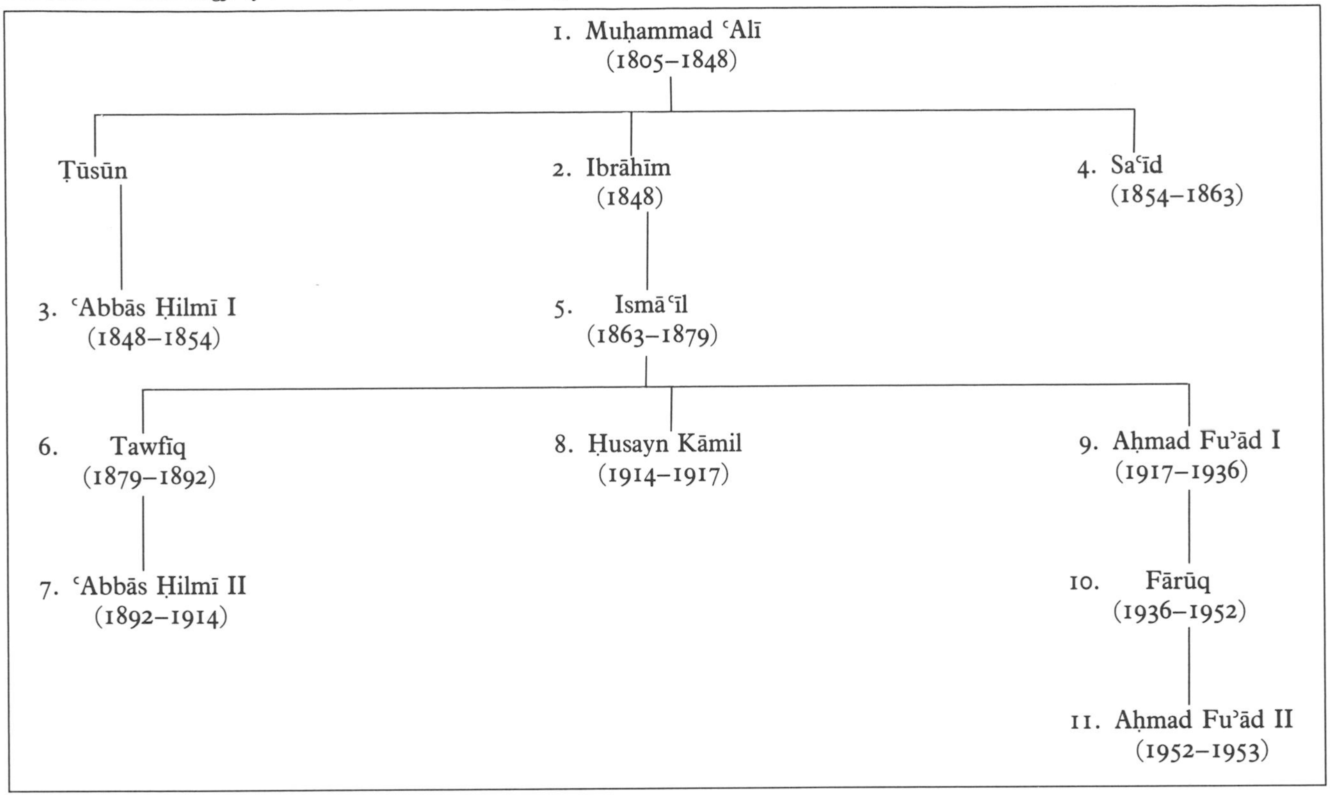

door to European exploitation. Ismāʿīl formally opened the Canal, promoted education and public works, and conquered a new African empire. But bankruptcy led to his deposition in 1879, followed by the ʿUrābī revolt, and the British occupation of 1882. Tawfīq was somewhat a tool of the British, and ʿAbbās II was an ineffectual rebel against the powerful British consul general, Lord Cromer.

Young ʿAbbās II and Fārūq squandered their initial popularity, and the dynasty's failure to come to terms with Egyptian nationalism in the twentieth century proved fatal. Fārūq was the first of the line to feel fully at home speaking Arabic. Fuʾād I cultivated al-Azhar (he harbored ambitions of becoming caliph) and founded Cairo University and other cultural institutions, but he is remembered best for his autocracy and his enmity toward the popular nationalist Wafd Party. By continuing his father's feud with the Wafd, Fārūq forfeited the possibility of becoming a nationalist rallying point like Sultan Muḥammad V of Morocco. Fārūq's private life became a national embarrassment and contributed to his overthrow. Because of the dynasty's alien origins, Gamal Abdel Nasser's claim to be the first indigenous ruler of Egypt since the pharaohs was not entirely fanciful.

[*See also* Egypt.]

BIBLIOGRAPHY

Colombe, M. "ʿAbbās Ḥilmī I" and "ʿAbbās Ḥilmī II." In *Encyclopaedia of Islam*, new ed., vol. 1, p. 13. Leiden, 1960–.

Jomier, Jacques. "Fuʾād al-Awwal." In *Encyclopaedia of Islam*, new ed., vol. 2, p. 934. Leiden, 1960–.

Kahle, Paul E. "Ibrāhīm Pasha." In *Encyclopaedia of Islam*, new ed., vol. 3, pp. 999–1000. Leiden, 1960–.

Marsot, ʿAfāf Luṭfī al-Sayyid. *Egypt in the Reign of Muhammad Ali.* Cambridge, 1984. Discusses individual reigns.

McLeave, Hugh. *The Last Pharaoh: Farouk of Egypt.* New York, 1970. One of several popular biographies of Fārūq.

Toledano, Ehud R. "Muḥammad ʿAlī Pasha." In *Encyclopaedia of Islam*, new ed., vol. 7, pp. 423–431. Leiden, 1960–.

Toledano, Ehud R. *State and Society in Mid-Nineteenth-Century Egypt.* Cambridge, 1990. Covers individual reigns.

Vatikiotis, P. J. "Fārūḳ." In *Encyclopaedia of Islam*, new ed., supp., pp. 299–302. Leiden, 1960–.

Vatikiotis, P. J. "Ḥusayn Kāmil." In *Encyclopaedia of Islam*, new ed., vol. 3, pp. 624–625. Leiden, 1960–.

Vatikiotis, P. J. "Ismāʿīl Pasha." In *Encyclopaedia of Islam*, new ed., vol. 4, pp. 192–193. Leiden, 1960–.

Vatikiotis, P. J. *The History of Modern Egypt: From Muhammad Ali to*

Mubarak. 4th ed. Baltimore, 1991. Discusses the rulers of the dynasty.

DONALD MALCOLM REID

MUHAMMADIYAH. The Javanese Islamic reformist movement known as Muhammadiyah has become one of the three or four most important religious, educational, and social movements throughout the islands of Indonesia as well as the most powerful current reformist movement in Muslim Southeast Asia.

By the fourteenth century Ṣūfī Muslim traders began arriving at Indonesian ports, and by the seventeenth century there were Islamic conversions occurring at numerous locations. The Ṣūfīs established schools, *pesantren,* that gave rise to a particular type of Indonesian purist Islam known as *santri* and dedicated to the Five Pillars: the affirmation of the faith (*shahādah*), commitment to the five daily prayers, the yearly tithe, the Ramaḍān fast, the pilgrimage to Mecca. This practice became polarized with a syncretic tradition fusing Islam with animism and elitest Hinduism.

The Dutch entered Java at Bantam in 1596 and eventually triumphed in a competition for colonialization. By the early twentieth century, increasing westernization had brought confusion and resentment that produced nativist reform and nationalist resistance movements. One of the most constructive of these movements was the Muhammadiyah, founded by Javanese *santri* in 1912.

By the late nineteenth century, modern Islam had called for a reforming return to the Qur'ān and the simplification of ceremony. It also called for modernization; toward that end, schools and organizations for women and youths were founded. For Indonesia, Malaysia, and Singapore, reform entailed rejection of syncretism, animism, Hinduism, and Sufism; reforming students founded schools, journals, and organizations that spread these ideas throughout Southeast Asia.

The Muhammadiyah emerged from among the *santri* of Java as a means of coping with the pressures and alienation of their recent history and recapturing a former sense of meaning. It established hundreds of branches with millions of members, missionary movements, clinics, orphanages, poorhouses, hospitals, books, magazines, newspapers, labor unions, farm cooperatives, factories, and schools. In spite of its position within Islam, it had to compete with numerous syncretic and political movements, including Indonesian nationalism and communism. It remains one of several important ideological and moral streams within a pluralistic society.

The Muhammadiyah was founded on 18 November 1912 in Jogjakarta by Kiyai Hadji Ahmad Dahlan (born Mohammad Darwisj). Dahlan came from a devout Muslim family; his father and maternal grandfather were mosque officials. After education in home, school, and mosque, he went to Mecca. His stay in Mecca lasted for several years and enabled him to study the Qur'ān, theology, astronomy, and religious law, including the works of the Egyptian reformist Muḥammad ʿAbduh. Upon his return he changed his name to Ahmad Dahlan and succeeded his father at the mosque. As he traveled throughout Java selling batik, he taught Islam and encouraged the improvement of Muslim communities. (This pattern of travel and trade remains a core of Muhammadiyah and *santri* life.) During this period he married his mother's brother's daughter, Siti Walidah, who remained his lifelong wife despite his marriages to four additional women whom he soon divorced.

By 1912, twelve individuals from among Dahlan's students and fellow teachers were urging him to form an organization, and thus the Muhammadiyah was begun. Dahlan dedicated the rest of his life to traveling and evangelizing for the mission of reformed and purified Islam in its struggle with syncretic mysticism, Hinduism, Buddhism, feudalism, and colonialism. Even when he became ill he continued to work, making seventeen trips during his last year and insisting, "If I work as fast as possible, what remains can be brought to perfection by another." At the age of fifty-nine, he died after delegating the continuance of his work to his friends and his brother-in-law.

Dahlan is described by his biographers in terms of the Javanese virtues of stoicism and tranquility; that is, he was able to engage in an outward struggle while maintaining inner peace. In this steadfast determination he was compared to the mythical hero Arjuna and became a paradigm for Muhammadiyah spirituality and culture.

Dahlan was able to undertake and continue his work throughout tumultuous times because the Dutch did not consider him a violent or revolutionary protester. He remained an official of the court mosque until his death and attempted no radical restructuring of traditional society. Today, the Muhammadiyah's survival can be partly attributed to its separation from politics.

Dahlan infused the Muhammadiyah with a rationalized form of mission and religious life combined with

Islamic traditionalism. This is especially conspicuous in his understanding of the role of women in religion and society. He was dedicated to the educational and organizational emancipation of women, encouraging them in independent teaching and public speaking; but, still suspicious of the sensual aspect of women, he intensified the traditional separation of the sexes in the Muhammadiyah itself and in the structuring of religious and social life. For instance, he fostered the medical education of women so that female physicians could take care of women patients; but he also commanded women to cease wearing jewelry and to cover their heads with scarves. He established a separate women's auxiliary within the Muhammadiyah, the Aisyiyah, which today remains one of the most dynamic Muslim women's movements in the world.

By 1930 the Muhammadiyah had established committees covering a wide spectrum of religious and social life: Islamic law, politics, women's affairs, youth, boy scouts, education, library and archives, celebrations and evangelism, social welfare and health care, economic development, and administration of property. It maintains a record of efficient organization, balanced budgets, and an uncorrupted leadership. Its membership of several million comes from the middle class, whose many activities for the Muhammadiyah are largely voluntary and unpaid. Although some changes have occurred since Indonesian independence (1945)—for example, the rising prominence of the Jakarta branch owing to its links to the national capital—both the basic structure and direction of the Muhammadiyah remain the same.

The Muhammadiyah has provided for almost a century a focused and practical theological vision, a moral system marked by clarity and specificity, and a system of order and meaning for a people whose culture, although rich and aesthetically satisfying, continues to experience rapid and often destructive changes.

[*See also* Indonesia.]

BIBLIOGRAPHY

Alfian. *Muhammadiyah: The Political Behavior of a Muslim Modernist Organization under Dutch Colonialism.* Yogyakarta, Indonesia, 1989.

Ali, A. Mukti. "The Muhammadijah Movement: A Bibliographical Introduction." Master's thesis, Montreal, 1957.

Noer, Deliar. *The Modernist Muslim Movement in Indonesia, 1900–1942.* London, 1973.

Peacock, James L. *The Muhammadijah Movement in Indonesian Islam: Purifying the Faith.* Menlo Park, Calif., 1978.

JAMES L. PEACOCK and
MARILYN TRENT GRUNKEMEYER

MUḤARRAM. The first month of the lunar Islamic calendar begins like the other months with the first sighting of the crescent moon. Muḥarram has a long tradition as a sacred month in Islam. For example, it was on 16 Muḥarram that the *qiblah* (the orientation of prayer) was shifted from Jerusalem to Mecca. Among Shīʿīs it is has special significance as the month when Imam Ḥusayn ibn ʿAlī, the grandson of Muḥammad, was martyred. In AH 81/680 CE, at the place known as Karbala on the banks of the Euphrates, the troops of the caliph Yazīd ibn Muʿāwiyah under the command of Ibn Ziyād laid siege to Imam Ḥusayn and his vastly outnumbered companions. The male members of his family, with the exception of his young son Zayn al-ʿĀbidīn, were killed, and the women were marched uncovered to the city of Damascus. Ḥusayn was decapitated and his body mutilated. Although Sunnī and Shīʿī Muslims alike recognize the tragedy of the sacrifice of Ḥusayn, for Shīʿīs it has special significance as the critical moment in the history of Islam, when the official Islamic regime murdered the only remaining grandson of the prophet Muḥammad.

In commemoration of Ḥusayn's martyrdom, the first ten days of the month are a period of intense ritual mourning during which Shīʿīs engage in lamentation assemblies, public processions, and other activities. These culminate on the actual date of Ḥusayn's martyrdom on 10 Muḥarram, also known as ʿĀshūrā'. The purpose of these activities is to evoke Karbala in an existential and dramatic manner and to induce tears of grief in the participants. These tears are a manifestation of devotional allegiance to Imam Ḥusayn, which is ultimately a sign of allegiance to both God and the Prophet and thus to Islam itself: for if Muḥammad is the beloved of God, and Ḥusayn is the beloved of Muḥammad, then love for Ḥusayn is the necessary corollary of love for Muḥammad and God. Those who cannot mourn for Ḥusayn are seen as deficient in their devotion to Muḥammad and to God.

Throughout the Islamic world there are a variety of performances connected with Muḥarram mourning. In Iran passion plays called *taʿziyah*s are performed. In India and Pakistan lamentation assemblies called *majlis* are occasions for often sophisticated discourses on Islam, followed by *ghamm* or lamentation, in which the congregation hears the story of Karbala and cries. The evocation and remembrance of Karbala in these performances provides believers with paradigms for proper behavior. The courage and discipline of Ḥusayn and his comrades provides a model to which all Muslims should aspire.

In the modern world, the story of Ḥusayn is retold not only in local *majlis* but also by means of cassette and video recordings. In this way discourses about Karbala have been made available to millions of listeners. Because the event of Karbala is seen as a paradigm of the oppression of the innocent at the hands of the unjust, its remembrance can provide the focus for sustained political agitation. For example, the circulation of cassette tapes in Iran containing speeches by Ayatollah Ruhollah Khomeini that equated the crimes of the shah with the actions of Yazīd and called on the people to identify with Ḥusayn were an important catalyst in the success of the Iranian revolution.

[*See also* ʿĀshūrāʾ; Ḥusayn ibn ʿAlī; Karbala; Martyrdom; Taʿziyah; *and* Cassettes.]

BIBLIOGRAPHY

Ayoub, Mahmoud M. *Redemptive Suffering in Islam*. The Hague, 1982.

Chelkowski, Peter, ed. *Taʿziyeh: Ritual and Drama in Iran*. New York, 1979.

Fischer, Michael M. J. *Iran: From Religious Dispute to Revolution*. Cambridge, Mass., 1980.

Schubel, Vernon. *Religious Performance in Contemporary Islam: Shīʿī Devotional Rituals in South Asia*. Columbia, S.C., 1993.

VERNON JAMES SCHUBEL

MUḤTASIB. A holder of the office of *al-ḥisbah*, an executive function falling roughly between the offices of *qāḍī* (judge) and *wālī al-maẓālim* (*maẓālim* court magistrate), the *muḥtasib* was charged with enforcing public morality, overseeing the public welfare, and supervising the markets, fulfilling thereby the community's collective obligation to command the good and forbid evil ("al-amr bi-al-maʿrūf wa-al-nahy ʿan al-munkar"). The *muḥtasib* had no jurisdiction to hear legal cases per se but only to settle common disputes and well-known breaches of the law in which the facts were obvious or where there was an admission of guilt. He was also vested with certain discretionary powers through which he could intervene in such matters as commercial fraud and public nuisances. In addition, he could levy discretionary punishments (*taʿzīr*) up to but not equaling the prescribed *sharīʿah* penalties (*ḥudūd*) for such indiscretions as private intermingling of the sexes or abuse of pack animals.

Early manuals on *al-ḥisbah* lay out precise (and extremely broad) jurisdictional boundaries. According to Ibn Taymīyah (d. 1328), however, the *muḥtasib*'s actual function was determined in large part by the time and place in which he operated as well as local custom and the political agenda of the particular ruler under whom he served. What belonged to the police (*shurṭah*) or to the courts in one place could fall under the jurisdiction of the *muḥtasib* in another. Prominent scholars and jurists are known to have held the office, but it was also known to have been occupied by merchants and other persons of surprisingly little legal training.

Later sources reflect a gradual evolution in the *muḥtasib*'s function from matters connected with public morality to a more restricted emphasis on policing the markets and overseeing the activities of merchants and artisans. In this capacity, in addition to his traditional duties of standardizing and inspecting weights and measures, the *muḥtasib* was often called on to collect certain taxes, for example, import and export duties, or to impose penalties on artisans and other guild-members found in violation.

By the nineteenth century, the office of the *muḥtasib* had all but disappeared in most parts of the Muslim world, its many functions being redistributed among various modern, secular jurisdictions. The Ottomans formally abolished the office in Istanbul in AH 1271/1854 CE, and it appears also to have disappeared in Persia around the same time. In the Indian subcontinent, the office had been in steady decline since the sixteenth century and enjoyed only a brief but futile revival under the Mughal ruler, Awrangzīb. Little is known about the impact of colonial rule on the office of the *muḥtasib*.

There remains today a few possible vestiges of the medieval office of the *muḥtasib* in certain parts of the Islamic world. In Morocco, for example, the *raʾīs al-maṣāliḥ al-iqtiṣādīyah* (chief of economic welfare), appears to be a possible descendent of the nineteenth-century *muḥtasib*, who, because of his intrusive tendencies, had acquired the nickname, *al-fuḍūlī* (busybody). The *niẓām al-ṭilbah* (system of appropriations) or *ḥalaqāt al-ʿazābīyah* (discipline corps) found among certain Ibāḍī communities in Algeria might also be considered a modern descendant of *al-ḥisbah*.

[*See also* Ḥisbah.]

BIBLIOGRAPHY

Cahen, Claude, et al. "Ḥisba." In *Encyclopaedia of Islam*, new ed., vol. 3, pp. 485–493. Leiden, 1960–.

Ibn Saʿīd, Aḥmad. *Kitāb al-taysīr fī ahkām al-tasʿīr*. Edited by Mūsā Laqbāl. Algiers, n.d.

Ibn Taymīyah, Aḥmad. *Al-ḥisbah fī al-Islām*. Beirut, 1387/1967.

Laqbāl, Mūsā. *Al-ḥisbah al-madhhabīyah fī bilād al-Maghrib al-ʿArabī.* Algiers, 1971.
Māwardī, Abū al-Ḥasan ʿAlī ibn Muḥammad al-. *Al-aḥkām al-sulṭānīyah.* Edited by Muḥammad ʿAbd-al-Qādir. Būlāq, Cairo, 1880. Translated into French by Edmond Fagnam as *Les statuts gouvernementaux, ou, Règles de droit public et administratif.* Paris, 1982.
Shayzarī, ʿAbd al-Raḥmān ibn Naṣr. *Nihāyat al-rutbah fī ṭalab al-ḥisbah.* Edited by Sayyid al-Bāz al-ʿArīnī. Cairo, 1946.

SHERMAN A. JACKSON

MUJĀHID. *See* Jihād.

MUJĀHIDĪN. [*This entry comprises articles focusing on Iran and on Afghanistan, the two countries where groups known as* mujāhidīn *have been active in the late decades of the twentieth century.*]

Mujāhidīn-i Khalq

The Sāzimān-i Mujāhidīn-i Khalq-i Īrān (Holy Warrior Organization of the Iranian People) is better known simply as the Iranian Mujāhidīn. It is a religious, but anticlerical, organization and constitutes the main opposition to the Islamic Republic of Iran.

The Mujāhidīn's ideology combines Shiism with Marxism. It interprets Islam, especially the Qur'ān, the *ḥadīths* (sayings of the Prophet and imams), and Shīʿī teachings, to be a divine message for social, economic, and political revolution. It also finds much of Marxism, but not dialectical materialism, to be an indispensible tool for analyzing politics, society, and history. As one of its handbooks declares: "We say 'no' to Marxist philosophy, especially atheism. But we say 'yes' to Marxist social thought, particularly to its analysis of feudalism, capitalism, and imperialism" (Mujāhidīn Organization, *Tārīkhchah, jiryān-i kūditā, va khaṭṭ-i kununī-yi Sāzimān-i Mujāhidīn-i Khalq-i Īrān* [Short History, the Coup Incident, and the Present Policy of the People's Mujāhidīn Organization of Iran], Tehran, 1978). Mujāhidīn ideas are so similar to those of ʿAlī Sharīʿatī, the famous contemporary thinker, that many commentators have jumped to the erroneous conclusion that Sharīʿatī inspired the organization. Actually, the two developed their ideas independently of each other. [*See the biography of Sharīʿatī.*]

The Mujāhidīn organization was created in the mid-1960s by a group of recent graduates from Tehran University, most from the Colleges of Engineering and Agriculture, who had also studied the Qurʾān and Imam ʿAlī's *Nāhj al-balāghah* (Way of Eloquence) with Ayatollah Maḥmud Ṭāleqāni [*see the biography of Ṭāleqāni*]. The founding leaders had been members of Mehdi Bāzargān's Nahẕat-i Āzādī-yi Īrān (Liberation Movement of Iran), but after the bloody demonstrations of June 1963, they found their parent party too moderate and too wedded to conventional politics. Even more important, they were all deeply impressed by contemporary guerrilla movements, especially those in Cuba, Vietnam, and Algeria. They concluded that the only way to challenge the Pahlavi regime was through armed struggle and heroic deeds of martyrdom. In their own words: "After June 1963, militants—irrespective of ideology—realized one cannot fight tanks with bare hands. We had to ask the question 'what is to be done?' Our answer was straightforward: 'armed struggle.' " (*Mujāhid* 4 [November 1974]). In their early discussion groups, they studied Che Guevara's *Guerrilla Warfare,* Lenin's *What Is to Be Done?*, Frantz Fanon's *Wretched of the Earth,* Regis Debray's *Revolution within the Revolution,* and most important of all, Amar Ouzegan's *Le meilleur combat.* Ouzegan, a former communist who had become the leading theoretician of the Algerian FLN, argued that Islam was a revolutionary socialist creed and that the only way to fight imperialism and its local lackeys was to resort to the armed struggle and appeal to the religious sentiments of the masses. The early Mujāhidīn adopted *Le meilleur combat* as their main handbook.

In the late 1960s, the Mujāhidīn collectively wrote a path-breaking book of their own entitled *Nahẕat-i Ḥusaynī* (The Husaynite Movement). In this book they argued that Imam Ḥusayn had taken up arms because the Ummayyad Caliphate was exploiting the masses and betraying the Prophet's true cause—the establishment of a classless society, which they termed *niẓām-i tawḥīdī* (unitary order). This became their battle cry first against the shah and later against the regime of Ayatollah Ruhollah Khomeini. The eternal message of the holy month of Muḥarram, when Ḥusayn was martyred, *Nahẕat-i Ḥusaynī* stressed, was that human beings, unlike animals, had the sacred duty to fight political oppression and class exploitation. The Shīʿī martyrs, the book concluded, were like Che Guevara: they accepted martyrdom as a revolutionary duty and considered the armed struggle against class oppression as their sacred obligation. In short, both the martyrs and Guevara had died for the cause of social equality. The Mujāhidīn developed similar ideas in pamphlets entitled *Takāmul* (Evolution toward Perfection), *Shinākht* (Knowledge), and *Iqtiṣād bih zabān-i sādah* (Economics in a Simple Language).

The Mujāhidīn also developed their own *tafsīr* (explanatory method) for understanding scriptural texts, especially the Qurʾān and the *Nāhj al-balāghah*. These texts, they argued, should be treated not as dead parchments, but as "guides" and "living inspirations for revolutionary action." They should be placed in their proper "historical context" and read for their "real radical essence." They further argued that the clergy had done to these texts what the reformist Social Democrats of Europe had tried to do to Marx and Engels—paid lip service to them, turned their teachings into harmless banalities, and emasculated their revolutionary essence.

These early works gave new meanings to old Islamic and Shīʿī terms. For example, the meaning of *mustaẕʿafān* changed from "the meek" to "the exploited masses" (as in Fanon's *Wretched of the Earth*); *ummah*, from "a religious community" to "a dynamic society in constant motion toward a classless society"; *jihād*, from "crusade" to "liberation struggle"; *mu'min*, from "the pious believer" to "the true fighter for social justice"; *shahīd*, from "religious martyr" to "revolutionary hero"; *mujāhid*, from "holy warrior" to "freedom fighter"; and most ironic of all, *imām*, from "religious leader" to "charismatic revolutionary leader." Some of these new meanings eventually found their way into Khomeini's own pronouncements.

The Mujāhidīn launched their guerrilla struggle in 1971 with a series of bombings and armed attacks. In the course of the next eight years, the organization gained a nationwide reputation for courage, determination, and efficiency. At the same time, however, it lost many of its leaders and cadres through arrests, executions, and street shootouts. Of the eighty-three Mujāhids who lost their lives from 1971 to 1979, almost all came from the ranks of the young intelligentsia in Tehran and the central Persian-speaking provinces. They were engineers, teachers, accountants, and most often, university students. By the mid-1970s, the Mujāhidīn, as well as the Marxist Fidā'īyān, were considered to constitute the main opposition to the shah.

Despite this success, the Mujāhidīn suffered a major schism in 1975. Some members declared themselves Marxist-Leninists and denounced Islam as a "conservative petit bourgeois ideology." Their religious disillusionment was caused by the discovery that Khomeini and the clergy, with the notable exception of Ṭāleqāni, refused to support their armed struggles. These Marxists later renamed themselves the Sāzimān-i Paykār dar Rāh-i Āzādī-yi Ṭabaqah-yi Kārgār (The Combat Organization for the Emancipation of the Working Class)—Paykār, in short. Ibrāhīm Yazdī, a Nahẕat-i Āzādī leader, argued that this schism so weakened the Mujāhidīn that it paved the way for the clergy to come to power. The split, he claimed, changed the whole course of Iranian history (*Ākharīn Talāsh-hā dar ākharīn rūz-hā* [Last Struggles in the Last Days], Tehran, 1984).

By late 1978 and early 1979 little remained of the Mujāhidīn—and those who were left were incarcerated in prison and led by Mas'ūd Rajavī, one of the few early members to have survived the executions and the armed confrontations. A graduate of Tehran University's law school, Rajavī had been arrested in 1972 and condemned to death. An international effort made on his behalf by his brother, a student in Switzerland, had persuaded the shah to commute Rajavī's death sentence to life imprisonment. Rajavī did not leave prison until late 1978, but when released, he promptly regrouped his followers, who then helped deliver the old regime its coup de grâce in the final street battles of February 1979.

In the two years after the Iranian Revolution, the Mujāhidīn grew rapidly into a major force. It established branches throughout the country. It rebuilt an underground armed network—much to the consternation of the new authorities. Its organ, *Mujāhid*, became one of the country's largest-circulation newspapers. Its parliamentary candidates drew substantial votes, in some constituencies posing serious challenges to the clerical favorites. Its electoral supporters included not only numerous trade unions, leftist organizations, professional associations, and regional parties—notably, the Kurdish Democratic party—but also an impressive array of prominent writers, lawyers, politicians, antishah politicians, and even some maverick clergymen. Its rallies drew tens of thousands—sometimes hundreds of thousands—of enthusiatic supporters. Gradually the Mujāhidīn became allied with Abol-Hasan Bani Sadr, the popularly elected president, who, after taking office, accused the clergy of monopolizing power and plotting to establish the "dictatorship of the mullatariat."

The Mujāhidīn grew for a number of reasons. It had a well-earned mystique of revolutionary martyrdom. It adhered to Shiism, but opposed Khomeini's brand of Islam. It denounced his concept of *vilāyat-i faqīh* (*wilāyat al-faqīh*, jurist's trusteeship) and his claim that the clergy had the divine right to rule. It dismissed as "medieval" his attitudes toward women and his interpretation of *sharīʿah*—especially on the questions of corporal punishment and laws of vengeance. The Mujāhidīn often cited Ṭāleqāni's famous warning that "the most dangerous form of tyranny is that of the clergy." It called for political pluralism, freedom of the press, elected councils in towns, villages, and workplaces, and complete equality for all citizens (men and women, clerics and nonclerics, Muslims and non-Muslims, Shīʿīs and Sunnīs alike). Moreover, the Mujāhidīn advocated far-reaching social changes, including land reform, literacy campaigns, medical services, low-income housing, work projects, income redistribution, nationalization of large companies, and worker's control of industrial factories. In short, the Mujāhidīn presented a radical but modernist intepretation of Islam.

The Islamic Republic's restrictions on the Mujāhidīn intensified as the latter's popularity increased—especially after Tāleqāni, who had tried to mediate between the two, suffered a fatal heart-attack. The regime labeled the Mujāhidīn *iltiqāṭī* ("eclectic") and *gharbzadah* (contaminated with the disease of Westernism). It barred Mujāhidīn spokesmen from the radio-television network; disqualified Rajavī from the presidential race; periodically closed down *Mujāhid* and its provincial offices; and stopped the ballot-count in constituencies where Mujāhidīn candidates were doing well. The Khomeini regime also refused to grant demonstration permits, and it used club-wielders, known as Ḥizbullāhīs (those of the Party of God), to break up Mujāhidīn rallies. More than seventy Mujāhids lost their lives in such incidents in 1980 and 1981—almost as many as had been killed in nine years of guerrilla warfare against the shah. Most of the victims were college and high school students. Finally, in June 1981, Khomeini pronounced the Mujāhidīn to be *munāfiqīn* ("hypocrites"), and cited the Qurʾān to argue that the "*munāfiqīn* were more dangerous than the *kāfir* [infidels]." The regime promptly declared the Mujāhidīn to be the "enemies of God" and ordered the revolutionary guards to execute summarily Mujāhidīn demonstrators, irrespective of age.

The Mujāhidīn countered state terror with its own brand of "revolutionary terror"—ambushes, suicide attacks, bombings, and assassinations. The regime, in turn, retaliated with a reign of terror unprecedented in Iranian history: mass arrests, torture, executions, and even public hangings. During the height of this terror—which lasted from June 1981 until September 1985—the Mujāhidīn suffered more than nine thousand dead. Most of them came from the young generation of the intelligentsia: they were teachers, civil servants, doctors, veterinarians, technicians, accountants, and most important, college and high school students. The dead also included some factory workers, especially ones with high school diplomas. In terms of geography, most came from Tehran, the Caspian region, and the Shīʿī and Persian-speaking regions of central Iran and northern Khurasan.

The reign of terror forced the leadership, especially Rajavī, to move into exile, first to Paris, then, after June 1986, to Iraq. In Paris, the Mujāhidīn created a broad coalition named the Shūrā-yi Millī-yi Muqāvamat (National Council of Resistance). Its avowed goal was to replace the Islamic Republic with a Democratic Islamic Republic. Initially the council included Banī Sadr, the Kurdish Democratic party, and a number of leftist and liberal organizations as well as prominent national figures. In Iraq, the Mujāhidīn set up training camps, a radio station named *Ṣadā-yi Mujāhid* (Mujahid Voice), and most important, the National Liberation Army—a well-equipped force of some seven thousand men and women. Moreover, the Mujāhidīn, using the National Council name, established public-relations offices in the United Nations and in many capitals—in India, Pakistan, Indonesia, as well as in the West. These offices hold press conferences, fax news bulletins, publish pamphlets, and circulate videos to convince their host publics both that the present Iranian regime is highly unstable and that the National Council is the only viable alternative to the Islamic Republic. In early 1986, for example, these offices collected signatures from more than five thousand public figures—including thirty-five hundred legislators in Western countries—denouncing mass executions and violations of human rights in Iran.

Although it remains a significant force in exile, the Mujāhidīn has lost much of its social basis within Iran. The open alliance with Iraqi President Saddam Hussein—especially during the Iran-Iraqi War—has alienated the general public. Important allies, notably Banī Sadr and the Kurdish Democratic party, have gone their separate ways. In fact, the National Council has been reduced to a mere front organization. The Mujāhidīn has lost some of its own cadres; some have dropped out of politics, others have created rival offshoots, yet others have made their peace with Tehran. The organization's denunciation of former allies as "traitors", "leeches," "garbage," and "parasites" has led many to wonder whether its version of Islam would be any more tolerant than that of Khomeini.

The Mujāhidīn has increasingly become an inward-looking religio-political sect. It has surrounded its leader with an intense personality cult, proclaiming that "Rajavī is Iran, and Iran is Rajavī." It has purged the half-hearted and denounced them as the enemies of Iran. It has ceased publishing intellectual works, serious analyses, and even regular newspapers. For some secular observers, it has become another sect—albeit an armed one—eagerly awaiting the New Revolution, much in the same way as the early Shīʿīs expected the Return of the Mahdi.

[*See also* Iranian Revolution of 1979.]

BIBLIOGRAPHY

Abrahamian, Ervand. *The Iranian Mojahedin.* New Haven, 1989.

Association of Committed Professors of Iranian Universities. *Facts and Myths on the People's Mojahedin of Iran: Examples of the Lies, Distortions, and Fabrications in Ervand Abrahamian's The Iranian Mojahedin.* N.p., 1990.

Irafani, Suroosh. *Revolutionary Islam in Iran.* London. 1983. Mujāhidīn critique of the Islamic Republic.

Mujāhidīn Organization. *The History of the People's Mojahedin Organization of Iran, 1965–1971.* Long Beach, Calif., 1981. Contains short hagiographies of the founding members.

Mujāhidīn Organization. *How to Study the Qoran?* Long Beach, Calif., 1981. Summary of the organization's method of exegesis.

Mujāhidīn Organization. *Massoud Rajavi.* N.p., 1981. Short biography of the organization's leader, together with its program in 1980–1981.

Mujāhidīn Organization. *List of Names and Particulars of 14,028 Victims of the Khomeini Regime's Executions.* N.p., 1987. The organization's book of martyrs since 1981.

Radjavi, Kazem. *La révolution iranienne et les Moudjahedines.* Paris, 1983. Authored by the brother of the organization's leader, it describes the Iranian Revolution from the Mujāhidīn perspective.

Shoaee, Rokhsareh. "The Mujahid Women of Iran: Reconciling 'Culture' and 'Gender.' " *Middle East Journal* 41 (Autumn 1987): 519–537.

Ervand Abrahamian

Afghan Mujāhidīn

The Afghan Mujāhidīn are guerrilla fighters who formed their groups in opposition to the communist government after the April 1978 coup. The Mujāhidīn movement is divided into an array of political parties, each following a different set of ideological, ethnic, clientelist, and sectarian loyalties. The first cleavage among the parties is based on ideological commitment: the Islamists advocate an Islamic revolution, and the "moderates," although committed also to the implementation of *sharīʿah,* rely on traditional elites and oppose the idea of Islamic revolution.

The Sunnī Islamist movement, influenced by the ideas of the Egyptian Muslim Brotherhood of the 1950s, was active in the late 1960s on Kabul college campuses. An urban movement, it recruited mostly among young intellectuals who considered Islam more a political ideology than a religion. This movement split into three parties: the most radical party, Ḥizb-i Islāmī, led by Gulbuddin Hekmatyar, a Pashtun and a former engineering student; a regionally influential party, also named Ḥizb-i Islāmī, led by Yunus Khales, a Pashtun mullah; and the relatively moderate party that is popular among Persian speakers, Jamʿīyat-i Islāmī, led by Burhanuddin Rabbani (Burhān al-Dīn Rabbānī), a Tajiki theology professor. From 1979 onward, the Islamist militants reentered Afghanistan (they had left in 1975) to lead the spontaneous armed rebellion that broke out after the communist coup of April 1978 and the subsequent Soviet invasion of December 1979.

The moderate parties were created after the communist coup: the Ḥarakat-i Inqilāb (Revolutionary Movement), led by Muḥammad Nabī Muḥammadī, a cleric, which recruits mostly among traditional Pashtun or Uzbek clerics; the Maḥāẕ-i Millī-yi Islāmī Afghānistān (National Islamic Front of Afghanistan), headed by Pir Aḥmad Gaylānī, a secular but charismatic leader of a Ṣūfī order, which recruits among traditional tribal, mainly Durrānī, leaders; and the Jabhah-yi Nahẕat-i Millī (National Salvation Front), led by Ṣibghatullāh Mujaddidī, a scholar and cleric from the Ṣūfī Naqshbandī order, which recruits among local traditional notables.

A seventh party, the fundamentalist Ittiḥād-i Islāmī (Islamic Union), led by ʿAbd al-Rabb Sayyāf, came into existence in 1982 as a front party for Arab Wahhābīs and Muslim Brotherhood groups. It has no sociological or ethnic base, because it recruits mainly by distributing weapons to local low-level commanders, whatever their party of origin.

These seven parties are all Sunnīs and have been united since 1985 in a loose Seven-Parties Alliance, based in Peshawar, Pakistan. This alliance constituted the core of the anti-Kabul Afghan Interim Government created in February 1988. The Jamīʿat slowly shifted toward the moderates, and the Ḥizb-i Islāmī of Hekmatyar has fought all the other parties, trying to seize power for itself through an alliance with the hardcore communists and Pashtun nationalists.

The division between Islamists and moderates is also found among Shīʿīs, who make about 15 percent of the Afghan population. Many of the Shīʿīs are members of the Hazara ethnic group. In 1984, the Islamist Shīʿīs, supported by Iran, were able to drive the moderates, organized within the Shūrā-yi Ittifāq (Islamic Council of Unity), out of Hazarajat Province. The Shīʿī Islamists were bound together in an Eight-Parties Alliance, based in Qom, Iran, which gave birth in July 1990 to the Ḥizb-i Waḥdat (Unity Party), headed by Shaykh ʿAlī Mazārī.

The civil war since 1978 has brought two considerable sociological changes: a new leadership has emerged in Afghanistan, and ethnicity is now more important than ever before. The major tribal leaders for the most part left the country or, more rarely, joined the communist regime, which implemented an active tribal policy, according to the traditional patterns of the relationship between central state and local powers. The new leadership of the Mujāhidīn is made up of either young, educated middle-class Islamists (i.e., Islamic militants) or traditional *ʿulamāʾ*, usually also rather young. The Islamist intellectuals do not have legitimacy according to traditional patterns (that is, as scions of influential families). They had to root themselves in the traditional society by using, on the one hand, new political patterns, such as affiliation with a political party, implementation of *sharīʿah*, or military efficiency; and by adopting, on the other hand, some traditional patterns of power, such as distributing weapons as a tool of influence, forging personal ties with the other leaders, and establishing a patron-client relationship with their followers.

In the course of the Afghan civil war, a general realignment did occur among the parties, from ideological feuds to ethnic splits: the war has accentuated the traditional segmentation of Afghan society by giving it political expression and by converting ethnic affiliations into a political issue. The Shīʿī Ḥizb-i Waḥdat shifted from a radical and ideological position to advocating a policy stressing ethnicity to the exclusion of other issues. It represents the Shīʿī Hazaras, rallying the former moderates and making an alliance with the Sunnī Persian speakers of Commander Aḥmad Shāh Masʿūd. For its part, the Ḥizb-i Islāmī became known as the forerunner of the hardcore Pashtun nationalists. Commander Masʿūd of the Jamīʿat, although himself committed to a multiethnic and Islamic Afghanistan, became the hero of the non-Pashtuns, who unanimously reject the two-century tradition of Pashtun political domination in Afghanistan. Further, the Peshawar-based interim government, established in 1988 under Pakistani and Saudi auspices, has been seen as mainly Pashtun, while the fall of Kabul in April 1992 has been viewed as the result of revenge-seeking efforts of the non-Pashtun commanders based inside Afghanistan. The war thus brought a new ethnic balance, in favor of the non-Pashtuns. If affiliation to a segmented group is the rule of the political game at the grass-roots level, ethnicity is now the foremost issue in nationwide politics, moreso than the confrontation between Islam and secularism.

The victory of the Mujāhidīn and collapse of the communist regime are likely to lead to the establishment of a conservative Islamic regime over a conservative society entailing the imposition of the veil, the prohibition of alcohol, the closing down of moviehouses, the enforcement of prayers, and the like. But widespread social or economic reforms are unlikely. The de facto model for Afghanistan is Saudi Arabia, not Iran, with all this implies in the way of status quo behavior on the part of the Afghan government in both domestic and foreign policies.

[See also Afghanistan; Ḥizb-i Islāmī Afghanistan; *and the biography of Hekmatyar.*]

BIBLIOGRAPHY

Bindemann, Rolf. *Religion und Politik bei den Schiʿitischen Hazara in Afghanistan, Iran und Pakistan.* Berlin, 1987. History and analysis of Shīʿī political dissent in Afghanistan during the nineteenth century, and of its links with the Iranian clergy.

Canfield, Robert, and M. Nazif Shahrani, eds. *Revolutions and Rebellions in Afghanistan.* Berkeley, 1984. Anthropological account of the reaction of the Afghan populations to the communist coup in 1978.

Dupree, Louis. *Afghanistan.* 3d ed. Princeton, 1980. Handbook on Afghanistan covering most fields, from geography to music, Islam, and recent history.

Roy, Olivier. *Islam and Resistance in Afghanistan.* 2d ed. New York, 1990. Analysis of the origins, ideology, and political activities of the Afghan Islamist movement, and of its adaptation to a traditional society.

OLIVIER ROY

MUJTAHID. *See* Ijtihād.

MUKHTĀR, ʿUMAR AL- (c. 1858–1931), Libyan resistance leader. ʿUmar al-Mukhtār ibn ʿUmar al-Minifī grew up in a religious family connected to the

Sanūsīyah Ṣūfī order in Cyrenaica (eastern Libya). He came from the ʿĀ'ilat Farḥāt branch of the Minifīyah, an independent client tribe. ʿUmar studied at the lodge of Zanzūr, moving on to the Sanūsī capital and university of Jaghbūb in 1887, then moving with the leadership to Kufra in the Libyan desert in 1895.

Two years later he was appointed shaykh of the al-Qaṣūr lodge in western Cyrenaica, in the territory of the unruly ʿAbīd tribe. ʿUmar was successful in solidifying the authority of the order in the region. His success noted, he was again called south in 1899, when the order was expanding into Borku (northern Chad). He was appointed shaykh of the ʿAyn Qalakkah lodge. Here he had his first military experiences fighting the French forces. In 1903 he moved back to al-Qaṣūr as shaykh of the lodge.

When the Italians invaded Libya in 1911, ʿUmar led the ʿAbīd in the ensuing *jihād*. By the time the first war ended in a truce in 1917, ʿUmar had gained great influence with the new leader of the Sanūsīyah, Muḥammad Idrīs. In 1923, the Italians reopened hostilities. Idrīs went into exile in Egypt and appointed ʿUmar as one of the leaders for the campaign in Cyrenaica. Already more than sixty years old, as *nā'ib al-ʿāmm* (general representative) he became a charismatic figure who inspired the tribes to join and maintain the struggle.

ʿUmar displayed considerable tactical skill and was able to lead the mostly tribal units in a campaign that for more than six years confounded the Italians in spite of their great numerical and material superiority. Eventually the guerilla forces started to be worn down, and in 1929, after a series of defeats, ʿUmar asked for truce negotiations. They led nowhere, and after three months he resumed fighting. But Italian superiority was now evident, in particular after they in 1930 began rounding up the bedouin population into concentration camps and cut off supply lines by closing the Egyptian border with barbed wire. ʿUmar's fighters became hunted groups, and on 11 September 1931, ʿUmar himself was captured in a chance encounter. He was brought to Benghazi and, after a summary trial, hanged on 16 September. After his death the resistance crumbled, ending within three months.

What made ʿUmar al-Mukhtār such a charismatic leader was a combination of religious authority and personal skill. While the forces he led were largely tribal, he himself came from a relatively minor, client tribe. His first military power was based on the ʿAbīd tribe, among whom he was the leader of the Sanūsī Ṣūfī lodge. With this basis he could use his political and military skill, which combined with a personal reputation for uprightness and incorruptibility formed a power strong enough to stand up to the Italian forces for almost a decade.

[*See also* Libya; Sanūsīyah.]

BIBLIOGRAPHY

Del Boca, Angelo. *Gli Italiani in Libia.* 2 vols. Rome, 1986–1988. Thorough study of the period from an Italian point of view.

Evans-Pritchard, E. E. *The Sanusi of Cyrenaica.* Oxford, 1949. Still the major study of the period in English.

Santarelli, Enzo, Giorgio Rochat, Romain Raniero, and Luigi Goglia. *Omar al-Mukhtar: The Italian Reconquest of Libya.* London, 1986. Concentrates on the last years of the war, using Italian sources in a critical perspective.

KNUT S. VIKØR

MULK. *See* Monarchy.

MULLABASHI. An institution designating a high religious functionary in Shīʿī Islam, which seems to have come into usage toward the very end of the Ṣafavid period (1501–1722), and slowly disapeared in the nineteenth century, *mullabashi* was intended to replace the more-established term Shaykh al-Islām, but it did not succeed in doing so. A passing reference to it is encountered as late as 1906 (Arjomand, 1988, p. 92). The term itself comes from a Perso-Arabic word, *mullā* ("mullah", a Muslim clergyman) and a Turkish word, *bāsh* (or *baş*, head or chief), thus having the general meaning of "head of the clergy." In point of fact, however, the *mullabashi* did not possess such an important function.

One of the earliest references to the term occurs in *Tadhkirat al-mulūk*, completed about 1726. The anonymous author states that the *mullabashi* was the chief *mullah,* foremost religious scholar, and had a privileged seat next to the shah on formal occasions. The duties of the *mullabashi* included soliciting pensions for students and men of merit, generally upholding virtuous conduct, and giving advice on legal matters. Thus, the *mullabashi* was more an adviser rather than an executive. The contemporary *Zubdat al-tavārīkh* makes the *mullabashi* sound more like the shah's boon companion, joining him in discussing literary problems and poetry and the preparation of dishes and medicines (Minorsky, 1943, p. 24).

Said Amir Arjomand (1988) has convincingly established that the office of *mullabashi* was "formally instituted" for Mīr Muḥammad Bāqir Khātūn-ābādī in 1712, disproving Minorsky's conjecture (1943, pp. 110 ff.) that the first occupant of the office was Mullā Muḥammad Bāqir al-Majlisī (d. 1699 or 1700), the most powerful Shaykh al-Islām of Isfahan toward the end of the Ṣafavid period. Abdul Hadi Hairi claims that "Madjlisī's title was changed to *Mullābāshī* on Sulṭān Ḥusayn's accession to the throne in 1106/1694" (*Encyclopaedia of Islam*, new ed., vol. 5, pp. 1086–1088, Leiden, 1960–).

The *mullabashi* had his rivals in the "*mujtahid* of the age," the Ṣadr, and the Shaykh al-Islām. There is some indication, however, that the *mullabashi* was the most powerful of them all. This is shown by the *Dastūr al-mulūk,* a work on the Ṣafavid administration from the same period as *Tadhkirat al-mulūk,* whose author refers to the *mullabashi* as the leader and most learned of the *ʿulamāʾ* (community of religious scholars).

The position of *mullabashi* became more of a public-relations office during the reign of Nādir Shāh Afshār (d. 1747). The shah, anxious to reach some kind of reconciliation between the Shīʿī Iranians and the Sunnī Ottomans, sent his *mullabashi,* Mullā ʿAlī Akbar, as his chief representative to the conference at Najaf in 1743 where he defended the Shīʿī views in lively conversations with Shaykh ʿAbd Allāh al-Suwaydī, an Iraqi Sunnī scholar, who was accepted by both sides as an impartial mediator. This reconciliation attempt ended in failure; in any case, it was essentially a political ploy by Nādir Shāh, who at the same time was actually at war with the Ottomans.

The office of *mullabashi* kept an attenuated existence throughout the Zand and Qājār periods. The incumbent often became tutor of the royal princes. At one time, "towards 1905, the buffoon of a governor of Kirmān figures in the rolls as *mullā-bāshī*" (Minorsky, 1943, p. 110, n. 5).

[*See also* Ṣafavid Dynasty; Shaykh al-Islām; *and the biography of* Majlisī.]

BIBLIOGRAPHY

Algar, Hamid. "Shiʿism and Iran in the Eighteenth Century." In *Studies in Eighteenth-Century Islamic History,* edited by Thomas Naff and Roger Owen, pp. 288–302. Carbondale, Ill., 1977. Discusses the Nādir Shāh period and draws attention to Shaykh ʿAbd Allāh al-Suwaydī's memoir, *Al-Ḥujaj al-Qaṭʿīyah li-Ittifāq al-Firaq al-Islāmīyah* (Cairo, 1323/1905).

Arjomand, Said Amir. "The Mujtahid of the Age and the Mulla-bashi." In *Authority and Political Culture in Shiʿism,* edited by Said Amir Arjomand, pp. 80–97. Albany, N.Y., 1988. Comprehensive treatment of the subject.

Dānishpazhūh, M. T., ed. "Dastūr al-Mulūk." In *Majallah-yi Dānishkadah-yi Adabiyāt va ʿUlūm-i Insānī.* Vol. 16, parts 1 and 2. Edition of the *Dastūr al-Mulūk,* a work on the Ṣafavid administration.

Gholsorkhi, Shohreh. "The Religious Policy of Nādir Shāh." Unpublished article, Princeton, n.d. Presents up-to-date research on religion and state in eighteenth-century Iran.

Minorsky, Vladimir, ed. and trans. *Tadhkirat al-mulūk: A Manual of Ṣafavid Administration (c. 1137/1725).* London, 1943. Standard work on Ṣafavid institutions before the fall of the dynasty in 1722.

MICHEL M. MAZZAOUI

MULLAH. A Persian construction probably from the Arabic *mawlā* ("master," "leader," "lord"), *mullah* is the title used to identify a religious functionary, a cleric, a learned man, or someone with religious education. The title is very much similar to *akhund* in the range of meanings it invokes.

From the Ṣafavid period (AH 907–1145/1501–1722 CE) onward, the term *mullah* began to be used for various clerical functionaries. During the Qājār period (1193–1342/1779–1925), the term was institutionalized as a designation of lower-ranking clerics. Beginning with the Constitutional Revolution in Iran (1906–1911), the term assumed an additional derogatory connotation, used by secular individuals to designate antimodern and reactionary tendencies.

The term *mullah* invariably refers to a male cleric, but in such constructions as mullābājī ("sister-mullah") it has been extended to female clerics, particularly to female teachers at girls' schools. The term *mullākhānah,* which has been used for traditional schools, indicates that at least since the Qājār period the word *mullah* has had an exclusive application to elementary teachers at traditional schools. The term *mullānuqaṭī* also refers to a person who is very particular about details (of punctuation, for example, and by extension other kinds of formalities). Probably because some high-ranking mullahs owned land, there are quite a number of small villages in Iran with the term *mullah* attached to a proper name, such as Mullā-Bāqir in Arāk, or Mullā-Budāq and Mullā-Pīrī in Zanjān.

In the Ṣafavid administrative apparatus, the term *mullabashi* referred to a high-ranking religious official in charge of a number of functions, including the religious education of the court (Muᶜallim Ḥabībābādī, 1362/1983, vol. 1, pp. 51–52). The office of *mullabashi* was subsequently developed into the most prestigious religious position at the Ṣafavid court (Arjomand, 1363/1984, pp. 154–155). [*See* Mullabashi.]

Among the clerics themselves, the term *mullah* is the highest expression of reverence for religious learning. Perhaps the most distinguished philosopher of the Ṣafavid period, Mullā Sadrā Shīrāzī (d. 1050/1640) received his name from the combination of *mullah,* here meaning "the most learned," and Sadr al-Dīn, his honorific title (Āshtīyānī, 1340/1963, pp. 1–3). Even in popular culture, the term *mullah* has strong connotations of learning and erudition. The verb *mullāshudan* (lit., "to become a mullah") in Persian means "to become learned." (For various popular expressions to that effect see Dihkhudā, 1363/1984, vol. 4, p. 1731).

During the Qājār period the term *mullah* was applied as an honorific title to a number of teachers at the court. Mullah ᶜAlī Aṣghar Hazārjarībī, known as "Mullahbashi" (d. 1213/1798), was a teacher of the celebrated Qājār prince ᶜAbbās Mīrzā and a number of other princes. The most distinguished philosopher of the Qājār period, Ḥājj Mullāh Hādī Sabzawārī (d. 1289/1872) also carried the honorific title of mullah (Muᶜallim Ḥabībābādī, 1983, vol. 2, p. 466).

After the Constitutional Revolution in Iran the derogatory implications of the term in secular contexts increased. To call someone a mullah is to accuse him of reactionary ideas. Opposition to the establishment of new schools during the constitutional period in Iran, for example, is identified with "the mullahs" (Kasravī, 1354/1975, pp. 38–39). The expression *mullākhūr* ("embezzled by the mullahs" or "edible by the mullahs") refers either to financial embezzlement or to fruits and vegetables that have become rotten and can be purchased for a cheap price. In Persian folklore, the term *mullah* appears most familiarly in the name of Mullah Naṣr al-Dīn, a legendary figure at the center of innumerable tales of either naive simplicity, or sometimes wit and wisdom.

As a self-conscious social group, the mullahs have performed a major role in the social history of Iran at least since the Qājār period. Their active participation during the Constitutional Revolution, both for and against it, continued well into the twentieth century. The Islamic Revolution of Iran in 1979 was largely led by Iranian mullahs. Beyond the crucial realm of politics, the mullahs are principally in charge of the religious functions and ceremonies in Iran. They are particularly visible in public places during the months of Muḥarram, Ṣafar, and Ramaḍān when their religious functions lead them into the mosques, markets, and other public places. As a class, also known as the *ākhūnd*s, the *ruḥānīyūn,* or the *ᶜulamāʾ*, they are the principal interpreters of the Islamic law for the Shīᶜīs. They preside over such crucial events in the life of a Muslim as circumcision, wedding, *hajj* pilgrimage, and burial. Their religious and juridical training is institutionalized in *madrasah*s (seminaries). The curriculum of a mullah's training includes the study of the Qurᶜān, the prophetic traditions, and the lives and sayings of the Shīᶜī imams (see Mottahedeh, 1985, *et passim*).

[*See* Ākhūnd.]

BIBLIOGRAPHY

Arjomand, Said Amir. *The Shadow of God and the Hidden Imam: Religion, Political Order, and Societal Change in Shīᶜite Iran from the Beginning to 1890.* Chicago and London, 1984.

Āshtīyānī, Jalāl al-Dīn. *Sharḥ-i Ḥāl va Ārāʾ-i Falsafī-yi Mullā Ṣadrā.* Mashhad, 1340/1963.

Dihkhudā, ᶜAlī Akbar. *Amsāl va ḥikam.* Tehran, 1363/1984.

Dihkhudā, ᶜAlī Akbar. *Lughatnāmah.* Tehran, n.d.

Kasravī, Aḥmad. *Tārīkh-i Mashrūṭah-yi Īrān.* Tehran, 1354/1975.

Mottahedeh, Roy P. *The Mantle of the Prophet: Religion and Politics in Iran.* New York, 1985.

Muᶜallim Ḥabībābādī, Mīrzā Muḥammad ᶜAlī. *Makārim al-Āsār dar aḥvāl-i rijāl-i dawrah-yi Qājār.* 6 vols. Isfahan, 1976–1985.

Muᶜīn, Muḥammad. *Farhang-i Fārsī.* Tehran, AH 1356–1358/1977–1979 CE.

HAMID DABASHI

MURĪDĪYAH. The best known of the Ṣūfī brotherhoods in Senegal, both within and outside of the country, is the Murīdīyah. Its name comes from *murīd,* the postulant who seeks the path to spiritual knowledge. The word was already in use when the French and the followers of the founder of the order, Amadu Bamba M'Backe, came into conflict in the 1890s in western Senegal.

Amadu Bamba (c. 1850–1927) was born into a family of itinerant scholars who moved through the Wolof kingdoms of Baol, Cayor, and Jolof, states that disintegrated rather rapidly in the late nineteenth century under the impact of internecine wars, French penetration, and opportunities provided by the cultivation of peanuts in the sandy soil of the Sahel. His father Momar Antassali had close attachments to the royal dynasty of Cayor and particularly to the ruler or *damel,* Lat Dior, and it was in a combination of court settings and rural retreats that Amadu Bamba acquired his apprenticeship in Islam and Senegalese politics.

By the 1880s he had achieved a significant reputation as a poet, scholar, and spiritual advisor in his own right. Bamba was able to maintain a growing following, particularly among the *ceddos* or slave warriors of the courts and other people who were increasingly marginalized with the decline of the kingdoms and growing violence. He affiliated with Qādirīyah shaykhs in Mauritania, although later his particular approaches to Islam often caused the Murīdīyah to be categorized as an autonomous if not separate order.

In the dramatically changing situation of late nineteenth-century Senegal, Bamba was careful to keep his distance from both the traditional courts, which were failing in their efforts to resist European conquest, and the Europeans themselves, who were working from coastal bases such as St. Louis and Dakar. In Senegalese lore he is closely identified with the defeat and death of Lat Dior in 1886, but in fact he did not advise the king to resist; Bamba was able to maintain his following on the fringes of areas of French control for several more years. The regime in St. Louis finally captured him in 1895, conducted a summary trial, and sent him into exile in Gabon for a period of seven years. Bamba spent a great deal of time during his exile in meditation and the writing of poetry, and the period has become enshrined in the memories of his followers as a series of constantly retold miracles of escape from French entrapments.

Some of Bamba's family and friends, particularly his brother Shaykh Anta and his lieutenant Ibra Fall, were quite active on his behalf during his exile; they actively encouraged the pattern of peanut cultivation and the acquisition of property in both rural and urban settings. The Senegalese deputy to the French Assembly, François Carpot, played a role in gaining the return of Bamba from exile in 1902, but the anxiety of the French and their Senegalese chiefs alike provoked a second exile (1903–1907), this time to Butilimit and the home of a close Mauritanian friend of the colonial regime, Sīdīyā Bābā. From 1907 to 1912 the French kept Bamba in a remote area of Jolof in northern Senegal before finally allowing him to move to Diourbel, near the headquarters of the Murīdīyah but still under close surveillance.

During all this time of exile Bamba's family and friends continued to develop their interests in peanut farming and in closer ties with the French administration. By World War I, in the midst of French needs for troops and endorsement of their cause, Bamba himself was ready to give his blessing to this tissue of cooperation. When he died in 1927, the French played a significant role in ensuring the succession of his son Muhammad Mustapha against the claims of Bamba's brother Shaykh Anta. They continued the close relationship with another son, Falilu, who served as successor or khalifa general from 1945 until his death in 1968, and the Senegalese government has enjoyed generally good relationships with the M'backe successors since.

Bamba was a man of great scholarly acumen and spirituality, and many of his descendants and associates have had the same orientation. Many Murīd followers, however, had little or no education in matters Islamic, and they were encouraged by the leaders to work hard, particularly in the cultivation of peanuts, and to allow the marabouts, the Islamic authorities, to carry out intercession on their behalf. This has been particularly true of the group called the Baye Fall, followers of Ibra Fall who were always ready to carry out any physical task for their leaders. Recently, however, Murīd cells throughout Senegal and in major French urban centers have modified this image of the "unlettered Murīd" by their zeal for learning the teachings of Islam and the heritage of the founder.

[*See also* Senegal.]

BIBLIOGRAPHY

Behrman, Lucy C. *Muslim Brotherhoods and Politics in Senegal.* Cambridge, Mass., 1970. Discussion of the *ṭarīqah* in its broader political context.

Cruise O'Brien, Donal B. *The Mourides of Senegal: The Political and Economic Organization of an Islamic Brotherhood.* Oxford and New York, 1971. The most complete study of the order.

Marty, Paul. *Les Mourides d'Amadou Bamba.* Paris, 1913. Early pioneering French work which had an influence on developing French scholarship and policies.

Robinson, David. "Beyond Resistance and Collaboration: Amadu Bamba and the Murids of Senegal." *Journal of Religion in Africa* 21 (1991): 149–171.

DAVID ROBINSON

MŪSĀ, NABAWĪYAH (1886–1951), feminist and pioneer in women's education. Born in Zagazig, Egypt, the daughter of Mūsā Muḥammad, an army captain who died before her birth, Nabawīyah was raised in Cairo by her mother. Beginning her education at home with the help of her older brother, Nabawīyah entered the girls' section of the ʿAbbās Primary School, receiving her certificate in 1903. She began teaching at ʿAbbās in 1906, after completing the Teachers' Training Program at the Sanīyah School. Mūsā resolved to obtain a secondary school diploma when she discovered that male teachers with this degree received higher pay. But, in the absence of government secondary school for girls, Mūsā prepared at home for the state baccalaureate examination. Overcoming objections from colonial education officials, she successfully completed the exam in 1907. She became the first woman to teach Arabic in the state school system, incurring the wrath of religiously trained shaykhs, who monopolized Arabic instruction. In 1909 she was appointed principal of the Girls' School in Fayyūm, an oasis west of Cairo, the first Egyptian woman to hold such a post. The following year she became principal of the Women Teachers' Training School in Manṣūrah. In 1915, Mūsā was principal of the Wardīyān Women Teachers' Training School in Alexandria. Nine years later she was appointed chief inspector of female education in the Ministry of Education. She incurred numerous adversaries as an efficient and strong-willed administrator who enforced a strict moral code among teachers and students, and was dismissed from the ministry in 1926. She then founded and ran two private schools for girls, al-Tarqiyah al-Fatāh primary school in Alexandria and Banāt al-Ashrāf secondary school in Cairo.

Mūsā's feminism and nationalist aspirations were expressed in her everyday life. Discreetly unveiling around 1909, in full awareness that concealing the face was not an Islamic prescription, Mūsā remained fastidious about covering her hair and wearing modest clothing. When the Egyptian University opened in 1908 Mūsā was refused enrollment, but the following year was invited to lecture in the university's special extracurricular program for women. During the Egyptian national independence movement of 1919–1922, Mūsā maintained the operation of her school, rather than demonstrating and risking closure, considering this a political act in itself and insisting that education was the strongest weapon against colonial domination. In 1920 she published *Al-mar'ah wa-al-ʿamal* (The Woman and Work), promoting education and work for women as a means of individual and national liberation within the framework of Islamic modernism. In 1923, the year after Egyptian independence, Mūsā joined the Egyptian Feminist Union, attending the Rome Conference of the International Woman Suffrage Alliance as a member of the union's delegation. However, Mūsā soon rejected movement feminism, preferring the mode of everyday activism within the context of her profession as an educator. She also sustained advocacy through her writings, including *Al-āyah al-bayyinah fī tarbiyat al-banāt* (The Clear Model in the Education of Girls), *Dīwān al-fatāh* (The Young Woman Collection of Poems), and *Riwāyah Nabhutub* (Nabhutub: A Novel). In 1937 she founded *Majallat al-fatāh* (The Magazine of the Young Woman), which published through 1943.

Mūsā's educational career came to an end in 1942 when she was imprisoned for publicly protesting the Egyptian government's conciliatory policy regarding national sovereignty in the face of British pressure. She died in retirement in 1951. Four decades later the Egyptian state honored her by issuing a commemorative stamp. Mūsā is claimed as a foremother by feminists and Islamists alike.

[*See also* Feminism.]

BIBLIOGRAPHY

Badran, Margot. "Expressing Feminism and Nationalism in Autobiography: The Memoirs of an Egyptian Educator." In *De/Colonizing the Subject*, edited by Sidonie Smith and Julia Watson, pp. 270–293. Minneapolis, 1992.

Badran, Margot. "From Consciousness to Activism: Feminist Politics in Early Twentieth-Century Egypt." In *Problems of the Middle East in Historical Perspective*, edited by John P. Spagnolo, pp. 27–48. London, 1992.

Badran, Margot. *Feminists, Islam, and Nation: Gender and the Making of Modern Egypt*. Princeton, 1995.

Kāẓim, Ṣāfīnāz Muḥammad. "Al-Rā'idah Nabawīyah Mūsā wa-Inʿāsh Dhākirat al-Ummah" (The Pioneer Nabawīyah Mūsā and Reviving the Nation's Memory). *Al-hilāl* (January 1984): 116–119.

Mūsā, Nabawīyah. *Dhikrayātī* (Memoirs). Serialized in *Majallat al-fatāh* (The Magazine of the Young Woman) from 1938 to 1942. Other works by Mūsā are cited in the text.

MARGOT BADRAN

MUSIC. Music of the Islamic world can be studied from a wide variety of perspectives, as a historical legacy extending back to the middle ages and antiquity, as a performing art, as a branch of science, and as a medium of spiritual devotion. In the Middle East, its domain spreads throughout North Africa and eastward to include the Arabian Peninsula, Arab countries east of the Mediterranean, Turkey, and Iran. Furthermore, certain patterns of musical culture can be found in various parts of the Islamic world, including countries of the African Sudanic regions, Central Asia, Pakistan, and North India. For more than a millennium, Islamic ways of life have provided a framework for the creative contributions of individuals from diverse ethnic, racial, and religious backgrounds.

Musical outlooks have been influenced by Islamic beliefs and institutions. Although the Qurʾān contains no strictures against music, the *ḥadīth,* which consists of sayings attributed to the prophet Muḥammad and his companions, presents numerous statements that caution against music and musical instruments. In Islamic history, however, music has played an extensive role and emerged as an art form of extraordinary popularity and significance. To begin with, the formal strictures appear to have addressed music primarily as a secular profession, thus exempting the various folk and ritualistic expressions, including religious genres, generally considered outside the domain of "music" proper. Furthermore, music acquired special recognition and prestige through medieval court patronage. Following the Muslims' exposure to ancient Greek philosophy, science, and cosmology, music also developed as a speculative branch of knowledge, *ʿilm al-mūsīqá,* literally "science of music." Meanwhile, music gained distinct prominence and spiritual meaning through the practices of the various Ṣūfī, or mystical Islamic, orders.

In Middle Eastern life, folk music appears in a wide variety of regional contexts. Throughout history, music has been incorporated into religious festivals and used in conjunction with manual labor and events associated with the human life cycle, including birth, circumcision, and marriage. Today, folk musical expressions, although often connected with social and religious events and with dance, differ in terms of performance style, instrumentation, and textual subject matter. Examples are: the group-performed *fjirī,* or pearl-diving songs of the Arabian Gulf; the heroic and love-related songs of the *shāʿir,* or bedouin nomadic poet-singer, who accompanies himself on the *rabābah,* a single-string upright fiddle; and the Anatolian *aşik,* or bard, who performs songs of moral and devotional themes while accompanying himself on the *saz,* a long-necked plucked lute. A further example is the music played on a large double-sided drum and an oboe type of wind instrument, together known in Turkey as *davul* and *zurna* and in some Arab countries as *ṭabl* and *zamr.* In many Middle Eastern communities, this combination accompanies folk dance, particularly at village weddings. Also songs, as well as dramatic representations, appear in the *taʿzīyah,* or passion play, held during the Islamic month of Muḥarram in Shīʿī communities, for example in Iran, Iraq, and India, to commemorate the martyrdom of early religious saints.

Islamic liturgical and devotional forms with musical components are numerous. As a rule, Qurʾānic chanting, or the reciting of the divine text of the Qurʾān, is soloistic, unmetered, governed by established rules of enunciation (*ʿilm al-tajwīd*), and melodically improvised, usually in accordance with the tradition of melodic modes, known as *maqāmāt* (sg., *maqām*) in certain parts of the Arab world. In the *adhān,* or "call-to-prayer," traditionally performed from minarets to announce the daily times of prayer, the text is usually delivered in a stylized, semi-improvised, melodic format.

Islamic mysticism, which became prevalent throughout the Islamic world since the thirteenth century CE, has generally treated music and dance as vehicles for spiritual transcendence. Expounded by early Ṣūfī scholars such as Abū Ḥāmid al-Ghazālī (1058–1111), the notion of spiritual music as a mode of attaining divine ecstasy was expressed through the concept and practice of *samāʿ,* literally "listening," or "auditioning." Today, music and dance constitute essential components within the rituals of various Ṣūfī sects. In many cases, the liturgies incorporate sections of *dhikr,* literally "remembrance" or "reiteration," in which religious phrases repeated by the chorus form an ostinato, or repeated pattern, that accompanies vocal improvisations and precomposed hymns, as well as rhythmic body movement. Meanwhile, the Mevlevî order, established by Jalāl al-Dīn Rūmī in Konya, Turkey in the early thirteenth century, is particularly known for its elaborate musical performances, the use of musical instruments such as the *ney,* or reed flute, and a type of religious dance consisting of circular motion, or "whirling." In India and Pakistan, Ṣūfī-related musical expressions include the Urdu *ghazal,* and the *qawwālī.* These and other comparable genres are often performed by highly skilled and widely admired vocalists. In addition to these religious expressions, there are numerous liturgical and semi-liturgical traditions belonging to various non-Islamic communities, for example, Christian groups such as the Copts of Egypt, Maronites of Lebanon, and Assyrians of Iraq, and Jews from different parts of the Middle East.

In the realm of secular music, certain traits appear widely prevalent, although tend to vary in detail and application from one context to another. Generally speaking, the melodic component is highly intricate and embraces distinct embellishments, such as the *taḥrīr*, commonly used by Iranian classical singers. The textures include solo, unison, octave-doubling, the occasional use of a drone or ostinato for accompaniment, and heterophony (when subtle differences in detail are created within two or more coexisting, essentially similar, parts). Specific melodic intervals are recognized and applied, including certain types of whole-tones, half-tones, and "neutral-tones," or microtonal steps created when notes are partially flattened or sharpened. Intervals are measured in various ways. In Turkey, for example, the *comma* (roughly one-ninth of a Pythagorean whole-step) is used as a unit for determining the size of scalar intervals. Melodic modes, namely schemes encompassing individual scales, notes of emphasis, and usually general modalities of execution, serve as foundations for precomposition and improvisation in many traditions in the Middle East, Central Asia, and India. In the case of the Arab *maqām* and Turkish *makam* modal systems, a musician, for example when performing an instrumental improvisation (*taqsīm* in Arab music and *taksim* in Turkish music) may shift between modes in the middle of a performance. In the case of the Iranian *dastgāh*, the performance (for example, an improvisatory *āvāz*) may pass through *gushes*, namely inner, or subsidiary, modes that are intrinsic to each of the twelve *dastgāhs* and are part of the entire *radīf*, or recognized modal repertoire. With some exceptions, modal improvisations in various Islamic traditions are nonmetric, in other words, not bound by regular-beat structures.

The rhythmic component is usually organized in terms of patterns, or modes. A rhythmic mode, or meter, incorporates a specific number of beats and rests. As illustrated by regional variants, such as the *mīzān* in the Andalusian, or Moorish derived, music of Morroco, the Arab *īqāʿ*, and the Turkish *usul*, rhythmic patterns are traditionally played on percussion instruments and serve as building frameworks for metric compositions, such as the Ottoman classical instrumental *peşrev* and the vocal *beste*. Meanwhile, compound, or "suitelike," forms are very common. As illustrated by the North African Andalusian *nawbah*, the Turkish *fasıl*, and the Iraqi *maqām*, such forms traditionally consist of individual sections that share the same melodic mode but differ in such areas as rhythm and structure.

Musical instruments similarly reflect patterns of consistency and variety. Numerous types of reed flutes, double reeds (oboes), fiddles, plucked lutes, cylindrical and frame drums can be found throughout the Islamic world. At the same time, the *ʿūd* (lute), *qānūn* (zither), and *nāy* (flute) are typical of urban centers, particularly in Arab countries and Turkey. In Ottoman classical music, we encounter such instruments as the *tanbūr* (long-necked fretted lute) and *kemence* (upright fiddle). Typical of the Iranian classical ensemble, however, are the *santūr* (hammer-dulcimer), the *tār* and the *setār* (both long-necked lutes), the *kamanchah* (upright spike-fiddle), the *ney* (reed flute), and the *dumbak* (hand drum). Further variety is represented by such instruments as the Afghani *rubāb*, a plucked lute which, like the North Indian *sarod*, has sympathetic, or unplucked resonating, strings and a face partially covered with skin. Meanwhile, a relatively recent acquisition, namely the Western violin, is fully adapted to local idioms and is prevalent throughout the urban Islamic world.

During the last two centuries increased contact with the West generated new interest in music as a "fine art" and led to the gradual assimilation of Western musical concepts and techniques. In Egypt, following the Napoleonic conquest (1798–1801), Muḥammad ʿAlī (r. 1805–1848), founder of the Khedive dynasty, established military schools in which Europeans taught military-band instruments according to Western methods of instruction. Later on, Khedive Ismāʿīl (r. 1863–1879), who sponsored Egyptian local celebrities such as ʿAbduh al-Ḥāmūlī (1843–1901), built the Cairo Opera House and invited foreign ensembles to Cairo, where Verdi's *Rigoletto* was presented in 1869, followed by *Aida* in 1871. In Turkey, Sultan Mahmud II (r. 1808–1839) abolished the Janissary army, and by extension the *mehter*, or the indigenous military-band tradition, and brought in Western composers to teach Western military-band instruments in Turkish military schools. Such efforts to assimilate European cultural and artistic models continued throughout the nineteenth century. Comparable importations of Western culture occurred in Persia, where the French Alfred J. B. Lemaire (1842–1902) established a musical institution for teaching Western military-band instruments. By the turn of the century, a number of influential Middle Eastern composers, theorists, and music educators were already well versed in European music theory, notation, and conservatory-based pedagogical methods.

The twentieth century witnessed further and more extensive musical developments. Governments in various parts of the Islamic world continued the process of modernization and europeanization, an example being the systematic efforts of Mustafa Kemal Atatürk (1881–

1938), the first president of the Turkish republic, to outlaw Ṣūfī orders, to ban Ottoman classical music, and to encourage folk and Western-derived musical forms. Meanwhile, the modern mass media made a tremendous impact upon the various musical traditions. In the first decade of the century, sound recording led to a growing mass audience in Cairo, Istanbul, and other Middle Eastern cities, and to the rise of new popular musical forms. Also the popularity of the musical theater in early twentieth-century Egypt and the musical film, first appearing in Cairo in 1932, led to the development of new musical expressions, for example the short eclectic film-songs of Muḥammad ʿAbd al-Wahhāb (c. 1901–1991). Later, the expanding domain of radio in the mid-1930s, the rise of L.P., and, even later, cassette recording, enhanced the broad dissemination of music, for example, recordings of live concerts by Egypt's recording celebrities such as Umm Kulthūm (c. 1904–1975). In later decades studio recording contributed further to the creation of new styles, sonorities, and orchestral blends. Moreover, in large cities such as Istanbul, Damascus, and Cairo, older compositions are sometimes performed by large modern ensembles with mixed choruses and large accompanying orchestras. Also, Western-trained composers have created symphonic works in which indigenous folk themes are incorporated. Meanwhile, the last few decades have witnessed a significant degree of musical interaction among the various cultures of the Islamic world. For example, Cairo's urban musical model, with its lush orchestration, multilayered unison and octave texture, and characteristic intonation, has been emulated in various urban traditions in North Africa, the Arabian Peninsula, and the East Mediterranean world. Furthermore, Cairo's influence is distinctly apparent in the *arabesk,* Turkey's newly developed and extremely popular urban genre. Other categories, however, use Western, particularly electronic, instruments and musical techniques somewhat prominently, for example the Algerian *rai,* whose appeal has extended to musical audiences in Europe and North America.

[*See also* Devotional Music.]

BIBLIOGRAPHY

Farhat, Hormoz. *The Dastgāh Concept in Persian Music.* Cambridge, 1990. Thorough and systematic explanation of the twelve Iranian melodic modes on the basis of current theory and performance practice.

Farmer, Henry George. *A History of Arabian Music to the XIIIth Century.* London, 1929; reprint, 1973. Classic historical work on the music of medieval Islam by a major and highly prolific writer on the subject.

Farmer, Henry George. "The Music of Islam." In *The New Oxford History of Music,* edited by Egon Wellesz, vol. 1, pp. 421–477. London, 1957. Detailed coverage of both music theory and practice in medieval Islam.

Nelson, Kristina. *The Art of Reciting the Qurʾān.* Austin, 1985. Pioneering and well-documented study of Qurʾānic chanting based on fieldwork in Egypt.

Nettl, Bruno. *The Radif of Persian Music: Studies of Structure and Cultural Context.* Champaign, Ill., 1987. The most detailed and encompassing work on Persian music and musical culture by a well-known ethnomusicologist and expert in the area.

Racy, Ali Jihad. "Music in Contemporary Cairo: A Comparative Overview." *Asian Music* 13 (1981): 4–26. Penetrating analysis of music and musical attitudes in modern Cairo, with special reference to other Middle Eastern cities.

Racy, Ali Jihad. "Creativity and Ambience: an Ecstatic Feedback Model from Arab Music." *The World of Music* 33 (1991): 7–28. First-hand study of how traditional Arab musicians perform, with specific reference to improvisation, creativity, and the ecstatic state experienced by performers and initiated listeners.

Sadie, Stanley, ed. *The New Grove Dictionary of Music and Musicians.* New York, 1980. Authoritative and extensive multivolume reference work. Includes entries, often several pages long, on the music of various Middle Eastern countries, ethnic groups, instruments, and genres written by different musical experts.

Signell, Karl. *Makam: Modal Practice in Turkish Art Music.* Seattle, 1977. Rare, in-depth discussion in English of the modal music theory of Turkey.

ALI JIHAD RACY

MUSLIM BROTHERHOOD.

[*This entry comprises five articles:*

An Overview
Muslim Brotherhood in Egypt
Muslim Brotherhood in Syria
Muslim Brotherhood in Jordan
Muslim Brotherhood in the Sudan

The introductory article provides an overview of the origin, ideological development, and geographical spread of the movement; the companion articles focus on four countries where the Muslim Brotherhood has played an active role in religious, social, and political life.]

An Overview

Founded in Ismāʿīlīyah, Egypt, in 1928 by Ḥasan al-Bannāʾ (1906–1949), the Muslim Brotherhood (al-Ikhwān al-Muslimūn) is the parent body and the main source of inspriation for many Islamist organizations in Egypt and several other Arab countries, including Syria,

Sudan, Jordan, Kuwait, Yemen, and some North African states. The movement was initially announced as a purely religious and philanthropic society that aimed to spread Islamic morals and good works. Its emergence, however, was part of a widespread reaction to various alarming developments that were sweeping through the Muslim world. The Arabs had been divided into spheres of influence by the European powers, and the attempted restoration of the caliphate, abolished in Turkey in 1924, failed in 1926. Western influence also appeared to be making serious inroads into the Islamic culture of the region. Not only did writers such as Salāmah Mūsā and Ṭāhā Ḥusayn propagate openly secularist ideas, but even some al-Azhar scholars adopted apparently Western approaches in analyzing "Islamic" issues, a trend that reached its most disconcerting point with the publication in 1925 of ʿAlī ʿAbd al-Rāziq's book on Islam and government in which he denied that Islam was in any way concerned with politics. [*See the biographies of Ḥusayn and ʿAbd al-Rāziq.*]

As a teacher and gifted orator, al-Bannā' was able to attract to his movement various members of the local intelligentsia, as well as some artisans and a few workers. The Ikhwān became increasingly interested in public affairs, developing a distinctive conception of the comprehensiveness of Islam, which contrasted with that of both the established clergy and the existing conventional philanthropic charities. Al-Bannā' called for a total and activist Islam. He perceived the Islamic state as a significant ingredient of the desired Islamic order, but the Ikhwān leaders probably did not consider the assumption of political power an imminent possibility at the time. At such an early stage in the group's formation and development, the tasks of moral reform (*iṣlāḥ al-nufūs*) and of agreeing on an Islamic approach and "methodology" (*minhāj Islāmī*) must have appeared more appropriate for the requirements of that phase. Too much emphasis on government might also have subjected the society to even more official suspicion.

The Ikhwān did not identify itself as a political party, although it acted very much as if it were. Its activities began to acquire a distinct political character around 1938. The weekly *Al-nadhīr* (The Warning) was started, and occasionally threatened to "fight any politician or organization that did not work for the support of Islam and the restoration of its glory." Its concept of absolute obedience (*al-ṭāʿah*) to the leader and its tight organizational pattern, which linked the highest level of the Guidance Council to the most basic level of the *usrah* ("family" or cell) and included all the technical sections and committees as well as the consultative council, have been likened by some observers to those of fascist organizations.

By now the Ikhwān had more than three hundred branches advocating its ideas, although it had been careful so far not to antagonize the Palace, and to avoid confrontation with the British at any price, while building up its own organizational and paramilitary capacity. A special "secret apparatus" was established within the movement (its membership is believed to have reached 75,000 by 1947), and special "phalanges" were formed, sometimes under the guise of ranger scouts (*jawwālah*). The Ikhwān also built its own companies, factories, schools, and hospitals, and infiltrated various organizations, including the trade unions and the armed forces, to such a degree that by the end of the 1940s it almost represented "a state within the State." By this time it also had escalated terrorist attacks on British and Jewish interests in Egypt, in which many Egyptians were inevitably killed or injured. The government was forced to respond by dissolving the brotherhood; the confrontation between the two reached its peak late in 1948 and early in 1949 with the Ikhwān's assassination of Prime Minister Maḥmūd Fahmī al-Nuqrashī and the government's assassination of the leader of the Ikhwān, al-Bannā' himself. Membership of the brotherhood had by now reached its peak, including nearly a half million active members (*ʿuḍw ʿāmil*) and another half million sympathizers, spread among some 200,000 branches throughout Egypt.

New Political Emphasis. The disappearance of the charismatic leadership of al-Bannā' in 1949 and, more specifically, the confrontation between the Ikhwān and the new revolutionary regime in Egypt in the 1950s caused it to raise the "political" to a much higher rank within its order of concerns. It should be noted that the Muslim Brothers were no strangers to the Free Officers who launched the 1952 revolution. Their various contacts with the officers enabled them to escape the fate of dissolution after the coup, since they were classified as a "movement" or a "society," not as a political party. Many brothers, including the new "general guide" (*al-murshid al-ʿāmm*) Ḥasan al-Huḍaybī, seem to have hoped that given the affinity between the two movements, the Free Officers would be prepared to allow the Ikhwān direct participation in government after the revolution. When this hope was frustrated, relations between them deteriorated, resulting in two bloody confrontations (in 1954 and 1965), repeated imprisonment, and severe torture. It was this confrontational atmosphere that eventually effected a shift in the thinking of the Ikhwān associate Sayyid Quṭb, a shift that subsequently colored the ideas of most of the regiments of radical political Islam in Egypt and the Arab world.

On a general ideological level, the detention of Quṭb and his colleagues led to an overall revision of the movement's thought, the major part of which now was affected by a hatred for the state and the regime. The Quṭbian ideas that have come to influence most of the contemporary movements of political Islam are mainly the ones to be found in the writings he produced between his two periods of imprisonment. The key concept in this later Quṭbian discourse is undoubtedly *jāhilīyah* (total pagan ignorance). Inspired partly by Ibn Taymīyah but most specifically by Sayyid Abū al-Aʿlā Mawdūdī, and influenced by the fascist ideas of Alexis Carrel, Sayyid Quṭb extracted this concept from any historical or geographical context, giving it a universal validity that covers all contemporary societies, Muslim ones included. The way out of such *jāhilīyah,* as prescribed by Quṭb, is also simple: a declaration of the total sovereignty and rulership of God *(al-ḥakīmīyah).* Strongly affected by such ideas, the imprisoned brothers in their anguish and isolation and with the ever-present memory of their martyrs, were to create an alternative to Nasserism, a "counterproject" that reflected the maturation of the contradictions between the brotherhood and the Nasserist state (and, indeed, between Islamists and all similar "modernizing" projects such as Baʿthism and Bourguibism). This contradiction in fact has become, since the late 1970s, the main ideological confrontation in the Arab world. [*See* Nasserism *and the biography of Quṭb.*]

From its inception, the Muslim Brotherhood in Egypt attracted a membership drawn principally from among the urban and recently urbanized *afendīyah* strata of lower- and middle-level officials, clerks and school teachers and from among the "traditional" artisans and merchants; from its beginning, too, it has had a fringe of professionals (lawyers, accountants, and doctors). In the 1940s, it managed to make serious inroads into the industrial proletariat. The splinter groups that have broken away from the brotherhood since the 1960s are characterized by their radicalism, their generally younger age, and a more scientific and technical slant in their educational backgrounds. A similar membership profile seems to characterize the brotherhood in other countries, although the relative importance of various social groups differs from one country to another, with, for example, the intelligentsia more heavily represented in a country like Jordan, the merchants and artisans in a country like Syria, and the students and professionals in a country like Sudan. However, the exact relationships, in terms of personnel, organization, and strategy, among the older Muslim Brotherhoods and the newer militant groups (often functioning under such names as Tanẓīm al-Jihād (The Jihād Organization) or Al-Jamāʿat al-Islāmīyah (The Islamic Group) are far from entirely clear. [*See* Jamāʿat al-Islāmīyah, al-.]

Pan-Arab Activities. Soon after its founding, the Muslim Brotherhood movement spread into the countries adjacent to Egypt; today it remains the main Pan-Arab Islamic movement. Its basic charter stipulates that it is a "universal Islamic assembly" *(hay'ah islāmiyah jāmiʿah)* rather than an Egyptian or even an Arab organization. It actively established branches from the mid-1930s onward, following a number of working visits to Syria, Lebanon, Palestine, Jordan, Iraq, Yemen and elsewhere, and set up special tents in Mecca during the pilgrimage seasons in the 1940s and 1950s to greet, entertain, and convert pilgrim delegates from all over the Muslim world. Several Sudanese and other Arab students, attracted to the movement while studying in Egypt, carried their ideas back to their countries. A number of fellow associations were also established, initially not always under the same title of the Muslim Brothers. The Pan-Arab activities of the Ikhwān were stepped up during the Palestine War of 1948, to which it contributed with voluntary personnel. From that time onward, the Ikhwān did its best to give support to its fellow movements from other Arab countries when they came under persecution, an activity that was soon caught up in the dynamics of inter-Arab politics. For example, the Syrian brothers gave support to their Egyptian colleagues (and perhaps even acted as the main regional headquarters, under the leadership of Muṣṭafā al-Sibāʿī) following the ordeal of the Egyptian Ikhwan in 1954. The Syrian brothers in turn received support from their Jordanian colleagues (and some say from the regime as well) after their ordeal at the hands of the Syrian government in 1981. The movement also had some appeal in North Africa, especially in Morocco (where it had close relations with the Istiqlāl Party and with Muḥammad ʿAllāl al-Fāsī), and was not completely unknown in Tunisia, Algeria (where it maintained cordial relations with the *ʿulamā'*) and in some regions of the Horn of Africa, such as Eritrea and Somalia. Sympathetic groups, with somewhat similar orientations, have also existed in places as far away as India, Malaysia, Indonesia, the Philippines, and of course Pakistan where the Jamāʿat-i Islāmī shares the Ikhwān ideology. In cooperation with such organizations the Muslim Brothers are believed to exercise a certain degree of influence over the Islamic World Congress (Mu'tamar al-ʿĀlam al-Islāmī). [*See* Istiqlāl; Jamāʿat-i Islāmī; *and the biographies of Sibāʿī and Fāsī.*]

Government circles in several Arab countries believe that there exists at present a "Muslim Brotherhood International" that coordinates activities and finances among the various countries' branches. According to unconfirmed reports, this organization's structure includes, in addition to the highly authoritative position of the General Guide, a General Guidance Bureau (GGB, Maktab al-Irshād al-ʿĀmm) and a General Consultative Council (GCC, Majlis al-Shūrā al-ʿĀmm), both of which provide a distinct advantage to the Egyptian brothers. The members of the GGB are the Egyptian General Guide, eight more Egyptians, and one representative each from Syria, Jordan, Lebanon, Algeria, and Kuwait, guaranteeing the Egyptian brothers an automatic majority. A similar pattern obtains in the GCC, the legislative branch of the organization, which has a minimum required membership of thirty: thirteen members from the personnel of the GGB, the guide himself and three persons appointed by him; three members from Syria, and two each from Jordan, Kuwait, Saudi Arabia, and Yemen; and one each from Bahrain, Qatar, the United Arab Emirates, Iraq, Lebanon, Somalia, Tunisia, Algeria, Europe, and the United States. In 1989 the GCC had thirty-eight members including twelve Egyptians and nine from the Gulf region; the Egyptians and the Gulf members (representing numerical weight and financial means) had an automatic majority within the Council.

Although meetings and exchanges among Ikhwān leaders from various countries certainly occur, and some transfer of funds likely takes place, the coordination of activities and finances is probably not as well planned and tightly executed as the authorities sometimes imply. For one thing, some of these movements (for example, in Sudan, Tunisia, and the Gaza Strip) have acquired a certain degree of autonomy in their intellectual and political outlook that noticeably distinguishes them from the conventional Muslim brothers' position. Most of them (with the partial exception of Sudan) are underground or opposition movements that have sufficient problems of their own in their own territory. And though the possibility of some Saudi Arabian financing is sometimes mentioned, many of the brothers have acquired part of their financial resources through working personally in the Arabian oil-exporting countries. Furthermore, the Gulf crisis of 1990–1991 reportedly has led to further divisions, not only among the brotherhoods from various countries but sometimes within the Muslim Brotherhood movement of one country.

A relatively recent development has been the electoral success and the participation in government by Muslim Brother elements in a number of Arab countries (notably Egypt, Sudan, Jordan, and Kuwait). The main question that follows from this is: will such a measure of success turn the Muslim Brothers into a milder, "legal" political force that accepts the rules of the game within their specific countries, or will it prompt them into a more radical, Pan-Islamist line in the belief that the universal triumph of political Islam lies virtually at hand?

[*See also* Pan-Islam *and the biography of Bannā'.*]

BIBLIOGRAPHY

ʿAbd al-Ḥalīm, Maḥmūd. *Al-Ikhwān al-Muslimūn.* 3 vols. Alexandria, 1979–1985. Very detailed account (including testimony) of the history of the brotherhood from 1928 to 1971, by a member of its Constitutive Body.

Ayubi, Nazih N. *Political Islam: Religion and Politics in the Arab World.* London and New York, 1991. Includes reviews of the political thought of al-Bannā', Quṭb, and the Jihādists, and studies on the role of the Muslim Brotherhood in Egypt, Syria, the Sudan, Jordan, and other Arab countries.

Bayyūmī, Zakarīyā S. *Al-Ikhwān al-Muslimūn wa al-Jamāʿāt al-Islāmīyah* (The Muslim Brothers and the Islamic Groupings). Cairo, 1974. Good study, especially on the shades and multiplicity within the Brotherhood and its relations with other Islamic groups.

Carré, Olivier, and Gérard Michaud. *Les Frères Musulmans, 1928–1982.* Paris, 1983. Good account of the brotherhood in Egypt and Syria.

Centre for Political and Strategic Studies. *Al-Taqrīr al-Istratījī al-ʿArabī* (The Arab Strategic Report). Cairo, 1991. Part 2, section 1.ii, includes a detailed account of the "Muslim Brotherhood International."

Harris, Christina. *Nationalism and Revolution in Egypt: The Role of the Muslim Brotherhood.* The Hague, 1964. Useful study of the interplay between religious and secular influences in the development of Egyptian nationalism.

Husaynī, Isḥāq Mūsā al-. *The Moslem Brethren.* Translated by John F. Brown et al. Beirut, 1956. Useful, detailed study, although now somewhat dated.

Mitchell, Richard P. *The Society of the Muslim Brothers.* London,

1969. Still the best account of the brotherhood in Egypt to the mid-1950s.

Nafīsī, ʿAbd Allāh F. al-. *Al-ḥarakah al-Islāmīyah* (The Islamic Movement). Cairo, 1989. Analysis and self-critique by a Kuwaiti Islamist of the aspects of unity and division within the Islamic movement in the Arab world.

Zahmūl, Ibrāhīm. *Al-Ikhwān al-Muslimūn: Awrāq tārīkhīyah* (The Muslim Brotherhood: Historical Papers). N.p., 1985. Sympathetic account with useful material and some information on the brotherhood outside Egypt.

NAZIH N. AYUBI

Muslim Brotherhood in Egypt

Contemporary Islamic social and political activism in Egypt is rooted in the founding in 1928 by Ḥasan al-Bannā' of Jamʿīyat al-Ikhwān al-Muslimūn (Society of Muslim Brothers; also known as the Muslim Brotherhood or the Ikhwān). From the beginning, the Ikhwān's goals were both social and political, promoting the causes of benevolence, charity, and development, on the one hand, and nationalism, independence, and Islamism, on the other. Throughout the Ikhwān's nearly seventy-year history, "Islamism" has consistently meant the reform of society. More recently, this goal has been expanded to include the full establishment of *sharīʿah* (Islamic law). To achieve such goals, the tactics used by various groupings within the Ikhwān have ranged from activism and proregime political accommodation to militancy and antiregime assassinations and violence; from philanthropy and economic institution building to accommodation with opposition political parties.

Although Islamism and nationalism theoretically should be seen as mutually exclusive, in fact the Ikhwān has pursued both simultaneously. According to the Ikhwān, Egypt is "a part of the general Arab nation [*waṭan*], and when we act for Egypt, we act for Arabism, the East, and for Islam" (Mitchell, 1969, p. 264).

Ḥasan al-Bannā' and the Founding of the Ikhwān. Ḥasan al-Bannā' was born in October 1906 in Buhayrah Province, northeast of Cairo. His father was imam and teacher at the local mosque. By his early teen years, al-Bannā' was committed to Sufism, teaching, organizing for the cause of Islam, nationalism, and activism. As an organizer, he worked with various societies. At the age of twelve, in his hometown of Maḥmūdīyah, he became the leader of the Society for Moral Behavior and soon thereafter, a member of the Ḥaṣafīyah Ṣūfī order. At age thirteen, he was named secretary of the Hasafīyah Society for Charity, whose goals were to preserve Islamic morality and resist Christian missionaries. Aḥmad al-Sukkarī, head of the order, later helped al-Bannā' develop the idea of the Ikhwān.

Al-Bannā' came of age as Saʿd Zaghlūl and his Wafd Party agitated for independence from Great Britain and for a liberal political experiment. He entered Dār al-ʿUlūm (Teacher's College) in Cairo in 1923 and graduated in 1927 at the age of twenty-one. He received a modern education in the sciences, as well as a continuation of his classical Islamic learning. Combined with the extracurricular influences of Sufism, the thought of Muḥammad Rashīd Riḍā and the Salafīyah movement, nationalism, and his father's instruction, al-Bannā' developed a diverse intellectual basis for his own mission. This development continued with his first job, teaching Arabic in a primary school in Ismāʿīlīyah, the heart of the British-occupied Suez Canal Zone.

A teacher by day to schoolchildren, al-Bannā' was active at night instructing the parents and elders of Ismāʿīlīyah, especially laborers, small merchants, and civil servants. Beyond the school and mosque, al-Bannā' held discussion groups in coffeehouses and other popular meeting places. He was equally active in lobbying the power brokers of his new community, the *ʿulamā'*, shaykhs of Ṣūfī orders, leading families, and social and religious organizations or clubs.

Al-Bannā' was deeply troubled by the foreign presence in Ismāʿīlīyah. His nationalist sentiments were merged with anticolonialism, as he spoke against British military occupation, the Suez Canal Company, foreign control of public utilities, and the extreme gap between the luxurious lifestyles of foreign owners and managers and the miserable conditions of Egyptian employees and servants.

But it was in the capital where al-Bannā's service to the message of Islam would be most needed and where it had its greatest chance for success. In 1927, he supported the creation in Cairo of the Young Men's Muslim Association. In March 1928, in Ismāʿīlīyah, he founded his own Society of Muslim Brothers.

The first four years of the organization's existence were used to solidify support in and around Ismāʿīlīyah. Al-Bannā' and fellow members toured the countryside preaching the message of Islam in mosques, homes, the workplace, clubs and coffeehouses. Branches were established in Port Saʿīd and Suez City, and other contacts were made in Cairo and parts of the Nile Delta. A headquarters was established, and separate schools for boys and for girls were built, along with mosques, clubs, and small home industries.

Al-Bannā' was denounced by various groups as a communist, a Wafdist, an antimonarchist republican, and a criminal violating civil-service regulations governing the collection of money. However, he was consistently cleared of the allegations of criminal misconduct leveled against him, some by dissidents in his own organization. In 1932, he was transferred to Cairo, where he joined his brother, ʿAbd al-Raḥmān al-Bannā', and his Society for Islamic Culture. The two brothers merged their operations to form the first branch of the Ikhwān in Cairo.

The 1930s was a time for organization building, honing the message of the Ikhwān, and developing print media to spread the message throughout and beyond the membership. It was also a time of political activism, as al-Bannā' began to communicate directly with kings (Fu'ād and Farouk [Fārūq]), prime ministers (particularly Muṣṭafā al-Naḥḥās Pāshā), and heads of all Arab governments. The message was one of reforming government and society in the spirit and letter of Islam. The Ikhwān also became active in raising funds to aid Palestinian Arabs in their resistance to Zionism, in particular to maintain the Arab Strike of 1936–1939.

In the 1940s, the Ikhwān was the most popular and respected of the nationalist forces in fighting against British imperialism and military occupation and in the growing struggle against Zionism in Palestine. The Wafd and the palace, having been too closely associated with the British, were by now discredited as nationalist forces.

Beyond al-Bannā'. The leaders and theoreticians of the Ikhwān are among the most influential of Egypt's twentieth-century political figures. After his assassination by police on 12 February 1949, Ḥasan al-Bannā' was succeeded as general guide *(murshid ʿāmm)* by Ḥasan al-Huḍaybī (1949–1972), a judge and an outsider to the Muslim Brotherhood. His son, Ma'mūn al-Huḍaybī, has been the official spokesperson of the Ikhwān since the mid-1980s, although the supreme leadership remained with ʿUmar al-Tilimsānī (1972–1986), the third general guide, and Ḥamīd Abū al-Naṣr, his successor.

The most famous theoretician of the brotherhood is Sayyid Quṭb, who joined the Ikhwān after al-Bannā's assassination in 1949, was chief spokesman for the brotherhood after its second dissolution in 1954, and was himself executed by the regime of President Gamal Abdel Nasser in 1966. Quṭb was influenced by the Pakistani theologian, Sayyid Abu al-Aʿlā Mawdūdī, and in turn influenced the thoughts of Ayatollah Ruhollah Khomeini of Iran, as well as such Egyptian militant groups as al-Takfīr wa al-Hijrah and al-Jihād, the latter responsible for the assassination of Anwar el-Sadat in 1981. Quṭb's principal concern was for the use of *jihād* (struggle), against Jāhilī (ignorant or pagan) societies, both Western and so-called Islamic ones, that were in need of radical transformation. Having lived in the United States for two years in the late 1940s, he had become disenchanted with what he saw as the moral decadence of Western civilization and its anti-Arab bias. He moved into a leadership role in the Ikhwān and paved the way for confrontation with the Nasser regime.

The Free Officers and other army officials had strong contacts with the Ikhwān well before the 1952 coup. Sadat had been the principal liaison between the two groups until the early 1940s and was replaced in 1942 by ʿAbd al-Munʿim ʿAbd al-Ra'ūf, who was both a dedicated member of the Ikhwān and a Free Officer. The 1954 assassination attempt against Nasser, purportedly by a member of the Ikhwān, put a quick and final end to the accommodation between the two groups. It also allowed Nasser to displace General Muḥammad Neguib, titular head of the Free Officers, whose name was linked with the Ikhwān. The brotherhood was disbanded and its activities prohibited by Nasser. Thousands of brothers were imprisoned. Several were hanged in 1954, and several more in the 1960s. Many remained in prison for seventeen years.

Sadat, after succeeding Nasser in 1970 and in need of support against leftists in his government, rehabilitated the Ikhwān and sought its support. He released members of the brotherhood in 1971, including al-Tilimsānī, whom Nasser had imprisoned. Yet Sadat refused to grant the Ikhwān unconditional legal status as a political party or as a *jamʿīyah* (private voluntary organization [PVO]) registered with the Ministry of Social Affairs. In 1979, in the midst of increasing criticism by the brotherhood of his peace initiative with Israel, Sadat offered to confer PVO status on the Ikhwān, as well as to appoint al-Tilimsanī to the Shūrā Council (upper chamber of parliament), on condition that the brothers moderate their criticism of his policies. Al-Tilimsānī rejected this overture, as it would have placed his society under direct governmental control and given the Ministry of Social Affairs the ability to dissolve the organization at will, confiscate its properties, and change its board of directors. Al-Tilimsānī would also have been beholden to the president rather than a voting membership or public.

Al-Tilimsānī and the other top leaders of the Muslim Brotherhood were among the approximately 1,500 arrested by Sadat in September 1981. Two-thirds of this total were from the brotherhood and other Islamic groups. The leadership was released after Sadat's assassination on 6 October. The Ikhwān was not implicated in that violence and had by this time established itself as a nonviolent opposition movement. With this new image and reality, al-Tilimsānī made a concerted effort to move the organization into the mainstream of political and social life in Egypt. Under his leadership, the brotherhood accepted political pluralism and parliamentary democracy. Unable to form its own party because of Egypt's party law, the Ikhwān formed an alliance with the Wafd Party in the 1984 parliamentary elections. This alliance gained 65 seats (out of 450), seven of which were earmarked for Muslim Brothers. This victory made these often uncomfortable allies the primary opposition group against the ruling party, President Hosni Mubarak's National Democratic Party (NDP).

By 1987, the coalition collapsed and the Muslim Brotherhood formed a new Islamic Alliance with the Socialist Labor Party and the Liberal Party to contest that year's parliamentary elections. The brotherhood had the dominant position in this alliance. The first priority in the Ikhwān's ten-point platform was the implementation of *sharīʿah* (divine law). The only campaign slogan for the alliance was "al-Islām huwa al-ḥall" ("Islam is the solution"). The brothers also reached out to Egypt's Coptic Christian community. The second of their ten points called for "full equal rights and obligations between Muslims and their Coptic brothers." Moreover, the only Copt at the top of any party list and elected in 1987 was on the Islamic Alliance list. (The Ikhwān joined with most of the other opposition parties in boycotting the 1990 elections.) This political moderation and willingness to approach constitutional reform through gradual means have placed the Ikhwān in the forefront of public debate over the most crucial issues in Egypt, especially the question of the appropriate role of religion in politics and society.

The publications of the Ikhwān over the years have also had a significant impact on the course of public debate. Ḥasan al-Bannā' knew the importance of communication, both to spread his message and to refute official or other adversarial reports about him and his organization. Since 1933 and the publication of *Majallat al-Ikhwān al-Muslimūn* (Magazine of the Muslim Brothers), the society has struggled against government censorship and internal divisions to produce a host of newsletters, magazines, and journals. These include: *Al-nadhīr* (The Warner; 1938–1939); *Al-manār* (The Lighthouse; 1939–1941), previously the organ of the Salafīyah movement and Muḥammad Rashīd Riḍā; *Al-Ikhwān al-Muslimūn* (The Muslim Brothers; 1942–1948), first a biweekly then a daily newspaper; and *Al-shihāb* (The Meteor; 1946–1948), a research journal. The last two were suspended in 1948 when the Muslim Brotherhood was dissolved for the first time.

Al-daʿwah (The Call) appeared from 1951 to 1956, struggling in the last two years in an atmosphere of government censorship and, finally, the official disbanding of the Ikhwān. In 1976, *Al-daʿwah,* along with other religious and oppositional publications, were allowed to publish again, as Sadat sought to demonstrate to Western supporters his commitment to political as well as economic liberalization. In addition to a campaign against the Camp David peace process, which was portrayed as humiliating and degrading to Egypt, and against Sadat's reform of family law and women's rights, *Al-daʿwah* kept up a steady campaign for the more general goals of Islamic renewal of society and full implementation of *sharīʿah.* Sadat banned this publication in September 1981 during his infamous crackdown on opposition leaders and others. In the mid-1980s, the Ikhwān launched another effort, *Liwā' al-Islām* (The Banner of Islam), a weekly publication. This would-be successor to *Al-daʿwah* was also banned (temporarily) during the 1990–1991 Gulf War, owing in part to its criticism of Egypt's participation in the U.S.-led coalition against Iraq.

Connections with Other Groups. The Muslim Brotherhood has had its share of internal disputes, some of which have resulted in the branching off of some members to form other Islamic groups. The only such split (though there were several disputes) in al-Bannā's time was the founding, in 1939, of Jamʿīyat Shabāb Sayyidinā Muḥammad (Society of Muhammad's Youth). In 1945, after the passage of Law 49 governing PVOs, the society divided itself into two parts: the politically active section that continued under al-Bannā's leadership and a section concerned with welfare and social services that had its own leadership and structure. This charitable section continued to receive governmental assistance for its efforts in running schools, technical institutes, small industries, social work, hospitals, clinics, and dispensaries. Earlier, in 1942–1943, al-Bannā' had established *al-niẓām al-khāṣṣ* ("special section"), a secret apparatus inspired by the notion of *jihād* and used as an instrument for the defense of Islam and of the society itself against police and various governments.

Other Islamist groups in Egypt either are offshoots of the Ikhwān or share its general goals of Islamic reform and implementation of *sharīʿah*. Whether these groups are direct descendants of the Muslim Brotherhood, as some argue, or are independently founded and administered, most would agree that the Society of Muslim Brothers is the theological, if not political, grandparent of the numerous Islamist groupings in Egypt. They differ mainly in tactics, not goals. Many advocate violence and militancy, although the Ikhwān, since the 1970s, has advocated gradualism and working within the system in order to change it. (Still, there are divisions within the society over this issue.) The various Islamist groups include: al-Jihād (Holy Struggle), Jund Allāh (God's Troops), Jaysh al-Taḥrīr al-Islāmī (Islamic Liberation Army), Jamʿīyat al-Tablīgh (Society of Islamic Propagation), al-Takfīr wa al-Hijrah (former Ikhwān-member Shukrī Muṣṭafā's Society of Muslims), and al-Jamāʿat al-Islāmīyah (Islamic Groups), among others. [*See also* Takfīr wa al-Hijrah, Jamāʿat al-; Jamāʿat al-Islāmīyah, al-.]

Many Egyptians claim to have no formal relationship with the Muslim Brotherhood yet support their goals and ideals. One of the more prominent of these is the popular religious leader Shaykh ʿAbd al-Ḥamīd Kishk (b. 1933), who was a strong critic of Sadat's government, its dependence on the United States, and its peace with Israel. His Friday sermons have been widely attended and distributed through tape recordings. As critical as he is of the government, he is equally supportive of the Ikhwān and other Islamic PVOs that provide affordable health care, day care, education, job training, development projects, access to credit, and other programs to help Egyptians. Kishk praises these efforts as he criticizes the government for its inability to provide for the needs of the vast majority of the Egyptian people. [*See the biography of Kishk.*]

Zaynab al-Ghazālī (b. 1917), the most prominent woman associated with the Ikhwān and a regular contributor to *Al-daʿwah,* is a fierce opponent of the feminist movement and a promoter of traditional Islamic values for women and men. She maintains that women can have an important public role as long as it is in the defense of Islam and traditional Islamic values. [*See the biography of Ghazālī.*]

The Muslim Brotherhood has mass appeal. Students, professors, doctors, lawyers, and other professionals have demonstrated their support for the organization in numerous elections on campuses and especially in syndicate and union elections.

The Ikhwān has had considerable influence beyond the borders of Egypt as well. There are or were strong branches of the Muslim Brotherhood in Palestine (founded in 1946), Jordan (licensed in 1953), Syria (c. 1935), Sudan, and Iraq. Egypt's Ikhwān also had significant influence on other Islamist organizations not formally known as Muslim Brotherhood groups, most notably the Islāmī Jamīʿat-i Ṭulabā (Islamic Society of Students), a wing of the Jamāʿat-i Islāmī (Islamic Party) of Pakistan.

Although various governments—monarchical and republican—have outlawed and restricted its activities, the very success and continuing popularity of the Ikhwān demonstrates to Egyptians and their government that Islamic groups in general can derive legitimacy from the positive influence they exert on the daily lives of the population. The government has thus resolved to deny legal recognition to the Ikhwān as either a political party or a *jamʿīyah,* but its de facto existence is accepted. The Ikhwān works within the present political and economic systems but must still work through other legal organizations—whether political parties or once-legal economic enterprises, such as al-Rayan Investment Company—to pursue its dual goals of socioeconomic development and political influence.

[*See also* Egypt *and the biographies of Bannā' and Quṭb.*]

BIBLIOGRAPHY

Ayubi, Nazih N. *Political Islam: Religion and Politics in the Arab World.* London, 1991. In its numerous case studies of Islamic movements, this book provides analysis of the Brotherhood in Egypt, Syria, Sudan, Jordan, Palestine, and Arabia.

Baker, Raymond William. *Sadat and After: Struggles for Egypt's Political Soul.* Cambridge, Mass., 1990. Chapter 8 deals with the Muslim Brothers in the 1970s and 1980s.

Bannā', Ḥasan al-. *Mudhakkarāt al-daʿwah wa-al-dāʿīyah.* N.p., c. 1951.

Esposito, John L. *Islam and Politics.* 3d ed. Syracuse, N.Y., 1991. Extensive analysis of the development of the Brotherhood as an alternative to secular nationalism in Egypt and beyond.

Hoffman, Valerie J. "An Islamic Activist: Zaynab al-Ghazālī." In *Women and the Family in the Middle East,* edited by Elizabeth W. Fernea, pp. 233–254. Austin, 1985.

Ḥusaynī, Mūsā Isḥāq al-. *Al-Ikhwān al-Muslimūn: Kubrā al-ḥarakāt al-Islāmīyah al-ḥadīthah.* Beirut, 1952. Translated by John F. Brown et al., *The Moslem Brethren.* Beirut, 1956.

Ibrahim, Saad Eddin. "Egypt's Islamic Activism in the 1980s." *Third World Quarterly* 10.2 (April 1988): 632–657.

Kepel, Gilles. *Muslim Extremism in Egypt.* Berkeley, 1985. Compares the neo-Muslim Brotherhood with the original leadership of the Ikhwān and with leaders of other contemporary Islamic organizations in Egypt.

Mitchell, Richard P. *The Society of the Muslim Brothers.* London, 1969. The most detailed and authoritative account of the founding, development, and program of the Ikhwān.

Quṭb, Sayyid. *Al-ʿadāla al-ijtimāʿīyah fī al-Islām.* 3d ed. N.p., n.d. Translated by John B. Hardie as *Social Justice in Islam.* Washington, D.C., 1955.

Ramadan, Abdel Aziz. "Fundamentalist Influence in Egypt: The Strategies of the Muslim Brotherhood and the Takfir Groups." In *Fundamentalisms and the State,* edited by Martin Marty and R. Scott Appleby. Chicago, 1993.

Sivan, Emmanuel. *Radical Islam.* New Haven, 1985. General comparison between the Egyptian and Syrian Muslim Brotherhood.

Springborg, Robert. *Mubarak's Egypt: Fragmentation of the Political Order.* Boulder, 1989. Section on Islamicist opposition analyzes its strengths and weaknesses, generally, and the factionalization of the Brotherhood, in particular.

Zuhur, Sherifa. *Revealing Reveiling: Islamist Gender Ideology in Contemporary Egypt.* Albany, N.Y., 1992. Important discussion of the Ikhwān's attitudes toward a host of gender-specific issues, such as birth control, polygamy, divorce, female education, veiling, and associational activity.

Denis J. Sullivan

Muslim Brotherhood in Syria

Throughout its fifty years of activity in Syria, the Muslim Brotherhood has been principally an opposition movement that has never held political power. The brotherhood traces its origins to the 1930s, when the Syrian people were engaged in their struggle to achieve national independence from French rule. The structural changes that Syria experienced during the interwar years were especially disruptive in the town quarters. Small merchants and artisans suffered under the weight of expanding European trade. The laboring classes found it increasingly difficult to feed their families because of the high inflation rates of the period. Uprooted rural dwellers in growing numbers entered the peripheral quarters of the towns, having been pushed off the land by drought or, more commonly, by indebtedness to absentee landowners and moneylenders. All sought the support of local leaders who could help them articulate their grievances and meet their needs. By this time, the leaders of the national independence movement had become increasingly distant from their urban constituencies, owing to their preoccupation with negotiations with the French Mandate authorities. This distance enabled newer, more radicalized groups to begin to challenge the leadership of the veteran nationalists.

To address the pressing social and psychological needs of the urban masses, the vast majority of whom belonged to the Sunnī Muslim rite, there arose in the towns a variety of socially and politically active organizations, some of which were religious beneficent societies (*jamʿīyat*) headed by men who had received formal religious training in Islamic law. The House of al-Arqam in Aleppo was one of these societies. On the eve of Syria's independence, the House of al-Arqam moved its headquarters to Damascus, the Syrian capital, where it became known in 1944 as the Muslim Brotherhood (al-Ihkwān al-Muslimūn). It is generally thought that the Muslim Brotherhood in Egypt, which had been established in 1928, influenced the emergence of the Muslim Brotherhood in Syria. Some Syrian students who had studied in Cairo became familiar with the ideas of Ḥasan al-Bannā', the Egyptian organization's founder. One was Muṣṭafā al-Sibāʿī, the Syrian brotherhood's first general supervisor (*al-muraqib al-ʿamm*), who became acquainted with al-Bannā' in Cairo. Others were inspired by a tour of Syria made by members of the Egyptian Muslim Brotherhood in the mid-1930s.

The earliest goals of the Muslim Brotherhood were to spread Muslim education and ethics and to inculcate anti-imperialist feelings among the urban populace. It was through schools and magazines associated with the brotherhood that such ideas were disseminated. Its first published program in 1954 failed to offer a detailed strategic plan, dwelling instead on the goals of combating ignorance and deprivation and establishing a political regime based on Islamic law. For a period after Syria gained independence, the brotherhood put forward a vague notion of Islamic socialism but eventually abandoned it. Unlike the Muslim Brotherhood in Egypt, the Syrian organization has never produced a systematically articulated set of principles and program of action. The closest it came to this achievement was the 1980 proclamation of the Syrian Islamic Front to which the Syrian Muslim Brotherhood belonged.

The Arab military defeat in Palestine in 1948 enabled the brotherhood to expand its following in the Syrian towns, especially in Damascus where its members controlled roughly a fifth of the parliamentary seats allotted to the capital and its environs in the 1950s. In this period, the brotherhood competed with Communists, Baʿthists, Nasserists, and other opponents of the veteran nationalists who had governed Syria since independence in 1946. The challenge posed by the Nasserist movement to the brotherhood was particularly effective because the two movements shared the same political constituency, the Sunnī Muslim urban trading classes. Not surprisingly, the brotherhood supported Syria's secession in 1961 from the Egyptian-dominated United Arab Republic, established in 1958. [*See also* Nasserism.]

The Baʿth Party's seizure of power in 1963 focused the Muslim Brotherhood's opposition squarely on the radical, secular, nationalist regime's socialist policies and its introduction of large numbers of rural peoples into the state bureaucracy. These measures not only upset the interests of urban absentee landowners, merchants and industrialists, middle-level bureaucrats, and the liberal professions, but also threatened the positions of the urban artisan and small trading classes that formed the main constituency of the Muslim Brotherhood. Religious leaders associated with the brotherhood promoted civil disobedience against the Baʿthist regime's secular policies. But in the aftermath of Syria's military defeat in the 1967 war with Israel and the establishment of Hafez al-Assad's Baʿthist government in 1970, a schism developed within the brotherhood. Militants in Aleppo and Hama pressed for a policy of armed struggle against the Assad regime but they were countered by the Damascus followers of ʿIṣām al-ʿAṭṭār, a religious shaykh in the Syrian capital who had replaced Muṣṭafā al-Sibāʿī in 1961 as general supervisor of the brotherhood. The ʿAttar wing of the organization had identified a certain convergence of interests between the urban artisan and trading classes that supported the brotherhood in Damascus and the Assad regime's gradual adoption of economic liberalization and its willingness to attract to Syria investments from the Arab oil-producing states of the Persian Gulf.

The Syrian regime's honeymoon with the Damascus branch of the Muslim Brotherhood did not last long. President Assad's secular constitution of 1973 provoked widespread protests in the Syrian towns led by the brotherhood and forced him to amend the constitution to require that the president had to be Muslim. By the mid-1970s, the northern militants in the brotherhood had gained the upper hand over the Damascus branch; during the next seven years they escalated the level of violence against the Assad regime. This phase in the Muslim Brotherhood's struggle against the Syrian government was closely identified with the leadership of ʿAdnān Saʿd al-Dīn, a teacher and writer from the central Syrian town of Hama, who had become the brotherhood's newest general supervisor. Several factors prompted the brotherhood to adopt a strategy of armed struggle (*jihād):* the Syrian government's intervention in 1976 in the Lebanese civil war against the Palestinians and their Lebanese Muslim allies; growing corruption stemming from the government's economic liberalization policies; and, above all, the increased power that the president's own rural-based community of ʿAlawīs, a religious minority who constituted only 10 percent of the Syrian population, had achieved at the expense of the country's Sunnī majority, and especially the Sunnīs of the towns. From this time onward, the brotherhood's opposition was defined as one of Sunnī majority against ʿAlawī minority and of town against countryside.

The Muslim Brotherhood's tactics at first focused on assassinating ʿAlawī officials but soon expanded into armed attacks on prominent institutional symbols of the Assad regime including Baʿth Party offices, police stations, and army units. Most notable were the June 1979 killing of eighty-three ʿAlawī artillery cadets in Aleppo, large-scale demonstrations and boycotts in Aleppo, Hama, and Homs in March 1980, and an attempt to assassinate Assad himself later that year. Those who carried out the violence against the regime and its supporters tended to be university students, school teachers, and members of the liberal professions. Their leaders were also engineers, dentists, and teachers who came from small trading families and the middle levels of the Muslim religious establishment.

To counter this violent opposition, the Syrian government decreed in July 1980 that any association with the Muslim Brotherhood was punishable by death. It began to crack down on the brotherhood with its formidable military resources, in particular its dreaded security forces composed almost exclusively of ʿAlawīs. Under this pressure, the Muslim Brotherhood regrouped under the banner of the Syrian Islamic Front (al-Jabhah al-Islāmīyah fī Sūrīyah), a broad-based alliance of Islamic opposition groups established in October 1980 and headed by the brotherhood. Shaykh Muḥammad al-Bayanūnī, a member of the religious establishment in Aleppo, became the Islamic Front's secretary-general, but its strongman was ʿAdnān Saʿd al-Dīn, the brotherhood's general supervisor. The front's chief ideologue was Saʿīd Ḥawwā, a religious figure from Hama who, with Saʿd al-Dīn, had been a leader of the northern militant faction that had taken control of the brotherhood in the mid-1970s.

The culmination of five years of terror and counterterror was a showdown between the Muslim Brotherhood and the Syrian regime in February 1982 in the socially conservative Sunnī stronghold of Hama. There the brotherhood sparked an armed uprising and seized control of the town in its strongest bid ever to challenge the Assad regime's legitimacy. Within two weeks, the regime had restored its authority over Hama, but not before its military forces killed between five thousand and twenty thousand inhabitants of Hama and razed large sections of this ancient town. Assad's regime had dealt a devastating blow to the brotherhood and in so doing put all its political opponents on notice that it would not countenance any challenges to its rule. The lesson of Hama appears to have been taken to heart for little has since been heard from the Muslim Brotherhood.

Unlike the Muslim Brotherhood in Egypt that struck roots in both town and countryside, in Syria the brotherhood was exclusively urban based. This can be explained in part by the fact that the Syrian countryside was to a large extent populated by heterodox sects such as the ʿAlawīs, Druze, and Ismāʿīlis. The Syrian brotherhood specifically appealed to townsmen from the class of small tradesmen and artisans. This class has long been closely intertwined with the Sunnī religious shaykhs attached to the neighborhood mosques that are located in the heart of the local *sūq*s or bazaars where small tradesmen and artisans work and live. The religious shaykhs provided the brotherhood with many of its leaders over the years and with the strong religious values to which its membership subscribed. Because many shaykhs from the middle rungs of the religious establishment also earned their livings as traders, they, like their followers, supported free enterprise and thus stood in opposition to the socialist and quasi-socialist reformism of the Baʿthist governments that have ruled Syria since 1963.

In the 1970s, when the Muslim Brotherhood became the most visible and powerful opponent of the Assad regime, it attracted to its ranks large numbers of students, school teachers, engineers, and other members of the liberal professions, many of whom came from small urban trading families. These elements contributed to the organization's increased militancy in this period and to a noticeable generation gap between its younger, better educated militant youth and their elders. Only rough estimates exist for the size of the Muslim Brotherhood. Although its numbers have fluctuated widely over the decades, it probably reached its maximum size of around ten thousand during the late 1970s. The Syrian government's efforts to destroy the organization by military and legal means reduced its ranks to fewer than five thousand on the eve of the Hama uprising in 1982 and to far fewer afterward. Since then the leadership of the Muslim Brotherhood has been in exile and its rank and file underground in Syria.

The ideological orientation of the Muslim Brotherhood is best summed up in the Islamic Front's proclamation of November 1980. Although it was designed to appeal to all political opponents of the Assad regime, the proclamation nonetheless pointed to several specific positions that the brotherhood had adopted over the years. It raised the prospects of civil war along Sunnī-ʿAlawī lines unless the leaders of the ʿAlawī community rejected Hafez al-Assad's political leadership. It emphasized the Syrian people's right to regain their basic political and civil liberties, which were described as being as important as the people's right to basic economic security, of which they had also been stripped. It called for an independent judiciary and for a government based on the rule of law and on the Islamic principle of mutual consultation (*shūrā*). And it emphasized the importance of *jihād* (struggle in the name of Islam) as a means for ending sectarianism and establishing an Islamic state in Syria. Many of the values and directions highlighted in the proclamation were not exclusively Islamic in character, particularly those that emphasized natural rights and liberties. In this sense, the brotherhood was in step with a wide variety of opposition groups throughout the Middle East that had already made individual freedoms their highest political priority as they struggled against the authoritarian governments that dominated the region.

Economic policies were also stressed in the proclamation. It insisted on the reintroduction of the ownership of private land and on giving workers ownership rights of public industries. The emphasis was clearly on buttressing private enterprise and reducing state controls over the movement of capital and the running of industry. The Islamic Front's economic orientation closely corresponded to the defined interests of the Sunnī trading and manufacturing classes in the Syrian towns, major contributors to the membership and coffers of the Muslim Brotherhood. They strongly opposed the government's economic favoritism toward the military, workers in modern industries, and rural minorities, especially the ʿAlawīs.

Since the Muslim Brotherhood's crushing defeat in Hama in 1982, its political prospects have not been promising. The strategy of armed struggle proved to be a major blunder from which the organization has yet to recover. Divisions within its leadership over whether to continue or abandon its militant tactics and over the Islamic Front's relations with neighboring states also contributed to its fragility. Outside support has not been forthcoming. Soon after coming to power in Iran, Ayatollah Khomeini disappointed the brotherhood when he made it clear that his government supported the Syrian regime because it was the only major Arab state to side with Iran in its war with Iraq that began in 1980. Iraq's victory over Iran in 1988 briefly freed the rival Baʿthist regime of Saddam Hussein to resume its efforts to destabilize the Assad regime, but Iraq's defeat in the Persian Gulf war in early 1991 has, for the time being, drastically reduced its threat to Syria. The best prospects for external support have come in recent years from Jordan where Islamic movements have expanded their political influence.

Ultimately, the Muslim Brotherhood's ability to resume its leadership of the Syrian opposition will depend on how successfully President Assad and his ʿAlawī supporters continue to wield the carrot and the stick. In the new post–cold war era, the Syrian regime no longer enjoys the patronage and protection of the former Soviet Union. American pressures on Syria to negotiate a less than advantageous settlement with Israel, especially in the aftermath of the Palestinian-Israeli peace initiative of 1993, and the continued fragility of the Syrian economy may well reduce the Assad regime's already narrow base of support, encouraging its opponents to resume their struggle. The visible but limited political successes registered by Islamic movements in other Arab countries offer Assad's opponents some hope. These are the kinds of conditions that may enable the Muslim Brotherhood to reemerge in Syria.

[*See also* Syria *and the biography of* *Sibāʿī*.]

BIBLIOGRAPHY

Abd-Allah, Umar F. *The Islamic Struggle in Syria*. Berkeley, 1983. The most comprehensive study of modern Syrian Islamic movements available in the English language.

Batatu, Hanna. "Syria's Muslim Brethren." *MERIP Reports* 12.9 (November–December 1982): 12–20, 34, 36. Penetrating social analysis of the Muslim Brotherhood in Syria.

Carré, Olivier. *Les frères musulmans: Egypte et Syrie, 1928–1982*. Paris, 1983. Comparative study of the Muslim Brotherhood in Egypt and Syria over a fifty-year span.

Commins, David D. *Islamic Reform: Politics and Social Change in Late Ottoman Syria*. New York, 1990. Informative study of the Islamic societies and movements that were precursors of the Muslim Brotherhood.

Dam, Nikolaos van. *The Struggle for Power in Syria: Sectarianism, Regionalism, and Tribalism in Politics, 1961–1978*. London, 1979.

Dekmejian, R. Hrair. "Syria: Sunni Fundamentalism against Baathi Rule." In *Islam in Revolution: Fundamentalism in the Arab World*, pp. 109–125. Syracuse, N.Y., 1985. Insightful analysis of the Muslim Brotherhood's struggle for power and the nature of its leadership.

Hinnebusch, Raymond A. "The Islamic Movement in Syria: Sectarian Conflict and Urban Rebellion in an Authoritarian-Populist Regime." In *Islamic Resurgence in the Arab World*, edited by Ali E. Hillal Dessouki, pp. 138–169. New York, 1982. Excellent overview of the place of Islamic movements during the past three decades.

Kelidar, Abbas. "Religion and State in Syria." *Asian Affairs* 61 (February 1974): 16–22. Useful account of the conflict of religion and state at the time of the Syrian constitutional crisis in 1973.

Khoury, Philip S. *Syria and the French Mandate: The Politics of Arab Nationalism, 1920–1945*. Princeton, 1987. Comprehensive study of interwar politics and society in the period when the Muslim Brotherhood first emerged.

Mayer, Thomas. "The Islamic Opposition in Syria, 1961–1982." *Orient* 24 (December 1983): 589–609. Useful examination of the conflict between the Baʿthist regime and the Muslim Brotherhood over a twenty-year span.

Mitchell, Richard P. *The Society of the Muslim Brothers* London, 1969. Remains the best study of the Muslim Brotherhood in Egypt.

Perera, Judith. "The Shifting Fortunes of Syria's Muslim Brothers." *Middle East* (London) (May 1985): 25–28.

Reissner, Johannes. *Ideologie und Politik der Muslimbrüder Syriens*. Freiburg, 1980. Unique study of the intellectual origins and ideological development of the Muslim Brotherhood in Syria in the 1940s and 1950s.

Seale, Patrick. *Asad: The Struggle for the Middle East*. Berkeley, 1988. Fascinating biography of Syrian president Hafez al-Assad based on a wide variety of sources, including extensive interviews with the subject.

Seale, Patrick. *The Struggle for Syria: A Study of Post-War Arab Politics, 1945–1958*. London and New York, 1965. Remains the most perceptive account of Syrian politics in the postindependence period.

PHILIP S. KHOURY

Muslim Brotherhood in Jordan

An enduring feature of Jordanian political life for more than fifty years, the Muslim Brotherhood in Jordan was created as part of an effort by the leader of the Muslim Brotherhood in Egypt, Ḥasan al-Bannā' (1906–1949), to form additional bases of support for his movement. In the early 1940s, members of the Egyptian Muslim

Brotherhood were sent to both Palestine and Jordan to establish new branches.

In 1946, the first Jordanian branch was founded in the town of Salt; further centers were then established in the capital, Amman, and the towns of Irbid and Kayak. The leaders of the new movement registered the organization under the Jordanian Charity Societies and Clubs Law. The leadership of the Muslim Brotherhood was indigenous, and the first head of the organization was a prominent cleric, Ḥājj ʿAbd al-Laṭīf al-Qurah (d. 1953). Ḥājj al-Qurah led an eight-member *majlis* (ruling council), which directed organizational aspects of the new movement. This leadership structure mirrored that of the Muslim Brotherhood in Egypt.

In addition to legal registration, Ḥājj al-Qurah sought official approval from the Jordanian monarch for his fledgling organization. King Abdullah (r. 1946–1951) extended tacit approval to the organization but warned that benefaction would be rescinded if the activities of the Muslim Brotherhood strayed from the spiritual and became identifiable with Jordanian political affairs. At this point, the Muslim Brotherhood was essentially a religious organization. The steady politicization of Islamic clerics, which began in Egypt in the nineteenth century, was barely discernible in Jordan in the 1940s. Nevertheless, the very founding of the Muslim Brotherhood at this time indicated that a new generation of politically active Muslim clergy was ascendant.

The Islamic Message. The functional religious role of the Muslim Brotherhood permitted the movement to promote its ideology to all sectors of Jordanian society. Through its charitable activities, including the provision of health and welfare facilities in the kingdom, the new movement was able to disseminate its Islamic message. The Muslim Brotherhood's message was a direct reflection of the prevailing philosophy it had embraced. Members should strive to educate society and encourage a return to Islamic values.

From 1946 until the outbreak of the war between the Arabs and Israel in 1948, the Muslim Brotherhood in Jordan remained essentially unchanged. Following the war and the Jordanian annexation of the West Bank area of Palestine in 1950, the number of branches of the Muslim Brotherhood increased, as existing Islamic organizations active in the West Bank, including Anṣār al-Fāḍil and al-Iʿtiṣām, were absorbed. As a result of this new, expanded base of support in the West Bank, the leadership and cadres of the Muslim Brotherhood became increasingly politicized.

Political Consolidation. Following the death of Ḥājj al-Qurah in 1953, a new leader was appointed for the movement. On assuming his new post, ʿAbd al-Raḥmān al-Khalīfah (an attorney) approached the Jordanian prime minister, Tawfīq Pāshā Abū al-Hudā, with an application for an expansion of the mandate regarding the activities of the Muslim Brotherhood to facilitate the political and cultural propagation of the movement's Islamic message. The license permitting the Muslim Brotherhood to be a general and comprehensive Islamic grouping was subsequently granted by the authorities.

What was most striking about the development of the Muslim Brotherhood under al-Khalīfah was its relatively close relations with the ruling regime and the monarchy. During the period when the Muslim Brotherhood in Egypt was being repressed by the state, the conservative Jordanian regime found in its own branch of the Muslim Brotherhood a useful ally against the leftist movements sweeping through the region. However, the relationship between monarch and movement has been characterized by peaks and troughs and is for the most part motivated by political pragmatism rather than Islamic idealism.

The attitude of the regime toward the Muslim Brotherhood was further emphasized in 1957 when King Hussein issued a decree proscribing all political parties. The Muslim Brotherhood was exempted because the organization was officially registered as a charity, although in practice its activities were indistinguishable from those of any political party. Thus, the Muslim Brotherhood was free to continue with its own political agenda. Throughout this period it fielded individual candidates in elections to the bicameral legislative assembly. In 1962, the Muslim Brotherhood was the only organization to defy a West Bank boycott of the general election.

By 1964 the Muslim Brotherhood had also formed an umbrella organization called the Islamic Charitable Society, described by al-Khalīfah as a charity rather than a political party. Nonetheless, the activities of the charity included the dissemination of Muslim Brotherhood ideology. By this time, the program of the Muslim Brotherhood in Jordan was almost identical to that of the organization in Egypt.

Pawns and Politics. Following the Arab-Israeli War of 1967, in which Jordan lost the West Bank and the Palestine Liberation Organization established strongholds among the refugee community of the East Bank, the relationship between the Muslim Brotherhood and the monarchy was strengthened. A relationship of dependency was forming, and during times of crisis, such as Black September in 1970, when the Jordanian army fought Palestinian guerrillas, the king was able to rely on the Muslim Brotherhood to be among his staunchest allies. However, by the end of the decade, the king was using the Muslim Brotherhood as a pawn in his foreign policy.

In 1980, as part of a continuing dispute between Jordan and Syria, the king encouraged al-Khalīfah to establish paramilitary bases in the north of Jordan for the purpose of training members of the Syrian Muslim Brotherhood in a campaign to undermine the rule of President Hafez al-Assad. By allowing this training to occur on Jordanian soil, the king increased diplomatic and military tensions with Syria, resulting in a state of near-war, as Syrian and Jordanian troops were moved to the common border between the two countries.

The role of the Muslim Brotherhood during the crisis with Syria served to increase the political profile and legitimacy of the movement domestically. Support from local and foreign sponsors—including the Gulf states—for the organization's charitable activities, such as the building of an Islamic hospital in Amman, increased. In the sphere of political activities, the Muslim Brotherhood began to criticize openly aspects of the regime; corruption within the ruling elite, public immorality, and insensitivity to religious life were the main issues around which the Muslim Brotherhood organized its protest. However, the movement miscalculated the king's response to this critique.

In 1985 the king publicly distanced himself from the Muslim Brotherhood in response to indirect attacks on his legitimacy as monarch and (more important) as political ruler. In a political climate of improved relations with Syria, King Hussein identified "Islamic elements" as responsible for the crisis in relations in 1980. He alleged that he had been misled by the Muslim Brothers and that their activities had been guided by foreign and hostile influences. He issued orders against the Muslim Brotherhood as a show of political strength. Muslim Brothers found themselves targeted by the Jordanian intelligence services as potential threats to the stability of the regime and witnessed government action against leaders of the movement; members of the movement were arrested, lost their jobs, or had their passports confiscated by the Jordanian intelligence services. It was the intention of the king to send a very clear message to the leadership of the Muslim Brotherhood: he was willing to permit and even tacitly encourage a legitimate Islamic presence within the kingdom, but he was not willing to tolerate the Muslim Brotherhood if it sought to undermine the legitimacy of his rule in any way.

Democratization and Political Pluralism. The deterioration of relations between the regime and the Muslim Brotherhood was resolved by the end of the 1980s, followed by a discernible improvement in relations. It became apparent that rather than isolate the movement the king had decided on a policy which would ultimately coopt the Muslim Brotherhood into the ruling strata of the regime. This policy was facilitated by the king's decision in 1989 to hold the first full elections in over twenty-two years.

The call for the election was precipitated by a severe economic crisis within the kingdom which culminated in riots against government-imposed price rises on basic foodstuffs. The crisis was the result of decades of economic mismanagement within Jordan, and genuine hardships were thrust on the poorer sections of society. The Muslim Brotherhood's critique of the early 1980s proved justified, a matter which took on added significance in view of the fact that its base of support was among the rural and urban poor, who were being asked to pay for the economic incompetence of the ruling oligarchy.

The king's decision to hold elections as a response to the riots came as a surprise. It indicated that the Jordanian monarch was willing to institute democratization and political pluralism. It also meant that the king was, at least publicly, willing to surrender his monopoly of control over political life.

The Muslim Brothers perceived the general election as an opportunity to increase their political stake in the regime. The organization mounted a comprehensive election campaign under the slogan, "Islam is the solution." The Muslim Brotherhood started the campaign with advantages over its political rivals. It had a constituency of support among the urban and rural poor. The brotherhood also appealed to the religiously conservative educated class, which was frustrated because of a lack of job opportunities and real prospects for social advancement. Furthermore, the Muslim Brotherhood had been politically active for decades, while its adversaries in the elections remained proscribed and repressed.

The results of the election, therefore, should not have been surprising. Nevertheless, there was consternation in the kingdom when it was announced that the Muslim Brotherhood had won enough votes for twenty-two out of eighty seats in the parliament and that its Islamist counterparts had won an additional twelve; this total of thirty-four seats comprised the largest parliamentary bloc. The king's policy of political cooptation had thus resulted in an Islamic majority in the country's legislative assembly. The future stability of the regime was called into question, yet many failed to take into account the fact that the king still possessed the ultimate authority over the legislature (and therefore the Muslim Brotherhood): he could dissolve parliament at any time.

The Muslim Brothers greeted their election success with characteristic zeal. They set about forcing their political agenda through the legislature and into the statute books. Large amounts of parliamentary time were devoted to specifically Islamic issues, such as the banning of the production of alcohol. In essence it appeared that the Muslim Brotherhood's response to the opportunities presented by its new political power was to concentrate on the areas of policy making that it knew best; thus, the Muslim Brotherhood lobbied for cabinet posts covering social, educational, and religious affairs. There did not appear to be any concerted attempt to tackle such issues as the economy, defense, or foreign affairs.

The outbreak of the Gulf War in 1990 signaled historic changes and challenges for the Muslim Brotherhood. The conflict presented the organization with the most difficult political dilemma in its history centering around the conflicting pressures from local constituents and financial backers in the conservative Gulf regimes. The Muslim Brotherhood initially condemned Saddam Hussein's invasion of Kuwait, but popular Islamic sentiment expressed in the streets of Amman soon persuaded the movement to alter its policy and support the Iraqi leader. This policy jeopardized the Muslim Brotherhood's relationship with Kuwait and Saudi Arabia, which had provided the bulk of its funding.

The fact that the king and the "loyal opposition" in the Muslim Brotherhood were on the losing side in the war has altered only regional rather than domestic political arrangements. The Muslim Brotherhood preserved and further legitimated its popular support. The Islamic message remains a broadly popular one and ensures an enduring future for the organization. However, in the final analysis, such endurance will always be dependent on King Hussein, and this factor makes the Jordanian movement unique with respect to any other branch of the Muslim Brotherhood.

[*See also* Jordan.]

BIBLIOGRAPHY

Abidi, Aqil H. H. *Jordan: A Political Study, 1948–1957*. London, 1965. Dated but worthwhile account of Jordan in the 1950s.

Aruri, Nasser Hasan. *Jordan: A Study in Political Development, 1921–1957*. The Hague, 1972. Introduction to the Jordanian political system.

Bailey, Clinton. *Jordan's Palestinian Challenge, 1948–1983*. Boulder, 1984. Perceptive book addressing the issue of Jordanian Palestinians, who account for 50 percent of the kingdom's population.

Gubser, Peter. *Jordan: Crossroads of Middle Eastern Events*. Boulder, 1984. Interesting account of Jordan's regional role.

Kīlānī, Mūsā Zayd al-. *Al-Ḥarakāt al-Islāmīyah fī al-Urdun* (The Islamic Movements in Jordan). Amman, 1990.

Milton-Edwards, Beverley. "A Temporary Alliance with the Crown: The Islamic Response in Jordan." In *Islamic Fundamentalisms and the Gulf Crisis*, edited by J. P. Piscatori, pp. 88–108. Chicago, 1991. Insight on Jordan during the Gulf crisis.

Wilson, Rodney, ed. *Politics and the Economy in Jordan*. London, 1991. Collection of essays on the inextricable relation between political and economic development in the Hashemite kingdom.

BEVERLEY MILTON-EDWARDS

Muslim Brotherhood in the Sudan

The Muslim Brothers originated among Sudanese students in Cairo in the 1940s. Jamāl al-Dīn al-Sanhūrī and Ṣādiq ʿAbdallāh ʿAbd al-Mājid were among its earliest propagators; in 1946 they were sent by the Egyptian movement to recruit members in the Sudan. They succeeded in setting up branches in several small towns in 1947–1949 but were barred from acting openly unless they declared their independence from the Egyptian Brothers, who were at the time illegal.

Another early recruit was al-Ṣā'im Muḥammad Ibrāhīm, a former teacher at Ḥantūb secondary school, who founded the Islamic Liberation Movement (ILM or Ḥarakat al-Taḥrīr al-Islāmī) at Gordon College in 1947 in order to combat communism. Its leaders, Bābikr Karrār and Muḥammad Yūsuf, called for the establishment of a socialist Islamic state. Early adherents came primarily from the rural areas of the northern Sudan and were deeply committed to Ṣūfī Islam and opposed to communism. The ILM enabled them to adopt a modern Islamic ideology without cutting their ties with their families, who were mostly Khatmīyah adherents. This dual loyalty did not disturb the Khatmīyah because it did not regard the Muslim Brothers as political rivals.

The Sudanese Muslim Brothers were officially founded at the ʿĪd Conference on 21 August 1954. Al-Rāshid al-Ṭāhir, one of the Brothers' most prominent student leaders, later became the movement's *murāqib al-ʿam* (general supervisor). A politician and lawyer, al-Ṭāhir established close relations with the Free Officers, especially with Ṣalāḥ Sālim, their coordinator with the Sudan, and supported the pro-unionist camp. This changed following Egyptian president Gamal Abdel Nasser's attempted assassination in October 1954, when Egypt turned against the Muslim Brothers. The Sudanese Brothers forsook union with Egypt and joined forces with the Anṣār-Ummah bloc, advocating the Sudan's independence.

After the 1958 military takeover led by General Ibrāhīm ʿAbbūd, the Muslim Brothers were at first allowed to continue their activities as a religious movement. On 9 November 1959 al-Ṭāhir attempted to overthrow the regime, aided by an illegal cell of Muslim Brothers, communists, and others within the army. The plotters were arrested, and the Muslim Brothers lost their cadres in the army as well as their freedom to act.

The next important stage in their history began in 1964 when Ḥasan al-Turābī and several leading brothers returned from their studies abroad. Turābī, who had joined the brothers while an undergraduate at Khartoum University College in 1954, emerged as their most effective university spokesman and started promoting a peaceful settlement in the south. Most of the mass gatherings in October 1964, which ultimately led to the civilian revolution and the downfall of ʿAbbūd, were led by the Muslim Brothers in the university.

In October 1964 the Muslim Brothers founded the Islamic Charter Front (ICF) with Turābī as secretary general. Concerned that they would remain a small elitist group lacking the broader support enjoyed by the communists, they decided that a front organization advocating an Islamic constitution was likely to gain support among Ṣūfīs and Anṣār. Moreover, Turābī was a pragmatist whose prime concern was political rather than ideological, so the purist tendencies of the older Muslim Brothers were overshadowed. The ICF provided an ideal platform for his dynamic leadership. In the years 1965–1968 the ICF cooperated with Ṣādiq al-Mahdī's wing of the Ummah party in its anticommunist drive and in promoting an Islamic constitution. The battle was waged first on university campuses, contesting student elections against the communists. Campus politics provided the launching pad for broader political action; the ICF—allied with the Anṣār, the Khatmīyah, and others—succeeded in having the Communist Party of the Sudan outlawed in 1965. The ICF also succeeded in formulating an Islamic constitution, in alliance with the Anṣār, but it was not implemented because of the May 1969 coup led by Jaʿfar al-Nimeiri (al-Numayrī) and his Communist allies.

Following the coup some of the brothers' leaders, including Turābī, were arrested. Others escaped to Aba Island, where some died in the uprising of the Anṣār in March 1970; a few made their way to Egypt or other countries. ʿUthmān Khālid represented the Muslim Brothers as secretary general of the National Front (NF) of Opposition Parties, founded in London in 1970 under the leadership of the DUP and Ummah parties. Turābī, who was not exiled, met President Nimeiri following the abortive procommunist coup of July 1971 and asked for permission to resume the brothers' activities. In 1972 their new campus organization, the Students Unity Front, gained control of the Khartoum University Students' Union.

Although the NF, including some of the brothers' leaders, continued to advocate armed struggle from exile, the majority of the brothers, led by Turābi, preferred pragmatism. He concentrated his efforts on restructuring the party in such a way that the old guard of brothers lost what influence they still had while his followers, who had joined in the 1960s, assumed the top positions. Turābī and the brothers who remained in Sudan were thus well prepared for Nimeiri's move toward an "Islamic path" in the mid-1970s. Lack of democracy did not trouble Turābī and his colleagues because they realized that they could not rely on the traditionalist parties, the Ummah and DUP, in their fight for an Islamic state. It seemed reasonable to cooperate with Nimeiri, who was seeking their support, influenced by President Anwar el-Sadat's accommodation with the Egyptian Brothers in the early 1970s.

The Sudanese Brothers decided to join forces with the regime following the failure of an anti-Nimeiri coup led by the Anṣār in July 1976. The appointment of Rāshid al-Ṭāhir, a former leader of the Muslim Brothers, as deputy president and prime minister in that year was also an indication of change. Al-Ṭāhir, though no longer a member, was popularly identified with the brothers. Once national reconciliation became official policy in July 1977, the brothers were well prepared and grasped whatever positions the government offered. Turābī himself was appointed attorney general in 1979, and many of his colleagues accepted positions in the judiciary, the educational and financial systems, and the Sudan Socialist Union (SSU). The brothers also managed to infiltrate the Anṣār-dominated western regions, helped by Muslim Brothers who had become teachers in Kordofan and Darfur.

A noteworthy outcome of the brothers' close collaboration with Nimeiri was their improved organization and finances, which partly explains their success in the 1986 elections. The National Islamic Front (NIF) was founded in April 1985 and came in a close third after the Ummah and the DUP. The NIF's financial supremacy can be attributed to the fact that beginning in the early 1970s it had taken control of the Islamic banking system, first through its connections in Saudi Arabia and later through collaboration with Nimeiri. The establishment of the Fayṣal Islamic bank in 1978 enabled the Muslim Brothers to infiltrate the new system as employees and investors and gain access to credit and to a share in profits. The bank also opened doors to economic and social advancement for the movement's young adherents and enabled the NIF to establish international financial contacts, primarily in the Arabian Peninsula. Following a June 1989 coup the NIF enhanced its domination of the banks, the building industry, transport, and the media. Since roughly 90 percent of the banks' income was invested in import-export ventures, the NIF has dominated that field at the expense of the Khatmīyah supporters who had controlled it in the past. The appointment of ʿAbd al-Raḥīm Ḥamīd, a prominent NIF member, as minister of finance and economy leaves little doubt as to the NIF's overwhelming dominance of the state's chief financial institutions.

Another factor in the NIF's success in the 1986 elections was its supremacy among the Graduates' constituencies. Sudanese university graduates living abroad were allowed, for the first time, to vote for any constituency they chose. The NIF exploited this departure by instructing its supporters to vote en bloc for candidates in marginal seats, capturing 23 out of 28 Graduates' seats. This victory, however, emphasized an inherent weakness of the NIF: its main support even at this stage was among university students and graduates. Since the June 1989 fundamentalist coup the NIF has further strengthened its hold over all institutes of learning. Ibrāhīm Aḥmad ʿUmar, an NIF member, became minister of higher education. He dismissed the university's president and deans and reorganized higher learning in the five public and private universities, doubling the number of students. This enabled NIF members, who were mostly graduates, to benefit from the increased employment opportunities, which included senior academic posts as well as diplomatic, economic, and political positions abroad.

The Muslim Brothers first attempted to infiltrate the Military College in 1955, helped by Abū al-Makārim ʿAbd al-Ḥayy, an Egyptian army officer who had commanded the Muslim Brothers' Special Apparatus. He had escaped to Sudan following the attempt on President Nasser's life in October 1954. The abortive coup of 9 November 1959, initiated by Rāshid al-Ṭāhir with the participation of both Muslim Brothers and other supporters within the army, was a clear indication of future intentions. The next stage started in the military camps in Ethiopia, Eritrea, and Libya in the early 1970s, where young Sudanese Muslim Brothers were trained by Egyptian officers, under the command of Ṣalāḥ Ḥasan, an Egyptian Muslim Brother. Following national reconciliation, in July 1977, many of them joined the Sudanese army. Its members were put in charge of courses in "Islamic ideology and instruction" for senior army officers, enabling them to infiltrate the officer corps. Four members of the military council that has ruled the Sudan since the June 1989 coup, including its leader ʿUmar Ḥasan al-Bashīr, attended these courses. Following Nimeiri's deposition the NIF further strengthened its support within the army by openly supporting the army's demands for better pay and equipment, while the Ummah and the DUP remained hesitant. The post-1989 regime is an indication that the NIF's infiltration of the army has paid the expected dividends.

The Muslim Brothers' policy on the "southern question" changed in the 1970s. Rejecting the liberal attitude of Turābī and his followers in 1964/1965, some now advocated partition, claiming that as long as the Sudan remained united an Islamic state would be impossible. The majority continued to insist on an Islamic state within a united Sudan, which would become the bastion of Islam in Africa. The NIF founded the African Islamic Center to undertake its missionary work among the non-Islamic majority in the south; in 1982 the Association of Southern Muslims was set up to establish Islamic schools and villages there, funded by Kuwait and the Gulf Emirates and stimulated by a mass influx of Muslim refugees from Uganda following Idi Amin's defeat in 1979. The close relations between the NIF and southern Muslims helped the party in the 1986 elections in the south and explain the importance of this issue in the NIF's election campaign.

In January 1987 the NIF published its National Charter, in which it elaborated on its special relation with the south and explained its program of islamizing it. Turābī proposed that the Muslim Brothers act as the Islamic vanguard in the south, with the traditionalists forced to follow suit. A major concession was the NIF's acceptance of the right of all citizens, regardless of religion, to hold any public office. The charter promised freedom of conscience and equality before the law, stating that in a federal state, non-Muslim regions would be allowed to opt out of the Islamic legal system based on the *sharīʿah*. However, the NIF consistently rejected any compromise entailing secularism, and the June 1989 coup can be partly attributed to the NIF's adamant opposition to accommodating the Sudan People's Liberation Movement.

The Sudanese Muslim Brothers remained independent of their Egyptian namesakes and offered a unique Sudanese version of the brothers' ideology. They compared their relationship to that between the Sudanese Ashiqqā' and the Egyptian Wafd; both propagated unity of the Nile Valley, but under separate identities. An additional reason for their insistence on their own identity was their fear that a united front with the Egyptian Brothers would alienate the anti-Egyptian Anṣār, their most cherished allies. The brothers' attempt to exploit front organizations that were less suspect to moderate Sudanese was regarded as a way to reach broader circles, especially among Khatmīyah supporters, and is reminiscent of communist practices. Similarly, the brothers tried to infiltrate other parties. Rāshid al-Ṭāhir attempted to become an Ummah candidate in the 1957 elections; Muddaththir ʿAbd al-Raḥīm and ʿUthmān Jaddallāh managed to join the editorial board of *Al-jihād*, the Khatmīyah newspaper. The rift between those declaring their affinity with the Egyptian Brothers and those opposing it was never really healed. Some of the older leaders, such as al-Ṣādiq ʿAbdallāh al-Mājid and Jaʿfar Shaykh Idrīs, continued to attack Turābī's strategy from their exile in the Gulf states throughout the Nimeiri years. They were closely associated with the Egyptian Muslim Brothers, and after Ḥasan al-Huḍaybī's release from prison, in 1973, they suggested joining the world organization of Muslim Brothers under his leadership. Politically they criticized Turābī's un-Islamic views with regard to the role of women in society and censured his intimacy with Nimeiri and his regime. Their proposals were defeated in the *shūrā* council; although ʿAbd al-Mājid was offered the deputy leadership upon his return to the Sudan in the late 1970s, he declined and formed an independent movement of Muslim Brothers that challenged the NIF unsuccessfully in the 1986 elections.

The Islamic constitution proposed by the Muslim Brothers in 1956 sought the establishment of an Islamic republic with a Muslim head of state and a parliamentary democracy based on Islamic law and legislating in accordance with the *sharīʿah*. Its Muslim citizens would be able to shape their lives in accordance with the dictates of their religion and to uproot social evils and corruption. Discrimination on the basis of race or religion would be forbidden, and non-Muslim citizens would enjoy all rights granted under Muslim law.

A more pragmatic approach developed following the October 1964 revolution and al-Turābī's rise to prominence. The newly formulated Islamic Charter proposed a presidential rather than a parliamentary system for the sake of greater stability and put greater emphasis on minority and regional rights. It undertook a complete revision of personal law in order to grant equal rights to women. The religion of the head of state was not mentioned in the Charter, a clear gesture to non-Muslims. The Charter proclaimed that even though all Muslims constituted one community, this Muslim state would encompass only Sudanese. Resident non-Muslims would be citizens with equal standing, guaranteed freedom of religion, decentralization, and public rights, namely, the right to determine their own way of life in the regions in which they constituted the majority, as well as the right to establish their own public institutions, be they traditional or modern.

Turābī advocated a gradual, nonviolent approach based on education and opposed the implementation of the *ḥudūd* (mandatory punishments) at this stage, claiming that they should be applied only in an ideal Muslim society. The NIF's later support of the *ḥudūd* imposed in September 1983 by Nimeiri was justified on the ground that the *ḥudūd* were part of an educational process whereby the state hoped to improve the morals of its citizens. The NIF continued to support the implementation of these laws after Nimeiri's removal and the military coup of June 1989. Al-Mikāshfī Ṭāhā al-Kabbāshī, a leading NIF jurist, was a member of the committee assigned to revise the laws in accordance with the *sharīʿah* and has headed the Supreme Court of Appeal in Khartoum since 1984. In a book on the implementation of the *sharīʿah* in the Sudan Kabbāshī justified the implementation of these Islamic laws, including the January 1985 execution of Maḥmūd Muḥammad Ṭāhā, leader of the Republican Brothers, for apostasy, in which he was personally involved as president of the Court of Appeal. For Kabbāshī and others in the NIF there was never any doubt as to the Sudan's Islamic identity, which implied the Jāhilī status of all non-Muslims. The Sudan's Islamic army would fight the enemies of Islam, "Communists, Crusaders, Zionists, Free Masons" or their Sudanese supporters, under the banner of Islam. However, regions in which non-Muslims were in the majority would be allowed to opt out of the Islamic legal system, provided the Sudan became a federation.

The brothers' attitude toward democracy, as formulated by Turābī, was based on both pragmatic and ideological considerations. Since the establishment of an Islamic state was the primary aim, the means of achieving it became secondary. Ideologically, there were several differences between Western democracy and Islamic *shūrā*. First, the West separates democracy from religion, which contradicts the *shūrā*. Second, the *shūrā* provides a system whereby the life of all believers is fully coordinated, whereas Western democracy is limited to politics. Third, *shūrā* grants democratic rights only insofar as these agree with the *sharīʿah,* whereas in Western democracy human rights are not limited by religious considerations. Fourth, Western democracy distinguishes between political passions and human morals; in Islam the two are inseparable. Finally, the *shūrā* provides greater guarantees for the unity of believers than does Western democracy. The *shūrā* accordingly can become a popular process based, unlike secular democracy, on the sovereignty of God and Islamic morality and free from secular distortions and manipulations. *Shūrā* can be applied by any group of people and is not limited by constitutional considerations. Military regimes can therefore apply the *shūrā* as well as elected parliaments as long as they fully implement the *sharīʿah.* [*See* Democracy.]

Renewal and revival *(tajdīd)* are among Turābī's most cherished ideas. He believed that Islam had to be rethought constantly and was open to radical change by the Muslim community—not necessarily by learned reformers. There were indeed eternal principles in Islam, but *fiqh,* the classical exposition of Islamic law, was a mere human endeavor which might be reevaluated in accordance with present requirements. For many generations *fuqahāʾ* (jurists) had neglected to rethink and redefine the role of the state and of the public in the formulation of Islamic law. Modern *fiqh* should concentrate on social rather than individual issues, since the former were hardly tackled in a largely individualistic society. The reopening of the doors of *ijtihād* was also advocated by the Muslim Brothers. With a few exceptions regarding the eternal components of divinity, everything was open to review and reinterpretation. The methodology suggested by Turābī was based on his formulation of *tawḥīd,* which involved a union of the eternal divine commands with the changing conditions of human life and a demand for harmony between reason and revelation. *Tawḥīd* should therefore lead to a single comprehensive methodology of reinterpretation, embracing all human knowledge—religious, natural, and social—absorbed through the filter of Islamic understanding.

[*See also* Anṣār; Khatmīyah; Revival and Renewal; Sudan; Ummah-Anṣār; *and the biography of Turābī.*]

BIBLIOGRAPHY

Aḥmad, Ḥasan Makki Muḥammad. *Ḥarakat al-Ikhwān al-Muslimīn fī al-Sūdān, 1944–1969.* Khartoum, 1982.

ʿAlī, Ḥaydar Ibrāhīm. *Azmat al-Islām al-siyāsī: Al-jabhah al-Islāmīyah al-qawmīyah fī al-Sūdān namūdhajan.* Rabat, 1991.

El-Effendi, Abdelwahab. *Turabi's Revolution: Islam and Power in Sudan.* London, 1991.

Kabbāshī, Al-Mukāshifī Ṭāhā al-. *Taṭbīq al-sharīʿah fī al-Sūdān bayna al-ḥaqīqah wa-al-ʿithārah.* Cairo, 1986.

Köndgen, Olaf. *Das Islamisierte Strafrecht des Sudan: Von seiner Einführung 1983 bis Juli 1992.* Hamburg, 1992.

Ṭaha, Ḥaydar. *Al-ikhwān wa-al-ʿaskar, Qiṣṣat al-jabhah al-Islāmīyah wa-al-sulṭah fī al-Sūdān.* Cairo, 1993.

Turābī, Ḥasan al-. "The Islamic State." In *Voices of Resurgent Islam,* edited by John L. Esposito, pp. 241–251. New York and Oxford, 1983.

Turābī, Ḥasan al-. "Al-shūrā wa-al-dīmūqraṭīyah: Ishkālāt al-muṣṭalaḥ wa-al-mafhūm." *Al-Mustaqbal al-ʿArabī* 8.75 (May 1985): 13–20.

Wolf, Susanne. "The Muslim Brotherhood in the Sudan." Master's thesis, University of Hamburg, 1990.

GABRIEL R. WARBURG

MUSLIM-CHRISTIAN DIALOGUE. Intentional, structured encounters between Muslims and Christians are generally termed "Muslim-Christian dialogue." Interfaith dialogue is a conversation in which two or more parties seek to express their views accurately and to listen respectfully to their counterparts. During the second half of the twentieth century, organized dialogue meetings have proliferated at the local, regional, and international levels. The meetings vary significantly in their organization, focus, and venue, as well as in the composition of participants.

Several motives have propelled the dialogue movement. These include desires to foster understanding, to stimulate communication, to correct stereotypes, to work on specific problems of mutual concern, to explore similarities and differences, and to facilitate means of witness and cooperation. The pragmatic need for better understanding and cooperation among adherents in the world's two largest communities of faith—Christianity and Islam—is particularly acute. Together Christians and Muslims comprise approximately half the world's population, so the way in which they relate is bound to have profound consequences for both communities and for the world.

The dynamics of interfaith encounter between Muslims and Hindus, Muslims and Jews, or Muslims and Christians are distinctly different. Their historic relationships as well as their major theological, social, and political concerns vary markedly. Contemporary initiatives in Muslim-Christian dialogue can be understood best when seen in the larger context, which can be established by a brief overview of dominant themes in Muslim-Christian encounter.

Historical Background. Muslim-Christian dialogical encounter dates to the rise of Islam in the seventh century. Rooted in the monotheistic tradition of the patriarch Abraham, Muslims and Christians share a common heritage. For more than fourteen centuries these communities of faith have been linked both by their theological understandings and by living in close proximity. The history of Muslim-Christian interaction includes periods of great tension, hostility, and open war as well as times of uneasy toleration, peaceful coexistence, and cooperation to achieve shared goals.

Islamic self-understanding incorporates an awareness of and direct link with the biblical tradition. Muḥammad, his companions, and subsequent generations of Muslims have been guided by the Qur'ān, which they have understood as a continuation and completion of God's revelations to humankind. The Qur'ān speaks of many prophets *(nabī;* pl., *anbiyā')* and messengers *(rasūl;* pl., *rusul)* who functioned as agents of God's revelation. Particular emphasis is laid on the revelations through Moses (the Torah) and Jesus (the Gospel) and their respective communities of faith or people of the book *(ahl al-kitāb).* [*See* People of the Book.]

The Qur'ān includes positive affirmations for the people of the book, including the promise that Jews and Christians who have faith, trust in God and the Last Day, and do what is righteous "shall have their reward" (2.62 and 5.69). The different religious communities are explained as a part of God's plan; if God had so willed, the Qur'ān asserts, humankind would be one community. Diversity among the communities provides a test for people of faith: "Compete with one another in good works. To God you shall all return and He will tell you (the truth) about that which you have been disputing" (5.48).

The Qur'ān makes clear that "there shall be no compulsion in religious matters" (2.256). Peaceful coexistence is affirmed (106.1–6). At the same time, the people of the book are urged to "come to a common word" on the understanding of the unity of God *(tawḥīd)* and proper worship (e.g., 3.64, 4.171, 5.82, and 29:46) Christians, in particular, are chided for having distorted the revelation of God. Traditional Christian doctrines of the divinity of Christ and the Trinity are depicted as compromising the unity and transcendence of God (e.g., 5.72-75, 5.117, and 112.3) There are also verses urging Muslims to fight those who have been given a book but "practice not the religion of truth" (9.29).

While the Qur'ān provides a framework for Muslims' understanding of Christians and Christianity, particular political, economic, and social considerations have shaped the encounter in each setting. Christians living under Islamic rule normally were treated as "protected peoples" *(dhimmī);* the practical implications of *dhimmī* status fluctuated from time to time and from place to place. Even in the best of circumstances, however, it was difficult for Christians and Muslims to engage one another as equals in dialogue. [*See* Dhimmī.]

With few exceptions, most Islamic literature focused on Christianity has been framed in the language of polemics. The writings of the celebrated fourteenth-century Muslim scholar Ibn Taymīyah (d. 1328) illustrate the point. In his book *Al-jawāb al-ṣaḥīḥ li-man baddala dīn al-Masīḥ* (The Correct Answer to Those Who Changed the Religion of Christ), Ibn Taymīyah catalogs the major theological and philosophical points of contention between Muslims and Christians: altering the divine revelation, propagating errant doctine, and grievous mistakes in religious practices.

The advent of Islam presented major challenges to Christians. In the short space of a century, Islam transformed the character and culture of many lands from northern India to Spain, disrupted the unity of the Mediterranean world, and displaced the axis of Christendom to the north. Islam challenged Christian assumptions. Not only were the Muslims successful in their military and political expansion, their religion presented a puzzling and threatening new intellectual position.

John of Damascus (d. c.750) provided the first coherent treatment of Islam. His encounter with Muslims in the Umayyad administrative and military center of Damascus led him to regard Islam not as an alien tradition but as a Christian heresy. Subsequent Christian writers, particularly those not living among Muslims, were even harsher. Most tended to focus on malicious and absurd distortions of the basic tenets of Islam and the character of Muḥammad. This trend is especially evident in Europe following the Crusades.

The Crusades, launched at the end of the eleventh century (1906), cast a long shadow for many centuries. In the midst of their stories of chivalry and fighting for holy causes, medieval writers painted a picture of Islam as a vile religion inspired by the Devil or Antichrist. The prevailing sentiment in Europe is illustrated in Dante's *Inferno,* where a mutilated Muḥammad is depicted languishing in the depths of Hell because he was "a fomenter of discord and schism."

There were a few more positive voices among medieval Christians. St. Francis of Assisi (d. 1226), who visited the sultan of Egypt in the midst of the Crusades, instructed his brothers to live among Muslims in peace, avoiding quarrels and disputes. Deep animosity toward Islam was pervasive, however. Martin Luther (d. 1546) wrote several treatises attacking Islam, the Qur'ān, and Muḥammad, motivated in part by the threat of Ottoman Turks advancing on Europe. Luther reflected the longstanding view that Islam as a post-Christian religion was false by definition.

Nineteenth and Twentieth Centuries. Several developments in the nineteenth and twentieth centuries set the stage for contemporary Muslim-Christian dialogue. First, constantly improving means of transportation and communication facilitated international commerce and unprecedented levels of migration. Second, the academic study of religion propelled scholars to gather a wealth of information on the world's various religious practices and belief systems. Although Western studies of Islam and other religious traditions in the East tended to be far from objective, significant changes have occurred. With more accurate information in hand, many non-Muslim scholars concluded that Muḥammad was sincere and devout, challenging the prevailing Western view of Muḥammad as a shrewd and sinister charlatan. Similarly, the scope and reliability of information on Christianity has broadened the horizons of many Muslim scholars during the past century. [*See* Islamic Studies, *article on* History of the Field; Orientalism.]

A third major factor contributing to the new context arose from the modern missionary movement among Western Christians. The experience of personal contact with Muslims (and other people of faith) led many missionaries to reassess their presuppositions. Participants in the three twentieth-century world missionary conferences (Edinburgh in 1910, Jerusalem in 1928, and Tambaram in 1938) wrestled with questions of witness and service in the midst of religious diversity. These conferences not only stimulated debate, they also paved the way for later ecumenical efforts at interfaith understanding under the auspices of the World Council of Churches or WCC, founded in 1948.

Dialogue Movement. The dialogue movement began during the 1950s when the WCC and the Vatican organized a number of meetings and consultations between Christian leaders and representatives of other religious traditions. These initial efforts resulted in the formation of new institutional structures. In 1964 Pope Paul VI established a Secretariat for Non-Christian Religions to study religious traditions, provide resources, and promote interreligious dialogue through education and by facilitating efforts by Catholics at the local level. In 1989 the Secretariat was reorganized and renamed the Pontifical Council for Interreligious Dialogue.

The WCC established its program subunit for Dialogue with People of Living Faiths and Ideologies (DFI) in 1971. As with the Vatican, Muslim-Christian relations were a primary focus from the outset. The DFI concentrated on organizing large international and smaller regional meetings, providing educational materials, working with the more than three hundred WCC member churches, and facilitating Christian theological reflection on religious pluralism. The WCC and the Vatican publish books, articles, reports, working papers, and reviews by both Christians and Muslims.

By the 1980s and 1990s, many other regional and international bodies had participated in or developed their own formal and informal programs for dialogue between Muslims and Christians. The Muslim World League, the World Muslim Congress, and the Middle East Council of Churches are among the organizations active in this process.

At the local level, hundreds of interfaith organizations have organized or taken part in Muslim-Christian dialogue programs. These programs are difficult to characterize because they vary substantially, even within a given setting. Detailed information and analyses of activities in specific countries and organizations is accessible through the periodical resources listed in the bibliography; the following examples illustrate the breadth of activity.

In India and the Philippines, Christian institutions study Islam, and Christians and Muslims have pursued dialogue programs for many years. Over the decades these academic programs have stimulated particular initiatives by churches and Muslim organizations.

The Muslim community in Great Britain numbers approximately two million. The large influx of Muslims since 1950 has led to the creation of numerous local and national Islamic organizations, many of which are engaged with their Christian counterparts in local churches or through programs of the British Council of Churches. Focal concerns range from local education and health care to Middle East peacemaking.

Diverse groups of Muslims and Christians have lived together in the area of Mt. Lebanon for more than a millennium. The unique history and political structures of Lebanon were central factors in the multisided civil war that plagued the country from 1975 to 1992. In the midst of the strife, religious and political leaders, scholars and neighbors continued to meet, exchange views, and even negotiate ceasefire agreements across confessional lines.

Muslim-Christian dialogue programs can be found throughout North America, in Nigeria, Indonesia, Tunisia, France, Tanzania, and elsewhere. While the nature of the encounter differs from place to place and over time, most organized efforts fall within the scope of one or more identifiable types of dialogue. Meeting together on equal footing in order to improve understanding is a worthwhile goal. As the interfaith dialogue movement developed, however, organizers and participants have developed several distinctive, yet interrelated modes.

"Parliamentary dialogue" is the term used for the large assemblies convened for interfaith discussion. The earliest example was the 1893 World's Parliament of Religions in Chicago. Such gatherings became more frequent in the 1980s and 1990s under the auspices of multifaith organizations such as the World Conference on Religion and Peace and the World Congress of Faiths. These sessions of several hundred participants tend to focus on better cooperation among religious groups and the challenges of peace for people of faith.

"Institutional dialogue" refers to the organized efforts to initiate and facilitate various kinds of dialogue meetings. In addition to the immediate focus, this approach also seeks to establish and nurture communication between institutional representatives of religious organizations. Institutional dialogue encompasses much of the work carried out through the Vatican and the WCC, with numerous variations at the local level.

"Theological dialogue" includes structured meetings in which theological and philosophical issues are the primary focus of discussion. Muslims and Christians, for example, may concentrate on their respective understandings of God, Jesus, the nature of revelation, human responsibility in society, and so forth. Theological dialogue can also refer to the wider discussion of the meaning of one's own religious tradition in the context of religious pluralism. Here, as with most other types of dialogue involving several participants, the dialogue occurs both within and between Muslims and Christians.

"Dialogue in community" and "the dialogue of life" are inclusive categories concentrating on practical issues of common concern—for example, the proper relationship between religion and the state, the rights of religious minorities, issues arising from interreligious marriage, appropriate approaches to mission and witness, or religious values and public education. Frequently this type of dialogue is designed to encourage common action. Another important function of dialogue focused on life in community is difficult to measure: organizers often express the hope that it will stimulate more intentional and informal interaction between Muslim and Christian neighbors in daily life.

"Spiritual dialogue" is concerned with developing, nourishing, and deepening spiritual life through interfaith encounter. Here too there is considerable latitude for exploration. The least threatening approach might include observing the worship of others or sharing perspectives on the meaning of fasting or prayer for Muslims and Christians. A more radical approach might include participation in joint worship experiences.

Obstacles. The organized dialogue movement represents a new chapter in the long history of relations between Muslims and Christians. Intentional efforts to understand and cooperate with one another are a hopeful sign, particularly for religious communities whose interaction frequently has been characterized by mistrust, misunderstanding, and mutual antipathy. Muslims and Christians who advocate and engage in dialogue still face many obstacles.

Many Muslims are wary of the entire enterprise owing both to the long history of enmity and the more recent experiences of colonialism. Contemporary political machinations involving the United States or other major Western powers also create problems for many would-be Muslim participants. Still other Muslims suspect that dialogue is a new guise for Christian missionary activity.

Although the primary impetus for organized dialogue originated largely with Christians and church-related bodies, many conceptual and theological obstacles remain. Some Christians argue that dialogue weakens or undermines Christian mission and witness. For many, the perception of Islam as inherently threatening is deeply ingrained; they are unwilling or unable to move beyond stereotypes or to distinguish between sympathetic and hostile counterparts in the other community.

The newness of dialogue and the absence of conceptual clarity has required a good deal of experimentation. Questions about planning, organization, representation, and topics require thoughtful consideration and careful collaboration. Through trial and error, advocates of interfaith dialogue in Asia, Africa, Europe, and North America have continued to refine the process. Many local, regional, and international dialogue groups have developed and published guidelines to address common concerns and avoid pitfalls.

[*See also* Christianity and Islam; Muslim-Jewish Dialogue.]

BIBLIOGRAPHY

Brown, Stuart E., comp. *Meeting in Faith: Twenty Years of Christian-Muslim Conversations Sponsored by the World Council of Churches.* Geneva, 1989.

Centre for the Study of Islam and Christian-Muslim Relations, Research Papers. Birmingham, ca. 1975–. Series sponsored by the Centre, and a primary source for contemporary research and reflection. Other Centre publications focus on Europe and Africa.

Cragg, Kenneth. *The Call of the Minaret* (1956). 2d rev. ed. New York, 1985. Pivotal book challenging Christians to take Islam seriously and on its own terms.

Current Dialogue. Geneva, 1980–. Publication by the World Council of Churches, featuring articles, reports, reviews, and bibliographies.

Encounter: Documents for Muslim-Christian Understanding. Rome, 1965–. Publication of the Pontifical Council for Interreligious Dialogue.

Ibn Taymīyah, Aḥmad. *A Muslim Theologian's Response to Christianity.* Edited and translated by Thomas Michel. New York, 1984.

Islamochristiana. Rome, 1975–. Scholarly annual journal produced by the Pontifico Instituto di Studi Arabi e d'Islamistica. Articles, notices, and reviews are in English, French , and Arabic.

Kimball, Charles A. *Striving Together: A Way Forward in Christian-Muslim Relations.* New York, 1991. Brief, accessible introduction to major obstacles and opportunities in dialogue.

The Muslim World. Hartford, Conn., 1911–. Indispensable quarterly journal devoted to the study of Islam and Christian-Muslim relations past and present.

Rousseau, Richard W. *Christianity and Islam: The Struggling Dialogue.* Scranton, Pa., 1985. Collection of twelve major articles and reports by Christian participants in dialogue.

Southern, Richard W. *Western Views of Islam in the Middle Ages.* Cambridge, Mass., 1962. Highly readable survey by a noted historian.

Watt, W. Montgomery. *Christian-Muslim Encounters.* London and New York, 1991. Contemporary reflections by a prominent scholar.

CHARLES A. KIMBALL

MUSLIM-JEWISH DIALOGUE. Relations between Jews and Muslims have been extensive and often cooperative throughout history, whereas Jewish-Muslim dialogue has not yet achieved a respected status. The creation of the state of Israel and the displacement of millions of Palestinians since 1948 have precluded the launching of a successful Jewish-Muslim dialogue.

Although the parameters of dialogue from an Islamic perspective as stipulated by the Qur'ān may seem ambiguous, they are the product of the context of revelation when the Muslim community was establishing itself. The pronouncements regarding Jews are framed in the Qur'ān in the context of the establishment of the Muslim community in Medina, where several Jewish tribes resided, and they furnish a sufficient basis of theological dialogue between Muslims and Jews. One can deduce theological commonalities between Jews and Muslims (and, of course, Christians) on the basis of the following key Qur'ānic terms: *ahl al-kitāb* (people of the book); *umm al-kitāb* (the mother of all books, *al-lawḥ al-maḥfūẓ* (the preserved tablet). From this perspective, the Qur'ān is just one link in a long chain of revelations given to earlier people, including but not confined to Jews and Christians. In certain surahs, the Qur'ān speaks of the Jews as a community of faith. Politically speaking, however, the Qur'ān documents an increasingly negative relationship between Jews and Muslims in Medina. Fazlur Rahman argues:

> Jews, like Christians, had been recognized as a community, possessing a revealed document and called "People of the Book". They were asked to live by the Torah. As such, they had religious and cultural autonomy. Yet, the Qur'ān continued to invite them to Islam. . . . Thus, at the reli-

gious level, the relationship is somewhat ambiguous, although there is no doubt that Jewish religious and cultural autonomy was respected. ("Islam's Attitude Toward Judaism," *The Muslim World* 72.1 [January 1982]: 5.)

The relationship between Jews and Muslims has evolved over time and taken different shapes. There is an almost unanimous Arab and Muslim opinion that Jews fared better under Islam than they did under Christian Europe. Jewish scholarly opinion is divided on the matter, but, on the whole, it indicates that Muslim-Jewish coexistence was possible in most instances. Bernard Lewis, for example, concludes in a recent article, "There is in medieval and even modern Christianity a vast literature of polemics, written by Christian theologians, to persuade Jews of the truth of the Christian dispensation. The theologians of Islam felt no such need. There are few Muslim polemics against Judaism, and most of them are efforts at self-justification by recent converts from that religion" ("Muslims, Christians, and Jews: The Dream of Coexistence," *The New York Review of Books* 39.6 [26 March 1992]: 48). A different view stipulates that Jewish-Muslim dialogue was impossible because of the "darker side of Jewish life under Islam, which redefined the erstwhile conception of Islamic 'toleration' as having been more problematic than could before have been imagined." (Ronald L. Nettler, *Past Trials and Present Tribulations: A Muslim Fundamentalist's View of the Jews,* New York, 1987, p. ix). According to this view, Muslims have developed a sophisticated and rich doctrine of hatred toward Jews since the foundation of the Islamic state during the Prophet's time in Medina in 622, and this "emotional hatred" is best represented by the ideology and activities of Islamic revivalists.

In the few Jewish-Muslim dialogue meetings taking place in Europe and the United States, one is struck by the similarities in themes often raised by Jewish and Muslim scholars and thinkers. These include the emergence of the modern West as a world power with the spread of colonialism and westernization; the emergence of Zionism as a national movement for the liberation of Jews in Europe; the Holocaust and its aftermath; the creation of the state of Israel; and the displacement of the Palestinian people.

Jewish scholars usually focus on the Holocaust as one of the major events still affecting Jewish relations, with other groups: "For contemporary Jews, the overwhelming experience of suffering is the Jewish Holocaust, the death of six million Jews and the attempted annihilation of our entire people. Interpretation of the event is omnipresent, though insights are diverse and often controversial" (Marc H. Ellis, *Toward a Jewish Theology of Liberation,* Maryknoll, 1988, p. 11).

Muslims and Jews maintain fundamental, and perhaps unbridgeable, differences over the meaning of Israel. To most Jewish theologians and thinkers, especially those affected by the Holocaust, the creation of Israel has been a divine sign that God is on the side of a victimized people. To the majority of Arab and Muslim thinkers, those same Jewish theologians are not sensitive to the plight of the displaced Palestinians, who are usually treated as the nonexistent other. The 1967 Israeli victory and the annexation of Jerusalem were seen by some Jewish theologians as a symbol of "the presence of God and the continuation of the [Jewish] people" (Marc H. Ellis, *Beyond Innocence and Redemption: Confronting the Holocaust and Israeli Power,* New York, 1990, p. 16), whereas it was seen by Arabs and Muslims as a great tragedy, and by some as God's testing of Muslim faith or punishment for veering away from the true faith.

Perhaps Ismāʿīl R. al-Fārūqī's ideas, as expounded in his *Islam and the Problem of Israel,* best summarize the modern Islamist position toward dialogue with Jews and Judaism. Al-Fārūqī contends that Islam and Judaism are theologically compatible in that they both affirm the divine principle of *dīn al-fiṭrah* or *religio naturalis* and are united by the principle of revelation and the same religious tradition of Noah, Abraham, Jacob, and Isaac. Islam, in the opinion of al-Fārūqī, not only recognized Judaism as a religion *de jure*—which no other religion or political system did before the Enlightenment—but it further demanded the observance of the Torah and gave rabbinic courts in Muslim lands the executive power to manage the internal religious and cultural affairs of the Jewish community there. Al-Fārūqī presents the following theses in summarizing of the positions of modern-day Islamists. First, the Jewish question, as it was termed in Europe before the Holocaust, is an exclusively European, Christian problem, and as such, it must be understood against the religious, social, and historical background of Medieval and modern Europe. Second, in the same vein, Zionism was created in Europe as the result of the unique circumstances the Jewish people there faced in the nineteenth and early twentieth centuries. Third, Israel is a unique and aggressive form of Western colonialism in Muslim lands. Finally, the danger posed by the existence of a settler-colonial state like Israel is enormous: far from endangering Palestinian society alone, Israel poses a real threat to the security and safety of Arabs and Muslims at large. Al-Fārūqī writes: "The problem of Israel confronting the Muslim world today has neither precedent nor parallel in Islamic history. The Muslim world has tended to regard it as another instance of modern colonialism, or at best, as a repetition of the Crusades. The difference is not that Israel is neither one of these; but that it is both and more, much more" (*Islam and the Problem of Israel*, London, 1990, p. 1).

Jewish-Muslim dialogue, as an academic discourse, has been confined in the main to a handful of scholars and thinkers from both sides. The stumbling block continues to be the clashing interpretations given to the meaning of the state of Israel and the Palestinian question. Another difficulty associated with Jewish-Muslim dialogue lies in the different nature of the two communities. Applied to the American scene, what that means is that for Jewish-Muslim dialogue to succeed, Muslim and Jewish institutions, and not merely a handful of individuals, should assume a leading role. Although "American Islam" is in the process of growth and expansion, it is doubtful that American Muslims, who are such a diverse and dynamic group, have caught up with the high level of economic progress and political organization American Jews have achieved over the past several decades. Therefore, at least theoretically speaking, there are many issues that need to be discussed by both sides in a spirit of critical dialogue.

[*See also* Judaism and Islam; Muslim-Christian Dialogue.]

BIBLIOGRAPHY

Abu Amr, Ziyad. *Islamic Fundamentalism in the West Bank and Gaza: Muslim Brotherhood and Islamic Jihad*. Bloomington, 1994.

Abu-Rabiʿ, Ibrahim M. "Israel and the Palestinians: Muslim and Jewish Perspectives." *Islamic Studies* 31.2 (Summer 1992): 235–245.

Arkoun, Mohammed. "New Perspectives for a Jewish-Christian-Muslim Dialogue." In *Muslims in Dialogue: The Evolution of a Dialogue*, edited by Leonard J. Swidler, pp. 345–352. Lewiston, N.Y., 1992.

Bretton-Granatoor, G. M., and A. L. Weiss. *Shalom/Salaam: A Resource of Jewish-Muslim Dialogue*. New York, 1993.

Ellis, Marc H. *Ending Auschwitz: The Future of Jewish and Christian Life*. Louisville, Ky., 1994.

Gordon, H. "The Lack of Jewish-Arab Dialogue in Israel and the Spirit of Judaism: A Testimony." In *Muslims in Dialogue: The Evolution of a Dialogue*, edited by Leonard J. Swidler, pp. 389–401. Lewiston, N.Y., 1992.

Haddad, Yvonne Yazbeck. "Islamists and the 'Problem of Israel': The 1967 Awakening." *Middle East Journal* 46.2 (Spring 1992): 266–285.

Haddad, Yvonne Yazbeck, and Adair T. Lummis. *Islamic Values in North America*. New York and Oxford, 1987.

Hertzberg, Arthur. *Jewish Polemics*. New York, 1992.

Kattānī, Idrīs al-. *Banū Isrā'īl fī ʿahd al-inḥiṭāṭ al-ʿArabī*. Rabat, 1992.

Rahman, Fazlur. *Major Themes of the Qur'ān*. Minneapolis, 1980.

IBRAHIM M. ABU-RABIʿ

MUSLIM LEAGUE. This organization is the successor in Pakistan of the All-India Muslim League, which spearheaded the movement for the creation of Pakistan. The latter, established in 1906 in Dhaka, articulated three objectives—the protection of Muslim political rights in India, the attainment of self-government appropriate to India, and cooperation with the All-India National Congress. In its first phase (1906–1930) Mohammad Ali Jinnah, the President of the League, emphasized the creation of a separate Muslim province in Sindh, political reforms in the North-West Frontier Province and Baluchistan, and representation for the Muslims in the Punjab and Bengal provinces in proportion to their populations, with 30 percent of the seats in the central legislature of India reserved for Muslims. However, he failed to convince the Congress that these demands were equitable.

By 1930 public opinion in the Muslim-majority provinces had changed to demand Muslim self-determination in India, rather than seeking autonomy within the Indian Federation. This transformation was reflected by Muhammad Iqbal's presidential address to the All-India Muslim League in Allahabad in 1930, when he articulated the Two Nation Theory. At the annual meeting of 1940, the League under Jinnah adopted the so-called Pakistan resolution. Seven years later, Pakistan became a reality.

The Muslim League ruled Pakistan intermittently from 1947 to 1958 and then again for short periods during the 1960s, 1980s, and 1990s, and gave birth to practically all contemporary political parties in Pakistan with the exception of the Jamāʿat-i Islāmī. Jinnah died in September 1948; immediately afterward the Muslim League and its provincial branches became involved in the struggle for power, financial corruption among their leaders, and conflict with the newly created central government. This political instability led to military takeovers of the government, in 1958 by Field Marshal

Ayub Khan (1958–1969) and in 1978 by General Zia ul-Haq (1978–1988).

Under Ayub Khan political parties were reorganized, while the Muslim League split into two factions; the Council Muslim League opposed the Ayub regime, while the Conventionist Muslim League (now called the Pakistan Muslim League) supported him. In the 1965 election, Ayub was declared president with 63.3 percent of the total vote. His opponent, Fatimah Jinnah, lost the election but had overwhelming support in East Pakistan, now the nation of Bangladesh.

After the secession of East Pakistan in 1971, Prime Minister Zulfiqar ʿAli Bhutto came to power with the support of the Pakistan Peoples Party, an offshoot of the All-Pakistan Muslim League. The Bhutto government lasted until 5 July 1977, when General Zia ul-Haq, chief of the army staff, staged a coup. Declaring martial law, Zia suspended the 1973 constitution and banned all political activity.

In February 1985, Zia appointed Muhammad Khan Junejo as prime minister; he resurrected the political parties banned by Zia and himself became president of the All-Pakistan Muslim League. In May 1988 Zia dismissed Junejo, accusing his government of corruption and mismanaging the national economy.

On 17 August 1988, General Zia died in the crash of a Pakistan Air Force craft in the Punjab. Immediately, Ghulam Ishaq Khan, chairman of the Senate, was sworn in as acting president, and he arranged elections in November 1988.

Ishaq Khan appointed leader of the Pakistan People's Party (PPP), Benazir Bhutto, prime minister in December 1988, and he himself was elected to a five-year term as president. In this election, the Islamic Democratic Alliance of nine parties, led by the Muslim League, won the majority of the legislative seats in the Punjab Legislative Assembly, bringing a leader of the Muslim League, Mian Mohammed Nawaz Sharif (chief minister of the Punjab, 1985–1988), into the leadership of the Muslim League.

In August 1990, President Ishaq Khan dismissed the National Assembly and the government of Prime Minister Benazir Bhutto and announced fresh elections. In the 1990 elections, the Islamic Democratic Alliance and the Muslim League captured the majority of seats in the Federal Legislature, and its leader Mian Mohammed Nawaz Sharif became the prime minister of Pakistan.

President Ishaq Khan dismissed the Nawaz Sharif government in 1993, accusing him of corruption and mismanagement, although this action was declared unconstitutional by the Supreme Court. Fresh elections were held, and the PPP won the majority in the Federal Legislature; its leader, Benazir Bhutto, became prime minister once again.

There seem to be no ideological differences between the policies of the PPP and the Muslim League. The personal charisma of the leaders maintains tenuous cohesion within the ranks of these parties. The struggle between the PPP and the Muslim League indicates that if martial law is not declared again, Pakistan may yet evolve a two-party system.

[*See also* All-India Muslim League; Pakistan; *and the biography of Jinnah.*]

BIBLIOGRAPHY

Gopal, Ram. *Indian Muslims: A Political History*. Bombay, 1959.

Ikram, S. Mohamad. *Makers of Pakistan and Modern India*. Lahore, 1950.

Malik, Hafeez. *Muslim Nationalism in India and Pakistan*. Washington, D.C., 1963.

Noman, Mohammed, ed. *Our Struggle, 1857–1947: A Pictorial Record*. Karachi, n.d.

Qureshi, Ishtiaq Husain. *The Muslim Community of the Indo-Pakistan Sub-Continent*. The Hague, 1962.

Rajput, A. B. *Muslim League Yesterday and Today*. Lahore, 1948.

Saiyid, Matlubul Hasan. *Mohammad Ali Jinnah: A Political Study*. Lahore, 1953.

Wolpert, Stanley. *Jinnah of Pakistan*. Oxford and New York, 1984.

HAFEEZ MALIK

MUSLIM WORLD LEAGUE. Founded in AH 1381/1962 CE at the height of the Egyptian-Saudi political crisis, the Muslim World League (Rābiṭat al-ʿĀlam al-Islāmī) was the product of a meeting of 111 Muslim scholars, intellectuals, and politicians held in Mecca on the occasion of that year's pilgrimage. They convened to discuss the affairs of the Islamic *ummah* in view of the threats posed to it by "communism" in general and the "irreligious" Egyptian president Gamal Abdel Nasser in particular. On 18 May 1962 they inaugurated the Muslim World League as a new transnational Islamic organization, describing it as a "Muslim cultural organization" and an "Islamic peoples' organization," "serving the whole *ummah* and not acting as an agent of any government."

With its head office in Mecca, the League was at first represented by a constituent council (*al-majlis al-taʾsīsī*) only. The conference at Mecca chose twenty-one scholars, intellectuals, and notables as members of the council, which met for the first time in December 1962. The number rose to some sixty members in the early 1990s. From the start, the composition of the council demonstrated that the League was trying to bring together four mainstreams of contemporary Islamic ideology and theology: the council was headed by the grand *muftī* of Saudi Arabia, Muḥammad ibn Ibrāhīm Āl al-Shaykh (d. 1969), ensuring a minimum of Wahhābī control; eight scholars, among others Abūlḥasan ʿAlī al-Nadvī from Lucknow in India represented the classical Salafīyah; Saʿīd Ramaḍān (Egypt), Abū al-Aʿlā Mawdūdī (Pakistan), and ʿAllāl al-Fāsī (Morocco) were among the partisans of the divergent currents of the neo-Salafīyah; and finally, the first secretary-general, the Meccan merchant Muḥammad Surūr al-Ṣabbān (1898/99–1972) spoke in the name of the Ḥijāzī neo-Wahhābīyah. Nearly half of the members of the council had already been in contact with the General Islamic Conference founded in Jerusalem in 1953 (a reservoir of Muslim Brotherhood tendencies). This general proportional representation has been maintained since the League's founding. Correspondingly, the Wahhābī scholar ʿAbd al-ʿAzīz ibn ʿAbdallāh Ibn Bāz took over the presidency of the constituent council after the grand *muftī*'s death, and Ḥijāzian intellectuals have been in control of the administration of the League.

The Muslim World League, on the one hand, has acted as a mouthpiece of the Saudi Arabian Government, which has financed the organization since its inception. On the other hand, the different currents represented by the League have been able to develop an identity of their own so that the activities of the League have sometimes been directed against Saudi interests.

Nevertheless, according to statute, the League's secretariat is headed by a Saudi Arabian citizen (Muḥammad Surūr al-Ṣabbān, 1962–1972; Muḥammad Ṣāliḥ al-Qazzāz, 1972–1976; Muḥammad ʿAlī al-Ḥarkān, 1976–1983; and ʿAbd Allāh ʿUmar Nāṣīf [Abdullah Omar Nasseef], since 1983). During the early phase of its history, the Muslim World League succeeded in subjecting to its control other competing transnational organizations, such as the General Islamic Conference of Jerusalem, the Islamic World Congress (Karachi), and the International Islamic Organization (Jakarta). In its covenant of December 1962, the League stated its intention to promote the message of Islam, to fight conspiracies against Islam, and to discuss all problems relevant to Islam. In addition, in article four of the covenant and in accordance with the politics of Islamic solidarity heralded by King Fayṣal, the League promised to work for the cooperation of all Islamic states and argued in favor of an Islamic bloc taking a stand against pro-Nasserist and Baʿthist regimes.

After the end of the Arab cold war—a term coined by Malcolm Kerr to characterize the political split between Egypt and Saudi Arabia from 1957 to 1967—the Muslim World League gradually changed its objectives. Following the foundation of the Organization of the Islamic Conference in 1968–1972, the League stressed its supranational, independent identity and concentrated on establishing a network of Islamic cultural and political organizations.

The League upgraded the role of the constituent council and abolished the so-called General Islamic Conference (which met in 1962, 1965, and, exceptionally, in 1987). It founded twenty-two branch offices and bureaus in countries where Muslims constitute a minority (primarily in Africa) and affiliated itself with local Islamic organizations and agencies.

During the 1970s, the League gradually expanded its activities in the fields of coordination *(tansīq), daʿwah,* jurisprudence, and social welfare. In 1974, it invited 140 delegations to a conference of Islamic organizations and decided to establish continental councils (in 1985, five), local Islamic councils in twenty-eight Muslim minority communities, and a coordination committee. One year later, in 1975, the League set up a World Council of Mosques, which specialized in the coordination of *daʿwah* activities; it controls several regional and numerous local mosque councils. Since the League's beginnings, the faction of Wahhābī scholars has argued for the establishment of a jurisprudence council entrusted with the elaboration and control of internationally accepted standards of Islamic law. Internal disputes postponed this project; in 1976, however, the League opened the Islamic Fiqh Academy with which other academies in Europe and in other parts of the world were associated. The decisions taken at the annual meetings of the *fiqh* council have acquired some authority. Finally, the International Islamic Relief Organization was made responsible for the League's activities in the field of social welfare. Together with several Islamic universities in Saudi Arabia, Egypt, and the Gulf states, the League's training center for *dāʿīs* (missionaries) supervizes the education of official or semiofficial *daʿwah* workers. From 1973 to 1990, the number of *daʿwah* workers increased from 49 to 816.

The League has gradually developed a publication program: in 1963, the headquarters began to publish the monthly journal *Majallat Rābiṭat al-ʿĀlam al-Islāmī*, called *Al-rābiṭah* since 1987. After several disappointing attempts, the League in 1973 succeeded in editing an English-language journal called *Journal of the Muslim World League;* in addition, the press office has published a weekly called *Akhbār al-ʿĀlam al-Islāmī* (after 1991, named *Al-ʿĀlam al-Islāmī*). After the death of the secretary-general in 1976, the former Saudi Arabian minister of justice and new secretary-general al-Ḥarkān, who had stressed the League's activities in the field of jurisprudence, and his successor in office, Nāṣīf, himself an academic (rector of King ʿAbdalʿazīz University in Jeddah in 1981), both emphasized the importance of media and of education.

[*See also* Daʿwah, *articles on* Institutionalization *and* Modern Usage; Organization of the Islamic Conference; Saudi Arabia.]

BIBLIOGRAPHY

Landau, Jacob. *The Politics of Pan-Islam: Ideology and Organization.* Oxford, 1990.

Schulze, Reinhard. *Islamischer Internationalismus im 20. Jahrhundert: Untersuchungen zur Geschichte der Islamischen Weltliga.* Leiden, 1990.

Sharipova, Raisa M. *Panislamiza Segodnia: Ideologia i praktika Ligi Islamskogo Mira.* Moscow, 1986.

REINHARD SCHULZE

MUSTAḌʿAFŪN. Revolutions tend to popularize egalitarian, romantic, and utopian ideas that often mesmerize the masses. In revolutionary Iran, Ayatollah Ruhollah al-Musavi Khomeini (d. 1989) popularized the concept of the *mustaḍʿafūn*, which literally refers to the lower classes, the downtrodden, the meek, and to all those who are deprived of the opportunity to develop their full potential.

Khomeini's sympathy with the plight of the *mustaḍʿafūn* was rooted in both political and religious grounds. Politically, it enlarged significantly his popular base of support. Although in his writings prior to the Islamic Revolution he had championed the cause of the poor, it was only after the collapse of the *ancien régime* in 1979 that he explicitly spoke of the two diametrically opposed versions of Islam; the Islam of the *mustakbarūn* (the rich and the arrogant) and the Islam of the *mustaḍʿafūn*. His mission was to institutionalize the latter, which he labeled as the authentic Islam. He consistently maintained that the Islamic Revolution was made by the *mustaḍʿafūn* and must serve their interests.

Immediately after the collapse of the Pahlavi regime in 1979, a fierce competition began among many rivals for the control of the state. Khomeini's historic victory in that struggle became possible partly because he won the allegiance of the lower classes, or what he called the "barefooted," which constituted the largest block of the urban population. He declared that the most important characteristic of the Islamic Revolution was "that it is Islamic and its slogans and goals are compatible with the [needs] of the *mustaḍʿafūn*." In the early days of the revolution in 1979, he publicly pressured Mehdi Bāzargān's Provisional Revolutionary Government to provide free electricity, water, and housing for the poor. The goal should be, he emphatically declared, "to create a system in which there are no hungry people." In that spirit and in a symbolic gesture, Khomeini renamed the Pahlavi Foundation, a conglomeration of dozens of industrial and commercial enterprises, the Mustaḍʿafūn Foundation. Sayyid Hādī Khusrawshāhī, appointed by Khomeini to direct the foundation, was quick to promise that in "three years all the poor will be provided with free housing, or you can kill us." Of course, not all the poor were given free housing.

Khomeini effectively used the Qur'ān, Islamic history, and the chiliastic and apocalyptic overtones of Shiism to justify his sympathy for the *mustaḍʿafūn*. He often cited the Qur'ānic verse, "And we wish to show favor to those who have been oppressed upon earth [*mustaḍʿafūn*], and to make of them leaders and inheritors" (surah 28.5), which is also used in the Constitution of the Islamic Republic of Iran to justify the state's commitment to support "all oppressed and deprived people throughout the world" (Article 3, Section P).

In his writings and sermons, Khomeini pointed out that the poor were the prophet Muḥammad's most dedicated supporters. The Prophet was forced out of Mecca, he said, by the rich and returned there with the backing of the poor. Imam ʿAlī ibn Abī Ṭālib (r. 656–661) followed the Prophet's tradition of befriending the poor. Khomeini often cited Imam ʿAlī as saying that, as a caliph, he could not sleep comfortably if he knew there was someone poor or deprived under his rule.

Khomeini's support for the *mustaḍʿafūn* paid off, because they were his largest and most loyal followers. In the age of mass politics, this critical support helped Ayatollah Khomeini consolidate his rule and leave a legacy as the champion of the *mustaḍʿafūn*.

[*See also* Bunyād.]

BIBLIOGRAPHY

Khomeini, Ruhollah al-Musavi. *Kalām-i Imām: Mustaẓʿafūn va Mustakbarūn*. Tehran, 1984. *Kalām-i Imām: Inqilāb-i Islāmī*. Tehran, 1984. These two volumes contain Ayatollah Khomeini's declarations on the Islamic revolution and the *mustaḍʿafūn*.

Milani, Mohsen M. *The Making of Iran's Islamic Revolution*. 2d ed. Boulder, 1994. Discusses the context in which Khomeini popularized the notion of *mustaḍʿafūn*.

MOHSEN M. MILANI

MUṢṬAFĀ, SHUKRĪ (1942–1978), Egyptian Islamist militant who worked for the moral reformation of society. The Islamist movement in Egypt is characterized by internal divisions. The Muslim Brotherhood represents the more accommodationist groups who work to reform the system by working within it. Al-Jihād is the most famous of the antiregime elements while al-Takfīr wa al-Hijrah epitomizes the antisociety Muslim groups. The last was founded in the early 1970s by Shukrī Muṣṭafā, who defected from the Muslim Brotherhood in protest over that group's willingness to work with the secular regime. Muṣṭafā and his group sought, instead, to focus on the reform of society first before attempting to revolutionize the state system. Society was seen by Muṣṭafā as corrupt, decadent, and sinful and thus in need of a moral reformation.

Al-Takfīr wa al-Hijrah is not the real name of the organization, formally the Society of Muslims. This informal title was given to it by the state and the Egyptian press. It suggests the group's tactics. *Takfīr* means, in essence, to excommunicate the infidels from society. *Hijrah* means "flight" and evokes the prophet Muḥammad's flight from Mecca to Medina to abandon the immoral society in order to establish the new, faithful order. Here, it refers to the way in which this contemporary group separated itself from Egyptian society and formed a communal living arrangement, living in caves in Upper Egypt and cramped flats in Cairo.

Shukrī Muṣṭafā was born in 1942 in Asyut Province in Upper Egypt. He attended Asyut University's Faculty of Agriculture and in 1965 was arrested for distributing Muslim Brotherhood leaflets on campus. First incarcerated in Tura prison, he was transferred to Abū Za'bal concentration camp in 1967. He was released from prison in 1971 as part of President Anwar el-Sadat's general amnesty of many Islamists in Sadat's quest to garner their support against his leftist opponents.

Muṣṭafā returned to Asyut University to complete his studies. He also began to build his Society of Muslims by preaching throughout the province. Impressed by Sayyid Quṭb's *Signposts on the Road*, which declared the whole of Egyptian society as Jāhilīyah (a state of infidelity, decadence, and ignorance as in pre-Islamic Arabia), Muṣṭafā built his Society of Muslims by preaching that Egyptian society must be declared to be unfaithful to God and Muḥammad's teachings. This Society of Muslims (i.e., true believers) must then withdraw, take flight, and separate itself from society as a whole. Muṣṭafā attracted a following that eventually totaled a few thousand highly committed members.

Ostensibly, the group sought no confrontation with the state until it had won over and transformed society into a truly pious Islamic community. Then it would seek the immediate destruction of the secular system to establish the Islamic state reflective of the new Islamic society. But in transforming society and in attempting to prevent defections from its ranks, Muṣṭafā used violence, and this brought him into conflict with the state. Muṣṭafā felt that quitting his group was equivalent to quitting Islam, an apostasy punishable by death. In 1976, he led a raid against dissidents who had quit his group to join rival Islamists. Egyptian police caught many of his loyalists, but Muṣṭafā escaped. In July 1977, his group kidnapped Muḥammad al-Dhahabī, a former minister of *awqāf* (religious endowments; sg., *waqf*), in order to exchange him for their captured brethren. With Sadat on a visit to Morocco, the political leaders left in charge failed to respond to the demands of Muṣṭafā. Hearing no response, Muṣṭafā had the ex-minister killed. The government now responded. A manhunt for Muṣṭafā and other leaders of the group resulted in scores dead and wounded and hundreds arrested and tried. Muṣṭafā and four other leaders of al-Takfīr were sentenced to death. Others were imprisoned for five to twenty-five years. Shukrī Muṣṭafā was executed in 1978 at the age of thirty-seven.

Although the group apparently collapsed with the death of its leaders, many of the members of al-Takfīr simply joined other antisociety and antiregime groups, including al-Jihād, which became very active after 1977.

[*See also* Takfīr wa al-Hijrah, Jamāʿat al-.]

BIBLIOGRAPHY

Ansari, Hamied. "The Islamic Militants in Egyptian Politics." *International Journal of Middle East Studies* 16.1 (March 1984): 123–144.

Ayubi, Nazih N. *Political Islam: Religion and Politics in the Arab World*. London and New York, 1991.

Esposito, John L. *Islam and Politics*. Syracuse, N.Y., 1984.

Guenena, Nemat. *The Jihad: An "Islamic Alternative" in Egypt.* Cairo, 1986.

Ibrahim, Saad Eddin. "Anatomy of Egypt's Militant Islamic Groups." *International Journal of Middle East Studies* 12 (December 1980): 423–453.

Ibrahim, Saad Eddin. "Egypt's Islamic Activism in the 1980s." *Third World Quarterly* 10.2 (April 1988): 632–657.

Kepel, Gilles. *Muslim Extremism in Egypt: The Prophet and Pharaoh.* Berkeley, 1985.

Stowasser, Barbara, ed. *The Islamic Impulse.* Washington, D.C., 1987.

Voll, John Obert. "Fundamentalism in the Sunni Arab World: Egypt and the Sudan." In *Fundamentalisms Observed,* edited by Martin E. Marty and R. Scott Appleby, pp. 345–402. Chicago, 1991.

DENIS J. SULLIVAN

MUTʿAH. A pre-Islamic tradition, *mutʿah* ("temporary marriage") still has legal sanction among the Twelver Shīʿīs, residing predominantly in Iran. It is often a private and verbal contract between a man and an unmarried woman (virgin, divorced, or widowed). The length of the marriage contract *(ajal)* and the amount of consideration *(ajr)* given to the temporary wife must be specified; temporary marriage may be contracted for one hour or ninety-nine years. The objective of *mutʿah* is sexual enjoyment *(istimtāʿ),* that of permanent marriage *(nikāḥ)* is procreation *(tawlīd-i nasl)* (Ṭūsī, 1964, pp. 497–502; Ḥillī, 1968, pp. 515–528; Khomeini, 1985, p. 116; Muṭahharī, 1974, p. 38).

Presently, *mutʿah* is a marginal urban phenomenon, popular primarily around pilgrimage centers in Iran. This pattern, however, is changing owing to the Islamic regime's support of and advocacy for the institution. A temporary marriage need not be registered or witnessed, although taking witnesses is recommended (Ṭūsī, 1964, p. 498). In addition to the four wives legally allowed all Muslim men, a Shīʿī Muslim man is permitted to contract simultaneously as many temporary marriages as he desires, a practice disputed by Ayatollahs Ruhollah Khomeini (1982, p. 39) and Murtaẓā Muṭahharī (1974, p. 50). A Shīʿī Muslim woman is permitted only one temporary marriage at a time. No divorce procedure exists in a temporary marriage, for the lapse of time specified in the contract automatically dissolves the temporary union. After the dissolution of each temporary union, no matter how short, the wife must undergo a period of sexual abstinence *(ʿiddah);* in case of pregnancy, *ʿiddah* serves to identify a child's legitimate father. Herein lies the legal uniqueness of temporary marriage, distinguishing it, in Shīʿī law, from prostitution, despite their striking resemblance.

The reciprocal obligations of temporary spouses are minimal. The man is not obliged to provide the daily maintenance *(nafāqih)* for his temporary wife, as he must in a permanent marriage. Correspondingly, the wife is under minimal legal obligation to obey her husband, except in sexual matters (Haeri, 1989, p. 60).

Mutʿah of women was banned in the seventh century by the second caliph, ʿUmar, who equated it with fornication *(zinā).* For the Sunnī Muslims, therefore, temporary marriage is legally forbidden, although in practice some have resorted to it occasionally (Benson, 1992, pp. 5–8).

The Shīʿīs have maintained all along the legitimacy of temporary marriage based on the Qur'ān (4.24) and on the absence of specific prohibition by the Prophet Muḥammad, not withstanding some Sunnī *ḥadīth*s to the contrary. The legitimacy of temporary marriage has continued to be a point of chronic disagreement, passionate dispute, and, at times, animosity between Sunnīs and Shīʿīs (for a contemporary exposition of this ongoing dispute, see Kāshif al-Ghiṭāʿ, 1964; Shāfa'ī, 1973: Murata, trans., 1987, pp. 51–73).

During the Pahlavi regime (1925–1979) the custom of temporary marriage, though not illegal, was perceived negatively. The Islamic regime (since 1979), on the contrary, has made a concerted effort to resuscitate the custom publicly. Following the ideological legacy of Ayatollah Muṭahharī (d. 1979), many of the Islamic regime's thinkers and theologian/bureaucrats, most notably President Hashemi Rafsanjani (Hāshimī Rafsanjānī), have lauded the institution of temporary marriage as a desirable approach to relationships between men and women in a modern Islamic society (Ṭabāṭabā'ī, 1977, 1985; Bahunar, 1981). They specifically see temporary marriage as an ethically and morally superior alternative to the "free" relations between the sexes prevalant in the West.

Despite the religious and legal rehabilitation of *mutʿah,* most urban, educated middle-class Iranians view it with some moral and emotional ambivalence. *Mutʿah* marriage has never won the unequivocal approval of permanent marriage among the Iranians (Haeri, *Law of Desire,* 1989).

[*See also* Inheritance; Iran; Marriage and Divorce, *article on* Modern Practice; Women and Social Reform, *article on* Social Reform in the Middle East.]

BIBLIOGRAPHY

Bahunar, Muḥammad Ja'far, et al. *Taᶜlīmāt-i dīnī* (Religious Education). Tehran, 1981. A high school textbook, published after the revolution, in which the benefits of temporary marriage for youth was first discussed.

Benson, Linda. "Islamic Marriage and Divorce in Xinjiang: The Case of Kashgar and Khotan." *Association for the Advancement of Central Asian Research* 5.2 (Fall 1992): 5–8. On the legitimacy of temporary marriage among Chinese Sunnīs.

Gourji, Abu'l-Qasim. *Temporary Marriage (Mutᶜa) in Islamic Law.* Translated by Sachiko Murata, N.p., 1987. Very competent summary of the major Shīᶜī sources of jurisprudence on *mutᶜah.*

Haeri, Shahla. *Law of Desire: Temporary Marriage in Shīᶜi Iran.* Syracuse, N.Y., 1989. First major ethnography on the institution of temporary marriage.

Ḥillī, Najm al-Dīn Abū al-Qāsim Ja'far. *Sahrayᶜ al-islām* (Islamic Law), vol. 2. Translated from Arabic to Persian by A. Aḥmad Yazdī and M. T. Dānishpazhūh. Tehran, 1968. Excellent compendium on Shīᶜī marriage and divorce by the thirteenth-century Shīᶜī scholar.

Kāshif al-Ghiṭāᶜ, Muḥammad Ḥusayn. *Ā'īn-i mā* (Our Custom). Translated by Nasir Makarim Shirazi. Qom, 1968. Contains a major chapter on temporary marriage, refuting some of the Sunnī allegations.

Khomeini, Ruhollah. "Non-Permanent Marriage." *Mahjuba* 2.5 (1982): 38–40. English translation of his position on temporary marriage.

Khomeini, Ruhollah. *The Practical Laws of Islam.* 2d ed. N.p., 1985. Abridged version of his *Tawẓīḥ al-masā'il* (Clarification of Questions).

Muṭahharī. Murtaẓā. *Niẓām-i ḥuqūq-i zan dar islām* (Legal Rights of Women in Islam). 8th ed. Qom, 1974. One of the more comprehensive writings on the rights of women in (Shīᶜī) Islam.

Shāfa'ī, Muḥsin. *Mutᶜah va aṣar-i ḥuqūqī va ijtimāᶜī-i an* (*Mutᶜah* and its Legal and Social Effects). 6th ed. Tehran, 1973. Extensive, if apologetic, treatment of *mutᶜah.*

Ṭabāṭabā'ī, Muḥammad Ḥusayn. *Shīᶜite Islam.* Translated by Seyyed Hossein Nasr. Albany, N.Y., 1977. Major contribution to understanding Shīᶜī theology and philosophy.

Ṭabāṭabā'ī, Muḥammad Ḥusayn, et al. *Izdivāj-i muvaqqat dar islām* (Temporary Marriage in Islam). Qom, 1985. Edited volume on temporary marriage; includes an article by Rafsanjani.

Ṭūsī, Abū Ja'far Muḥammad. *Al-nihāyah.* Translated from Arabic to Persian by M. T. Dānishpazhūh. Tehran, 1964. One of the four major sources of Shīᶜī jurisprudence, compiled in the tenth century.

SHAHLA HAERI

MUṬAHHARĪ, MURTAẔĀ (1920–1979), Iranian religious scholar and writer, one of the closest associates of Ayatollah Ruhollah Khomeini. Born in a village in northeastern Iran to a scholar who was also his first teacher, Muṭahharī began his formal schooling at the age of twelve in the great shrine city of Mashhad, where he discovered the great love for philosophy, mysticism, and theology that was to remain constant throughout his life. The core of the religious curriculum, however, consisted of *fiqh* (jurisprudence). To study this subject under the principal authorities of the day, Muṭahharī moved to Qom in 1937. In Qom he made the acquaintance of Khomeini, renowned at the time mainly for his mystically tinged lectures on ethics. Significant, too, were the links Muṭahharī developed with ᶜAllāmah Muḥammad Ḥusayn Ṭabāṭabā'ī (d. 1981), the well-known exegete and philosopher. In 1952 Muṭahharī left Qom for Tehran, where he began teaching at the Madrasah-yi Marvī and, two years later, at the Faculty of Theology at Tehran University. The scope of his activity expanded still further when he began collaborating with Islamic organizations founded by religiously inclined laymen, the most important of these being the Ḥusaynīyah-yi Irshad, founded in 1965. Many of the lectures he gave under the auspices of these organizations were later published in book form.

Muṭahharī was imprisoned for forty-three days in the aftermath of the uprising led by Khomeini in June 1963. After his release, he participated actively in organizations that sought to maintain the momentum the uprising had created, most significantly the Jamīᶜah-yi Rūḥānīyat-i Mubāriz (Society of Militant Clergy). He remained in touch with Khomeini during the ayatollah's fourteen-year exile, visiting him repeatedly in Najaf and, during the revolution of 1978–1979, at Neauphle-le-Château near Paris. A sign of the trust in which Khomeini held Muṭahharī was his appointment to the Shūrā-yi Inqilāb-i Islāmī (Council of the Islamic Revolution), which functioned as interim legislature after the victory of the revolution in February 1979. A few months later, on 1 May 1979, Muṭahharī was assassinated in Tehran by adherents of Furqān, a group preaching a radically modernistic and anticlerical reinterpretation of Shīᶜī doctrine, which regarded Muṭahharī as its most formidable intellectual opponent. Muṭahharī was eulogized as "a part of my flesh" by an atypically weeping Khomeini and buried in Qom.

Although the Iranian Revolution gave Muṭahharī visibility as a political figure, it is his writings, vigorously promoted by the revolutionary authorities, that constitute his chief legacy. The most substantial of his works is, perhaps, his philosophical critique of materialism, *Uṣūl-i falsafah va ravish-i rī'alism* (The Principles of Philosophy and the Method of Realism, 4 vols., Qom, 1953–1971), based largely on discussions held in the circle of ʿAllāmah Ṭabāṭabāʾi. A more polemical approach to the same subject, paying particular attention to the cultural disorientation of Iranian society, was *ʿIlal-i girāyish bā māddīgari* (Reasons for the Turn toward Materialism, Qom, 1971). Other works were also conceived in a spirit of addressing urgent contemporary concerns, most notably *Niẓām-i ḥuqūq-i zan dar Islām* (The System of Women's Rights in Islam, Qom, 1966). Taken as a whole, the works of Muṭahharī demonstrate how leading figures among the Iranian *ʿulamāʾ* concerned themselves, against a background of traditional learning, with the problems of the modern age, and thereby contributed to creating the intellectual climate of the Iranian Revolution of 1979.

[*See also* Qom; Shīʿī Islam, *article on* Modern Shīʿī Thought; *and the biographies of Khomeini and Ṭabāṭabāʾi.*]

BIBLIOGRAPHY

Hoda, M. *In Memory of Martyr Mutahhari.* Tehran, 1982.

Khurāsānī, Muḥammad Vāʾiẓzādah. "Sayrī dar zindagī-yi ʿilmī va inqilābī-yi ustād-i Shahīd Murtaẓā Muṭahharī." In *Yādnāmah-yi ustād-i Shahīd Murtaẓā Muṭahharī,* edited by ʿAbd al-Karim Surūsh, pp. 319–380. Tehran, 1981.

Muṭahharī, Mujtabā. "Zindagī-yi pidaram." *Ḥarakat* (Tehran) 1 (n.d.): 5–16.

Muṭahharī, Murtaẓā. *Fundamentals of Islamic Thought: God, Man, and the Universe.* Translated by R. Campbell. Berkeley, 1985.

HAMID ALGAR

MYANMAR. At the time of the most recent published census (1983), the Muslim population of Myanmar (formerly Burma) accounted for only 3.9 percent of the country's 34 million people. This proportion has remained stable since records began last century. The overwhelming majority are followers of Sunnī Islam, but they are divided into three distinct Muslim communities, each having a very different relationship with the majority Buddhist society and the government.

The longest-established Muslim community, with its roots in the Shwebo area in the central plains near the precolonial capitals of the Burmese kings, can trace its origins back to the thirteenth and fourteenth centuries when their ancestors came to the country as court servants, mercenaries, and traders from the west. By the 1930s these well-assimilated Burmese Muslims accounted for less than a third of the Muslim community. Nearby, in the Shan State bordering China, there were also a small number of Muslims of Chinese descent.

The most recently established section of the Muslim community arrived following the colonization of Myanmar by the British in the nineteenth century. By making British Burma a province of India until 1937, the colonial government encouraged significant numbers of immigrants and casual laborers, as well as traders and civil servants, to settle mainly in and around Yangon, the colonial capital and entrepot. These Indian Muslims, who by the 1930s accounted for more than a third of those who followed Islam, maintained strong links with the religious and cultural practices of their homelands. This often brought them into conflict with the Buddhist majority and the Burmese Muslims over matters of marriage and property law as well as the role of Islam in Myanmar's political life.

The third Muslim community is settled in the Myanmar state of Arakan or Rahkine, which borders Bangladesh. Prior to 1784, when it was finally destroyed by a Burmese army, Arakan had been an independent Buddhist monarchy, though the rulers used Islamic designations. Its position was weakened not only by the rise of Burmese power to the east, but also by Mughal power to the west. After its absorption into British Burma, Arakan received large numbers of Bengali immigrants. The largest proportion of Muslims in Burma are of Bengali descent, and the majority of these reside in Rahkine State.

Indian immigration and the rise of nationalism generated significant tensions among the three Muslim communities in Burma, as well as between them and the Buddhist majority. While many of the Indian Muslims became involved in organizations and societies with their origins in the Indian subcontinent, the long-established Burmese Muslim population tended to identify with the Burmese Buddhist majority and supported the Burmese nationalist movement. The Rahkine Muslims remained detached from both and have continued to develop their own history separate from the other two communities.

Following the independence of Myanmar in 1948 the roles of the three communities continued to be divided. The Burmese Muslims found places in the government of the devout Buddhist Prime Minister U Nu, and many continued to serve in the military and socialist governments of General Ne Win after the coup of 1962. The more outward-looking and commercially oriented Indian Muslims found life more difficult after independence and sought political alliances with Burmese politicians or returned to India and Pakistan. Following the wholesale nationalization of the economy by Ne Win's Revolutionary Council government in 1963, several hundred thousand South Asians, including many Muslims, returned to the countries of their ancestors. A significant Muslim community, however, remains in Yangon (Rangoon) and other cities in southern Myanmar.

The position of the Rahkine Muslims has been the most difficult. As the poorest and the least established of the three communities, they have been buffeted by war, dislocation, and civil strife. During World War II several thousand fled into Bengal when Burmese-Bengali strife developed in the area. After the war, some Muslims in the area demanded that the northern part of the region be included in Pakistan. There ensued armed conflict between the so-called Mujahid and government troops until 1961. Since that time conflict over land and access to resources has remained a problem in the area. The Mujahids, arguing that they were Rohinga (the name of the mixed Bengali, Urdu, and Burmese language that was the language of their poetry and songs of Arabic and Persian origins) became especially active again in the 1970s and 1980s. Encouraged by the economic decline of Myanmar and the rise of Pan-Islamic movements elsewhere in the world, they championed the cause of the tens of thousands of Bengalis who had settled in Rahkine during and after Bangladesh's war with Pakistan. In 1978 the Myanmar authorities forced many of these settlers back into Bangladesh. After negotiations and the assistance of the United Nations High Commissioner for Refugees, many were resettled in Rahkine, but similar conflicts erupted in 1989–1990, with many thousands of persons seeking refuge in camps in Bangladesh.

[*See also* Islam, *article on* Islam in Southeast Asia and the Pacific.]

BIBLIOGRAPHY

Chakravarti, Nalini R. *The Indian Minority in Burma: The Rise and Decline of an Immigrant Community*. London, 1971.

Taylor, Robert H. *The State in Burma*. London and Honolulu, 1987.

Yegar, Moshe. *The Muslims of Burma: A Study of a Minority Group*. Wiesbaden, 1972.

R. H. Taylor

N

NAHḌAH. The Arabic word *nahḍah* may be translated "rising," "awakening," "revival," or "renaissance" and refers commonly to the revival, or renaissance, of Arabic literature and culture in the Levant and Egypt from about the middle of the nineteenth century to World War I. This revival began with the work of writers such as Nāṣīf Yāzijī (1800–1871) and Buṭrus al-Bustānī (1819–1883) in Syria and Lebanon and Rifāʿah Rāfiʿ al-Ṭahṭāwī (1801–1873) in Egypt, who sought to revive classical forms of Arabic, to develop the language in new ways appropriate to modern times, and to make their compatriots aware of the new ideas coming from Europe. These concerns are exemplified by two of al-Bustānī's main achievements, his Arabic dictionary *Muḥīṭ al-muḥiṭ* (Circumference of the Ocean) and his uncompleted *Encyclopaedia*. There was also a concern to develop a common patriotism that would transcend sectarian differences. Initially this was limited to Syria or Egypt, but in time it was to develop into a Pan-Arab sentiment.

The Nahḍah expressed itself partly through cultural societies, the first of which was formed in Beirut in 1847, and later in political societies, of which the first was a secret society in Beirut in 1875 that called for the autonomy of Syria and Lebanon and the recognition of Arabic as the official language. Also important were newspapers and periodicals, beginning in 1870 with al-Bustānī's review, *Al-jinān* (The Shield).

In later years activity shifted mainly to Cairo, where there was greater freedom of expression. A number of newspapers were published, largely by Syrians and Lebanese, including *Al-muqtaṭaf* (The Selection, 1876), *Al-ahrām* (The Pyramids, 1876) and *Al-hilāl* (The Crescent, 1892), the last edited by Jurjī Zaydan, an important author in his own right. Among the contributors to *Al-muqtaṭaf* was Shiblī Shumayyil (1850–1917), the preacher of Darwinism. Although the Naḥḍah had begun in Christian circles, and to a degree under the stimulus of Western missionaries, it was predominantly Muslim by the end of the century.

Although the Nahḍah is commonly considered to have ended by World War I, it laid the basis for the Arab national movement to follow. The word may also refer to the Arab and/or Islamic revival of the whole modern period, and Abdallah Laroui speaks of a "second Nahḍah" dating from the mid-1960s as Arab intellectuals have attempted to rethink their positions (1976, p. 92). In 1989 the Islamic Tendency Movement in Tunisia changed its name to the Renaissance Party (Ḥizb al-Nahḍah), and *Al-nahḍah* is the name of the journal of the Regional Islamic Daʿwah Council of Southeast Asia and the Pacific (RISEAP). In all these uses the term implies a historical sequence of past greatness, recent decadence, and a current effort to revive greatness. It therefore encapsulates a picture of history and ideological presuppositions that are widely shared among both Arabs and other Muslims today.

[*See also* Arab Nationalism; Revival and Renewal.]

BIBLIOGRAPHY

Amin, Samir. *The Arab Nation: Nationalism and Class Struggle*. Translated by Michael Pallis. London, 1978.

Antonius, George. *The Arab Awakening*. New York, 1965 (foreword dated 1938). Classic study of the period, though now dated in many ways.

Hourani, Albert. *Arabic Thought in the Liberal Age, 1798–1939*. London, 1962 (reprinted with a new preface in 1983). The most important study of Arabic political and social thought for the period.

Laroui, Abdallah. *The Crisis of the Arab Intellectual: Traditionalism or Historicism?* Translated by Diarmid Cammel. Berkeley and Los Angeles, 1976.

The Renaissance Party in Tunisia: The Quest for Freedom and Democracy. Washington, D.C., 1991. Collection of materials by party supporters. For the term *nahḍah,* see especially the preamble to the constitution (pp. 181–183).

WILLIAM E. SHEPARD

NAHDATUL ULAMA. Established in 1926, the Nahdatul Ulama (or Nahdlatul Ulama, abbreviated NU; from Ar., *nahḍat al-ʿulamāʾ*) is one of the two largest

Islamic social organizations in contemporary Indonesia. It embodies the solidarity of traditionalist *ʿulamāʾ* and their followers who hold to one of the four schools of Sunnī Islam, among which the Shāfiʿī school has been dominant. The social basis of NU has been and still is largely the *pesantren* or traditional institution of Islamic learning, where *santri* (religious students) live and learn classic Arabic texts *(kitab kuning)* under the tutelage of a *kyai* (the head of *pesantren,* and a respectful Javanese term for a spiritual leader). There are reportedly about six thousand *pesantren,* with more than one million *santri,* mostly in rural areas throughout the country. Most *pesantren* are affiliated with NU, and almost all of them follow orthodox Sunnism. The best-known NU *pesantren* are largely concentrated in eastern and central Java. The NU's presence over the past three generations, with members and supporters currently estimated at thirty million, is a testimonial to the resilience, adaptability, and vitality of Islamic traditionalism in Indonesia.

The name of the organization—"awakening of *ʿulamāʾ*"—reflects two aspects of its origin. It was part of the wave of nationalist awakening spearheaded by Sarekat Islam (SI), which was formed in 1912. Abdul Wahab Hasbullah (1888–1971), a later cofounder of NU, is said to have formed a branch of the SI in Mecca in 1913. Upon returning to Indonesia, he established an educational organization named Nahdlatul Wathan ("awakening of the nation") in Surabaya in 1916, and this became a forerunner of the NU.

At the same time, the challenge of reformism represented by Muḥammad ʿAbduh of Egypt was influencing Indonesian *ʿulamāʾ* in the form of the Muhammadiyah, the second major Islamic organization in twentieth-century Indonesia. The abolition of the caliphate in Turkey and the fall of the Hejaz to the Wahhābī Ibn Saʿūd in 1924 caused open conflicts in the Indonesian Muslim community. These changes profoundly disturbed the mainstream Javanese *ʿulamāʾ* to which Hasbullah belonged. For him and like-minded *ʿulamāʾ*, recognizing and taking measures against these threats of *bidʿah* (improper innovation) was an urgent need. Hasyim Asyʿari (1871–1947), *kyai* of the *pesantren* of Tebu Ireng, Jombang, East Java, who was then the most revered of Javanese *ʿulamāʾ*, approved their request to form the NU in 1926 and became its first president or *rois akbar*.

The NU's original charter of 1926 stated its purposes as follows: to enhance the relationships among *ʿulamāʾ* of the various Sunnī schools; to examine textbooks to determine whether they are appropriate for *ahl al-sunna wal-jamaʿa* (people who follow the customs of the Prophet and the Muslim community) or constitute *bidʿah;* to propagate Islam based on the teachings of the four schools; to establish *madrasahs*; to manage mosques, prayer houses, and dormitories *(pondok);* to look after orphans and the poor; and to organize bodies for the advancement of agriculture, trade, and industry that are lawful in Islamic terms.

The emblem of the NU, adopted in 1927 explicitly symbolizes its traditionalism. A large star over the globe represents the prophet Muḥammad; four small stars, two on each side of the large one, stand for the four Rightly Guided Caliphs, and four small stars beneath indicate the four schools of Sunnī Islam; these nine stars together also signify the nine saints *(wali songo)* who first spread Islam in Java. The green globe is to remind humanity of its origin, earth, to which it will return and from which it will eventually be recalled on the day of judgment. The golden rope surrounding the globe with ninety-nine twists represents the ninety-nine beautiful names of God through which the worldwide Muslim community is united. Thus the emblem embraces the NU's Sunnī traditionalism, Sufism, and specifically Javanese Muslim elements.

The NU has had distinct features from the beginning that reflect the subculture of *pesantren* on which it is based. Central is the charisma of the *kyai* as a spiritual leader inheriting the authority of the Prophet. This authority derives primarily from the *kyai*'s intellectual and spiritual powers—his command of Arabic, often acquired during a long stay in Mecca, and his profound classical scholarship, usually exemplified by his memorization of the entire Qur'ān and several other texts, his ability to quote from them relevant phrases or passages in Arabic, and his eloquence in interpreting and explaining them in the vernacular. Buttressing these abilities is his biological and/or spiritual genealogy *(isnād, silsiah),* often going back to the Prophet himself through a series of renowned *ʿulamāʾ* or Ṣūfī masters *(mursyid;* Ar., *murshid),* from whom he has received the authority to teach *(ijāzah).* His genealogy also often includes local cultural heroes such as the Javanese nine saints or indigenous rulers. He is not only learned in Islamic science *(ilmu;* Ar., *ʿilm)* but is also regarded as endowed with divine power *(keramat;* Ar., *karāmah).* Generally, the lifelong loyalty of a *santri* to his *kyai* is established in the *pesantren,* while absolute obedience of a disciple *(murid;* Ar., *murīd)* to his master is formed in a *pesantren* operated by a Ṣūfī brotherhood *(tarekat;* Ar., *ṭarīqah).*

The *kyai*'s role as spiritual leader is not confined to the compound of the *pesantren.* He usually serves the local community at large, giving Friday sermons and public lectures and leading ritual prayers on major festivals of the Islamic calendar. If he is a Ṣūfī *murshid,* he leads prayers *(doʿa;* Ar., *duʿā')* and recitations *(dzikir;* Ar., *dhikr)* on such occasions as Manaqiban—a monthly gathering in praise and commemoration of ʿAbd al-Qādir al-Jīlānī, the founder of the Qādirīyah order—and *haul,* the anniversary of the death of the founder of the *pesantren.*

The blessing of God *(barakah)* possessed by the *kyai* is overwhelming in the eyes of ordinary Muslims. They join in these gatherings in hundreds and thousands to receive God's blessings through him. Kissing the hand of a *kyai* to obtain a share of his *barakah* is customary in the NU. He also receives a constant stream of visitors requesting advice *(nasehat;* Ar., *naṣīḥa)* and legal judgment *(fatwā)* on such personal matters as seeking marriage partners for their children, solving family dispute over inheritance, and improving business.

In appreciation of the *kyai*'s guardianship, villagers and parents of *santri* usually contribute rice and other food, poultry and livestock, fuel and building materials, and cash. Often land and buildings are donated to a *pesantren* as *wakaf* (Ar., *waqf*). Thus most *pesantren* are financially independent.

The NU has instituted an organizational framework to tap and augment popular religiosity under a *kyai*'s guidance. One of its primary activities is the *lailatul ijtimāʿ,* a monthly meeting hold by the *kyai* on the eve of the fifteenth day of every lunar month; this begins with *salat ghaib* (ritual prayers) for the recently deceased of the local community, followed by speeches explicating the NU's policies and activities, and a session for questions and answers. The NU thus provides a forum for personal piety and spiritual solidarity through face-to-face communication. These activities centering on the local *kyai* reflect the grass-roots character of the NU, embedded in close-knit interpersonal relationships imbued with the ethics of mutual help among neighbors. Each *kyai* thus has his own *umat (ummah),* or local Muslim community under his spiritual guardianship.

The *kyai* is independent of secular rulers, standing on his own religious authority and economic resources. Secular rulers, however, often ask for his consent and support to enhance their legitimacy and control of social order. In this situation, he often assumes the role of mediator or broker between secular rulers and his *umat.* This relationship gives bargaining power to the *kyai* vis-à-vis secular rulers. In turn, secular rulers often reward the *kyai* by giving him position or wealth. This adds to his resources for patronage within the *umat.* Nonetheless, unless he maintains his charisma in religious terms, political or economic patronage alone is usually insufficient to support his power; moral corruption of *ʿulamā'* by association with secular rulers is one of the most despised situations in Sunnī tradition. The NU is thus ultimately a federation of independent realms of *kyai*s with distinctive characteristics of autonomy, independence from secular rulers, and populism.

From 1930 until the outbreak of World War II the NU grew rapidly, not only as a movement to counter the advance of reformism, but also as an agent for the internal transformation of the *pesantren.* Most prominent in this effort was Wahid Hasyim (1900–1957), son of Hasyim Asyʿari, who introduced a modern educational system of *madrasahs* with graded classes and girls' education into the *pesantren;* he also established NU's youth (Ansor) and women's (Muslimat) organizations. He represented the NU in the MIAI (Majlisul Islamil A'laa Indonesia), a federation of Islamic organizations formed in 1937; Hasyim Asyʿari served as its chairman. Through Wahid Hasyim the NU also joined a political campaign initiated by secular nationalists in 1939, demanding parliamentary representation for Indonesian people. Through these activities the NU organization grew nationally, extending its membership to the Outer Islands.

In the brief but turbulent years of the Japanese occupation (1942–1945) the NU, together with other Islamic organizations, experienced a major change in its relationship with the government—from being the object of hostile colonial control by the Dutch to acting as a tool of mass mobilization for the Japanese. After an initial period banning their activities, the Japanese military authorities not only allowed the NU and the Muhammadiyah to operate but actually encouraged them to mobilize their members and followers in support of Japanese war efforts. The MIAI was soon transformed into Masyumi (or Masjumi; Majlis Syuro Muslimin Indonesia), a comprehensive federation of Islamic organizations that vowed to wage a *jihād* against the Allies under Japanese leadership. Officially, Hasyim Asyʿari continued to head Masyumi.

Masyumi organized its own paramilitary corps, Hizbu'llah, while recruiting a number of young Muslim activists to join the voluntary military troops or PETA. Japanese soldiers provided military training. The Japanese military government also restructured the Dutch Bureau of Native Affairs into the Department of Religious Affairs, and to head it appointed first Djajadiningrat, a Dutch-educated scholar, and later Hasyim Asyʿari.

Toward the end of the Japanese occupation, Islamic leaders, including NU representatives, joined secular nationalist leaders in the preparation of a constitution for an independent Indonesia. Islamic leaders argued for an Islamic state under the *sharīʿah*, but they finally agreed on the formula of the Pancasila (Five Pillars), in which belief in the one and only God was the first element. The constitution was promulgated on 18 August 1945, the day after the declaration of Indonesia's independence. Islamic leaders had attained remarkable ascendancy in administration and politics during the Japanese occupation.

In the war of independence fought between 1945 and 1949, regular troops of the new Republic were drawn mostly from former PETA forces, while irregulars and militia were largely recruited from the Masyumi's Hizbu'llah units whose commanders included a number of NU *ʿulamāʾ*. In addition to their military contribution, NU *ʿulamāʾ* inspired Republican troops in October 1945 by issuing a *fatwā* calling on all able Muslim men to join the war as a holy war *(jihād fī sabīl Allāh)* of individual obligation *(farḍ ʿayn)*. This *fatwā* encouraged the Republican forces in their first major battle against the incoming Allies in Surabaya in November 1945. A fierce war of independence, in which "Allāhu Akbar" was a common war cry, continued until 1949 when the Dutch finally recognized Indonesia's sovereignty.

In the war of independence, Islamic forces were united under the Masyumi Party, which had been an umbrella group for all Islamic organizations, including the NU, since November 1945. In 1952, however, the NU withdrew from the Masyumi party to become an independent political party because of disagreement over the status and role of the *ʿulamāʾ* in the party. The NU wanted to empower the council of *ʿulamāʾ*, the Syuriyah, as the highest decision-making body of the party; however, the majority of the party leadership, most of them secularly educated, refused to recognize such a special position for the *ʿulamāʾ*.

In the first parliamentary general elections and the elections for the Constitutional Assembly in 1955, the NU party received 18.4 percent of the total vote, emerging as one of the top four parties alongside the Nationalist Party (PNI), the Masyumi Party, and the Communist party (PKI). This was an unexpected show of popular support for the NU, which previously had only a handful of individuals prominent in national politics. The election results were also unexpected for other reasons. Not only did the Masyumi party, which had formed the core of a series of coalition cabinets, fail to maintain its pre-election dominance in national politics; in addition, the total votes cast for the Islamic parties fell short of a majority, only 43.9 percent, even though the overwhelming majority of Indonesian people professed to be Muslims.

In the Constitutional Assembly, the NU and other Islamic parties endeavored to adopt a new constitution that would make Indonesia an Islamic state. The PNI, PKI, Christian, and other minor parties preferred a secular state based on the Pancasila. The assembly failed to produce a consensus on the constitution. Meanwhile, rebellions in the name of Darul Islam (Islamic State) continued in West Java, Aceh, and South Sulawesi. Moreover, several leaders of the Masyumi party joined the rebels and formed a countergovernment in 1958. President Sukarno dissolved the Constitutional Assembly, and banned the Masyumi party and the PSI (Socialists) for their involvement in the rebellion. He decreed a return to the 1945 constitution and formed the so-called NASAKOM government, a coalition of nationalists, religious forces (including the NU), and Communists.

In all this the NU recognized Sukarno, in terms of *fiqh* (Islamic jurisprudence), as the legitimate head of state to whom Muslim loyalty was due. Since the early period of the Republic the NU had joined a series of coalition cabinets, thus developing a number of its own politicians, the most prominent being Idham Chalid (b. 1921), who occupied ministerial positions beginning in 1952 when he was first appointed vice-premier. The position of minister of the Department of Religion was occupied by NU leaders from 1949 to 1972, making the department a basis for its political patronage. In the NASAKOM government (1960–1965), the NU's share of power became much greater than before, leading to its deeper entrenchment in the religious bureaucracy.

An unsuccessful Communist-inspired coup attempt in late 1965 transformed the situation. The NU supported the mainstream of the army under Suharto in expelling the Communists and radical nationalists from the national and local political scenes. The NU's parliamentarians were instrumental in banning the PKI and pressing for the presidents' accountability for the coup attempt. Suharto replaced Sukarno in 1967 and ushered in the so-called New Order.

The NU party participated in the 1971 general elections as the only major party of the big four of the 1955 elections to have survived the 1965 turmoil. The NU party, through a vigorous campaign headed by Hasbullah, obtained 10.5 million votes (18.3 percent of the total), thus apparently retaining its 1955 strength; it secured the second position behind Golkar, the newly formed government party, which received an overwhelming 63 percent majority.

The 1971 elections were, however, the last time NU campaigned as an independent political party. From then on the New Order government denied the NU its share of power. No longer were any cabinet seats given to it. Moreover, the government took a drastic measure to secure political stability—the reduction of political parties to only three, Golkar, the Development Unity Party (PPP), and the Indonesian Democratic Party (PDI). At the same time, day-to-day political party activities below the regency *(kabupaten)* level were forbidden. The NU Party was forced to fuse with the PPP, while the latter's top leadership was directly controlled by the government. It vigorously promoted the depoliticization of Islam.

After the advent of the New Order, the government implemented programs for rapid economic development with a massive influx of Western capital and technology. This created a number of social problems, including the concentration of wealth among the urban elite and the weakening of indigenous entrepreneurs. The PPP, and its NU faction in parliament in particular, increasingly assumed the role of channeling popular grievances against the negative effects of economic development. Moreover, blatant attempts at the infringement of Muslim rights—for example, the Marriage Law bill of 1973—and the favoring of Javanese indigenous religion over Islam in 1978 roused widespread resentment in Islamic organizations. As a result, the PPP, under the leadership of the NU's elderly Bisri Syamsuri (1886–1980), the last survivor of its founding fathers, even staged a walk-out in parliament. The critical stance of the NU and other Islamic organizations vis-à-vis the government was manifest toward the end of the 1970s.

Annoyed by this Islamic militancy, the government initiated comprehensive measures to eliminate potential threats to political stability arising from the revival of Islamic political forces. In 1982 it adopted a policy of imposing the Pancasila as the sole foundation of all political and social organizations. After tense negotiations and some bloodshed, it finally won in 1985 by passing new laws to that effect.

The NU's consultative assembly of *ʿulamāʾ* accepted the new government policy as early as 1983 with remarkable positiveness. At the same time, they proposed that the NU severe its relationship with the PPP and return to its original character as a religious, educational, and social organization, with the slogan "Return to the 1926 Principle (Khitthah 1926)." The new direction was to bring the demise of the NU politicians exemplified by Idham Chalid. The National Congress of the NU in 1984 ratified the decisions of the *ʿulamāʾ*s assembly of the previous year.

The most articulate formulator of the new direction was Ahmad Siddiq (1926–1990), who was elected president of the Syuriyah at the Congress. He argued that the Pancasila was not a religion and could not replace religion. The pillar of belief in the one and only God was in accordance with the Islamic creed of *tawḥīd* (oneness of God) and represented the Muslim commitment to practice Islam in Indonesia. Therefore, there was nothing in the Pancasila that interfered with Muslim religious faith and Islamic law. The NU should accept the Pancasila as a manmade state philosophy and as a foundation of its organization within the framework of the Republic of Indonesia while retaining Islam as the basis of its members' religious faith. By stating this, Ahmed Siddiq made it clear that Islam should not confront the state and that the Republic of Indonesia under the Pancasila was the final form with which Indonesian Muslims were to live.

Alongside Ahmad Siddiq's presidency, the 1984 NU Congress elected Abdurrahman Wahid (b. 1940), son of Wahid Hasyim and grandson of Hasyim Asyʿari, as chairperson of the Tanfidziyah or executive council, while denying Idham Chalid's effort to regain power. The Ahmad Siddiq–Abdurrahman Wahid team went on to enforce strictly the decision of the Congress severing its organizational ties with the PPP by forbidding NU officers to be PPP officers simultaneously. The active effort to withdraw the NU from practical politics reached a peak when it staged a "deflation campaign" against the PPP in the 1987 general elections. As a result, the latter suffered a drastic decrease in votes. In spite of complaints from dislocated NU politicians and some *ʿulamāʾ*, the team of Ahmad Siddiq and Abdurrahman Wahid was reelected for another five-year term in the 1989 Congress, indicating the strong support they enjoyed among the majority of the *ʿulamāʾ* and local activists.

Meanwhile, Abdurrahman Wahid attempted to explain the NU's policies and behavior in theological terms. According to him, the NU was not opportunistic nor accommodationist, as it was often labeled by outsiders. The tradition of Islamic doctrine to which the NU adhered combined both worldly and other-worldly dimensions of life in one ongoing organic whole, thus forming an effective defense against secularism. The NU's political behavior was to be understood in this perspective. The NU did not recognize the existence of Islamic alternatives outside the status quo. Constant and gradual improvement of a given situation without endangering the existing order was the religiously enjoined guideline for the NU's behavior, including politics. In NU circles, disagreements in opinion did not endanger the integrity of the organization, for conflicting views were acknowledged as equally valid. Consensus, including agreeing to disagree, was always sought. This decision-making pattern had great bearing upon national unity and integration because it excluded a confrontational approach in pursuit of political alternatives.

The NU is faced with enormous social transformation as the twenty-first century approaches. Industrialization and urbanization are reducing the proportion of rural population and changing rural ways of life at a rapid rate, while the expansion of modern national education is affecting the continuity of traditional Islamic scholarship based on *pesantren* education. The shape of Islam in the future of Indonesia, as well as that of Indonesia itself, in turn seems to depend much on the direction and behavior of the NU in responding to these challenges. A new generation of NU leadership personified by Abdurrahman Wahid is endeavoring to respond to them by transforming the NU into a massive social movement for a more democratic, prosperous, and religiously harmonious Indonesia.

[*See also* Indonesia; Masjumi; Partai Persatuan Pembangunan; Pesantren; Sarekat Islam; *and the biography of Abdurrahman Wahid.*]

BIBLIOGRAPHY

Abdurrahman Wahid. "The Nahdlatul Ulama and Islam in Present Day Indonesia." In *Islam and Society in Southeast Asia,* edited by Taufik Abdullah and Sharon Siddique, pp. 175–85. Singapore, 1986. A systematic explanation of NU's orientation and behavior in terms of its religious foundations by its current top leader.

Benda, Harry. *The Crescent and the Rising Sun: Indonesian Islam under the Japanese Occupation 1942–1945.* Leiden, 1983. A classical study describing the ascendancy of the Islamic movement, including the NU, in Indonesian politics and administration through the Japanese occupation.

Bruinessen, Martin van. "Indonesia's Ulama and Politics: Caught between Legitimising the Status Quo and Searching for Alternatives." *Prisma* (English edition) 49 (1990): 52–69. A useful survey on the recent political trends among Indonesian *ʿulamāʾ* in the widest sense of the term, for example, inclusive of Western-Educated intellectuals.

Bruinessen, Martin van. "Kitab Kuning: Books in Arabic Script used in the Pesantren Milieu." *Bijdragen tot de Taal-, Land- en Volkenkunde* 146. 2–3 (1990): 226–269. A report of extensive survey on the so-called "Yellow Books," that is, textbooks in Arabic script, used in the *pesantren* in Indonesia today.

Bruinessen, Martin van. "The 28th Congress of the Nahdlatul Ulama: Power Struggle and Social Concerns." *Archipel* 41 (1991): 185–199. An informative field report on the 1989 NU National Congress.

Geertz, Clifford. *The Religion of Java.* New York, 1960. Presents a now-classic "traditionalist" versus "modernist" dichotomy of Indonesian Islam observed in East Java in the early 1950s.

Geertz, Clifford. "The Javanese Kijaji: The Changing Roles of a Cultural Broker." *Comparative Studies in Society and History* 2 (1960): 228–249. Places Javanese *ʿulamāʾ* as a mediator between the Jakarta-centered state power and local communities.

Johns, Anthony H. "Indonesia: Islam and Cultural Pluralism." In *Islam in Asia: Religion, Politics, and Society,* edited by John L. Esposito, pp. 202–229. New York, 1987. A readable historical overview on the development of Indonesian Islam against the background of nationalism since the turn of the century and a penetrating analysis of ongoing dialectic between Islamic forces and the state power since the advent of the New Order.

Jones, Sidney. "The Contraction and Expansion of the 'Umat' and the Role of the Nahdatul Ulama in Indonesia." *Indonesia* 38 (1984): 1–20. Reports on the encroachment of the NU constituency by the New Order government.

Mansurnoor, Iik Arifin. *Islam in an Indonesian World: Ulama of Madura.* Jogjakarta, 1990. An anthropological study of *ʿulamā* in the island society of Madura, northeast of Java, an NU stronghold.

Nakamura Mitsuo. "The Radical Traditionalism of the Nahdlatul Ulama in Indonesia: A Personal Account of the 26th National Congress, June 1979, Semarang." *Tonan Ajia Kenkyu (Southeast Asian Studies)* 19.2 (1981): 187–204. An attempt at understanding organizational features of the NU, in which *ʿulamāʾ* play a decisive role, and their political implications.

Noer, Deliar. *The Modernist Muslim Movement in Indonesia 1900–1942.* Kuala Lumpur, 1973. A standard work on the development of modernist Muslim organizations up to the outbreak of the World War II, in which the NU is depicted mostly reactive and reactionary.

Ward, Ken E. *The 1971 Election in Indonesia: An East Java Case Study*. Clayton, Victoria, 1974. One of the earliest reports on the militancy of NU's criticism against the New Order government.

Zamakhsyari, Dhofier. "Kinship and Marriage among the Javanese Kyai." *Indonesia* 29 (1980): 47–58. A detailed description of kinship and marriage networks among leading *ʿulamāʾ* families in Java since the late nineteenth century.

NAKAMURA MITSUO

NĀʾĪNĪ, MUḤAMMAD ḤUSAYN (1860–1936), the leading theoretician of the 1905–1909 Persian constitutional movement and the leading clergyman who granted legitimacy to the rule of Reza Shah Pahlavi. His life can be divided into three periods. During the first, he was actively engaged in bringing about the Constitutional Revolution and wrote a famous treatise. During the second period, he was an important lecturer and became one of the most important Shīʿī *mujtahids*, clergymen entitled to exercise *ijtihad* (individual inquiry into legal matters). He led the Iraqi nationalists against the British and worked actively for independence. During the last period, he lost his fighting spirit, devoted his life to teaching, and acquiesced to the powers that be.

Nāʾīnī studied in Samarra, Iraq, with Muḥammad al-Fishārakī al-Iṣfahānī (d. 1899) and Muḥammad Ḥasan Shīrāzī (d. 1896), whose secretary he became. After his master's death, he moved to Karbala and studied with Mullā Muḥammad Kāẓim Khurāsānī (d. 1911). Both Shīrāzī and Khurāsānī played important roles in political events in Iran. Nāʾīnī drafted the telegrams that Khurāsānī sent to Iran during the Constitutional Revolution. He was heavily involved in the planning of *ʿulamāʾ* (religious scholars) involvement in the politics of Iran. However, he and other constitutionalists became disillusioned with subsequent events. Nāʾīnī therefore concentrated on teaching, became involved in Iraqi politics at the outset of World War I, and led the Iraqi opposition against the subsequent British mandate. This latter action led to his departure from Iraq in 1923. Nāʾīnī was then drawn into Iranian politics, namely, the campaign to establish a republic in that country. Together with ʿAbd al-Karīm Ḥāʾirī Yazdī (d. 1936) and Abū al-Ḥasan Iṣfahānī, he was able to convince Reza Khan to give up this idea in 1924. Reza Khan assisted in the return of Nāʾīnī to Iraq by first arranging compensation for the British insult against him in expelling him in the first place, followed by an invitation to return to that country. Nāʾīnī showed his gratitude by sending a letter plus portrait of Imam ʿAlī ibn Abī Ṭālib to Reza Khan, thus conferring legitimacy on his regime. One year later, he and Iṣfahānī jointly sent a letter depicting those opposing Reza Khan's rule as enemies of Islam. This opened the road to the deposing of the Qājār dynasty (1785/97–1925). On Reza Khan's accession to the throne, Nāʾīnī sent a telegram of congratulations to the shah and continued to send him similar messages on holy festival days. The remainder of his years he spent teaching in Najaf, Iraq.

Nāʾīnī's most famous work was *Tanbīh al-ummah va tanzīh al-millah dar asās va uṣūl-ī mashrūṭīyat* (An Admonition to the Nation and an Exposition to the People Concerning the Foundations and Principles of Constitutional Government), written in 1909. It is still the most detailed and coherent justification of constitutional government from a Shīʿī point of view. It aims to reconcile the impossibility of legitimate rule (in the absence of the Hidden Imam) with the practical need for government that promotes the well-being of the Shīʿī community, but in a way that is not too much at odds with the dictates of religion. In his book, Nāʾīnī does not advocate actual administration of government by the *ʿulamāʾ*, but he embraces an islamization of constitutionalist principles, and he accepts certain principles of democracy that are in conformity with Islam. The importance of the book, even for modern times, is emphasized by the fact that its third edition (1955), with notes, was prepared by Ayatollah Maḥmud Ṭāleqāni (d. 1979), a major religious figure who played an important role in the Iranian Revolution of 1979.

[*See also* Constitutional Revolution; *and the biographies of Ḥāʾirī Yazdī and Pahlavi.*]

BIBLIOGRAPHY

Arjomand, Said Amir. "The State and Khomeini's Islamic Order." *Iranian Studies* 13.1–4 (1980): 147–164. Contains a pertinent summary of Nāʾīnī's doctrinal justification for supporting the Constitutionalists (see especially pp. 150–152).

Bayat, Mangol. *Iran's First Revolution*. New York, 1991. Minimizes the importance and originality of Nāʾīnī's ideas (see especially pp. 256–258).

Hairi, Abdul-Hadi. *Shīʿism and Constitutionalism*. Leiden, 1977. Full treatment of Nāʾīnī's thought and activities in Shīʿī Islam and Iran.

WILLEM FLOOR

NAJAF. A religious center of the Shīʿīs since the eighth century, Najaf is located in Iraq, south of Baghdad and 6 miles west of Kufa. It is the site of the *mash-*

had of the first Shīʿī imam, ʿAlī ibn Abī Ṭalīb, whose gravesite was revealed to the public in the early ʿAbbāsid period by Jaʿfar al-Ṣādiq (d. 765) during one of his visits to Kufa. Under al-Sadiq and his disciples, Najaf also became heir to the Shīʿī learning that had flourished in Kufa, where in the grand mosque, al-Ṣādiq's *ḥadīths* (reports) were disseminated among some nine hundred teachers of traditions.

Following the founding of Baghdad (754–775), a number of Shīʿī scholars from Kufa migrated to this new capital. Some others chose the *mashhad* at Najaf as the base from which to teach and spread Shīʿī traditions. Although Kufa retained its importance as the locus of Shīʿī activities until fifteenth century, Najaf gradually replaced it. During this transition, Najaf's *mashhad* and the *madrasah* (seminary) attached to it found much-needed patronage from Shīʿī rulers. The ruler of Tabaristan, Muḥammad ibn Zayd al-ʿAlawī (d. 900), ordered the construction of the dome and the Ṣūfī *zāwiyah* (cells). The Būyid sultans added the arched halls and hospices that provided residence for the students who came to study in Najaf. During his visit to Najaf in 1336, Ibn Baṭṭūṭah noted the existence of a number of *madrasahs*, hospices, and Ṣūfī convents attached to the shrine.

In the eleventh century, Shaykh al-Ṭā'ifah al-Ṭūsī (d. 1067), a great Shīʿī scholar and leader of the community, migrated from Baghdad to Najaf and established his own school based on a text-oriented Shīʿī curriculum. The present-day Shīʿī *mujtahids* regard themselves as the intellectual descendants of al-Ṭūsī's *madrasah*, but in the twentieth century, Najaf lost its leadership of Shīʿī learning. With the establishment of Shiism as the state religion of Iran under the Ṣafavids in the early 1500s, there was a flow of Shīʿī scholars from Iraq and Lebanon to Isfahan and other places in Iran. [*See* Ṣafavid Dynasty.] Nineteenth-century Iraq and Iran witnessed the modernization of educational and political institutions along with the development of an intense nationalism that created a different challenge for the *mujtahids* in Iran. Under the leadership of Ayatollah ʿAbd al-Karīm Ḥā'irī Yazdī (d. 1937), the religious hierarchy in Iran found it appropriate to establish a *madrasah* in Qom that would respond to the growing needs of the times and would equal and even surpass Najaf as the hub of Shīʿī religious sciences. Moreover, the highly centralized religious leadership of the *marjaʿ al-taqlīd* had passed on to prominent *mujtahids* of Qom, overshadowing the apolitical leadership of Najaf in the growing turmoil of the 1950s and 1960s. It was not until the rise of Ayatollahs Khomeini (d. 1989) and Muḥammad Bāqir al-Ṣadr (executed 1980) that Najaf reversed its tradition of shunning politics and actively sought to combat the secular ideology of the Baʿthists in Iraq.

There are several historical sites in the vicinity of Najaf that form an important part of Shīʿī piety. One of the most sacred places is the grand mosque of Kufa where ʿAlī was assassinated. In Shīʿī estimation, the Kufa mosque is equal in status to the mosques of Mecca and Medina. The other important spot of pilgrimage is the Sahlah mosque, where the Shīʿīs believe that the twelfth imam appears every Tuesday evening to perform the sunset prayer. Accordingly, a large crowd of pious Shīʿīs assembles in Sahlah that evening in the hope of meeting the Hidden Imam.

[*See also* Mashhad; Shrine; Ziyārah; *and the biography of ʿAlī.*]

BIBLIOGRAPHY

Algar, Hamid. *Religion and State in Iran, 1785–1906: The Role of the Ulama in the Qajar Period.* Berkeley, 1969. Covers Najaf and its religious establishment, and the politics of the *ʿulamā'* and Muslim powers.

Ayoub, Mahmoud M. *Redemptive Suffering in Islam: A Study of the Devotional Aspects of ʿĀshūrā' in Twelver Shīʿism.* The Hague, 1978. Discusses *mashhad* rituals in Shīʿī piety.

Mottahedeh, Roy P. *The Mantle of the Prophet: Religion and Politics in Iran.* New York, 1985. Covers the curriculum and methodology of the religious sciences at the *madrasah* in Shīʿī centers of learning.

ABDULAZIZ SACHEDINA

NAMES AND NAMING. "Choose for your children pleasant and beautiful names," the Prophet is reported to have said, and, as a measure of how significant names could be, he changed the name of an individual whose name he thought improper. This care about names has perhaps developed from the sensitivity to God's beautiful names in the Qur'ān (17.110) and the great piety with which the ninety-nine names of God are recited.

In general, Muslims in the Islamic heartlands have followed naming practices established early in Islamic times: the only name "given" is the first name, because the Qur'ān instructed, "Call them after their true father's names" (33.5), thereby dictating that the second name will be the father's, while the third may well be the grandfather's. There has seldom been variation in this rule because Muslim inheritance laws depended on it and claims had to be validated according to it. The requirement applied to both boys and girls; girls legally retained their patronymic even after marriage. This basic structure, however, has been considerably adapted, particularly under modern influences.

The naming of a child need not occur until the moment of registration, which may be delayed for a considerable period, especially if the actual birthdate of the child is not held to be auspicious or if important family members are absent. This stay allowed the family to discuss the given name and provided the opportunity to assess the child's personality or health to determine what a given name should be. During this interim, a male child was called "Muḥammad" and a female one "Fāṭimah" as recommended in certain prophetic traditions. Once the decision has been made, however, quite elaborate celebrations usually herald the event. South Asian Ismāʿīlīs perform a ceremony called a *chanda,* a sprinkling of blessed water over the child at a special rite in the *jamāʿat-khanah;* the names, dates of birth, and professions of the parents are registered at the same ceremony.

Because of its importance for identity, the greatest variation has taken place within the first name *(ism).* As might be expected, religious conviction has been a fundamental determinant: Sunnīs have preferred the names of Muḥammad and the first three rightly guided caliphs, while Shīʿīs have opted for those of ʿAlī and other figures important in their history. Favorite names for girls have been less clearly sectarian, with the possible exception of *ʿĀʾishah,* since the wives and daughters of the Prophet are universally appealing. Also broadly acceptable are combinations reflecting religious resonances—names attributed to God, prefixed with "slave of," as *ʿAbd al-Raḥmān,* or to religion, as *Quṭb al-Dīn,* "pole of religion." Family experience has also played a role. Among Arabs, if a family had previously lost boys, they might give a new son the name of a girl as a way of deflecting the attention of evil powers and ensuring his survival. Such a name could follow him into adulthood. Ethnic or heroic popularity sometimes overcame religious influences, as witness *Timur* among Turkish-speaking peoples. Children could be given a name that anticipated a characteristic, as in *Fayṣal* (signaling the hope that the individual will be an arbiter or peacemaker) or *Saʿīd* ("happy"). Girls could also be named for a fond hope, such as Umm al-Saʿādah ("mother of happiness"). Throughout Islam, where parents gave a religious name, they customarily added to it a local name or nickname. Thus Muslim children in the heartland could have long given names. The recent trend is away from this toward the simple and straightforward. Modernity has had other dramatic impacts on first names. The attractiveness of traditional Muslim names in Turkey, for example, has dropped off in interesting correlation with secular reforms. Since the 1970s a wide variety of names have appeared that have no connection with Islam, for instance *Lenin* and *Russa,* indicating political orientation, or *Misra* and *Mecca,* for favored places. Now children may be named after a great performer like Umm Kulthūm or a leader like Nāṣir.

The patronymic has also undergone some modification over time. The *kunyah* or honorific name goes back to pre-Islamic times among the Arabs and was sometimes given as a mark of special recognition by the caliph. It could also indicate one's tribe, birthplace, or even legal school. The honor was often linked to the father's name and became part of the legal name of the child. Special linkage phrases amplified the underlying relationship, utilizing the the prefixes *ibn* ("son of") or *abū* ("father of") in Arabic or the suffixes *-zādeh* or *-oghlu,* both also meaning "son of" in Persian and Turkish, respectively. Magnifiers were also added, such as *Magdī* "my glory" added to a father's or grandfather's name. Officially, one's name always included the *kunyah.* Eventually these could become part of a perpetually retained ancestral name.

Other elements of naming are to be found. Where an individual's given and ancestral names are quite conventional and liable to be confused with identical names, another name, called *laqab* in Arabic, serves as a special indicator. Indicator names may refer to profession (*al-Naqqāsh* "the painter"), to a concept (*al-Mulk* "of the kingdom"), or to a physical characteristic, (*al-Aʿmā* "the blind"). Conventionally, the assignment of a place-name *(nisb)* did not occur until the individual became famous and was associated with a location, for example Dhū al-Nūn al-Misrī ("Dhū al-Nūn of Egypt").

Names marking special recognition have been popular in most Muslim countries. These include titles like *shaykh, agā,* or *beg;* descriptors like *ḥājjī* or *ḥājjah,* denoting someone who has completed a pilgrimage, usually to Mecca; and respectful designators like *shāh* ("saint," when a prefix to a name). These may become part of the individual's official name, especially if the person is of some status.

Under pressure to adapt to Western ways, professionals in Muslim countries shorten their names to the given name and an indicator name, although locals will know the physician merely by the professional title and given name. Muslims coming to the West have had considerable trouble with these traditions. Early immigrants were often assigned "Western-sounding" names, for example *Sid* for *Saʿīd*. Anglicization has affected the spelling of Muslim names in India and Pakistan, and names in African countries influenced by various European languages. Indigenous languages also affected the form of names adopted from Arabic; thus in Kiswahili, *Fāṭimah* became *Fatuma* and *Abū Bakr* became *Bakāri*.

Among the Hui of China, only surnames reflect Muslim ancestry. Early in the expansion of Islam into China, *Muḥammad* was shortened to *Ma*, perhaps because it sounded much like existing common names, and the name became recognizably Muslim, as did *Bai*, perhaps from Turkish *bey*. Since Muslim law has not applied to Chinese Muslims, their first names did not need to carry the individual's prime identity, so first names follow local traditions. Names like Fāṭimah are maintained, however, in sinicized form. Similarly, in Indonesia, Muslim identity has depended less on naming practices; recognizing God's beneficence in a child's name may indicate religious conviction, but not necessarily Muslim. The presence or absence of Muslim law appears to be a factor in maintaining naming traditions.

Nevertheless, Muslim naming protocols continue to be important identity markers. Converts throughout the Muslim world are given Muslim names chosen as fitting the individual, perhaps by the convert's own choice, and keeping in mind the new believer's position within the community. Recently, Serbian pressure on Bosnian Muslims to europeanize their names was important in hardening Muslim resistance in former Yugoslavia. Black Muslims in the United States have been very active in adapting Muslim names; one of their most famous converts, Malcolm X, had six names before his death as Malik al-Shabazz.

BIBLIOGRAPHY

A helpful overview of Arab traditions carried on into Islam is Frederick Mathewson Denny, "Names and Naming," in *The Encyclopedia of Religion*, edited by Mircea Eliade, vol. 10, pp. 300–307 (New York, 1987). Naming trends are covered in two important articles by Richard W. Bulliet: "Conversion to Islam and the Emergence of a Muslim Society in Iran," in *Conversion to Islam*, edited by Nehemia Levtzion, pp. 30–51 (New York, 1979), on medieval Iran; and "First Names and Political Change in Modern Turkey," *International Journal of Middle East Studies* 9 (1978): 489–495. G. W. Murray's *Sons of Ishmael: A Study of the Egyptian Bedouin* (London, 1935) is an older source with useful ethnographic materials. Finally, Dale F. Eickelman, a foundational writer on modern Moroccan Islam, covers the topic in "Rites of Passage: Muslim Rites," in *The Encyclopedia of Religion*, edited by Mircea Eliade, vol. 12, pp. 380–403 (New York, 1987), and *Moroccan Islam: Tradition and Society in a Pilgrimage Center* (Austin, 1976).

EARLE H. WAUGH

NAQSHBANDĪYAH.

NAQSHBANDĪYAH. One of the most widespread and vigorous of the Ṣūfī orders, the Naqshbandīyah is found in most regions of Muslim Asia (although rarely among Arabs) as well as in Turkey, Bosnia-Herzegovina, and the Volga-Ural region. Originating in Bukhara in the late fourteenth century, the Naqshbandīyah began to spread to contiguous areas of the Muslim world within a hundred years. New impetus was given to its expansion by the rise of the Mujaddidī branch, named after Shaykh Aḥmad Sirhindī Mujaddid-i Alf-i Thānī ("Renewer of the Second Millennium," d. 1624), which by the close of the eighteenth century was virtually synonymous with the order as a whole throughout South Asia, the Ottoman lands, and most of Central Asia. The leading characteristics of the Naqshbandīyah are strict adherence to the *sharīʿah,* a sobriety in devotional practice that results in the shunning of music and dance and a preference for silent *dhikr,* and a frequent (although by no means consistent) tendency to political involvement.

History. Most Mujaddidī Naqshbandīs of the past two centuries traced their initiatic descent through Ghulam ʿAlī (or Shāh ʿAbdullah Dihlavī (d. 1824), because in the early nineteenth century India was the chief intellectual and organizational center of the order. Ghulam ʿAlī's *khānaqāh* (hospice) in Delhi drew followers not only from all parts of the subcontinent but also from the Middle East and Central Asia. The *khānaqāh* has continued functioning down to the present (with a hiatus occasioned by the British sack of Delhi in 1857), but what might be termed its Pan-Islamic function was inherited largely by representatives and successors of Ghulam ʿAlī who were established elsewhere in the Muslim world. Particularly important were *shaykh*s resident in Mecca and Medina: the holy cities served to disseminate the Naqshbandī order in many Muslim lands until the Wahhābī conquest of the Hejaz in 1925 resulted in the proscription of all Ṣūfī activity. Thus Muḥammad Jān al-Makkī (d. 1852), Ghulam ʿAlī's representative in Mecca, initiated many Turkish and Bashkir pilgrims who established new branches of the Naqshbandīyah in their homelands. The first successor of Ghulam ʿAlī at the Delhi *khānaqāh,* Shāh Abū Saʿīd, spent a period in the Hejaz dispensing initiations, and Abū Saʿīd's son and successor, Shāh Aḥmad Saʿīd, chose to settle in Medina after the events of 1857, transferring the direction of the Indian Naqshbandīyah temporarily to the Hejaz. Aḥmad Saʿīd's three sons jointly inherited his legacy: two left for Mecca, where they attracted a circle of Indian and Turkish followers, while the third, Muḥammad Maẓhar, remained in Medina administering a following of religious scholars and students from India, Turkey, Daghestan, Kazan, and Central Asia. Most significant among Muḥammad Mazhar's initiates was, however, an Arab, Muḥammad Sāliḥ al-Zawāwī, who did not share the disdain generally shown by the indigenous *ʿulamāʾ* to non-Arabs in their midst. As a teacher of Shāfiʿī *fiqh,* he had special access to the Malays and Indonesians who congregated in the Hejaz, and it is to al-Zawāwī and his disciples that is owed the first serious implantation of the Naqshbandīyah in Southeast Asia. There alone, in Pontianak on the west coast of Kalimantan, does any trace persist today of these various Naqshbandī lineages that emanated from the Hejaz.

The impetus that has carried the Naqshbandīyah forward into modern times came from another successor to Ghulam ʿAlī Dihlavī, Mawlānā Khālid al-Baghdādī (d. 1827). Such is his importance in the development of the order that his initiatic descendants are known as Khālidī, and he is sometimes regarded as having been the "renewer" *(mujaddid)* of the thirteenth century of the Islamic era, just as Sirhindī was seen as the renewer of the second millennium. The Khālidīyah has not differed markedly from its Mujaddidī antecedents: new, however, was Mawlānā Khālid's attempt to create a centralized and disciplined order, focused on his own person by means of the devotional practice known as *rābiṭah* ("linkage") or concentration on the mental image of Mawlānā Khālid before engaging in *dhikr.* This attempt was connected in turn to an activist political stance, aimed both at securing the supremacy of the *sharīʿah* within Muslim society and at repelling European aggression. No centralized leadership existed after Mawlānā Khālid's death, but the political attitudes that had underlain the attempt have indeed survived.

Born in the Shahrazur district of Southern Kurdistan in 1776, Mawlānā Khālid spent about a year with Ghulam ʿAlī in Delhi before returning to his homeland with "complete and absolute authority" as his representative in 1811. Before leaving Delhi, Mawlānā Khālid had told his preceptor that his supreme goal was to "seek, this world for the sake of religion"; from his three successive places of residence—Sulaymaniya, Baghdad, and Damascus—he accordingly set up a network of 116 representatives, each with a carefully delineated geographic area of responsibility. His initiates included not only members of the Ottoman religious hierarchy but also a number of provincial governors and military figures. Particularly important in advancing the prestige of the Khālidīyah was Mawlānā Khālid's second representative in Istanbul, ʿAbd al-Wahhāb al-Sūsī, who recruited Makkizada Muṣṭafā ʿAsim, the *shaykh al-Islām* of the day, into the order. The attempt at gaining influence on Ottoman policies that these efforts implied was never fully successful, but something of an alignment between the Khālidīyah and the Ottoman state took place during the reign of Sultan Abdülhamid II, who associated with the leading Khālidī *shaykh* of Istanbul, Ahmed Ziyaüddin Gümüşhanevî (d. 1893). Gümüşhanevî's importance by far transcended the political: his numerous writings on Sufism in general and the Naqshbandīyah in particular represent the last major flowering of Ottoman Ṣūfī literature. Thoroughly opposed to Abdülhamid by contrast, was another prominent Naqshbandī *shaykh,* Muḥammad Asʿad of Irbil in northern Iraq.

Mawlānā Khālid's impact was perhaps most immediately visible in his Kurdish homeland. The branch of the Naqshbandīyah he introduced there thoroughly eclipsed the Qādirīyah, previously the most prominent order in Kurdistan, and gave rise to a number of families which, as hereditary leaders of the order, came to exercise a leading role in Kurdish affairs. The gradual intertwining of these Naqshbandī lineages with Kurdish separatism and later nationalism is first seen in the great Kurdish uprising of 1880 led by Shaykh ʿUbayd Allāh of Shamdinan, which succeeded in temporarily freeing most of Iranian Kurdistan from Iranian control. A similar uprising against the nascent Turkish Republic was led in 1925 by Shaykh Saʿīd of Palu in eastern Anatolia. The Barzānī family was likewise enabled to dominate the expression of Kurdish nationalism in Iraqi Kurdistan for several decades through its inherited Naqshbandī prestige.

The Khālidīyah also took swift and permanent root in Daghestan, the mountainous region lying at the junction of the Caucasus with southern Russia. This region had made its first acquaintance with the Naqshbandīyah in the late eighteenth century, but it was the arrival of the Khālidīyah that made it Naqshbandī territory while Mawlānā Khālid was still alive. The dual emphases of the Khālidīyah in Daghestan were the substitution of the *sharīʿah* for non-Islamic customary law and resistance to the imposition of Russian rule. The first Naqshbandī leader of the Daghestanis, Ghāzī Muḥammad, was killed by the Russians in 1832, and his immediate successor met the same fate two years later. By contrast, Shaykh Shāmil, who next assumed leadership of the movement, was able to hold the Russians at bay until 1859—one of the most prolonged and celebrated instances of Muslim resistance to European imperialism. The Naqshbandī influence in Daghestan proved ineradicable; Naqshbandīs were active in the uprising of 1877 and provided the leadership for the short-lived Imamate of Daghestan and Chechenia that flourished in the interval between the collapse of tsarist Russia and the establishment of Soviet rule.

Another Russian-ruled area of Muslim population that proved receptive to the Khālidīyah was the Volga-Ural region (corresponding to present-day Tatarstan and Bashkiria). Mawlānā Khālid's representative in Mecca, Abdullah Makkî (or Erzincanî), initiated at least one disciple from Kazan, Fäthüllah Menavuzi; however, it was a Bashkir follower of Gümüşhanevî, Shaykh Zäynüllah Räsulev of Troitsk, whose influence proved decisive. Originally the initiate of a Mujaddidī line that went back to Bukhara, Räsulev transferred his loyalties to Gümüşhanevî after a visit to Istanbul in 1870. On his return he swiftly set about the propagation of the Khālidīyah, thereby arousing both the hostility of rival *shaykh*s and the suspicions of the Russian authorities; this led to a period of imprisonment and banishment. Free again in 1881, he consolidated and expanded his following to the extent that he brought under his influence hundreds of mullahs not only in the Volga-Ural region but also in Kazakhstan and Siberia. On his death in 1917 he was eulogized as "the spiritual king of his people," and his prestige seems to have echoed posthumously in the Soviet period: three of the heads of the Spiritual Directorate for the Muslims of European Russia and Siberia that functioned under Soviet supervision had been among Räsulev's disciples.

Finally, the Khālidīyah also secured the permanent implantation of the Naqshbandīyah in the Malay-Indonesian world. Abdullah Makkî had a disciple from Sumatra, Ismail Minangkabawi. After a lengthy residence in Mecca, Minangkabawi settled at Penyengat in the Riau archipelago at the tip of the Malay Peninsula. There he gained the allegiance of the ruling family, which had already been introduced to the Naqshbandīyah by emissaries sent from Medina by Muḥammad Maẓhar. He also traveled in Malaya as far north as Kedah, propagating the Khālidīyah wherever he went. His efforts were, however, those of a pioneer, and were superseded by the activities of two Khālidī *shaykh*s resident in Mecca—Khalīl Ḥamdī Pāshā and Shaykh Sulaymān Zuhdī. The fact that these two were rivals, denouncing each other for alleged deviations from Naqshbandī principles, suggests how rich the Malay-Indonesian world had become as a source of recruits for the Naqshbandīyah. Shaykh Sulaymān Zuhdī was in the long run more successful than his rival, to the extent that Jabal Abi Qubays in Mecca, where he resided, came to be regarded in Southeast Asia as the fountainhead of the entire Naqshbandī order. Among the numerous disciples of this *shaykh* who established the Khālidīyah at various centers in Sumatra, Java, and Sulawesi, the most significant was perhaps Syaikh Abdul Wahab Rokan (d. 1926). He was dispatched from Mecca in 1868 with the mission of spreading the Khālidīyah throughout Sumatra, from Aceh to Palembang, a mission he fulfilled with great success from his *pesantren* (teaching center) at Bab al-Salam, Lengkat; a three-year sojourn in Johore enabled him to extend his influence farther in the Malay Peninsula.

Naqshbandī practice in the Malay-Indonesian world has from the very beginning been distinctively marked by the ritual known as *suluk*, a retreat of variable length accompanied by a partial fast; the origins of this practice, greatly at variance with Naqshbandī tradition, are unknown. The severance of links with Mecca following the Wahhābī conquest of the Hejaz has tended further to endow the Naqshbandīs of Malaysia and Indonesia with specifically regional characteristics.

Political Role. Not all formative developments concerning the Naqshbandīyah were connected with Ghulam ʿAlī Dihlavī and his descendants. One branch of Shaykh Aḥmad Sirhindī's progeny established itself at Shur Bazar in the suburbs of Kabul in the mid-nineteenth century, and members of this branch played important roles in Afghan affairs down to the formation of the first post-Communist administration in 1991. Elsewhere in Central Asia, Naqshbandīs of various lineages were prominent in resistance to the Russian conquest and its aftermath. Thus the defense of Göktepe by the Akhal-Tekke Türkmen was directed by a Naqshbandī, Qurban Murad, and the great Andijan uprising of 1898 was led by another, Muḥammad ʿAlī Īshān (Dukchi Ishan). Naqshbandīs also headed rebellions against Chinese rule in Xinjiang in 1863 and 1864 and in Shaanxi and Gansu between 1862 and 1873.

The distinctively militant character that such activities seem to indicate has often been invoked to describe the role of the Naqshbandīyah in several modern states, most notably Turkey. Precisely in Turkey, however, Naqshbandī resistance to secularism has always been passive (with the single exception of the uprising of Shaykh Saʿīd); the depiction of the Menemen incident in 1931 as a Naqshbandī conspiracy for which Shaykh Muḥammad Asʿad (Mehmed Esad) was justly punished by execution has now been discredited. A number of Naqshbandī leaders have been particularly important as spiritual and intellectual teachers: Mahmud Sami Ramazanoğlu (d. 1984), a successor to Shaykh Muḥammad Asʿad; Mehmed Zahid Kotku (d. 1980), a spiritual descendant of Gümüşhanevî, together with his successor, Esad Coşan (still living); and Maḥmūd Ustaosmanoğlu (still living) and Reşit Erol (d. 1994). The teaching activities of these and other *shaykh*s have naturally had political implications, tending however to Naqshbandī integration into the structures of the Turkish Republic rather than rejection of them. It was significant that several Naqshbandī leaders were in prominent attendance at the funeral of Turkish president Turgut Özal in 1993.

No uniform picture can be drawn of Naqshbandīs, their numerical strength and intellectual orientation, in the present-day Islamic world. Their influence is strongest, perhaps, in Turkey and the Kurdish lands, and weakest in Pakistan. In the Soviet period much was made of Naqshbandī influence on the "underground Islam" of the Caucasus and Central Asia, but the end of Soviet rule has not seen any noteworthy surfacing of Naqshbandīs. What is certain is that the order has not produced in the twentieth century a leader of notable gifts that would give him broad universal appeal and reinvigorate the order as a whole. Instead, groups varying in size, influence, and emphasis operate separately across the Islamic world, from the Balkans to Indonesia.

[*See also* Sufism, *article on* Ṣūfī Orders; Sufism and Politics; *and the biography of Sirhindī.*]

BIBLIOGRAPHY

Algar, Hamid. "Some Notes on the Naqshbandi *tariqat* in Bosnia." *Die Welt des Islams* 13 (1972): 168–203.

Algar, Hamid. "Der Nakşibendi-Orden in der republikanischen Türkei." In *Jahrbuch zur Geschichte des Vorderen und Mittleren Orients*, edited by Jochen Blaschke and Martin van Bruinessen, pp. 167–196. Berlin, 1985.

Algar, Hamid. "Bagdādī, Mawlānā Kāled." In *Encyclopaedia Iranica*, vol. 3, pp. 410–412. New York, 1987.

Algar, Hamid. "A Brief History of the Naqshbandi Order" and "Political Aspects of Naqshbandi History." In *Naqshbandis: Cheminements et situation actuelle d'un ordre mystique musulman*, edited by Marc Gaborieau et al., pp. 3–44, 123–152. Istanbul and Paris, 1990.

Algar, Hamid. "Shaykh Zaynullah Rasulev: The Last Great Naqshbandi Shaykh of the Volga-Ural Region." In *Muslims in Central Asia: Expressions of Identity and Change*, edited by Jo-Ann Gross, pp. 112–133. Durham, N.C., 1992.

Bruinessen, Martin van. "The Origins and Development of the Naqshbandi Order in Indonesia." *Der Islam* 67.1 (1990): 150–179.

Fletcher, Joseph. "Les 'voies' soufies en Chine." In *Les ordres mystiques dans l'Islam*, edited by Alexandre Popovic and Gilles Veinstein, pp. 13–26. Paris, 1986.

HAMID ALGAR

NĀṢIF, MALAK ḤIFNĪ (1886–1918), feminist and writer known as Bāḥithat al-Bādiyah (Searcher in the Desert). Daughter of a scholar and littérateur, Nāṣif entered the ʿAbbās Primary School when the state opened a girls' section in 1895. Receiving her diploma in 1901, she began to teach while enrolled in the Teachers' Training Program at Sanīyah School, where she received her certificate in 1905. She left her teaching post two years later upon marriage to ʿAbd al-Sattār al-Baṣṣāl, a bedouin chief, and settled with him in Fayyūm oasis. Although obliged by the Ministry of Education as well as personal circumstances to stop teaching after marriage, Nāṣif continued to write, publishing under the name Bāḥithat al-Bādiyah. She spoke in the women's lecture series begun in 1909 and held at the Egyptian University and in the offices of the liberal newspaper, *Al-jarīdah.* Her essays, newspaper articles, and speeches were collectively published in *Al-nisāʾīyat* (Women's/"Feminist" Pieces), a pioneering feminist book.

A reformer in the Islamic modernist tradition focusing on gender, Nāṣif inveighed against men's abuses relating to divorce and polygamy. Appropriating a male Muslim nationalist forum, the Egyptian Congress meeting in Heliopolis in 1911, she sent a list of feminist demands insisting specifically that women be allowed to participate in congregational worship in mosques, to study in all fields, and to enter all occupations and professions, and, more generally, that women be permitted to develop themselves (as enjoined by Islam upon all believers) and to contribute to the welfare of the *ummah* (the community and nation). She also called for reform of the Muslim Personal Status Code. Unswerving in her goals but cautious in her methods, Nāṣif did not advocate uncovering of the face (although she knew this form of veiling was not ordained by Islamic religion) until society was better prepared to accept this change. Following the Italian invasion of Libya in 1911, Nāṣif initiated a program in Cairo to train women as nurses. In 1914 she participated in founding the Women's Refinement Union (al-Ittiḥād al-Nisā'ī al-Tahdhībī) and the Ladies Literary Improvement Society (Jamᶜīyat al-Raqy al-Adabīyah lil-Sayyidāt al-Miṣrīyat). When Nāṣif died in 1918 at the age of thirty-two, women and men alike paid her homage. In commemorating the life and work of Malak Ḥifnī Nāṣif, future feminist leader Hudā Shaᶜrāwī publicly pledged to continue her struggle on behalf of women.

[*See also* Feminism *and the biography of Shaᶜrāwī.*]

BIBLIOGRAPHY

Badran, Margot. "From Consciousness to Activism: Feminist Politics in Early Twentieth-Century Egypt." In *Problems of the Middle East in Historical Perspective*, edited by John P. Spagnolo, pp. 27–48. London, 1992.

Badran, Margot. *Feminists, Islam, and Nation: Gender and the Making of Modern Egypt*. Princeton, 1995.

Nāṣif, Malak Ḥifnī. *Āthār Bāḥithat al-Bādiyah Malak Ḥifnī Nāṣif, 1886–1918* (Works of Bāḥithat al-Bādiyah). Edited by Majd al-Dīn Ḥifnī Nāṣif. Cairo, 1962.

Ziyādah, Mayy. *Bāḥithat al-Bādiyah: Dirāsah naqdīyah* (Bāḥithat al-Bādiyah: A Critical Research) (1920). Beirut, 1983.

MARGOT BADRAN

NASR, SEYYED HOSSEIN (b. 1933), Iranian philosopher, philosopher of science, theologian, and traditionalist. A prolific writer, Seyyed Hossein Nasr is one of the most visible exponents in the West of an understanding of traditional Islam. He was born in Tehran on 7 April 1933; his father was a physician and educator. Nasr went to the United States for his higher education, receiving his B.S. degree from the Massachusetts Institute of Technology in 1954 and going on to Harvard to work in geology and physics. His longstanding interest in the traditional disciplines, however, led him to change his field to philosophy and the history of science; he received his Ph.D. in 1958. Nasr's broad classical education spans Eastern and Western history, philosophy and social science, Muslim and Christian historical and contemporary theological materials, and the development of Islamic mysticism, spirituality, art, and culture.

In 1958 Nasr returned to Iran to teach at Tehran University, continuing his own education with some of Iran's foremost religious authorities. At the time of the Iranian revolution in 1979 he was director of the Imperial Iranian Academy of Philosophy. Since leaving the country at the fall of the shah, he has remained an advocate of Ṣafavid Islam as representing the real essence of Islamic, and particularly Shīᶜī, thought. In the 1990s he was University Professor of Islamic Studies at George Washington University in Washington, D.C.

The underlying theme of Nasr's recent work has been the perception that persons in the contemporary world, especially in the West, can no longer understand and appreciate the sacred—that they have lost sight of what is essential and eternal. His Gifford Lectures, given in 1981 and published as *Knowledge and the Sacred,* reveal his hope of reviving what he calls the sacred quality of knowledge as opposed to secularized reason. He is an articulate opponent of such contemporary ideologies as modernism, rationalism, secularism, and materialism, and advocates instead the immutable principles best illustrated in traditional Islam. His writings clearly show his related aims of interpreting Islamic civilization to a skeptical Western audience and attacking the secularizing forces that have alienated Westerners from their faith and are threatening to do the same to Muslims.

Always concerned for the integration of science, philosophy, and art, Nasr is devoted to an explication of the essential unity of all things as reflecting the unity of God. He sees the secularization of the natural sciences and the destruction of the earth's equilibrium evident in today's ecological crisis as illustrations of the essential disruption of the relationship between human and divine. This he compares with the *scientia sacra* of traditionalist Islam, in which there is a sacred relationship of the terrestrial and the celestial, and of human and sacred history.

A student of and advocate for the classical schools of Islamic mysticism, Nasr has recently focused on spiritual disciplines as expressed in the arts of architecture, music, and poetry, and on the particular role of Shiism within Islamic history and thought. He has tried to show that some Muslims are posing falsely as traditionalists, suggesting that they are really duplicating some of the mistakes made by the modern West rather than learning from them. He sees Western individualism as the opposite of the true freedom expressed in Islamic philosophy and Sufism—a freedom consisting not in action but in understanding one's essential relationship to God.

BIBLIOGRAPHY

Chittick, William C. "The World of Seyyed Hossein Nasr through His Fortieth Birthday." *Research Monograph* (University of Utah, Salt Lake City), no. 6 (1977): 7–12.

Nasr, Seyyed Hossein. *Islam and the Plight of Modern Man.* London, 1981.

Nasr, Seyyed Hossein. *Knowledge and the Sacred.* New York, 1981.

Nasr, Seyyed Hossein. *Traditional Islam in the Modern World.* London, 1981.

Nasr, Seyyed Hossein. *Islamic Art and Spirituality.* Albany, N.Y., 1987.

Nasr, Seyyed Hossein, et al., eds. *Shīʿism: Doctrines, Thought, and Spirituality.* Albany, N.Y., 1988.

Smith, Jane I. "Seyyed Hossein Nasr: Defender of the Sacred and Islamic Traditionalism." In *The Muslims of America*, edited by Yvonne Yazbeck Haddad, pp. 88–95. New York and Oxford, 1991.

JANE I. SMITH

NASSER, GAMAL ABDEL (1918–1970), more properly, Jamāl ʿAbd al-Nāṣir, Egyptian soldier and statesman and proponent of Arab nationalism. Leader of the group of Free Officers which overthrew King Farouk (Fārūq) in 1952, Colonel Nasser became chairman of the Revolutionary Command Council in 1954 and was elected president of the Egyptian Republic in 1956, a post which he held until his death in 1970. He was one of the generation of Third World leaders who had to face the demands of ruling postcolonial countries in the age of the superpowers and the cold war, while at the same time coping with the problems of economic development in poor overpopulated countries. In addition, Egypt under Nasser became the center of the Arab world and Arab nationalism, and Nasser was seen as the leader who would unite the Arabs in the struggle to eliminate both the last vestiges of imperialism in the Middle East and the ally of the West, Israel.

Nasser came into office with no firm ideology or plans and made several attempts to provide a broader base of legitimacy for his rule. He lit on socialism as the best solution and in the Arab Socialist Union tried to establish a vehicle to put his ideas into practice. Socialism, he believed, would foster development and provide a political framework for the country.

In the Charter of 1962 he set forth guidelines for Egypt's future. His ideas were strongly influenced by the then widely held principles of Marxism. In the charter, religion is mentioned hardly at all, Islam only once as the historical determinant of Egypt's thought and spiritual development. Yet Nasser was not a Leninist atheist or a secularizing Atatürk. He valued Islam as an essential part of Egyptian life which should be enlisted to further the ends of the socialist revolution. Nothing he proposed conflicted with deeply held religious principles, yet he did not want these principles to be allowed to hinder the development of a progressive, modernizing society. Islamic values were to be used positively to reinforce the legitimacy of the state political system.

Presumably in order not to offend Christian Egyptians, the charter underlined the "eternal moral values of *religions*," not solely of Islam: "All religions contain a message of progress. Their essence is to assert man's right to life and freedom" [*italics added*]. But the religious leaders of al-Azhar University went further, stressing that the aims of Islam and socialism were precisely similar—the achievement of social justice, equality, freedom and dignity, and the elimination of want. Al-Azhar served as an organ of state propaganda and Nasser himself used mosque pulpits as a platform from which to proclaim his policies. After the Arab defeat in the 1967 Arab-Israeli War, when it seemed that Arab nationalism and socialism had failed, Nasser appealed more strongly than ever to Islamic values. Traditional Islamic themes and symbols were revived, and he made frequent references to Allāh in his speeches. By the time of his death he was trying to set Egypt on a different course, less socialist, more accommodating, in which religion would play a greater role.

[*See also* Arab Nationalism; Arab Socialism; Egypt; Nasserism.]

BIBLIOGRAPHY

Hopwood, Derek. *Egypt, Politics and Society 1945–90.* 3d ed. London and New York, 1991. An introductory survey.

Rejwan, Nissim. *Nasserist Ideology, Its Exponents and Critics.* New York, 1974. Good coverage of the subject.

Stephens, Robert. *Nasser, a Political Biography.* London, 1971. An early but comprehensive work.

Vatikiotis, P. J. *Nasser and His Generation.* London, 1978. A good study by a keen observer of the scene.

Vatikiotis, P. J. *The Modern History of Egypt.* 4th ed. Baltimore, 1991. The standard history of the whole period.

DEREK HOPWOOD

NASSERISM. As a political movement transcending Egypt's frontiers, Nasserism began developing after Gamal Abdel Nasser achieved full power in Egypt in 1954. It stood for the liberation of the Arabs and all Afro-Asian states colonized or dominated by the Western powers, with Egypt playing a key role at the coincidence of the Arab, African, and Islamic circles, according to Nasser's tract *The Philosophy of the Revolution* (1959). Nasserist ideology received fresh impetus from the Afro-Asian Bandung Conference of 1955, and its influence grew as Nasser led opposition to the pro-Western Baghdad Pact, bought Soviet arms, and declared neutrality in the cold war and defiance of the old colonial powers. Nasserism attained new heights after the Anglo-French humiliation in the 1956 Suez crisis.

In the 1960s, Nasserism was the most potent political force in the eastern Arab world; its influence was much less in the Arab Maghreb apart from Libya. At its peak, it was considerably more powerful than Baʿthism, which had similar Pan-Arab aims. Nasserism's weakness was its association with one political leader. Non-Egyptian Nasserists were necessarily accepting of Egyptian leadership in the struggle for Arab unity and the liberation of Palestine. After Egypt's shattering defeat in the 1967 Arab-Israeli War, Nasserism inevitably declined, although it did not disappear, as evidenced by the Nasserist coup in Libya in 1969 and the survival even after Nasser's death in 1970 of self-proclaimed Nasserist groups in Lebanon, Yemen, and elsewhere.

Nasserism was essentially a secular Pan-Arabist movement. Initially, Nasser's most formidable opponents were the Muslim Brothers, who had expected to lead and control the antimonarchist revolution in Egypt. But Nasserism never stood for the total separation of religion and state or the establishment of a secular republic on the model of Kemalism in Turkey. Nasser aimed to mobilize all but the most extreme Muslim sentiment to his revolution. He imposed state control over the religious authorities and the mosques in order to incorporate them into the political system rather than to isolate them. While Nasserism was dominant in Egypt the secular/religious divide was submerged and Muslim/Christian tension was less than in subsequent years.

The socioeconomic component of Nasserism developed later than, but in harness with, its ideology of Pan-Arab nationalism. This component was predominantly concerned with Egypt and was expounded in the 1962 National Charter after Syria's secession from the United Arab Republic pushed Nasser to concentrate on Egypt's problems.

Marking a shift to the left, the National Charter prescribed the political system of the Arab Socialist Union for Egypt. Half of all elected seats were reserved for farmers and workers from local councils up to the National Executive. Although the charter had obvious Marxist influences, it denied the class struggle and retained private ownership of property and land under stringent limits. It also repudiated atheism but generally ignored Islam without showing hostility toward it. The essence of the Nasserist creed was that without socialism to provide economic security and equality of opportunity, democracy would be a pure facade.

[*See also* Arab Nationalism; Arab Socialism; Egypt; Muslim Brotherhood, *article on* Muslim Brotherhood in Egypt; *and the biography of Nasser.*]

BIBLIOGRAPHY

Haykal, Muḥammad Ḥasanayn. *Nasser: The Cairo Documents*. London, 1972. Unique insight by a major contributor to the development of Nasserism.

Mansfield, Peter. *Nasser's Egypt*. Harmondsworth, 1969. Firsthand account of Nasserism in action.

Nasser, Gamal Abdel. *The Philosophy of the Revolution*. Buffalo, 1959. Statement of the ideas that influenced the formation of Nasser's general policies and attitudes.

Nutting, Anthony. *Nasser*. New York, 1972. Sympathetic but critical survey of Nasser's policies.

PETER MANSFIELD

NATION. In modern times, nationalism emerged first in Europe and then on other continents. It was the ideological expression of complex political, economic, and social developments. By the eighteenth century English nationalism had already manifested itself in the works of Milton and Locke and later in those of Blackstone and Burke. It was with the French Revolution, however, that a truly national state was created. Political and social institutions were secularized and transformed to serve the purpose of a national state. In other parts of Europe, Italians, Poles, Germans, Greeks, and Slavs in the Balkans gained national feeling and consciousness and strove toward creating, maintaining, and increasing the power of the national state.

The emergence of national consciousness and nationalism in a politically meaningful way among the Muslim peoples dates to the late nineteenth century; the formation of national states to the early twentieth century. Although linguistic, racial, and territorial notions regarding political entity, similar to Western perceptions, were known to Muslims earlier, the integrating factors remained their common identity as Muslims and their allegiance to dynastic rulers—sultans/caliphs. During medieval times, Muslims considered themselves members of the *ummah,* all brothers and sisters belonging to the community of Islam, even though the political philosophy of the state was based on distinct social estates with mutual obligations between themselves and the ruler. Christians and Jews lived in Muslim lands as *dhimmī*s, protected members of the society, and had formal legal status.

In the Ottoman Empire (c.1300–1918), the most powerful of the Muslim empires, the social estates or *erkân-ı erbaa,* the division of the society into occupational groups, formed the economic and social foundations of the state. Concomitantly, from the rule of Mehmed II (r. 1451–1481) until the nineteenth century, the population was divided into religious-communal organizations or *millet*s. By the end of Mehmed II's reign, Orthodox Christian, Jewish, Armenian, and Muslim *millet*s were organized. Each *millet* was headed by its own highest ranking religious leader—the Greek Orthodox patriarch, chief rabbi. Armenian patriarch, and *şeyhülislam,* respectively. The heads of the *millet*s and other officials were elected by their constituents; their positions were confirmed by the Ottoman government. *Millet*s had the right to decide on matters related to religion and personal status and establish their own social and cultural institutions. The system covered the entire empire. [*See* Millet.]

The Ottoman Empire gradually declined beginning in the seventeenth century. Political and economic developments, both outside and within the empire, and European military successes affected the traditional social structure. By the end of the eighteenth century, the social estates had disappeared. In response to these changes, the Ottoman government first restructured its army and then reformed its educational institutions. Beginning early in the nineteenth century the reforms intensified and, with the Hatt-ı Şerif of Gülhane (The Rescript of the Rose Chamber) in 1839, the Ottomans entered the period of Tanzimat or Reorganization.

The Hatt-ı Şerif, which promised security of life, honor, and property for all and equality among Muslims and non-Muslims, ushered in fundamental administrative, educational, and financial reforms. Particularly after the Crimean War (1853–1856), it also furthered European influence and interference in Ottoman affairs. This often undermined the relations of the Porte with its non-Muslim subjects. The protection granted to Christians and the favorable economic privileges given to them by European powers subjected this segment of the population to different socioeconomic forces than those affecting the Muslims. The Hatt-ı Hümayun (Imperial Edict) of 1856 reaffirmed the rights of all Ottoman subjects, Muslim and non-Muslim, and brought in further reorganization. The reforms also changed the structures of the *millet*s so that the laity gained ground at the expense of the clergy, and particular ethnic affiliation and the use of the vernacular slowly overcame the universalist ideas of the church and its language. Thus secular ideas and increasing awareness of ethnic identity gave rise to nationalist ideals and movements first among Christian Ottomans.

Paradoxically then, the Tanzimat had created cultural and political crises. The Ottoman government, by issuing the law of nationality and citizenship in 1869, attempted to establish the concept of Ottomanism as the legal basis of the empire. The first cohesive response of the Muslim intelligentsia came through the Young Ottomans (1856–1876). Within the framework of Islamic precepts and Ottoman historical experience, they formulated a concept of fatherland *(vatan;* Ar. *waṭan)* and nation. In their writings, the liberal intellectuals İbrahim Şinasi (1824–1871), Ziya Paşa (1825–1880), and Namık Kemal (1840–1888) criticized the Tanzimat and argued that many of the reforms along Western lines had undermined basic Islamic values. They pointed out that the reforms had not answered the needs of the empire and demanded a constitutional system. [*See* Waṭan; Tanzimat; Young Ottomans; *and the biographies of Şinasi and Kemal.*]

The constitution of 1876, promulgated by Abdülhamid II (r. 1876–1909), emphasized Ottomanism as the ideological basis of the empire. The chamber, which held only two sessions in 1877–1878 before it was prorogued, included deputies from all peoples of the empire. Yet it was during Abdülhamid II's reign that various Balkan provinces were lost and some other territories came under European control. This, combined with the influx of Muslims from Russian territories into the Ottoman lands, changed the composition of the population heavily in favor of Muslims.

These developments, along with increasing Western financial and political dominance, helped transform the ideology of the state. Ottomanism, which no longer appeared viable, gave way to Muslim nationalism. Increasingly, Islam became the social and political basis of the empire. Although the legal system, which recognized all subjects as equal, remained in effect both in theory and practice, Abdülhamid II's policies generated solidarity through Islam. [*See the biography of Abdülhamid II.*]

Early criticism of Abdülhamid II's repressive policies came from the Young Ottomans, but most of them were exiled by the end of the nineteenth century. Then new opposition was formed by students from military and military-medical schools as well as young bureaucrats, together known as the Young Turks, who would later establish the Committee of Union and Progress.

Moreover, by the beginning of the twentieth century the coastal regions of the Fertile Crescent had experienced economic and social development closely resembling that in the Balkans a few decades earlier. This gave rise to ethnic and linguistic awareness. The graduates of the new schools established in the major cities in Syria and Iraq had been exposed to new ideas and had gained political consciousness as well as pride in the Arabic language and history. Soon they expressed particularist and nationalist sentiments.

The Young Turk Revolution of 1908 brought about fundamental changes. In the newly established Ottoman parliament, the Union and Progress Party under the control of the Young Turks pursued secularist and, in certain important programs such as education, pro-Turkish policies. In addition, the Young Turks efforts to centralize caused serious concern among Arab leaders who favored decentralization and even nurtured aspirations of independence. The Arab revolt of 1916 against the Istanbul government during World War I clearly charted the course of nationalism in the Middle East. Arab nationalism, though still lacking cohesive expression and clear territorial definition, had taken root. It would lead to the formation of independent national states of Syria, Iraq, Lebanon, and Jordan after the British and French mandates of the interwar period.

Despite the emphasis Young Turks placed on Turkish identity, the ideology of the state remained Ottomanist within an Islamic framework. Whereas Balkan nationalism did not inflame Turkish nationalism, the nationalist movements of non-Turkish Muslims, such as Albanians and Arabs, did; they influenced the emergence of Turkish nationalism with secular tendencies, which received sustenance from its chief ideologue, Ziya Gökalp (1876–1924), a sociologist. Early in the Turkish War of Independence (1919–1922), the "National Pact" (1920), although still couched in Ottoman terms, with its territorial definitions and expressions of popular will, set the agenda for the formation of a Turkish state, the Republic of Turkey, in 1923. [See Young Turks; Turkey; *and the biography of Gökalp.*]

In the development and expression of nationalism and the formation of nations among the Muslim peoples, two trends can be observed. First, certain economic and social formations are reached in order to allow nationalism to develop as an ideological force. As the medieval socioeconomic system disintegrated and modern conditions developed, individuals' identification with a particular social group lessened. The result of this process, with variations, is indeed similar to nationalism in the West. Second, in the Muslim world, nation building received great impetus from religion, particularly from the anti-imperialist tendencies of Islam. As religious groups extensively participated in the nationalist movements from the Maghrib and Egypt to India and Indonesia, Islam lent a driving force to nation building. Thus, although the *ummah* was transformed into nations, Islam continued to be one of the major components of the ideologies of independent Muslim nations.

BIBLIOGRAPHY

Ahmad, Feroz. *The Young Turks.* Detailed study of the formation and activities of the Committee of Union and Progress and the Young Turks.

Berkes, Niyazi. *The Development of Secularism in Turkey.* Montreal, 1964. Provides a penetrating analysis of intellectual currents in the Ottoman Empire in the nineteenth and early twentieth centuries.

Davison, Roderich. *Reform in the Ottoman Empire, 1856–1876.* Princeton, 1963. Irreplaceable work on Tanzimat reforms, which are discussed in detail.

Dawn, C. Ernest. *From Ottomanism to Arabism.* Urbana, Ill., 1973. Contains the author's well-balanced articles on Arab nationalism.

Ghayasuddin, M., ed. *The Impact of Nationalism on the Muslim World.* London, 1986. Provides an Islamic view of the concept of nationalism in theory and practice.

Haddad, William W., and William Ochsenwald, eds. *Nationalism in a Non-National State.* Columbus, Ohio, 1977. Contains eleven articles on various issues related to nationalism in the former Ottoman territories.

Hourani, Albert. *Arabic Thought in the Liberal Age, 1798–1939.* London, 1962. Excellent work on the intellectual history of the Middle East.

Lewis, Bernard. *The Emergence of Modern Turkey.* 2d ed. London and New York, 1968. One of the best accounts of Ottoman/Turkish history.

Karpat, Kemal, ed. *Political and Social Thought in the Contemporary Middle East.* London, 1968. Contains selections from the writings of the major contributors to intellectual developments in the Middle East, with the author's analysis of the resulting political and social trends.

Mardin, Şerif. *The Genesis of Young Ottoman Thought: A Study in the Modernization of Turkish Political Ideas.* Princeton, 1962. The best account of the Young Ottomans and their arguments.

A. ÜNER TURGAY

NATIONAL ISLAMIC FRONT. *See* Muslim Brotherhood.

NATIONAL SALVATION PARTY. *See* Refâh Partisi.

NATION OF ISLAM. The migrations of African Americans from the rural South to the urban North after World War I provided the background for the development of one of the most militant and separatist black religious movements in America, the Nation of Islam. Although it uses the term *Islam* as part of its official name, the movement is essentially "proto-Islamic" in that it utilizes some of the symbols and trappings of Islam, and its central message is one of black nationalism. The Nation of Islam, however, has had an important role in the development of Islamic orthodoxy among African Americans.

In the summer of 1930, a friendly but mysterious peddler appeared among the impoverished southern migrants in Paradise Valley, a black ghetto of Detroit, selling raincoats, silks, and other sundries but also giving advice on health and spiritual development. He told the poor residents that their true religion was not Christianity but the "religion of the Black Men" of Asia and Africa. Using both the Bible and the Qur'ān in his messages, he began teaching in the private homes of his followers, later renting a hall that became known as the Temple of Islam. This mysterious stranger often referred to himself as Farrad Mohammed, but he was also known as Wali Farrad, Wallace D. Fard, Professor Ford, or, to the faithful, Master Fard. In 1931, Fard was recognized by his followers as the Great Mahdi ("savior"), who had come to bring a special message to the suffering African Americans in the teeming ghettos of America.

Fard taught his followers about a period of temporary domination and persecution by white "blue-eyed devils," who had achieved their power by brutality, murder, and trickery. As a prerequisite for black liberation, he stressed the importance of attaining "knowledge of self." He told his followers that they were not Americans and therefore owed no allegiance to the state. He wrote two manuals for the movement, *The Secret Ritual of the Nation of Islam,* which is transmitted orally to members, and *Teaching for the Lost-Found Nation of Islam in a Mathematical Way* (Lincoln, 1961), which is written in symbolic language and therefore requires special interpretation. By 1934, Fard had established the Temple of Islam, which had its own worship style and rituals; a school, the University of Islam, to propagate his teachings; the Muslim Girls Training group, which taught home economics and proper Muslim behavior to female acolytes; and the Fruit of Islam, an elite group of male members that provided security for Muslim leaders and enforced disciplinary rules.

The Honorable Elijah Muhammad. One of the earliest officers of the movement and Fard's most trusted lieutenant was Robert Poole (1897–1975), also known as Elijah Poole, who was given the Muslim name Elijah Muhammad (Perry, 1991, p. 143). The son of a rural Baptist minister and sharecropper from Sandersville, Georgia, Poole migrated with his parents' family to Detroit in 1923, and he and several of his brothers joined the Nation of Islam in 1931. Although he had only a third-grade education, Elijah Muhammad's shrewd native intelligence and hard work enabled him to rise through the ranks rapidly, and he was chosen by Fard as the chief minister of Islam, presiding over the daily affairs of the organization.

Fard's mysterious disappearance in 1934 led to an internal struggle for the leadership of the Nation of Islam among several contending factions. As a result of the severity of this struggle, Elijah Muhammad moved his family and close followers several times. In 1936, Muhammad's group settled on the south side of Chicago and established Temple of Islam No. 2, which would become the national headquarters of the movement. Throughout the 1940s, Elijah Muhammad reshaped the Nation of Islam and gave it his own imprimatur. He established firmly the doctrine that Master Fard was Allāh, proving that God is a black man, and that he, the so-called Honorable Elijah Muhammad, knew Allāh personally and was anointed the Messenger of Allāh. Muhammad continued the teachings of Fard, but he infused the lessons with a strong dose of the black nationalism voiced by such earlier movements as Marcus Garvey's United Negro Improvement Association and Noble (Timothy Drew) Ali's Moorish Science Temple.

Under Muhammad's guidance, the Nation of Islam developed a two-pronged attack on the problems of the black masses: the development of economic independence and the recovery of an acceptable identity. "Do for Self" became the rallying cry of the movement. The economic ethic of the Black Muslims was a kind of African American puritanism—hard work, frugality and the avoidance of debt, self-improvement, and a conservative life-style. The reputation of Black Muslims for discipline and dependableness helped many of them to obtain jobs or to start their own small businesses. During the forty-one-year period of Elijah Muhammad's leadership, more than one hundred temples and innumerable grocery stores, restaurants, bakeries, and other small businesses were established nationwide. The Nation of Islam also became known for its famous bean pies and whiting fish, which were peddled among African Americans to improve their nutrition and physical health. The movement also strictly forbade the use of alcohol or drugs and the eating of pork or an unhealthy diet, and Elijah Muhammad was prescient in his nutritional maxim, "You are what you eat," which he wrote in his book *How to Eat to Live* (1972). He also introduced his followers to the ritual of fasting, and he established December as the Nation's month of Ramaḍān in order to challenge the hegemony of the Christmas celebration among African Americans. In such small steps Muhammad's teachings had the unintended consequence of paving the way toward Islamic orthodoxy.

Muhammad's ministers of Islam found the prisons and the streets of the ghetto a fertile recruiting ground. The message of self-reclamation and black manifest destiny struck a responsive chord in the thousands of African American men and women whose hope and self-respect had been all but defeated by racial abuse and denigration. As a consequence of where they recruited and the militancy of their beliefs, the Black Muslims attracted many more young black males than any of the other black movements or institutions, such as the black churches.

In his book *Message to the Blackman in America* (1965), Muhammad diagnosed the vulnerabilities of the African American psyche as stemming from a confusion of identity and from self-hatred caused by white racism; the cure he prescribed was radical surgery, the formation of a separate black nation. Muhammad's 120 "degrees," or lessons, and the major doctrines and beliefs of the Nation of Islam, elaborated on aspects of this central message. The white man is a "devil by nature," unable to respect anyone who is not white, and he is the historic and persistent source of harm and injury to black people. The central theological myth of the Nation tells of Yacub, a black mad scientist who rebelled against Allāh by creating the white race, a weak hybrid people who were permitted temporary dominance of the world. But according to the apocalyptic beliefs of the Black Muslims, there will be a future clash between the forces of good (blacks) and the forces of evil (whites) in the not too distant future, a Battle of Armageddon from which black people will emerge victorious and recreate their original hegemony under Allāh throughout the world.

Minister Malcolm X. All of these myths and doctrines have functioned as a theodicy for the Black Muslims, an explanation and rationalization for the pain and suffering inflicted on black people in America. Malcolm X (1925–1965), formerly Malcolm Little, for example, described the powerful, jarring impact that the revelation of religious truth had on him in the Norfolk state prison in Massachusetts after his brother Reginald told him, "The white man is the Devil." The doctrines of the Nation deeply affected his thinking; the chaos of the world behind prison bars became a cosmos, an ordered reality. He finally had an explanation for the extreme poverty and tragedies his family suffered and for all of the years he spent hustling and pimping on the streets of Roxbury and Harlem as "Detroit Red." The conversion and total transformation of Malcolm Little into Malcolm X in prison in 1947 is a story of the effectiveness of Elijah Muhammad's message, which has been repeated many thousands of times over during the forty-one-year history of the Nation of Islam under Muhammad's leadership (Malcolm X and Alex Haley, 1965). Dropping one's surname and taking on an *X*, standard practice in the movement, was an outward symbol of inward changes: it meant ex-Christian, ex-Negro, ex-slave.

The years between Malcolm X's release from prison and his assassination, 1952 to 1965, mark the period of the greatest growth and influence of the Nation of Islam. After meeting Elijah Muhammad in 1952, Malcolm X began organizing Muslim temples in New York, Philadelphia, and Boston, in the South, and on the West Coast as well. He founded the Nation's newspaper, *Muhammad Speaks,* in the basement of his home, and he initiated the practice of requiring every male Muslim to sell an assigned quota of newspapers on the street as a recruiting and fund-raising device. He rose rapidly through the ranks to become minister of Temple No. 11 in Boston and was later rewarded with the post of minister of Temple No. 7 in Harlem, the largest and most prestigious temple in the Nation of Islam after the Chicago headquarters. Elijah Muhammad recognized his organizational talents and his enormous charismatic appeal and forensic abilities by naming Malcolm X his National Representative of the Nation of Islam, second in rank to the Messenger himself. Under his lieutenancy, the Nation of Islam achieved a membership estimated at 500,000. But like the other movements of this kind, the numbers involved were quite fluid, and the influence of the Nation of Islam refracted through the public charisma of Malcolm X greatly exceeded its actual numbers.

Malcolm X's keen intellect, incisive wit, and ardent radicalism made him a formidable critic of American society, including the civil rights movement. As a favorite media personality, he challenged Dr. Martin Luther King, Jr.'s central notions of integration and nonviolence. Malcolm X felt that the integrity of black selfhood and its independence was at stake, rather than the civil right to sit in a restaurant or even to vote. His biting critique of the "so-called Negro" and his emphasis on the recovery of black self-identity and independence provided the intellectual foundation for the "Black Power" and black-consciousness movements of the late 1960s and 1970s in American society. In contrast to King's nonviolence, Malcolm X urged his followers to defend themselves "by any means possible." He also articulated the pent-up anger, frustration, bitterness, and rage felt by the dispossessed African American masses, the "grass roots."

As a result of an internal dispute on political philosophy and morality with Elijah Muhammad, Malcolm X left the Nation of Islam in March 1964 in order to form his own organizations, the Muslim Mosque, Inc., and the Organization of Afro-American Unity. He took the Muslim name el-Hajj Malik el-Shabazz after converting to orthodox Sunnī Islam and participating in the *ḥajj* (the pilgrimage to Mecca). Malcolm was assassinated on 21 February 1965 while he was delivering a lecture at the Audubon Ballroom in Harlem.

From 1965 until Elijah Muhammad's death in 1975, the Nation of Islam prospered economically, but its membership never surged again. Minister Louis X of Boston, also called Louis Abdul Farrakhan, replaced Malcolm as the National Representative and the head minister of Temple No. 7 in New York. During this period, the Nation acquired an ultramodern printing press, cattle farms in Georgia and Alabama, and a bank in Chicago.

Imam Warith Deen Muhammad. After Elijah Muhammad died in Chicago on 25 February 1975, one of his six sons, Wallace Deen Muhammad (later Imam Warith Deen Mohammed), was named Supreme Minister of the Nation of Islam. However, two months later Muhammad shocked his Black Muslim followers and the world by declaring that whites were no longer viewed as devils and could join the movement. He began to make radical changes in the doctrines and the structure of the Nation of Islam and moved it in the direction of orthodox Sunnī Islam.

Warith Deen Mohammed dismantled the elite groups in the Nation, the Fruit of Islam and the Muslim Girls Training, and he lifted the dress code so that men would no longer have to wear suits and bow ties, and women did not have to wear long gowns and cover their heads. He also dispensed with the mythology of Yacub and opened the movement to white and immigrant Muslims. The traditional Muslim creed, the Shahādah, was restored, and the Qur'ān and the *sunnah* tradition were followed. The group's name and the name of its newspaper were changed several times: from the Community of al-Islam in the West and the *Bilalian News* to the American Muslim Mission and the *American Muslim Journal* and finally to individual mosques and *masjids* with no single name (or central organization) and the *Muslim Journal.* Although there is no longer a central organization, the followers of Warith Deen Mohammed still form an identifiable movement, studying Mohammed's teachings and attending his nationwide lectures. The movement still has not chosen a theological school of thought with which to align itself despite its gradual move to Sunnī orthodoxy. It is Mohammed's view that an American school of thought will eventually be developed in the United States, encompassing the contributions of both indigenous African Americans and immigrant Muslims. It is estimated that there are several hundred thousand followers of Warith Deen Mohammed, the largest group of orthodox African American Muslims.

Minister Louis Farrakhan. The changes introduced by Warith Deen Mohammed in 1975 led to a splintering of the movement, especially among the hardcore black nationalist followers. For example, Elijah Muhammad's brother John Muhammad formed a Nation of Islam group in Detroit, publishing a newspaper called *Muhammad Speaks*. Silas Muhammad set up another Nation of Islam in Atlanta. But the largest and most successful group was led by Minister Louis Farrakhan, a serious contender for the leadership post after Elijah Muhammad's death. After losing the post to Wallace Deen Muhammad, Farrakhan succeeded in resurrecting the old Nation of Islam in 1978. Farrakhan's Nation of Islam, based in Chicago, retains the black nationalist and separatist beliefs and doctrines that were central to the teachings of Elijah Muhammad.

Born in the Bronx, New York, in 1933, but raised in Boston by his West Indian mother, Louis Eugene Wolcott, a calypso singer and musician, was recruited by Malcolm X to the Nation of Islam in 1955 at the age of twenty-two. On successful completion of his trial period, Elijah Muhammad gave Louis the Muslim name Abdul Farrakhan. After serving a nine-month apprenticeship with Malcolm X at Temple No. 7 in Harlem, Louis X was appointed the head minister of Temple No. 11 in Boston.

Farrakhan displays much of the charisma and forensic candor of Malcolm X, and they have had similar career paths in the Nation. When Malcolm X defected from the Nation in 1964, Farrakhan was appointed head minister of Temple No. 7 and National Representative. Both men also founded newspapers for their movements. Malcolm X began *Muhammad Speaks*, and Farrakhan established the *Final Call*. In building his movement since 1978, Farrakhan has placed his imprimatur on the resurrected Nation of Islam by introducing changes, such as allowing his members to vote and to run for elected office. Under Elijah Muhammad the Black Muslims did not vote or participate in politics, since they felt that they did not owe any allegiance to the United States.

Farrakhan and the Nation gained national notoriety by their participation in Jesse Jackson's 1984 presidential campaign and by Farrakhan's sharp and controversial criticisms of the role of Jews and whites in the oppression of black people. Under Farrakhan's leadership, the Nation of Islam has provided security patrols for drug-infested areas, and it has set up its own AIDS awareness program. He has encouraged his followers to reestablish the economic base of the Nation through small businesses, such as the Nation's Power Pac cosmetics. He also repurchased the building of the former Temple No. 2, the old Nation of Islam's headquarters in Chicago, from Warith Mohammed and renamed it Mosque Maryam.

With the growth of urban poverty, Minister Farrakhan's message of black unity, self-knowledge, and independence and his critique of American society have struck a responsive chord among the African American masses. His message of black nationalism is again directed to those mired in the underclass, as well as to disillusioned intellectuals, through his lectures, the *Final Call* newspaper, and popular musical recordings by such rap groups as Public Enemy and Prince Akeem.

For more than sixty years, the Nation of Islam in its various forms has become the most enduring of the militant and separatist movements that have occasionally appeared in the history of black people in the United States. In addition to its crucial role in the development of the black-consciousness movement, the Nation of Islam is important for helping to build Islam into a fourth major religious alternative in American society, alongside Protestantism, Catholicism, and Judaism. More than 90 percent of the converts to Islam in the United States have been African Americans.

[*See also* Islam, *article on* Islam in the Americas; United States of America; *and the biographies of Elijah Muhammad and Malcolm X.*]

BIBLIOGRAPHY

Elijah Muhammad. *Message to the Blackman in America*. Chicago, 1965. Contains the central message of the Nation of Islam according to Elijah Muhammad.

Elijah Muhammad. *How to Eat to Live*. Chicago, 1972. Dietary advice and regulations for members of the Nation of Islam.

Essien-Udom, E. U. *Black Nationalism: A Search for Identity in America*. Chicago, 1962. Empirical case study of the Nation of Islam in Chicago.

Farrakhan, Louis. *Seven Speeches*. Chicago, 1974. The only collection of Minister Louis Farrakhan's speeches when he was National Representative and head minister of Temple No. 7 in Harlem.

Haddad, Yvonne Yazbeck, ed. *The Muslims of America*. New York and London, 1991. Diverse collection of essays on individuals, organizations, and issues for Muslims living in the United States.

Lincoln, C. Eric. *The Black Muslims in America*. Boston, 1960. The best social history of the Nation of Islam available, particularly on its early phase.

Lincoln, C. Eric. "The American Muslim Mission in the Context of Social History." In *The Muslim Community in North America*, edited by Earle H. Waugh et al. Edmonton, Alberta, 1983. Based on interviews with Warith Deen Muhammad; deals with the emergence of the American Muslim Mission.

Malcolm X. *Malcolm X Speaks*. Edited by George Breitman. New York, 1965. The best collection of speeches by Malcolm X.

Malcolm X and Alex Haley. *The Autobiography of Malcolm X*. New

York, 1965. Classic autobiography and the best source for Malcolm's views. Some of the best descriptions of religious conversion.

Mamiya, Lawrence H. "From Black Muslim to Bilalian: The Evolution of a Movement." *Journal for the Scientific Study of Religion* 21.2 (June 1982): 138–152. First scholarly analysis of the schism in the Nation of Islam movement, relating the socioeconomic position of its followers to the religious ideology of Louis Farrakhan and Warith Deen Muhammad.

Mamiya, Lawrence H. "Minister Louis Farrakhan and the Final Call: Schism in the Muslim Movement." In *The Muslim Community in North America*, edited by Earle H. Waugh et al. Edmonton, Alberta, 1983. Contains the first interview with Minister Farrakhan after he formed his own group.

Mamiya, Lawrence H., and C. Eric Lincoln. "Black Militant and Separatist Movements." In *Encyclopedia of the American Religious Experience*, edited by Charles Lippy and Peter W. Williams, vol. 2, pp. 755–771. New York, 1988. Overview of groups like Noble Drew Ali's Moorish Science Temple, Marcus Garvey's United Negro Improvement Association, and Elijah Muhammad's Nation of Islam.

Marsh, Clifton. *From Black Muslims to Muslims*. Metuchen, N.J., and London, 1984. Deals with Warith Deen Muhammad's attempt to move the Nation of Islam to Islamic orthodoxy, but completely misses the countermovement of Minister Louis Farrakhan.

Muhammad, Warith Deen. *As the Light Shineth from the East*. Chicago, 1980. Warith Deen Muhammad's criticisms of his father Elijah Muhammad and the reasons for his new path to orthodox Islam.

Perry, Bruce. *Malcolm: The Life of a Man Who Changed Black America*. Barrytown, N.Y., 1991. The only biography of Malcolm X, based on numerous interviews. Provides a corrective to aspects of the *Autobiography of Malcolm X*, but is neither as well written nor engaging.

Waugh, Earle H., et al., eds. *The Muslim Community in North America*. Edmonton, Alberta, 1983. Collection of essays on the Islamic experience in the United States and Canada.

LAWRENCE H. MAMIYA

NATSIR, MOHAMMAD (1908–1993), Indonesian intellectual, journalist, and politician. Natsir was among the first Indonesians to receive a modern European education. He attended Dutch primary and secondary schools where he acquired a solid grounding in European philosophy as well as fluency in Dutch and English. Like most educated Indonesians of his generation, Natsir was a fervent nationalist; he was also a Muslim idealist. Like the Egyptian reformer Muḥammad ʿAbduh, Natsir held that a return to the intellectual and scriptural traditions of classical Islam is essential for the modernization of Muslim societies.

Natsir was affiliated with Persatuan Islam, an exclusivist organization that combined modern education with Islamic fundamentalism and maintained cordial relationships with fundamentalist organizations in Saudi Arabia and Pakistan. He was a prolific author, writing more than ninety books and hundreds of articles. The tension between modernism and fundamentalism is apparent in many of Natsir's works as well as in his political career.

Natsir understood the nation-state as a tool for constructing an Islamic society. He emphasized the relationship between a just society and the rewards of heaven, arguing that the use of the Qur'ān and the *sunnah* of the prophet Muḥammad as a sociological model was the means through which both could be attained. Unlike naive fundamentalists, Natsir explicitly rejected the notion that the Qur'ān provides the basis for an administrative system. He played an active part in Indonesian politics from the 1920s until the dissolution of his political party (Masjumi) in 1958. From 1958 to 1961 he was affiliated with a Muslim-led insurrection centered in Sumatra. He was imprisoned between 1962 and 1966.

Following his release Natsir founded Yayasan Dewan Daʿwah, a missionary organization and publisher of books and periodicals promoting his theological and social agendas. Natsir devoted the remainder of his life to writing, preaching, and facilitating the construction of mosques and schools. He remained active in international Islamic organizations until his death in 1993.

Indonesians often distinguish between the young Natsir of the period before 1958 and the older Natsir of the post-1966 era. The young Natsir is revered for his devotion to Indonesian nationalism and development and his struggle to establish a more explicitly Islamic social system. Even those who hold vastly different theological views, including Nurcholish Madjid, recognize Natsir's enormous contributions to Indonesian Islam.

The older Natsir was the most outspoken and articulate proponent of fundamentalism in contemporary Indonesia. His theological rigidity limited his ability to respond creatively to the social and political realities of the modern Indonesia he had done so much to create. In his later years Natsir became increasingly anti-Christian, blaming Indonesia's Christian community for the establishment of Indonesia as a secular rather than an Islamic state. While Muslim fundamentalists continued to revere him as "the light of the Muslim community," many Muslim intellectuals felt that he had become too intransigent to contribute further to the struggle for an Islamic society. Yet however much younger intellectuals may criticize Natsir's theological and political programs, few would question his personal integrity or his devotion to Islam and Indonesia.

[*See also* Indonesia; Masjumi.]

BIBLIOGRAPHY

Burns, Peter. *Revelation and Revolution: Natsir and the Panca Sila.* Townsville, Australia, 1981. Analysis of Natsir's writings and political career of the pre-1958 period.

Federspiel, Howard M. *Persatuan Islam: Islamic Reform in Twentieth-Century Indonesia.* Ithaca, N.Y., 1970. Provides insight into Natsir's theology.

Noer, Deliar. *The Modernist Muslim Movement in Indonesia, 1900–1942.* London, 1973. Authoritative study of Indonesian Islamic modernism, which includes discussions and partial translations of Natsir's early works.

MARK R. WOODWARD

NATURAL SCIENCES. Under the impetus of Islamic teachings, a civilization grew up in the first two centuries AH that produced a dramatic change of outlook, arising from the integrated concept of knowledge (*ʿilm*) combining material and the spiritual aspects in a balanced whole. Starting from the commands to observe, to consider, and to reflect, the desire to acquire knowledge had become a deep-seated yearning. This movement for scientific knowledge and progress led by Muslims lasted for at least seven centuries (from 700 to 1400 CE) and produced more than one hundred men of genius recognized as having significantly changed the course of scientific thought (*Dictionary of Scientific Biography*, 1970–1976). Among the best known are Jābir ibn al-Ḥayyān (chemistry), Muḥammad ibn Mūsā al-Khwārizmī (mathematics), Muḥammad ibn Zakarīyā al-Rāzī (medicine), ʿAlī ibn al-Ḥusayn al-Masʿūdī (geography), Abū Rayḥān Muḥammad ibn Aḥmad al-Bīrūnī (physics and geography), Ibn al-Haytham (physics and scientific method), Ibn Sīnā (medicine), ʿUmar Khayyām (mathematics and astronomy), Abū al-Qāsim al-Zahrāwī (surgery), Abū al-Walīd Ibn Rushd (philosophy of science) and Ibn Nafīs (physiology).

Early Institutions. Possibly the first important institution for higher learning in Islam was the Bayt al-Ḥikmah founded by al-Ma'mūn in Baghdad in 830. It functioned as an academy, a translation bureau, a public library, and an observatory. Observatories of this time were also astronomy schools, just as public hospitals, which also made their first appearance during this period, served as centers for medical studies. But the first Islamic academy to make provision for the physical needs of its students and to become a model for later institutions of higher learning was the Niẓāmīyah, founded in 1065–1067 by Niẓām al-Mulk, the Persian vizier of the Seljuk sultans Alp Arslan and Malikshah and the patron of al-Khayyām. The Qur'ān and classical poetry formed the core of study in the humanities (*ʿilm al-adab*), precisely as the classics did later in European universities. Certain details of the academy's organization were copied by the early universities of Europe: one lecturer was appointed at a time; the lecturer had under him two or more repetiteurs (sg. *muʿīd*, "repeater") whose duty consisted of rereading the lecture after class and explaining it to the less gifted students—hence the designation "Reader" still current in some universities.

The mosques in almost all Muslim towns served as important educational centers. Through gifts and bequests, mosque libraries became especially rich in religious literature. Other libraries, established by dignitaries or men of wealth as semipublic institutions, accessible to scholars, housed collections of works on logic, philosophy, astronomy, and other sciences. The library (*khizānat al-kutub*) founded in Shiraz by the Būyid ʿAḍud al-Dawlah in 977–982 had its books arranged in cases and listed in catalogues and was administered by a regular staff. In the same century, Basra had a library whose founder granted stipends for scholars working in it.

Decline, Western Contacts, and Revival. This glorious phase was followed by a period of relative inactivity and even decadence that lasted for more than three hundred years (1400–1750), contemporaneous with the period when Europe was assimilating the scientific contributions of al-Khwārizmī, Ibn Sīnā, Ibn al-Haytham, al-Zahrāwī, and Ibn Rushd. One may perhaps agree with M. Bennabi's analogy that "the Qur'ānic impulsion being deadened, little by little the Muslim world came to a stop like a motor that had consumed its last litre of petrol. No temporal substitute, in the course of history, could replace this unique source of human energy, that is, faith" (1988, p. 9). There followed a period of considerable turmoil and rethinking for the Muslim world, precipitated partly by the political and then the economic and technological dominance of Europe (and later America) over Muslim countries. Bennabi writes:

> On the moral as well as on the social plane, the Muslim was obliged to seek a *modus vivendi* compatible with the conditions of a new life. From this obscure groping . . . stemmed the historic movements that would give the Mus-

lim world its present physiogonomy. These movements issued from two currents: the 'Reformist', linked to Muslim conciousness, and the 'Modernist', less profound, more fortuitous, and more particularly connected with the aspirations of a new social category, the issue of the Western School" (1988, p. 21).

Both these currents have been active—the first in promoting a philosophical rethinking leading back to original Islam, and the second in impelling Muslims of today to take up seriously the study of modern science and technology as a part of their own heritage, retransmitted to them by the West. The retransmission of modern science to Muslims began in the eighteenth century when Western colonial powers either conquered Muslim lands directly or subjugated their rulers. They needed raw materials for their industrial development and so local resources were surveyed and studied. To maintain continued occupation and supremacy the Western powers had to develop better transport, communications, and defense systems, and so they initiated training and education programs for the indigenous populations. Through this unavoidable transfer of science and technology Muslims became acquainted with the modern sciences. The only exceptions were Turkey and Egypt, which had already developed a definite base of modern technology as a result of commerce and sporadic warfare with European countries during the fifteenth and seventeenth centuries.

Scientific Resurgence. In individual countries there is evidence of modernization early in the eighteenth century, and of scientific activities by the end of the eighteenth century and the beginning of the nineteenth, with steady growth thereafter. Thus during the last decade of the eighteenth century, one scientific paper was published by a Muslim scientist in the Indian subcontinent, while the nineteenth century saw exponential growth, with fifty-two papers produced in the period 1890–1909. Thereafter, the growth of scientific activity in the subcontinent was very rapid, as documented by Mohammed Ataur-Rahim (1983).

In Egypt Muḥammad ʿAlī (r. 1805–1848) had initiated modernization by establishing schools for various sciences, but his policy was reversed by his grandson ʿAbbās I Ḥilmī (r. 1848–1854) as well as ʿAbbās's successor Saʿīd (r. 1854–1863). Only two nineteenth-century institutions survived, the National Library and the Royal Geographical Society of Egypt, which were founded by Ismāʿīl (r. 1863–1879). The era of modern science in Egypt effectively began at the end of the nineteenth century.

The Turkish adventure into modern science and technology was also catalyzed by the need to strengthen its military capability, which was essential for the Ottoman sultan to maintain his position. A revolution in military technology was marked by the Ottoman adoption of guns and gunpowder, and particularly in the enthusiastic development, production, and use of field and siege guns or cannon after the crucial war years 1440–1448 (Heywood, 1981). A century later, in 1547, the work of casting artillery was carried out in Istanbul by a crew of Germans. Thus began transfer of technology, with associated development of metallurgy and other sciences, which resulted in Turkey possessing a sizable science and technology structure earlier than most other Muslim countries, with some scientific research activity in the nineteenth century.

Islamic Tradition and Western Science. For an objective assessment of the interaction between science and Islam, it is necessary first to distinguish the mainstream of Islamic thought from its secondary components and minor issues. Islamic teaching is essentially based on obeying the commandments of God in the Qur'ānic injunctions and following the example of the prophet Muḥammad as reported in the *sunnah*. However, the actual practice as well as the teaching of the Islamic way of life has at various times been encumbered with several accretions. Thus, although Sufism, which may be seen as a form of mysticism, does attempt to trace its origins to the Qur'ān and the *ḥadīth*, in fact, as Hitti observes, "During and after the second Islamic century, [it] developed into a syncretic movement, absorbing many elements from Christianity, Neoplatonism, Gnosticism and Buddhism, and passing through mystical, theosophical and pantheistic stages" (1952, p. 433). S. F. Mahmood writes, "Many Sufi orders now [third century AH] made their appearance and people began to withdraw from the affairs of the world. . . . Convinced that this world was not a good place, they concluded, though fallaciously, that the world was not a reality. The real world, the new teachers began to say, was the world of God; the temporal world was a transient thing" (1960, p. 141). The pursuit of science and technology would be compatible with mainstream Islamic thought, but essentially incompatible with the otherworldliness of Sufism. It is of interest to note that, just as the rise of Islamic science and technology took place two to three centuries after the foundation of Islam, its decline began nearly three centuries after the spread of Ṣūfī doctrine in the Muslim world.

A similar phenomenon is discernible in the past three centuries, which saw three major reformist movements—the Wahhābīyah in Arabia, Shāh Walī Allāh in India, and the Zaydīyah in Yemen—reemphasizing *tawḥīd* and rejecting the accretions of Sufism. These were followed a century and a half later by the intellectual modernistic efforts of Muḥammad ʿAbduh (1849–1905) and Ismāʿīl (r. 1863–1879) in Egypt and of the Aligarh movement of Sir Sayyid Aḥmad Khān (1801–1891) in India, reinforced by the uplifting poetry and philosophy of Allāmah Muhammad Iqbal (1877–1938). The pattern that appears to emerge is that social and moral upsurge or stagnation precedes a corresponding scientific development or stagnation by a century or two and so presumably provides the basic motivation.

Modern Scientific Activity and Islam. Today the products of science and technology are to be found to some extent in all Muslim countries, but local development and assimilation of scientific and technological innovations are apparent in only twenty of the fifty-five members of the Organization of the Islamic Conference. Major scientific development and research is occurring in perhaps a dozen countries, with the top eight in 1980 being Turkey, Egypt, Iran, Malaysia, Pakistan, Sudan, Iraq, and Indonesia, which together had about 90 percent of all scientific and technical personnel (Moravcsik, 1983; Qurashi and Jafar, 1992), a total barely equal to the number in Germany and Japan alone.

In most Muslim countries, the scientists and the leaders of religion within the educational system are far apart; recently, however, a few authors have written on the subject of "Islamic science," or the development of science afresh from an Islamic perspective. Kaleemur Rahman (1987) has attempted a critical description of their efforts. Ziaʿuddin Sardar (1988) discusses the specific ideological and intellectual stands of four contemporary schools in this field: the Guenon/Schuon School of gnostic/mystical thought, represented by S. H. Nasr; the school of thought represented by P. Manzoor, M. A. Anees and Z. Sardar, who call themselves the "Group of Ijmal"; the Aligarh school of criticism of science, represented by M. Z. Kirmani, M. R. Kirmani, M. Kalimur Rahman, and Rais Ahmad; and scholars like S. Waqar Hussaini, Ali Kettani, Abdus Salam, and Z. R. el-Najjar, most of them actual practitioners of science and technology, who see science as a universal and objective pursuit of truth.

Although S. H. Nasr (1976, 1981) may well be credited with introducing the term "Islamic science", his view—which makes Islamic science akin to gnosticism or mysticism and implying that knowledge of everything (or almost everything) is available in the philosophical/scientific thought of the Muslims of the first four centuries AH—is too facile and one-sided, and it represents an extreme viewpoint. At the other extreme, the view of Abdus Salam, Ali Kettani, and certain other scientists and engineers defends present-day science as such without showing definite ways to reconcile it with Islam. Two facts stand out. First, more than two decades of intensive popularization of science at the grassroots level—in Pakistan, Bangladesh, and several other large Muslim countries—has hardly made a dent in scientific and technological deficiencies. We must ask why, and try to find workable solutions. Second, the problem of reconciling scientific thought with current religious thought still remains virtually unresolved. The problem appears to stem from the fact that there is no direct logical equivalency between the laws of the physical sciences and those of the spiritual disciplines. Accordingly, an extrapolation from one sphere to the other often leads to distressingly contradictory conclusions, and the practitioners of both disciplines retreat into their respective shells.

What is needed is a comprehensive study of the regions of overlap between the spheres, so as to develop a set of unifying principles. Three recent initiatives may lead toward such a synthesis. The Muslim Education Conferences held in 1971 (Mecca) and 1981 (Islamabad) attempted to define the role of education in the Islamic context and to lay down some basic rules for development of appropriate curricula. The islamization of social and natural sciences, as suggested by S. H. Nasr, has been attempted (for social sciences only) at the International Institute of Islamic Thought. Finally, the Islamabad Conference on Science in Islamic Polity (1983) took a coordinated look at the past, present, and future of science in the Muslim world and recommended positive interaction between scientists and religious scholars. Notable pursuant to this are the COMSTECH journal *Islamic Thought and Scientific Creativity* and recent articles by M. M. Qurashi and colleagues (1982, 1990, 1991, 1992). The future may see both the islamization of the social sciences and changes in current Islamic thought through interaction with the latest concepts of the physical, biological, and social sciences.

[*See also* Science; *and* Technology and Applied Sciences.]

BIBLIOGRAPHY

Ataur-Rahim, Mohammed. *Contributions of Muslim Scientists during the Thirteenth and Fourteenth Centuries Hijri in the Indo-Pakistan Sub-Continent.* Islamabad, 1983. Bibliography, alphabetically organized, of the widely scattered published work of Muslim scientists of this period, together with a tabular, decade-by-decade analysis.

Bennabi, Malek. *Islam in History and Society.* Translated by Asma Rashid. Islamabad, 1988. Presents an incisive and original analysis of the philosophical crisis facing the Muslim as well as the Western world.

Dictionary of Scientific Biography. 18 vols. Edited by Charles Coulston Gillispie. New York, 1970–1976. Includes 105 Muslim scientists whose contributions significantly altered the course of science.

Heywood, C. J. "Notes on the Production of Fifteenth-Century Ottoman Cannon." In *Proceedings of the International Symposium on Islam and Science, 1–3 Muharram, 1401 A.H. (10–12 November 1980)*, pp. 58–61. Islamabad, 1981.

Hitti, Philip K. *History of the Arabs.* 5th ed., rev. London, 1951.

Iqbal, Muhammad. *The Reconstruction of Religious Thought in Islam.* Reprint, Lahore, 1960. Contains a critique of modern philosophical thought and its impact on the future of Islamic culture, with emphasis on "The Principle of Movement in the Structure of Islam."

Mahmud, S. F. *A Short History of Islam.* Karachi, 1960. Intended to be "an account of Islam and not of Arabs or Persians, Turks, or Indians," clarifying several misconceptions.

Moravcsik, Michael J. "Scientific Manpower for the Islamic World." In *International Conference on Science in Islamic Polity*, 2+2 vols. *Science and Technology Potential and its Development in the Muslim World*, vol. 1, edited by M. Raziuddin Siddiqi, M. M. Qurashi, and S. M. A. Shah, pp. 340–354. Islamabad, 1983.

Nadvi, S. H. H. *Islamic Resurgent Movements in the Indo-Pak Subcontinent during the Eighteenth and Nineteenth Centuries: A Critical Analysis.* Durban, South Africa, 1987. Excellent comprehensive survey of several recent movements.

Nasr, Seyyed Hossein. *Islamic Science: An Illustrated Study.* London, 1976.

Nasr, Seyyed Hossein. *Knowledge and the Sacred.* Albany, N.Y., 1989.

Personalities Noble: Glimpses of Renowned Scientists and Thinkers of Muslim Era. Edited by Hakim Mohammed Said. Karachi, 1983. Provides concise, two-page accounts of the major scientific achievements of two dozen towering scientific and intellectual personalities of the early Muslim era (third to seventh centuries Hijrah).

Qurashi, M. M. "Muslim Contributions to Science" (Part 2). *Proceedings of the Pakistan Academy of Science* 19 (1982): 125–137. Contains an original analysis of the recurring peaks in scientific activity vis-à-vis intellectual activity over the first nine centuries AH.

Qurashi, M. M., et al. "A Basis for the Integration of Modern Scientific Studies with Islamic Thought," "Muslim Contributions to Pure Physics: A Critical Survey," "Semi-Quantitative Study of the Relationships between Islamic Worldview and the Physical and Biological Sciences." *Islamic Thought and Scientific Creativity* 1.1 (1990): 19–36; 2.4 (1991): 7–26; and 3.4 (1992): 7–19. Series of papers setting out "a basis for the integration of modern scientific studies with Islamic thought, in the light of basic concepts," including references to psychokinesis and extrasensory perception.

Qurashi, M. M., and S. M. Jafar. "Quantitative Study of Industrial R&D and Its Impact on Economic Growth." *Science, Technology & Development* 11.3 (1992): 5–23.

Rahman, M. Kaleemur. "Preface to Islamic Science." *MAAS Journal of Islamic Science* 3.1 (1987): 45–56.

Sardar, Ziauddin. "Where's Where? Mapping Out the Future of Islamic Science." *MAAS Journal of Islamic Science* 4.2 (1988): 35–63.

MAZHAR MAHMOOD QURASHI

NAWRŪZ. Literally "New Day," Nawrūz may be regarded as the foremost Iranian national festival. Although its origins are obscure, it is clear that it developed in a pastoral environment, as it has been observed on the first day of spring from the very earliest times. Both the Achaemenid and Sassanian kings celebrated the day by dispensing largesse and other observances. Its Zoroastrian features, which began to be secularized by the Sassanians, were finally completely neutralized with the coming of Islam, so that today Shīʿī Muslims in Iran associate the day with important events in their sacred history. According to the *Biḥār al-anwār*, it was on this day that the prophet Muḥammad designated his cousin and son-in-law ʿAlī ibn Abī Ṭālib his successor and *amīr al-mu'minīn* (commander of the faithful). According to the same source, it was also the all-important Day of the Primordial Covenant (*yawm alastu* or *yawm al-mīthāq*) recounted in the Qur'ān, surah 7.172. It was also the first day on which the sun rose and on which the sweet basil sprang forth and the earth blossomed; the day on which Noah's ark came to rest on Mt. Jūdī (Qur'ān, 11.44); the day on which Gabriel came down to the Prophet; the day on which the Messenger of God carried ʿAlī on his shoulders so that he could throw the idols of the Quraysh from the roof of the Sacred House and destroy them; the day on which Ibrāhīm (Abraham) destroyed the idols; and finally, the day on which the Qā'im will appear and defeat al-Dajjāl and crucify him at Kufa. All this information is relayed on the authority of the sixth imam of the Shīʿīs, Jaʿfar ibn Muḥammad al-Ṣādiq (d. 765). That the day has long been identified with joyfulness at the end of winter and the beginning of spring may be hinted at in the following quotation from al-Ṣādiq: "And there is no Nawrūz but that we have ordained that some divine felicity take place therein because it is one of our days and the days of our Shīʿa." Further, the imam acknowledges the importance of the Zoroastrian prelude to the Islamic period in Iran by saying that the observance of Nawrūz represents an ancient divine commandment that the Persians rightly preserved even though the Muslims had inadvertently neglected it.

Today the festival commences at the vernal equinox and lasts twelve days. An ancient association of the number seven with Nawrūz is preserved in the preparation and display during this holiday period of seven items whose names begin with the Persian letter *sīn*—the *haft sīn*. These are most commonly an apple, garlic, grass sprouts, silver coins, rowan berries, sumac, and vinegar. In addition, a table display is decorated with the Qur'ān, colored eggs, a mirror, a bowl of water, various fruits, herbs and sweets. It is a time for exchanging gifts and hospitality and perhaps most closely resembles Christmas in the manner it is observed and the mood its anticipation generates. Members of the household often don new clothing for the occasion. Nawrūz is also observed by Sunnī Kurds and Shīʿīs in Iraq and other places, in addition to other religious communities within Iran, and by the Parsi community of India. It is of some interest to note that Nawrūz is an official holy day in the Bahā'ī faith, so that with the spread of this religion this ancient Iranian festival is being observed in other locales throughout the world.

[*See also* Bahā'ī; Islamic Calendar.]

BIBLIOGRAPHY

Boyce, Mary. "Iranian Festivals." In *Cambridge History of Iran*, vol. 3, part 2, *The Seleucid, Parthian, and Sasanian Periods*, edited by Ehsan Yarshater, pp. 792–815. Cambridge, 1983.

Majlisī, Muḥammad Bāqir al-.Biḥār al-anwār, vol. 56, pp. 91–93. Beirut, 1983.

Patel, Manilel. "The Navraz: Its History and Its Significance." *Journal of K. R. Cama Oriental Institute* (Bombay) 31 (1937): 1–57.

Yarshater, Ehsan. "Now Ruz." *Iran Review* 4 (March 1959): 12–15.

B. TODD LAWSON

NEWSPAPERS AND MAGAZINES. Islamic journalism takes two forms: first, in general newspapers (Ar., *jarīdah, ṣaḥīfah;* Tk., *gazete;* Pers., *rūznāmah*) and magazines with certain sections or editorials about Islam and Islamic affairs; and second, in Islamic newspapers and magazines in which almost all the content deals with Islam. The latter may be either licensed or underground publications. Arabic-language journalism is the most important segment of Islamic journalism in terms of reputation and readership. The functions of the media in the Arab world are to convey news and information of general interest, to interpret and comment on events, to reinforce social norms and cultural awareness through the dissemination of information about culture and society, to provide commercial promotion and services, and finally to entertain.

The first newspaper in Egypt was established by Napoleon in 1798 after he invaded that country. *Courier de l'Egypte* was propagandistic in intent, designed to inform, instruct, and sustain the morale of the French expeditionary force.

On 20 November 1828, the first issue of the Turkish-Arabic *Al-waqā'iʿ al-Miṣrīyah* (Egyptian Events) was published in Cairo. It was the official newspaper of the Egyptian government headed by Muḥammad ʿAlī. In Beirut, Lebanon, *Hadiqat al-akhbar* (The Garden of the News) began publication in 1858, and was soon followed by *Cevâib* (Messages) in Turkey in 1860.

The development of Arabic magazines began in 1884 when Jamāl al-Dīn al-Afghānī and Muḥammad ʿAbduh, living in exile in Paris, published the monthly *Al-ʿurwah al-wuthqā* (The Firm). This was followed by *Al-azhar*, a monthly magazine published in Cairo in 1889.

The development of the Arab print media has been affected by a weak economic base, close ties to politics, and cultural factors. The most important newspapers published in the Arab world today are the Egyptian pro-government newspapers *Al-ahrām* (The Pyramids), *Al-akhbār* (The News), and *Al-jumhūrīyah* (The Republic); the Egyptian opposition journals *Al-wafd* (The Delegates) and *Al-shaʿb* (The People); *Al-nahār* (The Day) and *Al-anwār* (The Lights) of Lebanon; *Al-Sharq al-Awsaṭ* (The Middle East) and *Al-ḥayāh* (Life) of Saudi Arabia; *Al-anbā'* (The News) and *Al-qabaṣ* (The Beacon) of Kuwait; *Al-ʿālam* (The Flag) of Morocco; *Al-ra'y* (Opinion) and *Al-dustūr* (The Constitution) of Jordan; and *Al-ṣabāḥ* (The Morning) of Tunisia. Each newspaper usually carries unmistakably local content reflecting local conditions. Many items have a political message in the form of political commentaries and editorials, and the news media tend to report current events with a political perspective. Some of the Arabic newspapers with international distribution, such as *Al-ahrām*, *Al-Sharq al-Awsaṭ*, and *Al-ḥayāh*, endeavor to convey this kind of information and opinion to a mass audience throughout the world. There have been struggles both between national and opposition newspapers and between private ownership and government control.

There are several Islamic publications in Europe. *Al-ghurabā'* (The Strangers), a monthly magazine, was begun in 1972 in London, England, by the Muslim Students' Association. *Al-nadhīr* (The Warning Signal) was first published in 1979 by the Muslim Brotherhood. In addition, the Islamic Center in London has published the monthly magazine *Al-ṭalīʿah* (The Front) since 1983. All are Islamic newspapers serving Muslims from a specific point of view. In Germany, *ʿĀlam al-Islām* (The Islamic World) magazine was first published in 1913 and was followed by *Liwāʾ al-Islām* (Flag of Islam) in 1921. In Geneva, *Al-ʿurwahal-wuthqā* (The Firm Tie), a quarterly, was established in 1921. In 1982, *Ṣawt al-ʿUrūbah* (The Arab Voice) was published in Brussels. In Vienna, *Al-Kalimah al-ṭayyibah* (The Good Word) a monthly magazine, is published by the Islamic Union, which is influenced by al-Shawqīyūn, a conservative Islamic organization. *Aslafnā* (Our Ancestors) is a monthly magazine published by the Islamic Center in Vienna since 1991. In the Netherlands, *Al-usrah* (The Family), is published monthly by the Religious Endowments Association and covers Islamic affairs; *Al-insān* (The Human Being) a bimonthly established in 1990, is published in France. Several Islamic publications appear in Malta, including *Risālat al-jihād* (The Message of Holy War), first published in 1982, and *Mustaqbal al-ʿālam al-Islāmī* (Future of the Islamic World), a quarterly begun in 1991 at The Center of Islamic Studies, which is concerned with the major issues and social affairs of the Islamic world.

Newspapers and magazines for Turkic-speaking Muslims are not confined to Turkey alone but are also published in the Muslim nations of the former Soviet Union. Most are in Turkish or Kazakh. The Turkish press has historically been very influential throughout the Islamic world. In 1831, the first official newspaper, *Le Moniteur Ottoman,* was published in Constantinople. The development of the Turkish press was subject to turmoil when the Ottoman Empire ended; since then, journalism has greatly revived. Today the most serious and influential Turkish papers are *Milliyet* and *Cumhuriyet.*

Islamic journalism in the former Soviet republics of Central Asia is a recent development, begun through the efforts of two men, Ismail Bey Gasprinskii and Ahmed Bey Aghayef. The former founded *Turjuman* (Tataric Review) in 1879; it is still in publication. Ahmed Bey Aghayef founded the *Review Irshad* (Guidance) in Baku. In 1906, Jan El Barudi published *Al-dīn wa-a-adab* (Religion and Manners). Journals dealing with Islamic affairs were published in Arabic and Russian as well as in local languages.

In Iran, many newspapers were published early in the nineteenth century, such as *Iran* and *Sharaf* (Honor); these appeared irregularly and were devoted largely to praising princes and monarchs. Since the Islamic revolution of 1979 the government has allowed private ownership of periodicals, although publishers must obtain a license from the government; many Iranian papers publish articles reflecting disapproval of government policies. Several of the Islamic newspapers published in Iran, such as *Al-majālis* (The Councils), begun in 1906 in Tehran, and *Sūr-i Isrāfīl,* have reached a high level of circulation.

The history of Islamic journalism in the Indian subcontinent goes back to 1866, when Sir Sayyid Aḥmad Khān founded the oldest Indian review, *Aligarh Institute Gazette.* Throughout his life he continued providing this review with articles about politics and Muslim social issues. Two notable magazines are *Al-vaṭan* (The Nation), published in Lahore by Maulāy Inshā'allāh, and *Al-bashīr* (The Messenger), published by Maulay Bashīruddīn. There are also several English-language journals concerning Islamic affairs, such as the *Panjab Observer* in Lahore, *The Moslem Chronicle* and the *Comrade* in Calcutta, and *The Mohammadan* in Madras. Other periodicals covering Islamic affairs appear in Urdu; a very popular Urdu magazine for women is *Tahẕībunnisvān* (Manners of Women), published weekly in Lahore. In Pakistan some 125 daily papers are published; most are in Urdu and a significant number are in English. The news content of these papers is rather high. The most important Urdu dailes are *Jang,* the liberal *Ḥurrīyat,* the state-owned *Imroz* and *Mashriq,* and the conservative *Jasārat* and *Navā-i vaqf.* The most influential English-language daily is the state-owned *Pakistan Times. Akhbār-i Jahān* and *Takbīr* are very popular newsmagazines.

In Singapore two Arabic weekly journals are published, *Al-imām* (The Leader) and *Al-iṣlāḥ* (The Amendment). The latter was first published in 1912. In China there are more than a hundred newspapers and magazines for Muslims, most of them in Chinese, although there are several published in Arabic, Japanese, and English. Their content is related to Islamic affairs and current problems; most are published in Shanghai, Canton, or Hong Kong. *Uhowa* is considered the most important Islamic magazine and started in 1929.

Although the number of Muslims in Japan is relatively low, several Islamic publications have been established there. The most important magazines are

ChuKontu-Gibo (Middle East Magazine), published monthly by the Foreign Ministry, and *Arabo* (Arabs), dealing with Arabs and the Arab countries.

In North America, the development of Islamic newspapers and magazines was started by Lebanese and Syrians who immigrated to the United States at the beginning of the twentieth century. The most important of these today is a weekly bilingual newspaper, *Ṣadā al-waṭan* or *Arab American News*. The content is mainly Islamic affairs from a Shīʿī perspective; the newspaper is published in Dearborn, Michigan, with many subscriptions outside the state. *Al-rāyah* (The Banner) is another popular bilingual newspaper published in Philadelphia.

[*See also* Communications Media.]

BIBLIOGRAPHY

Drost, Harry. *The World's News Media*. New York, 1992. See pages 381–384.

Hartman, William, et al. *Al-jarīdah, aw, al-ṣiḥāfah ʿinda al-Muslimīn*. Beirut, 1984. See pages 37, 41, 125, 165.

Merrill, John C. *Global Journalism*. New York, 1983. See pages 107–109.

Napoli, James, and Hussein Y. Amin. "Press Freedom in Egypt." In *Communication and Press Freedom in Africa*, edited by William Jong-Ebot and Festus Eribo. Boulder, 1994.

Risālat al-Jihād. *Mawsūʿat al-ṣiḥāfah al-ʿArabīyah al-Islāmīyah* (Encyclopedia of the Arab-Islamic Press). Tobruk, Libya, 1991. See pages 186–193.

Rough, William A. *The Arab Press*. Syracuse, N.Y., 1979. See pages 1–8.

Waḥdān, Muḥammad S. "Al-ṣiḥāfah al-Islāmīyah fī Ūrbbā" (Islamic Journalism in Europe). Ph.D. diss., al-Azhar University, 1994.

HUSSEIN Y. AMIN

NEW YEAR. *See* Nawrūz.

NEW ZEALAND. *See* Australia and New Zealand.

NIGER. More than 90 percent of the 7,469,000 people of the Republic of Niger are Muslim (national census, 1988). Niger is situated in the Sahel region of Africa; its northern half is Sahara desert. Agriculture, including livestock rearing, is the primary economic activity of 85 percent of Niger's population. The two major droughts of 1973–1974 and 1984–1985 caused significant population displacement, forcing many nomadic groups to take refuge in towns. This accelerated Islamic reform as formerly marginal groups established links with Islamic associations or communities in the urban centers.

Niger is strongly multiethnic: the Hausa comprise 35 percent of the population, the Zarma-Songhay 21 percent, the Tuareg (Berbers) 11 percent, the Fulbe 10 percent, the Kanuri-Manga (Kanem-Bornu) 5 percent, and the Tubu, Arabs, and Gourmantche each less than one percent. All these ethnic groups have played major roles in the diffusion of Islam in the western Sudan. The Hausa, Songhay, and Kanuri states contributed significantly to early conversions to Islam (c.1100–1200 CE) during the course of territorial and political expansion. Much was also achieved through the establishment of local *madrasah*s in the spirit of *tajdīd,* or peaceful reform. Although some individual Fulbe were known for their contributions as *ʿulamāʾ*, the Fulbe and their affiliate group the Tukolor (or Torobe) are most noted for the reformist *jihād* movements that they carried out throughout West Africa in the early to mid-eighteenth century.

Some communities in Niger have historical ties to ancient Muslim communities such as the Dyula, Soninké, and Lamtuna Berbers who traveled the Saharan-Sahelian trade routes from the seventh to ninth century. Others were swept into Islam by forces unleashed by the Fulbe *jihād*s in the early nineteenth century. The region's first contact with Islam, however, occurred around 665 CE when the Arabs conquered the Berber territories under Uqba ibn Nafi al Fihri, who had founded Qayrawa at the northern edge of the Sahara desert and later traveled south to Kaouar.

In the eighth century the Iberkorayen, Berbers who had been islamized in the preceding century, began moving south. Approximately two centuries later, long-distance trade through the Soninké state of Ghana extended the influence of Islam through the western Sudan. The Songhay empire was first established along the eastern portion of the Niger River at Dendi, and today the eastern region of Niger is populated by many groups from Songhay who fled during the Moroccan invasions there in 1492–1510. Islamic theory and practice had already been diffused throughout the region before the invasion, and many communities had already drifted eastward into present-day Niger. During the era of the empire of Mali, founded by Sundiata Keita around 1200 CE, Islamic practice spread, especially among the elites. The Mali expansion encouraged the eastward movement of Songhay communities. Merchant/missionaries are said to have traveled eastward from Niani to the Hausa kingdoms to establish the practice of Islam there. Today more than 98 percent of Hausa people in Niger are Muslim. Among some contemporary Songhay and Zarma people in Niger, Islamic practice is syncretized with that of spirit possession, but this is not accepted by more purist Muslims in the country.

At the other geographical extreme of present-day Niger, the king of Kanem, Mai Houmé, is reported to have encouraged the practice of Islam during his reign (c.1085). He established the Saifawa dynasty, which later expanded to Bornu. Under Mai Idris Aloma the Tuba populations came under the Islamic influence encouraged by the state. Many Islamic reforms were established during his reign, and there was also great commercial activity. By the fifteenth century, scholarly communities were established throughout Kanem and Bornu.

At the beginning of the sixteenth century the Qādirīyah was introduced in Katsina (a Hausa area), Gao (Songhay), and the Air (Tuareg). Although Katsina now lies in northern Nigeria and Gao in eastern Mali, their influence as centers of Islamic philosophy and education are still felt in Niger today. An Islamic teacher from Touat known as Al Majhili is credited with introducing Mālikī tenets during this period, and this school is the most widely followed in the region now. With the fall of the Songhay empire to the Moroccans in 1591 and the extension of Malinké influence over the eastern Niger River area under the Mali empire, successive migrations took place from the Macina plains (including those of Fulbe dissenters with Shaykh Ahmadou) and from Gao and Koukia to the town of Say, which has since been a religious center. Say in southwestern Niger enjoyed a religious and cultural renaissance at the beginning of the nineteenth century with the arrival of the famous *walī* Alfa Mahamane Diobbo, who had in 1804 proclaimed a *jihād* against the Hausa king of Gobir in present-day Niger. He also supported similar *jihād*s in what are now northern Cameroon, northern Burkina Faso, and in Niger at Say, Lamordé, Torodi, and Lamordé Bitikiinkobé. This renaissance was encouraged by the great Fulbe Islamic leader Shaykh Usuman Dan Fodio, a member of the Qādirīyah.

Until the middle of the nineteenth century, the Qādirīyah was the only Islamic brotherhood among the nomads of Niger, as well as among the sedentary communities of Maradi, Dakoro, Tahoua and Zinder. During the later nineteenth century, the Tijānīyah brotherhood supplanted the Qādirīyah. Shaykh ʿUmar Tal, a native of Senegal important in Niger's history, is remembered for his promulgation of the Tijānīyah there. His influence was unsuccessfully resisted by the son of Usuman dan Fodio, Muhammad Bello, who died in 1837.

Today the Tijānīyah remains the most popularly represented order in Niger; its principal centers of adherence are in Say, Tessaoua, Zinder, Maradi, Gouré, and Dosso. There is also a brotherhood that derives from the Tijānīyah, that of the Mamalists, in Say and Lamordé. The Sanūsīyah has its largest membership among the Tuareg of Air and the Tubu of Bilma. Other brotherhoods include the Shādhilīyah, which has followers among the Tuareg of InGall and Zinder, and the strict sect of the Yan Koblé, with followers near Zinder and among the Fulbe of Gouré.

In 1981 an Islamic university was built in Say to commemorate its long history in Islamic learning, with funding contributed from numerous Islamic countries throughout the world. Muslims in Niger remain closely linked to the rest of the Islamic world; in fact, Niger hosted an international Islamic conference in 1982. Current international trends toward Islamic fundamentalism and other reformist movements are apparent in Niger today. Recently some dissent occurred in the Dosso region of Niger between adherents of the Association Izalatoul Bid'a wa Ikamatou Sunnah (Association for Elimination of Innovations in the Religion and for Reinforcement of the Sunnah, called "the Izal") and the Tijānīyah of that area. (The former association is believed by some observers to derive from the nineteenth-century reformist philosophy of Shaykh Muḥammad ibn ʿAbd al-Wahhāb.)

In the early 1990s there continued to be some unease among the various Islamic groups in the country. In Maradi major groups like the Tijānīyah, Qādirīyah, Zarrūqīyah, and Shādhilīyah experience less conflict among themselves than occurs between these orders and the Izal. The greatest reported difference between the Izal and the other groups is the emphasis among the Izal on prayers offered in homage to the Prophet Muḥammad, specifically what is locally called the "Salatoul Fatih" (prayers of the Fatih).

The coincidence of Islamic practice and philosophy with public ideology and state policy is not new in Niger. One of the major challenges is the development of a coherent judicial process that does not ignore customary and Islamic law on the issues of judicial rights, privileges, the protection of women and the family, and land tenure rights.

[*See also* Qādirīyah; Tijānīyah; *and the biographies of Dan Fodio and ʿUmar Tal.*]

BIBLIOGRAPHY

Dunbar, Roberta Ann. *Islam, Public Policy, and the Legal Status of Women in Niger*. Washington, D.C., 1992. Probably the most up-to-date information available on the status of women and Islamic practice in Niger.

Fugelstad, Finn. *A History of Niger, 1850–1960*. Cambridge, 1983. Presents a very good overview of Niger's history.

Hiskett, Mervyn. *The Development of Islam in West Africa*. New York, 1984. Excellent detailed accounts of the introduction of Islam in the western and central Sudan. Contrasts the views of various scholars.

Klotchkoff, Jean-Claude. *Le Niger aujourd'hui*. Paris, 1982. Not a scholarly work, but a good reference for important dates and figures of Islamic history in Niger.

Levtzion, Nehemia. *Ancient Ghana and Mali*. London, 1973. Concise and readable narratives of the history of the western Sudan, based on primary sources dating to the tenth century, including most of the well-known Arabic documents from the relevant historical periods.

Lovejoy, Paul. "The Role of the Wangara in the Economic Transformation of the Central Sudan in the Fifteenth and Sixteenth Centuries." *Journal of African History* 19.2 (1978): 173–193.

Republic of Niger, Ministry of Interior, Ministry of Plan. *National Census*, 1988, 1992.

Smith, M. G. "The Beginnings of Hausa Society." In *The Historian in Tropical Africa*, edited by Jan Vansina, Raymond Mauny and L. V. Thomas. London, 1964.

WENDY WILSON FALL

NIGERIA. A federal republic, Nigeria comprises thirty states plus a Federal Capital Territory at Abuja. The most recent census, in 1991, did not ask questions of religious or ethnic identity, but put the total population at about 90 million; however, several international organizations use population estimates for Nigeria ranging from 100 to 115 million.

Religious Identity and Demographic Patterns. The last official census that was accepted was in 1963, at which time questions of religious and ethnic identity were asked. The overall percentage of Muslim adherents was 49 percent, and of Christian adherents 34 percent; the remainder identified with traditional forms of religion. The major so-called ethnic identity groups were Hausa (Hausa-Fulani), Yoruba, and Igbo. Estimates of the number of language groups in Nigeria range from 350 to 400, with ten major groups accounting for about 90 percent of the population.

It is generally considered that Nigeria is about half Muslim and half Christian at present, since both major world religions have gained over the past twenty-five years at the expense of traditional religions. However, traditional customs still affect the variety of forms in both Christian and Muslim communities. To some extent there is a regional pattern of religious distribution, with high percentages of Muslims living in the states associated with the nineteenth-century Sokoto caliphate and its twentieth-century successor states, such as Sokoto (now Sokoto and Kebbi), Kano (now Kano and Jigawa), Katsina, Bauchi, Kaduna (including Zaria), Kwara (now Kwara and Kogi), and Gongola (now Adamawa and Taraba). In addition, the state of Borno (now Borno and Yobe) has been identified as a Muslim state for about a thousand years and was never conquered during the Sokoto reformist period. Borno has one of the longest traditions of affiliation as a Muslim state in all of Africa.

In the southwest, there has been an indigenous pattern of Islamic culture throughout the nineteenth and twentieth centuries, especially in the Yoruba-speaking states of Oyo, Osun, Ogun, and Lagos. However, Yoruba patterns of religious identification are "mixed," and even within the same extended family members may be Muslim, Christian, or traditionalist. City-state identities are generally regarded as the predominant factor in Yoruba political life.

The "middle belt" of Nigeria—including such states as Kogi, Plateau, Benue, and the Federal Capital Territory at Abuja—has witnessed a significant number of Muslim converts in the past several decades. The identity of "Three-M-ers" (Muslim, Middle Belt, Minority) has become highly visible in recent years because Ibrahim Babangida, president from 1985 to 1993, is from that area.

While the four geographical areas mentioned above form the bulk of the Muslim population in a zone stretching from northern Nigeria through southwest Nigeria down to the coast, Muslim immigrants or converts can be found throughout Nigeria, including the largely Christian southeast.

Much of the interpretation of these demographic patterns in relation to such factors as ethnicity, age, occupation, and education is a matter of speculation, since the period after the 1963 census has been one of considerable transformation in Nigeria. This includes the civil war of 1967–1970, the oil boom of the 1970s, the recession of the 1980s, and the preparation for return to civilian politics in the 1990s. It is not clear how the flow of peoples across national borders in west Africa has affected patterns of religious identity in Nigeria. For example, during the serious Sahelian drought in the mid-1970s, large numbers of Hausa-speaking Muslim people crossed from Niger into Nigeria and blended into one of the most rapid processes of urbanization in the world. The question "Who is a Nigerian?" was eased in 1992, when it was ruled legal for Nigerians to have more than one citizenship/nationality.

Religious Organization and Thought. Several recognizable subcategories of identity within the Nigerian Muslim community may be noted: Ṣūfī brotherhoods, anti-innovation legalists, adherents of the caliphal/Medina model, women's groups, and "big tent" national organizations. It should be added that there are a large number of Nigerian Muslims of all ages and backgrounds who simply identify themselves as "Muslim," without overt attachment to an organization or school of thought.

In the nineteenth century Qādirīyah affiliation became part of the identity of the Sokoto caliphal leadership. In addition, during the two decades after the death of Usuman Dan Fodio in 1817, the Tijānīyah brotherhood was spread in what later became northern Nigeria by ʿUmar Fūtī and his followers. Thus the Qādirīyah and the Tijānīyah became the two major Ṣūfī brotherhoods in the region, especially within the caliphal areas. By contrast, the leaders and scholars of Borno were not for the most part affiliated with Ṣūfī brotherhoods.

During the twentieth century the Tijānīyah spread extensively in Kano, the commercial and industrial capital of the north. Because of the social networks that extended out of Kano through the long-distance Hausa trading system, the Tijānīyah spread throughout Nigeria. A reformed version of Tijānīyah emerged that accommodated many of the modernizing developments of the era after World War II. The leader of this reform movement was Ibrahim Niass, of Kaolack, Senegal, but its Nigerian base was in Kano under the leadership of Tijjani Usman and others; the emir of Kano, Muhammadu Sanusi, eventually became the "caliph" in Nigeria.

After World War II, the Qādirīyah also experienced a reformation, associated with Shaykh Nasiru Kabara of Kano. He reauthorized (through his own chains of authority) many of the emirate notables who had been associated historically with Qādirīyah, and he also attracted large numbers of young people to study and

In the period leading to independence (1949–1960) and in the early period of independence (1960–1966), the Ṣūfī brotherhoods were major vehicles for religious organization and identity. The system of social networks allowed for the scale expansion of the Muslim community and facilitated interethnic contact. Importantly, the brotherhoods facilitated the high rates of rural-urban migration occurring in many Nigerian cities.

In the 1970s, with the oil boom providing dramatic changes in Nigerian educational opportunities, many of the younger generation became interested less in brotherhood affiliation and more in Western education and, at the same time, getting back to the basics of the Qur'ān and *ḥadīth*. Brotherhood affiliation is still significant, but it has been largely superseded by efforts to strengthen broader Muslim identity.

Another transformation during the oil boom of the 1970s, accompanying the enormous increase in higher educational opportunities, was the growth at Nigerian universities of Muslim student groups, especially the Muslim Students Society (MSS). Often these students were from families associated with brotherhood organizations, but the need to transcend Ṣūfī identities seemed imperative in the face of secular challenges to the whole idea of religious commitment.

Many of these students were influenced by Abubakar Gumi from Gumi village in Sokoto, who had been grand *kadi* (Ar., *qāḍī*) of Northern Nigeria during the first republic and had then retired to teaching from his home in Kaduna. Gumi had close connections with Saudi Arabian scholars and notables through his involvement in the pilgrimage process. He began to teach and preach a "return to basics"—the Qur'ān and *ḥadīth*—and came increasingly to regard Sufism as innovation.

Gumi formed a network called Izala (Izālah), which directly challenged many of the brotherhoods' leaders and practices, utilizing radio and television effectively. He was the first to translate the Qur'ān into Hausa; when he died in September 1992, it was estimated that his translation had sold millions of copies. His anti-innovation and legalist approach, combined with his emphasis on each person having direct access to the Qur'ān, became one of the major Muslim reformations in the 1970s and thereafter.

Even though the real impact of Gumi and the Izala may have been a "back to the Qur'ān" movement, it was not a literalist interpretation of classical precedents. He asked his students, many of whom were leaders in higher education, to interpret the Qur'ān in the light of modern times. A result in some quarters, however, was a revival of interest in recreating some approximation of the Sokoto caliphal model or the earlier Medina model in their personal lives or in the political communities of Nigeria. Many of the scholars and students who were exploring the ideals and relevance of the Sokoto caliphate and the early Medina model to the contemporary situation were at the major universities within the current boundaries of the Sokoto caliphal states—Ahmadu Bello University in Zaria, Bayero University in Kano, and Usmanu Danfodiyo University in Sokoto. In practice, many of these teachers and students participate in Nigerian affairs in various ways, but their classical training always creates a dynamic tension between present sociopolitical realities and the ideals of an earlier period.

Another outcome of the focus on original sources was to provoke a reassessment of the role of women in Muslim society. As students and teachers went back to the Sokoto caliphal model or to Qur'ānic sources in place of the inherited cultural patterns of the past two centuries, they became more aware of the Islamic emphasis on the education of girls and women. (Indeed, the daughter of Usuman Dan Fodio was a distinguished scholar in her own right.) The opportunities for women in Western education during the oil boom were also strong incentives to consider women's issues.

Muslim women in Nigeria have usually reflected the ethnolinguistic cultures of which they were a part. Thus, in the predominantly Hausa-Fulani emirates, urban women in the twentieth century have tended to be secluded. Muslim women in Borno have generally been less secluded and in recent years have been very active in educational and commercial pursuits. Muslim women in Yoruba societies have not been secluded and are virtually indistinguishable from non-Muslim Yoruba women in many respects. In the Muslim/Middle Belt/Minority areas women have tended to be educated, and they have no tradition of seclusion.

In the mid-1980s the impact of the spread of education began to be felt more clearly among Muslim women. Some participated in organizations such as Women in Nigeria (WIN), which was widely regarded in Nigeria as "feminist." Others, educated through the secondary or university level, began to reclaim their own sense of Muslim identity. One result of this trend was the organization of the Federation of Muslim Women's Associations in Nigeria (FOMWAN). This group was established in the 1980s to give coherence to Muslim women's organizations throughout Nigeria; it focused on the need to counteract the role of custom in Nigerian Muslim society. By the 1990s there were about four hundred member organizations in FOMWAN, distributed throughout Nigeria but with a majority in the Yoruba-speaking areas. Each state selects representatives to a national committee, which publishes a magazine, *The Muslim Woman*, and holds annual conferences on topics of special concern. The main language of communication is English, and FOMWAN acts as a liaison with other national and international Muslim women's groups. Many of the leaders of FOMWAN are also active in state and national affairs. Lateefa Okunnu of Lagos has served as president of FOMWAN and has also been presidential liaison officer in Lagos State. In October 1992 she was appointed by the president of Nigeria to be national organizer for one of the two political parties, the National Republic Convention, during the transition to civilian rule.

The emphasis on national-level activities reflects a widespread concern among Nigerian Muslims that they not be divided by sectarian loyalties. During the 1960s there was an attempt in northern Nigeria to form an ecumenical Muslim movement called the Society for the Victory of Islam (Jamatul Nasril Islam). Later, during the military periods, the ecumenical "big tent" approach was broadened to the national arena, mainly through the Supreme Council for Islamic Affairs (SCIA). The head of the Supreme Council was the sultan of Sokoto, the vice president was the shehu (shaykh) of Borno, and the secretary was a leading Yoruba Muslim lawyer. In a sense, this format reflected an emerging establishment with ties to the political, economic, and military sectors within Nigeria. With the succession of Ibrahim Dasuki to the sultanship in 1988 (partly because of his close association with the Supreme Council of Islamic Affairs) the council took on a new importance. It had to deal with a wide range of Nigerian Muslim identities and values and also try to serve as an effective liaison with its counterpart, the Christian Association of Nigeria (CAN).

Relationships to Transnational Patterns. The nationally based federations of Muslim groups, such as FOMWAN and SCIA, tend to mirror the existing international system and are often seen as an intermediate step toward closer cooperation within the global Muslim community *(ummah)*. It should be noted, however, that the Ṣūfī brotherhoods, the anti-Ṣūfī legalists, and the adherents of the classical model are also essentially transnational. How then do these groups relate to broader global trends?

The Ṣūfī brotherhoods include transnational and national forms of community organization. Because of their grassroots nature and their connection with long-distance trade, the branches of the Tijānīyah in particular have close ties throughout West Africa. (The reformed Tijānīyah is based on the mosque in Kaolack, Senegal.) The Tijānīyah in general is also connected to mosques in North Africa with Tijanī affiliation, such as the tomb of Aḥmad Tijānī in Fez, Morocco, or some of the clan mosques in Algeria. Likewise, the reformed Qādirīyah has ties to the Qādirī mosques in Iraq. Because of the traditional Nigerian pilgrimage routes through Sudan, there are connections to the Tijānī and Qādirī networks in Khartoum and elsewhere in Sudan.

Some members of the Sokoto caliphal dynasty had close ties to the Mahdi in the Sudan in the 1880s. Other members migrated to Sudan as a result of the British conquest of northern Nigeria at the turn of the twentieth century. In the late colonial period, the British actually encouraged contact between Nigeria and Sudan because the pilgrimage link was seen as a reinforcement of the policy of indirect rule. A number of distinguished Nigerian Muslim legalists studied the higher levels of Arabic in a school near Khartoum, and the Sudanese penal code was a model for reforms in northern Nigeria in 1959.

The anti-innovation legalists often have close ties to some of the official levels of religious activity in Saudi Arabia; Abubakar Gummi was central to this link. There is strong acceptance of the nation-state boundaries as appropriate units for international cooperation among Muslims, reflected in the model of the Organization of the Islamic Conference, which is often associated with a Saudi approach to international relations. On the other hand, the emphasis on non-Arabic Qur'ānic interpretation—especially through the Hausa language—creates a strong incentive for localism and Nigerian-based reforms rather than slavish imitation of Arab cultural models.

The adherents of the caliphal or Medina model have a strong sense of *ummah* or community of believers, but with due provision for trust *(amānah)* relations with people of the book and for tributary (i.e., taxation) relations with "pagans." Within the modern national state system, there is a strong sense of federalism with insistence on local autonomy, especially for Muslim communities that want to follow a *sharīʿah* model. Yet Nigerian Muslim links are clearly with the classical idealized past rather than with any particular contemporary community. Insofar as there are like-minded communities of believers throughout the world—whether in Africa, the Arab world, the Persian world, Asia, western Europe, or the Americas—there is a sense of solidarity that transcends nationalism and nation-state loyalties. The military regimes in Nigeria have often been suspicious of such adherents because of their obvious transnational loyalties.

The national umbrella organizations in Nigeria, including women's groups, seem to welcome the national focus of their activities. They appear at ease in dealing with a variety of other national religious groups and nongovernmental organizations. The leaders of such organizations tend to have higher education and to be fluent in English. The national nature of the annual pilgrimage seems to reinforce the appropriateness of the nation-state unit and of international organizations like the OIC. The strength and the weakness of such national umbrella groups are their closer identification with national-level sources of political power than characterizes the other types of Muslim organizations in Nigeria.

In conclusion, the large scale and complex nature of Nigerian society, combined with the rapid transformations associated with "riding the tiger" of an oil-based economy, make it difficult to generalize about the demographics, organizations, belief patterns, and international linkages of particular segments of the Nigerian Muslim community. What is clear is that a legacy of reformation continues as print and electronic media allow both vernacular languages and languages of wider communication to expand the awareness of all Nigerians with regard to the larger changes going on within the Muslim world and the global economy as a whole.

[*See also* Islam, *article on* Islam in Sub-Saharan Africa; Qādirīyah; Sokoto Caliphate; Tijānīyah; *and the biography of Dan Fodio.*]

BIBLIOGRAPHY

Clarke, Peter B. *West Africa and Islam.* London, 1982. Historical overview, with many case references to contemporary Nigeria.

Coles, Catherine, and Beverly Mack, eds. *Hausa Women in the Twentieth Century.* Madison, Wis., 1991. Historical and anthropological case studies that provide insight into Muslim women in northern Nigeria.

Gbadamosi, T. G. O. *The Growth of Islam among the Yoruba, 1841–1908.* London, 1978. Classic study by the Dean of Humanities, University of Lagos.

Hunwick, John O., ed. *Religion and National Integration in Africa: Islam, Christianity, and Politics in the Sudan and Nigeria*. Evanston, Ill., 1992. Contributions by scholars presented at a conference in May 1988.

Last, Murray. *The Sokoto Caliphate*. London, 1966. Classic study.

The Muslim Woman, 1990–. Journal of the Federation of the Women's Association in Nigeria (FOMWAN), available from the Federation at P.O. Box 29, Minna, Niger State, Nigeria.

Olupona, Jacob, and Tonin Falola, eds. *Religion and Society in Nigeria: Historical and Sociological Perspectives*. Ibadan, 1991. Selection of articles on religion and cultural life, human welfare, economics, politics, and nation-building.

Paden, John N. *Religion and Political Culture in Kano*. Berkeley, 1973. Early study of the Ṣūfī brotherhoods in northern Nigeria.

Paden, John N. *Ahmadu Bello, Sardauna of Sokoto: Values and Leadership in Nigeria*. London, 1986. Background on religious policies and developments in the 1950s and 1960s, especially reflecting power politics in Kaduna.

Sulaiman, Ibraheem. *A Revolution in History: The Jihad of Usman Dan Fodio*. London, 1986. Sympathetic but scholarly account of ideas of the nineteenth-century reformation that led to the Sokoto caliphate.

Usman, Bala, and Nur Alkali, eds. *Studies in the History of Pre-Colonial Borno*. Zaria, 1983. Conference papers from Ahmadu Bello University History Seminar, 1972–1973.

JOHN N. PADEN

NIᶜMATULLĀHĪYAH. Beginning as a Sunnī Ṣūfī order in the fourteenth century in southeastern Iran, the Niᶜmatullāhīyah became Shīᶜī in the fifteenth century. It established itself in India in the same century, returned to Iran in the eighteenth, and since the mid-1970s has spread into the West.

The Niᶜmatullāhīyah takes its name from Nūr al-Dīn Niᶜmat Allāh ibn ᶜAbd Allāh al-Kirmānī, better known as Shāh Niᶜmat Allāh Walī, a Ṣūfī and prolific author born around the year 1331. At the age of twenty-four Niᶜmat Allāh met his shaykh, ᶜAbd Allāh ibn Asᶜad al-Yāfiᶜī (d. 1367). Yafiᶜī's main lineage goes back to Aḥmad al-Ghazzālī (d. 1126), passes through Maᶜrūf al-Karkhī (d. 815), and ultimately derives from ᶜAlī ibn Abī Tālib (d. 661). Shāh Niᶜmat Allāh, a Sunnī, lived most of his life in Iran in the region of Kirman. After guiding his followers for nearly sixty years with teachings steeped in the thought of Ibn al-ᶜArabī (d. 1240), he died in 1430/31. His domed tomb in Mahan continues to be a pilgrimage site and is one of the marvels of Islamic art and architecture.

Soon after the passing of Shāh Niᶜmat Allāh, while Iran was still under Timurid rule, his son and successor Khalīl Allāh (d. 1456) moved the base of the order to India. During the rule of the Ṣafavids, by which time the order had become Shīᶜī, the Niᶜmatullāhīyah gradually died out in Iran. It returned, however, in 1775, when the ecstatic Maᶜṣūm ᶜAlī Shāh began gathering disciples. This Ṣūfī activity was seen as a threat by the Shīᶜī establishment, and in 1797/98 Maᶜṣūm ᶜAlī and subsequently his follower Nūr ᶜAlī Shāh-i Iṣfahānī were killed by Shīᶜī religious authorities.

Throughout the Qājār period the mutual dislike between Niᶜmatullāhīs and the Shīᶜī authorities gradually lessened. The order flourished, but after Majdhūb ᶜAlī Shāh (d. 1823) it divided into a number of branches. In the early 1990s the two most significant branches were known as the Gunābādī order and the Niᶜmatullāhī Ṣūfī order. The Gunābādī order, characterized by an emphasis on *sharīᶜah*-based practice, has as its current shaykh Riẓā ᶜAlī Shāh Sulṭān Ḥusayn Tābandah, who is known internationally for his *A Muslim Commentary on the Declaration of Human Rights* (London, 1970). The Niᶜmatullāhī Ṣūfī order, otherwise known as the Khāniqāhī Niᶜmatullāhī, the branch of Dhū al-Riyāsatayn, or the Mu'nisīyah order, emphasizes the universal, spiritual, and ethical aspects of Sufism and Islam while still following the *sharīᶜah*. Its membership has traditionally come from all strata of Iranian society, with the middle class being dominant. Since 1974 the order has expanded beyond its base in Iran into the United States, Europe, and Africa. Outside of Iran the membership of the order consists of both expatriate Iranians and converts to Islam. The shaykh of the order is Dr. Javād Nūrbakhsh, a retired psychiatrist, who lives in London; he has published numerous works on Sufism in both English and Persian and oversees the publication of a journal, *Sufi*.

Dr. Nūrbakhsh puts love ahead of intellect as the key to spiritual advancement. In addition, he emphasizes the need for devotees continuously to practice the silent remembrance (*dhikr*) of God while they are in the midst of productive activity in the world. It is also essential that devotees attune themselves to the shaykh. Traditionally this attunement, devotion to, or "passing away" (*fanā'*) in the shaykh has often been regarded as necessary for attaining the goal of Niᶜmatullāhī Ṣūfī practice, which is "passing away" in God and then "subsisting" (*baqā'*) in God.

BIBLIOGRAPHY

Algar, Hamid. "Niᶜmat-Allāhiyya." *Encyclopaedia of Islam*, new ed., vol. 8, pp. 40–43. Leiden, 1960–. A detailed article exclusively on the history of the order. Includes an extensive bibliography.

Gramlich, Richard. *Die Schiitischen Derwischorden Persiens*. Abhandlungen für die Kunde des Morgenlandes (AKM), 36.1, pp. 27–69. erster Teil: Die Affiliationen. Wiesbaden, 1965. AKM 36.2–4, zweiter Teil: Glaube und Lehre. Wiesbaden, 1976. AKM, 45.2, dritter Teil: Brauchtum und Riten. Wiesbaden, 1981. This masterpiece of thorough textual research contains much material not covered in English sources.

Nūrbakhsh, Javād. *In the Tavern of Ruin: Seven Essays on Sufism*. New York, 1978.

Nūrbakhsh, Javād. *In the Paradise of the Sufis*. New York, 1979. Emphasizing love as the path to the divine, both this and the previous work set forth the basic themes and methods of Nūrbakhsh's Niᶜö Nūrbakhsh, Javād. "The Nimatullāhī." In *Islamic Spirituality: Manifestations*, edited by Seyyed Hossein Nasr, pp. 144–161. New York, 1991. Largely Nūrbakhsh's own summary of Niᶜmatullāhī history, doctrine, and practice.

Pourjavady, Nasrollah, and Peter Wilson. *Kings of Love: The History and Poetry of the Niᶜmatullāhī Sufi Order of Iran*. Tehran, 1978. Written in an enjoyable conversational style, this work is scholarly yet easily read by the nonspecialist.

ALAN A. GODLAS

NIQĀBAH. The common contemporary Arabic for any association of those who earn their living by practicing a common profession or a profession within a common sector of the economy is *niqābah*. Like the French *syndicat* the term covers a range of occupations from the university-trained professions, such as medicine or law, to craftsmen, skilled workers, and industrial employees. It can refer to a union branch or local as well as to higher levels of associations, but it is not generally used for the highest level of institutional coordination of many subordinate branches or locals. That level, often referred to in the United States as the international union, is frequently called the *ittiḥād* in Arabic.

The use of the word *niqābah* for "professional association" in a general sense appears to have begun in the late nineteenth or early twentieth century. Earlier craft associations were usually referred to by the term *ṭā'ifah* and in Egypt an informal mutual aid association was called a *jamᶜīyah*. *Niqābah* appears to have been frequently used to indicate a more formal organization with a higher level of commitment from its members and a greater authority vested in its officials.

This usage of the word somewhat corresponds to an older, if somewhat uncommon, meaning. *Niqābah* appears in *Tāj al-ᶜArūs* (*naqabah* is given as the verbal noun) to have the meaning of guardianship or legal power and is a synonym for *walāyah* [*see* Walāyah]. The word appeared more commonly before the twentieth century for one who exercised such powers of trust, oversight, and responsibility, a *naqīb*. The appearance in modern times of the *niqābah* as an organization with powers that had previously only been seen as lodging in an individual thus marked a significant change in attitudes toward power, responsibility, and delegation of authority.

BIBLIOGRAPHY

Baer, Gabriel. *Egyptian Guilds in Modern Times*. Jerusalem, 1964.

Goldberg, Ellis. *Tinker, Tailor and Textile Worker*. Berkeley, 1986.

ELLIS GOLDBERG

NUBŪWAH. *See* Prophethood.

NUMEROLOGY. The science of interpreting numbers in a mystical or magical sense was very popular in the traditional Islamic world. By assigning each letter of the Arabic alphabet a number (*alif* = 1, *h* = 5, etc.) Muslims could easily derive dates from the sacred scripture by means of adding the values of the letters of key words or important phrases. This custom, very common in earlier days, is still practiced in some countries. However, the recent attempt of a Muslim numerologist to prove with the help of a computer that the entire Qur'ān is based on the number nineteen was rejected by the orthodox—perhaps because nineteen is also the sacred number of the Bahā'īs; it is the numerical value of the word *wāḥid*, "one."

As letters and numbers are interchangeable, numerologists could invent clever chronograms: when Stalin died, a Turkish theologian composed a chronogram stating "Satan was cast into Hell" that gave the *hijrī* date of his death. To display the date of a building by means of a fitting Qur'ānic *āyah* or a line of poetry was common in the Persian world until recently. The same device could be applied to date books; thus the Urdu story *Bāgh va bahār* (Garden and Spring) shows by its very title that it was completed in AH 1217/1803 CE.

As in other cultures, certain numbers occur frequently in Islamic belief and practice. Actions and formulas are often repeated three times because the Prophet reportedly practiced threefold repetitions. Four, the number of universal order, is reflected (perhaps coincidentally) in the four righteous caliphs, the four schools of law, and the four legal wives; five appears in the five pillars of Islam, the five daily prayers, and in the group of the *Panjtan,* the five holy persons Muḥammad, Fāṭimah, ʿAlī, Ḥasan, and Ḥusayn. Their names are often written on amulets as a protective formula, especially appropriate in amulets shaped like a hand with its five fingers. Seven is important in the *ḥajj* ceremonies (the sevenfold *ṭawāf,* running seven times between Ṣafā and Marwa, stoning Satan three times seven), and in Sufism where heptads of saints appear. The mystical path leads through seven steps or valleys. Seven plays a significant role in the Ismāʿīlī community, where prophets and their representatives, the prophetic cycles, and most aspects of life appear in heptads. The heptagonal fountain in the Ismāʿīlī Center in London well expresses the importance of seven.

The lunar number fourteen (at the same time the numerical value of *Ṭāhā,* surah 20 and one of the Prophet's names) and twenty-eight, the full lunar cycle and the number of the prophets mentioned in the Qur'ān, are well known. But the most important round number is forty, which in all religious traditions points to patience, trial, and maturity. Examples are the forty-day seclusion of the dervish, or groups of forty saints commemorated in names like *Kırklareli* (Land of the Forty). Impurity after childbirth lasts forty days, and the first memorial after a death is likewise on the fortieth day. Feasts are celebrated for forty days, and in folktales one encounters the forty thieves or women who give birth to forty children at once. In proverbs, forty years is the point where life changes and one matures.

The importance of such numbers may not be known to modern artists or writers but seems to be subconsciously alive in the structure of some literary and artistic works. The *One Thousand and One Nights* may also exert some influence—after all, 1,001 is an odd number, and "God is an odd number (i.e., One) and loves odd numbers." There are *tasbīḥ*s (rosaries) with 1,001 beads, but the usual number is 33 or 99; to repeat certain formulas thirty-three times is considered very useful. Dervishes may also count the numerical value of a divine name and repeat this name according to its numerical value: *Allāh* 66 times, *raḥmān* 299 times, or *ghafūr* 1,285 times.

[*See also* Divination; Geomancy; Magic and Sorcery; Mathematics.]

BIBLIOGRAPHY

Schimmel, Annemarie. *The Mystery of Numbers.* New York, 1993. Includes an extensive bibliography.

ANNEMARIE SCHIMMEL

NURCHOLISH MADJID (b. 1939), Indonesian scholar and advocate of religious tolerance. Nurcholish is among Indonesia's most daring theologians. His vision of Islam is pluralistic, tolerant, and intended to meet the spiritual needs of a modern urban population. Like other modernist thinkers, Nurcholish roots his theology in the doctrine of *tajdīd* or a return to the Islam of the prophet Muḥammad. Unlike other modernists he is more concerned with spirituality than with ritual and social behavior.

Born in east Java, Nurcholish is a scion of one of Indonesia's most celebrated families of Islamic scholars. He was educated at traditional Islamic schools *(pesantren)* and at the modernist school at Gontor, which emphasizes English and secular subjects as well as the traditional Islamic curriculum. He received a B.A. from the State Institute of Islamic Studies in Jakarta in 1968. From 1966 until 1971 he was chairman of the Indonesian Muslim Students Association. He studied with Fazlur Rahman at the University of Chicago, receiving his Ph.D. in 1984 with a dissertation on Ibn Taymīyah's understanding of the relationship between reason and revelation. In the early 1990s Nurcholish held positions at the State Institute of Islamic Studies in Jakarta and the Indonesian Academy of Sciences.

Nurcholish's thought is highly controversial. In the 1960s he challenged the "modernist" position that advocates a literal application of the Qur'ān and *ḥadīth* in contemporary society. As an alternative he advocated a return to the spirit or underlying principles of Islam as a guide for contemporary conduct. In 1970 he introduced the concept of "Islamic secularization." This does not mean secularization in the Western sense, but rather the desacralization of certain aspects of human life and knowledge, which, in view of the spirit of Islam, are not properly religious. During this period Nurcholish was influenced by two American scholars, the sociologist Robert Bellah and the theologian Harvey Cox. Older, *sharīʿah*-centered Indonesian modernists, including Nurcholish's mentor Mohammad Natsir, were outraged.

In numerous publications Nurcholish has emphasized the concept of Islamic brotherhood and has attempted to extend the boundaries of the Muslim community as broadly as possible. He is a strident opponent of all forms of sectarianism. In his dissertation and in Indonesian publications based on it he emphasizes the philosophically tolerant side of Ibn Taymīyah, who is better known for his polemical castigations of popular Islam.

He describes his work as an attempt to apply the universal Islamic values in the cultural and historical context of contemporary Indonesia. In a series of recent works Madjid has denounced sectarian and fundamentalist groups as cults and defined Islam as being nothing more nor less than submission to God—a definition that allows him to apply the word "Islam" in discussions of Christians and Jews.

Nurcholish's call for an inclusive, tolerant Islam and for dialogue with other faiths is a bold attempt to resolve the problems of bigotry and intolerance that plague not only Islam but also other major religions. Although he has many supporters among Indonesian intellectuals, the virulent polemics his works incite indicate that such an idealistic vision will be at best difficult to realize.

[*See also* Indonesia.]

BIBLIOGRAPHY

Barton, Greg. "The International Context of the Emergence of Islamic Neo Modernism in Indonesia." In *Islam in the Indonesian Social Context,* edited by Merle C. Ricklefs, pp. 69–82. Clayton, Australia, 1991.

Federspiel, Howard M. *Muslim Intellectuals and National Development in Indonesia.* New York, 1992. Includes biographical data and English summaries of Nurcholish's works.

Hasan, M. Kamal. *Muslim Intellectual Responses to "New Order" Modernization in Indonesia.* Kuala Lumpur, 1980. Critical analysis of Nurcholish's early works, including English translations.

Nurcholish Madjid. "The Issue of Modernization among Muslims in Indonesia from a Participant's Point of View." In *What Is Modern Indonesian Culture?,* edited by Gloria Davis, pp. 143–155. Athens Ohio, 1979. Autobiographical account of Nurcholish's student years.

Nurcholish Madjid. *Islam: Doctrin dan Peradaban* (Islam: Doctrine and Civilization). Jakarta, 1992. Collection of Nurcholish's major works.

MARK R. WOODWARD

NURCULUK. The modern Turkish religious movement known as Nurculuk takes its name from its founder and leader Bediüzzaman Said Nursî (1876–1960). He was born in the village of Nurs in the province of Bitlis in eastern Turkey in a region with a largely Kurdish population. In the 1870s the Ottoman government had only recently established centralized administrative structures in this area, replacing a flexible, decentralized system that relied on the local aristocracy. The fall from power of the local notables gave impetus to the growth of the fideist/fundamentalist Sunnī Naqshbandī (Tk., Nakşibendi) order, who took over local functions of conciliation among the tribes as the old system of law and order disintegrated. A branch of the Naqshbandīyah had established local seminaries and had spread from northern Iraq to Anatolia and to the Russian Empire in Kazan, the Caucasus, and Central Asia. It combatted the expansion of Russia and the spread of Russian Orthodox Christianity. Said Nursî was educated in a Naqshbandī circle; in Bitlis, however, his outlook was also shaped by the presence of an Ottoman administration modeling itself increasingly on western Europe. He realized that the Turkish modernization movement was establishing new criteria differentiating between the more modern Turks of western Anatolia and the Balkans and his own comparatively backward Kurdish region, and this moved him to take up the defense of his kin. An Islam that brought all Muslims under the umbrella of a common faith but added the advantages of Western technology and knowledge was his solution to this cultural bifurcation, which he considered to be a great danger for all Muslims. This foundation of his thought reappears in his later writings in diverse forms and also underlies his followers' self-assumed task of teaching advances in knowledge.

The Young Turk revolution of 1908 led Said Nursî to hope that his sociopolitical program could be carried out, but the new rulers' ambivalence toward Islam resulted in a series of conflicts in which he was temporarily exiled, although he later collaborated with the Young Turk regime. He eventually fought as an Ottoman patriot on the Caucasian front during World War I, and was taken prisoner by the Russians. Back in Turkey, he sided with the national resistance movement of Mustafa Kemal (later Atatürk), but he was forced into exile in Bitlis when his program of religious revitalization clashed with the aims of the founder of the Turkish Republic. Accused of complicity in the Kurdish uprising of 1925, he was sent to further exile in the province of Isparta. His proselytizing and the group of disciples he was able to influence resulted in yet further exiles to Kastamonu and Denizli. He was also imprisoned several times for contravening the Turkish Republic's laws against religious organizations. He died in 1960.

Said Nursî's disciples are known in Turkish as "Nurcu," or men of Nursî (or, alternatively, since *nur* [light] is an important symbol in the Qur'ān, "men of the light"). The Turkish authorities repeatedly accused Said Nursî of having established his own religious order, an action punishable under Turkish law since the dissolution of Ṣūfī orders in 1925. Both Said Nursî and his followers rejected this classification, indicating that their aims were the wider ones of the revitalization of Islam as a whole. Said Nursî's own writings, collected under the title *Risale-i nur* (Epistle of Light), seem to confirm this claim. The Nurculuk is better seen as a faith movement eventually having institutionalized none of the links between *shaykh* or pir (religious mentor) and *murīd* (disciple) that characterize Ṣūfī orders. The group, which originated as a religious movement in rural areas and provincial towns, has spread to larger cities and has gathered around it persons of increasingly high educational credentials, including university professors. It is extremely active in publishing the writings of Said Nursî as well as brochures explaining the foundation of modern science, and it has for many years published a newspaper, *Yeni Asya.* Divisiveness within the group has spawned a number of competing submovements; the rationales of these splinter groups are not easy to ascertain, and the factionalism appears to stem from leadership rivalries.

[*See also* Naqshbandīyah.]

BIBLIOGRAPHY

Bediüzzaman Said Nursî: Panel. Coordinated by Faik Bilgi. Istanbul, 1991. Proceedings of a conference on Said Nursî (in Turkish).

Bruinessen, Martin van. *Agha, Shaikh and State: On the Social and Political Organization of Kurdistan.* London, 1992.

Mardin, Şerif. *Religion and Social Change in Modern Turkey.* Albany, N.Y., 1989.

ŞERIF MARDIN

NŪRĪ, FAẒLULLĀH (AH 1259–1327/1843–1909 CE), more fully, Ḥājj Shaykh Faẓlullāh ibn Mullā ʿAbbās Māzandarānī Nūrī Tihrānī, a distinguished Iranian Shīʿī scholar. His father, Mullā ʿAbbās Nūrī, was a prominent jurist. Nūrī studied Shīʿī jurisprudence with Ḥājj Mīrzā Muḥammad Ḥasan Shīrāzī (d. 1312/1894) in Najaf. Shīrāzī is famous in nineteenth-century Iranian history because of his antitobacco edict during the Tobacco Revolt of 1891–1892. Finishing his studies in Najaf, Nūrī returned to Tehran and became a *marjaʿ al-taqlīd* ("source of exemplary conduct") in the Qājār capital. Among his writings is *Tadhkirat al-ghāfil wa-irshād al-jāhil,* which contained a harsh condemnation of proconstitutional ideas and forces (see Dabashi's translation of this text in Arjomand, ed., 1988, pp. 354–70; see also Hairi, 1977b).

Nūrī played an active but controversial part in the Constitutional Revolution of Iran (1905–1911). His role along with that of the entire clerical class has been debated extensively (for the nature of this debate, see Hairi, 1977a; cf. Lahidji's "Constitutionalism and Clerical Authority" in Arjomand, ed., 1988, pp. 133–158). Most historians of the constitutional period are critical of his anticonstitutional stands. Some, including Aḥmad Kasravī and Farīdūn Ādamīyat, are more moderate in their observations, although others, such as Nāẓim al-Islām Kirmānī, are extremely critical and even accuse him of greed and charlatanism (see Kirmānī, 1983, vol. 1, pp. 565–566; see also Qazvīnī, 1984, vol. 4, p. 880). A combination of religious convictions and personal and professional interests must have guided Nūrī's contradictory positions in this period. Initially, he appears to have been one of the most active supporters of constitutional government, but gradually he shifted his position and relentlessly opposed it (Kasravī, 1951, pp. 285–296; Kirmānī, 1983, vol. 2, pp. 535–537). Contrary to Sayyids Muḥammad Ṭabāṭabāʾī and ʿAbd Allāh Bihbahānī, the two prominent proconstitutional clerics, Nūrī became increasingly concerned with the dangers that he felt constitutional government posed for Islam in general and for Islamic law in particular. The phrase *mashrūṭah-yi mashrūʿah* ("constitutional government compatible with the Islamic law") is chiefly identified with Nūrī, who somewhat diffusely argued for tying the very foundations of a secular form of government to the requirements of Shīʿī law.

Historians of the constitutional period insist that personal rivalries between Nūrī and Bihbahānī were instrumental in Nūrī's opposition to constitutional government (Dawlatābādī 1983, vol. 2, p. 185; Kasravī, 1951, pp. 285–286; Ādamīyat, 1976, vol. 1, pp. 429–430). Ādamīyat holds that their opposing positions cloaked their personal rivalries and a struggle for power. He quotes Nūrī as having said: "Neither was I an absolutist nor were Sayyid Ābdullah and Sayyid Muḥammad constitutionalists. They were against me, and I was against them" (Ādamīyat, 1976, vol. 1, pp. 430–431). Kasravī, too, believes that none of the clerical antagonists "knew the precise meaning of constitutionalism, or the consequences of the propagation of European laws. They were not quite aware of the blatant incompatibility of constitutionalism with the Shīʿī faith" (Kasravī, 1951, p. 287).

Nūrī emphasized the necessity for Islam of both *salṭanat* (monarchy) and *nīyābat dar ʿumūr-i nabavīyah* (clerical viceregency in matters of prophethood; see Martin, 1989, pp. 28–29).

Because of his anticonstitutional activities, Nūrī was captured and executed by the constitutionalist forces on 13 Rajab 1327/31 July 1909. One of Nūrī's sons, Shaykh Mīrzā Mahdī, was, against the wishes of his father, a staunch proconstitutionalist. He is reported (Kirmānī, 1983, vol. 1, p. 566) to have been a militant advocate of constitutional government and was murdered by anti-constitutional forces in 1333/1914.

[*See also* Constitutional Revolution.]

BIBLIOGRAPHY

Ādamīyat, Farīdūn. *ʿIdi'ūlūzhī-yi Nahẕat-i Mashrūṭīyat-i Īrān*. 2 vols. Tehran, 1355/1976.

Arjomand, Said Amir, ed. *Authority and Political Culture in Shiʿism*. Albany, N.Y., 1988.

Dawlatābādī, Yahyā. *Ḥayāt-i Yaḥyā*. 4 vols. Tehran, 1362/1983.

Hairi, Abdul-Hadi. *Shiʿism and Constitutionalism in Iran*. Leiden, 1977a.

Hairi, Abdul-Hadi. "Shaikh Fazlullah Nuri's Refutation of the Idea of Constitutionalism." *Middle Eastern Studies* 23.3 (1977b): 227–239.

Kasravī, Aḥmad. *Tārīkh-i Mashrūṭah-yi Īrān*. Tehran, 1330/1951.

Kirmānī, Nāẓim al-Islām. *Tārīkh-i Bīdārī-yi Irānīyān*. 2 vols. Edited by ʿAli Akbar Saʿīdī Sīrjānīi. Tehran, 1362/1983.

Martin, Vanessa. *Islam and Modernism: The Iranian Revolution of 1906*. London, 1989.

Muʿallim Ḥabībabādī, Mīrzā Muḥammad ʿAlī. *Makārim al-āsār dar aḥvāl-i rijāl dawrah-i Qājār*. 6 vols. Isfahan, 1976–1985.

Nūrī, Faẕlullāh. *Lavāyiḥ-i Āqā Shaykh Faẕl Allāh Nūrī*. Edited by Humā Riẕvānī. Tehran, 1362/1983.

Qazvīnī, Muḥammad. "Ḥājj Shaykh Faẕl Allāh Nūrī." In *Maqālāt-i ʿAllāmah Qazvīnī*. 4 vols. Edited by ʿAbd al-Karīm Jurbuzah-dār. Tehran, 1363/1984.

HAMID DABASHI

NURSÎ, SAID. *See* Nurculuk.

NUṢAYRĪYAH. *See* ʿAlawīyah.

O

OMAN. Although a major component of its distinctiveness derives from Ibāḍī Islam, Oman is religiously, ethnically, and geographically complex. Its estimated 1992 population of 1,500,000 (17 percent noncitizens) included an Ibāḍī population of 40 to 45 percent; 50 to 55 percent were Sunnī; and no more than 2 percent were Shīʿī.

Roughly the size of Arizona, Oman was relatively isolated and underdeveloped until 1970, when the current ruler, Sultan Qābūs ibn Saʿīd, usurped his father, Saʿīd ibn Taymūr (r. 1932–1970), in a palace coup. Except for a few Sunnī bedouin tribes, the "inner Oman" of the northern interior, a string of oases separated from the coast by the imposing Ḥajar mountain range, remains almost exclusively Ibāḍī and Arab. In contrast, the towns and villages of the Bāṭinah coast, a narrow strip of oases 10 to 20 miles wide, are polyglot and multiethnic, with Arabs (Sunnī and Ibāḍī), Baluch (mostly Sunnī), Persians (mostly Sunnī and Shīʿī), and the Sindī- and Arabic-speaking Liwāṭīyah (who are Shīʿah) among the principal groups. The settled coastal population and the cattle-herding tribes of the mountainous interior of the southern province of Dhofar *(Ẓufār)* are almost exclusively Sunnī, as is the remote Musandam peninsula in the north.

From the mid-eighteenth to the mid-twentieth century, the major theme of Omani political and religious history was the conflict between dynastic rule by an Ibāḍī sultan and rule by an imam, a spiritual and temporal leader chosen by a consensus of Ibāḍī tribal notables and religious scholars.

Since the late eighteenth century, no sultan of the Āl Bū Saʿīd dynasty, which has ruled Oman continuously since 1744, has asserted the title of imam except for a brief interval from 1868 to 1871. From the mid-seventeenth century until Britain's ascendancy in the Persian Gulf in the early nineteenth century, Oman's domains included Zanzibar and the East African coast, and the energies of the Āl Bū Saʿīd dynasty were largely focused away from the Omani interior. By the late nineteenth century, however, the sultanate lost these possessions and entered an economic decline. On several occasions only British intervention prevented tribes from the interior acting in the name of the imam from overthrowing the dynasty.

In formal doctrine, the imamate was the ideal Muslim state. In principle, the *imām al-muslimīn* ("imam of the Muslims") ruled solely by Islamic law, legitimating actions according to precedents attributed to the prophet Muḥammad and his first two successors, Abū Bakr (d. 632) and ʿUmar (d. 634). In principle, imams were selected on the basis of their moral qualities, knowledge of the Qur'ān and Islamic tradition, and capacity for governing; in practice, their selection was the exclusive province of an oligarchic tribal elite. For example, the last imam on whom all tribes agreed, Muḥammad ibn ʿAbd Allāh al-Khalīlī (r. 1920–1954), who sold his personal estates to sustain the imamate as its resources dwindled, was the twentieth of a long line of imams selected from his immediate tribal group.

From 1913 until 1955, the northern interior was one of the world's last theocracies, ruled by a succession of imams. This arrangement, which did not rule out cooperation between the sultan and the imam (whom the sultan recognized only as a tribal leader) ended in 1955 when Saʿīd ibn Taymūr, backed by British troops financed primarily by an oil company, assumed direct control over the region. The imamate continued in exile in Saudi Arabia, and a Saudi-supported rebellion against dynastic rule (1957–1959) was suppressed with British support.

There is little overt sectarian friction in contemporary Oman, although the end of its isolation—in particular, that of the Ibāḍīyah—has brought major changes in how Islam is expressed and practiced. Until 1970, Oman was almost devoid of modern educational facilities, and Omanis who left the country for education were discouraged from returning. After 1970, the country's educational institutions developed rapidly, and mass communication permeated even remote villages.

The exposure of large numbers of Omanis to schooling and mass media has altered the style and content of Islam in Oman. For example, in "inner" Oman, only the imam gave regular Friday sermons until 1955. Beginning in the early 1980s, however, younger, educated Ibāḍīs began to ask for sermons like those delivered in Sunnī and Shīʿī congregational mosques. The government cautiously accommodated this request, setting up a committee to "guide" sermon content. Likewise, mosques named after Sultan Qābūs were constructed in larger towns—in Nizwā on the site of the imam's former mosque—and institutes were created to train religious teachers. Since 1970 Oman has also had an appointed *muftī*, or authoritative interpreter of religious doctrine. Although the post is formally unaffiliated with any sect, the first two *muftī*s have been Ibāḍī. The *muftī* speaks on public occasions, issues *fatwā*s (religious opinions), and represents the sultanate at international Islamic conferences.

The ruler's public addresses, like the content of Islamic studies in schools, scrupulously avoid sectarian issues. For instance, the *ḥadīth* (sayings of the Prophet) included in school texts are only those on which Sunnī, Ibāḍī, and Shīʿah agree. However, Oman's reentry into the wider Islamic world has led to a more-explicit discussion of religious doctrine and practice than was formerly the case. Thus, in late 1986, a leading Saudi religious scholar issued a *fatwā* accusing Shaykh Aḥmad ibn Ḥamad al-Khalīlī, Oman's *muftī* since 1975—and, by implication, all Ibāḍīyah—of *kufr* (heresy). In early 1987, al-Khalīlī replied in a two-hour television address, offering the first contemporary formulation of Ibāḍī doctrine in Oman. Another of the *muftī*'s talks, "Who is an Ibāḍī?" originated in a reply to an Omani student in the United States who requested guidance after "Sunnī brothers" questioned whether the Ibāḍīyah should lead Muslim prayers. These examples suggest how higher education and modern conditions have led Omanis, like Muslims elsewhere, to reformulate doctrine and practice.

[*See also* Ibāḍī Dynasty; Ibāḍīyah.]

BIBLIOGRAPHY

Eickelman, Christine. *Women and Community in Oman*. New York, 1984. Provides insight into women's religious practices in an oasis of "inner" Oman.

Eickelman, Dale F. "From Theocracy to Monarchy: Authority and Legitimacy in Inner Oman, 1935–1957." *International Journal of Middle East Studies* 17 (February 1985): 3–24. Describes the practical workings of the twentieth-century imamate and its assimilation into sultanate rule.

Eickelman, Dale F. "Ibadism and the Sectarian Perspective." In *Oman: Economic, Social, and Strategic Developments*, edited by B. R. Pridham, pp. 31–50. London, 1987. Discusses the changing meaning of "sectarianism" as Oman has lost its former isolation.

Eickelman, Dale F. "National Identity and Religious Discourse in Contemporary Oman." *International Journal of Islamic and Arabic Studies* 6 (1989): 1–20. Assesses how mass higher education and the mass media have changed Islamic thought and practice in Oman.

Khālīlī, Aḥmad ibn Ḥamad al-. *Who Are the Ibadhis?* Translated by A. H. al-Maamiry. Zanzibar, n.d. Although available only through research libraries, this booklet stands out as the most comprehensive expression in English of contemporary Ibāḍī belief in Oman.

Peterson, J. E. *Oman in the Twentieth Century: Political Foundations of an Emerging State*. London, 1978. The best overall introduction to contemporary Omani political history and religious development.

Wilkinson, John C. *The Imamate Tradition in OIan*. Cambridge, 1987. Difficult but essential reference by a former oil company geographer. Sociologically limited but comprehensive in use of Arabic and European sources.

DALE F. EICKELMAN

ORGANIZATION OF THE ISLAMIC CONFERENCE.

[*This entry comprises two articles. The first focuses on the political and historical context from which the organization arose; the second describes the institutional structure and activities of the group.*]

Origins

The Islamic theory of international relations centers around the Qur'ānic concept of *ummah*, the community of believers that spans all Muslims of various nations and races. Especially with the rise of modern nation-states, Islamic thinkers have debated whether the concept of a nation conflicts with the universality and unity of the Islamic community. Muhammad Iqbal asserted that Islam furnishes a model for human unity and that nationalism can coexist with it as long as Muslims believe in *tawḥīd* (the unity of God). Other scholars reject this view; thus ʿAlī Muḥammad Naqavi writes, "Nationalism and Islam have two opposite ideologies, schools and ideas and independent goals and programs" (*Islam and Nationalism*, Tehran, 1984).

Nonetheless, the modern world order has resulted in the suppression of two traditional vehicles of Islamic unity—empires with an integral clerical establishment, and conquest by *jihād*. Seeking a viable modern response to Western political and economic dominance, nineteenth-century reformers—notably Jamāl al-Dīn al-Afghānī (1839–1897), Muḥammad ʿAbduh (1849–1905), and Muḥammad Rashīd Riḍā (1865–1935)—developed the political theory of Pan-Islamism. The Pan-Islamist movement and its leading journal *Al-manār* began promoting the idea of Muslim congresses in 1898, but the first general Islamic conference was not held until 1926, with meetings in Cairo and Mecca. These meetings concerned themselves primarily with responses to Kemal Atatürk's abolition of the caliphate; a third congress in 1931 addressed the protection of Palestinian Muslims and the holy places of Jerusalem.

Saudi Arabia and the Muslim regions of the Indian subcontinent led attempts to establish an international Islamic body in the 1940s and 1950s, in the face of opposition from secularist regimes in Egypt, Turkey, and Iran. The first International Islamic Economic Conference met in Karachi in 1949, and the second in Tehran in 1950. A conference of Muslim religious scholars was held in 1952 in Karachi at the initiative of the grand *muftī* of Palestine, Amīn al-Ḥusaynī, who advocated Islamic unity: "Modern scientific research and discoveries have shortened distances. In these circumstances even the most powerful nations of the world cannot remain in isolation." Al-Ḥusaynī noted the unity of the Western and Communist blocs and lamented, "Only the Muslims in the face of so many difficulties and problems have so far failed to form themselves into an *ummah*." [*See the biography of Ḥusaynī*.]

Why had Muslims failed to translate their dream of an Islamic *ummah* into reality? There was no dearth of able thinkers and dynamic leaders, yet they had been unable to create a permanent international organization founded on Islamic ideology. Secularists, socialists, and regional nationalists were not yet prepared to rise above their differences and forge unity on the basis of their shared beliefs.

The movement for Pan-Islamic unity, however, was not without some results. Its tenacious adherence to the concept of a united world of Islam ultimately triumphed in the 1960s, when new and more vigorous attempts to develop bonds among Muslim countries emerged. The Saudi crown prince, later King Fayṣal, led this new effort, motivated by his desire to contain Egyptian president Gamal Abdel Nasser's Arab nationalism. He toured Pakistan, Iran, Jordan, Sudan, Turkey, Morocco, Guinea, Mali, and Tunisia advocating an Islamic *ummah*. In 1962 Saudi Arabia also established a philanthropic organization, the Muslim World League (Rābiṭat al-ʿĀlam al-Islāmī) to combat socialism and secularism. [*See* Muslim World League.]

The situation changed dramatically after the 1967 Arab-Israeli War in which Israel crushed Egypt, Jordan, and Syria and occupied large Arab territories. The entire Muslim world was shocked, especially by the occupation of Muslim holy places in Jerusalem—among them al-Aqṣā Mosque, the third holiest site of Islam. Amīn al-Ḥusaynī and King Fayṣal called for an Islamic summit conference, supported by other national leaders including Tunku Abdul Rahman of Malaysia. In their changed circumstances, Nasser and other former opponents could no longer ignore the initiatives of Saudi Arabia, Pakistan, and their allies. Finally, after an arsonist set fire to part of al-Aqṣā Mosque, the first Islamic summit was held in Rabat on 22–25 September 1969.

The leaders who assembled in Rabat were convinced that their peoples formed an indivisible *ummah* and were determined to exert united efforts to defend their legitimate interests. This resolve gave birth to the Organization of the Islamic Conference (OIC), formally proclaimed in May 1971. The OIC expresses the determination of Islamic nations to "preserve Islamic social and economic values" and reaffirms their commitment to the United Nations Charter. Its primary goals are to promote Islamic solidarity among member states; to consolidate cooperation among member states in economic, social, cultural, scientific, and other vital fields of activity, and to carry out consultations among member states in international organizations; to endeavor to eliminate racial segregation, discrimination, and colonialism in all its forms; and to support international peace and security founded on justice.

The highest policy-making function of the OIC consists in meetings of heads of state. These summit conferences enable the leaders of the Islamic world periodically to review both internal conditions and external political developments from an Islamic perspective. The next level of policy-making is the annual Conference of Foreign Ministers to consider international developments and their impact on the Islamic states with a view to defining common positions on global political and economic issues. The ministers have focused on such issues as the question of Palestine, the occupation of Afghanistan, the Iran-Iraq war, and the situation in South Africa, seeking equitable solutions to these problems.

The third and permanent component of the OIC's institutional structure comprises the General Secretariat based in Jeddah and OIC agencies and centers in a number of countries. The head of the Secretariat, the secretary-general, is elected for a four-year nonrenewable term by the Conference of Foreign Ministers; there are also four assistant secretaries and various other officials.

One important institution that has developed within the framework of the OIC is the Islamic Educational, Scientific and Cultural Organization (ISESCO), modeled on UNESCO. The need to advance education, particularly in science and technology, in contemporary Muslim countries can hardly be exaggerated. ISESCO has undertaken an ambitious program founded on two complementary objectives: to strengthen cooperation among member states in the fields of educational, scientific, and cultural research and to make Islamic culture the pivot of educational curricula at all levels; and to support genuine Islamic culture and to protect the independence of Islamic thought against cultural invasion, distortion, and debasement.

The OIC has been more successful in such cultural programs than in political matters, where Muslim countries are still far from achieving the cohesion and unity embodied in the OIC Charter. The Iran-Iraq war has perhaps been the most frustrating problem for the OIC among numerous regional and ethnic disputes. Despite such obstacles, however, the OIC in general provides a valuable forum in which Muslim countries are gathered for the first time in an official organizational setting. This is no small achievement after centuries of division and conflict within the *ummah*.

[*See also* Congresses; Pan-Islam; Ummah.]

BIBLIOGRAPHY

Aḥsan, ʿAbdullah al-. *OIC: The Organization of the Islamic Conference.* Herndon, Va., 1988. A detailed study of the origins, structure, and membership of the OIC.

Choudhury, Golam W. *Islam and the Contemporary World.* London, 1990. Chapters 5 and 6 explore the development of Pan-Islam and the structure and organization of the OIC.

Kramer, Martin. *Islam Assembled: the Advent of the Muslim Congresses.* New York, 1986.

Moinuddin, Hasan. *The Charter of the Islamic Conference: The Legal and Economic Framework.* Oxford, 1987. A detailed, constitutional study of the OIC.

GOLAM W. CHOUDHURY

Structure and Activities

The Organization of the Islamic Conference (OIC; Ar., Munaẓẓamat al-Mu'tamar al-Islāmī) extends its influence in the social, economic, and political spheres throughout the Islamic world. It reaches beyond Muslim nations as a forum in which they can coordinate their interactions with the rest of the world. To serve the OIC's many purposes, an elaborate organizational structure has been developed over the quarter-century of its existence.

Membership. The OIC currently has 50 members, including Palestine, four Central Asian republics, and Albania. Kazakhstan and Uzbekistan have observer status and the Turkish Cypriot community and the Moro National Liberation Front (MNLF) regularly attend meetings as observers. The MNLF applied unsuccessfully to join the OIC in 1987; the grounds for refusal were apparently that it was not a state. In addition, a number of intergovernmental organizations, such as the United Nations, the Organization of African Unity (OAU), and the Arab League, regularly send high-level observers. Observer status has also been granted to a number of nongovernmental organizations, but these normally have an Islamic flavor—for instance, the Muslim World League, the Tripoli-based Islamic Call Society, the World Muslim Congress, and the World Assembly of Muslim Youth.

Structure. The highest policy-making organ of the OIC is the meeting of heads of State, the summit. There have been six Islamic summits: Rabat (1969), Lahore (1974), Ṭā'if/Mecca (1981), Casablanca (1984), Kuwait (1987), and Dakar (1991). The summits review conditions in the Muslim world and consider international political developments. The second policy-making organ is the annual Conference of Foreign Ministers, which also reviews conditions in the Muslim world but tends to concentrate on international political, economic, social, and cultural questions.

In addition, there are three Standing Committees—for Information and Cultural Affairs, Scientific and Technological Cooperation, and Economic and Commercial Cooperation. The main functions of these committees are to monitor the implementation of resolutions passed by the OIC, to study means of strengthening cooperation among Muslim states, to draw up programs and submit proposals designed to increase member states' capacity in the fields indicated, and to study agenda items and submit draft resolutions before summit meetings and meetings of foreign ministers.

The Secretariat is based in Jeddah. It is headed by a secretary-general elected for a four-year renewable term by the Conference of Foreign Ministers. The present incumbent, Hamid Al Gabid of Niger, took office in January 1989. In accordance with an amendment to the Charter agreed at the Dakar summit in 1991, the secretary-general's term was extended for a second four-year term. The Secretariat has four assistant secretaries-general for Political Affairs; Jerusalem, Palestine, and Muslim minorities; Cultural and Social Affairs and the Islamic Solidarity Fund; and Economic, Administrative, and Financial Affairs.

OIC funding comes from contributions from member states. Originally it was agreed that the basis for assessing contributions should be per capita income. In practice, many states fail to make due payments, and the OIC is perennially short of funds. Indeed, the Secretary-General was reported in 1986 to be prepared to tell the 1987 summit that if members were not prepared to pay up, he and his staff would happily close the organization down and return to their former occupations. Hitherto, Saudi Arabia has bailed out the OIC when it is particularly short of funds, and it seems likely that this will continue. The Saudis have also given a former royal palace to house the Secretariat.

Agencies and Affiliates. The OIC has given birth to many subsidiary and affiliated bodies. Some, such as the Islamic Development Bank, are effective, others are less so, and some have yet to be established. Since the organization suffers from an acute shortage of funds, the development of new agencies, particularly the Islamic Court of Justice, may well be slow, but those already operating are unlikely to be allowed to die.

Among the specialized committees of the OIC is the Al-Quds (Jerusalem) Committee, which was established in 1975 and is based in Morocco. Its fourteen members meet twice a year under the chairmanship of King Ḥasan. It is charged with working for the liberation of Jerusalem, drawing the world's attention to the rights of Muslims and to Israeli defiance of UN resolutions, and implementing OIC resolutions relating to Jerusalem and the Palestine question. Allied to this committee is the Al-Quds Fund, established in 1976. Its objectives are to fight against the "israelization" of Jerusalem and to support the Palestinian struggle for liberation. Its income is derived from voluntary donations.

Important among the subsidiary organs of the OIC is the Islamic Solidarity Fund, created in 1974 to provide funds to meet the needs of Islamic unity, Islamic causes, and the enhancement of Islamic culture, values, and universities. The funds available have been used for a wide variety of charitable and relief purposes.

Economically oriented subsidiary organs have also been active. For instance, the Statistical, Economic, and Social Research and Training Center for the Islamic Countries was established in Ankara in 1978. It collects data and formulates economic policies, such as the "Ankara Economic Plan" adopted at the Ṭā'if summit of January 1981. It also publishes the *Journal of Economic Cooperation among Islamic Countries*. The Islamic Center for Vocational and Technical Training and Research, set up in Dhaka in 1977, is charged with the development of skilled manpower in Muslim countries; the Islamic Center for Development of Trade, based in Casablanca since 1983, encourages regular commercial contacts and investments among member states.

Perhaps the most important of the institutions within the OIC framework is the Islamic Development Bank. Established in Jeddah in 1974 to encourage economic development and social progress in member states and in Muslim communities elsewhere, it has been one of the fastest-growing aid agencies in the Third World. In July 1992, the bank agreed to double its subscribed capital from $2.9 billion to $5.8 billion. Less prominent but also noteworthy have been the International Islamic News Agency and the Islamic States Broadcasting Organization. The former, created in 1979 and based in Jeddah, issues daily news bulletins in Arabic, English, and French (the official languages of the OIC). The latter was established as a personal initiative of King Fayṣal in 1975 as a means of propagating Islam though radio and television. It makes and sells its own religious programs for the Muslim world and maintains a library of radio and television programs made in various Muslim countries. Copies are either lent or given to broadcasting organizations in all member states. The Islamic Educational, Scientific, and Cultural Organization, headquartered in Rabat, has since 1982 promoted cooperation among Muslim states in the cultural and educational fields.

Attitudes of Member States. Despite the high moral tone of the declaration issued by the first summit conference in 1969 following the fire at the al-Aqṣā mosque in Jerusalem, and of the OIC Charter, the organization has been predominantly a political one. During the early discussions on the drafting of the Charter, there was considerable argument about its proper aims. One faction argued that it should be entirely political, aimed at dealing with the problems of Jerusalem and Palestine. A second faction argued for something much wider and more nebulous and wished to emphasize closer cooperation in economic, cultural, social, scientific, and technological matters. Although the second faction was successful as far as the Charter went, the political side has in fact prevailed in practice. However, the plethora of nonpolitical subsidiary organizations established by the OIC is due in part to the strength of the nonpolitical group, whose members have generally taken the lead in proposing their establishment, in providing funding, and in giving the main impetus for their activities.

The attitudes of member states toward the OIC thus vary considerably. Saudi Arabia almost certainly sees it as a vehicle to bring influence to bear and as an institution in which it can reasonably hope to wield influence more actively and more widely than could be the case in other forums. In this, Saudi Arabia has been successful in that it has been able to use the nonpolitical aspirations of other members and the prospect of additional funding to further its own political objectives, sometimes in the face of more radical opposition. One example is the way in which Saudi Arabia used the OIC to legitimize its imposition of quotas on the number of Iranian pilgrims attending the 1988 *ḥajj*. Members agreed at the January 1988 meeting of foreign ministers in Amman to limit the number of pilgrims from member states to a maximum of 1,000 pilgrims per one million population. The ostensible reason was a Saudi plea for reduced numbers because of major construction works in the Ḥaramayn (holy places of Mecca and Medina). An equally striking example is the way in which Saudi Arabia led the campaign for the suspension of Egypt following the Camp David Accords; it later was able to force through the readmission of Egypt in 1984 in the face of strong opposition.

Saudi Arabia has, throughout the history of the organization, been a major contributor to funding for all purposes. This, coupled with the early Saudi success in ensuring an institutional framework for the organization and in making Jeddah the location of that framework pending the liberation of Jerusalem, has meant that Saudi Arabia has played a dominant role in the OIC. (Since 1975 when the Islamic Development Bank began operation, its president has been a Saudi.) Although this role has been reduced to some extent over the years by internecine strife, the wider interests of the larger membership, and the insistence of non-Arab members (the majority of members) on broader concerns, the development of the OIC can be seen as one of the success stories of Saudi foreign policy.

Pakistan's attitude is probably a combination of two strands. On the one hand, Pakistan has felt itself surrounded by potential enemies and therefore vulnerable. On the other hand, there is no doubt that the devotion of Pakistani elites to Islam is genuine: it therefore sees the OIC as a means of strengthening ties with other Muslim states and also as a vehicle through which to seek reassurance. A case in point is the manner in which Pakistan orchestrated pressure on the Soviet Union over Afghanistan through the OIC.

Arab members generally are more overtly political than others and have seized upon the organization as yet another means of publicizing their views on the Arab-Israel dispute and gaining support for their policies. Because of the common religious and cultural tradition and the importance of Jerusalem in Islam, the Arab states have been able to islamize the dispute in terms of rhetoric. However, there is little sign that non-Arab members are prepared to take any effective action.

Nigeria unexpectedly became a full member of the OIC in January 1986. It seems likely that the government's reasons were wholly domestic—an attempt to buy off its Muslim constituency—and that there were no foreign policy considerations. There is evidence that the government was lured into joining the OIC by influential Nigerian Muslims who persuaded it that there would be no political repercussions. There was, however, a serious Christian backlash, not surprising for a country in which Muslim/Christian tension is never far below the surface. After several unsuccessful attempts to find a compromise solution, Nigeria's membership is effectively in limbo, and although Nigeria continues to be represented in OIC deliberations, it takes little part in them. Zanzibar briefly acceded to the OIC in December 1992, ostensibly to gain access to Islamic Development Bank funds. However, the Tanzanian government deemed the accession unconstitutional and Zanzibar withdrew from the OIC in August 1993.

Iran's position is ambivalent. Before the revolution Iran probably shared the same perceptions as did Saudi Arabia, though it would have seen its role and influence as more significant. Since the revolution, Iran has consistently denounced the OIC as a front to further Saudi foreign-policy aims, the most notable case being the OIC endorsement of the *ḥajj* quota system in 1988. Iran also perceived the organization as biased in favor of Iraq, with which it fought a bloody war for eight years.

Yet at the Dakar summit in 1991, President Hashemi Rafsanjani used the occasion to promote Iran—at least rhetorically—as the chief guardian of the Palestinian *jihād*.

Iraq probably saw the OIC as a means to further its attempts to exert influence in the Arab and Third Worlds, and as a useful instrument in reducing its isolation. Throughout the conflict with Iran, Iraq sought to influence OIC deliberations and the activities of the Islamic Peace Committee in favor of the Iraqi version of events. However, the Iraqis boycotted the 1991 summit meeting, which came after their disastrous defeat in the war following the invasion of Kuwait. Although King Fahd of Saudi Arabia also stayed away from the meeting, the Iraqi government denounced the OIC as a Saudi institution sympathetic to Kuwait's wish to maintain sanctions against Iraq.

The poorer member states have undoubtedly seen the OIC as an additional channel through which to lobby for financial assistance, for extending the free flow of labor, and thus for maintaining and if possible increasing the flow of remittances from emigré workers, particularly in the Arabian Peninsula. As a result, despite routine grumbles about what they see as concentration on Arab issues, they are willing to acquiesce in the status quo in return for the benefits available.

The OIC is far from "fundamentalist" in attitude and tone (using the term as it is generally understood today). The member states are represented by their governments, not by religious leaders, and the organization does not have the establishment of a universal Islamic community or *ummah* as an eventual aim. Its relations with the outside world are based on cooperation, not confrontation, and during the Cold War it was much closer to the West than to the Soviet bloc. Nor is there any discernible fundamentalist influence within the Secretariat, whose officials are professional diplomats from member states. Nevertheless, the rise in Islamist challenges to the political establishments of several member states—Algeria, Tunisia, and Egypt, among others—has led to concern in certain official quarters over the "enemies within" and to anger at Iran for allegedly supporting them.

Activities. An examination of resolutions passed by the OIC over the years shows that the organization has become a natural forum in which to raise issues affecting the Muslim world or particular Muslim countries, and it has successfully engineered a broad consensus on a number of matters. However, it has been selective on the specific issues on which it seeks to take action beyond the passage of resolutions. In the political sphere, it has regularly called for Israeli withdrawal from Arab territories, recognition of the rights of the Palestinians and of the Palestine Liberation Organization as their sole legitimate representative, and the restoration of Jerusalem to Arab rule. It has also worked actively, though without much practical effect (through the Islamic Peace Committee established in 1981, initially chaired by the Secretary-General and later by President Jawara of Gambia), to try to bring an end to the conflict. It was also influential in coordinating international opposition to the Soviet invasion of Afghanistan. The annual resolution on this issue at the UN General Assembly was drafted by the Afghanistan Committee.

In other disputes, the secretary-general offered to mediate in the Somali civil war and denounced the Indian government's inability to protect Muslims in the wake of the destruction of the Babri mosque in Ayodhya in late 1992. Both acts, however, had no discernible effect. The Bosnian crisis has agitated Muslim opinion throughout the world, with Malaysia, Pakistan, and Iran particularly urging more decisive support, perhaps even military assistance, for the Bosnian Muslims. At a special meeting in Jeddah in December 1992, the OIC gave the Security Council a deadline of 15 January 1993 to take further measures in support of the Muslims or, failing that, unspecified Muslim collective action would be taken. At the Karachi Foreign Ministers' meeting in May 1993, a concrete plan for action once again failed to materialize. In July 1993, an emergency meeting of foreign ministers offered to contribute several thousand troops to the United Nations peacekeeping effort in the former Yugoslavia.

In the cultural field, the OIC has been active in support of education for Muslim communities throughout the world and, through the Islamic Solidarity Fund, has helped to establish Islamic universities in Malaysia, Niger, Uganda, and Bangladesh. It has also given support to publications on Islam in both Muslim and Western countries.

Assistance is also given to Muslim communities which have been affected by civil and other wars and natural disasters, largely in cooperation with UN agencies, particularly the UN High Commission for Refugees. Much of this aid has been concentrated in the Sahel region of Africa, though other deserving cases are also given help.

The OIC has also been active in support of Muslim minorities throughout the world, particularly those that are repressed or discriminated against. Thus it is active in support of the Muslim minorities in Bulgaria and the Philippines. Here as well, it is selective in the causes it actively supports, and although there have been contacts with China, it gives little practical support to the Muslim communities there, preferring to remain on reasonable terms with the regime.

Conclusions. Despite its wide range of activities, the OIC remains an essentially political organization to which the nearest analogue is probably the British Commonwealth. The differences of interest and emphasis between member states are likely to prevent a greater degree of solidarity than that existing today, and critics will continue to denounce it as a conservative, Saudi-controlled institution or an ineffective "talking shop"—or indeed both. Differences of interest among member states were particularly apparent during the Gulf crisis of 1990–1991. However, most members like members of the Commonwealth, see advantage in belonging to an organization, however loosely knit it may be, which facilitates a cohesive stance on certain issues without inhibiting disagreement and the pursuit of narrow national interests, and through which support for national policies on international issues can be sought.

Although the OIC has been in existence for only about a quarter-century, it has served to focus the attention of the Muslim world on the more important political, social, and economic issues of the day. It has developed a degree of muscle in all three fields, it has served to draw attention to the main concerns of a sizable proportion of the world's population, and it is taken seriously by other international organizations. Although writing before the momentous events in world politics associated with the end of the Cold War, a commentator on the 1981 summit in Mecca pointed to the OIC's importance in the following words:

> As an international organisation, the Islamic conference seems at least as dynamic as others for which the OIC has expressed strong support (e.g., the Non-Aligned Movement, the OAU and the Arab League). Strong support for the principles of the United Nations along with the appearance of the Secretary-General of the UN at the summit is proof positive that the OIC does not see itself as a restricted sectarian group but rather as an organisation with an important role to play in modern world politics.

[*See also* Islamic Development Bank.]

J. P. BANNERMAN

ORGANIZATION OF THE ISLAMIC JIHĀD.

Munaẓẓamat al-Jihād al-Islāmī (or simply Jihād al-Islāmī; the Organization of the Islamic Jihād) in Lebanon was formed out of Ḥizbullāh (Party of God), which came into being in June 1982 in the town of Baalbek in the Bekaa (Biqāʿ) valley. The Islamic *jihād* organization was used by Ḥizbullāh whenever it engaged in covert operations. To maintain that the Islamic *jihād* organization exists, however, does not mean that it has a separate structure from Ḥizbullāh.

The Organization of the Islamic Jihād claimed responsibility for bombing the U.S. embassy on 18 April 1983 and the U.S. Marine headquarters of the Multinational Forces (MNF) and the headquarters of the French contigent of the MNF on 23 October 1983. It was also behind the kidnapping of American and European nationals in Lebanon, beginning with the abduction of the acting president of the American University of Beirut, David Dodge, in July 1982. Although Dodge was released in July 1983 and other hostages were released later, the wave of hostage taking continued unabated from March 1984 until February 1988. The last American hostage was released in December 1991.

These operations were integral to the strategy pursued by the patrons of the Organization of the Islamic Jihād and Ḥizbullāh, namely, Syria and Iran. Syria has used the Organization of the Islamic Jihād to undermine Western influence in Lebanon and to dominate the country politically and militarily—an end achieved in June 1991. The continued barring of U.S. nationals from traveling to Lebanon is owed to the refusal of Syria to disarm Ḥizbullāh and the fear that the Organization of the Islamic Jihād could resume the campaign of hostage taking against U.S. nationals. From its support of the organization, Iran has gained the arms-for-hostages deals that were central to the Iran-Contra affair. Iran has also gained by having a foothold in Lebanon, which, despite the fact that it is not contiguous with Iran, has become its major sphere of influence.

The leadership of the Organization of the Islamic Jihād is basically identical to that of Ḥizbullāh. Prominent leaders of the latter, like the late ʿAbbās al-Musawī, have openly claimed some operations conducted by the organization as their very own. The use of violent means by the organization and by Ḥizbullāh has served many purposes other than the interests of Syria and Iran. These operations have given the Organization of the Islamic Jihād a high profile and tremendous prestige in its ability to challenge the United States and the West in general. Its goal has been clearly spelled out by its statements—to establish an Islamic state in Lebanon. Despite this, its support is limited to a segment of the Shīʿī community, which is a minority in Lebanon.

In respect to the Arab-Israeli conflict, the Organization of the Islamic Jihād is close ideologically to the two factions of the Palestinian Islamic Jihād organization, which refuse any compromise and are more rejectionist than the Palestinian Ḥamās group (Ḥarakat al-Muqāwamah al-Islāmīyah; Movement of the Islamic Resistance). The Palestinian and Lebanese *jihād* organizations have organizational links with each other and often coordinate their activities with the same patrons of Ḥizbullāh. This is especially true for the faction of the *jihād* organization led by Fatḥī Shiqāqī in Damascus.

[*See also* Ḥizbullāh, *article on* Ḥizbullāh in Lebanon; Hostages; *and* Lebanon.]

BIBLIOGRAPHY

Deeb, Marius K. *Militant Islamic Movements in Lebanon: Origins, Social Basis, and Ideology*. Washington, D.C., 1986.

Deeb, Marius K. "Shiʿa Movements in Lebanon: Their Formation, Ideology, Social Basis, and Links with Iran and Syria." *Third World Quarterly* 10.2 (April 1988): 683–698.

Al-Ḥarakah al-Islāmīyah fī Lubnān (The Islamic Movement in Lebanon). Beirut, 1984.

Marius K. Deeb

ORIENTALISM. Beginning as a field based on the study of original texts in Asian languages requiring a rigorous specialized training, Orientalism flourished in Western scholarship from the eighteenth century to well into the twentieth century. Through the critical philological study of cultural texts of Asian civilizations, it sought to uncover their allegedly essential features. Orientalism was not only a scholarly discipline deriving from European Enlightenment thought, but also an expression of the romantic exoticizing impulse of nineteenth-century European culture, which through its representation of other cultures permitted the exploration of other worlds, notably in art, literature, and music. This article is not concerned with Orientalism in this broader cultural sense.

Orientalism acquired a third meaning following twentieth-century movements of decolonization, when some scholars argued that the scholarly discipline of Orientalism could not be understood apart from the circumstances of its production, namely, Western imperialism. Thus was born the debate over Orientalism. This article cannot disentangle the multiple meanings of Orientalism; it can only suggest their many-layered intellectual and political realities. For these purposes, it is appropriate to first describe Orientalism as a product of Enlightenment thought, or, as it saw itself, as a science, and then to explain the debate over Orientalism. In fact, the epistemological relations of knowledge and power permit no such easy separation, for the reality is more complex.

Orientalism as a self-conscious scholarly discipline began to emerge in the eighteenth century as one stream of Enlightenment thought. Although Islamic science and philosophy attracted the interest of such scholars as Roger Bacon and Leibniz, earlier Western studies of Islam had been marked by Christian precommitment. Voltaire and Montaigne utilized Muslim locales to develop utopias and dystopias the better to criticize the European governments and propose reforms. But the field as an academic discipline centered on the philological study of allegedly formative texts of non-European cultures did not fully appear until the period of the French Revolution.

The Field and Its Development. The first institution whose mission it was to study Asian languages and civilizations was the École des Langues Orientales Vivantes, established in Paris in 1795. French Orientalists developed linguistic expertise in Arabic and other Islamic languages, and methods of instruction in Arabic and other Islamic languages were systematized at this time. A major product was the twenty-three-volume *Description de l'Egypte* (Paris, 1809–1828), which represents the first systematic effort to inventory the historical, cultural, and scientific patrimony of any Islamic country. Analogous surveys were later undertaken in Algeria and Morocco.

The trend toward institutionalization increased during the nineteenth century. Under Antoine-Isaac Silvestre de Sacy (1758–1838) and his students, the École became the leading orientalist institution in Europe, and philology attained the status of a science, the science of human culture. Its self-consciously secular object was to lay bare the principles by which civilizations operated: grounded in nineteenth-century empiricism, Orientalist knowledge stigmatized generalizations unsupported by the texts. While Orientalist scholars often vaunted the scientific character of their work, at no point were they insulated from the historical currents of their age.

Important figures in this period included the French scholars Armand-Pierre Caussin de Perceval (1795–1871), Étienne Quatremère (1782–1857), and Ernest Renan (1823–1892); the British Edward W. Lane (1801–1876), J. W. Redhouse, and W. Robertson Smith (1846–1894); the Germans Franz Bopp (1791–1867), Heinrich L. Fleischer (1801–1888), and Julius Wellhausen (1844–1918); the Austrian Joseph von Hammer-Pürgstall (1774–1856); and the Italians Michele Amari (1806–1889) and Leone Caetani (1869–1935).

Specialized journals, such as the *Journal asiatique* (1823), *The Journal of the Royal Asiatic Society* (1834), and the *Zeitschrift für deutsche morgenländische Gesellschaft* (1845), were published, and official scholarly societies were established to further the aims of Orientalism in most European countries and the United States. Dictionaries, grammars, catalogs of manuscripts, translations and editions of important texts, and narrative histories provided basic tools for further study. Based on these strong nineteenth-century foundations, Orientalism retained its raison d'être and coherence as a discipline well into the following century.

In the twentieth century Orientalism reached its height in power and influence. The establishment of the School of Oriental and African Studies in 1917 in Britain, and the establishment of new academic chairs and journals in France, notably at the Ecole des Langues Orientales, the College de France, the Sorbonne, and the Ecole des Hautes Études, inaugurated a new phase of brick and mortar Orientalism. In Germany, Russia, and Italy this period also saw the establishment of important new institutions of Orientalist scholarship.

At the same time, beginning in France where the emerging social sciences (which stressed precise observation of social phenomena) were furthest advanced, the Orientalist subject began to splinter as new disciplines emerged. An early publication that focused on the study of contemporary Islamic societies in implicit repudiation of Orientalist textualism was the *Revue du monde musulman* (1906–1923). It however succumbed to the increasing intellectual specialization and the professionalization of the field in the interwar period. The impact of the social sciences reached its height only after World War II.

A new field, Islamic studies, emerged in 1927 with the publication of the *Revue des études islamiques*, edited by Louis Massignon (1883–1962). This initiative was paralleled by the work of other scholars, especially Ignácz Goldziher (1850–1921), Christiaan Snouck Hurgronje (1857–1936), Carl Heinrich Becker (1876–1933), Carl Brockelmann (1868–1956), and Duncan Black Macdonald (1892–1925).

Following World War II the rise of area studies (especially Middle Eastern studies) and the dynamic growth of the social sciences accelerated the transformation of Orientalism as an academic subject. Among the leaders in this process were Claude Cahen (1909–1991), Philip K. Hitti (1886–1974), H. A. R. Gibb (1895–1971), Gustave E. von Grunebaum (1909–1972), and Giorgio Levi Della Vida (1886–1967). While contemporary Orientalist scholarship is still influenced by its philological origins, it has evolved in many directions in response to institutional, intellectual, and political currents.

Knowledge and Power. The contemporaneous independence movements of the Middle East and North Africa—especially the Algerian revolution—provoked a debate about Orientalist knowledge in which the interventions of Jean-Paul Sartre and Frantz Fanon were crucial. For Fanon, the anticolonial struggle was also a cultural struggle with liberation as its goal. The publication of Edward Said's *Orientalism* (1978) recast the terms of the debate. Following Michel Foucault, Said portrayed Orientalism as not just an academic discipline, but as an ideological discourse inextricably involved with European power. In the debate that followed, neither Said nor his critics were always careful to distinguish the elements of the critique or the complex epistemological issues involved: in part it is about the nature of Enlightenment thought and the epistemological underpinnings of scientific knowledge, in part about the connections between particular scholars and Orientalist institutions and imperialism.

Said argues that because all knowledge is the product of its age and necessarily contingent, there can be no knowledge unaffected by the auspices under which it comes to be. If this premise is accepted, it follows that there can be no knowledge which is fully objective: thus, Orientalism has no privileged claim to truth. However, Said and his allies go further, arguing that because Orientalism as a species of discourse was fatally entangled with imperialism, the knowledge it produced was inevitably distorted, if not willfully racist.

While there is much truth to these observations, they are lacking in complexity. Certainly, Orientalism as a discourse could not but reflect the views of the ambient culture in which it flourished. Thus, some Orientalists did place themselves in the service of European empires; the fortunes of the field were frequently linked to imperialism; European assumptions of superiority to non-Europeans and of the progressive role of imperialism were widespread. However, it is important to note that some Orientalists opposed imperialism or manifested a favorable attitude toward Islamic culture and society; that some Middle Eastern nationalists were themselves inspired by Western Orientalist writings; and that nationalist and Muslim theological positions have their own biases and assumptions.

It is undeniable that as a species of Enlightenment discourse, Orientalism has been a carrier of basic Western notions of the European self and the non-Western other which generated unfalsifiable propositions about the superiority of Europeans to non-Europeans. In this way, Orientalists participated in the elaboration of modern European cultural identity. However, it is only as a result of the subsequent development of Western thought that it is possible to raise these criticisms.

We can now see that modernity was a global process rather than a manifestation of European genius. This does not mean that Orientalism's claim to scientific status is void, but that like other forms of human knowledge, it is both contingent and subject to constant critique and reformulation as a function of changing perspectives on the past. It is only through the evaluation of these issues that one can understand Orientalism as a form of intellectual inquiry.

[*See also* Islamic Studies.]

BIBLIOGRAPHY

Abdel-Malek, Anouar. "The Crisis of Orientalism." *Diogenes* 44 (1964): 130–140.
Daniel, Norman. *Islam, Europe, and Empire*. Edinburgh, 1966.
Daniel, Norman. *Islam and the West: The Making of an Image*. Edinburgh, 1960.
Fanon, Frantz. *The Wretched of the Earth*. Paris, 1963.
Fück, Johann. *Untersuchungen zur arabischen Sprach- und Stilgeschichte*. Berlin, *Verlag* 1950.
Holt, P. M., and Bernard Lewis, eds. *Historians of the Middle East*. London and New York, 1962.
Hourani, Albert. *Islam in European Thought*. Cambridge, 1991.
Husain, Asaf, Robert Olson, and Jamil Qureshi, eds. *Orientalism, Islam, and Islamists*. Brattleboro, Vt., 1984.
Kerr, Malcolm H., ed. *Islamic Studies: A Tradition and Its Problems*. Malibu, Calif., 1980.
Laroui, Abdullah. *The Crisis of the Arab Intellectual*. Translated by Diarmid Cammell. Berkeley, 1976.
Reig, Daniel. *Homo orientaliste: La langue arabe en France depuis XIXe siècle*. Paris, 1988.
Rodinson, Maxime. *Europe and the Mystique of Islam*. Translated by Roger Veinus. Seattle, 1987.
Said, Edward W. *Orientalism*. New York, 1978.
Said, Edward W. *Culture and Imperialism*. New York, 1993.
Southern, Richard W. *Western Views of Islam in the Middle Ages*. Cambridge, Mass., 1962.
Tibawi, A. L. "English-Speaking Orientalists: A Critique of Their Approach to Islam and Arab Nationalism." *Muslim World* 53.3 and 53.4 (1963): 185–204, 298–313.
Waardenberg, Jean-Jacques. *Islam dans le miroir de l'Occident*. Paris, 1963.

EDMUND BURKE, III

OTTOMAN EMPIRE. Called by the Turks Osmanlıs, after the name of the founder of the dynasty Osman I (Ar., ʿUthmān), the Ottomans were Oghuz (Tk., Oğuz) Turks who came out of Central Asia and created a vast state that ultimately encompassed all of southeastern Europe up to the northern frontiers of Hungary, Anatolia, and the Middle East up to the borders of Iran as well as the Mediterranean coast of North Africa almost to the Atlantic Ocean.

Conquest, 1300–1600. The Ottoman Empire was created by a series of conquests carried out between the early fourteenth and late sixteenth centuries by ten successive capable rulers of the Ottoman Turkish dynasty. Starting as nomadic *gazis* (Ar., *ghāzī*, "raider"), fighting for the faith of Islam against the decadent Christian Byzantine Empire on behalf of the Seljuk Empire of Konya ("Seljuks of Rum"), Osman I and his successors in the fourteenth century expanded primarily into Christian lands of southeastern Europe as far as the Danube, while avoiding conflict with the Muslim Turkoman principalities that had dominated Anatolia after they defeated the Byzantine army at the Battle of Manzikert in 1055. These conquests were facilitated by policies that left the defeated Christian princes in control of their states as long as they accepted vassalage and provided tribute and warriors to assist further Ottoman conquests and that allowed Christian officials and soldiers to join the Ottoman government and army as mercenaries without being required to convert to Islam. This first Ottoman Empire incorporated territories that encompassed the modern states of Greece, Rumania, Bulgaria, Macedonia, Serbia-Montenegro, Bosnia, and Croatia; it bypassed the Byzantine capital Constantinople, which, despite the depopulation and despoilage inflicted by the Latin Crusaders early in the thirteenth century, held out as a result of its massive defense walls as well as the services provided by soldiers from Christian Europe, though its emperors for the most part accepted the suzerainty of the Ottoman leaders. Efforts by the Byzantine emperors to reunite the Orthodox church with Rome in order to stimulate the creation of a new Crusade to rescue their empire led to new internal divisions that prevented any sort of unified resistance to the Ottomans.

This initial period of Ottoman expansion came to an end during the reign of Bayezid I (r. 1389–1402) who, influenced by the Christian princesses and their advisers at the Ottoman court, replaced the *gazi* tradition of conquering Christian territories with seizure of the Turkoman Muslim principalities in Anatolia; at the same time he substituted Byzantine for Muslim practices in his court and administration. The Muslim Turkomans who had led the conquests into Europe as *gazi*s refused to participate in attacks on their Muslim coreligionists, however, particularly since the booty available was far less than in Europe, so the conquests to the East were accomplished largely with contingents furnished by Christian vassals. Many of the displaced Anatolian Turkoman princes fled to refuge with the Mamlūk sultans who since 1250 had displaced the Ayyūbids in Egypt and Syria, or with the rising Tatar conqueror of Iran and Central Asia, Tamerlane, where they sought assistance in regaining their territories. The Mamlūk Empire was then attempting to expand its influence north from Syria into Cilicia and the headwaters of the Tigris and Euphrates, but it was by this time too weak to provide substantial military assistance to the Turkomans. Tamerlane also preferred to move through Iran into India, but fearing that Ottoman expansion eastward past the Euphrates might threaten his rear, he mounted a massive invasion of Anatolia that culminated in his rout of the Ottoman army and capture of Bayezid I at the Battle of Ankara (1402). To ensure that no single power would rise up to dominate Anatolia and threaten his domains, he went on to ravage the peninsula and restore the surviving Turkoman princes before resuming his invasion of India.

Bayezid I died in captivity, but enough of his sons survived to contest for power during the Ottoman Interregnum (1402–1413) that followed. Initially Prince Süleyman, based at Edirne, managed to retain Ottoman power in Europe with the assistance of the Christian vassal princes of southeastern Europe. Ultimately, however, his efforts to restore Ottoman rule in Anatolia were defeated by his bother Mehmed, supported by the Turkoman *gazi*s who had remained along the Danube fighting against the Hungarians, and who had opposed Bayezid's expansion into the Muslim East as well as the Christian tendencies in his court. As Mehmed I (r. 1413–1421), he restored Ottoman rule between the Danube and the Euphrates, driving out Christian influences in the court and inaugurating a policy, continued by Murad I (r. 1421–1451) and Mehmed II (r. 1451–1481) "the Conqueror" *(Fâtih)* that instituted direct Ottoman administration in both Europe and Anatolia in place of the indirect rule through vassals which had characterized the previous century.

This restoration was accompanied in 1453 by Mehmed II's conquest of Byzantine Constantinople after a long siege. The city had been ravaged and largely depopulated since its occupation by Latin Crusaders in 1204. But Mehmed intended to restore it to its old splendor and prosperity so it could serve as the capital of the restored Roman Empire that he wished to create. Therefore, instead of following the Muslim tradition of sacking cities that resisted conquest, he used his army to rebuild it and then carried out a policy of forced immigration *(sürgün)* of peoples from all parts of his empire to repopulate it and restore its economic life as quickly as possible. Mehmed repopulated the new capital with Christians as well as Muslims and Jews, but because of his mistrust of his Christian subjects, who openly encouraged new crusades from Europe to "liberate" them from Muslim rule, he made special efforts to attract into his dominions the Sephardic Jews of Spain and the Ashkenazi Jews of western and central Europe who were then being increasingly persecuted by Christian movements soon to culminate in the horrors of the Inquisition. To this end he stimulated the newly established chief rabbi of Edirne, Isaac Tzarfati, himself an immigrant from Germany, to send messages to Jews throughout Christian Europe urging them to enter the Ottoman dominions, where, he said, there was no persecution and Jews could achieve peace and prosperity. As a result, even before the mass expulsion of Jews from Spain in 1492, thousands of them immigrated into the Ottoman dominions from all over Europe, providing substantial support to Mehmed's massive effort to rebuild Istanbul and to make it the political and economic center of a prosperous new empire.

The rapid expansion of the Ottoman dominions created severe financial, economic, and social strains. These were, however, successfully resolved during the long and relatively peaceful reign of Sultan Bayezid II

(r. 1481–1512), thus making possible substantial expansion in the first half of the sixteenth century beyond the boundaries of the first empire, across the Danube through Hungary to the gates of Vienna and eastward into the territories of the classical Islamic empires of the Umayyads and ʿAbbāsids. Sultan Selim I (r. 1512–1520) "the Grim" *(Yavuz)*, in response to the rise of the Ṣafavid empire in Iran starting about 1500 and its threat to conquer the increasingly weak and divided Mamlūk Empire of Syria and Egypt, first defeated the Ṣafavids at Chaldiran (1514) in eastern Anatolia, and then went on to conquer the Mamlūk dominions during a rapid campaign through Syria and Egypt in 1516–1517, soon afterward adding the Arabian peninsula to his domains. Sultan Süleyman "The Lawgiver" (*Kanuni;* called "The Magnificent" in Europe), who ruled from 1520 to 1566, supported by an alliance with France against their common Habsburg enemy, went on to conquer Hungary (1526) and to put Vienna under a siege (1529), which though unsuccessful was followed by the creation of a system of border *gazi* warriors who carried out guerrilla warfare with raids well into central Europe during the next two centuries. With the stalemate in land warfare, the struggle between the Ottomans and Habsburgs was transferred to the Mediterranean Sea. Süleyman created a powerful navy under the leadership of the pirate governor of Algeria, Grand Admiral Hayruddin Barbarossa; the commander not only brought Algeria into the empire as a province whose revenues were set aside in perpetuity for support of the Ottoman navy, but also made the entire Mediterranean into an Ottoman lake. Süleyman also expanded Ottoman power in the East; after conquering Iraq and the southern Caucasus from the Ṣafavids (1535), he built an eastern fleet that from bases in the Persian Gulf and Red Sea conquered the Yemen and broke European naval efforts to blockade the old international shipping routes through the Middle East and then went on to assist Muslim rulers in western India and Indonesia against the Portuguese and others.

Government and Society. The reign of Kanuni Süleyman marked the peak of Ottoman power and prosperity as well as the highest development of its governmental, social and economic systems. The Ottoman sultans preserved the traditional Middle Eastern social division between a very small ruling class (*osmanlılar*, or "Ottomans") at the top, whose functions were limited largely to keeping order and securing sufficient financial resources to maintain itself and carry out its role, and a large subject class of rayas (*reâyâ*, or "protected flock"), organized into autonomous communities according to religion (*millets*) or economic pursuit (*esnaf*, or "guilds") that cared for all aspects of life not controlled by the ruling class.

Ruling class. Membership in the ruling class was open to all who declared and manifested loyalty to the sultan, his dynasty, and his empire; who accepted the religion of Islam; who knew and practiced the Ottoman Way, a highly complex system of behavior including use of the Ottoman language, an artificial dialect derived from Turkish, Arabic, and Persian; and who knew and carried out the particular practices used by one or another of the groups into which the ruling class was divided. Those who failed to meet these requirements were considered members of the subject class regardless of their origins or religion. Thus ruling class members could be the children of existing members, but only if they acquired and practiced all the required characteristics. Members could also come from the *devşirme* system of recruitment among Christian youths, which was carried out on a large scale in the fifteenth and sixteenth centuries; the recruits were converted to Islam and educated in the Ottoman Way in the palace school established by Mehmed II and continued by his successors. Other members entered the ruling class as slaves or captives of existing members, or as "renegades" who came to the Ottoman Empire from all the nations of Europe, seeking their fortunes under the banner of the sultans. In general, all ruling class members who came from a Turkish or Muslim heritage, including the former members of the ruling classes of the Seljuk and Mamlūk empires and their descendants, formed a Turko-Islamic aristocracy; converts from Christianity formed a separate *devşirme* class. The two groups struggled for power and prestige, with the ruler usually balancing them with equal positions and revenues in order to control and use both.

Members of the ruling class were divided into "institutions" according to function. The Palace or Imperial Institution *(mülkiye)* in the Topkapı Sarayı palace consisted of two branches: the Inner Service *(enderûn)*, often called the Harem, was charged with producing, maintaining, training, and entertaining sultans, and as such comprised the sultans themselves, their wives, concubines, children, and slaves; the Outer Service *(birûn)* was led by the grand vizier *(sadr-ı azem)* and included other officials holding the rank of vizier and the title pasha *(paşa)* who met as the imperial council *(divan)* in the *kubbealtı* section of the second courtyard of the palace and were in charge of supervising and leading the remainder of the Ottoman system on behalf of the sultan. The Scribal Institution *(kalemiye),* constituting the treasury of the sultan and including all the "men of the pen" *(ehl-i kalem),* carried out the administrative duties of the ruling class, in particular assessing and collecting taxes, making expenditures, and writing imperial decrees and most other administrative documents. The Military Institution *(seyfiye)* included the "men of the sword" *(ehl-i seyf)* charged with expanding and defending the empire and keeping order and security: the *sipahi* cavalry, commanded for the most part by members of the Turko-Islamic aristocracy; the Janissary *(yeniçeri)* infantry, military arm of the *devşirme,* which comprised the most important part of the Ottoman army starting in the sixteenth century and constituted the principal garrisons and police of major cities and towns of the empire; the Ottoman navy, long commanded by grand admirals who were given the governorship of Algeria as well as control of the customs duties of most of the ports of the Mediterranean to provide them with necessary revenues; the artillery *(topçiyan);* and various other corps. Finally there was the Religious or Cultural Institution *(ilmiye),* led by the *şeyhülislam* (Ar., *shaykh al-Islām*) and composed of "men of knowledge" *(ehl-i ilm, ülemâ;* Ar. *ʿulamāʾ),* constituting not only the leaders of prayer *(imam)* and others serving in the mosques, but also the judges *(qadi)* and jurisconsults *(müfti),* and all others in the realm of culture; to these persons the title *efendi* was given, as it was to members of the scribal class, who also had to undergo religious training.

The Islam maintained by the Ottoman *ülema,* while basically Orthodox Sunnī in its official format, was in fact a syncretistic system. It combined orthodox beliefs and rituals with two other traditions—the practices brought into Islam by the heterodox Ṣūfī orders that had predominated among the pre-Ottoman Turkomans of Anatolia, and those of the indigenous Christian population, many of whom converted to Islam and were absorbed into the Ottoman melting pot.

Within the institutions of the Ottoman ruling class, organization was maintained largely in accordance with financial functions. Each position had certain sources of revenue, either taxes of varied sorts, fees levied in return for the performance of official duties *(bahşiş;* Pers., *bakhshish),* or salaries paid by the Treasury. In general, all revenues in the empire were considered to constitute the imperial wealth *(havâss-ı hümayûn)* of the sultan, who alienated it on occasion in perpetuity as private property *(mülk)* or for religious foundations *(vakıf, evkâf;* Ar., *waqf, awqāf)* or maintained it in financial/administrative units *(muqata'ât)* intended to produce revenues for the sultan and his ruling class. Out of the revenues that were left as *muqata'ât,* some were assigned as *emanet*s to collectors (*emin*s) who were paid salaries for carrying out their duties, for the most part consisting of collecting taxes or fees without additional functions; some were assigned to officials of the state or army who used the revenues entirely as their own salary (*timar*s) in return for performing functions in addition to collecting the revenues, as viziers in the imperial council or as officers of the *sipahi* cavalry or the artillery corps; and some were assigned as tax farms *(iltizam)* to tax farmers (*mültezim*s) as the result of bids won by those who promised to pay the treasure the largest share of their annual revenues, since unlike the *timar* holders they performed no other function than the collection of revenues. Regardless of the source of revenues, the holders of the *muqata'ât* were given only enough authority to make certain that taxable revenues were produced; the producers of the revenue, whether cultivators, artisans or merchants, maintained property rights to pursue their own occupations as long as they delivered the required taxes.

Subject class. All functions of society as well as of government and administration not dealt with by the ruling class were relegated to the *reâyâ* ("protected flock") or rayas, who constituted the subject class. For this purpose the *reâyâ* were organized into religiously based communities called at different times *cema'ât, tâ'ife* and, finally *millet,* as well as into guilds *(esnâf),* mystic orders of dervishes *(tariqât)* and other groupings that formed a substratum of Ottoman society.

Most important were the religiously based communities, most often called *millet*s, of which four were established by Mehmed the Conqueror soon after he made Istanbul his capital. The Greek Orthodox and Armenian Gregorian *millet*s were led by their patriarchs and staffed by the clerics organized in hierarchies under their authority. The former included, in addition to ethnic Greeks, all the Slavs and Rumanians living in southeastern Europe; the latter included not only Armenians, but also Gypsies, Nestorians, Copts, and other Eastern Christians. The Muslim *millet* was led by the Şeyhülislâm and the Cultural Institution and was thus the only *millet* with an organic connection to the ruling class. Mehmed II and his successor Bayezid II attempted to organize the Jewish *millet* like those of the Christians, appointing Moses Capsali, grand rabbi of Istanbul under the last Byzantines, as chief of all the rabbis and all Jews throughout the empire. There was, however, no religious hierarchy in Judaism comparable to those of the Christians. The Jews were moreover divided among those coming from Spain (Sephardim, or "Spanish"), the remainder of Europe (Ashkenazim, or "Germans"), and the classical Islamic empires of the Middle East (Musta'rab, or "Arabized") as well as those who had survived centuries of persecution by the Greek Orthodox church in the Byzantine empire (Romaniote). The early grand rabbis appointed by the sultans were therefore unsuccessful at controlling their followers so that the Ottoman effort to appoint grand rabbis was therefore abandoned after 1535, not to be resumed again until just three centuries later as part of the Tanzimat reforms that transformed the empire during the nineteenth century. The traditional Jewish *millet* therefore was composed of hundreds of small communities *(kahal, kehilla),* each surrounding a synagogue; relations with ruling class officials were therefore carried out not by *millet* leaders, as was the case with the Christian and Muslim *millets*, but rather by the individual rabbis or their lieutenants *(kâhya)* or by the wealthy and influential Jewish bankers and physicians who served the sultans and other members of the ruling class until late in the sixteenth century. [*See also* Millet.]

In the countryside, villages were for the most part constituted entirely of members of one *millet* or another. In the larger towns and cities, quarters (sg., *mahalle;* pl., *mahallât*), surrounded by walls and guarded by gates, were set aside for each *millet.* In sixteenth- and seventeenth-century Istanbul, for example, most of the Muslim quarters, each centered on a great imperial mosque, were located in what is known today as Old Istanbul. The Greek quarter was centered in Fener, on the Golden Horn, which was next to Balat, the principal Jewish quarter; the Armenians lived in Ayvansaray, next to Balat, as well as across the peninsula of Old Istanbul at Kumkapı on the Sea of Marmara. Most foreigners and many Ottoman Christians congregated across the Golden Horn at Galata and up its hill to Beyoğlu (Pera) as well as on the islands of the Sea of Marmara, while the Jews crossed the Golden Horn from Balat to Hasköy, immediately opposite. Later the Jews spread also into Galata and also, to get away from the Christians, they went up the Bosporus to Ortaköy and to its Anatolian shores at Kuzguncuk and Üsküdar.

There was no municipal government as such in traditional Ottoman society. Whether rabbis or bishops or imams, the religious leaders of each quarter or village carried out all the secular functions not performed by the ruling class, basing these duties on their own religious laws as interpreted in their religious councils and courts, and conducting their affairs in their own languages and in accordance with their own customs and traditions. Thus they organized and operated schools, old-age homes, and kitchens for the poor. They arranged to pave, maintain, and light streets. They organized security and police. Leaders of the different urban *millets* came together on occasion for specific functions that required general cooperation, such as the celebration of certain festivals or organization against attacks, plagues or fires; but for the most part each lived independently with little input either by members of the ruling class or by members of the other *millets*.

A major purpose of the *millet* system was to prevent the kind of conflict among people of different religions that has so bedeviled life in the recent Middle East and southeastern Europe. While this general objective was achieved by the sultans, the age-old Christian prejudice against Jews, which had caused so many of the latter to flee from Europe to the protection of the Ottomans, did result in hundreds of Greek and Armenian blood-libel attacks on Jews throughout Ottoman history. Such attacks were suppressed by the authorities only during the centuries in which the ruling class was strong enough to maintain order, but as its empire declined in later centuries, the attacks became endemic, with Muslims and Jews usually banding together to defend themselves against assaults conducted by local Christians, often with the assistance and support of the representatives of the Christian states of Europe resident in the Ottoman dominions.

Decline. The Ottoman Empire began to decline late in the reign of Süleyman. This decline continued in various forms until the empire's final decomposition as a result of World War I. The breakup of the empire resulted from a combination of multiple and interdependent factors, many of which were both cause and result. Domination of the ruling class by the *devşirme* class, starting about 1540, led to a decline in the quality of the rulers and to large-scale nepotism, corruption, and misrule of all elements of the population. Overtaxation by corrupt members of the ruling class caused cultivators to flee from the land, either to form robber bands or to migrate into the already overcrowded cities, where a shortage of work and food led to famine, disease, and urban anarchy. Capitulation treaties that allowed European subjects to live in the Ottoman dominions under their own laws, as enforced by their ambassadors and consuls, were transformed into instruments of semicolonial exploitation; this made it possible not only for Europeans, but also for the Greek and Armenian subjects of the sultan who accepted their protection, to dominate the Ottoman economic system and to drive out Muslims and Jews, who were as a result left in increasing poverty in the seventeenth and eighteenth centuries. The resulting suffering was alleviated for the mass of subjects by their *millet*s and guilds, which at least partially protected them from the worst results of the anarchy and misrule, though many still turned away from their official religious establishments toward mystic movements that offered more emotional solace and practical protection as conditions continued to worsen as the decline accelerated.

Reform and Modernization. Most members of the ruling class made little effort to reform the abuses, since they were able personally to profit far more from the anarchy than their predecessors had been able to do under the sultans' domination. It was only when the rising nation-states of Europe recognized the extent of Ottoman weakness and moved to conquer Ottoman possessions in Hungary and southeastern Europe in the seventeenth and eighteenth centuries that the ruling class accepted some sort of reform in order to preserve the empire on which their privileges depended. Under the leadership of Sultan Murad IV (r. 1623–1640) and the dynasty of Köprülü grand viziers placed in power during the later years of the seventeenth century by Sultan Mehmed IV (r. 1648–1687), efforts were made to reform the system in order to save the empire. This reform, however, was undertaken on the basis of the prevailing belief that Ottoman institutions and practices were superior to anything developed in Christian Europe; that therefore Ottoman weakness was due less to any inferiority of its institutions than to a failure to apply them as had been in the centuries of Ottoman greatness. Traditionalistic reform at this time therefore consisted of efforts to restore the old ways, executing corrupt and incompetent officials and soldiers. As soon as the government and army had been restored sufficiently to beat back the European attacks, however, the corruption returned and continued until the next crisis forced similar efforts. Increasing losses to Russia and Austria during the eighteenth century, however, forced the sultans to modify this traditionalistic reform, at least to the extent of acknowledging that European weapons and tactics were superior, and to accept at least partial reforms of the Ottoman military, which were introduced by a series of European renegades who entered Ottoman service. Inevitably, however, the older Ottoman military corps refused to accept this sort of change, because their status in the ruling class depended on their monopoly of the traditional techniques and practices. This compelled the sultans to allow the creation of separate modern infantry and artillery corps, which, however, could not for the most part be used because of opposition by the older corps, supported by members of the ruling class who also feared that the new forces would be used to eliminate them.

During the nineteenth and early twentieth centuries, the tremendously increased European threat to Ottoman integrity and direct intervention in internal Ottoman affairs stimulated and supported violent Christian nationalist uprisings to break up the empire in order to secure their independence. The resulting loss of territories and large-scale massacres of Muslim and Jewish subjects by the rebels as well as by the newly independent Christian states of southeastern Europe at last compelled the Ottomans to change their concept of reform to one of entirely destroying the old institutions and replacing them with new ones largely imported from the West. This sort of reform took place during the Tanzimat reform period planned under Sultan Mahmud II (r. 1808–1839), carried out under his sons Abdülmecid (r. 1839–1861) and Abdülaziz (r. 1861–1876), and brought to successful culmination under Sultan Abdülhamid II (r. 1876–1909). The traditional decentralized Ottoman system was replaced by an increasingly centralized one in which the central government extended its authority and activity to all areas of Ottoman life, undermining though not entirely replacing the *millet*s and guilds. Since functions were expanding, moreover, the traditional Ottoman governmental system in which the ruling class acted through the imperial council was replaced with an increasingly complex system of government, divided into executive, legislative, and judicial branches. The executive was organized into ministries headed by ministers (*vekil*s) who came together in a cabinet led by the grand vizier or, increasingly, an official called prime minister (*baş vekil*). The legislative function was given to deliberative bodies, culminating in a partly representative council of state (*şurayı devlet*) in the last quarter of the nineteenth century and in the democratically elected parliament introduced initially in 1876–1877 and then again in the Young Turk constitutional period (1908–1912) following the deposition of Abdülhamid II. Administration was turned over to a new hierarchy of well-educated bureaucrats (*memurs*) who dominated Ottoman governmental life until the end of the empire.

The reforms introduced during the nineteenth and early twentieth centuries transformed the Ottoman empire into a relatively well-governed and modern state, whose treatment of the mass of subjects was far more humane than that of most European states that its reformers sought to copy. Emphasis was laid, however, on institutional and physical reforms, with the centralized bureaucracy exercising far more control over the lives of the subjects than was the case in the traditional decentralized Ottoman system. As a result, liberal political movements, led by the Young Ottomans during the years of the Tanzimat and by the Young Turks during the reign of Abdülhamid II, demanded political and social reforms as well. In any case, however, the multinational state now was doomed to destruction by the spread of nationalism among its Christian minorities, encouraged by Russia and Austria, who sought to use these movements as vehicles to extend their influence within the Ottoman body politic and, ultimately, to replace Ottoman rule with their own. The arms, moral encouragement, and finances supplied to various Christian national movements led to violent uprisings, starting with the Greek revolution early in the century and continuing in Serbia and Bulgaria, and particularly in Macedonia as thousands of Muslims and Jews were slaughtered under policies subsequently called "ethnic cleansing," aimed at securing homogenous national populations for the new Christian states. The Ottoman military response was bloody, leading to the massacres and countermassacres that characterized the empire, with little break, during the last half century of its existence. The Armenian and Greek minorities remaining within the empire opposed reform and supported nationalist uprisings in order to secure their own independence. The Jewish minority, however, recognized the persecution to which Jews as well as Muslims were being subjected in the course of the revolts and following the creation of the new Christian states; they therefore strongly supported Ottoman integrity and opposed the efforts to gain their support, not only by Christian nationalists, but also by the Jewish Zionists who began their activities in the empire late in the century, though their efforts to secure Ottoman permission to establish a Jewish state in Palestine were rejected. At the same time, thousands of Jews fleeing persecution in Russia as well as Central Europe during the late years of the nineteenth century were encouraged to settle in other parts of the Ottoman Empire, particularly during the reign of Sultan Abdülhamid II, and they made significant contributions to the modernization of Ottoman agriculture, industry, and trade.

During the constitutional period (1909–1918) that followed, the Ottoman Empire experienced the most democratic era of its history, with a myriad of political parties electing deputies to the Ottoman parliament, which enacted major secular and liberal reforms. An initial period in which members of all the different nationalities worked to strengthen and preserve the empire was brought to an end by Austria's annexation of Bosnia and Bulgaria's conquest of East Rumelia. These events stimulated the Christian minorities to abandon their short-lived support of the empire and to resume violent and bloody revolutions, particularly in Macedonia and eastern Anatolia, with the forceful Ottoman military responses to restore order compounding the violence. Other factors were Italy's conquest of the provinces of Libya in the short Tripolitanian War (1911) and the victory of the newly independent states of southeastern Europe during the First Balkan War (1912), which pushed the Ottomans out of all their remaining European provinces and threatened their control of Istanbul itself. As thousands of Muslim and Jewish refugees from the Christian attacks flooded into Istanbul, and as the remaining parts of the empire fell into increasing despair and chaos, the Young Turk leaders Enver Pasha, Talat Pasha, and Kemal Pasha were in 1912 able to end the short-lived Ottoman democracy and establish an autocracy that successfully defended Istanbul and took advantage of disputes among the Balkan states during the Second Balkan War (1913) to regain Edirne and eastern Thrace, and that introduced major social and economic legislation. Despite the wishes of most of the empire's politicians and people to stay out of further conflicts, the Young Turk Triumvirate also brought the empire into World War I on the side of Germany and Austria, leading to its defeat and destruction along with that of its allies, with the remaining population devastated by a massive Russian invasion in the east as well as by an Allied naval blockade which caused large-scale famine and death as the war progressed. The Turkish War for Independence that followed (1918–1923) under the leadership of Mustafa Kemal Atatürk and İsmet İnönü, however, defeated the efforts of the victorious Allies to take over the territories occupied primarily by Turks, thus leading to the establishment of the Turkish Republic in Anatolia and eastern Thrace.

[*See also* Tanzimat; Turkey; Young Ottomans; Young Turks; *and the biographies of Abdülhamid II, Atatürk, and Enver Pasha.*]

BIBLIOGRAPHY

Ahmad, Feroz. *The Young Turks: The Committee of Union and Progress in Turkish Politics, 1908–1914*. Oxford and New York, 1969.

Alderson, A. D. *The Structure of the Ottoman Dynasty*. Oxford and New York, 1956.

Berkes, Niyazi. *The Development of Secularism in Turkey*. Montreal, 1964. Masterful analysis of secular modernization in the Ottoman Empire during the nineteenth and early twentieth centuries.

Braude, Benjamin, and Bernard Lewis, eds. *Christians and Jews in the Ottoman Empire*. 2 vols. New York and London, 1982. Articles by specialists on *millet* organization and operation.

Cahen, Claude. *Pre-Ottoman Turkey*. London and New York, 1968. Definitive study of the situation in Anatolia before the Ottoman conquest.

Davison, Roderic. *Reform in the Ottoman Empire, 1856–1876*. Princeton, 1963. Detailed study of Ottoman reforms following the Crimean War.

Evans, Laurence. *United States Policy and the Partition of Turkey, 1914–1924*. Baltimore, 1965. American involvement in the efforts to turn Turkish territories over to non-Muslim minorities during and after World War I.

Findley, Carter. *Bureaucratic Reform in the Ottoman Empire: The Sublime Porte, 1789–1922*. Princeton, 1980. Definitive study of nineteenth-century Ottoman bureaucratic reforms based on extensive archival research.

Gibb, H. A. R. and Harold Bowen. *Islamic Society and the West*, vol. 1, *Islamic Society in the Eighteenth Century*. London and New York, 1950–1957.

Goodwin, Godfrey. *History of Turkish Architecture*. London, 1972.

Inalcık, Halil. *The Ottoman Empire: The Classical Age, 1300–1600*. London and New York, 1973. Study of Ottoman society and administration in the classical period by the leading Ottoman historian of our time.

Karpat, Kemal. *Ottoman Population, 1830–1914*. Madison, Wis., 1985.

Kushner, David. *The Origins of Turkish Nationalism*. London, 1977. Turkish nationalism and Pan-Turkism in the late nineteenth century.

Lewis, Bernard. *The Emergence of Modern Turkey*. 2d ed. London and New York, 1968. Ottoman modernization and reform.

Mandel, Neville J. *The Arabs and Zionism before World War I*. Berkeley and Los Angeles, 1976. Important study of Ottoman-Zionist relationships based on Turkish as well as Zionist sources.

Mantran, Robert, ed. *Histoire de l'Empire Ottoman*. Paris, 1989. Most up-to-date general history of the Ottomans, written by leading French Ottomanists.

Mardin, Şerif. *The Genesis of Young Ottoman Thought*. Princeton, 1962. The Young Ottoman society during the later years of the Tanzimat.

McCarthy, Justin. *Muslims and Minorities: The Population of Ottoman Anatolia and the End of the Empire*. New York, 1983. Definitive study of Ottoman population movements in Anatolia based on exhaustive examination of Ottoman census records.

Quataert, Donald. *Social Disintegration and Popular Resistance in the Ottoman Empire, 1881–1908*. New York, 1983. Ottoman economic and social development under Sultan Abdülhamid II.

Ramsaur, Ernest. *The Young Turks: Prelude to the Revolution of 1908*. Princeton, 1957. The Young Turk movement before the Constitutional revolution in 1908.

Sanjian, Avedis. *The Armenian Communities in Syria under Ottoman Dominion*. Cambridge, Mass., 1957.

Shaw, Stanford J. *The History of the Ottoman Empire and Modern Turkey*, vol. 1, *Empire of the Gazis: The Rise and Decline of the Ottoman Empire, 1280–1808;* vol. 2 (with Ezel Kural Shaw), *Reform, Revolution, and Republic: The Rise of Modern Turkey, 1808–1975*. Cambridge, London, and New York, 1976–1977.

Shaw, Stanford J. *Between Old and New: The Ottoman Empire under Sultan Selim III, 1789–1807*. Cambridge, Mass., 1971. Study of Selim III's failure to establish a "New Order" *(nizam-i cedid)* while leaving the old military and social structure intact.

Shaw, Stanford J. *The Jews of the Ottoman Empire and the Turkish Republic*. London and New York, 1991.

Trumpener, Ulrich. *Germany and the Ottoman Empire, 1914–1918*. Princeton, 1968. The Ottoman-German alliance during World War I.

Wittek, Paul. *The Rise of the Ottoman Empire* (1938). Reprint, London, 1982. Pioneering study of Ottoman origins as a *gazi* state.

STANFORD J. SHAW

ÖZAL, TURGUT (1927–1993), eighth president of Turkey. Born in Malatya on 13 October 1927, Özal died in office in Ankara on 17 April 1993. He was the eldest of three sons of the banker Mehmet Sıddık (Sadık) Bey and the teacher Hafize (Doğan). He received an M.S. in electrical engineering from Istanbul Technical University in 1950 and studied advanced engineering economics in the United States on an A.I.D. grant (1952–1953). He worked for the Electrical Survey Administration from 1950 to 1965, rising to deputy director general; concurrently he served as secretary of the State Planning Commission (1958–1965) and as instructor in mathematics at Middle East Technical University (1960–1962). He became technical adviser to Premier Süleyman Demirel in 1966 and undersecretary at the State Planning Organization (1967–1971). He was a consultant to the World Bank from 1971 to 1973 in the US. After holding executive positions in various Turkish private firms from 1974 to 1979, he was appointed undersecretary in the Prime Ministry and acting undersecretary in the State Planning Organization, where he was the architect of Demirel's January 1980 Economic Liberalization Program. He became deputy prime minister under Bülend Ulusu after the September 1980 military intervention but resigned after twenty-two months.

In May 1983 Özal founded the Motherland (Anavatan or ANAP) Party, won the November 1983 elections, resulting in his serving as premier until elected president in October 1989. Turkey's democratic constitutional process weathered the shock of Özal's sudden death from heart failure after an exhausting eleven-day visit to the Central Asian Turkic republics and Azerbaijan. A smooth transition of power resulted in the election of Premier Demirel as president and the appointment of the new True Path Party leader, Madame Tansu Çiller, as prime minister.

Özal's greatest service was to transform Turkey into a free-market economy and to prepare it for the twenty-first century. His free-market economic program reversed decades-long, static import-substitution policies. Turkey enjoyed the highest growth rate among Organization for Economic Cooperation and Development (OECD) members—between 6 and 8 percent annually from 1986 onward. Rapid industrialization, urbanization, modern banking, convertible currency, a free press and elections, quintupled exports, telecommunications development, and investments in education surpassing those for defense annually since 1991, coupled with implementation of the vast Southeast Anatolian Development Project (one of the world's largest)—plus considerable inflation—are elements of these changes. His controversial, dynamic foreign policy involved active participation in the Organization of the Islamic Conference (OIC); prompt closing of Iraqi pipelines to Turkish ports after Iraq's invasion of Kuwait in 1990 (despite costing Turkey some $15 billion); the Black Sea Economic Cooperation Zone; openings to the new Turkic republics of the former Soviet Union; mediation in Azerbaijan, the Balkans, and Iran; and staunch membership in the North Atlantic Treaty Organization (NATO), the European Union, the Conference on Security and Cooperation in Europe, and other international agencies. These policies notably enhanced Turkey's global stature and key geopolitical and intercultural role as a stable bridge between Europe and the rest of Eurasia in an era of revolutionary change.

Özal's father was a *medrese* (Ar., *madrasah,* Islamic theological college) graduate later trained as a banker. His mother was a devout, enlightened primary school teacher and had made the *ḥajj*. His grandmother was partly Kurdish. Özal himself was an observant Muslim who kept the fast and prayed regularly, but he was also a strong secularist and tolerant ecumenist. He was an initiate of the Naqshbandīyah dervish order, his Ṣūfī mentor, Mehmet Zahit Kotku (d. 1980), who claimed descent from the Prophet, was buried in the grounds of Süleymaniye mosque in Istanbul, as was Özal's mother in 1988, both beneficiaries of special permits issued by the Council of Ministers.

Özal envisioned the twenty-first century as that of the Turks. He was extremely intelligent, with an analytic mind and retentive memory, friendly, smiling, open-minded, self-assured yet modest, remarkably persuasive, focused, and hard-working. He and his second wife, Semra Yeğinmen (m. 1954), who bore him a daughter, Zeynep, and two sons, Ahmet and Efe, were close confidants who usually ate together and walked hand-in-hand in public—a rare sight in Turkey. An indulgent father, he was criticized for nepotism. He became computer adept in his sixties and used and played with more than a dozen computers at home and work. He said, "I think world leaders should make more use of the technological marvels of our age in order to reach out to the masses in other countries to convey conciliatory messages and to build new understanding among peoples. . . . Tolerance and fraternal solidarity among peoples and faiths are the two main themes . . . in the planetary enterprise to build the next millennium on sound foundations of freedom, peace, progress and prosperity." His remarkable book *Turkey in Europe and Europe in Turkey* (1991) argues cogently that Anatolia (now most of the Turkish peninsula) has always been a contributor to and part of European civilization, and that the roots of so-called Western or Judeo-Christian civilization include Anatolia: consequently, a more accurate designation would be "Judeo-Christian-Islamic civilization." Unfortunately, this learned and eloquent book has received virtually no notice abroad except for a few reviews in French periodicals, notably *Le Monde.*

Many consider Turgut Özal Turkey's greatest leader since Mustafa Kemal Atatürk (president, 1923–1938), İsmet İnönü (president, 1938–1950), and Adnan Menderes (premier, 1950–1960). His bold, far-sighted and often successful policies appear more admired in death than in life. Özal dedicated himself unstintingly to improving the quality of life of all Turkish citizens and achieved remarkable results in a life whose untimely end prevented him from his hope of continuing to lead as president or possibly again as prime minister. He urged his compatriots to escape from "the tunnel of history" and to realize his dreams and plans for the next century, in which Turks would come into their true inheritance and achieve the status of an advanced society. He opened up new possibilities and challenging perspectives for every Turk that can stimulate his successors to even greater achievements. It is too early for any definitive assessment of his career, its impact on Turkey, and the world, but his legacy challenges all Turks.

[*See also* Anavatan Partisi; Turkey.]

BIBLIOGRAPHY

The reader may consult the following works by Turgut Özal:

"Türkiye'nin Kalkınmasında Görüşler" (Perspectives on Turkish Development). 1973. Thirty-five-page letter from Özal to Süleyman Demirel, written after Özal's two-year consultancy with the World Bank. The letter sets out a blueprint for Özal's later (1979–1980) free-market program, which introduced radical and positive changes in Turkey's economic structure. See *Değişim "Belgeleri,"* cited below, for Özal's three basic principles essential to Turkey's future (pp. 9, 19, 161–162).

"Kalkınmada Yeni Görüşün Esasları" (The Basic Elements of the New Perspective on Development). Speech delivered at the Minor Congress of the Nationalists, Ankara, April 1979 (published in *Değişim "Belgeleri"*).

Opening and Closing Speeches of Deputy Prime Minister and Minister of State Turgut Özal at the Second İzmir Economic Congress, İzmir, 2 and 7 November 1981. In Turkish. The first speech presents a historical analysis of Turkey's economic policies and growth since 1923. The second recommends basic principles to which Turkey must adhere to assure continuous socioeconomic development. Published in *Değişim "Belgeleri."*

Speeches by Prime Minister Özal, 1983–1989, and President Özal, 1989–1993, published periodically in Turkish by the Grand National Assembly, Ankara. See, for example, *Başbakan Turgut Özal'ın Yurtiçi–Yurtdışı Konuşmaları* (Prime Minister Turgut Özal's Speeches in Turkey and Abroad, 13 December 1988–31 October 1989). Ankara, n.d.

La Turquie en Europe. Paris, 1988. Translated and revised as *Turkey in Europe and Europe in Turkey*. Nicosia, Northern Cyprus, 1991. Traces the significant contributions of Anatolians to universal civilization during the past eight thousand years, underscoring Turkey's seminal interaction with and contributions to European/Western culture. Özal unmasks and refutes mistaken prejudices of Europeans regarding Turks and provides illuminating historical evidence to support Turkey's 1987 request for full membership in the European Community.

Değişim "Belgeleri," 1979–1992 ("Documents" on Change, 1979–1992). Istanbul, 1993. Posthumously published book containing four key documents from 1979, 1981, 1983, and 1992. The documents enunciate Özal's three basic freedoms (freedom of thought, freedom of conscience and religion, and freedom to engage in free enterprise) and his guidelines for shifting Turkey into a free-market economy, reorganizing and decentralizing government, amending the constitution, revitalizing education and health services, creating necessary infrastructures (including state-of-the-art fiber optics capability and telecommunications), sustained improvements in energy and water supplies, and environmental protection.

The Turkish weekly newsmagazine *NOKTA* (Istanbul) published a special supplement on Özal, *NOKTA Özal Ek TURGUT ÖZAL, 1927–1993*, distributed with the regular weekly issue for 25 April (Nisan)—1 May (Mayis) 1993, which contains a series of commissioned articles by former associates and informed specialists providing useful data and perspectives on the late president's career. The supplement is a useful addition to earlier books on various aspects of Özal's career, written in Turkish and undocumented, hence very hard to assess, despite the fact that a few have become best sellers in Turkey.

HOWARD A. REED

P

PAHLAVI, MUHAMMAD REZA SHAH (1919–1980), last ruling monarch of the Pahlavi dynasty of Iran. Born in Tehran, Crown Prince Muhammad was elevated to shah in August 1941 by the British and Russians who had invaded Iran and ousted his father in fear of growing German influence in Iran. The shah never managed to convince the Iranian people that he was their legitimate ruler. Throughout his rule, many perceived him to be serving foreign interests.

This view of the shah was heightened in August 1953 when the British and Americans staged a coup to oust Prime Minister Mohammad Mossadegh and restore the shah to the throne.

In 1963, the shah launched his White Revolution to accelerate social change and guarantee the security of his throne. At that period of social turmoil, Ayatollah Ruhollah Khomeini, a cleric with a burgeoning reputation based more on his political activism than religious scholarship, began to criticize the Pahlavis and their alleged worship of the West. The ayatollah was arrested and mass protests broke out in cities throughout Iran. Hundreds of his followers were shot. The ayatollah was released and rearrested but finally exiled in the fall of 1964.

With his most vociferous clerical opponent apparently silenced, the shah continued his reforms. But the reforms did not transform Iran as much as the sharp rise in oil prices of December 1973, which he did much to engineer. The result was an explosion of oil revenues and of government spending. Tehran experienced a massive building boom. Property speculation swept the country and inflation spiraled. Industries, universities and schools, hospitals and roads were all built. But the economic boom spawned chaos and social turmoil. Corruption was unchecked. The shah also had the wealth to realize another dream—to make Iran a major military power—and spent billions of dollars to buy U.S. arms.

After an article lambasting Ayatollah Khomeini appeared in the Iranian press in early 1978, demonstrations broke out in the religious city of Qom. Young clerics were killed by the police. The revolution was on. After a year of escalating violence, the shah fled Iran on 19 January 1979, never to return. Ayatollah Khomeini flew back in triumph to destroy the remnants of the shah's regime and create an Islamic republic.

No country would offer asylum to the shah, and he was shunned by his former friends. But when the cancer that had been diagnosed in the early 1970s began to burgeon, President Jimmy Carter relented and allowed the shah to enter the United States for medical treatment. The clerics in Tehran responded by urging their followers to seize the U.S. embassy and hold captive American diplomats. The ensuing hostage crisis was not to be resolved until 1981 and U.S.-Iranian relations were to be poisoned permanently.

The shah was no longer welcome in the United States and spent the remaining year of his life continuing to search for a home until his cancer finally killed him. He was buried in Cairo; not even his remains were welcome in the country that he had ruled for so many years.

[*See also* Iran; *and* Iranian Revolution of 1979.]

BIBLIOGRAPHY

Bill, James. *The Eagle and the Lion.* New Haven, 1988. Critique of U.S. foreign policy toward Iran, with important attention to the second Pahlavi shah.

Cottam, Richard. *Nationalism in Iran.* 2d rev. ed. Pittsburgh, 1979. Classic work on the subject, with major focus on the Pahlavi period.

Gasiorowski, Mark. *US Foreign Policy and the Shah.* Ithaca, N.Y., 1991. Emphasizes the client relationship between Iran and the United States during the second Pahlavi period and examines its impact on internal Iranian politics.

Lenczowski, George, ed. *Iran Under the Pahlavis.* Stanford, 1978. Essays on various aspects of politics, economics, and society by scholars generally sympathetic to the cause of the Pahlavis.

Zonis, Marvin. *Majestic Failure.* Chicago, 1991. Analysis of the shah, with emphasis upon the political psychology of the ruler and stressing the gap between an insecure monarch and the exigencies of his sovereign rule.

MARVIN ZONIS

PAHLAVI, REZA SHAH (1878–1944), Iranian monarch and founder of the Pahlavi dynasty. Of modest origins and without a formal education, Reza joined the Cossack Brigade at an early age. In February 1921, with the support or approval of the British military and civilian personnel in Iran, Reza (then a brigadier general and known as Reza Khan) launched a coup together with Sayyid Ẓiyā' al-Dīn Ṭabāṭabā'ī, a pro-British journalist who briefly became prime minister before being forced into exile. Following the coup, Reza Khan became war minister and commander of the army, and he concentrated his efforts on creating a unified standing army and consolidating his own position, eventually assuming the premiership in October 1923.

From the outset, Reza Khan betrayed a contempt for constitutional procedures and principles. In the face of mounting, primarily religious opposition, he abandoned the republican campaign which he had instigated in 1924 and concentrated instead on establishing a dynasty of his own. His success in suppressing regional contenders and rebellions enhanced his power to the detriment of his parliamentary opponents, who failed to block his assumption of the throne in late 1925.

Enjoying the support of a large section of the intelligentsia, Reza Shah embarked on reforms which embodied ideas that had long been in the air. The strengthening of the army and the centralized bureaucratic state proceeded, as did efforts to disarm and settle the pastoral nomadic population coercively. Public health care and secular primary and higher education received particular attention. Substantial reform in the institutions of justice, together with the promulgation of modern legal codes enabled the government to terminate the capitulations [*see* Capitulations]. Measures to expand urbanization, strengthen and modernize the Iranian economy, build factories and roads, extend electrification, modernize transportation and communications, and construct a trans-Iranian railroad, among other things, went hand in hand with the imposition of modern dress and headgear for men, the abolition of traditional honorific titles, the adoption of surnames, and the persianization of the calendar.

Many of these reforms, particularly the secularization of education and the legal system, directly encroached on the privileges of the *ʿulamā'* (community of religious scholars). The outlawing of the veil in January 1936 in defiance of religious and traditional sensibilities aggravated the situation. Reza Shah, however, tolerated no opposition. He was inspired by a nationalism which sought its mythological repository in the pre-Islamic era of Iranian history and affected the whole ethos of his rule.

Despite socioeconomic reforms, the power of the shah remained arbitrary and no institutions were developed to depersonalize the state. Parliamentary politics was reduced to a mere facade. Rarely courteous toward subordinates, the quick-tempered shah ruled by fear and by rewarding docile loyalty. Those whom he perceived to be capable of endangering his own power or his son's subsequent assumption of the throne often met a tragic end, even if they were his closest aides. Reza Shah was deeply suspicious of the Russians and particularly of the British; toward the end of his reign, with the outbreak of World War II, Iran's close economic ties with Germany, and refusal on the grounds of neutrality to expel German nationals, prompted the Allied occupation of the country in August 1941. Reza Shah abdicated and was exiled to South Africa, where he lived until his death. Reza Shah rarely made public speeches; he had a remarkable ability to absorb and remember details, was frugal, and was very keen on amassing a personal fortune, particularly through the acquisition of land. He was essentially pragmatic, espousing no coherent intellectual creed, and yet nationalism, étatism, anticlericalism, and a desire to modernize Iran were important elements in his political outlook.

[*See also* Iran.]

BIBLIOGRAPHY

No scholarly biography of Reza Shah exists in English. For a slightly dated but still useful account of developments during his reign, see Amin Banani, *The Modernization of Iran, 1921–1941* (Stanford, Calif., 1961). On his early political career and rise to power, see Houshang Sabahi, *British Policy in Persia, 1918–1925* (Portland, Ore., 1990), and Michael P. Zirinsky, "Imperial Power and Dictatorship: Britain and the Rise of Reza Shah, 1921–1926," *International Journal of Middle East Studies* 24.4 (November 1992): 639–663. See also E. Eshraghi, "Anglo-Soviet Occupation of Iran in August 1941," *Middle Eastern Studies* 20.9 (January 1984): 27–52.

FAKHREDDIN AZIMI

PAINTING. With very few exceptions, there is no tradition of figural imagery in a religious context in Islam. Religious structures have been lavishly decorated with nonfigural imagery in a variety of media, and religious texts are ornamented with illuminated frontispieces and chapter and verse headings. An exception to the general tendency against figural imagery in a religious context occurs with the illustration of manuscripts that contain religious subjects, such as particular events in the life of the Prophet, particularly the *miʿrāj* or miraculous journey. Lives of the saints, augury texts, and mystic poetry may also contain figural imagery. While the existence of religious painting has long been recognized by scholars of Islamic art, it has only recently begun to be studied in some detail.

Much more attention has been directed to the painting that is so much more prevalent in the art of the Islamic world: the illustration of manuscripts of histories, folktales, romances, epics, poetry, and animal fables, and the production of single page paintings that were collected and assembled into albums by individual patrons. This painting, almost without exception done in a miniature format on paper, was generally produced in a royal atelier or for elite patrons. Throughout Islamic history, artists associated with the courts were exposed to the foreign artists (Byzantine, European, or Chinese) who visited the courts as well as to the foreign works of art that found their way into royal collections. European prints and paintings in particular began to have an impact on miniature painting at the courts of the Ṣafavids, Qājārs, Ottomans, and Mughals. Artists at first confined themselves to experimentation with technical aspects of perspective and shading. However, as the artists of the Islamic world became more familiar with European painting, and as political and cultural contact between the two spheres increased more generally, nineteenth-century artists adopted other conventions of European painting that had a far-reaching effect on painting in the Islamic world.

Although it is generally true that painting in the Islamic world changed dramatically during the nineteenth century, it is impossible to discuss these changes in a meaningful way on a pan-Islamic level. Regional variations in painting style are extreme and are closely related to the political, economic, and cultural history of each individual region. The histories of Iran, Egypt, and Turkey, for example, and particularly of their contact with the European powers in the nineteenth and early twentieth centuries, vary so tremendously that it is misleading and uninformative to treat them as a single political or cultural entity. The same is true of the history of the art of each of these regions. Thus the art of each major cultural region must be considered separately to gain an understanding of painting in the modern Islamic world.

The art of the nineteenth-century Islamic world has only recently begun to be studied, and most work so far has concentrated on architecture, not painting. Developments in contemporary art may be reported in local publications throughout the Islamic world, but these publications, often produced by private galleries or banks, are difficult to obtain outside the region. Until quite recently there have been very few works in European languages about contemporary art in the Islamic world. An exception is modern Turkish art, which has been the subject of numerous publications, many in English, and which is thus the most accessible to the nonspecialist. Also, as a result of the long cultural relationship between France and North Africa, there are a number of French publications about contemporary art in North Africa. Finally, the journal *Arts and the Islamic World,* which first appeared in 1982, has made a concerted and successful effort to publicize contemporary art from all regions of the Islamic world. Articles about modern art in the Islamic world appear less regularly in other publications, such as *Aramco World, Asian Art News,* and *Arts of Asia.* The material presented in this article is necessarily limited by available source material as well as by space constraints. More attention is given to Turkish art, since that information is readily available, but the art of other regions and related issues in the study of modern Islamic painting are touched on briefly.

Ottoman painting in the classical tradition ends with the end of the eighteenth century; modern Turkish painting begins in the mid-nineteenth century, after a period of nearly fifty years from which very few examples of miniature painting have survived. The transitions between the two painting traditions are rarely discussed, yet a careful examination of eighteenth-century miniatures reveals the beginnings of experimentation with European painting conventions.

Abdülcelil Çelebi, or Levni, the best-studied of the eighteenth-century painters, is known particularly for the *Surname-i vehbi* (Book of Festivals) commemorating the circumcision of the sons of Ahmed III in 1711, and for a large number of single-figure studies. Situated comfortably within the Ottoman tradition, his painting is characterized by its complex compositions, clarity of representation, richness of detail, and technical competence. In his articulation of architectural and landscape elements and shading, we see rudimentary attempts to indicate depth and three-dimensionality.

A second, slightly younger contemporary of Levni's is Rafael, sometimes called Rafael the Armenian. Unlike

Levni's figures, Rafael's convey a sense of mass and three-dimensionality, an impression strengthened when we notice that they cast shadows. Formed by color, light, and shadow, not by line, they are compelling figures who establish direct eye contact with the viewer (see figure 1).

Rafael's work is unique in that his attention is focused solely on the figures he depicts, revealing the artist's interest in Western painting conventions; however, it is more often in landscape that we can detect the most obvious impact of European painting conventions of perspective and three-dimensionality. Ottoman artists had always taken a strong interest in the depiction of landscape, and its importance in Ottoman painting continues unabated throughout the eighteenth century, but its treatment began to change. In addition to the obvious differences in technique, the artists' intent is altered: the sixteenth-century artist was interested in conveying precise topographical information, but the eighteenth-century painter is much closer to the European romantic tradition of landscape painting.

FIGURE 1. *Woman with Bow and Arrows.* Rafael the Armenian, c.1747. Topkapı Sarayı, Istanbul.

After Ahmed III was deposed in 1730, the royal atelier barely survived. There is very little information available about artistic activity at the court in the first decades of the nineteenth century, and few manuscripts or albums survive from this period. Murals and other painted architectural decoration were the most viable of the visual arts in the late eighteenth century and the first decades of the nineteenth, and indeed this art form continued to be popular throughout the century.

The first works of modern Turkish painting emerge in the 1840s and 1850s. The modern artists are set apart from their predecessors on several grounds. Abandoning the miniature format, the nineteenth-century artists worked in oil or watercolor, at an easel. Their subject matter resembled that of their European contemporaries—landscapes, still-lifes, and genre scenes. No longer the products of a court atelier system, these artists were graduates of the new engineering and military academies set up by the government. Their training in sketching, draftsmanship, and engineering distinguishes them from the court painters of a century earlier. In addition, the majority of the artists were sent to Europe to complete their education and often were able to study in the studios of the famous European artists of the day. Upon their return to the Ottoman empire, nearly all of them worked as engineers, military officials, or government bureaucrats first, and artists second.

We know of at least forty artists who were active during the later nineteenth century, working in a variety of styles. Osman Hamdi Bey (1842–1910) is one of the best-known and most interesting Turkish painters of the nineteenth century. He spent twelve years in Europe, perhaps studying at some point in the studio of the Orientalist painter Jean-Léon Gerôme. In 1881 Hamdi Bey was appointed director of the Archaeological Museum and was responsible for the passage of the first antiquities law in the Middle East. He was also the first director of the newly founded School of Fine Arts, a post he held from 1883 until 1908. A very prolific, accomplished painter, his work in many cases resembles that of the Orientalist painters, with whom he was certainly familiar from his time in Europe (see figure 2). He often painted women in the harem and street or genre scenes, as well as single figures and landscape. The paintings of the nineteenth-century Orientalist artists are often interpreted generally as a reflection of the stereotyped view

FIGURE 2. *Girl Placing a Vase.* Osman Hamdi Bey, 1881. Istanbul Painting and Sculpture Museum.

of Middle Eastern society held by Europeans. To some extent this is a useful way of analyzing these works; however, Hamdi Bey and the other Turks painting in the European tradition do not fit neatly into this scheme, and in fact suggest the need for a more critical application of theories of Orientalism.

Twentieth-century visual artists have worked in a variety of styles and media, generally related to some extent to major art movements in Europe. Contemporary art in Turkey is supported by two major museums for painting and sculpture, one in Istanbul and one in Ankara, as well as by numerous private galleries and collectors. There are a number of highly regarded art schools that train younger artists in addition to providing a source of income for practicing painters and sculptors. Turkey's proximity to Europe and its long history of cultural interaction with the European art world has allowed Turkish artists to exhibit their work and communicate with a wide international audience.

The political and cultural history of Iran differs from that of Turkey in a number of important aspects, and those differences are apparent in the way in which modern Iranian painting evolved from Ṣafavid miniature painting. During the Ṣafavid period (1501–1732) Persian artists were exposed to quantities of European prints as well as to the artists who travelled to the Ṣafavid court from Europe. Royal palaces were decorated with large-scale mural paintings that illustrated primarily historical subjects and figures relaxing in landscape settings. Under the Qājārs (1779–1924) a distinctive style of painting emerged, similar in conception to the Ṣafavid murals but completely different in appearance (see figure 3). Intended as wall decoration, the

FIGURE 3. *Girl Dancing with Castanets.* Artist unknown, period of Fatḥ ʿAlī Shāh. Formerly in the Pahlavi collection.

paintings are large in scale, done in oil, and most often depict a royal prince or woman of the court. Scrupulous attention is paid to the representation of costume and jewelry, and the women are often shown as dancers, musicians, or servants. Although details of setting are minimal, the manner in which palace interiors or landscapes are depicted indicates that the Qājār artists were attempting to use a Western perspective system. The same style of painting was also used during the Qājār period to decorate lacquer bookbindings and pen boxes.

Although the art of the Qājārs has been studied to some extent, the painting of twentieth-century Iran is virtually unknown in the West. Persian publications on modern painting rarely reach North American libraries, and there have been few if any studies of the subject in European languages. Furthermore, it is unclear how the Iranian Revolution of 1979 and the subsequent dramatic change in the cultural climate of the country have affected the art world.

Within the Arabic-speaking world, the development of modern styles of painting has taken a variety of paths. In Saudi Arabia, for example, where there was no earlier painting tradition, modern art has emerged only in the past few decades. In other areas, particularly North Africa and Lebanon, where there has been significant contact with French culture and artists, Arab artists have worked to develop the cultural institutions necessary to support a modern art community. Exhibitions, public and private collectors, and publications—often on an international scale—testify to the importance of painting within contemporary Arab culture.

Throughout the history of Islamic art Egypt has had a pivotal role, and this is true of its place in the contemporary art scene. The first modern school of fine arts was established in Cairo in 1908, surviving today as the College of Fine Arts. The National Centre for Fine Arts oversees the operation of a number of centers of art education as well as museums of modern art and organizes a series of exhibitions each year. Egyptian painters work in diverse styles, and many enjoy international reputations, exhibiting their work in Europe and elsewhere.

South Asia has a long and rich tradition of painting in a variety of media in Hindu, Buddhist, and Islamic traditions. As a result of the long period of British colonial rule, Indian artists became very familiar with European painting styles. Elements from European painting traditions were added to the already eclectic mix of styles and subject matters that had long characterized the painting of the subcontinent. Since independence and partition, numerous traditional regional painting forms, such as story-telling murals, have flourished. However, there is also a strong contemporary art movement, supported by art colleges and galleries in the major cities of the subcontinent.

As painting in the Islamic world has moved from a private art form intended for the enjoyment of a small group of manuscript owners to a public art exhibited in galleries and museums, and as the practice of art has become more accessible, artists have begun to explore themes that were not part of the miniature tradition. For example, painting specifically concerned with Islamic religious values has an important place in contemporary art in most countries with a significant Muslim population. Many of the creators of these works observe the traditional prohibition against figural imagery alluded to in the *ḥadīth* and focus instead on painted calligraphic forms (see figure 4). A. D. Pirous, a contemporary Indonesian painter, is an excellent example of an artist whose work often reflects his Islamic identity and is a prominent figure in the contemporary Indonesian art world. He has travelled and studied art outside Indonesia and has exhibited both his prints and paintings widely. His experiments with calligraphic painting in the early 1970s and his more general interest in incorporating Islamic themes or motifs in his work have been an important influence on younger Indonesian artists.

Traditionally women had almost no role in the production of miniature painting in the Islamic world. Although the majority of the painters whose work has survived are anonymous, there is absolutely no evidence to suggest that any of these artists were women. With the introduction of fine-arts schools and the increasing accessibility of education to women beginning in the nineteenth century, women have become important members of the art community throughout the Islamic world. They have, however, faced the same barriers to success and recognition as their sister artists in the West throughout the nineteenth and twentieth centuries: restricted access to major centers of art training (particularly in the nineteenth century), much more limited exposure in gallery and museum collections, and a dramatically lower rate of inclusion in publications. For example, one recent work on contemporary Turkish painters included 148 artists, of whom only 13 were women (Başkan, 1991). A rough survey of the available literature indicates that the Turkish example is representative: women generally comprise about 10 percent of the artists discussed in an article or catalog. Exceptions occur rarely, as in an article entitled "The Emergence of Women on the Malaysian Art Scene" (*Arts and*

FIGURE 4. *A. D. Pirous, Working in His Studio.* Photograph taken before 1985.

FIGURE 5. *Painted Mural Commemorating the Pilgrimage to Mecca.* Upper Egypt, artist unknown, c.1980s.

the Islamic World, 1988), which is concerned solely with women artists and mentions a women-only exhibition and the role of women in the Malaysian art world as practicing artists, curators, and so on. Women are active artists and art professionals throughout the Islamic world, but at present they are nearly invisible owing to their absence from the published record. The difficulties that women face in gaining recognition in the art world are of course exacerbated by the feeling in some parts of the Muslim community that the public role of women should be limited.

Throughout the history of art in the Islamic world, painting has also taken place in contexts outside the courtly tradition. Unfortunately, these more popular art forms are nearly impossible to document, at least until around the beginning of the nineteenth century (see figure 5). However, the paintings that decorate ceramics, trucks, boats, houses, fountains, books, and innumerable other objects display the aesthetic values and cultural identity of large segments of the population, often demonstrating a juxtaposition of artistic and religious concerns that were not apparent in the art of the elite.

[*See also* Aesthetic Theory.]

BIBLIOGRAPHY

Arts and the Islamic World. London, 1982–. The most important publication on modern art in the Islamic world, appearing in two or three issues annually. Nearly every issue contains at least one article about contemporary art somewhere in the Islamic world, and a few issues have been devoted almost entirely to the art of a particular area.

Başkan, Seyfi. *Contemporary Turkish Painters*. Ankara, 1991. Bilingual publication (Turkish/English) organized as a series of short biographies of nineteenth- and twentieth-century artists in Turkey.

Bosworth, C. E., and Carole Hillenbrand, eds. *Qajar Iran: Political, Social, and Cultural Change, 1800–1925*. Edinburgh, 1983. Collection of essays on a variety of topics, all concerned with the Qājār period. The diversity of discipline and subject matter provides an excellent overview of the period.

Brosh, Na'ama, and Rachel Milstein. *Biblical Stories in Islamic Painting*. Jerusalem, 1991. Catalog published in conjunction with an exhibition of the same name held at the Israel Museum in Jerusalem.

Buchari, Machmud, and Sanento Yuliman. *A. D. Pirous: Painting, Etching, and Serigraphy*. Bandung, 1985. Bilingual (Indonesian/English) exhibition catalog, copiously illustrated, with essays on various aspects of the artist's work.

Falk, S. J. *Qajar Paintings: Persian Oil Paintings of the Eighteenth and Nineteenth Centuries*. London, 1972. The main publication on Qājār paintings, focused on a private collection in the possession of the empress of Iran at the time of publication.

Glassie, Henry. *Turkish Traditional Art Today*. Bloomington, Ind., 1992. Comprehensive survey of the subject, copiously illustrated, with many interviews by contemporary artists throughout Turkey.

Grant, Jean. "Saudi Art: A Fledgling about to Take Off." *Arts and the Islamic World* 4.1 (1986): 28–32. Brief overview of the development of modern Saudi art, with a discussion of several contemporary artists.

Renda, Günsel, et al. *A History of Turkish Painting*. 2d ed. Seattle, 1988. Comprehensive survey of Turkish painting, beginning with an overview of Ottoman miniature painting and continuing through the contemporary period.

Wright, Astri. *Soul, Spirit, and Mountain: Preoccupations of Contemporary Indonesian Painters*. Kuala Lumpur, 1994. First scholarly analysis of contemporary Indonesian art in English, containing a discussion of the work of numerous artists in its sociocultural context, based on interviews with the artists.

NANCY MICKLEWRIGHT

PAKISTAN. The Islamic Republic of Pakistan, with a population of 122.8 million (1993 estimate), is the second largest Muslim nation in the world. Although they belong to five distinct ethnic groups—Punjabi, Sindhi, Pathan, Baluch, and Muhājirs (Urdu-speaking immigrants from prepartition India)—the overwhelming majority (97 percent) of Pakistanis are Muslims. Non-Muslim minorities include Christians, Hindus, and Parsees. Among the Muslims, between 10 and 15 percent are Shīʿīs, the majority of these subscribing to the Ithnā ʿAsharī (Twelver) school of Shiism. Minority Shīʿī sects include Ismāʿīlīs, mostly in Karachi and the northwestern region of Gilgit, and Bohoras, whose spiritual headquarters are in Bombay, India. The overwhelming majority of Pakistan's Sunnī Muslims subscribe to the Ḥanafī school of law, although a small minority follow the Ḥanbalī school.

Origins. Pakistan, which came into being as a result of the partition of British India on 14 August 1947, is unique among Muslim countries in regard to its relationship with Islam: it is the only Muslim country that was established in the name of Islam. Hence Pakistan's political experience is integrally related with the struggle of Indian Muslims to find a new sovereign political center after their loss of power to the British in the early nineteenth century. Beginning with Sir Sayyid Aḥmad Khān's Aligarh movement of educational and religio-intellectual reforms and his insistence on separate political identity and rights for Indian Muslims, the resurgence of Indic Islam made its mark in such religious movements as the Mujāhidīn movement of Sayyid Aḥmad Shahīd and the Deoband movement of Maulānā Qāsim Nanautvi (1821–1880) and Maulānā Maḥmūdulḥasan (1851–1920). While the Mujāhidīn movement launched an armed *jihād* to restore Muslim political power in northwest India, the Deobandīs and other Islamic educational movements sought to help Indian Muslims keep their traditional Islamic heritage during their period of political subordination. The concept of a sovereign Muslim political domain was kept alive by Muḥammad ʿAlī (1878–1931) and Bahādur Yār Jang (1905–1944), and by the emergence of the Khilāfat movement in the 1920s under the leadership of the ʿAlī brothers. [*See* Khilāfat Movement.]

Earlier, in 1906, the Western-educated Muslim elite had established a political organization of their own—the all-India Muslim League—in Dhaka to champion the religious, cultural, political, and economic interests of Indian Muslims and to thwart attempts by the growing Hindu nationalist organizations to deprive Muslims of their rightful place in the India of the future. What galvanized the Muslims' search for a new political strategy, however, was the Hindu agitation against the partition of Bengal, which convinced the Indian Muslims of the need to protect their religio-cultural and political interests through a separate political organization. This drew support to the Muslim League and its platform for a separate system of Muslim representation in all political institutions. At about the same time, extremist Hindus started the Shuddhi and Sangathan movements aiming at the forcible conversion of Muslims. The Muslims reacted by organizing the Tanẓīm and Tablīgh movements to defend Islam and to launch their own missionary work.

After many years of persistent attempts to reach some reasonably acceptable settlement with the Hindu-dominated Indian National Congress, the Muslim League, under the leadership of Mohammad Ali Jinnah, realized that the religious, cultural, and political interests of the Indian Muslim community could not be safeguarded in a postindependence united India dominated by the Hindu majority. The Muslim League therefore adopted the goal of creating a separate state from the Muslim-majority areas of northwest and northeast India, to be known as Pakistan. The poet-philosopher Muhammad Iqbal also argued for centralizing "the life of Islam as a cultural force" in a specified territory through the creation of a "consolidated Muslim State" in Northwest India. He thought that for Islam such an autonomous state would mean "an opportunity to rid itself of the stamp that Arab Imperialism was forced to give it, to mobilize its laws, its education, its culture, and to bring them into closer contact with its own spirit and with the spirit of modern times."

The popular acceptance of the idea of Pakistan was made possible only through the Muslim League's success in politicizing the religious sentiments of Indian Muslims and in claiming that the struggle for Pakistan was the struggle for the preservation and glory of Islam. By the time the movement for the establishment of Pakistan came near the realization of its goals, its religious revivalist character had already been established. The revivalist character of the Pakistan movement had firm historical roots in such premodern fundamentalist movements as that of Shāh Walī Allāh of Delhi and Sayyid Aḥmad Shahīd of Bareilly. This revivalist impulse was also intertwined with the late nineteenth- and early twentieth-century Muslim modernist-nationalist tradition of Sir Sayyid Aḥmad Khān, Syed Ameer Ali, and Muhammad Iqbal on the one hand, and such diverse religious revivalist movements as the Tablīghī Jamāʿat of Maulānā Muḥammad Ilyās, the reform Ṣūfī movement of Maulānā Ashraf ʿAlī Thānvī, the Jamāʿat-i Islāmī of Maulānā Abū al-Aʿlā Mawdūdī, the Khilāfat movement of Maulānā Muḥammad ʿAlī Jauhar, and the Khāksar movement of ʿAllāmah ʿInāyatullāh al-Mashriqī. Although these movements differed on important religious and political issues and methods, their emergence during the most critical phase of the history of Indic Islam had the combined effect of directing the collective Muslim position on a parallel course with that of Hindus and of dividing the two religious communities—a division that ultimately resulted in the creation of the Muslim state of Pakistan. [*See* All-India Muslim League *and the biographies of Jinnah, Iqbal, Aḥmad Khān, Ameer Ali, and Mawdūdī.*]

Pākistān kā maṭlab kyā? Lā ilāha illa Allāh! ("What does Pakistan stand for? There is no god but God!") was a powerful popular slogan given to the Indian Muslims by the All-India Muslim League during the peak of its struggle for the establishment of a separate homeland. Especially since the creation of Pakistan in 1947, the question of the new nation's ideological character has been a subject of continuous debate among Pakistani intellectuals. Two distinct schools of thought have emerged on this issue: one contends that Pakistan was demanded and created in the name of Islam and therefore can exist only as an Islamic state; the other emphasizes that the country was created to safeguard the political and economic interests of South Asian Muslims and was in no way intended to be a religiously based, ideological state. Irrespective of the real motives and interests of the Muslim League leadership during the 1940s, there is ample evidence that the Muslim masses of India who formed the backbone of the struggle for Pakistan and voted in large numbers in favor of the Muslim League candidates wanted Pakistan to be an Islamic state. Maulānā Shabbīr Aḥmad ʿUs̱mānī and a few other *ʿulamāʾ* of Deoband who defied the majority support for Indian unity also justified their call for Pakistan in terms of its potential as an Islamic state. The same may be said of the Muslim League leadership, despite certain differences among the Western-educated Muslim League leaders, the traditional *ʿulamāʾ* who supported the Pakistan movement, and the Muslim masses, in regard to their respective visions and perceptions of an Islamic state.

The Muslim masses saw Pakistan as an Islamic state that would reflect the religious and social ideals of early Islam as practiced during the era of the first four rightly guided caliphs. However, this vision of an Islamic state was constitutive more of socioeconomic ideals of justice, equality, and brotherhood than of the specifics of the *sharīʿah*. The "religious" element in this vision was primarily a cultural framework that would encompass and, in some concrete way, create conditions in their new homeland for the realization of the socioreligious ideals of Islam. Building an Islamic state for the Muslim masses was thus synonymous with building a good society. Hence we see little if any reference to the introduction of specific Islamic laws, such as *ḥudūd* (Islamic penal laws prescribed in the Qurʾān), in the prepartition popular literature on Pakistan. Similarly, the speeches and statements of the leaders of the Muslim League do not indicate that the new state would be governed by the letter of the *sharīʿah*. If this had been the case, the majority of the *ʿulamāʾ* in India would not have opposed the establishment of a separate homeland for Muslims.

Almost the entire Deoband school of *ʿulamāʾ*, led by Maulānā Ḥusain Aḥmad Madanī, opposed the creation of Pakistan and allied itself with the All-India National Congress. Their religio-political organization, Jamʿīyatul ʿUlamāʾ-i Hind, campaigned vigorously against the Muslim League and accused its leadership of being ignorant of Islam and lax in the observance of Islamic rituals and practices. A *fatwā* (religious decree) was issued by Maulānā Madanī forbidding the Muslims of India to join the Muslim League and describing the League's Quaid-i-Azam, Mohammad Ali Jinnah, as "Kāfir-i-Aʾẓam" ("the great heathen"). Maulānā Mawdūdī, who founded the Jamāʿat-i Islāmī in 1941, opposed Muslim participation in the Indian National Congress but was equally emphatic in rejecting the concept of Pakistan. He also doubted the ability of the westernized Muslim League leadership to establish an Islamic state in Pakistan.

Nonetheless, the Muslim League leadership—least of all Mohammad Ali Jinnah—were not dishonest when they proclaimed that Pakistan would be an Islamic state; however, their vision of an Islamic state was sharply different from that of the *ʿulamāʾ*. Most of the Muslim League leaders were Western-educated, liberal-minded Muslim nationalists whose commitment to Islam was primarily defined in terms of the economic, political, and cultural uplifting of the Indian Muslim community. Their notion of Pakistan as an Islamic state included the restoration of Muslim political power in the subcontinent, or at least in a part of it; the revitalization of the cultural and intellectual tradition of Islamic civilization in a modern-day context; and the establishment of a modern, sovereign state for Indian Muslims where they would be free to practice their religion and pursue their economic and political interests without fear of domination by or competition from the Hindu majority. Although it was religion which provided the basis for all these concerns, it is obvious that their vision of Pakistan as an Islamic state was influenced by their political and cultural ideals and economic interests formed and conditioned, in part, by the ideas of modern nationalism. Thus the classical idea of the Islamic religious community living in its own, autonomous political domain under divine law, and the modern idea that culturally distinctive people are entitled to political self-determination were employed with equal emphasis in the Pakistan movement.

Although there is no doubt that the Pakistan movement was essentially a nationalist movement, its nationalism was firmly anchored in the Islamic consciousness and sentiments of the Muslim masses. The Muslim League's slogan "Islam is in danger" was a powerful stimulus to move the masses to political action. The "Two Nation Theory" of Mohammad Ali Jinnah further reinforced the Islamic basis of this nationalist movement. It is important to note that Jinnah did not define "nation" in terms of shared language or common territory, history, culture, and custom; rather, he stated that Islam and Hinduism are not religions in the strict sense of the word but are in fact distinct social orders and thus cannot evolve into a single nationality.

Both Jinnah and the poet-philosopher Muhammad Iqbal perceived Islam not in terms of the details of *sharīʿah* and the hair-splitting of *fiqh*, but at three broad and interrelated levels: (1) Islam as a faith, a religio-moral system whose cardinal beliefs identify its adherents as Muslims; (2) Islam as a culture, a way of life that would integrate Muslims into a nation-state; and (3) Islam as a political ideological system whose set of values could socialize Muslims into a viable, separate political community.

Early Years as a Nation. While the Muslim League leadership which assumed political power in independent Pakistan in 1947 saw Islam as a moral force and as an ideological base on which national unity and loyalty could be built, the *ʿulamāʾ* and the Jamāʿat-i Islāmī viewed the Islam-state relationship in terms of an Islamic constitituion, the introduction of the *sharīʿah*, and the restoration of traditional socioreligious institutions sanctified by medieval Muslim jurists. These contrasting visions became the major source of conflict between the so-called modernists and liberals on the one hand and the conservatives and fundamentalists on the other.

Although Pakistan has from the beginning faced critical economic, political, and ethno-regional problems which have shaped subsequent political developments and engendered its chronic sociopolitical instability, there is one issue that has generated maximum political conflict and intellectual controversy: the role of Islam in politics and the state. The ideological and political history of Pakistan has been marked by a continuous debate on the nature of the Islamic political system and its concrete manifestation in constitutional structure and socioeconomic policies. With the exception of the Islamic-oriented martial-law regime of General Muhammad Zia ul-Haq (1977–1985), this debate always took the form of fierce confrontation—sometimes violent and leading to serious political crises—between the state and organized religious groups. The ideological orientations and power imperatives of those who controlled the state—the higher echelons of the civil service, the military, the feudal landlords, and a section of the urban-based capitalist class—did not always coincide with those of the *ʿulamāʾ* and the fundamentalists.

In analyzing Islamic constitutional developments in Pakistan in the early 1950s, Leonard Binder has identified four distinct groups that were actively involved in the controversies associated with the Islamic state and constitution. These included the traditionalists, represented by the *ʿulamāʾ* of various schools of thought; the fundamentalists, represented by the Jamāʿat-i Islāmī; the modernists, represented by politicians, westernized businessmen, and professionals; and secularists, represented by "the most highly westernized" politicians, senior civil servants, and military officers.

With the exception of a few secularists, the majority of the political leadership of the new nation agreed that Pakistan's constitution and government should reflect the teachings and traditions of Islam. The problem was how to relate Islam with the needs of a modern state. The definition of an Islamic state formulated by the *ʿulamāʾ* and the fundamentalists assumed the application of the *sharīʿah* and an overarching authority of religious scholars in evaluating the Islamicity of all legislation, which was not acceptable to the modernists. The fundamentalists saw Islam as a guiding force that regulates every aspect of human life—social, economic, political, or personal. They insisted that existing laws and practices that were in conflict with the Qur'ān and the *sunnah* should be repealed or amended to conform with Islamic law.

In marked contrast were the views held by the Western-educated, Western-oriented politicians, civil servants, judiciary, and military. Though they did not seem to have abandoned the all-embracing concept of Islam, they nevertheless subordinated it to the intellectual approach of Western secular education and training with its assumption of the separation of state and religion. While the religious leaders defined and formulated the goals of the newly born state in terms of Islamic revivalism, very few politicians and administrators saw these goals as anything other than secular economic and social development. The only thing they could promise to the religious groups was that they would try to create conditions favorable for the realization of Islamic ideals. They would not, however, commit themselves to the actual legislation of these ideals. The terrestrial heaven was to be designed and built by the modern-educated Civil Service of Pakistan (CSP) officials and not by the *madrasah*-educated *ʿulamāʾ*. To the Western-educated politicians and administrators, the foremost task was the establishment of a viable civil order and the maximization of national production. They perceived public policy issues not in terms of their conformity to the *sharīʿah* but in terms of their relevance to national development goals.

Mawlānā Shabbir Aḥmad ʿUs̱mānī, a respected Deobandī *ʿalim* whose services were extremely effective in winning over the support of the *ʿulamāʾ* in east Bengal for the Muslim League and who was appointed to the prestigious position of Shaykh al-Islām of the new state of Pakistan, was the first to raise the demand that Pakistan become an Islamic state. However, it was Mawdūdī and his Jamāʿat-i Islāmī that played the central part in the demand for an Islamic constitution. Mawdūdī asserted that the Constituent Assembly must make an unequivocal declaration affirming the "supreme sovereignty of God" and the supremacy of the *sharīʿah* as the basic law of Pakistan. He also demanded that existing laws that were in conflict with the *sharīʿah* should be gradually repealed, and that the state should have no authority to transgress the limits imposed by Islam. The Jamāʿat launched a massive public campaign to seek popular support for these demands.

The majority of the *ʿulamāʾ* also joined the movement for Islamic constitution, although they differed with the fundamentalist Jamāʿat-i Islāmī on what the government should do to establish an Islamic way of life. They were primarily concerned about the preservation of orthodoxy under the guardianship of the *ʿulamāʾ*, implementation of the *sharīʿah* under their supervision, and the infallibility of the *ijmaʿ* (consensus) of classical jurists.

The first important result of the combined efforts of the Jamāʿat-i Islāmī and the *ʿulamāʾ* was the passage of the Objectives Resolution in March 1949. In their search for a compromise, Prime Minister Liaquat Ali Khan and the religious groups had come up with a formula that, at least on the surface, was good enough to satisfy all the groups. The resolution embodied "the main principles on which the constitution of Pakistan is to be based." It declared that "sovereignty over the entire universe belongs to God Almighty alone and the authority which He has delegated to the State of Pakistan through its people for being exercised within the limits prescribed by Him is a sacred trust." Further, "the principles of democracy, freedom, equality, tolerance and social justice, as enunciated by Islam shall be fully observed," and "the Muslims shall be enabled to order their lives in the individual and collective spheres in accord with the teaching and requirements of Islam as set out in the Holy Qur'an and Sunna." The Objectives Resolution has been successively reproduced as a preamble to the constitutions of 1956, 1962, and 1973. The Eighth Amendment to the 1973 Constitution, passed in 1985, made the Objectives Resolution an operable part of the constitution.

The Objectives Resolution was a classic case of compromise made possible by vague and indeterminate formulations. For the *ʿulamāʾ*, the acknowledgment of God's sovereignty meant the acceptance of the *sharīʿah* as the law of the land and the recognition of their role as its guardians and interpreters. The Jamāʿat-i Islāmī interpreted the resolution as a document that laid the foundation for an Islamic state as a "theodemocracy" in order to transform the entire spectrum of collective life in accordance with the teachings of the Qur'ān and *sunnah*. For the Western-educated politicians, the resolution recognized that God's authority had been delegated to the people and to no one else, and that it was up to the people to decide who would exercise that authority. The resolution further precluded the establishment of a theocratic state in Pakistan by incorporating the liberal principles of "democracy, freedom, equality, tolerance and social justice," and by guaranteeing fundamental rights including "freedom of thought, expression, belief, faith, worship and association."

When the first constitution was finally approved by the Constituent Assembly in March 1956, it was mainly a collection of modern secular laws for the administration of a parliamentary democratic form of government with broad Islamic ideology as its guiding but nonbinding basis. A synthesis of Islamic principles and the needs of a modern society, the constitution became a symbol of ideological victory for all the major contending groups, except of course for the secularists.

The preamble of the constitution reproduced the Objectives Resolution with an addition that Pakistan would be a democratic state based on Islamic principles. The Directive Principles of State Policy—which were not enforceable in courts of law but were expected to serve as a guide to the state authorities in the formulation of policies—included the elimination of gambling, drinking, prostitution, and parochial, racial, tribal, sectarian, and provincial prejudices; the elimination of *ribā* (usury) and the implementation of *zākat* (obligatory alms-tax); and promotion of Islamic teachings and moral standards. Article I of the constitution designated Pakistan an Islamic Republic; the president of Pakistan was required to be a Muslim.

Two other Islamic provisions were of a more substantive nature. The more important was Article 198, which stated that no law shall be enacted which is repugnant to the injunctions of Islam as laid down in the Qur'ān and *sunnah*, and that existing laws should be brought into conformity with such injunctions. However, contrary to what the *ʿulamāʾ* and the Jamāʿat-i Islāmī had been demanding, the constitution made the National

Assembly responsible for deciding whether any law was repugnant to the Qur'ān and *sunnah*.

The other Islamic provision related to the establishment of an Islamic research and instructional organization to assist in the "reconstruction of Muslim society on a truly Islamic basis." This provision led to the establishment of the Islamic Research Institute, later renamed the Central Institute of Islamic Research, which under the leadership of late Professor Fazlur Rahman emerged as a major component of Islamic modernism and an adversary of the *ʿulamāʾ* and the Jamāʿat-i Islāmī in the 1960s.

The constitutional victory of the religious groups was, however, short lived. The 1956 Constitution was abrogated by the martial-law regime of General Muhammad Ayub Khan in 1958. President Ayub announced a new constitution in 1962 that changed the name of the nation from the Islamic Republic of Pakistan to the Republic of Pakistan. Later, however, as a result of the intense pressure from religious groups, the constitution was amended to restore the word "Islamic." The new constitution retained most of the Islamic provisions of the 1956 constitution but did not make them mandatory. It also replaced the phrase "Qur'ān and *sunnah*" with the word "Islam," a change that the *ʿulamāʾ* thought was intended to deny the authority of *ḥadīth* as a source of Islamic law and to allow a liberal and modernist interpretation of Islam. The constitution stated that "no law should be repugnant to Islam" but gave to the legislature the responsibility for deciding about the repugnancy of proposed laws. Superior courts were not allowed to review the laws for their Islamicity. The constitution, besides retaining the Islamic Research Institute, provided for the establishment of the Advisory Council of Islamic Ideology, which was to recommend means by which Muslims could live in accordance with the tenets of Islam, and to advise the legislative or executive on any questions of the Islamicity of proposed laws.

Besides these constitutional issues, the major demands of the *ʿulamāʾ* and the Jamāʿat-i Islāmī, as always, had been the introduction of Islamic penal laws, the elimination of *ribā*, and the prohibition of drinking, gambling, and the free mixing of sexes—questions of little interest to President Ayub Khan. Unlike the military regime of Zia ul-Haq, which appointed fifty-three different commissions and committees to make recommendations on various aspects of Islamic reforms from 1977 to 1985, Ayub Khan's military government set up thirty-seven reform commissions and committees from 1958 to 1966 to review virtually all aspects of Pakistani society, economy, and government—none of them directly concerned with Islamic issues. In 1958 Ayub Khan appointed the Law Reform Commission to suggest how the administration of justice might be improved and how to restructure the laws of procedures and evidence, as well as to recommend changes in the legal system. It is indicative of the Ayub Khan regime's ideological orientation that the 368 recommendations of the Commission, not a single point dealt with the islamization of laws or legal procedures.

Islamic Resurgence after 1971. The traumatic events of the 1971 civil war and Pakistan's dismemberment at the hands of India had a psychologically unsettling effect on the people. The separation of East Pakistan and the emergence of Bangladesh as an independent state raised serious doubts about the Two Nation Theory as a foundation on which to base a modern nation-state. The serious questioning of Pakistan's ideology, nationalism, and statehood was no less critical than the physical assault on its integrity in 1971. In the midst of what many Pakistani authors described as an "identity crisis," there began a period of introspection and soul-searching. A renewed quest for authenticity and national identity caused by the Bengali separatism and defeat by India tended to reaffirm Islam as both a personal succor and a national ideology the 1970s and 1980s, the two decades identified with Islamic resurgence and islamization in Pakistan.

The Islamic groups seized on the opportunity and pointed out that East Pakistan was lost because the leaders betrayed the cause of Islam; the loss was not the result of Islam's failure to keep the country together but that of the ruler's un-Islamic policies and conduct. The experience of East Pakistan thus became a rallying point for many Pakistanis, especially the religious groups, to "return" to Islam as an ideological remedy to national malaise and to cultivate religious rejuvenation.

This post-1971 rediscovery of Islamic identity in Pakistan also had great impact on the new constitution promulgated in 1973. Spearheaded by Zulfiqar ʿAli Bhutto, a secularist, the 1973 constitution (which is still in effect) has been described as the most Islamic constitution in the history of Pakistan. Islam was declared to be "the state religion" for the first time. The Objectives Resolution, the pillar of the *ʿulamāʾ*'s success in the history of constitution-making in Pakistan, was retained as a preamble and later incorporated in the operable body of the constitution during General Zia's regime. While the 1956 and 1962 constitutions had made the office of president attainable only by a Muslim, the 1973 constitution made non-Muslims ineligible for the office of the prime minister as well. The constitution also made it obligatory for the president, prime minister, and certain other officials to take an oath in which the prophet Muḥammad was explicitly declared to be the final prophet. The constitution also commits government officials to "strive to preserve the Islamic ideology which is the basis for the creation of Pakistan." It states that steps shall be taken to enable the Muslims of Pakistan, individually and collectively, to order their lives in accordance with the fundamental principles of Islam, and to provide facilities "whereby they may be enabled to understand the meaning of life according to the Holy Qur'ān and *sunnah*." The constitution mandates compulsory Islamic studies in schools, promotion of the Arabic language, and publication of an "error-free" Qur'ān. The constitution provides that the state shall endeavor to secure the proper organization of *zākat* and *awqaf* and to eliminate *ribā*, the two tasks that became hallmarks of General Zia's islamization program in subsequent years. Another clause called for the preservation and strengthening of fraternal relations with all Muslim countries on the basis of Islamic unity. It was further required that all existing laws should be brought into conformity with Islam, and that no law should be enacted which is repugnant to Islamic injunctions. The task of reviewing existing laws was entrusted to the Council of Islamic Ideology, which was to make recommendations to the national and provincial legislatures. Later, during General Zia's regime, this task was shared by the Federal Shariah Court.

Prime Minister Zulfiqar ʿAli Bhutto's islamization went far beyond introducing an Islamic constitution and employing powerful Islamic religious imagery and symbolism in his public speeches and statements. A 1973 law created institutional procedures for the printing and publishing of an error-free Qur'ān. In 1974 Bhutto changed the name of the Pakistan Red Cross to the Pakistan Red Crescent. During the same year Bhutto granted the ultimate favor to the *ʿulamāʾ* and the Jamāʿat-i Islāmī: he amended the constitution to declare the Aḥmadīs a non-Muslim minority, a concession that even the devout Khvājah Naẓīmuddīn, Pakistan's prime minister during the first anti-Aḥmadīyah agitation of 1953, had refused. [*See* Aḥmadīyah.] Bhutto also established a separate federal Ministry of Religious Affairs to develop and supervise the teaching of Islamic studies, promote Islamic research, establish contacts with Islamic institutions in other countries, organize conferences and seminars on Islam, give advice to other government departments on Islamic religious matters, seek cooperation from the *ʿulamāʾ* for national development, formulate policies for the management of *awqaf*, and make arrangements for the annual pilgrimage to Mecca. Bhutto's other islamization measures included instituting Arabic language courses in school curricula; the liberal allocation of foreign exchange for those performing the *ḥajj;* initiating Islamic missionary activities in Africa; hosting the Second Islamic Summit Conference in Lahore in February 1974 (a turning point in Pakistan's renewed efforts to form new cultural, political, and economic ties with the Muslim Middle East); and hosting an international conference on the life of the prophet Muḥammad. In 1977, in order to appease the *ʿulamāʾ* and the Jamāʿat-i Islāmī—who had launched a mass movement to overthrow his government—Bhutto issued another package of Islamic reforms that included ban on alcoholic drinks, gambling, horse-racing, and dance and nightclubs. It has been rightly observed that in the realm of ideology, Zia ul-Haq, not Benazir Bhutto, turned out to be the true heir of Zulfiqar ʿAli Bhutto.

Although the Islamic measures introduced by Bhutto were piecemeal and peripheral to the core of his socioeconomic policies, their impact on subsequent Islamic development was quite significant and far-reaching. By incorporating extensive Islamic provisions in the 1973 constitution and by declaring the Aḥmadīs non-Muslims, Bhutto helped raise the expectations of the religious parties and prepared the ground for a full-blown islamization movement during Zia's regime.

General Zia's military government defined its mission as "laying down the foundations of the Islamic system in Pakistan." An orthodox Muslim himself, Zia was convinced that the success of the 1977 anti-Bhutto agitation provided him with a sufficient mandate to introduce "concrete steps and solid measures" designed to transform the country's socioeconomic and political structures in accordance with the principles of Islam.

Coming in the wake of worldwide Islamic resurgence, President Zia's islamization measures, introduced from 1977 to 1988 through a series of laws and executive decrees, were much more substantive than those of earlier regimes. Working in close cooperation with the *ʿulamāʾ* and the Jamāʿat-i Islāmī, Zia was able to create a network of state-sponsored institutional structures to translate the norms of the *sharīʿah* into public policies. First, federal, provincial and local institutions and committees were created for compulsory collection and distribution of *zākat* and *ʿushr* (an Islamic tax on produce of the land), a long-standing demand of the religious groups. Second, a Federal Sharīʿah Court was established with power to decide whether laws were consistent with the injunctions of Islam. Third and most important was the introduction of Islamic penal law *(ḥudūd)* with specific Islamic punishments (such as caning, stoning, or cutting off limbs) for drinking, theft, adultery, and false accusation of fornication. The law of evidence was amended in conformity with the *sharīʿah* to give lesser weight to women's and non-Muslims' evidence in courts of law. Fourth, some initial measures were taken to eliminate interest *(ribā)* from the banking system and the economy. Fifth, school textbooks were revised to reflect an Islamic bias, and an International Islamic University was established in Islamabad to promote higher Islamic learning. [*See* International Islamic University at Islamabad.] In 1988 President Zia issued a comprehensive Sharīʿah Ordinance encompassing most of his earlier Islamic reform measures and incorporating further moves toward islamization of economy, society, culture, and education. This ordinance was subsequently incorporated, with some changes, in the Sharīʿah Bill introduced by Prime Minister Nawaz Sharif in April 1991, providing for a series of legislative and administrative measures to islamize education, the mass media, the economy, the bureaucracy, and the legal system.

Most of the substantive Islamic measures introduced by the Zia regime were retained by the governments that came after him, although they showed no enthusiasm in implementing them. While Islamic groups were critical of the method, scope, and effectiveness of these reforms, other sectors saw the whole process of islamization by the military regime as a cynical exploitation of the religious sentiments of the Muslim masses for political goals.

The long-term consequences of Zia's islamization policies on Pakistani society have yet to be determined. However, because of the great gap between the heightened expectations of the people and the actual outcome of the Islamic reforms, especially in the socioeconomic sector, the early enthusiasm seems to have dissipated and Islam and Islamic issues have gradually receded to the periphery of national political discourse. One important fallout of the islamization process—sectarianism—continues to haunt Pakistani politics and society. The introduction of *zākat* and *ʿushr* and the enforcement of other sharīʿah laws have brought to the surface the old doctrinal and juristic differences between Shīʿīs and Sunnīs. The question of which interpretation of Islamic law should form the basis of public policy became a major source of conflict both between Sunnī and Shīʿī *ʿulamāʾ* and also among different schools of Sunnīs. These controversies have caused frequent violent incidents, including sectarian riots and the assassination of several prominent Sunnī and Shīʿī *ʿulamāʾ*. Sectarian politics has also given rise to such militant Shīʿī organizations as the Taḥrīk-i Nifāẓ-i Fiqh-i-Jaʿfarīyah (Movement for the Enforcement of Jaʿfarīyah Fiqh) and the Imāmīyah Students' Federation (a pro-Khomeini group that has been involved in several sectarian riots), as well as the *madrasah*-based militant Sunnī organization, Anjuman Sipāh-i Ṣaḥābah (Society of the Soldiers of the Prophet's Companion), a group that regards Shīʿīs as non-Muslims and demands that Shīʿī literature be proscribed and that Pakistan be declared a Sunnī state, barring Shīʿīs from holding public office.

Islam in Pakistan Today. At the sociocultural level, Islam is central to the life of most Pakistanis; but, as in other Muslim countries, Pakistan does not present a monolithic structure of Islamic beliefs, practices, and interpretation. There is considerable variation in the ways people articulate, interpret, and practice their faith and work out its implications in their individual and collective lives. For analytical purposes, one can discuss the religio-intellectual situation of Islam in Pakistan with reference to at least four distinct categories—orthodox, Ṣūfī, reformist/liberal, and revivalist/fundamentalist Islam.

Orthodox Islam is represented by the Sunnī *ʿulamāʾ*, who are regarded as guardians of the *sunnah* of the Prophet and the socioreligious institutional structures developed under the guidance of the classical jurists. Included in this category are three important schools: the orthodox Deobandī school, the Ṣūfī-oriented Barelwī school, and the extreme right-wing Wahhābī school of Ahl-i Ḥadīth. [*See* Deobandīs; Barelwīs; Wahhābīyah.]

The *ʿulamāʾ*, as the bearers of the legal and political tradition of latter ʿAbbāsid period, have four primary concerns: the unity and integrity of the Islamic *ummah* as a universal religious community; the integrity of the orthodox beliefs and practices of Islam as represented by Ashʿarī theology and the consensus *(ijmaʿ)* of the classical jurists; the implementation of the *sharīʿah* under their supervision, especially in matters pertaining to family law and religious rituals; and the preservation and dissemination of the Islamic religious sciences under their guidance. As the interpreters of the divine law, they resolve religious disputes and issue *fatwās*, providing the faithful with religious guidance on all kinds of issues. As religious functionaries, they organize and lead congregational prayers, supervise the celebration of Islamic religious occasions and festivals, and conduct marriage ceremonies and burial rituals.

The persistence of orthodox Islam as a significant cultural alternative and as the intellectual mode of a vital religious tradition is nowhere more salient than in the two central Islamic institutions, mosques and *madrasahs*, which constitute the base of the legitimacy, power, and authority of the *ʿulamāʾ*. A recent government survey estimated that there were more than 200,000 mosques of various sizes in Pakistan, staffed by approximately 350,000 religious functionaries—*imāms* (prayer leaders), *khātibs* (preachers), and *khādims* (caretakers). Unlike most Middle Eastern Muslim countries, the network of mosques and *madrasahs* in Pakistan operate outside state control and retain considerable autonomy, despite some recent moves by the state to weaken their independence. In many small towns and cities where there are no public halls or similar civic facilities, the mosque is not only a place of worship, it is also a forum in which to discuss public issues. A typical small town in Punjab, Sind, or the North-West Frontier Province will have at least four or five major mosques (*jāmiʿahs*) and at least one small mosque for each *muḥallā* (neighborhood). These small neighborhood mosques are closely identified with their congregations.

Madrasahs have long been the centers of classical Islamic studies and the guardians of orthodoxy in South Asian Islam. The *madrasahs* in today's Pakistan—estimated at more than two thousand at the intermediate and higher levels, with about 316,000 students—are a legacy of the spectacular resurgence of Islamic religious education in India during the late nineteenth century. Since then the *madrasah* system has played an important historical role by preserving the orthodox tradition of Islam, training generations of Islamic religious scholars and functionaries, by providing vigorous political leadership, and, more importantly, reawakening the consciousness of Islamic solidarity and the Islamic way of life among the Muslims of South Asia.

The *madrasahs* in Pakistan teach a curriculum known as *Dārs-i-niẓāmi*, a standard course of study in all Sunnī *madrasahs* of India, Pakistan, and Bangladesh. It consists of about twenty subjects, broadly divided into transmitted sciences *(al-ʿulūm al-naqlīyah)* and rational sciences *(al-ʿulūm al-ʿaqlīyah)*. Most madrasahs in Pakistan are private and are supported either by religious endowments *(awqaf)* or by donations from the faithful. The financial autonomy of the mosques and *madrasahs* has been a major source of the independent political power base of the *ʿulamāʾ* in Pakistan. It has also been responsible for thwarting the efforts of state authorities to introduce reforms in the *madrasah* system and to bridge the gap between the traditional systems of Islamic education and the modern, secular system.

Although the *ʿulamāʾ* have vigorously resisted state efforts to introduce changes in traditional religious practices, Muslim family law, and *madrasah* education, they are not frozen in legal, theological, and intellectual rigidity. Contrary to the general perception, the *ʿulamāʾ* have shown a remarkable flexibility in adapting to changing socioeconomic and political conditions, as is evident in the changes in their social organization and in their political role during the past hundred years. Although their system of education remains an exclusive and isolated phenomenon, there are nevertheless powerful social and political forces and institutions that cut across socioeconomic and cultural strata and tend to bind the traditional and modern sectors. These processual and institutional changes have become more significant in the postindependence era, as the changed political context has created a series of symbolic and institutional linkages (e.g., shared religious symbols; government-sponsored Islamic educational, cultural, legal research, and advisory institutions and *awqaf* organizations; political parties and legislative assemblies; and communication media, particularly the growing vernacular press) that facilitate increasing interaction between the *ʿulamāʾ* and the modern educated elite. These interactions (especially in the context of an increasingly mature democratic political process), have tended to create a measure of shared intellectual space and a common language of religious discourse between the *ʿulamāʾ* and the modern Muslim intellectuals.

The *ʿulamāʾ* are organized in several political groupings and have emerged as important actors in Pakistan's politics. The Barelwī-oriented Jamʿīyatul ʿUlamāʾ-i Pakistān (Society of Pakistani ʿUlamāʾ) enjoys a considerable following in the Urdu-speaking areas of urban Sind and in the rural areas and small towns of Punjab, where the influence of Islamic orthodoxy has not penetrated very deeply. Its religious ideology is based on folk Islam with an emphasis on populist Sufism, the festive display of syncretic religious rituals, and veneration of saints. [*See* Jamʿīyatul ʿUlamā'-i Pakistān.]

The ultra-conservative, orthodox *ʿulamā'* of the Deoband school are represented in Jamʿīyatul ʿUlamā'-i Islām (Society of the ʿUlamā' of Islam), a party that represents the core of Islamic orthodoxy and insists on strict adherence to the *sharīʿah* as interpreted by the founders of the four schools of Islamic law. Their political program consists of the enforcement of the *sharīʿah* under the strict guidance of the "righteous *ʿulamā'*," who will have the ultimate authority to determine whether a law passed by the parliament is in conformity with the *sharīʿah*. [*See* Jamʿīyatul ʿUlamā'-i Islām.] The third group, Jamʿīyat ʿUlamā-i Ahl-i Ḥadīth (Society of the ʿUlamā' of the People of the Ḥadīth) is heir to the extreme right-wing theocratic particularism of the Wahhābī movement. The party preaches uncompromising monotheism, rejects all notions of intercession by spiritual mentors, and condemns visitation of Ṣūfī shrines as polytheism. This is the only *ʿulamā'* organization that rejects modern democracy as antithetical to Islam and advocates autocratic rule by a "pious ruler" under the guidance of the *sharīʿah*. Among the non-political Islamic groups, the best-known is the Tablīghī Jamāʿat, a grassroots movement of lay Muslims and some *ʿulamā'* that strives for the moral and spiritual renewal of individual believers.

Ṣūfī Islam in Pakistan is represented at two levels. The first is the folk, populist Sufism of the rural masses, associated with unorthodox religious rituals and practices, belief in the supernatural powers of saints, a binding spiritual relationship between the shaykh or pir (master) and *murīd* (disciple), and pilgrimage to and veneration of shrines. The majority of Muslims in rural areas of Pakistan, where orthodox Islam has yet to penetrate successfully, identify themselves with some pir, living or dead, and seek his intercession for the solution of their worldly problems and for salvation in the hereafter. There is widespread belief in the magical powers of the saints and pirs, and legends about their miracles (*karāmah*) abound. Many pirs and *sajjādah-nishīns* (hereditary custodians of shrines) are either themselves big landlords or are associated with the traditional landowning interests. The pirs and *sajjādah-nishīns* of major shrines in Punjab and Sind thus exercise enormous spiritual and political influence over their followers throughout the country. Although most of the major shrines were taken over by the government in 1959 and 1961 as a part of President Ayub Khan's modernization program, the actual management of these shrines, the organization of their religious activities, and the dispensation of spiritual grace continue under the guidance of the original *sajjādah-nishīns*. The traditional triangular relationships between pir, landlord, and peasant have not been replaced by direct relationships between government bureaucrats and peasants despite state takeover of the shrines. Many of these pir families use their spiritual influence to gain election to the national and provincial legislatures.

The other strain is the scholastic or intellectual Sufism, a recent phenomenon based in urban areas and becoming increasingly popular in educated circles. Influenced by the writings of al-Ghazālī, Shāh Walī Allāh, and Shaykh Aḥmad Sirhindī, and by the spiritual experiences of the masters of the Suhrawardīyah and Naqshbandīyah orders, these young Ṣūfīs are rearticulating Islamic metaphysics as an answer to Western materialism. For them, Sufism is the heart of Islam, and Islamic revival means nothing if it does not begin with the spiritual reawakening of individual Muslims. They believe in an integral Islamic tradition and hence are critical of both Islamic modernists and Islamic fundamentalists. In recent years this trend toward intellectual Sufism was strengthened by the writings of the Iranian scholar Seyyed Hossein Nasr, the French Muslim thinker Réne Guénon, Martin Lings, and Frithjof Schuon, with their penetrating discussions of the metaphysical questions of Islamic gnosis.

Reformist or liberal Islam in Pakistan owes its origin to the writings of Sir Sayyid Aḥmad Khān (1817–1898) and to his educational reform efforts, represented by the Aligarh movement. Sir Sayyid emphasized the role of rational thinking in understanding the purposes of *sharīʿah* and maintained that *ijtihād* (independent reasoning) was permissible not only in matters of law but also in matters of doctrine. His main contribution, however, was in his efforts to persuade Indian Muslims to learn the modern scientific method, acquire new technological skills and ideas, and embody the spirit of liberalism and progress prevalent in the West. Islamic modernism also found expression in the writings of Sayyid Ameer Ali (d. 1928), who emphasized the essential compatibility between Islam and Western liberal values, and in the works of the poet-philosopher Muhammad Iqbal (d. 1938), one of the most eminent thinkers of twentieth-century Islam. Iqbal's vigorous plea to reactivate the "principle of movement" in Islam—*ijtihād*—to reinterpret the foundational legal principles of Islam in the light of modern conditions and ideas, and to work toward the reconstruction of Islamic religious thought has been a driving force for Islamic modernism in South Asia. The most ardent champion of Iqbalian ideas and the most profound and articulate spokesman of Islamic modernism in Pakistan was the late Fazlur Rahman (d. 1988), whose bold and often provocative reformulations of Islamic doctrines and sociolegal practices engendered intense religious controversies. As director of the Central Institute of Islamic Research during Ayub Khan's decade of development and modernization, he launched a vigorous intellectual assault against the conservative *ʿulamāʾ* and the fundamentalist Jamāʿat-i Islāmī and challenged the Islamic basis of their traditionally held views on the status of women, family and inheritance law, bank interest, the uncritical acceptance of *ḥadīth* as a source of Islamic law, *taqlīd* (blind following of the classical jurists), and a host of other doctrinal and jurisprudential issues. At the end, Fazlur Rahman was forced to resign from his position by the anti–Ayub Khan mass movement and intense pressure from the *ʿulamāʾ*. In 1969, he joined the faculty of the University of Chicago and remained there until his death in 1988. In line with Iqbal's ideas, Fazlur Rahman offers a devastating critique of traditional Islamic scholasticism, its rigid system of thought, and the educational system that was built on it. He contends that traditional interpreters of the Qur'ān have failed to see the universal principles underlying particular Qur'ānic passages and thus have not seen the Qur'ān as a unity. He believes that Muslims must return to the Qur'ān and reinterpret its precepts, reformulating them as general sociomoral principles that can be adapted to ever-changing conditions. [*See the biography of Rahman.*]

After Fazlur Rahman's departure from Pakistan, Islamic modernism was eclipsed as an intellectual movement. The Council on Islamic Ideology and the Central Institute of Islamic Research (later renamed the Islamic Research Institute) were reconstituted to reflect the conservative restabilization of sociocultural life and Islamic intellectualism during the Zia period. Despite Pakistan's rich tradition of liberal-modernist Islamic thought, the resurgent forces of Islamic revivalism and fundamentalism seemed to have overwhelmed this tradition since the 1980s. Many of the well-known liberals of earlier years in the universities, research institutions, and legal profession became champions of Zia's conservatism. The entire institutional framework created during the Ayub Khan era to rethink and reinterpret traditional Islamic doctrinal formulations and sociolegal precepts and practices was appropriated by the conservative *ʿulamāʾ* and the Jamāʿat-i Islāmī during the Zia period.

Revivalist/fundamentalist Islam in today's Pakistan is represented by the Jamāʿat-i Islāmī. Regarded as one of the most important and effectively organized religio-political movements of the Islamic world today, the Jamāʿat has been active in Pakistan's politics and has played a decisive role in Islamic constitution-making and in shaping Islamic intellectual and political discourse in Pakistan. The majority of its leadership consists of modern-educated lay Muslims who came to revivalist Islam via Mawdūdī's writings. Its support base is lower-middle-class Muslims from both the traditional petit bourgeoisie and the more modern economic sectors of Pakistani society. The Jamāʿat seeks Islamic revival through the establishment of an Islamic state with the Qur'ān and *sunnah* as its constitution and the *sharīʿah* as its law. It regards Islam as a comprehensive way of life that provides guidance in all human activities. Its political struggle has focused on making Pakistan an Islamic state and on capturing political power in order to implement the socioeconomic ideals of Islam. In the course of its intense ideological and political battles against secular liberalism, Communism, and Islamic modernism, the Jamāʿat has emerged as the most articulate spokesman of Islamic conservatism in socioreligious matters in contemporary Pakistan. Although its political influence and ideological impact on Pakistan's educational and cultural institutions has been considerable, the Jamāʿat has consistently fared poorly in national elections. It has about four thousand organization units in Pakistan with more than six thousand "full members," a select core group. The Jamāʿat has been closely associated with Islamic resistance movements in Afghanistan and Kashmir as well as with other Muslim causes such as Palestine and Bosnia. These developments have engendered growing radicalization of the Jamāʿat's foreign policy and have also strengthened its fraternal links with Islamic movements in other Muslim countries.

Although the Jamā'at remains the most powerful voice of Islamic fundamentalist revivalism in Pakistan, there have also emerged in recent years some splinter religious groups with considerable affinity to its ideology. Two of these groups are headed by former Jamāʿat followers whose intellectual indebtedness and ideological loyalty to Mawdūdī is evident in their writings and programs of action. One of these groups was launched by Israr Aḥmad under the name Tanẓīm-i Islāmī during the 1970s, with a program of Islamic moral and social revival aimed at the establishment of an Islamic *khilāfah*. Another such group was organized by Jāvid Aḥmad al-Ghāmidī, who claimed that he, not the Jamāʿat was Mawdūdī's true heir.

[*See also* Jamāʿat-i Islāmī.]

BIBLIOGRAPHY

Abbott, Freeland. *Islam and Pakistan*. Ithaca, 1968. A succinct study of the role of Islam in Pakistan's politics, culture, and society.

Ahmad, Aziz. *Islamic Modernism in India and Pakistan, 1857–1964*. London, 1967. Series of penetrating studies on modern intellectual and religious thought in India and Pakistan with an emphasis on the dynamic relationships between politics, socio-cultural change, and reformulation of religious ideas.

Ahmad, Aziz, and G. E. Von Grunebaum, eds. *Muslim Self-Statement in India and Pakistan, 1857–1968*. Wiesbaden, 1970. A valuable collection of writings by Indo-Pakistani Muslim intellectuals and religious and political leaders; an indispensable guide to the intellectual history of Islam in modern South Asia.

Ahmad, Mumtaz. "Pakistan." In *The Politics of Islamic Revivalism*, edited by Shireen T. Hunter, pp. 229–246. Bloomington, 1988. Examines the political, social and economic factors of Islamic resurgence in Pakistan during the 1980s and analyzes the political and social consequences of President Muhammad Zia ul-Haq's Islamization policies.

Binder, Leonard. *Religion and Politics in Pakistan*. Berkeley, 1963. A brilliant and perceptive analysis of early controversies with regard to Pakistan as an Islamic State, the role of Islam in Pakistan's constitution making and the divergent views of secularists, modernists, conservatives, and fundamentalists.

Ewing, Katherine. "The Politics of Sufism: Redefining the Saints of Pakistan." *Journal of Asian Studies* 42.2 (February 1983): 252–268. Examines the traditional role of Sufism in Pakistani society and the legislative and administrative moves by the state to control the sufi shrines.

Hussain, Arif. *Pakistan: Its Ideology and Foreign Policy*. London, 1966. Analysis of how Islamic ideological considerations shaped Pakistan's foreign policies toward India, Afghanistan, the Middle East, and the superpowers.

Ikram, S. M., and Percival Spear, eds. *The Cultural Heritage of Pakistan*. Karachi, 1955. Excellent collection of essays dealing with the cultural heritage of Pakistan and the ways in which it is reflected in its contemporary art forms.

Naim, C. M., ed. *Iqbal, Jinnah and Pakistan: The Vision and the Reality*. Syracuse, N.Y., 1979. Offers both the conventional and a revisionist view of the role of Islam in the creation of Pakistan.

Qureshi, Ishtiaq Husain. *The Muslim Community of the Indo-Pakistan Subcontinent (610-1967)*. The Hague, 1962. A valuable introduction to the history of the Indo-Pakistan Muslim Community with emphasis on religio-intellectual and ideological currents.

Qureshi, Ishtiaq Husain. *The Struggle for Pakistan*. Karachi, 1965. Traces the development of ideological and political forces that culminated in the creation of Pakistan.

Qureshi, Ishtiaq Husain. *Ulema in Politics*. Karachi, 1972. An excellent survey of the role of the *ʿulamā'* in politics of the subcontinent from the sultanate period to the creation of Pakistan.

Rahman, Fazlur. *Islam and Modernity: Transformation of an Intellectual Tradition*. Chicago, 1982. A passionate critique of contemporary Islamic intellectual thought and education with frequent references to Pakistani situation.

Sayeed, Khalid B. *The Political System of Pakistan*. Boston, 1967. Although dated, Sayeed's study is still the best introduction to Pakistani politics during its formative period; contains an excellent chapter on Islam and political culture of Pakistan.

Smith, Donald Eugene, ed. *South Asian Politics and Religion*. Princeton, 1966. Contains five important contributions by Freeland K. Abbot, Charles J. Adams, Fazlur Rahman, Khalid B. Sayeed, and Wayne A. Wilcox on several important aspects of the role of Islam in Pakistan's politics.

Smith, Wilfred Cantwell. *Islam in Modern History*. Princeton, 1957. Includes an excellent chapter titled "Pakistan as an Islamic State."

Syed, Anwar H. *Pakistan: Islam, Politics, and National Solidarity*. New York, 1982, Examines the role of Islam in Pakistan's political and ideological controversies.

MUMTAZ AHMAD

PALESTINE. *See* West Bank and Gaza.

PALESTINE LIBERATION ORGANIZATION. The recognized representative of the Palestinian people, the Palestine Liberation Organization (PLO) was established in 1964 in Jerusalem. Its first leader, the lawyer Ahmad Shuqayrī, was a close ally of Egyptian president Gamal Abdel Nasser, and the PLO was very much under the influence of Egypt during its earliest years. The PLO was founded in response to a number of factors, including the growing salience of the Palestine question in inter-Arab politics, the increasing friction between the Arab states and Israel over water diversion projects and other issues, and the growth of underground, independent Palestinian nationalist activity, which Arab governments, notably that of Egypt, wanted to preempt.

Very soon after its foundation, the PLO became the arena for much of this nationalist activity, which was increasingly directed at achieving independence of political action from the Arab regimes, in addition to the basic aim of liberating Palestine and securing the return of the approximately 700,000 Palestinians who had been made refugees in 1948. In the wake of the June 1967 war, and the attendant shattering of the prestige of these regimes, independent Palestinian political formations with a more radical program than that of the original founders of the PLO, most notably Fatah, took over the organization, and have dominated it ever since.

This change was signaled by the choice in 1969 of Fatah's leader, Yasir Arafat, as chairman of the Executive Committee of the PLO, the organization's guiding body. He has continued to hold this position since that time. In 1968, the PLO's charter was amended to reflect the ideology of militant groups like Fatah, which advocated "armed struggle" against Israel, initiated by the Palestinians themselves, as the main vehicle for the liberation of Palestine. This was in contrast to the original approach of Shuqayrī and others of his generation, who had accepted that the leading role in dealing with Israel must be played by the Arab states.

The new leaders of the PLO were younger, more radical, and generally of more modest social backgrounds than the old-line politicians from upper-class families who had dominated the organization, and Palestinian politics, until this point. They also came from disparate political backgrounds. Arafat and his closest colleagues in Fatah, such as Ṣalāḥ Khalaf (Abū ʿIyāḍ) and Khalīl al-Wazīr (Abū Jihād), were deeply influenced by the Muslim Brotherhood during their student days in Egypt. Others, such as Fārūq al-Qaddūmī (Abū Luṭf) of Fatah, or George Habash, leader of the Popular Front for the Liberation of Palestine, were closer to Baʿthist or other Arab nationalist ideologies. They agreed, however, on the principle of Palestinian agency, that Palestinians themselves must initiate political action and other forms of struggle, and shared a profound skepticism regarding the professed commitment of Arab governments to act in support of the Palestinians.

In the wake of the 1967 war, the PLO rapidly became the central focus of Palestinian political activity, and by 1974 was recognized as the sole legitimate representative of the Palestinian people by the Palestinians themselves, by the Arab and Islamic worlds, and by much of the rest of the world. As the "armed struggle" against Israel from within the Occupied Territories and across the frontiers flagged after 1970, the PLO scored more diplomatic and media successes, all the while developing into a "para-state," particularly in Lebanon.

At the same time, beginning in 1974 with the twelfth meeting of the Palestinian National Council (PNC), the highest representative body of the PLO, the organization began to move away from its original maximalist policy calling for the liberation of Palestine in its entirety, and toward a two-state solution that called for a Palestinian state alongside Israel. This evolution was completed with the resolutions of the nineteenth PNC meeting in 1988 and the Palestinian declaration of independence by the PNC in the same year, which firmly established the idea of a Palestinian state in the West Bank, Gaza Strip, and East Jerusalem (to be achieved via negotiations with Israel in an international forum) as the PLO's political objective.

This political evolution, while representative of majority Palestinian sentiment and welcome to most Arab states and much of the international community, met with the resistance of an important minority among Palestinians. Initially, the main advocates of this resistance were the so-called rejectionist groups of the PLO, backed by Arab regimes that claimed to be opposed to a negotiated settlement of the Arab-Israeli conflict or to the recognition of Israel. As these states waned in their opposition or their importance, and as the rejectionist trend within the PLO weakened, Islamic radical groups increasingly came to lead the Palestinian opposition to the PLO's policy of a negotiated, compromise settlement that would result in a West Bank/Gaza Strip state alongside Israel.

The most important of these Islamic groups, Ḥamās, founded in 1988 in the Gaza Strip, was an outgrowth of the Egypt-based Muslim Brotherhood, which had long been a political force among Palestinians. Ḥamās soon spread to the West Bank and other areas inhabited by Palestinians. Ḥamās was established in a response to several factors, including the outbreak of the Palestinian uprising in the Occupied Territories in December 1987, the growth of militant, independent Islamic formations such as Islamic Jihād, which strongly criticized the moderate line of the Muslim Brotherhood vis-à-vis the Israeli occupation, and the PLO's political shift toward a compromise solution with Israel. The PLO in turn responded to the formidable challenge posed by Ḥamās by on occasion attempting to cooperate with it, while at the same time pushing ahead with its own program, a strategy resulting in Palestinian acceptance of the U.S.-sponsored peace negotiations with Israel, begun in 1991.

Ḥamās rapidly became the main focus of the internal opposition to the participation in these negotiations by a Palestinian delegation operating under the leadership of the PLO, and the main challenger to the PLO for leadership of the Palestinian people. Beset by financial problems, many of them rooted in a withdrawal of funds by the Arab Gulf states (who resented the PLO's failure to support them during the Gulf War of 1990–1991), in September 1993 the PLO signed a Declaration of Principles with Israel in a ceremony in Washington, D.C. This surprise development appeared to rescue the PLO from a critical situation, while at the same time opening up prospects of a change in the status quo in the Occupied Territories and sparking new Palestinian opposition.

[*See also* Arab-Israeli Conflict; Ḥamās; Israel; West Bank and Gaza.]

BIBLIOGRAPHY

Abū ʿIyād [Ṣalāḥ Khalaf], with Eric Rouleau. *My Home, My Land: A Narrative of the Palestinian Struggle*. New York, 1981. A frank, first-person account by one of the founders of Fatah.

Brand, Laurie A. *Palestinians in the Arab World: Institution Building and the Search for State*. New York, 1988. Careful examination of some of the major constitutive organizations of the PLO.

Brynen, Rex. *Sanctuary and Survival: The PLO in Lebanon*. Boulder, 1990. Study of the PLO's "Lebanese era," from 1969 to 1982.

Cobban, Helena. *The Palestinian Liberation Organization: People, Power, and Politics*. Cambridge, 1984. Standard work on the history of the PLO during its first two decades.

Gresh, Alain. *The PLO: The Struggle Within; Towards an Independent Palestinian State*. London, 1985. Detailed and knowledgeable examination of the evolution of PLO policies.

Khalidi, Rashid. *Under Siege: P.L.O. Decisionmaking during the 1982 War*. Case study of how the PLO functioned during the Israeli invasion of Lebanon, based on primary sources.

Mishal, Shaul. *The PLO under ʿArafat: Between Gun and Olive Branch*. New Haven, 1986. Critical analysis of shifts in PLO strategy through the mid-1980s.

Quandt, William B., Fuad Jabber, and Ann Mosely Lesch. *The Politics of Palestinian Nationalism*. Berkeley, 1973. Valuable study of different facets of Palestinian nationalism.

Rouleau, Eric. *Les Palestiniens: D'une guerre à l'autre*. Paris, 1984. Acute analysis of the PLO and its leadership by a journalist who has closely followed its development.

Sahliyeh, Emile F. *The PLO after the Lebanon War*. Boulder, 1986. Assessment of the impact of the 1982 Lebanese war on the PLO and its strategy.

Shemesh, Moshe. *The Palestinian Entity, 1959–1974: Arab Politics and the PLO*. London, 1988. Examines the development of the idea of a Palestinian state up to 1974.

RASHID KHALIDI

PAMPHLETS AND TRACTS. Although religious pamphlets and tracts are a worldwide phenomenon in Islam, this article concentrates on their presence in the Arab world. To walk the streets of any city in the Middle East or North Africa is to be confronted by a world of pamphlets and booklets. At the same time, the transnational nature of culture generally means that some of the same pamphlets resurface in Western cities with large Muslim and arabophone populations. In these Western cities one will also find pamphlets with Islamic content produced in French, English, and other European languages. The greatest number of pamphlets are religious in nature, for several reasons beyond the fact that the Islamist movement may be one of the most significant intellectual and cultural forces in the region. Other trends have come together with this movement, including the increased arabization of previously francophone-dominated areas like North Africa, and the economic upsurge brought about by the oil boom in the Gulf states.

Pamphlets are normally packaged and sold for mass consumption, hence their low prices. In certain heavily islamicized city neighborhoods, for example in Fez, pamphlets are produced in offset editions, bound with simple covers, and distributed free (except to the unsuspecting Westerner, who invariably pays for them). In Tunisia, however, religious pamphlets are currently unavailable, the regime having clamped down on the activities of the Islamists.

Religious pamphlets cover a varied range of topics and are addressed to both genders. Although they are more often written by men (the names of the leading shaykhs, al-Shaᶜrāwī, Kishk, and al-ᶜUthaymīn, figure prominently here), women can still have a strong presence in this textual world. Thus one of the most popular religious pamphlets to date was written by a woman, Niᶜmat Ṣidqī; entitled *Al-tabarruj* (Female Adornment), this booklet has seen several editions and is as easily purchased in Saudia Arabia as it is in Morocco. Peddlers on busy streetcorners hawk individual surahs of the Qur'ān. The more adventurous reader can delight in miniature booklets setting forth advice on proper behavior, legal injunctions (*fatāwā;* sg., *fatwā*), or even mini-manuals to help one interpret dreams. A woman is told how to win her husband in the 67-page *Kayfa taksibīna zawjak*.

The appeal of these pamphlets goes beyond their content. Many sport brightly colored covers rich in semiotic significance. Like the stained-glass windows of a Christian cathedral, the covers tell a visual story as powerful in its own way as the verbal story within. Series like *Silsilat al-mar'ah al-Muslimah* (Series on the Muslim Woman) have their visual stamp on the cover, permitting buyers to spot them readily. The more astute connoisseur of pamphlets learns in time to recognize the distinctive visual style of certain artists (e.g., al-Zuhayrī) whose names are now important in the cultural segment of the Islamist movement. Like their counterparts in the more secularized culture of the contemporary Middle East and North Africa, they are helping to shape a new popular culture, transmitted through pamphlets.

BIBLIOGRAPHY

Douglas, Allen, and Fedwa Malti-Douglas. *Arab Comic Strips: Politics of an Emerging Mass Culture*. Bloomington, 1994. Discusses the visual world of Islamist artists.

Kepel, Gilles. *Les banlieues de l'Islam: Naissance d'une religion en France*. Paris, 1987. Includes analyses of some pamphlet literature in France.

Malti-Douglas, Fedwa. "An Anti-Travel Guide: Iconography in a Muslim Revivalist Tract." *Edebiyāt* 4.2 (1993): 205–213. Study of the iconographic and textual dimensions of an Islamist pamphlet.

FEDWA MALTI-DOUGLAS

PAN-ARABISM. *See* Arab Nationalism.

PAN-ISLAM. Since about 1878, the European appellation, for the ideology calling all Muslims to unite in support of their faith has been Pan-Islam. As a religious concept, it has existed since the early days of Islam; *ʿulamāʾ* and *fuqahāʾ* employed it repeatedly to encourage believers to cooperation and solidarity. Their ideal was the universally united Muslim community, that of the early days of Islam or of the extensive Muslim empire of past times. As Islam is a highly political religion, so was its Pan-Islamic element, chiefly since the 1860s and 1870s when European colonialism reached a peak. Then it became a defensive ideology, intended simultaneously to raise the morale of the foreign-dominated Muslims and to save the few remaining independent Muslim states from a similar fate. Of these, Afghanistan and Morocco were rather peripheral geographically; Iran, overwhelmingly Shīʿī, was hardly suitable to promote Pan-Islamic policy among preponderantly Sunnī populations. The Ottoman Empire, both centrally located and territorially the largest of the four, was decidedly more appropriate.

Turkish intellectuals had been discussing Pan-Islam (*ittiḥād-i Islām*) and writing about it, since the 1860s, as a potential political weapon capable of uniting all Muslims and saving the Ottoman Empire from fragmentation. However, only during the reign of Sultan Abdülhamid II (r. 1876–1909) did Pan-Islam become a favored state policy, adopted and promoted by some members of the ruling bureaucratic and intellectual elites of the empire. In reaction to the loss of Cyprus (1878), Tunisia (1881), and Egypt (1882), both orthodox and secular intellectuals in the Ottoman Empire energetically strove to formulate political ideologies aiming at a Pan-Islam directed against European political, military, economic, and missionary penetration. The best known was Jamāl al-Dīn al-Afghānī (d. 1897). Others were subsidized by Abdülhamid, whose agents spread Pan-Islamic propaganda, openly and covertly, within and without the Ottoman Empire. This sultan posed as the caliph, a would-be spiritual and temporal leader to whom all Muslims everywhere owed allegiance and obedience. The propaganda he fostered, intended to offset as far as possible the empire's military and economic weakness, had several policy objectives: to favor the central government over the periphery, and the empire's Muslims over its non-Muslims in education, office, and economic opportunities (particular attention being paid to Turks and Arabs, somewhat less to Albanians and Bosnians); to recruit the empire's Muslims and many outside it in response to the activities of some of the Great Powers, which were encouraging nationalist secessionist trends among sections of the empire's Muslims; to enable the sultan-caliph to threaten these powers with instigating Pan-Islamic activities among Muslims living under the rule of those Powers.

Actions based on Abdülhamid's Pan-Islamic policies were modest, confined to expressions of support and fund-raising, especially during wars, such as the conflict with Greece over Crete in 1897. His efforts, however, were taken seriously enough by several European powers, which refrained from attacking the Ottoman Empire while he reigned. It is no coincidence that only after his deposition (1909) and the general expectation that Pan-Islamic activities had come to an end, did Italy invade Tripolitania and the Balkan peoples annex Ottoman territories to bolster their own independence. The ruling Committee of Union and Progress (popularly called the Young Turks), less dedicated to Pan-Islam, did not hesitate to exploit it then and in World War I. The Ottoman declaration of war (11 November 1914) was accompanied by a proclamation of *jihād* and the pronouncement of five *fatwā*s enjoining all Muslims everywhere to unite and join, with life and property, the Ottoman Empire in the *jihād* against Russia, Great Britain, and France (which, along with the Netherlands, were then ruling most of the nonindependent Muslim populations).

But the intensive Ottoman Pan-Islamic propaganda, carried out with full German cooperation, failed to induce Muslims in the Allied forces to revolt, for several reasons: the limitations of Pan-Islamic organization; countermeasures by the Allied Powers; the reservations of Muslims, shocked by reports of the Young Turks' irreligiosity; the acquiescence of some Muslims (e.g., in India) in their foreign-dominated status; alternative priorities among some Muslims, such as Arab nationalist aspirations; and the alliance of the Ottomans with Christian powers such as Germany and Austria-Hungary.

The failure of Pan-Islam in World War I and the defeat and dismemberment of the Ottoman Empire brought Pan-Islam to an almost total standstill in the following generation. The abolition of the caliphate (1924) deprived it of its top leadership. Attempts at uprisings by Russia's Muslims (which had exhibited Pan-Islamic leanings since the late nineteenth century) were soon crushed by the Soviet armed forces. A Pan-Muslim mass movement in India, in the 1920s, the Khilāfat, petered out with hardly a trace. Five Pan-Islamic conventions (Mecca, 1924; Cairo, 1926; Mecca, 1926; Jerusalem, 1931; Geneva, 1935) had no follow-ups, highlighting organizational weakness. Further, Pan-Islam had to grapple with competing ideologies, universalist ones, like atheist communism in the Soviet Union and Pan-Arabism, and particularist ones, such as nationalism in Turkey and several Arab states, chiefly those that had adopted modernity and secularism as their creed and way of life.

Since the end of World War II, changing circumstances have again favored Pan-Islam. Rising Islamic fundamentalism comprised an element of Pan-Islam. The preaching of Muslim solidarity, as a step toward union, found ready ears. Newly independent Muslim states had the political means to promote the fulfillment of Pan-Islam, and several also had the economic capacity to do so. The latter, chiefly Saudi Arabia, set up Pan-Islamic international organizations for this purpose. The Muslim World League (founded 1962) serves as an umbrella organization for many nongovernmental Islamic associations and groups. The Organization of the Islamic Conference (established 1969) is an association of Muslim governments; it seeks to coordinate Islamic solidarity and promote Pan-Islamic political and economic cooperation internationally. The breakdown of the Soviet Union has afforded it new opportunities for co-opting the newly independent former Soviet republics.

The attempts of Saddam Hussein of Iraq in 1990–1991 and Muʿammar Qadhdhāfī of Libya in 1992 to recruit all-Muslim support against "foreign aggression" indicate that Pan-Islam is still considered an important political tool.

[*See also* Abdülhamid II; Congresses; Khilāfat Movement; Muslim World League; Organization of the Islamic Conference; Ottoman Empire.]

BIBLIOGRAPHY

Aziz, K. K., comp. *The Indian Khilafat Movement, 1915–1933*. Karachi, 1972. Documentary record.

Charmes, Gabriel. *L'avenir de la Turquie: Le panislamisme*. Paris, 1883. The first book informing Europe of Pan-Islam.

Chejne, Anwar G. "Pan-Islamism and the Caliphal Controversy." *Islamic Literature* 7.12 (December 1955): 5–23.

Gibb, H. A. R. "The Islamic Congress at Jerusalem in December 1931." In *Survey of International Affairs, 1934*, edited by A. J. Toynbee, pp. 99–109. London, 1935.

Keddie, Nikki R. "Pan-Islam as Proto-Nationalism." *Journal of Modern History* 41.1 (March 1969): 17–28. Important historical analysis.

Kidwai, Mushir Hosain. *Pan-Islamism*. London, 1908.

Kramer, Martin. *Islam Assembled*. New York, 1986. Pan-Islamic congresses.

Landau, Jacob M. "Al-Afghānī's Panislamic Project." *Islamic Culture* 26.3 (July 1952): 50–54.

Landau, Jacob M. *The Politics of Pan-Islam: Ideology and Organization*. Oxford, 1990. Contains a detailed bibliography (pp. 382–425).

Lee, D. A. "The Origins of Pan-Islamism." *American Historical Review* 47.2 (January 1942): 278–287. Brief, classic study of the subject.

Levtzion, Nehemia. *International Islamic Solidarity and Its Limitations*. Jerusalem, 1979. Useful survey of currently active Pan-Islamic organizations.

Mawdūdī, Sayyid Abū al-Aʿlā. *Unity of the Muslim World*. Lahore, 1967. Distinguished Pakistani's thoughts on Pan-Islam.

Qureshi, M. Naeem. "Bibliographic Soundings in Nineteenth-Century Pan-Islam in South Asia." *Islamic Quarterly* 24.1–2 (1980): 22–34. Systematic bibliographic survey.

JACOB M. LANDAU

PAN-TURANISM. The nationalist ideology known as Turkism or Pan-Turkism, and also called Pan-Turanism or Turanianism, began to emerge in Turkey during the Young Turk era (1908–1918) as a response to the failure of Ottomanism in the face of other nationalisms (Greek, Armenian, Arab) in the Ottoman Empire. Jacob Landau explains, "The guiding objective of this movement is to strive for some sort of union—cultural or physical, or both—amongst all peoples . . . of Turkic origins. . . . Turanism is a far broader concept than Pan-Turkism, embracing such peoples as the Hungarians, Finns, and Estonians . . ." (1981, p. 1).

The roots of this nationalism may be traced to the second half of the nineteenth century, when Turkish intellectuals came into contact with Pan-Slavism in tsarist Russia, as well as with national movements in western and central Europe. The works of European scholarship on the new discipline of Turcology increased Turkish consciousness by emphasizing the Turkish link with Central Asia and the role Turks had played in civilization. By the 1890s, especially following the victory in the Greco-Turkish war of 1897, the poet Mehmed Emin Yurdakul (1869–1944) could write with pride, "I am a Turk. My faith and my race are mighty," and "We are Turks, with this blood and with this name we live." This new sense of Turkishness was still linked closely with Islam and the Ottoman dynasty.

After the Young Turk revolution of 1908, Turkism came out into the open largely through associations like Türk Derneği (the Turkish Association) and Türk Ocakları (Turkish Hearths) and their publications. The date from which the Turkists became influential was August 1911, when the Türk Yurdu Cemiyeti (Turkish Homeland Society) was founded in Istanbul with *Türk yurdu* as its voice. Their stated purpose was "to raise the level of Turkish intellectual and cultural life and to serve those with wealth and initiative." In 1912 Ziya Gökalp's membership in Türk Yurdu and the serialization in 1913 of his seminal essay *"Türkleşmek, islamlaşmak, muasırlaşmak"* ("To be Turkish, to be Muslim, to be contemporary") signaled the Committee of Union and Progress's (CUP) active interest in Turkism. However, Gökalp had already acquired a reputation in nationalist circles for poems that glorified the Turks. In a poem published in 1911 he defined Turan:

> The country of the Turks is not Turkey, nor yet Turkistan,
> Their country is a vast and eternal land: Turan.

Up to this point the Turkist movement was essentially cultural, seeking to emphasize historical and linguistic elements common to all Turkic peoples. Even in the Ottoman Turkist movement the principal concern was how to lead the multiethnic, multireligious empire, even though the Turks were a minority in it. Following the territorial losses in the Balkan War (1912–1913), some intellectuals proposed the dual monarchy model of Austria-Hungary for the Ottoman Empire: just as the Hapsburg empire rested on the shoulders of Germans and Hungarians, the Ottoman Empire would rest on the shoulders of Turks and Arabs, with Islam as the uniting factor. Although this formula was never formally adopted, the government began to emphasize the importance of both Arabic and Islam in its ideology.

The impact of the Turkist movement was felt more directly in the area of economic reform. The Turkists spoke of the necessity of creating a national economy and a Turkish bourgeoisie in order to maintain their hegemony. Here the influence of Turks who had migrated from Russia was overwhelming. Men like Yusuf Akçura had been educated in St. Petersburg and Paris and had witnessed the role of European bourgeoisies in the modernization of their economies and societies. He issued the warning that "if the Turks fail to produce from among themselves a bourgeois class . . . the chances of survival of a Turkish society composed only of peasants and officials will be very slim." Therefore, capitalist economic development under state supervision and the creation of a capitalist class became the principal concern of the Turkists, and great progress was made during World War I.

Politically Turkism was overshadowed by Islam until 1917. Two grand viziers with Arab connections, Mahmud Şevket Pasha and Said Halim Pasha, governed from 1913 to 1917. They were appointed in large measure to mollify Arab/Islamic sentiment. When Turkey entered the war in November 1914, the proclamation of *jihād* gave primacy to Islam, but in the war against Russia, Turkism was also brought into play. For example, the Committee for the Defence of the Rights of Muslim, Turkish, and Tatar Peoples in Russia, headed by Yusuf Akçura and Hüseyinzâde Ali, issued a manifesto in January 1916. It demanded independence for the Khanates of Bukhara and Khiva, the union of Russian Turkistan and the Turcomans with these two khanates, political and administrative independence for the Kirghiz people, and the creation of a Crimean Khanate under the protection of the sultan of Turkey. During the war, however, the isolation of Anatolia increased awareness of local patriotism identified as Turkish Anatolian nationalism *(Türk Anadolu milliyetçiliği)*, and this became the ideology of the republic. [*See* Bukhara Khanate; Khiva Khanate; Crimea Khanate.]

Turkism peaked during the revolution in Russia in 1917–1918. There was hope that the Ottoman Empire would acquire a new basis by integrating the Turkic lands of a disintegrating Russia. The Congress of Russian Muslims held in Kazan in August 1918 demanded self-determination while Istanbul encouraged the delegates to seek the sultan's protection. The capture of Baku on 15 September was the high point of Pan-Turkist aspirations; as his forces advanced, Halil Pasha was welcomed with a ballad that began, "May God open your way to Turan." An editorial in *Tanin* (16 April 1918) predicted that Turkey would become a great power once again "if the strong moral force of Turkish culture was added to the spiritual force of Islam and the Caliphate." Here was the formula of what came to be described in the 1970s as the Turkish-Islamic synthesis. Enver Pasha's adventures notwithstanding, Pan-Turkist aspirations were dashed following the Ottoman collapse in 1918. [*See the biography of Enver Pasha.*]

The Kemalists abandoned all forms of irredentism as a chimera and focused their attention on creating a new Turkey within the boundaries of the National Pact of July 1919. Given the republic's good relations with the Soviet Union, all manifestations of Pan-Turkist irredentism were discouraged, even though cultural aspects like revisionist historiography and language reform were adopted into the nationalist ideology. Moreover, the Soviet Union made the task of the Turkists more difficult by fragmenting the Turkic peoples into separate republics, each with its own language. At the same time, Kemal Atatürk did not want another ideological focus competing with his own nationalism based on Anatolia. Therefore, the Turkish Hearths were dissolved in 1931 and replaced by the governing party's People's Houses (Halk Evleri). Thereafter political Pan-Turkism became dormant, to be awakened later during the cold war.

Turkism in the 1930s, influenced by Nazi ideology, tended to be secular and racialist and emphasized blood as the element of unity. When World War II broke out in 1939, there was a Pan-Turkist reassertion, especially after the Nazi invasion of Russia in 1941. Berlin financed and exploited Pan-Turkism and found many willing collaborators, though the Turkish government remained neutral. But once the tide turned against Germany and Soviet troops entered Ukraine in January 1944, the government arrested Turkist leaders. There were trials in September, and their organizations were dissolved. At the start of the cold war, however, charges against the Turkists were dismissed in higher courts and the movement was vindicated.

In the multiparty period after 1945, Turkism was again dormant, though it became an instrument of cold war propaganda. In the early 1960s it was revived to counter the challenge from the left, especially the Workers Party of Turkey, permitted under the constitution of 1961. The Turkists established a political platform in August 1965, when Alpaslan Türkeş (b. 1917), a member of the 1960 junta who had been tried for Pan-Turkist activities in 1944, took over the Republican Peasants Nation Party, renamed the Nationalist Action Party (Milliyetçi Hareket Partisi, MHP) in 1969.

Initially the party was secular and racialist, looking upon Islam as an Arab import alien to the Turkic genius. This alienated most of the party's supporters, and in 1969 Türkeş attempted to reconcile Islam and nationalism with the words, "We are as Turkish as Mount Tanri and as Muslim as Mount Hira; both philosophies are inherent in our character." But the party's ambiguous attitude toward Islam did not disappear totally, and Muslim voters preferred to support the National Salvation Party (Millî Selamet Partisi, MSP, later reformed as the Refâh Partisi or Welfare Party). After a weak showing in the 1973 elections, Türkeş turned more openly to Islam. He went on the pilgrimage to Mecca and acquired the honorific *Haci*. Meanwhile, a group of nationalist intellectuals and politicians had formed a group known as the Intellectuals' Hearth (Aydınlar Ocağı) whose aim, they claimed, was to create a synthesis between Turkic and Islamic values and culture. They also mediated between the political parties and played a role in the creation of the coalition governments of the seventies. Before the 1977 elections Türkeş won the support of some religious orders as well as the defection of Necip Fazıl Kısakürek, an important nationalist-Islamist publicist, from the MSP. He also appealed openly to the Sunnī, Turkish majority against minorities like the Kurds and Alevis, whom he described as the greatest threat to the Turks after communism. His party performed better in 1977, though it remained politically marginal. Its improved electoral performance resulted from the patronage it exercised as a coaliton partner after 1975 rather than from its Turkist platform.

The MHP was dissolved by the military junta that seized power in September 1980 and reappeared as the Nationalist Labor Party (Milliyetçi Çalışma Partisi). The Turkist movement declined in the 1980s while its top leaders were on trial for conspiracy to overthrow the state, but it received a boost when the Soviet Union collapsed in 1989. As in the period after 1918, the dream of a union of Turkic states was revived; it remains to be seen whether the dream will be fulfilled this time.

[*See also* Refâh Partisi; Young Turks; *and the biographies of Gökalp, Atatürk, and Kısakürek.*]

BIBLIOGRAPHY

Arai, Masami. *Turkish Nationalism in the Young Turk Era*. Leiden, 1992. Essential for an analysis of Turkist journals.

Berkes, Niyazi. *The Development of Secularism in Turkey*. Montreal, 1964. Probing analysis of Turkish nationalism, especially the socio-economic aspects.

Georgeon, François. *Aux origines du nationalisme turc: Yusuf Akçura, 1876–1935*. Paris, 1980. Fine monograph on Akçura and his ideas.

Gökalp, Mehmet Ziya. *Turkish Nationalism and Western Civilization: Selected Essays of Ziya Gökalp*. Translated and edited by Niyazi Berkes. New York, 1959. Essential for Gökalp's ideas, with an excellent introductory essay by Berkes.

Heyd, Uriel. *The Foundations of Turkish Nationalism: The Life and Teachings of Ziya Gökalp*. London, 1950. Remains an essential source on the subject.

Kushner, David. *The Rise of Turkish Nationalism, 1876–1908*. London and New York, 1977. Competent work on the origins of the movement.

Landau, Jacob. *Pan-Turkism in Turkey: A Study in Irredentism*. London, 1981. Most informative for the entire period; excellent bibliography.

Lewis, Bernard. *The Emergence of Modern Turkey*. 2d ed. London and New York, 1968. Authoritative account of intellectual trends, including Pan-Turkism.

Zenkowsky, Serge A. *Pan-Turkism and Islam in Russia*. Cambridge, Mass., 1967. A most readable, informative book, full of provocative ideas.

FEROZ AHMAD

PARADISE. *See* Afterlife.

PARTAI ISLAM SE-MALAYSIA. The antecedents of Partai Islam Se-Malaysia, better known by its Malay-Arabic acronym PAS, come from three distinct Malay groups, linked to a certain degree by Islamic concerns and Malay nationalism. In 1950 the leading Malay nationalist party in the country, the United Malays National Organization (UMNO), created a religious wing to satisfy the demands of its more religious Malay followers. Many of these were traditional Sunnī Muslims whose Islamic observances and way of life included a number of pre-Islamic practices, some of Hindu origin, derived from Malay *adat* (Ar., *ʿādāt;* custom).

When UMNO split in 1951, the religious wing decided to establish an independent Islamic political party. The meeting in November 1951 leading to the formation of PAS was heavily attended and influenced by former members of the Hizbul Muslimin, a reformist Islamic organization that had dissolved itself in 1948 to avoid being proscribed. It was decided at the meeting that PAS would be an Islamic welfare organization. It did not register as a political party, and its political goals were vague.

For the first few years, the party languished. However, it was gradually rejuvenated as alarm spread among Malays over UMNO's concessions to non-Malays during independence negotiations. A third group joined forces when a prominent Malay nationalist, Dr. Burhannuddin Al-Helmy, who was elected president in 1956, brought into PAS numerous old supporters of the disbanded radical Malay Nationalist Party (MNP), despite the fact that the MNP had been a secular party committed to socialism.

Ideologically, the three strands comprising PAS—the MNP, Hizbul Muslimin, and UMNO defectors together with anti-UMNO forces—represented both radical socialist and conservative feudal Malay nationalism, and both reformist and traditional Islam. During the decade after 1956 the party gave priority to radical Malay nationalism and Pan-Indonesianism. In the 1970s, the party symbolized conservative Malay nationalism coupled with support for the goals of traditional Islam. Since 1982, PAS has given priority to reformist Islamic goals and has downplayed Malay nationalism.

In 1955 PAS registered as a political party and won the only opposition seat in the election that year. In the first post-independence elections in 1959, PAS won the states of Kelantan and Trengganu in the heavily Malay-populated northeast. The party's slogan, "Bangsa, Ugama, Tanah Ayer" ("Race, Religion, Native Land"), had a powerful emotional attraction. Its nationalist appeal that "Malaya belongs to the Malays" was clear and unambiguous, and Islam was subordinated to it. The party advocated the formation of an Islamic state, but without defining the relationship between Islam and the structure of the state. Specifics were limited to areas where the reformists and traditionalists could agree, such as advocating the prohibition of alcohol and gambling.

Kelantan-born Datuk Asri bin Haji Muda became president of PAS in 1971. Under Datuk Asri, the party's main efforts shifted to the east coast and were devoted to governing in Kelantan. Despite advocating an Islamic state federally, the PAS Kelantan government made no effort to institute such a model there. Although Islam was often the idiom invoked, PAS's appeal still contained strong ethnic overtones.

In 1973, for a variety of reasons centering on retaining

control of the Kelantan state government, PAS joined the ruling Barisan Nasional coalition under UMNO's domination. PAS was then increasingly plagued by internal dissension. In December 1977, PAS quit the coalition, and in a state election the following year PAS was crushed, ending nineteen years of rule in Kelantan.

Datuk Asri's position in PAS was weakened considerably by the events of 1977–1978; this led to increasing influence by the reformist Islamists. The party shifted perceptibly to a greater priority on Islamic matters. PAS now called not just for a vague Islamic State, but for alterations in the federal constitution to bring it more in line with Islamic law and administration, and it criticized the government's policies as being devoid of spiritual values.

By 1982 an Islamic fundamentalist revival was sweeping Malaysia. Following a general election in which PAS failed to recapture Kelantan, at the PAS general assembly in October, under large posters of the Ayatollah Khomeini, Datuk Asri and a majority of the "old guard" were purged. The party came under the control of a group of young, largely Arabic-educated, Islamic reformists led by Haji Fadzil Noor of Kedah (who in 1989 became the president) and Haji Hadi Awang of Trengganu (who in 1989 became the deputy president), and a more powerful Council of Ulamak (Ar., *ʿulamāʾ;* religiously learned) to guide the party.

Despite energetic new leadership, PAS performed badly in the 1986 elections, partly because it aligned itself with "infidels" in an opposition front. Further, many Malays were alienated by the party's efforts to invoke pure Islamic values by calling for an end to ethnic preferences such as Malay Special Rights and the New Economic Policy.

For the 1990 elections PAS found itself in a promising opposition coalition made possible by a major UMNO split. The party's election manifesto advocated government based on the teachings of Islam and the promotion of *syariat* (Ar., *sharīʿah;* Islamic law) as the highest source of law in the country, but it made no specific mention of seeking an Islamic state. The manifesto also promised to protect the interests of non-Muslims.

The opposition coalition was decisively defeated, but PAS managed to recapture the state of Kelantan. The PAS Mentri Besar (chief minister) of Kelantan, a religious teacher, has gradually, but not without controversy, started to islamize the structures and laws of the state government.

Although PAS today is led by Islamic fundamentalists, its strength has always been based on rural Malay peasants and traditional village religious leaders who are not always receptive to fundamentalism. The party's old nationalist theme that UMNO had sold out the birthrights of the Malays is no longer very credible, and on moderate Islamic issues UMNO has in many ways "out-Islamed" PAS. While PAS has retained its traditional support, in the midst of a decade of prosperity for the Malays the PAS Islamic reformers have not been able to promote the hereafter sufficiently to win new support away from UMNO.

[*See also* Malaysia; United Malays National Organization.]

BIBLIOGRAPHY

Alias Mohamed. *Malaysia's Islamic Opposition.* Kuala Lumpur, 1991. This short, lightly footnoted book discusses the history and politics of PAS from the perspective of a Kelantanese critic.

Funston, N. J. *Malay Politics in Malaysia.* Kuala Lumpur, 1980. Good comparison of the origins and development of the two major Malay political parties.

Kessler, Clive. *Islam and Politics in a Malay State: Kelantan, 1839–1969.* Ithaca, N.Y., 1978. Interesting defense of PAS politics in Kelantan.

Marican, Y. Mansoor. "Malay Nationalism and the Islamic Party of Malaysia." *Islamic Studies* 16.1 (Spring 1976): 291–301. Explores the link between Malay nationalism, ethnicity, and Islam inside PAS.

Mauzy, Diane K. *Barisan Nasional.* Kuala Lumpur, 1983. Account of Tun Razak's coalition-building strategy that brought PAS and several other parties into the ruling Barisan Nasional coalition.

Means, Gordon P. *Malaysian Politics: The Second Generation.* Singapore, 1991. Comprehensive modern political history; very useful successor to his original *Malaysian Politics.*

Milne, R. S., and Diane K. Mauzy. *Politics and Government in Malaysia.* 2d ed., rev. Singapore and Vancouver, B.C., 1980. Includes detailed discussion of postindependence party politics and the political process.

Muzaffar, Chandra. "Introduction" to *The Universalism of Islam,* pp. 6–9. Penang, 1979. Points out the ethnic dimension in agitation by Malays for the establishment of an Islamic state.

Muzaffar, Chandra. *Islamic Resurgence in Malaysia.* Petaling Jaya, 1987. Discussion of the nature of the resurgence and its political ramifications.

Nagata, Judith. *Malaysian Mosaic.* Vancouver, B.C., 1979. Solid study of ethnicity in Malaysia; especially strong on the role of Islam.

Nagata, Judith. *The Reflowering of Malaysian Islam: Modern Religious Radicals and Their Roots.* Vancouver, B.C., 1984. Detailed investigation into and analysis of the Islamic resurgence and the groups leading it.

DIANE K. MAUZY

PARTAI PERSATUAN PEMBANGUNAN. The only Islamic political party in Indonesia today is the Partai Persatuan Pembangunan (Development Unity Party, abbreviated as Partai Persatuan, PPP, or P3), formed in 1973 through the fusion of the four preexisting Islamic parties: the traditionalist Partai NU (Nahdatul Ulama Party), the modernist Parmusi (Indonesian Muslim Party), and two other minor parties, the PSII and Perti. The fusion was imposed by the New Order government under General Suharto, who placed utmost priority on economic development, political stability, and national integration. The PPP was prohibited from pursuing an Islamic state as its goal and from using "Islam" or "Muslim" in its name. The government, to secure loyalty, also intervened in the formation of the PPP leadership.

In spite of these constraints the PPP became increasingly militant and confrontational vis-à-vis the government during the 1970s. The government had to withdraw its secular version of the Marriage Law bill in the face of Muslim criticism in 1973. Strong Islamic sentiments were mobilized in the 1977 general elections campaign for the PPP, who used the Kaʿbah as their party symbol. A number of charismatic *ʿulamāʾ* openly criticized the secularization, corruption, and inequality that the New Order had brought and urged Muslim voting for the PPP as religious obligation. The PPP received 29 percent of the national vote, obtaining the leading position in the capital city of Jakarta. The PPP staged a walkout from the parliament in 1978 in protest of the government promotion of Javanese mysticism over Islam. They maintained almost the same level of popular support (28 percent) in the 1982 general elections.

Alarmed by rising Islamic radicalism, the government instituted a law requiring all social and political organizations to stipulate the state philosophy of Pancasila (Five Pillars) as the sole foundation of their constitutions. The NU complied with this in 1983, followed by the PPP and others. The NU was, however, dissatisfied with the PPP leadership over the allocation of parliamentary seats and decided to withdraw its support from the PPP. In the 1987 general elections, the NU actively engaged in a "deflation campaign" against the PPP; the results showed a drastic reduction in votes for the PPP, which received only 16 percent of the total. The replacement of the Kaʿbah with a star as the party symbol also contributed to this demise, symbolizing the fact that its constitution and statutes had become less explicitly Islamic. It received 17 percent of the total votes in the 1992 general elections.

The decline of the PPP's strength has not, however, meant the departure of Islam from public life. Since the late 1980s, islamization of the bureaucracy has been visible. Now that all Muslim organizations have accepted the Pancasila as their sole foundation, the intensification of religious activities in government offices is no longer under scrutiny. Suharto himself has contributed to this trend by promoting the establishment of mosques all over the country and performing the *ḥajj* in 1991. The government party Golkar has also become manifestly Islamic in its orientation. A mainstreaming of Islam is under way. A number of goals previously pursued by the Islamic parties have been achieved without arousing political controversies. This new situation is blurring the distinctiveness of the PPP as an Islamic party, and its raison d'être is in question.

[*See also* Indonesia; Nahdatul Ulama.]

BIBLIOGRAPHY

English literature specifically on the PPP is scarce, but the following items provide basic information:

Haris, Syamsuddin. "PPP and Politics under the New Order." *Prisma* (English edition) 49 (June 1990): 31–51. Report by a close observer of the PPP through the 1980s.

Samson, Allan A. "Indonesian Islam since the New Order." In *Political Power and Communications in Indonesia*, edited by Karl D. Jackson and Lucian W. Pye, pp. 196–226. Berkeley, 1978. Detailed description of the early phase of the relationship between the New Order government and Islamic parties leading to the formation of the PPP in 1973 and its immediate aftermath.

NAKAMURA MITSUO

PATANI UNITED LIBERATION ORGANIZATION. A Muslim separatist organization in Thailand, the Patani United Liberation Organization (PULO) was established in 1968 by Tenku Bira Kotanila, who claimed to speak on behalf of Malay Muslims living in the four southern Thai provinces of Pattani (spelled Patani in Malay), Narathiwat, Yala, and Satun. Its goal is to detach these provinces from Thailand and combine them into an independent state based on Islamic principles. The creation of such a state is considered essential in order to preserve the "Malayness" and Islamic way of life of the local Malay Muslims, which are perceived to be threatened by the assimilationist policies of successive Thai governments. PULO also considers Thailand to be an occupying power from whom independence can be wrested only through the use of armed force.

PULO's emphasis on protecting the Malay and Islamic character of these Malay Muslims through achieving independence for the area serves as the basis for its political mobilization efforts, since the wide appeal of the agenda cuts across social classes and secular and religious boundaries; it has proved particularly attractive to younger, more militant Malay Muslims. It has also attracted moral, financial, and other support from Malaysian individuals and organizations associated either directly or indirectly with the Islamic Party of Malaysia (PAS), which draws most of its political support from Muslims in Malaysian states bordering Thailand. Another source of external support is the Middle East, where financial contributions are made to PULO, usually in the name of charity, by some governments, by organizations such as the Islamic Call Society in Libya, and by a few wealthy individuals. Furthermore, one faction of the Palestine Liberation Organization has provided training in Syria for small groups of PULO guerrillas.

PULO has a fairly sophisticated organizational structure with a central committee, headed by a chairman, at the top. Under the central committee is a secretariat with political, economic, military, and foreign sections. Policy-making headquarters are in Mecca, and operational headquarters are in Kelantan, Malaysia. Within Thailand, PULO guerrillas conduct both military and political activities.

In 1981 PULO claimed twenty thousand members, a figure that probably was exaggerated. Independent estimates of PULO guerrillas operating in three of the provinces (no separatist guerrilla activity has been noted in Satun) have previously ranged from around two hundred to six hundred. In the early 1990s, however, PULO's membership was smaller than before, and the number of guerrillas was thought to be fewer than a hundred. This is largely owing to the fact that in the mid-1980s Saudi authorities became disturbed by PULO activities such as openly issuing citizen identification cards, in the name of the Patani Republic, to Malay Muslim workers from Thailand in Saudi Arabia. PULO headquarters in Mecca were raided, some of the staff were arrested, about seven hundred PULO members were deported, and Tenku Bira Kotanila was replaced as chairman by Dr. Ar-rong Moorang. These developments left the organization in disarray, and it is still trying to regroup.

[*See also* Thailand.]

BIBLIOGRAPHY

Che Man, W. K. *Muslim Separatism: The Moros of Southern Philippines and the Malays of Southern Thailand.* Singapore and New York, 1990. Includes the most detailed information available to the public as regards the organization and activities of the Patani United Liberation Organization and other Muslim separatist groups in South Thailand.

Dulyakasem, Uthai. "The Emergence and Escalation of Ethnic Nationalism: The Case of the Muslim Malays in Southern Siam." In *Islam and Society in Southeast Asia*, edited by Taufik Abdullah and Sharon Siddique, pp. 208–249. Singapore, 1986. Perceptive examination of the factors explaining the emergence and development of ethnic nationalism and separatist organizations among the Malay Muslims of South Thailand.

Satha-Anand, Chaiwat. *Islam and Violence: A Case Study of Violent Events in the Four Southern Provinces, Thailand, 1976–1981.* Tampa, 1986. Discusses in some depth acts of violence in South Thailand involving Malay Muslim separatist organizations, including the Patani United Liberation Organization, and shows how Islam is used to rationalize political violence.

M. LADD THOMAS

PENAL LAW. *See* Criminal Law.

PEOPLE OF THE BOOK. Qur'ānic in origin, the term *ahl al-kitāb* refers mainly to Jews, Christians, and (less frequently) the Sabaeans as possessors of previous revealed books. It was sometimes applied also to other communities. Zoroastrians were most prominent here, although even polytheists were sometimes thus categorized.

In the case of the Jews and Christians, there were known books associated with them: *al-Tawrāh* (the Torah), *al-Zabūr* (the Psalms), and *al-Injīl* (the Gospel). Though considered by the Qur'ān to have been abrogated and in parts superseded by Muḥammad's book, as well as being corrupted, these books retained for Islam an aura of sanctity. Islam's attitude toward them was inherently ambivalent, therefore. For in this view, however much a book may have been altered, it was once (and must remain in part) God's word.

Like their books, the Jews and Christians were also treated with some ambivalence in the Qur'ān. The polemic against the Jews was stronger than that against the Christians, no doubt in part reflecting tensions between Muḥammad's people and the Jewish tribes in Medina. The Jews are even said to be the worst enemies of the believers along with the idolators, while the Christians are described as the most benign in intent toward the

Muslims. The worst transgressions of the Jews are corruption of their book, violation of the sabbath, persecution of their prophets, and defection from true monotheism. The Christians' main fault is doctrinal: the trinitarian idea and the divinity of Jesus. This is tantamount to *shirk*, associating something else with God, and thereby violating the monotheistic principle. Both Jews and Christians are threatened with hell. At the same time, there is a countercurrent of a more positive portrayal of the two peoples and religions, even, in the case of the Jews, some notion of their special relationship with God. Although the polemical elements in the Qur'ān seem dominant, the more irenic motifs have a voice which is not without effect. All this must be seen against the background of Islam's early development as a "new monotheism," possessing some of the themes of the older ones while striving to define itself as something truer to God's word than the others.

These ideas concerning the people of the book came into post-Qur'ānic Islamic thought and sources where they were explicated and developed, although remaining within the boundaries determined in the Qur'ān. In the modern period (from about the nineteenth century onward), the concept continued in the traditional form as part of Islam's religious and legal thought. But there was one great practical difference, which had a profound effect on the idea itself: the legal status of people of the book as *dhimmīs* (protected scriptural minorities), which Islam had designated for them and which had for centuries made possible a positive relationship between the parties, was either effaced or totally eliminated. This occurred as part of the disruption caused by Western presence or influence in Islam's Arab heartland, North Africa, Turkey, and Iran, where most of the *ahl al-kitāb* had lived for centuries. The Western powers themselves often had other notions of the proper status of minorities, which at times they attempted to impose; and the nation-states inspired by the powers continued in the same line. Then with Israel's creation in 1948 the next twenty years saw an almost total emigration of the ancient Jewish communities of the Arab Middle East, with most of them going to the Jewish state.

The classical idea of *ahl al-kitāb*, though remaining the same, now became almost wholly theoretical, having little or no demographic or legal reality in most places. This loss has been acutely felt in some modern circles. Thus certain trends of modern Islamic thought that propose a return to an idealized Islamic past as a way of meeting modern challenges consider the *ahl al-kitāb* living once again as *dhimmīs* to be an integral part of the true Islamic polity. And Islamic thought concerning the Palestine problem has sometimes envisaged the return of Middle Eastern Jews to their former places and status as a requirement in any solution to that conflict.

[*See also* Christianity and Islam; Dhimmī; *and* Judaism and Islam.]

BIBLIOGRAPHY

Lewis, Bernard. *The Jews of Islam*. Princeton, 1984. Good survey that includes a discussion of *ahl al-kitāb* and treats the modern period as well as earlier history.

Tritton, A. S. *The Caliphs and Their Non-Muslim Subjects: A Critical Study of the Covenant of ʿUmar* (1930). London, 1970. Still a basic and valuable book on the subject.

RONALD L. NETTLER

PERIODICAL LITERATURE. It is a prodigous, if not impossible, exercise to circumscribe "Islamic periodical literature." The tradition of Orientalist scholarship long employed the term "Arabic literature" as a synonym for "Islamic literature," extending this to a degree to literature in Turkish and Farsi. Urdu and Malay, however, did not receive the attention owed to the two major languages of nearly half the world's Muslims. For present purposes, we will define Islamic literature as the body of literature by Muslims, in any language, and not confined to theological subject matter.

Beyond Muslim literary production, Islam remains the religion most intensely studied by those outside its fold. Despite its innate ideological prejudices, it would be imprudent to ignore the corpus of Orientalism. Nonetheless simply being about Islam or Muslims does not intuitively make a work part of Islamic literature. In reckoning its ancillary status within that domain, it must be recognized that it lacks the inspiration of faith that characterizes the core works of Islamic letters. The following survey bears in mind the importance of that essential spirit in the vast body of Islamic periodical publication.

Islamic periodical literature made its debut with the publication of *Al-ʿurwah al-wuthqā*. Founded by one of the great Muslim reformers, Jamal al-Dīn al-Afghānī (1838–1897), its first issue appeared in Paris on 13 March 1884. As a symbol of Muslim resistance against colonialism, it infuriated the British, who convinced the Ottomans to prohibit its circulation; in India the ruling British imposed a hefty £100 fine and two years' imprisonment for possession of the newspaper, and Egypt ordered similar punishment. In the face of mounting pressure, the newspaper ceased publication on 17 October 1884, after seven months and eighteen issues. In recent times, a follower of Afghānī, Dr. ʿAbd al-Ḥakīm Ṭabībī, has kept Afghānī's memory alive by publishing from Geneva a bimonthly magazine of the same name. Afghānī's Pan-Islamic sentiment has further modern reflections in *Muslim World* (Karachi), published by Muʿtamar al-ʿĀlam al-Islāmī, and *Muslin World League Journal* (Makkah al-Mukarramah), published by Rābiṭat al-ʿĀlam al-Islāmī.

As a prologue to scholarly publishing by Muslims, *Islamic Culture* is an outstanding example. Appearing in 1927 under the patronage of the nizam of Hyderabad in Deccan, India, its first editor was Muhammad Marmaduke Pickthall, the famed English Muslim whose translation of the Qur'ān would later become a classic in its own right. After Pickthall's death the journal fell into the able hands of a Polish Muslim of Jewish ancestry, Muhammad Asad, whose translation of the Qur'ān and commentary on *Ṣaḥīḥ al-Bukhārī* would later earn him a respected position in the Muslim community. For nearly half a century *Islamic Culture* remained without peer; its publication has recently been suspended.

After the independence of Pakistan a number of journals rose to prominence, including *Islamic Literature, Islamic Studies, Iqbal Review,* and *Hamdard Islamicus. Islamic Literature* was unique in that it flourished through the enterprising spirit of its founder, Shaykh Muḥammad Ashraf, and died with him; he made a pioneering contribution to the diffusion of Muslim scholarly works. *Islamic Studies* and its sister journal in Urdu. *Fikr va naẓar* continue to fill the gap left by the loss of *Islamic Culture* and *Islamic Literature. Iqbal Review* has distinguished itself as the single most important source of research on the philosophy of ʿAllāmah Muhammad Iqbal. *Hamdard Islamicus* and its sister journal *Hamdard Medicus* reflect the unwavering dedication of Ḥakīm Muḥammad Saʿīd. Like *Türkiye Diyanet Vakfı* (Istanbul), they demonstrate that dissemination of knowledge through the time-honored Muslim tradition of publications funded by *waqf* is not outmoded. Some other prominent Pakistani titles include *Universal Message, Qur'ānulhudā, Islamic Order,* and *Mujāhidīn* (Peshawar).

Scholarly publishing in India is highlighted by such titles as *Islam and the Modern Age, Journal of Objective Studies, Aligarh Journal of Islamic Philosophy, Islamic Times, Radiance, ʿUlūm al-Qur'ān,* and *Al-risālah, Muslim India* is a remarkable publication that documents in detail problems of Muslims living in India as a minority. Another publication is *Kashmir Diary*.

For the past fifty years or so, *Glasnik* has been the sole voice of Bosnian Muslims and an indispensable source of reference for the history of Islam in the Balkans. The ongoing genocide of the Bosnian Muslims has made the continuation of this journal impossible. The same fate has befallen *Islamska Misao* (Sarajevo).

Turkey, officially a secular state, has seen an unprecedented growth of Islamic literature in the twentieth century. Bediüzzaman Said Nursî's *Nur* continues its long history of publication in the company of such titles as *İslamî araştırmalar-ı, Diyanet, Islam* (Istanbul), *Gene Akademi* and *Bilgi ve hikmet*. In Indoneisa, too, Islamic titles are flourishing, notably *Al-ḥikmah, ʿUlumul Qur'an, Kiblat, Bestari,* and *Adzan*.

A large number of periodicals arose out of the Islamic Revolution in Iran. They are distinguished by the consistency of their appearance in multilingual editions, such as *Al-tawḥīd, Maḥjūbah, Echo of Islam,* and *Message of Thaqalayn*.

Muslim Central Asia is coming to prominence with an expanding body of literature. *Journal of Central Asia* is perhaps the oldest in the trade. Other titles include *AACAR Bulletin* (a very useful biannual reference publication), *Central Asia, Central Asia Brief, Central Asia Monitor,* and *Central Asian Survey*.

Journal of Palestine Studies is the single most important source of scholarly articles on Palestine. *Washington Report on Middle East Affairs* is characterized by an even-handed approach. The United Nations Relief and Works Agency's *Palestine Refugees Today* is the official publication on refugees from Palestine. Other related publications are *Al-fajr, Human Rights Update, Israel and Palestine Political Report, New American View, April 17,* and *Breaking the Siege*. The Center for Policy Analysis on Palestine in Washington, D.C., issues occasional papers and reports.

In recent decades, Muslim minority communities have produced a substantial amount of periodical literature. The most prominent addition to this literature is a journal on Muslim minorities themselves, *Journal Institute of Muslim Minority Affairs* (Jeddah). Founded by the late Dr. Syed Zainul Abedin, it quickly rose to become one of the few Muslim journals of international repute.

In England and America, *The Muslim* and *Islamic Ho-*

rizons, respectively, were the forerunners of a number of currently appearing periodicals. From Canada, *Crescent International* is perhaps the oldest publication of its kind. Australian Muslims took the lead by bringing out *Insight* and later *Australasian Muslim Times. Impact International* (London) is among the oldest Muslim semi-academic publications that continues to have worldwide impact; *Islamic Quarterly* (London) has declined to irregular appearance. *Muslim Wise,* a new vibrant voice of Muslim youth, will be remembered in the history of Muslim journalism as a bold initiative. It was succeeded by another innovative but short-lived publication, *Muslim Update: Weekly Facsimile Edition.* Fortunately, *Q News,* a weekly by the same group of dedicated young writers, has shown greater resilience. *Muslim News* is another impressive new publication. Two now-defunct publications out of London must be mentioned—*Inquiry (Afkar)* and *Arabia;* both enjoyed a wide readership in many Muslim countries.

International Journal of Islamic and Arabic Studies (Bloomington, Indiana) is the first Muslim journal from America to achieve contemporary standards of scholarly publishing. Later the *American Journal of Islamic Social Sciences* appeared, with a slant toward the "islamization of knowledge." *Minaret, Inquiry,* and *Message* are now well-established community magazines, while *New Trend* maintains a loyal readership. *American Muslim* is a relatively new publication with wide appeal. *Muslim Media Watch Newsletter* is the first systematic attempt at media monitoring by Muslims. The African-American Muslim community has two important publications, *Muslim Journal* and *Final Call.* For the Arab-American community, *ADC Times* is essential reading.

For years, Muslim communities in Hong Kong, Singapore, Taiwan, Japan, Mauritius, and Reunion have faithfully published the *Hong Kong Muslim Herald, Muslim Reader, Islam in China, As-salam, La Croissant,* and *Al-Islam,* respectively. *Al-nahdah* (Kuala Lumpur) is famous for its in-depth coverage of the region.

Spanish Muslims are beginning to emerge on the publishing scene with titles such as *LamAlif, Bismillah boletin,* and *Ihsan.* South African Muslims have a strong publishing base. *Al-qalam, Majlis, Muslim Views, Al-ʿilm* (Dorban), and *Al-Islam* (Cape Town) are some widely circulated titles.

On Arabic language and literature, standard journals include *Al-Lisān al-ʿArabī, Journal of Arabic Studies* (Brunei Darussalam), *Journal of Arabic Literature, Revue de la lexicologie,* and *İslamî Edebivat* (Istanbul). Other titles include *Al-ʿArabīyah, Edebiyat,* and *Journal of Afro-Asiatic Languages. Muslim Musings* is a provocative new title on the literary scene.

There is a definite dearth of titles in the field of Islamic law. *Islamic and Comparative Law Quarterly* is the only journal of any distinction. Two journals started by the International Islamic University, Kuala Lumpur, *IIU Law Journal* and *Syariah Law Journal,* are now defunct. *Jurnal perundungan* (Kuala Lumpur) suffers from irregular appearance. *Jurnal syariah* has begun publication under the auspices of Universiti Malaya, Kuala Lumpur. Other titles are *Arab Law Quarterly* and *Arab Law and Society.*

Among specialized titles, foremost is the *Journal of Islamic Science.* It is the only publication of its kind that looks at modern science and technology from an Islamic perspective. Related titles are *Islam Today, Science and Technology in the Islamic World, Kesturi, İlim ve sanat, Journal of the Islamic Academy of Science,* and *Islamic Thought and Scientific Creativity.*

Only a few periodicals address the problems of Islamic education. *Muslim Education Quarterly* grew out of the first International Islamic Education Conference in Makkah al-Mukarramah (Mecca) in 1977 and has continued since then. The other is published in Kuala Lumpur under the title *Jurnal pendidikan Islam.* A new *Muslim Teachers College Journal* is published in the United States.

Recent interest in Islamic economies has resulted in a proliferation of literature on the subject. Prominent journals are *Journal of Islamic Economics, Pakistan Development Review, Humanomics, New Horizon, American Journal of Islamic Finance, Journal of Economic Cooperation among Islamic Countries, Middle East Business and Economic Review, Islamic Economic Studies* and *Journal of Islamic Banking and Finance.*

Islamic medicine is the subject of three leading journals—*Hamdard Medicus,* the oldest of the three, *Journal of the Islamic Medical Association of North America,* and *Journal of the Islamic Medical Association of South Africa. Islamic World Medical Journal* became defunct soon after it started publishing in London. *Medical Journal of the Islamic Republic of Iran* is a commendable addition. *Jihad wa Tauheed: A Publication About HIV/AIDS* is the only Islamic periodical on the subject.

Women's studies are not prominent in research and academic publishing in the Muslim world. However, titles such as *Maḥjūbah, Ummī, Al-wardah, Muslimah, Mother's Sense, Muslim Family, Soembike* (Kazan, Russia), *Islamic Sisters International,* and *Kadın ve aile* feature an Islamic approach to women and family problems. At least four titles are important for their coverage of Muslim women's affairs from a feminist perspective—*Shirkat Gāh Newsletter, Aḥfād Journal, Nimeye digar,* and *Women Living under Muslim Laws.*

Regrettably, Islamic arts, crafts, and architecture have remained among the most neglected areas in periodical publishing. The undisputed leader in Islamic art was *Arts and the Islamic World,* but after some twenty issues it has folded for lack of funds. *Eastern Art Report* has suffered the same fate. A useful source of reference, *IRCICA Newsletter,* is perhaps the last hope for scholars of the Islamic arts. *Mimar,* an acclaimed architecture journal, is now defunct. Another title is *Muqarnas.* In archaeology, a single title reigns supreme, *Archéologie islamique* (Paris).

There is discernible growth in the periodical literature on Interfaith studies. *Focus on Christian-Muslim Relations, Islamochristiana, Henry Martin Institute of Islamic Studies Bulletin,* and *Islam and Christian-Muslim Relations* are some of the pertinent titles.

In the area of reference periodical publishing, *Muslim World Book Review* remains one of a kind, rivaled only in part by the *Digest of Middle East Studies.* The *Index of Islamic Literature* that accompanies every issue of the *Muslim World Book Review* is a useful addition to Islamic bibliographic sources in English. For Arabic material, *ʿĀlam al-kutub* (Riyadh) is an excellent source. *Faṣl-i kitāb* is convenient for Farsi publications. *Periodica Islamica,* founded by Munawar Ahmad Anees, serves as the foremost source of current knowledge on Islamic periodical literature from a multidisciplinary perspective.

Finally, interdisciplinary studies are generating new journals. A few of the newest primary titles are *Al-qalam* (Lahore), *Al-aḍwā'* (Lahore), *Journal of Islamic Studies* (Oxford), *Jurnal IKIM* (Kuala Lumpur), *Muslim and Arab Perspectives* (New Delhi), *İzlenim* (Istanbul), *Fountain* (London), and *Intellectual Discourse* (Kuala Lumpur).

From the time of Afghānī to *ʿĀlam al-kutub,* Islamic periodical literature has matured into a tangible harvest. There are gaps in quality of production and editorial rigor; there are areas of outright neglect, and those where Muslim scholarship is heading for greater maturity. It is time for concerned scholars to examine critically the status of periodical publishing in the Muslim world.

BIBLIOGRAPHY

Aman, Muhammad M., ed. *Arab Periodicals and Serials: A Subject Bibliography.* New York, 1979. Lacks a title index.

Atram, M. A. al-. "*Al-Fihrist:* New Critical Study." *ʿĀlam al-Kutub* (Riyadh) 10.1 (AH 1409/1988 CE): 2–12 (in Arabic).

Auchterlonie, Paul, and Y. H. Safadi, eds. *Union Catalogue of Arabic Serials and Newspapers in British Libraries.* London, 1977. 1,011 titles from twenty-nine libraries.

Bachir. ʿImad, and Andrew Buxton. "The Information Content of Titles of Arabic Periodical Articles." *Journal of Information Science* 17 (1991): 57–63.

Behn, Wolfgang, ed. *Index Islamicus, 1665–1905.* Millersville, Pa., 1989. Covers Islamic periodical literature in Western languages since the appearance of the first article in 1665.

Bloss, Ingeborg, and Marianne Schmidt-Dumont, eds. *Zeitschriftenverzeichnis Moderner Orient (Stand 1979).* Hamburg, 1980. Lists holdings of the six largest periodical collections (Arabic, Persian, Turkish) in Germany.

Duman, Hasan, ed. *Istanbul Kütüphaneleri Arap Harflı Süreli Yayınlar Toplu Kataloğu, 1828–1928.* Istanbul, 1986. Union catalog of periodicals in Arabic script in the libraries of Istanbul.

Al-fihrist: Kashshāf ad-dawrīyāt al-ʿArabīyah. Annual. Beirut, 1981— Index of articles in selected Arabic periodicals, edited by ʿUbaydlī ʿUbaydlī.

Fihrist-i Maqālāt-i Fārsī dar Maṭbūʿāt-i Jumhūrī-i Islāmī-i Īrān. Quarterly. Tehran, 1982–. List of Persian periodical articles, edited by Īraj Afshar.

Index of Islamic Literature. Quarterly. Leicester, 1987–. Listings of articles in English only, issued as a supplement to *Muslim World Book Review.*

Islamic Book Review Index. Annual. Berlin, 1982–. Lists book reviews from nearly two hundred Western-language periodicals. Edited by Wolfgang Behn.

Pearson, J. D., et al., eds. *Index Islamicus, 1906–1955.* Cambridge, 1958. A classified list of articles in peridocials, collective volumes, and conference proceedings. Excludes Arabic and other Muslim languages. Sixth supplement, 1981–1985, London, 1990.

Periodica Islamica: An International Contents Journal. Quarterly. Kuala Lumpur, 1991–. Reproduces table of contents from more than eight hundred periodicals worldwide; multilingual. Edited by Munawar Ahmad Anees.

Sims-Williams, U., ed. *Union Catalogue of Persian Serials and Newspapers in British Libraries.* London, 1985. 640 titles from sixteen libraries.

Türkologischer Anzeiger. Annual. Vienna, 1975–. Listings of articles in all languages on Turkish and Ottoman studies.

Munawar Ahmad Anees

PERKIM. An acronym for Pertubuhan Kebajikan Islam SeMalaysia, or All Malaysia Muslim Welfare Association, PERKIM was founded in 1960 by the first prime minister of the newly independent nation, Tunku Abdul Rahman, as a religious and social welfare organization. Much of the original funding was provided by the Tunku's contacts with elites in the Muslim world, notably Saudi royalty, the Organization of the Islamic Conference, and a $12-million gift from Libya.

PERKIM's principal goal is the promotion of Islam as the national religion, with particular emphasis on the conversion of the non-Malay population, although without pressure or coercion. PERKIM's character as a noncommunal, or ethnic-bridging, religious organization is unique in multiethnic Malaysia; it was symbolically affirmed in the beginning by the ethnic identities of its cofounders, Haji Ibrahim Ma, Tan Sri O. K. Ubaidullah, and Tan Sri Mubin Sheppard, who are Chinese, Indian, and European Muslims, respectively.

Relatively inactive before 1970, PERKIM sprang to public attention during the 1970s following the ethnic and political conflicts of the late 1960s, which resulted in growing ethnic and religious polarization between the Muslim Malays and other groups. The New Economic Policy, enshrining strong affirmative action in favor of Malays, initiated two decades of Malay economic and constitutional assertiveness and tied economic and educational opportunity to Malay ethnic status, of which Islam is an essential cultural attribute. This was also the era of the Islamic resurgence in Malaysia, locally known as *dakwah* (Ar., *daʿwah*), whose activities were directed exclusively toward the Malay community.

In this social climate, PERKIM's distinctiveness lay in its continued attempts to create a multiethnic Islamic community and to reduce the perceived threat of a resurgent Islam among non-Malays. To these ends, PERKIM provides a wide range of support and services, including hostel accommodation and religious instruction for new converts and advice on personal problems arising from their conversion. Among its many educational services are preparation for government examinations, vocational courses, a variety of training schemes, and its own nondenominational kindergartens. PERKIM also sponsors clinics and drug rehabilitation schemes, which are important sources of new converts.

The total number of converts to Islam via PERKIM is hard to estimate precisely, partly because of an enthusiastic tendency toward overestimation during the early 1970s, and partly because of a subsequent high rate of recidivism; however, the total number of converts has probably never exceeded 120,000. During the early 1970s, the largest single constituency of converts to Islam via PERKIM consisted of working-class urban Chinese, who sought through Islam an assimilatory route to Malay ethnic and legal status, together with jobs and other privileges. For several years Tunku Abdul Rahman defended the Chinese converts' rights of access to occupational and other Malay quotas, both in parliament and in the Malay community at large, but he was ultimately unsuccessful. At this point, many Chinese Muslims were designated only as Saudara Bahru ("new brothers in the faith"), but not as Malays, and were relegated to a separate Chinese Muslims' Association. As a result, the rate of Chinese conversions has declined significantly to a level of less than one hundred annually, and many earlier converts have disappeared from view. More recent converts have tended to be young, male, and single, and to come from assorted Chinese, Indian, Eurasian, and European backgrounds; many of them are contemplating marriage with a Muslim, although a few still anticipate advantages in doing business with Malays. Finally, in 1979, PERKIM opened a settlement Pusan Pelarian Indochina (Indochina Refugee Center) in coastal Kelantan state specifically for Muslim (Cham) refugees from Cambodia.

The founding chapter and headquarters of PERKIM is the Balai Islam in the capital of Kuala Lumpur, with a further fifty or so branches throughout Malaysia, several of them supported by commercial and shopping complexes. In the East Malaysian states of Sabah and Sarawak, PERKIM's branches (USIA and BINA, respectively) have been particularly active among the non-Malay indigenous population, which accounts for another substantial category of recent converts.

PERKIM's publications include instructional books on Islam and social problems, as well as regular newsletters in three languages—*Suara PERKIM* (Malay), *Nur Islam* (Chinese), and the *Islamic Herald* (English).

BIBLIOGRAPHY

Mutalib, Hussin. *Islam and Ethnicity in Malay Politics.* Singapore, 1990.

JUDITH NAGATA

PERSIAN LITERATURE is a body of poetic and other literary works created principally, but not exclusively, in Iran. Beyond the present political boundaries of Iran proper, Afghanistan, the Indian subcontinent, Central Asia, and Turkey have been home to a rich body of literary work written in Persian.

In the context of Iran's full and multifaceted participation in and contributions to what has been called "the

Islamic civilization," Persian literature constitutes a rich, diversified, and autonomous aesthetic event to which the Iranian, or more accurately Persian-speaking, literati and their historical audiences have actively contributed. In its language and rhetoric, aesthetic and disposition, sensibilities and imagination, this literature is not, to any significant degree, reducible to fundamental tenets and doctrines of Islam. Although the majority of Persian poets and literati have been born to families and raised in environments in one way or another identifiable as "Islamic," their universe of imagination and literary production constitutes a reality sui generis, a space of aesthetic experience irreducible to any particular religious worldview. Zoroastrianism, Judaism, Buddhism, Hinduism, Manichaeism, Mazdakism, and all the major and minor sectarian divisions within Islam have invariably contributed to the Persian literary imagination. And yet the totality of that imagination is principally an aesthetic phenomenon irreducible to any one of its religious or nonreligious informants.

Perhaps the single most significant aspect of the Persian literary imagination, as it was delivered in a colorful panorama of formal styles and aesthetic sensibilities, is the noncanonical nature of its language. As it gradually developed after the Arab invasion of the early seventh century, modern Persian (as distinct from Pahlavi, or middle Persian, and Avestan, or old Persian) was a language in which no sacred text was believed to have been revealed. As opposed to Hebrew and Arabic, in which the Bible and the Qur'ān were revealed, Persian remained a constitutionally vernacular or, more accurately, secular language. The memories of the sacred language of the Avesta and the exegetical language of Pahlavi having been surpassed and superseded by the absolutist hegemony of the Arabic Qur'ān, Persian language occupied a noncanonical space in which secular events could occur beyond the doctrinal inhibitions of the sacred Arabic of the Qur'ān. It is crucial to remember that there were syncretic religious movements immediately after the Arab invasion, such as Khurramīyah and Bih-Afrīdīyah, that had occasional rhetorical claims to the revelation of a "Persian Qur'ān" (see Sadighi, 1938, *et passim;* Amoretti, 1975, pp. 489–490; Shahrastānī, 1979, vol. 1, p. 397). But with the political demise of such movements, the idea of a "Persian Qur'ān" never materialized. The Arabic Qur'ān remained the canonical text of all sacred imagination for Muslim Iranians who fully and productively participated in that imagination. The phrase "Persian Qur'ān" is later used by ʿAbd al-Raḥmām Jāmī (d. 1492), who called Jalāl al-Dīn Rūmī's *Maṣnavī* "the Qur'ān in Persian," meaning that Rūmī's text has the sacred sanctity of the Qur'ān expressed in Persian. Such hyperbolic expressions notwithstanding, the historical fact has always been that Persian remained a noncanonical language in which the literary imagination could be let loose.

The Persian literary imagination has been acted out in a conjunction of multiple sacred imaginings both domestic and foreign to Iranian communities. Zoroastrian, Manichaean, Mithraic, Mazdakian, Hindu, Buddhist, Judaic, Christian, Islamic, and a host of other less politically successful religions have emerged or arrived in historical succession and left indelible marks on Persian literary culture. But the very fact of their multiplicity, that they have come in succession and, in hostility or mutual tolerance, have coexisted together, has prevented any one of them from exercising absolutist, hegemonic power over the Persian literary imagination. Extensive scholarship (Muʿīn, 1959; Melikian-Chirvani, 1974, 1984 in particular) has established that Zoroastrian, Manichaean, and Buddhist imageries entered the aesthetic parlance of the Persian literary imagination and endured, even flourished, well into the Islamic period. Even within the Islamic context, sectarianized doctrinal differences continued to divide the active and passive loyalties of Persian literati throughout the ages. Whereas up until the fifteenth century the majority of Persian poets and literati could be identified as Sunnīs, after the establishment of the Ṣafavids (1501–1732), Shiism became at least the nominal faith of many poets and writers. Having theological/antitheological, philosophical/antiphilosophical, or so-called Ṣūfī/anti-Ṣūfī predilections further added to the divisive orientations that loosened the active absolutism of any one particular ideological force over the Persian literary imagination. As for the oral and literary sources of this imagination, Iranian, Indian, Chinese, Arabic, and Turkish material converged to create a multicultural literary universe that went beyond the confines of any particular politics. The world was home to the Persian poet as he or she sat to wonder on the nature and purpose of being.

The first textual evidence of a literary tradition in Iran is the royal inscriptions of the Achaemenid kings, Darius I (522–486 BCE) and Xerxes, his son, in particular. Inscribed in old Persian, these royal texts indicate a proud, self-confident, assertive, and theocentric imagination: "A Great God is Ahūrā Mazdā," reads one, "who created the earth, who created the sky, who created man, who created happiness for man, who made Darius the King" (quoted in Yarshater, 1988, pp. 5–6). Although theocentric, this royal self-conception is clearly conscious of an individual existence: "Says Darius the King, by the favor of Ahūrā Mazdā I am such a man who is friend to right. I am not a friend to wrong. It is not my wish that the weak man should have wrong done to him by the mighty; nor is it my wish that the mighty man should have wrong done to him by the weak" (*Ibid.*, p. 6). In these inscriptions, the king as narrator extends his authority from the supreme deity, Ahūrā Mazdā, and then acts as an individual full of moral and ethical convictions. With an authority extended from God, Darius the king is the man, the lawgiver, the monarch, the chronicler, and the historian of the Achaemenid's glorious deeds. In an inscription, Darius gives a rather full, boastful account of how he overthrew Gaumātā, a magian who had pretended to be the slain brother of Cambyses, Smardis. Darius's account is swift, concise, not devoid of narrative elegance.

From the royal inscriptions of the Achaemenids to Zoroaster's own hymns, the Gathas, there lies a vast arena of imaginative oral traditions that are distilled and barely visible through the Avestan prism. This oral tradition was perpetuated by Iranian minstrels, or *gosān*s who carried forward a fantastic tradition of narrative songs. As storyteller/magicians, *gosān*s had a central social function in ancient, particularly Parthian and Arsacid, communities (see Boyce, 1957). They sang songs, told stories, recited poems, delivered satires, mourned and celebrated on occasions, and carried forward a rich and rewarding tradition of songs and tales, legends and myths, stories and anecdotes (for a discussion of the Avestan literature, see Dale Bishop's article in Yarshater, 1988, chap. 2).

In the Avesta, the Gathas and the pre-Zoroastrian hymns Zoroaster remembered later, the Yashts, are the first, most comprehensive poetic narrative we have which remain principally subservient to the Zoroastrian sacred imagination. Gods, deities, and heroes, as well as their metahistorical relations to worldly being are the subjects of these sacred narratives in which the poetic plays a vital role. But the same poetic urge that partially subserved the sacred imagination of the Avesta was forcefully at work in the muscular epic narrative of ancient Iranians. As evident through the prism of the Avestan Yashts, a flourishing oral tradition had given epic proportions to legendary rivalries between the Iranian house of Kayānīyān and its perpetual enemies, the Turanians. Not until the time of Firdawsī (d. about 1025) do we have textual evidence of this effervescent oral tradition, which must have been active and widespread during the composition of the Yashts. Iranian minstrels must have transmitted various versions of these epics from generation to generation. Under the patronage of Parthians and the Arsacids (247 BCE–226 CE), this minstrel tradition was given enough political momentum to permit the extension of a folkloric narrative into a royal lexicon of cultural legitimacy. It has been suggested (Yarshater, 1988, pp. 10–11) that the overwhelming, and politically successful, Eastern (Zoroastrian) tradition overshadowed the receding memory of the legends and histories of the Persians and the Medes, and that by the time of the Sassanians (224–651 CE) only the Kayānīyān legends had been constituted as the legitimizing force at the disposal of courtly scribes.

The Sassanian emperors were the direct beneficiaries of both the sacred and the secular imagination that had informed much of the earlier Iranian communities. Certainly by the time of the composition of *Khwadāy-nāmag* (The Book of Lords) during the reign of Khusraw II (590–628 CE), the renarration of already ancient legends and stories had assumed legitimizing status. *Khwadāy-nāmag* represents the earliest extant fictive renarration of a legendary history that puts the poetic occasion at the service of ideological legitimation of the state apparatus. As the first man/king, Gayōmarth, in this narrative, presides over the creation and succession of the rendition of much older stories. As "the most important literary heritage of ancient Iran" (Yarshater, 1988, p. 10), *Khwadāy-nāmag* is a compendium of moral and philosophical injunctions as delivered through the Persian poetic imagination. As such, however, it is as much a distant memory of pre-Sassanian legends and stories as it is an immediate mirror of the moral and political imperatives of the Sassanian monarchy. As a supreme example of storytelling, *Khwadāy-nāmag* preserves some of the rhetorical features that have endured through subsequent variations in the epic genre.

The absence of textual evidence has permitted suggestions that pre-Islamic Persian literature lacked any significant secular literature. "This judgment," Ehsan Yarshater has suggested, "ignores two basic facts: that the secular literature of Iran prior to Islam was essentially oral, and that much of the early New Persian literature was in fact only a new recension or direct rendering of Middle Persian and Parthian creations" (1988, p. 10). As an example, Fakhr al-Dīn Asʿad al-Gurgānī's (d.

about 1063) eleventh-century modern Persian renditions of the love story *Vīs and Rāmīn* is our textual link to the Parthian version of the story available to al-Gurgānī in middle Persian and Georgian. As an adventurous love story, *Vīs and Rāmīn* reads in marked contrast to *Darakht-i asūrīg*, which, extant in middle Persian, provides one of the earliest examples of didactic dialogics in Persian poetry, in this case between a tree and a goat. Among an overwhelming body of religious verses that Manichaean and Zoroastrian priests produced in Parthian and Pahlavi, *Ayādgār-i zarīrān* and *Drakht-i asūrig* are among the few textual examples of a secular literary imagination. Indirectly, however, we know of a more elaborate secular literature. What in later sources is identified as *Fahlavīyat* refers to an elaborate body of beautiful poetic traditions—*Surūd, Chakāmah*, and *Tarānah* among them—with which even the later Persian poets, whose prosody was considerably arabicized, were familiar.

The Persian literature produced after the Arab invasion of the seventh century was thus both textually and orally heir to a substantial body of literature that, whether in direct (written or oral) tradition or in continuation of literary imagination, persisted well into the later periods. As it gradually emerged as a noncanonical language, Persian evolved into a literary language of monumental imagination. Always under the shadow of Arabic, modern Persian carried within its slanted relation of power to Arabic the debilitating memory of the decisive Battle of Qādisīyah (June 637) in which the Persians were defeated by the newly Muslim Arabs. In a remarkable division of creative imagination, the Persian scientific and philosophical writings were produced primarily, but not exclusively, in Arabic, while their literary output continued to flourish in Persian. Arabic then became the paternal language of the hegemonic theology, jurisprudence, philosophy, and science, while the maternal Persian, the language of mothers' lullabies and wandering singers, songwriters, and storytellers, constituted the subversive literary imagination of a secular and poetic conception of being.

As Iraq (Baghdad in particular) emerged as the cultural capital of the Arabic west, Khurasan (Nishapur in particular) emerged as the cultural capital of the Persian east. From the central heartland of Khurasan, Persian literature spread as far east as the Indian subcontinent, as far west as the Balkans, as far north as China, and as far south as the Persian Gulf. Contemporary Iranians, Afghans, Tajiks, Indians, Pakistanis, Turks, and Arabs have almost as equal a claim on the literary history of Persian as they have on Arabic and Turkish. Relations of power, the changing features of royal patronage, revolutions, wars, invasions, and conquests have had much more to do with literary productions than anything ethnic, racial, or linguistic. For Turkish warlords, in particular, Persian literature became the chief ideological legitimizer of their rule. As an apparatus of political legitimation, production of Persian literature functioned as one of the principal ideological forces at the disposal of the Ghaznavids (977–1186), the Seljuks (1038–1194), and even the Ottomans (1281–1924). As a courtly artifact, Persian poetry was equally present and instrumental in India, particularly during the reign of the Mughals (1526–1858). Exacerbated by the coming to power of the Shīʿī Ṣafavids (1501–1722), who, having substituted Shiism as the state ideology, had no particular need, penchant, time, or taste for Persian poetry, Persian and Indian poets found India a more congenial place than Iran. The result of this historical displacement is that any history of Persian literature in the sixteenth and seventeenth centuries ought to be traced to India rather than Iran. Whether self-consciously or not, dynasties that considered themselves Turkish, Persian, or Indian throughout the medieval period adopted the political apparatus of Persian poetry to fulfill the major ideological task of state legitimation in a space adjacent to other, principally Islamic modes and modalities of legitimacy.

The roots of Persian poetic imagination in the ideological apparatus of the Persian court is evident in the first, most successful form of its historical record, that is, the panegyrics (see Meisami, 1987). As it emerged in Khurasan between the tenth and twelfth centuries, Persian court poetry put itself at the disposal of the Samānids (819–1005) and the Ghaznavids, who consciously fashioned themselves after the enduring memories of the Sassanians. As Rūdakī (d. 940), Farrukhī (d. 1037), and Manūchihrī (d. 1040), among scores of others, marked the particular characteristics of Persian panegyric poetry, marks of chivalry and warfare, as symbolics of banquets and feasts, found their way into the operative repertoire of Persian aesthetics (for a full discussion of the prominent features of court poetry, see Jerome E. Clinton's article in Yarshater, 1988, chap. 4). But perhaps the most striking aspect of this poetry, best exemplified by Rūdakī's pictorial representations of nature, Farrukhī's penchant for exquisite physical details, and Manuchihrī's festive celebration of nature and particularly his joyous description of wine and wine drinking, is its worldly imagination, which has an unmitigated, direct, and spontaneous contact with the physicality of being. Thus, although Persian panegyrics developed into a highly stylized courtly form, its imageries and historical consciousness represent a wide spectrum of aesthetic and material sensibilities.

Rooted in the same political necessity, as well as in Persian folkloric traditions, is the epic poetry that comes to its fullest and aesthetically most sustained manifestation in Firdawsī's *Shāhnāmah.* Composed in some fifty thousand couplets over a period of thirty years, *Shāhnāmah* is a singular heroic narrative of a people's mythical, legendary, and historical memories. In *Shāhnāmah,* Firdawsī brings the diverse and scattered memories of a people he deliberately identifies as "Iranians" into the sustained imaginative force of a single poetic event. *Shāhnāmah* is self-consciously heroic, from its metrics to its diction. Firdawsī's epic narrative describes the heroic deeds of Rustam, the treacheries of Ẓaḥḥāk, the innocence of Siyāvush, the bedeviling attraction of Sudābah, the tragedies of Suhrāb and Isfandyār, the love stories of Bīzhan and Manīzhah, Zāl and Rūdabah. What holds these stories together is Firdawsī's self-conscious presence, his periodic interruptions of the epic narrative to dwell on the nature of human beings and their destiny, his unfailing moral gaze at the glories and atrocities of human existence. Firdawsī tells old stories with an unmistakably moral verve that operates in the towering imagination of a self-confident poet, fully conscious of his epic narrative (for two excellent essays on *Shāhnāmah,* see the articles by William L. Hanaway and Amin Banani in Yarshater, 1988, chaps. 5 and 6, respectively; for a good translation of a story from *Shāhnāmah,* see Firdawsī, 1933).

If epic poetry appealed to the heroic aspirations of both the changing monarchies and of folkloric traditions at large, a particular aspect of it, the romantic, catered to finer sensibilities of love and adventure. By the time Niẓāmī (d. 1209) composed his famous *Khamsah,* the Persian romantic tradition was already rich and diversified. Written about 1050, Gurgānī's *Vīs and Rāmīn* borrowed from pre-Islamic Iranian themes and constructed the first and most successful example of this genre. *Vīs and Rāmīn* of Gurgānī is one of the most brilliant examples of Persian narrative poetry, one in which pre-Islamic stories are resuscitated with powerful poetic imagination. The origin of *Vīs and Rāmīn* has been traced back to the Sassanian (226–652) or even Arsacid (250 BCE–224 CE) period. Gurgānī reports that he found the Pahlavi version of this story in Isfahan and, following the orders of Abū al-Fatḥ Muẓaffar al-Nīshāpūrī, rewrote it in poetic Persian with particular attention to the dramatic rhetoric of storytelling (for a comprehensive essay on *Vīs and Rāmīn,* see M. J. Mahjoub's introduction to his critical edition of the text, Gurgānī, 1959; for an excellent prose translation, see Gurgānī, 1972). In producing his version, Gurgānī took advantage of both written and oral accounts of the story, but he embellished and delivered it with particular attention to the details of dramatic delivery, a trademark of Persian narrative poetry. Adopting a number of Pahlavi words in his poetic rendition, Gurgānī produces a clear narrative with a stunning simplicity as its moving energy. Despite the brilliance of its poetic composition, *Vīs and Rāmīn* experienced a period of eclipse when its uncompromising celebration of physical love offended Islamic sensibilities. Nevertheless, *Vīs and Rāmīn* had a profound impact on subsequent Persian romances, not least on the master of Persian romantic narrative, Niẓāmī.

Niẓāmī's brilliant achievement in *Khamsah* (Quintet), however, brought the Persian romantic tradition to a height comparable to Firdawsī's achievement in epic poetry. In a masterful construction of a dramatic narrative, Niẓāmī, always personally present in his tales, constructs a literary humanism resting on nothing but the dramatic movement of his own power of storytelling. *Khamsah* consists of five narratives, each evolving around a thematic treatment of love and adventure. As evident in such stories as "Khusraw and Shīrīn" and "Laylī and Majnūn," Niẓāmī took full advantage of dramatic techniques to develop a particularly haunting narrative of love and adventure (for an excellent introduction to Niẓāmī's poetry, see Peter Chelkowski's article in Yarshater, 1988, chap. 10; J. C. Bürgel's article in the same volume, chap. 9, is a comprehensive introduction to the genre).

The romantic genre thus brought to full fruition by Niẓāmī soon unfolded into a rich tradition to which such gifted poets as Amīr Khusraw Dihlavī (d. 1325), Khwājū Kirmānī (d. 1352), and ʿAbd al-Raḥmān Jāmī (d. 1492) added dimension and brilliance, qualities never to reach the height of the master of the genre, Niẓāmī himself.

Whereas both the epic and the romantic genres demanded longer attention spans, the brevity of lyrical poetry tested the power of the Persian poets for the economy of their wording. From its origins in amorous occasions in the panegyric, epic, and romantic poetries, lyrical poetry emerged and found its most successful and enduring form in Persian *ghazal*. *Ghazal* became the functional equivalent of musical sonatas in Persian poetry. With sustained and implacable economy of wording, masters of Persian lyrics, principally Saʿdī (d. 1292) and Ḥāfiẓ (d. 1390), shed all extrapoetic functions of poetry and created perhaps the most artistically successful experience in the whole spectrum of Persian literature. *Ghazal* is the aesthetic challenge of brevity, the formal occasion of poetic mastery, a short space where the mosaics of words, sensibilities, and imageries demand the best in aesthetic creativity that a poet can command.

Although the origins of *ghazal* go back to such masterful practitioners as Sanā'ī (d. 1130) and Niẓāmī (d. 1209), it is with Saʿdī (d. 1292) that the miniaturesque composition of lyrics comes to its most brilliant fruition. Saʿdīs *ghazal*s are the very picture of beauty and subtlety. Rarely has a Persian poet had such a perfect, almost magical, command over words, with flawless harmony in their sound effects. The sheer musicality of Saʿdī's *ghazal*s defies all description. His *ghazal*s read and sound like a Chopinesque nocturne: crisp, clear, concise, brevity the very soul of their amorous movements. Saʿdīs works portray a human, physical, perfectly tangible love that registers with unfailing impact. The whole spectrum of Persian poetic repertoire, having come to perfection by the thirteenth century, is at the disposal of Saʿdī. Never after Saʿdī did classical Persian *ghazal* benefit from the ingenious powers of such a word magician. Saʿdī's lyrical humanism is arguably the zenith of Persian poetry and all its worldly possibilities (for a discussion of Persian lyric poetry, see Heshmat Moayyad's article in Yarshater, 1988, chap. 7).

Neither the romantic nor the lyrical possibilities of Persian poetry escaped the attention of Persian mystics. Devoted to a particular doctrinal reading of the Qur'ān and of the Muḥammadan message, the Persian Ṣūfīs joined their Arab, Turkish, and Indian brethren in a massive mystification of the physical world. Finalized in the doctrine of *waḥdat al-wujūd* (the Unity of Being), the Ṣūfīs collectively engaged in a radical mystification of both literature and love. Persian lyrical poetry in particular proved most appropriate for such a grand act of mystification. Three successive poets, Sanā'ī (d. 1130), ʿAṭṭār (d. about 1220), and Rūmī (d. 1273), are chiefly recognized as the master-builders of Persian mystical poetry.

With Sanā'ī we witness the decline of the court as the great patron of Persian poetry and the rise of religious sentiments to substitute the physical beauties that principally informed Persian poetry's imaginative repertoire. The substantial mystification of Sanā'ī by later Ṣūfīs is not borne out by the actual presence of religious sensibilities in his poetry. Sanā'ī professed that his worldly poetics did not in any significant way promote his station in life, and that consequently he decided to devote his talent to religious poetry. He blamed his contemporaries, a vague reference to his liaisons with the Ghaznavid court, for not having appreciated his poetry. He seems to have felt particularly humiliated by submitting his poetic gift to the brute taste of his patrons. He was the master of the world of words, he thought, and yet a servile slave to his brute masters. As a result, he informs us, he abandons worldly poetry and turns his attention to religious matters. But the conversion is not so dramatic as to abandon poetry altogether. He simply decides to attend to religious matters poetically. "My poetry shall be a commentary on Religion and Law / The only reasonable path for a poet is this." Despite his Shīʿī sentiment, Sanā'ī equally praised the first three caliphs, indicating a less than zealous religiosity (see Ṣafā, vol. 2, p. 560 for a discussion). Nevertheless, later Ṣūfīs took full advantage of this "conversion" and fabricated fantastic stories about it, turning Sanā'ī into a full-fledged Ṣūfī. As a poet, however, Sanā'ī remained singularly attached to religious matters, a fact best represented not only in his poetry but also in his pilgrimage to Mecca, which he undertook from Khurasan (for further details, see De Bruijn, 1983).

After his Mecca pilgrimage, a friend of Sanā'ī, a man named Khvājah ʿAmīd Aḥmad ibn Masʿūd, provided him with a home and daily sustenance and asked Sanā'ī to collect his own poems and prepare a *dīvān* (collection of poetry). Sanā'ī spent the rest of his life in this house in Ghaznīn and compiled his collected works, including his masterpiece *Ḥadīqat al-ḥaqīqah*. Sanā'ī's *dīvān*, masterfully edited in more than thirteen thousand verses by Mudarris Radavī, is a compendium of his secular and religious sensibilities. His *madā'iḥ* (panegyric praises) demonstrate Sanā'ī's mastery of the genre and are clear indications of a boastful awareness of his poetic gifts. *Ḥadīqat al-ḥaqīqah va sharīʿat al-ṭarīqah* (also known as *Ilāhī-nāmah*) is by far the most significant work of Sanā'ī, which he composed between 1129 and 1130 in ten thousand verses. Sanā'ī dedicated this *maṣnavī* couplet to the Ghaznavid warlord Bahrāmshāh (r. 1118–1152). *Ḥadīqat* begins with conventional salutations to God, the Prophet, and his companions, and then proceeds to poetic discourses on reason, knowledge, wisdom, and love. In his original version, something must have been in Sanā'ī's *Ḥadīqat* that caused the anger of contemporary religious authorities. He sent a copy of it to a prominent religious authority, Burhān al-Dīn Abū al-Ḥasan ʿAlī ibn Nāṣir al-Ghaznavī, in Baghdad and asked him to issue an edict in its support. In his letter, composed in the form of a poem, Sanā'ī went so far as to identify *Ḥadīqat* as "the Qur'ān in Persian," a phrase that has been used for other texts as well, particularly by Jāmī in reference to Rūmī's *Masnavī*. Immediately after the death of Sanā'ī, there was no complete version of *Hadīqah* extant. Muḥammad ibn ʿAlī al-Raffā', a Ṣūfī as judged by his introduction, prepared an edition of the text.

Kārnāmah-yi Balkh, another *masnavī* of Sanā'ī, thought to be the earliest poetic composition, is in an entirely worldly and humorous mode. Composed for the Ghaznavid ruler Masʿūd ibn Ibrāhīm, *Kārnāmah-yi Balkh* is full of praises for the nobility and poetic dialogues with his contemporary poets. *Sayr al-ʿibād ilā al-Maʿād*, *Ṭarīq al-tahqīq*, and *ʿIshq-nāmah* are three other of Sanā'ī's *masnavīs*.

ʿAṭṭār's *Manṭiq al-Ṭayr*, among his numerous other *masnavīs*, has been persistently read as a mystical allegory, foretelling Rūmī's *masnavī* to be composed later in the same century. ʿAṭṭār's story of a group of birds persuaded by the hoopoe (Hudhud) to look for a King is a simple didactic narrative. Thirty of the many birds thus persuaded to look for their King finally make it to their destination, where they meet *Sīmurgh* (the "thirty-bird," or simply a reflection of the thirty birds). (For a brilliant translation of this poem, see ʿAṭṭār, 1984.)

Sanā'ī and ʿAṭṭār's experimentation with didactic *masnavī* narrative for suggestion of mystical allegories ultimately reached Rūmī, in whose hands Persian mystical poetry achieves its height and most prolific potentials. Rūmī's *Masnavī*, dubbed "the Qur'ān in Persian" by Jāmī, is the highest achievement and the metalogical conclusion of Persian mystical poetry. Rūmī took equal advantage of Persian *ghazal* lyricism and supplanted his mystical love where the physical love of Saʿdī was. With slight poetic modifications in conceptual and aesthetic sensibilities, Rūmī gave full expression to a mystical narrative that postulated an all-loving God presiding over the worldly manifestation of his omnipresence. Man in Rūmī's narrative became a Man-God potentially endowed with the realization of all divine attributes. Rūmī's became a passionate quest inward, toward the realization of God within (for the English translation of Rūmī's *Masnavī*, see Rūmī, 1925–1940).

After Rūmī the colossal mystification of Persian lyrical and romantic poetry was so pervasive and powerful that not until the advent of modernity in the wake of the Constitutional Revolution of 1906–1911 did an alternative universe of poetic imagination have a literary space to emerge. The only exception to that massive mystification in premodern Persian poetry is in the lyrical poetry of Ḥāfiẓ and a whole new universe of aesthetic sensibilities that he created.

With Ḥāfiẓ (d. 1390), Persian lyrical poetry reached a new height, the refreshing space of a whole new poetic thinking. Ḥāfiẓ's poetic narrative, the physical beauty of his verses, is above and beyond anything achieved before or after in Persian lyrics (for a sample of his poems, see Ḥāfiẓ, 1897). In Ḥāfiẓ's poetry dwells an unrelenting engagement with the physical presence of life, with the stunning irreducibility of being. He comes after both Saʿdī and Rūmī, and in a remarkable way weds the worldliness of one to the passionate intensity of the other. Ḥāfiẓ's *ghazal*s defy the temptations of Rūmī's mysticism, confront the world directly, and shift Saʿdīs worldliness to a new, aesthetically more compelling, engagement with being. The overriding sentiments of Ḥāfiẓ's lyricism is the pivotal primacy of physical love necessitated by an existentially ironic and paradoxical conception of being. The two crosscutting senses of paradox and irony give Ḥāfiẓ's conception of love a critical sense of urgency:

> Seize the moment, you and I here together, Once
> The short trip over, and we shall never meet again.

And as for the promises of knowledge and wisdom to mediate any conception of being:

> Thank God, just like us, no faith no fidelity
> Was in he who was called the wise, the trustworthy!

Testing the power of brevity in Persian poets even more vigorously than *ghazal* was *rubāʿī* or *dū-baytī* (quatrains). Bābā Ṭāhir-i ʿUryān (d. about 1063) was the indubitable master of a stunningly beautiful, yet irreducibly simple, genre of quatrains most probably first comprised in Lorī dialect and then modified by later scribes to literary Persian (Ṣafā, vol. 2, p. 386).

> A farmer was once waiting in a pasture,
> Crying sadly while to his tulips he attended.
> "Alas," he said, as he planted his flowers,
> "That we should plant and leave them unattended."

Bābā Ṭāhir's imageries are drawn from daily observations, to which a twist of unexpected poetic significance is given. Reading and understanding Bābā Ṭāhir requires no grand leap of faith. He addresses simple but compelling realities that can immediately register with his readers. A feeling of the simultaneous beauty and brutality of life abounds in his poetry (for a translation of Bābā Ṭāhir's poetry, see Bābā Tāhir, 1902).

In ʿUmar Khayyām's (d. about 1129) quatrains, however, Persian literature finally recognized one of its greatest potentials: an autonomous poetic voice radically subversive of all metaphysics, of all unexamined sacred assumptions (the most deservedly famous translation of Khayyām is that of Edward FitzGerald; see Khayyām, 1859). The prevalence of historical references to Khayyām in Persian primary sources make the Orientalist assumption that prior to FitzGerald's translation, Khayyām was not significantly recognized or appreciated highly dubitable. Equally challenging that assumption is the still widespread presence of oral traditions of Khayyāmesque quatrains. In the Persian and Arabic primary sources (e.g., Niẓāmī ʿArūdī's *Chahār maqālah* or al-Qifṭī's *Akhbār al-ḥukamāʾ*) Khayyām is widely reported in association with quite a number of his prominent potential contemporaries. Ibn Sīnā (Avicenna, d. 1036), Abū Ḥāmid al-Ghazālī (d. 1111), Ḥasan al-Ṣabbāḥ (d. 1124), and Niẓām al-Mulk (d. 1092) are among historical characters associated, in fiction or in fact, with ʿUmar Khayyām. Whether identified as a philosopher, mathematician, astronomer, or poet, Khayyām was widely known, loved, and respected by his contemporaries. This wide contemporary recognition is crucial to an understanding of the centrality of ʿUmar Khayyām in the Persian literary imagination.

ʿUmar Khayyām's poems, marked principally by a frightful recognition of the fragile beauty of life, reject all intermediaries of human existential understanding. In these quatrains Khayyām confronts and celebrates reality—always with a fearful embracement that trembles with life and anxiety—without a moment of neglectful blinking. Khayyām's quatrains are as compelling, simple, and unadumbrated:

> Here with a Loaf of Bread beneath the Bough,
> A Flask of Wine, a Book of Verse—and Thou
> Beside me singing in the Wilderness—
> And Wilderness is Paradise enow.

as they are matter-of-factly subversive of all the metaphysics of the sacred:

> You are a compound of the elements four,
> The seven planets rule your fevered life.
> Drink wine, for I have said a thousand times
> That you will not return: once gone, you're gone.

In marked contrast to Khayyām's constitutional doubt is Nāṣir-i Khusraw's (AH 394–481/1003–1088 CE) propagational poetry, which he put fully at the disposal of his Ismāʿīlī faith. Nāṣir-i Khusraw, as one of the most significant figures in Iranian intellectual history, had a profound effect on Persian poetic imagination. As an Ismāʿīlī *dāʿī* (propagandist) he put his immense poetic power at the full service of his faith. In such philosophical treatises as *Jāmiʿ al-ḥikmatayn, Zād al-musāfirīn,* and *Khvān va ikhvān,* Nāṣir-i Khusraw expounded proto-Neoplatonic ideas in the Persian philosophical tradition. In his *Safar-nāmah* he demonstrated an uncanny capability for critical social observations. But it was chiefly in his poetry that he is observed as a staunch ethicist fully aware, proud even, of his poetic powers. Much of Nāṣir-i Khusraw's poetry is also autobiographical, in the sense that he gives a full and detailed account of his moral and intellectual dilemmas at various stages of his life. Although he ultimately put his poetic gift fully in the service of the Ismāʿīlī cause, Nāṣir-i Khusraw leaves a detailed trace of his doubts and uncertainties prior to his conversion to Ismāʿīlism. His poetry in fact gives a rather full account of all sectarian, juridical, theological, philosophical, and even interreligious divisions that divided his contemporaries (for a sample of his poetry, see Schimmel, 1993).

By the end of the thirteenth century, classical Persian poetry reached its zenith. ʿAbd al-Raḥmān Jāmī is universally recognized as the last master practitioner of the classical style of practically all genres, with the exception of the epic (for a sample of his poetry, see Jāmī, 1956). During the Ṣafavid period, Shiism functioned as the operative state ideology, and as a result the royal patronage of poetry considerably declined. Persian poetic imagination flourished in India and at the Mughal (1568–1858) court. Not until the middle of the eighteenth century did the Persian literary imagination take partial advantage of the Ṣafavid demise and begin to reassert itself. With the decline of the Ṣafavid in the mid-eighteenth century and the rise of the intervening dynasties of the Afshārs (1736–1795) and the Zands (1750–1794), the Shīʿī ideological grip began to loosen. Nādir Shāh Afshār (r. 1736–1747), in particular, weakened Shiism considerably when he contemplated its effective doctrinal elimination by reducing it to the fifth school of Islamic law (see Arjomand, 1984). The so-called Literary Revival (Bāzgasht-i Adabī) in the eighteenth century, and the relative prominence that such poets as Hātif-i Iṣfahānī (d. 1783) found in that movement, was a substantial response to the decline of Persian literature in the sixteenth and seventeenth centuries. This revival, however, could not and did not do much to put the Persian literary imagination on a new plane. Age-old imageries and sensibilities began to be resuscitated in the service of new dynasties. The Qājārs (1796–1925) succeeded the Zands as the penultimate variation on the theme of Persian monarchy. With very few exceptions, Qājār monarchs were deeply corrupt despots, overpowering against their own defenseless subjects, weaklings and servile in front of their powerful external adversaries. The so-called literary revival could only serve outdated and repleted imageries full of empty praises for deeply corrupt kings. Even the spontaneous zeal of the Bābī movement, led by Sayyid ʿAlī Muḥammad Shīrāzī (d. 1849), which produced a brilliant poet in one of its radical exponents, Ṭāhirah Qurrat al-ʿAyn (d. 1851), could not for long save Persian poetic imagination from futile redundancy. What Persian literature needed, and received, were two major political and poetic revolutions.

The Constitutional Revolution of 1906–1911 was the festive birth of Iran as a nation of self-conscious citizens mobilized to define their inalienable rights. The Constitutional poetry in particular became the tumultuous birth channel of the dominant ideas of nation and nationalization (see Aryānpūr, 1978). The occasion of the Constitutional Revolution, in which the absolutist monarchy of the Qājārs was forced to accept the central political authority of a national assembly *(majlis)*, gave full, colorful, and enduring expressions to hopes, fears, and aspirations of a nation in the making. In the hands of these revolutionary poets, Persian poetic narratives were recast into the formative mold of a whole new aesthetic self-conception. Persian language in effect was liberated from old and tired repetition of outdated sensibilities. Īraj Mīrzā's (d. 1925) brutal satire, ʿĀrif's (d. 1933) stunningly beautiful lyricism, Parvīn Iʿtiṣāmī's (1907–1941) quiet anger, and Farrukhī Yazdī's (d. 1939) radical socialism gave fresh and invigorating blood to Persian poetry.

The revolutionary effervescent created by the poetry of the Constitutional period continued well into the 1920s and 1930s. But the political momentum that the revolution had given to the Persian poetic imagination was not internal and strong enough to shed the shackles of tired, old formalities forever. Toward that end a revolution was needed from within the poetic imagination itself, a radical rethinking of the poetic act that would match the revolution without.

If the poetry of the Constitutional Revolution of 1906–1911 gave birth to the Iranian "nation," the Nimaic revolution in Persian poetics was commensurate with the birth of the Persian "individual." Nīmā Yūshīj (1897–1960), the indisputable founding father of "New" Persian poetic imagination *(shiʿr-i naw)*, gave full theoretical and poetic expression to a whole new universe of creative imagination in Persian poetry. There is no historical comparison to what Nīmā did in Persian poetics in the millennium-old history of Persian poetry. Through a sustained theoretical and practical rethinking of the very act of poetic imagination, Nīmā revolutionized Persian poetry to the marrow of its bones and opened a vast spectrum of creative reconception of poetic being. Against tremendous odds, antagonized by generations of hostile and mediocre contemporaries, Nīmā singlehandedly made a monumental case for a radical rethinking in the very constitutional configuration of sensibilities that make a particular narrative "poetic."

Nīmā radically questioned the very validity of all hegemonic prosodies and persuasively argued for what he considered the innate, "natural" musicality of the poetic narrative itself as it emerges from the creative imagination of the poet. Nīmā argued that the hegemonic dictation of no extrapoetic prosody should hamper that innate force and presence of the poetic narrative. Futile attempts have been made to trace the aesthetic origins of the Nimaic revolution to vague and conventional references to "The West." The fact, however, is that in his major theoretical manifesto, *Arzish-i iḥsāsāt dar zindagī-yi hunarmand* (The Significances of Sensibilities in the Life of [an] Artist), Nīmā makes as many references to Russian, French, and German poets and theorists as he does to classical Persian and Arab prosodists. His argument, theoretical as indeed the very reading of his poetic narrative, is sui generis. Undoubtedly Nīmā's knowledge of his contemporary Russian and French poetics was as much a part of his radical rethinking of the Persian poetics as his knowledge of his own classical heritage. But no amount of historical or geographical genealogy or archeology can account for the unprecedented individuality of his poetic revolution. Nīmā changed the landscape and the topology of Persian poetic imagination, the very terms and thrusts of its worldly engagements.

Nīmā had to suffer the consequences of his poetic genius. With few but crucial exceptions, his contemporaries had no taste or patience for his radical reconfiguration of Persian poetics. Powerful and influential neoclassicists vehemently opposed him. But a group of young but extremely talented poets picked up where he had left off. Chief among these young followers is Aḥmad Shāmlū (b. 1925), who pushed the Nimaic poetics to even fresher, physically more tangible, edges. The radical physicality of Shāmlū's poetry, and ultimately his unbelievably daring experimentations with the full potentialities of Persian language, his poetico-politics, gave a supremely elegant twist to every possibility of poetic materialism available in Persian. In his hand, and through the effervescent force of his creative imagination, Persian poetic drive was pushed to exhilarating edges of radical narrativity. In his poetry, all extrapoetic realities dissolve and rise obediently to meet the poetic.

Another major voice in the Nīmāic movement was the most eloquent feminine voice in the entire history of Persian poetry: Furūgh Farrukhzād (1935–1967). No woman had hitherto dared to subvert so much so publicly in such a short span of time. Furūgh's decidedly feminine voice settled a millennium-old account of suffocating silence imposed on the Iranian woman in her relentlessly patriarchal society. Furūgh's naked, exquisite, beautiful, and daring subversion of Persian cultural taboos was so radical that it would take generations of her readers to map out the range of physical sensibilities with which she dared to experiment (see Hillmann, 1987).

Mahdī Akhavān-i Ṣāliṣ (1928–1990) was yet another forceful poetic voice that successfully and convincingly combined the best and the most eloquent potentialities of the Khurasani poetic tradition with an unflinching political commitment to radical reutilization of the Persian poetic. The result was a nuanced and barely noticeable balance between a poetic narrative that had nothing but its own story to tell and a relentless engagement with the political. Akhavān's poetry is a nostalgic reading of a glorious past that may or may not have been there and yet was narratively put there to make the present read a particularly powerful song. His poetry then became the conscience of a whole generation of poetic politics: a poetry that took zest and momentum from life, a politics that was embedded in the humanizing force of poetry.

In the same category of the master lyricists of the "New" Persian poetic imagination is Suhrāb Sipihrī (1928–1980), who gave momentous, elegant, and stunningly beautiful expression to a radical physicality in his poetry. A painter-poet, Sipihrī utilized almost identical strokes of simple, articulate, and deceptively naive staccatos to create sheer astonishment at the awesome physicality of the mere act of living, of the forceful, absolutist, conception of existence.

In many respects a follower of Akhavān in poetic diction and sentiment is Ismāᶜīl Khū'ī (b. 1938) who, from an early romantic beginning, grew to fruition in the post-Islamic Revolution period as a poet of massive rhetorical skills put squarely in the service of a severe, almost debilitating, anticlerical sentiment. Khū'ī's poetry in the 1980s emerged as the most articulate voice of Iranian diaspora in total disillusion with the consequences of the Islamic Revolution in Iran (1978–1980).

Two unusually gifted poets—Aḥmad Riẓā Aḥmadī (b. 1940) and Manūchihr Yaktāᶜī (b. 1921)—took the Nīmāic revolution in poetic narrative to yet another direction. Fuller experimentations with the aesthetic possibilities of the poetic narrative became paramount in Aḥmadī's poetry. Having lived most of his adult life in New York, Manūchihr Yaktāᶜī, yet another painter-poet in the Nimaic tradition, has been in a state of almost obsession with narrative experimentation. Coming to him from a distance, as it were, has made the poetic narrative of Nīmā something of a linguistic fable for Yaktāᶜī, folding and unfolding itself in self-descriptive directions.

Closer to popular taste but with no particularly significant connection to these phenomenal revolutions in Persian poetics were a number of poets, such as Farīdūn Mushītī (b. 1926), Farīdūn Tavallulī (b. 1919), Hushang Ibtihāj (H. I. Sāyah, b. 1927), Sīmīn Bihbahānī (b. 1927), Nādir Nādirpūr (b. 1929), and Manūchihr Shaybānī (b. 1923). At times virtuoso performers of pictoral and mental imageries, these poets had no particularly powerful connection to their time and space and spoke mostly of outdated and even irrelevant sentimentalities. The effective shock of the Islamic Revolution had a considerable impact on some of these poets—for example, Hushang Ibtihāj and Sīmīn Bihbahānī—but not to such a degree as to cause a drastic, qualitative change in their poetic diction or the narrative force of their creative imagination.

The Islamic Revolution in Iran subjected Persian poetry to a major political shock. The leading poets of the early 1970s, whose level and mode of discourse was established by the political-poetic power of Aḥmad Shāmlū, fully participated in the course of the revolution so far as they thought it a monumental, secular event. In the wake of the revolution, Shāmlū moved to London and published *Īrānshahr,* a journal that took full political and intellectual account of the event. After the success of the revolution and the commencement of its islamization, Shāmlū moved back to Iran and started a new journal, *Jumʿah,* to which the leading secular intellectuals contributed.

With the successful islamization of the revolution, Persian poetic imagination went into a major period of hiatus characterized by effective neoclassical islamization (characterized by Ṭāhirah Ṣaffārzādah), silent secular commitment (represented by Aḥmad Shāmlu), and radical exilic defiance (best voiced in the most recent poems of Ismāʿīl Khū'ī).

In the meantime, a new generation of Iranian poets are coming of age and fruition—some inside Iran, others in exile. This generation is too young to remember with any degree of intensity the particular package of sensibility carried for long by the no longer so "New" poetry. The rising spirit that informs and animates this generation is bilingual to the soul of its apparition.

Modern Persian fiction received its greatest narrative and aesthetic impetus from Muḥammad ʿAlī Jamālzādah (b. 1892) and Sādiq Hidāyat (1903–1951). With such works as *Yakī būd, Yakī nabūd,* and *Sar-va tāh yik karbās,* Jamālzādah successfully brought earlier attempts at a simplified prose to an effective and promising conclusion. He built on decades of revolutionary, simplified prose from the Constitutional period and rescued the suffocating Persian prose from the shallow formalism of the Qājār period. While Jamālzādah's simple, effective, colorful colloquialism provided ample opportunity for Persian prose to cultivate expressions of diverse social types and groupings, Hedayat took that prose and drove it into the darkest and most unexplored corners of Iranian communal and individual sensibilities. Hidāyat's *The Blind Owl* is the first and the most successful attempt to reach for and achieve a literary narrative in frightful tune with irreducible (at times even ahistorical) anxieties of being. Publication of *The Blind Owl* in the early 1940s was followed by other novellas and short stories, chief among them *Ḥājjī āqā* (1945). Although many prominent writers—for example, Buzurg ʿAlavī (b. 1904), Ṣādiq Chūbak (b. 1916), Maḥmūd Iʿtimādzādah (b. 1915), and Jalāl Āl-i Aḥmad (1923–1969)—followed Hidāyat's socially conscious fiction, no other author matched, let alone surpassed, him in his existential insights in *The Blind Owl.* The only exception to this assertion is perhaps the brilliant achievements of Ibrāhīm Gulistān (b. 1922), who took up and developed a particularly compelling aspect of Hidāyat's legacy, namely, an unswerving penchant for the primacy of the aesthetic narrative. In such brilliant staccatos as "Az rūzgār-i raftah ḥikāyat" and "Jūī va dīvār-i tishnah," Gulistān created and sustained flawless sketches of a descriptive self-signification that always surpassed the traces of its own acts of significations. What exactly these highly stylized, flawlessly crafted, descriptions "meant" or "signified" almost fades under the dazzling brilliance of the aesthetic act of narrativity itself.

Standing exactly at the opposite side of Gulistān is Āl-i Aḥmad, who took Hidāyat's social realism and carried it to thinly fictionalized political mainfestos. Infinitely more effective as an essayist and an engagé intellectual, Āl-i Aḥmad's perhaps most successful fiction was *Nūn va al-qalam* (translated as *By the Pen*), in which he borrowed from traditional narratives to depict a revolutionary society in the wake of a popular uprising.

In the same generation, and somewhere between Gulistān's aesthetic narrativity and Āl-i Aḥmad's excessive realism, is Ṣādiq Chūbak, one of the most prolific writers. In such works as *Tanqsīr* and *Antarī kih lūtiash murdah būd,* Chūbak paid critical attention to the narrative realism of his art. Having been born and bred in southern Iran, Chūbak was chiefly responsible for introducing a whole new repertoire of southern sensibilities to modernist Persian fiction, a trend that was then successfully pursued by Aḥmad Maḥmūd in such works as *Hamsāyah hā* and *Zā'in dar zīr-i bārān.*

The more aesthetically serious work that commenced with Hidāyat and continued with Gulistān was subsequently picked up by perhaps the most brilliant contemporary writer, Hushang Gulshīrī (b. 1938). Gulshīrī's *Prince Iḥtijāb* reads in the same vein as Ḥidāyat's *The Blind Owl* and Gulistān's "Az rūzgār-i raftah ḥikāyat." Manipulating the tormented consciousness of a Qājār prince, Gulshīrī masterfully re-creates in *Prince Iḥtijāb* the social and psychological malaise of a whole cycle of corruption and decay. Love and loyalty, power and seduction, corruption and decay, are the undercurrents of a narrative labyrinth that weaves its own story around itself.

Sīmīn Dānishvar (b. 1921), Shahrnūsh Pārsīpūr (b. 1946), Munīrū Ravānīpūr, and Mahshīd Amīrshāhī (b.

1940) are the four leading women writers who have contributed massively to a strong, pronounced, and articulate feminine consciousness in modern Persian fiction (for a detailed study, see Milani, 1992). Dānishvar's *Savāshun* became the most widely read fiction in the entire history of the genre. Shahrnūsh Pārsīpūr's *Ṭūbā' va maʿna-yi shab* and *Zanān bi-dun-i Mardān* explored deeply into the labyrinth of a feminine consciousness in history and politics. Ravānīpūr's *Ahl-i Gharg* opened a whole new vista of southern mythical sensibilities in Persian fiction. In this respect, Ravānīpūr's fiction sided itself with a tradition that claimed Ṣādiq Chūbak and Aḥmad Maḥmūd among its founding members. Amīrshāhī's *Dar Haẕar* became a sensitive chronicle of a deep frustration with the religious and antisecular turns that the Iranian Revolution of 1979 took.

Publication of Mahmūd Dawlatābādī's ten-volume epic *Klidar* in the late 1970s must be considered a major event in the history of Persian fiction. Centered around a fictionalized version of a local hero in Khurasan, *Klidar* is a majestic narrative of legendary proportions. Dawlatābādī constructs a full-bodied epic in which love and adventure, atrocity and nobility are woven together and led toward a uniquely enobling tragedy.

From such local traditions as romance literature, *shāhnāmah-khvānī, taʿziyah, rū-ḥawẕī, siyāh-bāzī, khayāl-bāzī, ʿarūsak bāzī,* and *khaymah shāh bāzī,* in conjunction with widespread exposure to other theatrical traditions in the Arab world, India, Central Asia, China, Turkey, and eastern and western Europe, a thriving Persian drama emerged in the middle of the nineteenth century. In the wake of the Constitutional Revolution of 1906–1911, drama took center stage in the Persian creative imagination. Mīrzā Fatḥ ʿAlī Akhūndzādah (1812–1878) and Mīrzā Malkom Khān (d. 1908) were the forerunners of social realism and political satire in Persian drama. Translations from Russian, French, and English plays increased dramatically after World War II; and such talented actors as ʿAbd al-Ḥusayn Nūshīn gave institutional recognition to the genre. But a major culmination of Persian drama is to be seen in the 1960s and 1970s, when leading playwrights such as Ghulām Ḥusayn Sāʿidī (1935–1985) ("Gawhar-i Murād" was his nom de plume), Akbar Rādī, Bahrām Bayẕā'ī (b. 1938), and ʿAbbās Naʿlbandiyān, among many others, took full advantage of drama to address prevailing social and political issues. Sāʿidī, in particular, explored the deepest corners of anxiety (he was a trained psychologist) in local characters and cultures beyond the reach of Tehran-based café intellectuals. Bahrām Bayẕā'ī very soon linked his interest in theater to a brilliant directorial career in cinema and created a whole spectrum of dramatic and visual sensibilities entirely his own. Another playwright/director of considerable talent is Parvīz Ṣayyād (b. 1937), who successfully bridged a widening gap between premodern and modern, as well as between popular and avant-garde art (see Dabashi, 1992).

The Iranian Revolution of 1979 and its immediate islamization by the victorious faction introduced the combined forces of a triple imperative in the Persian literary imagination: the first formed by those who opted for an exilic life over the militant censorship of a theocracy; and the second shaped by those who ideologically, or as a matter of principle, chose not to oppose the political formation of a theocracy; and the third grouped by those secular intellectuals who preferred to stay inside Iran. Ismāʿīl Khū'ī and Ghulām Ḥusayn Sāʿidī are prime examples of Iranian literati who left their country and chose the bitter tongue of expatriate intellectuals. Ṭāhirah Ṣaffārzādah and Shams Āl-i Aḥmad (the brother of Jalāl Āl-i Aḥmad) are among those members of the literati who wholeheartedly celebrated the Islamic Revolution, remained in Iran, and continued to be productive in the new political environment. But not all who have remained inside Iran advocate or even accept the radical islamization of the literary imagination. Aḥmad Shāmlu, Aḥmad Riẕā Aḥmadī, Hushang Gulshīrī, Mahmūd Dawlatābādī, Sīmīn Dānishvar, Shāhrnūsh Pārsīpūr, and Bahrām Bayẕā'ī, among scores of other poets, novelists, playwrights, and filmmakers, continue to produce in active or tacit celebration of an autonomous creative imagination. In the meantime, the younger generation of poets, novelists, dramatists, and critics are charting their own separate ways into the future. Inside Iran the radical implications of an Islamic revolution have stirred up the deepest emotions and anxieties. A flood of literary and visual outputs marks the younger generation's creative response to a groundbreaking revolution, to unfathomable sacrifices during the eight-year war with Iraq (1980–1988), and to the continued anxieties of a collective imagination still not at peace with itself. Iranians live in exile in all parts of the world, and whatever the language of their host-culture, they try to teach their children Persian, and these children are growing up to express the particular configuration of their history and identity in Persian and in the language of their adopted culture. Young poets, such as Ru'yā Hakkākiyān, ʿAlī Zarrīn, and Ramīn

Aḥmadī (all outside their homeland) and Qāsim Ahanīn-Jān, Aḥmad ʿAlī-pūr, Mihrī Murādī, Bīzhan Jalālī, Zuhrah Khāliqī, and ʿAlī Mu'minī, among scores of others (all inside Iran), are the emerging signs, the dancing rays of a rising sun, whose full, shimmering proportion and colorful disposition, its nature and orientation, are not yet in full view.

[*See also* Devotional Poetry; Iran.]

BIBLIOGRAPHY

Amoretti, B. S. "Sects and Heresies." In *The Cambridge History of Iran,* vol. 4 *The Period from the Arab Invasion to the Saljuqs,* edited by R. N. Frye, Cambridge, 1975.

Arberry, A. J. *Classical Persian Literature.* London, 1958.

Arjomand, Said Amir. *The Shadow of God and the Hidden Imam: Religion, Political Order, and Societal Change in Shi'ite Iran from the Beginning to 1800.* Chicago, 1984.

Aryānpūr, Yaḥyā. *Az Ṣabā tā Nīmā.* 2 vols. Tehran, 1357/1978.

ʿAṭṭār, F. *The Conference of the Birds.* Translated by Afkham Darbandi and Dick Davis. New York, 1984.

Bābā Ṭāhir. *The Lament of Baba Tahir: Being the Rubaiyat of Baba Tahir Hamadani (Uryan).* Translated by Edward Heron-Allen and Elizabeth A. C. Brenton. London, 1902.

Bahār, Malik al-Shūʿarā Muḥammad Taqī. *Sabkshināsī.* 3 vols. Tehran, 1331/1952.

Bausani, Alessandro. *The Persians.* London, 1962.

Boyce, Mary. "The Parthian *gosan* and the Iranian Minstrel Tradition." *Journal of the Royal Asiatic Society* (1957).

Browne, Edward G. *A Literature History of Persia.* 4 vols. Cambridge, 1902–1924.

Dabashi, Hamid, ed. *Parviz Sayyad's Theater of Diaspora.* Costa Mesa, Calif., 1992.

De Bruijn, J. T. P. *Of Piety and Poetry: The Interaction of Religion and Literature in the Life and Works of Hakim Sana'i of Ghazna.* Leiden, 1983.

Ferdowsi, A. (Firdawsī). *The Legend of Seyavash.* Translated by Dick Davis. New York, 1993.

Furūzānfar, Badīʿ al-Zamān. *Sukhan va sukhanvarān.* Tehran, 1350/1971.

Gurgānī, F. A. *Vis va Ramin.* Edited, annotated, and with an introduction by M. J. Mahjoub. Tehran, 1959.

Gurgānī, F. A. *Vis and Ramin.* Translated by George Morrison, New York, 1972.

Ḥāfiẓ, S. *Poems from the Divan of Hafiz.* Translated by Gertrude M. L. Bell. London, 1897.

Hammer-Purgstall, J. F. von. *Geschichte der Schönen Redekünste Persiens.* Vienna, 1818.

Hillmann, Michael C. *A Lonely Woman.* Washington, D.C., 1987.

Jāmī, A. *Salaman and Absal.* Translated by Edward FitzGerald. Cambridge, 1956.

Karimi-Hakkak, Ahmad. *An Anthology of Modern Persian Poetry.* New York, 1978.

Khayyam, Omar (ʿUmar Khayyām). *Rubaiyat.* Translated by Edward FitzGerald. London, 1859.

Levy, Reuben. *An Introduction to Persian Literature.* New York, 1969.

Literature East and West 20 (1976). Special issue: Major Voices in Contemporary Persian Literature, edited by Michael C. Hillmann.

Meisami, Julie Scott. *Medieval Persian Court Poetry.* Princeton, 1987.

Melikian-Chirvani, A. S. "Le legs littéraire du Bouddhisme iranien." In *Le monde iranien et l'Islam,* edited by J. Aubin, vol. 2, pp. 1–71. Paris, 1974.

Melikian-Chirvani, A. S. "The Buddhist Ritual in the Literature of Early Islamic Iran." In *South Asian Archaeology,* edited by B. Allchin, pp. 272–279. Cambridge, 1984.

Milani, Farzaneh. *Veils and Words: The Emerging Voices of Iranian Women Writers.* Syracuse, N.Y., 1992.

Muʿīn, Muḥammad. *Mazdayasnā va adab-i Fārsī.* 2 vols. Tehran, 1338/1959.

Rūmī, Jalāl al-Dīn. *The Mathnawi of Jalalu'ddin Rumi.* Edited, translated, and annotated by Reynold A. Nicholson. London, 1925–1940.

Rypka, Jan. *History of Iranian Literature* (1956). Dordrecht, 1968.

Sadighi, G. H. *Les Movements religioux iraniens au II et au III siecle de l'hegire.* Paris, 1938.

Ṣafā, Zabīḥ Allāh. *Ḥamāsah sarā'ī dar Īrān.* Tehran, 1321/1942.

Ṣafā, Zabīḥ Allāh. *Tārīkh-i adabīyāt dar Īrān.* 5 vols. Tehran, 1338–1364/1959–1985.

Schimmel, Annemarie. *A Two-Colored Brocade: The Imagery of Persian Poetry.* Chapel Hill, N.C., and London, 1992.

Schimmel, Annemarie, trans. *Make a Shield from Wisdom: Selected Verses from Nasir-i Khusraw's Divan.* London and New York, 1993.

Shafīʿī-Kadkanī, Muḥammad Riẓā. *Ṣuvar-i khayāl dar shiʿr-i Fārsī.* Tehran, 1349/1970.

Shahrastānī, ʿAbd al-Karīm al-. *Al-milal wa al-niḥal.* Tehran, 1358/1979.

Southgate, Minoo, ed. and trans. *Modern Persian Short Stories.* Washington, D.C., 1980.

Yarshater, Ehsan, ed. *Persian Literature.* Albany, N.Y., 1988.

Yūsufī, Ghulām Ḥusayn. *Chashmah-yi rawshan.* Tehran, 1369/1990.

HAMID DABASHI

PESANTREN. A type of school in Southeast Asia offering second-level training in Islamic subjects is termed *pesantren* on Java, *surau* on Sumatra, *pondok* on the Malay Peninsula, and *pandita* ("school") in the Philippines. *Pesantren* derives from the sixteenth century, when learning centers known as the "place of learning for the Islamic faithful (*santris*)," were established. *Surau* was a place for worship in early Southeast Asia, while *pondok* derives from the travelers' inns (Ar., *funduq*) of the Middle East. *Pandita* was the local term for a holy man in the Philippines.

By the seventeenth century the *pesantren* on Java had become alternate centers of authority to the princely courts. The courts stressed elaborate lifestyles based on Old Javanese values of refinement, while the *pesantren* stressed pious conduct and the hereafter. Each rival, however, usually recognized the legitimacy and societal role of the other. In Minangkabau the *surau* was likewise a center of authority outside the traditional communal units of society. In other places there seems to have been less social division between the court and the learning centers than existed in Java and Minangkabau.

In earlier times the *pesantren, surau, pondok,* and *pandita* schools were a rural phenomenon, interacting with local communities. Scholars provided education, gave advice to villagers, and legitimized local ceremonies. Some scholars were regarded as "blessed" and were consulted for cures and supernatural assistance during their lives and after death by cults at their tombs. Villagers supported *pesantren* with food and labor; in some places a poor tax, alms, and pious endowments were also given. In Malaysia support networks of parents provided assistance, and in all places learners often worked in the fields of the *pesantren,* since fees were seldom taken for learning per se. Today some *pesantren* are located in urban areas, and many rely on fees.

Pesantren are private ventures by scholars—called *kyai* on Java, *guru* on the Malay Peninsula, *pandita* in the southern Philippines, and *ʿālim* in most other places—usually with the assistance of their families. Many schools do not survive the founder, but others continue through several generations, with sons and sons-in-law succeeding to control and ownership. Prestige is gained by scholars through good contacts with other scholar families, some in Arabia, and also through pupils who establish new *pesantren* recognizing the original scholars as progenitors.

Learners in earlier times remained at a *pesantren* until they felt they had learned enough and then returned to society. Committed learners, often sons of scholars *(gus),* moved among *pesantren* whose scholars had reputations for special knowledge. Such travel allowed a learner the opportunity to marry a daughter of an established scholar, ensuring himself a place to teach and perhaps to succeed the older scholar. Today, additional training is obtained in Southeast Asia, South Asia, and the Middle East, often at Al-Azhar University in Egypt [*see* Azhar, Al-].

Historically, the intense education and worship schedule led to deep involvement of learners with their scholar, which produced strong loyalties and respect. In school and after departing, scholars could rely on their learners to answer a summons for aid, a factor of political importance at certain moments in history. In the Second Javanese War (1826–1830), the Acehnese War (1873–1903), and the Battle of Surabaya (1946) during the Indonesian revolution, scholars led their *santri*s into armed conflict against enemies who they believed threatened the Muslim community. Contemporary Indonesian Muslim intellectuals have lauded the anti-Dutch stance of the *pesantren* scholars, recognizing them as preservers of Indonesian and Islamic values during the colonial period.

Learning in *pesantren* is based on the "old books" *(kitab kuning)* of prominent scholars from the Muslim Middle Period (ca. 1250 to 1850), usually from the Shāfiʿī school of legal scholarship. Study has always included Arabic grammar *(naḥw)* and conjugation *(ṣarf),* Qur'ānic recitation *(qirā'ah),* Qur'ānic exegesis *(tafsīr),* theology *(tawḥīd),* jurisprudence *(fiqh),* ethics *(akhlāq),* logic *(manṭiq),* history *(tārīkh)* and mysticism *(taṣawwuf).* The *weton* or *ḥalaqah* system was used, in which learners sat in a semicircle before a seated scholar who called on them in turn for recitation. Learners at all levels of competence sat together, and the more accomplished assisted the less learned with their readings.

Change occurred slowly. Some learners studied in Mecca before becoming scholars and were influenced by thinking there. In this way the Naqshabandīyah order, with its balance between mysticism and legalism, became popular in nineteenth-century Southeast Asia. Wahhābī purism was introduced through the Minangkabau *surau*s in the early nineteenth century, and in the early twentieth century some schools came under the modernizing and spiritual reform of the Manār school of Egypt. There was locally induced change as well, for example in the reforms of Hasyim Asy'ari (d. 1947), who introduced new techniques for the study of Arabic.

In the twentieth century *pesantren* came under pressure from society and governments to adopt current teaching techniques and to include nonreligious subjects; many responded favorably. In Indonesia the Modern Pesantren at Gontor, for example, expanded to include training from elementary grades to the university level, with a mixed curriculum. Other *pesantren* converted to *madrasah*s or *sekolah*s within the Indonesian education system. Still others offered specialized training in agriculture, crafts, and business alongside traditional religious subjects.

In the southern Philippines the *pandita* schools gave way to more organized *madrasah*s promoted by Egyptian religious teachers in the 1950s. In Thailand in the 1960s, the *pondok* schools were united into a state-run system with a mixed curriculum. Losing pupils to government schools, *pondoks* in Malaysia sought accommodation with revivalist *(daʿwah)* activists in the 1970s to renew interest in Muslim education.

Although the value-oriented education of the *pesantren* remains respected by Southeast Asian Muslims, the *pesantren* still appears to be waning as an educational choice. Muslims increasingly feel compelled to send their children to government schools with modern curricula, believing they will be better prepared for the job market. Even children of scholars, who earlier formed the cadre of young scholars and their wives, are drawn by nonreligious education, so that fewer scholars are being trained, and there is a long-term decrease in the number of *pesantren*.

[*See also* Education, *articles on* Religious Education *and* Educational Institutions; Madrasah.]

BIBLIOGRAPHY

Azra, Azyumardi. "The Rise and Decline of the Minangkabau Surau." Master's thesis, Columbia University, 1988. Context of the *surau* in changing Minangkabau society.

Dhofier, Zamakhsyari. "Contemporary Features of Javanese Pesantren." *Mizan* (Jakarta) 2.1 (1984): 26–31. Basic description of life in a *pesantren;* for the general reader.

Federspiel, Howard M. *Muslim Intellectuals and National Development in Indonesia*. Commack, N.Y., 1992. Contemporary views on the value of *pesantren* education and ways of improving it. See pages 171–184.

Mastura, Michael O. *Muslim Filipino Experience*. Quezon City, 1984. Philippine efforts to incorporate the *madrasah* into the public education system. See pages 93–107.

Nagata, Judith. *The Reflowering of Malaysian Islam*. Vancouver, B.C., 1984. Challenge to *pondoks* of nonreligious education in Malaysia. See pages 20–54.

Pitsuwan, Surin. *Islam and Malay Nationalism*. Bangkok, 1985. Transformation of the *pondoks* undertaken by the Thai government to integrate Muslim society into Thai culture. See pages 175–204.

Rahardjo, M. Dawam. *Pesantren dan Pembaharuan*. Jakarta, 1983. Leading Indonesian intellectuals outline the strengths and weaknesses of *pesantren* and suggest ways of making them vehicles for Indonesian modernization.

Steenbrink, K. A. *Pesantren, Madrasah, Sekolah*. Meppel, 1974. Development of Islamic education in twentieth-century Indonesia, with emphasis on the Islamic associations that were responsible for the principal changes.

HOWARD M. FEDERSPIEL

PHILIPPINES. In 1990 the Muslim population of the Philippines comprised between five and six million, or about 8.5 percent of the country's sixty-six million inhabitants. The vast majority of these Moros, as Philippine Muslims are called, live in the western and central parts of Mindanao island and the Sulu Archipelago. They are classified into twelve ethnolinguistic groups, the major ones being Maranao, Maguindanao, Tausug, Samal and Yakan. Agriculture and fishing are their main occupations. Some groups are noted for household industries such as brasswork and weaving as well as for trading activities. Their regions have practically no industrial base.

Muslim traders and preachers visited Sulu as early as the thirteenth century. Soon after, Muslim adventurers from the Malay region followed, intent on founding principalities in Sulu and Mindanao. When the Spaniards came to the Philippines in 1565 to establish a colony and convert the inhabitants to Catholicism, they were confronted by three Muslim principalities in the south: Sulu, Maguindanao, and Buayan. The Spaniards were able to capture Manila, a principality ruled by relatives of the sultan of Brunei, with comparative ease; but they were unable to conquer the southern sultanates.

In time the conquered inhabitants, named *indios* by the Spaniards, came to identify themselves as Catholics as well as subjects of the Spanish monarch. But the Muslims of the south, called *moros* by the Spaniards (because they had the same faith as the Moors of Spain), never shared this identity. Actually, in the more than three hundred years of intermittent warfare between Spaniards and Moros, the christianized natives invariably served in the military expeditions against Muslims.

In the latter half of the nineteenth century the Spanish colonial government abandoned its previous policy of conversion for one of merely imposing sovereignty over the Moros, in order to define its southern borders against possible encroachment by other Western powers. A decline in agricultural productivity, the disruption of traditional maritime commercial activities, the ravages of continuous wars, and gradual isolation finally induced the sultans and *datus* (chieftains) to enter into friendly treaties with the Spanish government—a process tending toward eventual absorption into the colony. But the Philippine revolutions of 1896 and 1898, which led the Spaniards to withdraw their troops from Muslim lands to concentrate them in the north, arrested this process. Subsequent Filipino revolutionary leaders' attempts to solicit Moro help against the Spaniards brought no tangible results, since the Muslims viewed both Spaniards and Christian Filipinos as their traditional foes.

Spain ceded the Philippines to the United States by

the Treaty of Paris of 1898. American military superiority forced recalcitrant *datus* to accept United States sovereignty. American officials left Islam and Moro customary law untouched unless they ran counter to the U.S. Constitution. When Filipinos started to be trained in self-government preparatory to eventual independence, sultans, *datus*, and Muslim religious leaders petitioned American officials for exclusion from the proposed independent state. They desired to remain distinct from Christian Filipinos, staying under American protection until they could have their own separate state. When the Philippine Republic was established in 1946, the Moros found themselves included in a political structure without their consultation or consent. In 1951 a Senate committee studying the causes of an alarming breakdown of law and order in Moro regions concluded that one factor was that most Moros did not identify themselves as Filipinos or agree with the national polity.

Meanwhile, stirrings of a heightened Islamic awareness were becoming more evident. Every year hundreds joined the *ḥajj* and returned to their communities with acquired prestige and increased religious fervor. New mosques and *madrasahs* were being built, often with aid from outside Muslim organizations. The Egyptian government offered scholarships for Moros to study at Al-Azhar University in Cairo. Some scholars transferred to other Cairo universities and the Egyptian military academy. Muslim teachers from abroad also came to teach for a few years. A new sense of pride and achievement arose among Moro youth, and a younger and better-educated local *ʿulamāʾ* emerged.

At the same time, conflict was being exacerbated by several factors: the increasing and unrestrained influx of Christian settlers to Muslim traditional lands, often with government support; continued national neglect of Moro economic and educational aspirations; subtle discrimination against Muslims' serving in top national offices; Moro leaders' loss of political power in their former bailiwicks; and severe land conflicts between Moros and Christian settlers. These forces progressively led to an increase in armed clashes between Christian and Muslim bands; the constabulary or army usually sided with the former. Moro cries of "genocide" elicited sympathy from the Muslim world. The proclamation of martial law by President Ferdinand Marcos in 1972, followed by military attempts to confiscate Moro arms, led to an open revolt. The most popularly supported liberation front was the Moro National Liberation Front (MNLF) with its military arm, the Bangsamoro Army (BMA) under the leadership of Nur Misuari, a former faculty member of the University of the Philippines. In 1977 it was given observer status in the Organization of the Islamic Conference (OIC).

Pressure from the OIC and mediation by Libya influenced the Philippine government and the MNLF to sign the Tripoli Agreement of 1976, which provided for some form of autonomy for thirteen provinces with sizable Muslim populations. But neither the autonomy granted by the Marcos regime in 1977 nor that under the administration of Corazon Aquino in 1989 have satisfied OIC expectations or MNLF demands. In early 1989 the MNLF renewed its demand for secession while seeking membership status in the OIC.

The Moro uprising, along with diplomatic pressure from Muslim countries, had nevertheless persuaded the government to grant various concessions. In 1973 Arabic was authorized as a medium of instruction in schools attended by Muslims, and the two ʿĪds were proclaimed legal holidays for Muslims. In 1977, a national Code of Muslim Personal Laws, with provision for a *muftī*, was promulgated, although not all of the *sharīʿah* district and circuit courts provided for have yet been established. The following year, the Philippine Pilgrimage Authority was created to regulate and facilitate the annual *ḥajj*; during the 1980s these pilgrimages involved an average of two thousand pilgrims yearly. By 1980 most of the top MNLF field commanders who had come to pledge their loyalty to the republic had been rewarded with political positions or economic opportunities. In 1981 a Ministry (now Office) of Islamic Affairs was created. Since 1982 there have been government efforts to upgrade the *madrasah* system while integrating some *madrasahs* into the national educational system. (Presently, there are about fifteen hundred *madrasahs*, but the majority do not go beyond the secondary level.) There was also an increase in state scholarships for Moro students and more appointments of qualified Muslims to top positions in the Justice and Foreign Affairs departments. Socioeconomic development projects and refugee rehabilitation, albeit modest, are an ongoing process. Firm guarantees that Islam will remain unmolested, as well as a more realistic form of autonomy, may further dilute the current agitation for secession on the part of the Moro population.

[*See also* Islam, *article on* Islam in Southeast Asia and the Pacific; Moro National Liberation Front; Organization of the Islamic Conference.]

BIBLIOGRAPHY

George, T. J. S. *Revolt in Mindanao: The Rise of Islam in Philippine Politics*. Kuala Lumpur, 1980.

Gowing, Peter Gordon. *Mandate in Moroland: The American Government of Muslim Filipinos, 1899–1920*. Quezon City, 1977.

Gowing, Peter Gordon. *Muslim Filipinos: Heritage and Horizons*. Quezon City, 1979.

Gowing, Peter Gordon, and Robert D. McAmis, eds. *The Muslim Filipinos: Their History, Society, and Contemporary Problems*. Manila, 1974.

Jocano, F. Landa, ed. *Filipino Muslims: Their Social Institutions and Cultural Achievements*. Quezon City, 1983.

Kiefer, Thomas M. *The Tausug: Violence and Law in a Philippine Moslem Society*. New York, 1972.

Majul, Cesar Adib. *Muslims in the Philippines*. Quezon City, 1973.

Majul, Cesar Adib. *The Contemporary Muslim Movement in the Philippines*. Berkeley, 1985.

CESAR ADIB MAJUL

PHILOSOPHY. From its genesis twelve hundred years ago to today, Islamic philosophy *(al-ḥikmah; al-falsafah)* has been one of the major intellectual traditions within the Islamic world, and it has influenced and been influenced by many other intellectual perspectives including scholastic theology *(kalām)* and doctrinal Sufism *(al-maʿrifah; ʿirfān)*. The life of Islamic philosophy did not terminate with Ibn Rushd nearly eight hundred years ago, as thought by Western scholarship for several centuries; rather, its activities continued strongly during the later centuries, particularly in Persia and other eastern lands of Islam, and it was revived in Egypt during the last century.

Islamic philosophy was born of philosophical speculation on the heritage of Greco-Alexandrian philosophy, which was made available in Arabic in the third century A.H./ninth century CE by Muslims who were immersed in the teachings of the Qur'ān and lived in a universe in which revelation was a central reality. In contrast to the Greeks, Islamic philosophers concentrated on "prophetic philosophy," which in turn influenced deeply the philosophical life of the other two members of Abrahamic monotheism, namely, Judaism and Christianity. The Qur'ān, as well as *ḥadīth*s, served as the central source of Islamic philosophical speculation for centuries. In later Islamic philosophy the sayings of the Shīʿī imam also played a major role, especially in the works of Ṣadr al-Dīn Shīrāzī (Mullā Ṣadrā). Far from being simply Greek philosophy in Arabic and Persian, Islamic philosophy integrated certain elements of Greek philosophy into the Islamic perspective, creating new philosophical schools. Although Islamic philosophy drew from the Greek sources, which Muslims considered to be the fruit of earlier revelations associated with such figures as the prophet Idrīs (Hermes), it belonged to an independent philosophical universe of discourse.

The Early Peripatetics. The early centuries of Islamic philosophy were marked by the appearance of several schools of thought. The most prominent school, which is often identified with Islamic philosophy as such in Western sources, is the *mashshā'ūn* (Peripatetic). This school is not simply Aristotelian, as the name might indicate, but marks a synthesis of Islamic tenets, Aristotelianism, and Neoplatonism. Its founder is Abū Yaʿqūb al-Kindī (d. around AH 260/873 CE), the "Philosopher of the Arabs." Some Islamic sources have spoken of the Persian philosopher Abū al-ʿAbbās Īrānshahrī as the first Muslim to have written on philosophy, but nothing survives of his works save a few fragments. In contrast, a number of al-Kindī's works have reached us, some only in Hebrew and Latin, for he was well known in the West. Al-Kindī, like most of the early Peripatetics, was at once a philosopher and scientist. Although much of his voluminous corpus has been lost, enough has survived to reveal his mastery in both domains. Al-Kindī was the first Islamic thinker to grapple with the problem of the expression of Peripatetic thought in Arabic. He also confronted one of the central problems of philosophy in the monotheistic world, namely, harmonization of faith and reason. Among his philosophical works his treatises on the intellect, *Fī al-ʿaql* (The Intellect), and metaphysics, *Fī al-falsafah al-ūlā* (On Metaphysics), were particularly influential in the Muslim world; *Fī al-ʿaql,* known as *De Intellectu* in Latin, also had a widespread influence in medieval Europe.

Most of al-Kindī's immediate students were more significant as scientists than philosophers, and his real successor on the scene was not among them; rather, this title must be given to Abū Naṣr al-Fārābī (d. 339/950), who hailed from Khurasan in Central Asia. Many consider al-Fārābī to be the real founder of Peripatetic philosophy, and it was he more than al-Kindī who formulated Arabic philosophical language and wrote about the relation between the Arabic language and the expression of Aristotelian logic. He commented on Aristotle's *Organon* and is the father of formal logic in the Islamic world. He also sought to synthesize the political philosophy of Plato and Islamic political thought in his masterpiece, *Kitāb arā' ahl al-madīnah al-fāḍilah* (The Book of the Opinions of the Citizens of the Virtuous City), and is considered to be the founder of Islamic political philosophy. Al-Fārābī also wrote of the harmony between the views of Plato and Aristotle and on various metaphysical and epistemological questions. He is, moreover, the first Islamic philosopher to systematize the emanation scheme *(fayḍ)* of the ten intellects from the One, by which Peripatetic philosophy is known.

After al-Fārābī, Khurasan gradually became the major center of philosophical activity, but throughout the fourth century AH/tenth century CE Baghdad continued as an important center, following the earlier activities of al-Kindī. In the second half of the tenth century, however, the philosophical scene in Baghdad turned mostly to the study of logic under the guidance of Abū Sulaymān al-Sijistānī, who was known as al-Manṭiqī ("the Logician"). Meanwhile Abū al-Ḥasan al-ʿĀmirī from Khurasan was developing the Fārābīan teachings further and adding a new chapter of his own to Islamic philosophy by attempting to incorporate certain pre-Islamic Iranian ideas into his political philosophy.

Early Peripatetic philosophy reached its peak soon after al-ʿĀmirī with another Persian philosopher, Abū ʿAlī al-Ḥusayn ibn ʿAbd Allāh ibn Sīnā (369–428/980–1037), usually known as Ibn Sīnā (Avicenna). Often considered the greatest Islamic philosopher, Ibn Sīnā created a vast synthesis of Peripatetic thought in his *Kitāb al-shifā'* (The Book of Healing), which dominated many dimensions of Islamic thought for centuries. His ontological distinction between *wujūb* (necessity) and *imkān* (contingency) became central to Islamic thought and also deeply influenced Jewish and Christian philosophy and theology, as did his integration of the study of the three kingdoms within the scheme of the great chain of being (that is, the scheme that places all creatures in a chain or levels of being stretching from the dust to the highest angel).

Ibn Sīnā's major works, which also included *Kitāb al-najāh* (The Book of Salvation) and his last philosophical masterpiece, *Kitāb al-ishārāt wa-al-tanbīhāt* (The Book of Directives and Remarks), were widely read by defenders and opponents of Islamic philosophy alike. Moreover, Ibn Sīnā also wrote certain "visionary recitals" and philosophico-mystical treatises that contain what he called *al-ḥikmah al-mashriqīyah* ("Oriental philosophy"), which is of great importance if one looks upon the later tradition of Islamic philosophy.

Ismāʿīlī Philosophy. Featuring an emphasis on *ta'wīl* (spiritual hemeneutics), the Ismāʿīlī school of philosophy, associated with the Ismāʿīlī branch of Shiism, saw philosophy as an esoteric knowledge associated with the inner meaning of religion. It drew its ideas from Islamic esoterism and Neoplatonism, as well as both Hermeticism and Neopythagoreanism. The first work of this school, the *Umm al-kitāb* (The Archetypal Book), belongs to the second century AH/eighth century CE and is supposed to be the record of conversations between the fifth Shīʿī imam, Muḥammad al-Bāqir, and his students. On the basis of this early Shīʿī gnosis, Ismāʿīlī philosophy developed during the next two centuries and reached its full flowering in the tenth and eleventh centuries with such figures as Abū Yaʿqūb al-Sijistānī, Ḥamīd al-Dīn al-Kirmānī (often called the Ismāʿīlī Ibn Sīnā), the author of *Rāḥat al-ʿaql* (Repose of the Intellect), and finally Nāṣir-i Khusraw (d. around 470/1077), perhaps the greatest of the Ismāʿīlī philosophers. The Ismāʿīlī philosophers played an important role in the rise of Persian as the second major philosophical language of Islam, and Nāṣir-i Khusraw, the author of the major work *Jāmiʿ al-ḥikmatayn* (The Sum of Two Wisdoms), wrote all of his works in Persian. Ibn Sīnā, however, was the pioneer in the use of Persian as a philosophical language, having written *Dānish-nāmah-yi ʿalā'ī* (The Book of Science Dedicated to ʿAlā' al-Dawlah), the first work of Peripatetic philosophy in Persian.

The *Rasā'il* (Treatises) of the Ikhwān al-Ṣafā' (Brethren of Purity) is a collection of fifty-one treatises closely associated with Ismāʿīlī circles. These treatises, which appeared in the tenth century in Basra, have a strong Neopythagorean color. They were widely read by later philosophers and even theologians such as al-Ghazālī who wrote against the Peripatetics.

Independent Philosophers during the Early Centuries. Although Islamic philosophy is predominantly associated with schools which transcend the individual, the early centuries did produce a few independent philosophers who wielded some influence. The first among them is Muḥammad ibn Zakarīyā al-Rāzī (d. around 320/932), known in Latin as Rhazes, the greatest Muslim physician after Ibn Sīnā, who was also a philosopher known especially for his denial of the necessity of prophecy. He was strongly attacked by the Ismāʿīlīs for this view, as well as for positing "five eternal principles" consisting of the Demiurge, the Universal Soul, *Materia Prima*, Space, and Time. Another independent philosopher and one of Islam's greatest scientists, Abū Rayḥān al-Bīrūnī (d. 421/1030), held another philosophical view but admired al-Rāzī's scientific works. Al-Bīrūnī's most important philosophical contribution was his criticism of Avicennian natural philosophy, as well as his introduction of Hindu philosophy into the Islamic world. Finally, an important independent philosopher Aḥmad Ibn Miskūyah (Miskawayh; d. 421/1030) wrote the first major Islamic work on philosophical ethics, *Tahdhīb al-akhlāq* (Purification of Morals), as well as a book entitled *Jāvīdān khirad* (Philosophia Perennis).

Theologians against Philosophers. From the eleventh to the thirteenth century, the domination of Western Asia by Seljuks led to the eclipse of philosophy in the eastern lands of Islam. The caliphate, supported by the Seljuks, preferred the teaching of *kalām* in the *madrasahs* (Islamic schools) to philosophy, although *kalām* itself developed over time in a more philosophical form. During this period, the only notable philosopher in the eastern lands was the Persian poet and mathematician Omar Khayyám. The major theologians of this era, such as Abū Ḥāmid Muḥammad al-Ghazālī (d. 505/1111), Abū al-Fatḥ al-Shahrastānī (d. 548/1153), and Fakhr al-Dīn al-Rāzī (d. 606/1210), wrote treatises against Peripatetic and Ismāʿīlī philosophy.

The most famous attack against the *falāsifah* came from the great Ṣūfī theologian al-Ghazālī, who, however, dealt with philosophical themes himself and even composed treatises on formal logic. In his autobiography, *Al-munqidh min al-ḍalāl* (The Deliverance from Error), al-Ghazālī criticized the Peripatetic philosophers severely. Then he summarized their views in his *Maqāṣid al-falāsifah* (The Purposes of the Philosophers), which caused the Latin Schoolmen to think of al-Ghazālī himself as a Peripatetic. Finally, in his *Tahāfut al-falāsifah* (Incoherence of the Philosophers), he sought to demolish the views of the philosophers, accusing them of deviating from Islam in their denial of the createdness of the world, God's knowledge of particulars, and bodily resurrection. Al-Ghazālī's attack had the effect of curtailing the power of rationalism in Islamic philosophy, but it did not bring rational philosophy to an end, as some have thought. [*See the biography of Ghazālī.*]

The influence of Fakhr al-Dīn al-Rāzī on the technical discussions of later Islamic philosophy was even greater than that of al-Ghazālī. Al-Rāzī's most important attack against Peripatetic philosophy came in the form of his detailed criticism of Ibn Sīnā's *Kitāb al-ishārāt* in a work entitled *Shahr al-ishārāt* (The Commentary upon the Ishārāt), to which Naṣīr al-Dīn al-Ṭūsī (d. 672/1274) was to write the celebrated response that resuscitated Avicennian philosophy. In the fourteenth century this central debate was carried further by Quṭb al-Dīn al-Rāzī in his *Al-muḥākamāt* (Trials), in which he sought to judge between the commentaries of Fakhr al-Dīn al-Rāzī and al-Ṭūsī.

Islamic Philosophy in Spain. While philosophy was in eclipse in the eastern lands of Islam, it flourished in Islamic Spain. Islamic philosophy in the western lands of Islam actually began with the Ṣūfī philosopher Ibn Masarrah (d. 319/931), who profoundly influenced later thinkers. Another early thinker, Ibn Ḥazm (d. 454/1064), jurist, theologian, philosopher, and the author of one of the first Muslim works on comparative religion, also composed a famous treatise on Platonic love entitled *Ṭawq al-ḥamāmah* (The Ring of the Dove).

The first major philosopher in Spain and Morocco to follow the eastern *mashshāʾī* school was Ibn Bājjah (d. 533/1138), known both for his significant commentaries on Aristotelian physics and his philosophical masterpiece, *Tadbīr al-mutawaḥḥid* (The Regimen of the Solitary), which maintains that the perfect state can come about only through the perfection of individuals who can unite their intellects to the Active Intellect. His successor, Ibn Ṭufayl (d. 580/1185), who like Ibn Bājjah was also a political figure and scientist, is likewise known for one major opus, *Ḥayy ibn Yaqẓān* (Living Son of the Awake), which bears the name of Ibn Sīnā's visionary recital but with a different structure. The work deals in a symbolic language with the harmony between the inner illumination received by the intellect and the knowledge revealed through revelation. Ibn Ṭufayl's philosophical novel was translated immediately into Hebrew but not into medieval Latin until the seventeenth century, when it became famous in Europe as *Philosophies Autodidactus* and exercised wide influence in both philosophical and literary circles.

The most famous Islamic philosopher of the Maghrib, Ibn Rushd (523–595/1126–1198), known in Latin as Averroës, chief religious judge of Córdoba and a physician, wrote the most famous medieval commentaries on the Aristotelian corpus and was referred to in the West as "The Commentator." He set out to revive Peripatetic philosophy by responding to al-Ghazālī's *Tahāfut* in his own *Tahāfut al-tahāfut* (Incoherence of the Incoherence). In contrast to his image in the West as a rationalist "free-thinker" and author of the double-truth theory, Ibn Rushd was a pious Muslim who set out to harmonize faith and reason, especially in his *Faṣl al-maqāl* (The Decisive Treatise). His influence in the West, however, was greater than in the Islamic world, where the later destiny of philosophy was more closely associated with the name of Ibn Sīnā.

After Ibn Rushd, Islamic philosophy began to wane in the Maghrib but did not disappear completely. ʿAbd al-Ḥaqq ibn Sabʿīn (d. 669/1270) wrote a number of important treatises based on the doctrine of *waḥdat al-wujūd* (the transcendent unity of being), and the Tunisian ʿAbd al-Raḥmān Ibn Khaldūn (d. 780/1379) established the philosophy of history in his *Al-muqaddimah* (Prolegomena). The most important of these later figures from the Maghrib, however, was Muḥyi al-Dīn ibn ʿArabī (d. 638/1240), expositor of Ṣūfī metaphysics. Although not a philosopher in the sense of *faylasūf,* he is one of the greatest expositors of mystical philosophy in any time and clime, and he exercised a profound influence on Sufism as well as Islamic philosophy. [*See the biographies of Ibn Khaldūn and Ibn al-ʿArabī.*]

Suhrawardī and the School of Illumination. A new school of philosophy, which can more properly be called *theosophy* in the original sense of this term, was established by Shihāb al-Dīn Suhrawardī (d. 587/1191), who considered discursive philosophy as developed by Ibn Sīnā to be only the first, necessary step in the attainment of true philosophy, which must also be based on intellectual intuition or *ishrāq* (illumination). Suhrawardī integrated Platonic philosophy, Neoplatonism, the wisdom of the ancient Persians, especially Mazdaean angelology, and Avicennian philosophy in the matrix of Islamic gnosis to create a powerful new school of thought. His works, written in both Arabic and Persian, include many treatises written in a symbolic rather than discursive language, and they culminate in his masterpiece, *Ḥikmat al-ishrāq* (Theosophy of the Orient of Light). When he was executed in Aleppo, his followers went underground, but commentaries by Shams al-Dīn Muḥammad Shahrazūrī a generation later, followed by the better-known commentary of Quṭb al-Dīn Shīrāzī (d. 710/1311), revived the teachings of *ishrāq*. Henceforth, the school exercised a deep influence not only in Persia but also in Ottoman Turkey and the Indian subcontinent, and it continues as a living school of thought to this day.

Rapproachment between Various Schools of Thought. The period from the thirteenth to the sixteenth century marks the coming together of various schools of thought. The main arena of philosophical activity was Persia. Iraq and eastern Anatolia, which were closely related culturally to Persia, were also important centers. This period is witness to the revival of Ibn Sīnā's philosophy by Naṣīr al-Dīn al-Ṭūsī (d. 672/1273), who also wrote the most famous work on philosophical ethics in Persian, *Akhlāq-i nāṣirī* (The Naserean Ethics). Other notable figures of this rapproachment, such as Quṭb al-Dīn Shīrāzī, sought to integrate *mashshā'ī* and *ishrāqī* doctrines. These centuries also mark the spread of the doctrinal school of Sufism of Ibn ʿArabī, mostly through his foremost student Ṣadr al-Dīn Qūnawī and the latter's students and successors, such as Mu'ayyid al-Dīn al-Jandī, ʿAbd al-Razzāq al-Kāshānī, and Dā'ūd al-Qayṣarī. Likewise this period coincides with the spread of the school of *ishrāq* and philosophical *kalām* associated with such figures as Sayyid Sharīf Jurjānī.

During this era philosophers appeared who sought to synthesize these various schools together. One such figure is Ibn Turkah Iṣfahānī (d. 830/1427), who was at once an *ishrāqī,* a *mashshā'ī,* and an *ʿārif* of the school of Ibn ʿArabī. There was also a closer integration of philosophical activity and Twelver Shīʿī theology, as seen in the works of Naṣīr al-Dīn al-Ṭūsī, who, besides being a philosopher, was also the author of *Kitāb tajrīd al-ʿaqā'id* (The Book of Catharsis of Doctrines), which is the major work of Shīʿī *kalām*. The background was thus set for the synthesis associated with the Ṣafavid period.

The School of Isfahan. In the sixteenth century, with the establishment of the Ṣafavid dynasty in Persia, there began a new phase in Islamic philosophy associated with the School of Isfahan. Its founder, Mīr Dāmād (d. 1041/1631), taught in that city, although students came to him from all parts of Persia and many other lands. His most famous student, Ṣadr al-Dīn Shīrāzī (Mullā Ṣadrā; d. 1050/1640), is considered by many to be the greatest of all Islamic metaphysicians. In what he called the "transcendent theosophy" or *al-ḥikmah al-mutaʿāliyah,* he integrated the schools of *mashshā', ishrāq, ʿirfān,* and *kalām* in a vast synthesis which has influenced most Islamic philosophy to this day. The message of his magnum opus, *Al-asfār al-arbaʿah* (The Four Journeys), a veritable summa of Islamic philosophy, came to be known gradually as *al-ḥikmat al-ilāhīyah,* literally "divine wisdom" or "theosophy."

Mullā Ṣadrā and his followers exercised much influence in Persia, Muslim India, and Shīʿī circles in Iraq. His philosophy was taught in India and known to such figures as Shāh Walī Allāh of Delhi. It was revived in Qājār Persia by Mullā ʿAli Nūrī, Ḥājjī Mullā Hādī Sabzavārī, Āqā ʿAlī Mudarris Zunūzī, and others and has continued as a powerful intellectual tradition into the late twentieth century.

Islamic Philosophy in the Contemporary Islamic World. Islamic philosophy has continued as a living intellectual tradition and plays a significant role in the intellectual life of the Islamic world. Jamāl al-Dīn al-Afghānī, a student when in Persia of the school of Mullā Ṣadrā, revived the study of Islamic philosophy in Egypt, where some of the leading religious and intellectual figures, such as ʿAbd al-Ḥalīm Maḥmūd, the late Shaykh al-Azhar, have been its devotees. In the Indo-Pakistani subcontinent, Muhammad Iqbal was a student of Islamic philosophy, and even Mawlānā Mawdūdī, the founder of the Jamāʿat-i Islāmī of Pakistan, translated some of Mullā Ṣadrā's *Al-asfār* into Urdu in his youth. [*See the biographies of Afghānī and Mawdūdī.*]

In Persia Islamic philosophy has continued to play an especially important role despite the opposition of a sector of the Shīʿī *ʿulamāʾ*. Toward the end of the Qājār period a number of outstanding philosophers appeared, such as Mīrzā Mahdī Āshtiyānī and Mīrzā Ṭāhir Tunikābunī, who were active into the Pahlavi period, when such outstanding teachers as Sayyid Abū al-Ḥasan Qazvīnī, Sayyid Muḥammad Kāẓim ʿAṣṣār, and ʿAllāmah Ṭabāṭabāʾī came to dominate the scene. From the 1960s onward a veritable revival of Islamic philosophy occurred in the traditional schools as well as in circles of Western-educated Iranians, a revival that continues to this day. It must be remembered that Ayatollah Ruhollah Khomeini studied and taught *ḥikmat* for decades in Qom before entering the political arena and that the first head of the Council of the Islamic Revolution after the Iranian Revolution of 1979, Murtaẓā Muṭahharī, was a noted philosopher. Likewise in Iraq Muḥammad Bāqir al-Ṣadr, the well-known religious and political leader, belonged to the tradition of Islamic philosophy. [*See the biographies of Khomeini, Muṭahharī, and Ṣadr.*]

In most Islamic countries today there is renewed interest in various aspects of the Islamic intellectual tradition in which Islamic philosophy plays a central role. This philosophy is being studied and developed to an ever-greater degree to provide responses to the intellectual challenges from the West. It is also appealing to an ever-greater number of Western students, who are interested in it not only historically but as a living philosophy. In Islamic philosophy one can discover harmony between reason and revelation and the fruits of inner vision and ratiocination. Islamic philosophy is the repository of a knowledge that, on the basis of rational thought, leads ultimately to illumination and that is never divorced from the sacred.

[*See also* Theology.]

BIBLIOGRAPHY

Atiyeh, George. *Al-Kindī: The Philosopher of the Arabs*. Rawalpindi, 1966. Systematic treatment of the life, works, and main philosophical ideas of al-Kindī.

Corbin, Henry, in collaboration with Seyyed Hossein Nasr and Osman Yahya. *Histoire de la philosophie islamique*. Paris, 1986. Translated by Liadain Sherrard as *History of Islamic Philosophy*. London, 1992. Treats the whole of the Islamic philosophical tradition to the present day and in its relation to the Islamic revelation and various Islamic religious schools.

Corbin, Henry. *En Islam iranien*. 4 vols. Paris, 1991. Monumental work on Islamic philosophy, Shiʿism, and Sufism as they have developed in Persia up to recent times, including chapters on many important intellectual figures of the later period not treated in other books.

Cruz Hernández, Miguel. *Historia del pensamiento en el mundo islámico*. 2 vols. Madrid, 1981. Contains a particularly detailed account of Islamic philosophy in Spain and also late Islamic philosophy down to the present day in both the Arab and Persian worlds.

Fakhry, Majid. *A History of Islamic Philosophy*. 2d ed. New York, 1983. Systematic history of Islamic philosophy in its relation to theology, with emphasis on the early period of Islamic thought. Also contains a useful summary treatment of philosophical thought in the Arab world in the modern period.

Gutas, Dimitri. *Avicenna and the Aristotelian Tradition: Introduction to Reading Avicenna's Philosophical Works*. Leiden, 1988. Thorough, rationalist analysis of Ibn Sīnā's Peripatetic thought which, however, belittles his "Oriental philosophy." Opposes the views presented by Henry Corbin in his *Avicenna and the Visionary Recital*, translated by Willard R. Trask (Irving, Tex., 1980), and Seyyed Hossein Nasr, *An Introduction to Islamic Cosmological Doctrines* (Albany, N.Y., 1993).

Ha'iri Yazdi, Mehdi. *The Principles of Epistemology in Islamic Philosophy: Knowledge by Presence*. Albany, N.Y., 1991. In-depth analysis of the subject of knowledge by presence in Islamic philosophy from Suhrawardī to the present, with many comparisons to Western thought, the whole treatment being from the perspective of traditional Islamic philosophy.

Izutsu, Toshihiko. *The Concept and Reality of Existence*. Tokyo, 1971. Philosophical analysis of the structure of ontology in later Islamic philosophy as developed by Sabziwārī on the basis of the teachings of Mullā Ṣadrā.

Leaman, Oliver, and Seyyed Hossein Nasr, eds. *A History of Islamic Philosophy*. London, 1993. Detailed study of Islamic philosophy from its origin to the present and in relation to the Islamic revelation, the heritage of antiquity, and other related disciplines such as science and mysticism.

Mahdi, Muhsin. *Ibn Khaldun's Philosophy of History: A Study in the Philosophic Foundation of the Science of Culture*. Chicago, 1964. Thorough and critical study of Ibn Khaldūn's philosophy of history and its significance for Islamic thought.

Marmura, Michael E., ed. *Islamic Theology and Philosophy: Studies in*

Honor of George F. Hourani. Albany, N.Y., 1984. Contains a number of seminal essays in specific aspects of the philosophy of Ibn Sīnā and Ibn Rushd, as well as the first essay in English on Afḍal al-Dīn Kāshānī.

Morewedge, Parviz, ed. *Neoplatonism and Islamic Thought*. Albany, N.Y., 1992. Contains several in-depth studies of the relation of Neoplatonism to al-Fārābī, Ibn Sīnā, Naṣīr al-Dīn Ṭūsī, and the Ismāʿīlī philosophers, as well as certain Ṣūfī figures.

Mullā Ṣadrā. *The Wisdom of the Throne: An Introduction to the Philosophy of Mullā Ṣadrā*. Translated by James Winston Morris. Princeton, 1981. Careful translation of one of Mullā Ṣadrā's major works, with a long introduction on his school of thought and copious notes.

Nasr, Seyyed Hossein. *Three Muslim Sages*. Delmar, N.Y., 1975. Introduction to the Islamic intellectual tradition through the study of Ibn Sīnā, Suhrawardī, and Ibn al-ʿArabī.

Nasr, Seyyed Hossein, ed. *Ismaʿili Contributions to Islamic Culture*. Tehran, 1977. Contains essays on many different aspects of Ismāʿīlī philosophy and thought by such scholars as Henry Corbin, Wilferd Madelung, Pio Filippani-Ronconi, Alessandro Bansani, Aziz Esmail, and Azim Nanji.

Nasr, Seyyed Hossein. *Islamic Life and Thought*. Albany, N.Y., 1981. Contains chapters on Islamic hermeticism as well as later Islamic philosophy in Persia, particularly Mullā Ṣadrā and his school.

Netton, Ian Richard. *Allah Transcendent: Studies in the Structure and Semiotics of Islamic Philosophy, Theology, and Cosmology*. London, 1989. Analyzes the relation between the Qur'ānic doctrine of Allāh and how the problem of God and the emanation of the intellects is perceived by Islamic philosophers, from al-Kindī to Suhrawardī and Ibn al-ʿArabī. Author uses current semiotic theories of Western philosophy.

Netton, Ian Richard. *Al-Fārābī and His School*. London, 1992. Deals with al-Fārābī and his contemporaries and especially the epistemological substrate of al-Fārābī's philosophy.

Sharif, M. M., ed. *A History of Muslim Philosophy*. 2 vols. Wiesbaden, 1963–1966. Treats the whole of Islamic thought from its beginnings to the modern period, with greater emphasis on early Islamic philosophy and Islamic thought in the Indian subcontinent. The quality of the essays is rather uneven.

Urvoy, Dominique. *Ibn Rushd*. London, 1991. Thorough analysis of the various aspects of the philosophy of Ibn Rushd and its later significance.

Ziai, Hossein. *Knowledge and Illumination: A Study of Suhrawardī's Ḥikmat al-Ishrāq*. Atlanta, 1990. Analysis of the philosophy of Suhrawardī, emphasizing mostly his logic and epistemology.

SEYYED HOSSEIN NASR

PILGRIMAGE. *See* Ḥajj; Ziyārah.

PILLARS OF ISLAM. The foundations *(arkān)* upon which the religion of Islam rests are known as the five pillars, a belief based in a saying of the Prophet, reported in both Sunnī and Shīʿī *ḥadīth* tradition, "Islam is built upon five [fundamentals]." The five are the profession or witness *(shahādah)*. "There is no god except God and Muḥammad is the messenger of God"; regular observance of the five daily prayers *(ṣalāt);* the offering of the welfare alms *(zakāt);* performance of the *ḥajj* pilgrimage; and fasting *(ṣawm)* during the month of Ramaḍān.

Islam is a system of religious acts, obligations and intentions, service and human interactions. These essential principles are succinctly expressed in the terms *ʿibādāt* (rituals or acts of worship) and *muʿāmalāt* (human interrelations). The five pillars constitute the basis of worship, of the sacred law that governs social interrelations, and of theology.

The Qur'ān presents the five pillars not as a creed but as a framework of worship, a commitment of faith, and a moral responsibility. Thus, regular worship and the giving of alms (surah 2.43, 83; 4.77) are presented both as acts of worship and moral imperatives; prayers, the Qur'ān asserts, "dissuade from lewdness and indecency (29.45)," and almsgiving is also an act of purification (9.103).

Muslims believe that the five pillars were fully instituted during the Prophet's life. In a momentous Qur'ānic verse revealed after the farewell pilgrimage in which the Prophet led the Muslims shortly before his death, God says: "Today have I completed your religion for you, fully bestowed my favor upon you and accepted Islam as a religion for you (5.3)." The word *dīn* (religion) in this verse is taken to signify all the essential religious and legal institutions of Islam.

The five daily prayers are not strictly fixed in the Qur'ān; their times are only generally indicated (17.78, 11.114, 24.58). Frequent *zakāt* is enjoined but not fixed; but the fast of Ramaḍān and the *ḥajj* pilgrimage are clearly stipulated. The *shahādah* does not occur in the Qur'ān, but its early use is indicated by its inclusion in the call to prayer *(adhān)* and the five daily prayers.

Neither the Qur'ān nor the Prophetic tradition presents the five pillars together in a fixed sequence in any creedal definition of Islam. However, subsequent developments in the interpretation and application of the five pillars occurred in law, theology, and popular piety. Their centrality in the *sharīʿah* is evidenced by the general agreement of both Sunnī and Shīʿī legal schools (*madhhab*s) on the essential details of the duties *(farā'iḍ)* legislated in the five pillars. The Qur'ān distinguishes between *islām* and *īmān,* the former understood as the outward adherence to Islam and the latter as the inner faith of the heart (49.14). The Qur'ān also uses the term *islām* to designate a religious system that includes both faith and practice (3.19, 85). This seeming theological contradiction became an issue of great debate soon after the first generation of Muslims.

The crisis of succession following the Prophet's death and the vast conquests that resulted in the deterioration of the ideal of the caliphate into a monarchical autocracy, led to the rise of various sects and movements whose beliefs diverged from what came to be accepted as Sunnī orthodoxy. Chief among these were Shīʿīs, Khawārij, Murji'ah, and Muʿtazilah. Orthodox formulations of the five pillars, particularly the *shahādah,* were therefore attributed to the Prophet, or one of his prominent companions, and used as arguments against such religio-political movements.

In an early tradition reported by both Bukhārī and Muslim, the Prophet is said to have asserted: "I have been commanded to fight with all peoples until they say there is no god except God. When they say this, they protect from me their lives and their possessions except for what is due [as *zakāt*], and their final reckoning is with God." This tradition and other similar ones indicate that the five pillars very early served as a credal formula signifying a person's admission into the Muslim community. They were also used as polemical arguments against the Khawārij, who held that the profession of faith in God alone is not sufficient grounds for true Islam. In several important traditions reported by Bukhārī, the duties of Islam are defined as faith in God's oneness, observance of regular prayers, paying the *zakāt* alms, and fasting during the month of Ramaḍān. Some traditions add the duty of *jihād,* or fighting in God's way.

The rise of various schools and sects caused sharp disagreement among Muslims concerning the reality of *islām* and *īmān* as expressions of faith. The angel Gabriel, according to a well-known tradition reported by Muslim, came to the Prophet in human form and asked about *islām* and *īmān. Islām,* the Prophet said, "is to bear witness that there is no god except God and that Muḥammad is the messenger of God, to establish regular worship and give the *zakāt,* to observe the fast of Ramaḍān, and to perform the *ḥajj* if you are able to make your way thither." *Īmān* means "that you believe in God, His angels, His Books and messengers and the last day, and that you believe in Divine decree *(qadar),* be it good or evil." Belief in *qadar* was no doubt added later to counter the Muʿtazilī belief in free will and that human beings are alone responsible for their actions.

Through popular Ṣūfī piety, the five pillars were personally internalized as acts of devotion and spiritual exercises. Thus the *shahādah* became a constant recollection *(dhikr)* of God and the obligatory prayers became a life of continuous prayer and meditation.

Shīʿī tradition regards faith in God's oneness *(tawḥīd)* not as one of the foundations of Islam, but as its essence. Therefore, for Shīʿī Muslims, the fifth pillar is *jihād* or striving in the way of God, which can be realized fully only under the guidance of a divinely appointed imam. For Muslims of every legal school or theological persuasion, however, the five pillars have been the fundamental principles of both personal and collective faith, worship and social responsibility.

[*See also* Islam, *overview article;* Ḥajj; Ṣalāt; Ṣawm; Shahādah; Zakāt.]

BIBLIOGRAPHY

Primary Sources

Bukhārī, Muḥammad ibn Ismāʿīl al-. *The Translation of the Meanings of Ṣaḥīḥ al-Bukhārī.* 9 vols. 4th ed. Translated by Muhammad Muhsin Khan (with Arabic text). Beirut, 1405/1984. See especially volume 1, book 2, *The Book of Belief* (faith), and volume 9, book 93, *The Book of Tauhīd* (monotheism).

Muslim ibn Ḥajjāj al-Qushayrī *Ṣaḥīḥ Muslim* (with Nawawī's commentary). 3d ed. 18 vols. Beirut, 1978. Especially relevant is Nawawī's commentary on *Kitāb al-Īmān* (The Book of Faith), which heads Muslim's work. See also *Arkān al-Islām (The Pillars of Islam)* at the end of *Kitāb al-Īmān* in volume 1. *Ṣaḥīḥ Muslim* has also been translated into English by ʿAbdul Hamid Siddiqi (Lahore, 1972); see *Kitāb al-Īmān* (The Book of Faith).

Ibn Bābawayh al-Qummī, Muḥammad ibn ʿAlī ibn al-Ḥusayn (known as ash-Shaykh aṣ-Ṣadūq). *Iʿtiqādātu al-Imāmīyah (A Shīʿite Creed).* Translated by Asaf A. A. Fyzee. Tehran, 1402/1982. Important work, one of the earliest creeds, written by a foremost Shīʿī traditionist.

Secondary Sources

Cragg, Kenneth. "Worship and Cultic Life: Muslim Worship." In *Encyclopedia of Religion,* edited by Mircea Eliade, vol. 15, pp. 454–463. New York, 1987.

Cragg, Kenneth, and R. Marston Speight. *Islam from Within.* Belmont, Calif., 1980. Useful anthology of primary materials in English translation. See in particular chapter 2.

Wensinck, A. J. *The Muslim Creed: Its Genesis and Historical Development.* London, 1965. Very useful presentation of the genesis and development of the Islamic creed. Draws parallels and possible relations with Eastern Christian developments. See especially chapter 2.

MAHMOUD M. AYOUB

PIOUS FOUNDATIONS. *See* Waqf.

PIR. A word of Persian origin meaning "old man," the term *pir* (Ar., *pīr*) has been taken up into Ṣūfī discourse as a common title commonly for a Ṣūfī teacher, particularly in South Asia and neighboring areas. The pir is the revered elder who initiates disciples (*murīds*) into a Ṣūfī order. In popular practice, however, the term *pir* encompasses a complex and controversial array of social practices, relationships, and institutions that, though having their historical roots in Sufism, are regarded by some Muslims as distinct from it.

At certain periods in the history of Islam overt antagonism has existed between the modes of teaching and scholarship espoused by *ʿulamāʾ* and by Ṣūfīs. Major religious scholars have worked actively to reconcile and synthesize the two approaches, which are often distinguished as the external *(ẓāhir)* teachings of the Qurʾān, and the inner *(bāṭin)* teachings known through the spiritual experiences of the Ṣūfī master and spiritually transmitted from pir to disciple. In the modern period, reformist *ʿulamāʾ* such as those at the highly influential Deobandī school (see Barbara Metcalf, *Islamic Revival in British India: Deoband, 1860–1900*, Princeton, 1982), have also been pirs but have sought to eliminate from Ṣūfī practice what they regard as popular superstitions. [*See* Deobandīs.] In reformist discourse, which is common among urban middle-class Muslims today, the term *pīrī-murīdī* is often used in a derogatory sense to characterize forms of popular practice that are deemed to violate the Qurʾān and *sunnah* (practices of the Prophet) and to be typical of the uneducated. Reformists are highly critical of the pir who has no knowledge of Sufism as it is articulated in the literary Ṣūfī tradition but rather derives his status and his ability to confer the blessing *(barakah)* of God on disciples merely through descent from a pious Ṣūfī ancestor. The devotee of a pir may attribute supernatural powers to him and typically asks him to write amulets, cure diseases, and solve problems, often in return for a financial contribution to the pir or to the shrine to which he is attached. Reformist pirs, though retaining practices such as writing amulets for followers, place a heavy emphasis on *sharīʿah* in their teachings and stress that, when selecting a pir, the potential disciple should focus exclusively on the piety of the pir and his knowledge of and adherence to *sharīʿah*.

Pirs, their practices, and their links with shrines of past Ṣūfīs continue to be a focus of controversy, particularly in Pakistan, where the effort to articulate a relationship between Islam and the state is an ongoing struggle. Some of these hereditary pirs are major landholders and retain a considerable following, especially in rural areas, although direct control over the major shrines has been appropriated by the government (see Katherine Ewing, "The Politics of Sufism: Redefining the Saints of Pakistan," *Journal of Asian Studies* 42 [1983]: 251–268). Pirs have played an influential role in contemporary Pakistani politics, frequently taking a stance in opposition to efforts at social and religious reform by political parties such as the Jamāʿat-i Islāmī, who argue that the whole idea of a pir is against Islam and that all practices associated with pirs and shrines should be eliminated. Many concerned with modernization and development have also denounced popular belief in pirs, but even among the educated elite the search for a pir to be one's spiritual guide and the publication of Ṣūfī works appear to be widespread and even growing phenomena.

[*See also* Islam, *article on* Islam in South Asia; Sufism, *article on* Ṣūfī Thought and Practice.]

BIBLIOGRAPHY

Ewing, Katherine. "The Sufi as Saint, Curer, and Exorcist in Modern Pakistan." *Contributions to Asian Studies* 18 (1984): 106–114.

Lewis, P. *Pirs, Shrines, and Pakistani Islam*. Rawalpindi, 1985. Descriptive overview of popular beliefs and practices, including an eclectic treatment of recent scholarship.

Sherani, Saifur Rahman. "*Ulema* and *Pir* in the Politics of Pakistan." In *Economy and Culture in Pakistan*, edited by Hastings Donnan and Pnina Werbner, pp. 216–246. New York, 1991. Represents one Pakistani perspective which sharply distinguishes pirs from Ṣūfīs and is critical of the role of pirs in Pakistani society and politics.

KATHERINE P. EWING

POETRY. *See* Devotional Poetry; *and articles on specific languages and literatures.*

POLITICAL PARTIES. *See* Ḥizb.

POLYGYNY. The practice of one man simultaneously having several wives is a controversial issue in modern Islamic societies. Before the advent of Islam polygyny was practiced in many societies of Mesopotamia and the Mediterranean; some observers have attributed this pattern to the predominance of patriarchal systems in the region, but it should be noted that elsewhere in the world, polygyny may occur in nonpatriarchal societies. This traditional practice continued under Islam, where it is supported by the authority of the Qur'ān (4.3, 24, 25) and *sunnah.*

The religious justification for polygyny is found by some in the marriages of the prophet Muḥammad. He is said to have had a strictly monogamous relationship with his first wife, Khadījah, until her death in 619 CE. He subsequently married two women, Sawdā' and ʿĀ'ishah, and later took Ḥafṣah and Umm Ḥabībah as his *ʿaqdī* (concubines) Shīʿī tradition also offers the multiple marriages of certain imams in support of polygyny.

Polygyny has historically been practiced by both Sunnī and Shīʿī Muslims, with certain differences, primarily in the number of secondary wives permitted. In the Sunnī tradition the number of wives is restricted to four, but the Shīʿī tradition does not limit the number. Even among Sunnīs, rulers and other wealthy men often kept much larger harems.

Many modern Islamic nations have either outlawed or regulated polygyny; such laws were promulgated in Turkey (1917), Egypt and Sudan (1920, 1929), India (1939), Jordan (1951), Syria (1953), Tunisia (1956), Morocco (1958), Iraq (1959), Pakistan (1961), Iran (1967, 1975), and South Yemen (1974) (see Coulson and Hinchcliffe, 1978). In Iran, for example, modernizing legislation in 1967 attempted to create legal obstacles to men's unilateral exercise of the privileges of multiple marriage and of terminating marriages at will. The more conservative 1975 Family Protection Act provided that a man who wished to take a second wife must seek the permission of the court; furthermore, his first wife must either consent or be proven unwilling or unable to fulfill her conjugal responsibilities because of illness, imprisonment, or infertility. With the success of the Islamic Revolution, however, the 1975 act was repealed and the rules of the *sharīʿah* reinstated.

Beyond ordinary marriage, another form of polygyny exists in some Islamic societies in the form of *mutʿah,* a temporary relationship between a man and a woman based on mutual consent and certain contractual obligations. A form of concubinage, *mutʿah* requires exclusivity on the part of the woman for the duration of the contract and two months thereafter; the man provides her with financial support and a stipulated payment at the termination of the contract. *Mutʿah* has been the subject of ongoing legal and religious controversy in Iran: during the modernizing period attempts were made to ban it, but under the present regime it is not only permitted but actively promoted by the government.

[*See also* Family; Family Law; Marriage and Divorce; Mutʿah; Sexuality; *and* Women and Islam, *article on* Role and Status of Women.]

BIBLIOGRAPHY

Coulson, Noel J., and Doreen Hinchcliffe. "Women and Law Reform in Contemporary Islam." In *Women in the Muslim World,* edited by Lois Beck and Nikki R. Keddie, pp. 37–51. Cambridge, 1978.

Haeri, Shahla. "The Institution of Mutʿa Marriage in Iran: A Formal and Historical Perspective." In *Women and Revolution in Iran,* edited by Guity Nashat, pp. 231–252. Boulder, 1983.

Kusha, Hamid R. "Minority Status of Women in Islam: A Debate between Traditional and Modern Islam." *Journal Institute of Muslim Minority Affairs* 11 (1990): 58–72.

Matīndaftarī, Maryam. "Pīrāmūn-i āyīnnāmah-yi ijrā-yi mubārazah bā ʿbadḥijābī.' " *ĀZĀDĪ* 9 (Spring 1989): 30–43.

Muṭahharī, Murtaẓā. *Niẓām-i ḥuqūq-i zan dar Islām.* Tehran, 1986.

Vatandoust, Gholam-Reza. "The Status of Iranian Women during the Pahlavi Regime." In *Women and the Family in Iran,* edited by Asghar Fathi, pp. 107–130. Leiden, 1985.

HAMID R. KUSHA

POPULAR RELIGION.

[*To consider local beliefs and practices as they differ from mainstream Islamic traditions, this entry comprises six articles:*

An Overview
Popular Religion in the Middle East and North Africa
Popular Religion in Sub-Saharan Africa
Popular Religion in South Asia
Popular Religion in Southeast Asia
Popular Religion in Europe and the Americas

The first considers the principal forms of Muslim belief, ritual, narrative, and religious practice that have lent themselves to local and regional variation. The companion articles describe diverse modes of Muslim piety in various parts of the modern world.]

An Overview

The term "popular Islam" refers to the constellations of Muslim belief, ritual, narrative, and religious practice that flourish at particular points in time and space. They simultaneously islamize indigenous culture and popularize scripture. In some instances elements of pre-Islamic practices are given Islamic meanings, while in others particular interpretations of elements of the textual tradition are employed in the formulation of narrative, ritual, and social practice.

Popular Islams are as varied as contexts in which they are found, ranging from the austere, legalistic Islam of the Saudi Arabian Wahhābī sect to the ecstatic, charismatic cults of saints and Shīʿī imams characteristic of the popular Islam in South Asia and Iran. Despite this variety, popular Islams play similar mediating roles in Muslim religious life. They mediate between culturally specific patterns of social behavior and the idealized models for behavior expressed in the Qur'ān, *ḥadīth*, and *sharīʿah;* between the transcendentalism of Qur'ānic Islam and the deeply and widely felt need for direct and local access to the sacred; and between the limited, strict ritual requirements of textual Islam and the realities of human existence.

Islam, Custom and Culture. Scriptural Islam is more than religion. It is a detailed guide to human conduct, providing precise instruction in areas including personal hygiene, diet, dress, marriage, divorce, inheritance, taxation, and others. Particularly in the case of family law, the demands of the texts often clash with long-established cultural patterns. The problem is particularly vexing in matrilineal Muslim societies such as the Minangkabau of Indonesia. In many Islamic cultures a distinction is drawn between *sharīʿah* (Islamic law) and *ʿādāt* (custom). While *ʿādāt* is rarely recognized as entirely legitimate, many jurists tolerate deviation from *sharīʿah,* particularly in legal domains other than ritual performance. Others demand strict compliance with *sharīʿah* norms. The theoretical and highly demanding nature of *sharīʿah* has resulted in the recognition of a distinction between civil and religious law in many Islamic societies. [*See* Family Law; Adat.]

Qur'ānic Transcendence and Popular Piety. The doctrine of *tawḥīd* (the unity of God) is among the central teachings of Islam. The absolute power and majesty of God is a major theme in the Qur'ān and subsequent textual traditions. While understandings of *tawḥīd* range from transcendent monotheism to pantheistic assertions that all is God, textual traditions push God to the limits of the cosmos or, in mystical texts, to the depths of the human soul. In either case God is the sole object of devotion. [*See* Tawḥīd.]

Saint cults provide more direct, readily available access to the sacred and play important roles in most popular Islams. Saints are asked to intercede with God and are also sources of blessing *(barakah).* Pilgrimage to the tombs of saints *(ziyārah)* is among the most common Islamic devotional acts. They range from strictly local shrines to tombs of the founders of Ṣūfī orders and legal schools that attract pilgrims throughout the Muslim world. Muslims approach saints with requests ranging from desire for mystical knowledge to mundane problems of daily life. In Shīʿī communities imams and members of their families are the most important saints. Throughout the Muslim world, descendants of the prophet Muḥammad, religious teachers, and leaders of Ṣūfī orders are thought to be sources of blessing to whom devotees owe unquestioned obedience. Control of shrines and the equation of sainthood and kingship figure significantly in the legitimation strategies of many Muslim monarchies. [*See* Barakah; Ziyārah; Sufism, *article on* Ṣūfī Shrine Culture; *and* Authority and Legitimation.]

Ritual Practice. The five pillars of the faith, (the confession of faith, the five daily prayers, fasting during Ramaḍān, alms, and pilgrimage to Mecca) are described in the Qur'ān and *ḥadīth.* Legal texts describe the relative merits and mode of performance of these rites in great detail. The formal, orthoprax ritual system was devised by an urban scholarly elite, and its concern with ritual purity and the strict requirements for the fast of Ramaḍān make it difficult for those who must toil in fields and factories to comply. Pilgrimage to Mecca is greatly valued, but relatively few Muslims can hope to perform it. Lax observance of the formal ritual requirements of Islam should not, however, necessarily suggest impiety or secularism. While *sharīʿah* provides exemptions for those who find orthoprax ritual impossible, it does not provide alternatives. Popular Islamic practice fills this gap in the religious lives of many of the world's Muslims. [*See* Pillars of Islam.]

The comparative study of popular Islamic practice is underdeveloped. It has been largely ignored by Islamicists, and with few exceptions anthropologists have been reluctant to engage in comparative studies. Comparison of studies conducted in the Middle East, Africa, South Asia, and Southeast Asia reveals several common elements. Many of these are based on textual sources, particularly the *ḥadīth,* but adapt them to specific local contexts. Others are derived from the ritual systems of Ṣūfī orders, which played major roles in the conversion of non-Arab peoples to Islam.

The Mawlid al-Nabī that commemorates the birth and

death of the prophet Muḥammad is celebrated from Morocco to Indonesia and is frequently an element of Muslim imperial cults. Qur'ānic recitation, reproducing the speech of God, is performed at funerals, marriages, and other rites of passage, to cure the sick, to exorcise demons, and for numerous other purposes. The written text of the Qur'ān is used in charms and amulets. Modern developments include tape-recordings of famous Qur'ānic reciters and national and international recitation contests. *Dhikr* (remembrance of God) is the patterned recitation of Qur'ānic passages and the names of God, often involving the use of rosaries. Oral and written narratives concerning the lives and adventures of the prophet Muḥammad, members of his family, and other famous figures from Islamic history as well as saints and *jinn* circulate widely. *Jinn,* particularly those believed to have accepted Islam, are invoked for numerous magical purposes. *Jinn* and *shaiṭān* (devils) are often thought to be responsible for miraculous or unusual events. Ritual meals and the distribution of blessed food are especially common in the popular Islams of South and Southeast Asia. [*See* Mawlid; Qur'ānic Recitation; Dhikr; Magic and Sorcery.]

Puritanical Sects as Popular Islam. Owing to their insistence on the primacy of scripture, Wahhābīs and other fundamentalist/puritanical sects would appear to be exceptions to this view of the mediating function of popular Islam. Most fundamentalist programs include a deliberate rejection of aspects of popular Islam, particularly the cult of saints. However, fundamentalists base their religious lives on restricted readings of the textual tradition and maintain that their particular modes of ritual practice are the only source of God's blessing and mercy. Bruce Lawrence (*Defenders of God: The Fundamentalist Revolt Against the Modern Age,* New York, 1989) argues that fundamentalisms mediate between the demands of scripture and the intellectual and political contexts of modernity. In both senses fundamentalisms are contemporary popular Islams. [*See* Wahhabīyah; Fundamentalism.]

Islamic and Western Views. There is an enduring tension between popular and scriptural Islam that exists within most contemporary Muslim societies and is deeply rooted in Islamic scholarship. Islamic scholarly views have ranged from the intolerance of Ibn Taymīyah to al-Ghazālī's acceptance of a variety of modes of Muslim piety. The rise of scripturally oriented reform and fundamentalist movements in the twentieth century has increased the level of tension. Those who condemn popular Islams and those who are devoted to them share a conviction that their own understanding of Islam is the proper way of submitting to God—which is after all the meaning and purpose of Islam.

Western scholarship reflects this tension. Evaluations of popular Islams range from those of Orientalists who regard deviation from textual precedent as corruption or simply non-Islamic, to that of Reinhold Loeffler (*Islam in Practice: Religious Beliefs in a Persian Village,* Albany, N.Y., 1988) who argues that popular Islams are the means through which people who cannot possibly meet scriptural demands adapt the faith to local conditions. Most recent studies avoid questions of orthodoxy and corruption and focus instead on the ways in which Islam is understood and practiced in local contexts.

[*See also* Syncretism.]

BIBLIOGRAPHY

Antoun, Richard. *Muslim Preacher in the Modern World: A Jordanian Case Study in Comparative Perspective.* Princeton, 1989. Life history of a Jordanian village preacher.

Campo, Juan Eduardo. *The Other Sides of Paradise: Explorations into the Religious Meanings of Domestic Space in Islam.* Columbia, S.C., 1990. Explains the sacred character of domestic space in contemporary Egyptian Islam, including detailed references to the Qur'ān and *ḥadīth.*

Delaney, Carol. *The Seed and the Soil: Gender and Cosmology in a Turkish Village Society.* Berkeley and Oxford, 1991. Study of popular Islam in Turkey focusing on issues of gender, fertility, and domestic life.

Eickelman, Dale F. *Moroccan Islam: Tradition and Society in a Pilgrimage Center.* Austin, 1976. Study of the social and religious roles of Ṣūfī saints in Moroccan Islam.

Geertz, Clifford. *The Religion of Java.* Chicago, 1960. The most comprehensive account of popular Islam and its relationship to scriptural tradition and culture in Southeast Asia.

Geertz, Clifford. *Islam Observed: Religious Development in Morocco and Indonesia.* Chicago and London, 1968. One of the few comparative studies of popular Islam, this work also considers the impact of modernity on Islamic civilization in North Africa and Southeast Asia.

Lewis, I. M., ed. *Islam in Tropical Africa.* Bloomington, 1980. Collection of essays by leading Africanists and Islamicists concerning the popular Islams of Sub-Saharan Africa.

Martin, Richard C., ed. *Approaches to Islam in Religious Studies.* Collection of articles by leading Islamists combining theoretical approaches to the study of popular Islam with case studies of conversion, ritual, veneration of the prophet Muḥammad, ritual uses of the Qur'ān, and other topics related to popular Islams.

Metcalf, Barbara D. *Islamic Revival in British India: Deoband, 1860–1900.* Princeton, 1982. Study of one of the most important Islamic educational institutions in South Asia and its impact on Islamic thought and practice.

MARK R. WOODWARD

Popular Religion in the Middle East and North Africa

"Popular" Islam is the term used to describe the variations in belief and practice in Islam as they are understood and observed throughout the Muslim world. Religious leaders and spokespersons talk of the unity of Islamic belief and practice, but, as in other religions, there is considerable local variation. Muslims often implicitly assume that their local beliefs and practices are inherently Islamic because they are central to local tradition or to a given subgroup of society. These beliefs may include a special respect for claimed descendants of the prophet Muḥammad, the veneration of saints, possession cults *(zār)*, participation in religious brotherhoods (*ṭarīqah*s), or commemoration of the Prophet's birth *(mawlid al-nabī)*.

Traditionally educated religious scholars *(ʿulamāʾ)* and self-appointed contemporary Islamist spokespersons often dismiss as non-Islamic or "incorrect" local practices that they consider not in accord with central Islamic truths, even though the people who maintain such traditions consider themselves Muslims. Religious scholars usually pass over these understandings in silence unless they are held by members of weak or subordinate groups. Such practices include participation in religious brotherhoods (*ṭarīqah*s), *zār* cults in the Sudan, Turkish celebrations of the birth of the prophet Muḥammad *(mevlûd)* in which women play dominant roles, and the veneration of saints or "pious ones" *(al-ṣāliḥūn)* in North Africa.

Saints. A *ṣāliḥ* is a person, living or dead, who serves as an intermediary in securing God's blessings *(barakah)* for clients and supporters. In earlier centuries lineages of "pious ones" tied tribes to Islam and mediated disputes, and they are still thought to be particularly efficacious for those who have maintained long-term ties with them. In French usage, these saints are often called "marabouts" (Ar., *murābiṭ*, literally "tied one"). Most North Africans use the more ambiguous term "pious one" *(ṣāliḥ)* because it does not imply that God has intermediaries, a notion at odds with Qurʾānic doctrine but implicit in local beliefs. Many of the shrines associated with these saints are the focus of local pilgrimages and annual festivals. Some offerings—such as sacrifices at the annual festival of a saint—are annual obligations that ensure that the social groups involved "remain connected" with the marabout to secure his blessings. Festivals for major saintly figures attract tens of thousands of clients annually. [*See* Barakah.]

In addition to offering collective sacrifices to "remain connected," individuals give gifts or sacrifices for specific requests. For instance, it is common for women to go to certain shrines to ask for a saint's help in becoming pregnant. The woman may tear a strip of cloth from her dress and attach it to the door of a shrine as a reminder to the pious one. If the request is granted, she and her spouse give the promised payment.

Use of the term *ṣāliḥ* instead of "marabout" or "saint" evokes the multiplicity of the Moroccan concept. Participation in such a cult does not constitute evidence of an alternative, independent interpretation of Islam. Those who honor pious ones or seek their support are aware of the disapproval of some religious elites, but they nonetheless regard their vision of Islam as realistic and appropriate. Maraboutic shrines dot the landscape throughout North Africa, and the significance of saints is formally acknowledged in a variety of ways. In the Maghrib it is common for people going on the pilgrimage to Mecca first to visit local shrines or sanctuaries and to do so again on their return. Such ritual activities suggest that believers have an integrated vision of local religious practices and more universally accepted rituals such as the pilgrimage to Mecca. The Arabic word for pilgrimage *(ḥajj)* is not used to describe such local visits; the pilgrimage to Mecca is conceptually a separate phenomenon.

Belief in the efficacy of the *ṣaliḥūn* as intermediaries involves the implicit assumption that, whatever is formally stated about Islam, relations with the divine work in almost the same way as relations among humans. For a North African who implicitly accepts such beliefs, the main issue is not the existence of pious ones—that is taken for granted—but whether particular pious ones will exercise their powers on one's behalf. They are more likely to do so if a client can claim "closeness" *(qarābah)* to a pious one or his or her descendants. Offerings and sacrifices create a bond of obligation *(ḥaqq)* between the pious one and his client. [*See* Sainthood.]

Religious Orders in the Modern World. Religious brotherhoods (*ṭarīqah*s) and lodges (Ar., *zāwiyah;* Per., *khānqāh;* Tk., *tekke*), associated with mysticism, also figure in popular religious practices. As with the North African regard for pious ones, these orders are seen by many Muslims as complementing and enhancing the vitality of the Muslim community, although this view is subject at times to vigorous internal debate. In Iran, radical Islamist groups such as the Fidāʾīyān-i Islām incorporate Ṣūfī practices into their observances, and in

Morocco "fundamentalist" or Islamist groups adopt stylistic elements derived from Ṣūfī brotherhoods as a means of securing popular legitimacy. Even in Algeria, the scene of violent clashes between the government and Islamic radicals since the late 1980s, many radical groups have links with religious orders and local maraboutic families who have lost influence because of their suspected compromises with the French during the colonial era.

Such popular practices often reflect social differentiation. In North Africa, for instance, the Tijānīyah order had numerous government officials among its adherents, as did the Bektāshīyah order in Turkey. Other orders were associated with particular crafts or trades. Some were considered highly respectable; others, such as the Ḥamādshah and the Ḥaddāwah in Morocco, were associated with the use of drugs, trances, and other marginal activities.

Until the 1920s the majority of adult urban males and many villagers belonged to some brotherhood in most parts of the Middle East. A popular saying was, "He who does not have a Ṣūfī master as his guide has Satan to guide him." In recent times some of these orders are enjoying a revival, as religious traditions become "re-imagined." This is particularly the case in the newly independent states of Central Asia and in Cairo where, alongside the rise of Islamic radicalism, "neo-Sufism"—essentially a re-imagined tradition of Islamic mysticism purified of "non-Islamic" practices—has emerged as a significant religious force.

Zār Cults and the Birth of the Prophet. Sometimes popular religious practices are dismissed as little more than an affective complement to the formal side of Islamic practice and belief, and thus they are thought to be practiced more by women than by men. Such characterizations can be highly misleading. For example, *zār* cults are prevalent throughout Egypt, the Sudan, and East Africa and are associated with certain North African religious brotherhoods and some groups in the Arab Gulf and the Yemen. Because women often play a major role in these practices, some observers have speculated that they compensate for the often subordinate status women have in society. More recent studies suggest, however, that the elaborate array of spirits called up by participants in *zār* cults, which include *both* men and women, offer a conceptual screen against which villagers and others can imagine alternative social and religious realities, much like the veneration of saints, the "invisible friends" of early Latin Christianity.

Women also predominate in the ceremonies that mark the birth of the prophet Muḥammad, the *mevlûd*, in Turkey, while men predominate in activities that take place in mosques. Rather than seeing the *mevlûd* as primarily a women's activity, it is best to see it as complementary to mosque activities and an integral element of the way Islam is understood locally and practiced by both women and men acting as households.

Ritual and Community. Popular elaboration of ritual also distinguishes communities within the Muslim world. The ritual cycle of mourning for the betrayal of the Prophet's grandson Ḥusayn (d. 680) provides Shīʿī Muslims with a sense of self-renewal and victory over death and strengthens a sense of sectarian identity. On the tenth of Muḥarram, funerary processions in Shīʿī communities throughout Iran, Afghanistan, southern Iraq, Pakistan, and Lebanon reenact the last episodes of Ḥusayn's life and his burial. Central to these occasions is a mourning play (*taʿziyah*) about his martyrdom, its many versions being keyed to local circumstances. Since the audience knows the paradigm of the play, the drama does not rely on suspense but on how the scenes are enacted. Anachronisms abound; in some versions, European ambassadors rather than Sunnī Muslims betray Ḥusayn, and Old Testament figures are introduced. The final scene involves a procession with the martyr's coffin (or a severed head) to the court of the Sunnī caliph. On the way, Christians, Jews, and Sunnī Muslims bow before Ḥusayn. The intensity of such public performances, especially when they are elaborated in the context of other religious events, provide Shīʿī leaders with a means of mobilizing public opinion. In the last years of the Shah's rule, for example, political demonstrations were often planned to coincide with the cycle of Shīʿī religious activities.

The Alevi (Ar., ʿAlawī) Muslims of Turkey, Syria, and Lebanon illustrate another dimension of popular religious understanding, one which requires more elaboration than other examples of popular religious expression because Alevi religious beliefs are less well known. Until the mid-twentieth century the Alevi were primarily village-based and thus lacked a tradition of the formal religious scholarship and jurisprudence that produces the "authoritative" discourse that justifies a sect's divergence from other Muslim groups. Most Alevi villages in eastern Turkey lack mosques, and ritual practices also differ markedly in the interpretation of the "five pillars" of Islam. Alevis, like the Shīʿīs, emphasize the role of ʿAlī, the prophet Muḥammad's son-in-law, as much as they do the oneness of God and the prophecy of Muḥammad. Sunnī Muslims of the region's prevalent Ḥanafī rite pray five times daily, with a total of forty bowings (*rakʿas*). Alevis believe that two bowings annually in the presence of their spiritual leader (*dede* or *pīr*) suffice. Sunnīs fast for the entire lunar month of Ramaḍān; Alevis consider this a fetish and fast instead in the month of Muḥarram for twelve days in memory of the twelve imams. They call this fast *yas,* or "mourning" (for the martyrs of Karbala), not *ṣawm,* as the Ramaḍān fast is called. Alevis consider the pilgrimage to Mecca "external pretense"; for them the real pilgrimage takes place in one's heart.

From a Sunnī or Shīʿī perspective, Alevi interpretations of the Muslim tradition are unacceptable. Most scandalous of all from a Sunnī perspective is the Alevi feast of Ayin i Cem ("the day of gathering"). This feast is as important for the Alevis as the Feast of Abraham (Ar., ʿĪd al-Kabīr; Tk., Kurban Bayrami) is for Sunnī Muslims. Like the Shīʿīs, the Alevis practice *taqīyah,* the dissimulation of their beliefs and practices, and the Ayin i Cem, at least in Turkey, takes place when outsiders are not present. This is when community disputes are resolved, often with the mediation of the *dede.* Members of the community approach the *dede* in pairs, hand in hand, kneeling down and crawling on all fours to kiss the hem of his coat. This collective occasion is when the only obligatory annual Alevi prayer is performed. *Sema* music, accompanied by a *saz* (a sort of long-necked flute), is performed, and the men and women dance. Some dancers go into trance. Villagers recite mystical poetry commemorating the martyrs of the Alevi community; in Alevi gatherings outside Turkey, especially in Germany, the event is used to recreate or "reimagine" Alevi history in line with contemporary claims to identity. The climax of the festivity is the "putting out of the candle" *(mum söndürmek):* villagers throw water on twelve burning candles, representing the twelve imams and martyrs.

Alevi practices have thrived in western Germany because there the Alevis need not be concerned about government interference. Alevi migrants have been able to establish community-wide networks more easily in Germany than in Turkey, where state authorities have been suspicious of regional gatherings because many Alevis are Kurds. Since the 1970s these wider networks in the diaspora have also facilitated a greater sense of collective Alevi political identity.

Alevi beliefs and practices and the disapproval with which they are viewed by many Muslims serve as a reminder that orthodoxy and orthopraxy—conformity to standardized ritual—are situationally defined and linked to prevailing notions of dominance and religious authority. They also suggest the ongoing internal discussion and debate among Muslims of what constitutes common belief and practice.

The Alevis may be regarded as an extreme example, but similar ranges of popular perception and misperception prevail between Sunnī and Shīʿī, between the Ibāḍīyah of Oman and North Africa and their neighbors, and with the Aḥmadīyah in Pakistan. Indeed, after major riots against the Aḥmadīyah in 1953, an official government committee of inquiry concluded that the country's religious scholars were unable to agree on a definition of what a Muslim is.

The strength of the Alevi tradition and its capacity for self-renewal indicates the persistence of particularistic traditions within the Muslim community. The Alevi community, for the most part, lacks high scholarship and carriers of formal learning, but it compensates for this in the strength of shared local traditions and interpretations of Islamic belief and practice. These particularistic interpretations are not waning or becoming more homogenized in the face of modernization but maintain their vitality as much as do the Muslim traditions that have highly literate religious intellectuals to represent them. [*See* ʿAlawīyah.]

The Particular and the Universal. Carriers of a religious tradition often adhere to practices and beliefs that religious authorities, intellectuals, or scholarly observers see as contradictory because they cannot be reduced to a cohesive set of principles. Thus the late Fazlur Rahman (1919–1988), a leading Islamic scholar and reformist, dismissed the mystical and popular understandings of Islam that dominated in many parts of the Middle East and North Africa after the twelfth and thirteenth centuries as ideas and practices perpetrated by "charlatans" and "spiritual delinquents" who deceived the ignorant. An alternative view is that popular religious expression involves both explicit discussion and debate, and an implicit reimagination of belief and practice, which together contribute to a continuing reconfiguration of religious though throughout the world of Islam. In one dimension, opposing (or complementary) conceptions of Islam are particularistic and are significantly intertwined with the local social order. They often strengthen commitment to Islam. Thus the theologian Ibn Taymīyah (d. 1328) condemned all celebrations of the Prophet's birth as a harmful innovation *(bidʿah;)* many other theologians, however, tolerate it as an acceptable innovation *(bidʿah ḥasanah)* because it promotes reverence for the Prophet.

Other conceptions are universalistic, more amenable to generalization and application throughout the Muslim world, such as the pilgrimage to Mecca and ritual prayer. Some ideological expressions of Islamic doctrine, such as those characteristic of reformist Islam and the beliefs of many educated Muslims, tend to be universalistic in that they are explicit and more general in their implications. Others, including North African saint cults, are particularistic, in that they are largely implicit and tied to particular social contexts. These universalistic and particularistic strains are in dynamic tension with each other.

Islam's "New" Intellectuals. A major development in the popular understanding of Islam is associated with the rise of mass education and the decline of traditionally trained men of learning *(ʿulamāʾ)*. Not all Muslims regard a long apprenticeship under an established man of learning as a prerequisite to legitimize religious knowledge. Increasingly, the carriers of religious knowledge are those who claim a strong Islamic commitment, as is the case with many educated urban youths. Freed from traditional patterns of learning and scholarship, which have often been compromised by state control, religious knowledge is increasingly interpreted in a directly political fashion. Mimeographed tracts and the clandestine dissemination of sermons on cassettes have begun to replace the mosque as the vehicle for disseminating visions of Islam that challenge those sanctioned by the state.

The ideological spokespersons of most radical Islamist movements have received education in secular subjects, not religious ones. In the poorer quarters of Cairo or in the provincial capital of Asyut in Upper Egypt, the leaders of activist groups rely on pamphlets, books by journalists such as Sayyid Quṭb (1906–1966)—executed by Nasser and now regarded as a leading radical ideologue—and sermons on cassette rather than on direct study of the Qurʾān, *ḥadīth,* and other elements of the formal Islamic tradition. These understandings of Islam have become an important component of popular thought.

In the hands of radical Muslim thinkers such as Morocco's ʿAbd al-Salām Yāsīn, the militant argument provides an ideology of liberation. Yāsīn argues that contemporary Muslim societies have been deislamicized by imported ideologies and values, which are the cause of social and moral disorder. Muslim peoples are subjected to injustice and repression by elites whose ideas and conduct derive more from the West than from Islam. His argument is circumspect on how Muslims should liberate themselves from present-day polities, except to propose (ironically) that the state should allow militant Muslims *(rijāl al-daʿwah)* the right to speak to compensate for state-sponsored violence against them. His overall aim is to set coreligionists on the "right path" to a new era, not directly to confront the state.

The content of Yāsīn's sermons and writings and those of other new religious intellectuals suggests that their principal audience is educated and younger and already familiar with the imported, secular ideologies against which they argue. Their key terms, derived from Qurʾānic verses and religious slogans, are more evocative for their intended audience than the language and arguments of secular political parties. This language, in turn, has caused a transformation in how governments throughout the Muslim Middle East represent themselves, with many now stressing their religious credentials.

[*See also* Islam, *article on* Islam in the Middle East and North Africa; Sufism.]

BIBLIOGRAPHY

Boddy, Janice. *Wombs and Alien Spirits: Women, Men, and the Zār Cult in Northern Sudan.* Madison, Wis., 1989. Rich, evocative description and analysis of "possession" cults and how they relate both to Islam and to ideas of gender and person.

Chelkowski, Peter, ed. *Taʿziyeh: Ritual and Drama in Iran.* New York, 1979. Standard, accessible account of the ritual mourning of the death of Ḥusayn among Iran's Shīʿah.

Eickelman, Dale F. *Moroccan Islam: Tradition and Society in a Pilgrimage Center.* Austin, 1976. Thorough account of saints in a Moroccan context and the ambiguous tension between their veneration and other interpretations of Islam.

Eickelman, Dale F. *The Middle East: An Anthropological Approach.* 2d ed. Englewood Cliffs, N.J., 1989. Chapter 10 provides an extensive bibliographic description of "popular" religious practices throughout the region.

Fernea, Elizabeth W. *Guests of the Sheik.* Garden City, N.Y., 1965. Classic, accessible discussion of the mourning for Ḥusayn during the lunar month of Muḥarram among the Shīʿī of southern Iraq (pp. 194–208).

Geertz, Clifford. *Islam Observed.* New Haven, 1968. Classic account of how a world religion has taken root in Morocco and Indonesia.

Gilsenan, Michael. *Saint and Sufi in Modern Egypt.* Oxford, 1973. Good account of a modern Ṣūfī order.

Kepel, Gilles. *The Revenge of God: The Resurgence of Islam, Christianity, and Judaism in the Modern World.* Translated by Alan Braley.

Cambridge, 1994. The chapter on "The Sword and the Koran" offers insight into the "new" Muslim intellectuals and their appeal.

Mandel, Ruth. "Shifting Centres and Emergent Identities: Turkey and Germany in the Lives of Turkish *Gastarbeiter*." In *Muslim Travellers: Pilgrimage, Migration, and the Religious Imagination*, edited by Dale F. Eickelman and J. P. Piscatori, pp. 153–171. Berkeley and Los Angeles, 1990. Its account of how the Alevi Turks in Germany are regarded as more "progressive" than the Sunnī Turks can be usefully read in tandem with Yalman's earlier account (see below).

Mardin, Şerif. *Religion and Social Change in Modern Turkey: The Case of Bedrüzzaman Said Nursi*. Albany, N.Y., 1989. Fascinating study of a religious order that originated in late nineteenth-century Turkey and has become a significant transnational movement.

Reeves, Edward B. *The Hidden Government: Ritual, Clientelism, and Legitimation in Northern Egypt*. Salt Lake City, 1990. Excellent account of contemporary context of the veneration of saints in Upper Egypt.

Tapper, Nancy, and Richard Tapper. "The Birth of the Prophet: Ritual and Gender in Turkish Islam." *Man* 22.1 (March 1987): 69–92. Provides one of the best accounts of the complementarity of men's and women's religious practices for the entire region.

Yalman, Nur. "Islamic Reform and the Mystic Tradition in Eastern Turkey." *European Journal of Sociology* 10.1 (May 1969): 41–60. Although relatively inaccessible, this article remains a standard account of Alevi belief and practice.

DALE F. EICKELMAN

Popular Religion in Sub-Saharan Africa

During the nineteenth century, and to an even greater extent under colonial domination in the twentieth century, rapid and widespread islamization touched hundreds of African ethnic groups in West Africa, extending well into the forest zone, and in the interior of East Africa as far as Zaire and Malawi and South Africa. Previously many of these groups had only marginal contact with the Islamic world; in many places active Christian missionary efforts competed with the agents of Islam. As a result, popular expressions of piety in islamized Africa exhibit rich diversity, both within individual societies and in developments across time. Examples of popular religion in sub-Saharan Muslim societies can be grouped in three categories: culturally specific social behavior and religious ideas that include appropriations of Islamic motifs; the permeation of the Qur'ānic word into everyday life; and ritual practice.

Islam and Local Culture. The processes of islamization beyond the Sudanic belt in Africa that began during the nineteenth century and continue today are among the most dynamic in the Islamic world. Because of the rapidity of this process and because it occurs piecemeal, affecting some individuals and communities and leaving others untouched, it is frequently Islamic dress that most effectively distinguishes converts from non-Muslims living around them. That dress is generally a variation on the *jalabīyah* and cap (*kaffīyah*)—both sometimes bearing elaborate embroidery that may be an indicator of economic class—ornament in the form of talismans in leather amulet pouches tied to the arm or hung around the neck, *tasbīḥ* (prayer beads), and, for the traveler, a rolled prayer mat and a kettle of water carried for ablutions. To be so equipped is to be identified as a Muslim in sub-Sudanic African societies where specific local customs relating to diet, marriage, divorce, or inheritance may conflict with Islamic law or where the full weight of orthopraxy may not be felt. [*See* Dress.]

The decorative arts of local cultures across Muslim Africa, like their music and poetry, reveal great genius in the islamization of local motifs as well as in local appropriation of Islamic symbols. Islamic designs pervade local arts, exemplified by crescent designs on post-independence cloth prints, late colonial calabash engraving incorporating symbols of modernity alongside stylized *lawḥ* (wooden copyboards for Qur'ānic memorization), or elaborate nineteenth-century fans inscribed with one of Allāh's ninety-nine names. Islamic symbols and elements of Muslim material culture have also entered African arts in such forms as elaborately woven prayer mats, amulet-case designs in metal or leather, jewelry, and ornament in mask designs. No single symbol so remarkably conveys this appropriation of the Islamic tradition into folk arts in West Africa as does al-Burāq, the winged horse said to have carried the Prophet to Jerusalem. In sculpture cloth prints, amulets, masks, and drum stands, al-Burāq reappears across West Africa as one of the most enduring symbols of the mystical powers of the Prophet. Analogous to these representations in the arts are Islamic motifs in music and verse, woven into such diverse styles as Lagos juju music and—judging from the periodic denunciations by *ʿulamāʾ*—the unholy use of drumming as an integral part of Muslim marriage celebrations and performances on festival days.

Distinctive Islamic dress and Islamic motifs in the arts of many sub-Saharan African societies are the result of centuries of contact with Muslim lands. Beyond material culture, local cultures have also appropriated certain popular Islamic beliefs, perhaps most dramatically illustrated by the Mahdist expectations that have swept Sudanic Africa during the past two centuries. The popular belief was that the Mahdi would come from the east, just as the Antichrist Dajjāl would appear in the west. At least nine Mahdis are documented during the nineteenth century from the Senegal Valley and Futa Jalon in the west to Omdurman and Somalia in the east, and a like number of Mahdis appeared during colonial rule, as late as the 1940s. The Sudanese Mahdi Muḥammad ibn ʿAbd Allāh (1843–1898) was the most celebrated, inspiring a flurry of Mahdist claims (and colonial worries) during the opening decades of the twentieth century; well before this, however, each of the West African *mujāhid*s was obliged by his followers to explain why he was not the expected Mahdi. Less well-known are the Muslim communities in Niger, Nigeria, and Cameroon at the end of the nineteenth century where the reappearance of ʿĪsā (Jesus) was awaited as slayer of the Antichrist, a role for which he competed with the Mahdi in some traditions. Mahdist eschatology was popularly professed throughout the Sudanese communities during the nineteenth and early twentieth centuries. As late as the mid-twentieth century a Yoruba "Mahdi-Messiah" invented an amalgam of Christian and Muslim practice that inspired a thriving community of twenty thousand until his death in 1959. [*See also* Mahdi; Mahdīyah.]

An integral part of historical and contemporary Muslim life in sub-Saharan Africa is spirit-possession cults such as *sar* (from Gondar, Ethiopian *zar*, "origins") in East Africa, the Sudan, and parts of North Africa, and *bori* in Hausa-speaking West Africa and also in North Africa, sometimes seen as survivals of pre-Islamic practice. I. M. Lewis has argued persuasively that these cults—today largely urban, dominated by women and marginalized male migrant workers—hold special appeal to wives of the religiously minded who condemn the cults ("The Past and Present in Islam: The Case of African 'Survivals'," *Temenos* 19 [1983]: 55–67). These cults, varying in precise form from culture to culture but retaining the *sar* or *bori* appellation, thus become interwoven with orthopraxy, providing women and others alienated by locally constructed ideals of Islamic society with an avenue for participating in a counterculture whose definition is itself dependent upon Islamic orthodoxy.

Qur'ān and Popular Piety. The most pervasive example of Qur'ānic transcendence in popular usage throughout sub-Saharan Africa is the talisman or amulet industry, the products of which adorn babies, children, and adult men and women and hang in many a home and car. Talismans are mainly utilized for their therapeutic benefits or preventative powers, which underlines the important therapeutic attraction of Islam among peoples on the fringe of the Muslim world. The use of "washings" (typically inked or chalked verses from the Qur'ān, washed into a vial to be periodically drunk or dabbed on the body) to cure or at least mitigate a wide variety of ills has long been part of the repertoire of holy men and seers throughout Muslim Africa. In the same fashion talismans hung at a prescribed spot or worn on the body can serve a range of purposes: protection in armed conflict or everyday affairs, for individuals or whole communities; security for safe travel, avoidance of slander, or assurance of success or influence; advantage to protect pregnancies, cure disease, or promote intelligence; and punishment in the form of proactive measures against enemies.

Washings and talismans are at the juncture of medicine *(ṭibb)* and esoteric sciences *(baṭanīyah)* in Islamic learning, and these specifically Islamic cures compete with other therapeutic remedies readily available in most African societies. Murray Last notes that in Hausa society some Muslim holy men are known today for their success rate in prescriptions for physical illness just as others become specialists in social problems ("Charisma and Medicine in Northern Nigeria," in Donal Cruise O'Brien and Christian Coulon, eds., *Charisma and Brotherhood in African Islam,* Oxford, 1988, pp. 183–204). It is to those specialists in social problems that politicians and businessmen apply for formulas for success, and there are few heads of state, Muslim or Christian, who are not reputed to have a personal *mallam* or *marabout.* [*See* Magic and Sorcery.]

Esoteric sciences that complement the efficacy of washings and talismans are numerology and astrology, both of which emphasize, in I. M. Lewis's phrase, the "mystical defense system" popularly attributed to Islam in this region. Indeed, numerology is frequently the main science utilized in talisman production, and the propitious alignment of stars is as carefully watched by specialists in Sudanic Africa as by astrologers in the West. The significance of these practices lies not in the sciences themselves, nor in the fact that Islamic remedies are popularly understood to have therapeutic properties that compete favorably alongside non-Islamic medicines; rather, it lies in the symbolic power of the Qur'ānic scripture and the demonstrable function of the word in response to everyday needs. [*See* Numerology; Astrology.]

The Ṣūfī brotherhoods have long been the vanguard of islamization in sub-Saharan Africa, and with them have arisen popular attachments to individual shaykhs that are analogous to the special relation between shaykh and student in many other parts of the Muslim world. Pilgrimage to the tombs of saints may have therapeutic effects, most frequently for women to safeguard pregnancies. The desire for prayers of intervention on behalf of individuals has spawned a minor prayer industry for shaykhs in other settings. With this mediating role, most frequently played by Ṣūfī leaders, has come an iconization of both dead saints and living shaykhs. This is most vividly illustrated by the religious paraphernalia associated with the Murīdīyah in Senegal, where postcards and glass paintings commemorating events in the life of the patron saint, Ahmadu Bamba (d. 1927) can be found at most corner dealers in religious wares as well as adorning taxis and trucks driven by prudent followers. [*See* Murīdīyah.] Analogous marketing of local Tijānī shaykhs in Ghana, or of the Senegalese (Kaolack) Tijānī holy man al-Ḥājj Malik Sy in northern Nigeria, has become increasingly sophisticated during the past thirty years; today, few homes of the religious who can afford it lack a framed photo of their shaykh.

The Ṣūfī shaykh as a conduit between the supernatural and the common folk has long been an important fixture in the moral economy of Muslim communities. As with therapeutic matters, the shaykh's possession of at least a rudimentary knowledge of Arabic certifies his authority to mediate between scripture and supplicant in societies where Arabic is not spoken and access to the Qur'ān is thus quite restricted. Whether he is a writer of simple talismans or an accomplished jurist, a shaykh's authority rests largely on his near-monopoly over the scripture, but his *barakah* (blessing) may also be sought for its own sake. Where a local Ṣūfī *ṭarīqah* institutionalizes exploitive relationships between shaykh and student, it also makes popular religion a commodity. The Qādirīyah and Tijānīyah in West Africa, the Qādirīyah, Shādhilīyah and ʿAskarīyah in East Africa, and the Qādirīyah, Sammānīyah, Khatmīyah, and Mahdīyah in the Sudan, all fulfill analogous roles at one broad level of orthopraxy. Their ultimate meaning and local impact, however, depend heavily on individual shaykhs and their skills at mediating or manipulating the holy word. The title *"al-Shaykh,"* like the pilgrim's title *"al-Ḥājji,"* connotes local recognition of the religious, objects of veneration among their followers and subjects of snickers among their critics. In recent years inexpensive cassette tapes of sermons and readings by both Pan-Islamic notables and local preachers have become available on national markets in sub-Saharan Africa, providing an electronic form of mediation and translation of the word in local settings that now competes with the scripture in the economy of popular piety. [*See* Qādirīyah; Tijānīyah; Shādhilīyah; *and* Khatmīyah.]

Ritual Practice. Piety in most sub-Saharan African Islamic communities, as elsewhere in the Islamic world, is most publicly displayed at prayer and most effectively demonstrated on festival days. These are the occasions for new outfits for children, new gowns for adult members of the household, lavish displays of food for dependents, and generous dispensing of cash gifts—all widely accepted as indices of religiosity. Although the relative importance of individual festival days varies from region to region, ʿĪd al-Kabīr (widely known as "Tabaski" in West Africa) and ʿĪd Saghīr (or al-Fiṭr, also known as "Salla" in West Africa) at the end of Ramaḍān generally compete in importance; in East Africa ʿId al-Ḥajj replaces the first of these as a principal festival. Celebration of the Prophet's birth, the *mawlid,* is a minor holiday in parts of sub-Saharan Africa, although it has been appropriated by the Ṣūfī brotherhoods in many countries as an annual display of piety before saints' tombs. Large followings of some local saints have spawned individual festivals, exemplified by the annual Grand Maggal (Wolof, "to celebrate") in Touba, Senegal, when Murīd followers gather by the tens of thousands to observe the anniversary of the death of Ahmadu Bamba in a festive atmosphere.

The centrality of the visitation of saints' tombs varies across Africa's Muslim populations; in the northern Sudan such tombs are a chief source of *barakah* and popular sites of local pilgrimage. Across the continent in southern Mauritania, gravesites are modestly marked even for holy men, and although visitations take place they are not yet ritualized. Between these extremes, hundreds of African Muslim societies integrate local custom, generally heavily tinged with veneration of ancestors, with Islamic burial ritual. [*See* Ziyārah; Sufism, *article on* Ṣūfī Shrine Culture.]

Elements of life-cycle rituals in Muslim societies are popularly understood to be linked to Islamic prescriptions. In sub-Saharan Africa these focus on naming ceremonies (which frequently involve an imam or local shaykh and elaborate displays of hospitality), the acts of circumcision and clitoridectomy, the formalities and types of marriage (dowries, the degrees of proximity permitted in Islamic law, the number of wives, etc.) and divorce, and burial rites. In each islamized society compromise is negotiated among local custom, scripturally sanctioned practice, and orthopraxy in neighboring Muslim communities and lands. It is generally with respect to Islamic laws of inheritance and in particular land that local custom has proven most intractable. [*See also* Rites of Passage.]

Since the mid-twentieth century, as a result of increased communication between the Muslim heartlands and sub-Saharan Africa and also as a result of increasing numbers of African pilgrims traveling to the Hejaz, there has been a tendency toward a certain homogeneity within national Muslim cultures. This is most noticeable in ritual life, where the political influence of religious leaders has been recognized by national authorities and ritual reinforcement of that influence has been encouraged (in contrast to a definite wariness toward that same influence during colonial times). As a result, national Islamic political cultures have emerged in many countries. These tend to focus on annual rituals such as the *mawlid*, generally under the supervision of shaykhs in the local *ṭarīqahs* whose mediating roles increasingly extend into the political sphere.

BIBLIOGRAPHY

Bravmann, René A. *African Islam*. Washington D.C., 1983. Elegantly illustrated exhibition catalog with extended essays on the material culture of Muslim societies in sub-Saharan Africa.

El-Tom, Abdullahi Osman. "Drinking the Koran: The Meaning of Koranic verses in Berti Erasure." In *Popular Islam South of the Sahara*, edited by J. D. Y. Peel and Charles C. Stewart, pp. 414–431. Manchester, 1985. This collection also includes six contributions that address aspects of popular Islam in the Sudan, Nigeria, and Senegal.

Le Grip, A. "Le Mahdisme en Afrique noire." *L'Afrique et l'Asie* 18 (1952): 3–16. Remains one of the best, brief surveys of Mahdism in Sudanic Africa during the nineteenth and twentieth centuries.

Lewis, I. M., ed. *Islam in Tropical Africa*. 2d ed. London, 1980. Twenty-five years after its first appearance, this study remains one of the most succinct and comprehensive surveys of orthopraxy and popular piety in sub-Saharan African communities; includes an updated introduction.

Nimtz, August H., Jr. *Islam and Politics in East Africa*. Minneapolis, 1980. Surveys Ṣūfī brotherhoods in East Africa, with particular reference to Tanzania, and their gradual involvement in national politics.

Owusu-Ansah, David. *Islamic Talismanic Tradition in Nineteenth-Century Asante*. Lewiston, N.Y., 1991. Detailed study of a set of over five hundred folios of instructions on the manufacture of talismans recovered from a non-Muslim state on the Gold Coast in the early years of the nineteenth century.

Trimingham, J. Spencer. *Islam in West Africa*. Oxford, 1959. While the conceptual schema presented in this and other studies by the author may be contentious, the core of his ethnographic material collected on institutional Islam, Ṣūfī orders, and life cycles as observed in the mid-twentieth century remains useful.

Trimingham, J. Spencer. *The Influence of Islam upon Africa*. 2d ed. London, 1980.

CHARLES C. STEWART

Popular Religion in South Asia

A system of beliefs, rituals, practices, and attitudes among Muslims that deviates to some extent from the dictates of the *sharīʿah* has been a dominant element in South Asian Islam for centuries. Although Islam demands absolute conformity with the *sharīʿah* in all matters, public or personal, religious or mundane, and rejects compromise with non-Islamic culture, in reality it assimilated ideas, values, and symbols from different societies and traditions during its expansion. Often described as "rural," "folk," or "syncretic religion," popular religion in Islam does not in fact reflect only the values and perceptions of the illiterate masses, as opposed to the orthodoxy of the elites. Its sources are complex and varied and are not limited to a particular stratum of society. Even among highly educated urban Muslims, traces of popular religion are often conspicuous, especially in birth rites, marriage ceremonies, veneration paid to saints and shrines, and a host of other social ceremonies.

South Asian Islam demonstrates the multifarious character of popular religion and its ability to survive the pressures of orthodoxy, modernism, fundamentalism, and priestly ban. What sets South Asian Islam apart from the austere faith that emanated from Arabia in the sixth and seventh centuries CE is the unique mixture of Perso-Arabian norms and values, characterized as "authentic Islamic," with the various regional traditions and cultures of the subcontinent. More than five hundred years (1203–1757) of Muslim dominance in the region affected the lives of millions in various ways, yet this does not seem to have altered fundamentally the social and religious values and perceptions of the majority of Islamic converts. But indigenous traditions alone did not give shape and substance to popular religion in South Asian Islam; the individuals who introduced the faith in different parts of the region equally contributed toward its popular and unorthodox character.

Origins and Development. A basic problem in conceptualizing South Asian Islam is the tendency among scholars to overemphasize the impact of classical Islam in shaping a distinctive Muslim culture in the region. Such a view not only romanticizes the role of immigrant Muslims as the standardbearers of authentic Islam; it also minimizes the importance of the indigenous cultural traditions of South Asia in molding Islam in the region and ignores the fact that the great majority of South Asian Muslims (at least 90 percent have been converts from local tribes and castes, usually from the lower social strata).

Historically, Islam came to South Asia in several stages through traders, conquerors, and migrants. The small body of traders, many of whom settled in peripheral colonies along the south, west, and east Indian seaboards and in coastal Sri Lanka, came generally from Arabia, while the conquerors and migrants came mostly from Central Asia and Afghanistan (with the exception of the marginal conquest of Sind by the Arabs in 711 CE). Many came in search of fortunes, and others as religious missionaries. It was these immigrant Muslims who formed the core of early Islamic civilization in South Asia, to be strengthened later by the Turkic Mughals who ruled the subcontinent between 1256 and 1757, as well as a handful of Persians and Arabs who came at different times for different reasons.

It is easy to perceive that these Muslims from diverse social and cultural milieus could not have been the bearers of a single Islamic system. They each brought their own particular social norms, values, and traditions. Thus popular Islam in South Asia shows some strong Shīʿī influences even though it is generally Sunnī in character; there are widespread traces of tribal customs and ceremonies, including nomenclatures indicating past tribal affiliations (reflected in modern family names such as Khan, Malik, Mir, Mirza, or Yusufzai); and un-Islamic festivals like the Nawrūz (Persian New Year's festival) are celebrated. [*See* Nawrūz.]

Interaction with Hinduism also contributed to the creation of popular Islam. Though politically dominant for several hundred years, the Muslim elites constituted a small percentage of the total population and therefore relied heavily on the support of the Hindus. Many of them married into Hindu families, participated in local rites, rituals, and ceremonies, and even adhered to some of the social restrictions associated with the Hindu caste system. Perhaps many, especially the *ʿulamāʾ*, were concerned to guide the community strictly in accordance with the *sharīʿah*, but this could hardly be achieved. Aspects of indigenous culture became embedded in the Islamic tradition, inexorably altering its character. Islamic art forms in South Asia, social ceremonies, birth and marriage rituals, and many other practices bear strong marks of this interaction and assimilation. Nor was this a one-way process: Islamic cultural influence was equally felt at certain levels of Hindu society, encouraging the growth of syncretistic rituals and movements.

Not all the indigenous themes in South Asian Islam came from the Muslim elites' contacts with Hinduism. Through a slow process of acculturation, missionary efforts, and Ṣūfī influence—supported by the Muslim state—many of the region's other indigenous peoples were converted to Islam. Especially between the thirteenth and eighteenth century, millions of people from Bengal, South India, Sind, Punjab, Kashmir, and Nepal were absorbed into the expanding Islamic society. But the perceptions of the converts did not change overnight. They continued to live under the same social conditions, bound by the same caste rules that governed the lives of their Hindu neighbors; they followed the occupations particular to their caste groups, wore the same dress, and had similar names; they propitiated the same deities and sang hymns in praise of local gods and goddesses, even though some of them may have understood the basic dogmas of their new faith. Technically, they had converted to Islam, but this little affected their older way of life.

True to the traditions of peasant societies, the religious beliefs and rituals of the indigenous Muslims of South Asia—who generally belonged to the lower strata of the society and lived in rural areas—often reflected a concern for immediate problems. This is partly manifested in the unusual reverence paid to the village exorcist, who might be either a Hindu *ojha* or a Muslim pir, to the shrines of pirs or Ṣūfīs, and to the older mythical heroes, gods, and goddesses. To the average Muslim peasant, boatman, fisherman, or woodcutter, whose survival depended on the mercy of nature, belief in the miraculous powers of *ojha*s, pirs, *faqīr*s, and deities is but one way of seeking immediate protection against disaster. Thus, in the coastal districts of eastern Bengal, Pir Badr, legendary patron saint of sailors, was venerated by both Muslims and Hindus, much as many Sindhi Muslims observed the cult of Khvāja Khiẓr. A host of other cults—including those of Zindah Ghāzī, Mobrah Ghāzī, Shāh Mādar, and Pānch Priyas—formed part of the popular mythology of South Asian Islam and continue to play a role in the lives of millions.

Throughout history, the *ʿulamāʾ*, as self-proclaimed

guardians of orthodoxy, have consistently focused attention on the need of the community to conform to the Qur'ānic way of life, as they interpreted it, theoretically rejecting all compromises with local custom. The rural mullahs—whose own knowledge of Islam might well be inadequate—also attempted to purge un-Islamic beliefs and rituals from Muslim society. Pressure for rigid conformity to the Qur'ānic ideal progressively mounted in the nineteenth and early twentieth centuries with the rise of a number of Islamic revivalist movements. This had a powerful impact on average Muslims, gradually transforming their worldview in favor of a distinctive Islamic identity. Within popular religion, however, change was limited and at times contradictory. Villagers continued to cultivate the older forms of faith in songs, hymns, spells, and unorthodox rituals. A whole range of observances recognized by the orthodox as non-Islamic borrowings persisted, perhaps with an Islamic veneer, and often with approval from certain sections of the *ʿulamāʾ*, especially the rural mullahs and pirs. A notable example of the persistence of older customs was the practice of using amulets containing incantations for good luck or for the cure of specific illnesses. Now offered by the mullah or pir instead of the Hindu exorcist in exchange for money or a gift, the amulets merely replaced Hindu incantations with Qur'ānic verses. Likewise, the efficacy of vows and offerings to spirits or saintly figures of the past, which form part of popular Hindu mythology, was never seriously questioned. The Islamic veneer imparted to a host of local customs and practices thus did not imply a rejection of older forms of faith, but merely a reorientation of them.

Principal Features. One of the dominant features of popular religion in South Asian Islam is the veneration paid to pirs, living or dead, and to their shrines. Introduced by immigrant Muslims, the bases of pirism were strengthened further in South Asia by the Hindu-Buddhist notion of *guru* (preceptor) worship. Asim Roy (1983) has pointed out how a complex body of myths and legends became incorporated into the pir cult and institutionalized in the popular veneration of shrines holy to saints or pirs as well as those of mythical personages like Khvājah Khiẓr and Pir Badr, who are credited with specific supernatural powers and worshiped with offerings.

The pir is not merely a spiritual guide to millions of Muslims, both literate and uneducated, but someone semidivine. He commands blind obedience from his disciples and is credited with amazing virtues and powers. Occupying his position more often than not by accident of birth, the pir, in association with the village mullah, plies a lucrative trade in amulets and charms. A yearly gathering (*ʿurs*) at the site of the pir's residence (*dargāh*) or at the tomb (*mazār*) of a dead pir adds color to the system by a variety of rituals and observances not in conformity with the *sharīʿah*. This is particularly true of pirs who follow the tradition of certain non-*ṭarīqah* Ṣūfīs, often referred to as *galandaris*, in emphasizing unconventional forms of worship and make music, dance, and *dhikr* (chanting God's names in rhythm) the primary themes of their religious activity. Richard Eaton has shown in his pioneering study (1978) of Ṣūfīs in the Deccan that the rituals at many Ṣūfī shrines tend to draw on local vocabulary, customs, music, and dance, thus creating an Islamic milieu that transcends the formal boundaries of orthodoxy. [*See* Dhikr.]

Associated with pirism is the veneration paid to saintly shrines, genuine or mythical. Popular devotion to shrines, like obedience to pirs, is not limited to a particular region; it is pervasive all over South Asia, from Kashmir to South India and beyond. Almost every locality has its own *mazār* where people make offerings and vows. Susan Bayly mentions that in a south Indian coastal town twenty such shrines are believed by local Muslims to contain the remains of actual companions (Ṣaḥābah) of the Prophet and are held in high esteem (1989, p. 109) These and other shrines are frequented by pilgrims and devotees—educated and illiterate, rich and poor—to cure illnesses, to ward off malevolent influences, to fulfill cherished desires, or to gain ultimate salvation. Although the idea of worshiping the shrines themselves may not be clearly perceived by the devotees, some of the rituals performed there, such as paying obeisance, lighting candles, and offering flowers, are antithetical to monotheistic Islam. The degree to which people seem to depend on the miraculous powers of saints and shrines in effect renders the omnipotent God somewhat irrelevant (and ineffectual) in these nominal Muslim's lives. [*See* Sufism, *article on* Ṣūfī Shrine Culture.]

Among attendant practices mention may be made of Mawlid al-Nabī and Muḥarram. These festivals were not of South Asian origin but were imported from other Islamic lands. Mawlid al-Nabī is ostensibly a celebration of the Prophet's birthday, in which hymns recited in praise of the Prophet bestow on him an aura of divinity and suggest elevating him to a status rivaling God. The devotees' perception of the Prophet thus takes on the character of the Christian notion of Jesus; he becomes the intercessor as well as the protector. Likewise, the Muḥarram ceremony, commemorating the martyrdom of the Prophet's grandson Ḥusayn, reflects the popular tendency of hero worship. Despite its Shīʿī origins, Muḥarram has been equally popular with the Sunnī Muslims of South Asia. The tragedy at Karbala in the seventh century CE, when Ḥusayn was brutally murdered by the Umayyad caliph Yazīd, has always appealed deeply to South Asian sentiment. Until recently, elaborate commemorative festivals, in which Hindus also participated, were held during the first ten days of the first month of the Islamic calendar. Although it has diminished in importance lately, it is still an occasion for remembrance marked by festivities. The extreme veneration of Ḥusayn is also reflected in the homage paid to his mother, Bibi Fāṭimah, the Prophet's daughter. The idolization and glorification of Fāṭimah probably has nuances that go beyond the limits of Islam. [*See also* Mawlid; Muḥarram.]

Popular Islam in South Asia also features various rituals and practices associated with birth, circumcision, and marriage. The birth of a child is usually followed by a period in which the mother is regarded as unclean, which is basically similar to Hindu custom. The canonical ceremony of *ʿaqīqah* (naming of the child and seeking God's protection for him/her by animal sacrifice) is rarely observed, but when it is, it includes elaborate rituals, dancing, and singing. Circumcision, usually performed by a low-caste Muslim, is equally a social event that has little to do with the Islamic faith, although a mullah is invited to give it an Islamic touch.

It is the marriage ceremony that displays some of the most distinct local customs within popular Islamic culture. Although the actual marriage contract *(nikāḥ)* is administered Islamically by the *qāḍī*, a whole range of rituals and practices that precede and follow the *nikāḥ*, have transformed marriage into a social, nonreligious event; these include a large dowry given to the bridegroom by the bride's parents, an exchange of sweetmeats and gifts, dancing, singing, and feasting. Many customs associated with marriage ceremony—for example, welcoming the bride (especially in Bengal and parts of South India) with offerings of rice or wheat, and the ceremonial procession of festively attired women carrying gifts to the bride's home—have been inherited from the folk culture of South Asia. Muslims from affluent classes, however, make every effort to wrap an Islamic cloak around these ceremonies while denouncing others, especially the poor, for their un-Islamic conduct. [*See* Birth Rites; Circumcision; Marriage and Divorce.]

Finally, popular Islam in South Asia espouses some of the principal features of caste system, which divides society on the basis of birth. Although educated Muslims emphasize the egalitarianism of Islam, the role of caste in molding popular Islamic culture in the region can hardly be overemphasized. Variously termed *qaum*, *birādarī*, or *jātī*, these Muslim social divisions are modeled after the Hindu caste system. However, the rationale for rankings among Muslims in South Asia is generally based on claims of foreign ancestry, primarily Arab, Persian, Central Asian Turkic, or Afghan. Although the question of foreign descent has become somewhat irrelevant today owing to long years of intermarriage among indigenous converts and immigrant Muslims, even the flimsiest claim to such status can make a difference. Generally, those of "foreign" descent tend to consider themselves different from and superior to the indigenous Muslims and to maintain a conscious distance from them. The terms *ashrāf* ("noble") and *ajlāf* or *aṭrāf* ("lowly") are generally used to refer to the two categories. There are distinctions based on birth even at the level of *ashrāf* society, between *syed* (Ar., *sayyid;* supposedly, the descendants of the Prophet), *shaykh* (of Arab origin), *mughal* (descendants of Central Asian Turks), and *pathan* (of Afghan origin). However, it is mostly in the lower strata of Muslim society that caste restrictions are still common, based on Hindu notions of the purity and impurity of occupations. Many of the lower endogamous groups, like *dhobi* (launderer), *kalu* (oilpresser), *jolha* (weaver), and *hajjam* (barber), still maintain strict rules governing the conduct of their caste groups and will not intermarry or eat with others. The members of these groups maintain close contact with their respective clan even when they are away, and their "caste councils" play an important role in their communal life. This is particularly common among South Indian lower-caste Muslims. But even in the state of Uttar Pradesh, regarded as the heartland of South Asian Islam, caste groupings based on occupation exist to a considerable degree among the non-*ashrāf* Muslims.

Popular religion in South Asian Islam thus represents a tradition that is far from egalitarian, and that worships at the shrines of saints, believes in miracles, charms, and magic, and pays unquestioned obedience to the pir. As noted, beliefs and practices in *ashrāf* and educated society do not necessarily conform to Islamic dogma, but their practices generally have an Islamic veneer. Lower orders of the *ajlāf* society have never applied this veneer to many of their customs and rituals, which remain linked to local culture. Despite educated Muslim claims, popular Islam in South Asia thus still retains much of its older form, with minor modifications and adjustments. Whether Hindu cultural influence was the major source of this popular culture, or whether it was a natural consequence of years of interaction between indigenous Hindu-Buddhist culture and various Islamic traditions, are questions that remain open to discussion. But popular Islam has certainly proved closer to the hearts of millions than have the orthodox dogmas. The people's unquestioning affection for age-old practices reflects the close relationship with nature and the immediate environment common to popular traditions in all religions.

[*See also* Islam, *article on* Islam in South Asia; Pir; Syncretism.]

BIBLIOGRAPHY

Ahmad, Aziz. *Studies in Islamic Culture in the Indian Environment.* Oxford, 1969. Seminal work on the nature of interaction between Islam and Indian culture; essential for the study of popular traditions in South Asia.

Ahmad, Imtiaz, ed. *Caste and Social Stratification among Muslims in India.* 2d ed. New Delhi, 1973. *Family, Kinship and Marriage among Muslims in India.* New Delhi, 1976. *Ritual and Religion among Muslims in India,* Columbia, Mo., 1982. Useful collection of essays on Indian Muslim beliefs, rituals, practices, and society in different regional contexts.

Bayly, Susan. *Saints, Goddesses and Kings: Muslims and Christians in South Indian Society, 1700–1900.* Cambridge, 1989. Valuable survey on the growth and development of Islam in South India.

Eaton, Richard Maxwell. *Sufis of Bijapur, 1300–1700: Social Roles of Sufis in Medieval India.* Princeton, 1978. Pioneering study of Ṣūfīs in the Deccan, with a useful reading on their roles in propagating and popularizing Islam in South Asia.

Ewing, Katherine. "The Sufi as Saint, Curer, and Exorcist in Modern Pakistan." *Contributions to Asian Studies* 18 (1984): 106–114. Highly imaginative essay on the modern-day roles of pirs in Pakistan.

Ikram, Sheikh Mohamed. *Muslim Civilization in India.* Edited by Ainslie T. Embree. New York and London, 1964. Useful study of developments in South Asian Islam in the medieval period, which includes the Muslim perspective.

Mujeeb, Muhammad. *The Indian Muslims.* London, 1967. Provides valuable insight into the nature of developments in South Asian Islam. Essential for an understanding of Islamic culture in a non-Arab setting.

Roy, Asim. *The Islamic Syncretistic Tradition in Bengal.* Princeton, 1983. Excellent work on how the exogenous Islamic culture adjusted itself to the requirements of a specific situation, with a good deal of information on popular Islamic traditions in medieval Bengal.

Titus, Murray T. *Islam in India and Pakistan* (1929). Karachi, 1990. One of the earliest comprehensive surveys of Islam in South Asia.

RAFIUDDIN AHMED

Popular Religion in Southeast Asia

Nearly all Muslims in Southeast Asia form part of the Malay cultural region. This Muslim community is the largest in the world. It includes about 85 percent of Indonesia's 195 million people, about 11 million people in Malaysia, and several million in the southern Philippines. Underlying the many local differences in practice and belief are certain shared cultural features, including the use of Malay or Indonesian as a language of religious communication, forms of dress, food, and art associated with Islam, and a conception of gender relations that is relatively balanced in comparison with the gender relations codified in *sharīʿah.*

Since the late colonial period, Southeast Asian Muslims have also developed a Malay-language network of schools, publishing houses, and newspapers that crosses colonial and postcolonial boundaries throughout the archipelago. This network lends coherence to scholarly discussions occurring throughout the region, and these debates and exchanges among scholars have been brought into everyday dialogues about religious matters. For this reason, no clear line demarcates scholarly from popular forms of Islam in Southeast Asia, and "popular" henceforth is to be taken as meaning "as locally practiced." This articles focuses on the main ideas that have animated religious practices, interpretations, and debates among Muslims in Southeast Asia.

Spirit Transactions and Ritual Meals. Many of the practices that have lent a distinctive shape to Southeast Asian Islam involve exchanges or transactions with spiritual agents, including place spirits, ancestors, prophets, and God. The debates taking place over the last century among Muslims in the area have often turned on the legitimacy of certain transactions: appeals to spirits to heal, bless, or protect; sacrifices or offerings made to strengthen these appeals; or innovations in worship practice that have been made in the interest of clearer communication with God or to induce a benefit from God.

This emphasis on communicating with God and with diverse spirits has historically been supported by Ṣūfī teachings concerning the enduring ties between humans and God, by practices of meditation and the imitation of death, and by an emphasis on remembering spiritual ancestors. These ideas underlie the Ṣūfī orders in the region, but they also shape popular ideas of the power of speech and contribute to certain general cultural orientations such as the Javanist or *abangan* practices in Indonesia.

Central to most Southeast Asia Muslim cultures is the ritual meal, called *selametan* on Java and *kenduri* elsewhere in Indonesia and Malaysia. Participants at these meals generally burn incense, set out special plates of food that symbolize values of spirituality and purity, and deliver petitionary prayers to God, the prophet Muḥammad, and specific spiritual agents. Meals are held for a wide range of events, including life-crisis rituals of birth, circumcision, marriage, pregnancy, and death; annual celebrations of the Prophet's birthday, the completion of the fasting month (ʿĪd al-Fiṭr), and the Feast of Sacrifice (ʿĪd al-Aḍḥā); and occasional events such as leaving home, erecting a house, completing a recital of the Qur'ān, or resolving a dispute. Healing the sick and managing the agricultural cycle also involve special series of ritual meals.

Most such meals feature the recitation of one or more Qur'ānic verses, most commonly al-Fātihah or al-Ikhlāṣ. Special foods consumed at such meals include puffed rice (symbolizing the light qualities of spirituality), glutinous rice (symbolizing the strong ties among participants or with God), and small, flat pancakes called *apam* (usually associated with the dead). (Many of these elements are also found in South Asia.) Usually four, seven, or forty-four items are offered; the same numbers determine the intervals between the successive ritual meals held after a death.

Ritual meals give a religious meaning to a wide variety of events. They also provide a locally meaningful framework for interpreting broader Islamic ritual obligations, and many Southeast Asian societies observe Islamic feast-days and life-crisis rituals in the form of the *kenduri* or *selamatan*. [*See also* Rites of Passage; Islamic Calendar.]

The Power of Speech. Throughout the region Muslims have drawn on the powerful words of the Qur'ān to shape the world. Whether we classify them as spells or prayers, the speech forms usually labeled *doa* (Ar., *duʿā'*)—also called *donga* or *jampi*—are used to heal or ensorcel, to protect or attack, and to fortify or weaken other people, spirits, or objects. The substance of *doa* may range from the simple quotation of a Qur'ānic verse to a combination of Arabic verse, vernacular instructions, and semantically opaque syllables. *Doa* may be accompanied by accounts of how they came to be effective; thus, the power of a commonly found *doa* designed to ward off iron is understood as resulting from an original compact between God and iron. Speakers may also invoke the special qualities of a prophet, as by mentioning David's voice in a *doa* designed to attract a spouse. People may acquire the power to use a *doa* through meditation, possession, or visitation by a spirit or angel, or the words themselves may be sufficient to obtain the desired effect.

Many of the region's Muslims have regular recourse to particular verses of the Qur'ān as sources of help and strength in everyday life, but they may disagree about what reciting the verse does: does it bring about immediate, automatic aid? Or does it serve to strengthen one's heart against a difficulty? These beliefs and questions about the power of speech are not simply pre-Islamic remnants; often they are the topic of local commentaries that draw on Ṣūfī intellectual traditions identifying material reality as emanations from God and thus as susceptible to change through religiously inspired mental imaging and powerful speech.

The widespread use of Malay in the region also has meant that oral and written forms designed to transmit religious ideas have had wide distribution. These forms include historical works in verse or prose, such as the *Hikayat Raja-Raja Pasai* and the *Sejarah Melayu;* verse forms, especially the *syair* quatrain, which, born in sixteenth-century Aceh, became a major vehicle for the spread of Ṣūfī writings; and didactic texts, until this century written in the Arabic script and used across the region as basic texts in religious education. These texts have supplemented basic training in reading and reciting chapters of the Qur'ān. Children who complete their study of the Qur'ān are in many areas recognized at a *khatam Qur'ān* ceremony. [*See* Malay and Indonesian Literature.]

Popular Islam is not limited to oral means of learning, nor is it a fixed tradition. Muslims throughout the region have learned elements of Arabic, the Qur'ān, Islamic history, and ritual practice from shifting combinations of oral traditions, handwritten books of prayer and knowledge, and published texts regarding ritual practice, spells and prayers, and esoteric topics.

Healing. Powerful speech is particularly important in activities of healing. Southeast Asian healing practices may draw on ideas of possession (or "shamanism") or ideas of the susceptibility of spirits to direct control. Healers in many parts of Malaysia, for example, make frequent use of trance and spirit possession to investigate the nature of an illness. Malay séances are a form of public dramatic art in which shamans draw on Islamic prophets, spirits, and histories to explain an illness and to cure the patient of it. Although labeled non-Islamic (or pre-Islamic) by many Malay *ʿulamāʾ*, these practices draw on Islamic images and knowledge for their coherence and for their therapeutic effectiveness.

Other regional healing systems depend on the direct control of spirits. Sumatran Gayo healers, for example, speak directly to afflicting *jinn* and may then drive them out of the patient, but they never act as mediums. They expel spirits from persons by creating two parallel series of events: one series in the outer *(lahir)* world, where a rock smashes a citrus, and another in the inner *(batin)* world, in which the spirit has been captured in the citrus and is then expelled from it. Gayo reliance on a private form of exorcism, in contrast with Malay public séances, is consistent with their general social and cultural tendency to avoid public confrontations.

Most healing systems in the region share ideas of balance that derive from Islamic humoral theory. *Jinn* are held responsible for a wide range of illnesses, and imbalance between external and internal *jinn* or between qualities in the body may cause illness. Prophets, in particular Khidr, are called on to remove impurities from the body, such as those resulting from childbirth. [*See also* Medicine, *article on* Traditional Practice.]

Caring for the Dead. Of all the life-crisis rituals, the ways of caring for the dead have been of the greatest importance for Southeast Asian Muslims, possibly because of the importance of secondary burial in Southeast Asia prior to the coming of Islam. The scholarly debates published in the regional press beginning in the 1920s reflect a sharp conflict between local emphases on continued communication with the spirit after death and objections to those practices by modernist scholars. Several Islamic practices have become focuses for these arguments. One is the *talqīn*, the catechism read to the dead after burial; another is the set of recitation sessions held on successive evenings after a death.

Recitations feature forms of *tasbīḥ* (prayers for the glory of God), *salawat* (prayers for blessings on the prophet Muḥammad), *dhikr* or *tahlīl* (repetitions of "there is no god but God"), and *istighfār* (requests for God's pardon), along with the shorter Qur'ānic verses. Recitation leaders may deliver long prayers that include sections of the Qur'ān considered to be especially powerful, such as the Throne Verse (al-Baqarah, 255) or the chapter Yā Sīn. They learn these prayers by studying the pamphlets on prayer available throughout the region and by learning from older adepts.

Recitations are intended to create merit that can be transferred to the dead and to aid the spirit's passage from the community to the afterworld. Both objectives are shared with non-Islamic funeral practices in the region, and both Islamic and non-Islamic funerary ritual complexes feature a regular progression of feasts, with special weight placed on a feast held seven days after death. But the Islamic practices (especially the *talqīn* and *dhikr*) are also found elsewhere in the Muslim world. It is thus likely that similarities between Islamic and non-Islamic practices in Southeast Asia are in part the result of a convergence around quasi-universal ideas of death as transition, and not the simple result of the survival of pre-Islamic practices into the Islamic present. [*See also* Funerary Rites; Qur'ānic Recitation; Dhikr.]

Variations on Mainstream Rituals. Overreliance on an a priori distinction of official and popular religion risks obscuring the way in which mainstream religious forms become part of local religious systems. Worship ritual *(ṣalāt)*, for example, although an obligation all Muslims share, is also used as a way of distinguishing particular religious orientations. Because worship is considered prescriptively open to all who wish to attend, attempts to use it to create boundaries invariably occasion protest. In the 1970s, Muslim groups in Jakarta that wished to maintain a higher degree of personal purity sought to exclude all others from their worship services; these attempts at exclusion (not any differences in ritual form) led to popular protests and suppression of the group. On a more everyday level, some stratified societies, such as the Bugis of South Sulawesi, assign places in the mosque rows by social rank, thus reproducing a set of local distinctions through the medium of a generalized ritual form.

There are important resemblances among the ways other mainstream rituals are carried out across diverse Southeast Asian societies, and these resemblances may serve broadly to distinguish the region as a whole from South Asia or the Middle East. In much of Indonesia and Malaysia, for example, the sermons and symbols associated with the ʿĪd al-Aḍḥā emphasize the value of *ihklāṣ*, sincerely giving away something, as the central meaning of the ritual, rather than the sacrificial killing stressed in some other Muslim societies. Also throughout the region, this feast day has historically been given much less emphasis than has either the ʿĪd al-Fiṭr or the celebration *(mawlid)* of the birthday of the prophet Muḥammad. The latter is celebrated in a wide variety of ways, from elaborate social visiting to royal processions. [*See* ʿĪd al-Aḍḥā; ʿĪd al-Fiṭr; Mawlid.]

Personal Authority. The social organization of much Islamic practice in Southeast Asia is shaped by the idea that some persons are closer to God and therefore serve as channels to the divine. The idea of closeness is conveyed by the general term *walī* ("saint") but is realized in different forms. It is also shaped by older ideas of Malay and Javanese kingship, with the king at the ritual center of a sacred territory and at the highest point on a schema of social rank.

Religious orders *(tarekat;* Ar., *ṭarīqah)* may be centered on a founding ancestor. Orders are found throughout the region. Frequently found are local orders identifying themselves as Naqshbandīyah, sometimes also as Qādirīyah or Khālidīyah. These orders may have a single ritual center and more or less tightly knit networks of founders and disciples. Babussalam in West Sumatra is an example. Founded in 1883 by Syaikh Abdul Wahab Rokan, the village now serves as the center for a network of eighteen *syaikhs* (Ar., *shaykhs*) throughout Sumatra and Malaysia. Their followers attend an annual celebration at the founder's tomb. On Java orders may also be affiliated with the religious schools called *pesantren;* the important *pesantren* center Tebuireng in East Java, for example, is also the center for the Naqshbandīyah and Qādirīyah orders. The Javanese *kiyai* combines the prestige of the teacher with the spiritual authority associated with a genealogy, and prestigious *kiyai* offices are often handed down from father to son. [*See* Sufism, *article on* Ṣūfī Orders; Pesantren.]

Throughout the archipelago, graves or other sites associated with powerful ancestors define a sacred geography. Often these are the graves of men or women who founded a lineage or village, great healers, or teachers who founded religious orders. The sites may be the goal of regional pilgrimages or for regular visits by those seeking advice or assistance. (In this respect, Javanese practices of grave-visiting and meditation may be seen as accentuations of regionwide elements rather than constitutive of a distinct Javanist orientation.) Throughout Indonesia, the most powerful sacred gravesites are often those of men who brought Islam to the region, such as the Walī Songo on Java, or Syech Abdurrauf in Aceh. These sites may become the center for quasi-orders, loosely organized networks of adepts who venerate the tomb of the founder and consider themselves affiliates with an established *tarekat.* For example, the tomb of the late nineteenth-century figure Habib Muda in West Aceh is considered by his followers to be the "pole" *(quṭb)* for the west coast of the province. The founder's tomb is circumambulated each year on the tenth of Dhū al-Ḥijjah, as a "little *ḥajj.*"

Messianic figures have occasionally surfaced throughout the region, particularly in Malaysia, where Ṣūfī-like cults have combined meditation and trance dances with the veneration of a leader, sometimes referred to as the Mahdi. These cults may also encourage the practice of Malay martial arts *(silat),* an art form regionally associated with Islam that often incorporates worship or *dhikr* recitations.

Islam and *Adat*. Muslims everywhere conceive of a sphere of local custom designated by *ʿurf* or *adat* (Ar., *ʿādāt*) or other terms. But it is especially in Southeast Asia that *adat* has been developed as an alternative set of rules alongside *sharīʿah. Adat* is not merely local custom or practice; it is also worldview and culture, and in some places a legal code.

Southeast Asian Muslims by and large have constructed two perspectives from which to view the relation of *adat* to *sharīʿah.* From one perspective *adat* and *sharīʿah* appear as distinct, complementary spheres of social life—as tradition or custom contrasted with religion. Ideal constructions of Minangkabau (Sumatra) and Negeri Sembilan (Malaysia) societies, for example, link *adat* to the values of community and matriliny, and *sharīʿah* to the values of individuality and patriliny. Such holistic constructions also characterize the many descriptive and prescriptive pamphlets published in Malaysia, Singapore, and Indonesia on the *adat* of various Muslim peoples in the region, in which *adat* is typified by images of dress styles, marriage customs, and house forms.

From another perspective, however, *adat* and *sharīʿah* appear as providing distinct sets of norms regarding the same events: marriage, the transmission of property, and death ritual. Their relation may be complementary in some instances—*sharīʿah* stipulating the payment of a *mahr* at marriage, and *adat* elaborating on its form—but it may also be conflictual. *Adat* and *sharīʿah* may, in practice, provide conflicting ways of evaluating the same problem: how to divide an estate, how to celebrate a child's coming of age, or how to carry out a wedding. Such conflicts are particularly evident in the Malaysian *adat* law codes, but they also persist beneath the formal accommodation of the two systems elsewhere in the region. Of special importance have been conflicts over the division of an estate. Local *adat* norms may stipulate that all children (or all children remaining in their natal village) receive equal shares, or that males (or females) receive all the agricultural land, and they may allot to the village or lineage residual rights over land. Accommodations between *sharī'ah* and *adat* over this issue include figuring some property transfer as a gift or as a kind of *waqf*, and thus as distinct from the estate shares. [*See* Adat.]

Whereas the scholarship of the 1940s and 1950s generally portrayed Southeast Asian Islam as an overlay on a distinct, pre-Islamic substratum, more recent work has emphasized the Islamic character of many local practices, including those labeled as "pre-Islamic" by local *'ulamā'*. The central research activity has in effect shifted from distinguishing between Islam and non-Islam in popular religion to analyzing the debates within each society about the religious character of specific ideas and practices.

[*See also* Islam, *article on* Islam in Southeast Asia and the Pacific; *and the articles on individual countries in the region*.]

BIBLIOGRAPHY

Bowen, John R. *Muslims through Discourse: Religion and Ritual in Gayo Society*. Princeton, 1993. Detailed ethnography of rituals, and debates about their propriety in a Sumatran Muslim society.

Dobbin, Christine. *Islamic Revivalism in a Changing Peasant Economy: Central Sumatra, 1784–1847*. London, 1983. Superb history of religious and social change in an Indonesian society.

Ellen, Roy F. "Practical Islam in South-East Asia." In *Islam in South-East Asia*, edited by M. B. Hooker, pp. 50–91. Leiden, 1983. Insightful overview of the history of Islam and of colonial policies toward Islam in Southeast Asia.

Geertz, Clifford. *The Religion of Java*. Chicago, 1960. Classic, detailed study of Islam, culture, and society in Java.

Hefner, Robert W. "Islamizing Java? Religion and Politics in Rural East Java." *Journal of Asian Studies* 46 (1987): 533–554. Valuable update of Geertz's account.

Ibrahim, Ahmad, Sharon Siddique, and Yasmin Hussain, eds. *Readings on Islam in Southeast Asia*. Singapore, 1985. Useful collection of readings from past and present.

Laderman, Carol. *Taming the Wind of Desire: Psychology, Medicine, and Aesthetics in Malay Shamanistic Performance*. Berkeley, 1991. Includes material on Islamic sources for shamanism.

Lombard, Denys. "Les tarekat en Insulinde." In *Les ordres mystiques dans L'Islam*, edited by Alexandre Popovic and Gilles Veinstein, pp. 139–163. Paris, 1986. Insightful contrast of several orders in Indonesia.

Nagata, Judith. *The Reflowering of Malaysian Islam*. Vancouver, B.C., 1984. Good on older religious practices and the contemporary *da'wah* movement.

Siegel, James T.*The Rope of God*. Berkeley, 1969. Excellent study of changing social contexts for religious ideas in Aceh, Indonesia.

Snouck Hurgronje, Christiaan. *The Achehnese* (1893). Leiden, 1906. One of the best early accounts of religious life in a Muslim society.

Woodward, Mark R. "The Slametan: Textual Knowledge and Ritual Performance in Central Javanese Islam." *History of Religions* 28 (1988): 54–89.

JOHN R. BOWEN

Popular Religion in Europe and the Americas

Local Muslim belief and practice in non-Muslim countries reflect the historical experience of the community and the larger cultural environment within which it lives. Conversion and migration throughout the twentieth century have resulted in about eleven or twelve million Muslims living in Europe and America (the Muslim population figures tend to be estimates because of illiteracy, misunderstanding, and concealment of identity for fear of becoming entangled with the law). This large number has complicated the already complex relationship between Islam and the West. Islam is no longer "over there," in Asia or Africa; it is now a Western religion also.

To bring into relief the complicated processes at work in discussing popular Muslim belief and practice in the West, I will compare two Muslim communities: the Black Muslims in the United States and Muslims in Britain.

The range of belief and practice among these Muslims is wide, including fresh migrants from Muslim countries bringing their orthodox ways and local converts sometimes inventing their own. In some cases, the opposite is true: local Muslims have been notably correct in Islamic behavior and critical of Muslim visitors for being lax or improper. An interesting example, because it contains a paradox, comes from Cambridge University in 1991 when British Muslim students threatened members of the University's Pakistan society with physical violence if they went ahead with their plans for an ethnic folk-dance. Dancing, they said, was un-Islamic, and as Pakistan to them represented Islam, the Pakistani students needed to live up to their ideal.

Aghast at such challenges to their "Muslimness," the Pakistanis in turn complained that these British Muslims oscillated between two points: either very Islamic or very westernized. They have good-humoredly coined a name for local Muslims: BBCD or "British-Born Confused *Desi*" ("native"); in America, it is ABCD. For their part, the local Muslims call such Pakistanis TPs or "typical Pakistanis." Both labels contain negative connotations and reflect the inherent cultural tensions between Muslims in the West and those visiting from Muslim lands.

Developments in technology, transport, and communication—fueling the trend to globalization—in recent decades have ensured that no community can remain isolated, least of all Muslims; that all communities, however isolated in the past, are moving toward a defined uniformity. There are increasingly smaller chances for the survival of popular local religious practices in clashes with mainstream and orthodox Islam. Imams from Cairo and Medina, visiting scholars, audio- and video cassettes, ensure that the correct message is available as never before in history (Ahmed, 1988, 1992; Esposito, 1991; Nielsen, 1992; Shaikh, 1992).

Another factor in the decline of local customs is the dynamic and increasingly well-educated younger generation. Generally better educated than the previous one, it has higher hopes. Islam gives it an identity and pride. Young Muslims have wide and well-established networks in the academic world and jealously guard the frontiers of Islam.

Media interest in Muslims has been heightened by the growing notion in the West that Islam is the next major enemy after the collapse of communism. Discussion and debate around certain issues—the controversy around Salman Rushdie's novel, the Gulf War, the collapse of the Bank of Credit and Commerce International—have also forced onto Muslims an Islamic identity. In each case, this identity is reinforced in the community, as its members feel identified by their Muslimness regardless of their individual ideas. Muslimness is reinforced by a sense of deprivation, the feeling that as a community they have a long way to go in spite of numbers, education, and in many cases, wealth: there are still no Muslim members of Parliament in Europe or congressmen or senators in the United States.

Black Muslims. Perhaps the most dramatic example of how local Muslim belief and practice in the West differs substantially from orthodox Islam is provided by some of the Black Muslims in the United States. Although their membership was always a small percentage of the total U.S. Muslim population (about six million), their objectives, dedication, and the media's interest nonetheless gave them a high profile. In fact, they became the face of Islam in America as far as the media was concerned.

However, the Black Muslim movement cannot be understood without understanding the cultural environment in which it took root. Islam, however improperly and dimly understood, provided a genuine link with an atavistic past in Africa. It also provided a legitimate idiom in the fight for civil rights. Thus, the movement became inextricably linked with the struggle for civil rights, the need to combat slavery and racial discrimination, and the desire to locate dignity and pride in the face of ugly and massive racial prejudice.

Islam gave a coherent philosophy of life to many African Americans, and it provided a viable, ready-made role model in the form of the former slave Bilāl, one of the most ardent supporters of Islam in the seventh century and a great favorite of the prophet Muḥammad. Indeed, the Prophet appointed Bilāl as the first muezzin (Ar., *muʿadhdin;* the person who calls people to prayer at the mosque). The early African American Muslims called themselves Bilalians; Islam gave them a sense of honor and dignity.

However, there was much unorthodox thinking in the early Black Muslim movement. Although members of the Nation of Islam, founded in 1930 in Detroit, believed in the notion of one God called Allāh, they also believed that Elijah Muhammad was the last messenger of God. Heaven and hell were believed to exist on earth, and the number of stipulated prayers during the day was increased from five to seven. The month of December was fixed for fasting. Central Islamic beliefs, such as the finality of the Prophet, and accepted traditional practice, like the daily prayers or the month of fasting, were being challenged.

The belief in black supremacy, that the white race is intrinsically evil, was a major plank of the Nation of Islam's platform and reflected the racial situation in the United States. This philosophy was consciously inverting the form of racism that the African American community faced, especially in the southern states. There, some believed that blacks were congenitally inferior, their brains were smaller, their morals looser, and so on. Islamic belief and practice provided black groups with social cohesion, a sense of moral purpose, and above all, much-needed dignity. Also, a strict code of dress and conduct sought to stamp out drug and alcohol abuse in the community.

Hatred of white people, however, could not be justified in Islam. The Qur'ān emphasizes that all humanity—regardless of color—is equally the creation of God and among God's wonders. Indeed, this was conveyed in the last message of the Prophet at Arafat when he underlined that Arab and non-Arab, black and white, are all equal before God; only piety makes one person better than another.

Any Black Muslim seriously wishing to learn about Islam would confront many Nation of Islam teachings as un-Islamic and therefore ask questions. This is precisely what Malcolm X, one of the most charismatic of the Black Muslims, did. One of Elijah Muhammad's most trusted lieutenants, he had risen from the slums, knowing prison and drug abuse.

A pilgrimage to Mecca in 1964 opened Malcolm X's eyes to the true nature of Islam and changed his views dramatically. He expressed the change in his powerfully moving letters. He formally became a Sunnī and took the name El-Hajj Malik El-Shabazz. But by accepting orthodox Islam, he was challenging local belief and practice and therefore antagonizing his already-estranged group. Louis Farrakhan, once his friend, now demanded his death. A few months later, in 1965, Malcolm X was shot.

Spike Lee's film *Malcolm X* (1992) revealed the complexity and character of Malcolm X. It also revealed his continuing relevance to America today. The first American Muslim martyr, Malcolm X, ironically, has of late been recognized as a modern popular icon—not just a marginal black leader.

In the 1970s, important changes were taking place among the Black Muslims. After Elijah Muhammad's death in 1974, the succession of his son, Wallace (later Warith) Muhammad, the growth of the African American middle class, and the success of the Nation of Islam's chain of supermarkets, barber shops, and restaurants created a more relaxed community. Wallace Muhammad promptly dismantled the Fruit of Islam, the Nation of Islam's force of young men trained in martial arts and firearms use.

Postwar Muslim migrants from the Middle East and South Asia were also organizing Islamic societies which interacted with the Black Muslims and further drew them toward global Islam. Most important, increasing contact with and awareness of other Islamic movements outside the United States brought Black Muslim belief and practice more in line with international Islam. This occurred during the late 1970s, a time of increased international awareness of Islam, the era of King Fayṣal, of Saudi Arabia, General Zia ul-Haq of Pakistan, and Ayatollah Khomeini of Iran.

The pressures to reform split the Black Muslims in 1978 between Wallace Muhammad, who became head of the World Community of Islam, the U.S. component of which is the American Muslim Mission (present membership is about 150,000, but it has wide general support), and Louis Farrakhan, who revived the original Nation of Islam (membership about 50,000).

By reappraising the role of Elijah Muhammad—as a great teacher rather than a messenger—and adopting an international approach, the American Muslim Mission has reconciled with Sunnī sentiment. This link is further strengthened by the fact that the American Muslim Mission sends some members to study in Cairo and Medina.

Smaller groups, such as the Ḥanafī Muslims, whose leader, Abdul Khaalis, is accepted as an authority in about a hundred mosques, also split from the Black Muslims to move even more closely to mainstream Islam.

The beliefs and practices of Wallace Muhammad and Louis Farrakhan remain opposed: the former has opened membership to all races and moved toward the Sunnī position, the latter flaunts antiwhite sentiments, has recreated the Fruit of Islam, and rejects integration into the American political mainstream; indeed, he demands a separate African American state. Wallace Muhammad enjoys a degree of respectability in America never enjoyed before by a Black Muslim leader, but Farrakhan remains a figure of controversy. [*See* Nation of Islam *and the biographies of Elijah Muhammad and Malcolm X*.]

Muslims of the Outer Hebrides. The Muslim community in Stornoway on the Outer Hebrides, off the coast of Scotland, provides a dramatic contrast with the American Black Muslims. This group is almost invisible, grateful to be where it is, and earnestly working away to be accepted and integrated.

On Sundays the island is cut off from the world; there is no ferry or plane. No washing is hung out, and the parks are closed. The children's swings are chained and padlocked and so are the public toilets. This is high Presbyterian country, and Sunday is exclusively given to the Lord. No one in Stornoway would violate the cultural code that demands that people stay indoors, least of all the Muslim minority.

The group numbers about fifty and is mainly composed of Arain people from the Punjab in Pakistan (Ahmed, 1986). The Arain have specific social characteristics. They are generally small farmers from low-income groups. They tend to be thrifty, austere, and reflect the work ethic that made the Calvinists such a force in the drive toward Western capitalism (according to Max Weber's famous thesis).

In Stornoway, the Arain work ethic meets the Protestant work ethic, and the result is the success story of the small Pakistani community. The success, and the community's respectability, is reflected in the neat, gray suits, white shirts, sober ties, and clean-shaven appearance which the elders favor. Education is another area where the two ethics meet happily. Many of the young generation are pursuing advanced degrees.

The older generation did not build a mosque. There is no imam on the island. Indeed, they celebrate the religious festivals in a low-key manner, by taking an evening off on Saturday; both the work ethic and local cultural sensibilities are thus satisfied.

Muslim culture might seem subdued in Stornoway, but the sense of Muslimness is far from obliterated. In fact, there are many signs that the new generation is asserting itself in a much more distinctly Islamic manner than the previous one. A female Ph.D. candidate at Glasgow University, for example, is preparing for an arranged marriage in Pakistan. She has no qualms about this or her role as a Muslim wife; it is strange to hear this traditional Muslim speak in a strong Scottish accent. The living room of one of the Pakistani household heads is full of Islamic symbolism, of photos of Mecca and Medina; but it is a private room. We have in this Muslim group an example of a minority almost invisible and well integrated but showing signs of Islamic assertion under the surface. However, the harmony of the Outer Hebrides must not be taken as representative of the life of average British Muslims, which is fraught with change, tension, and challenge.

British Muslims. The main difference between Islam in the American and European contexts is the social and economic composition of the Muslim community. In the United States, the community is largely middle class; doctors, engineers, academics. This gives it a greater social confidence and a positive sense of belonging. In Europe, by and large, the community remains stuck in the underclass, still seen as immigrants. Its failure on the political scene is spectacular: although Britain has about two million Muslims, they have not been able to win a single seat in Parliament. Worse, their leaders tend to be divided and more interested in attacking each other than representing the community.

Another difference is that in the United States there is a greater geographical spread; Muslims are not seen as concentrating in one state or city. In Europe, there is a tendency to concentrate; Bradford, England, is an example. The concentration allows greater uniformity in belief and practice. During the Rushdie crisis, the leaders of Bradford were constantly consulted by the media. Concentration allowed the media to simplify questions of leadership, values, strategy, and organization among Muslims. Only subsequently did people realize that, although the Bradford spokespeople reflected broadly the general opinion of Muslims, they were by no means elected or unanimously accepted leaders of the entire Muslim community of the United Kingdom.

The concentration of Muslims in England has another consequence. The community can—and frequently does—import and perpetuate its sectarian and ethnic characteristics from home. The traditional sectarian tensions in Pakistan between the Barelwīs and Deobandīs, both mainstream Sunnī Muslims, were lifted en bloc to the United Kingdom. For the outsider, the differences between these sects would be confusing and difficult to understand. For example, the holy Prophet for the Barelwīs (or Barelvīs, who are mostly from the Pakistan province of Punjab) is a superhuman figure whose presence is all around us and at all times *ḥāẓir* (present); he is not *bashar* (material or flesh) but *nūr* (light). The Deobandīs, who also revere the Prophet, argue he was the *insān-i kāmil* (the perfect person) but still only a man, a mortal. This explains why Kalim Siddiqui in the United Kingdom, demanding the implementation of Khomeini's *fatwā* against Salman Rushdie for insulting the Prophet in his novel, found his most sympathetic audience among the Barelwīs. [*See* Barelwīs *and* Deobandīs.]

The known characteristics of British Muslims underline the differences between the community in the United Kingdom and in the United States: there is a greater concentration of the Muslim population in certain cities. There is the continuing pull of the old, home country. This has social implications. For instance, many Pakistani families still look for spouses in Pakistan. The larger political confrontation in South Asia between India and Pakistan, between Hindus and Muslims, is also reflected in the United Kingdom. An example is provided by the events following the destruction of the Babri mosque in Ayodhya, India, in December 1992. Hindu temples were attacked in the United Kingdom, and there was considerable tension between Muslims and Hindus in the traditionally peaceful Asian community.

However, there are also similarities between the United States and Europe. In both places, the mosque is an important center of social and political activity and has provided leadership in times of crises. In both places, the media have been involved in the Muslim debate, particularly in such cases as *The Satanic Verses* controversy. This in turn has united the community across sectarian and ethnic barriers.

The one major difference between the American and European situation is that in the United States a large percentage of Muslims are local or indigenous. So while the struggle in Europe is between Muslims attempting to establish a foothold, united in their foreignness, otherness, and alienness, in America, it is the move to find a balance between the local Black Muslims and mainstream Muslims from the rest of the Muslim world, between local practice and mainstream Islamic thinking and tradition.

The problem of an accurate population census of Muslims in both the United States and Europe remains. Therefore, not only populations but also percentages can only be estimates at best. Yet it is clear that the dynamics of Muslim belief and practice on the two different continents is affected by the percentage of immigrants in the Muslim population, which is overwhelming in Europe and much less so in the United States. However, this situation is beginning to change as a younger Muslim generation comes of age in Europe and sees itself as both Muslim and European. It is also changing in the United States as Black Muslims themselves move closer to the mainstream Muslim position recognized throughout the world.

Local belief and practice in Europe and the Americas have grown as a Muslim response to the larger non-Muslim community, echoing it. Over time, these beliefs and practices have been aligned more and more closely with the orthodox Islamic position. This process has been helped by the media, by international politics, by fresher migration from Muslim countries, and by a more educated and assertive younger generation. The reconciliation between the demands of local identity and those of universal Islam will be one of the great challenges for Muslims in Europe and America, a process fraught with excitement and, at times, tension.

[*See also* Islam, *articles on* Islam in Europe *and* Islam in the Americas.]

BIBLIOGRAPHY

Ahmed, Akbar S. *Pakistan Society: Islam, Ethnicity, and Leadership in South Asia*. Karachi and Oxford, 1986.

Ahmed, Akbar S. *Discovering Islam: Making Sense of Muslim History and Society*. London and New York, 1988.

Ahmed, Akbar S. *Postmodernism and Islam: Predicament and Promise*. London, 1992.

Esposito, John L. *Islam: The Straight Path*. Exp. ed. New York and Oxford. 1991.

Nielsen, Jørgen S. *Muslims in Western Europe*. Edinburgh, 1992.

Shaikh, Farzana, ed. *Islam and Islamic Groups: A Worldwide Reference Guide*. Essex, 1992.

AKBAR S. AHMED

POPULATION GROWTH. *See* Family Planning.

POTTERY AND CERAMICS. For nearly a thousand years ceramics has been one of the most creative fields of Islamic art. The needs and tastes of diverse Muslim societies have produced a great variety of forms, techniques, and decorative motifs. In addition, ceramic elements have been widely used in Islamic architecture.

Since the eighteenth century Islamic societies have undergone profound changes. Traditional economies were locally based, dominated by guilds of craftsmen and traders. Increasing contacts with industrial Europe dramatically transformed this system, especially in the provinces of the Ottoman Empire. Fine ceramics were imported from Meissen or Vienna, where manufacturers began producing special series for sale in the East, and even from Sèvres in France. In the nineteenth century a few, mostly short-lived porcelain factories were established in Iran and Turkey, notably at Incirli in 1845 and Yildiz in 1894. These enterprises used European manufacturing technology but adapted forms and designs to local tastes. During the same period the arrival of industrial products on the Eastern market at competitive prices made the middle classes increasingly dissatisfied with local products. The gradual disappearance of the guilds, which set standards for trades and trained apprentices, often brought a decline in quality, although this change did not reach the Maghrib until the twentieth century. Today the demand generated by tourism has created new outlets for Oriental ceramics, but the quest for maximum yield and steady profits is not always favorable to maintaining a high level of quality, let alone fostering creativity and innovation.

Fortunately, a few ceramists have devoted themselves to restoring the creative vision of past centuries through technical research or original designs; examples are the Chemla family in Tunis since 1880 and Lamali in Morocco beginning in 1920. At the same time, some contemporary artists have made ceramics their favored medium, while others, like the Algerian Baya, see it as an occasional support for their work. Various countries include ceramics in the curricula of their fine-arts academies, such as the programs at Istanbul and Baghdad. Furthermore, in the nineteenth and twentieth centuries some artists in Europe (Theodore Deck and Edmond Lachenal, for instance) and the Far East (Takuo Kato, the contemporary Japanese potter) have imitated or adapted Islamic styles and techniques with varying degrees of success.

Pottery is still produced in great quantity in most Islamic countries, where ordinary people use clay vessels to drink, cook, serve, store, and carry their food. These vessels remain cheap and popular, although they are gradually being replaced by plastic, aluminum, and enamelware. Various writers have addressed the rapid changes in ceramics materials, form, design, and production, making detailed studies of such key centers of the industry as Fez in Morocco, Nabeul in Tunisia, Fustāt and Luxor in Egypt, or Nain and Meybod in Iran.

FIGURE 1. *Large Plate, Ghotar.* Fez, Morocco. Photograph by Philippe Maillard.

Throughout the Maghrib two types of traditional pottery can be found—hand-built earthenware made by women, and turned pottery made by men. The first, produced in rural areas almost exclusively for local use, dates to Neolithic times and is today found mostly in northwestern Tunisia, in Algerian Kabylia, and in the Rif mountains of Morocco; production is very widely dispersed. Forms vary greatly; after a short firing, a piece may be glazed with a resin to make it watertight or decorated with vegetable or mineral dyes in a geometric design characteristic of the region. The second style is produced in urban potteries, primarily for sale rather than for personal use. Centers of production are less numerous, and the designs still reflect Andalusian and Ottoman influences. Ceramic architectural elements—glazed mosaics or excised terra cotta in Morocco and painted tiles in Tunisia—are common as facings *(zulayj)* throughout North Africa in religious schools, mosques, private homes, and official buildings.

Moroccan ceramics from the medieval period to the eighteenth century are poorly documented. Fez is the most famous center of production, but other potteries exist at Meknes, at Salé, and later at Safi. Ordinary clay is used, as in all of the Maghrib; a preliminary firing precedes the application of an opaque lead-tin glaze. A second firing fixes the decoration, blue or polychrome. Sometimes dots of minium (red lead) were added by retailers. Around 1850 the designs, either floral or geometric and often radiating from a central motif, grew denser, and the use of industrial pigments made the colors more enduring. Traditional forms are varied, including plates, covered dishes, and bowls, as well as oil or butter jars, inkwells, and lamps.

In Algeria pottery was never highly developed and virtually disappeared in the nineteenth century. Its porcelain and ceramics are imported primarily from the Netherlands, France, and Italy, or acquired through traditional trade with neighboring countries.

In the last two centuries, Qalliline, a suburb of Tunis, has continued to produce and export ceramic panels adorned with large floral or architectural patterns as those from Iznik or Damascus previously were. Its generously proportioned tableware is noted for vigorous, stylized decoration, often featuring such animal motifs as fish, birds, or lions. In the south of Tunisia, the island of Djerba, whose production of ceramics has been documented for centuries, is best known for its large,

FIGURE 2. *Wall Tiles.* Tunisia. Photograph by Philippe Maillard.

unglazed storage jars and the green and yellow ware that has recently been much in demand. At the beginning of the twentieth century a few Djerba potters established themselves in Nabeul on Cape Bon and began to produce glazed polychrome pottery that reflected their efforts at research and creativity. While Nabeul is presently the most important center of production, there are others in different parts of the country, including Moknine in the Sahel and Tozeur in the south.

In Egypt, despite a long and brilliant history, pottery and ceramics today are produced almost exclusively for utilitarian purposes. The poorest Egyptians use earthenware for a variety of everyday vessels such as water jugs and bowls. There are many potteries in Fustāt and Alexandria, and in Upper Egypt at Ballās, Qena, and Luxor. They rarely sell their wares directly, however, instead supplying peddlers at the local market and other middlemen. Most of the production is not very refined and is usually unglazed, although a few wares get a lead glaze, generally colored but occasionally opaque. The number of potteries is rapidly decreasing with the ongoing changes in rural life and the disappearance of ancient ways of life. In 1956 a new pottery center was created in Garagos in Upper Egypt, with the goal of developing a renewed popular art based on traditional pottery.

In Turkey during the golden age of the Ottoman Empire, the work of the court potteries at Iznik and Tekfur Sarayi dominated the field. Their collapse in the eighteenth century brought about a renaissance of production in the provinces. Among the most notable new products were those of Kütahya, whose tableware, architectural tiles, and religious objects were created primarily for the Armenian community. For everyday use, the pottery at Çanakkale on the Dardanelles produced designs that became nineteenth-century stereotypes. Today, in addition to the traditional studios, there is a steady flow of pottery imitating ancient Iznik, intended primarily for the tourist trade.

Nineteenth-century reports from diplomats and other foreign agents in Iran identify several cities as important centers of pottery and ceramics, including Kashan, Isfahan, Meybod, Shiraz, Nain, and others. A number of pieces with dates, identifying inscriptions, or signatures have been found to confirm these accounts. The techniques used are varied: bicolored black and blue, European-influenced polychromy, and a revival of lustre painting. Siliceous pastes are dominant here, and some workshops have made a kind of porcelain. The production of architectural tiles remains vigorous, primarily for garden pavilions as well as for the tourist trade. Folk pottery still yields such charming items as ceramic beehive covers. Copies of historical objects, like the overpainted *haft-rang* or *mīnāi,* lustre painted, and so-called Kubatcha wares are also widely produced.

Afghanistan and Central Asia saw far fewer nineteenth-century imports than their neighbors to the west. As a result traditional styles and techniques are well preserved, and ceramics produced today closely resemble those of earlier centuries: turquoise glazes with splashes of dark blue and purple, designs in colored *engobe,* and incised green-and-yellow ware that recalls a kind of earthenware produced in China under the Tang dynasty. Potteries are found near many cities, especially Bukhara, Dushanbe, and Khiva, renowned for the ceramic decorations of the many of their monuments. Here too the twentieth century has seen a decline in craftsmanship, despite massive public-works projects to restore many façades clad in brilliant tile.

In the Near East, the related art of glassmaking continued to develop from ancient times well into the fourteenth century, especially in Egypt and Syria and to a lesser degree in Iran, Iraq, and Turkey. Lustre glass, cut glass, gilt glass, and enameled glass were all produced. Since the sixteenth century, however, fine glassware has been imported, first from Venice and later from Bohemia and Silesia. Nineteenth-century Western artists like Emile Gallé and Joseph Brocard drew some of their ideas from Islamic glasswork.

As in the case of ceramics, the Ottoman government decided in the nineteenth century to build a glass factory on a European model. Situated at Beykoz near Istanbul, its most celebrated products, called *çaşmibülbül,* were often difficult to distinguish from Venetian glass. Today little fine glass is produced in the Islamic world, except in a few large cities like Cairo, Damascus, and Herat, where studios using recycled materials and kilns fired by gas or heating oil operate on a regular or occasional basis. Nevertheless, the skill of the craftspeople is obvious, even in pieces that have little or no decoration—a simple painted or enameled pattern, or just a thread applied to the surface. In addition to traditional pieces, apprentices make objects of personal adornment, especially glass beads and bracelets. Finding themselves threatened by a glass industry whose superior products are preferred by local buyers, these artisans are trying to adapt to meet foreign demand, both tourist and export, which recognizes the quality and particular value of handmade products, especially in the form of lamps and tableware.

BIBLIOGRAPHY

Ammoun, Denise. *Crafts of Egypt*. Cairo, 1991.

Bayramoğlu, Fuat. *Turkish Glass and Beykoz-Ware*. Translated by Leylâ Melek Kermenli. Istanbul, 1976.

Bel, Alfred. *Les industries de la céramique à Fès*. Algiers, 1918.

Boukobza, André. *La poterie marocaine*. 2d ed. Casablanca, 1987. Note especially the chapter on Lamali.

Bourdakoff, Nicolas. *Céramique de l'Asie Centrale*. St. Petersburg, 1904.

Brissaud, Philippe. *Les ateliers de potiers de la région de Louqsor*. Publication of the Institut Français d'Archéologie Orientale du Caire 78 (1982).

Centlivres-Demont, Micheline. *Faïences persanes des XIXe et XXe siècles: Nâîn et Meybod*. Bern, 1975.

Ceramics from Iran. London, 1977. Contemporary artistic pottery.

Chafiq, Imam, et al. "L'Artisanat du verre à Damas." *Bulletin d'Études Orientales* 27 (1974): 141–179.

Daoulatli, Abdelaziz. *Poteries et céramiques tunisiennes*. Tunis, 1979.

Dervize, G. *Keramika narodnykh masterov Sredney Azii* (Popular Contemporary Ceramics from the Masters of Central Asia). Moscow, 1974.

Gaulmier, Jean. "Note sur la fabrication du verre à Armanâz." *Bulletin d'Études Orientales* 6 (1936): 53–59.

Golvin, Lucien, et al. *Les potiers actuels de Fustât*. Publication of the Institut Français d'Archéologie Orientale du Caire 89 (1982).

Hakenjos, Bernd. *Marokkanische Keramik*. Stuttgart, 1988. Catalog of a recent exhibition on the subject.

Jones, Dalu. "Qallaline Tile Panels: Tile Pictures in North Africa." *Art and Archaeology Research Paper* (London) (December 1978): 1–30.

Lisse, Pierre, and André Louis. *Les potiers de Nabeul*. Tunis, 1956.

Marin, F. R. *Moderne Keramik von Zentralasien*. Stockholm, 1897.

Reut, Marguerite. "La verre soufflé de Hérat." *Studia Iranica* 2 (1973): 97–111.

Revault, Jacques. *Arts traditionnels en Tunisie*. Paris, 1967. See pages 77–103.

Soustiel, Jean. *La céramique islamique: Le guide du connaisseur*. Fribourg, 1985. Account of very interesting developments in Turkey, Iran, and Central Asia during the nineteenth and twentieth centuries.

Wulff, Hans E. *The Traditional Crafts of Persia*. Cambridge, Mass., 1966. See pages 136–171.

Zhadova, Larisa. *Sovremennaia keramika Uzbekistana* (Contemporary Folk Pottery of Central Asia). Moscow, 1963.

JEANNE MOULIERAC

Translated from French by Harry M. Matthews, Jr.

PRAYER. *See* Ṣalāt.

PROPERTY. Ownership is referred to in the Qur'ān many times: the Creator is the owner of everything; and he has made subject to human beings such creatures as the earth, the sun, the moon, the sea, the rivers, and so forth (see surahs 14.32–34, 16.12–14, 31.20, and 45.13). Vicegerency belongs to all the human race, the children of Adam who are required to act in accordance with the regulations set forth by the Real Owner. *Sharīʿah* (Islamic law) considers property rights as God given and God regulated.

In legal terms, personal property, which is referred to in many Qur'ānic surahs, is defined in *sharīʿah* as "an exclusivity over an object vesting the owner, alone and on owner's own behalf, with a legal authority of its use and enjoyment and of its disposal except when legally restricted" (Abbadi, 1974, vol. 1, p. 150). The object of personal property can be material or abstract, and it covers intellectual as well as financial properties. Under all circumstances, the object matter of personal property carries a moral and religious connotation according to Islamic law. For instance, since Islamic moral standards condemn alcoholic beverages and other intoxicating substances, these cannot be an object of personal property, that is, they cannot be owned by a Muslim. The same applies to swine and its products, as they are religiously prohibited in Islam. *Sharīʿah* makes exception for religious minorities inasmuch as their own moral standards permit. Thus, under Islamic law, property rights apply to alcoholic beverages owned by a Christian or a Jew and to swine owned by a Christian. Hence, an Islamic court can hear a dispute about them, although it cannot hear a dispute if those things belong to a Muslim.

The first and most important implication of the *sharīʿah* definition of property is that ownership in Islam is a right or collection of rights allowed by God, the Ultimate Lawmaker, not by society or its legislative authority. By no means do the society and its lawmaking organs have any legislative power to alter the basic rights laid down by God. Property rights are therefore granted by Allāh, they are not a societal function decided by society (Abbadi, 1974, vol. 1, pp. 426–39).

Second, private property is protected by *sharīʿah* itself. *Sharīʿah* in Islam is the divine law whose essential landmarks and principles are given in the divine revelation and whose details are worked out by human beings on the basis of the godly revelation as manifested in the Qurʾān and the traditions of the prophet Muḥammad. Therefore, a *sharīʿah* protection is an eternal protection, according to the Islamic system. This protection stands against any possible transgression from the government as well as from other persons.

Third, property rights entitle the owner full authority to use, benefit from, exploit, and dispose of the owned object. Muslim jurists usually use the rule "owners are absolute masters of their properties," which implies a wide range of economic freedom. This is, of course, within the limits of *sharīʿah,* which regulates private and public properties and forbids unfair exchanges.

Fourth, property rights are free of any prejudice on the basis of sex, religion, or ethnicity. The Islamic *sharīʿah* equalized men and women with regard to property rights, preceding most other legal systems and cultures.

From the point of view of the property owner, jurists distinguish between two kinds of property: private and public. Some Islamic writers like to add a third category, *waqf* (religious endowment) property. Although its use is restricted to the purpose designated by the donor, *waqf* property is considered owned by private parties (donor or beneficiaries) by most Muslim scholars. Some, however, believe that once designated for its philanthropic purpose, the *waqf* becomes a property of no one but God. [*See* Waqf.] Private property is individually owned by private persons.

Public property is owned collectively by the whole society or community. It covers things that benefit all members of a society or a majority of them, such as roads, rivers, forests, parks, lakes, natural springs and fountains, pasture lands not privately owned, and so forth. It also includes land not privately owned, land designated for community use around villages and towns, and mineral resources.

An Islamic government, according to *sharīʿah,* is the authority that administers public property on behalf of people and in their best interests. From the point of view of regulating governmental power in this regard, public property can be divided into three types (some jurists prefer a threefold classification to start with; accordingly, property can be private, state, or community):

1. *Public property designated for community use, such as roads, rivers, and mosques.* This type of public property cannot be sold or disposed of by the government nor can it be acquired or owned by private persons. However, if a community public property ceases to produce its desired benefit to the community and becomes deserted, the government can substitute it for a new property that can give similar benefit. Community property includes pasture and firewood lands surrounding villages.

In many African countries, community public lands still exist. They are related to a tribal social system. This is a dominant form of land ownership in pastoral areas, but it is also present in farming areas. This land, owned by tribal farming communities, is called *arāshī* land in Algeria and Tunisia. Usually, tribal customs and traditions determine the distribution of community-owned lands among families for cultivation, and except for *ʿushr*—10 percent of total agricultural products if the land is rain or river fed and 5 percent if it is irrigated by underground water, which is *zakāt* (alms) on agricultural products—there are no taxes or fees levied on families using collectively owned lands. *ʿUshr* is usually distributed to the poor and needy by tribal chiefs with the help of the village mosque's *imām* (prayer leader). [*See* ʿUshr.]

A special kind of community public property is called *ḥimā* ("protected") land. This is a lot of land appropriated by the government for a specific use, military or philanthropic. ʿUmar, the second caliph after the prophet Muḥammad, assigned certain lots for the army's horses and camels and for the cattle of the poor and needy.

2. *Nonused public land covers all lands that are not included in economic production.* In *sharīʿah* terms, this land is called *mawāt* ("dead"). Individuals have the right of *iḥyāʾ* ("revivification") of *mawāt* land, putting this public land into economic use, and this is considered a sufficient cause for earning private ownership of the land. The Islamic state can organize the exercise of this right, but it cannot eliminate it.

3. *State public property.* This category covers all other public properties whereby the only *sharīʿah* restriction on the behavior of the government is the criterion of serving the best interests of the people.

Sharīʿah recognizes six causes for personal property rights:

1. Lawful work in acquisition of unowned mobile things, such as obtaining water from a river in a container, hunting, and collecting firewood.
2. Revivification of nonused public land. Land revivification implies making it productive in agriculture, industry, or any other economic use. This means that mere acquisition of land by fencing or demarcation does not create a right of ownership.
3. Growth of an already owned property with or without labor involved. This growth includes fruits of owned trees and offspring of owned livestock. It also includes increments in value of owned merchandise.
4. Contractual relationships including exchange contracts, such as sale and hiring, contributory contracts, such as those involving gifts and last wills, and acceptance of religious and legal spending obligations, such as taking *zakāt* payment, alimony, money solemnly vowed to certain lawful purposes, and expiatory payments determined in *sharīʿah* for committing certain sins, such as breaking the fast in the month of Ramaḍān or making certain mistakes while performing *ḥajj* (pilgrimage to Mecca).
5. Tort liabilities which create a right of compensation.
6. Inheritance, where details of heirs and their shares are mostly given in the Qur'ān.

Noticeably, the first three causes create new property rights, while the last three transfer an existing property from one person to another.

There are three means of obtaining property which *sharīʿah* does not recognize: noncontractual acquisition of property belonging to others, including theft, swindling, plundering, looting, usurpation, acquisition by coercion, and fraudulent practices; acquisition of nonused land without its revivification (this kind of acquisition is usually done by demarcation and is called *taḥjīr* or "demarcation by stones"); and exchange relationships that are either invalid or prohibited in *sharīʿah*. Invalid relationships include contracts lacking some of the basic requirements, such as consent of contractors. Prohibited exchanges include: interest on loans, since the Qur'ān mentioned that a lender is only entitled to get the principal back and considers any increment as oppressive (surah 2.219); income from gambling (surah 5.90–91); bribery and similar exercises; and contracts whose object is condemned in *sharīʿah*, such as transactions of prohibited substances like alcoholic beverages, and prostitution.

Things acquired by prohibited means remain the property of their original owner and should be returned to him or her or to the rightful heirs. If owners or heirs do not exist, such things should be disposed of for charitable purposes on behalf of the true owners.

Sharīʿah distinguishes between two kinds of restrictions on property. The first kind of restrictions concerns the use and disposition of one's property. As the objective of property is the benefits and enjoyment derived from owned things, *sharīʿah*'s regulations aim at assuring that property fulfills its objectives. The Qur'ān ordains making one's best appearance and condemns those who prohibit adornments, beautiful living, and good things of sustenance (surah 7.31–32). At the same time, the Qur'ān forbids wastefulness, "for God loveth not the wasters" (surah 7.31), and considers spendthrifts as "brothers of the Satan" (surah 17.27). This led Muslim jurists to treat wasters and spendthrifts as legally incapable of using their own property and to subject them to legal guardians (Abbadi, 1974, vol. 2, pp. 86–96).

On the other hand, the use of one's property is constrained by others' rights. This means that extracting benefit and enjoyment of one's property must not be at the expense of the rights of other individuals or of the society as a whole. Islamic law disallows this kind of exercise regardless of personal intention and charges the harm-doer to compensate the injured. Examples of such actions are raising one's building to an extent that reduces the ventilation and sunshine reaching a neighbor's property (individual harm) and monopolistic practices (societal harm).

Another type of restriction on the use of one's property is related to inheritance and last will. Since the True Owner of all properties is God and private property is only a divine grant, the ownership right holds as long as the owner lives, but on death it goes back to the True Owner. The inheritance law in Islam is strictly founded on this principle. Shares are assigned to different heirs by God in the Qur'ān, and the owner has no right to change these shares under any circumstances. The heirs in *sharīʿah* are sons and daughters, parents and grandparents, spouses, brothers and sisters, uncles and aunts. Their respective shares are given according to a sophisticated chart dividing the estate. However, a person may make a last will, provided that it does not cover more than one-third of the estate and it does not alter the relative shares of the heirs. Permission to make a last will is called "a charity from God on us" by Abū Bakr, the most prominent companion of the prophet Muḥammad.

A fourth type of restriction on one's property is based on contractual relations, whereby through mutual consent and free will, an owner agrees to separate ownership of a property from its usufruct and surrenders one of them without the other.

The second kind of restrictions are rooted in conflict with the public interest. In recognition of philanthropic needs in any society, *sharīʿah* institutionalized a built-in financial obligation on personal property. This is called *zakāt* ("purification and growth"). It ranks as the third pillar of Islam after pronouncement of faith in God and his messenger and performance of prayers. This financial/religious obligation on property has, generally, a rate of 2.5 percent of the value of property with exemptions related to living expenses. The Qur'ān exclusively specifies eight categories of potential recipients and heads of expenditures for the proceeds of *zakāt,* and all but one are of a charitable and community service nature, the exception being the cost of collection and distribution of *zakāt* itself.

Besides this obligation, other financial duties or taxes on personal property are determined by the needs and interests of the society if the stream of public revenues coming out of public property proves to be insufficient. Such taxes are of temporal nature and are determined by the legislative branch of the state.

[*See also* Economics, *article on* Economic Theory; Inheritance; Land Tenure; Taxation; *and* Zakāt.]

BIBLIOGRAPHY

ʿAbbādī, ʿAbd al-Salām. *Al-milkīyah fī sharīʿah al-Islāmīyah.* Amman, 1974.

Abū Zahrah, Muḥammad. *Al-Milkīyah wa-naẓarīyat al-ʿaqd fī al-sharīʿah al-Islāmīyah.* Cairo, 1976.

Ahmed, Ẓiauddin, Munawar Iqbal, and M. Fahim Khan. *Fiscal Policy and Resource Allocation in Islam.* Islamabad, 1983.

Chapra, Mohammed Umer. *Towards a Just Monetary System.* Leicester, 1985.

Gulaid, M. *Land Ownership in Islam.* Jeddah, 1981.

Jalili, A. R. *Al-tharwah wa-al-milkīyah wa-tadakhkhul al-dawlah fī al-Islām.* 2 vols. Riyadh, 1988.

Muṣliḥ, A. al-. *Al-milkīyah al-khāṣṣah fī al-sharīʿah al-Islāmīyah.* Cairo, 1982.

Qaraḍāwī, Yūsuf al-. *Fiqh al-zakāh.* 2 vols. Beirut, 1973.

Rubi, R. al-. *Al-milkīyah al-ʿāmmah fī ṣadr al-Islām wa-waẓifatuhā.* Jeddah, n.d.

Samīḥ, Muḥammad ibn ʿAlī al-. *Mulkīyat al-arḍ fī al-sharīʿah al-Islāmīyah.* Riyadh, 1983.

Yūnus, ʿAbd Allāh Mukhtār. *Al-milkīyah fī al-sharīʿah al-Islāmīyah wa-dawruhā fī al-iqtiṣād al-Islāmī.* Alexandria, 1987.

Zuhaili, M. al-. *Iḥyāʾ al-ʾarḍ al-mawāt.* Jeddah, n.d.

MONZER KAHF

PROPHETHOOD. The commonest term for prophethood in the Islamic religious vocabulary is *nubūwah,* from the Arabic root *n-b-ʾ*, meaning "elevate" or "announce." The latter meaning is predominant in the Qur'ānic understanding of the prophet, *nabī*, as "one who announces." The first meaning is also employed by Islamic religious scholars to express the elevated status of the prophet among humankind or the elevating effect of the prophet's communication on those who receive it.

The Qur'ān uses the term "prophet" generically (pl., *nabīyūn* or *anbiyāʾ*) of persons called by God to communicate a divinely given message to humankind (*nas,* Qur'ān 16.44) and to the unseen world of the spirits (*jinn,* 46.29). A second term for prophet is *rasūl* (pl., *rusul*), derived from the Arabic root *r-s-l* meaning "send." Whereas *nabī* expresses the communicative nature of prophethood, *rasūl* emphasizes its emissary function of delivering the message in the language of a particular community (14.4, 16.36). Distinguishing these roles, which the Qur'ān often invests in a single person,

Muslim exegetes have considered the *nabī* to be a recipient of divine revelation in the form of general moral teaching, exemplified in the prophet's own life; *rasūl* denotes a prophet whose revelation contains God's specific commands and prohibitions in the form of an ethical code *(sharīʿah)* recorded in the scriptural form of a book *(kitāb)* as guidance *(hudā)* for a particular community in this world (5.48) and as the standard by which its members will be judged on the last day (10.47).

The Qur'ān presents belief in prophethood as the corollary of faith in God, the two being linked in the Muslim testimony of faith (Shahādah): "I testify that there is no god but God; I testify that Muḥammad is the messenger *(rasūl)* of God." Islamic religious thought deals extensively with prophethood as a mercy of God toward creation, given without obligation as the noblest expression of God's consistent guidance of humankind to the good. Prophethood meets an absolute human need and provides the means by which humans can respond individually and collectively to God in an active faith that "enjoins right conduct and forbids indecency" (3.104). The prophet is a witness *(shahīd)* of God's unity *(tawḥīd)*, an announcer *(mubashshir)* of the righteous conduct *(dīn)* God wills for this world, and the warner *(nadhīr)* of God's judgment on the last day. The messenger also has the eschatological role of being witness on the day of judgment in respect of the human community to which he was sent.

God's free initiative in revelation entails God's liberty to have chosen for prophetic responsibility any human being up to the prophet Muḥammad, whom the Qur'ān designates "the Seal of the Prophets" (33.40). Rationality of mind and sincerity of heart were the only human qualifications on which Muslim scholars insisted. To such men—and, some scholars such as Ibn Ḥazm argued, such women—God communicated through *waḥy*, the general Qur'ānic term for "revelation" (42.51). *Waḥy* embraces two dimensions: that of God's general inspiration *(ilhām)* of rational and nonrational creatures; more precisely, it signifies special revelation that God caused to descend *(tanzīl)* upon those God chose as prophets. These persons remain fully human but are elevated (note the first meaning of the Arabic root *n-b-'*) to the highest degree of intellectual and moral excellence, superior even to the angels, as exemplified especially in the character of the prophet Muḥammad (68.4).

The perfection of the prophets is expressed in the Islamic doctrine of infallibility *(ʿiṣmah)*, which, though nowhere explicit in the Qur'ān, was elaborated in the classical creeds of Islam. Infallibility applied to four defining attributes of prophethood: fidelity *(amānah)* to divine commands, veracity *(ṣidq)* respecting what God gave them to communicate, sagacity *(faṭānah)* in understanding its meaning, and the transmission *(tablīgh)* of the message itself. Classical Islam saw miracle *(muʿjizah)* as the external evidence of the elevated human qualities of prophets. In the prophet Muḥammad's case, however, the sole miracle the Qur'ān admits is that of the Qur'ān itself, an inimitable scripture in perfect Arabic that no human, least of all one presumed unlettered *(ummī*, 7.157), could emulate (2.23–24).

The Qur'ānic concept of prophethood turns on the twin principles of plurality and unity. The Qur'ān names many though not all prophets (40.78); Adam is implied to be the first (2.37) and Muḥammad is designated as the last (33.40). While nowhere enumerating the prophets, the Qur'ān teaches that every human community received its messenger in the medium of its own language (16.36). Equally it insists that, though many, the prophets were united in a single community of truth (23.52). Coming from the one and only God, the essence of revelation to all prophets was one and the same. The Qur'ān symbolizes the unity of prophethood in the concept of a prehistorical covenant *(mīthāq)* that God struck with the prophets before their human creation, that they would serve no god but God (3.81, 33.7). Historical prophethood is seen to be reiterative of this primordial covenant, elaborated in terms of moral teaching. Prophets therefore did not bring "new" revelations, nor was prophethood understood as a progressive unfolding of God's will. By this same covenant, however, the Qur'ān attests that all the prophets looked forward to the coming of Muḥammad as the final messenger who would confirm all that had been revealed to them (3.81) and universalize prophethood for the remainder of human history (21.107).

Prophethood is therefore always defined in terms of Muḥammad's experience, recorded in the traditions *(ḥadīth)*. The *waḥy* descended on him as "a heavy word," which he heard as a reverberating bell, causing him profuse sweating. Muḥammad also testified to the visual experience of seeing the angel Gabriel, who transmitted the revelation (2.97). Audition *(samʿ)* and vision *(ru'yā)* testify to an invasive power taking control of the human senses. It was in this state that Muḥammad is believed to have repeated the words dictated by the angel as a recitation *(qur'ān)*, thus reproducing the word of God.

Classical Islam favored an eschatological emphasis on the role of the prophet, particularly Muḥammad, as intercessor *(shafīʿ)* on behalf of believers—a doctrine which finds ambiguous sanctuary in the Qur'ān (10.3). Muḥammad's personal conduct *(sunnah)* was also emulated by pious Muslims as a way of expressing love for God, with the promised reward of God's reciprocal forgiveness (3.31). Resurgent Islam is today committed to the struggle of actualizing the content of Muḥammad's *nubūwah* in renewed Islamic community. Prophecy in this perspective is seen to be fulfilled in the political realm, as society conforms to the will of God.

[*See also* Muḥammad, *article on* Role of the Prophet in Muslim Thought and Practice; Revelation; Theology.]

BIBLIOGRAPHY

ʿAbduh, Muḥammad. *The Theology of Unity*. Translated by Ishaq Musaʿad and Kenneth Cragg. London, 1966. English translation of the treatise of the Egyptian Muslim modernist, Muḥammad ʿAbduh (d. 1905), entitled *Risālat al-tawḥīd*, containing an extended discussion of prophethood.

Gardet, Louis. *Islam: Religion et communauté*. Paris, 1967. Concise survey of major trends in classical Islamic religious thought.

Nasr, Seyyed Hossein. *Ideals and Realities of Islam*. London, 1966. Perceptive restatement of classical Islamic views of the fundamentals of the faith.

Rahman, Fazlur. *Prophecy in Islam: Philosophy and Orthodoxy*. London, 1958. Brilliant account of classical Islamic debates between theologians and philosophers about the nature of prophecy and its relationship to human intellect.

Ṭabāṭabāʾī, Muḥammad Ḥusayn. *Shīʿite Islam*. Translated from Persian and edited with an introduction and notes by Seyyed Hossein Nasr. Albany, N.Y., 1975. Modern Shīʿī statement of faith, with a useful discussion of prophethood in Shīʿī perspective.

Watt, W. Montgomery. *Islamic Revelation in the Modern World*. Edinburgh, 1969. Careful account of classical Islamic concepts of revelation and prophethood, with comparative Christian and psychoanalytic perspectives.

Wensinck, A. J. *The Muslim Creed: Its Genesis and Historical Development* (1932). London, 1965. History of the development of Islamic religious thought.

DAVID A. KERR

PUBERTY RITES. There is no specific Islamic ritual to mark the onset of puberty; Nevertheless, Muslims celebrate certain rituals to mark the initiation of sexuality, adulthood, and membership in the community. Following the work of Arnold van Gennep (1960), these rituals are usually considered Islamic "rites of passage." Rituals such as circumcisions and weddings are puberty rites in that the ceremonies in some way signal the end of childhood and the initiation into culturally and religiously defined roles of adulthood.

Male circumcision, or *khitān*, is the most widely observed "puberty rite" throughout the Muslim world. Despite its widespread observance, there is little mention or justification of *khitān* in the Islamic textual tradition. There is no mention of circumcision in the Qur'ān, and only scattered references are found in the *ḥadīth*. Male circumcision is mentioned in Bukhārī's collection of *ḥadīth* as a practice of pre-Islamic prophets such as Ibrāhīm (Abraham). There is little attention given to the practice in *fiqh* works, which usually state only its status as obligatory *(wājib)* or recommended *(sunnah)*. The role of circumcision as an Islamic rite of passage lies in the popular practices of Muslims.

A boy's circumcision occurs between the ages of three and fifteen years, depending on regional custom. The Islamic circumcision should take place at an age when the boy is aware and will retain memory of the operation. The circumcision may also follow some achievement such as the boy's first Qur'ān recitation from memory. Circumcisions are commonly held during the month of the Prophet's birthday. Locations of the ceremony range from the courtyard of a house, to a shrine, to a clinic or hospital. Throughout the Muslim world, the barber is traditionally the circumcisor. Often ties are established between the barber and the son's family, with gift exchanges long after the operation.

Festive celebration traditionally surrounds the boy's circumcision. Before the operation, the boy bathes, dons special clothing, and may have his head shaved by the barber. Qur'ānic recitation often accompanies the ceremony, along with music and a procession through the neighborhood or village. Both men and women from the boy's family and friends participate in the ceremony, which is preceded or followed by a large ritual meal including the exchange of gifts. After the boy's foreskin is removed by the barber, his movements, eating patterns, and dress are usually changed or monitored for close to a week.

Arnold van Gennep interpreted similar rituals as means of addressing periods of crisis or transition for the individual and the community. These "rites of passage," according to van Gennep, move the individual safely through a dangerous transitional stage by separating the person from the usual structures of life and reintegrating him or her with a new role into the community. The "puberty rite" does not necessarily mark the physiological changes of puberty, but rather the changes in social roles and behaviors when a child becomes an adult defined by certain cultural norms and behaviors.

In Muslim communities, circumcision may mark changes in role and status by signaling entrance into full participation in the Islamic ritual world or commencement of the study of Sufism. The circumcision might also signal the boy's entrance into the gendered world of men—his dress, social group, and behavior defined specifically by norms of men. The circumcision may also initiate the boy's sexuality, with the operation considered a crucial step before marriage.

Changes in dress most dramatically illustrate the elements of separation and reintegration in Islamic male circumcision. For example, in Egypt, Turkey, India, and Morocco the boy may be dressed in girl's clothing in the ceremony before the operation. This dress is often symbolic of the clothing worn by a bride. After the ceremony, the boy wears the typical clothing of the adult male or the dress of a learned religious leader. Among Javanese royalty, the boy's dress changes from that of a common man to that of a prince.

There is no puberty rite for girls that is so widely observed as male circumcision. Female circumcision is performed in some areas of Northeast Africa including Egypt and the Sudan, as well as in parts of North India and Southeast Asia. This operation varies in severity; often only a small portion of the clitoris is excised, but in some cases the female genitals are mutilated almost to seal the vaginal opening. Ensuring a girl's virginity before marriage is the justification most often cited for the operation. Female circumcision is a highly controversial practice and generally not sanctioned or condoned by the Islamic textual traditions or its authorities, and it is outlawed in certain countries. Female circumcision, *khafḍ*, is referred to in the *ḥadīth*, but it is considered a practice predating the rise of Islam.

It is not entirely clear that female circumcision is a "puberty rite." Often the operation is unmarked by celebration or attention. If the circumcision is celebrated, it is done so on a much smaller scale than is male circumcision and includes only female participants. Female circumcision often takes place at a very young age and is not generally followed by changes in roles or status.

Typically, a girl's menstruation is not mentioned or celebrated in any way. In certain South Indian areas, however, the appearance of the first menses is observed by ritual meals and special clothing and foods. The covering of a girl's hair could also be considered a puberty rite; the first wearing of the headscarf may follow the first menarche and signal the onset of a girl's sexuality.

The wedding is considered the equivalent puberty rite for the girl to the boy's circumcision. Traditionally, marriage has been arranged in a girl's early adolescence and marks her movement from girl and daughter to woman and wife. After marriage, the girl may move to the home of her husband's family, her movements may be restricted, and she may receive greater respect and authority. Processions, special clothing (in some areas the bride wears male dress until the ceremony), and feasts may also accompany the wedding.

Modernization in some areas carries significant changes in the practice of Muslim puberty rites. In urban and certain rural areas, a male nurse rather than a barber may perform the circumcision at a clinic or hospital rather than at a saint's shrine. Change in the participants and the locations may alter the relations and reciprocity formerly established between families and members of the community at the traditional circumcision ceremony. Furthermore, the role of marriage as a puberty rite for girls is unclear in certain urban areas marked by rapid economic and social change. Often marriage is delayed because of economic difficulties and the female assumes the role of a student or worker long before she is married.

[*See also* Circumcision; Clitoridectomy; *and* Rites of Passage.]

BIBLIOGRAPHY

ʿAmmār, Ḥāmid. *Growing Up in an Egyptian Village: Silwa, Province of Aswan*. New York, 1966. Ethnography, with descriptions and analysis of childhood in rural Egypt.

Delaney, Carol. *The Seed and the Soil: Gender and Cosmology in Turkish Village Society*. Berkeley, 1991. Primarily an ethnographic account of women's life in rural Turkey.

Geertz, Clifford. *The Religion of Java*. Chicago, 1960. See Chapter 5 of this ethnography for a comparison of circumcision and wedding ceremonies.

Gennep, Arnold van. *The Rites of Passage*. Translated by Monika B. Vizedom and Gabrielle L. Caffee. Chicago, 1960.

Jaʿfar Sharīf. *Islam in India, or, The Qānūn-i-Islām* (1921). Translated by G. A. Herklots. Reprint, London, 1972. Descriptive work primarily on South Indian Muslims; includes extensive sections on the ritual practices of Muslim women.

Lane, Edward W. *An Account of the Manners and Customs of the Modern Egyptians*. 5th ed. London, 1860. Late nineteenth-century British ethnography, including detailed descriptions of religious practices such as weddings and circumcisions.

Saʿdāwī, Nawāl al-. *The Hidden Face of Eve: Women in the Arab World*. Translated and edited by Sherif Hetata. Boston, 1980. Autobiographical and polemical work written by an Egyptian medical doctor, with description, information, and analysis of female circumcision.

Westermarck, Edward A. *Ritual and Belief in Morocco*. Vol. 2. London, 1926. Tremendously detailed information about ritual practices in diverse regions of Morocco.

Woodward, Mark R. *Islam in Java: Normative Piety and Mysticism in the Sultanate of Yogyakarta*. Tucson, 1989. Anthropological work on Islam in Javanese royal courts, including a brief but interesting account of male circumcision.

KATHERINE C. KOLSTAD

PUBLIC LAW. Concerned with the distribution and exercise of power by the state and the legal relations between the state and the individual, public law in the West is distinct from private law, which is concerned with the legal relationship between individuals. In Islamic law, the categories of public law and private law overlap, as some public law is civil and some happens to be criminal. On the whole, the primary purpose of Islamic public law provisions is the promotion of social objectives and the protection of collective rather than individual interest.

The notion of public law under sharīʿah (the divine law) hinges on the conception of sovereignty which belongs to God alone. The Qur'ān declares God as *mālik-al-mulk* (the sovereign of the entire universe) and *aḥkam al-ḥākimīn* (best of the judges). God has delegated the sovereignty to the *ummah* (Islamic community) and the *ummah* in its power constitutes state or government. Therefore the government that is representative of the *ummah* is administered on behalf of it and is subject to divine laws and is a trust for the benefit of the people. One of the main functions of state in Islam is to establish justice and righteousness. Since the government is to function according to *sharīʿah,* there is no struggle between state and church in Islam. A government or a ruler acts in his dual capacity as defender of the faith and governor of worldly affairs.

The people owe obedience to the government so long as it does not transgress the limits of sharīʿah. Despite a good deal of overlapping between public and private law, some distinction does emerge in the writings of prominent Muslim jurists *(fuqahā').*

The following areas are covered by public law in *sharīʿah:*

1. *Constitutional law.* The broad principles covered under constitutional law are the sovereignty of God as well as the delegation of that sovereignty to the *ummah* in the form of *khilāfah* (succession), *imāmah* (leadership), government, legislation, *shūrā* (consultation), administration of justice, and so forth. Since sovereignty belongs to God, the attributes of God's sovereignty appear in his names given in the Qur'ān, which are suggestive of one or other aspects of it (e.g., surahs 17.11, 59.2, 45.13, 21.22, 5.3, and 22.40). The word *mulk* signifies power in relation to what is concrete, that is, territory. *Mulk* has two shades of meaning in the Qur'ān and has an indirect connotation to territory (surahs 3.789, 5.123, and 67.1). The state is then a concrete entity in which the *ummah* attains righteousness. The government, therefore, is a representative of the *ummah* and is administered on behalf of God by principles of righteousness. Government is then a trust that God has placed in the hands of rulers.

The two main purposes of the government in Islam are trust and justice, as God is *ʿādil, ṣādiq,* and *sabbūḥ* (just, true and free from all taints). This requires justice and righteousness as its ends, and to this extent the state is theocratic, but it is entirely secular when its functions are taken into consideration.

The Islamic constitutional theory (caliphate) is based on consideration of *shūrā* and democracy. The caliph is bound to act according to the laid-down principles. As Māwardī has said in his *Al-aḥkām al-sulṭānīyah,* once the caliph disregards the principles, the people are absolved from obedience to him. The caliph in fact represents the Prophet in his dual capacity as the defender of faith and the governor of the world. The Shīʿī viewpoint concerning the *imāmah* is that he must also belong to the house of the Prophet *(ahl al-bayt),* while the Muʿtazilah and the Khawārij think that anyone may be elected a caliph based on a *ḥadīth:* "Listen and obey, even though the chief be a negro slave."

2. *Al-siyar (international or transnational law). Al-siyar* deals with war, peace, neutrality, and state relations with individuals or groups. Islamic ethics and law, as stated in the Qur'ān and explained by the *sunnah* (received custom) of the Prophet, embrace all moral and legal sociological rules of conduct which are enjoined on all Muslims. Therefore, the science of *al-siyar* began to be taught in institutions of learning as part of *fiqh* (jurisprudence) long before the works of Hugo Grotius, such as *De Jure Belli ac Pacis* (1625), were written. The Muslim jurist Muḥammad ibn al-Ḥasan al-Shaybānī gave an immense contribution to the field through writing *Al-siyar al-kabīr* (translated into English by M. Khadduri as *Islamic Law of Nations,* Baltimore, 1966). Islamic international law helped to rationalize relations with the outside world and discussed graphically the rights of non-Muslims under *sharīʿah.* The great jurists stood firmly for equality between Muslims and non-Muslims under Islamic law (except family law). *Diyah* (compensation) was imposed on a Muslim who murdered a non-Muslim. International treaties were gov-

erned with full consideration for all individuals within the state.

Al-siyar is divided into different branches and, by divorcing it from political science and law in general, the *fuqahā'* developed it as an independent subject and a separate science. It is amazing that the Muslim jurists thought of the rights, duties, and privileges of non-Muslims considering the fact that European jurists of Middle Ages, such as Grotius and Puffendorf, excluded completely the followers of all religions but Christianity. On the other hand, European international law originated in the necessity of regulating the relations of the new sovereign states for the purpose of achieving the temporal unity of Christendom.

3. *ʿUqūbāt (criminal laws).* Muslim jurists have laid down the principles of criminal law on the basis of the Qur'an and *sunnah,* which maintain that the commission of prohibited actions and omission of sanctioned actions create situations of injury to others called *jināyah. Jināyah* therefore means something injurious or wrongful, and it came to denote the action that is prohibited or unlawful, which was classified by Ibn Rushd as murder and injury that is wrongly done to a body or a person, defamation that is wrongly done to human honor, rape and adultery that is wrongly done to human decency, usurpation, theft and robbery that is wrongly done to property, as well as the related areas of cheating, fraud, embezzlement, and so forth; in other words, the violation of rights that relate to the person, owner, and property of others. *Jināyat* in *sharīʿah* can be both civil or criminal in nature, and therefore some may relate to public law and others to private law as in cases for which *diyah* and *qiṣāṣ* are provided, such as murder or bodily injuries which relatives of a victim can prosecute or pardon. The laws concerning major crimes are termed *ḥudūd* and the punishments *(ḥadd)* have been prescribed by the Qur'ān. The laws concerning minor crimes are known as *taʿzīr*. Islamic public law therefore deals also with the violation of public rights for which the remedy is granted by way of punishment. The wrong causing such a violation is called *nasiah.* The criminal administration of law under the general methodology of enforcement combines the principles of personality and territoriality and thus is applied and enforced on all criminals irrespective of their religious status. For the offenses for which *ḥadd* (fixed punishment) has not been set, chastisement is meted out through *taʿzīr. Taʿzīr* is inflicted for acts of an offensive nature and range from admonition, dragging the offender to the door and exposing him to scorn, imprisonment, to blows. Infringement on prayers, *zakāt* (giving alms), fasting, and the like are punished by *taʿzīr. Taʿzīr* may be combined with other kinds of penalties, such as *kaffārah* (expiation) or *diyah.*

4. *Taxation.* Under the fundamental principles of Islamic financial theory, there is no place for accumulation of wealth in the hands of the few or hoarding or profiteering. There should be no exploited or exploiting classes. The fragmentation of property owing to laws of inheritance and the operation of the laws of taxation, such as *zakāt* or *jizyah* (alms paid by non-Muslims), *kharāj* (land tax), *juʿl* (compensation for work, especially military service of a substitute), the chief beneficiaries of which are the poor, led to the establishment of a system that is more rational than contemporary communism or capitalism.

5. *Labor.* Labor laws include the idea that there is an employer-employee relationship about which the precept of the Prophet is, "give the worker his wages before his sweat dries" (Ibn Majāh, *Kitāb al-sunan,* II, 638). The employer is bound to pay the laborer a full wage and to protect the work environment and to provide full facilities for work.

6. *Municipal administration.* The functions of municipal administration and city authorities include safety of the people, health facilities, construction, gardening, public highways, markets, and so forth. Cleanliness and safety are subject to legal control. Traffic arrangements and footpath spaces are regulated. Thus, public places are controlled as public properties. The law of *waqf* controls religious endowments.

7. *Iḥtisāb.* A characteristic feature of public law is its injunction to create a public body with special powers of supervision, investigation, decision making, and enforcement in relation to a particular problem. The Qur'ānic injunction (surah 3.100) requires that public welfare work, as well as the supervision of similar functions, be done through the principles of *iḥtisāb.* The Qur'ān and *sunnah* offer guidance for the enforcement of good *(al-amr bi-al-maʿrūf)* and forbidding bad *(al-nahy ʿan al-munkar).* The office of the performance of *iḥtisāb* is called *ḥisbah,* and qualified officers are employed as *muḥtasibs* for proper enforcement of public morals, and those who violate *iḥtisāb* will be brought to the judicial department or the *qāḍī.* The duties of the *muḥtasibs* will revolve around what is owed to God or man, that is, for example, the enforcement of fasting in Ramaḍān or daily prayers. Other functions include

watching for corruption, bribery, nonpayment of debts, violation of public morals, and interference with public functions. The *muḥtasib* also has power over things related to fraud and deception and other offenses, such as road obstruction, unfair trade practices (including price control, smuggling, etc.), and the administration of juvenile and guardianship laws.

[*See also* Law.]

BIBLIOGRAPHY

Ibn Majāh. *Kitāb al-sunan*. Beirut, 1975.

Khadduri, Majid. *Islamic Law of Nations*. Baltimore, 1966.

Māwardī, ʿAlī ibn Muḥammad al-. *Al-aḥkām al-sulṭānīyah*. Cairo, 1960.

Shaybānī, Muḥammad ibn Ḥasan al-. *Al-siyar al-kabīr*. Cairo, 1967.

ABDUL RAHMAN I. DOI

PURDAH. *See* Seclusion.

PURIFICATION. A *ḥadīth* states, "Purity is half of faith." This terse statement related from the prophet Muḥammad underlines the importance of purity and purification in the Islamic tradition. The fundamental notion of purity is also reflected in the Islamic concept of *fiṭrah* (human nature). One famous *ḥadīth* enumerates the following elements of *fiṭrah:* circumcision, removing hair from under the armpits and pubic area, pairing the nails, proper cleanliness, and perfuming oneself. Each of these acts has direct relevance to notions of purity and purification in Islam. Accordingly, being human in Islam is in some sense reflected in maintaining purity.

The significance of ritual purity may be examined through the prism of the well-known Islamic division of the rights and duties accorded to God (*ḥuqūq Allāh*) and those accorded to the worshippers of God (*ḥuqūq al-ʿibād*). The duality is reflected in the purification obligations of the Muslim believer.

A state of purity is a precondition for worship (*ʿubūdīyah*). Every act of worship is an encounter with God, and the purification ritual is a form of preparation for this event. In fact, the purification ritual in Islam is one of numerous means by which sins and infractions are forgiven.

Purification rituals prepare for the journey that finally leads to closeness to God *(qurb)*. Physical purification rituals culminate in spiritual purity in acts of worship. Both the discipline of the ritual acts and their aesthetic dimensions contribute to the deepening of the purification process at the nonmaterial, spiritual level (Sayyed Ali Ashraf, "Inner Meaning of the Islamic Rites," in *Islamic Spirituality: Foundations*. pp. 111–130, edited by Seyyed Hossein Nasr, New York, 1987).

Purification norms and rituals also function on an entirely human level, facilitating human relations by setting off boundaries for interaction. Sexual relations between husband and wife, for example, are conditional upon a certain degree of ritual purity: menstruating women are ritually impure. Similarly, Muslims consider nonbelievers to be impure at one level or another. Traditional Shīʿīs consider non-Muslims spiritually impure to the extent that bodily contact with them necessitates a ritual bath (Khomeini, 1985, p. 20). Sunnīs also consider non-Muslims to be spiritually impure, based on the same verse in the Qur'ān (9.28), but they do not require a ritual purification in this case.

The Islamic legal tradition *(sharīʿah)* has set out rules and regulations for the successful fulfillment of purification rituals. I will now turn to the basic types of impurity, the reasons why these impurities must be removed, and the major rituals of purification in Islam. A discussion of some of the trends among Muslim peoples in the modern period will conclude the article.

A distinction is made in Islamic law between real (*ḥaqīqī*) and conceptual (*ḥukmī*) impurity. Real impurities include feces, urine, blood, semen, and alcohol, material impurities that defile objects or persons. In these cases, purity is attained by simply removing the defiling object by washing, rubbing, drying, or exposure to the sun. By contrast, conceptual (*ḥukmī*) impurities are states or conditions in which humans find themselves; they may or may not involve actual defilement by real impurities. Conceptual impurity arises through elimination, touching a corpse, disbelief, menstruation and postnatal bleeding, contact with the saliva of a dog, or touching any part of a pig. In such cases, purity can only be attained by special ritual acts after the defiling impurity, if any, has been removed.

The idea of removing impurities implies that purity is the natural human state. A person remains in a constant state of purity as long as this state is not nullified by any real or conceptual impurity. According to classical Arabic lexicons, moreover, "purity" (*ṭahūr*) is defined as the opposite of "menstruation." In Islamic tradition, maintaining purity reflects an ancient avoidance of menstrual bleeding; hence, a vast number of traditional rules of purity deal with the purity of women. The culture of purification has, however, expanded beyond this original idea. This association between purity in general and menstrual purity in particular may be understood in the sense that purity is an original state broken by temporary periods of impurity.

There are two major purification rituals in the *sharīʿah*—the bath *(ghusl)* and the ablution *(wuḍūʾ)*—and one minor ritual for exceptional circumstances. Both major rituals are accomplished through the use of water that is clean, colorless, and odorless and that has not been used for a previous ritual. Traditional manuals dealt extensively with the conditions under which wells and pools would be suitable for use and under what conditions they would be defiled. Jurists also stressed that water should be used sparingly.

The *ghusl* is a major ritual that becomes necessary under the following conditions: conversion to Islam, sexual relations, ejaculation, and for women, the end of the menstrual period or postnatal bleeding. According to Shīʿīs, the *ghusl* is also obligatory after having washed a corpse; there exists a difference of opinion among the Sunnīs on this issue, many believing that it is only recommended. In addition, both Sunnīs and Shīʿīs recommend *ghusl* for numerous other occasions like Fridays, the days of the two Muslim festivals (ʿĪd), the pilgrimage, and entering Mecca.

Like other acts of worship in Islam, the *ghusl* must be preceded by an intention to purify oneself. This is then followed by a general washing of every part of the body. Even though this would technically suffice for a *ghusl*, the following more elaborate procedure and order is recommended: (1) washing the hands; (2) washing the sexual organs; (3) performing the *wuḍūʾ*, (4) rubbing water into the roots of the hair; and (5) pouring water over the entire body, beginning from the right side. The washing of a corpse follows a similar procedure and must be performed by at least one person in the community; this duty is obligatory on society as a whole until one person performs it *(farḍ kifāyah)*.

There are other forms of defilement that reduce the conceptual purity of a person only to a limited degree. These are elimination, flatus, touching a person of the opposite sex (among some Sunnīs), irregular bleeding in a woman, and sleeping while resting against an object. In such a case, *ghusl* would not be obligatory; only the minor form of purification, *wuḍūʾ*, would be necessary to restore purity.

The essentials of the ritual of *wuḍūʾ* are washing the face, washing both arms up to the elbows, wiping part of the head, and washing both feet (Qurʾān, 5.6). In a different interpretation of the Qurʾānic verse, the Shīʿīs insist that the feet should be wiped, not washed. Like *ghusl*, *wuḍūʾ* also has a more elaborate procedure drawn from various prophetic recommendations. After an explicit intention is formed, the *wuḍūʾ* begins with washing the hands, followed by rinsing the mouth, brushing the teeth with a toothpick, and clearing the nostrils. The face is then washed, followed by the arms (first the right and then the left). The wiping of the head comes next, followed by wiping the ears, the neck, and in between the fingers. The final step is the washing (or wiping) of the feet up to the ankles. The *wuḍūʾ* is often concluded with the pious invocation, "O God! Place me among the repenters and place me among the pure."

In exceptional circumstances, a person may be unable to maintain the condition of purity for a sufficient time to fulfill the obligation of prayers or other necessary rituals. Such a person is called *maʿdhūr* ("excused") and may fulfill the duties of worship as long as the *wuḍūʾ* is performed on every occasion. A woman who bleeds irregularly is said to be in a state of *istiḥāḍah* and would also be considered excused.

The *sharīʿah* has also made provision for conditions when a person is ill and cannot use water, or when water is not available in the immediate vicinity. In such cases, the ritual of *tayammum* (dry ablution) may be substituted for either the *ghusl* or the *wuḍūʾ*. This ritual is performed by (1) making an intention to purify oneself; (2) placing the hands on clean dust and then blowing off excess small stones; (3) wiping the face with the hands; (4) repeating the application of dust and wiping the right arm and then the left arm up to the elbow.

A Muslim ought to maintain the basic minimum of ritual purity with a *ghusl*. Whenever any of the conditions exists that necessitates a *ghusl*, it must be performed immediately. As a form of motivation and warning, a *ḥadīth* reports that angels do not enter a home in which there is a person who requires a bath after sexual relations.

The *ghusl* is a precondition for all forms of worship in Islam. For example, entry to a mosque is permitted to a person without the *wuḍūʾ* level of purity but not to one without the *ghusl* level of purity. Thus, according to most Sunnī schools, women who are menstruating and who therefore require *ghusl* may not even pass through a mosque. Some Shīʿīs restrict this prohibition only to the great mosques in Mecca and Medina. Similarly, menstruation and postnatal bleeding preclude women from fasting during Ramaḍān. There is a difference of opinion whether menstruating women may recite the Qurʾān without touching it (Sabiq, 1985, p. 53). The state of *ghusl* is thus the first key to worship in

Islam; it opens the first door to an encounter with God.

In order to step into the immediate presence of God, however, even lesser impurities must be overcome. The *wuḍū'* is contained in the *ghusl,* but certain defiling acts partially reduce the pure state. Hence, acts like touching the Qur'ān, fulfilling the obligatory prayer *(ṣalāh),* and circumambulating the Kaʿbah *(ṭawāf)* must be performed in both states of purity. The *wuḍū'*, then, is a higher state of conceptual purity and is a precondition for intimate worship. Muslims often perform this act regularly before the abovementioned forms of worship. In fact, especially holy persons are often said to perform the night and morning prayer having made only one *wuḍū'*, indicating a night of vigil and contemplation.

Modern technological developments have had an impact on the conception and practice of Islamic purification. Advances in plumbing, sanitation, and the "sparkling clean" culture of advertising have intruded into the Islamic debate on purification. Traditional texts that deal at length with clean pools and wells have become obsolete for most Muslims living in towns and cities. Even the invention of the toothbrush has affected the way Muslims practice Islamic purification.

Most modernist and revivalist thought in matters concerning purity has incorporated what may be called the pseudo-Muʿtazilī view that real impurity *(ḥaqīqī)* is equivalent to conceptual *(ḥukmī)* impurity in Islam. Thus the Islamic taboo against the pig or the saliva of a dog becomes the object of ingenious scientific justification. The opposing Ashʿarī view that real impurity is subject to the laws of conceptual impurity persists in modern legal thought. However, the general tendency is to view the Islamic concern for ritual purity to be unique to Islamic civilization. In conformity with this trend, for example, reformist movements decry the actual filth around Muslim communities as contradictory to the essential teachings of Islam.

More traditional thinkers, however, have rejected this overt modernization. In the counterattack they have often accused the modernists of imitating the West in its impure ways. For example, in a popular *Kitaabut tahaarah* (Book of Purity) published by a council of *ʿulamā'* in South Africa, the modernists are castigated for adopting "unhygienic, disease-spreading, Western high-level toilets."

In another striking example, the *Kitaabut tahaarah* deals extensively with the tooth-stick *(miswāk)* of the prophet Muḥammad. Twenty-three of its 97 pages deal with the history, real benefits, and importance of the tooth-stick. The final paragraph rules out the toothbrush as a substitute even if the *miswāk* is not available. More particularly, the text reveals its intended target: "The argument of the modernist that the toothbrush today takes the place of the *miswāk* is fallacious and a good example of the apologetic attitude adopted by modern Muslims of today." In contrast, Sayyid Sābiq's *Fiqh us-Sunnah* (1985), a popular book on *sharīʿah* written from a revivalist perspective, deals very briefly with the tooth-stick and regards the toothbrush as a legitimate substitute: "This *sunnah* (prophetic practice) is fulfilled by using any object which removes yellow stains on the teeth and cleans the mouth, such as a toothbrush, and so on" (p. 29).

In modern thought, the Islamic legal injunctions are reduced in favor of keeping to the spirit and principles of purification. For example, concerning menstruation and bleeding after childbirth, Sābiq does not confirm the traditional three or ten fixed days for normal bleeding that appears in Islamic legal texts. He prefers to leave these matters to the individual experience of women themselves (p. 70). Similarly, women may pass through mosques in a state of impurity, and a person who performs the ablution may wipe over his socks where it was previously done over tight-fitting leather socks. For the most part, however, modern Islamic practice follows the standards established by traditional manuals. Islamic purification practice today is poised between traditional requirements and modern possibilities.

BIBLIOGRAPHY

Denny, Frederick Mathewson. *An Introduction to Islam.* New York and London, 1985. Contains a detailed section on the various purification rituals in Islam.

Ghazālī, Abū Ḥāmid al-. *The Mysteries of Purity: Being a Translation with Notes of the Kitāb Asrār al-Ṭahārah of al-Ghazzālī's Ihya ʿUlūm al-dīn.* Translated by Nabih A. Faris. Lahore, 1966. Translation of an early document of the inner and mystical significance of purity by one of the greatest scholars in Islamic history.

Khomeini, Ruhollah. *The Practical Laws of Islam.* 2d ed. Tehran, 1985. Abridged version of *Risālah-yi Tawẕiḥ al-masā'il.* Khomeini's juridical opinions on essential Islamic rules.

Lazarus-Yafeh, Hava. "Some Differences between Judaism and Islam as Two Religions of Law." *Religion* 14 (April 1984): 175–191. Good account of the general differences between classic Islamic and Judaic rules.

Sābiq, Al-Sayyid. *Fiqh us-Sunnah: Purification and Prayer.* Translated by Muhammad Sa'eed Dabas and Jamal al-Din M. Zarabozo. Indianapolis, 1405/1985. Partial translation of a very popular Arabic compendium of Islamic *sharīʿah* from a revivalist perspective.

ABDULKADER I. TAYOB

Q

QADHDHĀFĪ, MUᶜAMMAR AL- (b. 1942), Libyan military and political leader. When the monarchy in Libya was overthrown by a military coup between 31 August and 1 September 1969 by a group of "free unionist army officers," Muᶜammar al-Qadhdhāfī became the leader of the newly proclaimed Libyan Arab Republic. A Council of the Command of the Revolution took over the political future of the country. Qadhdhāfī was elected president and was promoted from captain to colonel on 13 September 1969. Qadhdhāfī's biography prior to 1969 is a synthesis of historical evidence, oral reports, and legendary elements, often fostered by his own cult of personality.

Life and Rule. Muᶜammar al-Qadhdhāfī was born in 1942 in the inland desert of the Sirte region, of a poor and illiterate family of bedouin belonging to the Qadhdhāfah tribe. Like most of his kin, as a very young boy he was a shepherd, but his father acknowledged the boy's intelligence and found for him (in 1949–1950) a teacher of classical Arabic and the Qur'ān from Fezzan. At the beginning of the 1950s Qadhdhāfī went to primary school in Sirte. Though very poor—he slept at the local mosque—he was a brilliant student and made up quickly for his late start at school. He then moved with his family to the Fezzan region and went to secondary school, where he met some of the people, including ᶜAbd al-Salām Jallūd, who would later join him in his seizure of power.

Qadhdhāfī at this time was fascinated by the personality of Egyptian President Gamal Abdel Nasser. In 1956 during the Suez War, he organized a demonstration supporting Egypt. The first group of the organization that carried out the coup of 1969 was created by him in 1958. The dates are not certain; however, in that period he was certainly actively involved in political activity opposing Western interference in the Arab world. For political reasons he was expelled from Fezzan; together with his family, he moved to Miṣrātah on the coast. He entered the Military Academy of Benghazi in 1964; there he organized the first underground structures of the movement that brought him to power.

From 1969 onward Qadhdhāfī's biography is coincident with the political stages of the Libyan Republic. On 18 September 1969 he drafted the main outlines of his political program; the following month he ordered foreign military forces to evacuate Libyan territory and called for neutrality and national and Arab unity. A few months later the main pillars of the economy (banks, clinics, oil, etc.) were nationalized. Qadhdhāfī met Nasser a few months before the latter's death (28 September 1970) and, in public opinion, he became the natural inheritor of Nasserism: political parties were banned, and in June 1971 the Arab Socialist Union was founded.

In 1971 Qadhdhāfī tried to reintroduce Islamic law in Libya. In 1973 the first steps of the "popular revolution" were taken, and this process led to the proclamation of the Arab Popular Socialist Libyan Jamāhirīyah. The Jamāhirīyah is supposed to be a new system of government: placing power in the hands of the masses, it is expressed by a peculiar structure of committees that represent the decision-making and executive bodies of the state. As a consequence, a division arose between power and revolution, until then united.

From 1977 onward there were two further important elements: the replacement of a rigid and repressive policy at home by a more moderate attitude, especially in economics; and the failure of Libyan foreign policy (in the case of Chad, for example). This second issue determined the marginal role played by Libya in the Arab world, although Qadhdhāfī is periodically identified by the United States as a symbolic enemy to be crushed at all costs. The latter response is due to his more or less active support of international terrorism by such groups as the Irish Republican Army, the Basques, and radical Palestinian groups.

Political and Social Thought. Qadhdhāfī's importance, however, is based more in the theory he has elaborated than in his practical accomplishments. The

"Third Universal Theory" that he drafted in his *Green Book* is composed of three different parts published in 1975, 1978, and 1980, laying out in turn his political, economic, and social conception of the world.

In his political philosophy, Qadhdhāfī considers society to possess a concentric structure from the minimal aggregation (the family) to the global aggregation (people/nation). The nation is held together by culture, religion, and language; the people are the preeminent political subject. The state is not a natural outcome, whereas social ties can be naturally converted into a conscious national identity. Democracy should express the real power of the people/nation. There should therefore be self-government of the people, and democracy must be direct and participatory, without the delegation of powers. These are the premises of the Jamāhirīyah. According to Qadhdhāfī, this form of government must be exported outside Libya, first within the Arab world. Thus Qadhdhāfī's attempts at federation with Arab countries (Egypt, Sudan, and Syria in 1970; Egypt and Sudan in 1971; Egypt in 1972; Tunisia in 1974; Syria in 1980; Chad in 1981; Morocco in 1984) acquire significance, even though they failed. They were not simply attempts to realize Nasser's idea of Arab unity, but the beginning of the new era of the masses, that is, of the Jamāhirīyah. Qadhdhāfī's propaganda, especially in Africa, stresses the role of Arabic as a cultural anticolonialist element, Islam as an anti-imperialist religion, and the ethical duty to divide wealth and resources equally. Even though this model is not applied in Libya itself, it has important theoretical value, which can be seen in today's thriving fundamentalist movements.

Qadhdhāfī's ideal society rejects class struggle and is based on solidarity. In this perspective, the individuals' dignity is essential. Nothing can force humans into a condition of slavery—hence his rejection of salary-based work. Unconsciously promoting a "petit bourgeois" society, the social aspect of his theory has obtained relative success at home; he helps the less privileged components of society, such as women and youths, to take a more active role. Part of the support for his policy in Libya is based on this.

The problem of wealth is logically connected to Qadhdhāfī's ideas on society. Primary needs have to be fulfilled, and in this sense, it is possible to speak of a socialist approach to economics. Economic equality is the goal.

Role of Islam. Qadhdhāfī often speaks about the specific role of Islam, but no mention of it is found in the *Green Book*. Islam is considered as the natural religion for meeting the immediate needs of the individual and of humanity as a whole. Islam is therefore the framework of history. In practical terms, this means that only the Qur'ān can be the direct source of reference. Tradition and religious interpretations evolved over succeeding centuries cannot help the believer. Mysticism and asceticism are useless, as are religious hierarchies. Qadhdhāfī rejects the power of the *ʿulamā'* on the one hand, and of popular religious beliefs on the other. Ṣūfī *ṭarīqah*s such as the Sanūsīyah are considered dangerous because they were once allied to the monarchy, regardless of their anticolonial history.

Qadhdhāfī is a modernist; he goes back to the sources, but as a reformer. He denies legitimacy to any specific body of interpreters of the religious sources. He is convinced that his political, social, and economic theory corresponds to the real nature of Islam. His idea that a "national" state is the "Islamic" state, if correctly understood, is the opposite of what Islamist movements theorize today. He attempts to bridge the gap between his roots and modern needs while rejecting the westernization of Muslim societies.

[*See also* Libya.]

BIBLIOGRAPHY

Bianco, Mirella. *Gadafi: Voice from the Desert*. London, 1975. First but still reliable biography.

Blundy, David, and Andrew Lycett. *Qaddafi and the Libyan Revolution*. Rev. ed. London, 1988.

First, Ruth. *Libya: The Elusive Revolution*. New York, 1974. Classic early study of the social bases and political directions of the Qadhdhāfist state.

Harris, Lillian Craig. *Libya: Qadhafi's Revolution and the Modern State*. Boulder, 1986. Excellent analytical study of the Libyan revolution under Qadhdhāfī.

"Libya" entries in *Annuaire de l'Afrique du Nord* (Paris). Contains annual updates on Qadhdhāfī's internal and external policies.

BIANCAMARIA SCARCIA AMORETTI

QĀḌĪ. Throughout Islamic history authority to judge cases between Muslims under the *sharīʿah* was vested in the post of *qāḍī*, the single judge of the *maḥkamah* court. Unlike jurisprudents *(fuqahā')*, *qāḍī*s did not delve into the sources of the *sharīʿah* but referred to recognized law books on subjects considered to fall under religiously sanctioned law. Although the *qāḍī*'s jurisdiction was fairly general, certain areas such as serious criminal offenses often came instead under the secular jurisdiction of executive rulers.

Although a kind of hierarchy apparently existed within the judicial branch of Islamic governing authority, no institutions for appeal existed. The ʿAbbāsid caliph Hārūn al-Rashīd, around 800 CE, is said first to have recognized the *qāḍī* of Baghdad as the *qāḍī al-quḍāt* or "judge of judges." Such recognition did imply jurisdictional superiority but related more to administrative aspects of *maḥkamah* activities, especially the nomination and appointment of *qāḍīs*. Originally the *qāḍī al-quḍat* presented potential nominees for the caliph's consideration; later he assumed the responsibility of making appointments or dismissals himself.

Political breakup within the core Islamic region led to different claims of legitimacy in the appointment of *qāḍīs*. For example, as early as the establishment of Umayyad authority in Islamic Spain in the mid-eighth century, the post of *qāḍī al-jamāʿah* was created out of the already existing regional function of the *qāḍī al-jund* (*qāḍī* of a military command district). In time, especially after the Fāṭimid countercaliphate was founded in 969, the appointment of regional *qāḍīs* was assumed not only by regimes that rejected the Baghdad caliphs' responsibility but also by loyal but politically and dynastically distinct provincial regimes.

The process of differentiation was strengthened by the evolution of four different orthodox schools of Islamic law (*madhhabs*). Each school recognized the others as acceptable interpretations of Islamic law, but the preference of local political authorities might grant precedence to the *qāḍī* of the preferred school. Thus the Tunisian beys appointed *qāḍīs* committed to Mālikī law—a carryover from pre-Ottoman Ḥafṣid times. In such regions, the Ottoman Shaykh al-Islām would appoint Ḥanafī *qāḍīs* who might serve both in a second string of local *maḥkamahs*, but also alongside Mālikī judges on a court (known in Tunisia as the *majlis al-sharʿī*) responsible for deliberating on matters of Islamic law relating to government policies.

Beginning in the 1830s, the reforms of the Tanzimat introduced changes that gradually distinguished the areas of law susceptible to secular codification from Niẓāmīyah jurisdiction over civil matters (especially contracts for business or credit). Limitation of the *qāḍī*'s jurisdiction occurred at varying rates depending on regional political characteristics. At the Ottoman imperial level, conservative reformers around the head of the Tanzimat Council, Mustafa Reşid, would have preferred to use a somewhat eclectic model of Islamic legal precedents to design a general civil code (the Mecelle), thus maintaining a framework within which judges trained as *qāḍīs* could continue in a secularized and partially westernized system. Where the westernizing tendency was strongest, there arose secular alternatives to the *maḥkamah,* together with changes in the secular professional qualifications required of judges.

The clearest case is Egypt during and just after the Tanzimat period. In the 1860s a system of *majālis maḥallīyah* (local councils) assumed jurisdiction over a wide range of cases that—even though not yet covered by specific secular codes—were deemed inappropriate for religious judgment, whether that of the *qāḍī* or of the Jewish or Christian jurisdictions traditionally guaranteed under the Ottoman *millet* system. Early in this transition to alternative, and then to officially required non-*maḥkamah* jurisdictions, such *majālis* could include representatives of the Islamic religious community to consult on overlapping areas of law. Increasingly, however, separate jurisdictional authority over most civil and penal matters was extended throughout the Ottoman Empire. However, at least until drastic secular reforms were adopted by the Turkish Republic and imposed in other formerly Ottoman areas in the interwar period, personal status cases (for example, issues of marriage, divorce, and guardianship) remained under the *qāḍīs*' jurisdiction well into the twentieth century.

[*See also* Maḥkamah.]

BIBLIOGRAPHY

Antoun, Richard T. "The Islamic Court, the Islamic Judge and the Accommodation of Traditions: A Jordanian Case Study." *International Journal of Middle East Studies* 12 (1980): 456–467.

Escovitz, J. H. "Patterns of the Appointment of Chief Judges of Cairo during the Baḥri Mamluk Period." *Arabica* 30 (1983): 147–168.

Gibb, H. A. R., and Harold Bowen. *Islamic Society and the West.* Oxford and New York, 1962. See vol. 1, part 2, pp. 121–133.

Schacht, Joseph. "Law and Justice." In P. M. Holt et al., ed., *The Cambridge History of Islam.* Cambridge, 1970. See vol. 2, pp. 539–568.

BYRON D. CANNON

QĀDIRĪYAH. Among the better-known names in Islamic mysticism is that of ʿAbd al-Qādir al-Gīlānī (or Jīlānī or Jīlī), who is associated with the beginnings of the Qādirī brotherhood or *ṭarīqah* either as founder or as patron and sponsor. ʿAbd al-Qādir's birthdate is usually given as AH 470/1077–1078 CE and his date of death as 561/1165–1166. According to the biographer Muḥammad Ibn Shākir al-Kutubī, ʿAbd al-Qādir came from the Persian province of Gīlān, southwest of the Caspian Sea; his father was called Abū Ṣāliḥ ibn Jangīdūst. Coming as a young student to Baghdad, ʿAbd al-Qādir studied under a number of different masters but always remained a Ḥanbalī. These studies included traditions and Ḥanbalī law, at first under Abū Saʿd al-Mukharrimī, then under Shaykh Aḥmad (or Ḥammād) al-Dabbās, and later under a number of others. After a long period, including a time of wandering through Iraq, ʿAbd al-Qādir returned to Baghdad, where he began to win fame as a preacher *(wāʿiẓ)* at funerals and other public occasions.

At this time in his life ʿAbd al-Qādir was better known for his sermons and eulogies than for his asceticism or Ṣūfī activities; apparently his interest in mysticism came toward the end of his career. Ibn Shākir says that ʿAbd al-Qādir took the "Ṣūfī way" *(ṭarīq)* from al-Dabbās. Soon he acquired a great reputation as a holy person and as the "Imām of his Time and the Quṭb [leading authority] of his Period," and he was considered incontestably the "Shaykh of Shaykhs." Ibn Shākir claims that "by 521/1127, ʿAbd al-Qādir had a *majlis* and was acclaimed by the people." Seven years later ʿAbd al-Qādir had succeeded his old master al-Mukharrimī at his *madrasah* or religious school, "where he taught and gave *fatwā*s." Ibn Shākir closes his report by noting that ʿAbd al-Qādir had forty-nine children, twenty sons and twenty-nine daughters. Aged about eighty-eight, ʿAbd al-Qādir died in 561/1165–1166.

Although this short account from the *Fawāt al-wafayāt* of Ibn Shākir was written about 180 years after ʿAbd al-Qādir's death, the author gives a restrained description of this learned man. Unlike many later accounts, it is unencumbered with imaginary details and yields a sober portrait. Moreover, it emerges from the researches of Jacqueline Chabbi (1973) that ʿAbd al-Qādir was merely a Ḥanbalī jurist, a part-time *muftī* (jurisconsult), and a public preacher. Although there are signs that he was increasingly friendly at the end of his life toward Sufism—which at the end of the twelfth century was rising along an ascending curve—ʿAbd al-Qādir did not found or promote any sort of Ṣūfī organization. However, one of his authentic writings, *Al-ghunyah li-ṭālibī ṭarīq al-ḥaqq,* has a section at its end about the relations of Ṣūfī students (*murīd*s) and their shaykhs or *murshid*s.

After his death, however, interested people raised him to the rank of patron or original sponsor of the Qādirīyah, which assumed his name about 1200; very soon ʿAbd al-Qādir became the "founder" of the brotherhood. Chabbi shows in detail the remarkable differences between contemporary notices and comments written about ʿAbd al-Qādir during his public career, when he had many enemies (some of this hostility arising from his forty-year occupancy of a "chair" at the Mukharrimī *madrasah*), and the eulogies that circulated once he was dead. The latter are typified by their length, their fulsomeness, and the imaginative episodes they contain. These notices were soon amplified by his *karāmāt,* stories about his startling ability to cure the sick, and tales of how he helped Ṣūfī students and adepts (Chabbi, 1973, p. 84). Somewhat later ʿAbd al-Qādir was credited with writing a Qur'ānic commentary, and many of his conversations and aphorisms *(malfūẓāt)* were recorded. With the passing of time many of these stories became even more vivid and sensational: A. A. Rizvi notes that ʿAbd al-Qādir supposedly "crushed mountains, dried up oceans, and raised the dead to life" (1978–1981, vol. 1, p. 85).

The Qādirīyah doubtless had real organizational difficulties on ʿAbd al-Qādir's death, but it was assisted by two of his sons, ʿAbd al-ʿAzīz and ʿAbd al-Razzāq, and slightly later by his grandson Shams al-Dīn. One might guess that its numbers were still very small, but that it benefited from its alleged founder's burgeoning reputation. By the end of this obscure period it is likely that a *ribāṭ* or *zāwiyah* (hospice) for the group had been constructed, perhaps near the tomb of ʿAbd al-Qādir. This tomb would have been a simple monument, not the large and magnificent structure erected for ʿAbd al-Qādir by the Ottoman sultan Süleyman I in 1535; the earlier structure may well have been damaged in the Mongol sack of Baghdad in 1258. Yet there is thin evidence that by 1300, small groups of ʿAbd al-Qādir's followers existed in Syria and Egypt and perhaps also in Yemen.

ʿAbd al-Qādir had left no system, no instructions, and no "Ṣūfī way" of his own. Nevertheless, these gaps were soon filled by his sons, followers, and relatives, who elaborated a Ṣūfī order in his name. The arrangement was a loose one, yet it embodied charitable and philanthropic aspects wherever it spread—very quickly in some places. As a result, it would not be wrong to say that ʿAbd al-Qādir eventually became the most popular saint in Islam. The director of each local unit of the Qādirīyah, often called the *khalīfah,* could use *dhikr*s (ritual repetitions), prayers, and other liturgies (including *aḥzāb* and *awrād,* specialized prayers and invocations) as he liked. *Samā*ʿ (listening to music) was another widely used Ṣūfī technique. As for the saint himself, some groups saw him as a universal holy man, nearly divine, whereas others only manifested great reverence toward him. Probably by 800/1397 there was a Qādirī *zāwiyah* in Damascus, called the Dā'ūdīyah, and another Qādirī group could be found at al-Azhar in Cairo, holding their sessions in mosques or *madrasah*s, buildings originally designed for different purposes.

Not long after the demise of ʿAbd al-Qādir, it seems probable that Indian influences began to enter Sufism, including the Qādirīyah. Exactly when this occurred is still uncertain, but it is likely that around 1200, various breathing techniques and perhaps body movements were imported into Arabia, Central Asia, Iran, and Iraq, and then traveled farther west. In his *Manhal al-rawī al-rā'iq,* Muḥammad ʿAlī al-Sanūsī (1785–1859) gives an example of a Qādirī *dhikr.* He probably borrowed the details from an older book by Abū al-Baqā' Ḥasan al-Ujaymī (d. 1702), perhaps his *Risālah,* but the details given are much older.

> . . . As for the Qādiri brotherhood . . . its basis is the verbal *dhikr* in a congregational circle .. along with a gradual diminution of eating, and flight from human beings. . . . It should be accompanied at the start by the prayer *Jalāl Allāh wa ʿaẓamatihi* ["the glory of God and His majesty"]. For through that, the breath is suppressed and purified, and . . . the loosening by the *Jalāl* prayer is the quickest way to extricate one's self from frivolity.
>
> One sits crosslegged, grasping with the toes of the right foot . . . the large artery which lies behind the left knee joint. One puts one's hands open on the knees, so that they take the form of the word *Allāh.* Then one speaks the name of God, prolonging it for a time, and extending it with an emphatic pronunciation *(tafkhīm)* until the breath is cut off, making the words *ʿAẓamat al-Ḥaqq* ["the majesty of the True"] while exhausting the breath. . . . One continues that way until the heart is relaxed and the Divine Lights are revealed. Then one goes on with . . . the *dhikr* of absorption *(fanā')* and remaining *(baqā')* in God, ascribed to Shaykh Sīdī ʿAbd al-Qādir. It consists of sitting as described and turning the face toward the right shoulder and saying *Hā,* turning the face to the left, saying *Hū,* then lowering the head and expelling the breath while saying *Ḥayy,* and repeating this without stopping.

Whether the diffusion of the Qādirīyah can be credited more to their own proselytizing efforts or to the scattering effects of the Mongol attack on Baghdad, it is clear that by 1350, they possessed all the contemporary Ṣūfī techniques and practices: *dhikr* on a regular basis, local leaders, *khalīfah*s, and shaykhs.

As the Qādirīyah spread from Baghdad and other Middle Eastern centers, India was the early destination of many Qādirīs. In one of the first instances, the founder of another Ṣūfī group, Shāh Ni'mat Allāh Walī of Mahān in Iran, sent his nephew Mīr Nūr Allāh to India about 1425. The nephew, a Qādirī, settled at the court of the Bahmanid sultan Aḥmad I at Bidar in the Deccan, where the Qādirīs had considerable support and success. A similar success is recorded in Multan, where the founder of a local branch (a ninth-generation descendant of ʿAbd al-Qādir) called himself al-Ḥusaynī, claiming the status of a sayyid (descendant of the Prophet), which no doubt helped in gaining adherents. The order also spread into the Punjab and Sind, which was proselytized by members of the same family that had been in Multan earlier. This family order of the Qādirīyah then progressed to Agra and Delhi and to other local capitals, being taken up at the Mughal court on several occasions. Other branches of developing family groups of the Jilānī clan arrived in Gujarat and Malwa from Iraq via Iran and Afghanistan in the sixteenth century, founding *khānqāh*s, attracting large numbers of followers, and to a large extent becoming the local scholars, intellectuals, and clerics.

In the course of time, the Qādirīyah included some famous names, such as Shaykh ʿAbd al-Ḥaqq (1551–1642), a *muḥaddith* (expert in *ḥadīth*) and a translator of ʿAbd al-Qādir's Arabic writings into Persian as well as a distinguished theologian. Another famous Qādirī was the ascetic Miyān Mīr (1531–1635), renowned for his austerities and also largely for avoiding kings and other worldly notables, in true Ṣūfī fashion. In the mid-seventeenth century another Qādirī figure, Mulla Shāh Badākhshī, initiated the Mughal prince Dārā Shukūh into the order; Dārā Shikūh was executed by his brother Awrangzīb for heresy in 1659. During the eighteenth and nineteenth centuries the Indian Qādirīyah continued to to flourish on the subcontinent, and it exists in both India and Pakistan today.

In the Islamic West, oral tradition has the grandsons or other descendants of ʿAbd al-Qādir entering Spain from the East. Under pressure during the period of the Reconquista, Qādirīs fled Spain for North Africa around 1460. Some of these Qādirīs penetrated through Morocco into the Sāqiyat al-Ḥamrā' (Mauretania). One name often mentioned is that of Aḥmad al-Bakkā'ī al-Kuntī (d. 1504), who won many adherents. [*See the bi-*

ography of Bakkā'ī al-Kuntī.] Another allied to this group is Muḥammad al-Maghīlī (also d. 1504), a Qādirī who had influence in Hausaland and adjoining regions; he was also involved in the persecutions of Jews. In the eighteenth century the Kunta branch of the Qādirīyah was rejuvenated by al-Mukhtār ibn Aḥmad al-Kuntī (d. 1811), a prolific author and master of many *karāmāt*. Al-Mukhtār ibn Aḥmad had direct influence on Usuman Dan Fodio (d. 1817), the leader of the Fulani Jihād in northern Nigeria, who was also a Qādirī. For a time in the early nineteenth century, the Mukhtārīyah Qādirīyah was very influential. In the mid-nineteenth century there was a bloody Qādirī-Tijānī contest in Mali, Guinea, and Senegal, involving the famous Tijānī jihādist al-Ḥājj ʿUmar Tal (d. 1864). One of the most recent offshoots of this West African cluster of branches (including the Fāḍilīyah) is the Murīdīyah, led by Aḥmadu Bamba (d. 1927). The Murīds, now less active than previously, were famous for their peanut growing and their subservience to French colonial control. [*See* Tijānīyah; Murīdīyah; *and the biographies of Dan Fodio and ʿUmar Tal.*]

In parts of North Africa, particularly Algeria and Tunisia, there are numerous Qādirī groups. In the nineteenth century one of the better known was the *zāwiyah* of the Algerian register Amīr ʿAbd al-Qādir at Mascara. From here and elsewhere in western Algeria the amīr led a successful war against France until 1847, when the local resistance was crushed. The Tunisian Qādirīs included the eighteenth-century Manzalīyah at Jerba, Safaqis, and Qabes. At Al-Kef there was a *zāwiyah* of the Mazūnīyah, founded in the nineteenth century by Muḥammad al-Mazūnī and related through its *silsilah* (chain of authority) to the Manzalīyah. The Moroccan Qādirī group called the Jilālah originated in Spain in the middle or late fifteenth century: according to J. S. Trimingham, a Qādirī *zāwīyah* was established at Fez in 1693 (1971, p. 272). A number of other smaller groups in Fez and elsewhere are mentioned by Mehmed Ali Aynî (1967, p. 252).

In the eastern Sudan, the fire of ʿAbd al-Qādir was lit by Tāj al-Dīn al-Bahārī about 1550. He stayed for a time in the Jazīrah, leaving behind a number of *khalīfah*s or deputies who spread the order. In the seventeenth and eighteenth centuries it gained many adherents and became popular, as it remains today.

In ʿAbd al-Qādir's homeland of Iran, the order spread widely between the time of his death and the appearance of the Ṣafavid regime in 1501, when many Ṣūfī orders were expelled from the country—the Ṣafavīyah and two or three other Shīʿī orders being exceptions. According to I. P. Petrushevsky (1985, p. 296), Qādirīs were especially numerous, but they were forced to depart from Iran because "ʿAbd al-Qādir was a Sunnī Ḥanbalite and fiercely antagonistic to the Shi'ites." Petrushevsky also claims that the color green was the symbol of this Ṣūfī organization, that the Qādirīs were "pantheistic," and that ʿAbd al-Qādir "was deified in secret" (p. 296).

In neighboring Afghanistan Qādirīs apparently reappeared after the downfall of Ṣafavid Shiism in 1722. About 1828, for example, one of the numerous descendants of ʿAbd al-Qādir, Saʿd Allāh Gīlānī, moved from Baghdad to Herat. Like others in his family, he was skilled in Qur'ānic commentary and prophetic traditions, attracting many students as a result. He managed to marry a descendant of the former Afghan ruler Aḥmad Shāh Abdālī (or Durrānī). Eventually he and his descendants acquired a *khānqāh* in a village about 14 kilometers south of Herat called Siyāwshān. This suborder of the Qādirīyah, the Razzāqīyah, functioned for a long time during the nineteenth century and into the twentieth. (Sayyid Maḥmud Gīlānī, 1989, p. 131).

The order became established in Ottoman Turkey when a Qādirī called Pīr Ismāʿīl Rūmī or Pīrī Sānī (d. 1631), from Kastamuni, founded a "Qādirī house" (*kadirihana*) at Istanbul, followed by some forty others throughout Anatolia. He invented a special Qādirī cap made of white cloth in eight parts in a cylindrical shape; he also created a *dhikr* in which the participants, standing upright, grasped each others' arms, swaying back and forth in rhythmic fashion and balancing themselves first right, then left, shouting loudly as they did so—to the scandal of the conservative *ʿulamā'*. This Rūmīyah suborder was only one of many, including the Hindīyah, Khulūṣīyah, Nābulusīyah, and Waṣlatīyah. These Qādirī institutions, like many others, were shut down in 1924 by Kemal Atatürk, and the orders were outlawed. Nevertheless it seems likely that the Qādirīyah continued a clandestine existence despite these prohibitions, and that it still exists in Turkey, although with a diminished membership.

Qādirīs are also to be found in China, Central Asia, Kurdistan, Indonesia, Bosnia and Macedonia, Somalia and the Horn of Africa, the East African coast, Palestine, and elsewhere. Much useful information on them is provided by A. Popovic and G. Veinstein (1986).

[*See also* Sainthood; Sufism; Sufism and Politics; Zāwiyah; *the biography of ʿAbd al-Qādir; and entries on specific countries.*]

BIBLIOGRAPHY

ʿAbd al-Qādir al-Jīlānī. *Al-ghunyah li-ṭālibī ṭarīq al-ḥaqq.* 2 vols. in 1. Cairo, 1956.

Aynî, Mehmed Ali (Mehmet Ali Aini). *Un grand saint de l'Islam, ʿAbd al-Qādir Guilânî, 1077–1166.* Paris, 1967. Photographic reproduction of the 1938 edition.

Chabbi, Jacqueline. "ʿAbd al-Kadir al-Djilani, personnage historique." *Studia Islamica* 38 (1973): 75–106.

Gīlānī, Sayyid Maḥmūd. *Tajallī-yi ʿirfān-i Qādirīyah.* Islamabad, 1989.

Kutubī, Muḥammad ibn Shākir al-. *Fawāt al-wafayāt.* Vol. 2. Cairo, 1951.

Petrushevsky, I. P. *Islam in Iran.* Albany, N.Y., 1985.

Popovic, Alexandre, and Gilles Veinstein, eds. *Les ordres mystiques dans l'Islam: Cheminements et situation actuelle.* Paris, 1986.

Rizvi, S. A. A. *A History of Sufism in India.* 2 vols. New Delhi, 1978–1983.

Sanūsī, Muḥammad ibn ʿAlī al-. *Kitāb al-manhal al-rawī al-rāʾiq fī asānid al-ʿulūm wa-uṣūl al-ṭarāʾiq.* In *Majmūʿāh al-mukhtārah.* Beirut, 1968.

Trimingham, J. Spencer. *The Sufi Orders in Islam.* Oxford, 1971.

BRADFORD G. MARTIN

QĀJĀR DYNASTY. The last of a series of tribal (or tribally based) dynasties that ruled Iran since the tenth century, the Qājārs (1796–1925), like the Ṣafavids, ruled a territory roughly coterminus with contemporary Iran. Most historiography, both Western and Iranian, has stressed negatives about the Qājārs, saying, with much justice, that they accomplished little reform or modernization and did little to hold off British and Russian incursions. Some recent historiography has been more positive, stressing the overwhelming obstacles facing the dynasty and its attempts to overcome some of them. The Qājārs did succeed in recreating a centralized state and quelling separatist revolts. Its avoidance of colonial conquest, however, was more a result of the Anglo-Russian rivalry than its own strength.

The Qājār dynasty began as a tribal federation in northwest Iran that engaged in a rivalry for power with another federation under the southwestern Zand rulers. A Qājār leader castrated in boyhood, Āghā Muḥammad Khan, was captured and kept under house arrest by the Zands, but on the death of a Zand ruler, he returned to lead his tribal forces, taking most of Iran by 1790. Becoming shah in 1796, he was known for cruelty and was assassinated in 1797. He was succeeded by a nephew, Fatḥ ʿAlī Shāh, who ruled until 1834. Qājār unification ended the civil strife of the eighteenth century.

Fatḥ ʿAlī was brought into European diplomacy by the British and French, who at different points in the Napoleonic period wanted Iran as an ally against Russia. Russia wanted Iranian-held territory in Georgia, Armenia, and North Azerbaijan, and in the first Russo-Iranian War (1804–1813), it took much of this territory. The Treaty of Gulistan (1813) ratified Iran's losses to the Russians.

European presence and the Russian war led Crown Prince ʿAbbās Mīrzā, who ruled in Azerbaijan, to try Western training of his forces, and he sent students abroad to improve the military. His chief minister continued reform efforts when he joined the central government after ʿAbbās Mīrzā's death in 1833. This death deprived the Qājārs of their last devoted reformer. Reform was harder in Iran than in, say, Egypt or Turkey, owing to size and difficulty of communications, the heavy presence of nomadic tribal groups tied to old ways, and the much smaller presence of Europeans and European trade, given Iran's distance from the West.

Disagreements over interpretation of the Treaty of Gulistan and agitation by some *ʿulamāʾ* (religious scholars) led to a second Russo-Iranian War (1826–1828). The Russian victory in 1828 was incorporated into the Treaty of Turkomanchai, which gave Russia more territory, a cash indemnity, extraterritorial rights, and a 5 percent limit on import tariffs, with no internal duties allowed. These provisions, similar to those exacted in the nineteenth century by Western powers on other undeveloped countries, put Iranian merchants, who had to pay internal duties, at a disadvantage. In later decades these provisions were extended to the other European powers by "most favored nation" clauses in treaties.

The killing by an *ʿulamāʾ*-inspired crowd of the Russian envoy Griboyedov in 1829 has been variously interpreted, but clearly it involved a major antiforeign incident and showed independent power by the *ʿulamāʾ*. Under the reign of Muḥammad Shāh (1834–1848), Western influence grew; there was a revolt by the Ismāʿīlīs, who left for India with their leader, the Aga Khan; and a more important heretical movement, the Bābīs, began in the 1840s. The succeeding shah, the teenaged Nāṣir al-Dīn (1848–1897), brought with him from Tabriz his chief minister, Amīr Kabīr, Iran's main reforming leader. Amīr Kabīr led in suppressing Bābī uprisings after the death of Muḥammad Shāh, and the Bāb was executed in 1850. Amīr Kabīr, also initiated major reforms, such as creating a defense industry to support the military, strengthening the Western training of troops, and forming the first Western-style advanced school for the training of military and governmental figures, the Dār al-Funūn. He also cut sinecures and pensions. He made enemies among vested interests, including the powerful queen mother. His enemies convinced the shah to have him removed from office in 1851 and to have him killed in 1852. Most of his reforms were reversed, and the few later reformers were also largely unsuccessful. [*See* Ismāʿīlīyah; Bābism.]

Although some historians are now sympathetic to Nāṣir al-Dīn Shāh, he did not reverse Iran's increasing dependence on Britain and Russia. His next reforming minister, Mirzā Ḥusayn Khān Sipāhsālār, in the early 1870s, tried to reorganize ministries and the military but foundered on his belief that foreigners must develop the Iranian economy. He was, along with another reformer, Malkom Khān, one of those who convinced the shah to accept the all-encompassing Reuter Concession of 1872, giving control of most of Iran's assets to a British subject. [*See the biography of Malkom Khān.*] Returning from abroad, Sipāhsālār and the shah were greeted by an opposition group uniting the shah's favorite wife, some courtiers, and *ʿulamāʾ*, and Sipāhsālār was dismissed and the concession abrogated on a pretext. Concession granting resumed in the 1888–1890 period, culminating in a mass movement led by *ʿulamāʾ* and merchants that forced the shah to cancel a monopoly tobacco concession to a British subject in 1892. Nāṣir al-Dīn Shāh was assassinated by a follower of Jamāl al-Dīn al-Afghānī in 1897 and was succeeded by his sickly son Muẓaffar al-Dīn Shāh. Weakness without major reform encouraged revolt.

Popular discontent, backed by the *ʿulamāʾ*, merchants, and a growing group of progressive intellectuals, spread in the early twentieth century and culminated in the Constitutional Revolution (1905–1911), which resulted in a written constitutional and a parliament (Majlis). Muẓaffar al-Dīn Shāh died in 1907; his counterrevolutionary son, Muḥammad ʿAlī Shāh, was deposed by the constitutionalists in 1909 and followed by the boy shah, Aḥmad, under a regent.

With British and Russian troops occupying Iran during World War I, and the British after, and Iran being a battleground for the Turks, Iran's government had little freedom of action, and the shah was a cipher. In 1919, the British negotiated a treaty with three ministers amounting to protectorate status for Iran, but the Majlis never ratified it. Facing a government stalemate, the head of the British troops in Iran encouraged an eager colonel in the Cossack Brigade, Reza Khan (Riẓā Khān), to lead a coup, supported by the pro-British journalist, Sayyid Ẓiyā al-Dīn Ṭabāṭabāʾī. The latter was soon forced out by Reza, who, after an abortive attempt at a republic on the Turkish model, got the Majlis to approve the ending of the Qājār dynasty and the establishment of the Pahlavi dynasty in 1925. Thus ended the century of the Qājārs, who, while hardly illustrious, did help keep Iran together and accomplished some change, chiefly in the direction of gradual centralization and bureaucratization of the government and partial acceptance of constitutional reform.

[*See also* Iran *and the biography of Pahlavi.*]

BIBLIOGRAPHY

Algar, Hamid. *Religion and State in Iran, 1785–1906*. Berkeley, 1969. The first book-length treatment of the *ʿulamāʾ* in Qājār times, which takes an optimistic view of their influence and motivation.

Arjomand, Said Amir. *The Shadow of God and the Hidden Imam*. Chicago and London, 1984. Revisionist scholarly view of *ʿulamāʾ*-state relations from the beginning to 1890.

Avery, Peter, et al., eds. *The Cambridge History of Iran*, vol. 7, *From Nadir Shah to the Islamic Republic*. Cambridge, 1991. Contains articles on the Qājār period by Gavin Hambly, Nikki R. Keddie and Mehrdad Amanat, Stanford J. Shaw, F. Kazemzadeh, Rose Greaves, Ann K. S. Lambton, Richard Tapper, Charles Issawi, Hamid Algar, Peter Chelkowski, and Peter Avery.

Bakhash, Shaul. *Iran: Monarchy, Bureaucracy, and Reform under the Qajars, 1858–1896*. London, 1978. Analytic study of the efforts at governmental reform under Nasir al-Din Shah.

Bayat, Mangol. *Mysticism and Dissent: Socioreligious Thought in Qajar Iran*. Syracuse, N.Y., 1982. The only serious Western-language study of nineteenth-century thinkers, stressing their roots in older Iranian thought as well as in new Western ideas.

Bosworth, C. E., and Carole Hillenbrand, eds. *Qajar Iran: Political, Social, and Cultural Change, 1800–1925*. Edinburgh, 1983. Festschrift for the late L. P. Elwell-Sutton, with far more internal consistency and substance than many such volumes.

Garthwaite, Gene. *Khans and Shahs: A Documentary Analysis of the Bakhtiari in Iran*. New York and Cambridge, 1983. Rare tribal history, showing the political importance of the main tribal confederations in Qājār Iran.

Lambton, Ann K. S., ed. *Qajar Persia: Eleven Studies*. Austin, 1988.

NIKKI R. KEDDIE

QĀNŪN. *See* Law.

QARAMANLI DYNASTY.

A Turkish dynasty founded by the original Qaramanlı, Ahmed Bey, controlled Ottoman Tripolitania and, intermittently, Cyrenaica and Fezzan, from 1711 to 1835. Ahmed Bey had been appointed to a subprovincial administrative position and took advantage of disorders within the Ottoman military to usurp power. Efforts by Sultan Ahmed III to install a new governor were rebuffed, and Ahmed won recognition as pasha by 1722.

From this point to the end of the century, two Qaramanlı successors, first Ahmed's son Mehmed (r. 1745–1754) and then Mehmed's son Ali (r. 1754–1793), obtained recognition of their control over Tripolitania. They gained even broader authority from their ability to suppress local uprisings in neighboring Cyrenaica and the Fezzan. Apparently this ability was based on different sources of military support for the Qaramanlıs, including remaining imperial Janissary units as well as mercenary forces of diverse nationalities. At the same time, Tripoli became a base for pirates who, by contributing to the pashas' coffers, enjoyed Qaramanlı patronage. Symbiotic relations with pirates played an important role in Qaramanlı history from the end of Ali's reign to the dynasty's fall four decades later.

Already under Ahmed Pasha, efforts had been made to secure trade relations with European powers. France and England, specifically, signed several bilateral agreements with Tripoli. By superseding Ottoman capitulations the rulers of Tripoli already held, such treaties in effect recognized the independence of the Qaramanlıs. To maintain benefits offered by bilateral treaties, Tripoli often had to press protected pirate factions not to attack maritime traders operating under the flags of signatory nations. This led to diplomatic clashes with victims of Tripoli-based piracy, particularly from neighboring Italian states and, most notably in 1800, the United States.

It was factors such as these that gradually weakened Qaramanlı control. In 1790 the assassination of Ali Pasha's heir apparent precipitated a succession struggle. Two sons and a total outsider from Algiers vied for Ali's post. Expanding intrigues brought Hamuda Bey of the Ottoman Regency of Tunis into the succession struggle on the side of the Qaramanlı family. Conflicting claims between Ali's two sons Ahmed and Yusuf, and then among Yusuf's descendants, continued to plague Qaramanlı rule over the next few decades. At each stage of infighting one finds external sponsorship for one or another of the candidates for the Tripoli governorship. From Napoleonic times until his abdication in 1832, Yusuf Pasha clearly preferred French sponsorship. His error was to offer France a formal treaty in 1830, soon after the French occupied the Algiers Regency. Alarmed critics of France's advance into Algeria, led by the British, tried to undermine Yusuf's pro-French posture by championing an heir who would reverse the Tripoli-Algiers-Paris alignment. When Yusuf attempted to pass his governorship on to his son Ali in 1832, his grandson Mehmed Bey counted on British support to thwart his grandfather's preference for Ali.

After Istanbul failed to obtain Britain's recognition of an imperial *firman* granting the succession to Ali, Sultan Mahmud II finally decided in 1835 to send an armed force to proclaim the end of Qaramanlı ascendancy. The return to direct imperial rule was in part tied to pressures by Britain to oppose a Qaramanlı successor who was openly receptive to French overtures. It is also likely, however, that the Ottoman sultan was reacting to another, more serious threat from Tripoli's dominant neighbor to the east; this threat had taken form in 1831 when Muḥammad ʿAlī, governor of Egypt, had expanded his control across Sinai in Syria.

[*See also* Libya; Ottoman Empire.]

BIBLIOGRAPHY

Abun-Nasr, Jamil M. *A History of the Maghrib in the Islamic Period*. Cambridge and New York, 1987.

Bono, Salvatore. *I corsari barbaeschi*. Turin, 1961.

Mantran, Robert. "Le statut de l'Algérie de la Tunisie et de la Tripolitaine dans l'Empire Ottoman." In *Atti del primo congresso internazionale di studi nord africani*. Cagliari, 1965.

Rossi, Ettore. *Storia di Tripoli e della Tripolitania: Dalla conquista araba al 1911*. Rome, 1968.

BYRON D. CANNON

QATAR. *See* Gulf States.

QIṢĀṢ. *See* Criminal Law.

QOM. A small provincial town south of Tehran, Qom (or Qum) is the site of Ḥaẓrat-i Maʿṣūmah, the shrine of Fāṭimah, sister of the eight Imam, the second most important Shīʿī shrine in Iran, and the leading center of Shīʿī theological seminaries in Iran. The gold-domed shrine and its spacious New or Atabegi Courtyard are filled daily with pilgrims. Entry to the shrine is through a mirrored portal from the Atabegi Courtyard, built in 1883, along the sides of which are graves of nobles and ministers of the Qājār dynasty. The present dome was constructed under the Ṣafavids and gilded by the Qājārs. Four Ṣafavid shahs are buried in a mosque behind the main shrine as are three leaders of the Qom seminaries. Behind the shrine is the new blue-domed Aʿẓam or Borujerdi Mosque, a major teaching space for the highest level of study, the *dars-i khārij*. Two Qājār shahs are buried to the right of the shrine in the Old Courtyard, behind which are two more courtyards, turned by the Ṣafavids into the Dār al-Shifā' and Faydīyah Seminaries, centers of political activity in 1963, 1975, and 1977–1979. The shrine courtyard and the Borujerdi Mosque are important places for leading communal prayers and sermons. The shrine has been an economic and state institution; a focus of endowments and commercial rents dedicated to its upkeep, as well as a symbolic site whose opening and closing each day is accompanied by state-appointed guards chanting the sovereignty of the reigning government under Allāh.

Economically, with little modern industry, the town depends on its farming hinterland, produces some fine carpets, but primarily provides services to pilgrims, religious students, and the religious establishment. Although Qom has a *madrasah* (seminary) tradition that can be traced back a thousand years, the current set of *madrasahs* are only some fifty years old and provided a major center of resistance to the Pahlavi monarchy. When Ayatollah Ruhollah al-Musavi Khomeini returned to Iran to lead the Islamic Revolution of 1979, he went immediately to Qom. Although Khomeini, as head of state, later moved to Tehran, Qom remained a key seat of educational and political organizations of the *ʿulamā'* (clergy). Qom's history provides a microcosm of currents in Iran's state-clergy relations, from the time of the establishment of Islam and then of the struggles to establish Shiism.

Qom's historians revel in its reputation as an obstreperous Shīʿī center, tracing this posture back to the early Shīʿī resistance to the Umayyads. Abū Mūsā al-Ashʿarī, a representative of the first Imam, ʿAlī, visited Qom in AH 23/644 CE, but Qom remained Zoroastrian and paid *jizyah* (the tax on protected minorities) for some time. The great Sassanian ritual fire in the nearby village of Mazdiajan was extinguished only in AH 288/899 CE by the governor of Qom, Bayram Türk. Qom, however, became a refuge for opponents of the Umayyads during this early period. After Muṭraf ibn Mughīrahs revolt against the governor of Iraq, Ḥajjāj ibn Yūsuf al-Thaqafī, failed in AH 66–67/685–687 CE, a group of his followers, the Banī Asad, came to settle in a village outside of Qom, called Jam Karan (now an important secondary shrine of the area). A decade later refugees from the unsuccessful *jihād* of ʿAbd al-Raḥmān ibn Muḥammad al-Ashʿath (governor of Seistan) against Ḥajjāj also came to Qom (c. 78/697). ʿAbd al-Raḥmān's army had included seventeen *tābiʿīn* (disciples of the Prophet's companions), and among the refugees who came to Quom were the sons of Ṣaʿib who had fought with Mukhtār in the unsuccessful attempt to revenge Ḥusayn in Kufa under the banner of his brother, Muḥammad ibn al-Ḥanafīyah. The first of ʿAbd al-Rahmān's followers to arrive in Qom were the brothers ʿAbd Allāh and Ahwas Ashʿarī. They were welcomed by the Zoroastrian, Yazdān Fizar of Abrastigān Qom, and were given a village, Muḥammadan, apparently in recognition of aid the Ashʿarīs had previously given Qom in efforts to stay independent of the Daylamīs. The alliance was short-lived, however: a quarrel broke out, the Ashʿarīs were asked to leave; instead they slaughtered the leading Zoroastrians. The other Zoroastrians began to leave or converted to Islam. Among the Ashʿarī sons were twelve *rāwī* (transmitters of *riwāyat* or *ḥadīth*) of Imam Jaʿfar al-Ṣādiq, the twelfth Imam.

From these beginnings, Qom next developed a reputation for resisting Sunnī governors and their tax demands. Ḥusayn Mudarrisī Ṭabāṭabā'ī (1350/1975) lists five occasions in the ninth century alone when the town had to be militarily reduced before taxes could be collected. In contrast, a Shīʿī governor was given so much cooperation that he was removed by the caliph lest he claim independence. During the ninth century there were 266 Shīʿī *ʿulamā'* and 14 Sunnī *ʿulamā'* in the town; among the former were the Bābūyah family and their most renowned son, counted now as a *marjaʿ al-taqlīd* (supreme guide in religious matters), Shaykh al-Ṣadūq ibn Bābūyah. On these grounds, Qom lays claim to being an older *ḥawzah-i ʿilmī* (center of religious learning) than Najaf (in southern Iraq), although the scholarly tradition had periods of virtual disappearance.

It was to this Shīʿī town that Fāṭimah, the sister of the eighth Imam, ʿAlī al-Riḍā, came when she fell ill in Saveh (then a Sunnī town) en route to visit her brother in Mashhad. She died in Qom, and over the years her grave has come to be the second most important shrine of Iran: the shrine of Ḥaẓrat-i Maʿṣūmah, Fāṭimah. The first *mutawalli* (administrator) of the shrine appears to have been a representative of the eleventh Imam, and was of the Ashʿarī family, Aḥmad ibn Isḥāq Ashʿarī. The first dome was constructed over the grave in the sixth century, and the shrine apparently served as a pilgrimage site for Sunnīs as well as Shīʿīs. The dome was redone in the Ṣafavid period and was gilded in the Qājār period. Fāṭimah's sister has a smaller shrine in the village of Kohak, a place that at times competed with Qom for predominance.

By the ninth/fifteenth century Qom's identity had begun to crystallize: it became, in addition to a Shīʿī center and a shrine, a place of royal interest. Jahān Shah, Uzun Hasan, Sultan Yaʿqūb, Alvand Sultan, and Sultan Murad all used Qom as a winter hunting capital (Uzun Hasan was visited here by envoys from Venice), Sultan Muḥammad Bahādur briefly established a semi-independent state centered on Qom. Jahān Shah Karakoyunlu issued the earliest extant *firmān* (royal order), dated 867/1462, naming Aḥmad Niẓāmuddīn as *mutawalli* of the shrine and *naqīb* (local head) of the sayyids. He also sponsored *majlis wāʿiz* (preachments) in Qom. From later *firmān*s it becomes clear that the two jobs of *naqīb* and *mutawalli* always went together and were assumed to be hereditary in the Razavī sayyid family of Mūsā Mubāqah, which had come to Qom in the ninth century. (This family has a large set of mausoleums on the edge of town.)

The Ṣafavid shahs Ismāʿīl and Ṭahmāsp continued the tradition of using Qom as a winter capital. But the Ṣafavids built Qom into something much grander than it had ever been. The tombs of Shahs ʿAbbās II, Ṣafī, Sulaymān, and Sultan Ḥusayn were placed here, near the shrine of Fāṭimah, Ḥaẓrat-i Maʿṣūmah. The shrine was refurbished and two of its four courtyards were turned into the Madrasah Faydīyah with a small hospital behind for pilgrims, the Dār al-Shafa. Important teachers were brought: Mullahs Muḥsin Fayd, ʿAbd al-Razzāq Lāhījī, Ṣadrā Shīrāzī, and Ṭāhir Qummī and Qāḍī Saʿīd. Several administrative arrangements were tried: for a while the governor was the *mutawalli;* for a while there were three *mutawalli*s, one each for the tombs of Fāṭimah, Shah ʿAbbās II, and Shah Ṣafī. But the main *mutawalli* was Mīrzā Ḥabīb Allāh ibn Mīr Ḥusayn Khātim al-Mujtahidīn and later his descendants; he had been brought from Lebanon by Shah Ṭahmāsp with his father and two brothers. The two brothers were made *mutawalli* of the Shah ʿAbd al-ʿAẓīm shrine in Rey and the Shah Ṣafī shrine in Ardebil. These jobs remained hereditary until 1965 when Shah Muhammad Reza Pahlavi ousted them. Whether the custom is older is unclear, but under the Ṣafavids the shrine became a place of *basṭ-nishīn* (sanctuary), where one could take refuge from the law until a judgment thought to be unfair could be sorted out. At times this legal recourse tended to degenerate into a device used mainly by debtors.

The Qājārs continued the tradition of placing royal and noble mausoleums at the shrine of Fāṭimah, with the tombs of Fatḥ ʿAlī Shah, Muḥammad Shah, and the many Qājār ministers: Qā'immaqām and Mīrzā ʿAlī Akbar Khān among others. They rebuilt sections of the shrine, the grand Ṣaḥn-i Jadīd (New Courtyard) being built by Amīn al-Sulṭān in 1883. The *bast* tradition continued despite efforts by the prime minister, Mīrzā ʿAlī Akbar Khān, to abolish it. The *madrasahs*, however, lost their vitality after the death of the scholar Mīrzā Qummī in 1231/1804, although several of them were rebuilt under Fatḥ ʿAlī Shah (1797–1834), and the Jānī Khān Madrasah was rebuilt under Nāṣir al-Dīn Shah (1848–1896).

In the twentieth century two social vectors became increasingly important and contested: first, the *ḥawẓah-i ʿilmī* was reestablished in Qom, but this time not through royal or aristocratic patronage; second, the Pahlavi state began to eliminate or reduce the spheres of influence claimed by the religious leaders: law, education, endowments, registry of contracts, and through control of television and radio even the dissemination of religious propaganda.

The year 1920, when Shaykh ʿAbd al-Karīm Ḥā'irī-Yazdī arrived from Arak (Soltanabad) after leaving Iraq, is usually given for the modern founding of the *ḥawẓah-i ʿilmī* of Qom. Ḥā'irī-Yazdī arrived as part of the exodus back to Iran by Shīʿī leaders who were concerned that the uncertain transition between Ottoman and British rule in Iraq might jeopardize their position in the *ʿatabāt* (shrine towns of Iraq). Shaykh Murtaẓā Anṣārī earlier had sent Mīr Muḥammad ʿAlī Shushtarī Jazāyirī to reconnoiter Qom and Mashhad. Then in 1916 Ayatollah Fayd Qummī, joined later by others, returned to Qom to restore the old *madrasahs* to their original purpose. Shops and storage areas had to be converted back to student rooms in the Madrasah Faydīyah. Even wheat bakeries had to be set up. Over the course of a full century—since the death in 1815 of Mīrzā Qummī, author of the *Qawānīn* (Laws)—Qom's *madrasahs* had fallen into disuse and ruin and the town had suffered "an intellectual famine" (Rahimi, 1339/1961). After establishing a minimal basis for a *ḥawẓah-i ʿilmī*, Ayatollah Mīrzā Maḥmūd Rūḥānī and Shaykh Ḥusayn Qummī were dispatched to Arak to invite and persuade Ḥā'irī-Yazdī to come. He did so, bringing with him a large following, including those who were to succeed after his death (in 1935): Ayatollahs Muḥammad ʿAlī Ha'irī Qummī (d. 1939), and Muḥammad Ḥujjat Kūhkamarī came immediately, as did Khomeini and Muḥammad Riẓā Gulpāygānī; Aḥmad Khusārī came in 1923, Shihāb al-Dīn Marʿashī and Muḥammad Kāẓim Sharīʿatmādārī in 1924, and Ayatollah Ṣadr al-Dīn Ṣadr in 1930. Almost immediately on the reestablishment of the Qom *ḥawzah*, it was able to play host to refugees from Iraq: Shīʿī resistance to the British caused for short periods both the voluntary and nonvoluntary exile of students and teachers.

How much of a change the growth of the *madrasah*s made to life in Qom can only be estimated from a series of incidents: the campaign of Ayatollah Bāfqī to keep men from cutting their beards, the staging by Nūr Allāh Iṣfahānī in Qom of calls for the ousting of the dictator Reza Shah (1925), the clash between Bāfqī and Reza Shah over the veiling of the royal women in the shrine, the burning of wine shops, opposition to modern schools, opposition to the enfranchisement of women, student harangues against the Tudeh (Communist) party, and opposition to the introduction of cinema and television. Not all the acts of the religious leaders, however, were conservative in this sense as can be seen in their leadership in building hospitals, welfare systems, libraries, and flood walls. Indeed some of the conservatism was reaction to Pahlavi-government-led anticlericalism. Some of the *ʿulamāʾ* had helped with the establishment of modern schools at the turn of the century, but by the 1930s people who grew up in Qom told stories of having to dodge heckling *ṭalaba* (religious students) on their way to school, especially the girls. The ambivalence of the *ʿulamāʾ* had to do with the growth of government regulatory functions in education and in the administration of endowments (a key source of revenues). Secular education beyond elementary school did not exist until 1935, but a coeducational school opened that year, adult education was offered by the government, and fifteen more schools were opened in the next two years; by 1937 there were three high schools.

These were years of great pressure against the religious establishment. The great struggle over dressing like Europeans and unveiling women came in 1935–1936. Attempts were made to license those who had a right to wear religious garb (i.e., traditional dress), and the number of *ṭalaba* began to decline, reaching a low of 500 or fewer at the end of Reza Shah's reign in 1941 (Rāzī, 1332/1954, vol. 2, p. 119). When Ḥā'irī-Yazdī died in 1935, not only were laws in effect against *rawẓah khvānī* preachments, but a formal death memorial for him was disallowed (though the inpouring of people to Qom to chant in the streets could not be prevented). In 1938 the government tried to introduce exams for the religious students to regulate their progress and to formalize procedures for exemption from the army. The examinations were evaded by a plea from the *ḥawzah* leadership that the date set had fallen on the death anniversary of Shaykh Muḥammad ʿAlī Qummī and the students had to convene a memorial service. The government acquiesced and did not try to reinstitute the examinations. In 1975 those who were at least middle-level students and had six years of secular education could ask a committee of *ḥawzah* teachers to certify to the Office of Education that they were students in good standing, and this was forwarded with a request for deferrment to the gendarmerie. Direct control over religious students thus was abandoned in favor of informal surveillance. Resistance to open procedures had led to expansion of covert procedures. Similarly, rejuvenation of the shrine with its endowments as a state-linked religious center and the expansion of control by the Office of Endowments over all religious endowments in Qom were viewed by the religious establishment as parts of a process directed against its claims to leadership in all religious and moral matters.

As tensions intensified, Qom became a site of increasing resistance to the policies of the Pahlavi state. In June 1963 and again in June 1975 there were major demonstrations in Qom that were direct precursors to the revolution of 1977–1979. In 1963 Khomeini was arrested for leading the opposition to the enfranchisement of women, the Local Council Election Bill of 1962, land reform, the six-point White Revolution, and a major military loan from the United States, which was tied to immunity from Iranian law for American service personnel. Three months earlier demonstrations by religious students had led to the occupation of the *madrasah*s of Qom by security forces. On the fifteenth of Khurdād (5 June), a date that was to become a symbolic anniversary thereafter, which fell at the end of the emotional first ten days of Muḥarram that year, Khomeini was arrested, and resistance among the religious students in the central Madrasah Faydīyah was quelled, a number of students losing their lives by being tossed by gendarmes from the roof of the madrasah into the dry riverbed below. Within two hours of Khomeini's arrest in Qom, crowds had also gathered in front of the Tehran bazaar; by 10:00 A.M. troops had fired on them. For three days disturbances continued in Tehran, Qom, Mashhad, Isfahan, and Shiraz; thousands are said to have died.

Twelve years later, the fifteenth of Khurdād 1975 fell just after the new single-party (Rāstakhīz party) state had been declared, during the registration for the first elections under the new party. Khomeini, who had been in exile since 1963, had smuggled into Iran pamphlets denouncing the new party as merely a tool for tightening the dictatorship. At the same time the anti-inflation campaign was moving into high gear, with many arrests of businesspeople. Students in Madrasah Faydīyah began to recite twenty thousand blessings (*ṣalavāt*) on the defenders of Islam (Khomeini) and curses (*laᶜnat*) on the enemies of Islam (the shah), keeping count on their prayer beads. Crowds gathered. The police and elite army units moved in. The disturbances went on for three days.

In 1975 there were 6,414 students listed in the seminary registers. Only a quarter of these were unmarried. There was a small sprinkling of international students from Pakistan, Afghanistan, India, Lebanon, Tanzania, Turkey, Nigeria, Kashmir, and Indonesia. By social background, the two major sources of students were sons of farmers and sons of clerics. There were some fourteen traditional style *madrasahs* and four innovative new ones attempting to introduce modern teaching methods and subjects. The *madrasahs* and associated activities were roughly grouped into three major establishments around the three *marjaᶜ al-taqlīds*: Sharīᶜatmādārī, Gulpāygānī, and Marᶜāshī Najafī. These establishments put out religious journals and books, sent missionaries abroad (to London, to India, to the Persian Gulf states, to Africa, etc.), and maintained a bureau of itinerant preachers who could be sent out to small villages.

During the revolution of 1977–1979 Qom, of course, remained a focus of activity, and after the revolution it has continued to play an important role in the affairs of the state and society. It is as well the home not only of those religious leaders and lower-rank personnel who guide and support the religious leadership of the state, but also of several important figures who have criticized the state from within the ranks of Islamic ideology.

[*See also* Iran; Shrine.]

BIBLIOGRAPHY

Fischer, Michael M. J. *Iran: From Religious Dispute to Revolution.* Cambridge, Mass., 1980.

Rāzī, Shaykh Muḥammad. *Ganjīna-i dānishmandān.* 5 volumes. Qom, Piruz. 1352–1353/1973–1974.

Ṭabāṭabā'ī, Ḥusayn Mudarrisī. *Qum dar qarn-i nuhum-i hijrī.* Qom, 1350/1971.

MICHAEL M. J. FISCHER

QUR'ĀN. [*This entry focuses on the scripture of the Muslim community. It comprises three articles:*

History of the Text
The Qur'ān as Scripture
The Qur'ān in Muslim Thought and Practice

The first article gives a brief history of the origin, collection, and structure of the text. The second presents the Qur'ān as a unique communication from God and provides a survey of modern exegesis of the text. The third discusses the central role of the Qur'ān in Muslim piety. For further discussion of the teachings of the Qur'ān, see Islam, *overview article.*]

History of the Text

The Qur'ān is a unique phenomenon in human religious history. It is held by its adherents to exist beyond the mundane sphere as the eternal and immutable word of God, "a glorious *qur'ān* [preserved] in a well-guarded tablet" (85.21–22). It is also an earthly book whose history is intimately tied to the life and history of an earthly community.

Although it was shaped by the Muslim community, the Qur'ān in fact created that community and remains the foundation-stone of its faith and morality. Many of its verses were circumstantially determined by the social and religious conditions and questions of the Prophet's society; yet the Qur'ān is believed to transcend all considerations of time and space.

Revelation. The Qur'ān is for Muslims the literal word of God revealed to the prophet Muḥammad. Like a number of pious Arabs, known as *ḥanīfs*, who rejected the idolatrous and immoral ways of their people, Muḥammad periodically left his home for solitary prayer and meditation (*taḥannuth*) in a cave on Mount Ḥirā' in the vicinity of Makkah (Mecca). During one such retreat in his fortieth year an awesome person, later identified as the angel Gabriel, appeared to Muḥammad as he sat one evening wrapped in deep meditation. Taking hold of him, the angel pressed Muḥammad so hard that he thought he was dying. This he repeated three times with the command "Read" or "Recite" (*iqra'*). Muḥammad asked, "What shall I read?" The angel then recited the first five verses of surah 96, which are traditionally considered to be the first revelation of the Qur'ān.

According to other reports, when the Prophet saw Gabriel he was frightened; he ran home and asked his family to cover him up. In that state of fear and trepidation revelation came down, ordering him to "rise and warn" (74.1–2). After a period of uncertainty lasting somewhere between six months and two years during which revelation was temporarily interrupted, the Prophet was reassured that the revelations he was receiving were from God, and that the spirit he encountered was an angel and not a demon. Thereafter revelation continued without interruption until his death in AH 10/632 CE. The formative history of the Qur'ān was therefore coterminous with the Prophet's life.

Qur'ān and Prophet. Tradition reports that when revelation came to the Prophet, he fell into a trancelike state. During such times he is said to have seen Gabriel either in human guise or in his angelic form. At still other times the Prophet heard sounds like the ringing of a bell; these sounds he apprehended as words that he remembered and communicated to others. The normal mode of revelation, however, was direct communication *(waḥy)* by the angel Gabriel.

During the Prophet's life many of his companions, as well as some of his wives, had their own partial collections *(maṣāḥif;* sg., *muṣḥaf)* of the Qur'ān, which they used in their prayers and private devotions. Other collections were made by the Prophet's amanuenses, known as the scribes of revelation.

These early collections differed in important respects, such as the number and order of the surahs and variant readings of certain verses, words, and phrases. With the spread of Islam outside Arabia, private collections and hence variant readings multiplied. Furthermore, as different codices gained popularity in particular regions of the expanding Islamic empire, the need soon arose for an official codex.

Collection of the Qur'ān. The crystallization of the Qur'ān was a long process, and its early stages were shrouded in political, theological, and juristic exigencies. Each of the four rightly guided caliphs has been credited with either initiating or forwarding this important process. Historians and traditionists are, however, unanimously agreed that an official codex was adopted under the aegis of the third caliph, ʿUthmān (r. 644–656), within twenty years of the Prophet's death.

The difficult task of eliminating rival codices was gradually but never fully achieved; many peculiarities of the early codices have survived in the official variant readings of the Qur'ān. By the third/ninth century a universally accepted orthography and system of vocalization of the ʿUthmānic codex was fixed. This helped to reduce a multitude of variant readings to only seven equally valid ones. Among these, the reading of ʿĀṣim (d. 744), transmitted by Ḥafṣ (d. 805), predominates in most areas of the Muslim world today. The royal Egyptian edition of 1924, which follows this reading and has itself become a standard text has further contributed to its popularity.

Structure and Internal History. The Qur'ān is a rather small book, consisting of 114 surahs or chapters varying in length from three to 286 verses. The surahs were arranged roughly by length, which means that the earliest and shortest surahs were placed at the end, and the latest and longest ones at the beginning.

Very early commentators classified Qur'ānic materials into Meccan and Medinan surahs. On the basis of such internal evidence as change in style, idiom, and subject matter of the revelations, modern Western scholarship has divided the Meccan period into early, middle, and late periods.

In spite of such efforts to construct a broad chronology of the Qur'ān, this goal remains impossible, because the sacred text itself provides no reliable framework for the history of its revelation. Nevertheless, knowledge of its chronology is crucial for an understanding of the early history of the Muslim community.

The Qur'ān makes numerous references to particular events and situations in the life of the Prophet and his society. On the basis of such allusions an important field of Qur'ānic study known as "occasions" or "causes *(asbāb)* of revelation" was developed. This subject is closely related to another field, the study of the abrogated and abrogating verses of the Qur'ān. Both fields are, moreover, of great significance for the developments of law and theology. But because law and theology have been inexorably bound to the political and sectarian realities of Muslim history, the study of the chronology of the Qur'ān has likewise been deeply affected by political and sectarian considerations.

In itself, the Qur'ān has been a closed book since the death of the Prophet; but the Qur'ān has continued to interact with the history of the Muslim world. From the beginning Muslims have dedicated their best minds, voices, and musical talents to the exegesis and recitation of the Qur'ān. While Western scholarship has subjected the Qur'ān to the full rigor of modern historical and literary criticism, contemporary Islamic scholarship has limited itself to the criticism of the Qur'ānic sciences. As for the Qur'ān itself, it remains the criterion by which everything else is judged.

BIBLIOGRAPHY

Bell, Richard. *Bell's Introduction to the Qur'ān*. New ed., revised by W. Montgomery Watt . Edinburgh, 1970. Basic English study, and still useful, but too speculative and inconclusive.

Burton, John. *The Collection of the Qur'ān*. Cambridge, 1977. Through a thorough analysis of classical juristic, *ḥadīth*, and exegetical sources, Burton arrives at the opposite conclusion from that of Wansbrough. The so-called ʿUthmānic codex was in fact, Burton asserts, the *muṣḥaf* used during the Prophet's life. Thus it was not ʿUthmān, but Muḥammad who first collected the Qur'ān.

Goldziher, Ignácz. *Die Richtungen der islamischen Koranauslegung* (1920). Leiden, 1970. Classic work on Qur'ānic exegesis, beginning with a very useful discussion of the history of the Qur'ānic text.

Jeffery, Arthur, ed. *Materials for the History of the Text of the Qur'ān*. Leiden, 1937. Important piece of research into the codex fragments preserved in classical works on the subject.

Khū'ī, Abū al-Qāsim al-. *Al-Bayān fī Tafsīr al-Qur 'ān*. Beirut, 1975. Al-Khū'ī (or al-Kho'i; d. 1993) was the supreme authority *(marjaʿ)* in legal and religious matters for the Twelver Shīʿī community. Long before Burton, he arrived at essentially the same conclusion. His thesis is that "ʿUthmān did not collect a *muṣḥaf*, but rather united the Muslim community upon an already existing and generally excepted *one*." The work also deals with many important issues in Qur'ānic studies.

Nöldeke, Theodor. *Geschichte des Qorāns* (1860). Revised and enlarged by Friedrich Schwally. 2 vols. Leipzig, 1909. Revised and enlarged by Gotthelf Bergsträsser and Otto Pretzl. 3 vols. Leipzig, 1905–1938. Rev. ed. Hildesheim, 1964. Basic work on the history of the Qur'ān.

Saʿīd, Labīb al-. *The Recited Koran*. Translated by Bernard G. Weiss et al. Princeton, 1975. Muslim response to Western critical scholarship on the Qur'ān.

Wansbrough, John. *Quranic Studies*. Oxford, 1977. Using biblical critical methods in the study of the Qur'ān, Wansbrough concludes that the sacred book did not attain its present state until the third century. Similar arguments are presented in his *Sectarian Milieu* (Oxford, 1978).

Welch, Alford T. "Ḳur'ān." In *Encyclopaedia of Islam*, new ed., vol. 5, pp. 400–432. Leiden, 1960–. Welch remains one of the few committed proponents of Bell's theories. The article provides a useful overview of Western Qur'ānic studies and a number of the author's own conclusions.

MAHMOUD M. AYOUB

The Qur'ān as Scripture

The term Qur'ān, most often translated as "reading" or "recital," has been linked etymologically to Syriac *qeryānā* ("scripture reading, lection") and to Hebrew *miqra'* ("recitation, scripture"). Some Muslim commentators have also proposed that it comes from the Arabic verb *qarana*, "to put together" or "bind together," thus giving the approximate translation of "a coherent recital" or "a scripture bound in the form of a book." As a verbal noun *(masdar)* of the form *fuʿlān*, *qur'ān* carries the connotation of a "continuous reading" or "eternal lection" that is recited and heard over and over. In this sense, it is understood both as a spiritual touchstone and a literary archetype. As a title, *al-Qur'ān* refers to the revelation *(tanzīl)* "sent down" *(unzila)* by God to the prophet Muḥammad over a period of twenty-two years (610–632 CE). In its more universal connotation, it is the self-expressed *umm al-kitāb* or paradigm of divine communication (13.39). For all Muslims, the Qur'ān is the quintessential scripture of Islam.

The term "the Noble Qur'ān" (*al-Qur'ān al-Karīm*, 56.77) is often used to stress the extraordinary nature of this text. Since its divine source makes the Qur'ān a sacred and therefore unique form of communication, its meaningfulness is dependent on the prior acceptance of a faith claim that posits specific assumptions about its historical and metahistorical contexts. Consequently, the Qur'ān's significance for the pious Muslim is entirely different from that seen by the non-Muslim or Islamic secularist. Because each and every written word and recited sound of the scripture is revered by believers in Islam as part of a divine lection, an interpretation of the Qur'ān solely according to the canons of literary criticism or philology can only do violence to the revelation in terms of its meaning to its audience. For this reason, many scholars in the West have ceased speculating on the "actual" origins of the Qur'ān or the historicity of its text and have devoted themselves instead to evaluating the Qur'ān's undeniable surplus of meaning in a combination of literary, cultural, and historical contexts.

As a communication from God, the Qur'ān is the prime theophany of Islam. Because its text consists of divine rather than human speech (*kalām Allāh*, 9.6), its significance for Muslims is similar to that of the *logos* (divine word) in Christianity. However, unlike the normative Christian view of the Bible as a divinely inspired discourse (but closely akin to Jewish attitudes concerning the holiness of scripture), the words of the Qur'ān are regarded by most Muslims as divine in and of themselves. Although the fully divine nature of Qur'ānic "speech" is difficult for the secular reader to understand, the importance of this concept should not be underestimated. Modern Muslims still demonstrate their reverence for the Qur'ān by approaching it in a state of ritual purity. At times it may also be treated as a prized artifact—as evidenced by the production of hand-decorated, calligraphic copies *(maṣāḥif)* and the popularity of Middle-Period Qur'ān manuscripts in collections of Islamic art. Ṣūfīs have long regarded the Qur'ān as a paradigm for all of God's communication with his creation. In the thirteenth century the great Andalusian mystic Ibn ʿArabī (d. 1240) organized the entirety of *Al-futūḥāt al-Makkīyah* (The Meccan Inspirations), his magnum opus, in conformity with the discourses and "signs" of the divine text.

Structure. The text of the Qur'ān is divided into 114 segments or surahs (Ar., *sūrah;* pl., *suwar*), each of which contains from three to 286 or 287 *āyāt* (sg., *āyah*). Although it has been common for Westerners to translate *āyah* as "verse," this is misleading. In the first place, the biblical concept of "chapter and verse" does not fully apply to the Qur'ān. Particularly in the case of the longer segments, the surahs may not always discuss themes whose consistency is easily apparent from title to final *āyah*. Indeed, the names of the surahs themselves may refer only obliquely to the main point of the discourse, and in several cases they have been changed at different times in Islamic history. This process continues even today, despite the increased standardization brought about by the mass printing of official renditions. Surah 17, for example, might be called *Banū Isrā'īl* (Children of Israel) in Pakistan and Saudi Arabia, while in Egypt and Iran it is likely to be known as *Al-isrā'* (The Night Journey). Each of these names refers to a different theme discussed in the same surah. Furthermore, while it is certainly correct to view the Qur'ān as a collection of divine discourses, a single surah may contain more than one discourse. On other occasions (as in the story of Mūsā/Moses), the same discourse may be continued in two or more noncontiguous surahs.

The most important reason for not referring to *āyah* as "verse," however, comes from the Qur'ān's own use of the term. The words *āyah* or *āyāt* are employed nearly four hundred times throughout the text. Most frequently, *āyah* refers to evidences *(āthār)* in nature that demonstrate the existence of God. At other times it may refer to a miracle confirming the truth of a prophet's message, a revealed message *(tanzīl)* in general, or even a fundamental "point" in a particular surah's discourse. Because of its multivalency, *āyah* can be seen to correspond quite closely to the concept of "sign" in Saussurean linguistics. An important proof of this assertion lies in the fact that "sign" *(ʿalāmah)* is the most commonly accepted synonym for *āyah* in Ibn Manẓūr's (d. 1311/1312) *Lisān al-ʿArab* and other influential lexicons of the Islamic Middle Period.

When inscribed in a written Qur'ān or recited on a believer's tongue, *āyah* is best understood as "a statement in the speech of God." The totality of these statements, along with a number of non-Qur'ānic inspirations known as *ḥadīth qudsī* (holy reports), constitute the divine "speech" *(parole)* as revealed to the prophet Muḥammad. Yet each statement of the Qur'ān was also revealed as a "remembrance" or "recollection" (*dhikr* or *dhikrā*, 38.8), whose purpose is to awaken human beings and cause them to look up from the written or recited text, so that they may see the existence of God through his creation. In this case, each *āyah* of the Qur'ān is also a sign—in the symbolic or semiotic sense—that points to another level of reality that in turn reaffirms the message of revelation. The believer who seeks to develop a sense of the sacred must thus learn two distinct levels of "language" *(langue)* at the same time—the Arabic text of the Qur'ān itself and the "language" of nature, which is also a manifestation of the speech of God. God created the world as a book; his revelations descended to Earth and were compiled into a book; therefore, the human being must learn to "read" the world as a book. This aspect of spiritual intellection is exemplified in the Qur'ān by the figures of Ibrāhīm/Abraham, who discerned the One God in the multiplicity of heavenly phenomena (6.75–79), and Sulaymān/Solomon, who was inspired to understand the "discourse of the birds"(*manṭiq al-ṭayr*, 27.16).

Theology and Anthropology. As an expression of theology, the Qur'ān is first and foremost a demonstration *(bayān)* of the existence of God. In this guise it acts as a criterion of discernment *(furqān* or *mīzān)*: "And We gave Moses the Book and the *furqān* so that you might be guided" (2.55). This discernment—the same as that given to Muḥammad, Abraham, Jesus, and all the other biblical and non-biblical prophets mentioned in the Qur'ān—leads humankind to perceive a single, absolute truth (the only noncontingent reality) that transcends the world of phenomena. This truth is God, whose essence, being unique and exalted, lies beyond the limits of human imagination: "Say: He is Allāh the Only; Allāh the Perfect beyond compare; He gives not birth, nor is He begotten, and He is, in Himself, not dependent on anything" (112). This purely monotheistic expression of divine simplicity is complemented, however, by a more monistic image of a complex deity who is immanent in the world by virtue of being the source of existence itself: "He is the First and the Last, the Outward and the Inward; And He is the Knower of every thing" (57.3). Between these two poles of monotheism and monism stands *tawḥīd,* the recognition of transcendent oneness that constitutes the theological premise of Islam and the fundamental message of the Qur'ānic discourse.

Despite the radically monotheistic nature of Islamic theology, the discourse about God in the Qur'ān fluctuates repeatedly between transcendence and immanence, the abstract and the concrete, the logical and the analogical: God is one and not a trinity (5.75); lord of the east and the west (55.17); he sends rain and revives the earth (29.63); his "face" will abide forever (55.27). Out of these distinctions arises the tradition of the ninety-nine *asmā' Allāh al-ḥusnā* or "excellent names of God" (7.180), which for later Muslim thinkers expressed the discursive field in which *tawḥīd* was conceptualized. The central or medial figure who straddles these perspectives (and in Sufism actualizes the excellent names according to his or her ability and destiny) is the human being (*insān,* masc. pl. *nās,* fem. pl. *nisā'*). The Qur'ān's use of this generic term demonstrates that both men and women are rational and ethically responsible creatures who occupy an intermediate position in respect to all the oppositions (e.g., true and false, necessary and contingent, or real and unreal) that characterize the Qur'ānic discourse. As such, the most meaningful duty in the life of every person is to submit the ego and intellect to the criterion *(furqān)* of manifest truth as given in the divine revelation. This act of choice, in turn, is the *furqān* that separates *islām* (surrender and submission to the one God) from *kufr* ("covering up" or denying the reality and moral implications of *islām*).

Human accountability is epitomized in the Qur'ān by a generic covenant (33.72) in which preexistent humanity, despite its creaturely limitations, assumes responsibility for the heavens and the earth. This moral and ecological commitment constitutes another *furqān* by which human actions are assessed. Also called " God's covenant" (*ʿahd Allāh,* 2.27), this pact was created to distinguish male and female hypocrites *(munāfiqūn)* and those lost in contingent reality *(mushrikūn)* from the believers *(mu'minūn)* who maintain their trust in the absolute (33.73). The human being who trusts in God and is true to God's trust by not breaking this covenant in thought, word, or deed actualizes God's vicegerency (*khilāfah,* 2.30–33), through which one is able to exercise choice and maintain covenantal responsibility. The society made up of such believing individuals thus constitutes a normative or "axial community" *(ummatan wasatan),* which acts collectively as a witness to the truth (2.143). This society appears in history as a "community in a state of surrender to God" (*ummah muslimah,* 2.128) and is exemplified in its penultimate form by the paradigmatic *ummah* created by the prophet Muḥammad and his companions in Medina (622–632 CE).

Qur'ān and Bible. References in the Qur'ān to the stories of biblical and extrabiblical prophets and their communities must be viewed from the perspective of the *ummah muslimah* in order to become intelligible to the Western reader. The historical discourses of the Qur'ān are linked together thematically rather than chronologically, and thus the revelatory concept of the book or divine communication *(kitāb)* employed in this text has more in common with the genre of wisdom traditions (cf., *al-Kitāb al-Ḥakīm* [X, 1]) than with that of European historiography or Aristotle's *Poetics.* For this reason students of Islam whose view of scripture is based on Judeo-Christian models are likely to be confused or even put off by what at first seems to be an incoherent scattering of biblical accounts and apocrypha. If, however, the text of the Qur'ān is read according to its own instructions to Christians and Jews—as a reminder *(dhikr)* and reaffirmation *(muṣaddiq)* of universal truths and the essential points of biblical discourse (5.44–48)—its lack of historical detail becomes less of a problem, and the logic of the Qur'ān's self-described complementarity to previous revelations (41.43) is easier to understand. As with every other sign, the purpose of a biblical reminder is to stimulate intellectual awareness, not to provide an exhaustive discussion of a particular person or topic. In the Qur'ān these reminders revolve around the quintessential unity of the Abrahamic tradition and include exemplary and cautionary narratives detailing humanity's acceptance or rejection of the divine message.

Despite the Qur'ān's apparent advocacy of an intertextual approach to scriptural analysis (5.47–51), a later preoccupation with abrogation *(naskh)* made the comparative study of revelation more difficult at precisely the time (ninth century CE) when the vocalization of the consonantal text of the Qur'ān fixed its discourse so that a true hermeneutic could become possible. The jurist al-Shāfiʿī's (d. 820) insistence that the Qur'ān was the primary source *(aṣl)* for Islamic law meant that its prescriptive *(muḥkam)* *āyāt* abrogated similar statutes in the Hebrew Bible and the Christian Gospels. Subsequent scholars expanded on al-Shāfiʿī's comments and claimed that the words of the Qur'ān constituted a blanket abrogation of the texts of all previous holy books. This opinion was reinforced by the doctrine of the "inimitability of the Qur'ān *(iʿjāz al-Qur'ān)*. Originating as part of a debate over the Qur'ān's challenge to unbelievers to produce a work of comparable eloquence and substance (2.23), by the time of the theologian al-Bāqillānī (d. 1013) this concept had evolved into the idea that the Qur'ān was completely unlike anything that had been revealed before. As a result, contemporary Muslim arguments against the doctrines of other "peoples of the book" still tend to recycle earlier polemics against Christianity and Judaism that are found in the Qur'ān itself or in the works of Middle-Period theologians. Only rarely does a Muslim exegete overcome the influence of tradition and undertake a serious study of modern Judaism or post-Reformation Christianity. This is even more the case in regard to polytheistic or nontheistic scriptural traditions, such as those of China and India.

Translations. A hallmark of twentieth-century exegesis *(tafsīr)* is the translation of the Qur'ān into local and regional vernaculars. As early as the eighth century the jurist Abū Ḥanīfah (d. 767) claimed that it was permissible for non-Arabic speakers to recite *al-Fātiḥah,* the opening surah of the Qur'ān, in Persian. Although other jurists disputed this view as contradicting the Qur'ān's own assertion of its Arabic linguistic identity (cf. 12.2, 16.23), a nativist *(shuʿūbī)* cultural revival on the Iranian plateau led to Persian translations of the complete text by the eleventh century. These works, however, did not have ritual value. The consensus of *ʿulamā'* has long held that a direct translation of divine speech is impossible. Vernacular editions of the Qur'ān are thus classified as commentaries or interpretations *(tafsīr* or *tafhīm*) to distinguish them from the Arabic original. This monadist opinion was authoritatively reaffirmed in the present century by the Syrian Pan-Islamist Muḥammad Rashīd Riḍā (d. 1935), who strongly rebutted Kemalist attempts to make Turkish a language of worship in the 1920s.

Important contemporary translations of the Qur'ān include those of the Indian modernist ʿAbdullāh Yūsuf ʿAlī (in English), the Pakistani reformer and politician Sayyid Abū al-Aʿlā Mawdūdī (in Urdu), and the Indonesian scholar, poet, and independence activist Hamka (in Bahasa Indonesia). In each of these cases the purpose of translation was twofold: to promote the related causes of Islamic preaching *(daʿwah)* and reform by making the text of the Qur'ān accessible to non-Arabic-speaking audiences, and to counteract translations of the Qur'ān in vernacular or European languages by non-Muslim missionaries and orientalist scholars working for colonial regimes. Of the translators mentioned above, Yūsuf ʿAlī is the least inclined to believe that rendering the words of God into another language implies a decisive departure from the original text. Although he asserts that his desire is to provide an "English interpretation" *(tafsīr)* of the Qur'ān, the final product (variously entitled *The Glorious Qur'an, The Holy Qur'an,* or *The Holy Qur-an,* 1934) is more commonly thought of by Muslims as an annotated translation rather than an exegetical work *per se.* This is primarily because the commentaries are introduced as footnotes or bracketed additions to the translated text. In fact, Yūsuf ʿAlī's avowed goal of making "English itself an Islamic language" has very nearly been realized. His work is at present the most widely available Qur'ān translation in English and forms the basis of the semiofficial *Muṣḥaf al-Madīnah al-Nabawīyah* printed in Saudi Arabia in 1990.

Mawdūdī's *Tafhīm al-Qur'ān* (1942–1979), although superficially similar to Yūsuf ʿAlī's work, is indisputably an example of *tafsīr.* In both his rendering of the original Arabic into Urdu and his extended discussions of each surah, the author's explicit intent is to amplify and clarify a unitary "Islamic message" for *daʿwah* purposes. Part of this clarification entails transforming the structure of the Qur'ān into paragraphs rather than leaving its text (either in Arabic or Urdu) in the traditional single-*āyah* format. This innovation is coupled with an analysis of the divine revelation according to the doctrines of the Jamāʿat-i Islāmī, which Mawdūdī founded in 1941. According to this party's point of view, the Qur'ān is both a revolutionary manifesto and a manual for missionaries; its message calls for the reconstruction of human society into an ideologically motivated community of virtue and social activism. As such, its text provides a blueprint for transcending sectarian and legalistic divisions and uniting humanity into a single brotherhood. As an implicitly political work, *Tafhīm al-Qur'ān* has much in common with *Fī ẓilāl al-Qur'ān,* an equally influential *tafsīr* in Arabic by the Egyptian ideologue Sayyid Quṭb (d. 1966). [*See the biography of Mawdūdī.*]

Vernacular translations of the Qur'ān in Southeast

Asia first appeared in the 1920s but did not become fully accepted until the 1960s. In most texts the vernacular rendition (in Bahasa Melayu, Indonesian, Sundanese, or Javanese) follows or is parallel to the Arabic original of each *āyah* and is referred to as an "interpretation" (Malay, *terjemah, tafsir*). Prefatory discussions are commonly added, and exegetical material is usually found in the form of extended footnotes, as in Yūsuf ʿAlī's and Mawdūdī's translations. *Tafsir al-Azhar,* the translation and exegesis by the West Sumatran scholar and Indonesian independence activist Hamka (Hadji Abdul Malik Karim Amrullah, d. 1981) is notable because of its nationalistic tone. Written in Bahasa Indonesia, this important work is a semi-official *tafsīr* of the Indonesian Muhammadiyah organization and has been widely disseminated throughout the Malay-speaking world. Hamka is distinctive among Southeast Asian commentators for his use of interlineal exegesis (a technique common in the Arabic tradition) and his reliance upon recent Indonesian history to illustrate specific points in the Qur'ānic discourse. [*See the biography of Hamka.*]

Modern Arabic Exegesis. Modern exegesis of the Qur'ān begins with the writings of Muḥammad ʿAbduh (d. 1905), an Egyptian essayist, jurisconsult, founder of the Salafīyah movement, and rector of al-Azhar University in Cairo. ʿAbduh's exegetical corpus consists of four works: *Tafsīr al-fātiḥah* (1901), *Tafsīr sūrat al-ʿaṣr* (1903), *Tafsīr Juz' ʿamma* (1922–1923), and the twelve-volume *Tafsīr al-Qur'ān al-Ḥakīm* (sometimes called *Tafsīr al-manār,* 1927–1935), which was completed after his death by Rashīd Riḍā. As a neotraditionalist scholar who felt an affinity for Muʿtazilī rationalism, ʿAbduh was influential in reviving the earlier genre of reason-based exegesis *(tafsīr bi'l-ra'y),* which except for the writings of certain Ṣūfīs had lain dormant for centuries. Also an avowed Spenserian social evolutionist, he saw the regulatory *āyāt* of the Qur'ān as corresponding to natural law, and he characterized the process of evolution as part of "God's *sunnah* " (*sunnat Allāh,* 48.23) or unchangeable pattern of conduct. He generally rejected the possibility of miracles as contradicting this principle but excepted the Qur'ān, whose miraculous uniqueness serves to awaken human reason to the truth of Muḥammad's prophecy. Claiming to follow the noted theologian al-Ghazālī (d. 1111), ʿAbduh asserted that even the ambiguous *(mutashābihāt) āyāt* should be open to analysis using the tools of modern thought. Once Islam was understood through the light of modern knowledge, the rectification of religious practice demanded that Muslims also take on the reformation of society as a whole. As a justification for this position ʿAbduh cited the first part of *āyah* 13.11: "God will never change the condition of a people until they change what is in themselves." [*See the biography of ʿAbduh.*]

A direct successor to the ʿAbduh-Riḍā *tafsīr* is Sayyid Quṭb's (d. 1966) *Fī ẓilāl al-Qur'ān* (In the Shade of the Qur'ān). Written for the most part between 1954 and 1964 during the author's longest period of imprisonment, this posthumously published work adopts many of the positions—both explicit and implicit—of ʿAbduh's earlier *tafsīr.* This reflects the fact that Quṭb's mentor, the Egyptian reformist and political activist Ḥasan al-Bannā' (d. 1949), was a student of ʿAbduh's disciple Muḥammad Rashīd Riḍā. Like its predecessor, *Fī ẓilāl al-Qur'ān* is also an example of *tafsīr bi al-ra'y.* Despite numerous appeals to the precedent of the Prophet and his companions, Sayyid Quṭb rivaled ʿAbduh in his faith in modern science as a universal criterion for knowledge, going so far as to quote British scientific journals in his exegesis. Both authors also distinguished themselves as advocates of social and intellectual reform and were equally fond of citing *āyah* 13.11 as a justification for sociopolitical activism.

Sayyid Quṭb differed from his predecessor, however, over the degree to which change dictates compromise with alien sociocultural systems. Although ʿAbduh maintained a traditional aura of legitimacy as an Islamic scholar and jurisconsult, he was also a political accommodationist who regarded British administration and scientific positivism as evolutionary advances over a decayed and ignorant Muslim society. Sayyid Quṭb by contrast, as a member of the Muslim Brotherhood, was a committed anticolonialist and anti-imperialist who sought to revive a Qur'ān-based "Islamic system" *(al-niẓām al-Islāmī)* that remained true to the cultural and social values established by God and Muslim consensus. While fully modern in his belief in the unitary message of the Qur'ān and skeptical of the accuracy of many prophetic traditions *(ḥadīth),* Sayyid Quṭb nonetheless rejected the examples of both the Uniteds States and the Soviet Union as societies where man is either made a commodity or reduced to little more than a machine. Western imperialism, he asserted, had created a "new ignorance" *(jāhilīyah)* in the Muslim world, where an original, faith-based consciousness of God *(taqwā)* was replaced by a "*jāhilī* consciousness" characterized by immorality, political corruption, and a servile reliance on Western paradigms. As the title to his *tafsīr,* "In the Shade of the Qur'ān," indicates, the Qur'ān serves Muslims not only as a source of guidance but also as a refuge from destructive influences. [*See the biography of Quṭb.*]

Apart from translation, the most important hallmark of modern exegesis of the Qur'ān has been the tendency to view each surah as a unified discourse. In itself this approach is not new. As early as the eleventh century it was followed by the influential Ṣūfī al-Qushayrī (d. 1073) in his exegesis *Laṭā'if al-ishārāt* (The Subtleties of Symbolism). In the following century the Andalusian legist Abū Bakr ibn al-ʿArabī (d. 1148) bemoaned the lack of interest in intratextual hermeneutics *(ʿilm al-munāsabāt),* and the subject was brought up again in the fourteenth-century *tafsīr* of Badr al-Dīn al-Zarakhshī (d. 1391). Until the twentieth century, however, such opinions were rare, and the usual approach was to view each surah as an atomistic collection of discontinuous narratives. In recent times Western attacks on the coherence of the Qur'ān have led to an apologetic defense of the text that vindicates its present structure by demonstrating the existence of thematic unities.

Although this approach is now followed by most modern commentators, one of the clearest examples of *ʿilm al-munāsabāt* can be found in *Al-mīzān fī tafsīr al-Qur'ān* (The Balance of Judgment in the Exegesis of the Qur'ān, 1973–1974), an influential Shīʿī *tafsīr* in Arabic by the noted Iranian philosopher and theologian Sayyid Muḥammad Ḥusayn al-Ṭabāṭabā'ī (d. 1981). He begins his exegesis of each surah by identifying its central theme, which he calls its "purpose" or "intent" *(gharad).* This theme is discovered by examining the surah's opening, its end, and the general flow of discourse. The actual commentary is then divided into subtexts, which correspond to discursive changes in the divine speech.

It is important to note, however, that Ṭabāṭabā'ī does not impose an artificial unity on the Qur'ān, nor does he conceive of his exegesis as an example of *tafsīr bi al-ra'y.* As a scholastic theologian and strict follower of the *uṣūlī* (source-oriented) jurisprudential tradition of Twelver or Imāmī Shiism, he prefers to let the Qur'ān "explain itself by itself" *(tafsīr al-Qur'ān bi'l-Qur'ān)* following a statement of Imam ʿAlī: "One part of the Qur'ān explains another, and one part witnesses to the other." Rejecting the concept of reason-based exegesis as a matter of principle, Ṭabāṭabā'ī first tries to explain ambiguous *āyāt* by syllogistically referring to others whose meaning is apparent. Next he turns to the extensive corpus of exegetical traditions left behind by the Shīʿī imams. When using a purely scholastic approach, as in his discussions of grammatical points, semantics, or human nature, Ṭabāṭabā'ī takes great pains to ensure that his conclusions are in overall agreement with the consensus of previous Imāmī scholarship. [*See the biography of Ṭabāṭabā'ī.*]

Qur'ān and Modernism. In recent years the Qur'ān has become a touchstone for controversy as well as piety. Nowhere has this been more the case than in modernist polemics, many of whose practitioners view the Qur'ān through the lens of ideological precommitment. Particularly prominent is the debate over the empowerment of Muslim women, who have become both combatants and prize in the struggle between Western critics of Islam and their Muslim opponents. A recent discussion of the Qur'ān from a womanist point of view is Amina Wadud-Muhsin's *Qur'ān and Woman* (1992). First published in Malaysia, it is presently used as a manifesto by the "Sisters in Islam" movement in that country. In her approach to the Qur'ān the American Wadud-Muhsin attempts to lay the groundwork for nontraditional *tafsīr* from a scripturally legitimate perspective. Borrowing heavily from the semantic analyses of the Japanese Qur'ānic scholar Toshihiko Izutsu and the modernist exegesis of the Pakistani Islamicist Fazlur Rahman (d. 1988), she postulates a distinction between the historically and culturally contextualized "prior text" of the Qur'ān and a wider metatext that conveys a more tolerant and universalistic worldview. Her conclusion is that while the Qur'ān indeed acknowledges functional gender distinctions based on biology, it does not propose essential or culturally universal roles for males and females. In fact, the assignment of gender distinctions based on early Arabian precedent would eliminate the transcendental nature of the Qur'ān by reducing it to a culturally specific set of discourses. Wadud-Muhsin argues her point by demonstrating the Qur'ān's stress on the "primal equality" of men and women, examining the issue of equity in the afterlife, and semantically analyzing Qur'ān-based legal terminology relating to women and the family.

Another use of the concept of "prior text," although with very different results, can be found in *Al-risālah al-thāniyah min al-Islām* (The Second Message of Islam) by the radical Sudanese modernist Maḥmūd Muḥammad Ṭāḥā (d. 1985). Essential to Ṭāḥā's doctrine is a distinction between two categories of the prophet Muḥammad's followers—the *muslim* (one who submits himself fully to God) and the *mu'min* (one who acknowledges the truth of the Qur'ān and the Prophet's message). During Muḥammad's lifetime the Prophet himself was the only true *muslim,* since he alone could submit himself to God completely. For this reason the community that the Prophet created in Medina was composed only of *mu'minūn*—those who followed the historically and culturally contextualized example of Muḥammad. This early stage of faith *(īmān)* is exemplified by the Medinan surahs of the Qur'ān and constitutes the "first message of Islam." As a formal religious tradition, it is characterized by the *sharī'ah.* Because it reflected its era and culture, however, the resulting "nation of believers" was unsuited to modern social and intellectual conditions.

The coming age of *islām,* by contrast, will be characterized by humankind's readiness to comprehend fully the universal message of the Qur'ān, which appears in the Meccan revelations. Not limited by an outdated "prior text" like the Medinan surahs, which modern conditions have abrogated, the Islam of the Meccan period is open-ended and subject to further elaboration. Consequently, the "nation of Muslims" born under the influence of this era will be one of tolerance, gender equality, social democracy, and a science-oriented approach to knowledge. Not content to be bound by the *sunnah,* Ṭāḥā, the "teacher" *(ustādh)* of this "second message of Islam," affirms the continuity of divine guidance by proclaiming himself a post-Muḥammadan "messenger" *(rasūl)*: "one to whom God granted understanding from the Qur'ān and is authorized to speak" (p. 42).

Surprisingly, given the radical and even heretical nature of Ṭāḥā's doctrine, it still reflects exegetical issues that have occupied practitioners of *tafsīr* since the very beginnings of the genre. Although the universality of the prophetic *sunnah* is seldom debated, the question of its applicability to contemporary conditions has always been important. The historical study of Qur'ānic exegesis continually reveals how much the discipline of *tafsīr* depends on prior methodologies. Muḥammad 'Abduh's and Sayyid Quṭb's reliance on *tafsīr bi al-ra'y,* for example, reprises the approach utilized by the influential Middle-Period commentator al-Ṭabarī (d. 923). Even Amina Wadud-Muhsin's undeniably modern use of semantic and "prior text" analyses echoes (albeit unintentionally) more mystically minded commentators such as Ibn 'Arabī and al-Qushayrī. Undoubtedly certain methodologies, such as translation and intratextual hermeneutics, have become more prominent in recent times; this is only natural given the increasingly non-Middle-Eastern demographic profile of the Muslim world and the resulting demand for a crosscultural discourse. Yet the very fact that many new commentaries recall previous approaches highlights the authority of tradition in Islam and the continued self-referentiality of Muslim exegesis. After all that has been accomplished, one threshold of Qur'ānically legitimate exegesis remains to be crossed—a systematically comparative approach to scriptural analysis.

[*See also* Tafsīr.]

BIBLIOGRAPHY

Ayoub, Mahmoud M. *The Qur'an and its Interpreters.* 2 vols. to date. New York, 1984–. Synopsis of Middle Period exegeses of the Qur'ān through surah 3 *(Āl 'Imrān).* The introduction to volume 1 covers the history of *tafsīr.*

Chodkiewicz, Michel. *An Ocean without Shore: Ibn 'Arabi, the Book, and the Law.* Translated by David Streight. Albany, N.Y., 1993. Superb discussion of the Ṣūfī approach to the Qur'ān in Ibn al-'Arabī's *Al-Futūḥāt al-Makkīyah.*

Cragg, Kenneth. *The Pen and the Faith: Eight Modern Muslim Writers and the Qur'ān.* London, 1985. Introduction to the importance of the Qur'ān in modern Islamic thought, for the nonspecialist.

Gätje, Helmut. *The Qur'ān and Its Exegesis: Selected Texts with Classical and Modern Muslim Interpretations.* Translated and edited by Alford T. Welch. Berkeley, 1976. Thematic exposition of classical and modern *tafsīr,* more useful for its examples than for a history of the genre.

Greifenhagen, F. V. "Traduttore Traditore: An Analysis of the History of English Translations of the Qur'ān." *Islam and Christian-Muslim Relations* 3.2 (December 1992): 274–291. Excellent overview of polemical and nonpolemical translations in English , with a very useful bibliography.

Hawting, G. R., and Abdul-Kader A. Shareef, eds. *Approaches to the Qur'ān.* London and New York, 1993. Useful overview of traditional and modern approaches to exegesis.

Izutsu, Toshihiko. *God and Man in the Koran: Semantics of the Koranic Weltanschauung* (1964). New York, 1980. One of the classics of Qur'ānic studies, and the best semantic analysis of this text written in the modern period.

Jeffery, Arthur. *The Foreign Vocabulary of the Qur'ān.* Baroda, 1938. Classic philological study of Qur'ānic terminology as it relates to other religions and cultural systems. Especially useful for the advanced student of Arabic.

Jeffery, Arthur , ed. *Materials for the History of the Text of the Qur'ān: The Old Codices.* Leiden, 1937. The only in-depth study of variations in the Qur'ānic text in early Islamic history. Requires knowledge of Arabic.

Mawdūdī, Sayyid Abū al-A'lā. *Towards Understanding the Qur'ān.* Translated by Zafar Ishaq Ansari. Leicester, 1988–. Excellent English translation of *Tafhīm al-Qur'ān,* by the director of the Islamic Research Institute in Pakistan.

McAuliffe, Jane Dammen. *Qur'ānic Christians: An Analysis of Classical and Modern Exegesis.* Cambridge and New York, 1991. Interesting study of the portrayal of Christians and Christianity in the Qur'ān.

Quṭb, Sayyid. *In the Shade of the Qur'ān*. Vol. 30. Translated by M. Adil Salahi and Ashur A. Shamis. London, 1979. Competent translation of the last part of *Fī Ẓilāl al-Qur'ān*.

Rahman, Fazlur. *Major Themes of the Qur'ān*. Minneapolis, 1980. One of the better modernist approaches to the Qur'ān, best read as an apologetic response to polemical scholarship.

Ṭabāṭabā'ī, Muḥammad Ḥusayn. *The Qur'ān in Islam: Its Impact and Influence on the the Life of Muslims*. London, 1987. Discussion of Ṭabāṭabā'ī's *tafsīr* methodology and a useful introduction to Imāmī Shīʿī exegesis. His *Tafsīr al-Mīzān* is presently being translated into English.

Ṭāhā, Maḥmūd Muḥammad. *The Second Message of Islam*. Translated and edited by ʿAbd Allāh Aḥmad Naʿīm. Syracuse, N.Y., 1987. Journey to the outer limits of Qur'ānic exegesis.

Wadud-Muhsin, Amina. *Qur'an and Woman*. Kuala Lumpur, 1992. The most effective Muslim response to the feminist critique of Islam yet written.

Welch, Alford T., and J. D. Pearson. "Ḳur'ān." In *Encyclopaedia of Islam,* new ed., vol. 5, pp. 400–432. Leiden, 1960–. Useful introduction to the history of the Qur'ān for the nonspecialist, although the philological and Orientalist approach of its author is outdated.

VINCENT J. CORNELL

The Qur'ān in Muslim Thought and Practice

Because Muslims view the Qur'ān as the very word of God, it naturally occupies the central place in their religious life. It is the one means for discovering the will of God and for measuring the success of a life lived in accordance with it. The Qur'ān has shaped the individual and collective lives of Muslims in many ways.

The Qur'ān was revealed to Muḥammad not all at once, but in large and small parts over some twenty-two years (610–632). Furthermore, the revelations it contains are related to the situations in which they were revealed. Thus the revelations, taken together, become a record of the society of Muḥammad's time and constitute the most important source for tracing the historical development of Islam from its origins in Mecca to its full maturity in Medina. The significance of the intermittency of revelation can be appreciated if, as Malek Bennabi suggests (1977), one asks what would have happened if the Qur'ān had been revealed all at once. In that case, Bennabi remarks, all those passages that console Muḥammad and his followers at times of distress, encourage them at times of difficulty, or guide them at times of uncertainty would not have the immediacy and freshness they otherwise do. The first thing to note about the Qur'ān, therefore, is its dual role as record and guide.

These two roles are important for understanding not only the times of the Prophet but also much of the later religious history of Muslims. Early Islamic history (even allowing for sectarian and other differences in periodizing and interpreting it) has paradigmatic value for Muslims, and the event of the Qur'ān is universally admitted to be central to that history. It is not surprising that all later movements, whether of radical reform or of moderate change, whether originating at the center or at the periphery of the Islamic world, have sought to ground themselves in the Qur'ān or at least to seek support from it. A typical instance is the Khārijī movement during the caliphate of ʿAlī. Displeased with ʿAlī's decision to accept arbitration (*taḥkīm*) as an alternative to a military solution of the dispute with Muʿāwiyah, the Khawārij appealed to the Qur'ān, saying that only its verdict was acceptable, and not the verdict of human arbitrators. For their part, the troops of Muʿāwiyah had, in order to avert imminent defeat, already impaled copies of the Qur'ān on their spears and waved them on the battlefield, practically forcing ʿAlī's camp to accept arbitration.

Arabian culture was oral; its transformation from preliterate to literate was due mainly to the Qur'ān. The notions of "writing," "reading," "pen," and "book" are found in some of the early revelations. For instance, the very first revelation, according to the generally accepted view, consisted of the first five verses of what is now surah 96: "Read in the name of your Lord Who created: He created man from a clinging matter. Read, and your Lord is Most Gracious, the One who taught by means of the pen: He taught man what he did not know." According to some scholars, the second to be revealed was surah 68, *al-Qalam,* which takes its name "Pen" from the opening verse. The Qur'ān as a whole is called a "book" in numerous verses. The Qur'ān repeatedly insists on writing down the details of a loan extended (2.282–283) and enjoins that the manumission contract be made in writing (24.33). A large number of scribes were employed by Muḥammad to preserve the scriptural text. Reading and writing were encouraged in general; it is interesting in this regard that the prisoners taken by the Muslims in the Battle of Badr were given the opportunity to win their freedom by teaching a certain number of Muslims how to read and write. A fundamental transformation was thus brought about in the consciousness of the Arabs, a nonliterate culture rapidly becoming a literate one.

An important element of the new consciousness was

the notion of book as law, for law now came to be identified with something more than custom and tradition passed down orally from earlier times; it came to mean something written down or laid down in writing. Surah 98.3 represents a coalescence of the notions of book and law; the word *kutub* in it means "laws, regulations."

The idea of the Qur'ān as a book of law, or indeed as a code of life, was to have further important consequences. Directly or indirectly it gave rise to the major disciplines of Islamic learning and led to the proliferation of literature in each. *Ḥadīth* (prophetic tradition), or rather the *sunnah* (path) of Muḥammad embodied in *ḥadīth,* is regarded as the authoritative explication of the Qur'ān. The sciences of the Arabic language, from lexicography to grammar to rhetoric, were developed with a view to arriving at a precise and accurate understanding of the Qur'ānic text. The need to understand the legislative content of the Qur'ān gave rise to both Islamic law and legal theory. The fundamental theological issues in Islam understandably revolve around certain verses of the Qur'ān. Historiography originated with the aim of elaborating the Qur'ānic view of religious history, according to which Adam was the first bearer of the divine message and Muḥammad the last.

Many Muslim scholars believe that not only the growth of religious sciences but also of learning in general was due to the inspiration of the Qur'ān. They point to its repeated urgings to study the universe, which is regarded as furnishing *āyāt* (signs) that point to the creator of the universe. A connection is thus established, the argument runs, between science and religion: the study of nature becomes a sacred pursuit; acquisition and dissemination of knowledge of all kinds takes on a religious significance; and a spirit of empirical inquiry and investigation is engendered that expresses itself in various areas of scholarly activity. Surah 2.164 may be taken as typical in this regard:

> Indeed, in the creation of the heavens and the earth, and the alternation of night and day, and what God has sent down from the sky in the form of water—reviving by means of it land after it has become barren, and spreading in it animals of all kinds—and the causing of the winds to blow in different forms, and the clouds that are held under control between the heavens and the earth, there are signs for those who would exercise reason.

The Qur'ān plays a central role in the larger world of Muslim society in at least five realms. First, as the fundamental text of Islam, it is cited as the ultimate authority in all matters pertaining to religion. Thus the Qur'ān furnishes the basic tenets of Islam, the principles of ethical behavior, and guidance in general or specific terms for social, political, and economic activities. Second, the Qur'ān is used in liturgy. In each of the five obligatory prayers of the day, the opening surah of the Qur'ān, *al-Fātiḥah,* is recited with other portions. During Ramaḍān, the month of fasting, the Qur'ān is recited in special prayers *(tarāwīḥ)* offered congregationally every night after the fifth and last prayer, usually with the goal of completing a recitation of the entire Qur'ān during the month.

The Qur'ān is also a basic vehicle of education. A large majority of the world's Muslim population is non-Arabic-speaking, yet in most Muslim societies the first alphabetical system children learn is the Arabic alphabet, in order to be able to read the Qur'ān. Beginning with a primer, young students work up to reading through the Qur'ān, usually under the guidance of the local imam of the mosque. The completion of a child's reading of the Qur'ān is often celebrated publicly, with the child receiving gifts and being the center of attention. Special importance is attached to completing the first reading of the Qur'ān at an early age, and even in Western countries it is not unknown for a Muslim child to complete his or her first Qur'ān-reading before entering public school at the age of five. The Qur'ānic education of children is not confined to mere reading of the text; it often includes inculcation of basic scriptural teachings.

The Qur'ān is an element of many nonliturgical social events. It is used to invoke the blessing of God *(tabarruk)* on various occasions. Thus to complete a recitation of the Qur'ān *(khatm al-Qur'ān)* at the death of a loved one—survivors, relatives, and friends get together for the purpose—is a custom in several parts of the Muslim world. The Qur'ān is often recited at the beginning of public political or social meetings, at conferences, and sometimes also at government or official functions, including cabinet meetings. Finally, the Qur'ān has artistic uses. The art of reciting Qur'ānic verses in a beautiful voice *(tajwīd)* and the art of Qur'ānic calligraphy are among the most highly developed skills in Islamic culture. Most mosques have inscriptions from the Qur'ān, and *tajwīd* competitions at different levels are popular events, with good reciters often becoming celebrities. [*See* Qur'ānic Recitation; Calligraphy.]

As noted above, even in non-Arab Muslim societies an attempt is made to teach children the Qur'ānic Arabic script, even though most people never learn the Arabic language. The concern that all Muslims be able to read at least the text of the Qur'ān derives from the fact that the Qur'ān is regarded as the very word of God. As such, the act of reciting the divine word is a good and pious act that brings blessings *(barakah)*. The disjunction between recitation and understanding produces the curious result that even in parts of the Muslim world that do not have a long history of distinguished Islamic scholarship, the art of recitation may be very highly developed; Malaysia and Indonesia are perhaps the most notable examples. On another level, the doctrine of *iʿjāz* (the inimitability or matchlessness of the Qur'ān) determines standards of linguistic excellence and makes an intimate knowledge of the Qur'ānic text—displayed in the ability to recognize a Qur'ānic quotation or to cite verses appositely—a mark of good education.

In modern times renewed emphasis has been placed on the Qur'ān as the fundamental source of guidance, though this has received more than one interpretive expression. Some distinguish between the kernel and husk of Islamic tradition, identifying the Qur'ān as the kernel and denying the normative value of the other religious sciences. Others seek to reassert the primacy of the Qur'ān in the hierarchy of Islamic sciences, pointing out that although theoretically the Qur'ān has always been the most important source of Islam, in practice *ḥadīth* and sectarian *fiqh* have relegated it to a secondary position, usurping its rightful position. Still others maintain that the masses need to be educated Islamically and that Qur'ānic learning should form the most important part of this religious training. In the eighteenth century Shāh Walī Allāh of India, defying opposition, translated the Qur'ān into Persian, after which it was rendered into many regional and local languages of India. His primary aim was to make the Qur'ān accessible to the common man, and his legacy in this regard has been an enduring one.

In whatever terms the primacy of the Qur'ān is asserted today, it remains a fact that a number of modern Muslim reformist thinkers have made the Qur'ān their main reference point. This is true of Sayyid Aḥmad Khān and Abū al-Kalām Āzād of India, Abū al-Aʿlā Mawdūdī of Pakistan, Sayyid Quṭb of Egypt, Muḥammad Rashīd Riḍā of Syria, and Ibn Bādīs of Algeria. All these writers chose the medium of Qur'ānic commentary to present their thoughts and ideas. What sets these commentators apart from others is the fact that, besides explaining the Qur'ānic text in a general way, they make a conscious response to modernity by developing an argument based on a careful selection and systematic interpretation of key Qur'ānic terms and concepts. Mawdūdī and Sayyid Quṭb, for example, develop the Qur'ānic notion of the conflict of Islam and Jāhilīyah at length, extrapolating the notion from the Arabian context and presenting it as an enduring truth of history. In doing so they aim to show the relevance of the Qur'ānic message for the present and to motivate Muslims to play their role in history. [*See* Jāhilīyah *and the biographies of all the figures mentioned in this paragraph.*]

The centrality of the Qur'ān in modern Muslim thought is also evident from the importance attached by scholars in law and other fields to developing a new Qur'ānic hermeneutic. Fazlur Rahman has in several works stressed the need to take a fresh approach to the Qur'ān, for only such an approach can take Muslims out of the intellectual morass in which they find themselves. In *Islam and Modernity* (1982) he proposes a process of Qur'ān interpretation that "consists of a double movement, from the present situation to Qur'ānic times, then back to the present" (p. 5). The important point here is not the details of this "double movement" but Fazlur Rahman's view of the pivotal role the Qur'ān can play in reorienting Muslim life and rejuvenating Muslim thought. [*See the biography of Rahman.*] This is a view on which Muslim scholars, for all their conceptual and methodological differences, would be found in agreement.

BIBLIOGRAPHY

Bennabi, Malek. *Le phénomène coranique*. Damascus, 1397/1977. Translated into English as *The Qur'ānic Phenomenon*. Salimiah, Kuwait, 1983.

Cragg, Kenneth. *The Pen and the Faith: Eight Modern Muslim Writers and the Qur'ān*. London, 1985.

Denny, Frederick Mathewson. "Qur'ān and Ḥadīth." In *The Holy Book in Comparative Perspective*, edited by Frederick M. Denny and Rodney M. Taylor, pp. 84–108. Columbia, S.C., 1985. See especially pp. 94–97.

Denny, Frederick Mathewson. "Qur'ān Recitation Training in Indonesia: A Survey of Contexts and Handbooks." In *Approaches to the History of the Interpretation of the Qur'ān*, edited by Andrew Rippin, pp. 288–306. Oxford, 1988.

Nelson, Kristina. *The Art of Reciting the Qur'ān*. Austin, 1985.

Rahman, Fazlur. *Major Themes of the Qur'ān*. Minneapolis, 1980.

Rahman, Fazlur. *Islam and Modernity: Transformation of an Intellectual Tradition*. Chicago, 1982.

Ṭabāṭabā'ī, Muḥammad Ḥusayn. *The Qur'ān in Islam: Its Impact and Influence on the Life of Muslims*. London, 1987.

MUSTANSIR MIR

QUR'ĀNIC RECITATION. The name for the Islamic revealed scripture, *al-Qur'ān,* means "the recitation," in both informative and performative senses. With respect to the first, the Qur'ān is a "message" *(risālah)* that has been communicated to humankind through Muḥammad, the "Messenger" *(rasūl).* But the recitation is also oral performance of the text in worship, meditation, and sublime aesthetic enjoyment. Muslims learn, preserve, transmit, and celebrate the Qur'ān through combining its informative and performative modes in a potent piety that also finds expression in calligraphy of the Arabic text. Thus the Qur'ān guides and empowers Muslims through intellectual, oral-aural, and visual modalities.

The Qur'ān has been handed down as both written and recited text; the combined effect has bound Muslims together into a vast community with a common creed, liturgy, and moral/legal system. Until the present, in many places the Qur'ān has served as the basic textbook for literacy, religion, and morals. Young children have learned the Arabic text through both rote memorization of chanted passages and copying out the letters on tablets of clay or slate or on paper.

Muslims speak many different languages, but even though Arabic speakers are a minority of Muslims worldwide, the Arabic Qur'ān is treasured and recited in study and worship by many millions for whom Arabic is an acquired and often not fully understood tongue. Yet the beauty of the recited Arabic Qur'ān (and it may be recited only in Arabic), coupled with a reliable translation, helps Muslims feel a close kinship with their fellows worldwide while applying the message to their own lives and conditions.

Readings and Recitation. The Qur'ān has since earliest times existed in a variety of readings of the Arabic text. These variants are not different messages but rather reflect slight dialectal differences that were followed in different regions. All were based on the ancient recension completed under the caliph ʿUthmān, which has been the received text until now and is believed to be free from error and admixture in its essentials. (The names, numbering, and arrangement of the surahs are considered additions to the divinely transmitted text.) There are seven principal readings of the Qur'ān, although additional ones are also known. The science of variant readings, known as *ʿilm al-qirā'āt,* is difficult and exacting; Egypt and Saudi Arabia are its principal centers.

Although the Qur'ān's major divisions are by chapter-like surahs, 114 in all, arranged roughly according to their diminishing length, liturgical divisions also exist. The most common arrangement is into thirty equal parts, which matches the number of days in the holy month of Ramaḍān, when Muslims like to complete a recitation of the whole Qur'ān. Another arrangement is into seven parts, for completing the whole within a week. When a complete recitation *(khatmah)* of the Qur'ān is achieved, the reciter normally then recites the first surah ("the Opening") and the first five verses of the second surah ("the Cow"), which assures believers that they are among the rightly guided who will be successful.

If the Arabic text of the Qur'ān can be rendered authentically in oral form, so also must any oral performance be amenable to accurate transcription. It is important to note, however, that authentic live recitation is more complete, because the bare written text does not contain the rhythm, sounds, modes, and fine points of pronunciation that the performed text exhibits. Although the Qur'ān is believed by Muslims to derive from a "preserved tablet" in heaven, it was revealed strictly orally to Muḥammad, who (it is believed) could neither read nor write. Thus the priority of the recited Qur'ān is evident.

The technical skills of recitation as performance have been handed down from teacher to student in chains of transmission that start with Muḥammad, who received the message from God through the archangel Gabriel. A reciter *(qāri'*; sometimes *muqri'* for a readings specialist) who has mastered the seven readings earns a certificate displaying his lineage. Written manuals, or indeed the written Arabic Qur'ān itself, cannot be understood from the performance perspective without a living teacher who has been properly trained in the ancient tradition of correct recitation.

The art of reciting the Qur'ān is known in Arabic as *ʿilm al-tajwīd,* "the science of embellishment" by means of correct intonation, pronunciation, and rhythm. The term *tajwīd* most often means the entire science of Qur'ānic recitation as performance, although it sometimes is taken to mean, more narrowly, the highly embellished, dramatically moving, quasimusical chanting performed by the most advanced reciters. The latter is more often called the *mujawwad* style. The rules of *tajwīd* can be traced back to the prophet Muḥammad in their rudiments, although it was some time before *tajwīd* manuals began to appear.

The word *tajwīd* does not occur in the Qur'ān; however, another Arabic term, *tartīl,* does occur in surah 73.4, where it means recitation in "slow, measured rhythmic tones" (according to the translator ʿAbdullāh Yūsuf ʿAlī). Learners start with the simpler *tartīl* style, which itself admits of wide variation and levels of artistry. *Tartīl,* known also as *murattal,* is the style used by the vast majority of Muslims. It must be performed according to the rules of *tajwīd* but without the high vocal artistry often displayed in the *mujawwad* style. In no sense is the *tartīl/murattal* style considered inferior to the more musical type of chanting. Yet another term for Qur'ānic recitation is *tilāwah,* which combines the notions of reading, reciting aloud, and following the commands of the Qur'ān.

The *tajwīd* manuals speak of different acceptable tempos of recitation: slow and deliberate, moderate, and rapid. Whichever tempo is used—moderate is most common—the rules of *tajwīd* must be observed. This can be difficult if not impossible with the rapid tempo, which is nevertheless useful to professional reciters whose memories need frequent practice in a sort of "fast forward" mode.

Prophetic Sayings and Basic Rules. A famous *ḥadīth* has it that "He is not one of us who does not chant the Qur'ān" (Bukhārī). The urge to excellence in recitation is found in another *ḥadīth:* "Adorn the Qur'ān with your voices" (Ahmad et al.; tr. Karim). The reciter should not seek admiration for vocal skills. The Prophet, when asked "who had the most beautiful voice for the Qur'ān and whose recitation was most beautiful, . . . replied, 'The one of whom you think when you hear him recite that he fears God' " (Darimi; tr. Robson). Loud chanting was characterized by Muḥammad as being "like him who gives charity openly, whereas he who recites the Qur'ān quietly is like him who gives charity discreetly" (Tirmidhi). On the other hand, God listens most attentively when a *prophet* recites in a beautiful, sonorous voice (Bukhārī and Muslim). As for musical sources and styles for Qur'ānic chanting, a celebrated *ḥadīth* reads: "Recite the Qur'ān with the melodies and tones of the Arabs, but steer clear of the tunes of the love poets and the airs of the People of the two Books [Jews and Christians]" (Baihaqi).

This command is carefully obeyed with the result that the sound of Qur'ānic recitation is like no other in the world. Part of the powerful appeal of the twentieth-century Egyptian popular singer Umm Kulthūm was the vestigial *tajwīd* from her childhood training in Qur'ānic recitation. Only a person as admired and respected as she could have escaped censure for this sort of crossover in singing style. In any event, while borrowing from *tajwīd* to serve art song may be tolerated, the converse is reprehensible.

There are a number of points of etiquette for recitation, of which a selection follows. The Qur'ān may be recited from the written text or touched only by persons in a ritually pure state, although it is permitted to recite from memory without first performing ablutions. Recitation is meritorious at all times, but certain times are particularly recommended: during the daily prayers (*ṣalāt*), at night, before dawn, after sunrise, on the day of the standing ceremony at Mt. ʿArafah near Mecca, on Fridays, Mondays, and Thursdays, during the fasting month of Ramaḍān (especially the last ten days, during one of which the Qur'ān first descended), and during the first ten days of the pilgrimage month.

The reciter should sit in a dignified and humble posture, facing the *qiblah* (direction of Mecca). Recitation from the written text is preferable to reciting from memory. One should not hurry the recitation. One should not complete a recitation of the entire Qur'ān in less than three days. Recitation always should begin by first uttering the formula "I take refuge with God from the accursed Satan," followed by "In the Name of God, the Merciful, the Compassionate." Recitation should be ended with the phrase "God Almighty has spoken truthfully." At certain points in the text, prostration (as in the *ṣalāt*) is required. It is preferable to proceed in the order of the text, without mixing passages together haphazardly. The reciter should not eat, although it is thought permissible by some to sip a drink during pauses, as when reciters in a group session (*maqra'ah*) take turns. If the reciter is greeted by someone during his performance, the greeting should not be returned, because recitation is like being at prayer (*dhikr*) and is higher in merit than greeting with the *salām.* When frightening portions about judgment and suffering are recited, a tearful voice should be used. When concentration wanes, then the recitation should be terminated. After recitation is a propitious time for sincere supplication.

The etiquette of the listener includes such prescriptions as worshipful silence, refraining from greeting or returning greetings, not eating, attentive reflection on the message being recited, and avoiding conversation or levity. In actuality, listeners, whether as individuals or groups, vary in their deportment. In Egypt there are often excited emotions, with listeners rocking rhythmically back and forth on their haunches, providing sighs, pious ejaculations, and other signs of pleasure or awe. In Indonesia, by contrast, listeners remain silent and restrained.

The Qur'ān and Islamic Education. The traditional Qur'ānic school, known in Arabic as *kuttāb,* still exists in villages and rural areas of the Muslim world, but it has been widely supplanted by modern schools with secular or mixed religious and secular curricula. However, Qur'ānic education is widespread in alternative programs, such as after-school sessions in mosques and other places. In Indonesia many boys and girls still attend traditional *pondok pesantren*s, residential Qur'ānic schools, mostly in rural areas. For Muslim children and youth attending secular government schools, evening, weekend, and vacation Qur'ānic schools are available. One of these ventures is called "Express Pesantren" and is held on college and university campuses during vacations. Muslims in North America have organized weekend and vacation Qur'ānic schools, too, and the movement is growing. [*See* Pesantren.]

In Cairo, adults have varied opportunities to improve their knowledge of the Qur'ān and to attain a modicum of recitation skill. A typical program met weekly for two hours in a mosque room of a corporation. Participants included engineers, university students, a laborer, a housewife, businesspersons, a physician, and others of both sexes. The teacher was a venerable *muqri'* who at the time was supervisor of professional reciters in Egypt's mosques.

Reciters (except for some stars) do not make much money at a single job, so they frequently supplement their incomes by serving the instructional needs of individuals and groups, both in private residential and public settings. Reciters are also in demand for celebratory functions such as weddings, funerals, business grand openings, government functions, conferences, and other events. Opinions vary on the matter of remuneration in connection with teaching and reciting the Qur'ān, but most appear to agree that it is not the Qur'ān that is being exchanged for money, but human services. Some famous reciters earn a great deal of money through private performances and commercial recordings. One prominent Egyptian reciter was known to assure questioners that it was not the holy Qur'ān he was selling for such a high fee, but his voice.

There are many voluntary charitable associations throughout the Muslim world dedicated to the propagation of Qur'ānic knowledge. For example, a physician in the North Sumatran city of Medan has endowed a Qur'ānic school for children and oversees its operations while making creative pedagogical contributions of his own. Although he is not a professional reciter, his knowledge and skills in the practice are recognized as being of the highest standard owing to his years of dedicated study.

Despite the attention paid above to professional recitation, it would be a mistake to conclude that the practice at its best is limited to that. Muslims of all walks of life take seriously the Prophet's exhortation that: "The best among you is the one who has learned the Qur'ān and taught it" (Bukhārī). Nowadays it is possible to learn as well as enjoy the recited Qur'ān by means of home study recordings and radio programs (there is a full-time Qur'ān station in Cairo, featuring a roster of regular reciters). [*See* Radio and Television.]

Finally, there are Qur'ān reciting competitions in many countries. Among the most famous is the national Musabaqa Tilawatil Qur'ān ("Contest in the Recitation of the Qur'ān") held every two years in Indonesia. This ambitious effort is linked with Islamic education and youth citizenship training as a "national discipline." Reciters in various categories—girls, boys, men, women, handicapped, memorizers—compete at local, regional and provincial levels before the national finalists meet at a designated city for some ten days of scored competition in recitation, interspersed with popular Qur'ān quiz shows for youth, Islamic fashion shows, and educational exhibits centering on Islamic missions *(daʿwah).* The daily events are reported on the national media and the gala opening and closing ceremonies may feature processions, music and dance performances, and social events attended by the president, cabinet, and dignitaries from Indonesia and abroad. At the center is Qur'ānic recitation, which is listened to respectfully, but with occasional outbursts of applause or other expressions of pleasure (and pride, in the case of regional supporters of a favorite contestant). The winners receive trophies and other rewards and are enthusiastically welcomed on their return home with motorcades and audiences with the provincial governor and other high officials. There are also major local and regional competitions, such as one sponsored by the main television station in Surabaya, Indonesia, which features interludes of lively but wholesome Islamic rock music performed by attractive young female and male students from the local Islamic teachers' college. This odd combination, probably unique to this California of the *ummah,* is an attempt to reach out to youth and help them toward the "straight path" in a confusing world of secular temptations.

BIBLIOGRAPHY

Abdul-Fattah, Ashraf, with Aladdin Hassanin and Salah Saleh. *Tajwīd-ul-Qur'ān: A New Approach to Mastering the Art of Reciting the Holy Qur'ān*. London, 1989. Clear and comprehensive introduction; transliterated phonetic aids are used only in the early chapters, so a basic knowledge of the Arabic script is essential. Includes two sound cassettes.

Denny, Frederick Mathewson. "Exegesis and Recitation: Their Development as Classical Forms of Qur'anic Piety." In *Transitions and Transformations in the History of Religions: Essays in Honor of Joseph M. Kitagawa*, edited by Frank E. Reynolds and Theodore M. Ludwig, pp. 91–123. Leiden, 1980.

Denny, Frederick Mathewson. "The *adab* [etiquette] of Qur'an Recitation: Text and Context." In *International Congress for the Study of the Qur'an*, series 1, edited by A. H. Johns and S. Husain M. Jafri, pp. 143–160. Canberra, 1981. Treats recitation sessions in Cairo.

Denny, Frederick Mathewson. "The Great Indonesian Qur'an Chanting Tournament." *The World and I* 1.6 (June 1986): 216–223. Illustrated.

Denny, Frederick Mathewson. "Qur'an Recitation: A Tradition of Oral Performance and Transmission." *Oral Tradition* 4.1–2 (January–May 1989): 83–95.

Khaṭīb al-Tibrīzī, Muḥammad al-. *Mishkāt al-Maṣābīḥ*. 4 vols. Translated by James Robson. Lahore, 1964–1966. Varied *ḥadīths* on the Qur'ān and its recitation, a compilation of the medieval Muslim scholars al-Baghawī and al-Khaṭīb al-Tibrīzī (see vol. 2, pp. 446–470). The same text is available in a different arrangement, published under the title *Al-Hadis: An English Translation and Commentary of Mishkat-ul-Masabih*, 4 vols., translated by Fazlul Karim (Lahore, 1939; see vol. 2, pp. 663–702). This version contains a detailed introduction about the Qur'ān and facing Arabic text of the *ḥadīths*.

Nelson, Kristina. *The Art of Reciting the Qur'ān*. Austin, 1985. Epoch-making study focusing on contemporary Egypt and ethnomusicological aspects, and based on extensive field research.

Quasem, Muhammad A. *The Recitation and Interpretation of the Qur'an: Al-Ghazālī's Theory*. Bangi, Selangor, Malaysia, 1979. English translation, with notes and commentary, of the medieval theologian Abū Ḥāmid al-Ghazālī's (d. 1111) treatise on the recitation and interpretation of the Qur'ān, as contained in his famous "Revival of the Sciences of Religion" *(Iḥyā' 'ulūm al-dīn)*, Book 8.

Sa'īd, Labīb al-. *The Recited Koran: A History of the First Recorded Version*. Translated and adapted by Bernard G. Weiss et al. Princeton, 1975. Contains much information on readings as well as recitation, and offers an unusual glimpse into the world of Qur'ānic preservation and propagation in Cairo.

Surty, Muhammad Ibrahim H. I. *A Course in the Science of Reciting the Qur'ān*. Leicester, 1408/1988. Clearly organized and comprehensive textbook, with useful background on recitation as a religious practice. Includes Arabic script with Roman transliteration and two sound cassettes with practice texts.

FREDERICK MATHEWSON DENNY

QUṬB, SAYYID (1906–1966), more fully, Sayyid Quṭb Ibrāhīm Ḥusayn Shādhilī, literary critic, novelist, poet, Islamic thinker, and Egypt's most famous Islamic activist of the twentieth century, exceeding in reputation even the founder of the Muslim Brotherhood, Ḥasan al-Bannā' (1906–1949). His passionate writings contain powerful images of the maladies of contemporary Islamic societies and an idealization of the faith through the words of the sacred texts. In his overall standing as an Islamic thinker and activist, he may be compared with Turkey's Bediüzzaman Said Nursî (1873–1960), Pakistan's Abū al-A'lā Mawdūdī (1903–1979), and Iran's 'Alī Sharī'atī (1933–1977) and Ayatollah Ruhollah al-Musavi Khomeini (1902–1989).

Life. Born on 9 October 1906 in the village of Musha near the city of Asyut in Upper Egypt, Quṭb was partly of Indian extraction. He was the oldest of five children, two brothers and three sisters. His father, al-Ḥājj Quṭb Ibrāhīm, was a member of Muṣṭafā Kāmil's Nationalist Party (al-Ḥizb al-Waṭanī) and a subscriber to its newspaper, *The Banner (Al-liwā')*. Quṭb's family was in economic decline at the time of his birth, but it remained prestigious owing to his father's educated status.

Quṭb was a frail child, which may have influenced his tendencies toward deep spirituality. He is reported to have memorized the entire Qur'ān by the age of ten. Although he attended the village *kuttāb* (religious school), he soon transferred to the government school, from which he graduated in 1918. Quṭb moved to al-Ḥulwān (a suburb of Cairo) in either 1919 or 1921. He is said to have lived with a journalist uncle from 1921 until 1925, enrolled in a teacher's training college in 1925, and graduated in 1928. He apparently attended classes informally in 1928 and 1929 at the Dār al-'Ulūm (established in 1872 as a modern Egyptian university on the Western model). In 1930 he was formally admitted to this institution and graduated in 1933 with a B.A. in arts education. In recognition of his accomplishments, he was appointed instructor at the Dār al-'Ulūm, but he mainly earned his living between 1933 and 1951 as an employee of the Ministry of Education, where he later held the post of inspector for some years.

During the 1930s, Quṭb wrote works of fiction, literary criticism, and poetry. He was influenced by such modernists as Ṭāhā Ḥusayn, 'Abbās al-'Aqqād, and Aḥmad al-Zayyāt. Al-'Aqqād in particular introduced him to editors of various newspapers, and he wrote scores of articles over the course of his career for the Egyptian press. Ṭāhā

Ḥusayn, who was a major adviser of the Ministry of Education, also encouraged him, at one time introducing his lectures to the Officers' Club after the July 1952 coup that overthrew the monarchy. However, Quṭb turned against both al-ʿAqqād, whose writings he deemed overly intellectualized, and Ḥusayn, on account of his Western orientations. Eventually, Quṭb left the Ministry of Education owing to disagreements with the government's educational policies as well as its submissiveness to the British. Quṭb joined the opposition Wafd Party of Saʿd Zaghlūl but eventually abandoned it to enter the breakaway Saʿdist Party on its emergence in 1937, only to break with it in turn in 1942.

In 1948, still in the ministry's employ, Quṭb was dispatched to the United States to study Western methods of education. He studied at Wilson's Teachers' College (currently, the University of the District of Columbia), at the University of Northern Colorado's Teachers' College, where he earned an M.A. in education, and at Stanford University.

Quṭb spent about three years abroad, leaving America in summer 1950 and visiting England, Switzerland, and Italy on his way back to Egypt in 1951. His trip to the United States was a defining moment for him, marking a transition from literary and educational pursuits to intense religious commitment. Although he acknowledged the economic and scientific achievements of American society, Quṭb was appalled by its racism, sexual permissiveness, and pro-Zionism.

Back in Egypt, Quṭb refused a promotion to adviser in the Ministry of Education and began writing articles for various newspapers on social and political themes. In 1953, Quṭb joined the Muslim Brotherhood and was appointed editor of its weekly paper, *Al-ikhwān al-muslimūn*. Not long afterward, he became the director of the Muslim Brotherhood's Propaganda Section and was chosen to serve on its highest bodies, the Working Committee and the Guidance Council.

It is said that Quṭb was a key liaison between the Muslim Brotherhood and the Free Officers, who overthrew the monarchy in 1952—some of them, including Gamal Abdel Nasser, visited his house just before the coup, and Quṭb was the sole civilian to attend meetings of the Revolutionary Command Council (RCC) after the seizure of power. He agreed to be an adviser to the RCC on cultural matters and briefly headed the Liberation Rally, the government-sponsored mass-mobilization organization.

However, relations between the Free Officers and the brotherhood soon deteriorated as it became clear that each side had a different agenda. The brotherhood called for a referendum on the new constitution, anticipating that Egyptians would demand an Islamic fundamental law, but the RCC refused. The Muslim Brotherhood condemned the RCC's agreement with Britain in July 1954 to end the occupation because that agreement allowed the British to return their troops within seven years if they perceived a threat to their interests. The brotherhood demanded a plebiscite on the agreement, but it, too, was rejected out of hand. A tense standoff prevailed until October 1954, when shots were fired at Nasser during a speech.

The Muslim Brotherhood has always maintained that this incident was a provocation engineered deliberately by the Free Officers to justify a sweeping crackdown against it. Quṭb, whom the regime had already detained for three months in early 1954, and then released, was caught in the net of arrests. Although he suffered from poor health, Quṭb was brutally tortured. In May 1955 he was transferred to the prison hospital. In July, the court sentenced him to fifteen years in prison, most of which he spent in the hospital. He witnessed continued torture against his colleagues in jail, with perhaps the worst episode occurring in 1957 when more than a score of the Muslim Brotherhood inmates were killed outright and dozens injured. Accordingly, Quṭb set in motion ideas for the creation of a disciplined secret cadre of devoted followers whose task originally was limited to self-defense. Without declaring it publicly, however, Quṭb came to believe in using violence against the government if it used force against his organization. Still later, he came to the view that violence was justified even if the regime were merely deemed unjust and refused to alter its behavior.

Owing to intervention by Iraqi president ʿAbd al-Salām ʿĀrif, Quṭb was released in May 1964. But in August 1965, he was rearrested on charges of terrorism and sedition. The trial was a fiasco. The authorities initially permitted media coverage, but when the defendants talked about their torture, the proceedings were held behind closed doors. Incontrovertible evidence against Quṭb was apparently not presented, as his revolutionary tract, *Maʿālim fī al-ṭarīq* (Milestones; 1964)—the chief document on which the prosecutors relied—did not explicitly call for armed overthrow of the state. Rather, it urged resistance by turning away from existing society and creating a model *ummah* (community of believers) which eventually would establish true Islam. Despite great international pressure, the government executed Quṭb and two colleagues on 29 August 1966. Ever since, he has been regarded as a martyr by his supporters.

Thought. Perhaps more than any other post–World War II Sunnī Muslim thinker, Sayyid Quṭb personifies the determination of Islamist movements to oppose both the West and leaders in Islamic societies whom they see to be disregarding Allāh's law. Quṭb regarded the leaders of Islamic societies of which he disapproved, and the societies that went along with them, to be living in a state of *jāhilīyah* (lit., ignorance of revelation's truths), which can be considered anything that is inimical to Islam. His most important political work, *Milestones,* contains trenchant attacks against *jāhilīyah,* which he perceives to pervade contemporary life throughout the Islamic world. [*See* Jāhilīyah.] Quṭb's writings have been translated into Persian, Turkish, Urdu, English, and other languages. Their availability in Iran during the 1960s and 1970s is a matter of public record. Indeed, ʿAli Khamene'i, who was to succeed Khomeini as the "revolutionary leader," translated into Persian parts of Quṭb's Qur'ānic commentary, *Fī ẓilāl al-Qur'ān* (In the Shade of the Qur'ān).

Quṭb's writings show his uncompromising commitment to the sacred text. It is self-evident to Quṭb that if the Qur'ān contains a message, then human beings must implement that message. Quṭb was so clear on this in his own mind that it never occurred to him that Muslims, living in historical time, reinterpret their traditions and their past in the context of their contemporary historical circumstances. Quṭb plainly held the view that Islam is a timeless body of ideas and practices. Thus, there is no excuse, in his mind, for people's failure to adhere to it. This failure is a matter of brazen, self-conscious refusal to accept God's word and not a question of hermeneutical discourse.

Quṭb thought of Islam as a comprehensive way of life. Islam thus provides model solutions to all aspects of human existence. In his most sustained exposition of his views, *Khaṣā'iṣ al-taṣawwur al-Islāmī wa-muqawwimātuh* (The Characteristics and Constitutive Elements of the Islamic Conception; 1962), Quṭb elaborates on the themes of the oneness of Allāh, Allāh's divine nature, the permanence of Allāh's order, its all-encompassing nature, the balanced interplay between what can be known and what must remain unknown, the positive quality of Allāh's construction of the universe, and the real, practical engagement by man in this universe. It is sufficient to say here that ultimately these qualities range Islam, in Quṭb's perspective, along an axis of social commitment and activism.

One key to Quṭb's overall social and political program is its organicism and connotations of corporatism. This is interesting in view of his explicit rejection of Greek thought and Islamic Neoplatonic philosophy, themselves steeped in corporate and organic assumptions about society. More specifically, Quṭb believes that Muslims cohere in a quiddity which he calls *al-tajammuʿ al-ḥarakī* ("dynamic concrescence"). This entity is in fact the embodiment of the *ummah,* which is reified into a living organism with attributes of thought and behavior. The success of this dynamic concrescence lies in its acceptance of the trust given to it by Allāh to master the world and benefit from its resources, but the purpose of this mastery is to obey the sovereign commands, the *ḥakīmīyah,* of Allāh. Quṭb holds that although the dynamic concrescence is a very real phenomenon acting in society and the world, and that it experiences change, has practical purposes, and is thoroughly enmeshed in the immediacy of everyday existence, the sources for its existence and behavior lie entirely outside itself and are rooted in revelation (cf. esp. Binder, 1988, pp. 178–179).

Quṭb is not an advocate of the majesty of human reason. The apprehension of knowledge is not a matter of intellectual activity but of the reception of truths that are absolutely divine in their origins. In his perspective, the workings of discursive logic or inductive analysis are not necessary for, and are actually inimical to, the triumph of mankind in Allāh's universe. Rather, that triumph is vouchsafed by the ability and willingness of the human mind to absorb self-evident truths whose secrets are unlocked by divine texts.

Reflecting the ideas of Mawdūdī, Quṭb focused on the so-called *ḥakīmīyah* verses of the Qur'ān (5.44, 45, and 47): "those who do not judge according to what Allāh has revealed are unbelievers . . . oppressors . . . sinners." Quṭb, in what his opponents regard to be a reprehensible innovation *(bidʿah),* given centuries of precedent set by commentators on the Qur'ān, reinterpreted these verses by changing the meaning of the verb *yaḥkumu* from "judge" to "rule," thereby implicitly sanctioning collective action to dismiss a ruler who failed to apply Allāh's revelations. Muslims who are actively engaged in the dynamic community of faith are thus mandated not only to apply Allāh's laws as he has revealed them, but they are authorized and even commanded to replace any leaders who fail to do so. Invoking authoritative opinions of jurists from earlier centuries, especially those of Taqī al-Dīn Aḥmad ibn Taymīyah (d. 1328) against the Mongol ruler of the time, Quṭb and his supporters came to the view that Islam made armed resistance to nominally Muslim rulers who were deemed to be anti-Islamic not only permissible or laudatory but mandatory.

Among the movements that Qutb's writings have inspired are the Egyptian groups known as al-Fannīyah al-ʿAskarīyah (The Technical Military Academy Group), Jamāʿat al-Takfīr wa al-Hijrah (Pronouncing Unbelief Upon Infidels and Emigration to Islam), al-Jihād, the group that claimed responsibility for the assassination of President Anwar el-Sadat in 1981, and al-Jamāʿat al-Islāmīyah (the Islamic Group). A reading of *The Absent Precept (Al-farīḍah al-ghā'ibah)* (1981), the pamphlet written by Muḥammad ʿAbd al-Salām Faraj, and the revolutionary pronunciamento of *Al-jihād*, reflects al-Jihād's indebtedness to Quṭb's ideas about *jāhilīyah*, *ḥakīmīyah*, and *jihād*. Groups outside Egypt have claimed the Quṭb legacy as well. His writings are frequently read by Sunnī opposition groups, such as the Jabhat al-Inqādh al-Islāmī (Islamic Salvation Front) in Algeria, the Tunisian Islamic Tendency Movement (al-Ittijāh al-Islāmī; now called the Ḥizb al-Nahḍah), and the Muslim Brotherhood in Sudan, Syria, and Jordan, and Ḥamās in the West Bank and Gaza Strip. Shīʿī groups, including Ḥizbullāh in Lebanon, the Ḥizb al-Daʿwah in Iraq, and even the Iranian clerical establishment have taken certain cues from Quṭb, although they disagree with him on the question of leadership. It can thus be concluded that Quṭb's role in inspiring Islamic revivalist movements since the late 1960s might be even greater than that of Ayatollah Khomeini. [*All of the groups named above are the subject of independent entries. For al-Jihād, see* Jihād Organizations.]

Ultimately, Quṭb's worldview rests on a manifest ahistoricity. He is not interested in a historically grounded analysis of the development of law in Islam, for example. Rather, one finds repeated references to the primary sacred texts, overwhelmingly the Qur'ān, and to a much lesser extent the *ḥadīth*s Quṭb does not acknowledge that Qur'ānic and *ḥadīth* texts might not be self-evident and that, as they are interpreted over the centuries, people might come to different conclusions as to their meanings.

The tone of his writings is exhortatory and didactic. As a professional educator, Quṭb stresses the pedagogic role of the tutor instructing students in the verities of the true faith. The enemy is at the gates in the form of international neo-Crusaders seeking to destroy the identity of the Muslims and domestic despots who set up their own laws in defiance of what Allāh has revealed. Although Quṭb witnessed first hand the scientific and technological advances of the West, he regarded the West as spiritually bankrupt and implacably opposed to Islam. He attacked Marxism as tantamount to the enslavement of human beings.

Despite this unreconstructed rejection of Western thought, Quṭb, as is often the case with other twentieth-century Islamic thinkers, does not hesitate to invoke concepts rooted in the Western tradition. He does not acknowledge the Western provenance of such ideas, reaching into the early Islamic period to argue that they in fact are endemic to Islam, but in fact, many of these concepts derive either from the ancient Greek tradition or otherwise emanate from the period of the Enlightenment and the French Revolution and its aftermath.

An example of Western roots to Quṭb's thought can be seen in his concept of democracy. No Arabic word for this term exists, so the cognate *al-dimuqraṭīyah* has been devised. Despite Quṭb's sensitivity to language issues, he never asks why Muslims use the word in this Western cognate form. Quṭb is satisfied to find two brief references to *shūrā* ("consultation") in the Qur'ān (3.159 and 42.38) from which he constructs an edifice or system that he refers to as "democracy." Although commentators of the Qur'ān for centuries have understood these two verses to mean something different from the modern notion of political democracy in its twin attributes of individual freedom and social equality as institutionalized in representative bodies endowed with sovereign authority, Quṭb is not deterred from vindicating the Islamic roots of democracy. [*See* Democracy.]

The same can be said of social justice. It was not until the twentieth century that the phrase *al-ʿadālah al-ijtimāʿīyah* ("social justice") was even used by jurists in Islamic law, although medieval writers, such as Abū Bakr al-Ṭurṭūshī (d. 1127), Najm al-Dīn al-Ṭūfī (d. 1316), Ibn Taymīyah, and Abū Zayd ʿAbd al-Raḥmān ibn Khaldūn (d. 1406), focused on the justice and the injustice of rulers and the requirement that the state pursue justice to ensure the *maṣlaḥah* (general interest) of the Muslims. [*See* Maṣlaḥah.] Quṭb's method is to find verses in the Qur'ān referring to Allāh bidding people to "justice" (16.90) or verses pertaining to the perfection of Allāh's words in "justice" (6.115). The view of justice that emerges from the scripture is a highly abstract and idealized interpretation of what can be termed "divine justice," perceived without regard to social reality.

By contrast, social justice, as understood in modern discourse, comes from the tradition of natural law and the philosophy of law, which are anthropocentric. The very phrase "social justice" implies equity considerations in the context of the development of human societies in historical time, rather than a reified category which is theocentric at its very core. Accordingly, the phrase "social justice," so important for Quṭb, contains within it the subversion of his project, which is based on the belief that truth is to be found immediately in revelation, not by reference to human endeavors in history. [*See* Justice, *article on* Social Justice.]

Notwithstanding, as would be the case with Sharīʿatī, a critique of Quṭb that remains at this level misses the point. His advocacy of revolutionary change to restore a pure Islamic order has resonated powerfully among those disgusted with the system that the leaders of the Muslim world have erected. Quṭb's evocations and invocations of concepts that seemingly come from Western traditions are apparently one of the ironies of the Islamic resurgence that has inhered during the last generation. But the measure of Quṭb's contributions will no doubt be the impact that he has had in the past two or three decades among Islamists as the nonpareil exemplar of collective protest against those deemed to be the enemies of Islam.

[*See also* Muslim Brotherhood, *article on* Muslim Brotherhood in Egypt.]

BIBLIOGRAPHY

For a comprehensive bibliography of the works of Sayyid Quṭb, see Muḥammad Ḥāfiẓ Diyāb, *Sayyid Quṭb: Al-khiṭāb wa-al-aydiyūlūjiyā* (Sayyid Quṭb: His Discourse and Ideology), pp. 155–189, 2d ed. (Beirut, 1988). For critical evaluations, consult the following:

Akhavi, Shahrough. "Sayyid Quṭb: The 'Poverty of Philosophy' and the Vindication of Islamic Tradition." In *Cultural Transitions in the Middle East,* edited by Şerif Mardin, pp. 130–152. Leiden, 1994. Examines Quṭb's indebtedness to concepts from Western political and social traditions.

Barakāt, Muḥammad Tawfīq. *Sayyid Quṭb: Khulāṣat ḥayātihi, manhajuhu fī al-Ḥarakah, al-Naqd al-Muwajjah Ilayh* (Sayyid Quṭb: A Summary of His Life, the Dynamics of His Method, and a Critique). Beirut, 197?. Particularly useful for certain biographical information.

Binder, Leonard. "The Religious Aesthetic of Sayyid Qutb." In *Islamic Liberalism,* pp. 170–205. Chicago, 1988. Sophisticated and incisive analysis of Quṭb's writing in the context of a sympathetic critique of the liberal dimension in contemporary Muslim thought.

Haddad, Yvonne Yazbeck. "The Qur'anic Justification for an Islamic Revolution: The View of Sayyid Quṭb." *Middle East Journal* 37.1 (Winter 1983): 14–29. Important essay delineating Quṭb's political activism by reference to the sacred texts of Islam.

Haddad, Yvonne Yazbeck. "Sayyid Qutb: Ideologue of Islamic Revival." In *Voices of Resurgent Islam,* edited by John L. Esposito, pp. 67–98. New York and Oxford, 1983. Assessment of Quṭb's writings in the broader context of activist Islamist movements.

Jansen, J. J. G. *The Neglected Duty.* New York and London, 1986. Noteworthy work that includes an assessment of the ideas of the "al-Jihād" organization, focusing on their revolutionary tract, *Al-Farīḍah al-Ghā'ibah,* itself influenced by Quṭb's ideas.

Kepel, Gilles. *Muslim Extremism in Egypt: The Prophet and Pharaoh.* Berkeley, 1985. Contains important information on Islamic groups influenced by Quṭb's ideas.

Khālidī, Ṣalāḥ ʿAbd al-Fattāḥ. *Sayyid Quṭb, al-Shahīd al-Ḥayy* (Sayyid Quṭb, the Living Martyr). Amman, 1981. One of the most reliable works on Quṭb's life.

Mitchell, Richard P. *The Society of the Muslim Brothers.* London, 1969. Classic work on the Muslim Brotherhood, including references to Quṭb's role.

Moussalli, Ahmad S. *Radical Islamic Fundamentalism: The Ideological and Political Discourse of Sayyid Quṭb.* Beirut, 1992. Sustained analysis of Quṭb's ideas by a keen observer, stressing the progressiveness of Quṭb's writings in the context of fundamentalist and modernist thought.

Quṭb, Muḥammad ʿAlī. *Sayyid Quṭb: Al-Shahīd al-Aʿzal* (Sayyid Quṭb: The Unarmed Martyr). Cairo, 1974. Appreciation of Quṭb's work by his brother.

Sivan, Emmanuel. *Radical Islam.* New Haven, 1985. Places the thought of contemporary radical Islamists in the context of the history of ideas.

SHAHROUGH AKHAVI

R

RĀBIṬAH, AL-. *See* Muslim World League.

RADIO AND TELEVISION. Communication patterns in the Islamic world have undergone considerable change since the advent of broadcasting in the twentieth century. When broadcasting systems were introduced to many parts of the world between 1910 and 1930, only a few Islamic countries were independent and thus able to launch their own national communication infrastructures. However, the growth of radio and television in the Islamic world has steadily accelerated since World War II and the close of the colonial era. The development of broadcasting systems in Islamic countries has been propelled by several factors, including the rise of the modern nation-state system and nationalism, Islamic revivalism and cultural identity, and the expansion of communication technologies as instruments for social and political mobilization.

In the 1930s Egypt, Iran, and Turkey were among the first Islamic countries to develop their own radio broadcasting and to utilize it mainly as a tool of national integration, government news and information, and state propaganda and ideology. Kemal Atatürk in Turkey and Reza Shah Pahlavi in Iran used the mass media, particularly radio, to promote nationalism. As more Islamic lands in Asia and Africa gained their independence, broadcasting systems were established as distinctive symbols of national and political power to promote Muslim cultural values and at the same time to maintain national identity in the face of economic, political, and social change. In the 1950s leaders such as Gamal Abdel Nasser of Egypt and Sukarno of Indonesia combined their strong personal leadership with radio as an instrument of national policy. Prime Minister Mohammad Mossadegh in Iran and his one-time political partner, the major religious leader Ayatollah Abol-Qāsem Kāshāni, combined radio broadcasting with traditional communication channels such as the mosques and the bazaar to wage successful campaigns for the nationalization of the Iranian oil industry. Since the demise of Western-style development in Iran and the Islamic revolution of 1978–1979, broadcasting systems with a great degree of Islamic identity have developed in many Islamic countries.

Television, which was introduced into a number of Islamic countries in the late 1950s and the early 1960s, has also become a potent medium of information, education, and entertainment. The introduction of television has added a new dimension to the traditional means of communication in the Islamic world. Mosques have used both radio and television to broadcast sermons and other religious events in order to reach greater audiences with their messages. In addition, coffeehouses and marketplaces have remained social centers where information is newly disseminated through group observance of radio and television events. The amplification of the human voice in Qur'ānic recitals by microphones, radio, and television, as well as the production of such recitals on cassettes distributed along with other religious materials, have brought new dimensions of communication to the Islamic world. In addition, through a combination of traditional channels and electronic media, religious leaders and Islamic groups have maintained their ability to voice their opinions to the public.

In the Islamic world, radio and television in general served to diffuse Islamic culture in pursuit of state legitimacy but refrained from the diffusion or propagation of anti-Islamic practices. One important feature of broadcasting media in the Islamic world is that they are being integrated into the vast and complex system of traditional and oral channels of communication. The substance and strategy of contemporary Islamic movements around the world are new, and so is the realizations that in Islamic societies such as Iran, Algeria, Indonesia, and Pakistan, control of modern communications media does not guarantee political control. Radio and television achieve the power and penetration of traditional channels of communication when they are used as social, political, and economic tools. Conventional analyses of radio and television in the Islamic world are too limited if they focus only on the conventional Western definition and ignore traditional organizational and group channels peculiar to Muslim culture, through which the modern mass-media messages are filtered. For example, the Friday prayer ceremony, a forum for both religious and political topics, attended by thousands, is broadcast and covered extensively in the press of many Islamic countries.

Although there are diversities within the Islamic world and their systems of broadcasting, Islamic moral and ethical criteria have considerable influence on the content, production, and distribution of modern communications media, especially radio and television; these values are the bases for common communication patterns among Muslims throughout the world. This value system applied to communication laws and regulations makes broadcasting in the Muslim world highly distinctive.

A number of technical as well as economic and political factors have inhibited broadcasting from realizing its full potential in the Islamic world. The most significant of these factors is an overall lack of economic resources and investment in communications infrastructure. A second factor has been the limited number of educational and training institutions that can provide expertise and technical personnel for radio and television programming and operation. Linguistic diversity combined with centralized broadcasting is a third factor in the slow expansion of radio and television, preventing program exchanges among Islamic countries. However, in the countries of the Middle East and North Africa where Arabic is the common language, radio and television have become powerful channels of communication in the hands of governments and commercial organizations both domestic and foreign. The Islamic countries have also encountered some technical difficulties in the implementation of their television systems. After television was introduced to various Islamic regions during the 1950s and 1960s, each country devised its own plans without consideration for the development of the region as a whole. Since different countries often chose incompatible systems such as PAL or SECAM, exchange of programs became difficult and expensive and inhibited the development of an Islamic regional network. Technological advances with satellites now largely overcome such barriers to information flow across borders.

The Islamic world has received a significant amount of international broadcasting owing to its vast and diverse geographical area. The Voice of America and the British Broadcasting Corporation (BBC) have been among the many international sources that for years have beamed programs in Arabic, Persian, and other languages to Islamic countries. Many Islamic countries' broadcasting systems have not only served immigrants and diverse linguistic groups from abroad, but have also attempted to reach their own nationals who live and work in foreign countries. As a result, many of these broadcasting systems have programs in such languages as Persian, Turkish, Urdu, Malay, or Swahili as well as in European languages.

The most substantial period of growth in broadcasting in the Islamic world occurred between the 1970s and the 1990s, when the number of radio and television transmitters doubled in most countries. The distribution of receivers also increased, especially in the Persian Gulf states and in Southeast Asia. Because of the Muslim tradition of group listening, broadcasting audiences in the Islamic world are much larger than the actual number of receivers.

Political developments, including the resurgence of Islam as a revolutionary force, have had considerable influence on the international broadcasting of several Islamic countries. Iran and Egypt are among the world's foremost international broadcasters. Iran's external Arabic-language programming exceeds any other initiated in the Islamic world. In terms of weekly program hours broadcast to the Islamic world, Egypt and Iran rank respectively third and fourth among major international broadcasters, following the United Kingdom and Russia.

Both radio and television systems in Islamic countries have generally been state-owned and controlled. Advertising has been one source of revenue for broadcasting; however, many governments have tried to avoid raising revenue through commercial methods that they believe might encourage further development of commercialism in their societies. In a number of cases, such as Bahrain, Lebanon, and Malaysia, privately owned commercial broadcasting systems have been allowed to coexist with government-operated networks. Control of broadcasting systems by the state has been justified on the grounds of national unity and the prevention of unwanted messages and foreign influence. Most countries in the Islamic world import 40 to 60 percent of their television programs, the majority of which consist of entertainment from Europe and the United States—a source of controversy and debate over foreign cultural domination. Some countries have felt the encroachment of Western-dominated programming and have sought to maintain their autonomy through a comprehensive communication policy of investment in the expansion of locally produced cultural programs.

Since the process of secularization and the separation of church and state have not taken firm roots in the Islamic countries, there has been no need or attempt to establish independent religious broadcasting networks like those in Europe and the United States. The Islamic world has developed a broadcasting policy that combines civic and religious programs. In the case of radio, however, special religious stations have occasionally been developed and devoted solely to the Qur'ān, for instance in Egypt in the 1960s.

Satellite technology has further widened dissemination of news and religious ceremonies, such as the *ḥajj*. In addition to the International Telecommunications Satellite Organization's (INTELSAT) worldwide satellite network, which has been available to all Islamic countries, two major satellite systems—the PALAPA of Indonesia and the ARABSAT of the Arab countries—have been particularly designed to serve the needs of Southeast Asia, the Persian Gulf region, and North Africa. Other countries such as Iran and Algeria have been considering launching their own national satellite systems. Program exchanges and technical cooperation in communication in the Islamic world have been carried out through a number of regional organizations, including the Islamic States' Broadcasting Organization (ISBO), the Arab States Broadcasting Union, and Gulf Vision serving Arab countries of the Persian Gulf. ISBO was established in 1975 in Jeddah, Saudi Arabia, in accordance with a resolution adopted by the Sixth Islamic Conference of Foreign Ministers. Its goals are to disseminate Islamic principles, to acquaint people with the objectives of Islam, to explain Islamic social, political, and economic solidarity, and to develop cooperation among Islamic technical organizations and institutions of member states in the field of broadcasting.

In the Islamic countries of Southeast Asia, where different ethnic and language groups spread over vast areas, as in Indonesia and Malaysia, privately owned radio stations have been allowed, but television has remained a government monopoly. The low literacy rate coupled with traditionally high dependence on oral communication has made radio the ideal medium of modern mass communication in Muslim Africa. In Africa, where many countries cover vast areas and where physical obstructions abound, reception areas of radio and television are geographically limited. The cost of equipment and the great number of languages are among the problems facing the expansion of broadcasting in these countries.

A growing phenomenon in the Muslim world is the development of transnational communications media, especially in the fields of radio and broadcasting. The increasing population of Muslims in Europe and America with their well-developed communication infrastructures, combined with the acceleration of movement across national boundaries, have resulted in the establishment of many international communication centers in London, Paris, New York, and Washington, D.C. Because of rapid innovations in information services and technologies, the Islamic world has found it increasingly difficult to control or enforce laws regulating the transnational use of satellite communications and broadcasting. Since the Persian Gulf War in 1991, the demand for satellite receiving dishes has skyrocketed in the Persian Gulf states and North Africa. Videocassette recording using television technology has had a similar impact on the Muslim world. The lack of government control over VCRs and videocassettes has created further problems for national communications policy. Within the changing international climate, the greatest communication challenge to the Islamic world is the rapid development of modern broadcasting technologies and the trend toward globalization of the media.

[*See also* Communications Media.]

BIBLIOGRAPHY

Boyd, Douglas A. *Broadcasting in the Arab World: A Survey of Radio and Television in the Middle East*. Philadelphia, 1982.

Kamalipour, Yahya, and Hamid Mowlana, eds. *Mass Media in the Middle East: A Comprehensive Handbook*. Westport, Conn., 1994.

Katz, Elihu, and George Wedell. *Broadcasting in the Third World: Promise and Performance*. Cambridge, Mass., 1977.

Mowlana, Hamid. "The Islamization of Iranian Television." *Inter/Media* (London) 17.5 (October–November 1989): 35–39.

Mowlana, Hamid, George Gerbner, and Herbert Schiller, eds. *Triumph of the Image: The Media's War in the Persian Gulf; a Global Perspective*. Boulder, 1992.

Ugboajah, Frank Okwu, ed. *Mass Communication, Culture, and Society in West Africa*. New York, 1985.

UNESCO World Communication Yearbook. Paris, 1989.

Varis, Tapio. *International Flow of Television Programmes*. Reports and Papers of Mass Communication, UNESCO, 100. Paris, 1985.

HAMID MOWLANA

RAHMAN, FAZLUR (1919–1988), Pakistani philosopher and educator and prominent liberal reformer of Islam. Born in what is now Pakistan in 1919, Fazlur Rahman received a master's degree in Arabic from Punjab University, Lahore, in 1942, and a doctorate in Islamic philosophy from Oxford University in 1949. He was lecturer in Persian studies and Islamic philosophy at Durham University from 1950 to 1958, associate professor at McGill University's Institute of Islamic Studies from 1958 to 1961, visiting professor at Pakistan's Central Institute of Islamic Research from 1961 to 1962, and that Institute's director from 1962 to 1968. He left Pakistan under criticism for his reformist views and was appointed visiting professor at the University of California, Los Angeles, in spring of 1969. That fall he went to the University of Chicago as professor of Islamic thought. In 1986 he was named Harold H. Swift Distinguished Service Professor at Chicago, a title he held until his death in July 1988.

Rahman first achieved international renown with the publication of *Avicenna's Psychology* (1952), in which he demonstrated the influence of the Muslim philosopher-physician Ibn Sīnā (d. 1037) on the medieval Christian theologian St. Thomas Aquinas (d. 1275). An expert in medieval philosophy, Rahman wrote two more books on Ibn Sīnā (*Prophecy in Islam,* 1958, and *Avicenna's De Anima,* 1959), but he was best known for his pioneering work in Islamic hermeneutics (*Islamic Methodology in History,* 1965) and educational reform (*Islam and Modernity: Transformation of an Intellectual Tradition,* 1984).

Rahman believed that contemporary Muslim conservatives, in trying to maintain the status quo in religious tradition, and fundamentalists, in interpreting the Qur'ān literally, are as misguided as secularists who deny Islam's relevance to the political and economic spheres. Both conservatives and fundamentalists have failed to distinguish the prescriptive or normative elements of revelation from the merely descriptive elements that are pertinent only to the time and place in which revelation occurred. In order to make Islam relevant to today's specific circumstances, he believed, Muslims must go beyond a literal or traditional interpretation of the Qur'ān to an understanding of its spirit. They must study the background or "occasions" of each verse in order to find the true essence of revelation. Muslims must also study in detail the specific circumstances of their own time in order to be able to apply the principles derived from revelation.

Overall, he was convinced that the disarray of the modern Muslim world was caused by inadequate understanding of Qur'ānic teachings. This he attributed to stagnation in Islamic education, beginning in the early middle ages and incorporated into traditional formulations, including Islamic law. He therefore devoted himself to educational reform and the revival of Islamic interpretation (*ijtihād*) through his later writings and teaching.

Rahman was greatly respected by other Islamic reformers such as ʿAbd Allāh al-Naʿīm of Sudan. He was, however, criticized by those he considered fundamentalist as being overly liberal in his interpretation of the Qur'ān, the *sunnah,* and classical Islamic law. In Pakistan his detractors referred to him as "the destroyer of *ḥadīths*" because of his insistence on judging the weight of *ḥadīth* reports in light of the overall spirit of the Qur'ān. However, he believed his reformist views would eventually be vindicated; he felt that contemporary Islamic fundamentalism was a defensive and temporary posture taken in response to the political and economic setbacks experienced by the Muslim world.

BIBLIOGRAPHY

Works by Fazlur Rahman

Avicenna's Psychology. Edited and translated by Fazlur Rahman. London, 1952.

Avicenna's De Anima (Arabic text). Edited by Fazlur Rahman. London, 1959.

Islamic Methodology in History. Karachi, 1965.

Intikhāb-i maktūbāt-i Shaykh Aḥmad Sirhindī (Selected Letters of Shaykh Aḥmad Sirhindī). Edited by Fazlur Rahman. Karachi, 1968.

Philosophy of Mullā Ṣadrā. Albany, N.Y., 1975.

Islam. 2d ed. Chicago, 1979.

Major Themes of the Qur'an. Minneapolis, 1979.

Prophecy in Islam, 2d ed. Chicago, 1979.

Islam and Modernity: Transformation of an Intellectual Tradition. Chicago, 1984.

Health and Medicine in the Islamic Tradition: Change and Identity. New York, 1987.

Works on Fazlur Rahman

Sonn, Tamara. "Fazlur Rahman's Islamic Methodology." *Muslim World* 81 (July–October 1991): 212–230.

Tamara Sonn

RAMAḌĀN. For the duration of Ramaḍān, the ninth month of the Muslim lunar calendar all Muslims are required to abstain during the daylight hours from eating any food, drinking any liquids, or engaging in sexual activity. Fasting (*ṣawm;* pl., *ṣiyām*) means abstention;

through heightened awareness of their own bodily needs Muslims come to greater awareness of the presence of God and acknowledge their gratitude for God's provisions in their lives. Abstinence during Ramaḍān, first prescribed in the second year of the Hijrah, is required of all Muslims except children, those who are ill or too elderly, those who are traveling, and women who are menstruating or have just given birth or are breastfeeding. In such cases one may make up the days of fasting in a later month.

The month of Ramaḍān during which the fast takes place starts with the announcement of the first sighting of the waxing moon and concludes when the moon is first seen for the next month, Shawwāl. If the moon cannot be seen, it ends with the completion of thirty fasts. On each day of Ramaḍān the fasting starts at dawn—defined as the moment when a white thread can be distinguished from a black one by the human eye—and concludes at dusk. Because the Muslim calendar is lunar, the month of Ramaḍān rotates through the months of the solar calendar. This means that fasting sometimes takes place in winter when the daylight hours are few, easing the stringency of the abstention, while at other times the day of fasting may be as long as twenty hours.

Like many other obligations of Islam, fasting during the month of Ramaḍān serves to enhance the sense of community as Muslims across the world join together in performance of this ritual. It is a deeply symbolic time: for a whole month Muslim men and women of all races, nationalities, and ethnic identities join together in an experience of global unity, brotherhood, and sisterhood. Following the example of the prophet Muḥammad, Muslims generally break their fast by taking dates and a glass of water. This is followed by the sharing of a common meal in which people join in expressing gratitude for God's provisions to them.

The Qur'ān traces the origins of fasting as a spiritual exercise to the time of the early prophets and understands it to be an integral part of the teachings of revealed religions (2.183). The month of Ramaḍān itself is particularly sacred to Muslims because it was during that time that the first revelation of the Qur'ān was received from God by the prophet Muḥammad: "During the month of Ramaḍān the Qur'ān was sent down as a guidance to the people with clear signs of the true guidance and as the criterion [between right and wrong]" (2.185). The particular night on which the first revelation came to the Prophet, Laylat al-Qadr (Night of Power) is referred to in several verses of the Qur'ān. The whole of surah 97 is devoted to this crucial event. It is marked by special celebrations, Qur'ānic recitation competitions, and vigils on odd nights, during the last ten days of Ramaḍān.

Ramaḍān also happens to be the month in which two decisive battles were fought and won by the early Muslim community, namely, the Ghazwat Badr (Battle of Badr, AH 2/624 CE) and the Fatḥ Makkah (Conquest of Mecca, AH 8/630 CE).

Both the historical and the communal dimensions of Ramaḍān are manifested in the fact that each year, over the course of the month, the Qur'ān is recited from beginning to end, just as it was received by the early Muslim community in Makkah and al-Madīnah (Mecca and Medina) fourteen centuries ago.

Ramaḍān is also the time when the ethical responsibilities of being Muslim are highlighted. Abstention from food, drink, and sex is understood to help develop self-control through awareness of God *(taqwā)*, which is considered the backbone of religious discipline in Islam, and to aid the believer in feeling the sufferings of others who hunger and thirst: "Believers, fasting is enjoined upon you, as it was enjoined upon those before you, that you become Allāh-conscious" (2.183). The external observation of the fast is merely a reflection of the internal intention to live a life of ethical and moral integrity. Ramaḍān is therefore the month in which the qualities of God-consciousness *(taqwā)*, striving for the good *(khayr)*, practicing virtue *(maʿrūf)*, and demonstrating piety *(birr)* become the norms both for the individual and for the Muslim community as a whole.

The prophet Muḥammad stressed that Ramaḍān is not simply a time to cease from indulging in the pleasures of the body, but a month in which the range of ethical responsibilities incumbent on Muslims should be given special attention. "If someone does not stop telling lies and promoting falsehoods during the fast, then know, Allāh does not want a person simply to stop eating and drinking" (Bukhārī, vol. 1). Even the concept of abstinence itself takes on a dimension beyond mere fasting. "If a person is fasting and someone tries to fight with him or abuse him, he should not react but should rather abstain from fighting and foul language by saying, 'I am fasting'" (*Ṣaḥīḥ Muslim*, vol. 1, *Bāb faḍl al-ṣiyām*).

The Prophet stressed that fasting is not intended to be a hardship on people as such, and he certainly did not indicate that enjoyment of food and drink or sex in itself, at appropriate times, is not desirable. He urged the taking of a regular meal *(suḥūr)* before starting the fast and enjoying a moderate repast at the time when the fast is broken each day *(ifṭār)*. Fasting is intended to be regulated according to the ability of humans to perform it. The Prophet is reported to have said that "if someone were to fast all the time [i.e. without a break] he would not be considered a faster" (Bukhārī, vol. 1, *Kitāb al-ṣawm*). Another *ḥadīth* suggests that one must avoid keeping two or more fasts together without having proper nutrition in between. The Qur'ān itself says that sexual activity with one's wife is permitted at the appropriate time: "Permitted to you on the night of the fasts is the approach to your wives, for they are your garments and you are their garments" (2.187).

Contemporary Muslim interpreters have emphasized the following advantages of fasting during Ramaḍān. It draws people out of their habitual behavior into a fresh state of mind; it is good for physical health; it helps people appreciate the sufferings of others; it provides discipline of the will and training in patience; and it is a means for purifying the soul.

[*See also* Islamic Calendar; Pillars of Islam; Ṣawm.]

BIBLIOGRAPHY

ʿAlī, ʿAbdallāh Yūsuf, trans. *The Holy Qur'ān*. New rev. ed. Brentwood, Md., 1989.

Bukhārī, Muḥammad ibn Ismāʿīl al-. *The Translation of the Meanings of Sahih al-Bukhari*. 9 vols. Translated by M. M. Khan. 3d rev. ed. Chicago, 1979.

Mawdūdī, Sayyid Abū al-Aʿlā. *Let Us Be Muslims*. Translated and edited by Khurram Murad. Leicester, 1981.

Mawdūdī, Sayyid Abū al-Aʿlā. *Towards Understanding the Qur'an*. Vol. 1. Translated by Zafar Ishaq Ansari. Leicester, 1988. Translation of *Tafhīm al-Qur'ān*.

Murad, Khurram. *Istiqbāl-i Ramaẓān*. Lahore, 1990.

Muslim ibn al-Ḥajjāj al-Qushayrī. *Ṣaḥīḥ Muslim*. 4 vols. Translated by ʿAbdul Hamid Siddiqi. Lahore, 1976.

Nadvī, Abulḥasan ʿAlī. *The Four Pillars of Islam*. Translated by Mohammad A. Kidwai. Lucknow, 1978.

Nu'mani, M. Manzoor. *Meaning and Message of the Traditions*. Translated by Mohammad A. Kidwai. Lucknow, 1979.

Plessner, M. "Ramaḍān." In *Shorter Encyclopaedia of Islam*, edited by H. A. R. Gibb and J. H. Kramers, pp. 468–469. Leiden, 1953.

Ṣadruddīn, Iṣlāḥī. *Islam at a Glance*. Translation of *Islām Ek Naẓar Men* by M. Zafar Iqbal. Delhi, 1985.

Von Grunebaum, G. E. *Muhammadan Festivals*. New York, 1951.

ANIS AHMAD

RASHĪD RIḌĀ, MUḤAMMAD (1865–1935), Islamic revivalist and reformer.

Muḥammad Rashīd Riḍā was born in a village near Tripoli, then Syria, to a family that claimed a line of descent from the prophet Muḥammad. After his early education in a traditional religious school, Riḍā attended an Islamic school established by an enlightened scholar, Shaykh Ḥusayn al-Jisr (d. 1909), who believed that the way to the progress of the Muslim nation was through a synthesis of religious education and modern sciences. Riḍā thus acquired a thorough education in the doctrine and traditions of Islam and a fair knowledge of the natural sciences and languages (Turkish and French). He studied the works of al-Ghazālī (d. 1111) and Ibn Taymīyah (d. 1328), which inspired him with the need to reform the declining conditions of Muslims and purify Islam from degenerate Ṣūfī practices.

By the end of the nineteenth century, a broader movement of reform, the Salafīyah movement led by Jamāl al-Dīn al-Afghānī (d. 1897) and Muḥammad ʿAbduh (d. 1905), was underway in Egypt. This movement, provoked by the stagnant and vulnerable conditions of the Muslims, sought to reinvigorate Islam; it stressed the need for the exercise of reason and the adoption of modern natural science, for agitation against tyranny and despotism and resistance to foreign domination, and the promotion of Muslim solidarity. The tenets of this movement were expounded in *Al-ʿurwah al-wuthqā* (The Indissoluble Bond), which al-Afghānī and ʿAbduh published in Paris in 1884. Instilling new ideas such as freedom, independence, unity, and the rights of the ruled into the minds of its Muslim readers, *Al-ʿurwah* made a deep impact on Riḍā; it broadened his idea of reform and brought him to a new stage in his intellectual life.

In 1897, Riḍā left for Egypt to join ʿAbduh and he soon became one of his close associates and leading disciples. In Cairo, Riḍā published his own magazine, *Al-manār* (The Lighthouse), which first appeared in 1898 as a weekly and, subsequently, as a monthly until his death in 1935. The objectives of *Al-manār* were to articulate and disseminate the ideas of reform and preserve the unity of the Muslim nation. Riḍā was a prolific writer, producing more work than ʿAbduh and al-Afghānī. Besides editing most of the articles that appeared in *Al-manār,* he wrote several books on various Islamic issues.

Riḍā, as did ʿAbduh, believed in the compatibility of Islam and modernity. ʿAbduh emphasized *ijtihād* (independent judgment) in an effort to reinterpret Islamic doctrines and give Islam a new vitality, but Riḍā, faced with more ominous challenges, insisted on certain criteria for Islamic reform. Riḍā's time witnessed the disintegration of the Islamic caliphate, the fragmentation of the Muslim world, and the ascendancy of the advocates of wholesale adoption of Western models, who tried to take ʿAbduh's reinterpretations of Islamic doctrines to secular conclusions (probably contrary to his intentions).

Concerned with the unity of the Muslim community and the preservation of its identity and culture, Riḍā viewed the original Islamic sources, the Qur'ān, *sunnah,* and *ijmā'* (consensus of the companions of the Prophet) as the basis of reform. Riḍā, however, distinguished between acts of worship *(ʿibādāt)* and matters concerning interaction with others *(muʿāmalāt).* Since the *ʿibādāt* organize human behavior, were revealed in the Qur'ān, and were laid down by authentic *ḥadīth,* they cannot be changed. But human relations, in the absence of an explicit, authentic, and binding text can be reinterpreted according to the interest *(maṣlaḥah)* of the community. *Ijtihād* can be exercised in light of achieving the common good of the Muslim community. By emphasizing *maṣlaḥah* and *ijtihād,* Riḍā allowed room for human legislation.

Throughout his intellectual career, Riḍā was preoccupied with the issue of reform. He believed the decline of the Muslim nation was due to the stagnation of its scholars and the tyranny of its rulers. He viewed European dominance over the Muslims as a result of the latter's weakness, which he attributed to the Muslims' inability to master the sciences, form organized political institutions, and restrict the power of their governments. Considering education a precondition for political reform and independence, Riḍā urged the Muslim peoples to acquire the commendable aspects of Western civilization, such as science, technical skill, and wealth. His emphasis on education was manifested in his founding of the School of Propagation and Guidance in 1912; here Riḍā attempted to combine modern education with religious teachings.

Central to Riḍā's scheme of thought was the concept of the caliphate and its indispensability to the coherence of the Muslim community. On the eve of the breakup of the Ottoman caliphate in 1923, Riḍā wrote a treatise, *The Caliphate or the Supreme Imamate,* which included an elaborate discussion of the caliphate and a plan for its restoration. Realizing the obstacles surrounding the revival of a proper Islamic caliphate of *ijtihād,* Riḍā proposed a caliphate of necessity, a temporary one, to preserve the solidarity of the Muslims. Essential to this caliphate were the issues of *shūrā* (consultation), *ahl al-ḥall wa-al-ʿaqd* ("those who bind and loose"), and *ijtihād* to ensure the adaptability of Islamic laws and the sovereignty of the Muslim nation.

Riḍā's ideas, particularly in the interwar period, gave an Arab emphasis to the Islamic reform movement. As a result of the repressive policies of the Turkish government in 1911, Riḍā held the non-Arab peoples, namely the Turks, responsible for the decline of the Muslim world. Glorifying the role of the Arabs in history, he placed them at the center of a revived Islamic state; Riḍā also participated in several parties and associations advocating Arab independence and freedom.

Riḍā contributed greatly to the preservation and dissemination of the ideology of Islamic reform. He perceived clearly the challenges and threats that led to the disintegration of the Muslim nation and constituted a link between al-Afghānī and ʿAbduh and the succeeding generations of Muslim activists and thinkers who appeared in the third decade of the twentieth century. He developed his own thought and attempted to elaborate a specific and systematic doctrine of Islamic laws and policies. Riḍā's ideas shaped modern Islamic thought with moderate and activist features that influenced later Muslim thinkers.

[*See also* Modernism; Salafīyah; *and the biographies of ʿAbduh and Afghānī.*]

BIBLIOGRAPHY

Adams, Charles C. *Islam and Modernism in Egypt: A Study of the Modern Reform Movement Inaugurated by Muhammad ʿAbduh.* London, 1933. Classic biographical source on Rashīd Riḍā and the Manār school.

Arslān, Shakīb. *Al-Sayyid Rashīd Riḍā wa-ikhā' arbaʿīn sanah* (Rashīd Riḍā and Forty Years of Brotherhood). Damascus, 1937. Excellent biographical source on Rashīd Riḍā by one of his close friends.

Enayat, Hamid. *Modern Islamic Political Thought.* Austin, 1982. Excellent analysis of Rashīd Riḍā's perceptions of the Islamic state and the caliphate.

Hourani, Albert. *Arabic Thought in the Liberal Age, 1798–1939.* London, 1970. Provides indispensable background to Rashīd Riḍā and his thought.

Kerr, Malcolm H. *Islamic Reform: The Political and Legal Theories of Muḥammad ʿAbduh and Rashīd Riḍā.* Berkeley, 1966. Thorough analysis of Rashīd Riḍā's interpretations of legal doctrines and the caliphate.

Khadduri, Majid. *Political Trends in the Arab World: The Role of Ideas and Ideals in Politics.* Baltimore and London, 1970. Introduction to the basic intellectual components of the school of Islamic revival.

Al-manār (1898–1935). Riḍā's periodical and a necessary source for understanding his thought and the political and intellectual currents of the time.

Rashīd Riḍā, Muḥammad. *Al-khilāfah, aw, al-Imāmah al-ʿUẓmá* (The Caliphate, or, The Supreme Imamate). Cairo, 1923.

Rashīd Riḍā, Muḥammad. *Tārīkh al-ustādh al-Imām al-Shaykh Muḥammad ʿAbduh* (The Biography of Imam Muḥammad ʿAbduh). 3 vols. Cairo, 1931. Excellent biography of Muḥammad ʿAbduh and a significant source on the Islamic reform movement.

Rashīd Riḍā, Muḥammad. *Mukhtārāt siyāsīyah min majallat Al-manār* (Political Selections from *Al-manār*). Introduction by Wajīh Kawtharānī. Beirut, 1980. Excellent analysis of Rashīd Riḍā's thought and well-selected texts from *Al-manār*.

Safran, Nadav. *Egypt in Search of a Political Community*. Cambridge, Mass., 1961. Critical and contextual study of Rashīd Riḍā and his intellectual contributions.

Shahin, Emad Eldin. "Muḥammad Rashīd Riḍā's Perspectives on the West as Reflected in *Al-manār*." *Muslim World* 79.2 (April 1989): 113–132.

EMAD ELDIN SHAHIN

RASSEMBLEMENT CONSTITUTIONEL DEMOCRATIQUE. *See* Destour.

RAWẒAH KHVĀNĪ. One of the foremost characteristics of Shīʿī Muslims is the veneration they express for the family of the Prophet and his martyred grandson, Imam Ḥusayn. These expressions take various forms the most common of which are public mourning ceremonies such as the *rawẓah khvānī* (narrative accounts of the martyrdom of Imam Ḥusayn), *taʿziyah* (passion plays) and *dastah* (processions). The *rawẓah khvānī*, specifically, is the remembrance through recitations and chanting of the suffering and death of Imam Ḥusayn and other Shīʿī martyrs at the battle of Karbala on the tenth of Muḥarram (ʿĀshūrā') in AH 61/680 CE, while fighting against the forces of Yazīd whom the Shīʿī consider an illegitimate, oppressive usurper of the caliphate.

These recitations are performed at various types of religious gatherings weekly throughout the year, especially on the anniversaries of the death dates of the Imams and other saintly figures such as Fāṭimah, the daughter of the Prophet and wife of ʿAlī, the first Imam. The rituals of lamentation reach their pinnacle of significance during the months of Muḥarram and Ṣafar when gatherings are held in mosques, *ḥusaynīyah*s, and in the courtyards of the bazaar and private homes to express grief over a death seen not only as a tragic event in itself but as an act of self-sacrifice on behalf of justice and truth.

The name *rawẓah khvānī* is derived from the title of the *Rawḍat al-shuhadā'* (Garden of Martyrs), the most comprehensive Shīʿī martyrology of its time (1502 CE), although its author, Ḥusayn-i Vāʿiẓ Kāshifī, was a Sunnī Muslim. This work and similar later ones, such as Jawharī's *Ṭūfān al-bukā* (Tempest of Tears) or the *Asrār al-shahādāh* (Mysteries of Martyrdom) by Ṭabāṭabā'ī are part of a literary genre known as *maqtal*, a development from a broader genre of eulogizing (*manāqib*) and elegizing (*marāthi*) poetry. These and still more recent works form the basis of the material used by the reciters (*rawẓah khvān*) in preparing their narrations.

The *rawẓah*, as it is popularly known in Iran, varies in length from about two hours to sessions lasting through the night. The usual format begins with the reading of verses of the Qur'ān followed by a sermon given by a preacher (*vā'iẓ*) who offers comments and advice on moral, religious, and social issues and/or the recitation of religious poetry by a panegyrist (*maddāḥ*) who eulogizes the family of the Prophet and the Imams. The eulogy leads into the *rawẓah khvānī* proper, at the conclusion of which is the chanting of dirges (*nawḥah*). Narrators are paid for their services and informally ranked on the basis of their rhetorical skills and the degree to which they can evoke intense emotional responses from their audiences. The *rawẓah khvān* recounts explicit details of the agony and torment suffered by Imam Ḥusayn and his followers, all the while emphasizing their human compassion, kindness, and love for their families. This elicits profuse weeping, cries of lamentation, and not uncommonly (especially among the lower classes) ecstatically induced rhythmic chest-beating.

Many of the *rawẓah* are sponsored in thankfulness to God for the fulfillment of a vow and to ensure further blessings since sponsoring or participating in such an event accrues religious merit (*savāb*). Weeping for Imam Ḥusayn, in particular, is believed to ensure his intercession on the Day of Judgment. Tears shed for the Imam are also believed to have curative powers and some individuals collect tears in small bottles that are used to cure various afflictions.

Women also sponsor and participate in gatherings where a *rawẓah* is performed, often by a professional woman narrator. The most popular such occasion is known as a *sufrah* (a ritual meal held to express gratitude for the fulfillment of a vow) especially that dedicated to ʿAbbās (also known by his epithet Abū al-Faẓl) who was also martyred at Karbala. The *rawẓah* associated with this event focuses in detail on ʿAbbās's sufferings on the battlefield; participants weep and beat their breasts in sympathy with his tribulations. In return for their pity and empathic compassion ʿAbbās is believed to act as an intercessor and mediator in the granting of wishes or responses to prayers.

With greater literacy and religious understanding, many of the practices associated with the *rawẓah* are undergoing reevaluation by the lay public, and many are criticizing them as un-Islamic and "ignorant" customs. Some of these attitudes reflect the political position taken by Reza Shah (r. 1921–1941) in his ban on what he felt were religious anachronisms incompatible with a modern nation-state; but such attitudes are also an aspect of a reformist Islam that seeks to purify the faith of folk beliefs and practices.

All rituals, however, are polysemic and have many broader social, economic, or political implications. Despite criticism of such practices by the majority of the *ʿulamāʾ*, the *rawẓah* has served them well over the centuries with its ability to evoke and maintain intense emotional passions often used to arouse mass opposition to tyrannical governments, repression, and injustice. Abū Muslim, who led the movement to overthrow the Umayyad dynasty in the eighth century, encouraged his followers by recounting the injustices suffered by Ḥusayn and the family of the Prophet. In the period preceding the Iranian Revolution of 1979, religious gatherings *(hayʾat-i mazhabī)* were organized daily within the quarters of the city by neighborhood groups and associations or by the guilds within the bazaar. Although they were intended to fulfill various religious goals, they almost always ended in a *rawẓah khvānī,* the not so latent message of which was opposition to the government. In fact, the ubiquity of *rawẓah khvānī* gatherings was instrumental in arousing the populace against the Shah, leading to his downfall and the establishment of the Islamic Republic of Iran.

The *rawẓah* is thus a vitally important religious ritual embodying the very ethos of Shiism with its focus on tragedy, oppression, suffering, intercession and final redemption; themes which also lend themselves to multiple meanings. Comparable gatherings of lamentation and mourning are found in most Shīʿī communities throughout the Muslim world. They have different names and differing sociopolitical functions depending on the local context. In Lebanon and Iraq, for example, it is known as a *taʿziyah majlis* (literally "mourning gathering") or *dhikra;* in Iraq women's *rawẓah* assemblies are referred to as *qarāyā;* and among the Shīʿīs of India, Pakistan, and the Indo-Muslim diaspora it is known as *majlis-i aʿẓa* or simply *majlis.*

[*See also* ʿĀshūrā; Ḥusayn ibn ʿAlī; Ḥusaynīyah; Imāmzādah; Martyrdom; Muḥarram; Taʿziyah.]

BIBLIOGRAPHY

Ayoub, Mahmoud M. *Redemptive Suffering in Islam: A Study of the Devotional Aspects of ʿĀshūrāʾ in Twelver Shīʿism.* The Hague, 1978. Important study of the theological and folk beliefs associated with Imam Ḥusayn's martyrdom.

Chelkowski, Peter. "Popular Shīʿī Mourning Rituals." *Al-Serāt* 12.1 (1986): 209–226. Excellent article by one of the leading authorities on popular Shīʿī ritual practices.

Mahdjoub, Mohammad-Djaʾfar. "The Evolution of Popular Eulogy of the Imams among the Shiʿa." In *Authority and Political Culture in Shiʿism,* edited by Said Amir Arjomand, pp. 54–79. Albany, N.Y., 1988.

Neubauer, Eckhard. "Muharram-Bräuche im heutigen Persien." *Der Islam* 49 (1972): 249–272. Excellent overview of Shīʿī mourning rituals in contemporary Iran.

Qureshi, Regula B. "Islamic Music in an Indian Environment: The Shiʿa Majles." *Journal of the Society for Ethnomusicology* 25.1 (1981): 41–71.

Thaiss, Gustav. "Religious Symbolism and Social Change: The Drama of Hussein." In *Scholars, Saints, and Sufis,* edited by Nikki R. Keddie, pp. 349–366. Berkeley, 1972. Study of the organization of religious gatherings, especially those of the guilds, in modern Tehran, and their role in facilitating the Iranian Revolution of 1979.

GUSTAV THAISS

REFÂH PARTİSİ. The Turkish Islamist political organization known as the Refâh Partisi (Welfare Party, RP) was established in 1983. It is the heir to two former parties, Millî Nizam Partisi (National Order Party, MNP) and Millî Selamet Partisi (National Salvation Party, MSP), both of which were banned from political activity. All three parties have functioned under the leadership of Necmettin Erbakan.

Millî Nizam Partisi was founded in 1970. Its program emphasized the encouragement of technological innovation, rapid industrialization, and the construction of a moral society. The latter goal would involve the recreation of a historical consciousness that the party saw as dormant in the national character, yet weakened by republican westernization. Although the party was careful not to include an explicit Islamist element in its program because of existing legislation that outlawed the use of religion for political purposes, it was nevertheless clear that both its ideology and its leadership were inspired by Islamist discourse. The MNP did not get a chance to compete in elections. It was closed down by a decision of the Constitutional Court in 1972, following its first congress, on the grounds that the slogans used by the delegates to the congress violated legal provisions forbidding the inclusion of religious themes in party propaganda.

The MNP was succeeded by the Millî Selamet Partisi, which was founded in 1972 by the MNP leadership. The MSP's program, like the MNP's, was critical of the republican road to development, which it saw as an unsymmetrical course of imitating Western culture without succeeding in attaining the technological and industrial levels of the West. The MSP program pointed out that the recreation of a powerful nation would require a reinterpretation of history to show that the greatness of the Ottoman Empire lay in its contributions to Muslim civilization, and that its decline started with the penetration of foreign cultural influences. In the MSP's view, the republican infatuation with Western civilization was at the root of the anomie facing family and social life, the bases of which no longer rested on morality and faith. Hence the MSP argued that rapid industrial development could not be achieved through the limited vision of the centrist parties that Erbakan colorfully called "members of the Western Club." Rather, economic development was dependent on a return to indigenous cultural sources, which only the MSP was equipped to regenerate.

Millî Selamet Partisi competed in two general elections, in 1973 and 1977, and received 11.8 and 8.6 percent of the votes, respectively. It participated in three coalition governments between 1973 and 1978, with Erbakan as deputy prime minister in all three. The first coalition was between the MSP and Cumhuriyet Halk Partisi (Republican People's Party, CHP), with the CHP leader Bülent Ecevit, as prime minister; it was formed in January 1974 and lasted until September 1974. It symbolized a significant success for the MSP, given CHP's historical role in defending the militant secularism of the Turkish Republic. The second coalition (April 1975–June 1977) was between the MSP, Adalet Partisi (Justice Party, AP), Cumhuriyetçi Güven Partisi (Republican Reliance Party, CGP), and Milliyetçi Hareket Partisi (Nationalist Action Party, MHP), under the name "Nationalist Front," with the AP leader Süleyman Demirel as prime minister. The third coalition (July 1977–January 1978) was between the MSP, AP, and MHP, under the name "Second Nationalist Front," with Demirel again as prime minister. This experience in governing bolstered the image of the MSP and legitimized Islamist politics, even though the MSP leadership acted less as power-holders and more as spokesmen for the opposition. The MSP was able to leave very little imprint on its electorate, although, as its leadership repeatedly emphasized, it held the "key to government."

All existing parties, including MSP, were closed down after the 1980 coup d'état. Its leader, Necmettin Erbakan, shared the fate of other party leaders as they were arrested and banned from political activity for ten years under a provisional article of the 1982 constitution, which later was deleted by a referendum. Unlike the others, the MSP leaders were also tried in military courts but were acquitted.

The MSP was succeeded by the Refâh Partisi with the return to competitive politics in 1983. The RP's ideology has significantly deviated from that of its two predecessors, MNP and MSP, both of which had rested their vision on rapid economic development based on a new Islamic ethics. With the socioeconomic changes of the 1980s, which opened the Turkish economy to world markets through the adoption of a free-market model and export-oriented growth, RP leadership began to view industrial growth as inimical to the interests of its traditional supporters, who were drawn mostly from small-business circles geared to the internal market. Hence the previous emphasis on rapid economic development has been replaced by a critique of the capitalist system and the world economic order; however, this critique verges on a paranoid interpretation of history and of economic models as shaped by Zionist aims. In the new RP perception, the collapse of the Ottoman Empire and the outbreaks of two world wars were part of a Zionist plot to establish the state of Israel with the aim of eventual world domination. Zionism is alleged presently to be seeking the means of establishing a federal Israeli state including Turkey, Syria, Iraq, and Egypt; the final aim is to establish a new world order based on the victory of capitalism and therefore under the command of Zionist interests.

In line with this revisionist history, RP is critical of capitalist development in Turkey, which, in its view, integrates the Turkish economy with world markets and thus with Zionist economic and military aims. The party literature argues that as both producers and consumers, working people pay a large portion of their income to the Israeli war industry through the financial transactions of local capitalists and governmental payment of external debts, which end up in Zionist banks in New York. In the RP analysis, a complex network of economic relations between systems integrated with the world economy serves to strengthen Israel's power.

This interpretation of capitalism as the vehicle of Zionism includes the RP view that an important consequence of Turkish integration with the world economy has been the destruction of the ethical values of an Islamic society. Party propaganda reiterates the MNP/MSP criticism of modern life as decadent and dictated by the logic of the market, where everything is up for sale. The name that the party gives to the new world order is *"köle düzeni"* ("the slave order"), which is contrasted with the RP's *"adil düzen"* ("just order"), whose outlines are given in general terms. Its major premise is to disengage Turkey from world capitalism and its international organizations by instituting an economic system without bank interest and taxes, establishing a "United Muslim Nations" to replace the UN, founding a "Defense Organization of Muslim States" to replace NATO, and creating a "Common Market of Muslim Countries" with a common currency to replace the European Community. The political, economic, and military cooperation of Muslim countries is envisioned as a significant step toward the cultural unification of the Muslim world. The RP promises a leadership role for Turkey in the creation of this alternative Muslim order.

The Refâh Partisi has competed in two general elections since its founding, in 1987 and in 1991, receiving 7.2 and 17.1 percent of the votes, respectively. However, it entered the 1991 elections on a common ticket with two smaller parties on the right, an electoral coalition to ensure that it would be able to muster enough votes to pass the 10-percent barrier imposed by the Election Law of 1983, under which the RP was unable to qualify in 1987. It currently has forty deputies in the four-hundred-member Grand National Assembly. Since 1983 it has also competed in four municipal elections, polling 9.8 percent of the votes in March 1989, 10.3 percent in June 1990, 18.5 percent in August 1990, and 24.1 percent in November 1992; the percentages represent votes cast in the limited number of constituencies where elections were held.

[*See also* Turkey *and the biography of Erbakan.*]

BINNAZ TOPRAK

REFERENCE BOOKS. Islamic civilization has always attached the greatest importance to the written word, and to books as vital sources of knowledge and guidance. But systematic access to this knowledge requires not just texts for reading, but also works which can be consulted for answers to specific questions and guidance to relevant material elsewhere. Such reference works were developed on an unprecedented scale in the classical periods of Muslim civilization, and the tradition has continued into modern times. The development of Islamic studies in the West, by Orientalists and others, has also led to the creation of research tools for scholarly reference; some have been adopted or adapted by Muslim scholars or have inspired the further development of reference materials.

Scripture, Traditions, and Law. The first and most important work of reference in Islam is of course the Qur'ān itself. The widespread practice of memorizing the text has traditionally enabled relevant passages to be cited by scholars and others in any given situation. In recent times, however, the relative decline of this practice has necessitated other means of access, and concordances and glossaries of Qur'ānic words and phrases have appeared. One of the earliest was *Nujūm al-furqān* by Muṣṭafā ibn Muḥammad Saʿīd, compiled in Mughal India, first published in Calcutta in 1811, and reprinted several times in the nineteenth century, despite its errors and omissions. In 1842 the German Orientalist Gustav Fluegel published his own famous concordance under the same Arabic title, more commonly known as *Concordantiae Corani Arabicae* (Leipzig, 1842; reprinted several times, most recently in Lahore, 1978). This has remained a standard rapid reference tool. The Arabic words are arranged under their root letters, with references to surah and verse numbers; however, it lacks contextual quotations, a deficiency made good by later compilations. Notable among the latter is Muḥammad Fu'ād ʿAbd al-Bāqī's *Al-muʿjam al-mufahras li-alfāẓ al-Qur'ān al-Karīm* (Cairo, 1945; reprint, 1987), which is probably now the most widely used of the monoglot Arabic concordances; unlike Fluegel, it refers to the standard Egyptian recension of the text. Arranged on somewhat different principles is Maḥmūd Rūḥānī's *Al-muʿjam al-iḥṣā'ī li-alfāẓ al-Qur'ān al-Karīm* (A Statistical Dictionary of Qur'anic Words, 3 vols., Mashhad, 1987–1990), which includes separate indexes for the Meccan and Medinan surahs, with word frequency counts, and is arranged in alphabetical order of the forms in the text, rather than by root letters.

The need of millions of non-Arabs for access to the Qur'ānic text has given rise to the compilation of concordances and indexes in foreign languages, both Muslim and non-Muslim. In Urdu, for instance, there is

Maẓhar al-Dīn Multānī's *Miftāḥ al-Qur'ān* (Lahore, 1970), and in Indonesian, Nazwar Syamsu's *Dictionary al-Qur'an* (Jakarta, 1977). For English readers, Altaf Ahmad Kherie's *A Key to the Holy Quran: Index-cum-Concordance* (Karachi, 1974–) is thematically arranged and refers to the edition and translation of Abdullah Yusuf Ali; in Hanna E. Kassis's *A Concordance of the Qur'ān* (Berkeley and Los Angeles, 1983) the Arabic words are given in romanization, arranged by roots, with English meanings, followed by references to and contextual quotations from Arberry's English translation, and alphabetical indexes of English terms at the end. In Arabic, English, and Urdu is Ahmad Shah's *Miftáh-ul-Qurán* (Benares, 1906, 2 vols.; recently reprinted in Lahore, n.d.).

Many readers of the Qur'ān also need dictionaries and glossaries to enable them to understand certain words. In Arabic there is the important *Muʿjam alfāẓ al-Qur'ān al-Karīm* (Cairo, 1953–1970, 2 vols.), prepared by the Arabic Language Academy in Cairo: this gives all the words, arranged by roots, with both definitions and contextual quotations. Most other Arabic glossaries have concentrated on difficult, unusual, or foreign vocabulary. English-speaking readers can consult John Penrice's *A Dictionary and Glossary of the Kor-ân* (London, 1873; reprinted several times, most recently in Delhi, 1987), as well as the second part of Ahmad Shah's *Miftáh-ul-Qurán,* mentioned above. More extended didactic treatment of selected words and phrases is given in two recent English-language compilations: Mustansir Mir's *Dictionary of Qur'ānic Terms and Concepts* (New York, 1987) and Faruq Sherif's *A Guide to the Contents of the Qur'an* (London, 1985).

The great works of exegesis *(tafsīr)* are traditionally regarded as essential to an understanding of the Qur'ān. There is also a concordance to the Qur'ānic verses as they appear in two of the greatest of these commentaries: Daud Rahbar's *Indices to the Verses of the Qur'ān in the Commentaries of al-Ṭabarī and al-Rāzī* (Hartford, 1962).

Concordances as such may eventually be rendered redundant by the development of electronic handling of the Qur'ānic text. The Islamic School in Cleveland, Ohio, provides the complete text on-line, accessible via the main networks, and there are several other such projects underway both in the Muslim world and elsewhere. They can provide the facility, either by on-line database or on disks, to search for any word or group of words, which can then be located in their contexts. This can apply equally to the Arabic text and to translations. An English version of the Qur'ān with subject indexes has been published on CD-ROM in Faisalabad, Pakistan.

The other great canonical source of authority for Muslims, after the Qur'ān, is the *ḥadīth,* or record of sayings and deeds of the Prophet. The vital need for concordances and indexes to this large body of texts was met in earlier times by a number of compilations; the modern reader is most likely to turn to Arent Jan Wensinck's *Al-muʿjam al-mufahras li-alfāẓ al-hadīth al-nabawī/Concordance et indices de la tradition musulmane* (Leiden, 1936–1988, 8 vols.; reprint, Leiden, 1992) and the same author's more abbreviated English manual, *A Handbook of Early Muhammadan Tradition, Alphabetically Arranged* (Leiden, 1927; Arabic version, *Miftāḥ kunūz al-sunnah,* Cairo, 1934). An elaborate set of indexes to these works is provided by Muḥammad Fu'ād ʿAbd al-Bāqī in his *Taysīr al-manfaʿah* (Cairo, 1935–1939, 8 vols.). The four great Shīʿī collections are indexed in Muḥammad al-Mahdī al-Kāẓimī's *Miftāḥ al-kutub al-arbaʿah* (Najaf, 1967). The famous compilation of sayings of Imām ʿAlī, especially important for Shīʿīs, has likewise been provided with a concordance: Muḥammad Dashtī's *Al-muʿjam al-mufahras li-alfāẓ Nahj al-Balāghah* (Beirut, 1986, 1460 pp.). There are also computerized databases for *ḥadīth,* both on disk and on-line. For the literature of *sīrah,* or biographies of the Prophet, there is now a multivolume compendium in English: *Muhammad: Encyclopædia of Seerah,* edited by Afzalur Rahman (London, 1981–).

The great traditional codifications of the Islamic law, the *sharīʿah,* based on Qur'ān and *sunnah,* are in a sense themselves reference works, but modern Muslims and others needing practical guidance on Islamic legal matters often require easier access. In Arabic there is the great Egyptian encyclopedia of jurisprudence, *Mawsūʿat (Jamāl ʿAbd al-Nāṣir) fī al-fiqh al-Islāmī* (Cairo, 1966–), which is alphabetically arranged. In English there are smaller handbooks of personal and family law: David Pearl's *A Textbook on Muslim Personal Law* (2d ed., London, 1987) and Keith Hodkinson's *Muslim Family Law: A Sourcebook* (London, 1984), as well as a compendium of specifically Qur'anic laws—Muhammad Valibhai Merchant's *A Book of Quranic Laws: An Exhaustive Treatise with Full Quranic Texts* (Delhi, 1981). A useful reference guide to the sources of Shīʿī law is Hossein Modarressi Tabātabā'ī's *An Introduction to Shīʿī Law: A Bibliographical Study* (London, 1984).

Biographical Dictionaries, Encyclopedias, and Historical Tables. The systematic compilation of biographical dictionaries for reference is a long-established practice among Muslims, and the tradition has continued into modern times. Good examples are Khayr al-Dīn al-Ziriklī's *Al-aʿlām* (3d ed., Beirut, c. 1970, 11 vols. in 13) and Zakī Muḥammad Mujāhid's *Al-aʿlām al-sharqīyah fī al-mi'ah al-rābiʿah ʿasharah al-hijrīyah* (Cairo, 1949–1963, 4 vols.). In English there is Yaacov Shimoni's *Biographical Dictionary of the Middle East* (Jerusalem and New York, 1991), which contains about five hundred biographies of present and recent personalities, mostly rulers and politicians. These are also covered in *Political Leaders of the Contemporary Middle East and North Africa: A Biographical Dictionary*, edited by Bernard Reich (New York, 1990). For Iran there is a major biographical dictionary covering the last three centuries, Mahdī Bāmdād's *Sharḥ-i ḥāl-i rijāl-i Īrān dar qarn-i 12 va 13 va 14-i hijrī* (2d ed., Tehran, 1978–1979, 6 vols.).

There also exist a great many biographical dictionaries, classical and modern, of specific categories of Muslims. Special mention must be made of the favorite category, authors and intellectuals, of whom there are some notable modern bio-bibliographical dictionaries, such as Mehmed Tahir Bursalı's (d. 1926) *Osmanlı müellifleri* (Istanbul, 1915–1924, 3 vols.; reprint, Farnborough, 1971, and on microfiche, Chicago, 1973; modern Turkish ed., Istanbul, 19[71?]–1975) for Ottoman Turkish authors, and ʿUmar Riḍā Kaḥḥālah's *Muʿjam al-mu'allifīn* (Damascus, 1957–1961, 15 vols.) for Arab ones. An index to the Arabic works in this field is provided by Khaldūn al-Wahhābī's *Marājiʿ tarājim al-udabā' al-ʿArab* (Baghdad and Najaf, 1956–1962, 4 vols.). Shīʿī authors can be found in Aḥmad al-Najāshī's *Fihrist asmā muṣannifī al-Shīʿah* (Qom, 1978), and a wider biographical dictionary of Shīʿīs is the massive *Aʿyān al-Shīʿah* (Beirut, 1951–1960, 7 vols.) by Muḥsin ʿAbd al-Karīm Amīn. A related field is the study of Arabic/Muslim names, of which a noteworthy dictionary and encyclopedia is *Mawsūʿat al-Sulṭān Qābūs li-Asmā' al-ʿArab/Sultan Qaboos Encyclopedia of Arab names* (Muscat and Beirut, 1991, 8 vols.); there is also an international project for a computerized database of Arabic onomastics and prosopography called *Onomasticon Arabicum,* coordinated at the Institut de Recherches et Histoire des Textes in Paris.

Much biographical information is also to be found in general encyclopedias of Islamic history and civilization, of which a number are now available. The genre originates in the classical Islamic period, but in modern times the initiative was taken by European Orientalists, who in 1908 launched the *Encyclopaedia of Islam* (Leiden/London, 1908–1938, 5 vols. including Supplement; reprinted, Leiden, 1987; also published in French and German editions). This is a detailed scholarly reference work on all aspects of Islamic religion, history, thought, and civilization, but it inevitably reflects the non-Muslim, European style of scholarship of the period. In the 1950s a new edition was started (first fasc., Leiden, 1954–), on a much larger scale, which is still in progress: this now includes some contributions by Muslim scholars, written from a Muslim standpoint, but the overall editorial policy is still rooted in the Western Orientalist tradition. Nevertheless, several major encyclopedias prepared and published in the Muslim world are translations or adaptations of it: in Arabic, the *Dā'irat al-maʿārif al-Islāmīyah* (Cairo, 1933; reprint, 1969, 16 vols.) and Aḥmad ʿAṭīyat Allāh's *Al-qāmūs al-Islāmī* (Cairo, 1963–1979, 5 vols.); in Turkish, the *İslâm ansiklopedisi* (Istanbul, 1940–1988, 13 vols.); and in Urdu, the *Urdū dā'irah-i maʿārif-i Islāmīyah* (Lahore, 1959–, in progress).

In the late twentieth century new initiatives have been launched in Muslim countries to prepare original large-scale encyclopedias by and for Muslims. In Iran an institute was established in 1983 to compile and edit such a work in Persian; ten years later it had a staff of about two hundred and had produced the first five volumes of the *Dā'irat al-maʿārif-i buzurg-i Islāmī/The Great Islamic Encyclopædia* (Tehran, 1989–, in progress), which will eventually be completed in about forty volumes. In 1991 the first volume of an Arabic edition appeared (*Dā'irat al-maʿārif al-Islāmīyah al-kubrá,* Tehran 1991–, in progress), and an English version is being prepared at the University of Cambridge. A similar enterprise in Turkey is the *Türkiye Diyanet Vakfı İslâm ansiklopedisi* (not to be confused with the *İslâm ansiklopedisi* mentioned above), which likewise is based in a well-resourced research institute; its first volume was published in 1988, thirty volumes are envisaged, and an English version may eventually appear. These two encyclopedias, unlike the *Encyclopaedia of Islam* and its derivatives, have been written from the outset from Islamic standpoints (Shīʿī and Sunnī respectively), but great care has been taken in both cases to ensure that they embody careful research and high scholarly standards.

As well as these large-scale works, there have also

been a number of encyclopedias on a smaller scale, usually devoted to one or more aspects of Islamic studies. The *Shorter Enyclopaedia of Islam* (edited by H. A. R. Gibb and J. H. Kramers, Leiden, 1953, reprinted 1991) contains articles from the first edition of the *Encyclopaedia of Islam* on religious and legal subjects; these are likewise the main themes of Cyril Glassé's *The Concise Encyclopædia of Islam* (London, 1989), although this does also contain some historical and geographical entries. Even more concise is I. R. Netton's *A Popular Dictionary of Islam* (London, 1992), a scholarly quick-reference source covering a wide range of Islamic (mostly Arabic) terms and names. For the modern Middle East there are a number of encyclopedias covering recent history, politics, and current affairs, such as Mehdi Heravi's *Concise Encyclopaedia of the Middle East* (Washington, 1973) and *An A to Z of the Middle East* (London, 1990) by Alain Gresh and Dominique Vidal.

Particular Muslim peoples are also covered in some large-scale encyclopedias, notably the *Encyclopaedia Iranica* (edited by Ehsan Yarshater, London, 1982–, in progress), *L'Encyclopédie berbère* (Aix-en-Provence, 1984–, in progress), and *Türk ansiklopedisi* (Ankara, 1946–, in progress). For the Arab world, there is the *Concise Encyclopaedia of Arabic Civilization* (Amsterdam, 1959–1966, 2 vols.) by Stefan and Nandy Ronart, with the emphasis on history.

Useful for historical reference are tables of Muslim dynasties such as the classic and indispensable work of Eduard de Zambaur, *Manuel de généalogie et de chronologie pour l'histoire de l'Islam* (Hanover, 1927, 2 vols.; reprinted, Osnabrück, 1976; Arabic version, *Muʿjam al-ansāb wa-al-usarāt al-ḥākimah fī al-tārīkh al-Islāmī*, Cairo, 1951, 2 vols.); a more handy modern guide is C. E. Bosworth's *The Islamic Dynasties: A Chronological and Genealogical Handbook* (rev. ed., Edinburgh, 1980). Equivalent dates in the AH and CE calendars are supplied by a number of published tables, of which the most popular and convenient is probably G. S. P. Freeman-Grenville's *The Muslim and Christian Calendars* (2d ed., London, 1977). Computer programs for calculating dates and prayer times are also available on-line from the American Arab Scientific Society (AMASS) Software Library in Boston, Massachusetts.

Atlases, Gazetteers, Directories, and Surveys. Most atlases of the Muslim world concentrate on historical aspects. Well-known examples are the *Historical Atlas of the Muslim Peoples* (Amsterdam, 1957) by Roelof Roolvink and others, and W. C. Brice's *An Historical Atlas of Islam* (Leiden, 1981); also, in Arabic, Ḥusayn Mu'nis, *Aṭlas tārīkh al-Islām/Atlas of the History of Islam* (Cairo, 1987). There are also cultural "atlases"—in fact mainly pictorial essays—covering both history and the modern scene: Francis Robinson's *Atlas of the Islamic World since 1500* (Oxford, 1982) and Ismaʿīl R. al-Fārūqī and Lois Lamyā' al-Fārūqī's *The Cultural Atlas of Islam* (New York, 1986). An atlas of the modern Islamist movement is *Atlas mondial de l'Islam activiste* (edited by Xavier Raufer et al., Paris, 1991). But most of those covering the geography and economics of the modern Muslim world are confined to certain regions, particularly the Middle East, for example, *The Cambridge Atlas of the Middle East and North Africa* (Cambridge, 1987) and *Atlas of the Middle East* (edited by Moshe Brawer, New York and London, 1988). This is true also of a massive German project, the *Tübinger Atlas des Vorderen Orients* (Tübingen, 1972–, in progress), which includes not only detailed maps but also major historical, toponymic, and geographical studies.

There are numerous directories and surveys of the modern Muslim world or parts of it. Especially noteworthy is *Muslim Peoples: A World Ethnographic Survey* (edited by R. V. Weekes, 2d ed., revised and expanded, Westport, 1984, 2 vols.). Academic and other educational institutions, libraries, museums, and so on in each country are listed in the *International Directory of Islamic Cultural Institutions/Al-dalīl al-duwalī lil-mu'assasāt al-thaqāfīyah al-Islāmīyah* (revised and enlarged ed. by Acar Tanlak and Ahmed Lajimi, Istanbul, 1989); international organizations can be found in *Arab and Islamic International Organization Directory* (Munich, 1984). For economic and financial information, useful works include J. R. Presley's *Directory of Islamic Financial Institutions* (London, 1988) and *Economie du monde arabe et musulman* (4th ed., Cachan, 1992), and for the Middle East only, the *Middle East Economic Handbook* (London, 1986), *Major Companies of the Arab World and Iran* (London, 1976–, periodic) and the *MEED Middle East Financial Directory* (annual, London, 1976–1990). There is even an *Islamic Transport Directory* (Colchester, 1987).

The annual Europa surveys and directories of the *Middle East and North Africa* (London, 1948–) and the *Far East and Australasia* (London, 1969–, including Muslim countries of South and Southeast Asia) provide much current information on those regions. There is also a useful *Middle East Studies Handbook* by Jere L. Bacharach (new ed., Seattle and Cambridge, 1984), and

The Middle East: A Political Dictionary by Lawrence Ziring (new ed., Santa Barbara and Oxford, 1992). More specialized, but of great importance for modern Muslims, is Ziauddin Sardar's *Science and Technology in the Middle East: A Guide to Issues, Organizations and Institutions* (London, 1982).

Language Dictionaries and Reference Grammars. Arabic lexicography has a venerable history, and the many great classical dictionaries cannot be enumerated here. The one most used by modern Arabs and Muslims is probably Ibn Manẓūr's *Lisān al-ʿArab* (new ed., Beirut, 1968, 65 parts in 15 vols.); an abridged and modernized version commissioned by a number of academies and universities has been published under the title *Lisān al-ʿArab al-muḥīṭ* (Beirut, 1970, 3 vols.). Another popular modern monoglot dictionary is *Al-munjid* (25th ed., Beirut, 1975). The classic Arabic-English dictionary is E. W. Lane's *Arabic-English Lexicon/Madd al-qāmūs* (London, 1863–1893, 8 vols.; reprint, Beirut, 1968, and, in 2 vols., Cambridge, 1984), continued by *Wörterbuch der klassischen arabischen Sprache* (Arabic-German-English, Wiesbaden, 1970–, in progress); the standard modern work is Hans Wehr's *A Dictionary of Modern Written Arabic* (edited by J. Milton Cowan, 4th ed., Wiesbaden, 1979). For Persian, the monumental monoglot *Lughat'nāmah* by ʿAlī Akbar Dihkhudā (Tehran, 1946–1981, about 260 parts; reproduced on microfiche, University of Chicago Library) must be mentioned, and there are also a number of bilingual dictionaries, as there are for most other Muslim languages.

Glossaries of Islamic terminology are provided by Syed Ali Ashraf's *A Glossary of Islamic Terms* (Cambridge, Islamic Academy, 1985), and on a larger scale, *A Glossary of Islamic Terminology* by Bassam Sulaiman Abughosh and Waffa Zaki Shaqra (London, 1992). There is also a good English-language dictionary of proverbs—*A Dictionary of Arabic and Islamic Proverbs* by Paul Lunde and John Wintle (London, 1984).

There are many Arabic reference grammars, both classical and modern. For Anglophone students the best is probably William Wright's *A Grammar of the Arabic Language* (3d ed., Cambridge, 1896–1898, 2 vols.; many reprints) for classical Arabic, and Vincente Cantarino's *Syntax of Modern Arabic Prose* (Bloomington, 1974, 3 vols.) for the modern language. Other Muslim languages are generally less well served, but for Turkish there is Geoffrey Lewis's *Turkish Grammar* (Oxford, 1967, reprint, 1985).

Bibliographies and Guides to the Literature. Islamic studies have been relatively well served by enumerative bibliographies, and only those of the highest importance can be mentioned here. Some bibliographies of the bibliographies are listed in the bibliography below.

A good basic guide to the most important material in most languages is *Middle East and Islam: A Bibliographical Introduction* (edited by Diana Grimwood-Jones, rev. ed., Zug, 1979; *Supplement 1977–1983*, edited by Paul Auchterlonie, Zug, 1986) although it is now in need of updating. For the great corpus of classical Arabic writings on all subjects, the fundamental work is still Carl Brockelmann's *Geschichte der arabischen Litteratur* (2d ed., Leiden, 1937–1949, 5 vols. incl. Supplement; Arabic version, *Tārīkh al-adab al-ʿArabī*, Cairo, 1974–1977, 6 vols.). A more recent and more comprehensive account of much of the earlier literature is Fuad Sezgin's *Geschichte des arabischen Schrifttums* (Leiden, 1967–1984, 9 vols.; Arabic version, *Tārīkh al-turāth al-ʿArabī*, Cairo, 1977–, and Riyadh, 1983–). At a much more elementary level, the Anglophone reader in need of a judicious classified selection of major works can consult N. A. Baloch's *Great Books of Islamic Civilization* (Islamabad, 1989). Shīʿī literature is minutely enumerated in Arabic in the massive *Al-dharīʿah ilá taṣānīf al-Shīʿah* by Muḥammad Muḥsin al-Ṭihrānī (Najaf and Tehran, 1936–1978, 25 vols.). Printed editions of Arabic literature with biographies of the authors, up to the early twentieth century, are listed in Yūsuf Aliyān Sarkīs's *Muʿjam al-maṭbūʿāt al-ʿArabīyah wa-al-muʿarrabah* (Cairo, 1928–1931, 2 vols.; reprinted, Baghdad, 1965). Much modern Arabic literature can be traced in Yūsuf Asʿad Dāghir's *Maṣādir al-dirāsāt al-adabīyah* (Sidon/Beirut, 1950–1983, 4 vols. in 5.); English translations are enumerated in Margaret Anderson's *Arabic Materials in English Translation: A Bibliography of Works from the Pre-Islamic Period to 1977* (Boston, 1980). Arabic periodical articles are listed retrospectively in ʿAbd al-Jabbār ʿAbd al-Raḥmān's *Index Arabicus 1876–1984/Kashshāf al-dawrīyāt al-ʿArabīyah* (Baghdad, 1989, 4 vols.) and currently in *Al-kashshāf al-Islāmī* (Nicosia, 1989–, quarterly).

Classical Persian literature is recorded in C. A. Storey's *Persian Literature: A Bio-bibliographical Survey* (London, 1927–, in progress); a more general basic retrospective bibliography of Iranian studies is the *Bibliographical Guide to Iran: The Middle East Library Committee Guide* (edited by L. P. Elwell-Sutton, Brighton, 1983). Turkish literature is less well served, but there is a comprehensive annual current bibliography of Turkish studies, *Turkologischer Anzeiger/Turkology Annual* (Vienna, 1984–, as separate publication; previously in *Wiener Zeitschrift für die Kunde des Morgenlandes*, 67–75, 1975–1983). Published Urdu literature is covered in *Qāmūs al-kutub-i Urdū* (Karachi, 1961–1975, 3 vols.).

For European-language studies of Islamic subjects there are a number of major bibliographies. The *Index Islamicus* (Cambridge and London, 1958–) has provided a register of articles published since 1906 and monographs since 1976; it continues as a current bibliography of books, articles, and reviews, and is published quarterly and annually in London. Another *Index Islamicus* volume (by W. H. Behn, Millersville, 1989) lists articles from 1665 to 1905. A useful bibliography of significant English-language publications on Islam as a religion and a civilization is David Ede's *Guide to Islam* (Boston, 1983), and a current register of such material is the *Index of Islamic Literature* (Leicester, 1986–, quarterly). The very important contributions of German-language scholarship are recorded in the *Bibliographie der deutschsprachigen Arabistik und Islamkunde von den Anfängen bis 1986* by Fuat Sezgin and others (Frankfurt a.M., 1990–1993, 18 vols.).

[*See also* Book Publishing; Periodical Literature.]

BIBLIOGRAPHY

ʿAbd al-Raḥmān, ʿAbd al-Jabbār. *Dalīl al-marājiʿ al-ʿArabīyah wa-al-muʿarrabah: Fihrist bibliyūghrāfī* (Guide to Arabic Reference Books: An Annotated Bibliography). Basra, 1970. Arranged thematically.

Amīn, ʿAbd al-Karīm, and Ibrāhīm Zāhidah. *Dalīl al-marājiʿ al-ʿArabīyah*. Baghdad, 1970. Another guide to Arabic reference works, thematically arranged.

Anees, Munawar Ahmad, and Alia N. Athar. *Guide to Sira and Hadith Literature in Western Languages*. London, 1986. Takes a rather negative view of the contributions of Orientalists.

Auchterlonie, Paul. *Arabic Biographical Dictionaries: A Summary Guide and Bibliography*. Durham, 1987. Includes a section on modern works.

Auchterlonie, Paul, ed. *Introductory Guide to Middle Eastern and Islamic Bibliography*. Oxford, 1990. Very useful annotated bibliography of the main bibliographies and reference works.

Besterman, Theodore. *World Bibliography of African Bibliographies*. Revised and updated by J. D. Pearson. Oxford and Totowa, N.J., 1975. Includes bibliographies covering North Africa and other Muslim areas.

Besterman, Theodore. *World Bibliography of Oriental Bibliographies*. Revised and updated by J. D. Pearson. Oxford and Totowa, N.J., 1975.

Geddes, Charles L. *Guide to Reference Books for Islamic Studies*. Denver, 1985. The most comprehensive bibliography available, with extensive annotations and index, but marred by numerous inaccuracies and misreadings.

Ghālī, Wajdī Rizq. *Al-muʿjamāt al-ʿArabīyah: Bibliyūjrāfīyah shāmilah mashrūḥah* (Arabic Dictionaries: An Annotated Comprehensive Bibliography). Cairo, 1971. Supplement in *Mélanges de l'Institut Dominicain d'Études Orientales* 12 (1974): 243–287. Thorough listing of 707 Arabic dictionaries: monoglot, diglot, and polyglot.

Grimwood-Jones, Diana, et al., eds. *Arab Islamic Bibliography: The Middle East Library Committee Guide*. Hassocks, 1977. Important comprehensive listing of reference materials, but in need of updating. Includes sections on bibliographies; encyclopaedias and reference works; Arabic grammars; genealogy, biographical dictionaries, and who's whos; the press and periodicals; maps and atlases; Arabic geographical names; Festschrifts and commemorative volumes; scientific expeditions; Orientalism and Orientalists; institutions; Arabic manuscripts; Arabic papyri; archives; Arabic epigraphy; Muslim numismatics; Arabic printing and book production; libraries; booksellers.

Haywood, John A. *Arabic Lexicography: Its History, and Its Place in the General History of Lexicography*. 2d ed. Leiden, 1965. Informative and readable account.

Hazai, György, and Barbara Kellner-Heinkele. *Bibliographisches Handbuch der Turkologie: Eine Bibliographie der Bibliographien vom 18. Jahrhundert bis 1979*. Vol. 1. Budapest and Wiesbaden, 1986. Lacks index, which may eventually appear in a later volume. Covers all Turkish- and Turkic-speaking areas.

Meiseles, Gustav. *Reference Literature to Arabic Studies: A Bibliographic Guide*. Tel Aviv, 1978. Unannotated.

Pearson, James D. *Oriental and Asian Bibliography: An Introduction with Some Reference to Africa*. London, 1966. Valuable description of the main sources, but now rather dated.

Selim, George D. *Arabic-English and English-Arabic Dictionaries in the Library of Congress*. Washington, D.C., 1992.

Siddiqi, Muhammad Z. *Ḥadīth Literature: Its Origin, Development and Special Features*. Edited and revised by Abdal Hakim Murad. Cambridge, 1993. Detailed account of the development of the main bodies of texts and reference works relating to them.

Siddiqui, Abdur Rashid. *Islamic Studies: A Select Guide to Bibliographic and Reference Material*. Leicester, 1979. Brief, annotated list of English-language material, for the benefit of Muslim readers.

Strangelove, Michael. *The Electronic Mystic's Guide to the Internet: A Complete Bibliography of Networked Electronic Documents, Online Conferences, Serials, Software, and Archives Relevant to Religious Studies*. On-line database, University of Ottawa, 1992. Contains details of various Islamic and Arabic reference materials available online (see volume 1, chapter 12: "Islamic Studies"). A printed version of this chapter may be found in *MELCOM International Newsletter* 2 (1993): 7–16.

Tasbīḥī, Ghulām-Ḥusayn. *A Comprehensive Survey of Persian Bibliographies in the World/Nigarishī-i jāmiʿ bar jahān kitāb-shināsī-hā-yi Īrān*. Tabriz, 1986.

Urdū men ḥavāle kī kitāben. Karachi, 1965. Classified bibliography of Urdu reference books.

Vesel, Živa. *Les encyclopédies persanes: Essai de typologie et de classification des sciences*. Paris, 1986. Includes an introduction in Persian.

Geoffrey Roper

REFORM. *See* Iṣlāḥ.

REFUGEES. In a Muslim context, the term "refugee" is related to formal concepts of migration and flight that are central to the history of Islam. When the prophet Muḥammed and his followers fled from hostile Mecca to friendly Medina (622 CE), they undertook what became known as the Hijrah (migration). This event constitutes the genesis of Muslim society and marks the beginning of the Islamic calendar. Thus *hijrah,* a generic Arabic term for migration, came to symbolize an exodus from a land of infidelity or oppression to the land of Islam. Later, the influential Wahhābī school of thought traced its own genesis to the *hijrah* of its founder, Muḥammad ibn ʿAbd al-Wahhāb, in the mid-eighteenth century.

Hijrah was prominent in early Islamic writings. Some Muslim scholars perceived Hijrah as a singular historical event; others, especially in the late medieval period, held that all Muslims who lived under conditions where Islam could not be practiced must migrate to the Muslim realm. Commonly understood as a collective, physical movement, *hijrah* was also interpreted, mainly by Ṣūfī scholars, as spiritual withdrawal from a hostile society.

As long as the Islamic realm was expanding, *hijrah* was of secondary importance. When Christian states started to conquer Muslim lands, however, the doctrinal obligation to flee appeared in stark terms. When Granada fell in 1492, many Muslims left the Iberian peninsula for North Africa, either in obedience to Islamic doctrine or because of persecution and eventual expulsion by the Christians. In the early nineteenth century thousands of Algerians left before the advancing French colonialists to settle in nearby Libya, in some cases after failed uprisings. Simultaneously, the Russians pressed against the Ottoman Empire from the North, generating a flood of Muslim refugees heading toward the interior regions of Ottoman rule. Some left their ancestral homes in accordance with *hijrah* precepts to live under the Ottoman Muslims rather than the Russian Orthodox czars; economic opportunity also beckoned. After 1812, Russian authorities increasingly sought to rid themselves of the Muslim population in colonized lands by encouraging or forcing emigration.

Elsewhere in the Islamic world, hijrah was infrequently undertaken despite growing conflict with non-Muslims. In the late eighteenth century the legendary founder of the West African Sokoto caliphate, Usuman dan Fodio, rallied Muslims against the "infidel" Hausa king by raising the twin banners of withdrawal and attack—*hijrah* and *jihād.* Later Sokoto leaders invoked similar concepts when fighting the British. [*See* Sokoto Caliphate.]

Hopes that the Ottoman Empire could roll back European colonialism took on a concrete and extreme form only in India. The Khilāfat movement, started after World War I by nontraditional Islamic scholars, was essentially a protest against the British power that weighed heavily on the Muslim world. Calling for self-determination for Indian Muslims and, simultaneously, the preservation of the Ottoman sultan as the temporal and spiritual head of the entire Islamic world, some 18,000 Muslims proclaimed a *hijrah* and started marching to neighboring Afghanistan. Hundreds died from exhaustion on the way, and when turned back at the border by Afghan militia, more succumbed on the return journey. While no friend of the British, the Afghan king Amānullāh declined the invitation to spearhead a *jihād* in India, nor would he give the marchers land in Afghanistan, as the Khilāfat leaders had led their destitute followers to believe. [*See* Khilāfat Movement.]

By the early twentieth century, the steady retrenchment of Muslim power had left millions of Muslims under Christian or Buddhist rule. For most, the formal obligation to migrate was not a realistic option. Instead, as the century progressed Muslims started to migrate into the Christian, industrialized states in search of economic advancement. At the same time, wars or oppression in the Middle East led many to seek asylum in Europe and North America.

The term *hijrah* remained in use for refugee situations from South Asia to the Balkans. The Central Asian Muslims who settled in Afghanistan during the 1920s after their failed rebellion against Russian, later Soviet, power in Turkestan were known locally as *muhājirūn,* those who perform *hijrah.* Indian Muslims who moved to Pakistan after the partition of India in 1947 called themselves *muhājir,* and their descendants in Karachi still use it as self-identification. Many Afghans who fled to neighboring countries following the Marxist revolution in 1978 and Soviet intervention in 1979 did the same. As in the case of the Prophet, flight was seen as a precondition for struggle; hence the Afghans used the terms *muhājirīn* and *mujāhidīn* (holy warriors) equally.

The Islamic model for granting asylum to refugees is the unreserved welcome that the people of Medina accorded the Prophet and his followers. The obligations of the hosts *(anṣār)* are stated in the Qur'ān, surah 4.100: "He who emigrates in the path of God will find frequent refuge and abundance."

The principal Islamic political entity in contemporary history, the Ottoman Empire, held liberal standards. Early Muslim migrants were accepted from a sense of religious duty, but this reflected also a traditional Ottoman practice of granting asylum freely to Muslims and non-Muslims alike. This was codified in the 1857 immigration law (Muhacirin Kanunnamesi), which made no distinction between migrants and refugees but used the *muhājir*-derived term for both. New arrivals were given plots of state land and were partially exempt from tax and military service. A commission (Muhacirin Komisyonu) was established to receive them. Between five and seven million arrived between 1860 and 1940; in 1860–1878 alone, the Ottoman population rose by about 40 percent.

The basis of the liberal immigration policy was partly economic. The Turkish heartland was thinly populated, and new arrivals provided needed labor. In some areas, Muslim settlers were especially welcome. The religious element in the policy became more pronounced toward the end of the century. Claiming that the lives of Muslims under foreign rule had become intolerable, the sultan's religious advisers persuaded him to declare the empire open to all Muslims who wanted to come and settle. The decree enhanced the position of the Ottoman Empire as a haven for all Muslims and the sultan as its center. The religious elites, notably from Central Asia, Afghanistan, and the Caucasus, brought the *hijrah* to its ultimate conclusion by immigrating instead to Mecca and Medina.

For the contemporary Islamic world, the fate of the Palestinians became a defining element of the refugee concept. The Arab exodus from the parts of Palestine that came under the control of Jewish forces in 1948–1949 numbered about 700,000 persons. Another quarter of a million were displaced by the war of 1967. The Gulf War of 1990–1991 produced further displacements as most of the 350,000 to 400,000 Palestinians working in Kuwait fled or were expelled to Jordan.

By 1990–1991 the Palestinian population of nearly six million fell into three major categories. Israel proper had about 730,000 Palestinians of whom 150,000 were displaced persons, but none had refugee status under the United Nations Relief and Works Agency (UNRWA), the special UN agency mandated to help the Palestinian refugees. In the Israeli-occupied territories of the West Bank and Gaza the Palestinian population was about 1.6 million, of whom 900,000 had UNRWA status and one-third were in refugee camps, especially in Gaza. In the diaspora, Jordan had the largest concentration, with 1.8 million Palestinians. Half of them had UNRWA status, and about one-third of those lived in camps. Syria and Lebanon had a combined population of 600,000; most were UNRWA-registered, and more than half lived in refugee camps. Smaller numbers were found in other Arab states and the West.

To skirt the intractable political issues that had produced Palestinian refugees in the first place, UNRWA adopted a need-oriented criterion to define refugees. Despite their material dependence on UNRWA, the Palestinians viewed it with suspicion. The agency was part of the system whose decision for the partition of Palestine was at the root of their tragedy, and the United States used it to promote resettlement.

The Palestinians have in principle rejected resettlement and local integration in exile—two standard solutions to international refugee problems. Instead, they have upheld the right to return, as initially stated in UN Resolution 194 (1948). The continued prevalence of refugee camps has served to underscore this claim, and the symbolism of the refugee camp may also be seen elsewhere. For example, during the war in Afghanistan after 1978, both Afghan refugees and their Pakistani hosts refused local integration on grounds that it would compromise the right to return. Many Palestinians in the diaspora have not been locally integrated. Only Jordan, originally an underpopulated state, readily issued passports to all Palestinians in its territory.

As the Palestine refugee question entered a new phase with the Israel-PLO agreement in 1993, another Muslim refugee population moved to the forefront of international attention. War in the republics of the former Yugoslavia led to large-scale and forcible expulsion of ethnic minorities. In 1992, the Muslims of Bosnia became the principal target as Serbian, and later Croatian, forces sought to create ethnic homogeneity within their respective and enlarged domains. In pre-war Bosnia-Herzegovina, Muslims had constituted 44 percent of the population, or 1.89 million people. By the end of 1993, slightly more than one million were left; the others had been driven into exile, mainly to neighboring Croatia and western European states, or killed. As the war continued during 1993, Bosnia's remaining Muslims had become concentrated in small enclaves, besieged by Serbian and Croatian forces although nominally under UN protection. Unlike Serbs and Croats who also were subjected to "ethnic cleansing," the Muslims had no equivalent of a "homeland" and hence were sometimes called "the new Palestinians."

At the beginning of the 1990s there were about 18 million international refugees worldwide, of whom perhaps two-thirds were Muslims. Africa had the largest share, including sizable concentrations in the heavily Muslim Horn. From the 1970s onward, war, drought, and environmental damage had turned millions into refugees. In many cases Muslim refugees sought asylum in Muslim areas, but cross-border ethnic ties, politics, and geographic proximity were also important in determining patterns of flight and protection. In the Sudan, for instance, the Islamist government equally received Christian and Muslim refugees from Ethiopia; Kenya, with only a small Muslim population, gave liberal asylum to Muslims from neighboring Somalia.

African Muslim states, like African states generally, have signed the UN legal instruments for protecting refugees (notably the 1951 Convention or its 1967 Protocol). Additionally, African states have separate and stronger legal instruments to protect refugees (the 1969 Convention of the Organization of African Unity, OAU), and the special OAU administrative apparatus for dealing with refugees. To provide supplies to mass inflows of refugees, however, African states are heavily dependent on the UN High Commissioner for Refugees (UNHCR). Individual states, including the Islamist-ruled Sudan, generally work closely with UNHCR and western aid organizations to receive and distribute relief supplies.

The Middle East had by the early 1990s several groups of refugees besides the Palestinians. Two groups were numerically small. An older and gradually disappearing generation of refugees and stateless persons of European origin (mainly White Russians and Armenians) were scattered from Egypt to Morocco; most were assisted by the UNHCR, and their legal status was often precarious. A limited number of Islamic militants in exile, often associated with the Muslim Brotherhood, appeared throughout the region, usually protected and supported through Islamic organizational links or by friendly states (notably Saudi Arabia).

Refugees from war or violent social upheavals typically appeared in large numbers to seek protection in friendly neighboring states. In the Middle East, this often meant that Muslim refugees sought asylum in Muslim states. Because of their numbers, these flows constituted the greatest challenge and potentially the heaviest burden. Yet, in contrast to the industrialized north, but in common with most of Africa, asylum was rarely refused except in the traditionally restrictive Arab Gulf states. Yemen, facing the Horn of Africa, took in thousands of Ethiopians and Somalis before they moved on. Algeria accommodated for more than a decade about 200,000 Ṣaḥrāwīs, partly to express its support for the Polisario Liberation Movement in the western Sahara. Thousands of victims of war and drought in Mali and Niger were also allowed entry. Demonstrating Tehran's interest in Afghan affairs, Iran accepted 2.3 million Afghan refugees after 1978. These were mainly fellow Persian-speaking Shīʿī Muslims who were permitted to settle, work, and utilize social services on an equal footing with Iranian citizens.

Geographic location and political aspirations made the Kurdish refugees more problematic. In Iraq alone, their persistent autonomy struggle generated large, cross-border flows in 1974–1975, 1987–1988, and in the aftermath of the Gulf War in April 1991. The Kurds of Iraq are mainly Shāfiʿī Sunnīs or members of Naqshbandī orders, and thus distinct from the Ḥanafī Sunnī Turks, the Shīʿī Iranians, and the Ḥanafī Sunnī Arabs who are their neighbors. Politics and not religion, however, determined the asylum policy of neighboring states: Turkey had rebellious Kurds of its own, and Iran was pursuing a long-standing rivalry with Iraq. Both governments initially sought to limit foreign aid organizations, including UNHCR, in order to implement an independent refugee policy.

Iran first opened, then closed the border to Kurdish refugees and militia in 1975. The border was reopened for refugees in 1987–1988, but foreign aid organizations were excluded. When a new emergency arose in 1991 as about one million Kurds fled into Iran, the Islamic Republic of Iran reversed its previous policy and worked closely with UN agencies to provide emergency relief. Economic constraints had similarly led the government reluctantly to approach UNHCR for assistance to Afghan refugees in 1984.

Turkey was consistently restrictive toward Kurdish refugees, closing the border in 1975 and permitting only temporary safe haven in 1988. UNHCR and foreign aid organizations were kept out. In 1991 Turkey successfully insisted that about 400,000 Kurds who crossed be given asylum on the Iraqi side of the border.

The Arab Middle East has been weakly tied to the international refugee regime. Except for Tunisia, Algeria, and Morocco in the west, and Sudan in the east—which had all benefited from UN support for refugees—none of the Arab states signed the 1951 UN Convention on refugees or its 1967 Protocol. Rich Arab Gulf states gave only symbolic contributions to the global operations of UNHCR. Signs of change in the late 1980s were accelerated by the Gulf War. UN agencies played a prominent role in helping the huge refugee flows generated by the war in and from Iraq and Kuwait. As a result, the Saudi-initiated Organization of the Islamic Conference (OIC) resolved to strengthen its cooperation with UNHCR in all matters concerning refugee assistance within the Muslim world. Two OIC-related agencies, the Islamic Development Bank and the Islamic Educational, Scientific and Cultural Organization, concluded agreements of cooperation with UNHCR.

Refugees from the Middle East have also moved out of the region because of war (Lebanon, 1975–1976 and in the 1980s) or revolution (Iran). An estimated two million Iranians fled or remained abroad as the fall of the shah (1979) ushered in revolution and war with Iraq. Mostly secularized or Western-oriented, these Iranians generally sought asylum in western Europe and North America. Only a few (perhaps one-fourth) were given formal refugee status, but Western states rarely returned asylum-seekers to the Islamic Republic of Iran, which they viewed as hostile and oppressive. Many Iranians (estimated to be about 800,000 in 1987) were in Turkey, where they were tolerated but not recognized as refugees.

Turkey was also a source of refugees. Both Turkish Kurds and other Turkish dissidents constituted a principal category of asylum-seekers in western Europe throughout the 1980s. As antiforeign sentiments hit Muslims and other groups in western Europe, asylum was tightened. By 1992 European states were very reluctant to accept refugees from the war in former Yugoslavia, including Muslims driven out by Serbs.

In Asia, on the outer rim of the Islamic world, Muslim refugees appeared as oppressed or rebellious minorities confronted by centralized state power (e.g., the Arakanese Muslims in Burma, the Moro in the Southern Philippines, or the Kazakhs in China). Closer to the Muslim heartland, in South and West Asia, refugees were generated as Muslim states were created (Pakistan) or experienced major social upheaval (Afghanistan). Established as a homeland for India's Muslims in 1947, Pakistan remained open to all Muslims in the Indian subcontinent until 1952. After that, the door was closed, even to the oppressed Bihari Muslims who wished to leave the former East Pakistan after it seceded to become Bangladesh in 1971. Pakistan did, however, provide exceptionally liberal asylum to more than three million Afghan refugees. The asylum decision reflected political interest in the Afghan *jihād* as well as deep sympathy for fellow Muslims in need. Iranian refugees who simultaneously asked for protection in Pakistan received an official cold shoulder. To aid the Afghan refugees, Pakistan worked closely with UNHCR, other UN agencies, and numerous non-governmental organizations (NGOs) from both Western states and the Muslim world.

National Red Crescent societies have worked actively throughout the Muslim world to aid refugees, sometimes alongside NGOs run by Christian churches. Among the Red Crescent organizations, only the Saudi has a reputation for prosyletizing.

[*See also* Hijrah; *and* International Relations and Diplomacy.]

BIBLIOGRAPHY

Eickelman, Dale F., and J. P. Piscatori, eds. *Muslim Travellers: Pilgrimage, Migration, and the Religious Imagination.* Berkeley and Los Angeles, 1990. Principal source on the origins and evolution of Islamic concepts of refugee and migration. See especially Kemal Karpat, "The *hijra* from Russia and the Balkans: The Process of Self-Definition in the Late Ottoman State" (pp. 131–152), on refugee migration to the Ottoman Empire in the nineteenth and early twentieth century; and Muhammad Khalid Masud, "The Obligation to Migrate: The Doctrine of *hijra* in Islamic Law" (pp. 29–49), on the theological discourse on refugee migration from its inception to the present.

Holt, P. M., et al. *The Cambridge History of Islam.* Vol. 2A. Cambridge, 1980. Contains a good section on the Khilāfat movement.

Meier, Fritz. "Über die umstrittene Pflicht des Muslims, bei nichtmuslimischer Besetzung seines Landes auszuwandern." *Der Islam* 68.1 (1991): 65–86. Definitive study of Muslim "religious refugees" by a leading scholar.

Shaw, Stanford J., and Ezel Kural Shaw. *History of the Ottoman Empire and Modern Turkey.* Vol. 2. Cambridge, 1977. Contains a good section on a classic pattern of receiving refugees in the nineteenth-century Muslim world.

There is no separate literature dealing with refugees in the contemporary Muslim world. Information must be culled from general sources or case study material:

Brand, Laurie A. *Palestinians in the Arab World.* New York, 1988. Outstanding analysis of Palestinians in the diaspora.

Bruinessen, Martin van. "Kurdish Society, Ethnicity, Nationalism, and Refugee Problems." In *The Kurds: A Contemporary Overview*, edited by Philip G. Kreyenbroek and Stefan Spearl, pp. 33–67. London, 1992. Balanced overview of a major, intractable refugee problem in the Muslim world.

Center for Policy Analysis on Palestine, Washington, D.C. *Facts and Figures about the Palestinians*. Washington, D.C., 1992. Updates figures on population distributions.

Holborn, Louise W. *Refugees: A Problem of Our Time*. 2 vols. Metuchen, N.J., 1975. Classic compilation of data about global refugee populations after World War II, including many in the Muslim world.

Marchal, Roland. "Production sociale et recomposition politique dans l'exil: Le cas érythréen." *Cahiers d'Études Africaines* 27.3–4 (1987): 393–410. Exceptionally fine case study on asylum practices for Muslim and non-Muslim refugees in a contemporary African Muslim state, Eritrea.

Olcott, Martha. "The Basmachi or Freeman's Revolt in Turkestan, 1918–24." *Soviet Studies* 33 (July 1981): 352–369. Early modern refugee movements in Central Asia.

United Nations, General Assembly, Executive Committee of the High Commissioner's Programme. *Overview of UNHCR Activities*. Annual report, published in Geneva, with detailed information on refugee flows and conditions in particular countries.

United States Committee on Refugees. *World Refugee Survey*. New York, 1980–. Annual report, with aggregate data and descriptive material on global refugee flows.

Viorst, Milton. *Reaching for the Olive Branch: UNRWA and Peace in the Middle East*. Washington, D.C., 1989. Analytical overview of the functions and politics of UNRWA.

Zolberg, Aristide, Astri Suhrke, and Sergio Aguayo. *Escape from Violence*. New York, 1989. Comprehensive analysis of contemporary refugee movements, with sections on refugees in Muslim Africa, West Asia, and South and Southeast Asia.

ASTRI SUHRKE and VEMUND AARBAKKE

REGIONAL ISLAMIC DAʿWAH COUNCIL OF SOUTHEAST ASIA AND THE PACIFIC. The nongovernmental nonprofit organization RISEAP, as its name indicates, operates in Southeast Asia and the Pacific region. Formed in 1980, RISEAP was established in response to a need to bring together Muslims in the area and to coordinate their Islamic *daʿwah* (missionary) activities. While the Mecca-based Rābiṭat al-ʿĀlam al-Islāmī (Muslim World League) addressed the general welfare of Muslims worldwide, the new organization was intended to concentrate on this particular part of the world.

Malaysia, through the work of its ex-premier Tunku Abdul Rahman and the Malaysian Muslim Welfare Organization (PERKIM), was largely responsible for the establishment of RISEAP, although the Rābiṭat also had a hand in its formation. RISEAP's headquarters are in Kuala Lumpur, and the organization has been funded mainly by the host country and Saudi Arabia.

RISEAP's central concern is to forge links among the various voluntary Islamic organizations in the spirit of *muaakhat* (brotherhood) and to coordinate their policies and actions for the betterment of Muslims in the region. Its responsibilities include supervising *daʿwah* activities, training individuals for Islamic social work, and providing experts to teach Islam. In its efforts to promote international Islamic cooperation, the organization gives special attention to the establishment of mosques and Islamic centers, the publication and distribution of Islamic literature, and related activities.

The 1980s saw RISEAP actively catering to the needs of Muslims who live in segregated areas or as isolated communities. RISEAP's objectives, which are cast in broad terms, appeal to national governments in its region, or at least are not in conflict with government interests; this partly explains RISEAP's success. Over the years it has held *daʿwah* training courses in such countries as Fiji, Australia, Thailand, and Japan. Under its auspices *ustadh*s or Islamic teachers work in remote regions such as the Solomon Islands to propagate the Muslim faith, or visit distant areas such as Yunnan in the People's Republic of China to establish contact with Muslim communities there, RISEAP's Department of Information and Welfare, which publishes the quarterly journal *Al-nahdah*, has undertaken to translate Islamic books, mainly for use by Muslim children. Although RISEAP concentrates on translating these works into Malay, English, Japanese, and Chinese, it has also set its sights on speakers of Korean, Thai, and Tagalog. One notable achievement was the production of a fifty-minute documentary film called "The Book of Signs," which attempts to explain modern science from the Qur'ānic perspective; based on the work of Dr. Maurice Buccaille, a French scientist, it was widely acclaimed.

Muslim minorities are also a focus of RISEAP's attention. They are part of an evolving Islamic presence that includes new converts to the faith. In this connection RISEAP has assisted them by providing prayer leaders (imams), religious teachers, and advisors, and by securing places for their children in universities abroad. The Muslim minorities of Papua New Guinea and Tonga are among the beneficiaries of this program. RISEAP has also been instrumental in arranging pilgrimages to Mecca from places such as Fiji, Hong Kong, and Japan. Since 1981 the Malaysian Pilgrims Management and Fund Board (Tabung Haji) has assisted RISEAP by making its facilities available to these potential pilgrims.

In 1986 RISEAP established its Women's Movement, further augmenting its *daᶜwah* base. Convinced that the Muslim woman has an equally important role to play in the development of the *ummah* of the Southeast Asian and Pacific region, the organization's first president, Tunku Abdul Rahman, envisaged that through the participation of women much could be done to alleviate the suffering of Muslims, particularly of Muslim women themselves. Although the Women's Movement is guided by the same overall objectives subscribed to by the parent organization, it pays special attention to families, the upbringing of children, and the general welfare of Muslims. Its main concern is with Muslim families in areas where Muslims constitute a minority and find it difficult to cope because of differences in lifestyle, eating habits, and clothing. RISEAP's role is to help these Muslims emphasize the Islamic basis of life, to facilitate their observance of religious rituals and customs, and to create a hospitable environment for them.

Despite its regional focus, RISEAP has not been insensitive to the problems faced by Muslims in other parts of the world. It has been vociferous in articulating concern over the plight of suffering Muslims whenever possible. This dimension of RISEAP was clearly evident when it called upon other countries to overcome problems faced by Muslims in the former Yugoslavia, Bulgaria, and Albania. For *Al-nahdah* has been highlighting the struggle of Muslims all over the world in its attempt to stir Islamic consciousness among its readers. The recent appearance of the *RISEAP Newsletter* has further bolstered the image of the organization.

In 1988, RISEAP elected a new president, Haji Taib Mahmud. By then RISEAP had grown in strength: the Islamic Association de Macao, the Western Samoan Muslim League, and Pembina Imam Tauhid Islam of Indonesia were admitted as full members, while the Centre of Islamic Studies of Sri Lanka became a new associate member. Overtures have been made to bring the Chinese Muslim Association of the People's Republic of China into the fold. In 1990 a RISEAP General Assembly was held for the first time outside Malaysia, when members met in Sydney, Australia, for their biennial conference. The gathering was hosted by the Australian Federation of Islamic Councils. The meeting also saw RISEAP taking up the cause of the Sri Lankan Muslims who were facing persecution at the hands of Tamil separatists. By 1992 RISEAP's membership had risen to fifty groups.

The RISEAP-PERKIM linkage has always been strong, and it was through the latter's influence and material help that RISEAP was able to make its presence felt during its early years. Financial support from many Muslim countries enabled RISEAP to operate. In addition to Saudi Arabia, Libya also has been generous in giving aid. Working funds have also been obtained from contributions made by Islamic associations.

RISEAP's achievement in the field of transnational *daᶜwah* has primarily been due to its being a nonpolitical body championing the cause of voluntary Islamic organizations. Its particular brand of Islamic evangelism has struck an accommodation with many Muslim governments. RISEAP's First General Assembly was attended by representatives from about sixty Islamic organizations from sixteen different countries and territories of the Southeast Asian and Pacific region. Throughout its existence it has dealt with issues that invoke the loyalty of Muslims of all political shades. What has resulted is therefore at least a semblance of mutual cooperation among the countries and territories involved.

[*See also* Daᶜwah, *article on* Institutionalization; Muslim World League; PERKIM.]

BIBLIOGRAPHY

Ilias Hj. Zaidi. "Muktamar DakwaH Islamiyyah Serantau Bermula Di Kuala Lumpur Hari Ini." *Utusan Melayu*, 11 Januari 1980.

Al-nahdah (a quarterly journal of the RISEAP). See vol. 6, no. 3 (1986); vol. 8, nos. 3–4 (1988); and vol. 10, nos. 3–4 (1990).

RISEAP Newsletter, vol. 1, nos. 1–2 (1992).

Wahba. "Dakwah Di Asia Tenggara Akan Lebih Teratur." *Utusan Zaman*, 20 Januari 1980.

MOHAMAD ABU BAKAR

RELICS. The remains of holy persons may serve as a focus for devotional practices in Islam. These relics include the physical remains of holy persons—the prophet Muḥammad, saints, and martyrs—and objects with which they were associated. It is commonly believed that contact with such relics may result in the transference of blessing *(barakah)*. Purported relics of the Prophet—for example, hairs, teeth, and clothing—can be found in many parts of the Muslim world.

The veneration of relics is most commonly expressed in pilgrimage *(ziyārah)* to tombs. The model for this is the pilgrimage to the Prophet's tomb in Medina, an act highly recommended by all schools of thought in Islam. Among Shīᶜī Muslims, *ziyārah* extends to pilgrimage to the tombs of the imams as well. Undoubtedly the most common form of tomb visitation in the Muslim world is *ziyārah* to the tombs of purported Ṣūfī saints. The great saints *(awliyā')* are understood to be the direct vice-regents (*khalīfahs*) of the prophet Muḥammad and the spiritual governors of this world. Their tombs serve as their courts *(dargāh)*, where—like the Prophet in his tomb in Medina—they continue to exist in a spiritual state. From these *dargāhs* they may intercede with God on behalf of their devotees, and so tombs are often seen as sites of miracles. People go to tombs for many reasons: to fulfill vows, to gain blessings for themselves or their families, to seek cures for illness or relief from misfortune, to obey a command by a living shaykh or a spiritual command received in a dream, or simply to show love and devotion to the person buried within.

Such devotion reflects a long tradition of personal allegiance in the Islamic tradition. From its onset Islam challenged people to give allegiance not only to the message of Islam revealed in the Qur'ān, but also to its messenger. Love and devotion toward the prophet Muḥammad was a necessary corollary of embracing Islam. That devotional allegiance extended logically to those persons seen as the legitimate successors to the Prophet. For the Shīʿīs this means the imams and the Prophet's family in general. Visitation to their tombs is therefore seen as an act of devotion and love toward persons loved by God and the Prophet. The Sunnī tradition has maintained this tradition of devotional allegiance in the practice of visiting Ṣūfī tombs.

Visitation to tombs has long been a target of criticism by Islamic reformers. Scholars such as Ibn Taymīyah have objected to it as a form of *shirk* or the association of others with God, the most heinous sin in Islam. In the modern world numerous Muslim reform movements have maintained this criticism. In the nineteenth century Wahhābīs attempted unsuccessfully to stop visitation even of the tomb of Muḥammad. In Egypt the Muslim Brotherhood is critical of festivals (*mawlids*) at Ṣūfī tombs. In South Asia the reformist Deobandīs, drawing on the writings of Shah Walī Allāh, have counseled against this practice as well. Some Muslim reformers have objected to tomb visitation on the grounds that it is irrational and superstitious and an impediment to progress. Western scholars like Gustave Von Grunebaum have shared this perspective and criticized tomb visitation as a non-Islamic intrusion into Islam. However, it should be remembered that the Muslims who visit tombs do not see their devotions as non-Islamic. Indeed, there are Muslim organizations, including the Barelwīs in South Asia and numerous Ṣūfī orders (*ṭarīqahs*), that explicitly defend tomb visitation on the basis of Qur'ān and *ḥadīth*.

[*See also* Barelwīs; Deobandīs; Ḥajj; Mawlid; Sainthood; Sufism, *article on* Ṣūfī Shrine Culture; Ziyārah.]

BIBLIOGRAPHY

Goldziher, Ignácz. *Muslim Studies*. Vol. 1. Albany, N.Y., 1971. Goldziher's discussion of tomb visitation, entitled "The Veneration of Saints in Islam," is typical of the critical Western accounts.

Metcalf, Barbara D. *Islamic Revival in British India: Deoband, 1860–1900*. Princeton, 1982. Provides an interesting discussion of a reformist group critical of tomb visitation, with material on the Barelwīs.

Reeves, Edward B. *The Hidden Government: Ritual, Clientelism, and Legitimation in Northern Egypt*. Salt Lake City, 1990. Provides a detailed description of tomb visitation in Egypt.

Troll, Christian W. *Muslim Shrines in India*. Delhi, 1989. Contains excellent discussions of tomb visitation and its critics in the South Asian context.

VERNON JAMES SCHUBEL

REPENTANCE. The Arabic term *tawbah* literally means "return." When used with reference to humans it means the individual's return to God after falling into sin or error; when used with reference to God, it means that divinity has turned to the penitent with compassion.

Repentance is an informal act in Islam and does not require atonement or ecclesiastical confession. The most comprehensive expression of repentance is essentially a moral one. The penitent should be convinced that a sin did occur, show remorse, and resolve to abstain in the future. If the sin committed involves the violation of a fellow human being's rights, then restitution is a precondition to repentance. If it does not infringe on others' rights but involves an offense against God, then penitence, remorse, and a resolution to abstain are sufficient.

Classical scholars saw sin and repentance as related to the individual; in modern writings there is a notable shift in emphasis relating these to questions of morality and social reform. This trend is noticeable in the writings of the nineteenth-century reformers and culminates with their recent revivalist successors.

The Egyptian reformer Muḥammad ʿAbduh (1849–1905) and his disciple Muḥammad Rashīd Riḍā (1865–1935) stress the dimension of public acknowledgment of sin as a vital part of the act of repentance. This stems from the Qur'ān, surah 2.160, where the accent is on repentance, making amends, and acknowledging the truth by disavowing sin and error. However, the same verse concludes with the statement, "And I am the most Forgiving and the Dispenser of grace," in which God personalizes repentance. Reformist scholars understood repentance to be society's moral crusade against evil. Failing to repent means being an accomplice to wrong. The notion of repentance was harnessed as part of the project of social reform. While individual repentance was not rejected, it became subordinate to broader social concerns.

In the writings of revivalist leaders like Abu al-Aʿlā Mawdūdī (1904–1979) and Sayyid Quṭb (1906–1966), the notion of repentance as social reform takes on another guise. According to their analysis, societies have fallen into a state of modern "barbarity" that can only be remedied by the implementation of the Islamic penal code. Repentance both individual and social takes place *after* the expiation of the sin by the law. Contrast this to the traditional view of al-Shafiʿī (d. 819) that a penal sanction (*ḥadd*) lapses if it is preceded by an act of repentance. This is also the view espoused by most modernist scholars.

Contemporary revivalist and even modernist discourses on repentance are polemical and consistently oppose Christian doctrine of original sin. Individual repentance is posited as the antithesis of the crucifixion and its accompanying salvation. While these polemics are primarily directed at Christianity, they indirectly serve as a puritan countermeasure to certain strains of popular Islam in which salvation through the intercession of saints features prominently. The subtle influence of doctrines of salvation in cultures that coexist with Islam is clearly distinguishable in the notion of repentance. Both Mawdūdī and Quṭb present repentance as a doctrine of hope and describe the Christian doctrine of original sin as a doctrine of despair.

Reformist and revivalist expressions of Islam maintain that genuine repentance means a renewed commitment to the faith followed by sincere and virtuous deeds. Traditionalists part company from the other expressions of Islam by arguing that faith alone can lead to salvation after expurgatory punishment has been suffered. According to this belief, a nominal believer will not suffer perpetual damnation. Other schools of thought contend that faith and action together constitute an acceptable definition of Islamic belief.

Twentieth-century writers on repentance also derive explanations from psychology and sociology. Sayyid Quṭb, commenting on surah 25.70 regarding the one who "repents, attains to faith and does righteous deeds, God will change the evil of such persons into good," says that by a process of "positive substitution" sinful impulses are replaced by virtuous ones. Others view the Qur'ānic concept of *tawbah* not as repentance from singular identifiable violations, but rather as the transformation of personality. This resembles the Ṣūfī attitude toward repentance, in which the term denotes spiritual conversion. Whereas traditionalists insist on the confession of sin and the declaration of the truth as a precondition for repentance, modernists following the Ṣūfī tradition emphasize a change in personality as the goal of repentance. In Sufism any recollection of sin or thought of remorse is wrong; for to remember sin is to forget God and a cardinal sin. The Qur'ān constantly exhorts believers to return to God, and the prophet Muḥammad is said to have sought God's forgiveness several times a day.

[*See also* Sin.]

BIBLIOGRAPHY

Denny, Frederick Mathewson. "The Qur'anic Vocabulary of Repentance: Orientations and Attitudes." *Journal of the American Academy of Religion* 47, Supplement (December 1979).

Maudūdī, Sayyid Abū al-Aʿlā. *The Meaning of the Qur'an*. Lahore, 1978.

Muḥammad Shāfiʿ. *Maʿārif al-Qur'ān* (Urdu). Karachi, 1969.

Nicholson, Reynold A. "Tawba." In *First Encyclopaedia of Islam*, vol. 7, p. 704. Leiden, 1913–.

Quṭb, Sayyid. *Fī Ẓilāl al-Qur'ān*. Cairo and Beirut, 1981.

Rashīd Riḍā, Muḥammad. *Tafsīr al-Manār*. Beirut, n.d.

EBRAHIM MOOSA

REPUBLIC. The political label of "republic" or *al-jumhūrīyah* is one without great apparent controversy in the Islamic world. The reason for this is twofold. First, although the term might be assumed to be a Western or an alien one, as is "democracy" (*dīmuqrāṭīyah*), its root meaning in fact exists in Arabic. Lane's *Arabic-English Lexicon* (1865) defines *jumhūr* as "the generality, or main part, of men or people; the eminent, elevated or noble of them, i.e. the majority and the most eminent of them." In addition, the Arab concept of republic was also nominally compatible with the Sunnī Islamic theory of rulership, which stipulated that the ruler not be hereditary and that he be selected on the basis of consensus of the ruled by the practice of *bayʿah* or agreement of the governed. Furthermore, it is clear from the foregoing that the meaning contains assumptions of consultive elitism *(shūra)* that are quite compatible with Islamic theory and Arab political culture.

The second reason for absence of controversy is that the specific form of *al-jumhūrīyah* was poised to be utilized in the practical world of politics in the twentieth century. The Ottoman Turks had already begun to use the term to denote the Italian city-states with which they were in direct contact in the eighteenth century and earlier (Lewis, 1960–); but with the advent of colonialism in the Middle East in the nineteenth century, it was constitutional monarchy rather than republic that became the preferred modern political form.

Al-jumhūrīyah has now become the common political label of Middle Eastern revolutions in the twentieth century. In the two great modern political convulsions of the Middle East, secular in Turkey and religious in Iran, a republican form of government was adopted without great internal or external controversy. In the case of Turkey, the Ottoman Empire and the institution of the sultanate had reached their nadir during World War I. Atatürk, personally and without consultation, declared the new Turkey to be a republic in 1924, and there was little criticism from abroad. The ending of the sultanate therefore lacked significant controversy, unlike Atatürk's subsequent abolition of the caliphate, which was to call forth anger and indignation from all over the Muslim world.

Azerbaijan, in the interval between its independence from the Russian Empire in November 1918 and its absorption into the Soviet Union, became the first Muslim country to become a republic. It was followed by Lebanon in May 1926, and Syria in May 1930.

Iran tested the concept by referendum in March 1979, when its Shīʿī population registered 98.2 percent popular approval of the abolition of the monarchy and its replacement by a republic (Matthee, 1982). This was a reversal of the Iranian *ʿulamā*'s historical support of the monarch, but it is noteworthy that the new Iranian republican constitution continued to place ultimate political sovereignty with God in the doctrine of *vilāyat-i faqih* (Ar., *wilāyat al-faqīh;* the guardianship of the jurist). The latter formulation is one particular to Shiism, but nonetheless the term "republic" now appears in the formal names of the Sunnī Arab states of the Arab Republic of Egypt and the Syrian Arab Republic. The Iranian revolutionary slogan *nah gharbī, nah sharqī, jumhūrī-yi Islām* ("neither Western nor Eastern, but an Islamic republic") sums up the point that the term "republic" today is without significant controversy and is in fact understood nearly as an indigenous concept in a Muslim world presently reasserting its Islamic identity.

[*See also* Democracy; Islamic State; Nation.]

BIBLIOGRAPHY

Atatürk, Mustafa Kemal. *A Speech Delivered by Ghazi Mustapha Kemal, President of the Turkish Republic, October 1927*. Leipzig, 1929.

Enayat, Hamid. *Modern Islamic Political Thought*. Austin, 1982.

Lewis, Bernard. "Djumhūriyya." In *Encyclopaedia of Islam*, new ed., vol. 2, pp. 594–595. Leiden, 1960–.

Matthee, R. "Iran: From Divine Monarchy to Divine Republic." *Orient* 23 (December 1982): 540–556.

Osman, Fathi. "The Contract for the Appointment of the Head of an Islamic State: Bai'at al-Imam." In *State, Politics, and Islam*, edited by Mumtāz Aḥmad, pp. 51–85. Indianapolis, 1986.

Louis J. Cantori

REPUBLICAN BROTHERS. In 1945 a small group of Sudanese led by Maḥmūd Muḥammad Ṭāhā organized the Republican Party to oppose both the establishment of a Mahdist monarchy in Sudan and the unification of Sudan with the Kingdom of Egypt. The party's manifesto also called for an Islamic resurgence. Following the 1969 revolution led by Colonel Jaʿfar Nimeiri, all political parties in Sudan were banned. Ṭāhā's followers consequently changed their organization's name to the Republican Brothers or, alternatively, the New Islamic Mission. They continued to advocate a new understanding of Islam to address contemporary personal and world problems as well as to meet modern, rational-scientific concerns.

Ṭāhā was born in 1909 or 1911 in Rufa'a on the Blue Nile. By 1936 he had completed his engineering education at Gordon Memorial College (now Khartoum University). An active nationalist, he was twice arrested by the British colonial government and served more than two years in prison. After a period of seclusion and prayer that ended in October 1951, Ṭāhā emerged with his version of the "Second Message of Islam." He spread his ideas through speeches, newspaper articles, pamphlets, and books until he was arrested and hanged on 18 January 1985 by the Nimeiri government, after a grossly unfair trial.

In their writings, Ṭāhā and the Republican Brothers define religion as a behavioral system of morals employed to attain peace, genuine freedom, and ever-growing, eternal happiness. They claim that Islam combines the materialism of Judaism and the spirituality of Christianity into a single religious experience. They stress the importance of achieving inner personal peace through religion as the necessary prerequisite to achieving national and international peace.

Ṭāhā and the Republican Brothers became politically controversial by opposing President Nimeiri's policy of imposing the *sharīʿah* on Sudan's diverse peoples. They charged that the traditional *sharīʿah* based on fundamental political, economic, and social inequalities, could not be reconciled with modern constitutional government. For the Sudan, they advocated a federal democracy with economic socialism and equal political rights for all, regardless of gender or religious preference.

The Republican Brothers' argument follows from Ṭāhā's belief that the Qur'ān contains two divine messages—the First and the Second, based on the Medinese and Meccan texts, respectively. They believe that the portion of the Qur'ān revealed to Muḥammad at Mecca over a thirteen-year period directed the Prophet to call people to God by wisdom and good admonitions, not by compulsion. Muḥammad was enjoined to preach the equality before God of men and women and of people of all stations. The ruling Meccan class, fearing the economic and political consequences of these ideas, rejected this message and persecuted the Prophet. God's later messages were tailored to the specific socioeconomic and political problems that faced Muḥammad in Medina and were thus less universal. Although they greatly improved social conditions of the time, they were less egalitarian than the Meccan messages that they replaced. They legitimized compulsory conversion as well as the principles of sexual and religious inequality. The Prophet, however, continued to exemplify in his private life the high moral and social precepts embodied in the Meccan texts.

Because Islamic laws up to the present continue to be based on the allegedly inferior Medinese texts, the Republican Brothers claim that all Muslims must now turn back to the Meccan texts, or Second Message. Through *ijtihad* they must reinstitute a religion and law based on fundamental principles of racial, ethnic, sexual, and religious equality. The historic *sharīʿah,* as advocated by the Muslim Brothers of Sudan, Egypt, and Syria and the governments of Iran, Saudi Arabia, and Libya, is a primitive level of law suited to an earlier stage of cultural development.

In the early 1980s the Republican Brothers had a few hundred hard-core members of both sexes and more than a thousand sympathizers. Many members were highly educated; some were university professors. They were widely respected by Muslim moderates and Sudanese non-Muslims, but were strongly opposed by the Muslim Brothers and other Muslim fundamentalists. After Ṭāhā's execution the Republican Brothers movement fell dormant in the Sudan, which continued to be ruled by military-backed fundamentalist governments.

[*See also* Sudan.]

BIBLIOGRAPHY

Magnarella, Paul J. "The Republican Brothers: A Reformist Movement in the Sudan." *Muslim World* 72 (January 1982): 14–24. General overview of the movement, based in part on interviews with one of its leaders.

Stevens, Richard P. "Sudan's Republican Brothers and Islamic Reform." *Journal of Arab Affairs* 1 (October 1981): 135–146. Excellent general treatment.

Ṭāhā, Maḥmūd Muḥammad. *The Second Message of Islam.* Translated and Introduced by Abdullahi Ahmed An-Na'im. Syracuse, N.Y., 1987. Ṭāhā's major writing with an informative introduction by one of his important followers.

PAUL J. MAGNARELLA

RESURRECTION. *See* Eschatology; Afterlife.

REVELATION. At the basis of Islam is the idea that God periodically reveals his will, providing precise information to guide human affairs and to lead to a happy afterlife. The term *waḥy,* from the Arabic verb *waḥa,* "to put in the mind," is sometimes understood as "inspiration"; the Qur'ān uses this term not only for divine inspiration to humans but also for spiritual communication between other created beings.

Revelation, however, refers specifically to the *waḥy* that is divine inspiration given to select humans, known as prophets, for the purpose of guidance. Beginning with the first human and prophet, Adam, this process of revelation has continued throughout human history until the message of the revelation was finally preserved intact in the form of the Qur'ān.

Muslims accept not only the Qur'ān but also the Torah, the Psalms of Dāwūd (David), the Gospels of Jesus, and other works as links in the chain of divine revelation. They believe that each contains the same basic message; however, the cultural, historical, and linguistic terms of particular revelations correspond to the time and place in which each was revealed. It is the ultimate principles within the revelation that transcend time and place to provide a message of universal significance to humankind.

Understanding revelation requires careful consideration of both the particulars of context and the universals of the message for humankind. Since revelation is given to guide human affairs, then intellectual understanding and practical implementation through a reliable example are also necessary. Thus the prophets were both messengers and models.

Recent Muslim thinkers have expressed the need to free interpretation of the Qur'ānic revelation from narrow literalism and the verse-by-verse, atomistic methods of earlier exegetes. This has led to a new hermeneutics that addresses the universal relevancy of the revelation in a world of rapid and radical change. Such hermeneutics agree with the traditional opinion that revelation is a special body of knowledge linking the divine creator to humans who possess free will and an independent capacity for reasoning.

Throughout Muslim history debates have raged over the relative value of knowledge received from divine revelation and knowledge arrived at through independent reasoning. According to some philosophers, human reason can be sufficient to guide affairs and therefore equal to revelation on occasion. If the Qur'ān is revelation of God's will, however, it must be unchallengeable and without equal. Orthodox Islam—although by no means denying the reasonableness of revelation—opposes the idea that all things can be known by human reason alone. Humanity requires revelation for clear information about such areas as the unseen—the hidden mysteries of existence that inform us of the relationship between the absolute and the manifest.

No amount of literal and philological analysis can reveal information about the inner dimension of divine-human exchange. Since such information—which cannot be known through empirical means or through logical, sense-based reasoning—is nevertheless considered vital to correct guidance, humanity cannot come to know the ultimate truths except through divine revelation. Thus revelation is considered a unique and necessary area of knowledge.

[*See also* Prophethood; Theology.]

BIBLIOGRAPHY

Arberry, A. J. *Reason and Revelation*. London, 1967. As the title suggests, a thorough discussion of the subject.

Izutsu, Toshihiko. *A Comparative Study of the Key Philosophical Concepts of Sufism and Taoism: Ibn ʿArabi and Lao-Tzu, Chuang-Tzu, Part One*. Tokyo, 1966. Revised as *Sufism and Taoism*. Berkeley, 1984. Thorough linguistic analysis of Ibn al-ʿArabī's philosophical outlook. With regard to revelation, it includes a discussion of the dilemma of communication between the transcendant and the materially manifest world.

Qadir, C. A. *Philosophy and Science in the Islamic World*. London, 1988. Critical and historical overview of philosophy and science as sources of knowledge in Islam.

ĀMINA WADŪD-MUḤSIN

REVIVAL AND RENEWAL. The Arabic terms *iḥyāʾ* (revival) and *tajdīd* (renewal) are often used in the context of modern Islamic movements, but they also have important premodern roots. Premodern renewal was usually associated with a specifically designated purifier who, according to the *ḥadīth*s (Prophetic traditions), would come at the "head of each century" to renew the faith and practice of Muslims. Many puritanical reformers were, as a result, identified by their followers as the designated renewer or *mujaddid* of the era. Revival had a stronger sense of a strengthening of the spiritual dimensions of faith and practice, as seen in the writings of Abū Ḥāmid al-Ghazālī. In the modern era the terms refer to the attempts by Islamic modernizers and Salafīyah advocates to introduce more Islamic influences into the lives of Muslims who have been subject to Western currents of thought and practice particularly in the wake of the Napoleonic invasion of Egypt. Shaykh Ḥasan al-ʿAṭṭār, an Egyptian cleric who worked closely with the French experts who accompanied Napoleon, may have been one of the first reformists/revivalsts when he said: "Our countries should be changed and renewed [*tatajaddada*] through knowledge and sciences that they do not possess." A distinction should be made here between the strict and orthodox Salafīyah trend and the reformist trend championed by people such as Muḥammad ʿAbduh.

The call for revival and renewal emanated from the detection of symptoms of backwardness and stagnation by religious thinkers in Muslim societies in the nineteenth century (and in the eighteenth century in the case of Muḥammad ibn ʿAbd al-Wahhāb, founder of the Wahhābīyah). Islamic thinkers realized that something must be done to achieve a degree of progress commensurate with the fast pace of development in Europe. Islam was not seen as the cause of the problem but as the problem's solution provided that Muslims approached religion in a new way. Two major movements designed to meet this challenge were the strict Salafīyah movement and the reformist movement.

The orthodox Salafīyah movement (as represented by the Wahhābīyah doctrine) did not concern itself with competing with the West. Far from that, Ibn ʿAbd al-Wahhāb worried about the very survival of religion in the face of dangerous *bidʿah* (innovations that are religiously impermissible). The Wahhābiyah aimed at cleansing religious practice and thought from all its alien elements to save the Muslim people from divine wrath. Ibn ʿAbd al-Wahhāb believed that Muslims in his time were worse than the *kāfirs* (infidels), because they strayed very far from the right path of Muḥammad's *sunnah* (exemplary life). The solution of Ibn ʿAbd al-Wahhāb, who came from the oasis-nomad society of the Arabian Peninsula, resided in returning to the simplicity of early Islam and to the *nuṣūṣ* (religious texts) and their classical interpretations.

The Salafīyah sought to revive Islam's role in society through an emphasis on *tawḥīd* (unity of God's qualities). Ṣūfī manifestations in Arabia, such as visitations of tombs and veneration of saints, were dismissed as un-Islamic and, more seriously, as polytheistic (polytheism is the only unforgivable sin in Islam). The movement stressed that Islam alone should guide the life of Muslims, and it did not see a need for reinterpretation of texts to adapt to the modern life that was already affecting Middle Eastern societies. Yet the Wahhābīyah, like the Sanūsīyah in North Africa and the Mahdīyah in Sudan, is considered a Salafīyah movement, because it sought and attained dramatic changes in society and politics according to its idealization of the lives and religious practices of the *salaf* (the Muslim predecessors, some of whom were companions of Muḥammad).

The movement for revival and renewal is more closely associated with the reformist strand represented by Muḥammad ʿAbduh, Jamāl al-Dīn al-Afghānī, Khayr al-Dīn al-Tūnisī, ʿAbd al-Raḥmān al-Kawākibī, and many others. The thrust of the movement centered around the realization that Muslim society was failing to catch up with the advances and progress in all facets of life that were proceeding in Europe. Many of the reformers traveled to Europe, and some mastered foreign languages. The reformist/revivalist movement did not call for westernization. In fact, al-Afghānī and ʿAbduh bitterly criticized those in the Muslim world whom they accused of blindly imitating Western ways. The movement wanted to restore dignity and greatness to Muslims and Arabs through a rejuvenation of Islamic thought and practice.

Revival, in the minds of nineteenth-century Islamic reformers, was a response to the challenges posed by contact with Europe. Muslims became aware of their underdevelopment and of the cultural stagnation that prevailed in much of the Islamic world. Although Islamic reformers were willing to acknowledge the existence of acute social and political problems in the Arab world, they strongly rejected some Orientalist arguments which attributed manifestations of backwardness to Islam. Not only did al-Afghānī and ʿAbduh deny the incompatibility of science and Islam, but they believed that progress in Europe was the result of contributions from Arab/Islamic civilization. Islamic reformers also refused to blame Islam itself for problems afflicting the lives of Muslims.

The reformist movement aimed, in the tradition of Ibn Rushd, at recognizing the role of reason in people's lives. Muḥammad ʿAbduh and al-Afghānī refused to accept that reason is incompatible with *īmān* (belief). They believed that the revivalist movement would fail if Muslim clerics continued to preach the virtues of *taqlīd* (imitation of the thought and practice of early Muslims). *Taqlīd* was rejected because it was seen as a major factor in perpetuating the cultural stagnation of the Arab world and because it made the believer entirely dependent on ancient interpretations of texts. Renewal, in the eyes of the reformists, entailed renewing religion itself, not, however, because Islam had any inadequacies—they would not argue that—but because interpretations and reinterpretations of texts were part of a continuous process.

Reformists would not accept the notion that *ijtihād* (individual inquiry in legal matters) was no longer acceptable or necessary. They believed that the need for continuous *ijtihād* was dictated by the prevalent stagnation—modern problems required modern answers. Islam was seen as flexible and creative enough to adapt to the modern times.

Reformists also rejected the Salafīyah's opposition to Sufism. ʿAbduh and his students made a distinction between those Ṣūfī orders that flourished in Mamlūk and Ottoman times and the classical Ṣūfī teachers, such as Ibn al-ʿArabī. The Ṣūfī orders that were obsessed with rituals and visitations of tombs were criticized by the reformists, because they were seen as part of the problem. Many of them were also either politically passive or compromising, as was the case with Algerian Ṣūfīs, who collaborated with the French. The classical Sufism of Ibn al-ʿArabī was appreciated, because it was less ritualistic and more philosophical. Ibn al-ʿArabī's Sufism was predicated on eliminating mediators between Allāh and the believers.

Advocates of renewal and reform gained momentum after the elimination of the caliphate in 1924. Some reformers, such as ʿAbd al-Raḥmān al-Kawākibī, associated renewal in religion with major political reform. The creation of an Arab caliphate was considered necessary in order to lead the process of change and reform. Religious thinkers have always associated religious reform with political reforms, because Islam, in their opinion, covers in its major texts all facets of life. The restoration of the caliphate was—and is—seen as a step toward bringing about the unification of Muslim ranks.

Some reformers also intended to improve the status of women in society. Muḥammad ʿAbduh and, in the twentieth century, Shaykh Muḥammad al-Ghazālī have refused to attribute the legal and social inferiority of women in the Arab world to Islam. They believe that the oppressive conditions of women in most Muslim countries are the product of ignorance and of the misinterpretation of Islamic texts. ʿAbduh wanted to apply the criterion of *maṣlaḥah ʿāmmah* (public interest) to the application of laws, including religious laws. By his criterion, the abolishment of polygamy, which is sanctioned in the Qur'ān, could be rationalized. Similarly, the Islamic ban on usury could also be overcome.

Another concern for those who preached revival and renewal was in the area of education in general, and Islamic education in particular. Reforms of educational systems were viewed by ʿAbduh and others as the vehicle through which the Muslim world would revitalize itself. Reform of education entailed the absorption of sciences and discoveries that obscurantist Islamic scholars (some of whom occupied high positions at al-Azhar in ʿAbduh's time) refused to incorporate into the curricula of Islamic institutions of learning. There were calls for modernizing civil education in order to contribute to national progress and to undermine the role of Christian missionary schools. Furthermore, educational reform required, in the mind of ʿAbduh, an overhaul of the structure of al-Azhar University. Al-Azhar itself was viewed as an obstacle to the goals of revival and renewal. [*See* Azhar, al-; *and* Education, *article on* Educational Reform.]

Revival and renewal was also predicated on the belief that the subservience of clerics to the political authorities is harmful to the interests of Muslims. In the context of Islamic reform, revival and renewal are equated with the needs of a group of *ʿulamāʾ* (religious scholars) who owe their allegiance to God only, not to political authorities who control important segments of the clerical establishment and pay their salaries. Advocates of revival and renewal are often praised for the independence of their minds and for their resistance to political pressures.

Revival and renewal are often understood in national terms. During the heyday of Arab nationalism, the terms were used in reference to the Arab nation and to the interests of its people. For Islamic fundamentalists, the unit of analysis became the Islamic *ummah* (community) in general. For both the Pan-Islamists and the Arab nationalists, revival and renewal have elements of national independence and national resistance. The major names in the contemporary history of revival and renewal are associated with struggle against foreign control and occupation. In other words, revival and renewal have internal and external dimensions, and the two dimensions should be approached simultaneously.

The two terms are often used in the political literature of present-day Islamic fundamentalists. For Ḥasan al-Turābī, the influential Sudanese Islamic fundamentalist leader, *tajdīd* is required by the need for a "total revival in all aspects." Revival here is not understood to mean modernization along Western lines. The revival of the *ummah* is seen as a means toward the establishment of a new society where *sharīʿah* (Islamic law) is applied. Renewal then becomes a prerequisite for the islamization of all aspects of life. In specific terms, advocates of religious renewal call for the creation of a new system of thought and a new epistemology which is free of "corrupt" Western influence and is rooted in Islam. Turābī calls for renewing *uṣūl al-fiqh* (the fundamentals of jurisprudence) to meet the needs of the community and to provide a foundation for renewal. At times, however, Islamic fundamentalist thinkers and leaders are short on details. Islamist political literature advocates renewal and revival, but it tends to lack programmatic specifics.

A discussion of revival and renewal should also take note of the emerging consensus about political reforms. Islamic fundamentalists express dissatisfaction with the prevailing political conditions in the Muslim world, and public demands for political liberalization are sometimes articulated in the fundamentalist literature. Renewal here is related to the notion of *shūrā* (deliberation) in the Qur'ān. Fundamentalists do not condone political repression, and they express their firm belief in the efficacy of *shūrā* arrangements. Turābī calls for *tajdīd* to cover the area of political reforms by devising a mechanism for introducing a system of *shūrā*. [*See the biography of Turābī.*]

The political popularity of movements and leaders calling for revival and renewal stems from Arab public awareness of the depth of social, economic, and political problems that afflict the region. Successive military defeats at the hands of Israel have only augmented the calls for revival and renewal, because people often draw analogies to the era of the Crusades when stagnation gives way to a revival that achieves victory over enemies. What the various movements and leaders agree on is that change is needed in all facets of life in the Arab and broader Islamic world. There is no consensus on the nature of change and ways to achieve it.

The increased influence of the West, especially the United States since the demise of the Soviet Union, fuels the calls for revival. Fears abound of total control by the United States over the region and its affairs. For people to refrain from revival and renewal, according to reformists, the people of the region must willingly accept their subjugation. The open dependence by several Arab governments on U.S. military and political support increases the fears of the masses regarding attacks against the culture and religion of the region. Only through revival and renewal can the region achieve its progress without undermining its religious foundations and without losing its *aṣālah* (authenticity).

[*See also* Fundamentalism; Iṣlāḥ; Salafīyah; Wahhābīyah; *and the biographies of* ʿ*Abduh, Afghānī, Ibn* ʿ*Abd al-Wahhāb, and Kawākibī.*]

BIBLIOGRAPHY

Dessouki, Ali E. Hillal, ed. *Islamic Resurgence in the Arab World.* New York, 1982.

Esposito, John L. *Islamic Revivalism.* Washington, D.C., 1985.

Esposito, John L. *Islam and Politics.* 3d ed. Syracuse, N.Y., 1991.

Hunter, Shireen, ed. *The Politics of Islamic Revivalism.* Bloomington, 1988.

Kerr, Malcolm H. *Islamic Reform: The Political and Legal Theories of Muḥammad ʿAbduh and Rashīd Riḍā.* Berkeley, 1966.

Levtzion, Nehemia, and John Obert Voll, eds. *Eighteenth-Century Renewal and Reform in Islam.* Syracuse, N.Y., 1987.

Voll, John Obert. "Renewal and Reform in Islamic History: *Tajdid* and *Islah.*" In *Voices of Resurgent Islam,* edited by John L. Esposito, pp. 32–47. New York and Oxford, 1983.

AsʿAD AbuKhalil

REVOLUTION. In contemporary Islamic discourse, there are various terms that bear on the social-science concept of revolution as a rising up against constituted authority. However, from a classical Muslim point of view, revolution has pejorative connotations, since it signifies impious attempts to overthrow the order established by believers who are following the commands of Allāh. Among the terms frequently employed by Islamists to refer to revolution in this negative sense are *fitnah* (temptation, trial, sedition, dissension against Allāh), *maʿṣīyah* (disobedience, insubordination, refractoriness, revolt), and *riddah* (a turning away or back from, i.e., apostasy from Islam).

Modern Islamists often cite Qur'ānic verses condemning the *fitnah* of the Prophet's early enemies: "fight those who fight you wherever you find them and expel them who had expelled you, for *fitnah* is worse than killing" (surah 2.191), and "fight them until *fitnah* comes to an end and Allāh's religion prevails" (surahs 2.193 and, with a minor variation, 8.39). The term *maʿṣīyah* appears twice in the Qur'ān (8.58 and 8.59), in both cases in reference to those who are in rebellion against the Prophet. The term *riddah* is not found as such in the Qur'ān, but it does appear in one of its verbal forms (*irtadda/yartaddu*) in surahs 2.217 and 5.54 ("whosoever among you turns away from his religion"), and in surah 47.25 ("and those who have turned back [from Islam] after guidance had been shown them"). For its part, *riddah* came into use shortly after Qur'ānic revelation had ceased, and it referred to the defection of the Arab tribes after the death of the Prophet in 632 and their forcible return to the Islamic fold.

Another term that signifies rebellion against Islam but which only appeared after the end of the revelations is *khārij* (pl., khawārij; lit., "to go out"), which referred to the first schismatics in Islam during the caliphate of ʿAlī ibn Abī Ṭālib (r. 656–661). *Khārij, fitnah, maʿṣīyah,* and *riddah* are employed by Islamists as antonyms for the word *jihād* (striving for the sake of Allāh). *Jihād* therefore always appears as a positive value in Islamic discourse.

Until the modern period, those few writers who justified rebellion against the ruler of the *ummah* (community) (e.g., al-Jāḥiẓ [d. 868/69] and Ibn Taymīyah [d. 1328]) did so on grounds of the impiety of that ruler, rather than on the abstraction that he was a bad ruler and his government was bad. But impiety itself is a relative term. Thus, Ibn Taymīyah ruled that Muslims should rise up against the Mongols for their extraordinary abominations against the faith (such as considering

Chinggis Khan the son of Allāh). Yet Ibn Taymīyah held his counsel in regard to the Mamlūk rulers of his time, whose behavior could be considered at least as intolerable as some of the contemporary rulers whom Islamists today declare to be unbelievers.

This reluctance to advocate resistance in all but the most reprehensible instances of misrule is instructive. Resistance could lead to *fitnah,* creating disorder in the *ummah.* But the doctrine of salvation requires the integrity of that *ummah,* for people must not only believe in Allāh's laws but establish and maintain the community which is the institutionalized expression of those laws. Accordingly, most jurists advised against behavior that would put the *ummah* at risk. Those jurists who served through appointment by putatively wrongdoing rulers have had to be particularly careful in their *fatwā*s (authoritative opinions) in regard to questions of obedience. Thus, in 1981 the grand *muftī* of Egypt, Shaykh Jād al-Ḥaqq ʿAlī Jād al-Ḥaqq, ruled in the wake of the assassination of President Anwar el-Sadat that Muslims were obliged to do everything in their power peacefully and through persuasion to return an unjust ruler to the true path and to abjure violence.

The modern terms for revolution, all of Arabic derivation, are: in Arabic, *thawrah* (from a root meaning a stirring up [of dust]); in Persian, *inqilāb* (from a root meaning overturn); and, in Turkish, *ikhtilal* (from a root meaning disturbance, confusion) and *inkılab.* They mainly came into use after the French Revolution and generally have positive connotations when used by nationalists resisting the despotism of unjust secular rulers, although some Turkish writers, critical of revolutionary developments in France, did employ *inkılab* in a pejorative sense. Of these four terms, only *thawrah* appears to have antedated the French Revolution in its active participial form *(thāʾir)* to refer to those who had either rebelled against established Muslim rulers or who had replaced them once they had fallen.

In the modern period, beginning with the Wahhābī movement in the mid-eighteenth century and continuing through a variety of revivalist movements in West, North, and East Africa, the Middle East, and Asia, Islamic movements arose to condemn what they perceived to be heretical deviations from Islam. In most cases, these movements were spurred by deep antipathy to Western colonialism and imperialism, which began as armed intervention or economic penetration but inevitably involved political and cultural threats to the integrity of the *ummah.*

Although disgruntled secular officials of the Ḥusaynid, Muḥammad ʿAlī, Ottoman, and Qājār dynasties played a major role in coining and elaborating on such terms as *thawrah, inqilāb/inkılab,* and *ikhtilal,* these terms have also sometimes been appropriated by certain members of the *ʿulamāʾ,* such as Jamāl al-Dīn al-Afghānī (1838/39–1897).

Interestingly, some Muslim jurists referred not to the Muslims but to the British as the "rebels" in the events known in the West as the great Sepoy Rebellion of 1857–1858 in India, because the British were seen to be violating the terms of the agreements that they had earlier contracted with representatives of the *ummah* on the subcontinent. Colonel Aḥmad ʿUrābī's rebellion in Egypt in 1881–1882 was glossed by contemporaries as a *thawrah,* as were the anti-British uprisings of the Egyptian people in 1919. The insurrection of southern Iraqis in 1920 was viewed as a *jihād* by that movement's clerical leaders, but because the Sunnī areas did not join, it would be misleading to term it as a general *jihād* of Muslims against the infidels.

In Iran during the Constitutional Revolution of 1905–1909, the term *inqilāb* was in some use, but even more current was the neologism *mashrūṭah,* ("to make conditional," i.e., to lay down stipulations [on the autocratic rule of the shah]). In other places, the terms *qiyāmah* and *nahḍah* (Pers., *qiyām* and *nihzat;* lit. a "rising up") have acquired currency, as has the more metaphorical word, *ṣaḥwah* (a coming to consciousness, awakening). These three words, along with such terms as *maʿrakah* and *niḍāl* (both of which may be translated as "struggle"), have come into increasing use, frequently to connote fighting on behalf of righteous or progressive causes.

One of the costs of the profusion of terms is a certain diffusion of meaning. The use of *thawrah* to refer to phenomena as divergent as simple coups d'état, extensive urban insurrections, and profoundly transformative social revolutions has done little to help provide analytical clarity. In any case, Islamists try to avoid the use of terms like *thawrah,* because they have been until recently the virtually exclusive preserve of secular nationalists. Islamist Arabs, however, refer to the Iranian Revolution of 1979 as *al-thawrah al-Īrānīyah,* so this generalization about reluctance to employ words closely associated with secular movements must be qualified.

Any discussion of revolution in the Islamic world must account for the prominent role in the nineteenth century of Ṣūfī movements. In North Africa, Sudan, and Egypt, the great Ṣūfī shaykhs, Muṣṭafā ibn ʿAzzūz (d. 1866), ʿAbd al-Qādir (d. 1883), Muḥammad al-Mahdī (d. 1885), Abd el-Krim (Muḥammad ibn ʿAbd al-Karīm al-Khaṭṭābī, d. 1920), ʿAbd al-Ḥamīd ibn Bādīs (d. 1940), and Ḥasan al-Bannā' (d. 1949), all took up the banner of revolt against colonialist rule. Their counterparts in Central and South Asia, often inspired by the examples of their fellow Muslims elsewhere, also followed this pattern. The Qur'ānic term *jihād* suffused the discourse of these leaders in their efforts to mobilize the Muslims in anticolonialist struggles. Also relevant in this connection is the term *tajdīd* ("renewal"), which came increasingly into use, although it designates essentially reformist movements often unaccompanied by widescale collective protest. [*See the biographies of ʿAbd al-Qādir, Abd el-Krim, Ibn Bādīs, and Bannā'; for al-Mahdī, see* Mahdīyah.]

More recently still, collective protest against ruling regimes became the *cri de coeur* of Abū al-Aʿlā Mawdūdī (1903–1979) in India and Pakistan, Sayyid Quṭb (1906–1966) in Egypt, and ʿAlī Sharīʿatī (1933–1977) and Ayatollah Ruhollah al-Musavi Khomeini (1902–1989) in Iran. In the cases of Mawdūdī and Quṭb, the key word was *jihād,* and the point of reference was Ibn Taymīyah's *fatwā* against the Mongols. Although Quṭb modeled his thinking greatly on Mawdūdī's, Mawdūdī stopped short of pronouncing *takfīr* (unbelief) on Muslims, whereas Quṭb extended it to those he believed were nominal, hence "false," believers. [*See the biographies of Mawdūdī and Quṭb.*]

Somewhat in contrast to Quṭb and Mawdūdī are the Shīʿī activists, Sharīʿatī and Khomeini. Although the word *jihād* was revered by them both, they (especially Sharīʿatī) also employed the apparently passive term, *intiẓār* ("waiting"), to powerful effect in mobilizing the faithful of the Hidden Imam. In this way Sharīʿatī called on devotees to take the initiative against injustice and thus prepare the way for the Mahdi. He termed this activism *intiẓār-i muṣbat* ("positive waiting") and invidiously contrasted it with *intiẓār-i manfī* ("negative waiting"). [*See* Intiẓār; *and the biography of Sharīʿatī.*]

Of course, no account of the concept of revolution in Islamic literature would be complete without mention of Ayatollah Khomeini of Iran. He repeatedly used the phrase *inqilāb-i Islāmī* (Islamic revolution) to refer to the movement that overthrew the shah in 1979 and established rule by the clergy (Pers., *vilāyat-i faqīh;* Ar., *wilāyat al-faqīh*), led by himself. Khomeini purported to find the doctrinal basis for clerical rule in a *ḥadīth* attributed to the sixth Shīʿī imam, Jaʿfar al-Ṣādiq (d. 765) regarding the *ex ante* appointment of judges to arbitrate technical disputes over debts or inheritance. Deliberately conflating the differences between the role of judges to arbitrate and that of sovereign rulers to govern, Khomeini claimed that the imam's *ex ante* appointment was the key legal basis for contemporary jurists to take over executive authority in the modern state. Having come this far, however, it is intriguing that Khomeini demurred from advocating an anticolonial *jihād* against the United States or the West, for all of his animosity toward them. [*See* Wilāyat al-Faqīh; *and the biography of Khomeini.*]

Since the execution in 1966 of Sayyid Quṭb by the Egyptian government of Gamal Abdel Nasser, a variety of radical groups have emerged among Sunnīs, inspired by Quṭb's last book, *Milestones* (1964). These groups advocate violence to overthrow existing regimes and to apply immediately what they believe to be *sharīʿah* (the holy law of Islam). The radical Sunnī movements include various groups in Egypt, such as al-Fannīyah al-ʿAskarīyah (The Technical Military Academy Group), Jamāʿat al-Takfīr wa al-Hijrah (Pronouncing Unbelief on Infidels and Emigrating to Islam), al-Jihād, and al-Jamāʿat al-Islāmīyah (the Islamic Group); and Ḥamās in the Gaza Strip and the West Bank. [*See* Takfīr wa al-Hijrah, Jamāʿat al-; Jihād Organizations; Jamāʿat al-Islāmīyah, al-; *and* Ḥamās.]

Other groups that began more moderately but have become more radicalized because of suppression include certain supporters of the leader of the Sudanese Muslim Brotherhood, Ḥasan al-Turābī; the Syrian Muslim Brotherhood leader, Saʿīd Ḥawwā; Rāshid al-Ghannūshī of the Tunisian Nahḍah; and ʿAbbāsī Madanī, the leader of the Algerian Jabhat al-Inqādh al-Islāmī (Islamic Salvation Front). The Tunisian and Algerian organizations are ironically better known by their French nomenclature, the Tendence Tunisien and the Front Islamien du Salut (FIS), respectively. [*See* Muslim Brotherhood, *articles on* Muslim Brotherhood in the Sudan *and* Muslim Brotherhood in Syria; Ḥizb al-Nahḍah; Islamic Salvation Front; *and the biographies of Turābī, Ghannūshī, and Madanī.*]

In Afghanistan, this form of radicalism among some Islamic groups evolved in the course of the devastating internal war fought against Soviet occupying forces between 1979 and 1989. The Shīʿī world also has seen the emergence of revolutionary groups intent on overthrowing the regimes in Iraq and Lebanon, where the groups are called, respectively, Ḥizb al-Daʿwah and Ḥizbullāh. [See Mujāhidīn, *article on* Afghan Mujāhidīn; Ḥizb al-Daʿwah al-Islāmīyah; *and* Ḥizbullāh, *article on* Ḥizbullāh in Lebanon.]

The common denominator for all these modern movements of collective protest in the Islamic world would appear to be the determination that Islam is both *dīn wa dawlah,* both religion and state. [*See* Dawlah.] If it is true that there is no separation of religion from politics in Islam, then protesting against political injustices becomes a religious duty *(farḍ al-kifāyah).* Apart from the Prophet himself and, for Shīʿīs, Imam Ḥusayn (d. 680), the authority most often mentioned by contemporary Islamists to justify their actions is Ibn Taymīyah. As he put it: "It must be known that governing the people [*wilāyat amr al-nās*] is one of the most important tasks of religion. Indeed, there is no establishment of religion without it. Men's interests will only be secured by coming together because they need each other. And upon coming together, they must have a leader" (1963, p. 74).

As already noted, Ibn Taymīyah did not protest against the impiety of the Mamlūks. It is clear, however, that revolution is no longer considered invariably harmful to the interests of the *ummah.* For some contemporary Islamists, the classic view that *fitnah* must be avoided at all costs has lost its compelling force and even come to be seen as a recipe for conniving with unjust rulers in their suppression of the Muslims.

[*See also* Fitnah.]

BIBLIOGRAPHY

Arjomand, Said Amin. *The Turban for the Crown.* New York, 1988. In-depth study of the religious and political causes of the revolution.

Ibn Taymīyah, Aḥmad ibn ʿAbd al-Ḥalīm. *Al-siyāsah al-sharʿīyah fī iṣlāḥ al-rāʿī wa-al-raʿīyah* (The Politics of the Holy Law of Islam in Reforming the Leader and His Subjects). Cairo, 1963. Inquiry into the relationship between religion and politics in Islam, by the canonical jurist of contemporary Islamists.

Jansen, J. J. G. *The Neglected Duty.* New York and London, 1986. Important examination of the ideologies and policies of radical Islam in Egypt since the June 1967 war.

Kepel, Gilles. *Muslim Extremism in Egypt.* Berkeley, 1985. Another significant study of radical Islamic groups in Egypt since the 1970s.

Khomeini, Ruhollah al-Musavi. *Islam and Revolution: Writings and Declarations of Imam Khomeini.* Translated and edited by Hamid Algar. Berkeley, 1981. Valuable compendium of Ayatollah Khomeini's major speeches and writings, including his most famous work, *Islamic Government.*

Lewis, Bernard. "Islamic Concepts of Revolution." In *Revolution in the Middle East,* edited by P. J. Vatikiotis, pp. 30–40. London, 1972. Illuminating overview of the evolution of terminology employed by Muslims to refer to collective protest.

Peters, Rudolph. *Islam and Colonialism: The Doctrine of Jihad in Modern History.* The Hague, 1979. Incisive exploration of the classic formulation of *jihād* doctrine, and its pertinence to a variety of cases of anticolonial rebellion in the modern period.

Quṭb, Sayyid. *Milestones.* Beirut, 1978. Handbook of contemporary radical Islamists, advocating the creation of countersocieties in the Muslim world which then would overthrow their governments.

SHAHROUGH AKHAVI

RIBĀ. *See* Interest.

RIḌĀ, RASHĪD. *See* Rashīd Riḍā, Muḥammad.

RIFĀʿĪYAH. The Sunnī Ṣūfī order known as the Rifāʿīyah played an important role in the institutionalization of Sufism. In all likelihood, until the fifteenth century it was the most prevalent Ṣūfī order. Thereafter the popularity of the Rifāʿīyah continued in the Arab world, where at the end of the nineteenth century and the beginning of the twentieth the Rifāʿī order possessed the greatest number of *tekke*s. Since then the order experienced a decline until recent years, when Rifāʿī activity began to increase.

The shaykh most responsible for its early renown was Aḥmad ibn ʿAlī al-Rifāʿī (1106–1182), who spent nearly his entire life in southern Iraq's marshlands. His Ṣūfī lineages include both Junayd al-Baghdādī (d. 910) and Sahl al-Tustarī (d. 896). In 1145 al-Rifāʿī became shaykh of the order when his uncle (who was also his shaykh) appointed him to be his successor. Al-Rifāʿī then established his center in Umm ʿAbīdah, a village in the district of Wāsit, where he later died. Under his guidance the order flourished. The spreading of the order beyond Iraq was due to disciples who fanned out throughout the Middle East. New Rifāʿī branches and even distinct orders were formed by these disciples who initially had been affiliated with al-Rifāʿī. The most important of these new orders were the Badawīyah, Dasūqīyah, and Alwānīyah. In time, branches of the Rifāʿī order increased, with the position of shaykh generally becoming hereditary.

Although existing elsewhere, the Rifāʿī order is most significant in Turkey, southeastern Europe, Egypt, Palestine, Syria, and Iraq, with a nascent presence in the United States. In late Ottoman Turkey the Rifāʿīyah was an important order, with Rifāʿīs comprising about seven percent of those affiliated with Ṣūfī orders in Istanbul. At that time one of the most important branches of the Rifāʿī order was the Ṣayyādī branch, which owed its significance to Shaykh Abū al-Hudā Muḥammad al-Ṣayyādī's (1850–1909) influence on the Ottoman sultan Abdülhamid II (r. 1876–1909). More recently in Turkey, Kenan Rifaî (d. 1950) was a Rifāʿī shaykh whose circle included many highly cultured and educated Turks, among them women and Christians. He taught a Sufism of universal love. This tendency has been modified of late by Samiha Ayverdi—who after Rifāʿī's death has guided those devoted to his teachings—with her publication of a sharply political work, *Let Us Be Not Slaves but Masters* (Istanbul, 1979).

In the modern period in southeastern Europe, the Rifāʿīs have been active in Albania, Bulgaria, Greece, and Yugoslavia. Beginning in 1936 the Albanian Rifāʿīs joined a coalition of Albanian Ṣūfī orders called Drita Hyjnore (The Divine Light). In the former Yugoslavia, of its nine Ṣūfī orders in 1985, the Rifāʿī order was third in importance, having centers in Skopje (Macedonia), Kosova, and Sarajevo. The Rifāʿīs of the Prizren *tekke* in Kosova became well known through the UNESCO audio recording of their *dhikr* as well as three documentaries of the ritual. In the early 1990s numerous dervishes of the Rifāʿī order have been killed fighting the Serbs' "ethnic cleansing."

In the Arab world, the Rifāʿī order has a significant presence in Egypt, Palestine, Lebanon, Syria, and its birthplace Iraq. In the early part of the nineteenth century in Egypt, there was no central authority among the Rifāʿīyah. As of 1970, however, the supreme head of the Rifāʿī order in Egypt was Maḥmūd Kamāl Yā Sīn, although he was also head of the ʿAmrīyah branch of the order. The Egyptian Rifāʿīs, like most Egyptian Ṣūfīs, feel that one of the factors that make the Ṣūfīs distinct from other Muslims is their devotion to the Prophet and his family. In Palestine, in 1981 the main active Rifāʿī shaykhs were Kāmil al-Jaʿbarī of Hebron and Naẓmī ʿAwkal of Nablus. The Rifāʿīs of Tripoli, Lebanon, were active as of 1984; at that time there were five well-known *zāwiyah*s where the ritual of the *dhikr* was still practiced. In Syria the Rifāʿī order, after the Naqshbandī, is probably the most widespread and dynamic of the orders. As of the early 1980s the most significant Syrian branch was that of ʿAbd al-Hakīm ʿAbd al-Bāsiṭ al-Saqbānī; he and those affiliated with him have published numerous writings of Rifāʿī shaykhs. The chief branch of the Rifāʿī order in Iraq has been headed by the al-Rāwī family. Recently, under the direction of Shaykh Khāshī al-Rāwī of Baghdād, the Rifāʿīs of Iraq—like those of Syria—have published a number of older Rifāʿī texts.

There are currently at least three Rifāʿī branches in the United States. Shaykh Taner Vargonen, based in Northern California, has a Qādirī-Rifāʿī lineage deriving from Muḥammad Anṣārī (d. 1978) of Istanbul. Since 1992 another Turkish Rifāʿī, Mehmet Çatalkaya (Şerif Baba), has overseen the establishment of *tekke*s in Chapel Hill, North Carolina and in Manhattan; Şerif Baba's shaykh was Burhan Efendi of Izmir. The third Rifāʿī branch is located in the state of New York. Dr. Muhyiddin Shakoor, a counseling psychologist, writes about his involvement with them in *The Writing on the Water* (Dorset, Great Britain, 1987). His shaykh is connected by lineage to Rifāʿīs of Kosova.

As an example of Aḥmad al-Rifāʿī's teaching, Shaʿrānī (d. 1565) notes that he spoke of traditional Ṣūfī stations *(maqāmāt)* such as piety *(waraʿ)*, worship *(taʿabbud)*, love *(maḥabbah)*, gnosis *(maʿrifah)*, and unification *(tawḥīd)*. These would give rise, respectively, to abandonment of calamities *(āfāt)*, constant striving *(ijtihād)*, melting *(dhawabān)* and rapture *(haymān)*, passing away *(fanāʾ)* and effacement *(maḥw)*, and the affirmation *(ithbāt)* and presence of the Divine *(ḥuḍūr)* (*Al-ṭabaqāt al-kubrā*, Cairo, 1954, vol. 1, p. 141).

Among the practices of the Rifāʿīs their distinctive *dhikr* is noteworthy. On account of it they were known as the "howling dervishes." Formerly some Rifāʿīs were notorious for including in their rites practices such as piercing their skin with swords and eating glass. Such practices traveled with the Rifāʿī order as far as the Malay archipelago, but in recent times the Rifāʿī order has been known for its rejection of any practices that are alien to Islam. This rejection of *bidʿah* is what attracted ʿAbd al-Salām Muḥammad ʿAmrīyah (1965), the shaykh of Maḥmūd Kāmil Yāsīn, to the Rifāʿīyah. One soundly Islamic practice found among some Rifāʿīyah, occurring during the initiation rite, is that the spiritual director may inculcate the *dhikr "Lā ilāha illā Allāh"* (No god but God) in the devotee. This may also take form as a vocal *dhikr* recited regularly by the Rifāʿīs in their *zāwiyah*. In some Rifāʿī branches the devotees recite various litanies and invoke names of God such as *Allāh*, *Hū* (He), *Ḥayy* (Living), *Ḥaqq* (Real), *Qayyūm* (Self-subsistent), *Raḥmān* (Compassionate), and *Raḥīm* (Merciful). Finally, in certain branches of the Rifāʿīyah devotees must go into seclusion and undertake a spiritual retreat *(khalwah)* for a least a week at the beginning of the month of Muḥarram.

The Rifāʿī order exhibits a wide variety of practices and teachings that scholars have not yet adequately studied. Although the presence of the Rifāʿīyah is threatened in the Balkans and has only a foothold in the United States, it is indeed significant in Turkey as well as in much of the Arab world.

BIBLIOGRAPHY

Bannerth, Ernst. "La Rifāʿiyya en Egypte." *Mélanges: Institut Dominicain d'Études Orientales du Caire* 10 (1970): 1–35. Limited in scope, but no other Western secondary source covers the Egyptian Rifāʿīyah.

De Jong, Frederick. *Ṭuruq and Ṭuruq-Linked Institutions in Nineteenth Century Egypt*, Leiden, 1978. References on the organization of the Rifāʿīyah are found throughout the work.

Najjār, ʿĀmir. *Al-Ṭuruq al-Ṣūfīyah fī Miṣr*. Cairo, 1978. Contains a chapter on the Rifāʿīyah and includes discussion of Rifāʿī practices.

Öztürk, Yaşar Nuri. *The Eye of the Heart*. Translated by Richard Blakney. Istanbul, 1988. An abridged translation of *Tasavvufun Rûhu ve tarîkatlar*. Istanbul, 1988. Contains a short chapter on the Rifāʿīyah.

Popovic, Alexandre, and Gilles Veinstein. *Les Ordres Mystiques Dans L'Islam: Cheminements et situation actuelle*. Paris, 1986. This indispensible collection supplements Trimingham and contains articles by a number of scholars on the Ṣūfī orders in the modern world. For the Rifāʿīyah see especially the contributions of F. de Jong, Popovic, and Kreiser.

Trimingham, J. Spencer. *The Sufi Orders in Islam*. London, 1971. Despite gaps it is the most comprehensive work on the Ṣūfī orders. It is out of print.

Wāsiṭī, ʿAbd al-Raḥmān al-. *Ṭiryāq al-muḥibbīn*. Cairo, 1887–1888. Contains the earliest hagiography of Aḥmad al-Rifāʿī.

Alan A. Godlas

RIGHTLY GUIDED CALIPHS.

Sunnī Muslims see the first four successors of the Prophet as caliphs who were "rightly guided" or "following the right path," and refer to them by the appellation *al-khulafā' al-rāshidūn*. (Shīʿīs in general reject the legitimacy of the first three successors.) The usage was adopted from the dominant Sunnī tradition by modern writers, and consequently the period between the death of the Prophet and the accession of the Umayyad dynasty in 661 CE is often referred to as that of the Rightly Guided Caliphs. Those caliphs are Abū Bakr (r. 632–634), ʿUmar ibn al-Khaṭṭāb (634–644), ʿUthmān ibn ʿAffān (644–656), and ʿAlī ibn Abī Ṭālib (656–661). For Sunnīs this period, at least up to the middle of ʿUthmān's caliphate, was a golden age when the caliphs were consciously guided by the practice of the Prophet.

Externally the period saw the establishment of Arab Muslim rule over the heartlands of the Middle East. By about 650 Syria, Iraq, Egypt, and western Iran were under Arab control, and the way was prepared for the expansion of the next century or so. The conquests outside Arabia followed the unification of Arabia under Islam by the Riddah (Apostasy) wars during the caliphate of Abū Bakr.

For the internal history of the nascent Muslim state during the period of the Rightly Guided Caliphs we are dependent entirely on Muslim tradition as it was compiled in works written at a significantly later date. Because that tradition often reflects the views of the different groups, such as the Sunnīs and Shīʿīs, that were developing as it was being formed, it is often difficult to distinguish between actual events and subsequent interpretations.

The origins of the institution of the caliphate itself are shown to have resulted from a series of ad hoc decisions not really distinguished from the recognition of individual rulers. ʿUmar is reported to have been the first to use the title caliph *(khalīfah)* in a self-conscious way. All the Rightly Guided Caliphs had been prominent companions of the Prophet and belonged to the tribe of Quraysh, but each obtained office in a different manner—there was no accepted procedure of appointment or election. Shīʿī tradition argues that the Prophet designated his cousin and son-in-law ʿAlī as his successor, but the historical tradition in general reflects the Sunnī view that the Prophet died without leaving instructions for the succession.

ʿUmar is portrayed as the dominant personality among these caliphs. Not only is he shown to have been instrumental in securing the appointment of his predecessor Abū Bakr, there is also a tendency to attribute to him many of the fundamental institutions of the classical Islamic state. ʿUthmān, who is generally reported to have been responsible for the formation of the text of the Qur'ān as we know it, is described as personally pious but lacking the character needed to withstand the demands made on him by his unscrupulous relatives.

The murder of ʿUthmān by malcontents from the garrison of Fustat in Egypt in the summer of 656 opened a period known as the Fitnah (civil war). The fourth caliph ʿAlī had to face opposition from several different quarters and was himself murdered early in 661. In tradition the Fitnah brings about the disintegration of the previously united community, the takeover of the caliphate by the Umayyad family, and the end of the time when Islam had its center in Arabia. Although Muslim tradition tends to focus on the personalities of the protagonists, modern scholars have sought the deeper political, economic, and social tensions resulting from the development of the Muslim state under the Rightly Guided Caliphs.

[*See also* Caliph; Fitnah; Muḥammad, *article on* Life of the Prophet; *and the biography of* *ʿAlī ibn Abī Ṭālib*.]

BIBLIOGRAPHY

Kennedy, Hugh. *The Prophet and the Age of the Caliphates: The Islamic Near East from the Sixth to the Eleventh Century.* London and New York, 1986. See pages 50–81.

Levi della Vida, Giorgio. "ʿOmar ibn al-Khaṭṭāb" In *Encyclopaedia of Islam,* vol. 6, pp. 982–984. Leiden, 1913–.

Levi della Vida, Giorgio. "ʿOthmān b. ʿAffān." In *Encyclopaedia of Islam,* vol. 6, pp. 1008–1011. Leiden, 1913–.

Madelung, Wilferd. "Imāma." In *Encyclopaedia of Islam,* new ed., vol. 3, pp. 1163–1169. Leiden, 1960–. Summary of discussions about the legitimacy and status of the caliphs.

Vaglieri, Laura Veccia. "ʿAlī b. Abī Ṭālib." In *Encyclopaedia of Islam,* new ed., vol. 1, pp. 381–386. Leiden, 1960–.

Von Grunebaum, G. E. *Classical Islam: A History, 600–1258.* London, 1970. See pages 49–63.

Watt, W. Montgomery. "Abū Bakr." In *Encyclopaedia of Islam,* new ed., vol. 1, pp. 109–111. Leiden, 1960–.

G. R. HAWTING

RISALE-I NUR. *See* Nurculuk.

RITES OF PASSAGE. Rituals conducted at different stages of life, from conception until death and after, are means through which human beings live and act religiously. The terms "life-cycle rituals" or "*rites de passage,*" as described by Arnold van Gennep, embrace ritualistic ceremonies associated with conception, birth, puberty, marriage, death, and other significant events.

The transformative effect of rites of passage reinforces the religious worldview at both the individual and communal levels of experience. As vehicles for the transmission of religious symbols, values, self-understanding, and culture, the rites reconstruct and renew life. Thus they play an important role in the religio-cultural framework of a community.

The rites of passage of Islam provide Muslims with meaning as they progress through different life-stages. In this article, the term refers to rites other than the religious practices known as the Five Pillars of Islam.

Islamic rites of passage are the products of the encounter between the worldview of Islam and cultures within and outside Arabia. Contrasting elements of uniformity and variety in these rituals highlights the distinction between normative and popular Islam and reflects the cultural diversity of the Muslim world. As a system of symbol and action, the Islamic rites of passage play an important role in reaffirming the Islamic worldview at both the ideational and experiential dimensions of life, thought, and culture.

The prophet Muḥammad selectively adapted certain pre-Islamic rites of passage of Arabia to conform with the main beliefs of Islam. With the spread of Islam, the islamized life-cycle rituals of Arabia played a determining role in reshaping the non-Arabian rites of newly converted Muslim communities around the world.

Islam, like all religions, addresses questions concerning the existential dimension of life. The Qur'ān views the purpose of life as *ʿibādah*—serving God through submission and thanksgiving (Qur'ān, 2.21, 51.56). Hence the rites of passage of Islam are acts that symbolize this belief at all stages and in various dimensions of life. Generally, in terms of religious experience, life-cycle rituals are often perceived as a medium for enhancing Islamic spirituality and cultivating purity of intention for God alone.

Islam perceives sexuality as a natural dimension of life, subjected to ethical principles and rules aimed at maintaining social morality. The Qur'ān and the *sunnah* regard sexual relations between married partners as an expression of love and also as the means of human regeneration. They also contain recommendations concerning the rules and etiquette of conjugal relations. In order to maintain psychological balance between spirituality and corporeality, the two natural dimensions of humanity, the couple recite the following prayer while engaging in lovemaking: "In the name of Allāh, O Allāh, protect me and what you will bestow upon us (our offspring) from Satan" (*Ṣaḥīḥ al-Bukhārī,* vol. 7, section 62, chapter 67). Sexual intercourse must be followed by the *ghusl* or ritual bath, involving thorough washing of the whole body. This is a symbolic act of restoring a normal state of physical cleanliness necessary before engaging in rituals such as prayer and fasting.

At the birth of an infant, the *adhān* (call to prayer) is recited in its right ear, and the *iqāmah* (call to establish prayer) in its left. The infant is given a name, preferably derived from those of the prophets, their wives, or their companions. Alternatively, the name may be formed from the prefix *ʿAbd* ("servant") and an attribute of God; for example, the name ʿAbd al-ʿAzīz means "servant of the Almighty." On the seventh day the infant's hair is shaved, and the *ʿaqīqah,* an ancient Arab ritual of sacrificing a goat or sheep, is performed. The *ʿaqīqah* is perceived as an act that symbolically expresses gratitude to God and happiness for the birth of a child. The prophet Muḥammad islamized the pre-Islamic Arabian ritual of *ʿaqīqah* by associating its meaning with Abraham's willingness to sacrifice his son Ismāʿīl. It symbolizes gratitude to God. The meat of the sacrificed animal is distributed among the poor, neighbors, and relatives.

Khitān (circumcision), the surgical removal of the foreskin of the penis, is an ancient Arabo-Semitic practice. Though not mentioned in the Qur'ān, *khitān* is traditionally identified as an act dating back to the time of the prophet Ibrāhīm (Abraham). *Khitān* is a *sunnah*—a custom, and not a legal obligation. Unlike the case of Judaism, circumcision has no doctrinal significance in Islam. It is viewed by Muslims as an act of *ṭahārah* (hygiene) and a method for prevention of diseases of the urinary tract. In the past there were elaborate ceremonies associated with male circumcision, each reflecting the diversity found in the Muslim culture. Some of these ceremonies are still observed in rural areas, particularly in regions of West and South Asia and also the western and northern portions of Africa. Circumcision has traditionally been performed between the ages of three and seven years, or before reaching puberty. In rural areas it is normally performed by a barber; however, with the spread of modern medicine, most male infants are now surgically circumcised in hospitals, either on the second day after birth or before puberty. In modern times the ceremonial dimension of circumcision has also been greatly diminished. Being a custom, circumcision is not obligatory for adult converts to Islam.

The ancient Arabs also practiced *khafḍ,* a slight excision of the clitoris. *Khafḍ* was tolerated during the early years of Islam but gradually fell into disuse; it is no longer practiced in the heartland of Islam. *Ḥadīth* texts indicate that Muḥammad expressed reservations about its practice. *Khafḍ* is not clitoridectomy, which involves removal of the female genital organs of the labia minora, labia majora, and the clitoris, a pre-Islamic rite found among the peoples of North and Northeast Africa (particularly the Sudan, Egypt, Ethiopia, and Morocco), and in Java. Clitoridectomy has survived among the Muslim communities of these countries. In modern times, however, the continuing practice of clitoridectomy has led to protests against it and calls for reform in the Sudan, Egypt, and Morocco.

Neither male nor female circumcision have any doctrinal basis in Islam. Sociologically, they symbolize passage into adulthood and define and reinforce gender roles.

Puberty represents entrance into the state of adulthood. In the official Islamic perspective, it also marks the beginning of religious and social responsibility. Upon attaining puberty one is obliged to perform the religious rituals of Islam—*ṣalāh,* the daily prayers, and *ṣawm,* fasting during the month of Ramaḍān. Since the performance of these obligatory rituals requires that one should be in a state of physical cleanliness, children are instructed early on how to perform the rituals of cleansing oneself. These rituals include *wuḍū,* an ablution before the daily prayers, and *ghusl,* a ritual bath or washing of the whole body after a nocturnal ejaculation, menstruation, or sexual intercourse, conditions that cause one to enter into a state of *janābah* or being physically unclean. Muḥammad is reported to have said, "Purification is half of faith."

Nikāḥ (marriage) in Islam is a contract between two consenting partners. It is not a sacrament. Marriage is the appropriate means through which one channels one's sexual urges and raises a family. Since sexuality is an integral part of humanity, Islam encourages marriage and discourages celibacy. Marriage shields against irresponsible sexual behavior and thus helps preserve social morality. The prophet Muḥammad recommended marriage to those who could afford it and fasting to those who could not, for fasting helps attenuate passion. As with other rites of passage, marriage customs in the Muslim world are varied, with local customs playing an important role. The variety found in Muslim marriage ceremonies has been the subject of several studies in cultural anthropology.

The Arabic word *mawt* (death) means "cessation of breathing." Death is considered a transitional stage from life in this world to life in the hereafter. Normally, the dead person is to be buried on the day of death. The rituals of the *janāzah* (funeral) are based on the practice of Muḥammad, differing slightly from country to country according to cultural factors. *Ghusl* or bathing of the corpse is performed in order to remove physical impurities such as blood and excrement; it is an essential part of the funeral ceremony. The corpse is bathed by persons of the same gender. Care is taken not to expose the nakedness of the corpse, in order to respect the dignity of the dead. The corpse is then wrapped in a *kafan,* a white shroud consisting of three pieces for a man and five for a woman, which covers it completely. *Ṣalāt al-janāzah,* the funeral prayer for the dead, is performed in the mosque following any of the prescribed daily prayers, with the bier placed in front of the congregation. The funeral prayer is led either by a relative of the deceased or by the imam, the prayer leader of the mosque. The prayer is performed in a standing position and does not involve bowing or prostrations. It acknowledges the reality of death and seeks of God's mercy for the dead. The corpse is carried to the graveyard for burial in a procession consisting of relatives, friends, and other members of the community, who recite the *shahādah,* the attestation of faith. The corpse is placed in the grave with its face turned toward the Kaʿbah. Every participant in the funeral ceremony is expected to contribute three handfuls of earth toward the filling of the grave, reminding the participant of death and reinforcing humility.

In Iran, Africa, and Southeast Asia there are no social prohibitions against women joining in the funeral ceremony or visiting the graveyard; however, in the patriarchal societies of Arabia and South Asia, women are not permitted to join in either function.

In Southeast Asia, relatives of the dead distribute money among the people attending the funeral ceremony as an act seeking expiation for the sins committed by the dead person. This is probably owing to the influence of the Buddhist notion of "merit-making." In the Indian subcontinent, the Fātiḥāh, a ceremonial communal meal, is served by the bereaved family as an act of charity on behalf of the dead and seeking God's mercy and forgiveness. This ceremony for the dead is held every Thursday night for a period of forty days after the occurrence of a death. It involves collective recitation of the first chapter of the Qur'ān at the end of the meal. Indian and East African Muslims also observe the ceremony of *khatm al-Qur'ān,* congregational recitation of the whole of the Qur'ān, also held every Thursday night for forty days after the *ʿishā'* (night prayer) with the similar intention of seeking God's mercy and compassion for the dead. Such localized Islamic rites of passage for the dead are viewed with disdain by Islamic orthodoxy.

In modern times, contributions to Islamic thought and literature have also focused on the role of Islamic life-cycle rituals. While reiterating the main theme that the aim of Muslim life is submission and thanksgiving to God, they illustrate the tensions between tradition and modernity in the Islamic world. The culturally varied role of Islamic life-cycle rituals in shaping modern Muslim life, thought, and culture has also been a theme of various novels and films produced in the Muslim world.

ʿAlī Sharīʿatī (d. 1977), a modern Islamic thinker, discusses this theme in his philosophical discourse on the anthropology of Islam. For Sharīʿatī, passage through the various stages of life involves a dialectical struggle between *al-rūḥ* (God's own spirit/breath), which God has instilled in all human beings, and *turāb* (dust) or *ṣalṣāl* (clay), the physical elements that make up a human body (Qur'ān, 15.29, 32.9, 38.72). According to him, salvation lies in triumph over the struggle between the spiritual and material components that make up human personality, witnessed in the submission and gratitude to God expressed symbolically at various stages of the life cycle.

[*See also* Birth Rites; Circumcision; Clitoridectomy; Funerary Rites; Marriage and Divorce; Names and Naming; Puberty Rites; Purification.]

BIBLIOGRAPHY

Abdalati (ʿAbd al-ʿAṭī), Ḥammūdah. *The Family Structure in Islam.* Indianapolis, 1977. Detailed study of the institution of family in Islam.

Abu-Lughod, Lila. *Veiled Sentiments: Honor and Poetry in a Bedouin Society.* Berkeley, 1986. Excellent anthropological study of the relationship between life-cycle rituals and gender in the Arab world.

Abu-Lughod, Lila. "Islam and the Gendered Discourses of Death." *International Journal of Middle East Studies* 25 (1993): 187–205. Anthropological analysis of the gender dimension of discourse on death in Arabia.

Abu Zahra, Nadia. "The Comparative Study of Muslim Societies and Islamic Rituals." *Arab Historical Review for Ottoman Studies* 3–4 (December 1991): 7–38. Study of burial practices in Egypt and Tunisia.

Aswad, Sayyid al-. "Death Rituals in Rural Egyptian Society: A Symbolic Study." *Urban Anthropology and Studies of Cultural Systems and World Economic Development* 16 (1987): 205–241. Analysis of funerary rituals in rural Egypt.

Bouhdiba, Abdelwahab. *Sexuality in Islam.* London, 1985. Excellent and provocative study of sexuality and gender in the Muslim world.

Bukhārī, Muḥammad ibn Ismāʿīl al-. *Ṣaḥīḥ al-Bukhārī.* Vols. 2 and 7. Translated by M. M. Khan. Beirut, 1980. Contains *aḥādīth* pertaining to funerary and marriage customs in early Islam.

Denny, Frederick Mathewson, and A. A. Sachedina. *Islamic Ritual Practices: A Slide Set and Teacher's Guide.* Asian Media Resources, 7. New York and New Haven, 1983. Excellent tool for a basic introduction to Islamic ritual customs.

El Guindi, Fadwa. *El Sebouʿ: Egyptian Birth Ritual*. Los Angeles, 1987. Documentary film portraying childbirth rituals in Egypt.

Gennep, Arnold van. *Les rites de passage*. Paris, 1909. Translated by Monika B. Vizedom and Gabrielle L. Caffee as *The Rites of Passage*. Chicago, 1960. Classic study of life-cycle rites.

Kane, Hamidou. *Ambiguous Adventure*. New York, 1963. A novel by an African Muslim illustrating tensions between tradition and change in colonial Africa.

Laye, Camara. *The Dark Child*. New York, 1969. A novel highlighting the blending of African and Islamic life-cycle rituals.

Metcalf, Barbara D. *Perfecting Women*. Berkeley, 1990. Annotated translation of a popular Urdu marriage manual, *Bihishtī Zevar*, by Mawlānā Ashraf ʿAlī Thānavī, featuring Muslim marriage customs of the Indian Subcontinent.

Muslim ibn al-Ḥajjāj al-Qushayrī. *Ṣaḥīḥ Muslim*. Translated by ʿAbdul Hamid Siddiqi. Lahore, 1976. Muslim's *Al-jāmiʿ al-ṣaḥīḥ* is the second most important canonical collection of *aḥādīth* in Sunnī Islam.

Ṣāliḥ, Al-Ṭayyib. *The Wedding of Zein and Other Stories*. London, 1968. African novelist's treatment of the tensions between sensuality and spirituality in Islamic life.

Schuler, Margaret, ed. *Freedom from Violence*. New York, 1992. Commendable collection of articles about contemporary women's issues worldwide.

Sharīʿatī, ʿAlī. *On the Sociology of Islam*. Berkeley, 1979. Philosophical discourse on the anthropology of Islam by an outstanding Islamic thinker of the modern age.

Smith, Jane I., and Yvonne Yazbeck Haddad. *The Islamic Understanding of Death and Resurrection*. Albany, N.Y., 1981. Comprehensive study of Islamic discourse on death and dying during the classical and modern periods.

Smith, W. Robertson. *Kinship and Marriage in Early Arabia*. Cambridge, 1885. Classic study of the institution of marriage in Arabia.

Turner, Victor W. *The Ritual Process: Structure and Anti-Structure*. Chicago, 1969. Classic anthropological study of the role of life-cycle rituals in human societies.

IMTIYAZ YUSUF

RUSHDIE AFFAIR. On 26 September 1988, Viking Penguin published *The Satanic Verses* in London. The author, Salman Rushdie, was already a well-known and esteemed writer. On 5 October, the Indian government, acceding to the requests of its Muslim deputies, forbade the sale and distribution of the book in India. This decision was followed by similar actions in a number of countries, such as Pakistan and South Africa. There had not yet been a reaction from Iran. On 8 November, *The Satanic Verses* won Britain's Whitbread Prize. On 11 November, Margaret Thatcher, the British prime minister, rejected an appeal, put forward by the Union of Muslim Organisations, to prosecute Rushdie and Penguin under the Public Order Act (1986) and the Race Relations Act (1976); the Home Office said that no change would be made to British law against blasphemy, which applies only to Christianity. Later, on 22 July 1989, the Paris Court also rejected a Muslim request to banish *The Satanic Verses*. There were protests and demonstrations in England and elsewhere, but reaction to the book did not become dramatic until 14 January 1989, when Muslims in the northern city of Bradford, England, burned copies of the book. Tension grew, and events took a deadly turn on 12 February when six persons were killed and a hundred others were injured during protest demonstrations in Islamabad, Pakistan. After the last events, Ayatollah Ruhollah Khomeini passed his celebrated 14 February death sentence against Salman Rushdie. The situation thus became truly international, entering history as the Rushdie affair.

The *fatwā* (formal legal opinion) of Ayatollah Khomeini read as follows:

> In the name of God Almighty; there is only one God, to whom we shall all return; I would like to inform all the intrepid Muslims in the world that the author of the book entitled *The Satanic Verses* which has been compiled, printed and published in opposition to Islam, the Prophet and the Koran, as well as those publishers who were aware of its contents, have been sentenced to death. I call on all zealous Muslims to execute them quickly, wherever they find them, so that no one will dare to insult the Islamic sanctions. Whoever is killed on this path will be regarded as a martyr, God willing. In addition, anyone who has access to the author of the book, but does not possess the power to execute him, should refer him to the people so that he may be punished for his actions. May God's blessing be on you all.

Shortly after Khomeini's *fatwā*, the Organization of 15 Khurdād (the date of Khomeini's first rebellion against the shah's regime in 1963) put a price of $1 million on Rushdie's head. Fearing for his life, Rushdie went into hiding. Khomeini's *fatwā* also provoked a huge reaction worldwide. The European Economic Community's ministers of foreign affairs met in Brussels on 20 February 1989 and condemned the death sentence and recalled their ambassadors from Tehran. However, on 20 March, the same ministers, meeting again in Brussels, decided to return their ambassadors to Tehran.

On 24 February, the Indian police shot and killed twelve Muslim anti-Rushdie demonstrators in Bombay (Rushdie's birthplace). On 2 March, Javier Pérez de Cuellar, secretary general of the United Nations, declared (in India) that "we must respect all religions. At the same time we must respect the freedom of expression." On 4 March, the Holy See, through the *Osservatore Romano,* criticized the ingredient of "irreverence and blasphemy" in Rushdie's book, underscoring at the same time that the "sacred character of the religious conscience cannot prevail over the sacred character of the life of the author." On 6 March, the president of the United States, George Bush, condemned Khomeini's *fatwā* and held Tehran accountable. On 13 March, the foreign ministers of forty-six Muslim countries, members of the Organization of the Islamic Conference (OIC), met at Riyadh and judged *The Satanic Verses* blasphemous, because it "transgresses all norms of civility and decency and is a deliberate attempt to malign Islam and the venerated Islamic personalities." The OIC, however, did not endorse Khomeini's death edict.

Despite Khomeini's death on 3 June 1989, the Iranian Islamists remained intransigent; Ḥujjat al-Islām ʿAlī Akbar Hāshimī Rafsanjānī (elected president of Iran in July 1989), declared on 23 October that "the Islamic Republic's view and politics concerning Salman Rushdie is the same as it was under Imam Khomeini." Furthermore, on 9 February 1990 Ayatollah ʿAli Khamene'i, the new leader of the Islamic Republic, reiterated the late Khomeini's decree and called for its implementation.

Meanwhile, Salman Rushdie, in an attempt at conciliation with the Muslim community, converted to Islam (Christmas 1990 after having previously proclaimed himself non-Muslim. Later regretting his conversion, he again became a non-Muslim.

In 1991, because of the Gulf War and its aftermath, the Rushdie affair was almost neglected. After the end of the war and particularly after the liberation of the last Western hostages in Lebanon, Rushdie, whose case was no longer connected with the fate of the hostages, began to mobilize Western public opinion, hoping that Western governments would put more pressure on Iran to obtain an annulment of the famous *fatwā*.

Despite Rushdie's multiple efforts, his situation did not improve. On the contrary, in November 1992, the Iranian Islamists, furious at Rushdie's television interviews, raised the price on his head to $2 million and even more "in case a member of Rushdie's family will do the job." Furthermore, Ḥujjat al-Islām Aḥmad Khomeini, the son of the late ayatollah, has reiterated that "Imam Khomeini's death edict remains unchanged and will never be cancelled" (*Tehran Times,* 9 November 1992). As a result, Western sympathy for Rushdie grew, and he was received by several Western leaders, including the British prime minister, John Major (on 11 May 1993) and U.S. president Bill Clinton (on 25 November 1993).

There are two main issues in the Rushdie affair, namely, blasphemy and freedom of expression. In Islam there is no exact term for blasphemy, which comes from the Greek *blasphemia* (an offense against divinity). The Qur'ānic phrase *kalimat al-kufr* ("statement of impiety and infidelity" (surah 9.74–75) is close in meaning to blasphemy. According to the Qur'ān, blasphemy consists of *riddah* (apostasy) and *kufr* (infidelity), but it decrees no concrete punishment apart from encouraging the Prophet to "struggle with the infidels [*kuffār*] and the hypocrites [*munāfiqūn*]" (surah 9.73). The Qur'ān in general minimizes the act of blasphemy and infidelity. Moreover, it offers infidels and hypocrites the way of "return from their error" (surah 9.74–75).

The Sunnī and Shīʿī attitudes in regard to blasphemy are almost identical. The differences are based on, among other conditions, the sex of the apostate and whether he or she is *fiṭrī* (born a Muslim) or *millī* (converted to Islam). In general, both groups punish apostates and infidels with the death penalty, although a trial is imperative (for example Hallāj and ʿAyn al-Quzāt's trials in 922 and 1131, respectively). However, some Shīʿī religious authorities have executed the accused persons on their own initiatives; in some cases (for example, Muḥammad Bāqir Shaftī in the early nineteenth century) with their own hands.

Muslims convinced of the book's blasphemous nature have criticized Rushdie principally on the following points: when choosing the provocative title *The Satanic Verses* for his book, it was in reality *The Qur'ānic Verses* that the author had in mind. By doing that, Rushdie offended the Holy Qur'ān; Rushdie has made ironic remarks about Islam's most sacrosanct principles, such as *tawḥīd* (the concept of divine unity) and *nubūwah* (prophecy in general and the prophecy of Muḥammad in particular); the wives and the companions of the Prophet have not been spared Rushdie's derisive and airy comments. In short, these Muslims feel that the basic principles of their religion have been insulted.

Confronted with such severe accusations, Rushdie has based his defense essentially on the three following arguments: *The Satanic Verses* is essentially a work of fiction, "an imaginative text," and hence could not be blasphemous (interview with Rushdie, *Far Eastern Economic Review* [2 March 1989]); freedom of expression condones the work—as Rushdie has written, "What is freedom of expression? Without the freedom to offend, it ceases to exist. Without the freedom to challenge, even to satirise all orthodoxies, including religious orthodoxies, it ceases to exist" (*The Guardian,* 4 February 1990); finally, Rushdie defends himself against the accusation of apostasy by saying that he is not a Muslim, and "where there is no belief, there is no blasphemy" (*The Satanic Verses,* p. 380). Furthermore, he refutes the accusation of being an apostate, because "I have never in my adult life affirmed any belief, and what one has not affirmed one cannot be said to have apostatized from" (*The Guardian,* 4 February 1990).

Muslim reactions were varied and can be divided into three categories: those who considered Rushdie an apostate and so put a price on his head; those who concurred with the West; and those who took a more moderate attitude.

The first group did not wait for Khomeini's call to react. Several months before, the Muslim minority in England (1.5 million) demonstrated against Rushdie in early October 1988, only a few days after the book's publication. Khomeini's call was in fact a response to these and other reactions. After Khomeini's death edict, there was no lack of volunteers to carry out this mission. Numerous Iranians (including Iran's ambassador to the Vatican), Lebanese, and Palestinians (such as Aḥmad Jibrīl, leader of the Popular Front for the Liberation of Palestine—General Command) volunteered to kill Rushdie (*Le Monde,* 13–14 August, and *The Guardian,* 6 March 1989).

The second group, composed essentially of Muslim intellectuals residing in Western countries, vigorously condemned Khomeini's *fatwā* and approved of the book by putting their signatures to various petitions in the name of freedom of expression. The most significant of these petitions is signed by fifty Iranian intellectuals living abroad.

The third group, which included personages otherwise known for their lay views—among them Shabir Akhtar, member of Bradford's Council for Mosques, and Nobel laureate Naguib Mahfouz—condemned Khomeini's call but also criticized Rushdie's book. While Mahfouz accused Khomeini of "intellectual terrorism," he nevertheless declared that *The Satanic Verses* "is not an intellectual work . . . and a person who writes a book like this does not think; he is merely seeking consciously to insult and injure" (*Le Monde,* 9 March 1989).

[*See also* Fatwā, *article on* Modern Usage; *and the biography of Khomeini.*]

BIBLIOGRAPHY

Appiganesi, Lisa, and Sara Maitland, eds. *The Rushdie File.* London, 1989. Good documentary book that provides a chronology of events up to 1989.

Aubert, Raphaël. *L'affaire Rushdie.* Paris, 1990. Review of events and an analytical essay.

Easterman, Daniel. *New Jerusalem: Reflections on Islam, Fundamentalism and the Rushdie Affair.* London, 1992. A collection of essays and occasional pieces previously published by the author, added by the review of other authors' works.

Ibn Taymīyah, Aḥmad. *Majmūʿ fatāwā Shaykh al-Islām Aḥmad ibn Taymīyah.* 37 vols. Edited by ʿAbd al-Raḥmān ibn Qāsim. Riyadh, 1963.

Khomeini, Ruhollah. *Kashf al-Asrār.* [Tehran, 1943?] Probably the first book written by Ayatollah Khomeini, and a refutation of the "blasphemous statements" of some Iranian writers.

Khomeini, Ruhollah. *Risālah-yi tawẓīḥ al-masā'il.* [Tehran, 1980?] Authoritative *Risālah* of Ayatollah Khomeini.

Mozaffari, Mehdi. "La conception Shiʿite du pouvoir." Ph.D. diss., Sorbonne, 1971. The first work (in a Western language) on political Shiism.

Mozaffari, Mehdi. "The Rushdie Affair: Blasphemy as a New Form of International Conflict and Crisis." *Terrorism and Political Violence* 2.3 (Autumn 1990): 415–442. Comprehensive analysis of the different dimensions of the Rushdie affair.

Muḥaqqiq al-Ḥillī, Jaʿfar ibn Ḥasan. *Sharā'iʿ al-Islām.* Tehran, 1360/1981. Excellent collection of the classical Shīʿī laws and rules.

Pour Rushdie. Paris, 1993. One hundred Arab and Muslim intellectuals express their opinion on the Rushdie Affair.

Rushdie, Salman. *The Satanic Verses.* London, 1988.

Tunkābunī, Mirzā M. *Qiṣaṣ al-ʿulamā'.* Tehran, n.d. Excellent and probably unique work on the biography of the prominent Shīʿī *ʿulamā'* throughout history.

Tuthven, Malise. *A Satanic Affair: Salman Rushdie and the Rage of Islam.* London, 1990. Examination of arguments against Rushdie and the West.

Webster, Richard. *Salman Rushdie: Sentenced to Death.* New York, 1990. A critic of Western insensitivity toward Islamic culture and values.

Mehdi Mozaffari

S

SACRIFICE. The ritual and symbolic practice of sacrifice also has socioeconomic and political connotations in modern Islam. In its ritual facet, the notion of sacrifice is important in the outward practice of Muslim religiosity. Islamic sacrificial rituals may resemble superficially those found in other religious traditions. The most common form is the compulsory slaughter of an animal as part of the obligatory pilgrimage (*ḥajj*) and the optional slaughter by nonpilgrims on the occasion of ʿĪd al-Aḍḥā (the Festival of Sacrifice), viewed as a commemoration of the sacrifice of the prophet Abraham. Muslim lore has it that Abraham's son Ismāʿīl was the original token of sacrifice demanded by God but was miraculously replaced by a lamb.

In pre-Islamic times these practices were forms of blood sacrifice, but in Islam they acquired more symbolic meanings. The Qur'ān states, "And as for the sacrifice of cattle, We have ordained it for you as one of the symbols set up by God, in which there is much good for you" (22.36); and further, "[But bear in mind], never does their flesh reach God, and neither their blood: it is only your God-consciousness (*taqwā*) that reaches Him" (22.37).

In more recent times sacrifice has been interpreted as fulfilling the needs of social welfare and charity. The meat of the sacrificial animals slaughtered during the annual *ḥajj* is transported over long distances to feed the poor and hungry in disadvantaged communities. Formerly the meat was buried because it could not immediately be consumed or preserved, but modern technology has made such preservation possible. A portion of the food derived from the sacrifice by nonpilgrims is also given in charity to the disadvantaged groups in their local communities.

The consideration for welfare was always part of the wisdom of sacrifice, although it was primarily a ritual and only secondarily a charity. Nowadays, however, the early ritual and symbolic rationales are being rapidly replaced by the socioeconomic one. Contemporary Muslims tend to justify the practice of sacrifice by stressing that charity, welfare, and poor relief are its primary ends in the modern context. This is of special significance in light of the increasing criticism against this Muslim practice by animal-rights groups in various parts of the world. The social context understandably plays a major role in shaping the welfare dimension of this ritual, and the social function of sacrifice is coming to be emphasized above its significance as a ritual.

There are also other occasions of sacrifice. Among the more popular ones in many parts of the Muslim world is the tradition of *ʿaqīqah,* the sacrifice of two animals for a baby boy and one animal for a girl. This sacrifice, which is supported by the prophetic traditions, is reported to protect the child from potential harm in the future. The *ʿaqīqah* may be seen as a rite of passage into family life, but it is an optional practice, more prevalent in regions where local custom reinforces it. With the rise of evangelical and revivalist tendencies in modern Islam, many adherents see it as fulfilling the scriptural requirements. Animal sacrifice may also be made in fulfillment of a vow or as expiation of a sin during the pilgrimage. [*See also* Birth Rites.]

The notion of sacrifice may also carry strong political undertones. This is observable in the literature of political Islam during the anticolonial struggles in the Muslim world and also during the Islamic resurgence in contemporary times. Modern Islamic movements frequently urge adherents to strive for martyrdom (*shahādah*) when pursuing a political cause legitimized by religious ideology. Martyrdom is viewed as the highest form of personal sacrifice (*taḍḥīyah*). These political subthemes feed off the historical ritual and symbolic motifs of sacrifice.

A modern commentator, Muḥammad ʿAlī (1874–1951), points out that the act of sacrifice itself is connected with righteousness, humility, patience in suffering, and the awe of the divine. In the midst of the verses of sacrifice (Qur'ān 22.34–35) appear verses that ask believers to be patient when experiencing trials and hardships in the path of God (22.39). Thus ritual sacrifice points to a higher sacrifice. Believers are encouraged, says Muḥammad ᶜAlī, to "realize that if they have sacrificed an animal over which they have control, it is their duty to lay down their own lives in the path of Allāh." The symbiotic relationship between the abstract and the actual, the spiritual and the material significations to which the theme of sacrifice lends itself, is quite obvious. Similar interpretations were also made by the Egyptian reformer Muḥammad Rashīd Riḍā (1865–1935); in his commentary of the Qur'ān, Riḍā explains that the promotion of truth involves "fortitude, patience and sacrifice."

One of the more visible ideologues of Islamic Iran, ᶜAlī Sharīᶜatī (1933–1977), lavishly interprets the symbolism of the pilgrimage in terms of political metaphors. Sacrifice expressed as the slaughter of an animal, he explains, is an allegory for the extinction and demise of the ego. "It means to abstain from, and struggle against the temptations of the ego." The symbol of sacrifice has didactic value in the hands of intellectuals like Sharīᶜatī and Muḥammad ᶜAlī. Woven into the texture of their meditations is a propensity to reach deep into the Muslim psyche in order to discover and realize the latent implications of sacrifice. If the ego can be freed from the servitude of materialism to a higher consciousness, Sharīᶜatī argues, then the possibility of a peaceful political order becomes real. For his part, Muḥammad ᶜAlī draws on the mystical impulse of the theme: the sacrifice of an animal is in reality the sacrifice of the animal within the human being. If this perception is socialized within the community, it ought to lead to the development of an ethos of self-sacrifice in society at large.

It becomes clear that the symbolic and ritual meanings of sacrifice extend into the realm of the practical in important ways. Both social context and individual imagination play a crucial role in determining the range of meanings of this theme.

[*See also* Ḥajj; ᶜĪd al-Aḍḥā; Rites of Passage.]

BIBLIOGRAPHY

ᶜAlī, Muḥammad. *The Religion of Islam*. Lahore, 1983.

Bousquet, G.-H. "Dhabīḥa." In *Encyclopaedia of Islam*, new ed., vol. 2, pp. 213–214. Leiden, 1960–.

Sharīᶜatī, ᶜAlī. *Ali Shariati's Hajj: Reflections on Its Rituals*. Translated by Laleh Bakhtiar. Tehran, 1988. Related topics: patience; *taqwā; dhabīḥah*.

EBRAHIM MOOSA

SAᶜDĀWĪ, NAWĀL AL- (b. 1931), leading feminist of the Arab world. Al-Saᶜdāwī evokes more passion and controversy than any other Arab writer, male or female, inside or outside of the Middle East. At various times, she has been subject to governmental harassment and arrest, or, conversely, the recipient of special protective measures. Her diverse career as a writer, feminist activist, and physician has brought her international fame as well as political adversity in her native country of Egypt.

Born in 1931 in the village of Kafr Ṭaḥlah in the Egyptian Delta, al-Saᶜdāwī studied medicine in Cairo. As a physician she has practiced in the areas of public health, thoracic medicine, and psychiatry. In 1982, she founded the Arab Women's Solidarity Association (AWSA), with its official organ, *Nūn*, devoted to women's issues and feminist politics. She was appointed Egypt's minister of health in 1958, but was dismissed from that post in 1972 because of her frank writings on the sexuality of Arab women. In 1981, when the regime of President Anwar el-Sadat imprisoned numerous intellectuals of different political persuasions, al-Saᶜdāwī found herself sharing prison accommodations with both leftists and Islamists. More recently, her name has appeared on a death list drawn up by Islamic opposition groups. The assassination of the secularist Faraj Fawdah in 1992 sent shock waves through the Egyptian secular intellectual community and prompted government protection of intellectuals, al-Saᶜdāwī among them. That same year, she lost a court case contesting the governmental closing of AWSA and the diversion of its funds to the Association of the Women of Islam. *Nūn* had been shut down a few months earlier, thus censoring an important source of feminist theory and criticism.

These political setbacks have not kept al-Saᶜdāwī from indulging in her favorite activity: writing. The life of the pen has always had a greater attraction for the feminist physician than the life of the scalpel. Her extensive literary corpus covers a wide range of prose genres: novels, short stories, drama, travel and prison memoirs, and programmatic works. She wrote her first novel, *Mudhakkirāt ṭiflah ismuhā Suᶜad* (Memoirs of a Girl Called Suᶜād), at the age of thirteen. Her most recent novel, *Al-ḥubb fī zaman al-nafṭ* (Love in the Time of Oil, 1993), like all her writings, reflects her deep commitment to exposing gender inequality and the hardships endured by Arab women. Al-Saᶜdāwī tackles difficult subjects with a frankness few Arab writers display, forcefully illuminating sexuality, gender roles, and male/female relations in Arab society in a straightforward, accessible prose. Much in her fiction revolves around the body, and powerful physical images permeate her writings.

Al-Saʿdāwī has gained an international readership and is perhaps the most visible of modern Arabic writers. *The Hidden Face of Eve* is a classic in the West. Her popularity in the West has meant that many of her works have been translated into several European languages, and her novels have received a number of international awards. Consequently, she has been accused by some of writing for a Western audience. But anyone familiar with al-Saʿdāwī's writings recognizes that they only make sense within an Arab-Islamic cultural context. Her plots, her linguistic games, her literary allusions, her religious-legal intertextual references are part and parcel of what makes Nawāl al-Saʿdāwī a powerful Arab—and Arabic—writer.

[*See also* Feminism.]

BIBLIOGRAPHY

Malti-Douglas, Fedwa. *Woman's Body, Woman's Word: Gender and Discourse in Arabo-Islamic Writing*. Princeton, 1991. Discusses al-Saʿdāwī's fiction and sets it in the broader context of corporality and Arabo-Islamic prose, classical and modern.

Malti-Douglas, Fedwa. *Men, Women, and God(s): Nawal El Sadawi Writes Arab Feminism*. Berkeley, 1995. In-depth analysis of al-Saʿdāwī's literary writings.

Saʿdāwī, Nawāl al-. *The Hidden Face of Eve: Women in the Arab World*. Translated by Sherif Hetata. London, 1980. Classic work on the status of women and Arab feminism; originally published in Arabic as *Al-Wajh al-ʿĀrī lil-Marʾah al-ʿArabīyah*.

Ṭarābīshī, Jurj. *Woman against Her Sex: A Critique of Nawal el-Saadawi*. Translated by Basil Hatim and Elisabeth Orsini. London, 1988. Translation of a psychoanalytic work very critical of al-Saʿdāwī's positions, which appeared in Arabic under the title *Unthā ḍidda al-Unūthah*. Al-Saʿdāwī appended a response to the English translation.

FEDWA MALTI-DOUGLAS

ṢADR. Originally an Arabic honorific, *ṣadr* has been used informally since at least the tenth century to denote a prominent member of the *ʿulamāʾ* (community of religious scholars). It became a more institutionalized title in the late eleventh century, particularly in Islamic Central Asia and Iran. The title became hereditary in certain influential learned families, hence the survival of Ṣadr as a surname, particularly among Twelver Shīʿī Muslims. The title, however, was not originally confined to Shīʿī scholars; indeed, it seems to have first emerged in Sunnī Ḥanafī circles, as in, for example, the Āl-i Burhān family of Bukhara whose leader was first invested under the Seljuks (c.1105) with the title *ṣadr al-ṣudūr* (chief *ṣadr*)—a position with religious, fiscal, and political aspects.

Ṣadr as an official religious or political title occurs with significant variation according to regime and period, particularly in late medieval and early modern Iran, India, and Turkey. In early Mughal India, *qāḍīs* (judges) often held the title of *ṣadr,* while the *ṣadr al-ṣudūr,* initially the chief spokesman of the *ʿulamāʾ*, was the chief *qāḍī* and head of the judiciary, often with extraordinary powers. The emperor Akbar's appointment of six provincial *ṣadr*s (c.1581) was probably an attempt to curb the centralized authority of the *ṣadr al-ṣudūr*. In Iran, the *ṣadr,* already an important religious dignitary under the fifteenth-century Timurid dynasty, was made a political appointee by the first Ṣafavid ruler, Ismāʿīl I (r. 1502–1524), with the double aim of ensuring legitimacy for the new regime and controlling the religious establishment. Thus the *ṣadr*'s political influence under the early Ṣafavids was soon curtailed and his role eventually limited to supervision of the *waqf*s (religious endowments), with some juridical duties. The *ṣadārah* (office of *ṣadr*) was further weakened by its division into two positions around 1666 that were subordinate to the newly created *dīvānbagī* to whose decisions the two *ṣadr*s gave religious sanction. Eventually the *ṣadr*'s role in the Ṣafavid polity was eclipsed by that of *shaykh al-islām* and the new position of the *mullabashi* (chief mullah).

Meanwhile, under the nineteenth-century Ottoman Tanzimat (period of reform), the two *kazasker* (chief judges), who had already come under the jurisdiction of the grand *muftī* of Istanbul, were given the titles of *sadrı Rumeli* and *sadrı Anadolu,* while other chief *qāḍīs* were also known by the title of *ṣadr*. The title *ṣadr* was by no means limited to religious dignitaries, since the chief minister in Ṣafavid and Qājār Iran and in Ottoman Turkey held the title of *sadrı azam* (grand vizier).

The decline of the *ṣadārah* as an influential religious institution in Mughal India, Ṣafavid Iran, and Ottoman Turkey, reflects the policies of Muslim rulers. Such rulers sought the legitimacy flowing from the religious establishment, they transformed the *ʿulamāʾ* into official functionaries deprived of economic independence and the respect and support of their less-worldly colleagues and the wider Muslim community. This might explain the eventual rise of independent and more "authentic" *ʿulamāʾ* (e.g., *mujtahid*s in Iran) capable of criticizing the rulers.

[*See also* Muftī; Mullabashi; Qāḍī; Shaykh al-Islām; ʿUlamāʾ; Vizier.]

BIBLIOGRAPHY

Jackson, Peter, and Laurence Lockhart, eds. *The Cambridge History of Iran*, vol. 6, *The Timurid and Safavid Periods*. Cambridge, 1986. See chapter 6 and the index.

Lambton, Ann K. S. "Maḥkama: 3. Iran." In *Encyclopaedia of Islam*, new ed., vol. 6, pp. 11–22. Leiden, 1960–.

Savory, Roger Mervyn. *Iran under the Safavids*. Cambridge, 1980.

Shaw, Stanford J., and Ezel Kural Shaw. *History of the Ottoman Empire and Modern Turkey*. 2 vols. Cambridge, 1976–1977.

AHMAD SHBOUL

ṢADR, MUḤAMMAD BĀQIR AL- (1935–1980), innovative and influential Iraqi Islamic thinker and political leader. "An important figure not only in Iraq but in the life of the Shiʿi world, and indeed in the Muslim world as a whole" (Albert Hourani), Muḥammad Bāqir al-Ṣadr was both a prominent scholar of Islamic law and its contemporary applications and a political leader whose writ transcended his native country to reach Iran and the rest of the Middle East.

Thought. Muḥammad Bāqir al-Ṣadr's production is probably the most varied for a Muslim author of the twentieth century. Ṣadr wrote books on philosophy, Qurʾānic interpretation, logic, education, constitutional law, economics, interest-free banking, as well as more traditional works of *uṣūl al-fiqh* (principles of Islamic jurisprudence), compilations of devotional rites, commentaries on prayers, and historical investigations into early Sunnī-Shīʿī controversies.

As an innovative thinker on the issue of the desired shape and structure of a contemporary Muslim society, his most important work, which established his fame early on in his career, is a book on Islamic economics, which was published in two volumes in 1959–1961. This book, *Iqtiṣādunā* (Our Economics), probably remains the most scholarly twentieth-century study of Islamic economics as an alternative ideological system to capitalism and communism.

Methodologically, in *Iqtiṣādunā*, Ṣadr acknowledges that there is no scientific discipline in Islam which can be identified as economics and that the main elements in the approach to an Islamic economy must be derived from what he calls "the legal superstructure." The resultant process leads to the well-known operation of *ijtihād*, which is understood by Ṣadr in its wider definition as an intellectual endeavor into the law and jurisprudence of classical Islam and is consequently acknowledged as an exercise which is prone to human error. For Ṣadr, "Islamic economics is not a science" and will only stand as an original and serious discipline after a long process of legal discovery. Only after this research can one speak of an original Islamic discipline of economics, in which the moral imperative derived from the law is clear but in which, also, there is a difficult and patient scholarly investigation into the riches of the classical *fiqh* (jurisprudence) tradition.

From a substantive point of view, Ṣadr introduces in *Iqtiṣādunā* a detailed critique of Marxist socialism and Western capitalism before proceeding with the presentation of his alternative system. Because of the particular strength of communist ideology in Iraq at the time *Iqtiṣādunā* was composed, the book is devoted primarily to refuting various brands of Marxist socialism. Against capitalism, Ṣadr's arguments rest on the usual criticism of the hollowness of the concept of liberty when applied to unequal parties in economic exchange. Against socialism, Ṣadr develops a long-winded and informed argument demonstrating the fallacies of Marxist periodization of history, its overemphasis on the class struggle, and its unrealistic prescriptions against the basic (and natural) instincts of economic self-interest in mankind. Then, Islamic economics as a discipline is introduced by a series of principles, mostly of a methodological nature, which the author follows with a dirigiste (i.e., involving extensive state intervention) and generally egalitarian reading of the concept of property in a predominantly agricultural context.

Without going into the intricacies of his theory of landed property, Ṣadr's thesis can be presented as a call for the state's systematic intervention to ensure that land ownership depends as directly as possible on the actual laborer who works on it. The central concept of labor in *Iqtiṣādunā* requires an interventionist and welfarist operation of the ruler (called in that book *walī al-amr*), who combines two tools to redress "the social balance": one is the guidance of legal principles of property which connect ownership of land and means of production with labor; the other is "need," and the state is free, according to Ṣadr, to fill in the discretionary area with adequate measures in order to suppress what Ṣadr did not shy from calling, on the eve of the Iranian Revolution two decades later, "the exploitation of man by man."

Beyond these general principles, Ṣadr elaborately develops the guiding rules to property within the frame of what he calls "distribution in the phase that precedes production." Both in this phase and in the actual productive process, the most original dimension of *Iqtiṣādunā* appears in the method of discovering Islamic economics. By quoting classical jurists of the *fiqh* tradition, Ṣadr engages the field with the most serious such investigation among Muslim authors in the twentieth century, by basing it on the legal books of a millennium-old legal tradition. [*See* Property.]

The detour through classical law is also Ṣadr's path to a lengthy treatise on Islamic banking. Here again, he is a forerunner in a field which has become, a decade after his *Interest-Free Bank* was published in 1969, fashionable and controversial. Islamic finance is premised on a narrow interpretation of the ban on *ribā* (a word which for Ṣadr means interest), which has led Islamic banks to create operations allowing access to their coffers by depositors, in return for the bank's pooling these resources for investment operations that do not bear a predetermined and fixed rate of return.

The system devised by Muḥammad Bāqir al-Ṣadr needs to be appraised against the common practice of present-day Islamic institutions. If a deposit invested by an Islamic bank in a successful venture is profitable, the depositor and the bank (as entrepreneur) will share the profit according to a predetermined rate—for example, a 50–50 or 60–40 split. But the endeavor can also be a total failure, eating up the deposit as capital. In this case, under the classical contract of *muḍārabah,* which is also known as *commenda,* or partnership for profit and loss, the depositor has no recourse against the bank in normal circumstances.

Under classical Islamic law, *muḍārabah* operates as a two-party contract, with the agent-entrepreneur endeavoring to make money entrusted to him by the owner of capital. The operations of a modern Western bank, in contradistinction, involve as a matter of course three parties: the depositors, the bank, and the borrowers. The answers of present-day Islamic banks, although based in theory on the idea of *muḍārabah,* have to square the original two-party contract of *muḍārabah* with three parties. They sever the tripartite relationship by fictitiously considering the operation to consist of a double contract entered into by the bank on the one hand, and, on the other hand, the depositor and the borrower as separate parties. In the first contract, the depositor would be the owner of capital, and the bank the agent-entrepreneur. In the second contract, the bank would be the owner of capital, and the borrower the agent-entrepreneur.

Ṣadr has a more original and elaborate scheme in his book, *Interest-Free Bank:* he considers that the bank is actually only a mediator to a single *muḍārabah* contract between the pool of depositors and the pool of entrepreneurs. He goes on to elaborate on the rights and duties of each of the three parties and to provide interesting, if not altogether convincing, arithmetic formulas to assess the rate of profit and the resulting shares in the profits and losses of the three parties to the operation.

Beyond the rearrangements of contracts to avoid interest, the problem facing theoreticians and practitioners of Islamic banking can be summed up in the crucial question, can a bank refuse to tie itself down to a fixed interest rate offered to its depositors while guaranteeing the safety of these deposits? For present-day Islamic banks, the answer is generally negative. Guarantees on deposits cannot be offered, as the bank operates on the basis of a partnership for profit and loss. Ṣadr, in the main, partakes of this idea, although he seems to be inclined, in a treatise written ten years after his *Interest-Free Bank,* to acknowledge the necessity of preserving the depositor's capital, even if the venture it is used for is lost. [*See* Banks and Banking; Interest.]

A third area of innovation in Ṣadr's thought is related to the concept of an Islamic state: how would the constitution of such a state be conceived in theory and practice? Here, the influence of Ṣadr on the Iranian Revolution was remarkable, and there is an identifiable thread from his 1979 treatise on the subject to the constitution passed in the Islamic Republic of Iran a few months later.

The thrust of Ṣadr's idea appears in a two-tier separation of powers and in the Iranian Constitution: onto the traditional separation of powers between the three branches of government (executive, legislative, and judicial powers) was grafted an Islamic scheme which is derived from a combination of Shīʿī features of scholarship and the representation of the Platonic figure of the philosopher-king in the form of a jurist. The guardian of the city became the classical *faqīh* (a jurisprudent), hence the concept of *wilāyat al-faqīh* (guardianship of the jurisconsult), which Ayatollah Ruhollah Khomeini (1902–1989) had adumbrated in his Najaf classes of 1970 and which was brought into a more-precise constitutional rendering by Ṣadr in 1979. As for the Shīʿī imprint, it was obvious in the remodeling of the elaborate *marjaʿīyah* system in modern Shīʿī society, which recognizes a power of guidance at large to the most learned jurists of the tradition. These are called *marjaʿ*s (lit., "reference") represented by the top *mujtahids* (those who practice *ijtihād*, or *ʿulamāʾ* [scholars]) in the clerical system known for this reason as *marjaʿīyah*. In the Western world, the better-known word which stands for *marjaʿ* is ayatollah (Ar., *āyat allāh*). [*See* Wilāyat al-Faqīh; Marjaʿ al-Taqlīd; Ayatollah.]

But whether in Ṣadr's system or in the Iranian Constitution, the power of the ayatollahs was brought into the Islamic state alongside more Western-type offices, such as a president and parliamentarians who are elected under universal suffrage. The Iranian system has struggled with the two-tier separation of powers since its inception, although the inevitable tug-of-war had been best described, on the eve of the revolution, by Muḥammad Bāqir al-Ṣadr. [*See* Islamic State.]

Political Leadership. Considering the influence of his ideas in the Shīʿī milieu at large, it is not surprising to see the title of Ṣadr in 1979–1980 turning into the "Khomeini of Iraq." The sobriquet came as the result of a slow assertion of his leadership, first on the scholarly level and then directly on the political scene.

Ṣadr, who was born in 1935, showed early signs of intellectual superiority. His father, who died when he was very young, was, like his older brother and uncles, versed in traditional legal scholarship. Ṣadr grew up in the southern Holy City of Najaf in an Iraqi world which was witnessing a combination of mistrust toward a system perceived as corrupt and prone to Western influence and domination and a sharp rise in radical doctrines, most remarkably Baʿthism and communism.

It is against the tidal wave of communism that the *ʿulamāʾ* of Najaf, Ṣadr's seniors, were most exercised when the monarchy was overturned in 1958. But it was the Baʿth party which proved to be their most terrible nemesis. Ṣadr had countered the communist appeal by trying to expound a rational Islamic system, including such arcane topics as philosophy, banking, and economics. His more-direct political appeal can be traced back to the early and mid-1960s, in small circles of militant *ʿulamāʾ* who proved extremely influential across the Shīʿī world in the 1980s. With the accession of the Baʿth party of Aḥmad Ḥasan al-Bakr and Saddam Hussein to power in the summer of 1968, the relatively sheltered world of the schools of law and *ʿulamāʾ* in Najaf came directly under attack by a massive system of absolute repression which was combined with an increased "Sunnization" of the regime in Baghdad. Then started a cycle of repression which culminated, inside Iraq in 1980, in the execution of Ṣadr and his sister and, outside Iraq, in an all-out war against Iran.

The development of the antagonism between Saddam Hussein's Baghdad and Muḥammad Bāqir al-Ṣadr's Najaf between 1968 and 1980 has yet to be fully chronicled, but the occasion of ʿĀshūrāʾ (the yearly mourning day for the martyred Imam Ḥusayn in 680) proved often to be violent. Especially in 1974 and in 1977, and more abruptly after the accession of Khomeini to power in February 1979, the antagonism flared up in full-fledged rioting. It was reported that already during the 1977 riots, the security agents of the Baʿthist government would question those detained about their relationship with Ṣadr. Later, after Ṣadr was clearly turning into a major threat to the government, the rulers of Iraq moved directly to curb his activities and influence.

Ṣadr was arrested several times through the 1970s, but in June 1979, as he was reportedly getting ready to lead an Iraqi delegation to congratulate Khomeini in Tehran, he was forbidden to leave his home in Najaf. The tension continued to rise, until grenade attacks against leading Baʿthists in Baghdad led to the removal of Ṣadr from Najaf on the evening of 5 April 1980. He and his sister Bint al-Hudā were taken to Baghdad, where it is believed that they were killed on 8 April.

In the last years of his life, Ṣadr had tried to take advantage of the Shīʿī network to strengthen his appeal, but the organization was not sufficiently and effectively structured, and the government had been alerted by the success of the Iranian precedent. But his death marked the real beginning for the dissemination of his influence across the Middle East, in the midst of a confrontation between Tehran and Baghdad which turned into the bloodiest war in the Middle East of the twentieth century.

In Iran, both the debates on constitutional law and economics and banking saw the mark of Ṣadr's reasoning. In Iraq, Pakistan, and Lebanon, the Najaf network of Ṣadr's companions and students produced several leaders to whom the Shīʿī community looked up. But the intellectual influence of Ṣadr can also be seen in other areas of the Middle East, where his thought was received despite the skepticism of a Sunnī world toward Shīʿī legal scholarship. In Egypt and Jordan, his books were taught in universities, and critical works were published. In Algeria, where the Islamic movement lacked an original thinker to rest its views on, *Iqtiṣādunā*'s concepts could be found in the literature of the Front Islamique du Salut (FIS).

It is, however, in Iraq that Ṣadr will be remembered first and foremost. For a few days after the Gulf War, in March 1991, as Najaf was freed from Baʿthist rule, Ṣadr's pictures were paraded in his native city. The government of Saddam Hussein regained brutal control immediately afterward. But whatever the future of central rule in Baghdad, it is only a matter of time before Ṣadr gains the respect of all Iraqis for a legacy with which they may or may not agree from an ideological point of view, but which can only be acknowledged as formidable in modern Islamic thought.

[*See also* Iraq.]

BIBLIOGRAPHY

Works by Ṣadr

Iqtiṣādunā (1959–1961). New rev. ed. Beirut, 1398/1977. Available in English as *Our Economics,* 4 vols. (Tehran, 1982–1984), but a better translation of the most important sections of the text was serialized as "The Islamic Economy, I–VII," in the Shīʿī journal *Al-Sirat* from 1981–1985.

Khilāfat al-Insān wa Shahādat al-Anbiyā' and *Lamḥah Fiqhīyah Tamhīdīyah ʿan Mashrūʿ Dustūr al-Jumhūrīyah al-Islāmīyah fī Īrān.* Beirut, 1979. Constitutional pamphlets.

Falsafatunā (1959). 10th ed. Beirut, 1400/1980. Translated by Shams Inati as *Our Philosophy*. London, 1987.

Al-Majmūʿah al-Kāmilah li-Mu'allafāt al-Sayyid Muḥammad Bāqir al-Ṣadr. 15 vols. Beirut, 1980–. Ṣadr's collected works.

Al-Bank al-Lā-Ribawi fī al-Islām (1969). 8th ed. Beirut, 1403/1983. Ṣadr's book on the structure of an interest-free bank.

Works on Ṣadr

Mallat, Chibli. *The Renewal of Islamic Law: Muhammad Baqer as-Sadr, Najaf, and the Shiʿi International.* Cambridge, 1993.

Rieck, Andreas, trans. *Unsere Wirtschaft: Eine Gekürzte Kommentierte Übersetzung des Buches Iqtiṣādunā.* German edition of *Iqtiṣādunā,* which includes a good introduction by Rieck.

CHIBLI MALLAT

ṢADR, MŪSĀ AL- (1928–1978?), Iranian-born Shīʿī cleric of Lebanese descent who made an indelible mark on the Lebanese political scene. Mūsā al-Ṣadr is one of the most intriguing and fascinating political personalities to have appeared in the modern Middle East. He was an ambitious but tolerant man whose controversial career had an enormous impact on the Shīʿī Muslim community of Lebanon. His admirers describe him as a man of vision, political acumen, and profound compassion, while his detractors remember him as a deceitful, manipulative political chameleon. Mūsā al-Ṣadr was a towering presence in Lebanon's political history (literally as well as figuratively, as he was well over six feet tall). Though he disappeared in 1978, he still inspires his followers and dogs his enemies in Lebanon.

Ṣadr was born in Qom, Iran, in 1928, the son of Ayatollah Ṣadr al-Dīn Ṣadr, an important Shīʿī Muslim *mujtahid* (a Shīʿī jurisprudent qualified to make independent interpretations of law and theology). In Qom he attended primary and secondary school, and a Shīʿī seminary, and then he went on to Tehran University, where he matriculated into the School of Political Economy and Law of Tehran University, the first *mujtahid* to do so. He did not intend to pursue a career as a cleric, but on the urging of his father he discarded his secular ambitions and agreed to continue an education in *fiqh* (Islamic jurisprudence). One year after his father's death in 1953, he moved to Najaf, Iraq, where he studied under Ayatollahs Muḥsin al-Ḥakīm and ʿAbd al-Qāsim Khu'ī (Abol-Qāsem Kho'i).

He first visited Lebanon, which was his ancestral home, in 1957. During this visit he made a very positive impression on the Lebanese Shīʿah, including his relative al-Sayyid ʿAbd al-Ḥusayn Sharaf al-Dīn, the Shīʿī religious leader of the southern Lebanese coastal city of Tyre. Following the death of Sharaf al-Dīn in 1957, he was invited to become the senior Shīʿī religious authority in Tyre. Initially he spurned the invitation, but the urgings of his mentor Ayatollah al-Ḥakīm proved persuasive. In 1960 he moved to Tyre. In 1963 he was granted Lebanese citizenship, an early mark of his looming influence in Lebanon. Although he was a man of Qom, he understood Lebanon and the fundamental need for compromise in a land of sects, insecurity, and long memories. He emphasized ecumenicalism. His was an assertiveness laced with empathy.

One of his first significant acts was the establishment of a vocational institute in the southern town of Burj al-Shimālī (near Tyre), where Shīʿī youths could gain the training that would allow them to escape the privation which marked their community. The institute would become an important symbol of Mūsā al-Ṣadr's leadership; it is still in operation—now bearing his name—and provides vocational training for about five hundred orphans under the supervision of Ṣadr's strong-willed sister Rabāb (who is married to a member of the important Sharaf al-Dīn family of Tyre).

A man of keen intelligence, widely noted personal charm, and enormous energy, Ṣadr attracted a wide array of supporters, ranging from Shīʿī merchants making their fortunes in West Africa to petit-bourgeois youth. The Shīʿī migrants to West Africa, who had fled the poverty of Lebanon to seek their fortunes, proved to be an important source of financial support for Mūsā al-Ṣadr. Many of these men had done very well, and they were attracted to a man who promised to challenge the old system that had humiliated them and denied them a political voice. If there is an Arabic equivalent of "charisma," it is *haybah*—a word that describes the dignified presence and allure of this man from faraway Qom and Najaf.

Imam Mūsā—as he came to be called by his followers—set out to establish himself as the paramount leader of the Lebanese Shīʿī community, noted at the time for its poverty and general underdevelopment. He helped to fill a yawning leadership void which resulted from the growing inability of the *zaʿīm*s (traditional political bosses) to meet the cascading needs of their clients. From the 1960s onward, the Shīʿah had experienced rapid social change and economic disruption, and the old village-based patronage system, which presumed the underdevelopment and the apathy of the clients, was proving an anachronism.

Mūsā al-Ṣadr was able to stand above a fragmented and often victimized community and see it as a whole. Through his organizational innovations, his speeches, and his personal example, he succeeded in giving many Shīʿīs an inclusive communal identity. Furthermore, he reminded his followers that their deprivation was not to be fatalistically accepted, for so long as they could speak out through their religion, they could overcome their condition. He once observed, "whenever the poor involve themselves in a social revolution it is a confirmation that injustice is not predestined" (Norton, 1987, p. 40).

He shrewdly recognized that his power lay in part in his role as a custodian of religious symbols. He used the central myths of Shiism, especially the martyrdom of Imam Ḥusayn at Karbala thirteen centuries earlier, to spur his followers. The day of martyrdom is called ʿĀshūrāʾ, and it was a frequent motif of Ṣadr. The following excerpt from one of his speeches was reported by the newspaper *Al-ḥayāh* on 1 February 1974: "This revolution did not die in the sands of Karbala, it flowed into the life stream of the Islamic world, and passed from generation to generation, even to our day. It is a deposit placed in our hands so that we may profit from it, that we extract from it a new source of reform, a new position, a new movement, a new revolution, to repel the darkness, to stop tyranny and to pulverize evil."

Political Style. The record of his political alliances shows that Mūsā al-Ṣadr was—above all else—a pragmatist. It is both a tribute to his political skill and a commentary on his tactics that well-informed Lebanese should have commented that nobody knew where Imam Mūsā stood. According to reliable reports, Mūsā was friendly with both King Hussein of Jordan and President Anwar el-Sadat of Egypt, and he traveled regularly throughout the Arab world and Europe.

His followers today often characterize him as a vociferous critic of the shah of Iran, but it was only after the October War of 1973, when Iran supported Israel against the Arabs, that his relations with the shah deteriorated. In the autumn of 1973, he accused the shah of suppressing religion in Iran, denounced him for his pro-Israel stance, and described him as an "imperialist stooge." Although his Iranian citizenship was soon revoked, for more than a decade he had maintained close, even cordial, ties with the Pahlavi regime, and it seems that the shah provided financial subsidies to Imam Mūsā and his Iraqi cousin, the learned Muḥammad Bāqir al-Ṣadr.

Mūsā al-Ṣadr was a strong supporter of Ayatollah Ruhollah Khomeini; indeed, the last article he published was a polemic in *Le Monde* (23 August 1978), castigating the shah and praising Khomeini. Yet, Ṣadr's vision of Shiism was more moderate, more humanistic than Khomeini's. He was a friend of ʿAlī Sharīʿatī (d. 1977), the writer who propounded a liberal, modernist Shiism and thereby inspired many opponents of the shah (including, the Mujāhidīn-i Khalq, the organization that has proved to be the staunchest opponent of the Islamic Republic regime.) Mūsā al-Ṣadr's admiration for Sharīʿatī was rooted in the intellectual's commitment to confront tyranny and injustice through the renovation of Shiism, rather than through the rejection of faith. In Iran, Sharīʿatī's ideological message, with its stress on humanism, anti-imperialism, and self-reliance, appealed to the educated classes; while his emphasis on the martyrdom of Ḥusayn as a revolutionary exemplar appealed across socioeconomic lines. Absent from Sharīʿatī's writings and lectures was the vengefulness, the anger, and the intolerance that marked Iran's post-shah rulers. Many observers suspect that al-Ṣadr would have moderated the course of the revolution in Iran, if he were not consumed by it. [*See the biography of Sharīʿatī.*]

Political Alliances. Like the Maronite Christians, the Shīʿīs are a minority in a predominantly Sunnī Muslim Arab world, and for both sects Lebanon is a refuge in which sectarian identity and security can be preserved. Al-Ṣadr's message to the Maronites in the period before the Lebanese civil war of 1975–1976 was a combination of muted threat and impassioned egalitarianism. In his ecumenical sermons to Christian congregations, he won many admirers among his listeners. He was said to be the first Shīʿī *mujtahid* to visit the Maronite patriarch in his bastion at Bkerke. Many Maronites, not surprisingly, saw a natural ally in Imam Mūsā. He was a reformer, not a revolutionary, and he sought the betterment of the Shīʿah in a Lebanese context. He often noted, "For us Lebanon is one definitive homeland." The covenant or pact of the Movement of the Deprived, which al-Ṣadr wrote in 1974, emphasizes that the movement "adheres to the principles of national sovereignty, the indivisibility of the motherland, and the integrity of her soil." (See Norton, 1987, pp. 144–166, for the text of the pact.)

Mūsā al-Ṣadr recognized the insecurity of the Maronites, and he acknowledged their need to maintain their monopoly-hold on the presidency. Yet he was critical of the Maronites for their arrogant stance toward the Muslims, and particularly the Shīʿīs. He argued that the Maronite-dominated government had neglected the south, where as many as 50 percent of the Shīʿīs lived, since independence, and had made the Shīʿīs a disinherited class in Lebanon. Quoting from the Qur'ān, he often reminded his listeners that "He who sleeps while having a needy neighbor is not considered a believer."

He was anticommunist, one suspects not only on principled grounds but because the various communist organizations were among his prime competitors for Shīʿī recruits. He claimed to reject ideologies of the right and the left, noting that "we are neither of the right nor the left, but we follow the path of the just [*al-ṣirāṭ al-mustaqīm*]." Yet when the two branches of the Baʿth party (pro-Iraqi and pro-Syrian) were making significant inroads among the Shīʿīs of the south and the Beirut suburbs, he appropriated their Pan-Arab slogans.

Although the movement he founded, Ḥarakat al-Maḥrūmin (Movement of the Deprived), was aligned with the Lebanese National Movement (LNM) in the early stages of the Lebanese civil war Imam Mūsā found the LNM's Druze leader, Kamal Jumblatt, irresponsible and exploitative of the Shīʿīs. As he once noted, the LNM was willing "to combat the Christians to the last Shīʿī." According to Karīm Bakradūnī, a thoughtful militia figure, al-Ṣadr imputed to Jumblatt the prolongation of the war.

After the 1970 defeat of the Palestine Liberation Organization (PLO) in Jordan, the bulk of the PLO fighters relocated to south Lebanon where they proceeded to supplant the legitimate authorities. For their part, some PLO officials believed that Mūsā al-Ṣadr was a creation of the army's Deuxième Bureau (the Second [or intelligence] Bureau), or the CIA. Imam Mūsā prophetically warned the PLO that it was not in its interests to establish a state within a state in Lebanon. After he was gone, Shīʿī militiamen invoking his memory fought pitched battles with the PLO and its Lebanese allies, applauded the defeat of the *fidā'ī* at the hands of Israel in 1982, laid siege to their camps in 1985, and pledged never to permit the re-creation of the Palestinian state-within-a-state in Lebanon.

In 1967 the Chamber of Deputies (the Lebanese parliament) passed a law establishing a Supreme Islamic Shīʿī Council (SISC), which would for the first time provide a representative body for the Shīʿīs independent of the Sunnī Muslims. The council actually came into existence in 1969, with Imam Mūsā as its chairman for a six-year term—a stunning confirmation of his status as the leading Shīʿī cleric in the country, and certainly one of the most important political figures in the Shīʿī community. The council quickly made itself heard with demands in the military, social, economic, and political realms, including: improved measures for the defense of the South, the provision of development funds, construction and improvement of schools and hospitals, and an increase in the number of Shīʿīs appointed to senior government positions. The SISC quickly became a locus of action for the Shīʿī intelligentsia, the emerging middle class, as well as many of the traditional elites.

One year after the formation of the SISC, and following a string of bloody Israeli incursions and bombardments, Mūsā al-Ṣadr organized a general strike "to dramatize to the government the plight of the population of southern Lebanon vis-à-vis the Israeli military threat." Shortly thereafter, the government created the Council of the South (Majlis al-Janūb) which was capitalized at 30 million Lebanese pounds and was chartered to support the development of the region. Unfortunately, the Majlis al-Janūb reputedly became more famous as a cockpit of corruption than as a fount of worthwhile projects.

Kāmil al-Asʿad, the powerful Shīʿī political boss from

the south, quite accurately viewed al-Ṣadr as a serious threat to his political power base and opposed him at almost every move. For Mūsā al-Ṣadr and his followers, al-Asʿad was the epitome of all that was wrong with the *zaʿīm* system. Although the creation of the Council of the South was a victory for al-Ṣadr, it was the formidable al-Asʿad who dominated its operation.

On 17 March 1974, the *arbaʿīn*—the fortieth day after ʿĀshūrāʾ—Mūsā al-Ṣadr was in the Bekaa (Biqāʿ) Valley city of Baalbek at a now famous gathering. Standing before an estimated crowd of 75,000, Imām Mūsā declared the launching of the Ḥarakat al-Maḥrūmin. He ranged over Shīʿī grievances—poor schools, nonexistent public services, governmental neglect—and vowed to struggle relentlessly until the social grievances of the deprived were satisfactorily addressed by the government. He recalled that a Kūfan judge had accused Imam Ḥusayn of straying from the way of his grandfather, the Prophet, and noted that he too was now accused of abandoning his grandfather's way. But he refused to relegate himself to a life of quiet scholarship and prayer:

> The rulers say that the men of religion must only pray and not meddle in other things. They exhort us to fast and to pray for them so that the foundations of their reign will not be shaken, while they move away from religion and exploit it to hold on to their seats of power. . . . [Those in power] are the infidel of the infidels and the most atheist of the atheists. They want us to give ourselves up to them. (Cited in Ajami, 1986, p. 147.)

Civil War Erupts. Just one year later, al-Ṣadr's efforts were overtaken by the onset of civil war in Lebanon. By July 1975 it became known that a militia adjunct to Ḥarakat al-Maḥrumīn had been formed. The militia, Afwāj al-Muqāwamah al-Lubnānīyah (the Lebanese Resistance Detachments), better known by the acronym AMAL (which also means "hope"), was initially trained by al-Fataḥ (the largest organization in the PLO) and it played a minor role in the fighting of 1975 and 1976. Mūsā al-Ṣadr's movement was affiliated with the LNM and its PLO allies during the first year of the civil war, but it broke with them when the Syrians intervened in June 1976 to prevent the defeat of the Maronite-dominated Lebanese Front.

Impressive as Imam Mūsā's influence was, it is important not to exaggerate his impact in terms of the political mobilization of the Shīʿīs. The multiconfessional parties and militias attracted the majority of Shīʿī recruits and many more Shīʿīs carried arms under the colors of these organizations than under Amal's. Even in war the Shīʿīs suffered disproportionately; by a large measure they incurred more casualties than any other sect in Lebanon. Perhaps the single most important success achieved by al-Ṣadr was the reduction of the authority and the influence of the traditional Shīʿī elites, but it was the civil war, and the associated growth of extralegal organizations, that conclusively rendered these personalities increasingly irrelevant in the Lebanese political system.

Despite his occasionally vehement histrionics, Mūsā al-Ṣadr was hardly a man of war. (He seems to have played only an indirect role in directing the military actions of the Amal militia.) In a poignant effort to curtail the violence, he declared a hunger strike, but the combination of visceral fury and frustration, government impotence, and the strength of the emerging warlords dwarfed the gesture. His weapons were words, and as a result his political efforts were short-circuited by the war. In the months preceding the outbreak of mayhem Mūsā al-Ṣadr's star was still rising, but his political fortunes plummeted by 1976.

The Hidden Imam. Ironically, it was the still mysterious disappearance of Mūsā al-Ṣadr in 1978 that helped to retrieve the promise of his earlier efforts. In August 1978 he visited Libya with two companions, Shaykh Muḥammad Shihādah Yaʿqūb and journalist ʿAbbās Badr al-Dīn. The party has not been heard from since. Although his fate is not known, it is widely suspected that he died at the hands of the Libyan leader, Colonel Muʿammar al-Qadhdhāfī for reasons that remain obscure. The anniversary of his disappearance, 31 August, is celebrated annually with a national strike in Lebanon.

Mūsā al-Ṣadr has become a hero to his followers, who revere his memory and take inspiration from his words and his suffering. The symbol of a missing imam—reminiscent as it is of the central dogma of Shiism—is hard to assail, and even his blood enemies are now heard to utter words of praise. The movement he founded, now simply called Amal, has—since his disappearance—become the largest Shīʿī organization in Lebanon and one of the most powerful. Simultaneously, the more militant Ḥizbullāh (Party of God) claims the Imām al-Ghāʾib (or the Hidden Imam) as its forebear.

The competition for supremacy in Lebanon among the Shīʿīs is in large measure a matter of who is the rightful heir to the legacy of Mūsā al-Ṣadr. On the one side is Ḥizbullāh, under the strong influence of Muḥammad Ḥusayn Faḍlallāh, which emerged after the Israeli invasion of Lebanon and has been authoritatively associated with the kidnappings of foreigners. On the other side is Amal, still a reform movement, but an angrier, more vengeful one than it was under al-Ṣadr's leadership. Mūsā al-Ṣadr would probably recognize neither organization, but his message that deprivation or second-class citizenship need not be passively accepted retains its power.

[*See also* Amal; Lebanon.]

BIBLIOGRAPHY

Ajami, Fouad. *The Vanished Imam: Musa al-Sadr and the Shia of Lebanon*. Ithaca, N.Y., 1986.

Bulloch, John. *Death of a Country: The Civil War in Lebanon*. London, 1977.

Cole, Juan R. I., and Nikki R. Keddie, eds. *Shiʿism and Social Protest*. New Haven, 1986.

Khalidi, Walid. *Conflict and Violence in Lebanon: Confrontation in the Middle East*. Cambridge, Mass., 1979.

Mallat, Chibli. *Shiʿi Thought from the South of Lebanon*. Oxford, 1988.

Norton, Augustus Richard. *Amal and the Shiʿa: Struggle for the Soul of Lebanon*. Austin, 1987. (Arabic edition, Beirut, 1988.)

Pakradouni, Karim. *La paix manquée*. 2d ed. Beirut, 1984.

Salibi, Kamal S. *Crossroads to Civil War: Lebanon, 1958–1976*. Delmar, N.Y., 1976.

Sicking, Thom, and Shereen Khairallah. "The Shiʿa Awakening in Lebanon: A Search for Radical Change in a Traditional Way." In *Vision and Revision in Arab Society, 1974*, pp. 97–130. Beirut, 1975.

Theroux, Peter. *The Strange Disappearance of Imam Moussa Sadr*. London, 1987.

Wright, Robin. *Sacred Rage: The Crusade of Modern Islam*. New York, 1985.

AUGUSTUS RICHARD NORTON

ṢAFAVID DYNASTY. The Ṣafavid dynasty ruled Iran from 1501 to 1722, its end occasioned by the Afghan invasion. After 1722 a few members of the Ṣafavid family, particularly between 1729 and 1736 and between 1749 and 1773, were nominally shah, but in fact they were without real power. The Turkish-speaking Ṣafavids came from Azerbaijan, although they probably had ancient Kurdish origins. In the early years of the dynasty, the Ṣafavids settled in the western regions of the Iranian highlands. The first Ṣafavid capital was Tabriz, then Qazvin. From the time of Shah ʿAbbās I (1588–1629), however, the main Ṣafavid residence was in Isfahan, from which the dynasty controlled a territory corresponding more or less to that of modern Iran.

The origin of the Ṣafavid name is traceable to Ṣafī al-Dīn Isḥāq, who was the founder of the Ṣafawīyah (Ṣafavīyeh), a mystical and paramilitary order that had its center in Ardabil and spread to the southwest of the Caspian Sea. The birth of the Ṣafawīyah corresponds in time to the fall of the Baghdad caliphate under the pressure of the Mongol tribes and the consequent breakup of the Islamic East into different autonomous entities.

The history of Ṣafī al-Dīn's successors is connected to that of a series of tribal groupings and confederations, most of which were ethnically Turkish, that settled in the eastern regions of Anatolia and across the Caucasus mountains in the second half of the fourteenth century. Some of these tribal groupings, like the Kara-koyunlu and the Ak-koyunlu, were organized in statelike systems. Ismāʿīl, the first of the Ṣafavid shahs, entered Tabriz after having defeated the rival Ak-koyunlu. The main social characteristics of these groups and confederations were the preeminence of the nomadic element and the peculiar, substantial tendency to expansion that was normally associated with nomadism.

Coincidentally, the Ṣafavids were brought to power also because of the support of a few of these warrior tribes. These same tribes tried at that time to monopolize the power of the Ṣafavid state itself, but their influence was constantly reduced by Ismāʿīl's successors in favor of the more sedentary and rural social groupings of the Iranian highlands, and they gradually disappeared into the ethnic patterns of Iran. Other than the attitude bespeaking fighting potential that inhered in these tribes, what is of fundamental importance in defining them is their religious spirit. They fostered an extremist popular religious belief strongly suffused with syncretism—which was typical of the Anatolian and Caucasian context of that period. This was an environment in which Christian, pre-Islamic Turkish, and Muslim cults formed an intricate mixture, endowing practically all the local religious expressions of the time with Shīʿī themes of devotion to Imam ʿAlī and his family.

During the fifteenth century, the shaykhs of the Ṣafawīyah, one of whom was al-Junayd, promoted a singular political alliance with one of the former tribal groups, the Qizilbash. The Qizilbash represented a relatively homogenous tribal whole. The Ṣafavid alliance with them was one of the reasons for the Ṣafavid change from Sunnism to Shiism. In terms of doctrine, the Qizilbash cannot be defined as Shīʿī, especially Twelver Shiism, since their religious identity was too syncretic and extremist. But they did possess some distinguishing elements that identified them as Shīʿīs, for example, the twelve bands, representing the twelve imams of the Imāmī Shīʿī tradition, of their distinctive red headgear, which gave them the name "redcaps." They were at the same time an ideological and military movement that, together with ʿAlid devotion, was strongly focused on a messianic kind of expectation. Such religious fanaticism was concentrated on the leaders of the Ṣafawīyah.

Ismāʿīl's biography for the years preceding his seizure of power traces the commonplace hagiographic outlines of great charismatic leaders: his having been an orphan, his loneliness, persecution, the help of a few close friends. Nevertheless, he had some initial success, and this was interpreted as a proof of his "elected status." On the grounds of this success, he was able to make the most of the Qizilbash military force, and of the ideological impetus deriving from their worship of him as a god on earth. But Ṣafavid religious extremism soon ended for two main reasons.

The first reason lay in the necessity of obtaining a religious consensus in Iran. This need brought first Ismāʿīl and then—with greater determination—his successor, Ṭahmāsp (1524–1576), to cast off the theocratic form of power. They came to embrace a belief system that departed from leader worship by making Twelver Shiism the state religion. Iran at this time was mostly Sunnī, but ʿAlī's descendants and Shīʿī *ʿulamāʾ* had acquired a privileged role and were widely recognized by the masses. The second reason was the inevitable clash between the new Ṣafavid power and the Ottoman dynasty, which by then was firmly established and determined to maintain control over the whole of Anatolia, including the eastern regions. Although the Ṣafavid defeat at the Battle of Chaldiran (1514) permanently demolished Ṣafavid ambitions toward Anatolia, it also caused a crisis in Ismāʿīl's rule, diminishing his power by reducing the aura of his link to the divinity.

These conditions determined the subsequent fate of Iran. Shīʿī assumptions became the main distinguishing element of Iranian religious life, in comparison to the Sunnī Ottomans, on the one side, and the Sunnī Uzbeks and Mughals, on the other. At the same time, Iran became an imperative reference point for various Shīʿī dynasties that imposed their rule in various regions of the Islamic world: for example, the Deccan sultanates of the sixteenth and seventeenth centuries; Shīʿī social movements generally speaking; and the Shīʿī community in Iraq (probably the most homogeneous and well structured of them all).

The imperial yearning of ruling dynasties in Iran, beginning with the Ṣafavid era, was never to be appeased. This has great relevance even today. Iran, unlike other countries in the area, was already a national or protonational state in the sixteenth century. The confessional imprimatur that characterized Iran did not really change the country's multiethnic and multicultural structure. Despite the fact that just over a century later Shiism was the religion of the overwhelming majority, initially conversion to Shiism was slow. It came about gradually through the mechanism of the administration of justice. The rulers sought to import jurisconsults from Bahrain and Lebanon, especially the Jabal ʿĀmil region in southern Lebanon. From Iran, some of these jurists moved on to India and elsewhere.

Certain changes began to occur in the administrative realm, as the rulers increasingly centralized state power. This led to the replacement of the administrative apparatus that had been inherited from the Timurid tradition (1360–1460s). This process of centralization reached its peak under Shah ʿAbbās I. Clashes with former nomadic elements led to the creation of special military forces recruited mainly from the ranks of those with Georgian and Circassian origin, paid by the shah and answerable only to him.

The shah's continuing need for revenues to sustain his military expenditures led to a progressive transfer of landed property into the hands of the crown *(khāṣṣah)*. A consequence of this was the strengthening of the shah's power according to a historical pattern that was to repeat itself up to the Pahlavi dynasty, despite the monarchy's loss of political prestige. The transformation of the monarch into the country's largest landowner brought about the breakup of the traditional structure of the rural areas, where every family in a particular village had had the right to a plot of land to cultivate, to a certain amount of water to irrigate, and to free pasture areas. In spite of the relative opening up to the West, Ṣafavid Iran stayed anchored in the old economic dynamics, characterized by scarce displays of initiative, no entrepreneurial manpower, and an economic profile not far removed from autarky.

Another feature of the Ṣafavid dynasty was the ideological and religious nature of the state. Shiism came to be identified if not exclusively with Persia, then certainly predominantly, a development that entailed the scrapping of the memory of its Arab origins, both from the religious and political points of view. It is true that in the context of Iranian popular religion, with its historical memory of pre-Islamic cults and conceptions, the spread of Shiism was not traumatic. On the contrary, Shiism served as a means of islamizing certain religious attitudes. It is also true that Sufism, which was officially resisted at the end of the seventeenth century, was one of the principal vehicles of conversion to Shiism by virtue of nothing more than the importance of the family of ʿAlī and the practices of devotion directed toward it. By ascribing to themselves religious values by dint of a false descent from ʿAlī, the Ṣafavids' image was strengthened.

All this led to a literary and philosophical renaissance fostered by the growth and spread of the Shīʿī faith. It is this kind of renaissance that shaped the distinctively Persian element of Shiism in respect to neighboring countries. It is not a mere coincidence that it was at that particular stage (the mid-sixteenth century) that the juridical cleavage occurred between two groups. These were the Uṣūlīyah, those advocating *ijtihād* ("independent judgment"); and the Akhbārīyah, those according preference to tradition, rather than to the free interpretation of the religious sources.

It was the Akhbārīyah who, even though the more conservative in their theological and juridical approaches, were to give birth to some radical schools of modern Shiism. Thus the social and religious ferment of the nineteenth century was to foster the Bābī movement and the Bahā'ī religion. Religious vitality would bring about a progressive division between temporal and spiritual power, to the point that the mullahs and the jurisprudents would begin to organize themselves as a separate body with faculties similar to those of Western clergy, that is, many of the elements that characterize contemporary Iran have their roots in the Ṣafavid period. The religious policy of the Ṣafavid shahs was to be interpreted by ʿAlī Sharīʿatī (a contemporary ideologue to whom the Iranian Revolution of 1979 owes a great deal) as "regime Shiism," in contrast to the genuine ʿAlid Shiism of Imam ʿAlī. However, when the weakened Ṣafavid dynasty was followed by the Qājār dynasty (1785–1925), as well as in other times of crisis—for example, the already mentioned period of the Afghan invasion—at the popular level people sought after the Ṣafavid model. In so doing, they hoped that its reinstitution could guarantee the maintenance of the peculiar cultural physiognomy of modern Iran.

[*See also* Iran.]

BIBLIOGRAPHY

Arjomand, Said Amir. "Religious Extremism *(ghuluww)*, Sufism, and Sunnism in Safavid Iran, 1501–1722." *Journal of Asian History* 15 (1981): 1–35.

Aubin, Jean. "Šāh Ismāʿīl et les notables de l'Iraq persan." *Journal of the Economic and Social History of the Orient* 2 (1959): 37–81.

Aubin, Jean. "Révolution chiite et conservatisme: Les soufis de Lâhejân." *Moyen Orient et Océan Indien: XIVe–XIXe siècle* 1 (1984): 1–40.

Aubin, Jean. "L'avènement des Safavides reconsidéré." *Moyen Orient et Océan Indien: XIVe–XIXe siècle* 5 (1988): 1–130.

Bacqué-Grammont, Jean-Louis. *Les Ottomans, les Safavides et leurs voisins*. Istanbul, 1987.

Banani, Amin. "Reflections on the Social and Economic Structure of Safavid Persia at Its Zenith." *Iranian Studies* 11 (1978): 83–116.

Haneda, M. *Le châh et les qizilbâš: Le système militaire safavide*. Berlin, 1987.

Jackson, Peter, and Laurence Lockhart, eds. *The Cambridge History of Iran*, vol. 6, *The Timurid and Safavid Periods*. Cambridge, 1986. See, in particular, chapter 5 by H. R. Roemer (a historical survey), chapter 12 by Biancamaria Scarcia Amoretti, and chapter 13 by Seyyed Hossein Nasr, dedicated respectively to religion and spiritual movements.

Savory, Roger Mervyn. *Iran under the Safavids*. Cambridge, 1980.

Savory, Roger Mervyn. *Studies on the History of Safavid Iran*. London, 1987.

Scarcia, Gianroberto. "Intorno alle controversie tra Akhbārī e Uṣūlī presso gli Imamiti di Persia." *Rivista degli Studi Orientali* 33 (1958): 211–250.

BIANCAMARIA SCARCIA AMORETTI

ṢAḤWAH. *See* Revival and Renewal.

SAID HALIM PASHA, MEHMED (1864–1921), Islamic reformer and Ottoman grand vizier. Born in Cairo, Said Halim was the grandson of Muḥammad ʿAlī, the founder of modern Egypt. At the age of six he came to Istanbul when his father was exiled by Khedive Ismail. Tutors taught Said Halim Arabic, Persian, French, and English. Later he was sent to Switzerland where he read political science. On his return to Istanbul he was appointed to the Council of State in May 1888 and given the rank of a civil pasha. He continued to ascend the administrative ladder and gain new honors.

For an independent-minded and cosmopolitan intellectual, life under Abdülhamid (r. 1876–1908) was suffocating. Therefore, Said Halim withdrew to his villa on the Bosphorus and devoted his energies to the study of history and religion, concerned as he was about the decline and stagnation of the Muslim world vis-à-vis the West. An imperial spy denounced him as subversive, and he was exiled to Egypt and Europe. There he joined the Young Turks, supporting their activities financially.

He returned to Istanbul after constitutional rule was restored in July 1908.

Said Halim became a member of the inner circle of the Committee of Union and Progress (CUP) and leader of the Islamist faction. In December 1908 he was appointed to the senate and the Islamic Education Committee. He entered the cabinet in January 1912 as president of the Council of State; in January 1913, during the Balkan wars, he became foreign minister. He was appointed grand vizier on 11 June 1913 while retaining the foreign ministry. Niyazi Berkes notes that at a time when the Ottoman government "was accused of pursuing a policy of Turkification, its Sadrazam was an ardent Islamist who wrote only in French and Arabic." The appointment was designed to appease Arab/Islamic sentiment in the empire. Said Halim resigned on 3 February 1917 but remained in the senate, devoting himself to writing. The British who occupied Istanbul after the armistice of October 1918 arrested him in March 1919 and deported him to Malta. Released on 29 April 1921, he went to Rome, where he was assassinated by an Armenian nationalist on 6 December 1921.

Apart from his political role, Said Halim Pasha was also the secularly educated spokesman for the conservative Islamist faction of the Young Turks. His articles appeared in *Sırat-ı Müstakim* and *Sebil ürreşad,* but not in the radical *İslam mecmuası,* the organ of the Turkists. Between 1910 and 1921 he wrote influential essays later published in various editions under the title *Buhranlarımız* (Our Crises). Notable among these are "Islamic Fanaticism and Its Meaning, and Fanaticism" and "Our Imitations" (1910), "Constitutionalism" (1911), "Our Social Crisis" (1916), "Our Crisis of Ideas" (1917), "An Essay on the Decline of Islam" and "Islamization" (1918), and "Political Organization in Islam" (1921). The last essay was also published in French.

Said Halim was concerned with countering the West's criticism of Islam. He argued that Islam was a rational religion that encouraged scientific thought and did not regard science as inimical to faith. Since the problems of Western society were different from those of Islamic society, he thought it was damaging to imitate and borrow blindly ideas such as constitutionalism. The world of Islam should find its own answers to its own problems in the context of its own traditions and heritage, especially the *sharīʿah.* As for "Muslim fanaticism," he argued that the phrase reflected "in reality, not the Muslims' enmity towards Christians, but the West's inherent enmity towards the East."

[See also Ottoman Empire; Young Turks.]

BIBLIOGRAPHY

Ahmad, Feroz. *The Young Turks.* Oxford, 1969. Useful for the politics of the period 1908–1914.

Berkes, Niyazi. *The Development of Secularism in Turkey.* Montreal, 1964. Superb study of Ottoman/Turkish intellectual history.

Landau, Jacob. *The Politics of Pan-Islam: Ideology and Organization.* Oxford, 1990. Thorough study of an important subject.

Said Halim Paşha. "Notes pour servir à la réforme de la société musulmane." *Orient et Occident* 1 (January 1922): 18–52. French translation of Said Halim's last article.

FEROZ AHMAD

SAINTHOOD. The words "saint" and "sainthood" are used cross-culturally to describe persons of exceptional spiritual merit and the status attained by such persons. These terms are originally derived from Christian experience; it must not be assumed that all features of Christian sainthood are reproduced in Islam. Some similarities and differences are noted below.

The approximate equivalent in Arabic to "saint" is *walī* (pl., *awliyā'*); *wilāyah* or *walāyah* may be translated as "sainthood." The literal meaning of *walī* is "friend," "helper," or "patron." There is no passage in the Qur'ān that explicitly recognizes saints or sanctions the institution of sainthood. In fact, the message of the Qur'ān regarding *walī* is quite different. It repeatedly emphasizes that God and God alone is the *walī* of the believers and that there is no *walī* or helper but him (3.68, 2.107, 2.120, 9.116, 18.26, and many other verses). Humankind is sternly warned against taking "friends" or seeking aid from any but God (6.14, 42.9), as have the wrongdoers who take each other as friends (45.19, 8.73) and those who are the *awliyā'* of Satan instead of God (16.63, 4.76, 7.30). In addition, the Qur'ān disallows intercession *(shafāʿah)* by any but God (2.48, 74.48); there is neither *walī* nor *shafīʿ* (intercessor) except him (6.51).

Nevertheless, those who read *walī* as "saint" have found support in the scriptures. The revelation mentions that the believers may be "friends" to one another (5.55, 9.71), and some Ṣūfī exegetes have interpreted verse 62 of the tenth surah of the Qur'ān—"As for the friends *(awliyā')* of God, no fear shall come upon them, nor shall they grieve"—as referring to a class of persons selected by God for special favor, possessing esoteric knowledge, or even guarded from committing major sins. Ṣūfī exegesis has sometimes seized on qualifying phrases in verses banning intercession—for instance, "There is no intercessor *except by His permission*"

(10.3)—to suggest that there are indeed some granted special favor by God who may intercede on behalf of others. The Ṣūfīs also point to a number of *ḥadīth*s that describe the qualities and privileges of *awliyā*.

Sainthood in Islam is informal. Saints become saints by acclamation; there is no process of canonization and no constituted body to apply it, as in Catholicism. Consequently, there are many types of saints. Popular saints are the focus of local cults emerging from a stratum of pre-Islamic religion. These saints are associated with simple shrines or even natural objects such as springs or trees, and their veneration involves a variety of folk practices. A large number of such saints are found in North Africa, where they are known as *murābiṭ* ("he who watches [through the night over his soul]"; Fr., *marabout*). A host of popular saints was once venerated by the Arab population of Palestine, and similar figures are still a focus of folk religious life in present-day Lebanon. In Morocco, Palestine, Lebanon, Egypt, and Anatolia some saints were formerly shared by Jewish, Christian, and Muslim worshipers, but as political events and social developments have separated these religious groups, ecumenical saint-worship has declined.

Sufism has served in the past to absorb local customs and culture and to bring non-Islamic and peasant populations into the fold of Islam. Thus the majority of popular saints are also Ṣūfī saints. The tombs of such saints often serve as the focal point of the Ṣūfī lodges *(khānaqāh, ribāṭ, zāwiyah,* or *tekke)* in which members of the fraternities reside or meet and Ṣūfī ceremonies are performed. The anniversary of the birth or death of the saint *(mawlid)* may involve a more elaborate festival featuring songs and processions. Some Ṣūfī shaykhs, unlike Christian saints, are acclaimed as saints while still living; these may be called on to dispense advice and mediate disputes. Ṣūfī sainthood, in any case, has fulfilled and continues to fulfill an important social function, as saintly authority sometimes remains in one family through generations, and tribal and other social structures are reinforced through allegiance to particular saints.

Another category of saints is the past saints of Ṣūfī legend. Most of these are not identified with tombs; their memorials are contained instead in brief tales of their wise sayings, virtues, and miracles related in the biographical anecdotes that comprise an important part of Ṣūfī literature. (Some contemporary saints have been the subjects of more lengthy biographies.) A significant number of popular, Ṣūfī, and legendary saints are women. Muslim women, it seems, have found it easier to gain spiritual fame outside of mainstream Islam.

Finally, Ṣūfī mystical speculation presents an elaborate hierarchy of saints. These *awliyā'* comprise a divinely elected class, according to some accounts numbering several hundred. Their existence is said to be as necessary as that of the prophets, the chief of them being the "pole" *(quṭb)* around which the very universe revolves.

The mainstream Twelver Shīʿīs do not speak of saints, since the spiritual rank of *wilāyah* is already occupied by their imams who, much like the Ṣūfī saints, are God's elect, sustain the existence of the world, worked miracles in their lifetime, and continue to intercede for their followers with God. Iranian Shiism, however, does allow for a kind of lesser sainthood and absorption of local pilgrimage sites and folk practices by attaching these to relatives of the imams. There are many such *imāmzādah* ("related to the imams") shrines in Iran, some rather rudimentary and doubtful but nevertheless still active. A large and elaborate shrine has lately been constructed over the remains of Ayatollah Khomeini near the Bihisht-i Zahrā cemetery outside Tehran and is already a favorite place of pilgrimage. Khomeini has certainly become a "saint" in a practical, if not theological, sense; his charisma far outweighs that of any other deceased member of the religious hierarchy, and he may well become the only true Shīʿī saint apart from the imams and *imāmzādah*s. [*See* Imāmzādah.]

The chief function of the Islamic saints, similar to that of the Christian saints, is to intercede with God on behalf of those who appeal to them. The power the saints are granted to facilitate the affairs of their devotees and smooth their way to God is called *barakah* or "blessing." The tombs of the saints—or, during their lives, their residences—are the object of pilgrimage *(ziyārah)* by those who hope to obtain this *barakah. Barakah* is often thought to be transferred by physical touch from the tomb or person of the saint to the petitioner. Some popular saints are noted for dispensing particular kinds of favors: for instance, a female saint may be expert in granting children to the women who specially visit her or otherwise settling domestic matters. Allegiance to saints, saint pilgrimage, and seeking of *barakah* have lessened with modern times, particularly with the decline of Sufism; these practices, however, do survive, particularly among urban poor and rural populations. [*See* Barakah.]

Some Muslims have been opposed to sainthood as being un-Islamic in both conception and practice; the Qur'ānic texts referred to above enter into this controversy. Seeking intercession, belief in miracles, and pilgrimage to saints' tombs have been particularly disapproved; the dangers in these are thought to be violation of monotheism and setting up others as equal to the Prophet. An effort was made by the theologians to admit sainthood while protecting the position of the prophets by distinguishing the full-blown miracles *(muʿjizāt)* of the former from the mere "charismata" *(karāmāt)* of the latter. Some written creeds even listed belief in the *awliyā'* as an article of faith. Nevertheless, sainthood and saint-worship were frequent targets of the orthodox *ʿulamā'*. Ibn Taymīyah (d. 1328) was perhaps the most prominent critic of sainthood. He vigorously condemned the visiting of tombs and other popular practices as corruption of the true religion. Ibn Taymīyah has influenced many Islamic thinkers to seek a return to pure, "original" Islam, and they have also followed him in condemning sainthood. The present Saudi regime upholds Wahhābism, a movement originating in the Arabian Peninsula in the eighteenth century that also traces its spiritual descent to Ibn Taymīyah. The government and religious hierarchy of Saudi Arabia thus seek to suppress any manifestation of saint-worship; this is particularly significant since the Saudis have great religious influence in the Muslim world. A second type of criticism of sainthood is exclusively modern. This trend of thought sees saint-worship as a prime manifestation of the irrationality and obscurantism which has weakened the Muslim world. The Egyptian reformer Muḥammad Rashīd Riḍā (d. 1935) was one of those who expressed this opinion. The revered Pakistani thinker Muhammad Iqbal (d. 1938) and other subcontinental modernists have also considered the numerous local saints (called pirs, "elders") as founts of superstition and upholders of the feudal system and have thus called for the elimination of "pirism."

Saints and their shrines have often been centers of political power. Within the context of the modern nation-state, governments have tried either to suppress or to coopt saintly institutions. The secularizing measures of Mustafa Kemal Atatürk in the 1920s included suppression of the Turkish shrines and devaluing of saintly personality. In Pakistan various regimes have combined programs tending to strike at the economic and spiritual authority of living pirs with a conspicuous effort to make the state the overseer of the shrines and to patronize ceremonies associated with them. The pirs have responded to this by competing in the political system—for instance by influencing or putting up candidates—and have thus managed to maintain some independence and defend their interests. The Egyptian government has lately found it useful to patronize the saints and protect pilgrims and festivals in order to counter the Islamists who, in true fundamentalist fashion, abhor saint-worship; armed soldiers can be seen around some shrines at festival times. It seems that devotion to the saints is considered a politically safe diversion for the urbanizing masses.

[*See also* Pir; Popular Religion; Sufism, *article on* Ṣūfī Shrine Culture; Walāyah; Wilāyah.]

BIBLIOGRAPHY

Ansari, Sarah F. D. *Sufi Saints and State Power: The Pirs of Sind, 1843–1947*. Cambridge, 1992. Describes the functioning of the pir system in a modern political context and in the face of colonialism.

Biegmann, Nicolaas. *Egypt: Moulids, Saints, Sufis*. The Hague, 1990. A hundred color photographs, accompanied by text, convey the flavor of popular and Ṣūfī saint worship.

Canaan, Taufik. *Mohammedan Saints and Sanctuaries in Palestine* (1927). Jerusalem, 1979. Detailed description of popular shrines and folk practices in former Palestine.

Denny, Frederick Mathewson. " 'God's Friends': The Sanctity of Persons in Islam." In *Sainthood: Its Manifestations in World Religions*, edited by Richard Kieckhefer and George D. Bond, pp. 69–97. Berkeley, 1988. Treats the notion of sanctity throughout Islam, rather than confining it to saints.

Farīd al-Dīn ʿAṭṭār. *Tazkirat al-awliyā* (Memorials of the Saints). Selections translated by A. J. Arberry as *Muslim Saints and Mystics*. Chicago, 1966. The Persian mystical poet ʿAṭṭār's (d. c.1230) classic compilation of biographical notices of the saints.

Gellner, Ernest. *Saints of the Atlas*. Chicago, 1969. Specialized work, of particular interest to anthropologists and sociologists. Describes the social functioning of sainthood and *barakah* in the context of Berber settlements in Morocco; based on fieldwork done in the 1950s and 1960s.

Gilsenan, Michael. *Saint and Sufi in Modern Egypt: An Essay in the Sociology of Religion*. Oxford, 1973. Lively, imaginative, and readable account of modern Sufism and its underlying themes, written by a prominent anthropologist.

Goldziher, Ignácz. "The Veneration of Saints in Islam." In his *Muslim Studies*, vol. 2, pp. 255–341. Translated by S. M. Stern. London, 1971. Classic essay that presents sainthood, including veneration of the Prophet, as an accretion to original Islam. Many interesting popular practices are detailed, but the material (first published in 1890 in German) is now dated.

Lings, Martin. *A Sufi Saint of the Twentieth Century: Shaykh Aḥmad al-ʿAlawī, His Spiritual Heritage and Legacy*. 3d ed. Cambridge, 1993. Personal account of an Algerian Ṣūfī master and saint active in the first half of the twentieth century.

Memon, Muhammad Umar. *Ibn Taymīya's Struggle against Popular Religion*. The Hague and Paris, 1976. Includes an annotated translation of one of Ibn Taymīyah's polemics against sainthood.

LYNDA CLARKE

SALAFĪYAH. A reform movement founded by Jamāl al-Dīn al-Afghānī and Muḥammad ʿAbduh at the turn of the twentieth century, the Salafīyah has religious, cultural, social, and political dimensions. It aimed at the renewal of Muslim life and had a formative impact on many Muslim thinkers and movements across the Islamic world.

The term *salafīyah* is often used interchangeably with *iṣlāḥ* (reform) and *tajdīd* (renewal), which are fundamental concepts to Islam's worldview. For some, however, the term connotes reaction and rigidness because of the Salafīyah's strict adherence to the Qur'ān and *sunnah* and its exaltation of the past.

The word *salafīyah* is derived from the Arabic root *salaf,* "to precede." The Qur'ān uses the word *salaf* to refer to the past (5.95, 8.38). In Arabic lexicons, the *salaf* are the virtuous forefathers *(al-salaf al-ṣāliḥ),* and the *salafī* is the one who draws on the Qur'ān and the *sunnah* as the only sources for religious rulings (*Al-muʿjam al-wasīṭ,* vol. 1, p. 461).

The issue of who is considered a member of the *salaf* is a controversial one; however, most Muslim scholars agree that the *salaf* comprise the first three generations of Muslims. They span three centuries and include the companions of the Prophet, al-Ṣaḥābah, who end with Anas ibn Mālik (d. AH 91/710 CE or 93/712); their followers, al-Tābiʿīn (180/796); and the followers of their followers, Tābiʿ al-Tābiʿī (241/855). Aḥmad ibn Ḥanbal (164–241/780–855) is considered the last of the generation of the *salaf.* These three generations were highly esteemed by later Muslims for their companionship with the Prophet and proximity to his time and for their pure understanding and practice of Islam and contribution to it.

The chronological definition of the *salaf* is not sufficient to explain the term fully. The *salaf* are not confined to a specific group nor to a certain era. Muslims recognize later prominent scholars and independent figures as members of the *salaf,* including Abū Ḥāmid al-Ghazālī (d. 1111), Ibn Taymīyah (d. 1328), Ibn Qayyim al-Jawzīyah (d. 1350), Muḥammad ibn ʿAbd al-Wahhāb (d. 1792), and others. Moreover, the views of the members of the earliest Muslim generations were varied. The ideological components of the Salafīyah changed over the years in response to the challenges the Muslim community faced as its dedication to reform and revival persisted.

Origins. As Muslims began to expand beyond the Arabian Peninsula, they came into direct contact with different cultures, religions, and philosophical trends, among them Jews, Christians, Sabaeans, and Zoroastrians. They were also confronted with new situations and intellectual challenges for which they had to devise answers that reflected the ideals of the new faith. In addition to the Qur'ān, they used rational thought to present and explain Islamic concepts and doctrines, applying this technique to such issues as the existence of God, the divine attributes, the nature of the Qur'ān, and whether God is seen in paradise.

The violent conflicts that took place among Muslims over the caliphal succession following the death of ʿUthmān (d. 35/656) opened many controversies on such topics as the nature of faith, the status of the sinner, the nature of human acts, freedom and determination, and the imamate. Hence new intellectual currents and disciplines emerged within Islamic thought. Among the early developments was the discipline of *kalām* (theology). Its advocates addressed the aforementioned issues and resorted to subjective interpretations of the Qur'ān, using analogy and philosophy. The major representatives of this trend were the Qadarīyah, Jabrīyah, Ṣifatīyah, Khawārij, and Muʿtazilah. Several of these schools, particularly the first two, gained popularity and created divisions among the *ummah.* Some of their views represented a threat to the orthodox understanding of the issue of *tawḥīd* (the unity of God), the core concept of Islam. They also gave rationalist thinking and theological discussions prominence over revelation. [*See* Theology *and* Tawḥīd.]

Ibn Ḥanbal, Articulator of Classic Salafīyah. The diversity in opinions and fierce debate among the adherents of the theological schools gave rise to another intellectual trend that advocated a return by Muslims to pure and simple Islam and to the understanding of doctrine on the basis of the Qur'ān, the *sunnah,* and the *ḥadīth* traditions of the *salaf.* Aḥmad ibn Ḥanbal, the founder of the fourth school of Sunnī jurisprudence, was the major articulator of this trend. In his fight against the Muʿtazilah's doctrine of the creation of the Qur'ān, he laid out the tenets that later shaped the Salafīyah.

Ibn Ḥanbal's thought focused on several principles. The first is the primacy of the revealed text over reason. Ibn Ḥanbal saw no contradiction between reason and scripture. Unlike the *mutakallimūn* (scholastic theologians) who subjected the revealed text to reason, he dismissed *ta'wīl* (subjective or esoteric interpretation) of the texts and explained them in accordance with Arabic philology, *ḥadīth,* and the understanding of the Prophet's companions and their successors. The second principle is the rejection of *kalām*. The Salafīyah considered the issues raised by the theological schools as *bidʿah* (innovation) and confirmed the orthodox view of these matters. The third is strict adherence to the Qur'ān, the *sunnah*, and the consensus *(ijmāʿ)* of the pious ancestors. In line with the major Sunnī schools, Ibn Ḥanbal held the Qur'ān and the teachings of the Prophet to be the authoritative sources for understanding the matters of religion, from which the principles of the *sharīʿah* are derived. He set strict guidelines for the use of *ijtihād* (independent reasoning) and restricted the use of *qiyās* (analogical reasoning).

The Salafīyah approach evolved over the years to address new issues confronting the Muslim community. Taqī al-Dīn ibn Taymīyah, a follower of the Ḥanbalī school, jurist, and theologian, contributed greatly to the evolution of the Salafīyah. He combated accretions and innovations in religious practices and beliefs, particularly those introduced by the Ṣūfī orders (such as pantheism, syncretism, and saint-worship), and he criticized vehemently the different theological trends. His approach focused on confirming the creed of *tawḥīd*, proving the compatibility of reason and revelation, and refuting the ideological arguments of the theological schools, which he believed were influenced by Greek philosophy and terminology. Ibn Taymīyah regarded himself as a *mujtahid* within the Ḥanbalī school, but as a result of changes in time and conditions, he departed from it in some respects: he rejected *taqlīd* (adherence to tradition) and *ijmāʿ* and approved of the use of *qiyās*, and also maintained his own views on several jurisprudential issues. [*See the biography of Ibn Taymīyah.*]

Because of its emphasis on the restoration of Islamic doctrines to their pure form, adherence to the Qur'ān and *sunnah*, rejection of accretions, and maintaining the unity of the *ummah*, the Salafīyah has embodied the potential for reform and renewal, particularly at times of weakness and degeneration of the Muslim community. It has been a major influence on many movements that sought to reform their own communities on the basis of the original principles of Islam.

Premodern Salafīyah. In the eighteenth century several reform movements emerged to address the moral and social decay of the Muslim community. The Wahhābīyah is the most important. Its founder, Muḥammad ibn ʿAbd al-Wahhāb (1703–1792), drew on the teachings of Ibn Ḥanbal and Ibn Taymīyah in his drive to purify the Arabian Peninsula from un-Islamic practices and build an Islamic state modeled on that founded by the Prophet. The Wahhābīyah influenced other movements such as the Sanūsīyah and Mahdīyah, notwithstanding their Ṣūfī tendencies. [*See* Wahhābīyah.]

Similar movements surfaced beyond the Arab world, including the movement of Usuman Dan Fodio (1754–1817) in Nigeria, and the movements of Aḥmad Sirhindī (1564–1624), Shāh Walī Allāh (1702–1762), and Sayyid Aḥmad Barelwī (1786–1831) in the Indian subcontinent. They all advocated religious purification, moral and social reform, and unity among Muslims. However, they remained literalist in their reinterpretation of religion and tied to the past; they struggled not to build a viable model for the future but recreate the early model of the Prophet and his companions. Nonetheless, these movements left a legacy that inspired reform movements in the nineteenth and twentieth centuries. [*See the biographies of Dan Fodio, Sirhindī, Barelwī, and Walī Allāh.*]

Modern Salafīyah. The modern Salafīyah was established by Jamāl al-Dīn al-Afghānī (1839–1897) and Muḥammad ʿAbduh (1849–1905) at the turn of the twentieth century. Its prime objectives were to rid the Muslim *ummah* of a centuries-long mentality of *taqlīd* (blind imitation) and *jumūd* (stagnation), to restore Islam to its pristine form, and to reform the moral, cultural, and political conditions of Muslims. It is distinguished from the classic Salafīyah by its essentially intellectual and modernist nature and by the diversity and expanse of its objectives.

Against a legacy of stagnation, moral and social decay, political despotism, and foreign domination, the Salafīyah of Afghānī and ʿAbduh sought to revitalize Islam, to bridge the gap between historical Islam and modernity, and to restore Muslim solidarity and vigor. The writings of Afghānī and ʿAbduh—and of other reformist intellectuals such as ʿAbd al-Raḥmān al-Kawākibī (1854–1902), Muḥammad Rashīd Riḍā (1865–1935), and ʿAbd al-Ḥamīd ibn Bādīs (1889–1940)—focused on certain issues that constituted the ideological foundations of the modern Salafīyah. Among these were the causes of Muslim weakness, the reinterpretation of Islam, and comprehensive and institutional reform. [*See the biographies of Kawākibī, Rashīd Riḍā, and Ibn Bādīs.*]

The overwhelming supremacy of the West posed a dilemma for Muslim intellectuals, who probed the causes of Muslim weakness in an attempt to remedy them.

This issue has dominated the intellectual discourse of the reformist thinkers. It permeated the articles in *Al-ʿurwah al-wuthqā* (published by Afghānī and ʿAbduh in 1884 while in exile in Paris), Riḍā's periodical *Al-manār* (1889–1935), the writings of al-Kawākibī (particularly *Umm al-qurā*), and those of Ibn Bādīs.

They identified the roots of the evil not in the teachings of Islam but rather in the infiltration of alien concepts and practices, the disintegration of the Muslim community, and the practice of political despotism. Distortion of basic Islamic beliefs spread attitudes of predeterminism, passivity, and submission among Muslims, leading to stagnation and blind imitation by the traditionalist *ʿulama'*. They also precluded the advancement of Muslims and prevented them from pursuing power and independence. Thus they restricted the exercise of *ijtihād,* the force that preserves the vitality of Islam and links it to real life.

In the face of the threat of cultural submission to Western colonialism, the Salafīyah worked to assert the validity of Islam in modern times and to prove its compatibility with reason and science. They viewed it as a holistic message covering all aspects of life and as the driving force for advancement. For them, Islam provides Muslims with the foundations of progress. It honors humans and asserts their sovereignty on earth, blesses Muslims with the creed of *tawḥīd,* and sanctions the pursuit of knowledge and progress (Afghānī, 1973, pp. 136–139). Thus the reformist thinkers were trying to restore the pride of Muslims in their religion, to pave the way for reinterpreting Islam in a manner compatible with modernity, and to legitimize the acquisition of some Western scientific and technological achievements.

The reinterpretation of Islam constituted the second major principle of the modern Salafīyah. Like the classical thinkers, the modern Salafīs emphasized the importance of *tawḥīd* (ʿAbduh, 1897), purifying the Muslims' beliefs and practices from accretions, and restoring the unadulterated form of Islam. ʿAbduh summarized the objectives of the Salafīyah as follows: "To liberate thought from the shackles of *taqlīd,* and understand religion as it was understood by the elders of the community before dissension appeared; to return, in the acquisition of religious knowledge, to its first sources, and to weigh them in the scales of human reason" (cited in Hourani, 1962, pp. 140–141).

The modern reformers shared with classic Salafīyah the belief that the Qur'ān was the uncreated word of God, and they rejected any esoteric interpretation of its verses. Although they sought a return to the authoritative sources of Islam—Qur'ān, *sunnah,* and a few authentic *ḥadīth*—the modern Salafīyah went a step further in their attempt to devise a synthesis between text and reason. They considered revelation and reason to be in full consonance; whenever there seemed to be a contradiction between the two, they employed reasoning to reinterpret the text. In particular, ʿAbduh's and Aḥmad Khān's reinterpretations of some Qur'ānic verses sometimes went beyond the orthodox interpretations. For ʿAbduh, "reason is the source of unshakable truth about the belief in God, His knowledge, and omnipotence and the belief in His message" (*Islam and Christianity with Science and Modernity,* Cairo, 1954, p. 113). The Islamic reformists were well versed in theology and philosophy and utilized them in their discourse.

In their commentaries on the Qur'ān, the reformists tried to link the scriptures to modern-day conditions. This approach helped in reviving the Qur'ānic message, restoring its relevance, and making it understandable to ordinary Muslims. It offered an alternative to the literalism of traditionalist interpretations. The reformists' commentaries also suggested avenues for the renewal of Islamic disciplines and new approaches to jurisprudence, ethics, and law (Merad, 1960–, p. 147; Jurshī, 1991, pp. 212–213).

By emphasizing return to the fundamental sources of Islam, the Salafīyah thinkers aimed at unleashing the potential for exercising *ijtihād*. Their confidence in the ability of the Muslim mind to deal directly with revelation would eventually liberate Muslims from slavish obedience to traditionalist authorities. This, it was hoped, would give rise to a new jurisprudence and a positive rationalism that would eliminate the divisions among the different legal schools and draw on *ijtihād* without compromising the fundamentals of Islam.

To achieve this ambitious objective, the Salafīyah, following the line of Ibn Taymīyah, emphasized the distinction between the immutable and the mutable in religion. The former deals with matters of creed and rituals (*ʿibādat*), which have been prescribed in the Qur'ān and the authentic *sunnah;* any additions to them were condemned as unacceptable innovation. The Salafīs therefore launched fierce campaigns against the Ṣūfī orders, accusing them of introducing *bidʿah,* practicing alien rituals, and spreading submissive and superstitious attitudes.

The mutable part of religion (*muʿāmalat*) includes human transactions and laws governing social relationships. These were considered the domain of *ijtihād* that ought to be exercised in line with the requirements of modernity and scientific advancement. Al-Kawākibī interpreted the Qur'ānic statement, "Nothing have we omitted from the book" (6.38) as pertaining only to religious matters, not to worldly affairs. ʿAbduh issued several *fatwās* (legal opinions)—permitting Muslims to wear Western attire, eat meat slaughtered by Christians and Jews, and earn interest—that were considered departures from the traditionalist stand.

A third foundation of the modern Salafīyah is the comprehensive yet gradual nature of the reforms they proposed. Like most other Arab and Muslim countries, the Egyptian society in which the Salafīyah arose was already undergoing fundamental changes. Foreign laws had replaced supplemented indigenous laws; the educational system had bifurcated into Western and traditional; and the intellectual elite was split between advocates of the wholesale adoption of Western values and institutions and adherents to long-held traditions and practices.

The Salafīyah hoped to bridge the gaps within their respective societies by introducing sweeping reforms at the individual and institutional levels. Education was the cornerstone of their reform plan. The Salafīyah were convinced that no reform would be effective unless the moral and social values of Muslims were revived by education. They aspired to educate a new type of elite, combining Islamic and modern education, to close the gap between the conservatives and the westernized. They worked on restructuring the educational system and modernizing the curricula in traditional educational institutions, as well as establishing new schools that offered both Islamic and modern subjects.

Pertinent to the improvement of education was the reform of the Arabic language. As a result of an overall state of stagnation and imitation, the Arabic language had suffered for centuries from rigidity and artificial style. The reform of the language was intended to revive it and to liberate it from classical forms so that it could be easily understood and absorb modern terminology. The Salafīyah in the Arab world hoped thus to preserve their national identity and contain the spread of foreign languages.

The reform of law was another important aspect in the reformists' efforts to revitalize Islam. The Salafīyah reformers maintained that law should reflect the "spirit" of the nation, its dominant values and belief system. Imported or foreign law could never strike deep roots because it would always lack consensual acceptance and therefore legitimacy. Islamic *sharīʿah* should continue to regulate the legal and social affairs of Muslims. However, the reformers rejected the literal interpretation of law and advocated its reinterpretation on the basis of reason, *maqāṣid* (objectives), and *maṣlaḥah* (common good), particularly in areas where there was no Qur'ānic stipulation. On the institutional level, they directed efforts toward establishing specialized schools for *sharīʿah* judges, or reforming the existing ones, and to reforming the *sharīʿah* courts.

The Salafīyah viewed political reform as an essential requirement for the revitalization of the Islamic community. They denounced despotism and held autocratic rulers responsible for the spread of acquiescent political attitudes and the disintegration of the Muslim nation. Salafī intellectuals advocated a gradualist plan for political reform. They were convinced that political reform could not be achieved unless the people were educated about their rights and responsibilities.

Many reformist intellectuals attempted to reformulate Islamic concepts in the light of modern political ideals and practices. They reinterpreted such concepts as *shūrā* (counsel) and *ijmaʿ* (consensus) and equated them with democracy and a parliamentary system. In practice, they called for gradually increasing representation in administrative and political institutions.

European colonialism and the threat of cultural subjugation gave the modern Salafīyah a strong nationalist tone. The reformers, perhaps with the exceptions of ʿAbduh after his return to Egypt from exile in 1888 and of Aḥmad Khān, maintained an anticolonialist stance. They tried to promote a common awareness of Islamic nationalism and to preserve the solidarity of the *ummah*, advocating Pan-Islamism and the restoration of a form of political nucleus. Nonetheless, most of them had to compromise their idealist position to meet the realities of their time, accepting the imposed national divisions of the Muslim world.

Spread of Salafīyah. The teachings of the Salafīyah spread across the Arab and larger Muslim world, and wherever it took root, the Salafīyah acquired different expressions and emphasis. In Algeria, Ibn Bādīs focused his reform efforts on education as the means for countering the assimilationist policy of the French and preserving national identity, and on combating the Ṣūfī orders. He produced a commentary on the Qur'ān, and with other reformist religious scholars he established the

Association of Algerian ʿUlamāʾ, which played a prominent role in the struggle for independence.

Morocco had been exposed to the teachings of the Wahhābīyah since the eighteenth century. A neo-Salafīyah movement with a modernist orientation emerged in the nineteenth century under such reformist scholars as Abū Shuʿayb al-Dukkālī (1878–1937) and Muḥammad ibn al-ʿArabī al-ʿAlawī (1880–1964). Their ideas had a profound formative impact on many leaders of the Moroccan nationalist movements, notably ʿAllāl al-Fāsī, the leader of the Istiqlāl Party and a student of al-ʿAlawī. Al-Fāsī took the Salafīyah to new levels by linking Islamic reformism to the nationalist movement for independence and political liberalism. [*See* Istiqlāl; *and the biography of Fāsī.*]

The Salafīyah was introduced in Tunisia in the early years of the twentieth century; ʿAbduh visited in 1885 and again in 1903, and *Al-manār* was read there. The Salafī ideals were adopted by several Zaytūnī *ʿulamāʾ*, including Bashīr Ṣafar (d. 1937), a teacher of Ibn Bādīs; Muḥammad al-Ṭāhir ibn ʿĀshūr (b. 1879), who produced a commentary on the Qurʾān; and his son Muḥammad al-Fāḍil ibn ʿĀshūr (1909–1970). ʿAbd al-ʿAzīz al-Thaʿālibī (1879–1944), the founder of the Destour Party, was an advocate of the Salafīyah and Islamic reform.

Islamic modernists also emerged in Syria. Some were influenced by the Ḥanbalī orientation, such as Jamāl al-Dīn al-Qāsimī (1866/67–1914); others were disciples of Afghānī and ʿAbduh, such as ʿAbd al-Qādir al-Maghribī (1867–1956) and Shakīb Arslān (1869–1946).

In India, Sayyid Aḥmad Khān (1817–1898) founded a movement of Islamic modernism that had a profound impact on reform among Indian Muslims. Though a contemporary of Afghānī and ʿAbduh, Aḥmad Khān was distinguished by his acceptance of British rule, by his reinterpretation of the Qurʾān with a far more rationalist and naturalist approach than most Salafī intellectuals, and by his promotion of Western education through the educational institutions and journals he established. Another prominent Muslim modernist in India was Muhammad Iqbal (1875–1938); Combining Islamic and Western education, he attempted to reconstruct an Islamic intellectual model that would revive the Muslim community and address modern needs. [*See the biographies of Aḥmad Khān and Iqbal.*]

The Salafīyah principles also spread to Indonesia. In 1912, the reformist Muhammadiyah movement was established there as an educational and cultural organization that attracted a wide following.

Following the death of Afghānī and ʿAbduh, with a dearth of comparable thinkers, the course of the reformist Salafīyah began to change. Muḥammad Rashīd Riḍā represented a link between the reformist Salafīyah of Afghānī and ʿAbduh and the activist Muslim Brothers in Egypt. He continued to propagate the ideas of his mentors as well as his own in his periodical *Al-manār*, which had considerable influence on many Muslim intellectuals (known as the Manarists) throughout the Islamic world. Under increasing threats of political disintegration and cultural submission, Rashīd Riḍā drew the movement into more conservative and orthodox paths. The liberal and secular disciples of the reformist thinkers benefited from the rationalist approach of the Salafīyah in advancing secular nationalism and liberalism, as in the cases of Saʿd Zaghlūl in Egypt and Mohammad Ali Jinnah in India.

Influence on Modern Islamic Movements. The teachings of the Salafīyah continued to inspire later generations of Muslim activists. In the 1930s new Islamic movements emerged sharing many of the ideas of the Salafīyah. The most influential of these were Ḥasan al-Bannāʾs (1906–1949) Muslim Brothers in Egypt and Abū al-Āʿla Mawdūdīʾs (1903–1979) Jamāʿat-i Islāmī in the Indian subcontinent.

These movements too upheld the centrality of Islam to future progress and were convinced of its adaptability to modern life. However, they responded to different circumstances: continued Western occupation, anticolonial struggle, and the domination of secular political and social concepts. They therefore combined activism (*ḥarakīyah*) with their message of Islamic reform. They were more skeptical and critical of the West, and, while accepting modernity, they believed in the self-sufficiency of Islam as the basis for society and state (Esposito, 1991, pp. 152–160). They did not attempt to build on the intellectual venture the modern Salafīyah had undertaken in legal, political, educational reform, or to devise a systematic intellectual framework for reform. Instead, through their organizational structures and populist appeal, these movements focused on reforming the morality and beliefs of the Muslim individual as a precondition for the reform of the society as a whole. The Muslim Brothers and the Jamāʿat became an example for many subsequent movements; however, their ideological orientation, activism, and sometimes militant tendency distinguish them from the modern Salafīyah. [*See* Muslim Brotherhood; Jamāʿat-i Islāmī.]

Currently there are some groups and societies in the

Muslim world known as al-Jamāʿah al-Salafīyah or al-Salafīyun. They have more in common with the classic Salafīyah than with the modernist thought of Afghānī and ʿAbduh. Like the classic Salafīyah, they focus on matters of creed and morality, such as strict monotheism, divine attributes, purifying Islam from accretions, anti-Sufism, and developing the moral integrity of the individual (ʿAbd al-Khaliq, 1975; Ibn Bakr, 1990). These societies, however, remain very limited in following and in the extent of the reforms they propose.

Conclusion. The Salafīyah has taken different forms and expressions owing to changing conditions; however, throughout its different phases it has remained in essence a movement for reform and renewal. The classic or Ḥanbalī Salafīyah, to which several premodern reform movements belong, focused on issues of creed, the purity of Islam, and the restoration of a past Islamic model, and so it remained doctrinal and limited in its scope of reform.

While emphasizing the need to return to original Islam, the modern Salafīyah expanded the dimensions of reform to counter the threat of European colonialism and to accommodate the needs of modernity. While often criticized for being apologetic and conciliatory, they were nonetheless able to demonstrate to their coreligionists the adaptability of Islam and its relevance in modern times. Their intellectual efforts provided grounds for accepting and legitimizing change.

Despite its significant contribution to the revival of Islamic thought and noticeable impact on generations of Muslim intellectuals and activists, the modern Salafīyah stopped short of devising a solid framework for reform on which later followers could build systematically. Therefore, the continuation of the Salafīyah reformist message has depended on the individual efforts of Muslim intellectuals.

[See Modernism; Revival and Renewal; *and the biographies of ʿAbduh and Afghānī.*]

BIBLIOGRAPHY

ʿAbd al-Khāliq, ʿAbd al-Raḥmān. *Al-Uṣūl al-ʿilmīyah lil-daʿwah al-Salafīyah.* Cairo, 1975. Example of the ideological orientation of the contemporary Salafīyah.

ʿAbduh, Muḥammad. *Risālat al-tawḥīd.* Cairo, 1897. Translated by Ishaq Musaʿad and Kenneth Cragg as *The Theology of Unity*. London, 1966. Series of lectures on theology delivered at al-Madrasah al-Sulṭānīyah while in exile in Beirut.

ʿAbduh, Muḥammad. *Al-Islām wa-al-Naṣrānīyah maʿa al-ʿilm wa-al-madanīyah* (1905). Cairo, 1954. Excellent source for ʿAbduh's intellectual arguments on various issues.

Abun-Nasr, Jamil M. "The Salafiyya Movement in Morocco: The Religious Bases of the Moroccan Nationalist Movement." In *St. Antony's Papers,* no. 16, *Middle Eastern Affairs,* no. 3, edited by Albert Hourani, pp. 90–105. London, 1963.

Afghānī, Jamāl al-Dīn al-. "Risalat al-Radd ʿala al-Dahriyyin" (A Response to the Naturalists). In *Al-thā'ir al-Islāmī Jamāl al-Dīn al-Afghānī,* edited by Muḥammad ʿAbduh. Cairo, 1973. Al-Afghānī wrote this refutation in 1879 while in India, as a response to the threatened spread of materialist ideas.

Amīn, Aḥmad. *Zuʿamā' al-iṣlāḥ fī al-ʿaṣr al-ḥadīth* (The Leaders of Reform in the Modern Time). 4th ed. Cairo, 1979. Detailed biographies and study of several reformist intellectuals.

Amīn, ʿUthmān. *Muḥammad ʿAbduh.* Translated by Charles Wendell. Washington, D.C., 1953. Good introduction to ʿAbduh's life and thought.

Būṭī, Muḥammad Saʿīd Ramaḍān al-. *Al-Salafīyah: Marḥalah zamanīyah mubārakah, lā madhhab Islāmī* (Al-Salafīyah: A Blessed Period, Not an Islamic Doctrinal School). Damascus, 1988. Thorough study on the evolution and intellectual components of the Salafīyah.

Commins, David Dean. *Islamic Reform: Politics and Social Change in Late Ottoman Syria.* New York, 1990. Excellent analysis of Islamic reformism in Syria in the nineteenth and early twentieth century.

Esposito, John L. *Islam: The Straight Path.* Exp. ed. New York, 1991. Well-written introduction to Islam and contemporary developments in the Muslim world.

Fakhry, Majid. *A History of Islamic Philosophy.* 2d ed. New York, 1983. Excellent reference for the Muslim philosophical and theological schools.

Hourani, Albert. *Arabic Thought in the Liberal Age, 1798–1939.* London, 1962. Chapters on Afghānī, ʿAbduh, and Rashīd Riḍā provide detailed background and analysis of their life and views.

Ḥilmī, Muṣṭafā. *Al-Salafīyah bayna al-ʿaqīdah al-Islāmīyah wa-al-falsafah al-Gharbīyah.* Alexandria, 1991. Discusses the Salafīyah from Western and Islamic perspectives, its objectives and role.

Ibn Bakr, Abū Yūsuf. *Muḥāḍarāt fī al-Salafīyah* (Lectures on Salafīyah). Shibin al-Koum, Egypt, 1990. Sample of the intellectual orientation of contemporary Salafīyah.

ʿImārah, Muḥammad. *Tayyārāt al-fikr al-Islāmī* (The Trends of Islamic Thought). Cairo, 1982. Overview of the classic Islamic intellectual schools.

ʿImārah, Muḥammad. *Tayyārāt al-yaqaẓah al-Islāmīyah al-ḥadīthah* (The Trends of the Modern Islamic Awakening). Cairo, 1982. Overview of the Islamic reformist movements and modernist intellectual trends.

Jābirī, Muḥammad ʿĀbid al-. "Al-ḥarakah al-Salafīyah wa-al-Jamāʿah al-dīnīyah al-muʿāṣirah fī al-Maghrib" (The Salafīyah Movement and the Contemporary Religious Community in Morocco). In *Al-ḥarakah al-Islāmīyah al-muʿāṣirah fī al-Waṭan al-ʿArabī,* pp. 187–235. Beirut, 1989.

Jurshī, Ṣalāḥ al-Dīn al-. "Al-ta'thīrāt al-Salafīyah fī al-tayyārāt al-Islāmīyah al-muʿāṣirah" (The Influence of the Salafīyah on Contemporary Islamic Trends). *Ishkālīyat al-fikr al-Islāmī* (Islamic World Studies Center), no. 1 (1991): 203–230.

Kerr, Malcolm H. *Islamic Reform: The Political and Legal Theories of Muḥammad ʿAbduh and Rashīd Riḍā.* Berkeley, 1966. Thorough analysis of ʿAbduh's and Rashīd Riḍā's legal thought.

Khadduri, Majid. *Political Trends in the Arab World: The Role of Ideas and Ideals in Politics.* Baltimore, 1970. See pages 65–69.

Merad, ʿAlī, et al. "Iṣlāḥ." In *Encyclopaedia of Islam,* new ed., vol. 4, pp. 141–171. Leiden, 1960–.

Al-muʿjam al-wasīṭ. 3d ed. Cairo, n.d. See volume 1, page 461.

Shakʿah, Muṣṭafā al-. *Al-Islām bi-lā madhāhib* (Islam without Doctrinal Sectarianism). 5th ed. Cairo, 1976. Excellent study of Islamic sects, theological and intellectual schools.

ʿUthmān, Fatḥī. *Al-Salafīyah fī al-mujtamaʿāt al-muʿāṣirah* (The Salafīyah in Contemporary Societies). [Cairo, 1982?] Focuses on the Wahhābī movement and its influence on later Muslim thinkers and movements.

EMAD ELDIN SHAHIN

ṢALĀT. The Qur'ānic meaning of *ṣalāt* can be distilled from a number of verses that describe the characteristic features of worship and its ethical and social aims. In its Meccan phase, the Qur'ān associates *ṣalāt* with recitation, *tasbīḥ* (divine praise), *zakāt* (almsgiving), and *ṣabr* (patience). The Qur'ān commands the believers to, "Establish regular prayers at the sun's decline till the darkness of the night, [and to establish] the morning prayer and reading: for prayer and reading in the morning carry their testimony" (surah 17.78). Worshiping God can be adequately fulfilled only if the believer is guided by patience and perseverance. This was perhaps a historical necessity for the besieged Muslim community in Mecca in the first twelve years of Islam, "Nay, seek [Allāh's] help with patient perseverance and prayer: It is indeed hard, except to those who bring a lowly spirit" (surah 2.45).

In its shift from a doctrinal emphasis to a more behavioral one, especially with the Prophet's political triumph in Medina, the Qur'ān attaches additional meanings to *ṣalāt*. The Qur'ān seems to indicate that prayer in itself can be a valid mode of spirituality only if it is accompanied by a host of positive behavioral characteristics, such as commanding good, forbidding evil, and paying *zakāt*, "[They are] those who, if We establish them in the land, establish regular prayer and give regular charity, enjoin the right and forbid the wrong" (surah 22.41). Also, "Recite what is sent of the Book by inspiration to thee, and establish regular prayer: for prayer restrains from shameful and unjust deeds: and remembrance of Allāh is the greatest [thing in life] without doubt. And Allāh knows the [deeds] that ye do" (surah 29.45). In numerous Qur'ānic verses, *ṣalāt* is synonymous with *zakāt* (see Qur'ān 2.83; 2.110; 2.177; 9.18; 11.114; 17.78; and 58.13) Also, *ṣalāt*, as a concept as well as a practice, must reflect a deeply engrained attitude in man that manifests itself in acts of humility and patience. The Qur'ān tells us that the believers can succeed in this life and the hereafter only if they humble themselves in their prayers (surah 23.1, 2).

In general, the Qur'ānic meaning of patience (surahs 2.153; 13.22; and 22.35) reminds the believer of the necessity of constant perseverance and struggle against the evils of the self and life's hardships. To elevate the self to the level of obedience to the divine majesty, believers must observe *ṣalāt* on time, since it is a *kitāb mawqūt*—it is enjoined on believers at stated times (surah 4.103). It is clear from the above that the intention of the Qur'ān is not to merely prescribe prayer as a ritual or an institution, but as an immense personal and communal commitment to order, punctuality, change, and coherence. *Ṣalāt*, in a sense, is the meeting point between the sacred and the secular in Muslim life. It is a reflection of a divine desire to change the world in the direction prescribed by God in the Qur'ān.

Since one of the main goals of Islam is to establish an egalitarian and just moral and social order, the purpose of *ṣalāt* should be to enhance this outward political and social tendency. And in this regard, Imam Shāfiʿī defines worship as consisting of *qawl* (word), *ʿamal* (deed), and *imsāk* (abstension from the forbidden deeds) (Majid Khadduri, trans., *Islamic Jurisprudence: Shafiʿi's Risala*, Baltimore, 1961, p. 121). Humility, perseverence, devotion, remembrance of God and the Day of Judgment, are attributes of the believers who perform *ṣalāt*.

Origin of the Practice. One of the earliest and most elaborate sources on *ṣalāt* in Islam is the often-quoted *Ṣaḥīḥ* of the famous traditionist Imam Bukhārī (810–870). In the section, "The Book of Ṣalāt," Bukhārī recounts how prayer was made obligatory on Muslims. He relates that prayer was prescribed on the night of the Isrā' Ascension (surah 17) when Muḥammad was taken up by the angel Gabriel to the highest heaven. There Muḥammad met with Moses, Jesus, Abraham, Adam, and other celebrated personalities whom Muslims consider prophets. Muḥammad, Bukhārī tells us, was led to a mysterious spot in heaven where he heard the creaking of the pens, and there God enjoined fifty prayers on Muslims. When Muḥammad returned to earth, he passed by Moses, who asked him about the number of prayers imposed on the Muslim community. When Moses heard it was fifty a day, he asked Muḥammad to go back and ask God for reduction, "for your followers will not be able to bear with it." Muḥammad did as he was told, and God reduced the number by half, and

Moses once again informed him it was still too much. Muḥammad went back and forth between God and Moses until God granted him five daily prayers, which Muslims could tolerate. Bukhārī sums up this interesting anecdote by quoting a *ḥadīth qudsī* (a holy *ḥadīth* attributed to God): "These are five prayers and they all [equal to] fifty [in reward] for My word does not change" (Muḥammad ibn Ismāʿīl Bukhārī, *Ṣaḥīḥ al-Bukhārī,* translated by Muhammad Khan, Chicago, 1976, p. 213)

When Islam took its political, social, and legal shape in Medina, and more so in Arabia after the conquest of Mecca, Muslims focused their attention on three major elements of the new religion: prayer as an institution; the *qiblah* (direction of prayer); and the mosque as a place for both individual and congregational worship.

The act of prayer, although following certain well-defined movements, involves the following required steps: ablution *(wuḍūʾ* or *ṭahārah* or *ghusl),* intention *(nīyah),* bending the back *(rukūʿ),* and prostration *(sujūd).* To perform ablution adequately, one has to go through two intertwined processes: spiritual purity and physical cleanliness. In the first process, you cleanse your mind and heart from any thoughts related to this world and try to concentrate on God and the blessing he has bestowed on you. In the second, you wash the face, hands, mouth (unless you are fasting), feet, and forehead. You begin the ablution with recitation of the formula, "In the name of God, the Merciful, the Compassionate. I am proposing to perform ablution so that God may be pleased with me." When you complete it, you say, "I bear witness that there is no god but Allāh; He has no partner; and I bear witness that Muḥammad is His servant and Messenger." In its totality, the act of worship presupposes certain traits that Islam encourages: humility, knowledge, presence of the heart, wisdom, and devotion.

Because of the central position *ṣalāt* occupies in Islamic thought and life, Muslim jurists and theologians have discussed at length the act of individual and group prayer, the conditions surrounding it, who must pray or who can abstain from praying, characteristics of the prayers' leader *(imām),* significance of the Friday prayer, and prayer times and making up missed prayer. On the whole, Muslim jurists agree that *ṣalāt* is obligatory for sane Muslim men and women who have reached puberty. In the words of the thirteenth-century Sunnī jurist, Aḥmad ibn al-Naqīb al-Miṣrī, any person, growing up in a Muslim society, "who denies the obligatoriness of the prayer, *zakāt,* fasting Ramaḍān, the pilgrimage, or the unlawfulness of [alcohol] and adultery, or denies something else upon which there is scholarly consensus and which is necessarily known as being of the religion, thereby becomes an unbeliever" (al-Miṣrī, p. 109). Al-Miṣrī also gives the following description of the *arkān* (pillars) of prayer, which summarizes the opinion of the majority of Muslim jurists, both Sunnī and Shīʿī. He says that the pillars of prayer consist of the following seventeen items: (1) intention *(nīyah)*; (2) the opening "God is the Greatest" ("Allāhu akbar"); (3) standing *(wuqūf)*; (4) reciting the *fātiḥah* (the opening surah); (5) bowing *(rukūʿ)*; (6) remaining motionless a moment therein *(ṭumaʾnīnā)*; (7) straightening back up after bowing *(iʿitidāl)*; (8) remaining motionless a moment therein *(ṭumaʾnīnā)*; (9) prostration *(sujūd)*; (10) remaining motionless a moment therein *(iʿitidāl)*; (11) sitting back between the two prostrations *(al-julūs bayna al-sajdatayn)*; (12) remaining motionless a moment therein *(iʿitidāl)*; (13) the prayer's final Testification of Faith *(al-tashahhud al-akhīr)*; (14) sitting therein *(julūs)*; (15) the Blessings on the Prophet *(al-ṣalāt ʿalā al-Nabī)*; (16) saying "Peace be upon you" ("al-salāmu ʿalaykum"), the first of the two times it is said at the end of the prayer; and (17) the proper sequence of the above integrals (*ibid.,* pp. 153–154).

The above features of prayer have always made *ṣalāt* a distinctive Islamic practice and defined Muslims in a unique way. Thus, although Islam might share the same general spiritual aims of Judaism and Christianity, in that it seeks to establish an ideal state in both the believers' hearts and in this world, it has helped Muslims to set themselves apart from both Jews and Christians by just following certain rites and practices related to their performance of *ṣalāt.*

The Qur'ān discusses, somewhat at length, the meaning of *qiblah,* and the selection of Mecca as the place toward which Muslims turn their faces when praying. After the death of Muḥammad in 632 and the dramatic expansion of Islam beyond its Arabian origins, Muslims were in direct contact with people who held different religious and cultural views. Muslims accepted for a while the idea of worshipping in non-Muslim places of worship, that is, Christian churches, and recent research indicates that the early Muslim prayer was toward the east (Sulayman Bashear, "Qibla Mushariqqa and Early Muslim Prayer in Churches," *The Muslim World* 81.3–4 [July–October 1991]: 268; Tor Andrea, *Der Ursprung des Islams und Christentum,* Uppsala and Stockholm,

1926, p. 4; A. J. Wensinck, "Kibla" *Encyclopaedia of Islam,* new ed., Leiden, 1960–, vol. 5, p. 82). *Ṣalāt,* as the institution of worship, became one of the main manifestations of the power of nascent Islam. This can be corraborated by the Qur'ānic verse, "To Allāh belong the East and the West: Whithersoever ye turn, there is Allāh's countenance, for Allāh is All-Embracing, All-Knowing" (surah 2.115). In the opinion of Bashear, although the church, as a non-Muslim place of worship, was not favored by the Prophet as the place of worship for Muslims, he definitely did not prohibit Muslims from using it as such (*ibid.,* p. 274). With the further evolution of Islam and the establishment of a large empire in the eighth and ninth centuries, Muslims became more conscious of the need to establish their own separate places for worship, and thus the idea of praying in non-Muslim places was forsaken gradually. Bashear contends that "as far as the first century [seventh century CE] is concerned, one cannot speak of 'one original *qiblah* of Islam,' but rather of several currents in the search for one. It is also plausible that this search was eventually decided after Islam acquired a central sanctuary, prayer places, and religious concepts and institutions of its own" (*ibid.,* p. 382).

The Prophet's mosque in Medina, as the first Muslim place of worship, functioned as a gathering place for worship, meditation, and learning. Because of such quality invested in this Muslim sacred space, the mosque has exerted an ideological influence on the believers, and this might explain why modern Islamic movements have paid special attention to the social and intellectual significance of the mosque as a place from which the organization of society and state emanates.

Mystical Worship. Ṣūfī literature abounds in references to prayer, its virtues, and various characteristics. Great Ṣūfīs, especially those defining themselves as *ahl al-sharīʿah wa-al-ḥaqīqah* (followers of *sharīʿah* and the esoteric truth), have viewed the Qur'ānic verses of *dhikr* (invocation or remembrance of God), *duʿā* (supplication), and *taḍarruʿ* (beseeching God in great humility) as the heart of worship, without which *ṣalāt* becomes a meaningless ritual. According to ʿAbd al-Qādir al-Jīlānī (d. 1166), remembered by some as *al-quṭb al-aʿẓam* (the greatest [Ṣūfī] pole), when the remembrance of God is invoked, at any time of day or night, the heart of the believer hears the invocations and is "enlightened with the light of that which is remembered. It receives energy and it becomes alive—not only alive in this world, but alive forever in the hereafter" (ʿAbd al-Qādir al-Jīlānī, *The Secret of Secrets,* London, 1992, p. 48; see also Muḥammad ibn ʿAllān al-Bakrī, *Al-futūḥāt al-rabbānīyah ʿalā al-adhkār al-Nawawīyah,* Beirut, n.d.; Ibn ʿAṭā' Allāh, *Al-ḥikam al-ʿAṭā'īyah,* Cairo, 1969; and ʿAbd al-Ḥalīm Maḥmūd, *Al-madrasah al-Shādhilīyah al-ḥādithah wa-imāmuhā Abū al-Ḥasan al-Shādhilī,* Cairo, 1969). Being close to God and obedient to His injunctions should be the main goal of the Muslim. A true Muslim has to exert the necessary effort in order to bridge the gap or the chasm that may exist between him or her and God. Besides being the heart of Islam, *ṣalāt* is an obligatory duty that each Muslim woman and man has to perform five times a day. Although *ṣalāt,* as described above, involves a well-known ritual, its final aim is to transcend any formal barrier between God and a person. The Prophet expresses that clearly in one of his sayings: "God, most blessed and most high, says, 'Nothing brings humans near to Me like the performance of what I made obligatory for them. . . . Through works of duty, My servant comes ever nearer to Me until I love him, and when I have bestowed My love on him, I become his hearing with which he hears, his sight with which he sees, his tongue with which he speaks, his hand with which he grasps, and his foot with which he walks.' " Taken metaphorically, the righteous, those who follow the divine path, will be guided by the mercy and compassion of God.

Supplications are the heart of the Ṣūfī understanding of *ṣalāt.* The Qur'ān expresses that in a succinct fashion, "When My servants ask thee concerning Me, I am indeed close [to them]: I listen to the prayer of every suppliant when he calleth on Me: let them also, with a will, listen to My call, and believe in Me: that they may walk in the right way" (surah 2.186).

Ṣūfīs, from Abū Ḥārith al-Muḥāsibī (d. 857) to Abū al-Ḥasan al-Shādhilī (d. 1256), wrote beautiful poetry extolling the meaning, virtue, significance, and final goal of *ṣalāt.* The true Ṣūfī is in constant contact with the divine through daily, if not hourly, prayer. Ṣūfīs usually ask God to provide them with *yaqīn* (incontrovertible certainty), *tawḥīd* (unity), which is unassailed by *shirk* (association), and an obedience that no insubordination can confront. They also ask God to grant them neither love nor preference of any worldly thing and neither fear of or for any thing. Since one of the main goals of Ṣūfī worship is to converse with God through association with and comprehension of divine secrets (*asrār rabbānīyah*), there is a constant reminder of human fragility and imperfection. Ṣūfīs tend to often repeat the Qur'ānic verse, "O my Lord, I have indeed wronged my soul" (surah 27.45) A Ṣūfī meditative prayer might end by asking God to prescribe a way out from all sin, anxiety *(hamm)*, grief *(ghamm)* and anguish; from every carnal impulse, desire, alarm, involuntary thought, idea, will, and act; and from every divine decree and command. The supplicant, in the final analysis, cannot attain any of the above goals without divine mercy. The Ṣūfī, and the Muslim in general, remains hopeful, since God's mercy comprehends everything. In Islamic meditative practices, *ṣalāt* has been used as a means of healing and remover of worry and anxiety.

Changing Function: The View of Islamic Resurgence. Muslim revivalist movements in this century have looked for inspiration to the past, when Islam was in its strength and glory. Their main goal is socioreligious: to bridge the increasing gap between state and religion in modern Muslim society. They advance Islam as an all-encompassing ideology, and some contend that a true Muslim individual and family can exist only in a genuine Muslim state, that is, a state that is based on *sharīʿah*. The teachings of Ḥasan al-Bannā' (d. 1949) of Egypt, Abū al-Aʿlā Mawdūdī (d. 1979) of India/Pakistan, and Ruhollah Khomeini (d. 1989) of Iran, illustrate the new dynamic meaning given to *ṣalāt* and the mosque as a sacred place in modern Islam. All went about organizing their movements with ceaseless zeal and energy and preached the message of revolution and change. They viewed the mosque not merely as a place for worship, but as a place where radical transformation and renewal might take place. In this, they follow the Qur'ānic maxim: "The mosques of Allāh shall be visited and maintained by such as believe in Allāh and the Last Day, establish regular prayers, and practice regular charity, and fear none (at all) except Allāh" (surah 9.18).

In the view of modern Muslim revivalists, the mosque offers a multiplicity of functions. First, it is a place of worship; it links the people of this earth with the affairs of the heavens. In addition to reflecting man's spirituality, worship, in Ḥasan al-Bannā's view, for instance, reflects the social, political, and ethical values of the three major systems known to man: communism, dictatorship, and democracy. Bannā' captures the connection between Islamic prayer and the three systems in the following:

> Islamic prayer . . . is nothing but a daily training in practical and social organization uniting the features of the Communist regime with those of the dictatorial and democratic regimes. . . . the moment [the believer] enters [the mosque], he realizes that the mosque belongs to God and not to anyone of his creatures; he knows himself to be the equal of all those who are there, whoever they may be; here there are no great, no small, no high, no low, no more groups or classes. . . . And when the *muezzin* calls, "now is the hour of prayer," they form an equal mass, a compact block, behind the *imam*. . . . That is the principal merit of the dictatorial regime: unity and order in the will under the appearance of equality. The imam *himself* is in any case limited by the teachings and rules of the prayer, and if he stumbles or makes a mistake in his reading or in his actions, all those behind him . . . have the imperative duty to tell him of his error in order to put him back on the right road during the prayer, and the *imam* himself is bound to accept the advice and, forsaking his error, return to reason and truth. That is what is most appealing in democracy. ("New Renaissance," in *Political and Social Thought in the Contemporary Middle East*, edited by Kemal H. Karpat, New York, 1968, 121.)

In other words, the mosque, far from being an abstract metaphysical locus, is placed by Bannā' squarely within this world and its secular systems.

The mosque is the abode of the newly found religiosity. Here, secular domain and space ceases to exist. The mosque is also the criterion against which the religiosity of society is judged. It is the symbol of Islamic rule. "Mosques," in Ḥasan al-Bannā's words, "are the schools of the commoners, the popular universities, and the colleges that lend educational services to the young and old alike" (*Mudhakkirāt al-daʿwah wa-al-dāʿiyah*, Beirut, 1979, p. 128). Briefly, A mosque should have the triple function of being a place of worship for people; a place of education; and a hospital for the spiritually, mentally, and physically sick. In this Bannā' invokes the early experience of the Prophet in Medina when the latter saw the mosque as the concrete embodiment of Islamic belief and as a culmination of many of the ideals that he had preached in Mecca.

At the surface, modern Islamic revivalist movements use conventional Islamic terminology which is common to all who share the Muslim cultural space. Their use of the mosque as a key term is significant for the meaning it denotes and for the social and political functions it can render. The physical space, that is, the mosque, is interpolated with the cultural and religious space, or the mosque's functions. Thus they put emphasis on the mosque as a key term in order to demonstrate its usefulness and in order to cleanse it of the meaning other religious groups, especially the *ʿulamāʾ* (community of religious scholars), had attached to it. Above all, the mosque purifies the intentions, and physical outlook of the person in prayer, and initiates a new meaning of religiosity that compels the believer to conquer the secular domain of life.

In sum, Islamic revivalism elevates politics to the level of prayer. Sacred space is the center of political activity, and prayer is just one of its many expressions.

BIBLIOGRAPHY

Ghafūrī, ʿAlī. *The Ritual Prayer of Islam*. Translated by Laleh Bakhtiar and Mohammed Nematzadeh. Houston, 1982.

Ghazālī, Abū Ḥāmid al-. *Ghazālī on Prayer*. Translated by Kōjirō Nakamura. Tokyo, 1973. Reprinted as *Invocations and Supplications*. Cambridge, 1990.

Heiler, Friedrich. *Prayer: A Study in the History and Psychology of Religion*. Translated and edited by Samuel McComb. London, 1932.

Jeffery, Arthur, ed. *A Reader on Islam*. The Hague, 1962.

Miṣrī, Aḥmad ibn al-Naqīb al-. *The Reliance of the Traveller: A Classical Manual of Islamic Sacred Law*. Translated by Noah H. M. Keller. Evanston, Ill., 1993.

Muḥammad Zakarīyā Kāndhalavī. *Virtues of Salaat*. Lahore, 1982.

Muṭahharī, Murtaẓā. *Fundamentals of Islamic Thought: God, Man, and the Universe*. Translated by R. Campbell. Berkeley, 1985.

Nasr, Seyyed Hossein. *Ideals and Realities of Islam*. Boston, 1975.

Padwick, C. E. *Muslim Devotions*. London, 1961.

Rahman, Fazlur. *Major Themes of the Qurʾān*. Minneapolis, 1980.

Zayn al-ʿĀbidīn ʿAlī ibn al-Ḥusayn. *The Psalms of Islam (Al-Ṣaḥīfat al-Kāmilat al-Sajjādiyya)*. Translated by William Chittick. London, 1988.

Zwemer, Samuel M. *Studies in Popular Islam*. London, 1939.

IBRAHIM M. ABU-RABIʿ

SAMĀʿ. *See* Sufism, *article on* Ṣūfī Thought and Practice.

SANHŪRĪ, ʿABD AL-RAZZĀQ AL-. *See* ʿAbd al-Razzāq al-Sanhūrī.

SANŪSĪYAH. Founded by Muḥammad ibn ʿAlī al-Sanūsī (1787–1859), the Sanūsīyah is a Ṣūfī brotherhood based in Libya and the central Sahara. The Sanūsī brotherhood is well known for the role it played in the resistance to French and Italian colonialism, but it was formed as a strictly religious brotherhood based on the doctrine of the Shādhilīyah order. The founder, al-Sanūsī, was born near Mostaganem in Algeria. In his early life he studied Sufism and Islamic sciences including law and tradition in the reformist environment of Fez. In 1823 he moved to Cairo, and later to the Hejaz to prolong his studies there. In Mecca he met the very influential Ṣūfī teacher Aḥmad ibn Idrīs, and his Ṣūfī doctrine was from then on virtually identical to that of ibn Idrīs. When ibn Idrīs left Mecca for Yemen shortly afterward, al-Sanūsī was put in charge of his students in Mecca and built the first lodge at Abū Qubays outside Mecca in 1827. However, ibn Idrīs never formed a structured order around his teachings, and after his death in 1837 several of his students set up independent orders like the Khatmīyah and the Rashīdīyah. Al-Sanūsī moved back to North Africa, and after an apparent period of indecision he settled in Cyrenaica (northeastern Libya) in 1841, founding his new organization.

The Sanūsīyah is commonly known as a "revivalist" brotherhood, but its doctrine does not show great variation from traditional Sufism. It disapproves of excesses in ritual, such as dancing or singing. The founder put great emphasis on the role of the Prophet and on following his example. Al-Sanūsī was more controversial in his views on Islamic law; he wrote several books arguing for the right to *ijtihād*, the interpretation of dogma in the light of original sources. He put this into practice by incorporating elements commonly found in the Shāfiʿī school of law into the prayer ritual of the Sanūsīyah, while still maintaining his way to be a Mālikī one.

The brotherhood was typical of some newer orders of the eighteenth and nineteenth centuries in its internal organization. The structure was simple and centralized. The local lodge had very little autonomy and was ruled by three or four officials appointed by the center, each with specific tasks and answering to the center. Shortly before al-Sanūsī's death, a central lodge was established in Jaghbūb, on the Libya-Egypt border.

The Sanūsīyah was primarily a desert order. The core area was that of the Bedouin of Cyrenaica, and the larger part of the population there came to identify with the order. It was not confined to this area, however; the order also had a number of urban lodges, and it spread into non-bedouin areas like Tripolitania and Fazzan in western Libya, as well as in the Hejaz. Toward the end of the nineteenth century it spread across the Sahara to the area east (and partly northwest) of Lake Chad, where it gained adherents from among other population groups.

The brotherhood was in this period not at all militant; rather, it promoted learning and piety among its adherents. It also had a strong work ethic, in particular relating to the building and upkeep of new lodges and development through agriculture. The brotherhood became an important factor in the development of trans-Saharan trade. The lodges provided safety as well as a network of resting places and contacts for the traders, and many of them joined the order.

Through its structured internal organization and the increasing identification of the local population with the order, the Sanūsīyah acquired the capacity for political leadership in the eastern Sahara. In spite of this, there is no indication that the building and extension of the brotherhood was made with a conscious political objective. While relations with the Ottoman rulers of the region may have cooled toward the end of the nineteenth century, this was not the major reason why the center of the order was moved from Jaghbūb to Kufra, in the middle of the Libyan desert, in 1895. This was more likely a result of the order's increasing importance in the south, beyond the desert, and a wish to be closer to that region. However, the French, who were moving toward Lake Chad, saw the Sanūsīyah as an activist and inimical force and opened hostilities at the Bir al-ʿAlī lodge in Kanem in 1901. The Sanūsīyah were caught unaware and withdrew. However, they quickly took up arms, and the population in the region fought the French in the name and under the leadership of the brotherhood until the Sanūsīyah were forced to withdraw around 1913–1914.

At the same time, the Italians invaded Libya in 1911. They did not initially target the Sanūsī brotherhood as enemies, but when Turkey withdrew from Libya the following year, the Sanūsī leader Aḥmad al-Sharīf raised the call for *jihād* and led a largely bedouin force against the invaders. The Sanūsī held the Italians at bay for several years, but an attack on the British forces in Egypt (then allies of Italy) led to the brotherhood's defeat. Al-Sharīf was replaced by his cousin Muḥammad Idrīs, and a settlement was made whereby the Sanūsī retained large degree of autonomy. After the rise of fascism in Italy, the agreement broke down, and hostilities recommenced. At this stage, however, the struggle became a more purely bedouin one led by tribal leaders like ʿUmar al-Mukhtār, while the Sanūsī hierarchy led by Idrīs remained in exile in Egypt and became more a focus of identity than an actual strategic leadership. In the course of this struggle, which lasted until 1932, the Sanūsī organizational structure of lodges was largely destroyed. When the modern state of Libya was created, Muḥammad Idrīs was brought back as *amīr* of Cyrenaica and in 1951 was made king of Libya; he was removed by the coup of Muʿammar al-Qadhdhāfī in 1969. The order showed some signs of revival under his patronage, but essentially the religious brotherhood had become a monarchical order. Most of the organization was destroyed in the conflicts in Egypt and Chad as well as in Cyrenaica. Today the order is not tolerated in Libya, and outside Libya only a few lodges remain, including the oldest one at Abū Qubays near Mecca.

[*See also* Idrīsīyah; Libya; *and the biographies of Ibn Idrīs and Mukhtār.*]

BIBLIOGRAPHY

Ciammaichella, Glauco. *Libyens et Français au Tchad, 1897–1914: La confrérie senoussie et le commerce transsaharien.* Paris, 1987. Contains a number of documents.

Dajjānī, Aḥmad Ṣidqī al-. *Al-Ḥarakat al-Sanūsīyah: Nash'atuhā wa-numūwuhā fī al-qarn al-tāsiʿ ʿashar.* Beirut, 1967. The most complete Arabic study on the Sanūsīyah in print.

Evans-Pritchard, E. E. *The Sanusi of Cyrenaica.* Oxford, 1949. Classic anthropological study of the interaction of the brotherhoods with the bedouins. Its main thesis has been criticized by Peters, below.

Martin, B. G. *Muslim Brotherhoods in Nineteenth-Century Africa.* Cambridge, 1976. Contains a chapter on the Sanūsīyah.

O'Fahey, R. S. *Enigmatic Saint: Ahmad Ibn Idris and the Idrisi Tradition.* London and Evanston, Ill., 1990. Places al-Sanūsī in a Ṣūfī context.

Peters, Emrys L. *The Bedouin of Cyrenaica: Studies in Personal and Corporate Power.* Cambridge, 1990. Includes a criticism of the "structural" explanation of the Sanūsīyah in Cyrenaica.

Triaud, Jean-Louis. *Tchad, 1900–1902: Une guerre franco-libyenne oubliée? Une confrérie musulmane, la Sanūsiyya, face à la France.* Paris, 1987. Collection of documents from the African conflicts.

Triaud, Jean-Louis. *Les relation entre la France et la Sanūsiyya, 1840–1930: Histoire d'une mythologie coloniale; découverte d'une confrérie saharienne.* Paris, 1991. A most complete study of the French "creation" of the Sanūsīyah enemy.

Vikør, Knut S. *Sufi and Scholar on the Desert Edge: Muḥammad b. ʿAlī al-Sanūsī, 1787–1859.* Bergen, 1991. Discussion of the founder of the movement, with a survey of its organization in the early period.

Vikør, Knut S., and R. S. O'Fahey. "Ibn Idrīs and al-Sanūsī: The Teacher and His Student." *Islam et Sociétés au Sud du Sahara* 1.1 (1987): 70–83.

Ziadeh, Nicola A. *Sanūsīyah: A Study of a Revivalist Movement in Islam* (1958). Reprint, Leiden, 1983. Basic study of the brotherhood, though somewhat dated.

KNUT S. VIKØR

SAREKAT ISLAM. Indonesia's first mass political party, Sarekat Islam at one time claimed more than one million adherents. It was the successor to Sarekat Dagang Islam, a primarily commercial Muslim organization initially formed to oppose Chinese competition in the batik industry. Organizational difficulties and intraparty divisions led to the demise of the original association, and Sarekat Islam was formed in 1912 under the leadership of H. O. S. Tjokroaminoto.

A variety of factors was responsible for the rapid expansion of the organization during the second decade of the twentieth century. Economically, it was oriented toward anticapitalist views and more particularly against the economic power of the local Chinese community. It also built its early strength on Javanese nationalism, which interacted with its campaigns against the Chinese and Dutch colonialism. Central to Sarekat Islam's appeal to Indonesians was its emphasis on the unity of all Muslims in the Indies. Islam and demands for economic and social reform were also interlocked, as the party represented Islam as the solution to all the people's basic problems. It further attempted to speak for the Muslims of the Indies in international Pan-Islamic movements and organizations.

Although Sarekat Islam's leadership tended to reflect Islamic socialist and modernist views, the organization was never strongly centralized, and its various branches often reflected diverse patterns of economic, social, political, and religious interests. This diversity aided its expansion by drawing a wide range of members into the party. It was also a hindrance, since the radical statements and actions of some branches antagonized the Dutch colonial administration, and far-left elements contested with the religious socialist leadership for control of the party. In particular, Sarekat Islam became locked in a crippling struggle for dominance of the nationalist movement with the newly formed Communist Party of Indonesia, which controlled some Sarekat Islam branches.

Sarekat Islam reached its height in the years immediately after World War I, when it was the largest nationalist movement in the Indies. It had its own newspapers, national congresses, and membership in the colonial legislature, and was the target of Dutch colonial administrators who feared its influence and religious views. However, it declined throughout the 1920s because of internal divisions, poor organization, secular competition, and Dutch repression. It first changed its name to the Partai Sarekat Islam, then in 1929 to the Partai Sarekat Islam Indonesia to emphasize its move toward a more nationalist and less Muslim platform. By that time, however, it had only 1 percent of its former membership and was overshadowed by other nationalist and religious organizations.

The party became moribund only to be reinvigorated after World War II, but in the 1955 national elections it received only 2.9 percent of the vote. It continued to be active in Muslim politics as a splinter party. In the 1970s, when the Suharto government consolidated all Muslim parties into one coalition (the PPP or Partai Persatuan Pembangunan), it became a charter member of that organization.

[*See also* Indonesia; Partai Persatuan Pembangunan.]

BIBLIOGRAPHY

Blumberger, J. Th. Petrus. *De Nationalistische Bewegung in Nederlandische-Indie*. Haarlem, 1931.

Kuntowijoyo. "Islam in Politics: The Local Sarekat Islam Movements in Madura, 1913–1920." In *Islam and Society in Southeast Asia*, edited by Taufik Abdullah and Sharon Siddique, pp. 108–135. Singapore, 1986.

von der Mehden, Fred R. *Religion and Nationalism in Southeast Asia*. Madison, Wis., 1963.

FRED R. VON DER MEHDEN